39th Edition

Warman's®

Antiques&
Collectibles

Price Guide

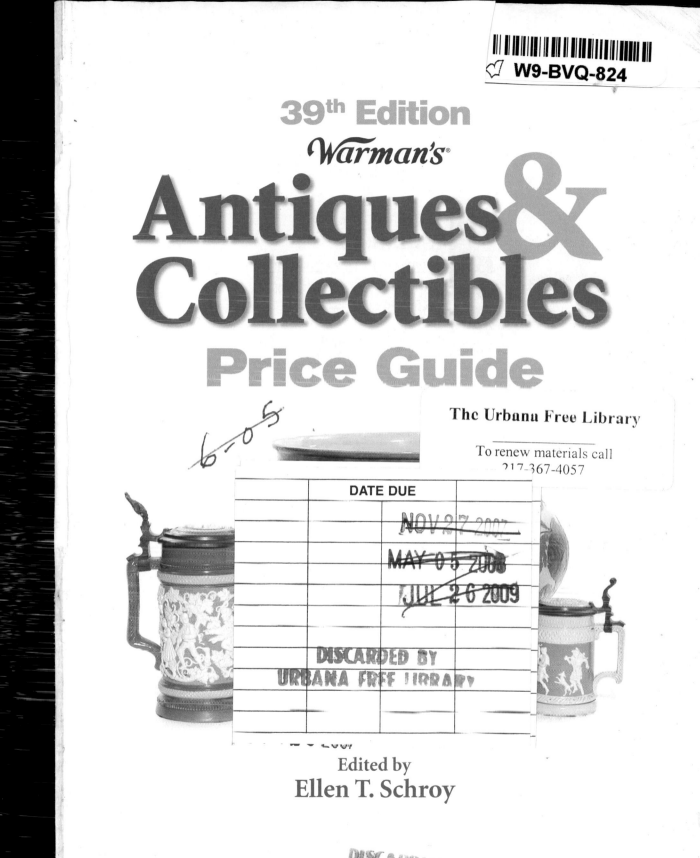

6-05

Edited by
Ellen T. Schroy

©2005 KP Books
Published by

kp books
An Imprint of F+W Publications

700 East State Street • Iola, WI 54990-0001
715-445-2214 • 888-457-2873

Our toll-free number to place an order or obtain
a free catalog is (800) 258-0929.

Library of Congress Catalog Number: 1076-1985

ISBN: 0-87349-990-5

Designed by Kay Sanders
Edited by Kristine Manty

Printed in the United States of America

On the front cover, from top left: Brooch/pin, Arts and Crafts, silver, enamel, opal, fresh-water pearl, c. 1900, shield-shaped plaque, stylized branchlike motif bezel-set with six small circular blue-green opal cabochons across top, enclosing large oval bezel-set opal with predominately red play-of-color, on a green plique à jour enameled ground, fresh-water pearl drop, reverse marked "DEPOSÉ," Fr import mark stamped on C-catch, attributed to Heinrich Levinger, Pforzhein (Germany), 1-1/4" w x 1-1/4" l, $1,200; carnival glass punch bowl, Northwood Grape and Cable, horehound/marigold, mid-size, part of a set with eight cups, $2,100; Gustav Stickley humpback rocking chair, Arts and Crafts, 1902, oak, original finish, small mark, seat cover replaced, 38" h, 28" w, $1,600-$1,800.
On the back cover: Roseville pottery, Gardenia vase, bulbous, golden tan, 684-8", $350-$400.

INTRODUCTION

Warman's: Serving the trade for more than 50 years

In 1994, *Warman's Antiques and Their Prices* became *Warman's Antiques and Collectibles Price Guide*. Longtime *Warman's* users will find a couple of new changes to this edition. The first and biggest change is the book is now in full color, which is exactly what you have been demanding. The second is the new smaller size, but the book is still packed with the same great information.

Individuals in the trade refer to this book simply as *Warman's*, a fitting tribute to E. G. Warman and the product he created. *Warman's* has been around for more than 50 years. We are proud as peacocks that *Warman's* continues to establish the standards for general antiques and collectibles price guides in 2005, just as it did in 1972 when its first rival appeared on the scene.

Warman's, the antiques and collectibles "bible," covers objects made between 1700 and the present. Because it reflects market trends, *Warman's* has added more and more 20th-century material to each edition. Remember, 1900 was more than 100 years ago—the distant past to the new generation of 20-something and 30-something collectors. The general "antiques" market consists of antiques (for the purposes of this book, objects made before 1945), collectibles (objects of the post-World War II era that enjoy an established secondary market), and desirables (contemporary objects that are collected, but speculative in price). Although *Warman's* contains information on all three market segments, its greatest emphasis is on antiques and collectibles. In fact, this book is the essential field guide to the antiques and collectibles marketplace, which indicates that *Warman's* is much more than a list of object descriptions and prices. It is a basic guide to the field as a whole, providing you with the key information you need every time you encounter a new object or collecting category.

'*Warman's* is the Key'

Warman's provides the keys needed by auctioneers, collectors, dealers, and others to understand and deal with the complexities of the antiques and collectibles market. A price list is only one of many keys needed today. *Warman's* 39th edition contains many additional keys including histories, marks, and reproductions. Useful buying and collecting hints also are provided. Used properly, there are few doors these keys will not open. *Warman's* is designed to be your first key to the exciting world of antiques and collectibles. As you use the keys this book provides to advance further in your specialized collecting areas, *Warman's* hopes you will remember with fondness where you received your start. When you encounter items outside your area of specialty, remember *Warman's* remains your key to unlocking the information you need, just as it has in the past.

Organization

Listings: Objects are listed alphabetically by category, beginning with Advertising and ending with Zsolnay Pottery. If you have trouble identifying the category to which your object belongs, think about what the object is made of, or who made it, what marks are visible, and use the index in the back of the book. It will guide you to the proper category. We have made the listings descriptive enough so that specific objects can be identified. We also emphasize items that are actively being sold in the marketplace. Some harder-to-find objects are included to demonstrate market spread—useful information worth considering when you have not traded actively in a category recently. Each year as the market changes, we carefully review our categories—adding, dropping, and combining to provide the most comprehensive coverage possible. *Warman's* quick response to developing trends in the marketplace is one of the prime reasons for its continued leadership in the field.

History: Collectors and dealers enhance their appreciation of objects by knowing something about their history. We present a capsule history for each category. In many cases, this history contains collecting hints or other useful information.

References: KP Books also publishes other *Warman's* titles. Each concentrates on a specific collecting group, e.g., American pottery and porcelain, Americana and collectibles, glass, and jewelry. Several are second or subsequent editions. Their expanded coverage compliments the information found in *Warman's Antiques and Collectibles Price Guide*. Many categories in the 39th edition feature the cover of a *Warman's* book where you can find more information and in-depth coverage on the subject. These books include *Warman's Advertising*, *Warman's American Furniture*, *Warman's American Pottery and Porcelain*, *Warman's American Records*, *Warman's Carnival Glass*, *Warman's Civil War Collectibles*, *Warman's Coins and Paper Money*, *Warman's Depression Glass*, *Warman's English and Continental Pottery and Porcelain*, *Warman's Glass*, *Warman's Jewelry*, *Warman's Native American Collectibles*, and *Warman's Pattern Glass*.

There are also several good publications collectors and dealers should be aware of to be knowledgeable about antiques and collectibles in general. Space does not permit listing all of the national and regional publications in the antiques and collectibles field; this is a sampling:

- *Antique & The Arts Weekly*, Bee Publishing Company, 5 Church Hill Road, Newton, CT 06470; http://www.thebee.com/aweb
- *Antique Review*, P.O. Box 538, Worthington, OH 43085
- *Antique Trader Weekly*, P.O. Box 1050, Dubuque, IA 52001; http://www.csmonline.com
- *AntiqueWeek*, P.O. Box 90, Knightstown, IN 46148; http://www.antiqueweek.com
- *Antiques* (The Magazine Antiques), 551 Fifth Ave., New York, NY 10017
- *Antiques & Collecting*, 1006 South Michigan Ave., Chicago, IL 60605
- *Maine Antique Digest*, P.O. Box 358, Waldoboro, ME 04572; http://www.maineantiquedigest.com
- *New England Antiques Journal*, 4 Church St., Ware, MA 01082
- *New York-Pennsylvania Collector*, Drawer C, Fishers, NY 14453

Reproductions: Reproductions are a major concern to all collectors and dealers. Throughout this edition, boxes will alert you to known reproductions and keys to recognizing them. Most reproductions are unmarked; the newness of their appearance is often the best clue to uncovering them. Specific objects known to be reproduced are marked within the listings with an asterisk (*). The information is designed to serve as a reminder of past reproductions and prevent you from buying them, believing them to be period. We strongly recommend subscribing to *Antique & Collectors Reproduction News*, a monthly newsletter that reports on past and present reproductions, copycats, fantasies, and fakes. Send $32 for 12 issues to: ACRN, Box 12130, Des Moines, IA 50312-9403; (www.repronews.com). This newsletter has been published for many years. Consider buying all available back issues. The information they contain will be of service long into the future.

Price notes

In assigning prices, we assume the object is in very good condition; if otherwise, we note this in our description. It would be ideal to suggest that mint, or unused, examples of all objects exist. The reality is that objects from the past were used, whether they are glass, china, dolls, or toys. Because of this, some normal wear must be expected. In fact, if an object such as a piece of furniture does not show wear, its origins may be more suspect than if it does show wear. Whenever possible, we have tried to provide a broad listing of prices within a category so you have a "feel" for the market. We emphasize the middle range of prices within a category, while also listing some objects of high and low value to show market spread. We do not use ranges because they tend to confuse, rather than help, the collector and dealer. How do you determine if your object is at the high or low end of the range? There is a high degree of flexibility in pricing in the antiques field. If you want to set ranges, add or subtract 10 percent from our prices.

Price research

Everyone asks, "Where do you get your prices?"

They come from many sources. First, we rely on auctions. Auction houses and auctioneers do not always command the highest prices. If they did, why do so many dealers buy from them? The key to understanding auction prices is to know when a price is high or low in the range. We think we do this and do it well. The 39th edition represents a concentrated effort to contact more regional auction houses, both large and small. The cooperation has been outstanding and has resulted in an ever-growing pool of auction prices and trends to help us determine the most up-to-date auction prices.

Second, we work closely with dealers. We screen our contacts to make certain they have full knowledge of the market. Dealers make their living from selling antiques; they cannot afford to have a price guide that is not in touch with the market. More than 50 antiques and collectibles magazines, newspapers, and journals come into our office regularly. They are excellent barometers of what is moving and what is not. We don't hesitate to call an advertiser and ask if his listed merchandise sold. When the editorial staff is doing fieldwork, we identify ourselves. Our conversations with dealers and collectors around the country have enhanced this book. Teams from *Warman's* are in the field at antiques shows, malls, flea markets, and auctions recording prices and taking photographs. Collectors work closely with us. They are specialists whose devotion to research and accurate information is inspiring. Generally, they are not dealers. Whenever we have asked them for help, they have responded willingly and admirably.

Board of advisers

Our board of advisers is made up of specialists, both dealers and collectors, who feel a commitment to accurate information. You'll find their names listed in the front of the book. Several have authored a major reference work on their subject. Our esteemed board of advisers has increased in number and scope. Participants have all provided detailed information regarding the history and reference section of their particular area of expertise, as well as preparing price listings. Many have furnished photographs and even shared with us their thoughts on the state of the market. We are delighted to include those who are valuable members, officers, and founders of collectors' clubs. They are authors of books and articles, and many frequently lecture to groups about their specialties. Most of our advisers have been involved with antiques and collectibles for more than 20 years. Several are retired, and the antiques and collectibles business is a hobby that encompasses most of their free time. Others are a bit younger and either work full time or part time in the antiques and collectibles profession. One thing they all have in common is their enthusiasm for the antiques and collectibles marketplace. They are eager to share their knowledge with collectors. Many have developed wonderful friendships through their efforts and are enriched by them. If you wish to buy or sell an object in the field of expertise of any of our advisers, drop them a note along with a SASE. If time permits, they will respond.

Buyer's guide, not seller's guide

Warman's is designed to be a buyer's guide, suggesting what you would have to pay to purchase an object on the open market from a dealer or collector. It is not a seller's guide to prices. People frequently make this mistake. In doing so, they deceive themselves. If you have an object listed in this book and wish to sell it to a dealer, you should expect to receive approximately 50 percent of the listed value. If the object will not resell quickly, expect to receive even less. Private collectors may pay more, perhaps 70 to 80 percent of our listed price, if your object is something needed for their collection. If you have an extremely rare object or an object of exceptionally high value, these guidelines do not apply. Examine your piece as objectively as possible. As an antiques and collectibles appraiser, I spend a great deal of time telling people their treasures are not "rare" at all, but items readily available in the marketplace. In respect to buying and selling, a simple philosophy is that a good purchase occurs when the buyer and seller are happy with the price. Don't look back. Hindsight has little value in the antiques and collectibles field. Given time, things tend to balance out.

Always improving

Warman's is always trying to improve. Space is freely given to long price descriptions to help you understand what the piece looks like, and perhaps what's special about it. With this edition, we've arranged some old formats, using more bold words to help you find what you're looking for. Some categories have been arranged so that if the only thing you know is how high, you can start there. Many times, identifying what you've got is the hardest part. Well, the first place to start is how big—grab that ruler and see what you can find that's a comparable size. You are still going to have to make a determination about what the object is made of, be it china, glass, porcelain, wood, or other materials. Use all your senses to discover what you've got. Ask questions about your object, who made it, and why, how was it used, where, and when. As you find answers to these questions, you'll be helping yourself figure out just what the treasure is all about.

Eager to hear from readers

At *Warman's* and KP Books, we're always eager to hear what you think about this book and how we can improve it. Write to either Ellen Schroy, *Warman's* editor, 135 S. Main St., Quakertown, PA 18951-1119 or e-mail at schroy@voicenet.com. The fine staff at KP Books can be reached at 700 E. State St., Iola, WI 54990. It's our goal to continue in the *Warman's* tradition and make it the best price guide available.

STATE OF THE MARKET

Every edition when I sit down to write this piece for *Warman's Antiques and Collectibles,* I happily travel back in time to the many wonderful auctions, exciting antiques shows, interesting shops, maze-like antiques malls, and many flea markets I have visited during the past months.

That travel last year was perhaps a little more difficult due to circumstances way beyond anyone's control—the weather! It played a huge impact on the economy in general and, by association, also the economy of many antiques and collectibles dealers. When you're battening down the hatches because of an impending storm, you're not out buying or selling. When you're moving things to high ground or out of the way of a potential forest fire, you've got bigger things on your mind. Add to that the worry about loved ones in harm's way, whether they are fighting for our freedom or tackling things here on the home front. Considering all of these "extra" influences, when time was spent enjoying the hobby of collecting, it was so much more enjoyable.

Several of the big auctions this year weren't only held at the "big name" auctioneers in major cities. Many of the smaller regional auction houses sold fine long-time collections, bringing today's collectors closer to those who practiced the same hobby years ago. The 2004 auction season certainly was one to delight collectors who wanted to add something interesting to their treasures, but also a piece with a well-known provenance. The term "provenance" in the antiques world is used to describe how the history of an item may increase its desirability and therefore value. In July, auctioneers at Early Auction Co., Ohio, offered exquisite glass objects from the collection of former premium dealer Maude Feld.

When I posed the question of how the provenance of a dedicated collector/dealer like Maude Feld may add to the value of an object, Steve Early of Early Auction Co. told me: "The greatest advantage of provenance is a guarantee of authenticity. The object also takes additional value from a respected collector's name by association depending on the status of the collector. Some of Mrs. Feld's items were extremely rare or one of a kind form or color. She didn't have the reference books of today, which elevates her status as one of the first and most astute dealer-collectors."

Platypus Antiques offered a booth full of fine country-oriented antiques at the March 2004 Atlantique City Antiques Show. Included in the booth were quilts, painted furniture, game boards, artwork, and accessories.

Dealer Paul Manning made sure this World War II German battleship gun sight was well polished before the March 2004 Atlantique City Antiques Show. The piece was priced at $25,000.

Being able to feel the softness of this nearly 10-foot square Tebrise Rug was part of the thrill of being at the March 2004 Atlantique City Antiques show. The smaller runner at the top was made of silk and while it was also soft, it was not as soft as the Tebrise, which was offered for $10,000 by Farsh, Inc

Conestoga Auction Co., Inc., Pennsylvania, offered the collection of Eugene and Dorothy Elgin, in April of 2004, where it established new prices for chalkware and redware and related primitives. The "buzz" created by this auction lasted for weeks among those who buy and sell primitives. In May of 2004, Green Valley Auctions sold the cup plate collection of the late John Bilane of Union, New Jersey. Mr. Bilane was a consummate cup plate dealer and collector who delighted in encouraging other cup plate collectors as well as those just entering the hobby. He was also a renowned researcher. His book, *Cup Plate Discoveries Since 1949*, was published in 1971 and built on the information previously documented by Ruth Webb Lee and James H. Ross.

When I asked Jeffrey S. Evans of Green Valley Auctions about Mr. Bilane and his collection, he said, "As a cup plate collector, John E. Bilane was an exemplar. He carried on the pioneering research efforts of his mentor James H. Rose, co-author of the 1948 standard reference

American Glass Cup Plates. Bilane's close attention to detail led to his discovery and identification of numerous new cup plate designs and variations. His 1971 publication *Cup Plate Discoveries Since 1949* was a much-needed update and sparked a renewal of interest among collectors. Mr. Bilane was extremely condition conscious and most of the plates in his personal collection were the finest examples available. This combined with his importance to the cup plate field, should prove to add a 10 percent to 20 percent premium in the future to plates with a Bilane provenance. It was a great honor to have the opportunity to catalog his collection."

The collection sold well and the catalog that Mr. Evans and his associates created for that auction will undoubtedly become part of future collectors' reference libraries.

To get another point of view on the subject of provenance, I posed the same question to author/appraiser Frank Farmer Loomis IV and he

Part of enjoying the experience at a big antiques show like Atlantique City is seeing the way dealers choose to display their items. Some, like Ella Diamond, like to add a little whimsy. Here she's displayed some interesting c1910-20 papier-mâché masks on top of Blackamoor pedestals.

One of the new dealers at the October Atlantique City show was Diann Walters. Her booth was filled with something that was pleasing to the eye, yet new to many of those who attended the show. Her artistic display of fruit baskets certainly helped to draw folks into her booth.

responded, "When you acquire an antique knowing its ownership, what a glorious windfall! Such positive energy practically renders the piece a cherished family heirloom. By realizing a fellow collector(s) shared the same joy for a beloved memento your new-to-you antique brings you even more joy."

Certainly 2004 was a year when the joy of collecting spread. And today, just as the early collectors did, we recognize the extra value that a good provenance can contribute to a particular piece. In his book, *The Secrets to Affordable Antiques,* (KP Books, 2004), Loomis discusses how collectors love to own something that was once owned by a famous person, whether it was Greta Garbo or Jackie Onassis. By subscribing to auction catalogs, reading them, and really studying the objects offered and their condition, Mr. Loomis feels those who attend and ultimately

buy at auctions are better-informed consumers. When the objects were formerly owned by someone famous or by a very dedicated collector, the object develops provenance, or its very own pedigree. To quote Mr. Loomis, "It is fascinating to observe how much a pedigreed provenance can increase the value of an antique. The more famous the former owner, the more expensive the object becomes."

While walking the aisles at the Atlantique City Antiques Fair held in March and October of 2004, I saw many tags that touted an item's provenance. Chatting with dealers usually led to even more information about how they had acquired some of the luscious items they were showing. One dealer had a beautiful folding screen that was completely covered with diecuts. When I stopped to inspect it a little more closely, the dealer explained how he bought it, that it was English, probably Victorian, and that it was only the second one he had ever seen. I am glad I stopped when I did as the screen easily found someone who adored it. The dealers at Atlantique City are always generous with their time when it comes to explaining the fine points of items in their booths. If collectors came to Atlantique City to add to their collections of vintage advertising, jewelry, textiles, or art pottery, they certainly weren't disappointed. If they were seeking an exquisite lamp or even something a little more on the funky 1950s side, it was there. Sports memorabilia collectors, glass collectors, and china collectors all could satisfy their yearnings for another wonderful piece. Atlantique City offers so many things by qualified dealers from all around the world, it truly can boast that it has something for everyone.

One new vendor at Atlantique City that caught my eye early was Diann Walters from S. Dennis, NJ. Her shop name, Basket Case Antiques & Collectibles, represents her love of fruit baskets. The interesting display she had created beautifully highlighted them. Each one was tagged with information about who made the basket, when, and, of course, the price. Some of the baskets have a small porcelain or china plate as the center, while others have glass plates. Each basket has a wirework frame that is surprisingly sturdy, despite it's fragile appearance. Diann, and her charming son, age 9, were more than glad to help me learn more about the fruit baskets displayed in her booth. She told me her inventory represented 20 years of collecting and she felt the time was right now to start to educate others as she sold some of them. Those attending the show must have agreed with her as she sold many prime

Diann Walters took time to tag each fruit basket with a description giving the name of the company, the approximate date of manufacture, and, of course, the price. Attention to detail like this made this booth popular with those who attended the October Atlantique City show.

examples. One merely needs to ask to have an opportunity to learn more about almost any object there, as the professional dealers that exhibit at Atlantique City are always glad to share information and provenance of their objects.

Prices from Atlantique City

Here is a sampling of items sold from last year's Atlantique City antiques shows:

- Dining room table, oak, carved legs, $450.
- Hatpin holder, carnival glass, Grape & Cable pattern, marigold, $200.
- Majolica, begonia leaf plate, $85.
- National Cash Register, Model 317, 1914, $1,300.
- Nautical-themed brass lamps, pair, $2,500.
- Oyster plate, scattered green florals, gilt trim, five shaped oyster depressions and center round well, Haviland, $375.
- Piano baby, crawling baby, white shirt with pink trim, holding basket, marked "Germany," $350.

- Portrait, young woman, pastels, green background, oval frame, $55.
- Quilt, striking red zig-zag on white ground, $200.
- Sarreguemines, fruit basket, white, blue decoration, $175.
- Silver-plated butler's tray, shaped for ease in carrying, $95.
- Sterling silver letter opener, $125.
- Slot machine, Mills, 1938, 25 cents, Bursting Cherry, $2,300.

FAKE AND CONFUSING MARKS ON NEW CHINA, POTTERY

by Mark Chervenka

Historically, collectors have relied on marks to authenticate and date antiques and collectibles. That process is becoming less reliable, though, as more reproductions are appearing with nearly exact copies of original marks.

Some old company names have been legitimately reregistered in America, but most marks on reproductions are deliberately designed to be confusing. In many cases, very slight variations—such as color, whether a mark is raised or impressed, whether the mark includes the country of origin—are all that separate vintage marks from the fakes.

Fake and confusing marks have become so widespread that marks alone should never be used as a single test of age or authenticity. Examine a variety of features on a piece including shape, colors, pattern and decoration before making a conclusion on age. Perhaps the best defense against fake marks is simply a healthy skepticism.

The marks shown here are typical of some of the confusing marks you'll find in the antiques and collectibles market today.

Brush-McCoy Pottery

The original Brush-McCoy Pottery operated between about 1911-1925. In 1925, the name was changed to Brush Pottery. Brush Pottery was among the first American potteries to produce cookie jars it made from 1929 until it closed in 1982.

The pre-1925 company named Brush-McCoy Pottery never made cookie jars; it was Brush Pottery, 1929-1982, which made cookie jars. Yet the market is being flooded with new jars marked Brush-McCoy.

At first, the confusing marks only appeared on reproductions of jars originally made by Brush Pottery. Now the mark also appears on jars by other vintage makers such as Shawnee Pottery and other vintage potteries. Most original Brush Pottery marks were impressed below the surface, not raised. So far, all the new Brush McCoy marks are raised molded marks.

A close up view of the raised molded Brush-McCoy mark found on reproduction cookie jars. No mark like this ever appeared before the late 1990s. It is only found on reproductions.

The Brush-McCoy mark on a new Mugsy cookie jar. Original Mugsy cookie jars were made by Shawnee Pottery.

There are two typical marks of Brush Pottery that appear on vintage cookie jars, ca. 1940s-1982. The closest original Brush Pottery mark to include a paintbrush was the palette mark, left. The "W" in authentic Brush-Pottery marks, right, indicates the jar was designed by Twin Winton Ceramics.

Bauer Pottery

The Bauer Pottery name has been registered again and new pottery is being marked with the Bauer Pottery name. New products, including copies of the popular "ring ware" line, are reproductions of original shapes manufactured in the 1930-1940s using vintage pieces as models.

The new company is hoping to help collectors avoid confusion by adding "2000" to the new marks. However, only about 20 percent of the new shapes include the 2000 mark. Company officials say the 2000 mark will be added to the other shapes as those molds are repaired or replaced.

All vintage Bauer marks are impressed, or incised, into the clay. Most, but not all, marks on new Bauer are raised.

New Bauer ring ware pottery. All pieces are marked Bauer Pottery.

A raised molded mark on new Bauer Pottery. All original Bauer marks are impressed, not raised

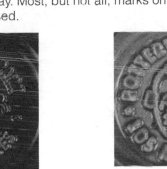

A raised molded mark of new Bauer Pottery with the number 2000. The 2000 appears on many but not all of the new Bauer to help collectors separate old from new.

Some pieces of new Bauer Pottery have impressed marks like this example on an 8-inch flower pot. This new mark is similar to incised marks on vintage Bauer

Delft

New "Delft" has been offered in antique reproduction wholesale catalogs virtually unchanged for more than 30 years. Most reproductions have elaborate fantasy marks to suggest age.

Detecting the fake marks is fairly simple. As a general rule, any mark that includes the word "Delfts" spelled with an "s" is new, and not more than 30-40 years old at most. One mark found on new Delft, that of a lion, appears on a wide variety of ceramic reproductions made in China.

The mark on new blue and white Delft reproductions, ca. 1960s-1970s. Note the letter "s" on the end of Delfts in the mark.

This mark appears on Delft reproductions made ca. mid 1970s to late 1980s. Note the use of the word "Delfts."

Reproduction Delft like this 16-inch plate has been sold since the early 1960s with confusing marks that suggest age.

This lion mark has been used since the late 1980s on a wide variety of reproductions such as Delft, Blue Willow, Pink Luster, Imari, Flow Blue and others.

McCoy Pottery

New pottery marked McCoy is one of the most common reproductions in today's market. The new McCoy marks are virtually identical to marks on originals. The marks appear on copies of specific McCoy originals as well as fantasy items never made by McCoy.

Reproductions that copy original McCoy shapes are the most difficult to identify. Since molds used to make the reproductions are taken from authentic samples, new and old shapes are almost impossible to separate. Questionable pieces should be carefully measured and compared to known originals in reference books. The reproductions are one-quarter to three-quarters of an inch smaller than the originals.

This wall vase/planter marked McCoy is a fantasy piece: no original was ever made by McCoy. A piece from another manufacturer was used to make a mold and a fake McCoy mark was added.

A new frog sprinkler marked McCoy USA. The frog is a direct copy of a McCoy original, but the original McCoy piece was made as a planter only, never as a sprinkler with a handle.

The raised molded "McCoy USA" mark on the bottom of the new frog sprinkler.

Nippon

Fake Nippon marks have appeared on new porcelain since the early 1990s. Although the wreath mark is the most common original mark, many different marks appear on authentic pre-1921 Nippon. There are now matching fake marks for most of the original variations.

No one rule can be used to detect all the new marks. What may be an indication of a fake in one mark, may not be of help when examining another mark. Most marks need to be examined on a case by case basis. Some of the most common faked marks are shown here.

This is a fake mark: the wreath is closed at the top, and there is a crude hand-painted appearance to the mark.

The wreath is open at the top; the letter "M" in the center. All lines are quite solid and distinct.

This is a fake mark: the wreath is turned upside down, and an hourglass was never used in the old mark.

This is a fake mark: the wreath is turned upside down, and the letter "K" was never used in old mark.

Keep in mind that reproduction wholesalers are using various fake Nippon marks on a wide variety of shapes and forms that have no old counterparts.

A fake RC mark entirely in green. RC is poorly formed and almost unrecognizable as English letters.

The words "Hand Painted" are in red; "RC" and "Nippon" appear in green. Letters RC are distinct.

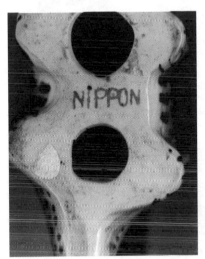

A fake Nippon mark in red block letters. This mark is found on the example shown at right.

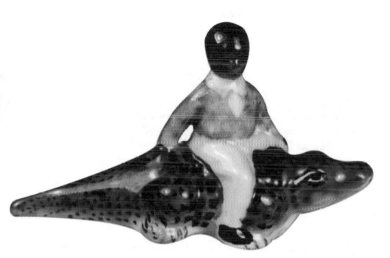

A new figural marked Nippon in red block letter; also found marked Occupied Japan. No pre 1921 original of this shape was ever marked Nippon.

Red Wing Stoneware

A company named Red Wing Stoneware Company begun in the mid-1980s uses markings similar to those found on vintage collectible stoneware.

Marks of the original Red Wing Stoneware Company established in 1876 never appear as a blue ink oval mark. The original blue oval trademark was not used until ca. 1906 by which time the original Red Wing Stoneware Pottery Company was known as Red Wing UNION Stoneware Company.

The mark of the new Red Wing Stoneware Company is easily confused with the mark of the old Red Wing UNION Stoneware Company shown at right.

The old mark of Red Wing UNION Stoneware Company that appeared with the red wing trademark, ca.1906-1930s.

Flow Blue

Reproductions of specific Flow Blue patterns with confusing new marks began appearing in the American market around late 2001. Some of the vintage patterns known to be reproduced include Touraine, Iris, Waldorf and Trentham. Many other pieces of new Flow Blue in various modern patterns are also appearing with confusing new marks that resemble marks used on vintage Flow Blue.

As a general rule, all vintage pieces should include "England" either within the mark or near the mark. The vast majority of Flow Blue reproductions are made in China, not England. That is not an absolute test, though, because some fake marks deliberately include England. Any suspicious mark should be carefully compared to known original marks found in reference books on Flow Blue.

This mark is found on new Touraine pattern Flow Blue. It is similar to the old Stanley Pottery Co. Touraine mark (at right), but without "England."

A mark on original Stanley Touraine with "England." Both old and new marks include the British Registration number 329815 issued in 1898.

The mark on reproduction Flow Blue with the Waldorf pattern. Notice that the new mark does not include "England."

The original mark on vintage pieces of Waldorf by New Wharf Pottery. The old mark includes "England."

This new mark on Flow Blue reproductions resembles the authentic ca. 1912 mark of T. Rathbone & Co. "Victor" appears as a pattern name. Very crude compared to the original at right. Although made in China, "England" is included in the new mark.

The genuine ca. 1912 mark of T. Rathbone & Co. A pattern name may or may not be included. "England" generally appears near or within the basic mark.

Roseville Pottery

Roseville Pottery has been reproduced in china since 1996. The majority of reproductions have a fake version of Roseville's Late Period mark, the word Roseville in script above a shape/size number. Original marks include U.S.A. between "Roseville" and the shape/size number. The comparable fake mark does not include U.S.A.

On some of the earliest reproductions you may find U.S.A in very faint weak letters like the example shown here. In original Late Period marks used 1935-1954, the U.S.A. is the same height and sharpness as Roseville and the shape/size number. The only exceptions are particularly small original shapes where there was no space for U.S.A.

Reproductions of Roseville's pre-1934 patterns have begun appearing with the mark shown here. Although this is a close copy of an authentic pre-1934 Roseville mark, it is easily detected. The original mark is impressed below the surface; the fake mark is molded and raised above the surface.

A typical authentic Roseville mark used during the Late Period, 1935-1954. Note that U.S.A is the same height and weight as Roseville and the shape/size number. If U.S.A. is missing or very faint in the Late Period mark, it is almost certainly a reproduction.

A fake raised mark used on reproductions of Roseville Middle Period patterns such as Jonquil and Luffa. Original Luffa and Jonquil never had raised marks. Original Luffa and Jonquil usually had paper labels only, never raised molded marks.

A typical fake mark found on the majority of Roseville reproductions made in China. This example is shown with the removable paper label as it arrives from the reproduction wholesaler. In fake marks, the letters U.S.A. are either missing or, as in this example, very faint.

Royal Doulton

Royal Doulton is still in business and has an active legal staff to defend its registered trademarks. As a result, few reproduction manufactures use copies of Royal Doulton marks. The fake Royal Doulton mark shown here appears on new Babes in the Woods plates.

A fake Royal Doulton mark found on a fake Babes in Wood plate. The lion's body is distorted, the crown is poorly shaped, and England is missing.

This is an authentic Royal Doulton mark. It has a clear distinct lion and crown, and "England" is very distinct. This mark is green, but colors of authentic marks may vary.

Hull

Compared to McCoy and Roseville, there are relatively few Hull Pottery reproductions. The new mark shown here is found on reproductions of Hull's Orchid pattern.

Mark Chevenka is the editor of *Antique & Collector Reproduction News*, a monthly newsletter on fakes and reproductions published since 1992 (www.repronews.com). For more information on marks on reproductions, see *Guide to Fake & Forged Marks* by Mark Chervenka, KP Books, $24.95, www.krause.com or phone: 888-457-2873.

This is the new mark on Hull Pottery reproduction. Note the script style of lettering which is particularly evident in the word Hull.

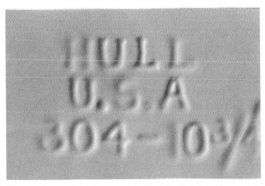

The mark on original Hull; note that the lettering is a block style, not script like the reproduction.

BOARD OF ADVISERS

Claire Lavin
P.O. Box 354
Cheltenham, PA 19019
(215) 663-9523
e-mail: clavin9036@aol.com
Halloween

Robert Levy
The Unique One
2802 Centre St.
Pennsauken, NJ 08109
(856) 663-2554
Web site:
Antiqueslotmachines.com
e-mail:
theuniqueone@worldnct.att.net
Coin-Operated Items

Clarence and Betty Maier
The Burmese Cruet
P.O. Box 432
Montgomeryville, PA 18936
(215) 855-5388
e-mail: burmeoocruel@erols.com
Burmese Glass, Crown Milano, Royal Flemish

James S. Maxwell, Jr.
P.O. Box 367
Lampeter, PA 17537
(717) 464-5573
Banks, Mechanical

Parker-Braden Auctions
Carlsbad, NM
(800) 748-3946
Web site:
www.parkerbraden.com

Bob Perzel
505 Rt. 579
Ringoes, NJ 08551
(908) 782-9361
Stangl Birds

Evalcno Pulati
National Valentine Collectors
Assoc.
P.O. Box 1404
Santa Ana, CA 92702
Valentines

John D. Querry
RD 2, Box 137B
Martinsburg, PA 16662
(814) 793-3185
Gaudy Dutch

Quinn's Auction Galleries
431 N. Maple Ave.
Falls Church, VA 22046
(703) 532-5632
Web site:
www.quinnsauction.com

David Rago
David Rago Auctions, Inc.
333 N. Main St.
Lambertville, NJ 8530
(609) 397-9374
e-mail: http://www.ragoarts.com
Art Pottery, Arts & Crafts, Fulper, Grueby, Newcomb

Remmen Auctions & Appraisal Services
P.O. Box 301398
Portland, OR 97294
(503) 256-1226
Web site.
www.remmenauction.com

Charles and Joan Rhoden
8693 N. 1950 East Road
Georgetown, IL 61846-6254
(217) 662-8046
e-mail: rhoden@soltec.net
Yard-Long Prints

Julie P. Robinson
P.O. Box 117
Upper Jay, NY 12987
(518) 946-7753
Celluloid, Mourning Jewelry

Jerry Rosen
15 Hampden St.
Swampscott, MA 01907
Piano Babies

Kenneth E. Schneringer
157 Holly Mill Village Drive
Canton, GA 30114
(707) 704-9913
e-mail: trademan68@aol.com
Catalogs

Susan Scott
882 Queen St. West
Toronto, Ontario Canada
M6K 1Q3
e-mail: SusanScottCA@aol.com
Chintz

Judy Smith
1702 Lamont St. NW
Washington, DC 20010-2602
(202) 332-3020
e-mail: judy@bauble-and-bibehs.com, judy@quilt.net
Lea Stein Jewelry

George Sparacio
P.O. Box 791
Malaga, NJ 08328-0791
(856) 694-4167
e-mail: mrvesta1@aol.com
Match Safes

Henry A. Taron
Tradewinds Antiques
P.O. Box 249
Manchester By-The-Sea, MA
01944-0249
(978) 526-4085
e-mail:
taron@tradewindsantiquoo.com
Canes

Lewis S. Walters
143 Lincoln Lane
Berlin, NJ 08009
(856) 719-1513
e-mail: lew69@erols.com
Phonographs, Radios

ABBREVIATIONS

The following are standard abbreviations, which we have used throughout this edition of *Warman's*.

ABP = American Brilliant Period
ADS = Autograph Document Signed
adv = advertising
ah = applied handle
ALS = Autograph Letter Signed
AQS = Autograph Quotation Signed
C = century
c = circa
Cal. = caliber
circ = circular
cyl. = cylinder
cov = cover
CS = Card Signed
d = diameter or depth
dec = decorated
dj = dust jacket
DQ = Diamond Quilted
DS = Document Signed
ed = edition
emb = embossed
ext. = exterior
eyep. = eyepiece
Folio = 12" x 16"
ftd = footed
ga = gauge
gal = gallon
ground = background
h = height
horiz. = horizontal
hp = hand painted
hs = high standard
illus = illustrated, illustration
imp = impressed
int. = interior
irid = iridescent
IVT = inverted thumbprint
j = jewels
K = karat
l = length
lb = pound

litho = lithograph
ll = lower left
lr = lower right
ls = low standard
LS = Letter Signed
mfg = manufactured
MIB = mint in box
MOP = mother-of-pearl
n/c = no closure
ND = no date
NE = New England
No. = number
NRFB = never removed from box
ns = no stopper
r/c = reproduction closure
o/c = original closure
opal = opalescent
orig = original
os = orig stopper
oz = ounce
pcs = pieces
pgs = pages
PUG = printed under the glaze
pr = pair
PS = Photograph Signed
pt = pint
qt = quart
RM = red mark
rect = rectangular
sgd = signed
S. N. = Serial Number
SP = silver plated
SS = Sterling silver
sq = square
TLS = Typed Letter Signed
unp = unpaged
vert. = vertical
vol = volume
w = width
yg = yellow gold

Grading Condition. The following numbers represent the standard grading system used by dealers, collectors, and auctioneers:

C.10 = Mint
C. 9 = Near mint
C.8.5 = Outstanding
C.8 = Excellent

C.7.5 = Fine +
C.7 = Fine
C. 6.5 = Fine – (good)
C. 6 = Poor

ADVERTISING

History: Before the days of mass media, advertisers relied on colorful product labels and advertising giveaways to promote their products. Containers were made to appeal to the buyer through the use of stylish lithographs and bright colors. Many of the illustrations used the product in the advertisement so that even an illiterate buyer could identify a product.

Advertisements were put on almost every household object imaginable and constant reminders to use the product or visit a certain establishment.

Additional Listings: See *Warman's Americana & Collectibles* for more examples.

For more information, see *Warman's Americana*, 11th edition.

Grading Condition. The following numbers represent the standard grading system used by dealers, collectors, and auctioneers.

C.10 = Mint
C. 9 = Near mint
C.8.5 = Outstanding
C.8 = Excellent
C.7.5 = Fine +
C.7 = Fine
C. 6.5 = Fine - (good)
C. 6 = Poor

Ashtray, Buster Brown, glazed china, figural hat, Buster gesturing towards Tige balancing steaming teapot on nose, 4-7/8" l, 1" h **165.00**
Bank, figural
Magic Chef, painted vinyl, 7" h **25.00**
RCA Nipper, light fuzzy flocked surface over metal, 6-1/4" h, C.8++ **230.00**

Blotter, unused
Cotton Overshirts, ivory white and black celluloid cover, bound at each corner by metal mount, two removable cardboard ink blotter ships, image of "Oppenheim, Oberndorf & Co.," 3" x 6" **28.00**
Eppens, Smith Co., NY, Coffee and Tea Importer, 1900 seasonal greetings, full-color celluloid, slight use **15.00**
Fairbanks Portable Pumping Outfit, graphics of metal vehicle, road paving machinery, 7-1/4" x 9-1/2" **10.00**
Booklet, Dutch Boy Paint, 20 pgs, 5" x 6" **12.00**

Bill clip, Priscilla Ware, Speaks for Itself, Leyse Aluminum Co., Kewaunee, WI, litho on aluminum, front with cameo of lady, spring clip on back, $25.

Bookmark, Rally Day, diecut celluloid, Spirit of '76 fife and drummers, large American flag, string tassel, early 1900s .. **25.00**
Box
Proctor & Gamble, 1873, wood **200.00**
Weideman Oak Flakes, 14 oz, cardboard, 6-1/4" x 4-1/4" **120.00**
Yanks Chewing Gum, counter display box, 20 orig packs of Yanks brand 5¢ Spearmint Chewing Gum, Gum Products Inc., Boston, MA 1" x 3-1/4" x 6-1/2" **190.00**
Broom holder, DeLaval Cream Separators, tin litho, black and white, orig adv envelope, 3-1/2" d, C.8 .... **450.00**
Calendar
Blue Ribbon Canned Foods, 1916, desk, ivory colored celluloid over tin, 3-1/5" x 4-1/2" **20.00**

Nevin's Candy, 1917, two-ply cardboard, wall type, 3-1/4" x 6-1/4" **15.00**
Red Goose Shoes, 1924, colorful print of mountain goat hunter titled "Getting His Goat," H. C. Edwards, artist, ads for Red Goose Shoes, Friedman-Shelby Shoe Col, Atlantic Shoes, Pacific Shoes, 8" x 19" wall type........... **25.00**

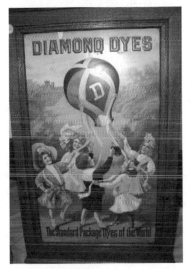

Cabinet, Diamond Dyes, oak, tin litho front panel with five children playing with balloon, complete, original Diamond Dye annual and direction booklet, **$2,250**.

Photo courtesy of Dotta Auction Co., Inc.

Candy pail
Novia Kiddie Pops, pail shape, image of pops and children and dog on both sides, 3-3/4" d, 3-1/4" h, C.7.5+........................ **675.00**
Three Pigs, Mayfair Candy Co., NY, tin litho, 3-1/8" x 3-3/8", C.8 .... **170.00**
Cigar box, Pittsburg's Finest, wood, colorful paper labels with uniformed police officer, 10-7/8" x 7-5/8" x 7-1/2", C.8+ **275.00**
Cigar tin, tin litho
Izaak Walton, image of Walton, hunting and fishing scenes in background, 5-3/8" x 5-3/8", C.8 .... **190.00**
King Midas, image of king on both sides, 5-1/8" x 6-1/8" x 4-1/8", C.8+ tin, lid fair **120.00**
Old Seneca Stogies, W. C. Kildow, colorful graphic Indian image, 5-3/4" x 4-3/8", C.8 .... **425.00**

Orcico Cigars, 2 for 5¢, colorful graphic Indian image, 5-1/2" x 6-1/8" x 4-1/8", C.8.5 .... **550.00**
Tobacco Girl, detailed image of trademark girl on both sides, 5-1/2" x 6-1/4" x 4-1/4", C.8.5 .... **3,300.00**
White Owl Brand, General Cigar Co., blue ground, white owl perched on smoking cigar, 5-3/4" x 5-1/2", C.8+ **675.00**

Clicker

Motorcycle Boy, litho tin, youngster in yellow motorcycling outfit wit ogles and neckerchief, riding red cycle, holding ice cream cone in one hand, 1930s **25.00**
Poll-Parrot Shoes, litho tin, red, yellow, blue parrot, yellow background, red lettering, 1930s **25.00**
Twinkie Shoes, litho tin, full-color art of elf character standing on mushroom, dark green background, tiny inscription for "Hamilton-Brown Shoes Co.," 1930s **30.00**

Clock

Calumet Baking Powder, Sessions clock, oak, wall-type, gold lettering, 39" x 18" x 5-1/2" **2,600.00**
Iroquois Beverages, Buffalo, NY, light-up, double bubble, 16" d **525.00**
None Such Mince Meat, Pumpkin-Squash, Like Mother Used to Make, ribbed cardboard, clock face shaped like pumpkin, tin back shaped like pie plate, easel, hanging hook, clock mechanism not working, 9-1/2" d **1,150.00**

Coffee tin

Daisy Fresh Coffee, Euclid Coffee Co., Cleveland, l lb, key wind, 3-5/8" x 5", C.8 .... **150.00**
Epicure Coffee, John Sills and Sons, 1 lb, image of butler serving cup of coffee, 6" x 4", C.8++ **725.00**
Fairway Coffee, 1 lb, key wind, colorful image of children in field, steaming cup of coffee in background, 4" x 5", C.8.5 .... **250.00**
First Pick Coffee, l lb, key wind, 4" x 5", C.8 .... **350.00**

Child's rocking chair, oak, pressback design of advertising character, the Yellow Kid, blowing horn, repair to back support, **$650**.
Photo courtesy of Dotta Auction Co., Inc.

Groub's Belle Coffee, Seymour, Connerville, 1 lb, colorful trademark girl, 6" x 4-1/8", C.8 .... **625.00**
Jipco Coffee, Beckers-Prentiss Co., Buffalo, NY, 1 lb, key wind, blue and white, buffalo on front, steaming cup of coffee and blossoms on back, 4" x 5-1/8", C.7 .. **250.00**
Loyl Coffee, Rochester Seed & Supply Co., 1 lb, 6-1/4" x 4", C.8.5+ **120.00**
Publix Markets Coffee, Lakeland, FL, 1 lb, key wind, grocery store image, 3-5/8" x 5", C.8 .... **200.00**
Red Turkey Coffee, Mailby's, Corning, NY, 1 lb, 5-3/4" x 4-1/4", C.8 .... **375.00**
Ten Eyck Coffee, Bacon, Stickney & Co., Albany, NY, 1 lb, pry lid, detailed image of Ten Eyck Hotel, 5-1/2" x 4-1/4", C.8 .... **375.00**
Turkey Coffee, Kasper Co., 1 lb, image of wild turkey on both sides, 5-3/4" x 4-1/4", C.8 .... **375.00**
Wake-Em Up Coffee, Anderson-Ryan Coffee Co., Duluth, MN, 10 lb, wooden handle, green and gold, trademark Indian on both sides, 13-1/2" x 9", C.8+ **475.00**

Chair, folding, blue and white enamel plaque on back, "Smoke Piedmont, The Cigarette of Quality," **$250**.
Photo courtesy of Alderfer Auction Co.

Yellow Bonnet Coffee, Springfield Grocer, 1 lb, key wind, white background, 4" x 5", C.7.5+/8- **325.00**

Crock, stoneware

Bowers Three Thistles Snuff, cobalt blue lettering, 14" x 9-1/2", few chips **450.00**
Heinz, detailed multicolored stone litho label, orig lid and closure, 8" x 4", C.8.5+ **675.00**

Diecut, litho cardboard

Colgate talcum powder, two-sided, seated baby in cap and romper, holding product, 1913, price for pr, 14" x 8-1/2", C.8 .... **675.00**
Johnson & Johnson talcum powder, baby on back playing with talc container, string hanger, 8-1/8" x 14-1/8", C-7.5 .... **575.00**
Larkin Boraxine Laundry Soap, cream-colored cat, red bow at neck, easel back, 12" x 9", C.8.5 .... **220.00**
Williard's Candy, 5¢ Nutritious, Wolf Co., Philadelphia Lithographers, blond boy in red sweater, blue shorts, easel back, 17" x 8-3/8" **400.00**
Williard's Candy, 5¢ Nutritious, Wolf Co., Philadelphia Lithographers, blond girl in blue blouse, red romper, easel back, 17" x 8-3/8" **675.00**

Counter display, Brown's Jumbo Bread, elephant shape, framed, 19" w, 17" h, **$300**.
Photo courtesy of Joy Luke Auctions.

Display cabinet, counter top

Blue Bird, A Man's Handerchief, tin litho, hinged top with glass insert, holds four early product boxes, 1920s, 6-3/4" x 11-1/2" x 8", C.8 .... **450.00**

Farnam's Famous Kalamazoo Celery and Pepsin Chewing Gum, wood, curved glass, gold lettering, 7-1/2" x 17" x 10" **5,600.00**

J & P Coats, thread spools **1,800.00**

Nestles, Hazelnut Chocolate Bars, adv labels inside glass lift top, 4-3/4" x 10-1/8" x 7 1/2", C.8 .... **600.00**

Tootsie Roll Candies, tin litho, 13" x 8-3/4" x 8-1/4", C.8 .... **700.00**

Van Haagen's Fine Toilet Soaps, German silver, curved corners, front glass etched with name, some denting to moldings **525.00**

Zeno Gum, wood, emb Zeno marquee with fancy filigree, 18" h, 10-1/2" w, 8" d ... **575.00**

Display cabinet, Shaeffer Fineline, pencils, semi-circular, 27" w, 14" h, **$250**.
Photo courtesy of Joy Luke Auctions

Display stand, Ask For Butter Nut Bread, child dressed as chef, diecut, **$16**.

Display

Red Goose Shoes, figural, papier-mâché, glass eyes, 10 1/2" x 9" x 4-1/2", C.7.5 .... **250.00**

Tennyson 5¢ Cigars Always Fresh, Mazer Cressman, tin litho, 8" x 5-3/4" x 5-3/4", C.8+ **400.00**

Door push

Canada Dry, multicolored bottle and slogan, emb tin litho, 9" x 3" **210.00**

Crescent Flour, Voight Milling Co., Grand Rapids, MI, emb tin litho, 9-5/0" x 3-3/4", C.8.5 .... **300.00**

Domino Cigarettes, emb tin litho, 14" x 4", C.8.5 ..... **100.00**

Edgeworth Tobacco, red, white, and blue, emb tin litho, 14" x 4" **170.00**

Ex-Lax, multicolored porcelain, 8" x 4" **375.00**

Fan, hand held

Alka-Seltzer, cartoon illus, late 1930s-40s, cardboard mounted on wooden rod, 8-1/2" x 9-1/2" **25.00**

Planters Peanuts, Mr. Peanut driving peanut shaped car, adv on back, 1940s, 5-1/4" x 8", C.8 .... **230.00**

Gauge, Standard Roller Bearing Co., 3" x 3" celluloid covers, diecut openings, inner disk wheels to use in determining precise measurements, requirements, etc. for ball bearings, c1920 .... **20.00**

Lapel stud

Alaska Stove Trimmings, brown and white celluloid, metal lapel stud fastener, stove lid lifter illus, plus inscription "Mama! Do You Use Alaska Stove Trimmings-Always Cold" **20.00**

Widow Jones Suits Me, 1-1/4", multicolored celluloid on metal, young lady in stylish gray outfit and hat, pale blue to white background, blue lettering, New England clothing store sponsor .. **40.00**

Display, tin litho, For Real Satisfaction Smoke a Pipe With This Trademark, WDC, gent smoking pipe and pointing to red triangular trademark, four pipes, easel back, c1910, **$145**.
Photo courtesy of Dotta Auction Co., Inc.

Lunch box

Dan Patch Cut Plug, Scotten Dillion Co., tin litho, bale handle, yellow, red, and black, 4-3/8" x 6-7/8" x 4-5/8", tin C.8+, lid C.7+ **325.00**

Green Turtle Cigars, Gordon Cigar Co., tin litho, turtle on rock smoking cigar, 5-1/4" x 7-1/2" x 4-1/2", from C.8-, back C.7 .... **350.00**

Match safe, Advance Farm Equipment, silvered brass, hinged, celluloid wrapper print in color, one side with medieval figure raising Advance banner on rocky height, opposite side with "Simple Traction Engine," two smaller panels each with lists of offices by city, early 1900s **115.00**

Tobacco tin, Buckingham Tobacco, 3-3/4" h, 4-1/2" d, **$75**.

Can, tin, paper label, twist lid, "Red Cow Coffee, Jos. Strong & Co., Terre Haute Coffee & Spice Mills, Terre Haute, Ind.," 1 lb., **$400**.

Tray, Campbell's Soup, tin, 9" x 14", **$15**.

Advertising plate, J. Palleys Hambone Sweets Cigar, hand painted, 10-1/4" d, **$90**.

Tobacco tin, "Light Hiawatha Fine Cut, Absolutely The Best," C. 7.5-8, round, 2" h, 8" d, **$212**.

Display stand, Wise Potato Chips, thin cardboard, image on front of boy and girl at store counter, boy holding up two fingers and smiling as retailer reaches for bags of potato chips from counter display, titled "A Wise Guy," door with logo "Eat Wise Potato Chips," easel back, copyright 1940 Wise Delicatessen Co., Burwick, Va. unused, 17" x 20-1/4", **$50**.

Photo courtesy of Hake's Americana & Collectibles

Mirror, pocket

Berry Bros Varnishes, celluloid, multicolored, little boy pulling dog in Berry Co. adv wagon, 1-3/4" x 2-3/4" **200.00**

I Wear Kleinert's Dress Shields, brown on cream, 2" d **45.00**

The Lincoln Savings Bank, blue on white, bright red center stripe surrounding profile of Lincoln above text "Vote for Lincoln As Your Bank," c1940, 2-1/8" d .. **30.00**

Oyster pail, Fresh Oysters, Schneier's Co., Akron, OH, 1 gal, orig lid, 7-3/8" x 6-5/8", C.8+ **250.00**

Paperweight, Southern Fruit Julep Co., glass, reverse adv on all four sides, five-year monthly scrolling calendar inside, 1-3/8" x 4" x 2-7/8" **325.00**

Peanut butter pail, tin litho

Armour's Veribest Peanut Butter, 2 lb, nursery rhyme characters, yellow ground, 4-5/8" x 4-3/8", C.7.5 ... **190.00**

Clark's Peanut Butter, Canadian, 1 lb, sporting images, 3-3/8" x 3-3/4", C.8++ **875.00**

Monarch Peanut Butter, Teenie Weenie, 1 lb, colorful image of children and giant peanuts, c1920, 3-3/4" x 3-3/8, C.8++ **300.00**

Lunch pail, Just Suits Tobacco, P. Lorillard Co., tin, red, gold text accented in black, lid hinged at right, clasp on left, wire handle on top, designed to be reused as lunch pail, bright glossy finish, gold luster, c1900, 7 3/4" l, 5-1/4" w, 4" h, **$90**.

Photo courtesy of Hake's Americana & Collectibles.

Lard pail, Swift's Silver-Leaf Pure Lard Kettle, red, black, and gold label, original handle and lid, some rust, **$25**.

O! Boy Peanut Butter, Stone Ordean Wells Co., Duluth, 1 lb, children eating sandwiches on front, seashore scene on back, 3-3/8" x 3-3/4", C.8+ ... **650.00**

Planters High Grade Peanut Butter, 25 lbs, 9-1/4" x 10-1/4", C.7.5 .... **575.00**

Squirrel, Canadian, 3 lb, pry lid, squirrel eating peanut, 4-3/4" x 5-1/8", C.8.5 ... **425.00**

Pencil clip

Ardee Flour, red, yellow, blue logo, celluloid on brass wire clip, Hubbard Milling Co., Mankato, Minn, sponsor, early 1900s **25.00**

Red Man Cigar Leaf, multicolored, tobacco pack mounted on brass wire spring clip, early 1900s **55.00**

The Metropolitan, black, white, and red celluloid, mounted on brass wire spring clip, sponsor store designates "Hats" and "Furnishings" **20.00**

Pinback button

Cherry-Ripe Ice Cream, two dark red cherries on green, c1940, 3-1/2" d **20.00**

Davis OK Baking Powder, multicolored, bottle flanked by slogans, black lettering, back paper, c1896 .... **20.00**

Empire Cream Separator, black and white image, blue letters, rim inscription "I Chirp for the Empire because it makes the most dollars for me," clicker hanging from bottom rim **50.00**

Farm Boy Bread, red, white, and blue, center bluetone photo of young farm lad posed next to cow and rooster, blue and red lettering, 1930s **15.00**

Hessler Rural Mailbox, illus of sample mailbox, "Approved By Postmaster General" **75.00**

Kar-A-Van Coffee, multicolored, loaded camel, early 1900s **20.00**

Lekko Scouring Powder, multicolored, image of product canister, and housewife on knees scrubbing floor, 1920s **35.00**

Mephisto Auger Bits, black and red lettering, white ground **15.00**

Metzer's Milk Infant Keeps Them Smiling, 1" d, tinted flesh-tone face, white background, blue and red lettering, c1930 .... **12.00**

O.I.C. Hogs, black and white art and inscription, patriotic red, white, blue, and silver outer rim, back paper with lengthy text for "Famous O.I.C. Hogs," c1900 ..... **50.00**

RCA Micro Mike, ivory white celluloid, red image and title, 3" d **18.00**

Stetson Hats Best in the World, multicolored logo, celluloid, oval **12.00**

Vote Betty Crocker, red, white, and blue litho, c1960 .... **12.00**

Widow Hoffman System-Boys Clothing-Harris Clothing Co., Baltimore, black and white celluloid, young lad in cap and jacket **15.00**

Wilbur's Cocoa, multicolored, cherub trademark stirring Wilbur mug, orig back paper, c1896 .... **20.00**

Plate, Season's Greetings, Gately & Fitzgerald Co., Allentown, PA, pretty red haired lady, white dress, red roses decoration, white ground, blue edge trim, **$35**.

Poster, F. H. Ayres Billiard Tables, Bagatelle Boards, scene of family playing billiards, framed, **$145**.

Plate, Old Barbee Whiskey, Vienna Art, center with peasants and cabin, tin litho, 10" d, C.8 .... **400.00**

Pot scraper, tin litho

MB Flavoring Extracts, Day-Bergwall Co., Milwaukee, Shonk Litho, slight wear, 2-7/8" x 3", C.7+ **375.00**

Nesco Royal Graniteware, 3-1/2" x 3" **500.00**

Print, 30" x 15", Falls City Clothing Co., Imperial Clothes, Louisville, Ky, titled *Elsie,* sgd B. Tichman, woman in red duster and bonnet, printed by Meek Co., Coshocton, OH, copyright 1908, framed **235.00**

Rolling pin, Royal Household Flour, Canadian, china body, wooden handles, blue and red printing, mkd "Hand-painted Nippon" on side 19-1/4" x 3" **230.00**

Print, Robert Smith Ale Brewing Co., Spread Eagle Inn, signed "J.P. 1908, Copyright 1909, Robert Smith Ale Brewing Co., original frame, 20" x 17", some staining, **$25**.

Photo courtesy of Michael Ivankovich Auction

Salesman's sample

Dilworth's Golden Urn Brand Coffee, Pittsburgh, tin litho, 2-1/2" x 2", C.8+ **150.00**

Goldsmith & Sons boxing gloves, leather, lace-up, two 4-1/4" x 2-1/2" gloves stamped "GoldSmith 01" in silver, 2-1/2" x 5-1/4" x 5-3/4" orig box **350.00**

Home plate, rubber, emb lettering, 4" x 4-1/8" **180.00**

Lawnmower, mkd "H. A. Daum, Locksmith" ... **3,950.00**

Toilet, Ariston Silent, Made of Durock, heavy ceramic bowl, orig hardware and seat, spider line to glaze on int., 7-3/4" x 14" x 7" **825.00**

Sharpening stone, Pike Mfg. Co., Pike, NH, gold luster finish metal case, pike fish passing through letter "P," rect whetstone, some wear to stone and luster **45.00**

Many dealers offered vintage advertising objects at the March 2004 Atlantique City Antiques Show. Shown here is part of the Signs of the Tymes booth, which was filled with quality advertising items.

Sign

Algo Spearmint Chewing Gum, cardboard, 4-1/2" x 7-3/4", C.8 .... **160.00**

Collins Honey Scotch Candy, Minneapolis, emb tin, 7" x 19-1/2" **210.00**

Continental Insurance, framed paper in three sections, left panel with Victorian Brooklyn, Continental Insurance Building with signage on front, right panel with New York Continental Insurance Building with multiple horse drawn carriages in front, center with Indian tribe watching as wild animals run out of burning forest, J. Ottoman litho, © 1895, some minor staining to orig matting, 34-1/2" h, 68-1/2" w.. **1,450.00**

Cracker Jack The More You Eat, The More You Want, F. W. Rueckheim & Bros., Chicago, mother holding child reaching for box, 1900, 14-1/2" x 10-3/4", C.8.5 .... **5,000.00**

Dakota Maid Flour, emb tin litho, yellow and blue, 9" x 19-1/2", C.8+ **120.00**

De Laval Cream Separators, tin, emb frame **2,800.00**

Drink Palmer's Root Beer, It's Better, Palmer Candy Co., Kaufman, TX, heavy porcelain, slightly curved, 14" x 21", C.8+ **300.00**

Drink Moxie, emb tin litho, 6-1/4" x 19", C.9 .... **220.00**

Elgin Watch, reverse painting on glass, trademark Father Time, gold on black, framed, 23-1/2" h, 17-1/2" w..... **500.00**

Enjoy Hires, it's always pure, emb tin litho, girl in red hat, 9-3/4" x 27-3/4", C.8+ . **475.00**

Enjoy Hires Healthful Delicious, 9-1/2" x 27-1/2", emb tin litho, C.7.5 ..... **250.00**

Everybody Likes Popsicle Refreshing Easy to Eat, emb tin litho, red, black, and yellow, 9-7/8" x 27-3/4", C.8+ **325.00**

Foster Hose Supporters, celluloid, 17" x 9" **425.00**

Gail Borden Col's Eagle Brand Condensed Milk, cardboard litho, puppy drinking from sleep baby's glass nursing bottle, 15" x 10-1/2", C.8- **450.00**

Georgia Stages, Inc. Ticket Office, Bus Station, porcelain, double-sided, graphics of bus, 1930s **10,500.00**

Can, tin, "Watkins Baking Powder, Purity Guaranteed, J.R. Watkins Co., Winona, Minn.," full, 1 lb, **$60**.

Container, paper, tin top/bottom, Gold Dust Scouring Cleanser, Lever Brothers Co., Cambridge, Mass., 14 oz, **$180**.

Festoon, cardboard, five pieces, Drink Dr. Pepper, Good For Life logo, 1930s-1940s, some cardboard missing, medium/heavy bends, C. 7-7.5, approx. 10' l, **$8,800**.

(Photo courtesy of Gary Metz, Muddy River Trading Co.)

Thermometer, Hills Bros. Coffee, porcelain, Beach, Coshocton, Ohio, dated 1915, 8-3/4" w, 21" h, **$825**.

Photo courtesy of Past Tyme Pleasures Auction.

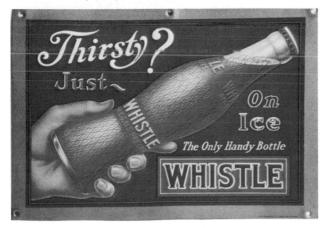

Sign, Thirsty, Just Whistle, embossed tin, litho by American Art Works, 9-3/4" l, 6-3/4" h, **$650**.

Photo courtesy of Past Tyme Pleasures Auction.

Sign, litho tin, yellow, red, white, and black, Columbia Records, Accredited Dealer, **$125**.

Sign, Fatima, A Sensible Cigarette, tin litho, multicolored pack of cigarettes, green background, 12" x 8-1/2", **$165**.

Photo courtesy of Dotta Auction Co., Inc

Good Humor Ice Cream, six-color porcelain, 1930s, 18" x 26", C.8+ **1,200.00**
John P. Squire & Co., self framed emb tin, pig in center, titled "Squires Arlington, Hams-Bacon-Sausage," © 1906, 24" h, 20" w ... **800.00**
Jersey Crème The Perfect Drink At Fountains, 5¢ Also in Bottles, two-sided tin litho flange, yellow and black, 6" d, C.9 .... **725.00**
Kis-Me-Gum, emb cardboard diecut, lady in diaphanous top, ©1905, framed, 8" h, 13" w **500.00**
Korbel California Champagne, tin litho over cardboard, 13" x 19", C.8 .... **250.00**
Lee Union-Alls, porcelain **2,800.00**
McCormick, The King of the Harvest, stone litho, image of well dressed farmer harvesting in field with team of horses, 15-1/2" x 21-1/2", C.8 .... **475.00**
Merry Widow Gum, cardboard, hanging type, 8" x 3", C.8 .... **375.00**

Sign, Buster Brown Bread – Branch of Golden Sheaf Bakery, featuring Buster Brown & Tige, self-framed tin, 30" x 22", **$1,500**.

Photo courtesy of Joy Luke Auctions.

Pearl Oil, flanged tin, diecut kerosene can shape **3,100.00**
Star Brand Shoes, self framed tin, bust of young lady with flowing hair, advertising "Women's Mayflower Shoe, $2.50," some overall spotting, 26" h, 19" w **300.00**
Sterling Super-Bru, Sterling Brewers, Evansville, IN, emb tin, trapezoid, 17-5/8" x 9-3/8", C.8.5+ **450.00**
Sunkist Grower, porcelain, black, white, and red, green border, 11-1/2" x 19-1/2" **375.00**
Tom Keene Cigar, curved corner type, heavy porcelain, orig Ingram-Richardson paper manufacturer's label on back, 15" x 14-3/4", C.8.5 ..... **575.00**
United Motor Service, porcelain, double sided **3,000.00**
Valentine's Valspar Varnish, It's The Coat That Makes The Boat, hanging, tin litho over cardboard, man varnishing 1920s wooden racing boat, 13" x 19", C.8+ **3,400.00**
Wonder Bread, porcelain, dark blue, red, and white, 8-5/8" x 20, C.8 .... **375.00**
Woolworth's, fiberboard, diamond-shape, "Woolworth's, Satisfaction Guaranteed, Replacement Or Money Refunded," white and black letters, red and white ground, some paint chipping and flaking **35.00**
W W W Rings, tin over cardboard, lady in vintage clothing at college football game, some damage, 9-1/4" h, 6-1/4" l **100.00**
Y & S Licorice, figural, pc of black licorice, orig paper label, hanging, 18" x 3-1/2", C.8- **275.00**

Zenith Radios, enamel, bright blue and white letters on red field, yellow background, "Long Distance Radio," 60" l, 18" w **200.00**

Spinner top
Hurd Shoes, black and white celluloid, wooden red spinner dowel, Parisian Novelty Co., maker name on rim curl, 1930s............................ **20.00**
Poll-Parrot Shoes, litho tin, wooden spinner dowel, red and yellow parrot striding between black shoes, yellow background, red rim, red star logo, 1930s.................. **25.00**
Woodmen of the World, blue lettering on white celluloid, wooden red spinner dowel, Parisian Novelty Co., maker name on rim curl, 1930s **18.00**

Store bin, tin litho
Beech Nut Chewing Tobacco, slant front, green ground, white lettering, 6" w, 10" l, 8" h **400.00**
Light Sweet Burley Tobacco, Spaulding Merrick, 10-3/4" x 8-1/4", C.8.................. **210.00**
Sure Shot Chewing Tobacco, graphic of Indian brave taking aim with bow and arrow, 6-1/2" x 15-1/4" x 10-1/4", C.8++ **950.00**
Sweet Cuba Tobacco, slant front, 10" l, 8" w **365.00**
Sweet Mist Chewing Tobacco, children in fountain, 11-1/2" x 8-1/4", C.8.................. **300.00**
Tiger Chewing Tobacco, Lorrilard Co., round, blue, 11-3/4" h, 8-3/4" d **850.00**

Tape measure
Fox's Guernsey Dairy, black lettering on yellow ground, red rim, four red carnations on black ground on reverse **25.00**
Sears, Roebuck & Co., white lettering, black ground, lightning bolt-style lettering for "WLS" (World's Largest Store,) red, white, blue, and green stylized floral design on back **15.00**

Thermometer
Calumet Baking Powder, wood, black, red, and white, yellow ground, 27" x 7-1/4", C.8+........................ **1,100.00**

Hills Bros. Coffee, porcelain, 1915, 8-3/4" w, 21" h ... **825.00**

Kentucky Club Pure Tobacco, painted metal, 38-1/2" x 8", C.8++ **200.00**

Wool Soap, black and white, metal case, glass front, 1895 copyright, 6" d **600.00**

Tins: left: Chicago Assortment, candy; Lady Churchill; Muriel 5 cent; Oceanic Cut Plug, the lot sold for **$130**.

Photo courtesy of Joy Luke.

Tin, miscellaneous

Busy Biddy Spice, Davies Strass Stauffer Co., red, white, and black, 3-1/8" x 1-3/4" x 1-1/4", C.7.5+ **120.00**

Cadette Tooth Powder, figural tin litho soldier, red cap and coat, full, 7-3/8" x 2-1/4" x 1-1/4", C.8 .... **625.00**

F. W. Cough Drops, Geo Miller & Co., Phila, "Cured My Cough," detailed graphics, 8" x 5-1/8" x 5-1/8", C.9 .... **1,400.00**

Planters Nuts & Chocolate Co., Egyptian design on lid and sides, c1919, 6-1/4" d, 4" h, C.8 .... **1,050.00**

Popeye Pop Corn, Purity Mills, Dixon, IL, pry lid, 4-3/4" x 3-1/4" x 2-1/8", C.8++ . **160.00**

W. Phillips Ltd., London, biscuits, Egyptian images on shaped hinged lid, 6" x 6-3/4" x 3-1/8," C.8- **90.00**

Tip tray, Cunard Lines, *Aquitania* ocean liner, tin litho, 4-5/8" x 6-5/8", C.8+ **350.00**

Tobacco tin, tin litho

Bulldog Smoking Tobacco, Lowville Buffington Co., vertical pocket, 4-1/2" x 3" x 7/8", C.8 .... **675.00**

Checkers, Weisert Bros, St. Louis, vertical pocket, white, black, and red, 4-1/2" x 3" x 7/8", C.8.5 .... **525.00**

C.H.Y.P. Inter-Collegiate Mixture, 2-1/4" x 4-1/2" x 3-3/8", C.8- **160.00**

Crane's Private Mixture, House of Crane, Indianapolis, vertical pocket, 4-1/4" x 3-3/8" x 1-1/4", C.8 .... **425.00**

Dixie Queen, canister, trademark girl in large hat on both sides, 6-1/2" x 4-1/4", C.8.5 .... **600.00**

Forest & Stream, Imperial Tobacco Co., Canada, vertical pocket, fisherman in canoe, 4-1/8" x 3" x 7/8", C.8 .... **475.00**

Guide Pipe & Cigarette Tobacco, Larus & Bros., vertical pocket, 4-1/4" x 3" x 7/8", C.8+ **230.00**

Long Distance, Scotten Dillon Co., pail, multicolored graphics with battleship, 6-1/2" x 5-1/2", C.8+ ... **170.00**

North Pole Tobacco, United States Tobacco Co., hinged box, 3-1/8" x 6-1/8" x 3-7/8", C.8+ **220.00**

Pat Hand, Globe Tobacco Co., vertical pocket, full, 2-3/4" x 2-1/2" x 1-3/8", C.8.5 .... **130.00**

Paul Jones, shield with Paul Jones on front, image of battleship on back, vertical pocket, 4-1/2" x 3" x 7/8", C.8+ **1,750.00**

Pipe Major, Brown & Williamson, vertical pocket, 4-1/2" x 3" x 7/8", C.8+ ... **325.00**

Princeton Mixture, Marburg Bros., paper label, 4-1/2" x 3" x 1-7/8", C.8+ **400.00**

Puritan, Phillip Morris, vertical pocket, 4-3/8" x 3" x 7/8", C.8.5 .... **300.00**

Seal of North Carolina, Marburg Bros., canister, multicolored graphic trademark on both sides, 6-1/2" x 4-7/8", C.8+ ... **375.00**

Trout-Line, vertical pocket, fly fisherman in stream, 3-3/4" x 3-1/2" x 1-1/8", C.8++ . **675.00**

Weyman's Cutty Pipe, canister, green ground, red and yellow lettering, 13-1/2" x 10-1/4" x 9-3/8", C.8.5 .... **1,400.00**

Whip, Patterson Bros., vertical pocket, rider in red coat, white pants, black boots, brown horse's head, 4-1/2" x 3" x 7/8", C.8- **850.00**

White Manor, Penn Tobacco, vertical pocket, 3" x 3-1/2" x 1", C.8++ **210.00**

Token, Sambo's Coffee, 1-1/2" d, wooden, printed in red on both sides, one side with patriotic design featuring coffee mug, inscription "What This Country Needs Is A Good 10 Cent Cup of Coffee-Sambo's Has It," reverse inscribed "Sambo's Restaurants Anywhere," late 1970s **10.00**

Toy, Oscar Mayer Wienermobile, plastic and vinyl body, bright orange, blue, white, silver, black, and red, **$225**.

Trade card, Jas A Armstrong, Druggist, Camden, NJ, Card No. 20, Design 1, framed, **$15**.

Trade card

Ayer's Sarsaparilla, "Ayer's Sarsaparilla Makes the Weak Strong," two gentlemen **18.00**

Child's & Staples, Gilbertsville, ME, young girl chasing butterfly, 2-3/4" x 4-1/2" **12.00**

Trade card, Metropolitan Life Insurance Co., "The Leading Industrial Insurance Company of America," little girl standing next to chair, branch addresses on other side, copyright 1902, scrolling borders, oversized, **$45**

Czar Baking Powder, black woman and boy with giant biscuit **25.00**

8th Wonder or Engle Clock, Capt J. Reid and his wife standing next to giant mechanical clock built by Hazelton, PA, jewelry and watchmaker, c1890, 3" x 5-1/4" **5.00**

Granite Iron Ware, three ladies gossiping over tea **25.00**

Heinz Apple Butter, diecut, pickle shape **60.00**

Hoyt's German Cologne, E. M. Hoyt & Co., mother cat and kittens **25.00**

J. & P. Coats, Best Silk Thread, "We Never Fade," black youngster and spool of thread **18.00**

New Essay Lawn Mower, scene of Statue of Liberty, New York harbor **35.00**

Norton Bros., sign and tin manufacturers, c1870, 2-3/4" x 4" **575.00**

Perry Davis, Pain Killer for Wounds, armored man of war ships battle scene **25.00**

Reid's Flower Seeds, two high wheeled bicyclers admiring flowers held by three ladies **25.00**

Scott's Emulsion of Cod Liver Oil, man with large fish over back, vertical format..... **20.00**

Singer Manufacturing Co., choir of children singing as birds listen **20.00**

Clark's O.N.T., set of four, multicolored image of pretty blond girl on front in various activities, light green border, blue promo text on back, 1883, each 3-3/4" x 6-1/2", **$30**.

Photo courtesy of Hake's Americana & Collectibles.

Solar Tip Shoes, Girard College, Philadelphia, Where Boys Wear Our Solar Tip Shoes........................... **20.00**

Thompson's Glove Fitting Corsets, lady and cupids **35.00**

White Sewing Machine Co., elves working at sewing machine **15.00**

Wall pocket, embossed multicolored stiff paper, woodland scene, text on pocket "Compliments of L. F. Harpel, General Merchandise, Richlandtown, Pa," **$35**.

Tray, tin litho

J. Leisy Brewing, Cleveland, OH, multicolored graphic of factory, horse-drawn delivery wagons, oval, 13-5/8" x 16-5/8", C.8+ **775.00**

Nova Kola, American Art Works, center graphic of well dressed couple clinging to world while raising glasses together, 13-1/4" x 13-1/4", C.8 .... **375.00**

Orange Julep, girl at beach, 1920s, 13-1/4" x 10-1/4" x 1-1/4", C.8+ **210.00**

Pabst Brewerys, black ground, gold dec, multicolored graphic of factory, rect, 12-1/4" x 17-1/4", C.8++ **550.00**

Robinson's Sons Pilsner Beer, 12" d, C.8.................... **575.00**

Stroh's Lager Beer, Detroit, heavy porcelain enamel center insert, 12" d, C.8+ **1,050.00**

Watch fob

Corby's Canadian Whiskey, silvered white metal frame, four large flower blossoms surround color insert of pretty woman reclining against stone wall, robe falling open, Whitehead & Hoag **175.00**

Savage Arms, emb metal, pointing Indian chief, painted head band, orig patina, 1-5/8" d **325.00**

AGATA GLASS

History: Agata glass was invented in 1887 by Joseph Locke of the New England Glass Company, Cambridge, Massachusetts.

Agata glass was produced by coating a piece of peachblow glass with metallic stain, spattering the surface with alcohol, and firing. The resulting high-gloss, mottled finish looked like oil droplets floating on a watery surface. Shading usually ranged from opaque pink to dark rose, although pieces in a pastel opaque green also exist. A few pieces have been found in a satin finish.

Bowl, crimped rim, Wild Rose shading, strong mineral staining, 8-1/4" d, 3-1/8" h, ex-Maude Feld, **$2,250**.

Photo courtesy of Early Auction Co.

Bowl

5-1/2" d, 3-1/2" h, waisted, crimped trefoil rim, overall mineral staining, ex-Maude Feld............................. **750.00**

8-1/4" d, 3-1/8" h, crimped rim, Wild Rose shading, strong mineral staining, ex-Maude Feld.......................... **2,250.00**

Celery vase, 6-1/4" h, satin, very heavy staining............. **8,960.00**

Cruet, 5-3/4" h, flat bottom **5,320.00**

Tankard pitcher, 8-1/2" h, tapering cylindrical body, Wild Rose with strong all over mineral staining, ex-Maude Feld **5,000.00**

Tankard pitcher, tapering cylindrical body, Wild Rose with strong all over mineral staining, 8-1/2" h, ex-Maude Feld, **$5,000**.

Photo courtesy of Early Auction Co.

Toothpick holder, tricorn, gold metallic tracery and mottling **645.00**
Tumbler, 3-3/4" h, gold tracery, peachblow ground, black splotches **635.00**
Vase
5" h, bowl shape, mottled blue mineral stain on matte ground, ex-Maude Feld....... **10,000.00**
7" h, lily, Wild Rose shading, mineral staining **700.00**
7-1/4" h, lily, shades from salmon pink to cream, ex-Maude Feld.............. **1,200.00**
10-1/4" h, Morgan, Wild Rose color, overall mineral staining, orig amber griffin holder, orig Maude Feld label, ex-Maude Feld.......................... **5,250.00**
Water pitcher, 7" h, amethyst staining framed with perfect gold, 5" crack to body..... **200.00**

AMBERINA GLASS

History:
Joseph Locke developed Amberina glass in 1883 for the New England Glass

Works "Amberina," a trade name, describes a transparent glass that shades from deep ruby to amber. It was made by adding powdered gold to the ingredients for an amber-glass batch. A portion of the glass was reheated later to produce the shading effect. Usually it was the bottom that was reheated to form the deep red; however, reverse examples have been found.

Most early Amberina is flint-quality glass, blown or pattern molded. Patterns include Diamond Quilted, Daisy and Button, Venetian Diamond, Diamond and Star, and Thumbprint.

In addition to the New England Glass Works, the Mount Washington Glass Company of New Bedford, Massachusetts, copied the glass in the 1880s and sold it at first under the Amberina trade name and later as "Rose Amber." It is difficult to distinguish pieces from these two New England factories. Boston and Sandwich Glass Works never produced the glass.

Amberina glass also was made in the 1890s by several Midwest factories, among which was Hobbs, Brockunier & Co. Trade names included "Ruby Amber Ware" and "Watermelon." The Midwest glass shaded from cranberry to amber, and the color resulted from the application of a thin flashing of cranberry to the reheated portion. This created a sharp demarcation between the two colors. This less-expensive version was the death knell for the New England variety.

In 1884, Edward D. Libbey was given the use of the trade name "Amberina" by the New England Glass Works. Production took place during 1900, but ceased shortly thereafter. In the 1920s, Edward Libbey renewed production at his Toledo, Ohio, plant for a short period. The glass was of high quality.

Marks: Amberina made by Edward Libbey in the 1920s is marked "Libbey" in script on the pontil.

Reproduction Alert:
Reproductions abound.

Additional Listings: Libbey, Mount Washington.

For more information, see *Warman's Glass*, 4th edition.

Basket, 10-1/2" l, wide flared rim, enameled and gilt dec florals, polished pontil, mounted with finely sculpted gilt bronze dragon form handle, Victorian **690.00**
Biscuit jar, 5" h, Diamond Quilted pattern, polished pontil, lid missing......................... **50.00**
Bonbon, 6-1/2" d, double reeded handles................. **90.00**

Bottle, 8" h, Coin Spot pattern, attributed to Libbey **375.00**
Bowl
5" l sides, 2" h, tricorn, amber base, Mt Washington.. **235.00**
5-1/8" h, crimson shading to amber, Diamond Quilted pattern, applied amber peaked overlay extends mid-length, orig Libbey paper label, ex-Maude....... **2,100.00**

Atomizer, cylindrical bottle, patterned amberina glass, pewter top for atomizer, 7-1/4" h, missing bulb, $250.
Photo courtesy of Alderfer Auction Co.

Celery vase, 6-1/2" h, cylindrical, tightly crimped thumbprint pattern **575.00**
Compote, 7-1/4" d, 8-3/8" h, catalog #3017, Libbey acid stamp mark, partial paper label, ex-Maud Feld............... **4,000.00**
Creamer, 4-1/2" h, Thumbprint pattern, polished pontil, Victorian **85.00**
Cruet
5-1/2" h, Inverted Thumbprint pattern, fuchsia trefoil spout, neck, and shoulder, Mt. Washington................. **435.00**
6" h, Inverted Thumbprint pattern, gilt dec, replaced stopper, wear to gilt...... **90.00**
6" h, Thumbprint pattern, replaced stopper, Victorian **95.00**
Decanter, 12" h, Optic Diamond Quilted pattern, solid amber faceted stopper **475.00**
Demitasse cup, 2-1/8" h, 16 optic panels, applied reeded handle **185.00**
Finger bowl, 5-1/2" d, crimped ruffled rim...................... **200.00**
Juice glass, 3-3/4" h, Coin Spot pattern **75.00**
Lemonade, 5" h, ribbed, applied amber ring handle, price for set of three........................... **425.00**
Miniature pitcher, 3" h, crimson sq mouth extends to amber bulbous body, Inverted Coin Dot pattern, applied reeded handle **400.00**

Mug, 3-7/8" h **1,000.00**
Nappy, 6" l, handle, enameled dec, polished pontil, Victorian **140.00**

Punch cup
  2-1/2" d, Optic Diamond Quilted pattern, fuchsia to amber body with 20 panels, applied ribbed handle, New England **185.00**
  2-3/4" h, Coin Spot pattern, reverse amberina.......... **50.00**
  3-1/2" h, Optic Ribbed pattern, applied reeded handle.......................... **100.00**
Shot glass, 2-1/4" h, faint Diamond Quilted pattern, attributed to Brayden Pairpoint **110.00**
Spooner, 4-3/4" h, Diamond Quilted pattern, crimped scalloped rim **250.00**
Sugar, 4-1/4" h, ovoid, Coin Spot pattern, two applied reeded handles **450.00**
Sweetmeat, 6" d, Baby Thumbprint pattern, applied colorless florals, feet, and rim, polished pontil **320.00**
Syrup pitcher, Hobnail pattern, orig pewter top std "Pat. Jan 29 84," Hobbs, Brockunier & Co., three hobs chipped......... **300.00**
Tankard pitcher, 4-1/4" h, New England, Optic Diamond Quilt pattern............................. **685.00**

Dish, expanded diamond pattern, 5" diameter, **$90**.
Photo courtesy of Joy Luke.

Toothpick holder, 2-1/4" h, sq mouth **250.00**
Tumbler
  3-3/4" h, Coin Spot pattern, ground rim **125.00**
  4" h, Coin Spot pattern, barrel shape.......................... **165.00**
Vase
  6-3/4" h, tri-fold lily blossom **250.00**
  8" h, Swirl pattern, applied amber rigaree around crown-form top, applied amber petal

feet, polished pontil, Victorian **150.00**
  8-1/4" h, swirled mold, enameled flowers, gilt scrolling, polished pontil, French, c1890............. **150.00**
  9-1/4" h, 4-1/4" w tri-fold lily blossom, 16 optic ribs, deep fuchsia and honey amber, attributed to Mt. Washington **485.00**

Water pitcher
  5-1/2" h, ovoid, sq mouth, Thumbprint pattern, faint optic ribbing at rim, applied reeded handle........................ **175.00**
  7" h, Coin Spot pattern, ftd, applied colorless reeded handle........................ **225.00**
  8 h, Optic Ribbed pattern, applied amber reeded handle **100.00**
  8-1/4" h, bulbous, tricorn mouth shades to amber Coin Spot patterned body, applied reeded amber handle. **295.00**
Wine, 4-3/4" h, Optic Ribbed pattern............................. **300.00**

AMBERINA GLASS, PLATED

History: The New England Glass Company, Cambridge, Massachusetts, first made plated amberina in 1886; Edward Libbey patented the process for the company in 1889.

Plated amberina was made by taking a gather of chartreuse or cream opalescent glass, dipping it in Amberina, and working the two, often utilizing a mold. The finished product had a deep amber to deep ruby red shading, a fiery opalescent lining, and often vertical ribbing for enhancement. Designs ranged from simple forms to complex pieces with collars, feet, gilding, and etching.

A cased Wheeling glass of similar appearance had an opaque white lining but is not opalescent and does not have a ribbed body.

Cruet, 7" h, high color, cut amber faceted stopper, applied amber handle, ex-Maud Feld.. **9,000.00**
Finger bowl, 51/2" d, ruffled, tightly crimped rim with 12 distinct ribs **5,750.00**
Lemonade, 5-1/4" h, applied amber handle, ex-Maude Feld **2,750.00**

Water pitcher, bulbous, deep mahogany extending to cream on lower body, 12 well defined protruding ribs, trefoil spout, applied amber handle, 7-1/2" h, ex-Maude Feld, **$14,000**.
Photo courtesy of Early Auction Co.

Pitcher, 8" h, very rare, one of three known, ex-Maude Feld **37,520.00**
Toothpick holder, 2-1/4" h **15,680.00**
Tumbler, 3-3/4" h, thin layered bottom with rare citron hue, ex-Maude Feld.................. **1,600.00**
Vase
  8" h, lily **4,480.00**
  9-5/8" h, lily, deep crimson shading to custard yellow, clear amber raised disc base, orig Maude B. Feld label **6,000.00**
Water carafe, 8-1/2" h, bulbous body, circular neck, 12 protruding amber ribs, orig New England Glass Works paper label, ex-Maude Feld. **42,000.00**
Water pitcher, 7-1/2" h, bulbous, deep mahogany extending to cream on lower body, 12 well-defined protruding ribs, trefoil spout, applied amber handle, ex-Maude Feld........... **14,000.00**

AMERICAN HAND-PAINTED CHINA

History: The American china painting movement began in 1876 and remained popular over the next 50 years. Thousands of artisans—professionals and amateur—decorated tableware, desk accessories, dresser sets, and many other items with floral, fruits, and conventional geometric designs and occasionally with portraits, birds, and landscapes. Some American firms, such as Lenox and Willetts Manufacturing Co. of Trenton, New Jersey, produced Belleek, a special type of porcelain that china painters decorated, but a majority of porcelain was imported from France, Germany, Austria, Czechoslovakia, and Japan.

Marks: American-painted porcelains bear foreign factory marks. However, the American style was distinctive, whether naturalistic or conventional (geometric). Some pieces were signed and dated by the artist.

Notes: The quality of the artwork, the amount of detail, and technical excellence—not the amount of gilding or the manufacturer of the porcelain itself—are key pricing factors. Unusual subjects and uncommon forms also influence value.

Bonbon box, 6" d, 3-1/2" h, dec with conventional design of three intertwined peacocks, baby blue base, burnished gold rims and foot, opal luster int., marked "T. & V. Limoges, France," c1892-1907 .... **95.00**

Dresser tray, hand painted pink and white roses, yellow highlights, green leaves, gold scalloped border, gold script on back: "For Mrs. J. Quincy Hunsicker, From Mrs. L. Pfizenmaier, A Merry Christmas, 1904." **$60**

Cake plate, individual, double-handled

7" d, dec with central conventional floral bouquet, sgd "IFP," marked "Schumann, Bavaria".... **20.00**

7-1/8" d, dec with conventional border design, burnished gold rim and handles, sgd "LMC," marked "MADE IN JAPAN," c1925 .... **22.00**

Chamber pot, scene of road and fence by lake, embossed scrolls with gold trim, unsigned, **$195**.

Photo courtesy of Dotta Auction Co., Inc.

Coffee pot, dec with conventional design in enamel, outline in raised paste covered with burnished gold, burnished gold finial and base, marked "CAC, BELLEEK," 1889-1906 .... **600.00**

Compote, ftd, 8-7/8" d, 4-1/4" h, interior dec with cluster of pink and white morning glories and pink butterfly, rim and foot dec with bands of conventional pink butterflies, burnished gold rim and foot, sgd and dated "CL, April 13th, 1881," marked "CFH" **200.00**

Cream soup cup, 4-3/8" d, double handled, dec with conventional border, burnished gold handles and rim, marked "Bavaria," c1900-1915 ...... **25.00**

Creamer and sugar, dec with conventional floral border design in blue and soft green on burnished gold band, burnished gold lips, spout, rims, and handles, ivory ground, sgd "Helen Hurley" **55.00**

Cup and saucer

Decorated with conventional Celtic border design in celadon, light blue border, ivory center, cup bottom and interiors, burnished gold rims and handle, sgd "L.E.S.," marked with crown in double circle, "Victoria, Austria," 1900-20 .... **30.00**

Decorated with conventional swag design of blue flowers, burnished gold rims and handle, sgd "Jane Bent Telin," marked "Favorite Bavaria," 1910-25 .... **45.00**

Dessert set, three pieces, 7-7/16" d plate, dec with forget-me-not clusters, cup and saucer, opal luster on cup interior, burnished gold rims and handle, plate marked with shield, "Thomas, Bavaria," cup and saucer marked "JAPAN," c1925-30 .... **40.00**

Jam jar, 4-3/8" h, 6-3/4" d plate, dec with border design of grapes and leaves, variegated blue enamels, burnished gold ground, yellow luster border band and knob, sgd "L. Vance Phillips, 1917," marked with Belleek palette, "Lenox" **350.00**

Pitcher, red and green grapes, green foliage and vine, shaded ground, gold rim, artist signed "E. Bennett," **$375**.

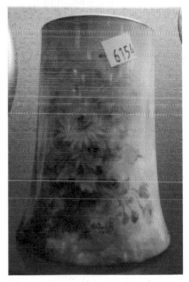

Vase, multicolored pastel strawflowers and foliage, gold rim, artist signed "E. B. John," marked "L Belleek" with palette mark, **$395**.

Vase, pink, yellow, and purple pansies, yellow domed flower frog, **$275**.

Milk pitcher and plate set, 5-11/16" h pitcher, 7-3/8" d plate, dec with conventional design of yellow wild roses, yellow ground, burnished gold rims, handle, and trim, sgd "M.S.C. '90," pitcher marked "H & Co., Limoges," plate marked "CFH/GDM" **75.00**

Olive or bonbon dish, 6" d, ring-handles, dec with conventional border motif in matt antique green, sgd "M.H. Butler," marked "Thomas Bavaria," c1908-15 .... **35.00**

Perfume bottle, stopper, 4-3/4" h, dec with daisies and greenery, ivory ground, burnished gold lip and stopper, marked "O. & E. G. Austria," 1896-1918 .... **45.00**

Pin tray, 5-3/4" l, 4" w, dec with border design of blue and burnished gold moths, connected by burnished gold and black band, ivory ground, burnished gold rim, sgd "E. ARRINDELL, 1-2-18," marked "MZ, Austria" **45.00**

Plate

6-5/8" d, dec with band of conventional style roses and leaves, ivory ground, pale green center, burnished gold rim, sgd "P. M. T.," marked "Bavaria," c1892-1914.. **20.00**

8-1/2" d, dec with clusters of sea shells and sea weeds, black green border band edged with burnished gold scrolls and rim, sgd "C.C.O.," marked with crown and crossed swords, "Bavaria," 1896-1906.................... **65.00**

Rose bowl, 2-7/8" h, dec with band of conventional-style violets and bands in burnished gold, marked "O. & E.G., Royal, Austria," c1898-1918 .... **30.00**

Salt and pepper shakers

3" h, dec with conventional blue-winged insects, burnished gold tops, 1905-20, price for pr **35.00**

4-3/4" w, 2-1/2" h, two-in-one shaker, dec with raised paste garlands cov with burnished gold, accented with turquoise enamel ivory ground, burnished gold tops, handle and foot rim, marked "Germany," c1891-1914 .... **45.00**

Teapot stand, 6-3/8" d, dec with border design of forget-me-not-clusters, burnished gold rim, c1900-1920 .... **45.00**

Vase, 7-7/8" h, dec with two Art Deco-style floral panels in various lusters and burnished gold, sgd "M.D.P. 1920" ... **85.00**

AMERICAN HAND-PAINTED CHINA JEWELRY AND BUTTONS

History: The American china painting movement began in 1876, about the time the mass production of jewelry also occurred. Porcelain manufacturers and distributors offered a variety of porcelain shapes and settings for brooches, pendants, cuff links, and shirt-waist buttons. Thousands of artisans painted flowers, people, landscapes, and conventions (geometric) motifs. The category of hand-painted porcelain jewelry comprises a unique category, separate from costume and fine jewelry. While the materials were inexpensive to produce, the painted decoration was a work of fine art.

Marks: American painted porcelain jewelry bears no factory marks, and is usually unsigned.

Notes: The quality of the artwork, the amount of detail, and technical excellence—not the amount of gilding—are the key pricing factors. Uncommon shapes also influence value.

Belt buckle brooch

1-11/16", x 2-1/4" oval, dec with white pansy, accented with white enamel, burnished gold ground, gold-plated bezel, 1900-17 .... **75.00**

2" x 2-1/2" oval, dec with horse chestnuts, baby blue ground, gold-plated bezel, 1900-17 .... **100.00**

Brooch

7/8" d, pink and ruby rose, leaves, polychrome ground, burnished gold rim, gold-plated bezels, price for pr **50.00**

Brooch, 1-1/2" w, 2" l, oval, violets, ivory ground, burnished gold border superimposed with black line border design of violets and vines, gold-plated bezel, **$75**.

All photos courtesy of Adviser Dorothy Kamm.

7/8" sq, diamond shape, dec with waterscape with water lilies, white enamel highlights, burnished with gold border, brass bezel, c1920-40.. **35.00**

1" d, dec with Colonial dame, burnished gold rim, brass bezel, c1890-1910........ **40.00**

1" x 1", cross-shape, dec with pink and ruby roses, polychrome ground, tips dec with raised paste dots, burnished gold gold-plated bezel with tubular hinge **80.00**

1" x 3/4" rectangle, Florida landscape in white on platinum ground, sterling silver bezel, c1920-40 .. **75.00**

1-1/4" x 1-4/8" oval, dec with woman's portrait surrounded by forget-me-nots, ivory ground, white enamel highlights, framed by burnished gold raised paste scrolls and dots, gold-plated bezel............................. **80.00**

1-7/16" x 1-7/8" oval, dec with pink roses, burnished gold border, sgd "Albrecht," brass bezel **65.00**

1-1/2" x 2", oval, dec with Art Nouveau-style woman's head and neck, poppies in her hair, gold-plated bezel **90.00**

1-1/2" x 2" oval, dec with stained glass-like conventional design in polychrome colors and burnished gold, gold-plated bezel, 1905-15 .... **65.00**

1-3/4" d, dec with daisy, burnished gold border, brass bezel, c1900-10 .... **45.00**

1-7/8" w, crescent shape, dec with dark pink roses, burnished gold tips, brass bezel, 1900-20 .... **45.00**

1-13/16" x 2-3/16" oval, dec with columbine and greenery, polychrome ground, burnished gold trim, gold-plated bezel **75.00**

1-9/16" x 1-7/8" oval, dec with pink roses and greenery on light blue and yellow, burnished gold ground, scrolls, and dots, sgd "E. GARDE," 1920s, gold plated setting **50.00**

1-11/16" x 2-1/8" oval, dec with a tropical landscape, burnished gold rim, sgd "OC" (Olive Commons, St. John's Island, FL, 1908-1920), gold-plated bezel **105.00**

2" x 1-5/8" oval, dec with Art Nouveau-style poppies, burnished gold border, brass bezel, 1856-1915 .... **75.00**

2" x 1-1/2" oval, dec with pink and ruby roses, solid dark blue ground, white enamel highlights, burnished gold border, brass bezel, c1940 .... **65.00**

2-1/16" d, dec with violets, burnished gold rim, brass bezel, 1900-1920 .... **65.00**

2-1/2" l, horseshoe shape, dec with violets, burnished gold tips, brass bezel . **100.00**

Cuff buttons, pr, 3/4" x 1" ovals, dec with lavender flowers, border of burnished gold dots and apple green jewels, burnished gold rims, c1890-1920 .... **40.00**

Shirt waist button, 1" d, with shank, conventional design in raised paste, pastel-colored enamel, cobalt blue ground, burnished gold rim, **$20**.

Dress set

Five pieces: 2" x 2-5/8" belt buckle brooch, oval brass bezel, pr 1" d shirt waist buttons with shanks, pr 1" d shirt waist buttons with sew-through backs, dec with forget-me-nots, black green scalloped borders rimmed in burnished gold, c1900-17 .... **400.00**

Four pieces: 3/4" d shirt waist collar button, three 5/8" d shirt waist buttons, dec with pink roses, white enamel highlights, burnished gold rims, shank backs **60.00**

Flapper pin, 1-5/8" x 2-1/8" oval, dec with stylized woman, burnished gold border, brass bezel, 1924-28 .... **75.00**

Hat pin, 3/4" wide by 1" oval medallion, 6" l shaft, dec with four-leaf clover on burnished gold ground, brass bezel, 1900-20 .... **115.00**

Pendant

1-5/8" x 2-1/8" oval, dec with violets, burnished bold border, brass bezel, c1880-1914.............................. **60.00**

1-3/4" x 1-3/4" oval, dec with forget-me-nots, white enamel highlights, burnished gold rim, brass bezel, c1900-20 .... **50.00**

Shirt-waist button

7/8" sq, with shank, dec with violets entwined around burnished gold fancy letter "J," burnished gold border, sgd with illegible cipher **20.00**

1-3/16" d, with eye, dec with single daisy, burnished gold ground **20.00**

1-3/16" d, with shank, dec with conventional floral design, burnished gold ground. **35.00**

Set, two 7/8" d, three 5/8" d, with shanks, dec with maidenhair fern, pastel polychrome ground, burnished gold borders, price for five-pc set................ **80.00**

AMPHORA

History: The Amphora Porcelain Works was one of several pottery companies located in the Teplitz-Turn region of Bohemia in the late 19th and early 20th centuries. It is best known for art pottery, especially Art Nouveau and Art-Deco pieces.

Marks: Several markings were used, including the name and location of the pottery and the Imperial mark, which included a crown. Prior to World War I, Bohemia was part of the Austro-Hungarian Empire, so the word "Austria" may appear as part of the mark. After World War I, the word "Czechoslovakia" may be part of the mark.

Additional Listings: Teplitz.

Organically shaped vase, four rounded handles above four reticulated flowers, jewel tone and gold, stamped "Amphora, Austria," 7-1/2" h, **$395**.

Photo courtesy of David Rago Auctions, Inc.

Center bowl, 2-1/8" h, incised dec outlined in black, enameled blue-green and pink cabochons, mottled tan matte ground, four legs, circular base **200.00**

Ewer, 14-1/2" h, pink, gold, and green floral dec, gold accents, salamander entwined handle, c1900 .... **575.00**

Lamp base, 12-1/2" h, stoneware, double handles ending in dragons, straw-colored glaze, China, T'ang period (618-920), drilled . **650.00**

Sugar bowl, cov, 6-1/4" d, 4-1/2" h, Art Deco enamel dec, polychrome birds and leaves, stamped mark "15449/30" **280.00**

Umbrella stand, 26-1/2" h, 15" d, emb gleaners, stylized indigo trees, lustered amber glaze, stamped "Amphora (crown) Austria," restoration to base **2,200.00**

Vase, Art Nouveau, body inverted amphora, molded with stylized pointed leaves, base spreading out and curling upward into gilt tendrils attached to the body, glazed in greens and pinks, Austria, early 20th C, 16" h, **$500**.

Photo courtesy of Skinner, Inc.

Vase

5-1/4" h, three buttressed handles dec with naturalistic leafy rose vines, rose hip clusters, matte green rose on mottled brown round, gilt highlights, imp mark and stamp on base **250.00**
6" h, flattened spherical form, shoulder dec with alternating large and small moths in shades of blue, pink, and yellow, raised gilt outline, relief spider webs and enameled disk centers, gilt highlights on green and blue ground, imp "Amphora" in oval, printed "R. S. & K. Turn-Teplitz Bohemia" with maker's device on base **900.00**

Vessel, covered, squatty, Art Deco-style enamel polychrome decoration with birds and leaves, stamped mark "15449/30," 4-1/2" x 6-1/4", **$300**.

Photo courtesy of David Rago Auctions, Inc.

6-1/4" h, 4" d, painted with portrait of Joan of Arc, eagle helmet, enameled garb, mkd "Amphora 1K" and red ink stamp mark **2,600.00**
11-1/8" h, pear shape, extended neck, two tri-part handles, mottled matte green and brown glaze, inscribed cipher, R. S. & K, Teplitz, Bohemia, c1900, crazing, base chip **1,035.00**

Wall plaque, 18-1/2" d, Moorish man and woman in relief, red ground, gilt molded frames, marked "Amphora," price for pr **900.00**

ANIMAL COLLECTIBLES

History: The representation of animals in fine arts, decorative arts, and on utilitarian products dates back to antiquity. Some religions endowed certain animals with mystical properties. Authors throughout written history used human characteristics when portraying animals.

The formation of collectors' clubs and marketing crazes, e.g., flamingo, pig, and penguin, during the 1970s increased the popularity of this collecting field.

Additional Listings: See specific animal collectible categories in *Warman's Americana & Collectibles*.

Cow, platter, blue and white transfer, marked "Victoria Ironstone," **$125**.

Barnyard

Carving, folk art, wood
7" l, peep, painted, c1900, with stand **9,545.00**
9-1/2" l, 2-1/2" w, 8" h, rooster, polychrome red, mustard yellow, and brown, base with indistinct pencil inscription, PA, c1840 .... **4,320.00**
17" l, 15" h, rooster, old cream-colored paint, 3/4 flat body, stand **460.00**

Chopper, 12" l, 7-1/2" d, 7-1/4" h, rooster, iron, fanciful silhouette, incised feather detail, mounted on wooden fragment, with stand, late 18th/early 19th C, lacks wooden handle **1,035.00**

Doorstop, lamb, polychrome glazed molded earthenware, attributed to J Eberly & Co., Strasburg, VA............. **34,100.00**

Figure, sewer tile
5-1/4" l, 5" h, frog on log, hand modeled, tooled bark, inscribed initials "H.S." on base, dark brown, slightly metallic glaze, traces of gold on one end of log **425.00**
7-7/8" h, pig, standing, wearing pants, vest, and bow tie, reddish-brown glaze, few spots of wear **320.00**

Hooked rug, owl in front of a full moon, oval, late 19th C ... **950.00**

Jar, cov, 6" d, 6-1/2" h, stoneware, figure of pig eating from trough on lid, German, some damage to base.... **115.00**

Lithograph, 10" x 7-1/2", *Prize Poultry*, from *Cassell's Poultry Book*, printed by Vincent, Brooks, Day & Son, each specimen titled including "Mr. Henry Belden's Pair of Golden Spangled Polish," etc., French matted, 21-1/8" x 18-1/2" ebonized and parcel gilt frames, England, late 19th C, price for set of eight **1,530.00**

Painting, gouache, 12-1/4" h, 20" w, sheep grazing in hilly pasture, sgd "H. I. Marlatt," (H. Irving Marlatt, Mt. Vernon, NY, 1867-1929, gouache sketch on heavy paper, matted, 22-1/4" h, 29-3/4" w frame, some edge wear **250.00**

Painting, oil on canvas, 29-1/8" h, 36-1/2" w, sheep and lamps in stable, nearby chickens, ornate frame with copper and gold repaint, rebacked on board, revarnished, minor touch up **920.00**

Pull toy, billy goat, gray fur, papier-mâché horns, leather harness, orig cream painted cart with gold and blue stripes, goat moves with rocking motion, one wheel knob replaced, wear, 23" l **815.00**

Tin, Dr. Daniels' Cow Invigorator, 18 oz pry lid tin litho, image of cow on each side, C-8+ .. **275.00**

Puzzle, flock of sheep, 75 pieces, 8-1/4" x 11-1/4", incomplete, no box, **$50**.

Birds

Architectural element, 18-1/2" h, owl, pottery, unglazed, traces of old silver paint, base imp "Owens and Howard, St. Louis, MO," minor hairlines **550.00**

Eagle, cast iron, painted, black with white spots, America, late 19th C, 11" l, 5-1/2" d, 3-1/2" h **250.00**

Figure, sewer tile, 10-1/2" h, horned owl, perched on round pedestal base, orange glaze **450.00**

Plaque, 7" x 4" sight, 11-1/2" x 8-1/2" ebonized frame, pietra dura, colorful parrot on perch, Italian, early 20th C **250.00**

Sculpture, 15-1/2" wingspan, 20" h, eagle, carved wood, standing, spread wings .. **395.00**

Trivet, parrot, pastel central figure with intricate flower and vine pattern, eight triangular feet, Rookwood marks, 1929, 5-3/4" sq **325.00**

Wall shelf, 16-1/2" w, eagle, carved wood, shaped shelf supported by eagle with spread wings, loss to gilt **475.00**

Cats

Bank, 11" h, chalk ware, seated, wearing red bow, minor loss **200.00**

Cane
34-1/2" l, 1-3/4" d x 1-3/4" h carved ivory ball handle with cat face emerging from one side, 1/0" sterling collar with Chester hallmarks for 1903, dark Malacca shaft, 3/4" brass ferrule **450.00**
36" l, 2" w x 3-1/2" carved wood head, nicely detailed features, when button on back is pressed, red eyes change to blue, long red tongue shoots out, 1-1/4" dec silver collar, Malacca shaft, 7/8" replaced brass ferrule, German, c1880 .... **2,020.00**

Figure
3-1/4" h, glass, cast, blue, sgd "Daum France," 20th C **185.00**
3-7/8" h, glass, cast, colorless, sgd "Baccarat," orig box **175.00**
9" l, sewer tile, reclining, hand-tooled eyelashes, white glazed eyes **360.00**
9-1/2" w, 7" d, 17-1/4" h, carved pine, fat cat, incised "E. Sweet," 20th C, cracks **435.00**
13-1/4" h, sewer tile, elongated form, head cocked to one side, curious look, hand tooled eyelashes, metallic glaze, Ohio **660.00**

Painting
Brown Tabby Kitten with a Rose Bow, John Henry Dolph, sgd "JHDolph" lower left, oil on board, 12" x 9", framed, scattered retouch **4,700.00**
Gray Tiger Cat with a Blue Bow, sgd "MABrown" lower right, American School, 19th C, oil on canvas, 17" x 21", framed, minor scattered retouch, varnish inconsistencies **2,000.00**
Sleepy Tabby, Franklin W. Rogers, sgd "F.W. Roger" lower right, label on reverse, oil on canvas, 21" x 17", framed, scattered retouch, varnish inconsistencies, craquelure **1,175.00**

Musical picture, tin figures of adult cat playing fiddle, kittens dancing, tin figures move in conjunction with music box attached to back, German, 8-3/4" x 12", missing key, losses to frame, **$10,450**.

Photo courtesy of Alderfer Auction Co.

The Sleeping Tabby, monogrammed and dated "JLC 1881" lower left, American School, 19th C, oil on canvas, 9" x 12", framed, scattered retouch, craquelure **3,300.00**

Stamp box, 4-3/4" l, carved fruitwood, figural cat lying inside shoe, glass eyes, hinged lid, early 20th C **225.00**

Dogs

Ashtray, Scottish Terrier, sq, porcelain, center black terrier, images of hounds and rabbits, green and white ground, Hermes **50.00**

Cane
35" l, 3-1/2" l x 1-1/2" h carved elephant ivory handle, pug family consisting of father, mother, three pups in line, 1" gold filled collar dec in "C" scrolls, orig owner's elaborate initials, ebony shaft carved with simulated thorns, 1-1/8" burnished brass and iron ferrule, English, c1890 .... **1,570.00**
35-1/4" l, 1-3/4" d x 4-3/4" h carved ivory handle, performing poodle, wearing toy soldier's cap, holding toy gun, 3/4" silver collar, tan Malacca shaft, 1" replaced brass ferrule, England, c1890 .... **1,120.00**
36-1/2" l, 2-1/2" w x 2" h purple quartz handle carved as French bulldog, upright ears, dec gold plated collar, ebony shaft, 1" brass and iron ferrule, Continental, c1890 .... **950.00**

Store display, collie, papier-mâché and synthetic fur, life size, **$850**.

36-7/8" l, 2" w x 2-3/4" h elephant ivory handle carved as mastiff emerging from seashell, brown glass eyes, maccassar ebony shaft, 1-1/2" white metal and iron ferrule, Continental, c1890... **1,680.00**
Figure, bronze, 5" l, 3-1/2" h, terrier with bone, bronze dog standing possessively over carved ivory bone on ground before him, oblong base, mold incised signature for Friedrich Gornik, founder's monogram AR **900.00**

Dog, boot scraper, bronze, dachshund shape, detailed, **$115**.

Photo courtesy of Dotta Auction Co., Inc.

Figure, clay
7" w, 3-1/2" d, 9-1/2" h, seated, freestanding front legs, yellow Ohio clay, mottled green glaze on dog, brown dec on dog, black eyes, blue ink stamp label "E. Houghton & Co. Dalton, Ohio, 1928," hairline in base **1,450.00**
7-1/4" l, 9-1/4" h, seated, freestanding front legs, gray clay, cream-colored glaze, brown and blue polka dots, long tail with brown, one ear brown, other blue, chips on base........................ **6,270.00**

8-1/8" h, Ohio white clay, seated, short ears and tail, long jowls, grown glaze, chip on back of base, small flake on ear **110.00**
10" h, Newcomerstown, Ohio, pottery, seated, unglazed clay, good detail, shallow front chip.......................... **3,750.00**
Figure, pearlware, 2-7/8" l, 3-1/4" h, long hair seated dog, white, brown and gold spots, minor flakes on base, short hairline **520.00**

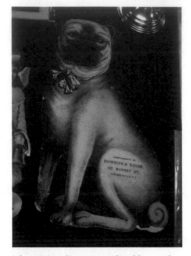

Advertising diecut, pug dog, blue neck ribbon with bell, printed "Compliments of Downing & Welsh, 197 Burnet St, New Brunswick, NJ," back plain, some wear and loss, 11" h, **$20**.

Figure, sewer tile
7-1/2" h, seated, hand modeled, tooled fur and facial features, mat glaze with metallic speckles, traces of white paint **110.00**
10-1/2" l, 5-1/2" w, 11-1/2" h, Collie, standing, reddish brown glaze, rect molded base, firing separations, small chips on ears.............. **935.00**
11" h, seated, molded with hand tooled details on ears and face, long eye lashes, glaze varies from light tan to dark reddish brown, Ohio, minor flakes on base .. **660.00**
Figure, stoneware, 13-1/2" h, Spaniels, tan and brown speckled matte glaze, glass eyes, oval bases, England, c1875, repair to base of one, glaze flakes, price for pr
.... **6,465.00**

Folk art painting, King Charles spaniel and her two pups, 8-7/8" x 11"............................. **2,800.00**
Jewelry, brooch
Micromosaic, recumbent King Charles spaniel, gold ropetwist frame, minor lead solder on verso........... **900.00**
Platinum and diamond, terrier, pave setting, green stone eyes **1,725.00**
Reverse painted crystal, standing boxer, oval 14k gold frame, sgd "W. F. Marcus" **920.00**
Painting, pastel on paper
13-1/4" x 17-1/4", naughty puppy worrying a piece of lace, unsigned, American School, 19th C, molded gilt frame, rippling **1,295.00**
12-1/2" x 17-1/4", puppy sleeping on green cushion, unsigned, American School, 19th C, gilt frame, small ear at center right edge..... **1,175.00**

Dog collar, leather, decorated with brass French boxer dog heads, early 20th C, 15" l, **$225**.

Photo courtesy of Wiederseim Associates, Inc.

Shaving mug, 4-1/8" x 3-3/4", hp, two hunting dogs, brown background, mkd "St. Louis Electronic Grinding Co., Barber Supplies," some wear to gold trim, crack in ring handle **120.00**
Vase, 10" h, Lenox, marked "Hunter Arms Co., First Prize, Class A," image of pointer in clearing, sgd "Delan," stamped Lenox logo **3,665.00**
Watch fob, four graduated round 14k gold plaques depicting dog's heads in repoussé, suspended by trace link chains, monogrammed, swivel clasp, 15.0 dwt **575.00**

Horses

Blanket, 68" sq, needlework design of horse, red ground, diamond design in field, black border with cross-stitched multicolored floral design, red yarn fringe, wool backing, reverse stitched with owner's name "Jacob Weber 1871," minor restoration, moth damage in backing **175.00**

Book, *Rodeo, A Collection of Tales & Sketches by R. B. Cunningham Graham,* selected by A. F. Tschiffeley, Literary Guild, 1936 .... **10.00**

Cane, 35-3/4" l, 4" l x 2-1/4" h elephant ivory handle carved as two riding horse heads, carved simulated leather tack, 1/2" sterling collar marked "Brigg," London hallmarks for 1897, ebony shaft, 7/8" brass and iron ferrule **1,350.00**

Condiment set, 5" l, 3-5/8" h, electroplate, base formed as horseshoe, spur-form handle, toothpick holder flanked by boot form castor, mustard pot with whip-form spoon, central jockey cap open salt, Elkington & Co., England, late 19th C **175.00**

Horse, award, crystal Tiffany vase, engraved "Pennsylvania Horse Breeders Association 1993 Iroquois Award, Pennfield Farms, Inc., breeder of Fleeced," $125.

Figure, carved and painted wood

7-1/2" h, laminated, stylized form, grommet eyes, orig glossy black paint, America, late 19th C, losses to tail **1,610.00**

10-1/2" l, 14-1/2" h, articulated circus figure with red textile shoulder girth, riding horse with glass bead eyes, attributed to Connecticut, c1900-10, stand, minor wear, paint imperfections.. **2,530.00**

Figure, porcelain

18" l, 20" h, man in colonial dress riding white horse **290.00**

18" l, 20" h, woman in colonial dress riding dappled brown horse **660.00**

Painting, oil on canvas, 18-1/4" x 24-1/4", portrait of horse standing in barnyard, sgd and dated "E. Corbet 1881" lower right, identified as Irish race horse by note on reverse, framed, small areas of paint loss, craquelure, varnish inconsistencies ,,,,,,,,,,,,,,,,,,,,,,,,,,,,,,,,,,,,,, **2,000.00**

Plate, Tally Ho pattern, Johnson Bros., price for service of 12, plus serving pieces and punch bowl, $950.

Pull toy, 11-1/4" l, painted and laminated carved pine, full stride, horsehair tail, wheeled platform base, America, early 20th C **635.00**

Sign, 14" x 20", The Stewart Clipping Machine, colorful image of horses in court room jury box, machine in center, cardboard litho, C.8.5 ..... **475.00**

Toy, Arabian Trotter, tin and composition wind-up, orig key, orig box **130.00**

Watch holder, 10" h, 5-3/8" d, figural, silver plated metal, detailed jockey and race horse figure, mkd "Reed & Darton," loss to orig silver plate **525.00**

Weathervane, 26 1/2" l, 16-1/2" h, full-bodied trotting horse, copper, verdigris surface, black metal stand, America, late 19th C, minor dents **1,325.00**

Wild animals

Bookends, pr, 5" h, rabbits, modeled poised on back legs, painted copper over plaster, red square bases, Aesthetic Movement, late 19th/early 20th C **300.00**

Cane

36" l, 2-1/3" w x 3-1/4" h elephant ivory handle carved as American bison, amber

glass eyes, finely fashioned features, 1/2" sterling collar with London hallmarks for 1920, heavy ebony shaft, 7/8" brass and iron ferrule **1,120.00**

36-1/4" l, 2" d x 3" h elephant ivory handle carved as six male lions, amber eyes, alternate with mouths open and closed, 1/3" ringed silver collar, thick Malacca shaft, 1-1/2" horn ferrule, English, c1890...................... **1,460.00**

Paperweight, crystal, two etched hippos, marked "Mats Jonasson, Sweden" on original label, $125.

Figure

Carved alabaster, reclining rabbit, full relief, rect base, 9" l, 5" d, 6" h............ **2,185.00**

Carved bone, elephant, carved bone, carved wooden armature overlaid with bone tiles in contrasting patterns, India, c1900, 24" l,.... **1,610.00**

Ceramic, white elephant figures, gray and pink enamel detailing, sq bronze bases with gilt rocaille scrollwork to sides, early 20th C, 10" w, 5-3/4" d, 10-1/2" h, price for pr **2,760.00**

Polychromed carved wood Deer, worn brown paint, white accents on nose and underbelly, green ground stand, America, 19th C, missing one antler and part of right foreleg, 18" l, 3-1/4" d, 17-3/4" h **3,450.00**

Kangaroo, Fred Alten, (1872-1945, Wyandotte, MI), body with traces of brown stain, red glass eyes, shaped base, 3-1/4" w, 7-1/4" h, with stand **575.00**

Sewer tile, recumbent, 15" l **3,800.00**

Shooting gallery target, 21" w, 7" d, 31-1/2" h, rabbit, MA, c1940, some paint remaining, with stand **815.00**

Tin, litho

Jumbo Peanut Butter, Frank Tea & Spice Co., one-lb size, 3-3/8" x 3-7/8".............. **775.00**

Red Wolf Coffee, Ridenour-Baker Co., Kansas City, one-lb size, vacuum pack, trademark wolf, 5" d, 4" h **575.00**

Tiger Bright Sweet Chewing Tobacco, P. Lorillard Co., vertical pocket size, 3" w, 7/8" d, 2-7/8" h **275.00**

ARCHITECTURAL ELEMENTS

History: Architectural elements, many of which are handcrafted, are those items which have been removed or salvaged from buildings, ships, or gardens. Part of their desirability is due to the fact that it would be extremely costly to duplicate the items today.

Beginning about 1840, decorative building styles began to feature carved wood and stone, stained glass, and ornate ironwork. At the same time, builders and manufacturers also began to use fancy doorknobs, doorplates, hinges, bells, window locks, shutter pulls, and other decorative hardware as finishing touches to elaborate new homes and commercial buildings.

Hardware was primarily produced from bronze, brass, and iron, and doorknobs also were made from clear, colored, and cut glass. Highly ornate hardware began appearing in the late 1860s and remained popular through the early 1900s. Figural pieces that featured animals, birds, and heroic and mythological images were very popular, as were ornate and very graphic designs that complimented the many architectural styles that emerged in the late 19th century.

Fraternal groups, government and educational institutions, and individual businesses all ordered special hardware for their buildings. Catalogs from the era show hundreds of patterns, often with a dozen different pieces available in each design.

The current trends of preservation and recycling of architectural elements has led to the establishment and growth of organized salvage operations that specialize in removal and resale of elements. Special auctions are now held to sell architectural elements from churches, mansions, office buildings, etc. Today's decorators often design an entire room around one architectural element, such as a Victorian marble bar or mural, or use several as key accent pieces.

For more information, see *Warman's Glass*, 4th edition.

Arch, 36" l, fragmentary, sandstone, carved figures, including Buddha seated on dais, central India, c15th/16th C **1,495.00**

Bird bath, 19" d, 33-1/2" h, cast iron, shallow basin, gadrooned rim mounted by two doves, fluted baluster form standard on circular base cast with pierced rose design **300.00**

Bird cage, 21" x 19-1/2" x 18", house form, grand entrance, front porch, bay windows, dormers, cupola, painted green, trimmed with red painted wooden buttons, knobs, and perches, some paint loss.................................. **230.00**

Bracket, 19-3/4" h, 10-1/2" d, carved wood, mermaids, gilded, bifurcated scrolled tails, America, 19th C, some loss, pr **4,230.00**

Capitals, 16" w, 10" d, 21" h, galvanized tin, flat tops, raised star and rope twist details, one stripped, other old gray and white paint, wear and split seams, price for pr.......... **250.00**

Catalog

Hudson Equipment Co., Chicago, IL, 1940, 256 pgs, 6-1/2" x 9-3/4", Hudson Barn Equipment Catalog No. B-31, stalls, stanchions, bull stall, etc................................ **30.00**

Morgan Sash & Door Co., Chicago, IL, c1953, 180 pgs, 8-1/2" x 11", Catalog & Price List No. 553, Morgan-Anderson Woodwork **35.00**

Chimneypiece, 96" w, 7" d, 72" h, carved pine, molded shelf above dentilled frieze with central roundel decorated with putto flanked by swags of flowers, jambs decorated with urns above scrolled brackets, acanthus leaves at feet, late Victorian or Edwardian, c1900 .... **1,800.00**

Bird or animal cage, wirework interior, ornate building structure with simulated brick and marble decoration, pediment over door, three stories, **$475**.

Photo courtesy of Dotta Auction Co., Inc.

Conservatory planter, oak, zinc liner **1,100.00**

Curtain tiebacks, mercury glass, grape dec, pewter collars, price for set of six, some chips, minor wear **175.00**

Door

27-1/4" w, 69-1/2" h, raised panel, pegged construction, orig red paint, wrought iron thumb latch, old corner chip **580.00**

31-1/2" w, 78-1/2" h, two molded recessed panels, grain painted to resemble exotic wood, attributed to Maine, early 19th C, very minor surface imperfections **920.00**

Doorknob, 2-1/8" d, brown pottery agateware, price for pr **90.00**

Door knocker, 4" w, 11-1/4" h, wrought and hammered copper, tulip shape, monogrammed "IGW," orig dark patina ... **175.00**

Door pull, 8" d, brass, Arts & Crafts, round, grimacing figure wearing head covering, holding ring in its mouth **270.00**

Eagle

12-3/4" w, 5" h, carved mahogany, bas-relief carving, perched on arrow, gilt highlights, America..... **530.00**

26" w, 31" l, 25" h, carved giltwood, perched on carved rockery, Pilot House type, America, c1875, old regilding, minor wear **2,415.00**

32-3/4" w, 19-1/4" h, gilded tin, outstretched wings, perched on rockery weighted base, holds scales In beak, metal manufacturer M. F. Frand Co., Camden, NJ, tag on lower base, late 19th C, imperfections **1,880.00**

Finials, pr

25" h, cast stone, cov urn draped with floral swags, fluted socle, sq base, 19th C, pr **1,800.00**

31" h, molded copper, star and crescent on ball above ring and baluster-form base, all-over verdigris surface, America, late 19th/early 20th C, purportedly from an Odd Fellows Lodge, minor dents **3,525.00**

Floor vase, 28-1/4" h, alabaster, urn form, scalloped rim, leaftip neck band, vertically fluted body with double leaftip stem, trumpet foot, plinth base, Classical Revival, late 19th C **325.00**

Fountain, verdigris bronze, nude boy with turtle, signed "H. Gonier," dated 1916, 48" h, **$33,000.**

Photo courtesy of Wiederseim Associates, Inc.

Garden bench, cast iron

36" w, 13-1/2" d, 28" h, openwork vintage design, scrolled seat, worn white paint, price for pr **350.00**

43-1/2" w, 15" d, 31" h, openwork fern design on back and legs, geometric cast designs on seat, old white repaint, two hairlines, chip near front corner . **325.00**

Fountain, bronze, mermaid and dolphin, wave-form base encrusted with turtle, crab, and shells, 38" d, 85" h, **$3,315.**

Photo courtesy of Sloans & Kenyon Auctions

Garden furniture, 36" h chair, 45" l x 18" d x 37" h settee, cast Iron, scrolled medallions on backs, scrolled arms, cast geometric stars on seats, Gothic style aprons, old white paint, price for two-pc set **1,495.00**

Garden ornament

10" l, 11-5/8" h, rabbit, cast iron, seated figure, traces of white, green, and red paint, late 19th C, wear **345.00**

16-1/2" l, 29-1/2" h, carved and painted wood and gesso, urn with flame, painted tan, putty, and white, traces of gilt, 19th C **2,185.00**

Garden seat, porcelain, 14-1/4" d, 19-1/4" h, detailed white relief floral and bird dec, dark blue ground, paneled sides with pierced dec on two sides and top, Oriental **425.00**

Garden table, 44" w, 26-3/4" d, 30-1/4" h, cast iron, painted white, ornate detail, openwork inserts on top, high cabriole legs, scrolled feet, foliage returns, one insert missing **520.00**

Griffins, winged, stone-cut, English, pr **4,200.00**

Hitching post, 31" h, cast iron, jockey, yellow, red, green, black, and white painted detail, wired for lantern **275.00**

Joint cap, 10-1/4" w, 12" l, composition, gilt, shell form, bases with tapering acanthus, Georgian, set of four **900.00**

Library steps, 28" w, 17-1/2" d, 17-1/2" h, metamorphic, mahogany, leather top, open position as rect low table, hinged to form four-tread library step, Regency style **900.00**

Lock, 8-1/2" w, 11" h, iron, rect plate with male and female silhouettes, key with quatrefoil terminal, 19th C, stand, minor surface corrosion **650.00**

Obelisks, pr, 13-3/4" h, black slate, parcel gilt, tapered form, front incised with pseudo hieroglyphics on gilt ground, stepped base, gilt metal feet, Egyptian Revival, late 19th C **940.00**

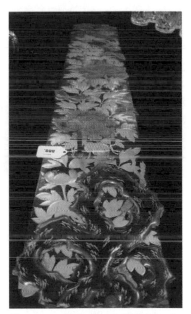

Plaque, rectangle, lacquered floral and butterfly design in gold and black, reverse with black speckled finish, top with rectangular aperture, bottom with two squared hooks, cracking, losses to lacquer, 6" w, 38" l, **$400.**

Photo courtesy of Alderfer Auction Co.

Pedestal, mottled salmon marble, turned columns, square top and base, 36" and 36-1/4" h, scattered chipping, break at base of shorter pedestal, price for pair, **$375**.

Photo courtesy of Alderfer Auction Co

Pedestal

27-1/2" h, carved walnut, turned top raised on figure of classical man, turned and bead-carved base, early 20th C **360.00**

27-1/2" h, 9-1/4" d, burled veneer, applied moldings on columns, stepped molded bases, paper label "Made in Italy," price for pr **250.00**

31" h, mahogany, circular top, turned standard, three paw feet, Victorian.............. **220.00**

31-1/2" h, 14" w sq top, copper and brass, twist-turned legs, paw feet, urn finial on base, Renaissance Revival **425.00**

40" h, Antico-verde marble, round and octagonal tapered revolving top, columnar pedestal carved with band of anthemion between beading, base with further beaded band, sq plinth base, Classical Revival, Italian, late 19th C **2,750.00**

40" h, 9-1/4" d top, white marble, dark gray striations, circular top, turned rings on column, octagonal base, small edge chips **450.00**

Planter, 22" l, 20" h, zinc, nautilus shell form, pr... **2,160.00**

Staircase and railing, oak, designed for the offices of Charles P. Limbert Co., Holland, Michigan, salvaged from building prior to demolition in 1990 .... **3,350.00**

Sundial, 17" d, 34" h, lead, circular, alpha numerics, terra cotta base shaped like three gargoyles, shaped plinth **850.00**

Terrarium, 17" w, 21-3/8" h, walnut and glass, rect body with four chamfered round uprights topped by turned finials, colorless glass sides, base with lead-lined interior, raised on bun feet, Victorian, late 19th C **600.00**

Topiary form, 13-1/2" w, 24" h, lyre-shape, wire, conical base, painted green, America, late 19th/early 20th C............. **150.00**

Urn, cast iron

14-3/4" h, double handles, flared rims, shell design on lower reservoir, round stems, painted black, repairs, price for pr **200.00**

19-1/2" h, flared rim, sq to round base, double handles, white paint, minor rim chip....... **420.00**

20-1/2" h, ribbed tops and columns, sq base, painted white, price for pr **120.00**

37-3/4" h, 30" w, fluting, relief acanthus leaves, raised cast scroll panels, pedestal base, removable handles, painted white **575.00**

Pair of cast iron garden cherubs, **$250**.

Wall plaque, pine, eagle and shield, carved in the manner of John Haley Bellamy, America, early 20th C, painted white, 48-1/4" w, 10-1/2" h **1,645.00**

Window frame, 35-1/2" w, 35" h, arched, mullions in gothic pattern, five small panes remaining, 20th C green paint **55.00**

Vault door, center plaque reads "Herring Hall Marvin Safe Co., Hamilton, OH," **$195**.

Photo courtesy of Alderfer Auction Co.

ART DECO

History: The Art-Deco period was named after an exhibition, "l'Exposition Internationale des Arts Déecorative et Industriels Modernes," held in Paris in 1927. Its beginnings succeed those of the Art-Nouveau period, but the two overlap in time, as well as in style.

Art-Deco designs are angular with simple lines. This was the period of skyscrapers, movie idols, and the Cubist works of Picasso and Legras. Art Deco motifs were used for every conceivable object being produced in the 1920s and 1930s (ceramics, furniture, glass, and metals) not only in Europe but in America as well.

Additional Listings: Furniture and Jewelry. Also check glass, pottery, and metal categories.

Aquarium, 41-1/2" h, 18" h stepped and paneled molded translucent yellow glass bowl, dec with six panels of stylized flowers, set in bronzed metal tripod stand, three enameled green handles, legs terminating in stylized dolphins, central light fixture, tri-part base, dark patina, c1925, chips, wear **2,415.00**

Armoire, 51-1/4" w, 19" d, 71" h, sycamore and fruitwood, interior fitted with top shelf over divided compartment, hardware fitted for wardrobe, flanked by two shelves, lollipop-shaped key, France, c1928 .... **1,650.00**

Ashtray, 12-7/8" h, Frankart, America, second quarter 20th C, white metal striding nude female figure, painted light green, green glazed square pottery ash receptacle on base, raised marks on base "FRANKART. INC. PAT. APPLD FOR," lacking ceramic cigarette box **450.00**

Bed, 82" l, single curvilinear bed frame with hanging shelf compartments, France, c1930, price for pr **1,410.00**

Bonbon dish, cov, 6-1/2" d, 1-1/4" h, colorless glass, relief etched dec of three nude mermaids on interior of cover, raised signature, Sabino Glass, Paris, France, 20th C, wear **295.00**

Bookends, pr, 8" h, bronze, cast as bust of woman, patinated, unmarked **360.00**

Cabinet, dressing, 68-1/2" w, 19-1/2" d, 66-7/8" h, rect curvilinear top, centered mirror over four drawers flanked on each side by full-length curvilinear cabinets, shaped foot skirt, France, c1925 ..... **1,100.00**

Cabinet, gentleman's, 28-1/2" l, 16-1/2" d, 40" h, burled veneer cabinet, Bakelite and chrome hardware, England, c1930 .... **940.00**

Center bowl, 16" d, 3-3/4" h, by Grace Helen Talbot, Roman Bronze Works, 1922, fluted bowl, four bronze nude female figures with arms outstretched, dark green-brown patina, signed and dated on base **5,875.00**

Chair, 27" h, tub, mahogany frame, upholstered seat, 20th C, price for pr **600.00**

Chandelier, 30" h, 19" d, colorless mold-blown and etched glass shade with stylized flowers and leaves, wrought iron frame with vine ornamentation, sgd "Degue 534," France, c1930 .... **600.00**

Cigarette case, 5-3/8" l, 3-1/8" w, silver, interior with vermeil wash, engraved "Fran," leather case **100.00**

Lamp, bronzed metal base with two figures, bright orange, white, and blue spatter globe shade, original wiring, **$250.**

Clock, table, 7-1/4" w, 6-1/4" h, Telechron, model 4F65, Ashland, Massachusetts, c1935, circular blue glass with Roman numeral dial raised on flat chromed metal bar with curvilinear foot, electric movement **750.00**

Coffee set, silver plated, Wilcox, design attributed to Gene Theobald, faceted 10-1/2" h coffeepot, and sugar container with Bakelite finials, matching creamer, 20" oblong tray, all marked "Wilcox S.P. Co/E.P.N. S./International S.Co./W. M. Mounts/1981N." **1,150.00**

Credenza, 61" l, 20-1/2" w, 82" h, beveled glass cabinet over rect marble top, two drawers over two cabinet doors in burlwood with metal mounts, c1930, wear, escutcheon missing **600.00**

Desk

30" x 44" x 22-1/2", Plycraft, double pedestal, four drawers on each side, single center drawer, stenciled #331 **350.00**

66-1/8" l, 36-1/8" d, 29" h, Leopold Corp, Burlington, IA, walnut veneered, semi-oval top over center drawer flanked by pull-out writing surface and two drawers, bronze handles, light brown finish, "Charles S. Nathan Office Equipment New York" distributor's metal tag in drawer, veneer loss, wear **900.00**

Drawings, 13-1/2" x 17", by Alexander Bronson, pencil drawings of two beds by Paul Frankl, other with pedestal table, sgd, mounted in natural wood frames, price for three-pc set **750.00**

Dresser box, 12" l, Egyptian Revival, bentwood Egyptian sarcophagus form, overlaid in emb copper with Egyptian motifs, blue opaque glass scarabs, sides trimmed in tooled leather, silk lining, dark rich patina with verdigris oxidation, c1925 .... **460.00**

End table, 16-1/2" w, 14" d, 29" h, mahogany and burlwood, orig marble tops over single drawers, one with two lower shelves, other with shelf and cabinet, raised rosettes on metal hardware, France, c1930, price for pr **1,400.00**

Figure, 9-1/2" h, molded opalescent glass, nude female figure, triangular base with raised and etched marks, paper label, Sabino Glass, Paris, France, 20th C **390.00**

Fireplace screen, 25-1/4" w, 35" h, wrought iron, diagonal grid with spade elements at intersections, dark patina, attributed to Raymond Subes, France, c1925 .... **4,200.00**

Lamp base, 21" h, etched brass, silver wash on ovoid brass form, etched nude female figures picking grape clusters from cascading grape vines, weighted round stepped base, France, c1925, wear, scattered corrosion **520.00**

Lamp, boudoir, Danse De Lumiere, 11" h, molded glass figure of woman with outstretched arms, bearing stylized feather drapery, oval platform base with internal light fixture, molded title and patent mark, c1930, mold imperfections **400.00**

Lamp, floor, 68" h, domical orange and blue mold-blown shade, wrought iron framework, conforming metal base, France, c1930 .... **3,290.00**

Lamp, hanging, 29" l, silvered metal, three arms with white etched glass shades attributed to Schneider, France, c1925 .... **800.00**

Lamp, table

19" h, 11" d concentric ribbed pink satin shade with stylized rosebud center, shade emb "Vleighe France 1137," nickel-plated brass base with emb geometric designs, minor flakes on shade **520.00**
19" h, 13" d shade, trefoil etched colorless glass shade, rosette and geometric designs, supported by wrought iron tripod with applied rosette accents and leaf motif, shade sgd "Degue," nicks and chips to shade **920.00**

Mirror

10-1/4" h, cast metal, circular plate supported by two figures with composition faces, stamped "Collection Francaise, made in USA" **360.00**
29" w, 15" d, 70-3/4" h, full-length mirror with arched top, asymmetrical rosewood base with geometric ivory inlay, France, c1925.......... **1,530.00**
36" w, 24" h, octagonal mirror in wrought iron frame, rose and leaf dec, France, 1930 .... **250.00**
36-3/4" h, oval beveled glass, wrought metal surround, France, c1928.......... **1,645.00**

Nightstand, 15-1/2" w, 15-1/2" d, 31" h, bird's-eye maple veneer, marble top, France c1930 .... **300.00**

Plaque, 12" x 9", cast aluminum, Love Birds, sgd "Rene P. Chambllen" lower right, dedicatory inscription verso, c1930 .... **920.00**

Poufee, 23" d, 13-1/2" h, floral upholstered round seat in gold, blue-gray, melon, and brown, four reeded legs that taper at base, France, c1925 .... **300.00**

Punch bowl and cordial set, eight-sided finial on paneled cov, 7-1/2" h, 8-1/2" d bowl dec with silver and red geometric design, six 2-1/2" d paneled cordials with similar dec, 14" d round glass tray with multiple star cuts on base, chrome sides, chrome ladle, imperfections **290.00**

Ring, lady's, rounded form bezel and bead-set with old European-cut diamonds, approx. total wt. 1.56 cts, millegrain accents, 18kt white gold mount **2,000.00**

Room divider, four panels, black lacquered arched frames inset with canvas, painted abstract gold and black pattern, each panel 24" w, 71-1/2" h, slight damage to hinges **1,725.00**

Perfume bottles, left: red skyscraper shape, black stepped stopper; right: slender green satin baluster, gold toned top, each **$125**.

Photo courtesy of Joy Luke Auctions

Salon chair, 28-1/2" w, 26-1/2" d, 24-1/2" h, U-shaped low chair, beige velvet and burlwood, metal tag on bases, "Hotel Le Malandre Modele Depose," c1945, price for pr **2,185.00**

Server, 55" w, 20" d, 36" h, stepped rect top, curvilinear ends over fitted cabinet doors, English, c1930 .... **1,880.00**

Sideboard, 76" l, 19-1/2" d, 50-5/8" h, walnut and burl book-matched veneer, Bakelite cabinet doors and drawer pulls, France, c1928................. **900.00**

Stand, 15" w, 18" d, 29-1/2" h, amboyna wood inlaid with stylized flowers in various fruitwoods and mother-of-pearl, attributed to Maurice Defrene, France, c1925, price for pr **2,235.00**

Table, dining

72" l, 43-1/2" w, 29-3/4" h, oval top with geometric inlay border with central medallion, angular center support, shaped platform base, US, c1930...................... **1,410.00**
79" l, 40" w, 29" h, burlwood oval top, fine ebony and ash inlay dec, four canted legs, accompanied by two conforming 16" leaves, France, c1930 .... **1,175.00**

Tea set, silver, wood handles, **$495**.

Photo courtesy of Dotta Auction Co., Inc.

Table, tea, 44" l open, 22" closed, 35-1/4" w, 28-1/4" h, walnut, rect top opens and swivels on U-shaped base, France, c1928............. **1,880.00**

Tea and coffee set, silver, 18-3/4" d oval tray, coffeepot, teapot, creamer and cov sugar accented by ebonized handles and finials, mkd "835," hallmarked, Germany, early 20th C, creamer handle restored, tray scratches **1,175.00**

Torchieres, 69" h, gilt bronze, skyscraper design raised on four stepped feet, US, c1930, price for pr **2,750.00**

Tray, 24" l, rect, two handles, hammered brass, stamped "M. Willig Freising Bavaria" ... **110.00**

Vase

8-1/2" h, cameo glass, black ground, stylized scene of three repeated terriers against bronzed and silvered ground, unsigned, French, c1925 .... **300.00**
8-1/2" h, citrine ground, stylized enameled flowers, sgd "Legras," minor heat check........................... **200.00**
9-1/2" h, frosted colorless glass angular bulbous body, octagonal rim, ftd, base, incised Sabino signature, France, c1930, edge nicks **275.00**
10-1/4" h, mold blown art glass, relief vine and leaf dec, remnants of silvered metal on interior, etched mark on base, France, c1930, interior rim ground **180.00**
11-3/8" h, ceramic, Boch Frères, extended rim, oval form, stylized light green blossoms, stems, and foliage, gold accents, turquoise ground, glossy glaze, painted "BFK/340," imp "708," minor crazing, minor light scratches, price for pr.................. **920.00**

12-1/4" h, 5-1/2" d, Wiener Werkstatte, bulbous, flaring neck, painted white and black geometric pattern, brown ground, stamped "WWW/ Made in Austria/HB" ... **125.00**

12-1/2" h, molded opalescent glass, Art Deco stylized scene of centaur and panther hunting gazelles, foliage background with blue patina, unmarked, attributed to Sabino **635.00**

Wall hanging, 63" w, 100" l, cotton velvet rose-colored curtain with multicolored crewel work design of stylized lanterns and trailing decoration, France, c1925 .... **1,470.00**

Wall sconces, pr, 20" l, colorless etched shades with vertical bands of flowers supported on bronze dore mounts, shades signed, by Heiter Vincent, France, c1925 .... **750.00**

Wash bowl and pitcher, graniteware, white ground, light brown and blue decoration, chips, **$150**.

Wristwatch, lady's

Baume & Mercier, center platinum rect dial framed by alternating rows of bead-set single-cut diamonds and channel-set rect sapphires, millegrain accents, 18k mesh band, 14kt closure... **1,410.00**

Concord Watch Co., 6-1/4" l, platinum, ivory tone dial with Arabic numeral indicators, 17 jewel Concord Watch Co. movement, bezel with bead-set single-cut diamond melee, 14k gold band with bead-set diamond accents........ **530.00**

D & L Co., rect ivory tone dial with Arabic numeral indicators, 17 jewel movement, bezel with bead-set single-cut diamonds and channel-set French-cut sapphires, 18k white gold case, adjustable platinum mesh band, case sgd **1,410.00**

ART NOUVEAU

History: Art Nouveau is the French term for the "new art," which had its beginning in the early 1890s and continued for the next 40 years. The flowing and sensuous female forms used in this period were popular in Europe and America. Among the most recognized artists of this period were Gallé, Lalique, and Tiffany.

The Art-Nouveau style can be identified by flowing, sensuous lines, florals, insects, and the feminine form. These designs were incorporated into almost everything produced during the period, from art glass to furniture, silver, and personal objects. Later wares demonstrate some of the characteristics of the evolving Art-Deco style.

Additional Listings: Furniture and jewelry. Also check glass, pottery, and metal categories.

Bowl, diamond shaped, green glass, white, yellow, and pink enameled orchids, gold tracery foliage, gold border trim, **$95**.

Photo courtesy of Dotta Auction Co., Inc.

Bud vase, 8-3/4" h, glass, deep crimson, cut back to citron . **100.00**

Candlestick, 11-3/8" h, patinated metal, figural, nymph standing on butterfly, holding flower form candle sconce, flower-form base, early 20th C **115.00**

Case, sterling silver, Tiffany & Co., rect, engraved on both sides, monogram "AJC," suspended from silver chain, brown leather interior with two pockets, orig silver retractable pencil, sgd **215.00**

Center bowl, 12" d, 9" h, purple iridescent threaded glass within green oil spot ground, tooled copper rim, Art Nouveau shaped metalwork sides framing faces, unsgd, Austria, early 20th C, possibly Loetz **650.00**

Clock

Desk, 3-3/4" w, 4-3/8" h, bronze, Chelsea Clock movement, gilt-metal and glass mount, red enamel dec devices, ftd base, circular face with Arabic chapters, imp "Chelsea Clock Co., Boston, USA, 155252" on inside clock works, worn patina......................... **460.00**

Figural, 12-1/2" h, enameled cast white metal, relief of woman's head, flowing hair, leaves, thistles, Seth Thomas movement, circular dial with Roman numerals, c1900, minor wear................ **300.00**

Wall, 24-1/2" w, 10" d, 38" h, carved walnut, two train movement, floral etched gilt metal dial sgd "Trilla, Barcelona," case topped by bust of young beauty on rocaille shell above iris flower, flanked by poppy roundels, case further carved with stylized florets, writing flower buds at corners, Spanish, early 20th C **490.00**

Desk lamp, 14-1/2" w base, two-light bypass fixture, base of colorless glass molded as ocean wave, top with gilt bronze figure of nubile mermaid, flanked by two lidded inkwells formed as fishing trap and whelk shell, flattened feet, early 20th C **1,360.00**

Door pull, 3" w, 15" h, bronze, whiplash handles, orig patina, Belgian, price for pr **1,150.00**

Fruit basket, center majolica type plate with violet poppies, green leaves, wire work basket, **$350**.

Floor vase, 21" h, glass, gray ground internally dec with streaked orange and mottled blue, blown-out into wrought iron armature with scrolled designs, stylized florals, Muller and Chapelle, c1910, glass damaged at base **1,100.00**

Garniture, centerpiece with bronze patina, female spelter figure of "L. Historie," flanked by spelter plinth with clock, enameled dial with painted Arabic numbers, sgd "L. Satre-A Pont. Aven," rect molded marble base with center bronze gilt neoclassical mounting, bronze gilded bun feet, pr of bronze patina spelter Louis XVI style urns, ribbons and swags centering figural medallion, sq marble base, bronze gilded feet **950.00**

Inkwell, double, scrolling foliate design, bronze, faces on ink bottle covers, two dolphins support raised pen rest, **$325**.

Jar, cut and etched jar, silver-plated lid, two-handled frame, 8-1/4" h, **$125**.

Photo courtesy of Joy Luke Auctions.

Inkwell, 7" x 13", bronze, double inkwells flanking shaped pen tray, raised leaf and berry motif, sgd "C.H. Louchet" **460.00**
Lamp, table, 18-1/4" h, opalescent shell held by arched foliage, supported by female figure in white metal, bronze patina, ruffled water-like base, early 20th C, imperfections **320.00**
Notebook, hammered sterling silver, Tiffany & Co., flying bird and branch dec, entwined

starfish on reverse, contains celluloid cards with days of week, sgd, additional hallmark for Shiebler **360.00**
Perfume bottle, 4-1/4" h, paneled slender baluster form bottle painted with blue and gold flowers, gilt-metal hinged lid enclosing glass stopper, lid with short chain **520.00**

Picture frame

4-7/8" h, sterling silver, oval, emb flowers and maiden, Unger Bros., Newark .. **175.00**
8-1/2" w, 11-3/8" h, wood, penwork and colored stained dec of stylized fruiting flowers, easel back **100.00**
Pitcher, 11-3/4" h, relief wheat dec, mottled blue, brown, and green, imp "Gres Mougin Nancy," by Joseph Victor Xavier, Nancy, France, c1900..... **865.00**

Plaque, tile by Johann von Schwarz, decoration in cuenca with lady in profile, yellow moon medallion, yellow irises on indigo ground, 11" x 17-1/2" tile mounted in original brass frame, incised "R/Q/8926," painted "A/b318/4," **$2,000**.

Photo courtesy of David Rago Auctions, Inc.

Plate, embossed Le Grand Paris, pretty maiden, green majolica glaze, French, faint stamp mark, 11" d, some abrasion, nicks to high points, **$195**.

Photo courtesy of David Rago Auctions, Inc.

Plaque, 12-3/8" x 9-5/9", Summer Maiden, possibly Limoges, late 19th C, enameled rect plaque depicting profile bust of brunette among sunflowers, bordered by poppy stems, sgd "Dorval," maroon velvet surround, 18-3/4" x 15-3/4" gilt metal frame mounted with flowering branches **4,410.00**
Stove, coal, 28-1/2" w, 22" d, 36" h, bronze and iron, shaped structure, pierced bronze plaque with "S"-scroll motifs centering pineapple, applied bronze medallions with female profiles, stamped "Deville Pailliette Forest, No. 17, Charlesville, Ardennes," c1900 .... **375.00**
Table, side, 24" w, 17" d, 30" h, scallop-edge rect top inlaid with poppies in exotic woods, fluted legs, cabriole feet, lower shelf with variation of poppy motif, orig finish, inlaid "Galle" signature **2,100.00**
Tea kettle, 11" h, sterling silver, floral repousse dec, curved handle, marked "J. E. Caldwell & Co., 925, Sterling, 1000, Philadelphia," 47 troy oz . **550.00**
Tumbler, 4" h crystal tumbler, acid stamped "WMF," hallmarked silver handled holders, set of four **175.00**

Thermometer, ornate scrolling Art Nouveau scrolls and flowers, brass, **$125**.

Photo courtesy of Dotta Auction Co., Inc.

Urn, 17-1/2" h, conical pottery body, large white and red spring garden flowers, painted blue shiny glazed body, artist sgd, Continental, triple griffin bronze holder base **475.00**

Vase

7-1/2" h, irid Bohemian glass, stylized floral metal frame **125.00**

8-3/4" h, glass, gray ground internally dec with mottled light and dark blue, blown-out into wrought iron reeded armature, base inscribed "Daum Nancy" and "L Majorelle," c1920 ..... **1,610.00**

17-1/2" h, suppressed circular body, extended tapering neck, everted rim, pink, blue, green irid finish, embedded threaded dec, attributed to Pallme-Koenig, minute rim nicks **700.00**

Wine cabinet, 46" w, 18" d, 68-1/2" h, carved walnut, panels elaborately carved with nymphs and grapevines, fitted with two pairs of doors and drawer, early 20th C **5,550.00**

ART POTTERY (GENERAL)

History: America's interest in art pottery can be traced to the Centennial Exposition in Philadelphia, Pennsylvania, in 1877, where Europe's finest producers of decorative art displayed an impressive selection of their wares. Our young artists rose to the challenge immediately, and by 1900, native artisans were winning gold medals for decorative ceramics here and abroad.

The Art Pottery "Movement" in America lasted from about 1880 until the first World War. During this time, more than 200 companies, in most states, produced decorative ceramics ranging from borderline production ware to intricately decorated, labor intensive artware establishing America as a decorative art powerhouse.

Listed here is the work by various factories and studios, with pricing, from a number of these

companies. The location of these outlets are included to give the reader a sense of how nationally based the industry was.

Additional Listings: See Clewell, Clifton, Cowan, Dedham, Fulper, Grueby, Jugtown, Marblehead, Moorcroft, Newcomb, North Dakota School of Mines, Ohr, Paul Revere, Peters and Reed, Rookwood, Roseville, Van Briggle, Weller, and Zanesville.

Notes: Condition, design, size, execution, and glaze quality are the key considerations when buying art pottery. This category includes only companies not found elsewhere in this book.

Adviser: David Rago.

For more information, see *Warman's American Pottery & Porcelain*, 2nd edition.

Arequipa, cabinet vase, squeeze bag decoration of white grape clusters and green leaves, matte pink ground, incised "AP 622," 3" h, 2-3/4" d, **$2,900.**
Photo courtesy of David Rago Auctions, Inc

Arequipa

Bowl, 6-1/2" d, 2-1/4" h, closed-in, emb eucalyptus branches, matte green and dark blue glaze, stamped mark, incised "KH/11" **800.00**

Vase, 10-1/2" h, 7-1/2" d, baluster, purple and brown mottled semi-matte glaze, incised "Arequipa California/404/JG/JJ" **1,600.00**
Vase, 13-1/2" h, 6-1/4" d, baluster, carved foliate design, sheer green and turquoise glaze, incised "G.B. Arequipa California" **2,500.00**
Vessel, 4-1/4" h, 4-1/4" d, squat, carved swirls, matte green and indigo glaze, stamped "Arequipa California" with potter **1,500.00**
Avon, Vance, vase, 5" d, 5-1/2" h, designed by Frederick Rhead, squeezebag stylized trees, orange and green ground, incised "Avon/WPTS.CO./174-1241" **920.00**
Bachelder, O. L., vase, 5" h, 3-3/4" d, bulbous, cobalt blue and teal sheer glossy glaze, incised "OLB/R," ink cipher **500.00**
Bennett, Edwin, vase, 8" h, 8-1/2" w, flat, Albion, painted squirrels on stonewall, pine bough above, 1895, E. Bennett Pottery/1895/AHB/Albion **2,400.00**

Bennett, John
Charger
14-1/2" d, dec with polychrome daisies and poppies enc within hearts, cobalt blue ground, black scroll design, sgd "J. Bennett/412 E24/NY/Oct 9/79," added inscription "Wed last 100 degs in shade" **4,600.00**
Vase, 3-3/4" d, 7-1/2" h, bulbous, painted burgundy phlox and honeybee, ivory ground, minute rim fleck, marked "BENNETT/W2E24/NJ/artist's cipher" **2,870.00**
Binns, Charles F., 7" h, 5-1/2" h, ovoid, amber, ochre, and chocolate brown hare's fur mirrored glaze, 1931, mkd "C.F.B. 1931" **3,250.00**
Cole, A. R., urn, 18-1/2" h, 9-1/2" d, hand-thrown, three fanciful twisted handles, mirror black glaze, unmarked, shallow scratches **400.00**
Denaura, Denver, vase, 5-1/2" h, 5" d, squat top, small opening, molded poppies, matte green vellum glaze, stamped "Denaura/Denver/169" **2,700.00**

Grand Feu, vase, 7" h, 4-1/4" d, corseted bulbous, purple and verdigris semi-matte crystalline glaze, stamped "Grand Feu Pottery, L.A. Cal, TT 154" **11,000.00**

Jervis, goblet, 4" h, 3" d, enameled green and white mistletoe, teal blue ground, vertical mark, few minute glaze flecks.......................... **2,000.00**

Merrimac, jardinière, squat, covered in green and gunmetal frothy glaze, paper label, listing of overglaze on bottom of interior, 5-1/2" x 9", **$1,100**.

Photo courtesy of David Rago Auctions, Inc.

Kenton Hills, vase

4-3/4" d, 7-1/4" h, cylindrical, white prunts cov in mirrored umber glaze, incised "Hentschel" for William Hentschel, imp "KH/124" **775.00**

6" d, 7-1/2" h, 4-sided, aventurine glaze, imp "KH/171" **650.00**

Norse, vase, 11-1/2" h, 7" d, applied salamander, verdigris and bronze glaze, stamped "Norse 25" **850.00**

Markham, vase, ovid, two low buttressed handles, green and orange dead matte glaze, incised "Markham 2923," few minor nicks, 7-1/4" x 7-1/2", **$700**.

Photo courtesy of David Rago Auctions, Inc.

Pewabic

Bookends, pr, 4" w, 4-3/4" h, emb animal, lustered blue and green glaze, stamped

"Pewabic," repair to small edge chip **415.00**

Miniature, vase, 2" h, crackled turquoise glaze, blue plumes, sgd "Pewabic/Detroit/PP" **265.00**

Plate, 9-1/4" d, white crackleware, rim dec with squeezebag yellow and red roosters on green field, stamped "Pewabic," some loss of glaze, chips on back **920.00**

Merrimac, urn, two handles, feathered matte green glaze, stamped "Merrimac" with fish, 6-3/4" x 6", **$815**.

Photo courtesy of David Rago Auctions, Inc.

Vase, 3" d, 3-3/4" h, cylindrical with squatty base, mottled and lustered purple and turquoise glaze, paper label, hand written "Anne/1942," small glaze scale at rim **265.00**

Vessel, 5-1/4" d, 5-1/2" h, bulbous, ribbed, glossy teal glaze, stamped "Pewabic/Detroit" **520.00**

Pisgah Forest

Tea set, Cameo Ware, wagon and landscape dec, dark matte green ground, raised mark and date 1943, 5-1/4" h teapot **950.00**

Vase, 4-3/4" d, 6-1/4" h, bulbous, white, blue, and yellow crystalline glaze, unmarked **460.00**

Vessel, 5" h, 5-3/4" d, spherical, amber glaze, white and blue crystals, raised potter's mark and date 1947 .... **350.00**

Poillon, Clara, pitcher, 5" d, 4-1/2" h, bulbous, medium green glaze, incised CPI monogram **365.00**

San Jose, charger, 15-1/2" d, cuerda seca dec, polychrome wagon train scene, green semi-matte ground, unmarked, small rim fleck **435.00**

Robineau, Adelaide, vessel, 3" h, 4-1/4" d, hemispherical, café-au-lait and verdigris crystalline glaze, carved "AB/184/5," opposing lines to rim **2,500.00**

Prang, vase, four-sided flaring form, frothy gunmetal, green, and Chinese blue flambé glaze, stamped "Prang," 8-3/4" x 3-3/4", **$900**.

Photo courtesy of David Rago Auctions, Inc.

Pewabic, vase, bulbous, applied blossoms on swirling stems, smooth matte green glaze, mark obscured by glaze, 6-1/4" x 4-1/2", **$4,320**.

Photo courtesy of David Rago Auctions, Inc.

Teco

Vase, 10-3/4" h, 3-1/2" d, cylindrical, organic buttressed handles, matte buff glaze, stamped "Teco," few base flakes **3,000.00**

Vase, 11-1/4" h, 5" d, buttressed handles, smooth matte green glaze, stamped "Teco," restored chip on handle..................... **1,300.00**

Vase, 11-1/2 h, 4-1/2" d, ribbed flaring neck surrounded by individual narrow leaves forming handles, matte green and charcoal glaze, stamped "Teco," restoration to two leaves, rim touch-ups **5,000.00**

Vessel, 4-3/4" d, 3-1/4" h, three handles, smooth matte green glaze, stamped "Teco," touch-up to rim bruise **490.00**

Vessel, 10" d, 14-1/2" h, corseted, four handles, smooth matte green glaze with charcoal highlights, stamped "Teco," incised 172, restoration................ **5,175.00**

Tiffany Pottery

Bud vase, 7" h, 2-1/2" d, emb tulips, Old Ivory glaze, Incised "LCT" **4,250.00**

Lamp base, 7" h, 8" d, collar rim, brown and gunmetal flambé glaze, incised "LCT" **2,400.00**

Volkmar, pitcher, 4" d, 4-1/2" h, bulbous, collared neck, cucumber green matte glaze, incised illegible inscription **265.00**

Walley, W. J., vase, 6-1/2" h, bottle shape, sheer light green and gunmetal glaze, imp "W.J.W." **535.00**

Walrath, vase, matte painted with full height stylized pink blossoms, green foliage, green mottled matte ground, incised "Walrath Pottery," 8-3/4" h, 4-1/2" d, **$7,000.**

Photo courtesy of David Rago Auctions, Inc.

Walrath

Cider set, 6-1/2" x 8" pitcher, five cups, painted with cherries on green and brown ground, incised Walrath Pottery, orig Handicraft Guild label on pitcher........ **4,250.00**

Sculpture, 4" h, 6" l, kneeling nude picking rose, sheer matte green glaze, yellow details, incised "Walrath" **300.00**

Vase, 6-3/4" h, 4-1/2" d, matte-painted green foliage trees, brown trunks, dark green ground, incised "Walrath Pottery" **4,250.00**

Wheatley

Lamp base, 14" d, 23" h, emb poppy pods, frothy matte green glaze, new hammered copper fittings, Japanese split-bamboo shade lined with new coral silk, stamped mark. **1,380.00**

Sand jar, 15" d, 24" h, high relief sculpted grape leaves and vines from rim, feathered medium green matte glaze, incised mark/722, several glaze nicks restored **2,415.00**

Vase, 6-3/4" d, 12-1/4" h, bulbous, three climbing lizards, feathered medium matte green glaze, remnant of paper label, restoration to drill hole on side **1,380.00**

White, Denver, vase, 6-1/2" d, 3-3/4" h, squatty, smooth matte gold and green glaze, incised "Denver/1916," small bruise under rim........................ **210.00**

ARTS AND CRAFTS MOVEMENT

History: The Arts and Crafts Movement in American decorative arts took place between 1895 and 1920. Leading proponents of the movement were Elbert Hubbard and his Roycrofters, the brothers Stickley, Frank Lloyd Wright, Charles and Henry Greene, George Niedecken, and Lucia and Arthur Mathews.

The movement was marked by individualistic design (although the movement was national in scope) and re-emphasis on handcraftsmanship and appearance. A reform of industrial society was part of the long-range goal. Most pieces of furniture favored a rectilinear approach and were made of oak.

The Arts and Crafts Movement embraced all aspects of the decorative arts, including metalwork, ceramics, embroidery, woodblock printing, and the crafting of jewelry.

Adviser: David Rago.

Additional Listings: Roycroft, Stickleys, and art pottery categories.

Box, hammered copper, strap hinges, riveted handles, from Dirk van Erp workshop, fine original patina, open box stamp mark, 2-1/2" x 7" x 3-3/4", **$2,300.**

Photo courtesy of David Rago Auctions, Inc.

Blanket chest, Greene & Greene, oak and yellow pine, unusually mortised corners fastened with sq dowel pegs, two lift-top doors, good orig finish, from Pratt residence, Ojai, CA, 65" l, 23-3/4" w, 18-1/2" h....... **22,500.00**

Bookcase, 37" w, 10-1/4" d, 47" h, gallery top, adjustable shelves, small cabinet with leaded glass door, orig finish, Liberty & Co. tag, c1900 .... **3,115.00**

Bookstand, 45-3/4" h, oak, four open shelves with cutout sides and through tenons......... **500.00**

Box, copper, 2-1/2" x 7" x 3-3/4", hammered, riveted handles and strap hinges, Van Erp Workshop, orig patina, open box stamp, few scratches **2,300.00**

Box, silver and enamel 3-7/8" w, 2-3/4" d, 2" h, rect, hinged lid cov with stylized enamel flowers and leaves in green, rose, blue, and white with applied wire and silver balls, raised artist's initials "EC," for Elizabeth Copeland, Boston, 1915-37 .... **14,100.00**

6-1/8" l, 4-3/4" w, rect, hinged, enameled plaque of sailboat with marsh grasses and waterscape, Liberty Tudric, imp "Tudric," numbered "083" **940.00**

Coal bucket, Dirk Van Erp, hammered copper, riveted brass bands, flame shaped brass finial, original dark patina, stamped open box mark, normal wear around rim, 10" d, 17" h, **$4,600**.

Photo courtesy of David Rago Auctions, Inc.

Candlesticks, pr
10-3/4" h, 8" d, brass, two-branch, conical holders set in spirals, bright finish, orig bobeches, Omicron, incised "Jarvie," small scratches and dents........................ **6,500.00**
11-3/4" h, 3-3/4" d, cast copper, imp "1797" with double cross, no patina, unmarked.................... **195.00**
Chair, dining room, Limbert, side, single broad vertical back slat, tacked-on brown leather, orig finish with heavy overcoat, branded mark, 17" w, 37" h, price for set of four................ **1,610.00**
Chair, side, L. & J. G. Stickley, Fayetteville, New York, c1916, oak, model no. 940, three vertical slats below crest rail, slip seat, double side stretcher, branded mark, price for set of six, 35-3/4" h **2,235.00**
Chamberstick, 6-1/4" h, hammered copper, cup-shaped bobeche, riveted angular handle, flaring base, stamped "OMS" for Onondaga Metal Shops, old cleaning and verdigris to patina **175.00**
Cigarette box, 2-1/4" x 5" x 4", hammered copper, riveted trim, emb circular medallions, cedar lining, natural patina, unmarked, attributed to England **260.00**
Clock, 14" w, 4-3/4" d, 21-3/4" h, New Haven, Japanese-style,

brass hands, keyed through-tenon sides, amber ripple glass, orig ebonized finish, paper label **490.00**
Coal scuttle, 15" x 22", hammered copper, repoussé floral motif, riveted seams, rolled rim, new patina, some dents to body, some replaced rivets **575.00**
Coffee and tea service, coffeepot, teapot, creamer, sugar, and tray, pewter, wicker handles, by Archibald Knox, stamped "Liberty/Tudric," price for five-pc set **3,115.00**
Compote, 8" d, 6-3/4" h, pewter, cluthra green glass liner with opalescent and gold swirls, Liberty Tudric, Archibald Knox **3,115.00**
Inkwell, 5-1/4" sq, 3-1/2" h, faceted copper, curled, riveted feet, enameled green, red, and black, spade pattern, orig patina, unmarked Arts & Crafts Shop, couple of nicks to dec **250.00**
Lamp, ceiling, 8-1/2" d, 11" h, polished hammered brass, four arms, flame-shaped opalescent glass shade with green pulled feather pattern, English **1,355.00**
Lamp, table, 21-1/2" h, 16-1/2" d shade, eight panels of textured white glass with exterior green paint within bronzed metal strapwork frame, three sockets with acorn pulls on bulbous verdigris base, unsigned, paint wear **1,060.00**
Lamp, student, 16" h, 13" d, Roycroft brass washed hammered copper base, Stickley Bros. copper and mica shades with silhouetted trees, orig finish, replaced mica, orb and cross mark **1,840.00**

Library table
47-1/2" l, 36-1/4" w, 28-1/2" h, double oval, flaring legs, cut-out stretchers, orig finish, branded Limbert mark, 1" cut off legs **7,475.00**
52" l, 24" w, 29-1/2" h, two arched drawers, corbels, one shelf, orig finish, Lifetime Paine Furniture Co. metal tag **2,300.00**

Magazine stand
18-1/4" w, 14" d, 50-1/2" h, gallery top, vertical slats all around, five tiers, fine orig dark finish, branded "CPM" **2,415.00**

24" w, 12" d, 41-1/2" h, three shelf, two short drawers, arched side rails over slatted sides, light finish, loose joints **630.00**

Lamp, ceramic, bulbous base, four arms, turtle shade inset with several green slag glass panes, matte green glaze, unmarked, Chicago, restored cracks to arms, 16-1/2" x 11", **$3,335**.

Photo courtesy of David Rago Auctions, Inc.

Lantern, hanging, Gustav Stickley, four sided, overhanging vented cap, pierced sides, hammered amber glass, die stamp compass mark, few scratches to original patina, 9" d x 4" h lantern, 21" l chain, **$3,400**.

Photo courtesy of David Rago Auctions, Inc.

Music cabinet, 21-1/2" w, 17" d, 42" h, attributed to G. M. Ellwood for J. S. Henry, c1900, English, mahogany, beveled top, paneled door inlaid with fruitwoods and mother-of-pearl, two drawers, brass hardware, good new finish **2,870.00**
Nut set, hammered copper, 8-1/2" d master bowl, six 3" d serving bowls, Benedict, some wear to patina, unmarked... **290.00**

Occasional table, 30" d, 29-1/2" h, circular top over flaring legs joined by cut-out stretchers, orig finish, branded Limbert mark, wear and stains to top **2,070.00**
Pagoda table, Limbert, corbels under sq top, flaring sides, arched apron, lower shelf, cut-out base, orig finish, heavy overcoat, paper label under top, 34" sq, 30-1/2" h **13,800.00**
Picture frame, 6" w, 9" h, hammered sterling silver, emb daisies, English hallmarks **750.00**

Mantel, custom-designed, oak, carved tree of life flanked by stylized floral stained glass cupboard doors, original finish, unmarked, 59" w, 14" d, 82-1/2" h, **$4,100.**
Photo courtesy of David Rago Auctions, Inc.

Server, Gustav Stickley, No. 818, overhanging top, backsplash, three drawers with oval iron pulls, lower shelf, red decal inside left drawer, refinished, repairs, 48" w, 20" d, 39" h, **$1,900.**
Photo courtesy of David Rago Auctions, Inc.

Pillow, 16" x 25", embroidered stylized orange and green poppies, beige linen ground **490.00**
Plant stand, Limbert, quarter-round corbels under sq top,

flaring sides, ovoid cut-outs, lower shelf, plank base, fine orig factory finish, factory edge repair to top, no visible mark, 20" sq, 29-1/2" h **6,900.00**
Room divider, 68" h, oak, grid-like top, three-panel, each panel cut-out with fern design, replaced linen panels, orig finish, unmarked, some minor chipping to edges **1,200.00**
Server, L. & J. G. Stickley, Fayetteville, New York, c1916, oak, rect top over single drawer, lower median shelf, branded mark, 32" w, 16" d, 33" h **1,410.00**
Sideboard, L. & J.G. Stickley, Fayetteville, New York, c1916, oak, plate rail on rect top, three central drawers flanked by two cabinet doors, over single long drawer, branded mark, 47" w, 19-3/4" d, 44" h **5,300.00**
String holder, 3-3/4" d, 3-1/2" h, sterling on bronze, bell shape, applied silver leaves and vines, orig patina, stamped "HAMS," Heintz **535.00**
Tablecloth, 39" d, circular, linen, embroidered red poppies, green leaves **860.00**
Table, dining
  Limbert, circular, extension, four-sided pedestal base, orig finish with heavy overcoat, 54" d, 27-1/4" h **2,300.00**
  Unknown maker, California, c1912, oak, rect board on board top, lower median shelf with through tenons, cutout sides, shoe foot base, deep brown restored finish, 83-1/2" w, 35-1/4" d, 29" h **3,200.00**
Tabouret, Limbert, sq top, box construction, sq cut-outs, top refinished, orig finish on base, branded mark, 16-1/2" sq, 18" h **2,615.00**
Trunk, 30-1/2" l, 16-1/2" d, 17-1/2" h, copper and iron, strapwork and pyramidal tack mounts, black paint, hinged slant lid revealing rect box **200.00**
Vase, 5" h, 6" d, bulbous, curtained copper, dimpled and folded sides covered in rare orig red finish, Dirk Van Erp, windmill/San Francisco mark with partial D'Arcy Gaw visible **2,760.00**
Wall sconces, pr, 6" d shade, 14-1/2" h, brass, emb stylized poppies, leaded glass period shades, English **2,530.00**

Table, book, L. & J. G. Stickley, vertical slats all around, square overhanging top, unmarked, base has enhanced original finish, top refinished, 27" square, 29" h, **$4,500.**
Photo courtesy of David Rago Auctions, Inc.

Window, leaded polychrome slag glass, arched top, windmill on hill in front of large puffy clouds, unmarked, wooden frame, from a Michigan home, few minor breaks, 41" w, 78 1/2" h, **$4,025.**
Photo courtesy of David Rago Auctions, Inc.

AUSTRIAN WARE

History: More than 100 potteries were located in the Austro-Hungarian Empire in the late 19th and early 20th centuries. Although Carlsbad was the center of the industry, the factories spread as far as the modern-day Czech Republic.

Many of the factories were either owned or supported by Americans; hence, their wares were produced mainly for export to the United States.

Marks: Many wares do not have a factory mark but only the word "Austrian" in response to the 1891 law specifying that the country of origin had to be marked on imported products.

Additional Listings: Amphora, Carlsbad, Royal Dux, and Royal Vienna.

Plate, yellow and pink flowers, green leaves, small pink twigs, gold trim, embossed swirls, **$25.**

Biscuit jar, cov, 6-1/2" h, two handles, small pink roses dec, mkd "MZ Austria" **200.00**

Bowl, 14" d, handles, marked "Imperial H&C Carlsbad Austria," numbers "2552" and "18," wear to gold edge, repaired chip..................... **50.00**

Celery tray, 12" l, scalloped border, pink roses, green leaves, gold trim **75.00**

Ewer, 11-3/4" h, 6" d, rococo gold scroll, hp pink and yellow wild roses, gold outlines, four ftd **125.00**

Figural group, bronze, cold painted, 13-1/2" w, 14-1/2" h, realistically modeled as small songbird perched on wide leaf in front of tall iris flowers, twig base, late 19th/early 20th C ... **1,840.00**

Compote, pierced rim hung with enameled drops over foliate embossed body, brown, green, and verdigris glaze, stamped "Teplitz, Made in Austria," restoration to three drops, 6-1/2" x 8-3/4", **$1,700.**

Photo courtesy of David Rago Auctions, Inc.

Luncheon plates

9-3/8" d, gilt, bead-molded shaped rim, body with cartouches of turquoise faux jewels on gilt ground, gilt scrollwork and quatrefoils with white jeweled points and mauve enameled centers, late 19th/early 20th C, set of 12 .... **1,300.00**

Carlsbad, "Austrian Plaque," 7" h, oval, portrait of Pope Leo XIII, c1900, imp "Karl Knoll, Carlsbad" **150.00**

Oyster plate, 9-7/8" d, porcelain, shell-shaped wells to center, scalloped rim, blue and gilt enamel flowers, fish, and birds dec, 19th C **175.00**

Perfume set, orange cut glass finials, angular opaque black glass vessels, metal mounts, enameled fan motif, all imp "Austria" on metal, two acid-etched "Austria," 6-1/8" h atomizer, 5-3/8" h perfume, 5" h cov box, imperfections ... **500.00**

Pin tray, 8-1/2" l, irregular scalloped shape, roses, green leaves, white ground, marked "Victoria Carlsbad Austria" **40.00**

Pokal, glass

17-1/2" h, green, detailed enameled cavalier holding empty stein, c1890 ..... **400.00**

18-1/2" h, green, detailed enameled scene of knight on horseback, colorful scrolled acanthus dec, c1890.. **400.00**

Table lamp, attributed to Wiener Werkstatte, in the manner of Susi Singer, ceramic, ovoid, flanked by two mermaid figures in high relief, fish, octopus, and starfish in relief, glossy aqua, orange, white, and irid glazes, textured mottled green and brown ground, gilt highlights, four patinated metal dolphins on stepped metal base, 22-1/4" h **375.00**

Trinket box, cov, 4-1/4" l, oval, the gilt metal box stamped with continuous bands of anthemion and torches, porcelain set lid with printed scene of two classical beauties on cobalt blue ground, velveteen lining, early 20th C **450.00**

Urn, 14-1/2" h, rose bouquet, shaded ivory ground, marked "Carlsbad Austria" **155.00**

Vase, bulbous, Amphora style, embossed with tall tree trunks in silhouette, covered in gold and brown glaze on white ground, stamped "PURN?EW Vienna, Made in Austria," 10-1/2" h, 6-1/2" d, base chip, **$800.**

Photo courtesy of David Rago Auctions, Inc.

Vase, 7-1/4" d, charcoal gray iridescent pottery body relief-decorated with iridescent green branches, orange wash glaze int., Turn-Teplitz, Austria, numbered 3517 .... **825.00**

AUTOGRAPHS

History: Autographs appear on a wide variety of formats—letters, documents, photographs, books, cards, etc. Most collectors focus on a particular person, country, or category, e.g., signers of the Declaration of Independence.

For more information, see *Warman's Americana & Collectibles*, 11th edition.

Abbreviations: The following are used to describe autograph materials.

Materials:

ADS	Autograph Document Signed
ALS	Autograph Letter Signed
AQS	Autograph Quotation Signed
CS	Card Signed
DS	Document Signed
FDC	First Day Cover
LS	Letter Signed
PS	Photograph Signed
TLS	Typed Letter Signed

Colonial America

Hancock, John, endorsement sgd, as Governor, approving sentences levied by garrison court martial against several convicts held on Castle Island, Boston, Aug. 3, 1790, three pgs, folds, minor browning .. **3,910.00**

Jefferson, Thomas, partially printed vellum DS, sgd as president, granting 327 acres on Northwest Territory to Martha Walker, countersigned by Secretary of State James Madison, small hand colored manuscript map on verso, showing location of plot near junction of Scioto and Whetstone rivers, Washington, Feb. 15, 1802, 10" x 12", minor fading **4,370.00**

Nicolls, Richard, DS, as British colonial governor, confirming Peter Stuyvesant's land grant to Egbert van Borsum, for first Brooklyn ferry house, NY, March 12, 1666, 1-1/2 pgs, separated at folds, some loss, wax seal intact **2,990.00**

Foreign

Bonaparte, Napoleon, LS, sgd "Buonparte," to President of Military Council, in French, 1 pg, small 8vo sheet, General in Chief of the Army of the Interior stationery, c1794 .... **1,610.00**

Disraeli, Benjamin, envelope, sgd "Disraeli," addressed to Lady Corneila Guest, 3" x 4" inches, matted and framed **80.00**

Eiffel, Gustave, TLS, Paris, April 19, 1889, sgd "G. Eissel" to E. Hippeau, in French, one page, single 8" x 10" sheet, business stationary, folds **375.00**

Leonov, Alexei, Cosmonaut, worn spacesuit............. **1,997.00**

Peron, Eva, PS, Buenos Aires, Oct. 10, 1950, bust portrait, sgd on mount beneath calligraphic inscription, 9" x 6-1/2" photo on 13-1/2" x 9-1/2" mount, signature light, framed................... **620.00**

General

Einstein, Albert, ALS, to his first wife Mileva, in German, regarding increase in monthly payments for son Tetel, praising his son Albert, acknowledging death of Dr. Zuercher, one page, Dec. 21, 1937 .... **5,060.00**

Ford, Henry and Edsel, TLS, congratulating Albert W. Howard as a new dealer, Dearborn, Aug. 1, 1939, Ford Motor Co. stationery, morocco folder with photograph **1,725.00**

Freud, Sigmund, newspaper photo sgd, "Sigm. Freud," 1932, framed, certificate of authenticity by Charles Hamilton, wax seal on verso of frame, 5-1/2" x 4", yellowed **1,955.00**

Lindbergh, Charles A., PS, inscribed, large close-up portrait in aviator's cap, Acme Newspictures, 13-1/2" x 19-1/2" **1,840.00**

Ruth, Babe

Baseball, graded C.9-9.5 .... **17,270.00**

Photo of Babe Ruth with golfer Rudy Jugan, sgd by Ruth **1,430.00**

Tiffany, Charles Louis, ALS, sgd "C. L. Tiffany" to George Wilson, NY Chamber of Commerce, sending check for dinner honoring Seth Low, one pg, New York, Oct. 5, 1867 .... **415.00**

Vanderbilt, William H., LS, to members of Special Committee of NY Chamber of Commerce, regarding railroad rate legislation, six pgs, New York Central & Hudson River Railroad Co. stationery, New York, Sept. 18, 1879, pin holes, inked stamp on first page **2,760.00**

Wright, Orville and **Wilbur**, check sgd by both, payable to B. F. Goodrich Co., Winters National Bank, 3" x 8-1/4", endorsement stamps on verso, cancellation perforation just above Orville's signature, Dayton, Jan. 26, 1911 .... **4,830.00**

ALS, Connie Mack, "...Felt that I had been in the game along time, am now going back to the game of Golf and am taking long walks which I did before giving up the management of the Athletics. You no [sic] I had given up Golf for a long time will have so much time on my hand,...," trimmed, identified in another hand, one page, 5-1/4" x 3", $290.

Photo courtesy of Historical Collectibles Auctions.

Literature

Aldrich, Thomas Bailey, poem sgd, titled "Three Flowers," inscribed to Bayard Taylor, 14 lines, 1876, one pg ... **260.00**

Browning Robert, ALS, granting permission to reprint two poems in volume edited by H. W. Dulcken, London, April 8, 1867 .... **865.00**

Dickens, Charles, ALS, to J. P. Harley, inviting him for a visit, Twickenham Park, Thursday night, c1838, 2 pgs, toned, soiled, tape repairs **1,035.00**

Frost, Robert, book, *The Best Poems of 1922*, sgd and inscribed by Frost to Carl Bernheimer above poem, The Witch of Coos, page 16, also sgd by Gwendolen Haste on page 57, and Leonora Speyer, page 58, custom slipcase, London, 1923................. **690.00**

Hawthorne, Nathaniel, clipped signature, mounted to another sheet, 1" x 3-3/4" **290.00**

Hemingway, Ernest, ALS, sgd "Papa," to Leonard Lyons, graphic letter describing injuries from plane crash and brush fire while on safari in Africa, Venice, April 8, 1954, two pgs.. **4,370.00**

Shaw, George Bernard, ALS, to Bruno E Kohn, declining request, The Hydro Hotel stationery, Torquay, Oct. 10, 1915, one pg **230.00**

Stowe, Harriet Beecher, quotation sgd "I know that my redeemer liveth," March 13, 1889, 4" x 5", trimmed **230.00**

ANS, hand written, written and signed by Abraham Lincoln, dated April 16, 1859, with card supporting authenticity, **$6,800**.

Photo courtesy of Joy Luke Auctions

Military

Beauregard, Pierre G. T., postcard sgd, thanking General for copies of order, congratulating him, New Orleans, Oct. 27, 1882, repaired tear, staining on verso from prior mounting **375.00**

Custer, George Armstrong, ALS, sgd "Armstrong," to his friend John Bulkley, regretting he declined position on Custer's staff, three pgs, orig envelope, Headquarters, 2nd Brigade, 3rd Div Cap Corp A.P., Summer, 1863, two minor tape repairs at folds **7,475.00**

Mussolini, Benito, PS, close-up bust portrait, looking downwards, sgd on sheet below image, red wax seal affixed to lower left corner, 11" x 7-1/2", minor creases in image, emb stamp on lower right corner of image, framed................. **520.00**

Pershing, John J., books, *My Experiences in the World War,* two volumes, publisher's cloth, author's autograph edition, one of 2,100 numbered copies, New York, 1931 .... **290.00**

Sherman, William T, PS, sgd "W. T. Sherman, General, New York, Feb. 8, 1889," standing 3/4 portrait, in uniform, 11-1/2" x 7" image size, matted, framed **2,300.00**

Thomas, Lorenzo, PS, "Brig Genl I. Thomas, Adj. Genl U.S.A.," bust portrait carte-de-visite by Frederick Gutekunst, orig photographer's mount, sgd on recto at bottom of image, bit yellowed and soiled, revenue stamp affixed on verso.... **260.00**

Music

Bernstein, Leonard, manuscript sgd, high school exam essay on religion and society, April, 1935, 3-1/2 pgs.......................... **520.00**

Caruso, Enrico, PS, inscribed, oval half-length portrait, 10" x 8-1/2" oval, framed **520.00**

Puccini, Giacomo, clipped signature, March 1916, framed, 1-1/2" x 6-1/2" **2,30.00**

Stravinsky, Igor, musical quotation, sgd and inscribed, 20 note tone row from The Flood, Hotel Pierre stationery, New York, May 4, 1962, framed, 7-1/4" x 10-1/4" **1,035.00**

ADS, Thomas McKean, signer of Declaration of Independence, ADS, vellum Pennsylvania land warrant for tract of 1099 acre land in Tioga County, dated June 1, 1806, signed by McKean as Governor, also signed by James Trimble as Deputy Secretary, 12" x 21", **$550**.

Photo courtesy of Alderfer Auction Co.

Presidents

Cleveland, Grover, ALS, to William Steinway, thanking him for grand piano given as a wedding present, three pgs, Executive Mansion stationery, orig envelope, Washington, Aug. 14, 1886 .... **490.00**

Eisenhower, Dwight D., typed quotation sgd, Presidential oath of office, Washington, Jan. 20, 1953, 7" x 5-1/4", framed. **815.00**

Grant, Ulysses, partly printed document, four language ship's papers to Captain West Mitchell for whaling voyage of the bark *Mount Wollaston,* countersigned by Secretary of State Hamilton Fish, Washington, July 8, 1872, one pg, folio **1,495.00**

Hayes, Rutherford B., Remarks of President Hayes, in Celebration of General Garfield's Election, inscribed and sgd "With compliments R. B. Hayes," orig Executive Mansion envelope addressed in Haye's hand to Hon. George K. Forster, postmarked Washington, Nov 17, 1880, 2-1/2 pgs......... **750.00**

Lincoln, Abraham, partially printed vellum DS, appointing Rowland C. Kellogg a Commissary with rank of Captain, countersigned by

Edwin Stanton, Washington, June 8, 1864, 17" x 14-1/2", faded, creased **4,140.00**

Nixon, Ford, Carter, Reagan, and Bush, PS, group portrait standing outside behind podium at dedication of Reagan Library, sgd in varying inks below image, Simi Valley, 1991, 7-3/4" x 10-3/4" **3,450.00**

Pierce, Franklin, ALS, to John E. Starr, asking about commission to investigate arms works at Springfield and Harper's Ferry, Washington, June 20, 1853, mourning stationery, three pgs **1,265.00**

Reagan, Ronald, book sgd, *Speaking My Mind,* sgd and dated on front blank, publisher's blue cloth backed boards, dust jacket, NY, 1989 .... **1,100.00**

Roosevelt, Theodore, TLS, to Sereno E. Pratt, editor of Wall Street Journal, White house Stationery, Washington, March 3, 1906, thanking him for article, 2-1/4 pgs **21,850.00**

Tyler, John, ALS, sgd "J. Tyler," asking for statement of accounts, Washington, April 1, 1842, 1-1/2 pgs **635.00**

Wilson, Woodrow, ALS, to W. A. Stein, request for autograph, Princeton, Feb. 4, 1901, one pg **320.00**

Posters, framed under glass: The Monkees, autographed by Davie Jones, Mickey Dolenz, Peter Tork and Michael Nesmith, 14-1/2" x 18-1/2", **$125**; Batman movie poster, autographed by Adam West, Burt Ward, Lee Merriweather and Frank Gorshin, 20" x 24", **$125**.

Photo courtesy of Joy Luke Auctions

Show business

Barrymore, John, scrapbook assembled by Barrymore for his daughter, sgd and inscribed to her on front pastedown, hundreds of newspaper and magazine clippings relating to his performance in Hamlet at the Haymarket Theatre, other material, oblong folio, orig morocco, London, 1925, some clippings loose **1,035.00**

Booth, Edwin, ALS, concerning availability of box seats for a performance, Dec. 1866, one pg, folded sheet.............. **210.00**
Holiday, Billie, PS, inscribed "To Norman Stay Happy," souvenir group photo taken in Chicago, showing "Lady Day" with five other people, sgd on mat above image, 5" x 7", presentation folder of Garrick Stage Bar, also inscribed by another, inscriptions in pencil **980.00**
Pavlova, Anna, PS, sgd and inscribed, silver print image by C Mishkin, en pointe, inscribed in blue ink on image, Jan 1907, 7-1/2" x 5-1/2", mounted in paper folder **635.00**

PS, Rudolph Valentino (1895-1926) from 1924 film "Monsieur Beaucaire," autograph at center bottom "sincerely Rudolph Valentino," matted, framed, 6" x 8", **$355**.
Photo courtesy of Sloans & Kenyon Auctions

Statesmen

Churchill, Winston, TLS, discussing upcoming General Election, one pg, 28 Hyde Park Gate stationery, London, Jan. 22, 1950, hole punched in upper left margin, minor toning **2,760.00**
Roosevelt, Franklin D., TLS, sgd as Acting Secretary of the Navy, March 27, 1919, on Dept of Navy letterhead, concerning investigation into collision between USS Lake Tahoe and scow W.T.C. #35, 10-1/2" x 8" **500.00**
Seward, William H, ALS, to Frederich Kapp, praising his German-language work on slavery, three pgs, folded, Washington, Dec. 7, 1852 .... **815.00**

Von Stauffenberg, Count, document of Cavalry Riding School, Hannover, Aug. 11, 1936, official school handstamp, 2-1/4" x 6-3/4" **1,925.00**

AUTOMOBILIA

History: Automobilia is a wide-ranging category. It includes just about anything that represents a vehicle, from cookie jars to toys. Car parts are not usually considered automobilia, although there are a few exceptions, like the Lalique radiator ornaments. Most sought after are automobile advertising, especially signs and deal promotional models. The number of items related to the automobile is endless. Even collectors who do not own an antique car are interested in automobile, bus, truck, and motorcycle advertising memorabilia. Many people collect only items from a certain marque, like Hupmobiles or Mustangs, while others may collect all advertising, like matchbooks or color brochures showing the new models for a certain year. Most material changes hands at automobile swap meets, and specialty auctions held throughout the year. Notably "hot" items on the market are service station and trucking company hat badges.

Advertising button

Auto dealership, Butzer Bros, purple on white, early touring car, early 1900s **25.00**
Best Buick Yet, litho of blue night sky studded by tiny white stars, slogan in white outlined in red, late 1930s **35.00**
Buick Fireball 8, graphic red, white, and blue design, for introduction of high-power engine, 1940s **45.00**
Colburn Automobiles, silver on blue, inscribed "Denver Made" **30.00**
Fisk Tires, black, white, and yellow, symbolic youngster ready for bed holding candle and automobile tire, slogan "Time to Re-tire, Get a Fisk," 1930s **20.00**

Flying Red Horse, red on white, symbol for Socony-Vacuum, 1940s............. **15.00**
Hyvis Motor Oil, black on white, center red figure for "Automobile Contest" sponsored by Kapisco Oil Co., Shakopee, Minn., 1930s **12.00**
Nash Airflytes, black inscription on gold, Nash's 50th anniversary year, 1952 .... **28.00**
Pyro-Action Spark Plugs, multicolored image of warrior in armor, orange rim inscribed "Crusade Against Spark Plug Paralysis-Sponsored by Robert Bosch," 1930s .. **10.00**
Advertising tab, 1-1/4" x 2-1/2", Ford Motors Merry Christmas, diecut thin metal tab, two gold lusters, red and green image of Santa in sleigh, red lettering, 1950s **50.00**
Air station, Gilbarco, hose and "Air" sign..................... **1,100.00**
Badge, attendent's uniform type 1-3/4" x 2-1/4", Texaco, inlaid cloisonné enamel **425.00**
2-7/8" x 2-1/4", Tydol Veedol Gasoline Motor Oil Serviceman, inlaid cloisonné enamel, orange and black on silver **675.00**

Calendar plate, 1910, pretty lady in red touring outfit, driving early auto, seasonal floral sprigs, calendar pages, gold text "W. P. Stellmach, Bottler, Schlitz Beer, Shamokin, PA," **$65**.
Photo courtesy of Dotta Auction Co., Inc.

Bottle, Charm Motor Oil, Lima, Ohio, emb, quart............. **440.00**
Calender, 3" x 5-3/4", Harley-Davidson, SD dealer, tin litho, detailed image of 1930s biker on Harley, full 1940 calendar pad, C.8 .... **525.00**
Cap, attendant's, never worn, Ashland patch **330.00**

Catalog

Buick Motor Co., Flint, MI, 1916, 16 pgs, 5-3/4" x 7-1/2", illus of models............ **100.00**
Curtis Aerocar Co., Inc., Coral Gables, FL, 1938, 8 pgs, 7-1/4" x 11-3/4"............ **40.00**
Harley-Davidson Motor Co., Milwaukee, WI, 1937, 12 pgs, 6" x 9", motorcycles, illus
.... **112.00**

Clock, Chevrolet dealer, "Chevy Time"............................ **2,800.00**
Compression tester, Hasting's Piston Ring advertising on dial, orig metal storage box...... **45.00**
Dealership sign, Dodge Plymouth, enameled porcelain, neon **4,000.00**

Display cabinet

Auto Lite Spark Plug, 18-1/2" h, 13" w, painted metal cabinet, glass front..... **125.00**
Schrader tire gauge cabinet, figural tire gauge, opens to reveal parts................ **350.00**

Emblem, Studebaker, red on white litho, late 1930s **20.00**

Gas pump globe

Atlantic, milk glass... **1,045.00**
Boron Supreme, plastic
.... **660.00**
British Shell, cased glass
.... **3,410.00**
White Eagle, eagle-shaped milk glass................ **2,750.00**

Gas pump nozzle, brass.. **110.00**
Island cabinet, Mobil, gargoyle type, 1920s, orig porcelain signs, replaced globe, restored
.... **1,045.00**

Keychain fob

Ford Tractors, dark gold plastic, showing key mechanism for "New Ford Select-O-Speed Tractors," reverse with "Greatest tractor advantage since hydraulics" and Ford logo, late 1940s
.... **12.00**
Shell Oil, silvered metal emblem, painted on reverse with instructions for return if lost, c1930 .... **10.00**

Key ring holder, 3-1/2" h, silvered metal, double ring holder, centered by applied miniature metal 7/8" h figure of smiling and saluting Esso Happy Oil Drop figure finished in porcelain white enamel, copper luster face, Esso logo on chest in red on silver, blue oval logo, 1960s **25.00**

AAA bumper insignia, White Rose Motor Club, York County, painted black and white, **$35.**

Lapel stud, brass, spoked automobile wheel, tiny inscription on tire wall "Albany Automobile Show, Feb. 15-22," center engraved "327," c1922
.... **15.00**
License plate, 1939 Wisconsin, ex-Chet Krause............ **2,000.00**
Lube tank, 43" x 17" x 29" h, double pump, oval, Texaco decals, mounted on wheels, restored........................ **4,510.00**

Oil can

Hudson Motor Oil, Kansas City, 5-1/2" x 4", quart, crimped seal, images of oil tanker, airplanes, and race cars, unopened, C.8.5 **275.00**
Sohio Hand Separator Oil, quart, full.................... **220.00**
Standard Eureka Harness Oil, gallon, full **275.00**

Folder, Chrysler Motors Five Star Show, New York World's Fair, 1940, red, white, and blue cover, rocket taking off from stylized rocket port, diagram of exhibit, products, bottom half with diecut stars denoting attractions, 3-3/4" w, 8-3/4" h, opens to 11-1/4" x 16-3/4", **$30.**

Photo courtesy of Hake's Americana & Collectibles

Oil carrier, wire
Esso, eight orig tall quart bottles with labels.... **2,100.00**
Mobiloil, eight matching embossed Mobil bottles, orig gargoyle spouts....... **4,100.00**

Texaco, eight matching quart bottles, labels, restored spouts, restored carrier
.... **965.00**
Oil carrier, wood, 16" x 12" x 16", Casto Penn Motor Oil, 12 matching tall quart bottles
.... **3,740.00**
Paperweight, Atlantic Richfield, 3" x 3" trapezoid, clear Lucite, small dark amber vial holding liquid "Crude Oil-Prudhoe Bay-North Slope, Alaska," and "Atlantic Richfield Co." with logo in internal blue lettering **15.00**
Pencil clip, Studebaker, diecut and rolled dark think brass with name diagonally across image of spoked automobile wheel, early 1900s **35.00**

Pocket mirror

2-1/4" d, shaded black and white photo, standing man, trees and railing in background, hand on hood of his Ford, license plate "NY 31"
.... **35.00**
2-3/4" x 1-3/4", celluloid, Oak Motoring Suits, man wearing suit standing in front of early car **240.00**
2-3/4" x 1-3/4", celluloid, Perfect Auto Finishing Co., colorful image of old woman and child.................... **130.00**

Two 1950s Ford promotional cars: one black, marked on top "EBY Auto Sales, Inc., Wakarusa, IN," one brown with key wind, **$150.**

Photo courtesy of Joy Luke Auctions

Pump

American Pump Co., octagon body, restored 10 gallon visible pump............ **2,640.00**
Erie, clock face type, Shell decals, restored, replaced globe **2,970.00**
Fry Mae West, 10-gallon visible pump, Shell decals, replaced globe, restored
.... **3,500.00**
Gilbert & Barker T-8 curbside pump, White Flash decals, restored **2,475.00**
Service Station Equipment Corp., Atlantic Richfield decals, twin 10 gallon visible tubes, restored, reproduced globes.................... **10,100.00**

Wayne, Model 60, digital computing, Gilmore decals, c1930, restored **3,190.00**
Wayne, non-visible self-measuring pump, c1912 .... **3,300.00**

Radiator water can
Charm Oil, The Radiant Oil Co., Lima, OH, half gallon **470.00**
Sinclair label, restored... **400.00**

Sales poster, International Harvester, friction drive tractor, 1907 .... **3,850.00**

Travel puzzle, two sided, The Continental Line, black and white illus, red, black, and white center logo, 40+ pieces, **$75**

Sign
Mobiloil, 37" x 32", lollipop style, flying red horse, some damage **500.00**
Pencoil Motor Oils, 14" x 42" wood frame metal **180.00**
Power-lube Motor Oil, Smooth as the tread of a tiger, orig condition, porcelain, 28" l, 20" h........................ **1,595.00**
Rest Rooms, black and white silhouettes of lady with hoop skirt and parasol and gentleman with cane .. **775.00**
Sinclair Clean Rest Rooms, 37" x 30", porcelain, orig condition...................... **415.00**
Solar Refining, Lima, Ohio, round, 30" d, rust and damage **1,870.00**
Sunoco, 14" x 22", double sided, porcelain, orig wrought iron hanging bracket, U-Gas-Um, porcelain, image of Indian boy, restored.... **600.00**
Willys Sales-Service, double sided, hanging type **3,800.00**

Stickpin, Kent Grease, diecut thin celluloid, tan and blue pennant on brass stickpin, 1920s **20.00**

Thermometer, Red Crown Gasoline, porcelain **1,265.00**

Tie bar, Sun Oil, 1939 award, silvered metal spring clip bar, chains suspending metal pendant formed in miniature replica of Sun Oil logo, bronze luster diamond logo inscribed "Bowling-Sun Oil-1939" **30.00**

BACCARAT GLASS

History: The Sainte-Anne glassworks at Baccarat in Voges, France, was founded in 1764 and produced utilitarian soda glass. In 1816, Aime-Gabriel d'Artiques purchased the glassworks, and a Royal Warrant was issued in 1817 for the opening of Verrerie de Vonâoche éa Baccarat. The firm concentrated on lead-crystal glass products. In 1824, a limited company was created.

From 1823 to 1857, Baccarat and Saint-Louis glassworks had a commercial agreement and used the same outlets. No merger occurred. Baccarat began the production of paperweights in 1846. In the late 19th century, the firm achieved an international reputation for cut glass table services, chandeliers, display vases, centerpieces, and sculptures. Products eventually included all forms of glassware.

Additional Listings: Paperweights.

For more information, see *Warman's Glass*, 4th edition.

Bonbon, 5-3/4" d, amberina, swirled mold, pedestal foot, emb "Baccarat" **150.00**
Candelabra, pr, crystal, 32" h, four light, diamond-cut baluster standard, four scrolling candle arms terminating urn-form sockets, etched glass globes hung with prisms.......... **2,000.00**
Cologne bottle, 6" h, Rose Tiente, matching stopper, price for pr **100.00**
Decanter, 11-5/8" h, flattened ovoid, scalloped edge, etched flat sides with hunter on horseback, forest animals, scrolling vine, neck with vine etching, similarly shaped and etched stopper, 20th C, price for pr **550.00**
Figure, porcupine, clear, trademark on base, 5" l, 3" h **150.00**
Finger bowl, 4-3/4" d, 6-3/4" d underplate, ruby ground, gold medallions and flowers dec **350.00**
Garniture, 22" h five-light candelabrum and four candlesticks, all hung with pendants..................... **2,275.00**

Obelisk, crystal, marked, **$45**.

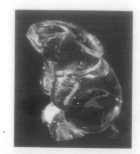

Paperweight, rabbit, crystal, marked, **$85**.
Photo courtesy of Joy Luke.

Lamp, 19-1/2" l, 24-1/2" h, central cut glass urn on short brass stem, two horizontal reeded candle arms, fan cut drip pans suspending cut prisms, ovoid glass knop stem, paneled trumpet foot cut with roundels, brass flat leaf base, one with collar at urn for further prisms, other with collars for two etched-glass shades, electrified, early 20th C, price for pr....... **2,875.00**

Paperweight, concentric multi-colored millefiori mushroom, green and white striped stem, light blue-over-white double overlay, multi-faceted top, six-faceted sides, flower-cut bottom, acid-etched insignia and date 1970 on base, 3-1/4" d, **$520**.

Photo courtesy of Alderfer Auction Co.

Paperweight, concentric millefiori, central pink cane, encircled by eight close packed rings of canes in yellow, pink, green, blue, and purple, outer-most ring extends in radiating canes on bottom of weight, acid-etched insignia on base, 3" d, **$350**.

Photo courtesy of Alderfer Auction Co.

Liquor set, 8-1/2" h decanter, 10 matching cordials, gilt dec Neoclassical motif........... **450.00**

Vase, 9-3/4" h, colorless, tapered cylindrical, slightly everted rim, vertical tapered flutes on body, press-cut, 20th C **165.00**
Wash bowl and pitcher, 12-1/2" h pitcher, 16-1/2" d bowl, colorless, swirled rib design, pitcher with applied handle and polished base, ground table ring on bowl, polished chip.... **250.00**

BANKS, MECHANICAL

History: Banks which display some form of action while accepting a coin are considered mechanical banks. Mechanical banks date back to ancient Greece and Rome, but the majority of collectors are interested in those made between 1867 and 1928 in Germany, England, and the United States.

Initial research suggested that approximately 250 to 300 different or variant designs of banks were made in the early period. Today that number has been revised to 2,000-3,000 types and varieties. The field remains ripe for discovery and research.

More than 80 percent of all cast-iron mechanical banks produced between 1869 and 1928 were made by J. E. Stevens Co., Cromwell, Connecticut. Tin banks are usually of German origin.

Reproduction Alert:
Reproductions, fakes, and forgeries exist for many banks. Forgeries of some mechanical banks were made as early as 1937, so age alone is not a guarantee of authenticity. In the following price listings, two asterisks indicate banks for which serious forgeries exist, and one asterisk indicates banks for which casual reproductions have been made.

Notes: While rarity is a factor in value, appeal of design, action, quality of manufacture, country of origin, and history of collector interest also are important. Radical price fluctuations may occur when there is an imbalance in these factors. Rare banks may sell for a few hundred dollars, while one of

more common design with greater appeal will sell in the thousands.

The mechanical bank market is being greatly affected by the on-line auctions found on the Internet. This past year has seen more examples of banks being offered for sale than has been seen in decades. Many of these previously unavailable examples are readily purchased by collectors. Because of large numbers of more common banks also coming into the market, this past year represents a drop in the price of many banks, especially those in the under $3,500 range, but recently the market appears to have stabilized on banks under $3,500. It looks like the market is now poised for potential movement upward on these lower priced banks. Additionally, there have been large sums of investment money coming onto the mechanical bank market, as of late, specifically directed at purchasing banks in the $20,000 to $100,000 and up levels per bank, causing an upward trend in these higher priced banks. It is my theory that much of this money has been moved into mechanical banks by non-collecting investors who have become fed up with the performance of the stock market and are searching for other directions of investment to protect their capital. I strongly suspect that this trend will continue.

The values listed here accurately represent the selling prices of mechanical banks in the specialized collectors' market. As some banks are hard to find, and the market is quite volatile both up and down in price structure, consultation of a competent specialist in mechanical banks, with up-to-the-moment information, is advised prior to selling any mechanical bank.

The prices listed are for original old mechanical banks with no repairs, in sound operating condition, and with at least 90 percent of the original paint intact. Banks that have touch-ups, flaws, repairs, or less than 90 percent of their original paint sell for much less than these prices. Banks with missing pieces often sell for as little as 10 percent to 20 percent of these prices.

Adviser: James S. Maxwell Jr.

Price note: Prices quoted are for 100 percent original examples with no repairs, no repaint, and which have at least 90 percent bright original paint. An asterisk indicates casual reproductions; † denotes examples where casual reproductions and serious fakes exist.

Always Did "Spise a Mule," boy seated on bench, missing trap door, 10" l, 6" h, **$990**.

Photo courtesy of Joy Luke Auctions.

†**Acrobat**...................... 1,200.00
African Bank, black bust, back emb "African Bank" 550.00
American Bank, sewing machine 950.00
***Artillery** 900.00
Automatic Fortune Bank, tin 3,700.00
Automatic Savings Bank, tin, soldier 270.00
Automatic Savings Bank, tin, sailor 250.00
†**Baby Elephant X-O'clock**, lead and wood 1,200.00
***Bad Accident** 1,650.00
Bear, tin...................... 280.00
†**Bear and Tree Stump** 1,000.00
†**Bear**, slot in chest 320.00
†**Bill E. Grin**.................. 500.00
†**Billy Goat Bank**........... 230.00
Bow-ery Bank, iron, paper, wood 2,000.00
Bowing Man in Cupola 1,800.00
†**Bowling Alley**........... 4,500.00
†**Boy and bull dog** 4,500.00
†**Boys stealing watermelons** 850.00
British Clown, tin 12,000.00
***Bull Dog**, place coin on nose 1,800.00
†**Bull and Bear**......... 75,000.00
†**Bull Dog**, standing 950.00
Bureau, Lewando's, wood 28,000.00
Burnett Postman, tin man with tray 2,580.00
†**Butting Buffalo**............ 850.00
†**Butting Goat** 1,200.00

***Cabin**, black man flips .. 575.00
Caller Vending, tin 2,800.00
†**Calamity**.................... 2,800.00
†**Called Out**................. 1,500.00
Calumet, tin and cardboard, with Calumet Kid............. 200.00
Calumet, tin and cardboard, with sailor 18,000.00
Calumet, tin and cardboard, with soldier................. 20,000.00
Calumet, tin only, with Calumet Kid 250.00
†**Camera**...................... 850.00
***Cat and Mouse**............. 775.00
†**Cat and Mouse**, giant cat standing on top......... 45,000.00
***Chief Big Moon** 1,080.00
Child's Bank, wood........ 450.00
Chocolate Menier, tin 950.00
†**Chrysler Pig**................ 950.00
Cigarette Vending, tin.... 420.00
Cigarette Vending, lead 1,200.00
†**Circus**, ticket collector . 375.00
†**Clown on Bar**, tin and iron 1,200.00
***Clown on Globe** 1,800.00
Clown with arched top, tin 150.00
Clown with black face, tin 675.00
Clown with white face, tin 125.00
Clown with white face, round, tin 3,700.00
Columbian Magic Savings, wood and paper 12,000.00
Cowboy with tray, tin 250.00
Crescent Cash Register 3,100.00
Crowing Rooster, circular base, tin 4,500.00

Creedmoor, hunter with gun firing into tree, 10" l, 6-3/4" h, **$675**.

Photo courtesy of Joy Luke Auctions.

†**Cupola**........................ 750.00
***Darktown Battery** 2,200.00
†**Darky Watermelon**, man kicks football at watermelon.. 8,500.00
Dinah, iron 300.00
Dinah, aluminum 200.00
†**Dog with tray** 450.00
***Eagle and Eaglettes**..... 750.00
Electric Safe, steel...... 1,200.00

***Elephant and Three Clowns** 850.00
***Elephant**, locked howdah 260.00
Elephant, man pops out, wood, cloth, iron 370.00
†**Elephant**, no stars 3,700.00
***Elephant**, pull tail........... 70.00
†**Elephant with tusks**, on wheels........................ 350.00
English Bulldog, tin....... 280.00
5 cents Adding 200.00
Football, English football 1,200.00
Fortune Teller, Savings, safe 1,320.00
†**Freedman's Bank**, wood, lead, brass, tin, paper, etc.. 55,000.00
Frog on rock 575.00
†**Frogs**, two frogs 650.00
***Gem**, dog with building 1,700.00
German Vending, tin... 1,200.00
†**Giant in Tower**............. 950.00
Girl Feeding Geese, tin, paper, lead 24,000.00
†**Girl in Victorian chair** 1,200.00
Guessing, woman's figure, iron 1,500.00
Guessing, woman's figure, lead 900.00
Hall's Liliput, with tray ... 200.00
Hartwig and Vogel, vending, tin 750.00
Highwayman, tin 400.00
***Hindu**, bust 450.00
|**Hold the Fort**, two varieties, each 750.00
Hoop-La 1,400.00
***Horse Race**, two varieties, each 1,200.00
†**Humpty Dumpty**, bust of clown with name on back, iron 1,680.00
***I Always Did 'spise a Mule**, black man on mule 750.00
***Indian and Bear** 950.00
†**Indian Chief**, black man bust with Indian feathered headdress, aluminum 575.00
†**Initiating Bank**, first degree 650.00
Initiating Bank, second degree 850.00
John R. Jennings Trick Drawer Money Box, wood 16,500.00
***Jolly Nigger**, American . 390.00
Jolly Nigger, lettering in Greek 225.00
Jolly Nigger, lettering in Arabic 1,200.00
***Jolly Nigger**, raises hat, lead 800.00

Jolly Nigger, wear, **$300**.

Jolly Nigger, raises hat, iron 1,320.00
Jolly Nigger, with fez, aluminum 450.00
Jonah and The Whale Bank, large rectangular base ... 1,200.00
†Jonah and The Whale Bank, stands on two ornate legs with rect coin box at center . 5,500.00
†Jumbo, elephant on wheels 300.00
Kick Inn Bank, wood... 1,500.00
†Leap Frog 1,320.00
Lehmann Berlin Tower, tin 350.00
Lehmann, London Tower, tin 350.00
†Light of Asia 425.00
Lion, tin......................... 400.00
†Lion and Two Monkeys 1,110.00

Lion and two monkeys, wear, **$850**.

*Little Joe Bank 570.00
Little Moe Bank 280.00
*Magic Bank, iron house 470.00
Magic Bank, tin 200.00
†Magician...................... 950.00
†Mama Katzenjammer 1,050.00

†Mammy and Child 1,050.00
*Mason 1,500.00
*Merry-Go-Round, mechanical, coin activates............... 1,400.00
†Merry-Go-Round, semi-mechanical, spin by hand 400.00
Mikado Bank.............. 5,500.00
†Milking Cow 1,600.00
Model Railroad Drink Dispenser, tin 15,500.00
*Monkey and Coconut .. 950.00
†Monkey Bank 500.00
Monkey, chimpanzee in ornate circular bldg, iron........... 575.00
†Monkey, slot in stomach 300.00
Monkey, tin, tips hat 270.00
Mule Entering Barn 775.00
Musical Church, wood... 450.00
Musical Savings, tin 300.00
Musical Savings, velvet-covered easel 270.00
Musical Savings, wood house 570.00
National, Your Savings, cash register........................ 1,680.00
*New Bank, lever at center 280.00
*New Bank, lever at left.. 240.00
†North Pole Bank 1,200.00
Old Mother Hubbard, tin 450.00
*Organ Bank, boy and girl 570.00
*Organ Bank, medium, only monkey figure 270.00
Organ Grinder and Dancing Bear 1,050.00
Owl, slot in head............ 220.00
*Owl, turns head............ 280.00
*Paddy and the Pig....... 950.00
Pascal Chocolate Cigarettes, vending, tin 1,080.00
Pay Phone Bank, iron . 1,680.00
Pay Phone Bank, tin 450.00
*Pelican, Arab head pops out 370.00
*Pelican, man thumbs nose 330.00
†Perfection Registering, girl and dog at blackboard ... 900.00
*Picture Gallery 1,400.00
Pinball Vending, tin..... 1,320.00
Pistol Bank, iron 250.00
Policeman, tin 350.00
Post Office Savings, steel 1,200.00
†Presto, iron building..... 570.00
*Presto, penny changes optically to quarter 575.00
Pump and Bucket....... 1,200.00
*Punch and Judy, iron 1,400.00
Punch and Judy, iron front, tin back 550.00
†Queen Victoria, bust, brass 1,500.00

Rex Rooster, some wear to original paint, 6-1/4" l, 6-1/4" h, **$550**.
Photo courtesy of Joy Luke Auctions.

†Queen Victoria, bust, iron 2,500.00
†Rabbit Standing, large 410.00
†Rabbit Standing, small 225.00
†Red Riding Hood, iron 1,650.00
Red Riding Hood, tin, vending 700.00
†Rival Bank.............. 1,950.00
Robot Bank, aluminum .. 390.00
Robot Bank, iron............ 620.00
Royal Trick Elephant, tin 2,200.00
Safe Deposit Bank, tin, elephant...................... 800.00
Sailor Face, tin, pointed top 1,920.00
Sam Segal's Aim to Save, iron 1,080.00
*Santa Claus................. 875.00
†Schley Bottling Up Cevera 585.00
School Teacher, tin and wood, American 750.00
Seek Him Frisk.......... 2,000.00
†Shoot That Hat Bank 1,600.00
†Shoot the Chute Bank 1,200.00
†Smith X-ray Bank 675.00
*Snap-It Bank 840.00
Snow White, tin and lead 475.00
*Speaking Dog 1,125.00

Speaking Dog, wear, **$875**.

Spring Jawed Cat, pot metal **120.00**
Spring Jawed Chinaman, pot metal **550.00**
Spring Jawed Felix the Cat, pot metal **3,700.00**
Spring Jawed Mickey Mouse, pot metal **13,500.00**
Spring Jawed Penguin, pot metal **120.00**
Springing Cat **2,350.00**
†**Squirrel and Tree Stump** **410.00**
Starkies Aeroplano, aluminum, cardboard **9,500.00**
Starkies Aeroplane, aluminum, steel **14,000.00**
Stollwerk Bros., two penny, vending, tin **840.00**
Stollwerk Bros., Victoria, spar-automat, tin **570.00**
*****Stump Speaker Bank** **1,200.00**
Symphonium Musical Savings, wood **1,200.00**
†**Tabby** **250.00**
*****Tammany Bank** **225.00**
Tank and Cannon, aluminum **1,200.00**
Tank and Cannon, iron **1,680.00**
†**Target Bank** **250.00**
†**Target In Vestibule** **570.00**
*****Teddy and The Bear** **990.00**
Tiger, tin **270.00**
Time Lock Savings **345.00**
*****Toad on Stump** **400.00**
*****Trick Dog**, six-part base **875.00**
*****Trick Dog**, solid base **400.00**
*****Trick Pony Bank** **750.00**
Trick Savings, wood, end drawer **400.00**
Try Your Weight, tin, mechanical **1,560.00**
†**Turtle Bank** **1,200.00**
Two Ducks Bank, lead **2,000.00**
†**U.S. and Spain** **850.00**
†**Uncle Remus Bank** **950.00**
†**Uncle Sam Bank**, standing figure with satchel **1,125.00**
†**Uncle Sam**, bust **280.00**
†**Uncle Tom**, no lapels, with star **255.00**
†**Uncle Tom**, lapels, with star **280.00**
†**Uncle Tom**, no star **260.00**
Viennese soldier **750.00**
Watch Bank, blank face, tin **120.00**
Watch Bank, stamped face, tin **90.00**
Weeden's Plantation, tin, wood **510.00**
Whale Bank, pot metal... **300.00**
*****William Tell**, iron........... **775.00**

William Tell, crossbow, Australian, sheet steel, aluminum **875.00**
Woodpecker Bank, large, tin, c1910 .... **450.00**
Woodpecker Bank, small, tin, c1930-1960 .... **50.00**
*****World's Fair Bank** **720.00**
Zentral Sparkasse, steel **720.00**
Zig Zag Bank, iron, tin, papier-mâché **4,120.00**
*****Zoo** **900.00**

BANKS, STILL

History: Banks with no mechanical action are known as still banks. The first still banks were made of wood or pottery or from gourds. Redware and stoneware banks, made by America's early potters, are prized possessions of today's collectors.

Still banks reached a golden age with the arrival of the cast-iron bank. Leading manufacturing companies include Arcade Mfg. Co., J. Chein & Co., Hubley, J. & E. Stevens, and A. C. Williams. The banks often were ornately painted to enhance their appeal. During the cast-iron era, banks and other businesses used the still bank as a form of advertising.

The tin lithograph bank, again frequently a tool for advertising, reached its zenith from 1930 to 1955. The tin bank was an important premium, whether a Pabst Blue Ribbon beer can bank or a Gerber's Orange Juice bank. Most tin advertising banks resembled the packaging of the product.

Almost every substance has been used to make a still bank—die-cast white metal, aluminum, brass, plastic, glass, etc. Many of the early glass candy containers also converted to a bank after the candy was eaten. Thousands of varieties of still banks were made, and hundreds of new varieties appear on the market each year.

Brass

Beehive, 4" h, 4-1/2" d, EOS, well detailed, base marked "A. B. Dalames Bank" **385.00**

Cast iron, reindeer, original gold paint, $150.
Photo courtesy of Dotta Auction Co., Inc.

Cast iron

Building, 2-3/4" to 4-3/4" h, Kyser & Rex, Town Hall and Log Cabin, chimney on left side, "Town Hall Bank" painted yellow, c1882 .... **260.00**

Cast iron, Presto Bank building, #485, original key, $225.
Photo courtesy of Dotta Auction Co., Inc.

Bungalow, 3-3/4" h, Grey Iron Ceiling Co., porch, painted **470.00**
Cab, Arcade, 7-3/4" l, Yellow Cab, painted orange and black, stenciling on doors, seated driver, rubber tires, painted metal wheels, coin slot in roof **935.00**
Cat with ball, 2-1/2" x 5-11/16", A. C. Williams, painted gray, gold ball........................... **190.00**
Circus elephant, 3-7/8" h, Hubley, colorfully painted, seated position **180.00**

Coronation, 6-5/8" h, Syndeham & McOustra, England, ornately detained, emb busts in center, England, c1911 .... **200.00**

Duck, 4-3/4" h, Hubley, colorfully painted, outstretched wings, slot on back **165.00**

Dutch boy and girl, 5-1/4" and 5-1/8" h, Hubley, colorfully painted, boy on barrel, girl holding flowers, c1930, price for pr **260.00**

Egyptian tomb, 6-1/4" x 5-1/4", green finish, pharaoh's tomb entrance, hieroglyphics on front panel **275.00**

Elk, 9-1/2" h, painted gold, full antlers **155.00**

Globe safe, 5" h, Kenton, round sphere, claw feet, nickeled combination lock on front hinged door **80.00**

Hall clock, 5-3/4" h, swinging pendulum visible through panel **110.00**

Horseshoe, 4-1/4" x 4-3/4", Arcade, Buster Brown and Tige with horse, painted black and gold **125.00**

Husky, 5" h, Grey Iron Casting Co., painted brown, black eyes, yellow box, repaired **365.00**

Jewel chest, 6-1/8" x 4-5/8", ornate casting, ftd bank, brass combination lock on front, top lifts for coin retrieval, crack at corner **90.00**

Kodak, 4-1/4" x 5" w, J & E Stevens, nickeled, highly detailed casting, intricate pattern, emb "Kodak Bank" on front opening panel, c1905 .... **225.00**

North Pole, 4-1/4" h, nickeled, Grey Iron Casting Co., depicts wooden pole with handle, emb lettering **415.00**

Mailbox, 5-1/2" h, Hubley, painted green, emb "Air Mail," with eagle, standing type **220.00**

Maine, 4-5/8" l, Grey Iron Casting Co., japanned, gold highlights, c1900 .... **660.00**

Mammy, 5-1/4" h, Hubley, hands on hips, colorfully painted **300.00**

Pagoda, 5" x 3" x 3", England, gold trim, c1889 .... **240.00**

Pershing, General, 7-3/4" h, Grey Iron Casting Co., full bust, detailed casting **65.00**

Pig, 2-1/2" h, 5-1/4" l, Hubley, laughing, painted brown, trap on bottom **120.00**

Professor Pug Frog, 3-1/4" h, A.C. Williams, painted gold, blue jacket, new twist pin **195.00**

Radio, Kenton, 4-1/2" h, metal sides and back, painted green, nickeled front panel in Art-Deco style **445.00**

Reindeer, 9-1/2" h, 5-1/4" l, A. C. Williams, painted gold, full rack of antlers, replaced screw **55.00**

Rumplestiltskin, 6" h, painted gold, long red hat, base and feet, marked "Do You Know Me," c1910 .... **210.00**

Cast iron, safe, Security Safe Deposit, black, gold toned dial, original combination taped to bottom, large size, **$125**.

Safe, 4-3/8" h, Kyser & Rex, Young America, japanned, intricate casting, emb at top, c1882 .... **275.00**

Sharecropper, 5-1/2" h, A. C. Williams, painted black, gold, and red, toes visible on one foot **240.00**

Spitz, 4-1/4" x 4-1/2", Grey Iron Casting Co., painted gold, repaired **165.00**

Steamboat, 7-1/2" l, Arcade, painted gold **190.00**

Stove, 4-3/4" h, Gem, Abendroth Bros., traces of bronzing, back marked "Gem Heaters Save Money" **275.00**

Tank, 9-1/2" l, 4" w, Ferrosteel, side mounted guns, rear spoke wheels, emb on sides, c1919 .... **385.00**

U.S. Mail, 5-1/8" h, Kenton, painted silver, gold painted emb eagle, red lettering large trap on back panel **180.00**

World Time, 4-1/8" x 2-5/8", Arcade, paper time-tables of various cities around the world **315.00**

Cast iron, dime register dime, well pump and bucket, partial label "No. 127 Pump Registering…," 5-3/4" w, 6-1/2" h, **$2,500**.

Photo courtesy of Joy Luke Auctions.

Glass, Bank of Independence Hall 1776-1876, 7 1/2" h, **$160**.

Photo courtesy of Joy Luke Auctions.

Cast iron, penny, Dolly Dimple, girl in bonnet with parasol, 4" w, 7-1/2" h, **$125**.

Photo courtesy of Joy Luke Auctions.

Chalk

Cat, 11" h, seated, stripes, red bow **200.00**

Winston Churchill, 5-1/4" h, bust, painted green, back etched "Save for Victory," wood base **55.00**

Glass

Charles Chaplin, 3-3/4" h, Geo Borgfeldt & Co., painted figure standing next to barrel slotted on lid, name emb on base ... **220.00**

Lead

Boxer, 2-5/8" h, Germany, head, painted brown, black facial details, lock on collar, bent in back **130.00**
Burro, 3-1/2" x 3-1/2", Japan, lock on saddle marked "Plymouth, VT" **125.00**
Ocean liner, 2-3/4" x 7-5/8" l, bronze electroplated, three smoking stacks, hinged trap on deck, small hole.............. **180.00**
Pug, 2-3/4" h, Germany, painted, stenciled "Hershey Park" on side, lock on collar **300.00**

Pottery

Acorn, 3-1/2" d, 4" h, redware, paper label reads "Tithing Day/ At The/First Methodist Episcopal Church/Sunday January 2nd 1916/In the Interest of the Improvement Fund" **220.00**
Bulbous, 3-1/4" h, redware, marked with initials "C.R.S.," 3-1/4" h, flakes on base .. **220.00**
Dresser, 6-1/2" w, 4" d, 4-1/2" h, redware, Empire chest of drawers shape, Philadelphia, PA, loss to feet, roughness on edges **220.00**
Hanging persimmon, 5" x 3", redware, yellow and red paint **90.00**
House, 7-1/2" h, redware, Georgian style house, brown glazed accents, good detail on windows and doorways, central chimney, Jim Seagreaves, sgd "JCS" **425.00**
Jug, 7-1/2" h, redware, bulbous, bird atop mouth, green and yellow sgraffito dev, Jim Seagreaves, sgd "JCS" .. **515.00**

Steel

Life boat, 14" l, pressed, painted yellow and blue, boat length decal marked "Contributions for Royal National Life Boat Institution," deck lifts for coin removal, over painted **060.00**
Postal savings, 4-5/8" h, 5-3/8" w, copper finish, glass view front panel, paper registering strips, emb "U.S.Mail" on sides, top lifts to reveal four coin slots, patent 1902 .... **95.00**

Stoneware

Dog's head, white clay, yellow glaze, two-tone brown sponging, 4" h, shallow flakes.......... **175.00**

Ovoid, brushed cobalt blue flowers, leaves, and finial, minor flakes at coin slot, 6" h . **6,875.00**
Pig, sitting, sgd in dark green "Delight M. Caskey Merry Christmas," 6-1/4" l **3,000.00**

Tin litho

Keene Savings, Kingsbury, bank building shape, 6-1/2" x 6" x 3", non-working tally wheels **70.00**

Tin, Popeye Daily Dime Bank, original closure, **$205**.

Photo courtesy of Dotta Auction Co., Inc.

Tin, monkey, tips his hat when coin is placed in slot, red jacket, gold and tan organ grinder box in front, tan hat, **$45**.

White metal

Amish Boy, seated on bale of straw, 4-3/4" x 3-3/8", U.S., painted in bright colors, key lock trap on bottom **55.00**
Cat with bow, 4-1/8" h, painted white, blue bow.............. **155.00**
Gorilla, colorfully painted in brown hues, seated position, trap on bottom **165.00**
Pig, 4-3/8" h, painted white, decal marked "West Point, N.Y." on belly **30.00**

Rabbit, 4-1/2" h, seated, painted brown, painted eyes, trap on bottom, crack in ear.......... **30.00**
Spaniel, seated, 4-1/2" h, painted white, black highlights **470.00**
Uncle Sam Hat, 3-1/2" h, painted red, white, and blue, stars on brim, slot on top, trap on bottom........................... **135.00**

Wood

Burlwood inlaid with exotic woods, top dec with geometric banding, front with sailing vessels, end panels with flags, Prisoner of War, late 19th C, 5" x 8" x 5-1/4", imperfections **1,150.00**

BARBER BOTTLES

History: Barber bottles, colorful glass bottles found on shelves and counters in barber shops, held the liquids barbers used daily. A specific liquid was kept in a specific bottle, which the barber knew by color, design, or lettering. The bulk liquids were kept in utilitarian containers under the counter or in a storage room.

Barber bottles are found in many types of glass—art glass with various decorations, pattern glass, and commercially prepared and labeled bottles.

Note: Prices are for bottles without original stoppers, unless otherwise noted.

Advertising

Koken's Quinine Tonic for the Hair, 7-1/2" h, clear, label under glass **195.00**
Lucky tiger, red, green, yellow, black, and gilt label under glass, emb on reverse.. **85.00**
Vegederma, cylindrical, bulbous, long neck, amethyst, white enamel dec of bust of woman with long flower hair, tooled mouth, pontil scar, 8" h **130.00**
Amber, Hobb's Hobnail .. **250.00**
Amethyst, Mary Gregory type dec, white enameled child and flowers, 8" h **200.00**
Cobalt blue, cylindrical, bulbous body, long neck, white enamel, traces of gold dec, tooled mouth, pontil scar, 7-1/4" h **100.00**

Emerald green, cylindrical bell form, long neck, orange and white enameled floral dec, sheared mouth, pontil scar, some int. haze, 8-1/2" h .. **210.00**

Latticino, cylindrical, bulbous, long neck, clear frosted glass, white, red, and pale green vertical stripes, tooled mouth, pontil scar, 8-1/4" h **200.00**

Milk glass, opaque white body, green fern decoration, black lettering, one reads "Bay Rum," the other "Toilet Water," worn gold trim, pontil marks, no stoppers, price for pair, **$165**.

Milk glass, Witch Hazel, painted letters and flowers, 9" h... **115.00**

Opal glass, squatty, blue and purple pansies dec, Mt Washington, numbered 1039, 7" h **100.00**

Opalescent
Coin Spot, blue........... **300.00**
Seaweed, cranberry, bulbous **465.00**

Sapphire blue, enameled white and yellow daisies, green leaves, 8-5/8" h **125.00**

BARBIE

History: In 1945, Harold Matson (MATT) and Ruth and Elliott (EL) Handler founded Mattel. Initially the company made picture frames but became involved in the toy market when Elliott Handler began to make doll furniture from scrap material. When Harold Matson left the firm, Elliott Handler became

chief designer and Ruth Handler principal marketer. In 1955, Mattel advertised its products on "The Mickey Mouse Club," and the company prospered.

In 1958, Mattel patented a fashion doll. The doll was named "Barbie" and reached the toy shelves in 1959. By 1960, Barbie's popularity was assured.

Development of a boyfriend for Barbie, named Ken after the Handlers' son, began in 1960. Over the years, many other dolls were added. Clothing, vehicles, room settings, and other accessories became an integral part of the line.

From September 1961 through July 1972, Mattel published a Barbie magazine. At its peak, the Barbie Fan Club was second only to the Girl Scouts as the largest girls' organization in the United States.

Always remember that a large quantity of Barbie dolls and related material has been manufactured. Because of this easy availability, only objects in excellent to mint condition with original packaging (also in very good or better condition) have significant value. If items show signs of heavy use, their value is probably minimal.

Collectors prefer items from the first decade of production. Learn how to distinguish a Barbie #1 doll from its successors. The Barbie market is one of subtleties.

Recently many collectors have shifted their focus from the dolls themselves to the accessories. There have been rapid price increases in early clothing and accessories.

Barbie is now a billion-dollar baby, the first toy in history to reach this prestigious mark—that's a billion dollars per year, just in case you're wondering.

For more information, see *Warman's Barbie Doll Field Guide*.

Accessories

Alarm clock, beige plastic, gold clock numbers, gold metal knobs on back, 1964, VG, nonworking **320.00**

Autographs book, black vinyl, graphics on cover, white and colored pages, age discolored rect sticker on upper left corner, 1961, NM/VG **125.00**

Barbie Teen Dream Bedroom, dated 1970, MIB, discoloration to orig box........................ **65.00**

Binder with pencil case, black vinyl covers, metal three-ring bidder, Dennison Webster's Notebook Dictionary, Study-Aids in Arithmetic, English Grammar, American History, General Science, 1962, NJ **400.00**

Lunch kit, black vinyl, thermos, cardboard insert, plastic handle, metal closure, 1962 .... **145.00**

Paper doll book, Whitman, uncut
Barbie's Boutique, #1954, dated 1973, NM............ **85.00**
Francie with Growing Pretty Hair, #1982, dated 1973, NM **35.00**
Midge, #1962, dated 1963, NM.............................. **145.00**

Play ring, adjustable, side view of Ponytail Barbie head surrounded by 10 clear rhinestones, clear plastic case with blue bottom, cardboard backing, pre-priced at .29, 1962, NRFC **135.00**

Snaps n' Scraps, blue vinyl covers, graphics on front cover, nine construction paper-type pages, black plastic binder with cord ties, 1961, VG **125.00**

Transistor radio, Vanity Fair, black vinyl case, Barbie graphics, metal closure, black velveteen liner, peach colored plastic radio, gold front, plastic dials, plastic and metal earphones, matching plastic case, 1962, VG **650.00**

Wallet, red vinyl, graphic of Barbie wearing Enchanted Evening, zipper closure on coin compartment, attached metal bead chain, four clear plastic photo holders, black and white photo of Perry Como and Maureen O'Hara, cream colored plastic change holder, mirror, snap closure, 1962, VG **120.00**

Barbie dolls

American Girl Barbie

Brunette, tan lips, fingernails painted, bendable legs, knit Pak dress, fringe trim, cord belt, pale no box, VG . **300.00**
Golden blond, beige lips, nostril paint, fingernails painted, orange one-pc swimsuit, no box, VG .. **350.00**
Light blond hair, peach lips, fingernails painted, bendable legs, Lunch Date, Barbie Pak, sleeveless dress, olive green skirt, green and white bodice no box, VG **450.00**
Titian hair, gold lips, fingernails painted, bendable legs, #1665 Here Comes the Bride outfit, white satin sleeveless gown, white tulle long veil, lace trim on gown and veil, ribbon bow accents, white nylon long gloves, blue nylon garter, white pointed toe shoes, box, VG **350.00**

Billions of Dreams Barbie, marked one billionth Barbie sold since 1959, #17641, box dated 1997, serial #00305, orig shipping box, NRFB, box slightly scuffed **225.00**

Bob Mackie design series

Goddess of the Sun, 8th in series, #14056, box dated 1995, orig shipping box, MIB, bottom box flap insert torn **80.00**
Madame du Barbie, #10 in series, #17934, box dated 1997, cardboard shipping box, MIB, top flap insert worn **200.00**

Bubblecut Barbie

Blond, coral lips, nostril paint, fingernails and toenails painted, straight legs, #1610 Golden Evening outfit, gold knit shirt, matching long skirt with gold glitter, gold belt with buckle, mustard open toe shoes, three-charm bracelet, no box, VG, loss to glitter **90.00**
Blond, white lips with pink tint, white nostril paint, fingernails painted, toenails with faint paint, straight legs, one-pc red nylon swimsuit, red open toe shoes, orig box with gold wire stand, no box, VG **225.00**
Brunette, red lips, fingernails and toenails painted lightly,

straight legs, Pak outfit, red and white striped knit shirt, blue shorts, no box, VG/G, frayed tag **135.00**
Light blond, pink lips, fingernails and toenails painted, straight legs, Best Bow Pak red dress, attached bow, floral print skirt, no box, VG **125.00**
Titian hair, coral lips, nostril paint, fingernails and toenails painted, straight legs, black and white striped one-pc swimsuit, pearl earrings, black open toe shoes, white rimmed glasses with blue lenses, black white stand, booklet, orig box, VG .. **200.00**

Spring in Tokyo Barbie, brunette, #19430, 1999, classic cream-colored suit from the City Seasons Collection, **$50.**

Color Magic Barbie

Lemon yellow hair, blue metal hair barrette, pink lips, cheek blush, fingernails painted, bendable legs, #1692 Patio Party, floral print nylon jumpsuit, blue and green satin overdress, blue pointed toe shoes, no box, NM **550.00**
Red hair, green metal hair barrette, pink lips, fingernails painted, bendable legs, nude, no box, VG **550.00**

Red hair, pink lips, cheek blush, fingernails painted, toenails with faint paint, bendable legs, nude, no box, NM/VG **525.00**

Summer in Rome Barbie, blond, #19431, 1999, white linen jacket, and halter top, chifon blue and white skirt and matching scarf, **$50.**

Fashion Queen, painted brunette hair, blue vinyl headband, pink lips, fingernails and toenails painted, straight legs, gold and white striped swimsuit, matching turban cap, pearl earrings in box with white plastic wig stand with brunette pageboy, blond bubblecut, and titian side-part wigs, black wire stand, MIB, orig box **400.00**
Growin' Pretty Hair, blond, peach lips, cheek blush, rooted eyelashes, bendable legs, pink satin dress, wrist tag, orig box with hair accessories, pink high tongue shoes, orig box, NRFB **475.00**
Hair Happenin's, titian hair, pink lips, cheek blush, rooted eyelashes, fingernails painted, bendable legs, nude, titan long hair piece braided with pink ribbon, no box, VG **225.00**
Happy Holidays, orig box 1988, #1, NRFB **230.00**

1989, NRFB, plastic window and box scuffed............ **70.00**
1990, NRFB, plastic window and box slightly scuffed **75.00**
1991, NRFB, box slightly scuffed and discolored. **45.00**
1992, NRFB, box slightly scuffed and worn.......... **35.00**

Living Barbie, brunette, pink lips, cheek blush, rooted eyelashes, bendable arms, bendable legs, rotating wrists, orig silver and gold one-pc swimsuit, orange net cover-up with gold trim, booklet, no box, NM **75.00**

Mackie, Bob

Gold Barbie, first in series, #5409, 1990, orig shipping box, NRFB **220.00**
Goddess of the Sun, eighth in series, #14056, 1995, certificate, stand, orig shipping box, NRFB **90.00**
Madame Du Barbie, tenth in series, #17934, 1997, certificate, stand, MIB **145.00**
Queen of Hearts, seventh in series, #12056, 1994, certificate, stand, shipping box, NRFB **85.00**

No. 2 Barbie, brunette ponytail, hoop earrings, black and white swimsuit, plastic box, #850, repainted, **$1,800.**

Ponytail

#1 ponytail
Blond, red lips, fingernails and toenails painted, straight legs, black and white striped one-pc swimsuit, silver loop earrings, black #1 open-toe shoes with holes, white rimmed glasses with blue lenses, pink cover booklet, reproduction #1 stand, box with replaced insert, VG **3,400.00**
Blond, reset in ponytail, red lips, nostril paint, fingernails painted, TL, straight legs, black and white striped one-pc swimsuit, gold hoop earrings, one black #1 open toe shoe with hole (unmarked), white rimmed glasses with blue lenses, pink cov booklet, VG, orig box with partial Marshall Field's sticker **3,200.00**

#3 ponytail, brunette, red lips, nostril paint, brown eyeliner, fingernails painted, straight legs, #976 Sweater Girl outfit, orange knit sweater, matching shell, gray skirt, black open toe shoes, pearl earrings, wooden bowl with orange, green and yellow yarn with two needles, metal scissors, *How to Knit* book, black pedestal with plastic base, pink cover booklet, white rimmed glasses with blue lenses, no box, VG/G, hair and banks no box and fuzzy **475.00**

#5 ponytail, brunette, orig set, red lips, nostril paint, fingernails and toenails painted, straight legs, Pak outfit, black and white striped knit shirt, red shorts, no box, NM/VG **225.00**

#6 ponytail
Brunette, orig ponytail top knot, coral lips, fingernails and toenails painted, straight legs, Japan market silver kimono, lavender lining, black and silver obi tied with silver and purple cord, attached bow, white nylon short gloves, black open toe shoes, silver and white purse with cord handle, VG.................. **550.00**
Titian hair, orig top knot, beige lips, fingernails and toenails painted, straight legs, blue two-pc pajamas with lace trim, button accents, no box, VG.............................. **325.00**

Presidential Porcelain Collection, Royal Splendor, #01078, #10950, 1993, NRFB **70.00**

Standard
Brunette, pink lips, cheek blush, fingernails painted, toenails with faint paint, straight legs, orig pink nylon swimsuit bottoms with plastic flower accent, #1804 Knit Hit blue and pink knit dress, pale blue high tongue shows, no box, VG...................... **150.00**
Light brunette, pink lips, cheek blush, fingernails and toenails painted, straight legs, nude, no box, VG, replaced rubber band **190.00**

Swirl ponytail
Brunette hair in orig set, coral lips, fingernails and toenails painted, straight legs, #1638 Fraternity Dance gown, pink satin skirt, pink chiffon overskirt, white lacy bodice, blue and green nylon waist scarf, brooch accent, rose colored open toe shoes, single pearl necklace, white nylon long gloves, orig box, VG/G **450.00**
Brunette hair in orig set, yellow ribbon, metal hair pin, coral lips, fingernails and toenails painted, straight legs, red nylon one-pc swimsuit, red open toe shoes, pearl earrings, wrist tag, box with gold metal stand, NM . **675.00**
Platinum hair in orig set, yellow ribbon, metal hair pin, white lips, fingernails painted, straight legs, nude, no box, NM-VG....................... **475.00**

Talking, brunette, ribbon bow ties, pink lips, cheek blush, rooted eyelashes, bendable legs, red nylon two-pc swimsuit with metal accent on bottoms, white and silver net cover-up with red trim, no box, VG, possible repairs to talker, working condition **275.00**

Twist 'n' Turn
Blond, pink lips, cheek blush, fingernails and toenails painted, bendable legs, multicolored one-pc knit swimsuit, wrist tag, clear plastic stand, booklet, NRFB **425.00**

Brunette, pink lips, cheek blush, fingernails painted, bendable legs, #1485 Gypsy Spirits outfit, pink nylon blouse, aqua suede skirt, matching vest, no box, VG **125.00**

Pale blond, pink lips, cheek blush, rooted eyelashes, fingernails painted, bendable legs, two-pc orange vinyl swimsuit, white net cover-up with orange trim, trade-in program doll, no box, VG **475.00**

Bubble Cut Barbie, brunette; #850; Ken, brown flocked hair, #750; Ponytail Barbie, platinum, #850; eight dolls three of which are shown, for **$5,175**.

Friends and family dolls

Allan, painted red hair, pink lips, straight legs, #1409 Goin' Hunting, red plaid shirt, denim pants, red socks, black boots, red plastic cap, hunting rifle, frayed wrist tag, VG **65.00**

Casey, blond hair, clear plastic headband, peach lips, cheek blush, two-pc hot pink nylon swimsuit, orig clear plastic bag, cardboard hanger, NRFP, orig price sticker **295.00**

Chris, Color Magic-type titian hair, green metal hair barrette, pink lips, cheek blush, bendable arms and legs, #3617 Birthday Beauties outfit, pink floral dress, white slip, white fishnet tights, white shoes with molded straps, gold wrapped present with white ribbon and pink flower accents, one pink crepe paper party favor with gold glitter, white paper invitation, orig box, VG.... **105.00**

Christie

Talking, red hair, pink lips, cheek blush, rooted eyelashes, bendable legs, wrist tag, clear plastic stand, NRFM, nonworking, box age discolored, scuffed, and worn **250.00**

Twist 'n' Turn, red hair, pink lips, cheek blush, rooted eyelashes, bendable legs, #1841 Night Clouds, yellow, orange and pink nylon ruffled night gown with ribbon straps, matching yellow nylon robe with ribbon ties and flower accents, no box, VG **115.00**

Nostalgic Reproductions, 30th anniversary Francie doll, 1996, **$45**.

Francie

Brunette, clear plastic headband, peach lips, cheek blush, two-pc yellow nylon swimsuit, orig clear plastic bag, cardboard hanger, NRFP, orig price sticker **250.00**

Brunette, pink lips, cheek blush, bent legs, ring earrings, Slightly Summery Pak dress, Barbie print top, green pleated skirt, VG **75.00**

Malibu, The Sun Set, blond, pink plastic sunglasses, plastic head cover, peach lips, painted teeth, bendable legs, pink and red nylon swimsuit, yellow vinyl waistband, orange terrycloth towel, box dated 1970, NRFB **235.00**

Twist 'n' Turn, blond, pink lips, cheek blush, rooted eyelashes, bendable legs, orig floral print outfit with lace trim, pink nylon bottoms, no box, VG **165.00**

Jamie, walking, Furry Friends Gift Set, Sears Exclusive, titian hair, pink lips, cheek blush, rooted eyelashes, bendable legs, green, pink, and orange knit dress, orange belt with buckle, orange furry coat with pink vinyl trim, orange boots, gray dot with felt features, pink vinyl dog collar with silver accents, leash, no box, VG **150.00**

Julia, talking, red hair, pink lips, cheek blush, rooted eyelashes, bendable legs, gold and silver jumpsuit with belt, wrist tag, clear plastic stand, NRFB, nonworking, box age discolored, scuffed, and worn **225.00**

Ken

Brunette flocked hair, beige lips, straight legs, red swim trunks with white stripe, wrist tag, booklet, yellow terrycloth towel, cork sandals in cellophane bag, black white stand, orig box, VG, oily face, worn wrist tag **155.00**

Brunette flocked hair, beige lips, straight legs, #790 Time for Tennis, white shirt and shorts, white sweater with navy and red trim, white socks and shoes, Tennis Rules book, tennis racquet and two balls, green plastic glasses, no box, NM **115.00**

Brunette painted hair, beige lips, straight legs, #0782 Sleeper Set, blue and white striped pajamas, wax honey bun, metal alarm clock, glass of milk, no box, VG **50.00**

Painted blond hair, peach lips, straight legs, #799 Touchdown red jersey with felt "7," red pants, white lacing closure, red socks with navy stripe, black cleats, red helmet, brown football, no box, VG **50.00**

Painted brunette, peach lips, straight legs, #790 Time for Tennis outfit, white knit shirt, white sweater with blue and red trim, white shorts, socks, and shoes, tennis racquet and ball, no box, VG **55.00**

Fashion Editor Barbie, suit dress with matching pillbox hat, camera, **$250**.

Talking, painted brown hair, peach lips, painted teeth, bendable legs, #1435 Shore Lines outfit, blue nylon jacket with zipper closure, blue shorts, vinyl side stripes, multi-print pants with zipper closure, yellow plastic face mask with elastic head strap, swim fins, no box, NM, nonworking, stretched elastic on mask **75.00**

Midge
Blond hair, pink lips, fingernails painted, white satin sleeveless shirt, bolero jacket, wrap skirt, hat with bow accent, white open toe shoes, no box, VG **85.00**
Titian hair, ribbon hair band, pink lips, fingernails painted, bendable legs, orig one-pc striped knit swimsuit, aqua open toe shoes, gold wire stand, orig box, VG..... **560.00**
PJ, talking, blond, beaded tie on left pigtail, replaced rubber-band on right pigtail, attached lavender plastic glasses, pink lips, cheek blush, rooted eyelashes, bendable legs, #1796 Fur Sighted outfit, orange jacket with fur trim, metallic gold tab and button closures,

matching pants, zigzag print knit sweater, orange hat with fur trim, metallic gold chin strap, yellow high tongue shoes, no box, NM/VG, non-working **155.00**
Ricky, painted red hair, peach lips, cheek blush, straight legs, striped jacket, blue shorts, cork sandals in bag, black wire stand, orig box with insert, NM, wrist tag torn........................... **155.00**

Skipper
Blond, pink lips, straight legs, /#1915 Outdoor Casuals, turquoise knit sweater, matching dickey with button closure, pants, white nylon short gloves, white socks, white flat shoes, red wooden yo-yo, no box, VG **55.00**
Color Magic-type dark red hair, pink lips, straight legs, #1902 Silk 'n' Fancy dress, red velvet bodice, white skirt, red lace underskirt, gold braid waistband, white nylon socks, black flat shoes, NM..... **90.00**
Color Magic-type titian hair, pink lips, straight legs, #1926 Chill Chasers, white fur coat, red cap with blue pompon, red flat shoes, no box, NM **120.00**
Pose'n Play, blond, blue ribbon ties, clear plastic headband, pink lips, cheek blush, bendable arms and legs, blue and white outfit with button accents, wrist tag, orig clear plastic bag, cardboard hanger, NRFP **85.00**
Quick Curl, blond hair, blue ribbon bow, pink lips, cheek blush, straight legs, blue and white long dress, orig clear plastic bag, NRFP **150.00**

Skooter
Blond, red ribbon bows, beige lips with tint of pink, cheek blush, straight legs, #1921 School Girl outfit, red jacket with pocket insignia, red and white pleated skirt, white shirt, red felt hat with red and white band and feather accent, white nylon socks, red flat shoes, brown rimmed glasses, arithmetic, geography, and English books, black book strap, red and natural wooden pencils, orig box, VG **90.00**
Brunette, hair in orig set with ribbons, pink lips, cheek

blush, straight legs, #1901 Red Sensation dress, gold button accents, white nylon socks, red flat shoes, white nylon short gloves, straw hat with ribbon band and bow accent, NM **70.00**
Brunette, retied with red cord, beige lips, cheek blush, straight legs, wearing Best Buy Fashions #9122, red plaid coat, black belt, matching cap with black ribbon accent, #9122 dress with red plaid skirt, black velveteen top, white nylon shirt, no box, VG **70.00**
Tutti, Me and My Dog, brunette, red ribbon bow, pink lips, bendable arms and legs, red felt coat, fur trim, white fur hat with ribbon ties, red tights, white flat shoes, white dog with felt features, attached red leash, no box, VG, leash worn and knotted **75.00**

Goddess of the Sun, #14056, 1995, gown encrusted with over 11,000 hand-sewn beads, Bob Mackie design, **$200**.

Outfits

Barbie
#934 black sleeveless dress, white collar, white hat with black ribbon accent, black open toe shoes, VG...... **65.00**

#957 Knitting Pretty, pink sweater, matching sleeveless shell, pink flannel skirt, pink #1 open toe shoes, metal scissors, How to Knit book, wooden bowl with two needles, yellow, red, and pale pink yarn, VG/G **160.00**
#958 Party Date, white satin dress, gold glitter accents, wide gold belt, gold clutch purse, clear open toe shoes, VG **95.00**
#968 Roman Holiday, sheath, red and white striped bodice, navy blue skirt, matching red and white striped coat, black open toe #1 shoes, white nylon shirt gloves, red woven hat with bow accent, white vinyl clutch purse, black rimmed glasses, white hankie, pink plastic comb, brass compact, VG **1,250.00**
#0873 Guinevere, royal blue velvet gown, embroidered and gold tri, attached chain belt, red and gold brocade slippers, red and gold brocade crown with navy blue and gold trim edging, attached gold nylon snood, red nylon armlets, NM/VG **105.00**
#0874 Arabian Night, pink satin blouse, pink chiffon long skirt, matching pink sari with gold trim, gold foil slippers, gold plastic lamp, gold and turquoise beaded necklace, gold drop earrings, gold and turquoise plastic bracelets, paper theater program, VG **95.00**
#1452 Now Knit, green, navy blue, and silver dress, matching green terry hat, blue nylon scarf with attached silver thread ring, NM/VG **50.00**
#1489 Cloud 9, pale blue nylon short nightie with satin bodice, matching long robe, satin slippers, VG **55.00**
#1593 Golden Groove, Sears Exclusive Gift Set, pink and gold lame jacket, matching short skirt, gold thigh-high boots, NM **145.00**
#1612 Theatre Date, NRFB **285.00**
#1615 Saturday Matinee, NM/VG **310.00**
#1617, Midnight Blue, NM-VG **150.00**

#1620 Junior Designer, turquoise dress with green design, green pointed toe shoes, metal iron with black handle, *How to Design Your Own Fashion* book, VG. **55.00**

Ponytail #3 blond, gold hoop earrings, black and white swimsuit, no holes in feet or shoes, **$3,500**.

#1622 Student Teacher, red and white dress, white bodice inset with button accents, red vinyl belt, red pointed toe shoes, black rimmed glasses with clear lenses, plastic globe, wooden pointer stick, geography book, VG/G **175.00**
#1629 Skater's Waltz, pink nylon skating suit, pink felt skirt, sheer nylon hose, white skates, pink fur muff, matching mittens, VG ... **45.00**
#1635 Fashion Editor, sheath, turquoise skirt, floral print bodice, glitter accents, matching jacket, green ribbon trim, turquoise cap with flower bud accent and ribbon bow, turquoise pointed toe shoes, plastic camera, NM **225.00**

#1637 Outdoor Life, blue and white checked coat, blue and white houndstooth print pants, blue nylon shirt, white hat, tennis shoes, VG **95.00**
#1644 On the Avenue, white and gold sheath with textured skirt, gold lame bodice, matching jacket, white nylon short gloves, cream-colored pointed toe shoes, gold clutch purse, NM/VG, jacket tag frayed, P condition belt **100.00**
#1645 Golden Glory, gold floral lame long dress, green chiffon waist scarf, matching gold lame long coat with fur trim, white nylon short gloves, green satin clutch purse, VG **120.00**

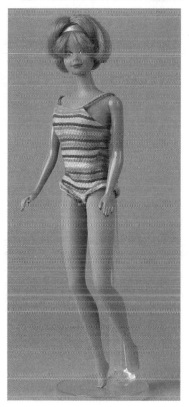

Midge, bendable leg, #1080, blonde, brunette, titan, striped swimsuit, **$450**.

#1649 Lunch on the Terrace, green and white checkered dress with polka dot bodice, matching hat with white net cover, VG **115.00**

#1650 Outdoor Art Show, VG **145.00**
#1652, Pretty as a Picture, VG **115.00**
#1656 Fashion Luncheon, VG/G **225.00**
#1663, Music Center Matinee, NM-VG **200.00**
#1678 Pan American Airways Stewardess, gray-blue jacket, attached metal wings, matching skirt, and cap, white shirt, white nylon short gloves, black pointed toe shoes, black vinyl shoulder bag, VG **700.00**
#1687 Caribbean Cruise, yellow jumpsuit with halter top, yellow flat soft shoes, NM **35.00**
#1695 Evening Enchantment, red taffeta and chiffon long dress, marabou trim, matching chiffon cape, red pointed toe shoes, VG **135.00**
#1792 Mood Matchers, paisley print nylon sleeveless blouse, matching pants, aqua nylon shirt, hot pink high tongue shoes, M **65.00**
#1814 Sparkle Squares, checkerboard pattern coat with ruffle trim, rhinestone buttons, matching dress with pleated white nylon skirt, white sheet stockings, NM **105.00**
#1848 All That Jazz, satin striped coat, matching dress with pleated skirt, beige sheer stockings, pink shoes with molded bows, VG **140.00**
#1880 Winter Wedding, cream colored brocade gown with fur trim, brocade and fur trimmed cap with attached metal headband and tulle veil, white pointed-toe shoes, VG **75.00**
#3428 The Zig Zag Bag, red and white zig zag pattern knit pants, orange terry cloth sleeveless shirt, zig-zag nylon shirt, red tennis shoes, M **185.00**
#4041 Color Magic Fashion Fun, NM/VG **145.00**
Dressed Up, Barbie Pak, dress with pale blue satin skirt, gold and white striped bodice, attached belt and buckle accents, pale blue pointed toe shoes, NM/VG **105.00**

Gala Abend, foreign market, white brocade gown, matching long coat with pale blue satin lining and fur collar, white nylon long gloves, white pointed toe shoes, VG **700.00**

Skipper, Barbie's little sister, #950, red and white sailor swimsuit, red flats, **$195**.

Francie

#1216 The Lace Pace, gold lame and pink coat cov with white lace, satin bow, matching dress with satin straps, pink shoes with molded bows, VG **105.00**
#1222 Gold Rush, orange satin dress, bright orange open toe shoes, VG **35.00**
#1232 Two for the Ball, pink chiffon long coat, black velvet waistband, long dress with pink satin skirt, pink lace overskirt, black velvet bodice, pink soft pumps, VG/G, coat tag frayed **45.00**
#3367 Right for Stripes, blue vest, blue and white striped pants, matching midriff top, floral print shoulder bag, aqua sneakers, VG **65.00**

Pancho Bravo, Francie Pak, blue, pink, green, and white poncho, blue ankle boots, lavender plastic glasses, label, NRFP, some age discoloration to cardboard backing, orig 99 cent price sticker **40.00**
The Bridge Bit, white knit sweater, green and blue stitching, royal blue stretch pants with metal accent, pink pillow with flower design, NM **65.00**

Ken

#788 Rally Day, NRFB .. **60.00**
#797 Army and Air Force, NRFB **220.00**
#799 Touchdown, NRFB, box in F/P condition........... **115.00**
#0770 Campus Hero, NRFB **130.00**
#0772 The Prince, green and gold lame coat, lace trim, rhinestone buttons, green velvet cape with gold lining, green nylon tights, green velvet shoes with gold trim, gold velvet hat with emerald, pearl, and feather accents, white collar with lace trim, velvet pillow with gold trim and tassels, paper program, VG............................... **150.00**
#0773 King Arthur, silver lame pants, shirt, and cap, red satin surcoat with gold griffin, gray plastic helmet and sword, brown scabbard, two red plastic spurs, cardboard shield, paper program, VG **95.00**
#0779 American Airlines Captain, NRFB............ **175.00**
#1404 Ken in Hawaii, VG **25.00**
#1416 College Student, VG **65.00**
#1417 Rovin' Reporter, red jacket, navy blue pants, white shirt, black socks and shoes, plastic camera, NM/VG **75.00**
#1419 TV's Good Tonight, red robe, blue trim, pocket insignia, cork sandals with red straps, brown plastic TV with metal antenna, VG, no tag on robe **50.00**
#1425 Best Man, VG-G **105.00**
Ricky, #1502 Saturday Show, NRFB **75.00**
Skipper
#1738 Fancy Pants, VG **50.00**

#1901 Red Sensation, NRFB **135.00**
#1912 Cookie Time, sleeveless dress, navy blue skirt, attached red belt, red flat shoes, miniature Barbie's Easy-As-Pie Cookbook, metal spoon with red plastic handle, gray bowl, Cookie Mix box, NM **70.00**
#1913 Me n' My Doll, pink and white gingham checked dress, ribbon ties, flower embroidered accent, white nylon socks, white flat shoes, miniature plastic Barbie doll with painted features, pink and white checked skirt, VG **75.00**
#1936 Sledding Fun, flower print jacket, fur collar, red sleeveless shirt, blue pans with sewn-on red socks, blue hat, one fur mitten, red boots, red and white plastic sled with cord handle, NM **85.00**
#1972 Drizzle Sizzle, pink and Kelly green knit dress, orange vinyl appliqué flowers, clear plastic raincoat, cap, and boots, VG **35.00**

BAROMETERS

History: A barometer is an instrument that measures atmospheric pressure, which, in turn, aids weather forecasting. Low pressure indicates the coming of rain, snow, or storm; high pressure signifies fair weather.

Most barometers use an evacuated and graduated glass tube that contains a column of mercury. These are classified by the shape of the case. An aneroid barometer has no liquid and works by a needle connected to the top of a metal box in which a partial vacuum is maintained. The movement of the top moves the needle.

21-1/2" l, wheel, Aneroid, Swedish, late 19th C, part ebonized, arch top with acorn finials, painted milk glass thermometer between turned uprights, open dial with printed enamel bezel signed "C.L. Malmsjo, Guteborg," within turned frame, acorn pendant finial **300.00**

Banjo, English, c1820, mahogany, broken arch pediment, ivory finial, convex mirror, 37-3/4" h, **$1,020**.
Photo courtesy of Alderfer Auction Co.

26-1/2" h, wheel, Georgian, mahogany, dial sgd "Dolland, London," rounded pediment over thermometer, urn inlaid central roundel line inlay throughout, early 19th C **1,840.00**
33" d, wheel, carved oak, foliage and C-scrolls, English, late 19th C **230.00**
34" l, stick, sgd E. Kendall, N. Lebanon, mahogany, etched steel face, mirrored well cov **550.00**
36-1/2" l, wheel, English, Georgian, early 19th C, mahogany, dial signed "Dolland, London," rounded pediment over thermometer, urn inlaid central roundel, line inlay throughout **1,840.00**
38" l, wheel, Scottish, mid-19th C, mahogany, swan's neck cresting over later German hygrometer, vertical thermometer, over painted roundel, signature roundel centered by level and sgd "F. Uago, Glasgow" **865.00**
38-3/4" h, banjo, mahogany, dial engraved "P. Nossi & Co. Boston," broken pediment cresting above shaped case with thermometer, circular barometer dial flanked by inlaid patera **690.00**

Banjo, English, George III, inlaid mahogany, baluster case inset with shell paterae, silvered thermometer and dial signed "J. Steele, Liverpool," 39" h, **$830**.
Photo courtesy of Sloans & Kenyon Auctions.

39" l, wheel, English, early 20th C, mahogany, broken pediment centered by finial, round hygrometer dial over vertical thermometer, convex mirror over barometer dial, ending in dial for level **815.00**
39-3/4" h, banjo, shell inlaid, painted black, Kirner Bros., Oxford, Victorian, mid-19th C **460.00**
40" l, wheel, rosewood veneer, onion top cornice with hygrometer dial over thermometer over convex mirror, large barometric dial, small level at base, English, mid-19th C **350.00**
42-3/8" l, wheel, rosewood case with thermometer over silvered barometer dial marked for J. Kienzly, Exeter, inlaid throughout with mother-of-pearl, abalone, and brass flowering vines, butterflies, and birds, Victorian, Anglo-Indian, late 19th C **1,410.00**
42-1/2" h, Louis XV-style, late 19th C, gray painted, parcel gilt, case topped by urn flanked by husk swag, floral painted thermometer, barometer dial mkd "Bourgeois, Paris"... **940.00**

50" h, barometer and wall clock, G. V. Mooney, NY, walnut, shaped backboard with molded wood and brass bezel framing paper dial and brass lever movement above printed paper dial "G.V. Mooney's Barometer Patented May 30th 1865—Sold by Arnaboldi & Co. 53 Fulton St. New York," mercury tube extending to the base with a molded wooden boss .. **1,880.00**

BASKETS

History: Baskets were invented when man first required containers to gather, store, and transport goods. Today's collectors, influenced by the country look, focus on baskets made of splint, rye straw, or willow. Emphasis is placed on handmade examples. Nails or staples, wide splints that are thin and evenly cut, or a wire bail handle denote factory construction, which can date back to the mid-19th century. Decorated painted or woven baskets rarely are handmade, unless they are American Indian in origin.

Baskets are collected by (a) type—berry, egg, or field; (b) region—Nantucket or Shaker; and (c) composition—splint, rye, or willow.

Reproduction Alert: Modern reproductions abound, made by diverse groups ranging from craft revivalists to foreign manufacturers.

Buttocks, splint, **$200**.

Cane and oak splint, round form, raised interior, banded top and base, bentwood handle, 10" d, 12" h, **$220**.
Photo courtesy of Alderfer Auction Co.

Elliptical, two rows of rose colored weave, flat wooden base, two small handles, 1950s, **$15**.

Half buttocks, woven splint, thick brown paint, bentwood handle, 8" w, 5" h............. **200.00**

Miniature

Bushel, painted cream-white over red, America, 19th C, 5-3/4" d, 3-1/4" h......... **760.00**
Woven splint, single handle, painted blue, 1-3/4" d, 2" h **550.00**

Nantucket Light Ship, America

3-5/8" h, round, carved wooden swing handle, turned wooden bottom with incised lines, stamped "Nantucket Mass.," paper label "Boyer 4 Federal Street Nantucket MA," America, 20th C, minor wear **900.00**
5-1/4" h, round, carved wooden swing handle, turned wooden bottom with incised lines, America, 20th C, minor wear........................... **675.00**
6-5/8" h, round, carved wooden bail handle, turned wood bottom with incised line dec, inscribed "Eldridge" on base, America, late 19th/early 20th C, losses............. **700.00**

8-1/8" h, round, carved wooden bail handle, turned wood bottom with incised line dec, America, late 19th/early 20th C **650.00**

Nantucket, oval, carved swing handle, oval wood base, 14-1/2" d, 7" h from base to rim, **$1,530**.
Photo courtesy of Skinner, Inc.

Native American

Covered, woven splint, attributed to New England Algonkian or Iroquois, early 19th C, round domed lid, round to square form, red and green flowering vine motif, side handles, 15-1/2" h, minor wear, fading............ **2,000.00**
Splint, Schaticoke Tribe, CT, 19th C, rect, two carved handles, decorative bands, polychrome blue, orange, green, and brown splints, 13" l, 10-1/4" w, 7" h . **1,725.00**

Oak

Peach basket shape, initials "CMT," 11-1/2" h, 14" d top **235.00**
Sewing, rect, compartments woven into one end, 21" l, 12" d, 6" h, minor cracking **250.00**

Painted woven splint, three-tier wall basket, graduating oval over rectangular baskets, terra-cotta colored paint, America, 19th C, 11-1/2" w, 6-1/2" d, 24-1/4" h, **$1,530**.
Photo courtesy of Skinner, Inc.

Rye straw

1-1/2" h, 4-1/4" d, child's, sewing, attached pin cushion **250.00**

2" h, 6-1/4" d, round, tapered sides, openwork rim ... **550.00**

3" h, 4-1/2" d, miniature, cov, openwork, woven hinges and latch **1,700.00**

3" h, 10-1/2" d, round triangular openwork rim, single coil base, attributed to Cumberland County, PA **660.00**

3" h, 19-1/2" d, round, drying **95.00**

3-1/4" d, 11 1/4" d, round, openwork, table **125.00**

3-1/2" h, 3-5/8" l, 2-1/2" w, miniature, oval, bend handle, wooden base, straw open work weave, Easter egg dated 1925 .... **385.00**

4" h, 9-1/4" d, round, openwork rim, color banding, attributed to Andrew Sheely, Hanover, York County, PA **990.00**

4" h, 12-1/2" l, 7-5/8" w, oval, openwork, attributed to unknown maker, Hanover, York County, PA **1,155.00**

4" h, 17-1/2" l, 13-1/4" w, oval, table, tapered sides, two handles **330.00**

4-1/2" h, 11" d, round, openwork, PA maker ... **770.00**

4-1/2" h, 10" l, 8-3/4" w, oval, fruit, two wove handles, looped openwork splint trim **500.00**

4-5/8" h, 11-1/2" l, 7-3/4" w, oval, table, painted green, woven handle **1,320.00**

4 3/4" h, 11-3/4" l, 7-1/4" w, oval, fruit or table, openwork, base, attributed to unknown maker, Hanover, York County, PA **3,850.00**

5-1/4" h, 13" d, cov, round, bread-rising, tapered sides, wooden finial............ **3,850.00**

6" h, 13" l, 8" w, oval, openwork, two woven handles, attributed to unknown maker, Hanover, York County, PA **1,045.00**

7" h, 12" l, 10-1/2" w, oval, cov, straight sides **1,320.00**

7" h, 13" l, 7-3/4" w, sewing, applied section for pin cushion, flared base rim, attributed to Hanover, York County, PA maker .. **10,725.00**

Round basket, high handle, brown stained finish, damage to rim, dry condition, $20.

8" h, 14-1/2" d, round, tapered sides, two attached bentwood handles **1,760.00**

8-1/2" h, 17" d, cov, bread rising, round, tapered sides, domed lid, wooden finial, two woven handles, attributed to PA maker **3,410.00**

8-1/2" h, 18" d, round, field, tapered sides, two woven handles **880.00**

9" h, 12" l, 8-1/2" w, oval, market, attached bentwood handle...................... **2,750.00**

10" h, 16" d, tapered, triple coil base **880.00**

10-1/2" h, 23" d, round, field, bentwood handles, cross supports in base......... **825.00**

11-1/4" h, 17" l, 10-1/2" w, market, oval, pinned bentwood handle..... **1,980.00**

11-1/2" h, 11-1/2" d, bulbous, flared rim,.................... **990.00**

12" h, 10-1/2" d, cov, hamper, bulbous, fitted lid and base **1,155.00**

12" h, 18" d, cov, painted salmon dec, wooden knob finial, attributed to unknown maker, Hanover, York County, PA **2,970.00**

13-1/2" h, 16-1/2" d, round, field, tapered sides, attached bentwood handle........ **500.00**

14-1/4" h, 32-1/2" l, 25" w, cov, oval, carved bentwood handles, attributed to Ephrata, PA maker **3,850.00**

15" h, 15" d, bee skep, ovoid, wood base............... **3,960.00**

15-1/2" h, 22" l, 17" w, cov, hamper style, oval ... **1,265.00**

19-1/2" d, serving tray, round, two woven handles..... **880.00**

20" h, 17" d, cov, hamper style, oval, hidden loss to inner rim..................... **770.00**

20" h, 22" d, cov, hamper style, bulbous **2,750.00**

22" h, 16" d, cov, hamper style, bulbous **1,760.00**

Square basket, high handle, brown stained finish, damage to handle, dry condition, $35.

Splint oak, kettle form, fixed handle, 12" d, 12" h, $150.

Photo courtesy of Alderfer Auction Co.

Splint

4" h, 8" d, oak, round, tapered sides, pine base, red stained rim and side banding, attributed to maker in Grantville, Dauphin County, PA **180.00**

8" h, 5" l, 3-5/8" w, oak, D-shape, hanger, rounded head nails, wooden base **470.00**

9-1/2" h, 6-3/4" l, 4" h, wall pocket, bentwood handle, painted brown **250.00**

13" h, 16-1/4" l, 10-1/4" h, oak, rect, market, tapered sides, bentwood handle, pinewood base, round head nails, attributed to Grantville, Dauphin County, PA, maker **990.00**

13-1/2" h, 14" l, 11-1/2" w, oval, market, bentwood handle, pine wood base, attributed to Grantville, Dauphin County, PA, maker **1,210.00**

Wooden
13" d, 17" h, stave construction, vertical wood staves taper down at base, fixed with wire, dark orig finish over varnish **250.00**
15" h, 15" l, 11-1/2" w, oval, painted green, wood slat and band construction, round head nails, metal support to bentwood handle..... **1,320.00**

BAVARIAN CHINA

History: Bavaria, Germany, was an important porcelain production center, similar to the Staffordshire district in England. The phrase "Bavarian China" refers to the products of companies operating in Bavaria, among which were Hutschenreuther, Thomas, and Zeh, Scherzer & Co. (Z. S. & Co.). Very little of the production from this area was imported into the United States prior to 1870.

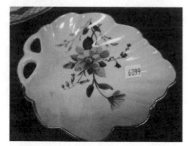

Bowl, hand painted tulip decoration, gold scrollwork, green mark, **$65**.

Coffee set, coffeepot, two cups and saucers, white and pink shaded roses, green foliage, gold tracery and borders, marked, **$145**.

Dinner service, Royal Heidelberg, multicolored floral design, gold rims, marked "Winterling, Germany, Bavaria," 106 pieces, **$225**.

Bowl, 7-3/8" l, 6" w, ovoid, reticulated sides, beaded rim, center and sides painted with scenic roundels en grisaille, blue ribbon cartouches with gilt detailing, scenes titled on underside "Badenburg," "Apolloscumpeil," and "Schloss Nymphenburg," late 19th C **325.00**
Celery tray, 11" l, center with basket of fruit, luster edge, c1900 .... **45.00**
Chocolate set, cov chocolate pot, six cups and saucers, shaded blue and white, large white leaves, pink, red, and white roses, crown mark . **295.00**
Creamer and sugar, purple and white pansy dec, marked "Meschendorf, Bavaria".... **65.00**
Cup and saucer, roses and foliage, gold handle **30.00**
Dinner service, King Cedric, service for eight, plus two platters **150.00**
Fish set, 13 plates, matching sauce boat, artist sgd **295.00**

Dinner service, Josephine, white ground, gold trim with monogram, green maker's mark, blue NY retailer's mark, **$650**.
Photo courtesy of Wiederseim Associates, Inc.

Plate, cherries spilling out of basket, gold fleur-de-lis border, green back stamp "Punch R. S. & Co. Bavaria," **$45**.

Grouping of nine miniature Bavarian glass tumblers, each with enameled decoration in different floral and foliate motifs, some with insects, gilt highlights, c1900, each 2-1/4" d, 3-1/4" h, two with chipped rims, **$1,380**.
Photo courtesy of Alderfer Auction Co.

Pitcher, 9" h, bulbous, blackberry dec, shaded ground, burnished gold lizard handle, sgd "D. Churchill" **125.00**

Portrait vase, 10" h, gold enameled flowers and leaves, hp portrait of Naomi, blue beehive mark and "TG Bavaria" mark **520.00**

Ramekin, underplate, ruffled, small red roses with green foliage, gold rim **45.00**

Salt and pepper shakers, pr, pink apple blossom sprays, white ground, reticulated gold tops, pr............................. **35.00**

Shaving mug, 3-5/8" x 3-5/8", hp, two colorful ducks at water's edge, mkd "J. & C Bavaria" **100.00**

Vase, 12" h, hp, red poppies, gold enamel dec, marked "Classic Bavaria" **260.00**

BEATRIX POTTER COLLECTIBLES

History: Helen Beatrix Potter was born in 1864 in London. Her favorite pets were a mouse, rabbit, and a hedgehog. As a child, she loved to sketch these creatures and by 1893, she had created the characters of Flopsy, Mopsy, Cottontail, and Peter Rabbit. By December of 1901, Beatrix published 250 copies of her first book, *The Tale of Peter Rabbit*, which included 41 black and white illustrations. She gave many of these books to friends and family as gifts, but did sell some for a halfpenny each. In 1902, Frederick Warne & Co. publisher the first trade edition of this book and it became an instant bestseller. Beatrix went on to write 23 more tales and each is still in print today and they have been translated into more than 35 languages.

Clearly a clever businesswoman, Beatrix designed and licensed her Peter Rabbit doll in 1903, making him one of the first licensed literary characters. Steiff produced its own version of Peter Rabbit in 1903. Grimwades Pottery, Stoke-on-Trent, England, was granted permission in 1922 to use Potter's illustrations on children's dishes. John Beswick obtained copyrights in 1947 to use Potter's storybook characters as figurines. The first set of nine figures, including Jemima Puddle-Duck, were an instant hit. In 1969, the Royal Doulton Group acquired Beswick and continued to produce the charming characters. Josiah Wedgwood and Sons began to use Peter Rabbit in its designs in the late 1950s.

Backstamps are useful in determining the date of Beatrix Potter figures. A gold circular backstamp is the earliest, dating to the 1940s-50s. Royal Albert backstamps were used only from 1989 to 1998. Some characters, Susan and Old Mr. Pricklepin, and Thomasina Tittlemouse, were produced by Royal Albert for a short six-week period and are much more sought after by collectors.

In 2002, an exhibition to celebrate the 100th anniversary of the first commercial publication was created by the Royal Ontario Museum and it has since traveled to other museums, like the Children's Museum in Indianapolis, delighting children of all ages.

Cup, Bunnykins figures, Royal Doulton, **$18.**

Baby bowl, Peter Rabbit, Grimwades, 1920s-30s ... **590.00**

Barbie, 2002 Peter Rabbit Centenary **29.95**

Book

> *The Roly-Poly Pudding*, Frederick Warne, NY, 1908 .... **80.00**
>
> *The Tailor of Gloucester*, Frederick Warne & Co., 1903, first US printing **130.00**

Egg-shaped covered jar, Benjamin Bunny standing on top, Mother Bunny attending at bed on base, **$65.**

> *The Tale of Peter Rabbit*, 1901, orig privately printed version **110,000.00**
>
> *The Tale of Peter Rabbit*, 1902-3, Frederick Warne, first edition, 2nd or third printing **18,500.00**
>
> *The Tale of Peter Rabbit*, 1904, American printing **450.00**

Chamber pot, Peter Rabbit, Wedgwood........................ **200.00**

Cup and saucer, Peter Rabbit, Wedgwood, 1958........... **140.00**

Dish, Peter Rabbit, jasperware, blue, Wedgwood, 1980s. **200.00**

Eggcup, Peter Rabbit, Grimwades, 1920s-30s ... **400.00**

Figure

> Duchess with Flowers, earthenware 1955-1967 .... **2,800.00**
>
> Duchess with Pie, earthenware 1979-1982 .... **4,255.00**
>
> Hunca Munca, Beswick, 2-5/8" h, 2-3/4" w......... **115.00**
>
> Jeremy Fisher, Royal Albert, 1st version, 2nd variation, modeled by Arthur Gredington, 3-1/2" h ... **135.00**
>
> Mr. Benjamin Bunny, Beswick, 4" h, 3-7/8" l, brown mark **75.00**
>
> Mrs Rabbit and bunnies, Beswick, 3-5/8" h, brown mark **75.00**

Mrs Rabbit with basket, F
Warne Co., Beswick, England,
4" h.................................. **35.00**
Mrs Ribby and the Patty Pan,
Royal Albert, modeled by
Martyn Alcock, 3-1/2" h **50.00**
Peter Rabbit, Beswick, sky
blue jacket, brown shoes, hp
"77" on base in brown and
"31" in black, 4-1/4" h, 1948
.... **120.00**
Pickles, earthenware 1971-
1982............................ **485.00**
Tailor of Groucester, Royal
Albert, 3-1/2" h.............. **35.00**
Game, Peter Rabbit's Race
Game **45.00**
Handkerchiefs, Peter Rabbit,
orig package.................. **385.00**
Pendant, F. Warne, made in Italy
Knitting bunny in rocking
chair, 3-1/4" h................ **30.00**
Moma mouse, babe in her
arms, 3-3/4" h **30.00**
Mr Pig, cane in hand, 3" h
.... **32.00**
Mrs Pig at the market, 3" h
.... **30.00**
Print, Squirrel Nutkin from *Tale of
Squirrel Nutkin,* published by F.
Warne, 1950s **25.00**
Tea set, Peter Rabbit, 17 pcs,
Grimwades.................. **5,100.00**
Watercolor, unpublished,
Building a Snowman, 1893
.... **75,000.00**

BELLEEK

History: Belleek, a thin, ivory-
colored, almost-iridescent porcelain,
was first made in 1857 in county
Fermanagh, Ireland. Production
continued until World War I, was
discontinued for a period of time,
and then resumed. The Shamrock
pattern is most familiar, but many
patterns were made, including
Limpet, Tridacna, and Grasses.

There is an Irish saying: If a
newly married couple receives a
gift of Belleek, their marriage will
be blessed with lasting happiness.

Several American firms made a
Belleek-type porcelain. The first
was Ott and Brewer Co. of Trenton,
New Jersey, in 1884, followed by
Willets. Other firms producing this
ware included The Ceramic Art
Co. (1889), American Art China
Works (1892), Columbian Art Co.
(1893), and Lenox, Inc. (1904).

Marks: The European Belleek
company used specific marks

during given time periods, which
makes it relatively easy to date a
piece of Irish Belleek. Variations in
mark color are important, as well
as the symbols and words.

First mark: Black Harp, Hound,
and Castle, 1863-1890.

Second mark: Black Harp,
Hound, and Castle and the words
"Co. Fermanagh, Ireland",
1891-1826.

Third mark: Black, "Deanta in
Eirinn" added, 1926-1946.

Fourth mark: Green, same as
third mark except for color,
1946-1955.

Fifth mark: Green, "R" inside a
circle added, 1955-1965.

Sixth mark: Green, "Co.
Fermanagh" omitted, 1965-
March 1980.

Seventh mark: Gold, "Deanta in
Eirinn" omitted, April 1980-
Dec. 1992.

Eighth mark: Blue, Blue version of
the second mark with "R" inside a
circle added, Jan. 1993-present.

Additional Listings: Lenox.

For more information, please see
*Warman's English & Continental
Pottery & Porcelain*, 4th edition.

American

Bowl

7" d, 4-1/4" h, double handles,
ruffled rim, gilt trim and
handles, gilt and rose-colored
flowers dec, brown Willets
mark............................ **275.00**
7-1/2" d, green ext., wide gilt
textured border, int. with hp
floral design, artist sgd "MS"
on base, brown Willets mark
.... **100.00**
Candy dish, 8" x 6", shell form,
ivory ground, hp floral dec,
ruffled gilt rim, marked
"Columbia Art Co., Trenton, NJ"
.... **80.00**
Chocolate pot, 10-1/4" h, ivory
ground, Art Deco rose design,
pale green and yellow wide
borders, gilt accents, green
Lenox pallet mark **135.00**
Cider jug, 6" h, hp, fruit dec, gilt
handle, green Lenox pallet mark
.... **50.00**
Cup and saucer, 2" cup, 5-3/4" d
saucer, hp, pale pink and green
beaded dec, gilt borders, brown
Willets mark...................... **60.00**
Jug, 5-1/2" h, hp, pale yellow
ground, floral dec, gilt rim and
handle, green CAC pallet mark
.... **110.00**
Mug, 4-1/2" h, pink luster and
enamel dec, continuous scene
of drunken taverners, artist sgd
"EMS '04," printed Ceramic Art
Co. mark, Trenton, New Jersey,
c1904 .... **150.00**
Pitcher, 7" h, hp, white ground,
geometric blue floral design, gilt
trim, artist sgd "G. L. Urban,"
green Willets mark **85.00**
Plate, 7-1/4" d, gilt foliate rim,
blue enamel beads, red Willets
mark, price for pr **45.00**

Irish creamer and kettle shaped bowl, Shamrock pattern, green castle with R mark,
$165.

Salt, 1-1/2" d

Gilt, ruffled edge, marked "CAC," price for set of six **45.00**
Pale green, hp pink enamel dec, artist sgd "E.S.M.," Lenox pallet mark, price for set of six...................... **135.00**

Swan, 8-1/2" h, ivory, open back, green Lenox wreath mark . **90.00**

Tankard, 5-3/4" h, hand painted
Brown and blue painted ground, poppy dec, sgd "LM '06," green CAC pallet mark **135.00**
Multicolored ground, foliage dec, sgd "B.M.A.," brown Willets mark **125.00**

Teapot, 6" h, blue glazed ground, gilt dec, brown Willets mark **135.00**

Vase

10" h, cylindrical, hand painted, egrets in landscape, artist sgd "A.MacM.F.," printed mark, Trenton, NJ, c1900........................... **215.00**
15" h, baluster, hp pine cone dec, artist sgd "A.E.G.," green Lenox pallet mark **450.00**

Irish

Basket, 6-1/2" x 4-1/2", four strand, applied flowers, Belleek Co. Fermangh Ireland pad mark, some repairs, petal missing **80.00**

Bread plate, 10-1/2" l, 9-1/4" w, Shamrock pattern, double handle, 3rd green mark **80.00**

Bowl, 4-1/2" h, Imperial Shell, modeled shell supported on shell adorned coral base, third black mark, c1930 .... **565.00**

Butter dish, cov, 6-1/2" d top, 8-1/2" d base, Limpet pattern, 1st black mark **475.00**

Cake plate, 10-1/2" d, mask with grape leaves pattern, four looped handles, pale yellow edge, 3rd black mark...... **155.00**

Compote, 6-3/4" h, shell modeled dish, triangular base set with three dolphin, first black mark, c1880, dish restored, slight rim chips................ **470.00**

Creamer

3-1/4" h, Lifford pattern, 3rd green mark **60.00**
3-1/4" h, Ribbon pattern, 3rd green mark **40.00**
3-1/2" h, Cleary pattern, 1st green mark **50.00**

4" h, Rathmore pattern, 3rd green mark **40.00**
4-1/2" h, Undine pattern, 3rd black mark................... **55.00**

Creamer and sugar, 3-1/2" h creamer, 2" h sugar, Lotus pattern, 3rd black mark, rim chip **70.00**

Cream jug, 5-1/2" h, Thorn Tea Ware, pale yellow relief dec, c1880, first mark **300.00**

Cup and saucer, 5-3/8" d saucer, Tea Ware, hexagon, pink tint, second black mark, early 20th C, price for pr.......... **460.00**

Figure

2-1/2" h, pig, 3rd green mark **90.00**
6" h, harp, 3rd green mark **70.00**

Flowerpot, 7" h, naturalistically modeled shell body, applied flowers and foliage, second black mark, c1900, chips to leaves............................ **940.00**

Font, 7" h, Sacred Heart, cross form, shaped font, 2nd green mark **50.00**

Lithophane, 5-1/2" l, rect shape with arched top, modeled as two ladies with bird, no visible mark, mounted in electrified shadow box, 19th C **715.00**

Mint tray, 8-1/2" l, shell form, pink highlights on rim, brown mark **70.00**

Mustache cup and saucer, 2-1/2" h cup, 6" d saucer, Tridacna, pink rim, 1st black mark **495.00**

Night light, 10-3/4" h, figural, lighthouse, pierced cover and insert pot, modeled rocky base, second black mark, c1900, restored rim on insert pot **1,410.00**

Pitcher, 9" h, Aberdeen, applied with flowers and leaves, second black mark, c1900, chips to leaves............................ **300.00**

Plate, 10-1/2" d, scalloped edge, woven, three strands, pad mark **200.00**

Spill vase

5" h, Shamrock, 2nd green mark............................. **50.00**
5-1/2" h, Shamrock Daisy, 3rd green mark **65.00**
8" h, owl, 2nd green mark **55.00**

Sugar bowl, 4" h, Shell, pink tinted edge and coral, first black mark, c1880, foot-rim chips **575.00**

American urn, spherical, two upright handles, four reticulated feet, red Oriental poppies decoration, light wear to gilting around rim, red O&B crown stamp, 8" x 6", **$1,725.**

Photo courtesy of David Rago Auctions, Inc.

Swan, 4" h, open back, yellow wings and head, brown mark **55.00**

Tea kettle, cov, 7" h, Thorn Tea Ware, pale yellow relief dec, c1880, first mark **350.00**

Tea set

Grass tea ware, 4" h covered teapot; 3-3/4" h cov sugar bowl; cream jug; first black marks, c1880........... **1,175.00**
Tridacna, 5-1/2" h cov teapot; 4-1/4" h cov sugar bowl; 3-1/4" h cream jug; 3" h waste bowl, each with third black mark; 15-1/2" l rect tray with second black mark, c1920-30 .... **1,120.00**

Tea urn, cov, 6-1/2" h, gilt, bronze and enamel dec, China man finial, first black mark, c1880, cover with hairline and chip, stand missing **4,410.00**

Tray, 14-1/2" sq, Thorn tea ware, scalloped rim, molded floral border, web interior with central spider, second black mark, c1900........................... **1,175.00**

Irish vase, applied flowers and leaves; black mark, 8" h, bowl, green mark, 4-3/4" d; vase, tree trunk shape, 6-1/4" h, **$150.**

Photo courtesy of Joy Luke Auctions.

Vase

4-1/4" h, six-sided pot, 3rd green mark **45.00**
4-3/4" h, 5-3/4" d, Cardium, shell form, coral and shell base, 2nd black mark... **80.00**
8" h, coral, pink tinted coral and shell int., 1st black mark, c1880...................... **1,150.00**
8-1/4" h, Dolphin, 1st black mark, chip on tail **775.00**
9" h, two scrolled and pierced handles, delicate applied bouquet of flowers, 1891 mark, price for pr **690.00**
12" h, tree trunk with three lower and three upper vase spouts, applied with flowers and leaves, bird perched atop arched branches above another bird in nest, second black mark, c1900, chips to leaves, hairline repair to lower trunk......................... **1,175.00**

BENNINGTON AND BENNINGTON-TYPE POTTERY

History: In 1845, Christopher Webber Fenton  joined Julius Norton, his brother-in-law, in the manufacturing of stoneware pottery in Bennington, Vermont. Fenton sought to expand the company's products and glazes; Norton wanted to concentrate solely on stoneware. In 1847, Fenton broke away and established his own factory.

Fenton introduced to America the famous Rockingham glaze, developed in England and named after the Marquis of Rockingham. In 1849, he patented a flint enamel glaze, "Fenton's Enamel," which added flecks, spots, or streaks of color (usually blues, greens, yellows, and oranges) to the brown Rockingham glaze. Forms included candlesticks, coachman bottles, cow creamers, poodles, sugar bowls, and toby pitchers.

Fenton produced the little-known scroddled ware, commonly called lava or agate ware.

Scroddled ware is composed of differently colored clays, which are mixed with cream-colored clay, molded, turned on a potter's wheel, coated with feldspar and flint, and fired. It was not produced in quantity, as there was little demand for it.

Fenton also introduced Parian ware to America. Parian was developed in England in 1842 and known as "Statuary ware." Parian is translucent porcelain that has no glaze and resembles marble. Bennington made the blue and white variety in the form of vases, cologne bottles, and trinkets.

The hound-handled pitcher is probably the best-known Bennington piece. Hound-handled pitchers were made by about 30 different potteries in more than 55 variations. Rockingham glaze was used by more than 150 potteries in 11 states, mainly in the Midwest, between 1830 and 1900.

Marks: Five different marks were used, with many variations. Only about 20 percent of the pieces carried any mark; some forms were almost always marked, others never. Marks include:
1849 mark (four variations) for flint enamel and Rockingham
E. Fenton's Works, 1845-1847, on Parian and occasionally on scroddled ware
U. S. Pottery Co., ribbon mark, 1852-1858, on Parian and blue and white porcelain
U. S. Pottery Co., lozenge mark, 1852-1858, on Parian
U. S. Pottery, oval mark, 1853-1858, mainly on scroddled ware

Additional Listings: Stoneware.

Flask, book, spine impressed "DEPARTED SPIRITS," spout with circle of raised dots, mottled brown Rockingham glaze, 5-5/8" h, **$350**.
Photo courtesy of Skinner, Inc.

Butter churn, stoneware, five gallons, J. Norton & Co., cobalt blue flowering cornucopia of flowers, original dasher guide, c1861, 19" h, very minor staining, 3" very tight line on side, **$8,250**.
Photo courtesy of Bruce and Vicki Wassdorp.

Bowl, 7-1/8" d, shallow, brown and yellow Rockingham glaze, Fenton's 1849 mark......... **775.00**
Candlestick, 8-1/4" h, flint enamel glaze **875.00**
Curtain tiebacks, pr, 4-1/2" l, 1849-58, Barrett plate 200, one chipped **185.00**
Figure, 8-1/2" h, 9" l, poodle, standing, basket in mouth, Barrett plate 367, repairs to tail and hind quarters **2,500.00**
Flask, book, flint enamel, title imp on spine, 1849-58, Barrett plate 411
5-3/4" w, 2-5/8" d, 7-3/4" h, brown and blue flint enamel glaze, "Bennington Battle" on spine........................ **3,300.00**
6" h, titled "Hermit's Life & Suffering" **980.00**
7" h, titled "Ladies Companion"............... **690.00**
Flowerpot, 3-1/8" h, molded shells, imp "Bennington Aug 16, 1877 Centennial," shallow flake **200.00**
Jug, 17-3/4" h, stoneware, cobalt blue leaf dec, imp mark "E. Norton & Co., Bennington, VT, 4," strap handle, stains, base flakes **300.00**

Dog, seated, molded base, Rockingham glaze, 8" w, 11" h, **$350**.
Photo courtesy of Dotta Auction Co., Inc.

Marble, 1-1/2" d, blue, some wear **90.00**
Paperweight, 3" h, 4-1/2" h, spaniel, 1849-58, Barrett plate 407 .... **815.00**
Picture frame, 9-1/2" h, oval, 1948-58, Barrett plate VIII, chips and repairs, pr **230.00**
Pitcher, 8" h, hunting scene, Barrett pate 26, chips **175.00**
Spittoon, 9-1/2" d, flint enamel glaze, rare 1849 mark   **450.00**

Inkwell, unsigned, five holes, formed column design, applied flint Bennington glaze, c1850, 3" d, 2" h, **$200**.
Photo courtesy of Bruce and Vicki Wassdorp.

Sugar bowl, cov, 3-3/4" h, Parian, blue and white, Repeated Oak Leaves pattern, raised grapevine dec on lid
.... **150.00**
Teapot, cov, flint enamel, Alternate Rib pattern, pierced pouring spout.................. **425.00**

Wash bowl and pitcher, flint enamel glaze **1,100.00**

Jug, stoneware, two gallons, ovoid, applied strap handle, ornate cobalt blue floral sprig decoration, impressed maker's marks, "J.NORTON & CO BENNINGTON VT," 1839-43, 14" h, **$600**.
Photo courtesy of Skinner, Inc.

Jug, stoneware, two gallons, ovoid, applied strap handle, ornate cobalt blue floral sprig decoration, impressed maker's marks, "J.NORTON & CO BENNINGTON VT," 1839-43, 14" h, $600.
Photo courtesy of Skinner, Inc.

Bennington-Type

Bank, 3-1/4" h, 3-3/4" h, chest of drawers shape, Rockingham glaze, Barrett plate 428, small chip to front top edge **150.00**
Creamer, 5-1/2" h, 6-3/4" l, figural, cow, Rockingham glaze, Barrett plate 378, chipped cov, repairs............................ **115.00**
Flask, 7-1/4" l, 7" h, boot, laced up one side, daubed Rockingham glaze, rare removable spout included, lip repaired......................... **450.00**

Spittoon, 8-1/2" d, scallop shell form, Rockingham glaze, 19th C
.... **175.00**
Toby bottle, 9" h, barrel, Rockingham glaze, mid-19th C, rim and base chips......... **175.00**

BISCUIT JARS

History: The biscuit or cracker jar was the forerunner of the cookie jar. Biscuit jars were made of various materials by leading glassworks and potteries of the late 19th and early 20th centuries.

Note: All items listed have silver-plated (SP) mountings unless otherwise noted.

For more information, see *Warman's Glass*, 4th edition.

Burmese glass, 9" h, raised gold oak leaves and pastel flowers, Mt. Washington, possibly replaced lid **450.00**
Cranberry glass, 9" h, 6-1/4" d, two applied clear ring handles, applied clear feet and flower prunt pontil, ribbed finial knob
.... **195.00**

Carlton Ware, Peony pattern, flowers decoration, silver-plated lid, **$295**.
Photo courtesy of Joy Luke Auctions.

Crown Milano
6" w, jeweled body, starfish dec, rust and cream colored body, Mt. Washington, non-matching lid............... **550.00**

Earthenware, Crown Ford, scenic decoration, desert scene with figures and camels, 9" h, **$200**.

Photo courtesy of Joy Luke Auctions.

10" h, rect, raised gold tracery and large chrysanthemums, emb metal lid with seashell design, stamped "M.W. 4413" **400.00**
Earthenware, 9" h, Crown Ford, scenic dec, desert scene with figures and camels **200.00**
Electroplate silver and glass, 9-1/4" h, ovoid, colorless liner cut with vertical flutes to center, set into frame with baluster uprights supporting patera rim, beaded base with four strapwork feet, domed lid with leaf band below berry vine offset with winged masks, spherule and beaded scroll finial, German, early 20th C, likely Wurttembergische Metallwarenfabrik (WMF) **200.00**

Glass

8-1/4" h, pale yellow ground, green, gold, and rose floral dec, tooled silver-plated cover, handle, and rim, unsigned, Mt. Washington, New Bedford, MA **150.00**

9-1/2" h, blue, black scenic dec, pewter lid and handle **175.00**

English, dark cobalt blue transfer of morning glories, brass lid with shaped finial, elaborately shaped handle, **$495**.

Nippon China, 7-1/2" h, 4-1/2" w, sq, white, multicolored floral bands, gold outlines and trim **110.00**
Opal glass, 11" h, shading from white to blue, purple and crimson stemmed flowers, attributed to Wavecrest... **325.00**
Porcelain

5-1/2" h, blue flowers on molded panels, four-footed **125.00**
7" h, panels of small pink flowers, cobalt blue border, gilding, ftd **150.00**
7" h, portrait panels and flowers, Tirchenreuth dec **175.00**
7-1/2" h, fruit dec, minor rim chips.......................... **90.00**
7-1/2" h, German, cityscape panel dec **175.00**
7-1/2" h, roses and leaves dec **120.00**
8" h, scenic panels dec, blue beehive mark, silver plated lid and handle **175.00**

9" h, unmarked, oriental landscape panels, silver plated lid and handle . **145.00**
10" h, Art Nouveau floral dec, silver plated lid and handle **230.00**
10" h, Crown Devon, molded panels, flowers dec, silver plated lid and handle . **145.00**

Satin glass, flowers and leaves decoration, non-matching silver-plated lid, **$125**.

Photo courtesy of Joy Luke Auctions.

Pottery, 9" h, blue morning glory flowers and leaves, silver plated lid and handle **150.00**
Royal Bayreuth, Poppy, blue mark................................. **650.00**
Satin glass, 11" h, floral dec, pewter lid and handle..... **175.00**
Wave Crest, 9" h, yellow roses, molded multicolored swirl ground, incised floral and leaf dec on lid, marked "Quadruple Plate" **410.00**

Wedgwood, jasper

5" h, green dip ground, applied white classical figure groups above acanthus leafs, SP rim, handle and cover, imp Wedgwood mark, late 19th C, footrim nick **400.00**
5-3/4" h, central dark blue ground bordered in light blue, applied white Muses in relief, banded laurel border, SP rim, handle and cover, imp mark, c1900, slight relief loss... **650.00**
5-3/4" h, yellow ground, applied black relief of Muses below fruiting grapevine festoons terminating in lion masks with rings, grapevine border to foot, SP rim, handle and cover, imp mark, c1930 .... **800.00**
6" h, central dark blue ground bordered in light blue ground, applied white classical relief, SP footrim, rim, handle and cover, imp mark, c1900, slight firing lines to relief **600.00**

Left to right: English, brown enameled decoration with white and light pink flowers, c1811, **$595**; Carlton Ware, multicolored flowers, ivory ground, c1904, **$875**; English, hand painted swallow and flowers, c1891, **$495**; English, embossed mold, hand painted flowers, ivory ground, c1891, **$595**.

Biscuit jars, from left: Wood & Co., pink and yellow flowers, gold trim, c1895, **$695**; Doulton Burslem, blue and gold flowers, ivory ground, c1891, **$595**; Carlton Ware, Poppy Ware, hand painted, first mark, c1890, **$795**; Taylor, monks, shaded gray ground, c1890, **$650**.

BISQUE

History: Bisque or biscuit china is the name given to wares that have been fired once and have not been glazed.

Bisque figurines and busts, which were popular during the Victorian era, were used on fireplace mantels, dining room buffets, and end tables. Manufacturing was centered in the United States and Europe. By the mid-20th century, Japan was the principal source of bisque items, especially character-related items.

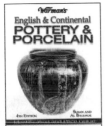

For more information, see *Warman's English & Continental Pottery & Porcelain*, 4th edition.

Bust, 12" h, female holding flower, green ribbons in hair, Cybis #471 .... **435.00**
Dish, cov, 9" x 6-1/2" x 5-1/2", dog, brown, and white, green blanket, white and gilt basketweave base **500.00**
Figure
7-1/2" h, hunters, dressed in Indian attire, riding on elephants, shooting attacking tigers, polychrome enameling, facing pair................... **350.00**
11-1/2" h, woman seated in chair, Cybis #298, issued 1968........................... **380.00**

Figure, court figure, white ground, gold trim, black and peach accents, painted facial features including blue eyes, **$195**.
Photo courtesy of Dotta Auction Co., Inc.

Hen on nest with basketweave, naturalistic colors, English, 8-1/2" h, 9-1/2" l, **$275**.
Photo courtesy of Joy Luke.

Figures, matched pair, girl cradling dove, boy holding rabbit, mauve, fleshtones, white, and gold, pink and green enameled flowers, price for pair, **$245**.

Box, covered, oval, two lambs on lid, applied coleslaw type grass and flowers, applied flowers on base, 5" l, 4-1/2" h, minor damage, **$95**.
Photo courtesy of Joy Luke.

14" h, modeled as young man and woman, each with light green bicycling attire, holding metal bicycle, Heubach Brothers, Thuringia, Germany, early 20th C, price for pr **1,175.00**
Match holder, figural, Dutch girl, copper and gold trim........ **45.00**
Planter, carriage, four wheels, pale blue and pink, white ground, gold dots, royal markings **165.00**
Salt, 3" d, figural, walnut, cream, branch base, matching spoon **75.00**
Wall plaque, 10-1/4" d, light green, scrolled and pierced scallop, white relief figures in center, man playing mandolin, lady wearing hat, c1900, pr **275.00**

Box, covered, oval, horse and dog on lid, 5-3/4" l, 6" h, **$230**.

Photo courtesy of Joy Luke.

Figure, semi-nude child seated on a stone plinth, mold incised "H. Dopping," German, early 20th C, 17-5/8" h, **$250**.

Photo courtesy of Skinner, Inc.

BLACK MEMORABILIA

History: The term "Black memorabilia" refers to a broad range of collectibles that often overlap other collecting fields, e.g., toys and postcards. It also encompasses African artifacts, items created by slaves or related to the slavery era, modern Black cultural contributions to literature, art, etc., and material associated with the Civil Rights Movement and the Black experience throughout history.

The earliest known examples of Black memorabilia include primitive African designs and tribal artifacts. Black Americana dates back to the arrival of African natives upon American shores.

The advent of the 1900s saw an incredible amount and variety of material depicting Blacks, most often in a derogatory and dehumanizing manner that clearly reflected the stereotypical attitude held toward the Black race during this period. The popularity of Black portrayals in this unflattering fashion flourished as the century wore on.

As the growth of the Civil Rights Movement escalated and aroused public awareness to the Black plight, attitudes changed. Public outrage and pressure during the early 1950s eventually put a halt to these offensive stereotypes.

Black representations are still being produced in many forms, but no longer in the demoralizing designs of the past. These modern objects, while not as historically significant as earlier examples, will become the Black memorabilia of tomorrow.

> Reproductions are becoming an increasing problem, from advertising signs (Bull Durham tobacco) to mechanical banks (Jolly Nigger). If the object looks new to you, chances are that it is new.

Autograph, Martin Luther King, Jr., 11" x 14" photograph, sgd "with best wishes Martin Luther King" **3,220.00**

Advertising figure, life-size, polychrome papier-mâché, figure posed in seated position, hands poised as if holding newspaper, white hat with red band, dark blue jacket, white shirt, vest, pants, and shoes, red necktie, America, late 19th/early 20th C, 20" w, 33" d, 48-1/2" h, minor paint wear, separations, **$5,900**.

Photo courtesy of Skinner, Inc.

Baseball cap, Kansas City Black Royals Negro League, white, gray pinstripes, worn black visor, large black "KC" stitched on front, c1920 .... **930.00**

Book
George Washington Carver, An American Biography, Rackham Colt, 1943, ex-library copy **5.00**

Aunt Jemima, cookie jar, salt and pepper shakers, range shakers, measuring cup, spice shakers, all plastic, **$250**.

Who's Who in Colored America, Volume I, J. Joseph Boris, ed., New York, 1927, first edition, portrait plates, small 4to, orig cloth **375.00**
Women of Achievement, Benjamin Brawley, Woman's American Baptist Home Mission Society, 1919, portrait plates, small 8vo, orig cloth **375.00**

Carte-de-visite

Colored Baptist Church, Petersburg, VA, Lazell & McMillin, Petersburg, photographers, 1966, ext. view, men and women sitting on front fence, pencil inscription "Church of Petersburg Negroes burned by rebels, given by Lottie, Feb. 9th, 1868," soil, wear, slight crimp **345.00**
Frederick Douglas, full-length portrait, c1860, erased pencil marks on top border ... **550.00**
Sojourner Truth, 3/4 view, seated at table, knitting, "I Sell the Shadow to Support the Substance," 1864, corners clipped, toning, light browning..................... **660.00**
Cigar box label, 6-1/4" x 10", glossy paper label, Booker T., Perfecto Cigars, black and white portrait of Booker T Washington, red, pale blue, and dark blue border, white stars, c1930s, unused **20.00**

Bank, Mammy, cast iron, slot in back, painted red hat, dress, white kerchief and apron, some loss to paint, **$85**.

Doll

12" h, Mammy, nut head, painted features, looped plush hair, whisk broom body, orig commercial assemblage, pink print dress, twin black babies in green print organdy outfits, early 20th C..... **635.00**
18" h, Mammy, stuffed cloth, hand-embroidered features, red trimmed dress, blue and white cap, wear, damage **220.00**
20" h, Golliwog, velveteen face, hands, and feet, applied felt eyes and mouth, inked nose, yellow checked shirt, golden crepe pants, red braid trim, removable gray and white checked wool jacket, c1930, some wear and soil **460.00**

Ephemera

Certificate of Freedom, for Thomas Chambers, resident of New York City, September 1814, partly printed document, sgd, small folio, docketed on verso...... **950.00**
Deposition of Thomas Cook, Shrewsbury, NJ, concerning slave trade and events on the sloop *Fanny,* Jan. 10, 1801, 12-1/2" x 8".................. **175.00**
Depositions concerning slave trade by sloop *Fanny* between Africa and North America, Oct 8, 1801, 17 pgs, 9-1/2" x 7-1/2" **550.00**
Notice, *The Charleston Daily Courier,* Jan. 5, 1858, regarding issuing of slave badges, giving prices for various trades.......... **1,380.00**
Receipt, "Negro Apprenticeship 2/0," printed, "Bought of the Anti-Slavery Society, Office, No. 18, Aldermanbury," (England) signed and dated by Francis Wedgwood, Society seal, dated 1838 .... **490.00**
Game, Jolly Darkie Ten Pens, McLoughlin Bros, 14-7/8" x 9-1/2" x 1-1/2" orig box, two wooden balls, ten 8" x 2-1/2" diecut cardboard black men figures on wooden bases, C.8 .... **1,000.00**
Nodder, 30" h, black boy, clockwork, head nods up and down, eyes roll, one arm extended upward, other extended forward in greeting manner, papier-mâché . **1,500.00**

Book, *Kemble's Coons*, John Lane, London, R. H. Russell & Son, New York, **$75**.
Photo courtesy of Michael Ivankovich Auction Co., Inc.

Perfume bottle, 4-3/4" to 6" h, Golliwogg, stylized faces, black and brown hair covering stoppers, bulbous frosted glass body, painted white collar, black round feet, raised maker's mark for DeVigny, one with partial paper label, c1919, price for three-pc set..................... **575.00**

Pinback button

Baltimore Elite Giants, Negro Leagues, red and white, glossy cello, c1940....... **45.00**
Gold Dust Washing Powder, multicolored trademark of Black twins seated in wash tub, white background, black letters.................... **60.00**

Plate, advertising, "Chocolate Drops" in gold, center design of Black child, white dress, yellow ribbons, gold rim, **$65**.

Pocket tin, 4-1/4" x 3-3/4" x 7/8", tin litho, vertical pocket type, image of black man smoking pipe on front, mkd "Record Pipe Tobacco" on back........... **625.00**

Print, 13-1/4" x 9-3/4", litho, *I'm Not to Blame for Being White Sir*, young white child holding out her hand for coins while passing stranger places coins in hands of black child, c1850, heavily toned **290.00**

Puzzle, 7-1/2" x 9-1/2" x 1-1/8", Darktown Fire Brigade, Parker Bros, c1890s, heavy cardboard pcs, wear to orig box **425.00**

Roly poly, Mayo's Roly Poly Tobacco, Mammy, litho tin, 7" x 5-1/4", two pcs, C-8+ **825.00**

Slave tag, 2" sq, copper, Charlestown, 1834
Porter, 171 .... **3,065.00**
Servant No. 205, wear, minor dents **1,175.00**

Target game, 15-1/2" x 8" x 1-5/8", McLoughlin Bros, image of black man holding musical instruments, C.8.5 .... **500.00**

Sign, tin litho, tan ground, black lettering, red trim, child eating slice of bread with honey, honey pail to right, "Honey, dat's all! Rocky Mountain Honey Co., Producers of Choice Honey, Silver City, New Mexico," red border, some wear, **$195**.

Photo courtesy of Alderfer Auction Co.

Textile, printed, 32-1/2" x 42", showing Little Black Sambo and tiger, earth tones of red, green, and dark brown, tan linen ground, folded, sewn seam with red ink label "WPA Handicraft Project #10235, Milwaukee, Wisconsin, Sponsored by Milwaukee County and Milwaukee State Teachers College, c1935-43" **1,350.00**

BOHEMIAN GLASS

History: The once independent country of Bohemia, now a part of the Czech Republic, produced a variety of fine glassware: etched, cut, overlay, and colored. Its glassware, which first appeared in America in the early 1820s, continues to be exported to the U.S. today.

Bohemia is known for its "flashed" glass that was produced in the familiar ruby color, as well as in amber, green, blue, and black. Common patterns include Deer and Castle, Deer and Pine Tree, and Vintage.

Most of the Bohemian glass encountered in today's market is from 1875 to 1900. Bohemian-type glass also was made in England, Switzerland, and Germany.

Reproduction Alert.

For more information, see *Warman's Glass*, 4th edition.

Basket

6-1/2" h, irid green, ruffled, applied reeded handle, gilt dragonfly and fern dec **175.00**

8" d, irid green body dec with amethyst straw marks, metal rim and handle, Wilhelm Kralik **150.00**

Bowl, 6" d, green ground, random ruby threading, c1910 .... **175.00**

Candlesticks, set of four, 10-1/2" h, cranberry flashed, cut to clear, wide drip pan cut with guilloche band accented with stars and roundels, similarly cut elongated egg-shaped stem, panel-cut domed foot, late 19th/ early 20th C **1,645.00**

Compote, 9-1/4" h, irid green, threaded glass trim on bowl, pedestal, and foot, c1900 .. **175.00**

Dresser bottle, 8-1/4" h, cut panel body, enameled dec, c1890 .... **90.00**

Ewer, 14" h, ftd, blue cut to clear, horizontal gray panels, dec with cameo carved white and blue grapes and leaves, price for pr **1,050.00**

Goblet, 6-3/4" h, white and cranberry overlay, thistle form bowl, six teardrop panels alternately enameled with floral bouquets and cut with blocks of diamonds, faceted knob and spreading scalloped foot, gilt trim........ **600.00**

Low bowl, 8-1/2" d, ftd, optic ribbed, blue, large enameled roses and foliage, three figural fish form feet, accented with jeweled eyes, and pointillism enamel, Harrach **1,500.00**

Cordial set, decanter and six matching cordial glasses, ruby stained, etched decoration, **$350**.

Decanter, ruby stained, cut grape decoration, **$125**.

Mantel lusters, pr, 12" h, trumpet shaped body cased in white, enamel dec floral sprays and gilt moss, cut to ruby flashing, crenellated edge and trumpet foot, hung with long faceted colorless lusters, late 19th C **650.00**
Mantel urns, cov, pr, 18-1/2" h, amber flashed, tapered octagonal bodies etched with continuous scene of deer in wooded landscape, domed lids with paneled baluster finials, faceted knop, trumpet foot with scalloped rim, star-cut base, late 19th C **2,500.00**
Portrait vase, 9-1/2" h, slender baluster-form cranberry flashed body over-enameled with gilt vines, one side with white cased oval painted with portrait of young lady, late 19th C ... **250.00**
Ramekin, 3" w, translucent yellow and clear, dec with red, green, yellow, and blue scrolling, white dotted and gold horizontal band, price for set of eight **100.00**

Rose bowl, 5" h, optic ribbed body, applied ruffled rim, cobalt blue, Harrach **110.00**
Toothpick holder, 2-1/2" h, tapering body, brass rim, threaded irid body, Pallme-Koening........................... **115.00**
Urn, 11" h, ftd, cranberry, medallion coal of arms, gold encrustations, polychrome floral scrolling, raised glass jewels, two jewels missing **175.00**
Vase
3-1/4" h, paneled shouldered body, irid dark olive green/brown............................ **35.00**
6" h, tapering ovoid body, blue cut to clear, notched rims, overlaid circular bases, clear floral pattern cutting, price for pr **200.00**
7-1/4" h, applied clear snake form **75.00**
7-1/2" h, bulbous stick, mottled red, colorful scrolling foliage, Graf Harrach propeller mark **350.00**
8-1/4" h, bulbous stick, quadra-fold rim, deep amethyst, irid blue oil spot finish **120.00**
8-1/4" h, bulbous stick, tri-fold rim, cranberry, overall gold oil spot finish, random threading at rim........................... **150.00**
9" h, cylindrical, tri-fold inverted rim, irid blue, white draped loops, Rindskopf **150.00**
10" h, cylindrical, shading from amber green to rose, Grenada Line, Rindskopf **175.00**
10-1/2" h, wide cylindrical, irid green, shades of blue and purple in undulating design **600.00**

Vases, cased, blue cut to clear, gilded decoration, 9" h, price for pair, **$900**.

Photo courtesy of Joy Luke.

12" h, cylindrical tapering body, irid citron, applied irid threading, Pallme-Koenig **400.00**
12-1/8" h, azure blue, tapered conical body with slightly flared rim, cut with daisy heads between navettes, cut and gilded chinoiserie hunting scenes and florals on smoked ground, paneled foot, early 20th C **250.00**
Water set, 11" h covered water jug, four matching 5" cups, cobalt blue ground, gilt bands, raised pink flowers, mkd "Made in Czecho-Slovakia"........ **125.00**
Wine bottle, 10" h, ruby flashed, engraved florals, matching stopper, c1890................. **90.00**

BOOKS, EARLY

History: Collecting early books is a popular segment of the antiques marketplace. Collectors of early books are rewarded with interesting titles, exquisite illustrations, as well as fascinating information and stories. The author, printer, and publisher, as well as the date of the printing, can increase the value of an early book. Watch for interesting paintings on the fore-edge of early books. These miniature works of art can greatly add to the value.

History of Lehigh and Carbon Cos, Pennsylvania, with Illustrations, 1884, **$225**.

Photo courtesy of Dotta Auction Co., Inc.

Aelianus, Claudis, *Claudis Aelianus His Various History*, translated by Thomas Stanley, London, Thomas Dring, 1665, first Stanley edition, small 8vo, modern 1/2 sheep gilt, first blank leaf missing, rubbed, some dampstaining in outer corners **130.00**

Armstrong, John, *The Art of Preserving Health: A Poem*, London, A. Millar, 1774, first edition, 134 pgs, 4to, modern 1/4 calf, title browned........ **70.00**

Bentley, Richard, *The Folly and Unreasonableness of Atheism...In Eight Sermons Preached at the Lecture Founded by the Honourable Robert Boyle, Esquire*, London, J. H. for H. Mortlock, 1693, eight parts in one volume, 4to, contemporary mottled sheep, rebacked......................... **410.00**

Bohn, Henry C., *A Catalogue of Books*, London, 1841, engraved frontispiece and title page, thick 8vo, contemporary 1/4 road, front cover detached, frontispiece adhere, heavy foxing **150.00**

Burke, Edmund, *Reflections on the Revolution in France*, London, J. Dodsley, 1790, second edition, second impression, 356 pgs, 8vo, contemporary calf, rebacked, hinges reinforced, cloth slipcase **165.00**

Burney, Frances, *Evelina* or *A Young Lady's Entrance into the World*, London, T. Lowndes, 1779, second edition, three volumes, 12mo, contemporary sheep, rebacked............. **130.00**

Dart, John, *Westmonasterium; or, The History and Antiquities of the Abbey Church of St. Peters Westminster*, London, John Coles, c1723, engraved titles, 148 of 149 plates, two volumes, folio, contemporary calf gilt, red and green morocco lettering pieces, joints cracked, foxing, 19th C armorial bookplate **350.00**

Norman Rockwell, Artist and Illustrator, white cover with classic self portrait illustration, Harry N. Abrams, 1970, original dust jacket, **$20**.

Dickinson, Emily, *Poems*, 1890, FE.................................. **6,500.00**

Fairbairn, James, *Fairbairn's Crests of the Families of Great Britain and Ireland, Revised by Laurence Butters*, Edinburgh and London, later 19th C, engraved titles, 148 plates, two volumes, 8vo, contemporary 1/2 levant gilt, rebacked retaining faded orig backstrips........ **70.00**

Fielding, Henry, *Amelia*, London, A. Millar, 1752, first edition, integral ad leaf at end of Volume 2, four volumes, 12 mo, modern beige calf gilt with morocco lettering pieces **490.00**

Gay, John, *The Shepherd's Week, In Six Pastorals*, London, Ferd. Burleigh, 1714, first edition, seven full-page etched illus by Louis Du Guernier, 8vo, modern 1/2 calf............... **865.00**

Gibson, Edward, *The History of the Decline and Fall of the Roman Empire*, London, A. Strahan and T. Cadell, 1782-88, six volumes, three engraved portrait, contemporary tree calf, map of Constantinople missing ... **320.00**

Godwin, William, *Things as They Are; or The Adventures of Caleb Williams*, London, B. Crosby, 1794, first edition, three volumes, 12mo, contemporary marbled boards with red morocco lettering, spines darkened, occasional light browning, armorial bookplates and signatures of SC rice planter Charles Izard Manigault (1795-1874)............................ **1,840.00**

Howell, William, *An Institution of General History; or The History of the World*, second edition with large additions, London, Thomas Bassett, 1680-80, four volumes in three, folio, modern 1/4 morocco......................... **435.00**

Hume, David, *The History of England*, London, A. Millar, 1754-59-62, six volumes, 4to, contemporary calf gilt with morocco lettering pieces, few joints cracked **980.00**

Johnson, Samuel, *Irene, A Tragedy*, London, R. Dodsley and M. Cooper, 1749, first edition, 8vo, joints rubbed............ **865.00**

Knight, Henrietta, Lady Luxborough, *Letters Written by the Late Right Honourable Lady Luxborough to William Shenstone, Esq.*, London, J. Dodsley, 1775, first edition, 416 pgs, 8vo, contemporary calf, rebacked......................... **375.00**

Really Babies, Elizabeth B. Brownell, green cover with gilt trim, oval portrait medallions, **$35**.

Photo courtesy of Alderfer Auction Co.

Lackington, James, *Memoirs of the First Forty-Five Years of the Life of James Lackington, the Present Bookseller in Chiswell-street, Moorfields, London, Written by Himself*, printed for and sold by the author, 1791, first edition, engraved frontispiece portrait, 344 pages, 8vo, modern tree calf gilt **215.00**

Milton, John, *Paradise Lost, Paradise Regain'd*, Birmingham, John Baskerville for J. and R. Tonson, London, 1760, together, two volumes, large 8vo, contemporary mottled calf, rebacked......................... **575.00**

Nicolay, John G. and John Hay, *Abraham Lincoln, A History*, 1909, two-volume set...... **460.00**

Priestley, Joseph, *Lectures on History, and General Policy*, London, J. Johnson, 1793, two folding engraved tables, two volumes, 8vo, contemporary calf gilt, joints cracked **200.00**

Sinking of the Titanic, The World's Greatest Sea Disaster, Official Edition, red cover, **$75**.

Photo courtesy of Alderfer Auction Co.

Shakespeare, William, *The Famous History of the Life of King Henry the Eight(h)*, extracted from the second folio, London, 1632, modern cloth, calf lettering piece, some foxing and minor stains, 18th C owner's signature on last page **460.00**

Thomas, Gabriel, *An Historical Account of the Province and County of Pensilvania and of West-New Jersey in America*, 1698 .... **27,000.00**

Unknown author

Confessions of a Medium, FE, London, 1882 .... **250.00**

Modern Magic: A Practical Treatise on the Art of Conjuring, FE, London, 1876 .... **2,000.00**

The Great Chinese Wizard's Handbook of Magic, Hurst & Co, NY, 1872 .... **275.00**

Walpole, Horace, *A Castle of Otranto, A Gothic Story*, London, William Bathoe and Thomas Lownds, 1765, second edition, 200 pgs, 8vo, contemporary calf, rebacked endpaper renewed **435.00**

BOTTLES, GENERAL

History: Cosmetic bottles held special creams, oils, and cosmetics designed to enhance the beauty of the user. Some also claimed, especially on their colorful labels, to cure or provide relief from common ailments.

A number of household items, e.g., cleaning fluids and polishes, required glass storage containers. Many are collected for their fine lithographed labels.

Mineral water bottles contained water from a natural spring. Spring water was favored by health-conscious people between the 1850s and 1900s.

Nursing bottles, used to feed the young and sickly, were a great help to the housewife because of their graduated measure markings, replaceable nipples, and the ease with which they could be cleaned, sterilized, and reused.

For more information, see *Warman's Glass*, 4th edition, and *Warman's Bottles Field Guide*.

A.M. Bininger & Co. 19 Broad St. N.Y. Distilled In 1848, Old Kentucky Bourbon 1849 Reserve, barrel shape, applied top, tubular open pontil, **$240**.
Photo courtesy of American Bottle Auctions

Beverage

A. M. Bininger & Co., 338 Broadway, NY, Distilled in 1848, Old Kentucky Bourbon, 1849 Reserve, true green, applied lip, iron pontil **6,000.00**

Beehive, pattern molded, Midwestern

7-1/2" d, 24 vertical ribs, single roll collar, light green, unusual lip **180.00**

9" h, 24 ribs swirled to right, open pontil, wear, light scratches **70.00**

Empire Soda Works, San Francisco, aqua, 1861-71 .... **400.00**

Excelsior Water, eight-sided, iron pontil, dug, uncleaned, some white paint on pontil **450.00**

Miller's Extra Old Bourbon, E. Martin & Co., light amber, c1871-75, placed bubbles on front **12,000.00**

Bitters, St. Drakes 1860 Plantation X Bitters, reverse embossed "Patented 1862," four logs, **$210**.
Photo courtesy of American Bottle Auctions

Napa Soda Natural Mineral Water, sapphire blue, "W" on base, needs int. cleaning, few scratches, wear **140.00**

Thos Taylor & Co., Virginia, Nevada, medium to deep reddish-chocolate color, c1874-80, few scratches **4,400.00**

Union Glass Works Phila Superior Mineral Water, deep cobalt blue, iron pontil, mug base, some int. stain, few scratches **350.00**

Williams & Severance San Francisco Calsoda Mineral Waters, light green, orig graphite **700.00**

Demijohn, blown, olive green, ovoid, pushed-I base, remnants of cork in neck, minor scratching, **$150**.
Photo courtesy of Alderfer Auction Co.

Cosmetic

Kickapoo Sage Hair Tonic, cylindrical, cobalt blue, tooled mouth, matching stopper, smooth base, 5" h **160.00**

Kranks Cold Cream, milk glass, 2-3/4" h................................ **6.50**

Pompeian Massage Cream, amethyst, 2-3/4" h **9.00**

Milk bottle, Martin Century Farm, quart, brown pyro decoration, **$85**.

Food, Cathedral, honey jar, light aqua, open tubular pontil, 6-1/4" h, **$120**.
Photo courtesy of American Bottle Auctions.

Food and household

Ink, Waterman's, paper label with bottle of ink, wooden bullet shaped case, orig paper label, 4-1/4" h.............................. **10.00**

Pickle

Cathedral, pale aqua, sq applied top, sticky ball type pontil, 12" h................ **190.00**

W. D. Smith, N.Y., deep squa, pint, applied lip, graphite pontil, 8-1/2"h........... **1,000.00**

Sewing Machine Oil, Sperm Brand, clear, 5-1/2" h **5.00**

Shoe Polish, Everett & Barron Co., oval, clear, 4-3/4" **5.00**

Nursing

Acme, clear, lay-down, emb **65.00**

Cala Nurser, oval, clear, emb, ring on neck, 7-1/8" h........ **12.00**

Empire Nursing Bottle, bent neck, 6-1/2" h.................... **50.00**

Mother's Comfort, clear, turtle type **25.00**

BRASS

History: Brass is a durable, malleable, and ductile metal alloy consisting mainly of copper and zinc. The height of its popularity for utilitarian and decorative art items occurred in the 18th and 19th centuries.

Reproduction Alert: Many modern reproductions are being made of earlier brass forms, especially such items as buckets, fireplace equipment, and kettles.

Additional Listings: Bells, Candlesticks, Fireplace Equipment, and Scientific Instruments.

Ash bucket, covered, urn form, original insert, English, mid-19th C, **$200**.
Photo courtesy of Wiederseim Associates, Inc.

Andirons, pr

17-1/2" h, acorn tops, seamed columns, cabriole legs, ball feet.............................. **220.00**

18" h, ring-turned columns, scalloped cabriole legs, ball feet.............................. **360.00**

Bed warmer

42-1/2" l, engraved lid with large central flower surrounded by scrolls, maker's touchmark "ST," turned maple handle with old refinishing, minor damage near hinges................ **215.00**

43-3/4" l, engraved lid with central flower surrounded by scrolls, turned wood handle with daubs of brown paint, wear, minor split in ferule **185.00**

Candlesticks, pr, 10-1/8" h, pricket, ovoid drip pan on double baluster stem, domed cast foot, Continental, 18th C **650.00**

Chandelier, 25" d, 20" h, cast, eight scrolled arms with torch shaped ends, each with small electric socket, simulated candle coverings, 20th C **250.00**

Chestnut roaster, 18-3/4" l, oval, pierced hinged lid, long handle **120.00**

Chimes, 18-1/2" w, 27-1/2" h, mahogany and rosewood frame, eight brass chimes, turned pilasters on either side, striker missing, 20th C **220.00**

Coal bin, 16-1/2" w, 15-1/2" d, 26" h, brass gallery, applied Wedgwood dec, paterae carved rosewood frieze, tilting bin, splayed legs, Aesthetic Movement, c1875 price for pr **4,410.00**

Clockwork jack, signed "John Linwood," **$175**; and brass chamber stick, unmarked, **$95**.
Photo courtesy of Wiederseim Associates, Inc.

Coal grate, 19-1/2" l, 10-1/4" d, 27" h, Neoclassical-style, late 19th C, back plate cast with scene of figures in revelry, grate with central horizontal bar over guillouche band, uprights with brass urn finials, rear plinth base, front tapered legs . **175.00**

Dresser mirror, 11" w, 18" h, French, gilt brass, mirrored glass, scrolls, floral pots, and garlands dec, cracks, loss to silvering............................ **525.00**

Easel, late 19th/early 20th C, 61-5/8" h, A-frame topped by girdled round finial **500.00**

Foot warmer, hexagonal, wedding presentation type, pierced and embossed body, hearts, flowers, and busts of man and woman, Dutch, 18th C, 8 1/2" d, 7" h, $2,530.
Photo courtesy of Pook & Pook.

Figure, 31-1/2" h, Bodhisattva, dark patina, 10 arms, eight faces, single body, walnut block base **450.00**

Fireplace fender, 47" w, 13" d, 9" h, pierced grapevines, applied bunches of grapes, rope twist detail, three cast brass paw feet **360.00**

Gong, 18" d, dragons and tokugawa mons designs, Japan, early 20th C...................... **325.00**

Ladle, brass bowl attached with copper rivets to wrought iron flattened handle, rattail hanging hook

> 11-1/4" l....................... **300.00**
> 16-1/4" l....................... **85.00**

Pipe mold, American, 18th C, 10" l, $575.
Photo courtesy of Pook & Pook.

Letter sealer, 2" l brass tube, 23 double-sided brass discs with various sentimental seals for wax, 19th C **100.00**

Oil lamp, 19-1/2" h, Bouillote, three-light, squat ovoid font with short arms, suspending three tools from chains, spreading foot

with ogee shaped rim, black tin frame, 19th C **420.00**

Palace jar, 17" d, 16" h, chased designs of various deities within scrolled field, India, 20th C **420.00**

Snuff box, top set with blue and white glazed tile of Emperor in profile, marked "Low Tile, Chelsea" and other worn lettering, $75.

Snuff box, oval, three dials having Roman numerals and arrows for combination, hinged lid, 3-1/2" x 2-1/2", denting, brass button for opening detached, $175.
Photo courtesy of Alderfer Auction Co.

Plant stand, 14-1/2" d, 35-1/2" h, old gilding, round top with leaf drops and three scrolls, scrolled supports, leaves, and large flowers, eagle talon feet, lacquered......................... **450.00**

Samovar, 19-1/2" h, worn partial marks, illegible from polishing, heavy cast base, replaced burner cover, damage to spout, repair.............................. **150.00**

Sconces, pr, 21" d, hammered, gilt carved wooden foo dogs accents **360.00**

Steam whistle, 2-1/2" d, 12" h, single chime, lever control **150.00**

Sundial, 12-1/2" l, 12" w, 8-3/4" h, engraved markings, scrolls, and lettering "Merton Londini Anno Dom 1675" and "I stand amid ye Summere flowers To tell ye passinge of ye houres,"

imp "Made in England," early 20th C **265.00**

Trump indicator, circular flat brass disk, green enamel top, celluloid rotating suit and no trumps indicator.............. **130.00**

BRIDE'S BASKETS

History: A ruffled-edge glass bowl in a metal holder was a popular wedding gift between 1880 and 1910, hence the name "bride's basket." These bowls can be found in most glass types of the period. The metal holder was generally silver-plated with a bail handle, thus enhancing the basket image.

Over the years, bowls and bases became separated and married pieces resulted. If the base has been lost, the bowl should be sold separately.

Reproduction Alert: The glass bowls have been reproduced.

Note: Items listed here have a silver-plated (SP) holder unless otherwise noted.

Cased glass, pink, ruffled rim, silver-plated pedestal stand with handle, 9-1/2" d, 11-1/2" h, $225.
Photo courtesy of Joy Luke Auctions.

6" d, 5-1/2" h, blue and white glass bowl, enameled floral dec, SP holder **250.00**

8-1/2" d, 12" h, amber, enameled berries and buds, SP holder **1,195.00**

9" h, white opal basket, cranberry ruffled rim, applied vaseline rope handle, no holder **95.00**

9-1/2" d, 12" h, satin, deep pink ruffled bowl, white ext., marked "Nemasket Silver Co." SP holder **275.00**

Opalescent glass, pink, ruffled rim, lattice design, silver-plated basket stand, 10-1/2" d, 11" h, **$395**.
Photo courtesy of Joy Luke Auctions.

9-3/4" h, opaline cased in pink, ruffled amber rim, married plated holder.............................. **150.00**
9-7/8" d, 3" h, 3-3/4" base, bowl only, peachblow, glossy finish, deep pink shading to pale **250.00**
10" d, 11" h, pink hobnail bowl, blue ruffled rim, SP holder dec with leaves **525.00**
10" w, sq, custard, melon ribbed, enameled daisies, applied Rubena crystal rim, twisted and beaded handle, ftd, emb SP frame, marked "Wilcox" .. **450.00**
10-1/2" h, peachblow, cased rose shading to pink ground, applied amber stem, green leaves, amber handle, four applied feet, some losses **200.00**
10-1/2" d, 12-1/2" h, sculptured Rubena verde vaseline shading to pink, yellow and green enameled flowers, Benedict SP holder............................... **460.00**
10-3/4" d, 3-1/2" h, bowl only, overlay, heavenly blue, enameled white flowers, green leaves, white underside, ruffled **215.00**

Vaseline hobnail bowl, ornate silver plated frame, **$500**.
Photo courtesy of Joy Luke.

Ruffled deep pink hobnail bowl with blue edge, ornate silver plated frame with leaves on handle, 10" d, 11" h, **$525**.
Photo courtesy of Joy Luke.

11" d, 7-1/2" h, satin, light beige shading to orange ruffled bowl, hp pink, purple and yellow flowers, green leaves, raised gold outlines, blue int., sgd "Simpson, Hall, Miller Co. Quad Plate" holder **895.00**
11-1/8" d, 3-3/4" h, bowl only, satin, brown shaded to cream overlay, raised dots, dainty gold and silver flowers and leaves dec, ruffled...................... **250.00**
11-1/4" h, opalescent Rubena verde, applied lime stepped flower feet, thorny twist handle, Victorian **425.00**
12" d, 7-1/2" h, white opaline, cased in pink, overall colorful enameled dec, emb Middletown plated holder, applied fruit handles, Victorian, minor losses **525.00**
13" l, 5" h, Crown Milano, ruffled edge bowl, heavy hand applied gold encrustation on mottled ground, pontil sgd with trademark..................... **2,000.00**

BRISTOL GLASS

History: Bristol glass is a designation given to a semi-opaque glass, usually decorated with enamel and cased with another color.

For more information, see *Warman's Glass*, 4th edition.

Initially, the term referred only to glass made in Bristol, England, in the 17th and 18th centuries. By the Victorian era, firms on the Continent and in America were copying the glass and its forms.

Bowl, light blue, Cupid playing mandolin, gold trim........... **45.00**
Box, cov, 4-1/8" l, 2-3/4" d, 3-1/2" h, oblong, blue, gilt-metal mounts and escutcheon ... **550.00**

Cordial compotes, deep blue, hand painted polychrome floral decoration, brass hinged mounts, original cordial glasses, wear to gold trim, price for pair, **$275**.
Photo courtesy of Wiederseim Associates, Inc.

Cake stand, celadon green, enameled herons in flight, gold trim **135.00**
Candlesticks, pr, 7" h, soft green, gold band **75.00**
Decanter, 11-1/2" h, ruffled stopper, enameled flowers and butterfly............................. **75.00**
Dresser set, two cologne bottles, cov powder jar, white, gilt butterflies dec, clear stoppers............................. **75.00**
Ewer, 6-3/8" h, 2-5/8" d, pink ground, fancy gold designs, bands, and leaves, applied handle with gold trim **135.00**
Finger bowl, 4-3/8" d, blue, faceted sides, early 20th C, eight-pc set.................... **500.00**
Hatpin holder, 6-1/8" h, ftd, blue, enameled jewels, gold dec **100.00**
Perfume bottle, 3-1/4" h, squatty, blue, gold band, white enameled flowers and leaves, matching stopper **100.00**

Vase, monumental, hp decoration, bird in flowering tree branches, polychrome on white ground, blue footed base, gilt leaf decoration, wooden reeded column base, 24-1/2" h vase, **$450**.

Photo courtesy of Alderfer Auction Co.

Puff box, cov, round, blue, gold dec **35.00**
Sugar shaker, 4-3/4" h, white, hp flowers.............................. **65.00**
Sweetmeat jar, 3" x 5-1/2", deep pink, enameled flying duck, leaves, blue flower dec, white lining, SP rim, lid, and bail handle **110.00**

Vase, white body, blue accents at ruffles, gold, black, and pink floral decoration, 9" h, **$35**.

Urn, cov, 17" h, pink opaque, hp bird and branch dec, base mkd "251" **150.00**
Vase, 11" h, bulbous stick, Delft windmill dec **100.00**

BRONZE

History: Bronze is an alloy of copper, tin, and traces of other metals. It has been used since Biblical times not only for art objects, but also for utilitarian wares. After a slump in the Middle Ages, the use of bronze was revived in the 17th century and continued to be popular until the early 20th century.

Notes: Do not confuse a "bronzed" object with a true bronze. A bronzed item usually is made of white metal and then coated with a reddish-brown material to give it a bronze appearance. A magnet will stick to it but not to anything made of true bronze.

A signed bronze commands a higher market price than an unsigned one. There also are "signed" reproductions on the market. It is very important to know the history of the mold and the background of the foundry.

Censor, foo dog, standing, three dimensional features, open mouth, removable section in back, 20" l, 21" h, loss to tip of mane, **$715**.

Photo courtesy of Alderfer Auction Co.

Basket, 10-1/4", trompe l'oeil, folded linen form, woven handle, applied florals and insects, Japanese, 19th C............ **350.00**
Bookends, pr, 9" h, daffodil silhouette, imp mark of G. Thew, 1928 .... **225.00**
Box, chaise lounge form, topped with monkey on pillows, lid lifts to reveal erotic scene of man and woman with carved ivory features, gilt and polychrome dec, marble base, 20th C **1,495.00**

Bust, 11-3/8" h, Napoleon, Sienna marble column with leaftip surround, plinth base, late 19th/early 20th C **1,410.00**
Candlesticks, pr, figural
6" h, owl, granite base **225.00**
10" h Don Quixote standing and holding a lance, 11" h Pancho Sanchez, riding a donkey and holding a staff, each with inverted helmet-formed sconce, both on tripod base, early 20th C **300.00**
Cauldron, 19" d, four flanges with geometric decoration, two with handles, tripod base, Central Asia, Seljuk period, 15th C **1,100.00**
Clock, 8" w, 3" d, 6-1/4" h, Chelsea Clock Co., Boston, silvered dial, round case, shaped rect base, ball feet, retailed by Tiffany & Co. . **650.00**
Clock garniture, parcel gilt bronze and slate, 20" h clock with two-train Hersant Freres chiming movement, case topped by griffin-handled urn, front set with female mask, raised front paw feet, pair of three-light 18" h candelabra, fruiting vine scrolled candle arms, similarly styled base, French, Renaissance Revival, late 19th C **1,175.00**

Figure sitting on top of tiered pedestal, gilt bronze, red pigment on steps, Southeast Asia, 19th C, 11-7/8" h, overall wear, tip of hair bend, **$350**.

Figure and sculpture

3-1/4" w, 2-1/2" d, 5-7/8" h, mythical beast, tail raised, supporting figure sitting on its back, table form base, Southeast Asia, 18th or 19th C, one leg loose.......... **175.00**

7-3/4" h, two Arabs, one man drawing water from well, other cooking, under grass roof, cold painted, Viennese, early 20th C, mounted with small electric bulb, early 20th C **2,350.00**

11-1/2" h, 12-1/2" w, hockey player, cast, green patina, base sgd "Joe Brown 1956" **1,150.00**

12-1/2" h, Shepherdess and her flock, woman in cape, standing with group of sheep by a stream, mold incised signature of Charles (Karl) Korschann, 15" w hexagonal green marble base .. **1,410.00**

13-1/2" d, gentleman reading newspaper, oblong base, indistinct mold incised signature, Continental School, dated 1903 .... **1,300.00**

14" h, Napoleon, standing by column, sq base with leaf-tip rim set with gilt eagle, late 19th C **940.00**

14" h, young Dionysus, standing, empty wine skin, after the antique, verdigris patination, early 20th C **500.00**

15" h, Allegorial Autumn, standing figure holding sheaf of wheat and flowers, holding staff, fluted black slate base, grand tour, late 19th/early 20th C **600.00**

20-1/2" h, seated woman with lyre resting on her lap, rect base with mold incised signature, for Georges Van der Straeten, Parisian foundry seal, late 19th C **1,650.00**

22-1/4" h, Nature Revealing Herself, standing woman in dore and pewter patinated robe, carved malachite scarab set at bodice, carved ivory bust, arms, and feet, mold incised signature "E. Barrias," Susse Freres foundry seal, slate and onyx base, 2-3/4" h stone base **11,200.00**

23-1/2" h, little girl covering giggle with her hand as she hides nosegay behind her back, medium brown patina, mold incised signature "Gaudez," (Adrien-Etienne Gaudez, 1845-1902) **3,525.00**

28" l, 13" h, cast from model by Vanetti, modeled as warrior in chariot drawn by three horses, rounded rect base, cast signature **3,150.00**

Figure, standing peacock with long tail, cold painted, Bergmann, Austrian, 12" l, loss to comb, **$150**.

Photo courtesy of Alderfer Auction Co.

Flower vessel, tightly curled lotus leaf resembling small boat, attached lotus blossoms, seed pods, crabs crawling to top, signed on rectangular reserve, Japanese, 19th C, carved wooden stand, 9-1/2" l, 3-1/4" h, **$2,450**.

Garden lantern, 4" h, jewel finials and eaves decorated with fish finials, pierced fire boxes, bases with cast foo dogs, Japan, 19th C, price for pr....... **2,115.00**

Jose stick holder, 4-3/4" h, attendant holding cloth with censer on top, opening in censer to hold joss stick, dark brown patina, China, Ming Dynasty, several holes................... **200.00**

Incense burner, 22" h, Oriental, circular base with relief birds and foliage, center medallions, applied handles, old clock set into one side which has a loose hand, some damage, soldered restorations **525.00**

Lamp, 68" h, designs of birds and flowers in high relief, Japan, Meiji period (1868-1911) **1,765.00**

Lamp base, 22" h, gilt bronze, candelabra, five flower-form serpentine candle arms, raised on fluted rouge marble stem set with figure of cherub, ovoid base, black painted wood plinth, Louis XVI-style, late 19th/early 20th C, electrified, price for pr **2,235.00**

Letter holder, 8-1/2" l, 2" d, 5" h, doré, Silvercrest, double tiered, overlay of sailing ship in waves accented by linear decoration, imp mark, numbered "2222" **300.00**

Parade helmet, cast

15-3/8" l, 11-1/4" h, 19th C, depicting Hercules battling the hydra with cityscape in background, borders of military motifs and emperors **460.00**

18" l, gladiator's, Continental-style, China, early 20th C, four-part hinged visor comprising two-piece pierced eye guard, over two-piece face guard cast as figures before prison gates, helmet with high relief battle scene, further Roman-style figures **690.00**

Powder jar, figural bronze cold painted woman in bonnet, marble base, **$70**.

Pen vase, 3-1/2" h, gilt, cylindrical vessel, flared base, ribbed swirled design, unsigned, attributed to Tiffany Studios, NY **175.00**

Plaque

5-5/8" sq, Flower Maidens, profile busts of long-haired beauties, incised titles "Marguerite" and "Mignon," set in 11-3/4" sq maroon velvet frames, Aesthetic Movement, late 19th/early 20th C, price for pr **715.00**

14" d, circular, high relief design of lion's head, early 20th C **1,300.00**
Scepter, 20-1/2" l, three cast faces, paneled rod, engraved swirled designs, crown finials, Oriental, possible brazed repair on rod **175.00**
Smoking tray, 6-1/4" d, Doré finish, applied scrolling on ash bowl, cigar rests, matchbox holder, unmarked, c1910 .. **70.00**

Tray, four corners embossed with cranes around whiplash center, impressed "FRIES," original dark patina, 9-1/4" square, **$300**.
Photo courtesy of David Rago Auctions, Inc.

Tray, 9" d, band of hammered designs, marked "Apollo Studios, New York" c1910. **45.00**
Urn, 11-3/8" h, cast, black patinated, everted reeded rim, central band of classical figures, two short handles with male masks, fluted foot, sq black marble base, Classical-style, late 19th/early 20th C, price for pr **2,530.00**
Vase, 13" h, enameled dec of figures in ancient Roman garb, dragons on shoulder, butterflies on rim, mark on underside, possibly Japanese, early 20th C, slight loss to enamel **175.00**
Wall sconces
    11-7/8" h, pr, cast, Louis XV-style, two-light, rocaille-shaped candle arms and backplate, floriform drip pans hung with faceted colorless glass lusters **150.00**
    21" h, set of four, each with two candle sockets on cornucipia-shaped stems bound by ribbons, drapery like wall plates with rosettes at top, gilded **700.00**

27-1/2" h, set of four, Neoclassical-style, gilt bronze, four-light, urns issuing four scrolling candle arms, back-plates inset with green jasperware medallions, hung throughout with floral swags, electrified, 20th C **13,145.00**

BUFFALO POTTERY

History:
Buffalo Pottery Co., Buffalo, New York, was chartered in 1901. The

first kiln was fired in October 1903. Larkin Soap Company established Buffalo Pottery to produce premiums for its extensive mail-order business. Wares also were sold to the public by better department and jewelry stores. Elbert Hubbard and Frank Lloyd Wright, who designed the Larkin Administration Building in Buffalo in 1904, were two prominent names associated with the Larkin Company.

Early Buffalo Pottery production consisted mainly of semi-vitreous china dinner sets. Buffalo was the first pottery in the United States to produce successfully the Blue Willow pattern. Buffalo also made a line of hand-decorated, multicolored willow ware, called Gaudy Willow. Other early items include a series of game, fowl, and fish sets, pitchers, jugs, and a line of commemorative, historical, and advertising plates and mugs.

From 1908 to 1909 and again from 1921 to 1923, Buffalo Pottery produced the line for which it is most famous—Deldare Ware. The earliest of this olive green, semi-vitreous china displays hand-decorated scenes from English artist Cecil Aldin's *Fallowfield Hunt*. Hunt scenes were done only from 1908 to 1909. English village scenes also were characteristic of the ware and were used during both periods. Most pieces are artist signed.

In 1911, Buffalo Pottery produced Emerald Deldare, which used scenes from Goldsmith's *The Three Tours of Dr. Syntax* and an Art Nouveau-type border. Completely decorated Art Nouveau pieces also were made.

Abino, which was introduced in 1912, had a Deldare body and displayed scenes of sailboats, windmills, or the sea. Rust was the main color used, and all pieces were signed by the artist and numbered.

In 1915, the manufacturing process was modernized, giving the company the ability to produce vitrified china. Consequently, hotel and institutional ware became the main production items, with hand-decorated ware de-emphasized. The Buffalo firm became a leader in producing and designing the most-famous railroad, hotel, and restaurant patterns.

In the early 1920s, fine china was made for home use. Bluebird is one of the patterns from this era. In 1950, Buffalo made its first Christmas plate. These were given away to customers and employees primarily from 1950 to 1960. However, it is known that Hample Equipment Co. ordered some as late as 1962. The Christmas plates are very scarce in today's resale market.

The Buffalo China Company made "Buffalo Pottery" and "Buffalo China"—the difference being that one is semi-vitreous ware and the other vitrified. In 1956, the company was reorganized, and Buffalo China became the corporate name. Today, Buffalo China is owned by Oneida Silver Company. The Larkin family no longer is involved.

Marks: Blue Willow pattern is marked "First Old Willow Ware Mfg. in America."

Abino Ware
Candlestick, 9" h, sailing ships, 1913 .... **475.00**
Pitcher, 7" h, Portland Head Light **700.00**
Tankard, 10-1/2" h, sailing scene **900.00**

Child's feeding plate, ABC's around outer rim, center with Dolly Dingle type scene of little boy comforting little girl with doll, marked "Semivitreous, (buffalo) Buffalo Pottery," edge chip, **$25**.

Advertising Ware

Jug, 6-1/4" h, blue and green transfer print, inscribed "The Whaling City Souvenir of New Bedford, Mass.," whaling motifs, staining **325.00**
Mug, 4-1/2" h, Calumet Club **90.00**
Plate, 9-3/4" d, Indian Head Pontiac **55.00**
Platter, 13-1/2" l, US Army Medical Dept., 1943 .... **60.00**

Deldare

Calling card tray, street scene **395.00**
Cereal bowl, 6" d, Fallowfield Hunt **295.00**
Chop plate, 14" d, Fallowfield Hunt **795.00**

Mug, Emerald Deldare, **$475**.

Cup and saucer, street scene **225.00**
Hair receiver, street scene **465.00**
Jardinière, street scene . **975.00**
Mug
  Fallowfield Hunt, 3-1/2" h **395.00**
  Three Pigeons, 4-1/2" h **350.00**
Pitcher, 12" h, 7" w, The Great Controversy, sgd "W. Fozter," stamped mark **320.00**
Powder jar, street scene **395.00**
Punch cup, Fallowfield Hunt **375.00**
Soup plate, 9" d, street scene **425.00**
Tankard, Three Pigeons **1,175.00**
Tea tile, Fallowfield Hunt **395.00**
Tea tray, street scene **650.00**

Ewer, covered, green shaded ground, pink roses, blue flowers, green leaves, embossed scrolls, gold trim, **$115**.

Pitcher, George Washington on horseback, blue and white decoration, 7-1/2" h, some staining and crazing, **$160**.

Photo courtesy of Joy Luke Auctions.

Vase, 7-3/4" h, 6-1/2" d, King Fisher, green and white dec, olive ground, stamped mark, artist signature **1,380.00**

Emerald Deldare

Creamer **450.00**
Fruit bowl **1,450.00**
Mug, 4-1/2" h **475.00**
Vase, 8-1/2" h, 6-1/2" h, stylized foliate motif, shades of green and white, olive ground, stamp mark **810.00**

Deldare, left: bowl, closed-in rim, Ye Lion Inn, restored chips; back: tray, Heirlooms, 10-1/4" x 13-3/4"; front: covered box, Ye Village Streets, all stamped, sold as lot, **$500**.

Photo courtesy of David Rago Auctions, Inc.

BUSTS

History: The portrait bust has its origins in pagan and Christian traditions. Greek and Roman heroes dominate the earliest examples. Later, images of Christian saints were used. Busts of the "ordinary man" first appeared during the Renaissance.

During the 18th and 19th centuries, nobility, poets, and other notable people were the most frequent subjects, especially on those busts designed for use in a home library. Because of the large number of these library busts, excellent examples can be found at reasonable prices, depending on artist, subject, and material.

Additional Listings: Ivory, Parian Ware, and Wedgwood.

7-1/2" h, bronze, Nubian Princess, Edrmann Encke, Gladenbeck foundry mark, short socle, marble base **415.00**

8-1/4" h, lady, carved facial features, ears, and hair style, stepped base with dentil carving, stamped dec, old surface, America, early 20th C **650.00**

8-1/2" h, Homer, bronze, dark brown patina, French, possibly Barbediene, 19th C **750.00**

9" h, bronze, winged cherub, seated on broken column, playing hornpipe, pair of doves perched opposite, after Mathurin Moreau, dark brown patination, green marble socle **250.00**

9-1/4" l, Gamin, polychromed plaster, Augusta Christine Fells Savage, (American 1892-1962), c1930, imp on verse .. **33,350.00**

9-3/4" h, bronze, Virgin, dark brown patina, Leon Pilet, French, 1836-1916, sgd **575.00**

10" h, black basalt, Cicero, waisted circular socle, imp title and Wedgwood & Bentley mark, c1775, chips to socle rim **2,300.00**

10-7/8" h, bronze, Watteau-style woman, tricorn hat, low décolletage, George (Joris) Van Der Straeten, Paris Bronze Society foundry mark, fluted marble socle, reddish brown and black patination **460.00**

11-1/4" h, bronze and marble, medieval woman, after Patricia by Roger Hart, young woman, sheer headdress, marked "Mino di Tiesole" on ovoid white marble base, 20th C **575.00**

11-1/2" h, bronze, Mercury, chocolate brown and parcel-gilt patina, short socle, sq base, after the antique, 20th C . **410.00**

Dante, bronze, back inscribed "Dante Original. Neapel Akt Ges: Gladenbeck Berlin," mounted on green and black marble base, 18" w, 12" h bronze, 16" h, **\$535**.

Photo courtesy of Alderfer Auction Co.

12-1/2" h, bronze, child, modeled as the head of a young child with curly hair, on cylindrical stone base, 20th C **635.00**

13-3/4" w, 9-3/4" d, 26" h, carved marble, Pharaoh's Daughter, John Adams-Acton, snake headdress, beaded necklace, tapered sq section base, carved on front with scene of the discovery of Moses and title, 13-3/8" w, 10-3/4" d, 39" h breche d'alep marble tapered sq section pedestal, England, late 19th C **16,100.00**

15-1/4" w, 6-3/4" d, 15" h, carved marble, Jeanne D'Arc, white marble face and base, pink marble bodice, incised title on front, early 20th C **700.00**

16-1/4" h, bronze, Ajax, after the antique, helmet, beard, parcel gilt toga, sq base, dark green patination, 20th C **865.00**

17-1/4" h, alabaster, woman in lace headdress and bodice, tapered alabaster socle, early 20th C **450.00**

19" h, Majolica, young boy, French colonial dress, marked "BU 677" **900.00**

Enid the Fair, bronze, George Frampton, 1907, signed, titled and dated in the mold, original dark patina, abrasion to nose, 20-1/2" x 9", **\$7,500**.

Photo courtesy of David Rago Auctions, Inc.

20" h, marble, lady with rose, incised "A. Testi," associated partial alabaster pedestal with spiral fluted stem **2,645.00**

20-1/2" h, bronze, Rembrandt, Albert-Ernest Carrier-Belleuse, silvered patination, bronze socle, marble plinth **2,300.00**

Lord Byron, parian, mounted on waisted circular socle, Copeland, England, c1870, impressed mark, 24" h, **\$1,775**.

Photo courtesy of Skinner, Inc.

22" h, bronze, gentleman, Leo F. Nock, brown-green patina, sgd on base "Leo Nock Sc," dated 1919, stamped "Roman Bronze Works, NY" **320.00**

24" h, bronze, cold painted, Bianca Capello, woman wearing classical clothing, Renaissance Revival motifs, sgd "C. Ceribelli," marble plinth **2,100.00**

26" h, marble, young pious woman, lace and flower bodice, hair in long braid, matching 6" h marble socle, Italian, late 19th C **7,475.00**

BUTTER PRINTS

History: There are two types of butter prints: butter molds and butter stamps. Butter molds are generally of three-piece construction—the design, the screw-in handle, and the case. Molds both shape and stamp the butter at the same time. Butter stamps are generally of one-piece construction, but can be of two-piece construction if the handle is from a separate piece of wood. Stamps decorate the top of butter after it is molded.

The earliest prints are one piece and were hand carved, often heavily and deeply. Later prints were factory made with the design forced into the wood by a metal die.

Some of the most common designs are sheaves of wheat, leaves, flowers, and pineapples. Animal designs and Germanic tulips are difficult to find. Prints with designs on both sides are rare, as are those in unusual shapes, such as half-rounded or lollipop.

Reproduction Alert:
Reproductions of butter prints were made as early as the 1940s.

Stamp, flowers with center fern leaves, coggled edge, one-piece wooden handle, $90.

Butter mold

3-1/2" d, sunflower, carved wood **125.00**
4-3/8" d, pineapple, carved wood **325.00**
5" x 8", roses, carved maple, serrated edges **165.00**

Top, carved wood, center handle, age crack, $65.

Photo courtesy of Wiederseim Associates, Inc.

Butter stamp

1-7/8" d, round, carved flower, one piece handle, 1-7/8" d **175.00**
2-3/8" x 1-3/4", rectangular, backward looking crested peafowl-type bird, sitting on flowering branch, turned inset handle, dark stains **250.00**
2-7/8" d, 4-1/2" l, carved fruitwood, strawberry **50.00**
3" d, speckled rooster, leafy foliage, one-piece handle, small chip on handle **275.00**
3-1/4" d, round, carved wide-eyed cow and fence, threaded insert handle with chip on end **200.00**

Pineapple carved butter print, round, single handle, age crack, $85.

Photo courtesy of Wiederseim Associates, Inc.

3-3/4" d, double sided, oval, peony on one side, tulip on other, carved print on handle, age crack **295.00**
3-3/4" d, stylized eagle with shield, natural finish, blue ink stain **110.00**
3-7/8" d, double sided, geometric design and initials, carved print on handle.... **250.00**

3-7/8" d, stylized eagle with shield, concentric circle rim, dry surface........................... **110.00**
4" d, nesting swan, threaded handle, old refinishing, some worm holes, minor edge damage **500.00**
4-1/4" d, pomegranate, concentric circle rim, one-pc handle, dark patina......... **100.00**

Heart and leaf design, semi-circular form with handle, 6-3/4" l, 4-1/2" h, $935.

Photo courtesy of Alderfer Auction Co.

4-1/2" d, eagle on laurel branch, star over its head, wavy feathers, one-pc handle, scrubbed surface........................... **395.00**
4-3/4" d, double sided, flowers, carved print on handle, dark patina **265.00**
4-3/8" d, round, carved primitive eagle, rayed sunbursts, dark patina, worn finish, large one-piece handle, 4-3/8" d **330.00**
4-1/2" l, 4-3/4" d, hexagonal, pineapple print, tall case, pewter straps, orig plunger **100.00**
4-1/2" d, round, carved strawberries and leaf, threaded handle, age cracks......... **110.00**

Leaf and vine design, round, single handle, $65.

4-3/4" d, 5-1/2" l, walnut, foliage and flowers **115.00**
5" d, round, carved tulip, good patina, PA, age cracks, 5" d **665.00**
6" l, lollipop style, carved pinwheel on one side, tulip with leaves on other **3,900.00**

6-1/2" l, lollipop style, carved heart and leaves, chip carved stars, soft worn finish, hold through handle for cord to hang **1,375.00**
6-3/4" l, sheaf of wheat, stylized design, notched rim band **200.00**

Carved rooster, chip carved border, round, single handle, **$95.**

7", lollipop style, eagle and shield, inscribed "Win Redmon 1820" **3,000.00**
8-3/4" l, 4-1/4" d, lollipop style, carved pine, six-pointed star on one side, foliate dec on back, rope border on side, carved handle **3,300.00**
9-3/4" l, 4-3/8" w, lollipop style, carved cherry, pinwheel design, serrated edges, aged patina **2,750.00**

CALENDAR PLATES

History: Calendar plates were first made in England in the late 1880s. They became popular in the United States after 1900, the peak years being 1909 to 1915. The majority of the advertising plates were made of porcelain or pottery and the design included a calendar, the name of a store or business, and either a scene, portrait, animal, or flowers. Some also were made of glass or tin.

Additional Listings: See *Warman's Americana & Collectibles* for more examples.

1906, Compliments of A. K. Clemmer, Kulpsville, PA, scattered florals and calendar pages **60.00**
1908, hunting dog, Pittstown, PA **40.00**

1908, pretty girl, calendar pages in center, gold lettering "Compliments of A. A. Eckert, General Merchandise, Packerton, PA," **$55.**
Photo courtesy of Dotta Auction Co., Inc.

1909, Compliments of John U. Francis, Jr., Fancy and Staple Groceries, Oaks, PA, multicolored transfer of roses and grapes, calendar pages around rim with holly leaves and berries, worn gold trim, mkd "Iron Stone China, Extra Quality" with lion and shield mark .. **35.00**
1910, pretty lady in red touring outfit, driving early auto, seasonal floral sprigs, calendar pages, gold text, mkd "W. P. Stellmach, Bottler, Schlitz Beer, Shamokin, PA" **65.00**
1911, Souvenir of Detroit, MI, months in center, hen and yellow chicks, gold edge **30.00**
1912, Winchester, rifle with grouse, autumn scene **75.00**
1913, boy in overalls, mkd "Our Art Dept, 1913" **65.00**

1913, holly and roses decoration, William F. Weber, Allentown, PA, gold-trimmed edge, **$95.**
Photo courtesy of Dotta Auction Co., Inc.

1915, black boy eating watermelon, 9" d **60.00**
1916, eagle with shield, American flag, 8-1/4" d **40.00**
1917, cat center **35.00**
1919, ship center **30.00**
1920, The Great War, MO . **30.00**

1916, pretty girl, calendar pages, blue birds, green ribbon garland on border, gold lettering "E. G. Hassler, Groceries, Dry Goods & Notions, 500 Schuykill Ave, Reading, PA," gold edge, **$80.**
Photo courtesy of Dotta Auction Co., Inc.

1917, pair of grazing deer, calendar pages on border and flags, gold lettering "Compliments of E. D. Reitter, Hoppenville, PA," **$65.**
Photo courtesy of Dotta Auction Co., Inc.

1921, bluebirds and fruit, 9" d **35.00**
1922, dog watching rabbit **35.00**
1969, Royal China, Currier & Ives, green, 10" d **40.00**

CALLING CARD CASES AND RECEIVERS

History: Calling cards, usually carried in specially designed cases, played an important social role in the United States from the Civil War until the end of World War I. When making formal visits, callers left their card in a receiver (card dish) in the front hall. Strict rules of etiquette developed. For example, the lady in a family was expected to make calls of congratulations and condolence and visits to the ill.

The cards themselves were small, embossed or engraved with the caller's name, and often decorated with a floral design. Many handmade examples, especially in Spencerian script, can be found. The cards themselves are considered collectible.

Note: Don't confuse a calling card case with a match safe.

Calling card case, hinged lid, base decorated with tortoiseshell and mother-of-pearl panels separated by silver inlay, push-button to open lid with tortoiseshell only and small vacant silver panel, rims fitted with ivory, cobalt blue velvet lining, Continental, early to mid 1800s, 2-5/8" w, 7/16" thick, 3-5/8" h, **$500**.

Photo courtesy of Gamal Amer.

Cases

Ivory, rect, wood inlay, block rows, center framed with diamond design rim band, 4" l **175.00**

Leather, sterling silver plaque depicting young woman in Renaissance costume, seed pearl accents, Art Nouveau, French hallmarks............. **300.00**

Silver, American, mid to late 19th C

  Coin silver, Albert Coles, engraved dec, monogram **350.00**

  Coin silver, pointed arched base, engraved dec, monogram **325.00**

  Sterling silver, goldwashed, fitted leather case, engine turned dec, monogram **250.00**

  Sterling silver, Gorham, engraved dec, monogram **325.00**

Ivory, Chinese, Qing dynasty, carved garden scene, 4-1/2" h, **$475**.
Photo courtesy of Sloans & Kenyon Auctions.

Silver, Chinese Export, rect, all-over hammered appearance, central monogrammed roundel, attributed to Tuck Chang & Co., late 19th/early 20th C, approx four troy oz, 2-7/8" x 3-7/8" **200.00**

Silver and ivory, silver filigree work over ivory panels, filigree depicts wild boar hunt n one side, cartouche with monogram framed by filigree border on reverse, engraved brass frame, 5-1/2" x 3", lid needs regluing, loss to int. **220.00**

Silver plate, quadruple silver plate, orig chain, Victorian, 3-1/2" x 3-3/4" **125.00**

Tortoiseshell with stylized floral plique, hinged metal lid, 19th C, 4" x 3"................... **110.00**

Wood, burl, Victorian, 3" l . **95.00**

Receivers

Bronze

  7" l, figural, bronze, monkey, Victorian..................... **135.00**

  9-1/2" l, 6" w, hammered, ovoid, emb comedy and tragedy masks, orig dark patina, crisp details, Gorham stamp mark................. **650.00**

Porcelain, 10" l, hand painted, roses, foliage, gold handles **45.00**

Silver plate, 7-1/4" l, 5-1/2" h, silver plate, marked "Meriden," wear to plating **60.00**

Tile, 5-1/4" x 6-1/2", emb monks, gun-metal glaze, raised AETCo medallion for American Encaustic Tiling Co., few edge nicks.................................. **95.00**

CAMBRIDGE GLASS

History: Cambridge Glass Company, Cambridge, Ohio, was incorporated in 1901. Initially, the company made clear tableware, later expanding into colored, etched, and engraved glass. More than 40 different hues were produced in blown and pressed glass.

  The plant closed in 1954 and some of the molds were later sold to the Imperial Glass Company, Bellaire, Ohio.

Marks: Five different marks were employed during the production years, but not every piece was marked.

For more information, see *Warman's Glass*, 4th edition.

Basket, Apple Blossom, crystal, 7".................................... **475.00**

Bonbon, Chantilly, crystal, Martha blank, two handles, 6" **35.00**

Bowl, Wildflower, flared rim, three-ftd, 9-3/8" d **85.00**

Butter dish, cov, Gadroon, crystal **45.00**

Candlestick

  Caprice, blue, Alpine, #70, prisms, 7" h................ **195.00**

  Doric, black, 9-1/2" h, pr **160.00**

  Rose Point, crystal, two-lite, keyhole, pr................... **95.00**

Candy jar, cov, Rose, green rose-shaped finial, 8" h **250.00**

Celery, Gloria, five-part, 12-1/2" l **70.00**

Champagne

  Adonis, crystal, #3500.. **35.00**
  Chantilly, crystal **30.00**
  Roxbury, crystal........... **30.00**

Cocktail
Apple Blossom, Gold Krystal,
#3130............................ **48.00**
Caprice, blue................ **55.00**
Chantilly, crystal............ **42.00**
Cocktail icer and liner, Adonis,
#968............................. **65.00**
Cocktail shaker, Chantilly,
crystal, glass lid.......... **250.00**
Comport, Honeycomb, rubena,
9" d, 4-3/4" h, ftd **150.00**
Cordial
Caprice, blue.............. **120.00**
Chantilly, crystal............ **75.00**
Rose Point, #3121........ **78.00**
Corn dish, Rose Point **88.00**
Cornucopia vase, Chantilly,
9-1/8" h.......................... **195.00**
Creamer
Chantilly, crystal, individual
size **22.50**
Tempo, #1029.............. **15.00**
Creamer and sugar, tray,
Caprice, crystal................ **40.00**
Cream soup, orig liner,
Decagon, green.............. **35.00**
Cup and saucer
Caprice, crystal **14.00**
Decagon, pink.............. **10.00**
Martha Washington, amber
.... **12.00**

Decanter set, decanter, stopper,
six-handled 2-1/2 oz tumblers,
Tally Ho, amethyst........... **195.00**
Flower frog
Draped Lady, dark pink,
8-1/2" h....................... **185.00**
Eagle, pink.................. **365.00**
Jay, green **365.00**
Nude, 6-1/2" h, 3-1/4" d, clear
.... **145.00**
Rose Lady, amber, 8-1/2" h
.... **350.00**
Seagull........................ **85.00**
Two Kids, clear **155.00**
Fruit bowl, Decagon, pink,
5-1/2"...................................... **5.50**
Goblet
Chantilly, crystal, #3600 **45.00**
Diane, crystal, #3122.... **45.00**
Roxbury, crystal............ **30.00**
Tempo, #1029/3700...... **15.00**
Wildflower, gold trim, #3121
.... **45.00**
Ice bucket
Chrysanthemum, pink, silver
handle........................... **85.00**
Wildflower, #3400/851 **225.00**
Iced tea tumbler, Chantilly
.... **45.00**
Ivy ball, Nude Stem, Statuesque
#3011/2, 9-1/2" h, 4-1/4" h d ruby
ball, 4" d base................ **500.00**

Jug
Gloria, ftd, 9-3/4" h...... **325.00**
Rose Point, Doulton **595.00**

Dinner plate, Cleo, **$45.**

Lemon plate, Caprice, blue, 5" d
.... **15.00**
Marmalade, sterling silver cover,
orig spoon, Rose Point, #68
.... **225.00**
Mayonnaise set
Chantilly, divided bowl,
underplate, ladle, #3900/111
.... **95.00**
Wildflower, bowl, underplate,
#3900/139..................... **55.00**
Oyster cocktail, Portia, crystal
.... **40.00**
Pitcher, cov, Forest Green,
#3400/107, 1931 .... **500.00**
Plate
Apple Blossom, pink, 8-1/2" d
.... **20.00**
Chantilly, #3900/22, 8" d
.... **18.00**
Dianthus, 7" d, pink, triangle C
mark.............................. **10.00**
Diane, 14" d, rolled edge,
#3900/166..................... **75.00**
Rose Point, crystal, 8" d, ftd
.... **70.00**
Relish
Apple Blossom, Gold Krystal,
five-part, 12" l, #3400/67
.... **125.00**
Caprice, club, #170, blue
.... **115.00**
Mt. Vernon, crystal, five-part
.... **35.00**
Wildflower, 8", three-part,
three handles................ **45.00**
Salt and pepper shakers, pr,
Wildflower, chrome tops, one
slightly cloudy................ **40.00**
Seafood cocktail, Seashell,
#110, Crown Tuscan, 4-1/2" oz
.... **95.00**
Server, center handle, Apple
Blossom, amber................ **30.00**
Sherbet
Diane, crystal, low **20.00**
Tempo, #1029.............. **12.50**

Sherry, Portia, gold encrusted
.... **60.00**
Sugar
Rose Point, gold encrusted,
#3900............................ **75.00**
Tempo, #1029.............. **15.00**
Swan, 3-1/2" h
Crown Tuscan.............. **60.00**
Crown Tuscan, gold
encrusted **125.00**
Crystal **40.00**

Vase, shell shape, Crown Tuscan,
Charlton decoration with roses, leaves,
gold trim, **$175.**

Torte plate, Rose Point, crystal,
13" d, three ftd **95.00**
Tray, Gloria, four part, center
handle, 8-3/4" d **70.00**
Tumbler
Adam, yellow, ftd **25.00**
Carmine, crystal, 12 oz **25.00**
Chantilly....................... **42.00**
Rose Point, 10 oz, #3500
.... **35.00**

Vase, opaline, classic baluster shape
original paper label, 16" h, **$90.**

Vase
Diane, crystal, keyhole, 12" h
.... **110.00**
Songbird and Butterfly, #402,
12" h, blue.................... **375.00**

Wildflower, #3400, 10-3/4" h
.... **175.00**
Whiskey, Caprice, blue, 2-1/2 oz
.... **225.00**

Wine

Caprice, crystal **24.00**
Diane, crystal, 2-1/2 oz. **30.00**

CAMEO GLASS

History: Cameo glass is a form of cased glass. A shell of glass was prepared, and then one or more layers of glass of a different color(s) was faced to the first. A design was then cut through the outer layer(s), leaving the inner layer(s) exposed.

This type of art glass originated in Alexandria, Egypt, between 100 and 200 A.D The oldest and most famous example of cameo glass is the Barberini or Portland vase found near Rome in 1582. It contained the ashes of Emperor Alexander Serverus, who was assassinated in 235 A.D.

Emile Gallé is probably one of the best-known cameo-glass artists. He established a factory at Nancy, France, in 1884. Although much of the glass bears his signature, he was primarily the designer. Assistants did the actual work on many pieces, even signing Gallé's name. Other makers of French-cameo glass include D'Argental, Daum Nancy, LeGras, and Delatte.

English-cameo pieces do not have as many layers of glass (colors) and cuttings as do French pieces. The outer layer is usually white, and cuttings are very fine and delicate. Most pieces are not signed. The best-known makers are Thomas Webb & Sons and Stevens and Williams.

Marks: A star before the name Gallé on a piece by that company indicates that it was made after Gallé's death in 1904.

Reproduction Alert.

Atomizer, 8" h, amethyst floral cutting on pumpkin orange ground, sgd in cameo "Ciriama," French **200.00**
Basket, 5" h, textured ground, cameo carved gold highlighted

green ferns, metal collar and handle, sgd with ship mark and initials "V.S.," French **250.00**
Biscuit jar, cov, Webb, 6" d, 7-1/4" h, white cameo dec, single-petaled blossoms, leafed branch, ruby red ground, silver plate fittings **2,950.00**
Bowl

4" d, Algues pattern, ovoid, three-pointed rim, underwater scene, sgd in cameo "Legras," slight chips to points **225.00**
7-3/4" d, 4-1/4" h, ftd, four pulled points, pale pink ground, light yellow-green and amber overlay, etched clusters of blossoms on leafy branches, sgd "Galle" among leaves, several bubble bursts and int. wear **690.00**
8" d, mottled yellow and amethyst-gray ground, overlaid with vitrified green, red, and yellow powders, cameo cut with stemmed leafy red berries, sgd in cameo "Daum Nancy" with Croix de Lorraine, c1900
.... **2,760.00**
10" d, 3-3/4" h, olive-green body, heavily etched and engraved Art-Deco swag and drapery design, fire polished, acid-etched "Legras" near base........................... **825.00**
Box, cov, 3" h, triangular form sloping from round opening, cameo cut and etched mountain landscape in blues and greens, sterling silver lid, cameo-etched "Lamartine" on side, int. rim nicks **360.00**
Cabinet vase, 3-1/2" h, opal, internally dec with mottled green and amber glass, finely etched dandelion flower heads, fluffy windblown seed pods, gilt highlights, sgd in gilt "Daum Nancy Croix de Lorraine"
.... **2,415.00**

Cologne bottle

3-3/4" l, lay down, teardrop shaped body, green ground, carved water lily, Webb
.... **1,900.00**
4-3/8" h, frosted cylindrical body, cameo cranberry floral relief, cut faceted stopper, Val St. Lambert **175.00**
7" h, mottled gray to yellow ground, cameo and enameled branching acorns silhouetted

against distant forested shoreline, sgd in cameo "Daum Nancy" with Cross of Lorraine **1,550.00**

Vase, Daum Nancy, snowy winter landscape with snow flecked bare trees outlined against mottled golden yellow graduating to mossy green, etched "Daum Nancy," 10" h, 3-1/8" d at top, **$3,500**.

Photo courtesy of Alderfer Auction Co.

Cruet, 6-1/2" h, ruby-red body, textured white enamel meadowland scene, Meadowlark on tall plant stalk, smaller scene on reverse, white rim, trefoil spout, clear frosted handle, teardrop- shaped stopper, pontil mark sgd "59," Florentine Art **50.00**
Decanter, 10-1/4" h, flattened oval body, upturned rim, conical stopper, frosted colorless and purple ground, overlaid in deep purple, etched iris, engraved "Cristallerie de Galle Nancy modele et decor deposes" on base........................ **2,530.00**
Epergne, 10-1/2" h, five 6" h etched cameo cylindrical flower holders, stylized naturalistic brass frame, Val St. Lambert
.... **1,800.00**
Ewer

7-1/2" h, cranberry ground, highlighted in gold, overlaid in deep purple, cameo cut grapevine motif, metal mount flip lid and handle, emb with matching grape dec, sgd in gold "Daum Nancy," c1895
.... **1,380.00**
10-1/2", textured translucent glass, gold highlighted ruby cameo with random trailing

flowers, silver-gilt emb collar, handle, and lid with raspberry finial, sgd in gold "Daum Nancy," c1895 .... **1,955.00**

Flask, 5-5/8" h, tapered cylindrical bottle, translucent colorless body cameo cut with violet blossoms, enameled purple, yellow, orange and white, gilt highlights, inscribed "Daum (cross) Nancy," mounted with bulbed silver cap with emb flower blossoms, engraved "Lola," small cup with raised leaf blade design, emb "SH" in diamond, cap loose **375.00**

Floor vase, 24" h, rose amber ground, overlaid in green, cameo cut towering trees above deep forested lake scene, sgd "Legras" in cameo, c1910, price for pr **4,025.00**

Incense burner, 7" h, bell shaped vessel, shading from citron to frosted, wine-red and amethyst floral cameo cutting, lower body sgd in cameo relief "D'Argental" **700.00**

Inkwell, 4-1/4" d, 3-1/2" h, mottled green and purple ground, cameo cut falling oak leaves, five jeweled carved insect and acorn cabochons, sgd "Daum Nancy," c1900 .... **1,265.00**

Lamp base

1" h, 4-1/2" w, flattened circular body, Prussian blue, detailed white opaque floral cameo relief, butterfly, three frosted feet, English.... **900.00**

16-3/4" h, blue-gray ground, overlaid with cinnamon and orange, cameo cut cascading leafy stemmed fruit, sgd "Galle" in cameo, lamp fittings **1,330.00**

Lamp, table

12-1/2" h, mushroom shape, yellow overlaid in dark brown, cut frosted lake scene and oak leaves, French, c1920 .... **600.00**

15" h, textured frosted ground, cascading crimson leafy vines, sgd in cameo "Legras" **250.00**

Pitcher, 7-1/2" h, vitrified fall color leaves, mottled earth tone ground, applied gold enameled bug and handle, base engraved

with block letters "Mueller Croismare" **2,700.00**

Tray, 9" w, triangular, inverted rim, frosted to orange, overlaid and cut large green stemmed oak leaves and acorns, sgd in cameo "Galle" **700.00**

Tumbler, 3-1/4" h, gray ground mottled in yellow and amethyst, cameo cut purple and yellow enameled flowers, green leafy stems, sgd in cameo "Daum Nancy" with Croix de Lorraine, c1900 .... **1,035.00**

Vase

4-1/4" h, conical, green ground, bands of stylized flower blossoms on etched and polished surfaces, gilt highlights, inscribed "Daum (cross) Nancy" on base, gilt wear **325.00**

4-1/2" h, gray ground internally dec with amber and frost mottling, cameo carved vitrified leaves, stemmed red bleeding hearts, sgd in cameo "Daum Nancy" with Croix de Lorraine, c1910 .... **1,100.00**

4-3/4" h, 5-1/2" w, pillow shape, scenic, snow covered barren trees against distant gray forest, mottled yellow ground, sgd in cameo "Daum Nancy" with Cross of Lorraine **2,450.00**

5" h, squatty, Prussian blue, cameo carved tropical design, bamboo tree trunks and palms, double banded rim, top band carved with arrow dec, Webb **600.00**

5-3/8" h, etched colorless body, white and pale yellow overlapping petals emerging from transparent green base, ftd, rolled base rim, rough pontil, sgd "L.C. Tiffany Favrile," numbered "4053D" **11,200.00**

5-3/4" h, ovoid cylindrical bulbous mottled green body, seven brown sailing ships, crimson and yellow sky, sgd in cameo "Daum Nancy" with Cross of Lorraine **1,200.00**

6" h, lemon yellow ground, cameo cut royal blue thistles, sgd "Richard" in cameo, c1915......................... **320.00**

Vase, Legras, square form, shepherd tending flock on rocky landscape, cameo signature, 5-1/2" h, **$650**.

6-3/4" h, tapering ovoid body, frosted with swirled amethyst, overlaid with detailed summer forest scene, circular base sgd "Lamartine," numbered "327-604"................. **1,000.00**

7" h, ovoid, cameo carved red lily on gold Aventurine internally dec ruby and yellow body, sgd "Desiré Christian Meisenthal Loth"...... **2,850.00**

7-1/2" h, frosted gray ground overlaid in chartreuse and white, cut with trailing leaves and seed pods, sgd "Galle" with star in cameo, c1900 .... **1,035.00**

8" h, baluster, camellias in polished red and orange, pale ground, sgd "Galle" in cameo **1,300.00**

8-1/4" h, triangular frosted blue body with blue mottling, cameo carved wisteria blossoms and vines, sgd in cameo "Legras".......... **675.00**

9" h, bottle form, martele frosted ground, amethyst gold highlighted cameo stemmed flowers, icicle body, sgd with Burgun Schverer thistle and cross monogram **3,950.00**

9-3/4" h, olive green cased to salmon and translucent colorless glass, cameo cut and etched leaves and pendant seed pods, sgd "Galle" in cameo on side, polished pontil, rim possibly ground, base wear **460.00**

10" h, cylindrical citron body, dark crimson and rose colored maple leaves and seed pods, sgd in cameo "D'Argental" **900.00**

10-1/2" h, shaded yellow ground, polished dark green blossoming branches, cameo sgd "Galle" **1,500.00**

Vase, Richard, oval, brown pinecones and branches acid-etched to orange, 1920s, side signed "Richard," 8-1/2" h, **$900**.

Photo courtesy of Skinner, Inc.

10-3/4" h, gray ground internally dec with mottled custard, overlaid in variegated orange and brown, cameo cut leafage and buds, inscribed "Degue," c1925............. **750.00**

11-1/2" h, swollen elongated neck, flared base, opaque orange glass overlaid in black, cameo cut and etched tall leafy stems, scrolled lower border, cameo-etched "Richard" **300.00**

11-3/4" h, dark amber ground, overlaid in plum and burgundy, cut cascading branches of seed pods and leaves, sgd "D'Argental" in cameo, c1910.......... **1,610.00**

12-1/2" h, ftd cylindrical matte finish amber body, long stemmed blue flowers and leaves, attributed to Mueller, engraved signature "Crois Mare" **1,500.00**

12-3/4" h, pale ground, red and orange polished trumpet vines, cameo signature "D'Argental" **1,800.00**

13" h, amber glass overlaid in orange and green, cut mountainous lake scene outlined with towering pine trees, sgd in cameo "Daum

Nancy" with Croix de Lorraine, c1910...................... **3,115.00**

Vase, Gallé, blown-out, naturalistic green and brown cherry branches, frosted pale amber ground, cameo signature, 11-1/8" h, **$7,000**.

Photo courtesy of David Rago Auctions, Inc.

Vase, D'Argental, polished red lilies on pale green ground, cameo signature, 8" h, **$950**.

Photo courtesy of David Rago Auctions, Inc.

13-3/4" h, frosted ground with flecks of orange and green, orange and burgundy orchid, Daum Nancy, signature on side, c1905.............. **3,525.00**

14-3/8" h, cylindrical, cameo cut trailing vines and flowers in green and brown over frosted ground, Foussin signature at side, 20th C **500.00**

Vase, Daum, carved wooded lake landscape, violet and green over pale ground, cameo signature, 12-1/2" h, **$1,800**.

Photo courtesy of David Rago Auctions, Inc.

21-1/2", gray ground, overlaid with amethyst, cameo cut mountainous lake scene and medieval castle, sgd "Richard" in cameo, c1915, drilled........................... **650.00**

22-1/2" h, gray and rose mottled ground, overlaid in amethyst, cameo cut shoreline castle between towering trees, distant mountains, sgd "Richard" in cameo, c1915.......... **1,495.00**

Whiskey jug, 10-1/2" h, textured translucent ground, cameo cut and enameled grapevine and leaves, metal lid and handle in form of knight's helmet, lion finial on flip lid, unsigned, c1895 .... **815.00**

CAMERAS

History: Photography became a viable enterprise in the 1840s, but few early cameras have survived. Cameras made before the 1880s are seldom available on the market, and when found, their prices are prohibitive for most collectors.

George Eastman's introduction of the Kodak camera in 1888, the first commercially marketed roll-film camera, put photography in the hands of the public.

Most collectors start with a general interest that becomes more defined. After collecting a broad range of Kodak cameras, a collector may decide to specialize in Retina models. Camera collectors tend to prefer unusual and scarce cameras to the most common models, which were mass-produced by the millions.

Because a surplus exists for many common cameras, such as most Kodak box and folding models, collectors are wise to acquire only examples in excellent condition. Shutters should function properly. Minimal wear is generally acceptable. Avoid cameras that have missing parts, damaged bellows, and major cosmetic problems.

Additional Listings: See *Warman's Americana & Collectibles* for more examples.

Adviser: Tom Hoepf.

Kodak, Anostigmet f:8.8 lens, original box, **$35**.

Agfa, Germany, Billy O, c1932-37, vertical folding camera, uses 127 roll film, Solinar f 3.9/75mm lens, Compur shutter **50.00**

American Optical Co., NY, Flammang's Patent Revolving Back View Camera, c1886, 5" x 7", tan red bellows, mahogany body with brass fittings, Prosh Triplex lens and external shutter .. **625.00**

E. & H.T. Anthony & Co., NY, Anthony 5" x 8" view camera, c1880, mahogany with nickel and brass fittings, folding bed, original "EA" stamped landscape lens **350.00**

Bell & Howell, Chicago, Dial 35, c1968, unusually configured half frame camera, spring-powered motor drive, f2.8/28mm Canon lens, molded plastic case. **35.00**

Foton, c1948, high quality 35mm rangefinder camera with spring-powered motor drive, Cooke Amotal f2/50mm lens **850.00**

Conley Camera Co., Rochester, MN, Conley Folding 3A Kewpie, 1916, vertical folding camera with square corners and red bellows **40.00**

Eastman Kodak, Rochester, NY. Kodak Petite, c1929 Vest Pocket Kodak Model B, light green, orig faded green bellows (also available in blue, gray, lavender and rose), matching hard case **150.00**

Kodak Cirkut Camera No. 10, Folmer & Schwing Division, c1917, large format camera for photographing panoramic pictures on film up to 10" w, outfit includes Turner Reich lens, tripod and gearbox **2,700.00**

No. 4 Folding Pocket Kodak camera, c1907-15, vertical folding camera, 4" x 5" exposures on roll film, red bellows, polished wood insets on bed **80.00**

Ordinary Kodak Camera, c1891-95, wooden box camera, loaded with 24 4" x 5" exposures on roll film, string set shutter **900.00**

Front view, Eastman Kodak, field type camera, large, **$125**.
Photo courtesy of Dotta Auction Co., Inc.

Franke & Heidecke, Germany, Rolleiflex 3.5F, c1961 twin lens roflex camera, Planar f3.5/75mm lens, light meter, excellent condition **900.00**

Heiland Photo Products, Premiere, c1957, 35mm non-range-finder camera, made in Germany, Steinheil Cassar f2.8/45mm lens, Pronto shutter **15.00**

Ica, Germany, Polyscop, c1911-25, stereo camera with rigid nonfolding body, Tessar f4.5 or 6.3 lenses **200.00**

Lionel Manufacturing Co., NY, Linex, c1954, cast metal subminiature stereo camera, f8/30mm lenses, for taking pairs of 16mm by 20mm exposures on roll film............................... **90.00**

Side view of camera above right, Eastman Kodak, field type camera, large, **$125**.
Photo courtesy of Dotta Auction Co., Inc.

Minolta, Japan, Autocord, c1955, twin lens reflex camera, Rokkor f3.5/75mm lens, Seikosha MX 1-500 shutter, non-metered **70.00**
Nippon Kogaku, Japan, Nikon S2, c1952, rangefinder camera, Nippon Nikkor f1.4/5cm lens, non-metered, chrome top, excellent condition **1,100.00**
Seneca Camera Co., Rochester, NY, Seneca No. 1, 4" x 5" folding camera, polished wood interior, red bellows, Wollensak Junior brass cased lens, carrying case containing two plate holders **95.00**
Spencer Co., Chicago, Falcon Flash Camera, inexpensive plastic miniature camera using 127 roll film, flash attachment, orig box **15.00**

Kodak, No. 14, Antographic Kodak Junior, original box, **$45**.

Voigtlander, Germany, Vitomatic IIa, c1959, 35mm viewfinder camera, outfitted with superior Ultron f2/50mm lens, Prontor 500 SLK-shutter **185.00**
Yamato Koki, Japan, Pax, c1952-55, small 35mm rangefinder camera styled after Leica, Luminor f3.5/45mm lens, YKK shutter **40.00**
Yashica, Japan
    Electro 35, c1974, 35mm rangefinder, Yashinon f1.7/45mm lens, screw-on telephoto and wide-angle adaptor lenses **50.00**
    Yashica Flash-O-Set, c1961, 35mm camera, f4/4cm lens, single-speed leaf shutter, built-in light meter, AG-1 flash unit **24.00**

Zeiss, Germany
    Contarex "Bull's-eye," c1959-66, 35mm camera, large round exposure meter window over lens, Tessar f2.8/50mm lens **425.00**
    Super Ikonta III, c1954-1958, folding rangefinder camera, Tessar f3.5/75mm coated lens, Synchro-Compur shutter to 1/500 .... **350.00**

CANDLESTICKS

History: The domestic use of candlesticks is traced to the 14th century. The earliest was a picket type, named for the sharp point used to hold the candle. The socket type was established by the mid-1660s.

From 1700 to the present, candlestick design mirrored furniture design. By the late 17th century, a baluster stem was introduced, replacing the earlier Doric or clustered column stem. After 1730, candlesticks reflected rococo ornateness. Neoclassic styles followed in the 1760s. Each new era produced a new style of candlesticks; however, some styles became universal and remained in production for centuries. Therefore, when attempting to date a candlestick, it is important to try to determine the techniques used to manufacture the piece.

Candelabras are included in this edition to show examples of the many interesting candelabras available in today's antiques marketplace. Check for completeness when purchasing candelabras; most are sold in pairs.

Candelabra

Brass
    14-1/2" h, three scrolled arms, center fruit finial, two Sevres-type blue porcelain pieces with white reserves filled with hand painted polychrome flowers, cast brass base with grape leaves and cherub faces **300.00**
    22-1/4" h, baluster stems, scrolled tripod bases, cov with highly detailed cast grape vines, center and two branching arms with cast

vines with leaves and bunches of grapes, leaves cover sockets, small dents on one, price for pr **1,155.00**

Candelabra, gilt bronze, urn form supporting five arms with single candle sockets, one central arm with single candle socket, floral foliage, garlands, figural details, 25" h, **$1,760**.
Photo courtesy of Alderfer Auction Co.

Bronze
    27" h, gilt bronze, shafts modeled as quivers rising from acanthus scrolled brackets, rouge marble plinths, columned feet, quiver tops emanating from scrolled arms, fluted candle socket, Napoleon III, French, c1855-70, pr **1,380.00**
    33" h, bronze and gilt bronze, Victory, winged figure in flowing gown, rising from caramel colored marble plinth, four scrolled arms with candle sockets, later conversion to electric lamp, French Empire, 19th C **980.00**
    41" h, gilt bronze, ftd base supporting altar from which a column of clouds mounted with winged angels looking up toward five-arm candelabra, French, 19th C **865.00**

Brass, rectangular base, push-up, ring handle, **$150**.
Photo courtesy of Wiederseim Associates, Inc.

Gilt metal

19-3/4" h, five-light candelabra centerpiece with scrolled foliate arms, colorless prisms supported on patinated baluster form shaft with gilt floral and foliate designs on black ground, two matching 16-5/8" h three-light candelabra, all on sq white marble bases, seam separation on shafts, lacking some prisms **360.00**
23" h, Victorian, Egyptian Revival style, scrolling candle arms supporting five candles, urn-shaped support, black marble plinth **360.00**

Glass

11-1/4" h, deep amethyst base and column with cut panels, cut stars around center, detailed brass castings include four branches, all with scrolled acanthus leaves and sockets, emb "Made in France," wear to silver plating, center finial missing **550.00**
20" h, 14-1/2" w, pressed colorless glass, two-light, center faceted prism above drip pan hung with faceted prisms, suspending two chains of prisms to a pair of spiral twisted scrolled arms, flanked by two scrolled candlearms, drip pans hung with further prisms, single knob stem, stepped sq base, late 19th C, bases drilled, price for pr **350.00**

Brass, Queen Anne, c1750, price for pair, **$750**.
Photo courtesy of Wiederseim Associates, Inc.

Candlesticks

Art glass, 4" h, iridescent gold, large disc foot and top separated with baluster stem, sgd "650 Nash" **350.00**

Brass

4-1/2" h, push-ups, saucer bases, tooled rings around columns, pr **175.00**
5-1/4" h, heavy stem threaded into saucer base, dings and scratches **320.00**
6" h, capstan base, damage, soldered repair **215.00**
8-3/8" h, push-rod, round base **90.00**
8-3/4" h, side push-up, threaded into domed base with scalloped edge ... **275.00**
9-1/0" h, mid drip pans, baluster stems, round spun base, finely detailed turnings with extractor holes in sockets, Dutch, 19th C copies of earlier style **230.00**
9-3/4" h, removable candlecup, beaded on rim, octagonal, baluster shaft, domed base with ruffled edges, remnants of silver plating, France, early- to mid-18th C **150.00**
10" h, removable candlecup, octagonal, baluster shaft, domed base with ruffled edges, remnants of silver plating, France, early- to mid-18th C **150.00**
Bronze, 10" h, patinated bronze, silvered and gilt sconces over rouge marble drip pans, classical male bust, tapered stem, round base, Italian, late 19th C **600.00**
Cast brass and wrought iron, 61" h, Gothic Revival, late 19th C, pricket, trefoil-edged drip pan, girdled multi-knopped cast brass standard, wrought-iron trefoil base with serpentine legs, acanthus knees and flowerhead scrolls, price for pr **1,610.00**
Glass, pressed, early
6-3/4" h, dark blue-violet, faint white swirls within base, hexagonal socket, circular base, wafer construction, Boston & Sandwich Glass Co., Sandwich, MA, 1835-50 .... **1,155.00**
7-1/2" h, canary, hexagonal, large base, wafer construction, Boston & Sandwich Glass Co., Sandwich, MA, 1840-60, socket flake, minor base flakes **190.00**
8" h, vaseline, hexagonal sockets, patterned hexagonal base, one pc construction, possibly European, second half 19th C, price for pr,

minute socket rim flake, minor base nicks **125.00**
10-1/2" h, alabaster/clambroth, petal socket, dolphin, single-step base, orig gilt dec shells on base, wafer construction, Boston & Sandwich Glass Co., Sandwich, MA, 1845-70 .... **1,155.00**

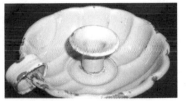

Graniteware, shell scalloped base, ring handle, light blue and white speckled finish, chips, **$95**.

Gilt bronze

10" h, base of sconce with acanthus, tapered stem with central guilloche band on fish scale ground, ovoid base with leaftip and patera roundels, Empire, French, early 19th C **900.00**
11-3/4" h, gilt metal, Gothic Revival, hexagonal sconce, drip pan with pierced trefoil rim, hexagonal stem with bulbous shaped knop, loaded floriform base enameled with lion shields and griffins on trefoils, ropetwist footrim, late 19th C **1,000.00**

Marble, red-brown mottled marble, turned pedestal bases supporting twisted standards, turned candle sockets, bases chipped, 11" h, **$250**.
Photo courtesy of Alderfer Auction Co.

Marble, 8" h, Empire-style, late 19th C, engine turned and beaded ormolu nozzles, gray marble columns hung with gilt-metal chains suspending acorns, stepped white marble base with flat leaf and beaded mounts, flattened ball feet, price for pr **350.00**

Pewter, 22-3/4" h, pewter, pricket, wide drip pan, double-baluster stem, shaped-tripartite base, three ball feet, Continental, 18th C **700.00**

Porcelain, 10-5/8" h, figural, male and female flower gatherers, against brocage, rocaille base, attributed to Samson, France, late 19th C, price for pr **450.00**

Sterling silver, 5-1/2" h, Neoclassical, England, first half 19th C, emb gadrooned nozzle, campana-shape stems, foliate festoons and acanthus dec, waisted pedestal base, emb arms and beaded rims, price for pr **280.00**

Pottery, Deldare Ware, Buffalo Pottery, faceted, 9" h, one factory drilled for wiring, restored foot ring on other, marked, price for pair, **$225.**

Photo courtesy of David Rago Auctions, Inc.

Tin

4-1/2" h, 7-1/2" d, pie plate base, ring handle..... **1,100.00**

5-1/2" h, 6" d, adjustable push-up rod, pie plate base, ring handle.................. **550.00**

7-1/4" h, 3-3/4" d, hog scraper, adjustable push-rod, decorative brass ring, illegible name stamped on push-rod handle.......................... **660.00**

Wrought iron

6-7/8" h, spiral, scrolled push-up, turned wood base... **300.00**

11-1/2" h, scrolled handle and feet, lip handle, notched push-up, price for pr .. **550.00**

CANDY CONTAINERS

History: In 1876, Croft, Wilbur, and Co. filled small glass Liberty Bells with candy and sold them at the Centennial Exposition in Philadelphia. From that date until the 1960s, glass candy containers remained popular. They reflect historical changes, particularly in transportation.

Jeannette, Pennsylvania, a center for the packaging of candy in containers, was home for J. C. Crosetti, J. H. Millstein, T. H. Stough, and Victory Glass. Other early manufacturers included: George Borgfeldt, New York, New York; Cambridge Glass, Cambridge, Ohio; Eagle Glass, Wheeling, West Virginia; L. E. Smith, Mt. Pleasant, Pennsylvania; and West Brothers, Grapeville, Pennsylvania.

Additional Listings: See *Warman's Americana & Collectibles* for more examples.

Notes: Candy containers with original paint, candy, and closures command a high premium, but beware of reproduced parts and repainting. The closure is a critical part of each container; if it is missing, the value of the container drops considerably. Small figural perfumes and other miniatures often are sold as candy containers.

Airplane, P-38 Lightning, orig wire clip, motors, and ground, no closure **200.00**

Auto, coupe, long hood, orig tan snap-on strip, orig gold stamped tin wheels, orig closure ... **120.00**

Barney Google, bank

Orig paint, orig closure **650.00**

Repainted, orig closure **450.00**

Baseball player, with bat, 50 percent orig paint, orig closure **500.00**

Bear, on circus tub, orig tin, orig closure **500.00**

Hen on basket, clear glass, no closure, $60.

Boat, USN *Dreadnaught*, orig closure **350.00**

Bulldog, 4-1/4" h, screw closure **60.00**

Bus

Chicago, replaced closure **275.00**

New York-San Francisco, orig closure........................ **375.00**

Victory Glass Co., replaced closure........................ **300.00**

Camera, tripod base, 80 percent paint............................... **200.00**

Cannon

Cannon #1, orig carriage, orig closure **375.00**

U. S. Defense Field Gun #17, orig closure................. **380.00**

Two-Wheel Mount #1, orig carriage, orig closure . **220.00**

Cat, papier-mâché, 3-3/4" h, seated, gray and white paint, pink ribbon, glass eyes, touch up and repairs **375.00**

Chick, composition, 5" h, cardboard, base, Germany **20.00**

Dog, by barrel, 90 percent paint, chip on base, orig closure **220.00**

Dog, papier-mâché, gray, painted and molded feathers, stamped "Made in Germany," repair at neck opening...... **50.00**

Elf on rocking horse, 3-1/2" h, pressed glass, no closure **160.00**

Felix the Cat, repainted, replaced closure............ **550.00**

Fire truck, with ladders **45.00**

George Washington, 3" h, papier-mâché, with tricorn hat, white ponytail and blue coat, standing beside cardboard cabin with deep roof and chimney, unmarked **195.00**

Rabbit, clear glass, no closure, $25.

Ghost head, 3 1/2" h, papier-mâché, flannel shroud **150.00**
Gun, 5-3/4" l, West Specialty Co. **20.00**
Horse and wagon, pressed glass **35.00**
Indian, 5" l, pressed glass, riding motorcycle with sidecar, no closure **350.00**
Kettle, 2" h, 2-1/4" d, pressed glass, clear, T. H. Stough, cardboard closure **50.00**
Limousine, orig wheels, orig closure, small chip **600.00**
Little boy, 6" h, papier-mâché head and hollow body, large pink nose, closed smiling mouth, painted brown eyes, molded and painted red vest, green jacket, yellow short pants, purple socks, black shoes, brown tie **210.00**
Locomotive, Mapother's 1892, orig closure **125.00**
Man on motorcycle, side car, repainted, replaced closure **525.00**
Mule, pulling two wheeled barrel with driver, 95 percent paint, orig closure **85.00**
Nursing bottle, pressed glass, clear, natural wood nipple closure, T. H. Stough, 1940-50 .... **20.00**
Puppy, 2-1/2" h, papier-mâché, painted, white, black muzzle, glass eyes **35.00**
Rabbit, glass
Rabbit pushing chick in shell cart, orig closure **500.00**
Rabbit with basket on arm, no paint, orig closure **120.00**
Rocking horse, small chips on rockers, no closure **180.00**
Rooster, 6-1/2" h, papier-mâché, pewter feet, orig polychrome paint, marked "Germany" **225.00**

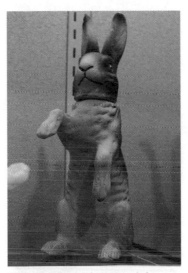

Rabbit, papier-mâché, original closure, $550.

Papier-mâché, four rabbits, two with exaggerated ears, other pair dressed as man and lady, German, $175.
Photo courtesy of Joy Luke Auctions

Sailor, 6" h, papier-mâché head and hollow body, large pink nose, closed smiling mouth, protruding lower lip, molded and painted sideburns and hair, molded gray fez, painted blue eyes, molded and painted blue sailor uniform, black belt with knife case and sword, black shoes, unmarked **275.00**
Santa Claus, by sq chimney, 60 percent paint, replaced closure **180.00**
Stop and Go, replaced switch handle, orig closure **440.00**
Submarine F6, no periscope or flat, orig super structure, orig closure **250.00**
Tank, World War I, traces of orig paint, no closure **90.00**
Telephone, small glass receiver **55.00**
Turkey, gobbler, small chip under orig closure **100.00**
Village bank, with insert, log-cabin roof **110.00**

Wagon, orig closure **90.00**
Wheelbarrow, orig wheel, no closure **35.00**
Windmill, five windows, ruby-flashed orig blades, orig closure **495.00**

CANES

History: Canes or walking sticks have existed through the ages, first as staffs or symbols of authority, and then items like religious ceremonial pieces. They eventually evolved to the fashion accessory that is the highly desirable antique prized by today's collector for its beauty and lasting qualities. The best were created with rare materials such as carved ivory, precious metals, jewels, porcelain, and enamel, with many being very high-quality works of art. They were also fashioned of more mundane materials, with some displaying the skill of individual folk artists. Another category of interest to collectors is the gadget canes that contained a myriad of hidden utilitarian objects, from weapons to drinking flasks, telescopes, compasses, and even musical instruments, to cite just a few.

Adviser: Henry A. Taron.

Carved elephant ivory, Abraham Lincoln, 3-1/4" h x 1-3/4" d handle, finely carved, 1" gold filled collar with "C" scrolls, initialed "E.G.B." for owner, refinished black Malacca shaft, 1" ivory ferrule, American, c1880, 34-1/4" l, **$1,008**.
All cane photos courtesy of Henry Taron.

Automata, 36-1/4" l, 4-1/3" h x 2-1/4" handle, carved wood full-bodied pug, brown glass eyes, sitting on top of stump, short curly tail swings upward, long red tongue protrudes when button activated, 2/3" smooth gold collar mkd "Brigg, London," mahogany shaft, 7/8" brass ferrule **3,640.00**

Bamboo, carved, 36" l, 1-1/2" h x 1-1/8" natural root handle, low relief carved shaft with leaves, insects, and moths, dark stained and chip carved background, 1" burnished brass ferrule, Japanese, c1900 .... **390.00**

Cameo glass, 35-3/4" l, 3-2/3" h x 1-1/3" w pistol handle, cameo-carved white palm trees on pale blue blown glass, 3/4" silver collar, rosewood shaft, 1-1/4" dark horn ferrule, English, c1895 .... **2,920.00**

Campaign, 36" l, 4-1/4" l x 1-2/3" w tau horn handle, hollow tin, top engraved "Patriotism, Protection, Prosperity," shaft engraved "Pat. Apl'd For, The Winfield Mf'g, Warren, O," oval shaped tin shaft with multiple small dents, capped end, McKinley, 1896 .... **450.00**

Damascene, 35-3/4" l, 6-1/2" l steel crook handle with gold damascene of dragons, flowers, geometric designs, ebony shaft, 1" burnished brass ferrule, England, handle imported from Toledo, Spain, c1890 ... **4,370.00**

Ebony, carved, 35-1/2" l, 5-1/4" h x 2" handle, grinning black man, wearing linked silver collar necklace, 1/4" elephant ivory ring collar, ebony shaft, 1-14" ivory ferrule, English, c1890 .... **785.00**

Enamel, 36" l, 1-1/2" h x 2-1/2" l duck handle, teal green enamel head, yellow glass eyes, painted yellow beak, 1/3" silver collar, black shaft, 1" horn ferrule, Continental, c1890 .... **1,010.00**

Gold, 33-1/2" l, 1-7/8" h x 7/8" d knob, chased and raised owner's initials on top, four standing Hindu gods in relief on side, single-pc elephant ivory carved to simulate thorns, 1-1/4" brass ferrule, Anglo/Indian, c1890 .... **3,360.00**

Gun, 33-1/2" l, 2-1/2" l "L" handle, black painted metal, opens 4-1/2" down shaft, bayonet-type socket for loading pin fire 12 mm cartridge,

hammer on top of barrel pulls back with thong, 3/4" removable ferrule/tampion, Continental, c1885 .... **1,100.00**

Ivory and shagreen, 1" h, 1-1/2" d elephant ivory knob handle, six-sided, orig owner's initials incised on top, very thin separator on wood shaft covered with pale green shagreen, 2" l ivory ferrule, Continental, c1890

.... **2,020.00**

Carved elephant ivory, 1-1/2" h x 3" l handle carved as terrier, brown glass eyes, simulated leather collar with buckle, thick furry coat, open mouth with fangs, 2-1/4" decorated silver collar with shield cartouche, inscribed "Presented to Sgt. W. O. Conway, R. A. as a token of esteem from his br. N. C. officers on his discharge from the Regiment. October, 1876," Malacca shaft, 1-1/4" burnished brass ferrule, English, 33-1/2" l, **$728**.

Ivory, carved

35-1/2" l, 2-1/4" h x 2" handle, covered wicker basket with four puppies, 1/3" silver collar with London hallmarks for 1883, Malacca shaft, 7/8" burnished brass ferrule
.... **3,100.00**

35-1/2" l, 2-1/3" h x 1-2/3" w handle, hand around face of young woman, curly tresses, lace collar, ebony shaft, 2/3" horn ferrule, English, c1885
.... **900.00**

36" l, 1-3/4" h x 4-1/3" l handle, semi-nude Cleopatra reclining on fancy divan, scratching dog's back while cat licking her foot, silver collar, heavy ebony shaft, 1-1/2" replaced white metal and iron antique ferrule, Continental, c1880, small chip on divan **10,640.00**

36" l, 5" h x 2" w octopus handle, long tentacles, yellow glass eyes, ebony shaft, 2-2/3" light horn ferrule, English, c1885 .... **3,910.00**

36" l, 2-3/4" h x 1-7/8" d, high relief carved forest scene with dinosaurs, thick honey-toned Malacca shaft, 1" burnished brass ferrule, Continental, c1870 .... **3,810.00**

36" l, 2" h x 3-1/2" l, well-carved donkey, brown glass eyes, 3/4" silver collar with London hallmarks for 1896, and button to activate ears and mouth, red tongue, dark bamboo shaft, 1" replaced brass ferrule, attributed to Brigg, London, 1896 .... **4,190.00**

36" l, 7-1/2" h x 2-1/8" w pistol grip handle, carved coat of arms with plumed knight's helmet, detailed shield, inscribed Latin mottos "honestas, equitas, virtus," 1/3" carved ivory ring collar, dark rosewood shaft, 3/4" ivory ferrule, German, student type, c1885 .... **2,690.00**

36-1/4" l, 2" h x 1" d Napoleon profile shadow handle, 2/3" silver collar, heavy ebony shaft, 1" horn ferrule, French, c1825 .... **2,020.00**

36-1/2" l, 3" h x 2" w handle, cat, articulating mouth, clear glass eyes, bow under chin, spring loaded lever in center of bow opens mouth, red tongue, 1/8" gold gilt collar, black enameled shaft, 1" horn ferrule, English, c1890
.... **1,680.00**

36-3/4" l, 2-1/5" h x 1-1/3" handle, clown wearing dec pointed hat, three pink coral buttons, ruffled collar, lips pursed, tears flowing from eyes, ebony shaft, 1" burnished brass and iron ferrule, Continental, c1895
.... **2,355.00**

37-1/4" l, 3-1/4" h x 1-2/3" w handle, hermit crab emerging from spiral shell, 1-1/3" silver collar dec with "C" scrolls and oval cartouche, heavy ebony shaft, 1-1/8" dark horn ferrule, English, c1910 .... **2,800.00**

37-1/3" l, 4" h x 2-1/2" handle, bearded troll kneeling on branch of oak tree, hand resting on rock hammer, 3/4" textured silver collar rimmed with two gold rings with gold tree trunk on side, worn Continental hallmark, ebony shaft, 1" replaced ferrule, German, c1800 .... **1,800.00**

37-1/2" l, 3-1/4" h x 1-1/3" ivory handle, pierced in center for cord, 3/4" scalloped and punch dec silver collar, orig thick full bark Malacca shaft, 4" brass ferrule, England, c1690........................ **3,585.00**
38-1/4" l, 2-3/4" h x 6-1/4" l handle, Turk head wearing turban, button and laced tunic, lower part of body as mythical fish tail, 1/3" horn separator, blond Malacca shaft, 1-1/4" ivory ferrule, Continental, possibly French, c1890...................... **2,465.00**

Ivory pique pomander cane, 1-7/8" l x 1-1/3" d elephant ivory handle, top unscrews to reveal shallow round compartment, round silver disc with holes, pique decoration with tiny hollow spherules, silver bars, four small round tortoiseshell inlays, thin scalloped silver collar, round silver eyelets, Malacca shaft, shaft stamped "Robert Gainsborough, 1724," English, 1" brass and iron Victorian replacement ferrule, 35" l, **$7,840.**

Ivory, hippo, carved, 38" l, 4-1/8" h x 1-1/4" d fluted mushroom shaped top, graceful hand with fringed cuff holding ivory top, 3/4" rope turned ivory collar, finely figured thin snakewood shaft, 1-3/4" horn ferrule, Continental, c1895
.... **1,010.00**

Ivory, walrus, carved
36" l, 4-1/2" h x 1-7/8" handle carved as young woman wearing fancy hat, blouse revealing breasts, opposite side inscribed "Madamd

Plaisir, Orleans," 3/4" rope turned silver collar, smooth partridgewood shaft, 1-1/2" white metal and iron ferrule, French, c1880.......... **4,480.00**
36-3/4" l, 5-1/4" h x 1-3/4" w handle with hunter leaning against tree with propped rifle, dog on hind legs sniffing game bag, hunter lighting pipe, 1" dec sterling collar with 1896 London hallmarks, tightly stepped partridgewood shaft, 7/8" replaced brass ferrule, made in England, imported German handle, 1896......................... **1,460.00**

Map, 34-1/2" l, American Legion Convention, 1940, 6-1/2" wooden crook handle, 3/4" white metal collar with slot, spring-loaded cloth street map of Boston with metal edge and grip, paper label "American Legion Convention 1940," picture of Paul Revere, text "Paul Revere rides again," 2/3" white metal ferrule **535.00**

Merchant's measure, 36-1/2" l, 2-1/2" h x 1-1/4" d ivory knob handle, rich yellow patina, unscrews to reveal long thing flexible Malacca rod with small round rosewood handle, 1 1/2" brass and iron tip, rod has line of dots to measure in one inch increments, 1" scalloped and punch dec silver collar, worn Malacca shaft, 3" brass ferrule, English, c1695 .... **4,700.00**

Gun curio type, 1-1/2" h x 3-1/3" L-shaped horn handle, breech opened with pull and quarter turn, 9mm, shaft covered with black and brown leather, French, c1890, 34-1/2" l, **$1,008.**

Music box, 34-3/4" l, carved from single pc of hardwood, possibly birch, 3" l, 2" h smooth "L" handle, carved brown pug dog sitting upright on top of music box on top of shaft, separate winding key, carved shaft with simulated thorns, Swiss, c1900
.... **6,440.00**

Nautical
32-1/4" l, carved whale ivory and whalebone, 2-1/4" h x 1-1/8" d whale ivory mushroom handle, inlaid on top with 1/3" sq piece of baleen with round mother-of-pearl spherule in center, thin baleen separator, fully carved whalebone shaft with section of sawtooth pattern, section of convex fluting, then concave fluting raised stringing turns to left followed by raised piece, uniform yellow patina, America, c1840 .... **2,800.00**
35" l, whale ivory and carved whalebone, 3" h x 1-1/2" d whale ivory handle, 1/3" round baleen spherule inlaid in flat top, three tin baleen spacers around two whale ivory spacers, whalebone shaft with angled twist carving, some age cracking, spacers cosmetically in-filled, American, c1850 ..... **2,240.00**

Ophthalmologist, 36" l, 1-1/2" elephant ivory ball handle, 1" brown glass eyes, 7/8" dec collar mkd "sterling," figured rosewood shaft, 1" black horn ferrule, America, c1890 .... **840.00**

Phrenology, 36-1/3" l, 2-2/3" h x 1-1/4" w handle with markings and clear decoder, yellow patina, 2/3" beaded and lined silver collar, stepped partridge-wood shaft, 1" burnished brass and iron ferrule, American, c1850........................... **3,360.00**

Pique, 36" l, 3-1/2" h x 1-1/2" d elephant ivory handle, scrolls and crossed, top inscribed in pique "A.R. 69," pierced handle with decorated eyelets, 3/4" scalloped and punch dec silver collar, honey-toned Malacca shaft, 4" brass and iron ferrule, English, dated 1669... **11,760.00**

Porcelain
English, 36-3/4" l, 1-1/2" d pale blue porcelain ball, painted jockey and horse jumping over water hazard, green wreath of foliage frames scene, 1/4" gold ring collar, heavy ebony shaft, 1" replaced brass ferrule, c1900 .... **500.00**

Royal Copenhagen, 2-1/4" h x 7/8" cylindrical handle, hand painted scene with sailboat, pale blue, green, gray, and pink, 1/2" gold wash collar, black enameled shaft, 7/8" horn ferrule, England, 1900 .... **1,345.00**

Presentation, 36-1/4" l, 18k gold, double gold quartz inlays, 4" h, 4" l, 1" thick tau handle, inlaid on each end is polished oval gold quartz stone, each matrix with gold flecking in gray/white background, inscribed fancy cartouches on handles, presenter's initials on side, receiver's name on shaft portion, dark tropical wood shaft, 1" white metal and iron ferrule, America, c1870 .... **6,160.00**

Quartz, 37" l, vermeil silver overlay, 2-3/4" h x 7/8" d pale pink rose quartz handle, internal crystalline fissures, two vermeil silver floral rings at top and bottom, three long classical columns topped with ferns, one column with French Minerva hallmark for 950 silver, ebony shaft, 1" burnished brass ferrule, French, c1900 .... **1,795.00**

Rock crystal
36" l, 2-3/4" h x 1" d rock crystal handle, reticulated overlay vermeil silver in diamond and swirled patterns, tiny French hallmarks, brown hardwood shaft, 7/8" horn ferrule, French, c1900.......... **1,345.00**
36" l, 3" h x 1" d rock crystal handle, top faceted like jewel, 14 long smooth panels on sides, 2/3" silver collar with blue guilloche enamel, custom 4-1/4" l red leather case mkd "Berthold Fuchs," jewelry from Bad Kissingen, Bavaria, lined with satin and velvet, ebonized hardwood shaft, 1" horn ferrule, c1900 .... **1,345.00**

Shooting stick seat, 34" l, birch and bamboo, iron slide fittings, two 6" x 4" folding seat, 3-1/2" pointed ferrule can be inserted into ground for stability, French, c1900 .... **500.00**

Silver
36" l, 3" l silver dog head with amber glass eyes, mkd "800," partridge wood, 7" crook handle, 1-1/4" brass and iron ferrule, c1895.............. **280.00**

Rock crystal, 1-1/3" d ball handle, carved in concentric swirls, 2/3" gold collar with worn London hallmarks, rosewood shaft, 1" replaced brass ferrule, English, c1890, 36-2/3" l, **$1,064**.

36" l, 3-1/4" h x 3-3/4" l "L" handle shaped like golf putter, oval cartouche with owner's initials, dec with fancy scrolls and flowers, mkd "Sterling," opens to gold washed cigarette case, figured snake-wood shaft, 1-1/2" burnished brass ferrule, American, c1895...................... **1,120.00**

Staghorn, 36" l, 2" h x 4" l polished staghorn handle carved as African elephant, amber glass eyes, 1" gold collar initialed "C.J.W.," dated 1906, hallmarked 12k gold, mkd "Brigg," honey-toned bamboo shaft, burnished brass ferrule **840.00**

Sunday stick, 37-1/4" l, tortoiseshell, 1-1/2" h x 3" l handle fashioned like golf driver, faux gold weight on side, inscribed "Good Luck," London hallmarks for 18k and 1905, mkd "Brigg," 7/8" gold collar, inscribed "Sir Louis Nuthsen," stepped partridge wood shelf, 1" burnished bras ferrule, storage bag **1,800.00**

Sword, 44-1/4" l, 2-1/2" h x 1-1/4" gold knob handle, ducal stallion engraved on top, engraved with scrolls and flowers, two swimming swans, orig owner's name "E. Barnard" engraved on lower edge, thick Malacca shaft with gold mounts and swing clevis 2-1/2" d down 30" l triangular sword, tight tongue, groove metal fitting, twin blood grooves, minor age pitting, 5-7/8" brass ferrule, English, c1760 .... **3,810.00**

Violin, 34" l, 2-3/4" h x 6-1/2" l mahogany tau handle, 1-1/3" lined nickel collar where handle unscrews, fitted chamber with fitted mahogany horsehair bow, dark horn and ivory dec, 21" l panel opens for removal, internal ebony seats, maple sounding board, ebony bridge, four tuning pins, separate old clock key for tuning, two other nickel bands secure panel on mahogany shaft for storage, 7/8" nickel and iron ferrule, recently professionally restored, America, c1860 .... **11,200.00**

Wood, carved from single piece of heavy tapered oak, flat top inlaid with round mother-of-pearl disc, top 12" of shaft carved with textured cartouche, foliage, and scrolls, raised fancy lettering "Robert A. Van Wyck, Mayor, Greater New York, 1898-1901," and "Auburn Prison 1898" where it was made, 3" burnished brass ferrule, 34" l, accompanied by custom wooden tube carrying case, **$784**.

Wood, double action automaton, 4-1/2" h x 2-1/4" handle of carved house cat sitting upright on plinth, yellow glass eyes, red nose, white facial features, back and tail painted black with white stripes, when button at back of plinth is pushed, cat's head swings to side and tail lifts sharply, brass collar, green stained hardwood shaft, 1" brass ferrule, Vienna, c1890, 34" l, **$4,480**.

Wood

33-2/3" l, carved Boer War P.O.W., Bermuda cedar, 2" h x 4-1/4" l "L" handle as horse leg and hoof, bone horseshoe, 1-3/4" tin collar hand cut with six holes for dec, carved raised letters on thin textured ribbon around shaft "C.M.S., P.O.W. Bermuda, 1902," 1-1/4" ferrule made from same soft material as collar with similar dec, Bermuda, 1902 .... **840.00**

34-1/2" l, 5-1/2" l x 3" d "L" handle, high relief carving of rifle and game shoulder bag with roping, shield with roping at bottom of handle, 2/3" coin silver collar inscribed "F.K. Murray, Captain US Navy, 1868," knobby hickory shaft, 1" brass and iron ferrule **360.00**

36" l, 3-1/2" l x 2-1/2" w carved half crook handle, single pc of ash, carved face of John Brown, revarnished, 2" iron ferrule, American, c1860 .... **1,120.00**

37-1/4" l, carved rosewood, 4-1/4" h x 1-1/3" w stylized bird handle, ivory and ebony eyes, ivory tail, two 1/2" ivory separators and one horn separator, 2-3/4" of reticulated silver at top of rosewood shaft, three more separators, thin ivory ferrule, Anglo-Indian, first half 20th C **400.00**

39-1/2" l, made from single piece of hardwood, perhaps birch, 4-3/4" l pistol grip handle carved as brown and white fox, stained dark brown shaft stepped to simulate bamboo, 1" white metal and iron ferrule, English, c1900 .... **1,010.00**

CANTON CHINA

History: Canton china is a type of Oriental porcelain made in the Canton region of China from the late 18th century to the present. It was produced largely for export. Canton china has a hand-decorated light- to dark-blue underglaze-on-white ground. Design motifs include houses, mountains, trees, boats, and bridges. A design similar to willow pattern is the most common.

Borders on early Canton feature a rain-and-cloud motif (a thick band of diagonal lines with a scalloped bottom). Later pieces usually have a straight-line border.

Early, c1790-1840, plates are very heavy and often have an unfinished bottom, while serving pieces have an overall "orange-peel" bottom. Early covered pieces, such as tureens, vegetable dishes, and sugars, have strawberry finials and twisted handles. Later ones have round finials and a straight, single handle.

Marks: The markings "Made in China" and "China" indicate wares that date after 1891.

Reproduction Alert: Several museum gift shops and private manufacturers are issuing reproductions of Canton china.

Basket, reticulated, oval, blue decorated rim and base, scene of pagodas and junks, 19th C, 9-3/4" l, 3-3/4" h, **$375**.
Photo courtesy of Alderfer Auction Co.

Bowl, covered, round, domed lid, blue flowering tree motif, 9-1/2" d, 5" h, **$700**.
Photo courtesy of Alderfer Auction Co.

Bowl, 9-1/2" d, cut corner, minor int. glaze imperfections, 19th C **900.00**

Box, cov, sq, domed top, cloud-and-rain border on lids, early 19th C, pr **6,270.00**

Coffeepot, 7-1/4" h, mismatched cover **750.00**

Cup, cov, 4" l, 3-1/2" h, handle, repaired lid **165.00**

Dish, leaf shape, 19th C, chips
6-3/4" l **145.00**
8-1/2" l **165.00**

Fruit basket

9-1/4" d, minor chips .. **690.00**
10-1/2" l, reticulated, undertray **1,100.00**

Bowl, covered, snail finial, blue and white decoration, **$295**.
Photo courtesy of Wiederseim Associates, Inc.

Milk pitcher, 6-1/8" h, very minor chips **575.00**

Miniature, tureen, underplate, 6-1/2" l, 5" w, 4" h **300.00**

Plate, early, c1820-30
6" d, bread and butter .. **65.00**
7-1/2" d, salad **85.00**
8" d, dessert **95.00**
9" d, lunch................. **115.00**
10-3/8" d, dinner, 19th C, price for set of six, one with rim chips **360.00**

Platter, octagonal, cut corners, blue underglaze landscape, white ground, Chinese Export, 13" l, 10-1/4" w, minor roughness on rim, **$250**.
Photo courtesy of Alderfer Auction Co.

Platter

14" x 17", dark blue, finely detailed scene with figure inside pagoda, bridge, trees, mountains, small sailboat, basketweave design around rim, glaze flakes **460.00**

14-3/8" x 17-1/4", octagonal, oblong, China, 19th C, small chip underside of rim . **350.00**

14-3/4" x 18", octagonal, oblong, China, 19th C, minor glaze imperfections **450.00**

17-1/4" x 20-1/4", octagonal, oblong, well and tree, Chinese Export, 19th C, rim chip and glaze wear **390.00**

Salt, 3-3/4" l, trench, chips, three-pc set **550.00**
Sauce boat, 6-7/8" w, 8" l, 3-3/8" h, lobed, applied bifurcated handles, rim chips, one handle cracked, price for pr **850.00**
Serving dish, 15-1/4" x 18-1/4", octagonal, 19th C **650.00**
Shrimp dish, 10-1/4" d, minor edge roughness, pr **690.00**
Tea caddy, cov, 5-1/2" h, octagonal, 19th C **2,645.00**
Tray
 9-3/4" l, 6-3/4" w, rect, 19th C **875.00**
 11-1/4" l, 8-1/4" w, lobed lozenge form, 19th C .. **875.00**

Platter, octagonal, cracked, **$95**.
Photo courtesy of Wiederseim Associates, Inc.

Tureen, cov, 14" l, 9-3/4" w, 7-3/4" h, stem finial, oval, ftd, hog snout handles **1,265.00**
Vegetable dish, cov, 9-1/2" w, 8" d, 3-1/4" h, diamond shape, scalloped edges, fruit finial, orange peel glaze, unglazed bottom **225.00**

CAPO-DI-MONTE

History: In 1743, King Charles of Naples established a soft-paste porcelain factory near Naples. The firm made figurines and dinnerware. In 1760, many of the workmen and most of the molds were moved to Buen Retiro, near Madrid, Spain. A new factory, which also made hard-paste porcelains, opened in Naples in 1771. In 1834, the Doccia factory in Florence purchased the molds and continued production in Italy.

Capo-di-Monte was copied heavily by other factories in Hungary, Germany, France, and Italy.

Reproduction Alert: Many of the pieces in today's market are of recent vintage. Do not be fooled by the crown over the "N" mark; it also was copied.

Basket, yellow, pink, and white roses, green foliage, tan basketweave base, marked with crown and "Capo-di-Monte, Made in Italy," **$75**.

Box, cov, 8" d, 4-1/4" h, round, domed lid molded with low relief figures of cherubs with flower baskets, sides similarly molded with cherubs at various artistic pursuits, gilt-metal rim mounts, int. painted with floral sprigs, late 19th C **475.00**
Casket, 13" l, 8" w, 5-1/2" h, molded opal body, cherubs in relief, detailed polychrome floral dec, gilt highlights, underglaze blue crown "N" mark, 19th C **2,400.00**
Creamer and sugar, mythological raised scene, dragon handles, claw feet, lion finial, 5-1/2" x 6" creamer, 6-1/4" x 6" cov sugar **250.00**
Dresser set, mythological raised scene, pair of 4" d, 7" h perfume bottles with figural stoppers, 5" d, 4" h cov powder jar, 30" l x 15" w tray **500.00**
Ferner, 11" l, oval, relief molded and enameled allegorical figures, full relief female mask eat each end **120.00**
Lamp, table, 25" h, figural Bacchus, female, and grapes **1,300.00**

Lamp, green jasper ware type base with white relief, **$150**.

Plate, 8-3/8" d, each with Capo-di-Monte crest at top, pair of swans, pair of cranes, crimson, blue, yellow, and burnt-orange flowers on border, gold trim, minor wear, price for eight-pc set **1,100.00**
Snuffbox, 3-1/4" d, hinged lid, cartouche shape, molded basket-weave and flower-head ext., painted int. with court lady and page examining portrait of gentlemen, gold mountings, c1740, minor restoration **1,650.00**

Plaques, pair, colored relief of Adam and Eve and The Adoration, conforming ebonized frames, mounted with gilt-bronze strapwork cartouche scrolls and marble medallions, blue crowned N marks, 20th C, 19-1/2" h, **$1,065**.
Photo courtesy of Sloans & Kenyon Auctions.

Plate, pedestal base, gilt decoration around foot, three mermaid figures supporting plate, gilding and raised allegorical figures around rim, center of plate decorated with coat of arms featuring cloak descending from crown with two rampant lions holding crest, surrounded by gilt scrollwork accented with black, marks on bottom of pedestal include under-glaze mark of N below crown in blue, bumblebee painted over glaze in gold, and words, "Napoleon and Josephine," 10-1/4" d, 5" h, **$115.**

Photo courtesy of Alderfer Auction Co.

Stein, 7-1/2" h, lion-hunt scene, lion on lid, elephant-trunk handle **400.00**

Table decoration, 8-3/4" h figural group of three female dancers on hexagonal base, 6-3/4" l four individual dancers, 6-1/4" l four kidney-shaped flower wells, gilt dec, 20th C, price for nine pcs **365.00**

Urn, cov, 21-1/8" h, ovoid, central-molded frieze of Nerieds and putti, molded floral garlands, gadroon upper section, acanthus-molded lower section, socle foot with putti, sq plinth base, applied ram's-head handles, domed cov, acorn finial, underglaze crowned "N" mark, minor chips and losses, pr **1,650.00**

CARNIVAL GLASS

History: Carnival glass, an American invention, is colored-pressed glass with a fired-on iridescent finish. It was first manufactured about 1905 and was immensely popular both in America and abroad. More than 1,000 different patterns have been identified. Production of old carnival-glass patterns ended in 1930.

Most of the popular patterns of carnival glass were produced by five companies: Dugan, Fenton, Imperial, Millersburg, and Northwood.

Marks: Northwood patterns frequently are found with the "N" trademark. Dugan used a diamond trademark on several patterns.

Notes: Color is the most important factor in pricing carnival glass. The color of a piece is determined by holding it to the light and looking through it.

For more information, see *Warman's Carnival Glass* and *Warman's Glass*, 4th edition.

Acanthus, Imperial, bowl, smoke, 8" d **115.00**
Acorn Burrs, Northwood
Punch set, ice blue, small flake on bowl **6,500.00**
Punch set, ice green, lightly iridized on exterior **8500.00**
Punch set, white **5,000.00**

Acorn, Fenton, bowl, ruffled, amethyst, $90.

Acorns, Millersburg, compote, six ruffles, marigold and Vaseline **3,750.00**
Apple Blossom Twigs, Dugan, plate, low, ruffled, purple, electric purple-and-blue highlights **225.00**
Basket of Roses, Northwood, bonbon, stippled, amethyst **475.00**
Beaded Cable, Northwood
Candy dish, ftd, amethyst **70.00**
Rose bowl, aqua opalescent **400.00**
Blackberry Block, Fenton, tumbler, blue **45.00**

Blackberry Spray, Fenton, hat, 6-1/2" h, Vaseline, sq, four sides up **40.00**
Blackberry Wreath, Millersburg
Bowl, 7-1/2" d, six ruffles, green **65.00**
Bowl, 10-1/2" d, three-in-one edge, green **165.00**
Ice cream bowl, 8" d, green, some wear to berries **85.00**
Ice cream sauce, 5-1/2" d, dark marigold **110.00**
Sauce, 6-1/4" d, six ruffles, green, satiny finish **65.00**
Blossomtime, Northwood, compote, marigold.......... **200.00**
Bouquet, Fenton
Tumbler, blue **55.00**
Water pitcher, marigold **150.00**
Bull's Eye & Beads, Imperial, vase, 7" h, flared, dark marigold **40.00**
Bushel Basket, Northwood, round, sapphire **1,350.00**
Butterflies, Australian, compote, stemmed, calver shape, purple, 7" **300.00**
Butterfly & Fern, Fenton
Tumbler, green **55.00**
Water pitcher, blue, radium finish **800.00**

Beaded Cable, Northwood, rose bowl, amethyst, $80.

Captive Rose, Fenton, plate, blue, 9" d **265.00**
Cherries, Dugan
Banana boat, electric blue, purple highlights, three ftd **275.00**
Sauce, low, ruffled, 6" d, purple **120.00**
Chrysanthemum, Nu-Art, chop plate, marigold................ **450.00**
Colonial Lady, Imperial, vase, marigold, 6" h.................. **600.00**
Concave Diamond, Northwood
Tumbler, celeste blue ... **30.00**
Tumble-up, russet green **900.00**

Vase, 6" h, celeste blue
.... **175.00**
Courthouse, Millersburg, ice
cream bowl, 7-1/2" d, amethyst,
lettered example **900.00**
Daisy Wreath, Westmoreland, 8-
1/2" d, ice cream bowl,
moonstone **110.00**
Dandelion, Northwood, tumbler,
purple............................. **55.00**
Diamond Points, Northwood,
vase, 10-1/4" h, aqua
opalescent, iridescent and
opalescent from top to base
.... **1,650.00**

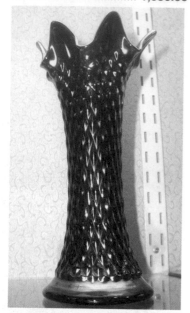

Diamond Point, Northwood, vase,
amethyst, 9" h, **$110**.

Diamond Rib, Fenton, vase,
9" h, purple....................... **40.00**
Diving Dolphins, Millersburg,
compote, Rosiland int., green
.... **1,700.00**
Dragon and Lotus, Fenton,
bowl, red **750.00**

Dragon and Lotus pattern, Fenton, low
ruffled bowl, amethyst, **$145**.

Drapery, Northwood, vase, marigold,
8" h, **$95**.

Drapery, Northwood, rose bowl,
aqua opalescent, light
butterscotch overlay **250.00**
Embossed Scroll
Bowl, 7" d, Hobstar & Tassel
exterior, electric purple
.... **400.00**
Sauce, 5" d, purple....... **45.00**
Embroidered Mums,
Northwood, plate, 9" d, ice green
.... **1,100.00**
Enameled Grape, Northwood,
water set, six pcs, blue, enamel
dec................................ **800.00**
Fanciful, Dugan, bowl, low,
ruffled, frosty white, pink, blue,
and green highlights **115.00**
Fashion, Imperial
Punch cup, marigold **28.00**
Tumbler, marigold......... **90.00**
Water set, marigold, seven-pc
matched set................ **150.00**
Fine Cut & Roses, Northwood,
rose bowl, purple **135.00**
Fine Rib, Fenton, vase
10" h, powder blue **60.00**
10-1/2" h, blue **85.00**
10-1/2" h, cherry red ... **225.00**
11-3/4" h, vaseline, marigold
overlay **70.00**

Fish Scale and Beads, Dugan, bowl,
marigold, **$40**.

Fishscale & Beads, Dugan
Plate, 7" d, electric purple
.... **575.00**
Plate, 7" d, marigold, satin irid
.... **45.00**
Plate, 7-1/2" d, low, ruffled,
purple **325.00**
Flowers, Fenton, rose bowl,
blue, multicolored irid **110.00**
Flute, Imperial, toothpick holder,
blue................................ **925.00**
Frosted Block, Imperial, rose
bowl, deep marigold......... **30.00**
Fruits & Flowers, Northwood,
bonbon, handled, lavender
.... **200.00**
Good Luck, Northwood, bowl,
ruffled, ice blue, 8-1/2" d,
three flutes missing **275.00**
Grape, Imperial
Decanter, electric purple,
stopper missing............ **85.00**
Punch set, marigold ... **300.00**
Water carafe, emerald green
.... **4,300.00**
Grape & Cable, Fenton, bowl,
6-1/2" d, smoky blue **40.00**

Grape & Cable pattern, Northwood,
dresser tray, purple, **$450**.

Grape and Cable, Northwood
Banana boat, purple... **195.00**
Cracker jar, cov, handles,
amethyst **275.00**
Humidor, amethyst...... **325.00**
Pin tray, blue **400.00**
Plate, ruffled, stippled,
sapphire **2,000.00**
Punch bowl set, bowl, base,
12 cups, marigold ... **2,300.00**

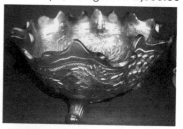

Grape & Cable pattern exterior, Persian
Medallion pattern interior, Fenton, bowl,
ruffled, footed, marigold, **$75**.
Photo courtesy of Dotta Auction Co., Inc.

Grape & Cable pattern, water set, pitcher, six tumblers, amethyst, **$650**.

Photo courtesy of Alderfer Auction Co.

Grape & Cable pattern, Fenton, bowl, footed, amethyst, **$85**.

Photo courtesy of Alderfer Auction Co.

Grape & Cable, Fenton, bowl, ruffled, green, **$45**.

Sweetmeat compote, cov, purple **170.00**

Grape & Gothic Arches, Northwood, tumbler, electric blue **45.00**

Grape Arbor, Northwood
Tankard pitcher, dark marigold, radium finish **575.00**

Tankard pitcher, purple, blue irid highlights, bronze highlights at base **400.00**

Grapevine & Lattice, Dugan, tumbler, white **225.00**

Grape Wreath, Millersburg
Bowl, 8-1/2" d, three-in-one-edge, green, radium finish **135.00**
Bowl, 9" d, six ruffles, marigold, blue radium finish **65.00**
Ice cream bowl, 8" d, amethyst, radium finish **155.00**

Grape Wreath Variant, Millersburg, bowl, 7" d, three-in-one edge, Feather center, purple, radium finish **115.00**

Greek Key, Northwood, plate, blue **400.00**

Hanging Cherries, Millersburg, ice cream bowl, amethyst, radium finish, 7" d **115.00**

Hearts and Flowers, Northwood, plate, lime ice green **3,000.00**

Heavy Grape, Imperial
Chop plate, 11" d, electric purple **400.00**
Chop plate, 11" d, helios green, flat, wear on high points **135.00**
Nappy, 5" d, electric purple **110.00**
Plate, 8" d, purple **65.00**

Heavy Iris, Dugan, tumbler, amethyst **75.00**

Heavy Pineapple, Fenton, bowl, ftd, 10" d, amber, satiny iridescence **500.00**

Hobnail, Millersburg, spittoon, marigold **700.00**

Hobnail Swirl, Millersburg, vase, 11" h, amethyst, radium iridescence **250.00**

Hobstar & Feather, Millersburg
Compote, round, clear . **75.00**
Compote, round, frosted **135.00**
Punch cup, crystal **25.00**
Tumbler, crystal, clear .. **65.00**
Tumbler, crystal, frosted **125.00**

Holly, Fenton
Compote, ruffled, lime green, marigold overlay **100.00**
Jack-in-the-pulpit hat, crimped edge, marigold **50.00**

Holly Sprig, Millersburg
Bowl, 6-1/2" d, deep, tight crimped edge, amethyst **120.00**
Nappy, tri-corn, handle, green **160.00**

Holly Whirl, Millersburg
Bonbon, Issac Benesch 54th Anniversary adv, marigold **150.00**
Bowl, 9-1/2" d, ruffled, marigold, radium finish . **85.00**
Nappy, two handles, deep, flared, amethyst, radium finish **100.00**

Homestead, plate, electric purple **2,300.00**

Horse Head Medallion, Fenton
Jack-in-the-pulpit bowl, ftd, marigold **75.00**
Plate, 7-1/2" d, crystal. **115.00**

Imperial Grape, Imperial, wine set, marigold, 7 pcs . **160.00**

Inverted Strawberry, Cambridge, sauce dish, 5" d, marigold **25.00**

Kittens, Fenton
Bowl, six ruffles, marigold **135.00**
Cup and saucer, marigold **245.00**
Toothpick holder, ruffled, marigold, radium finish **115.00**

Leaf and Little Flowers, Millersburg
Compote, flared, deep, green, radium finish with bright blue highlights **500.00**
Compote, flared, deep, marigold, radium finish **225.00**
Compote, six ruffles, amethyst **475.00**
Compote, six ruffles, dark marigold **300.00**

Leaf Columns, Northwood, vase, 10-1/2" h, radium green, multicolored irid, slightly flared top **135.00**

Grape & Cable, Northwood, banana boat, marigold, **$90**.

Photo courtesy of Seeck Auctions.

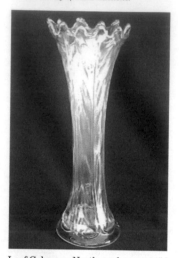

Leaf Columns, Northwood, vase, 10" h, white, **$300**.

Photo courtesy of Seeck Auctions.

Leaf Tiers, Fenton, tumbler, ftd, marigold **80.00**

Lotus & Poinsettia, Fenton, bowl, 10" d, ruffled, ftd, dark marigold **75.00**

Many Stars, Millersburg
Bowl, adv, Bernheimer Bros, blue **3,000.00**
Bowl, 10" d, blue **3,700.00**

Maple Leaf, Dugan
Tumbler, marigold **25.00**
Water pitcher, marigold
.... **90.00**

Morning Glory, Imperial
Funeral vase, 16-1/2" h, 4-3/4" d base, purple .. **250.00**
Vase, 6-1/2" h, olive green
.... **60.00**

Multi Fruits & Flowers, Millersburg, pitcher, marigold
.... **14,000.00**

Night Stars, Millersburg, bonbon, two handles, two sides, olive green, blue radium finish
.... **800.00**

Ohio Star, Millersburg
Cider pitcher, 11" h tankard, crystal **250.00**

Cider set, six pcs, 10" h tankard, crystal, chip on one tumbler **625.00**
Compote, 4-1/2" d, crystal
.... **35.00**
Punch set, 10 pcs, crystal
.... **1,550.00**
Toothpick holder, crystal
.... **115.00**

Open Rose, Imperial
Bowl, 8-1/2" d, electric purple
.... **85.00**
Plate, 9" d, marigold **45.00**
Rose bowl, electric purple int. and ext. **625.00**

Optic & Buttons, Imperial, rose bowl, marigold **30.00**

Orange Tree, Fenton
Bowl, 9" d, ruffled, Tree Trunk center, white, blue irid .. **90.00**
Plate, 9-1/2" d, Tree Trunk center, white, frosty irid
.... **185.00**
Powder box, cov, blue **115.00**
Punch set, punch bowl, stand, 12 cups, marigold **395.00**
Wine, blue **60.00**

Pansy, Imperial, pickle dish, green **145.00**

Peacock, Millersburg
Berry bowl, individual, 5" d, purple, radium finish... **115.00**
Berry bowl, master, 9" d, purple, radium finish, small nick **225.00**
Bowl, 10" d, three-in-one edge, green, radium finish, blue highlights **425.00**
Ice cream bowl, 5" d, marigold, satiny irid **200.00**

Peacock at Fountain, Dugan, tumbler, blue **35.00**

Peacock at Fountain, Northwood
Punch cup, white **20.00**
Tumbler, amethyst **25.00**
Water pitcher, amethyst
.... **250.00**

Peacock at Urn, Fenton
Compote, stemmed, celeste blue, marigold overlay **150.00**
Plate, marigold, 9" d ... **200.00**

Peacock at Urn, Millersburg
Berry bowl, master, 9" d, flared, marigold, radium irid with blue highlights..... **275.00**
Bowl, 8" d, blue **2,100.00**
Bowl, 10-1/2" d, six ruffles, green, satin finish, bee, no beading **250.00**
Compote, stemmed, ruffled, large, green **1,500.00**
Compote, stemmed, ruffled, large, marigold **2,300.00**

Ice cream bowl, 9-3/4" d, amethyst, radium finish, bee, no beading **225.00**
Sauce, 6" d, ruffled, blue, no bee, no beading **1,050.00**

Peacock Gardens, Fenton, vase, marigold **15,000.00**

Peacocks on Fence (Northwood Peacocks), Northwood
Bowl, aqua opalescent
.... **1,100.00**
Plate, ice green, 9" d .. **350.00**

Persian Medallion, Fenton
Bonbon, two handles, vaseline, marigold overlay
.... **140.00**
Chop plate, blue **195.00**
Plate, 6" d, marigold **25.00**

Peter Rabbit, Fenton, bowl, ruffled **1,800.00**

Poinsettia, Imperial, milk pitcher, purple **5,500.00**

Poppy, Millersburg, compote, flared, dark marigold **475.00**

Poppy Show, Northwood
Bowl, electric blue ... **2,300.00**
Plate, amethyst **750.00**

Leaf Chain, Fenton, bowl, amethyst, 9" d, **$135**.

Leaf Rays, Dugan, nappy, marigold, tricorn, clear ring handle, **$75**.

Rays & Ribbons, Millersburg
Bowl, 9-1/2" d, ruffled, crimped edge, Cactus exterior, purple, blue radium irid **175.00**

Octagon, Imperial, marigold, wine decanter, **$45**; two wine glasses, each **$20**.

Bowl, 9-3/4" d, three-in-one
  edge, marigold **140.00**
Ripple, Imperial, vase
  Green, 5" h **185.00**
  Purple, 8-1/2" h **95.00**
Rosalind, Millersburg
  Bowl, 10-1/2" d, six ruffles,
  amethyst **225.00**
  Jelly, stemmed, flared, deep,
  8-1/2" h, amethyst **3,500.00**
Rose Show, Northwood
  Bowl, ruffled, aqua
  opalescent **2,000.00**
  Bowl, ruffled, sapphire
  .... **3,500.00**
  Plate, blue **600.00**
  Plate, ice blue **2,100.00**
Rose Spray, Fenton
  Goblet, marigold **30.00**
  Jack-in-the-pulpit, celeste
  blue **65.00**
Round-Up, Dugan
  Bowl, low, ruffled, peach
  opalescent **250.00**
  Plate, 9" d, blue, basket-
  weave back, blue-and-pink
  highlights **275.00**
Rustic, Fenton
  Funeral vase, 18-1/2" h, blue,
  electric-blue highlights
  .... **675.00**
  Swung vase, 15" h, 4-1/4" d
  base, green, radium
  multicolored irid **110.00**

Open Rose, Imperial, rose bowl,
amethyst, **$25**.
Photo courtesy of Seeck Auctions.

Scroll Embossed, Imperial,
  bowl, plain back, purple,
  7-3/4" d **245.00**
Seacoast, Millersburg, pin tray,
  amethyst **550.00**
Seaweed, Millersburg
  Bowl, 10-1/4" d, three-in-one
  edge, marigold, satiny irid
  .... **350.00**
  Plate, 9" d, flared, marigold
  .... **1,600.00**
Stag & Holly, Fenton
  Bowl, 10" d, ruffled, ftd,
  powder blue, marigold
  overlay **200.00**
  Bowl, 10-1/2" d, crimped
  edge, ftd, marigold **125.00**
  Bowl, 11-1/4" d, ruffled, ftd,
  light-blue aqua base,
  marigold overlay **200.00**
Stippled Three Fruits,
  Northwood, plate, purple, 9" d
  .... **350.00**

Orange Tree, Fenton, fruit bowl, footed,
marigold, **$75**.

Peacock Tail Variant, Millersburg,
compote, ruffled, amethyst, **$125**.

Peacock at Urn, Fenton, bowl, ice cream
shape, amethyst, 9" d, **$200**.

Strawberry, Northwood
  Bowl, 8" d, pie crust edge,
  purple **90.00**
  Plate, 9" d, basket weave
  back, dark marigold, etched
  "St. Joe, Mich" **155.00**
  Plate, 9-1/4" d, basket-weave
  back, green **235.00**
Strawberry Wreath, Millersburg
  Bowl, 9" d, low-crimped
  ruffled, purple **185.00**
  Compote, six ruffles, dark
  marigold **175.00**
  Sauce, 5" sq, crimped edge,
  green **650.00**
Swirl Hobnail, Millersburg, rose
  bowl, purple **275.00**
Ten Mums, Fenton
  Bowl, 9" d, three-in-one edge,
  green **100.00**
  Bowl, 10" d, six ruffles edge,
  emerald-green base,
  multicolored irid **350.00**

Persian Medallion, Fenton, bon bon,
aqua, **$160**.
Photo courtesy of Seeck Auctions.

Persian Medallion, Fenton, bowl, blue,
8" d, **$45**; Peacock Tail, Fenton, bowl,
blue, 7" d, **$40**.
Photo courtesy of Joy Luke Auctions.

Three Fruits, Northwood
Bowl, eight ruffles, stippled, green **300.00**
Plate, stippled, amethyst
.... **300.00**
Tiger Lily, Imperial, tumbler, marigold **75.00**
Tornado, Northwood, vase, ice blue **8,000.00**
Tree Trunk, Northwood, funeral vase, 12-1/2" h at back, 10-1/2" h at front, green, radium finish
.... **425.00**

Scroll Embossed pattern, Imperial, small ruffled berry bowl, purple, **$40**.

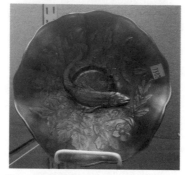

Ski Star, Dugan, bowl, large, ruffled, peach opal, **$265**.
Photo courtesy of Seeck Auctions.

CASTOR SETS

History: A castor set consists of matched condiment bottles held within a frame or holder. The bottles are for condiments such as salt, pepper, oil, vinegar, and mustard. The most commonly found castor sets consist of three, four, or five glass bottles in a silver-plated frame.

Although castor sets were made as early as the 1700s, most of the sets encountered today date from 1870 to 1915, the period when they enjoyed their greatest popularity.

Two bottles, mustard container, mottled blue, orange, tan, and gray decoration on white opaque body, silver stand with foliage, silver tops, **$250**.

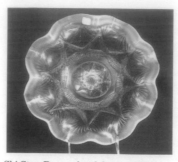

Singing Birds, Northwood, mug, stippled, blue, **$850**.
Photo courtesy of Seeck Auctions.

Trout and Fly, Millersburg
Bowl, 9" d, three-in-one edge, light amethyst **700.00**
Ice cream bowl, 8-1/4" l, marigold, satiny finish. **525.00**
Wild Flower, Northwood, compote, stemmed, light marigold **65.00**
Wild Rose, Northwood, rose bowl, ftd, stippled rays int., electric purple **650.00**
Wild Strawberry, Northwood, plate, 8" d, hand grip, basket-weave back, electric purple
.... **325.00**
Windflower, Dugan, plate, marigold, 9" d **65.00**
Windmill, Imperial
Bowl, deep, round, emerald green, 7" d **375.00**
Pitcher, marigold........... **65.00**
Tumbler, purple............. **75.00**
Wishbone, Northwood, bowl, low, ftd, ice blue **1,000.00**

Trout and Fly, Millersburg, bowl, ruffled, green, **$650**.

Wishbone, Northwood, plate, 9" d, footed, purple, **$220**.
Photo courtesy of Seeck Auctions.

Wishbone & Spades, Dugan, chop plate, 10-3/4" d, plain back, purple, with electric purple and blue highlights **900.00**
Wreath of Roses, Fenton, punch cups, Vintage interior
Blue **40.00**
Green........................... **40.00**
Zig-Zag, Millersburg
Bowl, 10" d, three-in-one edge, amethyst........... **400.00**
Bowl, tri-corn, crimped edge, amethyst **1,050.00**

Two interesting forms that graced sideboards years ago: left: sugar dish with bird finial, 14 spoons mounted around exterior, right: five-bottle caster set, silver-plated stand, each **$150**.
Photo courtesy of Joy Luke Auctions.

Two bottles, salt and pepper shakers, covered mustard, glass bases shaped so fit into base around looped handle, silver-plated mounts and round base, **$150**.

Photo courtesy of Joseph P. Smalley, Jr., Auctioneer.

2-bottle, Reed and Barton, Egyptian-style frame, two cranberry glass cruets and matching open salt elevated in center, 18" h **600.00**

3-bottle, Bohemian, three shouldered 14" h decanters, flashed blue, green, and cranberry, cut with circles,

etched Greek key band, silver-plated stand with tall central handle above three cylindrical wells, with geometric engine turning, borders with fruiting grapevine, three grapevine feet, late 19th C, 10-1/4" w, 20-1/2" h **865.00**

3-bottle, clear, Daisy-and-Button pattern, toothpick holder center, matching glass holder **125.00**

4-bottle, clear, mold blown, pewter lido and frame, domed based, loop handle, marked "I. Trask," early 19th C, 8" h. **320.00**

4-bottle, cranberry bottles and jars, clear pressed-glass frame, silver-plated look handle, two brass caps, one pewter, 9-1/2" h **275.00**

Seven-bottle, George III, c1800, Anglo-Irish cut glass shakers, ewers, etc with silver mounts, fitted oval tray with four feet, 11" h, 8-1/2" l, **$1,675**.

Photo courtesy of Pook & Pook.

Five bottles, silver plated stand with floral trim, clear bottles with engraved floral decoration, one bottle missing top, **$175**.

Five bottles, silver-plated stand with floral trim, clear bottles with matching engraved floral decoration, one with clear glass faceted stopper, rest with silver-plated tops, triangular motif handle, **$225**.

Porcelain, blue and white motif, two bottles with original stoppers in base with two holes for salt shakers, and two fixed napkin rings in base, no mark, **$95**.

4-bottle, ruby stained, Ruby-Thumbprint pattern, glass frame **360.00**
5-bottle, clear, New England Pineapple, two cruets with orig numbered cut and pressed panel hollow stoppers, two shakers with cut panel necks, period lids, mustard pot with period hinged lid, unmarked Brittania frame, 14-1/4" h, 7" d frame **330.00**
6-bottle, cut, diamond-point panels, rotating sterling-silver frame, all-over flowers, paw feet, loop handle, Gorham Mfg. Co., c1880, 11-1/2" h **2,500.00**
6-bottle, etched designs, revolving silvered metal stand, Victorian **175.00**

CATALOGS

History: The first American mail-order catalog was issued by Benjamin Franklin in 1744. This popular advertising tool helped to spread inventions, innovations, fashions, and necessities of life to rural America. Catalogs were profusely illustrated and are studied today to date an object, identify its manufacturer, study its distribution, and determine its historical importance.

Additional Listings: See *Warman's Americana & Collectibles* for more examples.

Adviser: Kenneth Schneringer.

A. B. See Electric Elev., New York, NY, 1908, 24 pgs, 8-3/4" x 10", stiff wraps **24.00**
A. Cutler & Son, Buffalo, NY, early 1900s, 86 pgs, 6" x 8", Catalog No. 12 .... **75.00**
Baraca & Philathea Supply Co., Syracuse, NY, 1923, 32 pgs, 3-1/2" x 6" **21.00**
Bullock & Crenshaw, Philadelphia, PA, 1857, 60 pgs, 5-3/4" x 9" **325.00**
Burstein-Applebee Co., Kansas City, MO, 1948, 114 pgs, 8" x 10-1/2", wraps **40.00**
Century Furniture Co., Grand Rapids, MI, 1927, 145 pgs, 5-1/2" x 8-1/4", hard cover. **24.00**
Champion Corp, Hammond, IN, c1929, 39 pgs, 7" x 9-1/2", vertical fold in center **35.00**

Jewett & Root, Buffalo, NY, 1877, 79 pages, 8-1/4" x 10-1/2", **$225**.

Crane Co., Chicago, IL, 1927, 28 pgs, 3-1/2" x 6-1/4" **15.00**
Crofts & Reed Co., Chicago, IL, 1916, 148 pgs, 7-3/4" x 10-1/2", Spring & Summer catalog. **37.00**
Detroit Dental Mfg Co., Detroit, MI, c1924, 11 pgs, 5-14" x 8-1/4", Gilmore Adjustable Attachments **15.00**
Distinctive Weathervane, York, PA, 1930s, 15 pgs, 6" x 9-1/4" **80.00**
Eli Lilly & Co, Indianapolis, IN, 1925, 295 pgs, 7" x 9-1/4", hard cover, Handbook of Pharmacy & Therapeutics, illus **48.00**
Erie Engine Works, Erie, PA, 1901, 48 pgs, 7-1/2" x 9-3/4" **190.00**
Ernst Heinrich Roth, US, 1924, 40 pgs, 6-1/2" x 9-1/2", photos of violins **50.00**
Fairbanks, Morse & Co., Chicago, IL, 1926, 24 pgs, 8-1/2" x 11", pictorial wraps **20.00**
Flaig Bros, Pittsburgh, PA, c1930, 24 pgs, 6-1/2" x 9". **22.00**
Fuller Brush Co., Hartford, CT, c1975, 12 pgs, 8-1/4" x 11", full color **10.00**
Geo. Delawrence, Berlin, WI, c1929, 25 pgs, 4-3/4" x 7". **12.00**
George C. Frys Co., Portald, ME, c1928, 78 pgs, 8" x 10", Cat. No. 162 .... **48.00**
Horace Partridge Co., Boston, MA, 1932, 92 pgs, 6-1/2" x 9-1/2", Catalog No. 139 ..... **85.00**
Howard Tresses, New York, NY, c1935, 30 pgs, 5-3/4" x 9". **16.00**
James B. Clow & Sons, Chicago, IL, c1911, 52 pgs, 9-1/4" x 12" **45.00**
James Manufacturing Co., Ft. Atkinson, WI, 1914, 255 pgs, 6-3/4" x 9-3/4", hard cover **55.00**

Liquid Carbonic Co., Chicago, IL, 1914, 72 pages, 6" x 9", **$85**.

King & Eisele Co., Buffalo, NY, c1928, 12 pgs, 9-1/2" x 12-1/4", two pgs illus, order form laid-in **55.00**
Krafft & Phillips Fashion, Philadelphia, PA, 1935, 20 pgs, 10-3/4" x 15", color **45.00**
Liquid Carbonic Co., Chicago, IL, 1914, 72 pgs, 6" x 9" **85.00**
Louden Machinery Co., Fairfield, IA, 1912, 50 pgs, 7-3/4" x 10-3/4", illus **42.00**
Luger Industries Inc., Burnsville, MN, 1971, 80 pgs, 8-1/4" x 11", in mail-out envelope **30.00**
Lyons Band Instrument Co., Chicago, IL, 1956, 256 pgs, 9" x 11", spiral bound **40.00**
Marshall Field & Co., Chicago, IL, 1932, eight pgs, 6-1/4" x 8-1/4", pocket folder of floor coverings **20.00**
Norlin Music Inc., Lincolnwood, IL, c1975, 12 pgs, 7-1/2" x 11" **15.00**
Northfolk Paint & Varnish, Norfolk Downs, MA, 1930, 26 pgs, 8-1/2" x 11" **10.00**
Oakwood Manufacturing Co., Springfield, OH, c1910, 32 pgs, 8" x 7-1/2" **18.00**
Ohio State Stove & Mfg Co., Columbus, OH, c1925, 12 pgs, 7-3/4" x 10-1/2", six illus, pages laid-in **26.00**
Old Town Canoe Co., Old Town, ME, 1956, 48 pgs, 6" x 8" .. **75.00**

Sears, Roebuck & Co., Chicago, IL, 1911, 34 pages, 7" x 9-1/2", **$100**.

Oskamp, Nolting & Co., Cincinnati, OH, 40 pgs, 8-3/4" x 11-3/4", wraps **65.00**

Pan-American Band Instruments, Elkhart, IN, 1930s, 3-1/4" x 6-1/4" **30.00**

Pass & Seymour Inc., Syracuse, NY, 1919, 107 pgs, 7-1/2" x 10-3/4", Catalog No. 25 .... **26.00**

Richmond Stove Co., Richmond, VA, c1920, 96 pgs, 3-1/2" x 6" **40.00**

Rock Island Stove Co., Rock Island, IL, 1929, 63 pgs, 7-3/4" x 10-1/2", Catalog No. 38 ..... **32.00**

Sayre & Fisher Co., New York, NY, c1895, 122 pgs, 6-3/4" x 10-1/2", hard cover........... **32.00**

Sealed Power Corp, Muskegon, MI, 1943, 32 pgs, 8" x 10-1/2" **14.00**

Sears, Roebuck & Co., Chicago, IL, 1911, 34 pgs, 7" x 9-1/2", automobiles **100.00**

Sears, Roebuck & Co., Chicago, IL, 1936, 19 pgs, 8-3/4" x 12-3/4", rugs and carpets **20.00**

Shakespeare Co., Kalamazoo, MI, 1959, 32 pgs, 7" x 10", Angler's Catalog................ **24.00**

Stewart & McGuire, New York, NY, eight pgs, 8-1/4" x 11", silver gilt highlights.................... **45.00**

Stover Mfg & Engine Co., Freeport, IL, c1939, 24 pgs, 8" x 9", folded vertical as issued **35.00**

Victor Safe & Lock Co., Cincinnati, OH, 1910, 200 pages, 6-1/2" x 9-3/4", wear at binding, **$110**.

Targ & Dinner, Chicago, IL, 1967, 472 pgs, 9" x 12", bound volume of catalogs............ **55.00**

The Cloak-Drummer Co., Chicago, IL, 1912, 86 pgs, 7" x 9-1/2", fall and winter **30.00**

United States Rubber Co., New Orleans, LA, 1940, 12 pgs, 9" x 12"................................ **32.00**

Victor Safe & Lock Co., Cincinnati, OH, 1910, 200 pgs, 6-1/2" x 9-3/4", wear at binding **110.00**

Weber Lifelike Fly Co., Stevens Point WI, 1938, 96 pgs, 6-1/4" x 9", No. 19 .... **60.00**

Westinghouse Machine Co., Pittsburgh, PA, c1895, three pgs, 6" x 9" **140.00**

Whitemore Associates Inc., Boston, MA, 1950, 160 pgs, 6" x 9"................................ **30.00**

Wright & Ditson, Boston, MA, 1928, 112 pgs, 5-1/2" x 8", Spring & Summer Sports Equipment...................... **100.00**

Wright Co., Inc., Atlanta, GA, 1928, 212 pgs, 8-1/2" x 11-1/4", kitchen equipment **125.00**

Yale & Towne Mfg Co., Stamford, CT, 1921, 450 pgs, 7-3/4" x 10-3/4", hard cover, Catalog No. 25................ **110.00**

CELADON

History: The term "celadon," meaning a pale grayish-green color, is derived from the theatrical character Celadon, who wore costumes of varying shades of grayish green in Honore d'Urfe's 17th-century pastoral romance, *L'Astree*. French Jesuits living in China used the name to refer to a specific type of Chinese porcelain.

Celadon divides into two types. Northern celadon, made during the Sung Dynasty up to the 1120s, has a gray-to-brownish body, relief decoration, and monochromatic olive-green glaze. Southern (Lung-ch'uan) celadon, made during the Sung Dynasty and much later, is paint-decorated with floral and other scenic designs and is found in forms that appeal to the European- and American-export market. Many of the southern pieces date from 1825 to 1885. A blue square with Chinese or pseudo-Chinese characters appears on pieces after 1850. Later pieces also have a larger and sparser decorative patterning.

Reproduction Alert.

Bowl, large, deep, lightly embossed pattern, hairlines, **$165**.
Photo courtesy of Wiederseim Associates, Inc.

Bowl
5-3/4" d, wide flaring form, dark gray-green color, traces of three spurs on base, surface entirely glazed, Korea, Koryo period, 12th C **600.00**
6-1/4" d, exterior carved with lotus petals, China, 14th C **365.00**
7-1/2" d, sea green color, inlaid in Sangam technique with clouds and phoenix, Korea, Koryo period, 12th C **875.00**
7-1/2" d, sea green color, inlaid in Sangam technique with branches and sprigs of flowers, Korea, Koryo period, 12th/13th C **475.00**

9-1/2" d, 4-1/2" h, cut corner shape, Rose Canton dec, hardwood stand, repaired **385.00**

10-1/2" d, scalloped rim, dec with exotic birds, butterflies, and flowers, repairs and gilt losses to edge **245.00**

15-1/4" d, Lung Chuan ware, interior with kylin and waves, China, 14th C **1,450.00**

Brush box, cov, 7-1/2" w, 3-1/4" d, 2-1/2" h, dec in Rose Medallion palette **400.00**

Center dish, 11-1/4" l, diamond shape, conforming foot, court scenes, central scene contained in vasiform device, Rose Canton pattern, China, 19th C, gilt wear **530.00**

Charger

10" d, Mandarin warrior, One Hundred Antiques border, China, 19th C **210.00**

13-1/2" d, Rose Medallion, court scene within medallion, Famille Rose border, minor glaze wear **725.00**

Dish, carved stoneware, flower center and foliate border under dark celadon glaze, Chinese, Ming Dynasty, 14th-15th C, 10" d, **$1,100**.

Photo courtesy of Alderfer Auction Co.

Ice cream tray, 7" x 13-1/4", rect, flange handles, Rose Canton motif, China, 19th C, minor gilt wear **600.00**

Incense burner, lid surmounted by Buddhist, lion base with lion mask feet, sea-green color, Korea, 12th C **8,000.00**

Plate

5-1/4" d, Rose Canton dec, China, 19th C **90.00**

10-1/4" d, river scene, butterfly and floral border, minor gilt and glaze wear **150.00**

10-1/4" h, Rose Canton motif, bird and butterflies around tree peony, underglaze blue sq mark, wear, some in-painting **210.00**

11" d, hexagonal, Lung Chuan ware, latticework center and floral rim, China, Ming period (15th-16th C) **1,175.00**

Platter, 13-1/4" x 15-3/4", oval, Rose Canton dec **650.00**

Rice bowl, cov, underplate, 7-1/2" d, 5-3/4" h, dec with various animals, figures, and flowers **390.00**

Sauce tureen, cov, undertray, gilt floriform finial, gilt handles, bird, butterfly, and floral motifs, China, 19th C, minor edge wear **600.00**

Plate, 10" d, multicolored floral and butterflies decoration, gold rim, Chinese, **$150**.

Serving dish, cov, 10" d, 6-1/2" h, domed lid, single handle, Rose Canton dec, imperfections **300.00**

Shrimp dish, 10-1/4" x 9-3/4", bird, butterfly, and floral motif, China, 19th C, minor glaze wear **650.00**

Soap dish, three part, 4-1/8" l, 5-1/4" w, 2-1/2" h, figures in garden on lid, Rose Medallion border, minor edge wear **265.00**

Vase

10-3/4" h, Maebyong form, carved floral sprigs on body and lotus petals at base, deep sea-green color, Korea, Koryo period, 12th/13th C, old repair to mouth **1,800.00**

12-3/4" h, hexagonal paneled form, two handles, bird and floral dec, handle chip, gilt wear **385.00**

CELLULOID ITEMS

History: In 1869, an Albany, NY, printer named John W. Hyatt developed and patented the world's first commercially successful semi-synthetic thermoplastic. The moldable material was made from a combination of camphor, the crystalline resin from the heart of a particular evergreen tree, and collodion, a type of nitrated-cellulose substance (also called Pyroxylin), which was extremely flammable. Hyatt and his brother, Isaiah, called their invention Celluloid, a name they made up by combining the words cellulose and colloid.

By 1873, the Hyatts were successfully producing raw pyroxylin plastic material at the Celluloid Manufacturing Company of Newark, NJ. In the early days of its commercial development, Celluloid was produced exclusively in two colors: flesh tone, for the manufacture of denture-base material, and off white, which was primarily used for utilitarian applications like harness trimmings and knife handles.

By the early 20th century, there were four major American manufacturers firmly established as producers of quality pyroxylin plastics. In addition to the Celluloid Company of Newark, NJ, there was the Arlington Manufacturing Company of Arlington, NJ, which produced Pyralin; Fiberloid Corporation of Indian Orchard, MA, makers of Fiberloid; and the Viscoloid Company of Leominster, MA. Even though these companies branded their plastic products with registered trade names, today the word "celluloid" is used in a general sense for all forms of this type of early plastic.

Celluloid-type plastic became increasingly popular as an alternative for costly and elusive natural substances. Within the fashion industry alone, it gained acceptance as a beautiful and affordable substitute for increasingly dwindling supplies of ivory and tortoise shell.

In sheet form, celluloid found other successful applications as well. Printed political and advertising premiums, pinback buttons, pocket mirrors, and keepsake items from 1890-1920 were turned out by the thousands. In addition, transparent-sheet celluloid was ornately decorated by embossing, reverse painting, and lamination, and then used in the production of decorative boxes, booklets, and albums. The toy industry also capitalized on the use of thin-celluloid sheet for the production of blow-molded dolls, animal toys, and figural novelties.

By 1930, and the advent of the modern-plastics age, the use of celluloid began to decline dramatically. The introduction of cellulose-acetate plastic replaced the flammable pyroxylin plastic in jewelry and toys, and the development of non-flammable safety film eventually put an end to its use in movies. By 1950, the major manufacturers of celluloid in the United States had ceased production; however, many foreign companies continued manufacture. Today, Japan, France, Italy, China, and Korea continue to manufacture cellulose-nitrate plastics in small amounts for specialty items such as musical-instrument inlay, knife handles, ping-pong balls, and designer fountain pens.

Beware of celluloid items that show signs of deterioration: oily residue, cracking, discoloration, and crystallization. Take care when cleaning celluloid items; it is best to use mild soap and water, avoiding alcohol- or acetone-based cleansers. Keep celluloid from excessive heat or flame and avoid direct sunlight.

Marks: Viscoloid Co. manufactured a large variety of small hollow animals that ranged in size from two to eight inches. Most of these toys are embossed with one of three trademarks: "Made in USA," an intertwined "VCO," or an eagle with a shield.

Adviser: Julie P. Robinson.

Manicure box, cream colored, printed winter scene on lid, embossed flowers, blue satin lining, fitted with original manicure implements, 5" x 7" x 2" h, **$115**.

All celluloid photos courtesy of Julie Robinson.

Advertising and souvenir-keepsake items

Badge, 2" d, printed with "P H" and two intertwined American flags, fraternal organization for Patrons of Husbandry—The Grange, Whitehead & Hoag Co., early 1900s, shaped metal pinbackframe **20.00**

Bookmark, 3 1/4" l, 1/4" w, folded top for slipping over a page, violets dec, "Greetings" on the long flat surface **20.00**

Card, 3-1/16" x 2", engraved "Baldwin & Gleason With Best Wishes," ivory-grained sheet cream-colored celluloid, deep-blue floral motif **30.00**

Compact, 1-3/4" d, imitation ivory-grained celluloid with gold Elk motif and "Third Annual Ball, BPOE, Leominster Lodge No. 1237, Jan. 26, 1917," produced by the Viscoloid Co. of Leominster, MA **65.00**

Fan, 4" h when closed, mottled turquoise and cream celluloid Brise fan, light blue ribbon, shows the Washington Monument and "Washington D.C." in goldtone paint **40.00**

Ink blotter, 4 1/8" x 2 7/8" ivory-grained celluloid, front and back covers w/ blotters inside, engraved scene of Black Diamond File Works, Philadelphia, PA, 1900 calendar, Baldwin & Gleason Co. **45.00**

Match safe, 2-1/2" x 1-1/2", ivory-grained safety-match holder, red outline, blue lettering, "Joseph's Economy Store, 406 Penn St. Reading, PA" **20.00**

Pin holder, 1-3/4" d, celluloid disc, metal framework, "F Krupps Steel Works, Thomas Prosser & Son, NY," front shows advertising, back shows small child, engraved ivory-grained celluloid **40.00**

Tape measure, 1-1/4" d, pull out tape, colorful pretty girl with flowers, adv for "The First National Bank of Boswell, The Same Old Bank in its New Home," printed by P.N. Co. (Parisian Novelty Co. of Chicago), Patent 7-10-17, emb in the side **65.00**

Animals

Viscoloid Co. of Leominster, MA, manufactured a variety of small hollow toy animals, birds, and marine creatures, most of which are embossed with one of these three trade marks: "Made In USA," an intertwined "VCO," or an eagle with shield. A host of foreign countries also mass-produced celluloid toys for export into the United States. Among the most prolific manufacturers were Ando Togoro of Japan, whose toys bear the crossed-circle trademark, and Sekiguchi Co., which used a three-petal flower motif as its logo. Paul Haneaus of Germany used an intertwined PH trademark, and Petticolin of France branded its toys with an eagle head. Japanese- and American-made toys are plentiful, while those manufactured in Germany, England, and France, are more difficult to find. English toys were made by Cascelloid and also marked "Palitoy." The most prolific manufacturer of German dolls was the firm Schildkrott, whose logo was a turtle or a turtle in a diamond.

Alligator, 3", green, white-tail tip, VCO/USA **18.00**

Animal set, six circus animals, garish bright colors, marked "Made In Occupied Japan," elephant, gorilla, giraffe, tiger, lion, and hippo, set **85.00**

Bear, 5" w, cream bear, pink and gray highlights, VCO/USA .. **20.00**

Bison, 3-1/4" l, dark brown, eagle-and-shield trademark **18.00**

Boar, 3-1/4" l, brown, Paul Haneaus of Germany/PH trademark **75.00**

Cat
  3-1/2" l, peach, flower trademark, Japan **30.00**
  5-1/4", cream, pink and black highlights, molded collar and bell, Made in USA trademark **50.00**

Chick, 7/8", yellow, black eyes and beak, no trademark **8.00**

Chicken, metal feet, no trademark **30.00**

Cow, 4-1/2", cream-and-orange cow; intertwined VCO/USA **25.00**

Dog
  Bulldog, 4-3/4" l, 2-1/2" h, spiked neck collar, translucent-green color, rhinestone eyes, intertwined VCO/USA **30.00**

Hound, 5", long tail, peach celluloid, gray highlights, crossed-circle Japan.... **20.00**
Scottie, 3-1/4" l, plaster-filled cream-colored celluloid, no detailing, marked JAPAN **20.00**
St. Bernard, 3-1/4", tan, black highlights, intertwined VCO/USA................ **18.00**

Donkey, nodder, made in Occupied Japan **35.00**

Duck, 2-1/4", standing, cream-colored celluloid, hand-painted eyes and bills, original paper label, Japan **20.00**

Elephant
3-3/4", nodder, trunk down, wide open ears, white, gray highlights, Japan **35.00**
6-3/4" x 4-3/4", gray elephant, tusks, USA **35.00**

Fish
2-1/4" l, bright red, USA.. **8.00**
2-7/8" l, yellow, brown highlights, molded scales, intertwined VCO, circle. **10.00**

Frog, 1-1/4", green or yellow, stripe on back, intertwined VCO/USA................................ **15.00**

Giraffe, cream, painted yellow and brown spots, eagle trademark, French............. **65.00**

Goat, 3", white, curled horns, flower, "N" in circle, Japan **18.00**

Hippopotamus, 3-3/4", pink, closed mouth, Japan **18.00**

Horse, 5" l, bending to eat grass on base, Occupied Japan **30.00**

Leopard, 4-1/2", white, orange highlights, black spots, Occupied Japan **20.00**

Lion, 5-1/4" l, nodder, fierce open mouth, full mane, Japan **30.00**

Lobster, 1-3/4", bright red, detailed shell, no trademark **55.00**

Penguin, 4-1/2" h, nodder, red, peach bill and feet, blue eyes, Japan **50.00**

Pig, 4-1/2", pink, painted eyes, USA..................................... **30.00**

Polar bear, 2-1/4" l, white, USA **12.00**

Ram, 4-1/2", cream, gray highlights, USA **18.00**

Rhino, 5", gray, fine detail, PH trademark, Paul Haneaus . **65.00**

Seal, 4-1/2", gray, balancing red ball, VCO/USA **60.00**

Squirrel, 2-7/8", brown, holding nut, USA............................. **45.00**

Stork, 6-3/4", standing, white, pink legs, flower mark, Japan **18.00**

Swan, 3-3/8", multicolored purple, pink, yellow, crossed circle **10.00**

Teddy bear, moveable arms and legs
4-1/4" h, bright pink, made in Occupied Japan........... **25.00**
6-1/2" h, light green **35.00**

Turtle, 1-3/8", brown top, yellow bottom, USA on foot.......... **12.00**

Decorative albums and boxes

Autograph album, 6" x 4", silver and violet clear celluloid-coated paper, central emb oval with beautiful lady in wide-brimmed hat, white dress and fur, maroon-velvet back and binding ... **95.00**

Collar box, 6" h, 6" d, covered in gold paper with pink, green, and yellow flowers, clear-celluloid overlay, central image of a pretty woman wearing ruffled dress with corsage **120.00**

Hankie box, 7" sq, 3" h, center vignette of pretty girl in hat and gown picking pink flowers, emb Greek-key design on sides, overall pale yellow, green, and blue grapevine with leaf design **120.00**

Necktie box, 12-1/2" x 4", emb script "Neckties," cream-colored celluloid, emb-circular design on sides **95.00**

Photograph album, 8" x 11", Gibson girl, lavender dress, hat with lavender plumes, emb corners, applied-gilt paint. **175.00**

Baby rattle, boy in Indian headdress, playing guitar, attached two-tone ball, intertwined "VCO/USA" trademark, 4-1/2" h, $60.

Kewpie doll, white feathers, silver and gold paper hat, molded white socks and red shoes, intertwined COH Made in Japan mark, 12" h, $55.

Dolls and toys

Baby rattle, 4-1/2", light blue, boy in Indian headdress playing guitar, attached two tone ball with amber ring, intertwined "VCO/USA" trademark on back **60.00**

Toy, boat, cream, red topped smoke stacks, red and green portholes, red base, German made by Dr. Paul Hunaeus, "PH" trademark, c1925, 5" l, $55.

Doll

3-1/4" black baby, strung arms and legs, unidentified lantern trademark, Made in Japan............................ **50.00**
7", molded, moving arms, molded bracelet on right wrist, mermaid in shield trademark on back, DRP Germany, mfg. by Cellba, Celluloidwarenfabrik Co. **95.00**

Roly Poly, 2-1/2", duckling, peach hat trimmed in flowers, jacket, necktie, green trim, cream celluloid, VCO trademark **85.00**

Toy, 5", ocean liner, gray and red, flag, intertwined PH ... **50.00**

Whistle, 3-1/4" l, 2-1/4" h, Nightingale bird, yellow celluloid, green and red highlights, VCO/ USA...... .... **25.00**

Fashion accessories

Bar pin, 2-1/2" l, ivory-grained rect shape, orange-brown swirled-pearlescent laminate, center hp florals **28.00**

Belt, 22" l, 3/4" x 1-1/2" rect mottled-green celluloid slabs linked by chain, applied silver-tone filigree dec **35.00**

Bracelet, bangle, ivory colored, embedded with center row of red rhinestones and flanked by outside rows of clear rhinestones **75.00**

Bracelet, link, 3" d, four oblong two-tone cream and ivory links, attached by smaller round cream links **65.00**

Brooch

1-1/4" d thin gold-tint metal frame, blue and white enamel floral embellishment, clear celluloid, designed to hold photo, safety clasp **25.00**
2-1/4", girl, molded red dress and bandana **30.00**

Comb and case, 2-1/4" l, folding molded case, emb-rose motif, imitation ivory **30.00**

Cuff links, pr, toggle back, realistic molded-celluloid lion heads, c1896 .... **95.00**

Dress clips, pr, molded-floral motif, semi-translucent cream celluloid, marked "Japan". **35.00**

Eyeglasses, Harold-Lloyd type, black frames **20.00**

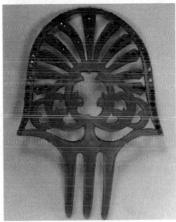

Hair comb, three prongs, 11 rays, semi-opaque amber, blue rhinestones, c1920, 4-3/4", **$55**.

Hair comb, 4" x 5-1/4", imitation tortoiseshell, 24 teeth, applied-metal trim studded with rhinestones and brad-fastened Egyptian-Revival pink and gold metal floral and beetle dec **145.00**

Hat pin, 4" l, elephant head, tucks, black glass eyes, imitation ivory **95.00**

Hat ornament, 3-1/2" h, Art Deco, pearlized red and cream half circles, rhinestone trim **65.00**

Necklace, 2" elegant Art Nouveau-filigree pendant, cream celluloid, oval cameo, profile of a beautiful woman, suspended from 20" cream celluloid-beaded necklace **110.00**

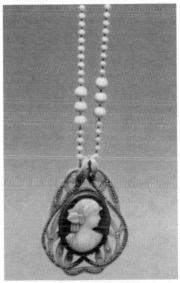

Pendant, Art Nouveau-style cameo-type imitation ivory pendant applied to faux shell, gold scrolled beaded mounting, 20" l imitation ivory celluloid beaded necklace, beads, **$110**.

Pendant, black, crystal rhinestones **35.00**

Purse frame, 4" l, black pointed-horseshoe shape, rhinestones, white-molded cameo clasp **95.00**

Purse, 4-1/2" x 4-1/2", basketweave, link-celluloid chain, mottled grain ivory and green............................... **185.00**

Holiday items

Angels, 1-1/2" h, set of three, one holding cross, star, or lantern, Japan, Mt. Fuji trademark **35.00**

Christmas decoration, roly poly-type house, opening in back for a small bulb, shows Santa approaching door, red and white, intertwined VCO/USA trademark **125.00**

Brooches, left: portrait of pretty lady with celluloid hair comb and mantilla in Gibson girl hair style, twisted metal work frame, C-clasp, c1890, oval, 2-1/4" l, **$65**; right: two round portraits of husband and wife, enameled blue forget-me-nots in center, twisted metal frames, C-clasp, c1890, 1" l, **$50**.

Christmas ornament

3-3/4" little boy on swing, all celluloid, dark-green highlights, holding onto string "ropes" for hanging on tree **95.00**

4" l, stripped green and white Christmas stocking filled with gifts including duck and kitten, crossed-circle trademark, Ando Togoro **125.00**

Figure

4-3/4" h, duck, standing, wearing tails and top hat, red and green paints **75.00**

8-7/8", Uncle Sam, stars on hat, USA..................... **150.00**

Halloween, roly poly, black cat on orange pumpkin, red trim, Viscoloid Co., Leominster, MA, intertwined VCO trademark, 3-1/4" h, **$200.**

Halloween favor, 4" l, orange horn, black witch and trim, intertwined VCO/USA...... **125.00**

Rattle, 3-3/4" l, standing black cat, orange bow, intertwined VCO/USA **185.00**

Reindeer, 3-1/2", white deer, gold glitter, red eyes and mouth, molded ears and antlers, USA **20.00**

Roly poly, 3-1/2", black cat on orange pumpkin, intertwined VCO/USA **235.00**

Santa

4", yellow or mint-green translucent celluloid, holding lantern and sack, Japanese, Mt. in circle trademark.. **55.00**

5" h, basket of flowers, fur-trimmed suit, nice detail, VCO/USA trademark **75.00**

Toy

2-7/8" l, Easter rabbit in harness, attached to cart full of eggs, "Made in Japan" on cart, "Pat.15735" on rabbit **95.00**

4-3/4" h, Paddy, riding pig, movable legs, little boy with dunce cap riding on back, Japan......................... **200.00**

Easter, chicken pulling cart with eggs and two chicks, made by Viscoloid Co, Leominster, MA, intertwined VCO trademark, 3" l, **$85.**

Novelty items

Letter opener

7 3/8" l, ivory grained, magnifying glass in top, coiled-metal snake, red-glass eyes around the handle **85.00**

8" l, blade top by intricately detailed full-figure lady holding a flask **80.00**

Pin cushion

2" h, rabbit with pin cushion baskets, marked "Germany" **130.00**

2-1/4" h, straight pin holder, brown hen on base....... **65.00**

Tape measure

1-1/4" d, basket of fruit, marked "Made in Germany" **150.00**

2-1/2" h, Billiken, cream celluloid, applied-brown highlights, marked "Japan" **185.00**

Utilitarian and household items

Bookends, pr, 4-1/4" h, 3-1/4" w, 2-1/4" d, mottled-pink celluloid, emb ornamental gold neoclassic drape, plaster weighted, no trademark, c1930............. **35.00**

Candle holders, pr, 5-1/4" h, cylindrical, round flared-weighted bases, unmarked **60.00**

Clock

3" sq, New Haven Clock Co., alarm, folding travel case, pearlescent pink laminated over amber celluloid..... **30.00**

5-1/2" x 3", classical Gothic cathedral design, round face, dark-yellow ivory-grained celluloid, Germany **45.00**

Crumb tray set, two dust pan-shaped trays, ivory celluloid, dark-blue dec border, monogrammed "T" in center of each tray **50.00**

Cutlery, solid imitation ivory grained-handle utensils, eight forks, eight knives in orig box, Standard Mfg. Co. **30.00**

Frame, 4" d, round, ivory grained, easel back.......... **25.00**

Napkin ring, 1-1/2" w, plain, pale-green celluloid **5.00**

String holder, round sphere on a weighted base, twist apart, center hole in top for string, imitation-ivory grain, no trademark **65.00**

Vase, 6" h, imitation ivory, conical, fluted weighted base, flange around top **25.00**

Watch holder, 6-1/2" l, pearlescent blue, green, and amber, wall-hanging banjo-clock style, Wilcox trademark, late 1920s **25.00**

Comb and brush set, light pink ground, delicate pink and white roses, green leaves, gold highlights, plaster filled celluloid brush, celluloid comb with hand applied roses and gold trim, c1930, **$35.**

Vanity items

Dresser boxes, pr, oval-shaped pearlized peach boxes, dec-shaped lids, marked "Amerith," Lotus Pattern, c1929......... **30.00**

Dresser set, 17-piece, Fairfax pattern, Fiberloid Company, mottled brown and gold, carved floral trim, comb, brush, mirror, powder box, hair receiver, nail file, scissors, button hook, and clothing brush, c1924 ..... **125.00**

Dresser tray, 7-1/2" l, 5" w, oval, pearlized cream color and amber framework, Normandy lace inserted between double-glass bottom, c1925 .... **30.00**

Hair receiver and powder box set, 4" d, ivory-grained set, scalloped lids laminated in Goldaleur, marked "The Celluloid Co." **45.00**

Hatpin holder, weighted base, 5" h center post, round circular disc on top, circular base, cream celluloid, cranberry-colored velvet cushion **90.00**

Manicure set, rolled-up leather pouch fitted with six imitation-tortoiseshell celluloid manicure tools, gold trim, pink-velvet lining **30.00**

Vanity set, amber, teal green pearlescent laminate surface, dresser tray, octagonal amber hair-receiver box with pearlized lid, nail buffer, scissors, and button hook, hp rose motif on all pcs, unmarked, c1930 ...... **45.00**

CHARACTER AND PERSONALITY ITEMS

History: In many cases, toys and other products using the images of fictional comic, movie, and radio characters occur simultaneously with the origin of the character. The first Dick Tracy toy was manufactured within less than a year after the strip first appeared.

The golden age of character material is the TV era of the mid-1950s through the late 1960s; however, some radio-premium collectors might argue this point. Today, television and movie producers often have their product licensing arranged well in advance of the initial release.

Do not overlook characters created by advertising agencies, e.g., Tony the Tiger. They represent a major collecting sub-category.

Additional Listings: See *Warman's Americana & Collectibles* for expanded listings.

Andy, litho tin wind-up, yellow derby, light blue jacket, red and tan striped trousers, Louis Marx & Co., **$320**.
Photo courtesy of Pook & Pook.

Character

Andy Gump, pinback button, 1-1/4" d, "Andy Gump For President/I Endorse The Atwater Kent Receiving Set," red, white, blue, and fleshtone **40.00**

Betty Boop
Book, *Betty Boop Cartoon Lessons*, Fleischer Studios, 1935, 12" x 9" **500.00**
Marble, 11/16", Peltier Glass Co., black and white swirl, black transfer of Betty, c1932 .... **175.00**
String holder, 6-1/2" w, 7-1/2" h, chalk, head and shoulders, orig paint... **625.00**

Brownies, Palmer Cox
Book, *The Brownies, Their Book*, Palmer Cox, NY, 1887, first edition, second issue, illus by Cox, 4to, pictorial glazed boards **230.00**
Child's fork and spoon, emb Brownies on handles **18.00**
Doll, set of 8" dolls, stuffed cloth, Uncle Sam, Indian, Highlander, Chinaman, German, Sailor, Soldier, Canadian, Irishman,

Policeman, John-Bull, and Dude, each has name stitched on back, colorful-printed outfits, marked "Copyright 1892 by Palmer Cox" on back of each, "Brownie's" on right foot of each, set of 12............ **775.00**

Buster Brown
Bench, child size bench, four seats divided by diecut animal shapes, one black and white lion, black and white zebra, and orange tiger, red background, detailed illus of Buster and Tige on ends **6,000.00**
Children's feeding dish, Buster and Tige, wear to gold trim............................... **115.00**
Figure, 2" h, bisque, red hat and suit, blue bow tie, black shoes, c1920 .... **100.00**
Sunday comics, 1914, *St. Paul Daily News*, full section **20.00**
Tray, Buster Brown Shoe's, brown grain painting, gold lettering, some wear, 13-3/8" d **65.00**

Campbell's Kids
Child's feeding plate, two Campbell kids, one holding doll behind back, Buffalo Pottery **45.00**
Doll, 16" h, boy, orig clothing, 1970...................... **35.00**
String holder, 6-3/4" h, chalk, incised "Copyright Campbell" **395.00**

Charlie the Tuna
Animation cel, 10 1/2" x 12" clear acetate sheet, centered smiling full-figured 4" image of Charlie gesturing toward 4" image of goldfish holding scissors, 10-1/2" x 12-1/2" white paper sheet with matching blue/lead pencil, 4" tall image of Charlie, c1960 .... **150.00**
Wristwatch, 1-1/2" d bright gold luster bezel, full-color image of Charlie on silver background, ©1971 Star-Kist Foods, grained purple leather band **60.00**

Dutch Boy, string holder, 14-1/2" x 30", diecut tin, Dutch Boy sitting on swing painting the sign for this product, White Lead Paint Bucket houses ball of string **300.00**

Tom Corbett Space Cadet, bedspread, chenille, white, red, black and yellow decoration, rocket ship, twin bed size, $150.

Elsie the Cow, Borden
Display, mechanical milk carton, cardboard and papier-mâché, figural milk carton rocks back and forth, eyes and mouth move from side to side, made for MN state-fair circuit, 1940s **500.00**
Lamp, 4" x 4" x 10", Elsie and Baby, hollow ceramic figure base, Elsie reading to baby nestled on her lap, brass socket, c1950 .... **125.00**

Felix the Cat
Figure, 1" h, dark copper-colored plastic, loop at top, 1950s **10.00**
Pinback button, 1" d, Herald and Examiner, c1930s .. **45.00**
Valentine, diecut, jointed cardboard, full color, "Purr Around If You Want To Be My Valentine" inscription, ©Pat Sullivan, c1920 .... **20.00**

Happy Hooligan
Figure, 8-1/4" h, bisque, worried expression, tin-can hat, orange, black, blue, and yellow............ **75.00**
Stickpin, 2-1/4" l, brass . **25.00**

Howdy Doody
Belt, suede, emb face .. **35.00**
Cake-decorating set, unused **40.00**
Pencil case, vinyl, red... **25.00**

Jiggs and Maggie
Pinback button, 3/4" d, *The Knoxville Sentinel*, black and white image of Jiggs, red bow tie, c1920 .... **15.00**
Salt and pepper shakers, pr, ceramic............ **48.00**

Katzenjammer Kids
Christmas card, 4-1/4" x 4-1/2", 1951, copyright King Features Syndicate....... **18.00**
Comic strip, Ovaltine ad on back............ **15.00**

Li'l Abner
Bank, Schmoo, blue plastic **50.00**
Pinback button, 13/16", Li'l Abner, *Saturday Daily News*, black litho, cream ground, newspaper name in red **20.00**
Little Annie Rooney, pinback button, 1-1/4" d, comic-strip contest button, serial-number type, c1930 .... **25.00**

Little Orphan Annie
Big Little Book, *Little Orphan Annie Secret of the Well*, No. 1417............ **85.00**
Book, *Little Orphan Annie and the Gila Monster Gang*, Harold Gray, Whitman Publishing, © 1944, licensed by Famous Artists Syndicate, 248 pgs, 5" x 8"............ **12.00**
Toothbrush holder, 4" h, bisque, back inscribed "Orphan Annie & Sandy, © F.A.S., #1565," bottom stamped "Japan," some wear to paint............ **165.00**

Orphan Annie, left: Ovaltine shaker, Beetleware, original shaker top, original decals, **$115**; right: mug, Ovaltine advertising, wear to original decal, **$65**.

Mr. Peanut
Ashtray, Golden Jubilee, 50th Anniversary, gold-plated metal, figural, orig attached booklet, orig box, 5" h, 5-3/4" h **130.00**
Bank, 8-1/4" h, green... **20.00**
Booklet, *Mr. Peanuts Guide to Tennis*, 6" x 9", ©1960, 24 illus pgs **20.00**
Mug, 3-3/4" h, green, c1960 .... **18.00**
Paint book, *Planter's Paint Book No. 2*, 7-1/4" x 10-1/2", © 1929, 32 pgs............ **35.00**
Toy, trailer truck, red cab, yellow and blue plastic trailer, 5-1/2" l............ **275.00**

Mutt & Jeff
Bank, 4-7/8" h, cast iron, orig paint............ **125.00**

Book, *The Mutt & Jeff Cartoon Book*, Bud Fisher, black and white illus by author, Ball Pub. Co., 1911 .... **100.00**
Doll, 6-1/2" h and 8" h, composition character heads, molded and painted features, molded mustaches, metal ball jointed body, composition hands, orig felt jackets, vests, ties, and pants, molded hat, Bucherer, price for pr . **500.00**

Popeye
Cereal bowl, plastic, white ground, red, blue, and black illus of Popeye and Olive Oyl **5.00**
Charm, 1" h, bright copper-luster plastic figure of Olive Oyl, 1930s **10.00**
Figure, 14" h, chalkware **150.00**
Mug, 4" h, Olive Oyl, figural **20.00**

Reddy Kilowatt
Hot pad, 6" d, laminated heat-resistant cardboard, textured top surface with art and verse inscription, "My name is Reddy Kilowatt-I keep things cold. I make things hot. I'm your cheap electric servant. Always ready on the spot," c1940............ **40.00**
Pinback button, "Please Don't Litter," blue and white, 1950s **15.00**
Stickpin, red enamel and silvered-metal miniature diecut figure, c1950 ..... **30.00**
Speedy Alka Seltzer, patch, colorful stitched image of smiling Speedy waving his wand, pixie dust accent, 1960s............ **35.00**

Yellow Kid
Cap bomb, 1-1/2" h, cast iron, c1898............ **185.00**
Pinback button, #2, 1894, orig paper label **60.00**

Personality

Amos and Andy
Photograph, framed black and white facsimile signed photograph and brochure **95.00**
Toy, Andy, litho tin wind-up, yellow derby, light blue jacket, red and tan striped trousers, Louis Marx & Co. **320.00**

Autry, Gene

Badge, 1-1/4" d, Gene Autry Official Club Badge, black and white, bright orange top rim, c1940 .... **50.00**

Child's book, *Gene Autry Makes a New Friend,* Elizabeth Beecher, color illus by Richard Case, Whitman Tell A Tale, 1952 .... **12.00**

Watch, orig band **145.00**

Ball, Lucille

Magazine, *Life,* April 6, 1953, five-pg article, full-color cover of Lucy, Desi Arnaz, Desi IV, and Lucy Desiree **30.00**

Movie-lobby card, 11" x 14", full color, 1949 Columbia Picture "Miss Grant Takes Richmond" **40.00**

Cassidy, Hopalong

Coloring book, 1950, large size **30.00**

Tablet, 8" x 10", color-photo cov, facsimile signature, unused **24.00**

Wallet, leather, metal fringe, multicolored cover, made by Top Secret **35.00**

Chaplin, Charlie

Candy container, 3-3/4" h, glass, Charlie and barrel, small chip **100.00**

Magazine, *Life,* April 1, 1966, Chaplin and Sophia Loren **10.00**

Dionne Quintuplets, booklet, *All Aboard for Shut-Eye Town,* Dr. Dafoe and Quints on cover, **$25**.

Photo courtesy of Sky Hawk Auctions.

Dionne Quintuplets

Advertisement, 5" x 7", Quintuplet Bread, Schultz Baking Co., diecut cardboard, loaf of bread, brown crust, bright red and blue letters, named silhouette portraits, text on reverse **70.00**

Booklet, *All Aboard for Shut-Eye Time,* Dr. Dafoe and Quints on cover **25.00**

Doll, 14" h, Dr. Dafoe, composition, painted blue eyes, single stroke brows, closed smiling mouth, gray mohair wig, jointed at shoulders and hips, orig two-pc doctor's uniform, hat, socks, and shoes, marked "Madame Alexander New York" on clothing tag, doll unmarked **525.00**

Fan, 8-1/4" x 8-3/4", diecut cardboard, titled, "Sweethearts of the World," full-color-tinted portraits, light-blue ground, ©1936, funeral director name on reverse **35.00**

Garland, Judy

Pinback button, 1" h, "Judy Garland Doll," black and white photo, used on c1930 Ideal doll, name appears on curl, also "Metro-Goldwyn-Mayer Star" in tiny letters **125.00**

Sheet music, "On the Atchison, Topeka, and the Sante Fe," 1945 MGM movie, "The Harvey Girls," sepia photo, purple, light pink, and brown cov **35.00**

Gleason, Jackie

Magazine, *TV Guide,* May 21, 1955, Philadelphia edition, three-pg article on the Honeymooners **18.00**

Pinback button, 1-5/8" d, "Jackie Gleason Fan Club/ And Awa-a-ay We Go!," blue on cream litho, checkered suit, 1950s **65.00**

Laurel & Hardy, movie poster, When Comedy Was King, 20th C Fox, Laurel and Hardy in center, **$25.**

Laurel & Hardy

Movie poster, When Comedy Was King, 20th C Fox, Laurel and Hardy in center **25.00**

Salt and pepper shakers, pr **175.00**

Lone Ranger

Coloring book, unused . **50.00**

Game board, target bull's eye **185.00**

Ring, Cheerios premium, saddle type, filmstrip missing **225.00**

Marx, Groucho, book, *Groucho and Me, Groucho Marx,* Bernard Geis, 1959, 22 photos **10.00**

Mix, Tom

Big Little Book, Whitman, *Tom Mix and The Stranger from the Sea,* Pete Daryll, 1936, #1183 .... **75.00**

Premium, Tom Mix Ralston Telegraph Set, 1940 ..... **95.00**

Ring, magnet, 1946.... **145.00**

Scarf, Tom Mix Ralston Straight Shooters **195.00**

Our Gang, Little Rascals, display sign, 23-1/4" x 32", heavy diecut cardboard, Felin's Meat Products, sign and individual 1-1/4" x 3" named figures, c1920 .... **4,700.00**

Rogers, Roy

Bank, Roy on Trigger, porcelain, sgd "Roy Rogers" and "Trigger" **200.00**

Charm, 1" h, blue plastic frame, black and white glossy paper photo.................. **35.00**

Ring, litho tin, Post's Raisin Bran premium, Dale Evans, ©1942.......................... **45.00**

Watch, Roy and Dale.. **120.00**

Shirley Temple, Sing with Shirley Temple, song album, **$15.**

Shirley Temple, book, *The Shirley Temple Edition of Susannah of the Mounties,* by Muriel Denison, Random House, New York, 1936, reprint orange cover with red and black lettering on front and end cover, original dust jacket, $20.

Temple, Shirley

Child's book, *The Shirley Temple Edition of Susannah of the Mounties,* by Muriel Denison, Random House, New York, 1936, reprint orange cover with red and black lettering on front and end cover, orig dust jacket
.... **20.00**
Doll, 18" h, composition, hazel sleep eyes, open mouth, orig mohair wig in orig set, jointed at shoulders and hips, dressed in tagged pajamas from Poor Little Rich Girl, orig shoes, mkd "Shirley Temple, Ideal, N & T Co." **575.00**
Figure, 6-1/2" h, salt-glazed
.... **85.00**
Handkerchief, Little Colonel, boxed set of three **200.00**
Magazine tear sheet, Lane Hope Chests adv, 1945 .. **8.00**
Pinback button, 1-1/4" d, brown-tone photo, light-pink rim, Ideal Dolls, 1930s .. **75.00**

Three Stooges

Autograph, letter, 4-1/2" x 5-1/2" mailing envelope, two folded 6" x 8" sheets of "Three Stooges" letterhead, personally inked response to fan, sgd "Moe Howard," March 10, 1964 Los Angeles postmark **200.00**
Badge, 4" d, cello, black and white upper face image of Curly-Joe on purple background, Clark Oil employee type **20.00**

Photo, 4" x 5" glossy black and white, facsimile signatures of Curly-Joe, Larry, and Moe, plus personal inscription in blue ink by Moe
.... **95.00**

Wayne, John

Magazine, *Life,* Jan. 29, 1972
.... **25.00**
Magazine tear sheet, 10" x 13", "Back to Bataan," black and white, 1945 .... **15.00**
Movie poster, "McLintock," 1963 .... **250.00**

CHILDREN'S BOOKS

History: Because there is a bit of the child in all of us, collectors always have been attracted to children's books. In the 19th century, books were popular gifts for children, with many of the children's classics written and published during this time. These books were treasured and often kept throughout a lifetime.

Developments in printing made it possible to include more attractive black and white illustrations and color plates. The work of artists and illustrators has added value beyond the text itself.

Additional Listings: See *Warman's Americana & Collectibles.*

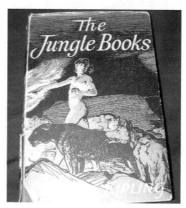

The Jungle Books, R Kipling, original orange and black dust jacket, wear, tears, **$45**.

A Child's Garden of Verses, illus by Myrtle Sheldon, Donahue Pub, 1916, 1st ed............. **25.00**

A Christmas Carol, Charles Dickens, Garden City Pub, ©1938, color and black and white illus by Everett Shinn, red cover, fancy gold trim **28.00**
Adventures of Tom Sawyer, Mark Twain, American Pub. Co., Hartford, CT, 1899, blue and gold cover **45.00**
Alice's Adventures in Wonderland in Words of One Syllable, Saalfield, ©1908, illus by John Tenniel, dj **18.00**
American Girl Beauty Book, Bobbs-Merrill, NY, 1945, illus
.... **9.00**
And To Think That I Saw It On Mulberry Street, Dr. Suess, Vanguard Pub., ©1937, 3rd printing **15.00**
An Old Fashioned Girl, Louisa M. Alcott, Robert Bros. Pub, 1870, 1st ed **35.00**
Bobbsey Twins At The County Fair, The, Grossett & Dunlap, 1922, 1st ed., dj **28.00**
Book of the Camp Fire Girls, Rev. Ed., 1954, paperback **6.00**
Boys Story of Lindbergh, The Lone Eagle, The, Richard Beamish, 1928, John C. Winston Co., dj **20.00**
Bunny Rabbit Concert, Lawrence Welk, illus Carol Bryan, Youth Pub. Sat Evening Post, 2nd printing, 1978 ..... **8.00**
By the Shores of Silver Lake, Laura Ingallis Wilder, illus Garth Williams, Harper Collins, 1953, dj
.... **10.00**
Christmas Eve on Lonesome and Other Stories, John Fox, Jr., Grosset & Dunlap, 1904 ... **15.00**
Eric & Sally and Other Stories, Johanna Spyrl, Grosset & Dunlap, 1932, 342 pgs **7.00**
Freckles, Grossett & Dunlap, 1904, illus by E. Stetson Crawford **8.00**
Girl Scout Handbook, Rev. Ed., 1930 .... **7.00**
Hardy Boys, Missing Chums, Franklin Dixon, illus by Walter Rogers, Grossett & Dunlap, 1928, 1st ed. **25.00**
Helen's Babies, John Habberton, J. H. Sears & Co., colorful illus by Christopher Rule **10.00**
How the Grinch Stole Christmas, Dr. Suess, Random House, ©1957, Grinch on red and green cover **25.00**

The Land of Long Ago, A Novel Picture Book For Children, **$125.**

Little Britches, Father and I Were Ranchers, Ralph Moody, illus Edward Shenton, Peoples Book Club, Chicago, 1950 .... **8.00**
Lullaby Land, Eugene Field, Scribner, 1897, 1st ed **35.00**
Magic Garden, The, Grossett & Dunlap, 1927, green cover **20.00**
Marcella Stories, Johnny Gruelle, M. A. Donohue Co., 1930s, color and black and white illus, dj **95.00**
Mary Frances Garden Book, Adventures Among the Garden People, The, Jane Fryer, illus by Wm Zivimer, John C. Winston, 1916, 7" x 9", 378 pgs **12.50**
Metropolitan Mother Goose, Elizabeth Watson, Metropolitan Insurance Co. promo, 1930s, 20 pgs **18.00**

Mother Goose, **$35.**

Mother Goose and Nursery Rhymes, Anthemum Pub., colored wood engravings by Philip Reed, 1963, 1st ed, Mother Goose and gander on orange cover **35.00**
Mother Goose or The Old Nursery Rhymes, Warne, c1900, 44 rhymes, Kate Greenaway illus, pictures on both front and back cov **45.00**

Moving Picture Boys and the Flood, The, Victor Appleton, Grossett & Dunlap, 1914, pictorial cover **15.00**
Mr. Winkle Goes to War, Theodore Pratt, 1943, Duell, Sloan & Pearce, 1st ed, dj .. **8.00**
Mrs. Appleyard's Year, Louise Andrews Kent, Hough. Mifflin, 1941, 195 pgs, rooster on cover **9.50**
Mrs. Wiggs of the Cabbage Patch, Alice Hegan Rice, Appleton Century Co., 1941, hard bound, lady in red dress on cover **10.00**

Peeps Into Fairy Land, Ernest Nigler, London, E. P. Dutton, New York, printed in Bavaria, **$140.**

My Very Own Fairy Stories, Johnny Grulle, P. F. Volland Co., 1917, 30th ed, color illus **65.00**
Mystery Hunters on Special Detail, #4, The, Capwell Wyckoff, Saalfield, 1936 .... **12.00**
Nancy Drew, The Password to Larkspur Lane, illus by Russell Tandy, Grossett & Dunlap, 1933, some fading to blue cover **65.00**
Nelly's Silver Mine, Helen Hunt Jackson, 1924, Little Brown & Co., illus by Harriet Richards and Henry Pitz, dj **20.00**

Book, *The Purple Prince of Oz,* by Ruth Plumly Thompson, Founded on and Continuing The Famous Oz Stories by Frank L. Baum, Illus by Jno. R. Neill, **$300.**

Now We Are Six, A. A. Milne, Dutton, 1927, 1st printing . **17.50**
Peter Rabbit and the Little Boy, Linda Almond, Platt & Munk, 1935 .... **15.00**
Raggedy Ann's Wishing Pebble, Johnny Gruelle, M. A. Donohue Co., 1930s, color and black and white illus, dj **85.00**
Riley's Songs O'Cheer, James Whitcomb, Bobbs Merrill Pub, 1905, six color illus, black and white illus by Will Vawter ... **35.00**
Six White Horses, Candy Geer, illus Leslie Bennet, M & W Quill Pub, 1964, 2nd printing **6.00**
Smoky The Cow Horse, Will James, Aladdin Books **8.00**

The 3 Little Kittens, McLoughlin Bros, copyright 1890, New York, linen, wear, **$20.**

Swiss Family Robinson, The, Johann Wyss, Illus by Lynd Ward, Grosset & Dunlap, 1949, Junior Library edition **8.00**
Tarzan and City of the Gold, Edgar Rice Burroughs, Whitman, 1952, dj **15.00**
The Cat In The Hat Comes Back, Dr. Suess, Random House, 1958, dj **185.00**
The New Our Friends, Dick and Jane, Scott Foresman, 1951 .... **38.00**
The Night Before Christmas, A Little Golden Book, Simon Schuster, 1946, illus Cornelius DeWitt **45.00**
Tom Sawyer Detective, Mark Twain, 1924, Grosset & Dunlap **15.00**
Uncle Remus His Songs and Sayings, Joel Chandler Harris, 112 illus by A. B. Frost, D. Appleton & Co., 1916 ...... **75.00**
Uncle Wiggily and the Runaway Cheese, Howard R. Garis, color illus by A. Watson, Platt & Munk, 1977, oversize **12.50**

When We Were Very Young, A. A. Milne, Dutton, 1924, 3rd printing **17.50**

CHILDRENS FEEDING DISHES

History: Unlike toy dishes meant for play, children's feeding dishes are the items actually used in the feeding of a child. Their colorful designs of animals, nursery rhymes, and children's activities are meant to appeal to the child and make meal times fun. Many plates have a unit to hold hot water, thus keeping the food warm.

Although glass and porcelain examples from the late 19th and early 20th centuries are most popular, collectors are beginning to seek some of the plastic examples from the 1920s to 1940s, especially those with Disney designs on them.

ABC plate

Aesop's Fables the Leopard and the Fox, black transfer print, pearlware, England, 19th C **175.00**
Crusoe Finding the Foot Prints, color enhanced brown transfer, pearlware, England, 19th C, minor discoloration **125.00**
Eye of the master will do no more than his hands, multicolored transfer ... **145.00**
Franklin's Provbs, (sic) black transfer print, pearlware, England, 19th C **175.00**

Old Mother Hubbard, brown transfer, polychrome enamel trim, alphabet border, marked "Tunstall," 7-1/2" d **200.00**
Take Your Time Miss Lucy, black transfer of money and cat, polychrome enamel, titled, molded hops rim, red trim, ironstone, imp "Meakin," 6" d **125.00**
Bowl, Sunbonnet girls dec, pale orange band, cream colored ground, marked "Roseville," slight wear, inner rim chip **200.00**
Butter pat, 3-1/4" d, "A Present For Ann," blue transfer medallion **125.00**

Buffalo Pottery, Grace Drayton children, worn image, chip on inner rim, $20.

Cereal set, Nursery Rhyme, amber, divided plate, Humpty Dumpty on mug and bowl, Tiara **125.00**
Creamer, three yellow ducks, yellow band with black outline, cream-colored ground, marked "R12" **125.00**
Cup, Raggedy Ann, Johnny Gruelle, 1941, Crooksville China **65.00**

Cup plate, 4-5/8" d, "Constant dropping wears away stones and little strokes fell great oaks," green transfer, polychrome enamel dec **90.00**

Feeding dish
Kiddieware, pink, Stangl **125.00**
Little Bo Peep, glass, divided, white, red trim **65.00**
Nursery Rhyme, green enamelware, marked "Made in Germany"................. **40.00**
Raggedy Ann, Johnny Gruelle, 1941, Crooksville China, 8-3/4" d.............. **85.00**
Sunbonnet babies, sweeping, 7-1/4" d **400.00**

Mug
1-7/8" h, pearlware, black transfer, girl jumping rope, England, early 19th C. **275.00**
2-3/8" h, pearlware, polychrome dec, "Leap Frog," England, early 19th C. **250.00**
2-3/8" h, pearlware, polychrome dec, "Elizabeth," scrolled foliate embellishments, England, early 19th C **275.00**
2-1/2" h, pearlware, black transfer dec, Dr. Franklin's Maxim's on Industry, England, early 19th C **345.00**
2-1/2" h, pearlware, black transfer dec, "G is for Giles with weary strides…" with farmer and work horse, int. rim alphabet border, England, early 19th C **315.00**
2-1/2" h, pearlware, black transfer dec, "Perish Slavery Prosper Freedom, England," early 19th C **295.00**
2-1/2" h, pearlware, blue transfer dec, "A Present for Charles," vine borders, England, early 19th C. **325.00**
2-1/2" h, pearlware, blue transfer dec, "A Pres-ent for Samuel," recumbent cow, England, early 19th C. **275.00**
2-1/2" h, pearlware, reddish-brown dec, "For loving a book," England, early 19th C **300.00**
2-5/8" h, pearlware, blue transfer dec of couple in boat in scene with deer, England, early 19th C, minor rim chip **195.00**
2-5/8" h, pearlware, brown transfer motto "Better be alone than in bad Company," England, early 19th C .. **265.00**

Assortment of children's feeding dishes, back shelf with mugs, most English, ranging in price from **$95** upward; feeding dishes in front with a variety of nursery rhymes, prices range from **$175** upward.

2-5/8" h, pearlware, dark red dec, poem for December, child with dog and cat pulling cart full of toys, England, early 19th C **295.00**
2-5/8" h, pearlware, green and black transfer dec, "Dr. Franklin's Poor Richard Illustrated," on industry, England, early 19th C . **285.00**
2-5/8" h, pearlware, green transfer dec, "The Orchard," England, early 19th C.. **235.00**
2-7/8" h, pearlware, maroon transfer, "Mr. Winkle's Horsemanship," England, early 19th C **295.00**

Baby plate, rolled rim, decal decoration, verse "Baby Bunting Runs Away, And joins the little pigs at play," wear to gold trim on border, marked "D. E. McNichol, East Liverpool, O, 1218," **$95**.

Plate

6" d, Buster Brown, 1910, mint center image **135.00**
8" d, nursery rhymes, glass, green **40.00**
8" d, "Where Are You Going My Pretty Maid, See Saw Margery Daw," three parts, transparent-green Depression-era glass ... **45.00**

CHILDREN'S NURSERY ITEMS

History: The nursery is a place where children live in a miniature world. Things come in two sizes: Child scale designates items actually used for the care, housing, and feeding of the child; toy or doll scale denotes items used by the child in play and for creating a fantasy environment which copies that of an adult or his own.

Cheap labor and building costs during the Victorian era encouraged the popularity of the nursery. Most collectors focus on items from 1880 to 1930.

Additional Listings: Children's Books, Children's Feeding Dishes, Children's Toy Dishes, Dolls, Games, Miniatures, and Toys.

Child's rocker, original paint decoration, **$200**

Photo courtesy of Dotta Auction Co., Inc.

Blocks, boxed set, ABCs, animals, litho of Noah and ark on cov, Victorian **185.00**
Boat, play, ice, 24" l, wood with iron runners, c1900 .... **460.00**
Bucket, 5-1/2" d, 4-1/4" h, wooden-stave construction, orig yellow paint, blue-painted tin bands, stenciled stars, chick, and eagle, wood and wire bale handle, int. has some crayon marks, bottom band replaced **660.00**
Carriage, 53" l, 37" h, wicker, brown and white hide-covered horse with glass eyes, leather tack, hair mane, horse-hair tail, two-wheeled vehicle pushed by handle, horse sets between shafts on three-wheeled frame, wire wheels with rubber tread, late 19th/early 20th C, some damage to hide, wear to paint
.... **1,380.00**

Chair

6" h, 24" h back, ladder-back, arms, leather seat, turned finials and legs, old blue-green paint **415.00**
8-1/2" h seat, 21-1/2" h back, attributed to New England, late 17th C, turned ash, two turned stiles flanking two horizontal and two vertical spindles with turned arms, projecting handholds continuing to slightly tapering legs with stretchers, old refinish, imperfections **2,820.00**
9-5/8" h seat, 20-1/8" h back, America, 19th C, pine, shaped crest rail over back splat with keyhole cut-out, shaped seat, splayed ring-turned legs, painted brown with polychrome floral dec on crest and splat, red and black striping, gilt accents, minor paint wear and cracks........................... **265.00**
Chest of drawers, child-size, Hepplewhite-style, curly maple, pine secondary wood, banded inlay around two-board top and base, four graduated dovetailed drawers with dark line inlay, and fans at corners, well-scalloped base, French feet, diamond-shaped escutcheons, emb brasses with cornucopia designs, 27" w, 17" d, 28" h **1,320.00**
Crib, 38-3/4" d, 69-1/2" h, orig 48" l rails, refinished bird, tapered high posts with incised line beading along edges, urn-shaped supports on all sides, narrow vertical slats added for stability **220.00**

Four baby feeding plates, all English, c1900-1910; left to right: center train motif, titled "Puff-Puff," **$325**; Shelley, center train motif, titled "Puff-Puff-Puff," **$350**; Baby's Plate, Carlton Ware, center train motif, titled "Puff-Puff-Puff," c1910, **$395**; Baby's Plate, English hunt scene, **$375**.

Cradle roll certificate, framed, partially printed, filled in, dated 1917, framed, some fading, **$35.**

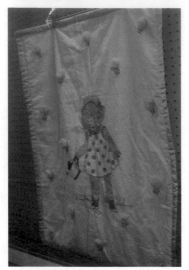

Child's coverlet, center with printed blond girl in blue and white polka dot dress, watering can in one hand, chenille-type pink flowers with yellow centers, printed green stems and leaves, pink binding and backing, **$95.**

Crib quilt, 40" x 41", central diamond, needlework heart and foliate black bound edges, Amish, Lancaster County, PA **4,675.00**

Desk, 22-3/4" w, 14-1/4" d, 27" h, Queen Anne, southeastern New England, 18th C, cherry and poplar, slant lid, int. with four compartments over drawers, sliding panel revealing well, case with single thumb molded drawers, bracket feet, replaced brasses, old refinish, restorations.... **4,120.00**

Doll bed, 28-5/8" l, 16" w, 15-3/4" h, Arts & Crafts, oak, rect headboard with two cartoon-like images of baby dolls, footboard with two sq form cut-outs, imperfections **230.00**

Doll carriage
30" l, 28" h, Heywood Wakefield, woven wicker, natural finish, diamond patternweave, steel wheels, rubber tires, clamshell hood, maker's label on underside, early 20th C **150.00**
30" l, 28" h, natural wicker wooden spoked wheels, original button-upholstered back, red cotton parasol on wire hook, late 19th C . **230.00**
32" l, 28" h, American, fringed top surrey, original dark green paint, gold stenciling, wooden wheels, platform top, fringe replaced, c1870 .... **350.00**

Doll cradle, 15" l, 8-1/4" w, 13" h, pine, sq and "T" head nails, footboard and part of hood are dovetailed, scrolled end rockers, layers of red paint, age cracks, wear, one rocker glued ... **150.00**

Doll crib, 16-1/2" l, 11-1/2" d, 11" h, poplar, orig reddish-brown painted dec, shaped head and footboards, rockers, turned posts with ball finials, edge wear, finial chips **320.00**

Doll crib quilt, embroidered cross-stitch nursery motif, yellow binding and backing, hand quilted, **$65.**

Game, ring toss, 16" d, green painted wood backplate set with small hooks, each with gold transfer printed number, four leather tossing rings, England, first quarter 20th C **175.00**

High chair, 22" h seat, 33" h back, pillow-back crest rail, rect splat flanked by raked stiles, scrolled arms, turned supports, rush seat, turned legs joined by stretchers, old beige paint, floral polychrome dec **1,000.00**

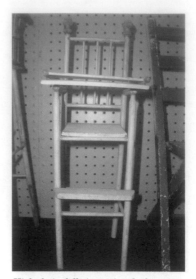

High chair, doll size, painted white, play wear, **$25.**

Horse, pull toy, 16-1/2" l, 6" w, 16" h, carved wood, painted white ground, black sponge highlights, horse hair mane and tail, applied saddle, bridle, and ears, metal wheel base, mid-1800s... **2,860.00**

Needlework picture, silk threads and watercolor on silk, titled "The Mother's Hope," young girl in landscape setting, MA, early 19th C, framed in oval format, minor scattered staining, small areas of fabric loss, replaced tablet............. **1,725.00**

Noah's Ark, 18-1/2" l, 5" d, 11-1/2" h, painted red, blue, orange, white, and green wood, roof and one side of base open to inner compartments, six carved and painted animals, Noah, two ladies, one glued leg, some edge wear............. **750.00**

Potty chair, 22" h, Windsor, attributed to New England, orig yellow paint, green and black striping, stenciled front on crest, potty chair hole in seat covered in old brown, green, and white chintz with large bird and foliage design, bamboo turnings, 10" h seat, 22" h back **250.00**

Push cart, 12" l, 5-1/4" h, red and blue, gold stenciled dec, sgd "Wm F. Goodwin's Patents, Jan. 22, 1867 & Aug. 25, 1868," black painted wheels, handles and undercarriage, corner joints need resoldering............ **250.00**

Lawn chair, red, yellow, green, gray, and white stripes, wood frame, **$55**; print of boy in red suit, **$6**; Ready Cut Village, original contents, **$28**.

Pull-toy, horse, leather hide, Germany, 12" h, **$200**.
Photo courtesy of Wiederseim Associates, Inc.

Paint set, Alice in Wonderland, tin litho box, some original paints, marked "Made in England." **$25**.

Rattle, 4" l, sterling silver, pink coral handle below knopped body with emb dec, five silver bells, whistle, maker's mark "E.S.B.," Birmingham, England, 19th C **475.00**

Rocking chair

7-3/4" h seat, 24" h back, Shaker, production, Mt. Lebanon, New York, 1880-1930, incised "O" with decal on rocker, old varnished surface, replaced tape seat, minor imperfections . **3,300.00**

8" h seat, 19" h back, plank seat, spindle back, salmon and brown paint, cheese-cutter rockers.............. **200.00**

Rocking horse, 45" l, 12" w, 26" h, wooden, mortised and dovetailed, tacked leather seat, mustard paint, arched, gouged-carved tail, Adams County, PA, use wear **6,380.00**

Schoolboy sketchbook, 6-1/4" x 7-3/4", Thomas Stapler, attributed to New England, 1803, booklet with pen and ink inscription on cover reading "Thomas Stapler's Book 1803," six pages with pen and ink and watercolor pictures of birds, one titled "The Gull," one page with perspective drawing of a Federal-style building, one page depicting a mathematical problem, toning, light stains **600.00**

Sled, 37" l, 12-1/4" w, 20" h, carved oak and wrought iron, carved horse head, traces of polychrome dec, PA, 19th C **3,110.00**

Rocking horse, carved and painted, base inscribed "E.F. Eggleston & Co. of 3 Fulton St. N.Y.," original red, blue and pumpkin swirl decoration, 46" w, 23-3/4" h, **$1,840**.
Photo courtesy of Pook & Pook.

Sleigh, 19" l, 13-1/2" w, 18" h, high sides, wooden runners, old repaint with scrollwork and foliage, red ground, yellow line borders, blue int., edge wear **365.00**

Tricycle horse, 39" l, 22-1/2" w, 33" h, painted wood horse model, glass eyes, suede saddle, velvet saddle blanket, single front wheel, two rear wheels, chain-driven mechanism, by Jugnet, Lyon, repainted.......................... **850.00**

Wheelbarrow, painted red, hand painted scenes with American eagle and flags **2,700.00**

CHILDREN'S TOY DISHES

History: Dishes made for children often served a dual purpose—playthings and a means of learning social graces. Dish sets

came in two sizes. The first was for actual use by the child when entertaining friends. The second, a smaller size, was for use with dolls.

Children's dish sets often were made as a sideline to a major manufacturing line, either as a complement to the family service or as a way to use up the last of the day's batch of materials. The artwork of famous illustrators, such as Palmer Cox, Kate Greenaway, and Rose O'Neill, can be found on porcelain children's sets.

Akro agate, green, two doll size cups and saucers, one child size cup and saucer, creamer in back, Interior Panel, green, **$65**.

Butter dish, white milk glass, File & Fan pattern, Westmoreland, **$40**.

Akro Agate

Tea set, octagonal, large, green and white, Little American Maid, orig box, 17 pcs............................. **225.00**

Water set, Play Time, pink and blue, orig box, seven pcs **125.00**

Bohemian glass, decanter set, ruby flashed, Vintage dec, five pcs **135.00**

Candlesticks, pr, 2" h, 1-3/8" d base, hexagonal, colorless, tiny socket hole, rough pontil mark, 1850-70 .... **50.00**

China

Cheese dish, cov, hunting scene, Royal Bayreuth.. **85.00**
Chocolate pot, Model-T car with passengers **90.00**
Cup and saucer, Phoenix Bird **15.00**
Dinner set, Willow Ware, blue and white, Japanese .. **200.00**
Tea set, Children playing, cov teapot, creamer, cov sugar, six cups, saucers, and tea plates, German, Victorian **285.00**
Tureen, cov, Blue Willow, 3-1/2" w, marked "Made in China" **60.00**

Tea set, pink roses, green leaves, small blue forget-me-nots, blue rim bands, white ground, teapot, creamer, covered sugar, three plates, one cup and saucer, marked "Made in Japan," **$45**.

Decanter, blown molded glass 2-3/4" h, colorless, ringed type III base, rough pontil mark, no stopper, Boston & Sandwich Glass Co., 1825-35 .... **220.00**
5" h, colorless, rayed and ringed type I base, rough pontil mark, pressed sunburst stopper, Boston & Sandwich Glass Co., 1825-40, quarter pint **450.00**

Depression glass, 14-pc set Cherry Blossom, pink . **390.00**

Tea set, pink roses, red and blue flowers, green leaves, gold filigree border, white ground, teapot, creamer, sugar (lid missing), six cups and saucers, six plates, marked "Japan," **$85**.

Laurel, McKee, red trim **355.00**
Moderntone, turquoise, gold **210.00**
Flat iron, 7/8" h, 1-5/8" l, light amethyst, Boston & Sandwich Glass Co., 1850-70, tip polished **150.00**

Tea set, blue, orange, and red flowers, green leaves, pale yellow rim border, white ground, creamer and covered sugar, six cups and saucers, ring handles, unknown maker, wear to enameled decoration, **$65**.

Plate

2-1/4" d, Lacy Diamond and Scroll with Concentric Rings, amethyst, 49 even scallop rim, rope table ring, Boston & Sandwich Glass Co., 1835-50, loss to one scallop **440.00**
2-5/8" d, Lacy Scroll and Diamond Point, colorless, plain rim, American or possibly Continental, rim spall, minor roughness . **25.00**

Tea set, original box, white ground, multicolored floral decoration, service for six, Japan, **$90**.

Tea set, pink Sunderland luster, teapot, lidded sugar, creamer, three cups, three saucers, handle-less cup and saucer, **$350**.
Photo courtesy of Joy Luke.

Tea set, partial, porcelain, Buster Brown and girl having tea decoration, mug and two plates shown from 16-piece set, wear, some damage, **$395**.
Photo courtesy of Joy Luke Auctions.

Tumbler

1-5/8" h, 1-1/2" d, Nine-Panel, canary, slightly rough pontil mark, Boston & Sandwich Glass Co., 1845-70 ..... **100.00**
1-5/8" h, 1-1/2" d, Nine-Panel, deep translucent starch blue, slightly rough pontil mark, Boston & Sandwich Glass Co., 1845-70 .... **110.00**
1-7/8" h, 1-5/8" d, Lacy Pointed Oval, brilliant teal, ten scallop base rayed underneath, faint pontil mark, Boston & Sandwich Glass Co., 1835-50 .... **525.00**

CHINTZ CHINA

History: Chintz china has been produced since the 17th century. The brightly colored exotic patterns produced on fabric imported from India to England were then recreated on ceramics. Early chintz patterns were hand painted and featured large flowers, fantastical birds, and widely spaced patterns. The advent of transfer printing resulted in the development of chintz dishes, which could be produced cheaply enough to sell to the masses. By the 1830s, a number of Staffordshire potteries were producing chintzware for everyday use. These early patterns are now starting to attract the interest of some chintz collectors.

Collectors typically want the patterns dating from roughly 1920 until the 1950s although some of the earlier un-named Royal Winton patterns are starting to become popular with longtime collectors. In 1920, A.G. Richardson "Crown Ducal" produced a range of all-over-transfer chintz patterns that proved to be very popular In North America, particularly the East Coast. Florida was the most popular of the Crown Ducal patterns in North America for collectors, but Pink Chintz and Peony have become increasingly popular.

From the late 1920s until the mid-1950s, Royal Winton produced more than 80 chintz patterns. In some cases, the background color was varied and the name changed: Hazel, Spring, and Welbeck is the same pattern in different colorways. After World War II, Royal Winton created more than 15 new patterns, many of which were more modern looking with large flowers and rich dark burgundy, blue, or black backgrounds—patterns such as May Festival, Spring Glory, and Peony. These patterns have not been as popular with collectors as 1930s patterns, although other 1950s patterns such as Florence and Stratford have become almost as popular as Julia and Welbeck.

Some of the more widely spaced patterns, like Victorian Rose and Cotswold, are now attracting collectors.

The 1930s were hard times in the potteries and factories struggled to survive. They copied any successful patterns from any other factories. James Kent Ltd. produced chintzes such as DuBarry, Apple Blossom, and Rosalynde. The most popular pattern for collectors is the white Hydrangea, although Apple Blossom seems to be more and more sought after. Elijah Cotton "Lord Nelson" was another factory that produced large amounts of chintz. The workers at Elijah Cotton were never as skilled as the Grimwades' workers, and usually the handles and spouts of teapots and coffeepots were left undecorated. Collectors love the Nelson Ware stacking teapots, especially in Black Beauty and Green Tulip.

Although a number of factories produced bone china after World War II, only Shelley Pottery seems to be highly desired by today's collector.

By the late 1950s, young brides didn't want the dishes of their mothers and grandmothers, but preferred the clean lines of modern Scandinavian furniture and dishes. Chintz gradually died out by the early 1960s, and it was not until the 1990s that collectors began to search for the dishes their mothers had scorned.

Reproduction Alert: Both Royal Winton and James Kent reproduced some of their more popular patterns. Royal Winton is reproducing Welbeck, Florence, Summertime, and Julia; in 1999 it added Joyce-Lynn, Marion, Majestic, Royalty, and Richmond, Old Cottage Chintz, and Stratford. The company added several new chintz patterns such as Blue Cottage and Christmas Chintz. James Kent reproduced Du Barry, Hydrangea, and Rosalynde, as well as creating several new colorways of old patterns. James Kent has discontinued the production of chintz ware. Elijah Cotton backstamp was purchased

and as well as reproducing Rosetime chintz the factory has issued a number of new chintzes with the new backstamp. Wade recently produced three chintz patterns—Butterfly, Thistle, and Sweet Pea. Two's Company and Godinger have also copied some of the Royal Winton patterns. Prices for vintage chintz seem to be rising again as new collectors have been attracted to the market but they are still well below the very high prices of the late 1990s. Inexperienced collectors often pay high prices for brand new pieces so check backstamps carefully.

Warning: Before you buy chintz, ask whether it is new or vintage. Ask to see a photograph of the backstamps if not examining the piece in person. The "1995" on the RW backstamp refers to the year the company was bought, and not the year the chintz was made. Compare old and new backstamps on www.chintz.net.com or in Susan Scott's *Charlton Standard Catalogue of Chintz*, 3rd edition, *New Chintz Section*.

Note: A newsletter devoted to Chintz is available, *Crazed Collector*, P.O. Box 2635, Dublin, CA94500. CrazedCollctr@aol.com, www.crazedcollector.net. For those who prefer on-line information, there is a free Chintz chat group: chintz-subscribe@yahoogroups.com.

Adviser: Susan Scott.

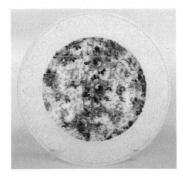

James Kent Ltd., Rochelle Ware, plate, luncheon, octagonal, Fenton, England, **$50.**

Elijah Cotton "Lord Nelson"

Bud vase, 5" h, Marina pattern
.... **65.00**
Creamer and sugar, Briar Rose
pattern **75.00**
Cup and saucer, Rosetime
.... **50.00**
Jug, 6" h, Bute shape, Pansy
pattern............................ **150.00**
Plate, 8", Briar Rose pattern
.... **50.00**
Sauce boat, undertray, Country
Lane pattern **95.00**
Teapot, stacking, totally
patterned, Marina **250.00**

Grimwades "Royal Winton"

Biscuit barrel, Rheims shape,
Hazel pattern **600.00**
Breakfast set, Somerset pattern
.... **700.00**
Bud vase, Royalty pattern
.... **115.00**
Candy dish, covered, Gordon
shape, Cotswold pattern. **175.00**
Cake stand, three-tier Sweet
Pea pattern **195.00**
Coffeepot, Albans shape, Julia
pattern............................ **400.00**
Cup and saucer, Chelsea
pattern............................. **75.00**

Royal Winton, bud vases, left: Floral Feast, **$125**; right: Old Cottage, **$65**.

Eggcup, footed, Bedale pattern
.... **90.00**
Hot water pot, Albans shape,
Royalty pattern................ **300.00**
Jug, 5" h, Duval shape, Majestic
pattern............................ **175.00**
Plate, 10" Ascot shape, Beeston
pattern............................ **165.00**
**Salt and pepper shakers on
tray**, Hazel pattern **115.00**
Teapot
Albans shape, Esther pattern
.... **350.00**

Stacking, Pekin pattern
.... **225.00**
Stacking, Stratford pattern
.... **875.00**
Toastrack, Stafford shape,
Summertime pattern ... **200.00**
Tray, 10" Ascot shape, June
Roses pattern **175.00**

Royal Winton, June, creamer and sugar on tray, **$225**.

Royal Winton, Evesham, stacking creamer, sugar, and teapot, **$450**.

James Kent Ltd.

Coffeepot, Granville shape, Du
Barry pattern................... **300.00**
Dish
12" l, octagonal, Milles Fleur
pattern **95.00**
12" x 8", ruffled, Chelsea Rose
pattern **75.00**
Plate
9" d, Crazy Paving pattern
.... **95.00**
10" d, Hydrangea pattern
.... **75.00**
Tray, 8" by 5", Apple Blossom
pattern.............................. **55.00**
Teapot, Square Diamond shape,
Mille Fleur pattern **200.00**
Vase, 2" h, Hydrangea pattern
.... **105.00**

A. G. Richardson "Crown Ducal"

Cake plate, 10", Peony pattern
.... **150.00**
Plate, 9" sq, Blue Chintz pattern
.... **65.00**
Sugar shaker, Primula pattern
.... **95.00**

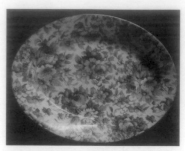

Royal Winton, Summertime, sauce dish, marked "Grimwades, England, Copyright Wright Tyndale, & Van Roden, Inc., Summertime," **$35**.

Teapot, Georgian shape,
Roseland pattern **350.00**
Teapot and trivet, Primula
pattern **295.00**
Vase
8" h, Florida pattern **145.00**
6" h, Ivory Chintz pattern
.... **125.00**

Shelley Potteries Ltd.

Biscuit barrel, Blue Pansy
pattern **235.00**
Cup and saucer
Henley shape, Countryside
pattern **165.00**
Henley shape, Summer Glory
pattern **125.00**
Miniature, Blue Pansy pattern
.... **1,860.00**
Ripon shape, Briar Rose
pattern **160.00**
Oleander shape, Rock
Garden pattern **105.00**
Pin dish, 3" round, Countryside
pattern **75.00**
Plate, 7" round, Oleander shape,
Primrose pattern **50.00**
Teapot, Henley shape, Summer
Glory pattern................... **375.00**
Toast rack, 5 bar Melody pattern
.... **115.00**

CHRISTMAS ITEMS

History: The celebration of Christmas dates back to Roman times. Several customs associated with modern Christmas celebrations are traced back to early pagan rituals.

Father Christmas, believed to have evolved in Europe in the 7th century, was a combination of the pagan god Thor, who judged and punished the good and bad, and St. Nicholas, the generous Bishop of Myra. Kris Kringle originated in Germany and was brought to America by the Germans and Swiss who settled in Pennsylvania in the late 18th century.

In 1822, Clement C. Moore wrote "A Visit From St. Nicholas" and developed the character of Santa Claus into the one we know today. Thomas Nast did a series of drawings for *Harper's Weekly* from 1863 until 1886 and further solidified the character and appearance of Santa Claus.

Reproduction Alert: Almost all holiday decorations, including Christmas, are now being skillfully reproduced. Only by knowing the source of a possible purchase, trusting the dealer, and careful observation can you be sure you are obtaining an antique.

Additional Listings: See *Warman's Americana & Collectibles* for more examples.

Wall pocket, embossed stiff paper, tan, blue, and rose, Nativity scene, text on pocket "Compliments of E. C. Fritz, Steam Bread and Cake Bakery, 19 S. Hellertown Ave., Quakertown, Pa., Post Office Address: Richland Center, Pa.," **$35.**

Advertising
Bank, molded rubber, Santa Clause holding a coin, toys in pack, marked "Christmas Club A. Corp, N.Y. 1972" **6.00**
Booklet, "When All The World Is Kin," 5" x 4", collection of Christmas stories, Christmas giveaway, Fowler, Dick, and Walker, The Boston Store, Wilkes-Barre, PA **7.00**
Catalog, Boston Store, Milwaukee, WI, 1945, 48 pgs, 8-1/2" x 11", "For An American Christmas" **20.00**

Display, 16-3/4" x 32", Santa in sleight with two reindeer, Snow King Baking Powder, diecut cardboard **675.00**

Pinback button
American Red Cross, red, green, and white celluloid, Santa carrying toy sack with Red Cross symbol, 1916 .... **60.00**
Eagle Tribune, 1991 Santa Fund, red, white, and blue portrait, two green holly sprigs **25.00**
Esso, red, white, and blue, centered Santa, 1940 ... **45.00**
Gilmore Brothers Santa, black and white portrait, fleshtone tinted face, red cap, black "Christmas Greetings-Gilmore Brothers," 1940s **60.00**
Josko Bros Santason is Here, litho, color design on yellow ground, Santa and child **60.00**
Macy's Santa Knows, red and white, 1950s **35.00**
National Tuberculosis Assn, Health for All, multicolored litho, Santa, 1936 .... **15.00**
Santa Claus at Schipper & Blocks, multicolored, Santa wearing holly leaf and berry crown, nestled by blond child, pale blue blending to white background, early 1900s **85.00**
Santa's Headquarters Namm's New Fulton Street Addition, Whitehead and I lag back paper, c1920, 1-1/4" d **125.00**
Spiegel Toyland Santa, multicolored litho, black lettering, 1930s **50.00**

The May Co. Santa, multicolored Santa surrounded by children in winter outfits, holly leaves and berries in background, red lettering "I Am At The May Co." **95.00**
Stickpin, diecut thin cello multicolored portrait of Santa on short hanger stickpin, back inscribed, "Meet Me At Bowman's," c1920 .... **48.00**
Trade card, child holding snowballs, "The White is King of all Sewing Machines, 80,000 now in use," reverse reads "J. Saltzer, Pianos, Organs, and Sewing Machines, Bloomsburg, Pa." **10.00**

Candy box
6" x 5", cardboard, pockethook style, tuck-in flap, Merry Christmas, Santa in store window with children outside, marked "USA". **15.00**
8" h, cardboard, four-sided cornucopia, Merry Christmas, Santa, sleigh, and roindoor over village rooftops, string bail, USA **35.00**
Candy pail, 2-7/8" x 2-7/8", tin litho, holiday greetings and adv on front, color graphics of children sledding and skating on back **525.00**

Children's books
A Certain Star, Pearl Buck, Herschel Levit illus, American Weekly, 1957 .... **5.50**
How Santa Filled the Christmas Stockings, Carolyn Hodman, color illus by F. W. Stecher, Stecher Litho Co., 1916, 13" x 71" **85.00**

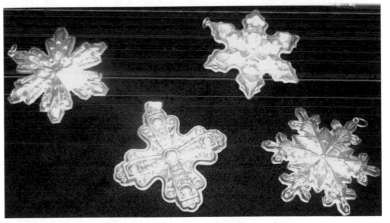

Snowflakes, Gorham, sterling silver, set of four, each different, **$100.**

Rudolph the Red-Nosed Reindeer, Robert I. May, Maxton Publishers, Inc., 1939 .... **12.00**
The Bird's Christmas Carol, Kate Douglas Wiggin, Hough Miffin, 1912, dj **7.50**
The Fireside Book of Christmas Stories, Edw Wagenknecht, Wallace Morgan illus, Bobbs Merrill 1945, 656 pgs **8.50**
The Littlest Snowman, Charles Tazewell, Grosset Dunlap, NY, 1958 .... **18.00**

Feather tree

6" h, red wooden base.. **35.00**
12" h, green wooden base **95.00**
26" h, red and green wooden base............................... **225.00**
4' h, green goose feather-wrapped branches with metal candleholders, painted white with green trim round wooden base, marked "Germany" **420.00**

Figures

Belsnickle

5-1/8" h, chalk, green-hooded coat with clear mica flecks, painted black base, feather tree missing, minor damage to base............................ **275.00**
8-3/4" h, composition, orig red, white, and black paint, gold mica flecks, green feather tree, blue pipe cleaner trim, minor wear on hood **980.00**

Father Christmas

7" h, composition, pink face, red-cloth coat, painted blue pants, black boots, mounted on mica-covered cardboard base, marked "Japan".. **90.00**
8" h, papier-mâché, hollow molded, plaster covered, white coat, black boots, sprinkled with mica..... **300.00**
Reindeer, 1" h, pot metal, marked "Germany"....... **20.00**

Santa Claus

3" h, cotton batting, red, attached to cardboard house, marked "Japan"............ **48.00**
3" l, celluloid, molded, one-piece Santa, sleigh, and reindeer **35.00**
5" h, hard plastic, Santa on green plastic skis, USA **120.00**

10" h, pressed cardboard, red hat and jacket, black boots **90.00**
Sheep, 3" h, composition body, carved wooden legs, covered with cloth or wool, glass eyes **40.00**

Christmas Card, 1951, slightly textured white paper, full-color Christmas caroling scene of Mickey, Minnie, and Donald standing in front of The Little House, two of Donald's nephews watching them while holding snowballs behind their backs, card opens to reveal two-panel scene of Susie the Little Blue Coupe pulling wheeled wagons containing many Disney characters such as Seven Dwarfs, Gus and Jaq, Bambi, Pinocchio, etc., each wagon has monthly calendar for 1952, back cover with illustrations of Robin Hood and Peter Pan, title "Coming Soon," 7" x 8", **$75**.

Photo courtesy of Hake's Americana & Collectibles.

Greeting cards

1892, "Sincere Good Wishes," purple pansy with green leaves, greeting inside, Raphael Tuck & Sons ... **12.00**
1910, "Loving Greetings," flat card, two girls pictured hanging garland, marked "Germany" **10.00**
1933, "Merry Christmas," series of six envelopes, decreasing in size, small card in last envelope, American Greeting Publishers, Cleveland, USA **12.00**

House, cardboard
2" x 2", mica covered, wire loop on top, marked "Czechoslovakia" **10.00**
4" x 5", house and fence, sponge trees, marked "USA" **12.00**

Lantern, 8" h, four sided, peaked top, wire bail, metal candleholder in base, black cardboard, colored tissue paper scenes, 1940s................... **25.00**

Magazine, *St. Nicholas*, bound edition of 1915 and 1916, color covers, ads, illus, story **15.00**

Carolers on sled, original boxes, marked "Japan," lot of three, **$30**.

Ornaments

Angel, 4" h, wax over composition, human-hair wig, spun-glass wings, cloth dress, Germany............ **60.00**
Ball, 2" d, silvered glass, any color................................ **4.00**
Beads, 72" l, glass, half-inch multicolored beads, paper label marked "Japan"..... **8.00**
Bulldog, 3" h, Dresden, three-dimensional, marked "Germany".................. **250.00**
Camel, 4" h, cotton batting, Germany..................... **160.00**
Cross, 4" h, beaded, two-sided, silvered, wire hanger, paper label marked "Czechoslovakia" **20.00**
Father Christmas on Donkey, 10" h, chromolithograph, blue robe, tinsel trim............. **25.00**
Kugel, 4-1/2" d, round, deep sapphire blue, brass hanger **120.00**
Mandolin, 5" h, unsilvered glass, wrapped in lametta and tinsel **45.00**
Parakeet, 5" h, multicolored glass, spun glass tail, mounted on metal clip.. **20.00**
Pear, 3" h, cotton batting, mica highlights, paper leaf, wire hanger, Japan **15.00**

Santa Claus in Chimney, 4" h, glass, Germany **75.00**
Swan, 5" x 6", Dresden, flat, gold with silver, green, and red highlights **150.00**
Tree top, 11" h, three spheres stacked with small clear glass balls, silvered, lametta and tinsel trim, attached to blown glass hooks **90.00**

Ornament set, 10 wood jointed Jaymar figures, goose, sailor, Betty Boop, Popeye, clown, bear, pig, Ed Wynn, Humpty Dumpty, Little Red Riding Hood, each with hook on top of head, text on lid "Hook These Ornaments Onto Your Christmas Tree. After Christmas, Detach Hook And You Have An Ornamental Gift Or Toy," some wear and loss to original 10-1/2" x 12-1/2" x 1-3/8" deep box, 1935, **$575**.

Photo courtesy of Hake's Americana & Collectibles.

Postcards, Germany
Christmas bells and snow scene, marked "Made in Germany," used, one cent stamp, 1911 .... **20.00**
"Happy Christmas Wishes," Santa steering ship **15.00**
"May Your Christmas Be Merry and Gay," photo card, sepia tones, Father Christmas peeking between two large wooden doors, wearing fur cap **20.00**

Putz
Brush tree, 6" h, green, mica-covered branches, wooden base **8.00**

Christmas-tree fence
Cast iron, silver, ornate gold trim, fifteen 10" l segments with posts, Germany... **600.00**
Wood, folding red and green sections, 48" l, USA **35.00**

Santa in cardboard candy box chimney, 1-1/4" x 1-3/4" x 2" h red and white cardboard box designed as chimney, wrapped in shiny string, 2-3/4" h composition Santa coming out of top wearing brown wool outfit, red felt arms, waist wrapped in brown string, black fabric legs, Charms Co., Newark, N.J., figure made in Japan, 1920s, **$50**.

Photo courtesy of Hake's Americana & Collectibles.

Toys
Horse and wagon, 21" l, 9" h, composition, hand-painted workhorse, gray dapping, remnants of leather harness with brass rosettes, partial paper label, red and yellow painted wagon with sign "St. Claus Dealer in Good Things," wear, wagon fork replaced **575.00**
Jack-in-the-box, 9-1/2" h, "Santa Pops," hard plastic, red-felt hat, orig box, Tigrette Industries, 1956 .... **30.00**
Merry-go-round, wind-up, celluloid, green and red base, four white reindeer heads, Santa sitting under umbrella, Santa spins around, stars hanging from umbrella bounce of bobbing deer heads, orig box, Japan **65.00**
Santa, 10" h, battery operated, metal covered with red and white plush suit and hat, soft-plastic face, holding metal wand with white star light, wand moves up and down and lights up while Santa turns head **90.00**

Tree stand, 9-3/4" sq, 4" h, cast iron, old worn green, gold, white, and red paint, relief tree trunk, foliage, and stairway design **110.00**

CLIFTON POTTERY

History: The Clifton Art Pottery, Newark, New Jersey, was established by William A. Long, once associated with Lonhuda Pottery, and Fred Tschirner, a chemist.

Production consisted of two major lines: Crystal Patina, which resembled true porcelain with a subdued crystal-like glaze, and Indian Ware or Western Influence, an adaptation of the American Indians' unglazed and decorated pottery with a high-glazed black interior. Other lines included Robin's Egg Blue and Tirrube. Robin's-Egg Blue is a variation of the crystal patina line, but in blue-green instead of straw-colored hues and with a less-prominent crushed-crystal effect in the glaze. Tirrube, which is often artist signed, features brightly colored, slip-decorated flowers on a terra-cotta ground.

Marks: Marks are incised or impressed. Early pieces may be dated and impressed with a shape number. Indian wares are identified by tribes.

Vase, four buttressed handles, Crystal Patina, celadon matte crystalline glaze, incised, 14" h, 9" d, **$2,500**.

Photo courtesy of David Rago Auctions, Inc.

Vessel, squat, after Indian Peublo Viejo tribe, Upper Gila Valley, Arizona, marked, 9" x 14", chip inside rim, **$395**.

Photo courtesy of David Rago Auctions, Inc.

Biscuit jar, cov, 7" h, 4-1/4" d, gray-brown ground, enameled running ostrich and stork, florals, bail handle **300.00**
Bowl, 9" d, Indian cooking ware, black glazed dec, marked, minor rim flake **150.00**
Creamer, Crystal Patina, incised "Clifton," dated................ **225.00**
Decanter, 11-1/2" h, rose shading to deep rose, purple flowers, gilt butterfly on neck, applied handle, marbleized rose and white stopper **150.00**
Jardinière, 8-1/2" h, 11" d, Four Mile Ruin, Arizona, incised and painted motif, buff and black on brown ground, imp mark and incised inscription, hairline to rim **400.00**
Pedestal, 20" h, Indian, unmarked, small chip to top and glaze **690.00**
Sweetmeat jar, 4" h, hp ducks and cranes, robin's egg blue ground, cow finial............ **375.00**
Teapot, 6" h, brown and black geometric design............ **200.00**
Vase
  6-1/2" d, 5-1/2" h, spherical, Crystal Patina, green and mirrored caramel glaze, sgd and dated 1906 .... **575.00**
  9-1/2" h, 4-1/2" d, bottle shape, Crystal Patina, incised "Clifton/158"................ **350.00**
  10" h, 7" d, angular handles, Crystal Patina, incised "Clifton"....................... **450.00**
Vessel
  5-1/4", gourd shape, Indian, swirl pattern, Arkansas, #216, marked....................... **380.00**
  7-1/2" x 10", bulbous, Indian, collared rim, geometric chain pattern, "Homolobi, #233," marked, few shallow scratches **925.00**

8" x 9", bulbous, Indian, dark birds in flight, "Homolobi, #235," marked **975.00**

CLOCKS

History: The sundial was the first man-made device for measuring time. Its basic disadvantage is well expressed by the saying: "Do like the sundial, count only the sunny days."

Needing greater dependability, man developed the water clock, oil clock, and sand clock, respectively. All these clocks worked on the same principle—time was measured by the amount of material passing from one container to another.

The wheel clock was the next major step. These clocks can be traced back to the 13th century. Many improvements on the basic wheel clock were made and continue to be made. In 1934, the quartz-crystal movement was introduced.

The first carriage clock was made about 1800 by Abraham Louis Breguet as he tried to develop a clock that would keep accurate time for Napoleon's officers. One special feature of a carriage clock was a device that allowed it to withstand the bumpy ride of a stagecoach. These small clocks usually are easy to carry with their own handle built into a rectangular case.

The recently invented atomic clock, which measures time by radiation frequency, only varies one second in a thousand years.

For more information, see *Warman's American Clocks Field Guide.*

Notes: Identifying the proper model name for a clock is critical in establishing price. Condition of the works also is a critical factor. Examine the works to see how many original parts remain. If repairs are needed, try to include this in your estimate of purchase price. Few clocks are purchased purely for decorative value.

> **Clock memorabilia of note**
> Skinners Auctions, Inc., sold an interesting piece of clock memorabilia at its June 6, 2004 auction. It was a 4-1/2" x 6" framed engraving on paper, titled "Directions for Putting Up the Timepiece," issued by Aaron Willard, June, Washington St., near Roxbury, MA, c1825. The engraving sold for a bid of $3,525.

Advertising

Chew Friendship Cub Plug, face of man with moving mouth chewing Friendship Tobacco to the tic of the clock, pat'd March 2, 1886, 4" h.................. **900.00**
Gruen Watch, Williams Jewelry Co. on marquee at bottom, blue neon around perimeter, 15" x 15" **600.00**
Hire's Root Beer, "Drink Hires Root Beer with Root Barks, Herbs," 15" d **250.00**
International Tailoring, Chicago, cast iron, emb design, bronzed, orig working clock, 12" w, 2-1/2" d, 16" h, C.8+ **1,000.00**
Longine's Watches, "The World's Most Honored Watch," brass, 18-1/2" d **300.00**
None Such Mincemeat, pumpkin face, 8-1/2" w, some wear **300.00**
Victrola Records, orig pendulum.................... **2,100.00**

Alarm

Attleboro, 36 hours, nickel-plated case, owl dec, 9" h **75.00**
Bradley, brass, double bells, Germany **40.00**
Champion, 30 hours, American movement, metal frame, ornamental feet, 9" h......... **75.00**
New Haven, c1900, 30 hours, SP case, perfume-bottle shape, beveled-glass mirror, removable cut-glass scent bottle, beaded handle **185.00**

Bracket

Louis XV, Corne Verte, c1735, gilt bronze mounts, bracket stamped "GOTER" and "JME," porcelain dial and backplate signed "F. cois Gilbert A. Paris," five turned pillar movement with silk suspension, recoil escapement with silk suspension, converted from verge escapement, eight-day time and strike movement with vertical striking, count wheel mounted on the back plate, 25-pc porcelain dial mounted on brass dial plate, Roman numeral hours and Arabic five-minute gradations, 11" w, 6" d, 26" h case, 12" w, 6-3/4" d, 12" h base **5,500.00**

Regency, Bennett & Co., Norwich, c1810, brass inlaid and gilt bronze mounted mahogany, dial and back plate sgd, oak leaf spandrels, case inlaid with scrolls, gadrooned bun feet, 17" h, chips **4,325.00**

Tiffany & Co., bronze, stepped rect-shaped top, four acorn finials, cast foliate frieze, four capitals with reeded columns, shaped and foliate cast base, beveled glass door and panels, circular face dial with Roman numerals, marked "Famiel Marti Medaillo...Paris 1900, Tiffany & Co.", 13" h **600.00**

Carriage, Benrus, eight-day, presentation inscription on top front panel of brass case, marked "Western Germany," **$95**.

Carriage

French, oval, brass, four beveled glass panels, fine cut flowers in border to sides, top oval glass panels initialed "M.E.H.," dial painted with woman and cupid, decorative D-shaped handle on top, 5-1/2" h **1,150.00**

Grande Sonnerie, brass, dial marked for "Muiron & Cia., Mexico," phases of the moon, subsidiary day, date, and seconds dial, all enamel, set into brass plate engraved with leafy scrolls and dragons' heads, repeater button, strike/silent quarter strike lever, title on movement engraved in Spanish, made for Mexican market, early 20th C, 7-1/2" h **7,475.00**

New Haven Clock Co., gilded brass case, beveled glass, gold repaint to case, orig pendulum and key, 11-1/2" h **315.00**

Japan, 19th C
  Brass works and case, floral engraving on rect case, surmounted by bell, stand missing, 6-1/2" h **3,000.00**
  Brass works, rosewood case, 7" h...................... **7,100.00**

Tiffany & Co., early 20th C, brass and glass, French half strike repeater movement marked for Souaillet Freres, enamel dial with Arabic numerals and subsidiary seconds dial, 3-3/8" w, 3" d, 7" h **950.00**

Carriage clock, LaCoultre Atmos, brass and glass, one panel cracked, 9" h, **$225**.

Photo courtesy of Wiederseim Associates, Inc.

Desk

American, shaped rect, brass case, white enamel bordering cobalt blue, stylized applied monogram, decorative brass corners, central dial with Arabic numerals, 4-3/4" h **150.00**

British United Clock Co., Ltd., Birmingham, England, 20th C, brass, bracket cut-out edges on diamond-shaped brass clock frame, four pierced diamond patterns, floral, bowknot, and fleur-de-lis punch dec, wire easel stand, printed and imp maker's marks, spotty corrosion, 6" w, 4-1/2" h **260.00**

Enameled, c1910, gilt bronze, tombstone shape, front enameled in translucent emerald green enamel on wavy engine turned ground, 4-1/4" h... **350.00**

Mantel, fake graining, yellow ground, black "smoke" type graining, circular dial flanked by two columns on each side, marble base, applied ormolu on sides, no markings, **$200**.

Mantel

Ansonia, French-style, rococo scroll dec, enameled face sgd "Ansonia," bronze-colored patina on spelter, orig pendulum, missing finial and key, 14-1/2" h **275.00**

Birge, Mallory, and Co., Bristol, CT, c1830, Classical, mahogany and gilt gesso, scrolled cornice with fruit-filled basket flanked by square plinths, glazed door enclosing white painted and gilt dial, seven-day brass strap weight-driven movement, mirror below, reverse-painted tablet below that, all flanked by gilded engaged and free-standing columns on ball feet, refinished, restoration, imperfections, 17" w, 5" d, 38" h **650.00**

Classical Revival, French, early 20th C, retailed by Theodore B. Starr, New York, two-train half-striking Japy Freres movement, ovoid case with beveled glass sides, dial with colorless paste-set bezel, pendulum centered by portrait miniature on ivory of lady in 18th C dress, double bezel of colorless pastes, 12-1/4" h **725.00**

French, Louis XVI-style, late 19th C, patinated metal, figural cherub painter with palette and wreath-draped easel, two-train half-striking movement with Japy Fils Medaille D'Argent seal, enamel dial with worn retailer's mark, set into beaded gilt-metal bezel, waisted black marble socle, 17-3/4" w, 7-1/2" d, 22" h **2,990.00**

George III, c1800, William Stephenson, London, maker, mahogany case, arch top with lifting handle, glass front and rear doors, side frets, brass bracket feet, two-train fusee striking movement, painted dial, 16-1/2" h **1,650.00**

Mantel, Herschede, hump back, original key and pendulum, **$150**.

Photo courtesy of Dotta Auction Co., Inc.

Gothic Revival, French, late 19th C, gilt bronze, two-train half-striking Japy Freres movement with pull repeater, retailed by Bourdin, Paris, case formed as pointed arch Gothic cathedral, central round dial, pierced curved arch revealing red glass panel at back, pair of columns, stacked plinth base, further ebonized wood platform, 20-3/8" h **2,350.00**

Jugendstil, oak, retailed by Liberty & Co., exposed bell on top, open sides, copper face emb with violets, purple and yellow slag glass window, orig finish, working condition, unmarked, 9-3/4" w, 14-1/4" h **1,840.00**

Leavenworth, Mark, Waterbury, CT, c1825, Federal, pillar and scroll, mahogany, scrolled cresting, three brass urn finials on sq plinths above glazed door, eglomise tablet showing house by lank flanked by freestanding columns, wooden dial with gilt dec housing thirty-hour wooden striking movement, cut-out valanced base, 16-1/2" w, 31-1/4" h, refinished, restoration to tablet **3,820.00**

Louis Philippe style, late 19th C, retailed by Hollin, ormolu, figural, Vincenti two-train chiming movement set in bale, topped by hat and bag of coins, figure of boy holding anchor, rect plinth base set with scene of cherub loading ship, another bookkeeping, trumpet feet, 11-3/8" h **1,880.00**

Louis XV, gilt bronze mounted, waisted ovoid tulipwood veneered case topped by rocaille urn and trimmed in rocaille C-scrolls, two-train half-striking movement, enamel dial with outer ring of seconds markers, 19" h **1,175.00**

Louis XVI style, French, late 19th C, figural, bronze painted white metal figure of classical woman, holding gilt metal and engine-turned orb movement on white metal rod from her upraised hand, onyx plinth base, 26" h **7,050.00**

Shreve, Crump & Low, late 19th C, Gothic Revival, carved mahogany, French two-train half-strike movement, engraved silver dial, case formed as Gothic pointed and trefoil arch, paneled turrets, blocked base, 19-1/2" h **850.00**

Terry, Samuel, c1825, Federal, pillar and scroll, mahogany, scrolled cresting, three brass urn finials on sq plinths above glazed door, eglomise tablet showing building in landscape, flanked by freestanding columns, wooden painted and gilt dial, thirty-day wooden movement, valanced cut-out base, 17" w, 4-1/2" d, 31-1/2" h, refinished, tablet replaced **1,530.00**

Mantel, Gothic, gilt metal case, central figural decoration flanked by fluted columns resting on stepped base, scrolling feet, mermaid type figures forming side handles, all surmounted by domed to with spires, 25-1/2" h, chips to glass front, **$500**.

Photo courtesy of Alderfer Auction Co.

Thomas, Seth, Plymouth Hollow, CT, Classical, c1825, carved mahogany and mahogany veneer, eagle and shield-carved scroll flanked by square plinths above glazed door with eglomise tablet showing public building with floral stenciled border, opening to wooden painted dial, 36 weight-driven movement, flanked by stencil decorated engaged columns on carved acanthus leaf and hairy paw feet, minor imperfections, 17" w, 4-3/4" d, 30" h **775.00**

Tiffany & Co., late 19th C, marble and patinated metal, two-train half-striking movement sgd by Tiffany & Co., pink marble temple form case, pediment set with patinated metal plaque of putti with goat, round bezel set to center of case flanked by patinated pilasters, plinth base mounted with central cartouche and laurel branches, 12-1/4" w, 5-7/8" d, 13-1/8" h **300.00**

Victorian, late 19th C, black, rect, two-train strike and bell movement, front with breche d'alep marble pilasters flanking round dial, plinth base with breche d'alep band and diamond inlay, gilt incised line dec, 9-3/4" w, 5-3/4" d, 10-3/4" h **425.00**

Waterbury, c1900, black lacquer, patinated metal scrolled feet, faceplate flanked by marbleized columns with patinated metal mounts, hourly chime, 15" l, 12" h **300.00**

Porcelain

Ansonia, Royal Bonn, shelf, blue and white case dec with flowers, open escapement, time and strike, 9-1/2" w, 15" h....... **920.00**

French, possibly Sevres, c1880, architectural stepped down form, roof with ormolu shell finial, ormolu mounted columns flanking central dial, figural garden scene over scrolled ormolu mounted base, 10 1/2" h, chips, crazing **700.00**

Shelf, Ansonia, eight-day movement, time and strike, lion heads on side panels, **$260.**

Photo courtesy of Joy Luke Auctions.

Shelf

Atkins Clock Mfg., Bristol, CT, c1855-58, rosewood, 30-day wagon spring movement (invented by Joseph Ives), case with hinged door, zinc painted dial framed by eglomise tablet above lower mirrored door, iron and brass "patent equalizing lever spring" movement, flanked by canted recessed paneled corners, backboard with maker's label
13-1/2" w, 4" d, 17-3/4" h **3,525.00**
13-1/2" w, 4" d, 17-3/4" h, refinished, dial repaired **2,235.00**

Birge and Fuller, Bristol, CT, c1845-50
Gothic, candlestick, double steeple, mahogany, wagon spring, orig painted tablets, painted zinc dial, eight-day time and strike, "J. Ives Patent Accelerating Lever Spring" movement, 13-3/4" w, 4" d, 26" h......................... **8,225.00**

Gothic, double steeple, wagon spring, case with orig painted tablets, painted zinc dial, 30 hour "J. Ives Patent Accelerating Lever Spring Movement," 11-1/2" w, 4-1/4" d, 24-1/4" h.... **3,300.00**

Brewster and Ingrahams, Bristol, CT, c1845, Gothic twin steeple, mahogany, peaked cornice, glazed door, stenciled gilt-green on white table showing love birds, enclosing painted zinc dial, double fusee brass movement, flanked by two turned finials and columns, flat base, 19" h, dial replaced, minor veneer loss.................. **1,100.00**

Forestville Manufacturing Co., J.C. Brown, Bristol, CT, Gothic, c1849, acorn, rosewood, shaped laminated case with orig reverse painted tablet, painted zinc dial and eight-day fusee movement, dial attributed to repainted, 10-1/8" w, 4" d, 20-1/4" h...................... **6,500.00**

New Haven, glass door, mirrored side panels, spelter standing cupids, walnut case with drawer at base, 24" h **490.00**

North, Norris, Torrington, CT, c1825, Classical, mahogany, flat cornice above glazed door, eglomise tablet of young woman flanked by engaged black paint stenciled columns, polychrome and gilt white painted dial, 30-hour wooden weight-driven movement, 23-3/4" h, 13-1/2" w, 5-1/4" d....................... **4,900.00**

Pomeroy, Noah, Bristol, CT, 1860s, mahogany veneer, movement marked "N. Pomeroy, Bristol, Conn," steeple frame encloses glass tablets, lower one with polychrome beehive imagery, 14-3/4" h, imperfections **1,150.00**

Terry, Eli and Sons, Plymouth, CT, c1810-15, Federal, paper label "Eli Terry and Sons," mahogany, scrolled pediment, wooden painted dial with gilt spandrels, wooden 30-hour movement, eglomise glass, curving case skirt, French feet, 31-1/4" h, restoration.... **1,955.00**

Thomas, Seth, Plymouth, CT, c1820, calendar, double dial, time, and strike, glass door, 14" w, 27" h................... **1,150.00**

Unidentified MA maker, c1805, Federal, mahogany, pierced fret over unsigned painted dial,

rocking ship and gilt spandrels, red, white, and blue shields, box base on feet, 38-1/2" h, restorations **12,650.00**

Willard, Aaron, Grafton, Massachusetts, c1775-1825, mahogany and mahogany veneer, flat rect cornice above hinged square veneered door with mitered corners, brass engraved dial with floral designs, mkd "A. Willard, Grafton," framed by ropetwist bezel with brass weight-driven thirty-hour movement, flanking ball top vase and ring-turned posts above lower section of flat mid molding, central pierced and mitered panel with flanking crossbanding and free standing tapering columns on square plinths and flat base, imperfections, 9-1/4" w, 3-1/2" d, 18" h **4,700.00**

Table

French, gilt bronze and enamel, case finely molded gilt bronze with hooved feet, translucent maroon panel enameled with cherubs and floral sprays, maroon enameled dial with circular florals, gilt numerals, surmounted by matching enameled dome, gilt acorn finial, works stamped "Etienne Maxant, Brevete, Paris made in France," c1900, 14" h **2,590.00**

French, gilt bronze and guilloche enamel, round clock, Swiss movement, enameled in translucent azure blue on engraved radiating ground, enameled and gilt chapter ring, gilt bronze case surmounted by petal forms, 19th C, 4" d . **600.00**

Wendell, "Mr. Clock," sq ribbon-mahogany box, tall verdigris-patinated copper legs, sgd and dated 1988, 24" x 6"..... **1,380.00**

Tall case, dwarf

Gilmanton, Noah Ranlet, NH, dial sgd "Noah Ranlet Gilmanton 1796," time and strike movement, pine, scrolled solid crest above bonnet that encloses sgd, painted dial, includes side lights, waist door, flanked by quarter-engaged columns above base box, later stenciled eagle dec, pine case with old refinish, 49-1/4" h, replaced crest, other imperfections **18,400.00**

French, 19th C, marble and agate, Egyptian revival style, ormolu anthemion corner pendants, female busts, swans, laurel wreaths, paw feet, 52" h **3,800.00**

Hingham, J. Wilder, c1810-15, dial face indistinctly sgd, reverse dial reads "J. Wilder Hingham" in period script, painted bowl of fruit in arch, gilt spandrels, eight-day timepiece with drop-off strike, mahogany and mahogany veneer, bonnet flanked by free-standing tapering columns above waist door with applied molding, cross-banded veneer box base, curving skirt and feet, 47-1/2" h, replaced crest, other minor imperfections ... **28,750.00**

Tower, Reuben, Plymouth, MA, c1820-30, alarm dial sgd "Reuben Tower Kingston," pine, pierced fret above bonnet flanked by free-standing mahogany columns, painted iron dial with spandrels and polychrome painted basket of flowers, fruit, and foliage above waist, box base over curing skirt, ogee feet, 40-3/4" h, refinished case, replaced crest and columns, some height loss **12,650.00**

Tall case

Brokaw, Isaac, Federal, mahogany inlaid, dial marked "Isaac Brokaw Bridge Town" (New Jersey), 1800-10, shaped hood with inlaid patera and book-end inlays above glazed door, painted dial, eight-day weight-driven movement, seconds hand, calendar aperture, waist door with serpentine top and elliptical inlay, oval and quarter-fan inlays on lower case, similar embellishments above the bracket feet, refinished, restored, 94-1/2" h...... **10,575.00**

Caldwell, J. E., late 19th/early 20th C, Georgian-Revival, mahogany, dial sgd "Caldwell," subsidiary seconds dial, cast scroll and cherub detailing, phases of the moon, two train chiming movement, hood with swan's neck cresting centered by urn, carved scroll detailing, glass front door flanked by tapering and partially reeded circular section columns, case with beveled glass front door flanked by engaged partially reeded columns, paneled plinth base centered by carved shell, front paw feet, rear ogee feet, 24" w, 15" d, 95" h **2,895.00**

Tall case, John Heilig, walnut case, bonnet with broken arch top with rosettes and full columns, case with quarter columns, label by David Rose, Reading, 1771, eight-day moon dial, signed by John Heilig, Germantown, (1801-50) sweep second hand, 98" h, hinges shimmed, replaced glass and feet, broken hour hand, **$7,000.**

Photo courtesy of Alderfer Auction Co.

English

George III style, works attributed to Elliott of London, retailed by Bigelow, Kennard, three-train movement, quarter striking and chiming, nine tubes, pierced brass spandrels, inlaid mahogany case with swan's neck cresting, three ball and spire finials, mid-case with glass door and engaged columns, inlaid with fan and urn, 91" h **5,600.00**

Victorian, dial painted with landscape scenes, sgd "Thompson of Huddersfield," two-train movement, oak case carved all over with flat foliage and lappets, swan's neck cresting, engaged columns, 95" h........................ **2,350.00**

Farquharson, Alexander, George III, mahogany, gilt bronze mounts, dial signed "Alexander Farquharson, Edinburgh," etched steel face with date aperture and seconds dial, case with broken pediment cresting, dentil molding, two columnar supports with gilt capitals, shaped long door and bracket feet, 89" h........ **2,760.00**

French, Provincial Renaissance style, quarter strike mobilier, 19th C, serpentine cresting above glass door, brass face depicting courting couple, single train movement with quarter chiming on two bells, hour strike on one bell, case carved with strap work and mask, 94" h **1,400.00**

Mulliken, Joseph, Concord, MA, c1800-10, Federal, cherry, hood with pierced fretwork joining sq plinths and brass ball finials above arched cornice molding, iron painted tombstone dial with bird and floral designs inscribed "J. Mulliken Concord," eight-day weight-driven movement, flanked by free-standing reeded columns, waist with molded rect door flanked by reeded quarter columns on base with inlaid stringing joining corner quarter fans on flat molding, 88-3/4" h, imperfections, lacks hood door and feet........................ **4,700.00**

Mulliken, Nathaniel, Lexington, MA, c1760, walnut, hood with molded flat cornice above arched molding, glazed tombstone door with flanking engraved columns, engraved brass dial with brass spandrel, boss in arch engraved "Nath Mulliken LEXINGTON" above chapter ring, seconds indicator, and calendar aperture, waist with thumb-molded door, base with applied thumb-molded panel, bracket feet, 87" h, refinished, restored...... **7,650.00**

Mulliken II, Nathaniel, Lexington, MA, c1770-75, attributed to, mahogany and cherry, hood with broken arched cornice molding, three sq plinths, tombstone glazed door with flanking engaged columns, brass dial with cast spandrels, silvered banner in arch engraved "Nath. Mulliken + Lexington," above the boss with engraved eagle on branch, silvered chapter ring, seconds indicator, calendar aperture, eight-day weight-driven movement, waist with thumb-molded door, molded base, 88" h, refinished, loss of height, restored **7,650.00**

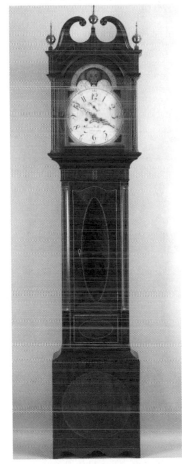

Tall case, New Jersey, Federal, c1800, mahogany, broken arch bonnet with line and oval inlays, white painted face, signed "Joakim Hill, Flemington," case with arched door flanked by fluted quarter columns over rectangular base, scrolled skirt and bracket feet in overall line, oval, and circular inlays, 93" h, **$14,950.**

Photo courtesy of Pook & Pook.

Munroe, Daniel, Concord, MA, Federal, c1810, mahogany, hood with pierced fretwork joining three reeded brass stop fluted plinths above arched cornice molding, glazed inlaid tombstone door enclosing polychrome iron moon phase dial with floral spandrels, polychrome indicator, calendar aperture inscribed "Daniel Munroe," eight-day weight-driven movement, flanked by reeded brass stop-fluted columns, rect inlaid waist door flanked by reeded brass stop-fluted quarter columns on inlaid base ending in molding, 85-1/2" h, feet missing, restored fretwork **17,625.00**

Nash, William, Bridge, England, George III, works signed, brass and steel face with date aperture and seconds dial, inlaid mahogany case with swan's neck cresting, columnar supports, cross-banded door inlaid with shell, bracket feet, 95" h **6,900.00**

Parke, Soloman, late 18th/early 19th C, Phila, cherry, replaced dial **7,700.00**

Read, A. Hepplewhite, country, cherry with old mellow refinishing, bonnet with turned front columns and reeded pilasters in back, broken arch pediment and chip carving on arch, waist with chamfered corners, lamb's tongues and molded edge door, molding between sections, cutout feet and apron, painted wood face labeled "A. Read & Co. Xenia, Ohio," polychrome flowers and vintage dec, wooden works replaced with electric movement, age crack in base, minor pierced repairs, 94-1/2" h **4,400.00**

Smith, Benjamin, Provincial, works signed by Benjamin Smith, Leeds, brass face, steel chapter ring, two-train movement, lunar arch, date dial and subsidiary seconds hand, pierced spandrels, inlaid oak case with broken arch cresting, checkered banding, inlaid with shell and fans, bracket feet, 96" h **7,495.00**

Taber, Elnathan, Roxbury, MA c1815, Federal, dial sgd "E. Taber, Roxbury," painted iron dial with calendar aperture, seconds hand, gilt spandrels, two ships, one flying American flag in the arch of dial, eight-day movement, mahogany veneer inlaid case with pierced fretwork,

fluted plinths, brass stop fluted free-standing columns flanking bonnet above waist door with applied moldings, flanked by engaged brass stop fluted quarter columns with brass capitols and bases, waist door opens to reveal early 19th C label "Directions for Setting Up a Clock" above box base with inlay in outline, curving skirt, French feet, 92" h, refinished, imperfections **48,875.00**

Unidentified American maker

Federal, Massachusetts, c1810-20, inlaid mahogany, upper case with three spire and ball finials, open fretwork cornice, arched door and painted metal face with flowerhead spandrels and portrait of Washington and flags in the arch, two-train movement and subsidiary seconds dial, mid case with rect door and brass stop-fluted quarter columns, plinth with flared French feet, inlaid checked banding throughout, restorations, 95" h **9,990.00**

Hepplewhite, cherry, inlaid, swan neck pediment with carved rosettes, vase finial, barber pole and vine and berry inlay on hood, barber pole, vine inlay, and inlaid oval a waist, 97" h.. **15,275.00**

Weiser, Martin, Northampton, Pennsylvania, Chippendale, softwood, painted red, brown arch pediment, spiral carved finials, carved rosettes, arched side lights, turned and reeded column supports, shaped pendulum door with wrought iron rattail hinges, reeded quarter columns, molded base with raised panel with carved oblong rosette and ogee bracket feet, 30 hour movement, illuminated dial with bird and floral motif, dated register, some minor in-painting on dial, minor repair to bonnet, 92" h.............. **13,750.00**

Willard, Benjamin, Lexington, MA, c1771, cherry, brass dial inscribed "Benjamin Willard Lexington," boss inscribed "Tempus fugit," cast brass spandrels, silvered chapter ring, second hand, calendar aperture, eight-day time and strike movement, pagoda style bonnet, fluted plinths above scalloped waist door, molded box base, 82" h, refinished case, restoration to bonnet.. **12,650.00**

Wall, Black Forest, carved, musical, cuckoo, deer head at center top above crossed long guns, clock face with hunting horn bezel, flanked by carved rabbit and bird, carved leaf details at sides, carved hunting bag below face, figural pendulum, 50" h, break to one antler, **$1,500**.

Photo courtesy of Alderfer Auction Co.

Willard, Simon, Roxbury, MA, c1800, Federal, dial indistinctly sgd, eight-day time and strike movement, mahogany inlaid case with pierced fret on bonnet, American dial with "S+N" on reverse, rocking ship flying two American flags in arch of dial, painted rose spandrels and gilt outline, flanked by brass stop-fluted free-standing columns above waist door with applied molding, cross-banded veneer, boxed inlaid base, sq feet, 93-1/2" h, refinished, height loss, replaced feet.............. **37,375.00**

Wismer, Henry, Plumstead, Bucks County, PA, c1820, cherry, hood with molded broken-arch resting, carved floral rosettes, three plinths with turned finials, glazed tombstone door, polychrome iron dial, basket of fruit in arch, seashell spandrels, calendar aperture signed "Henry Wismer B.C.," brass weight-driven striking pull-up movement, flanked by turned columns, waist with door flanked by four ring-turned columns, base with canted corners, flaring French feet, old surface, 95-1/2" h....................... **5,875.00**

Wood, David, Newburyport, MA, c1800-15, Federal, cherry and maple, hood with three reeded plinths above arched molding, glazed tombstone door, polychrome and gilt dial with fruit designs, seconds indicator, calendar aperture inscribed "D. Wood," brass weight-driven movement, flanked by reeded columns, cockbeaded waist door flanked by reeded quarter columns, cove molding, base with reeded band and cut-out feet, engraved label affixed to back of door "David Wood, watch and clockmaker," 89" h, refinished, imperfections................. **8,820.00**

Wall

Automaton movement, Friesland, arched hood, face painted with central landscape scene within chapter ring with hours and seconds, allegorical women in corners, arch with automaton figures of jumping dog, peddler, child on hobby horse, painted bracket case, 39" l................................ **765.00**

Banjo

Abbott, Samuel, Boston, MA, c1815-25, attributed to, Federal, mahogany, painted dial, "A"-shaped brass weight-driven eight-day movement, reverse painted throat glass flanked by gilded rope twist and brass side arms, lower eglomise glass depicting in polychrome "Lafayette the Friend of Liberty," 33-1/2" h, restoration **1,955.00**

Cummens, William, Boston, MA, c1820, Federal, dial sgd "warranted by Wm. Cummens," convex painted iron dial enclosed by convex glass and bezel topped by acorn finial, molded mahogany veneer case, T-bridge eight-day weight-driven movement, reverse painted throat glass, flanked by side arms, eglomise tablet marked "Patent" in box base, 34" l, restoration **6,325.00**

Currier, Edmund, Salem, MA, c1820, Federal, dial sgd "E. Currier Salem," eight-day weight-driven movement, throat glass panel reads "Patent," lower reverse painted glass reads "E. Currier Salem" above gilt

bracket, 41-3/4" h, restoration **3,335.00**

Curtis and Dunning, Concord, MA, c1815, Federal, dial sgd "warranted by Curtis and Dunning," eight-day weight-driven movement, mahogany case with brass bezel and convex glass, tapering throat with reverse painted glass flanked by brass side arms, box base with eglomise panel, rope twist giltwood in outline, 33-1/2" l, period throat glass broken............ **5,175.00**

Curtis, Lemuel, Concord, MA, c1815, Federal, brass eagle finials, mahogany and gilt gesso case, brass bezel, painted and gilt iron dial inscribed "warranted by L. Curtis," eight-day weight-driven movement, throat glass enclosing thermometer, inscribed "L. Curtis Patent," lower tablet showing figures in farm landscape, both framed by gilt spiral moldings, flanked by brass side arms, 33-1/4" h, restoration, imperfections........... **7,650.00**

Dyar, J., Concord, MA, c1815, Federal, mahogany, brass eagle finial above bras bezel, painted metal dial, reading "Warranted by J. Dyar," eight-day eight-drive movement, foliate throat glass reading "Patent," flanked by rope twist dec, brass side arms, lower tablet with eglomise naval battle framed by applied rope twist moldings, 32-3/4" h, lower tablet replaced, other imperfections........... **2,820.00**

Munroe and Whiting, Concord, MA, c1808-17, Federal, gilt mahogany, acorn-form finial, iron painted dial enclosing eight-day weight-driven movement, foliate throat glass flanked by side arms, lower panel depicting ship battle, both within rope twist dec frames, 33" h, lower tablet replaced, other imperfections.. **1,880.00**

Noyes, L. W., Nashua, NH, c1825, Federal, mahogany, brass belted ball finial, brass bezel, printed dial, eight-day weight-drive movement, throat glass flanked by brass side arms and tablet with foliate and eagle devices framed by half round moldings, 34" h, restoration including tablets **1,765.00**

Sawin, John and John W. Dyer, Boston, MA, c1825, Federal, giltwood and mahogany, dial sgd "Sawin and Dyer, Boston," acorn finial above convex glass and brass bezel, brass eight-day weight-driven movement, glass throat panel reads "Patent" flanked by brass side arms over lower glass eglomise tablet which depicts seaside hotel, reads "Nahant," 33" h, minor restoration **4,025.00**

Unidentified Concord Massachusetts maker, c1815, Federal, gilt and mahogany

Brass ball finial above brass bezel and dial, eight-day weight-driven movement, foliate throat glass reading "PATENT" flanked by brass side arms, lower tablet depicting battle between the *Constitution* and the *Guerriere,* both framed by applied rope twist dec, 35" h, imperfections **2,475.00**

Unsigned painted dial, Concord-type eight-day brass weight drive movement, carved wooden eagle finial, throat glass panel reading "Patent," flanked by brass side arms over reverse painted glass panel in box base, 33-1/2" h, restoration **2,875.00**

Wall, German, Viennese, with chimes, **$400.**

Photo courtesy of Dotta Auction Co., Inc.

Unidentified Massachusetts maker, Classical, c1825, mahogany and mahogany veneer, acorn finial, molded bezel, painted metal dial, brass eight-day weight-driven movement, lyre-form throat, rect pendulum box, both with eglomise tablets, molded bracket with acorn pendant, restored, 38-3/4" h ... **1,300.00**

Willard, Aaron, Jr., Boston, Massachusetts

Classical, c1825, carved mahogany, lyre, urn-turned finial above molded wooden bezel, painted metal dial inscribed "A Willard, Jr., Boston," eight-day weight-driven movement above acanthus leaf scroll carved throat and pendulum box, both with eglomise tablets, molded bracket, old refinish, old replaced tablets, accompanied by bill of sale dated 1946 for $200, 40-1/2" h **10,575.00**

Federal, c1820, mahogany case, molded brass bezel, painted zinc dial, brass eight-day weight-driven movement stamped "A Willard Jr Boston," above half-round molded throat and pendulum and eglomise tablets, imperfections, 28-1/2" h **1,645.00**

Willard, Simon, Roxbury, MA, Federal, c1805, mahogany, unmarked dial, eight-day weight driven T-bridge movement with stepped train, escapement in case with cross-banded veneer, brass side arms, reverse painted throat glass above lower eglomise tablet which reads "S. Willard's Patent," 33-1/2" h, restoration **10,350.00**

Girandole, J. L. Dunning, attributed to, Burlington, Vermont, c1818-20, Classical, carved mahogany, molded wooden bezel, painted iron dial inscribed "... Dunning," brass weight-driven movement above tapering molded throat with mahogany panel flanked by carved scroll side pieces, circular molded door with pierced mahogany panel, scroll carved acanthus leaf bracket, imperfections, 39" l **62,275.00**

Wall, gilt bronze, center panel mounted with shell flanked by two ebonized columns over round clock face, Roman numerals on dial, engraved Arabic numeral minute markers, ornamented by winged embossed ro heads and scrolled leaf decoration, figural winged angel ornament at base, conforming scroll and leaf decoration, 14" w, 33" h, **$1,540.**

Photo courtesy of Alderfer Auction Co.

Lyre, chandler, Abiel, Concord, NH, c1825, Classical, dial sgd "A. Chandler," striking brass eight-day weight-driven movement, leaf carved mahogany veneer case with bracket, 43" h, refinished, imperfections **17,250.00**

Mirror

Chandler, Abiel, Concord, New Hampshire, c1825, gilt gesso and wood, gilt and black painted split baluster door with stencil and painted tablet, mirror below, painted iron dial inscribed "A. Chandler," brass eight-day weight-driven movement, maker's label affixed to backboard, minor imperfections, 13-3/4" w, 4" d, 29" h **8,225.00**

Morrill, Benjamin, Boscawen, NH, c1825, late Federal, dial sgd "B. Morrill Boscawen, N.H.," c1825, eight-day wheelbarrow movement surrounded by gilded spandrels above mirror glass, flanked by gilded and painted split baluster columns, 31-3/4" h, restoration ... **3,740.00**

Unidentified, attributed to New Hampshire, c1825, giltwood and gesso, gilt split baluster framed door with eglomise tablet and mirror below, painted tin dial set into wooden frame enclosing a brass eight-day rack and snail movement, imperfections including replaced tablet, 13" w, 4-1/4" d, 29-1/2" h **1,800.00**

Wall, Ithaca, calendar, oak case, carved pediment (replaced), upper dial with Roman numerals, lower calendar dial with date, date and month, marked "H.B. Horton's Patents April 18, 1865 and August 28, 1866, Ithaca Calendar Clock Company, Ithaca, New York," 10-1/2" w, 4-1/4" d, 24" h, **$550**.

Photo courtesy of Alderfer Auction Co.

Spiderweb
Nelson, George, for Howard Miller, wood center, white enameled metal rays, black string, black Howard Miller decal, No. 2214, 18-1/2" d **1,150.00**

Watchman
Morrill, Benjamin, Boscawen, NH, 1860s, rect birch box case, painted iron dial marked "B. Morrill Boscawen," eight-day weight-driven brass movement, 54-1/2" h, imperfections **2,875.00**

CLOISONNÉ

History: Cloisonné is the art of enameling on metal. The design is drawn on the metal body, then wires, which follow the design, are glued or soldered on. The cells thus created are packed with enamel and fired; this step is repeated several times until the level of enamel is higher than the wires. A buffing and polishing process brings the level of enamels flush to the surface of the wires.

This art form has been practiced in various countries since 1300 B.C. and in the Orient since the early 15th century. Most cloisonné found today is from the late Victorian era, 1870-1900, and was made in China or Japan.

Box, cov, 4-3/4" d, 2-3/4" h, rounded form, butterflies among flowering branches, turquoise ground, Chinese, 19th C . **345.00**

Candlesticks, pr, 7-1/8" h, figural, brass, blue mythical animals seated on round dark red base with open work sides, three feet, each animal holds flower in mouth, red candle socket on back **200.00**

Cane, 36" l, 1-1/3" d x 9-1/2" l Japanese cloisonné handle, dark blue ground, long scaly three-toed Japanese dragon in shades of white, pale blue, black, and brown, 1/3" gold gilt collar, black hardwood shaft, 7/8" horn ferrule, fashioned in England, c1890............ **1,460.00**

Cup, 4" h, ftd, butterflies and flowers, lappet borders, Chinese, 19th C **100.00**

Desk set, brush pot, pen, pen tray, blotter, and paper holder, Japanese, price for set ... **130.00**

Figure, 11-3/4" h, Killin, riders atop their backs, one saddle blanket dec with house floating on clouds above waves, other with crane flying above mountainous landscape, Chinese, late 19th or early 20th C, losses to enamel, pr ... **800.00**

Incense burner, 19-3/4" h, globular, three dragon-head feet, high curving handles, scrolling lotus and ancient bronzes motif, openwork lid, dragon finial, raised Quinlong six-character mark, damage................. **815.00**

Jar, cov, 6" h, ovoid, even green over central band of scrolling flowers, dome lid, ovoid finial, marked "Ando Jubei," 20th C **230.00**

Jardinière, 13" d, 10" h, bronze, bands of cloisonné designs, golden yellow and blue triangles, polychrome geometric designs on dark blue, chrysanthemums on light blue, cast relief scene of water lily, turtle, and flowering branches on int., soldered repair at foot **220.00**

Vase, rectangular form, slender body, four panels profusely decorated with flowers, silver wire, dark blue enamel on shoulder and bottom, Japan, Meiji period, 7-1/4" h, light cracks on shoulder, chip at neck, **$850**.

Planter, 11" l, quatralobe, classical symbol and scroll dec, blue ground, Chinese, pr **200.00**

Scepter, 22" l, three cloisonné plaques inset with wooden cloud-carved frame, China, early 20th C **125.00**

Tea kettle, 10-1/2" h, multicolored scrolling lotus, medium-blue ground, lappets border, waisted neck with band of raised auspicious symbols between key-fret borders, floral form finial, double handles, Chinese, 19th C **690.00**

Teapot, 4-3/4" d, 3-1/4" h, central band of flowering chrysanthemums on pink ground, shoulder with shaped cartouches of phoenix and dragon on floral and patterned ground, lower border with chrysanthemum blossom on swirling ground, flat base with three small raised feet, single chrysanthemum design, spout and handle with floral design, lid with two writhing dragons on peach-colored ground, Japanese, late 19th/early 20th C **4,025.00**

Urn, 23-3/4" h, ovoid, slightly waisted neck, peony dec, black ground, base plaque marked "Takeuchi Chubei," Japanese, late-19th C, Shichi Ho Company, Owari **690.00**

Vase, Imperial Dragon, 18-1/4" h, **$265**.
Photo courtesy of Pook & Pook.

Vase

3" h, animal head handles, gilt rims and bases, China, 19th C, pr **375.00**

3-3/4" h, two birds taking flight from flowering tree, cluster of plants on back side, gold wire cloisons on dark blue ground, band of shippo designs on mouth rim and base, silver rims, bottom rim mkd "silver," base with Hayashi Kondenji inlaid mark, Japan, Meiji period **3,750.00**

6" h, surface of minuscule scrolling with scattered chrysanthemums, possibly by Namikawa, unsigned, Japan, Meiji period (1868-1911) **725.00**

16-1/2" h, lobed form, blue ground, design of phoenix, dragons, and flowers, China, late 18th/early 19th C **1,530.00**

CLOTHING AND CLOTHING ACCESSORIES

History: While museums and a few private individuals have collected clothing for decades, it is only recently that collecting clothing has achieved a widespread popularity. Clothing reflects the social attitudes of a historical period.

Christening and wedding gowns abound and, hence, are not in large demand. Among the hardest items to find is men's clothing from the 19th and early 20th centuries. The most sought after clothing is by designers, such as Fortuny, Poirret, and Vionnet.

Additional Listings: See *Warman's Americana & Collectibles* for more examples.

Note: Condition, size, age, and completeness are critical factors in purchasing clothing. Collectors divide into two groups: those collecting for aesthetic and historic value and those desiring to wear the garment. Prices are higher on the West coast; major auction houses focus on designer clothes and high-fashion items.

Afternoon dress

Dark gray silk, pleated skirt, black lace trim on bodice, c1880 .... **60.00**

Pale blue lawn, two-pc, white crocheted buttons, white dotted Swiss detailing on bodice, c1900 .... **95.00**

Rust silk, two-pc, train, fitted bodice trimmed with tan silk knotted fringe, silk covered buttons, c1880 .... **450.00**

White dotted tulle, two-pc, lace yoke, pin tucks, ruffles, lace cuffs, c1890 .... **75.00**

White lawn, white cotton embroidery, filet lace insertion, rows of mother-of-pearl buttons on front, c1910 .... **225.00**

White linen, elbow-length sleeves, fitted waistline, crocheted buttons up back of bodice, cotton floral embroidery and trim, c1900 .... **250.00**

Beaded dress, black silk crepe and silk chiffon over black taffeta, embroidered all over with black glass beads, black silk chiffon drape from waistline, labeled "Best & Co.," c1940 .... **200.00**

Bed jacket, pale blue quilted satin, c1950 .... **40.00**

Belt, 31" l, Hermes, wide beige leather belt, gold tone pyramidal hardware **200.00**

Dresses, left: Lillie Rubin gown, black silk embroidered all over with black glass beads, halter-style neckline, single strap on low back, labeled "Lillie Rubin, 100% silk, Made in China, Size 4," 1970s, **$175**; center: black velvet cape, embroidered on pockets with rhinestones and large black beads, black satin lining, single button closure at neckline, early 1950s, **$95**; right: dress, navy cotton crochet, elbow length sleeves, long fringe, deep scoop neckline, satin fringe hem, mid-1940s, **$115**.

Bonnet, child's, brown crochet work, silk ribbon ties, mid-1800s, **$65**.

Bonnet, sun type, gray denim with stitching, ruffles, and large box, early 1920s, **$45**.

Blouse

Black dotted net, long sleeves, pin tucks, lace insertion at neckline, c1910
.... **45.00**
Cream bobbin lace over net, Battenberg lace yoke, stand-up collar, elbow-length sleeves, c1900............. **90.00**
Ivory silk, gray satin floral embroidery, c1955........ **35.00**
White lawn, embroidery and lace insertion, c1890, minor edge damage to collar . **30.00**

Cape

Black velvet, modified Napoleon collar, single button closure, lined with black quilted satin, c1930 ...... **60.00**
Black wool, black silk lining, rows of black glass beads trim, c1900................... **35.00**
Rose silk velvet, fully lined with pale green silk crepe, wide collar, single button closure, c1920 .... **195.00**
Capelet, black, glass beaded trim, open work, fringe, c1890
.... **40.00**
Chemine, linen, ruffles and lace at cuffs, late 18th/early 19th C
.... **25.00**

Collar

Black net, attached yoke, elaborately embroidered with black glass beads, c1890
.... **30.00**
Black silk and velvet, steel beading, c1890 .... **25.00**

Coat, woman's

Black silk velvet, black silk appliqués, cream silk satin lining, black soutache on lapels, red wool appliqué and gold embroidery, labeled "Lazarus Bros, Wilksbarre, PA, c1910......................... **250.00**
Black wool cashmere, long sleeves, black satin lining, deep cape of black fur, labeled "Kraeler, Jeannette, Reading, Harrisburg," c1940
.... **900.00**
Brown wool, brown silk velvet trim on front, collar, capelet, and cuffs, padded, fully lined in brown silk, c1870...... **75.00**

Dress

Black cotton sleeveless, double breasted style, large collar, gray buttons **30.00**
Black silk crepe, scallops at sleeves, cream embroidered silk cuffs and collar, wrap style, labeled "Lucille Ltd., New York," c1915 .... **195.00**
Burgundy satin brocade, wrap style bodice with frogs,

mandarin collar, "Hand Made in Hong Kong, 100% Rayon Broade," c1955 .... **90.00**
Bustle, two-pc, brown silk damask and brown silk, ruching and ruffles on bustle skirt, tan shell buttons on front, c1870, later added collar.......................... **275.00**
Iridescent mauve and green silk, hand stitched, full skirt gathered at waistline with smocking, pagoda sleeves, rose silk braid and fringe, lace under sleeves, hidden inside pocket, c1850.............. **65.00**
Navy blue and white cotton calico wrapper, ruffle at hem, capelet effect at yoke, some old repairs, c1900 .... **25.00**
Rust silk crepe, detailed at bodice and hem with cream silk, embroidered with pink, tangerine, aqua, and green satin flowers, labeled "New York, Paris, Claire Gowns, Made by Starr and Herbert," c1920......................... **120.00**
Dressing gown, white voile, lace trim, blue and white flowers, c1950................................ **65.00**
Frock, tan cotton print, tangerine and blue paisley detailing, brown carved buttons, c1880, some old repairs, minor fading
.... **65.00**

Evening wear, from left: Gown, sea foam green silk chiffon, long sleeves, illusion yoke, several layers in flowing A-line style, label "Rizkallah for Malcolm Starr," late 1960s, **$85**; fuchsia floral print silk chiffon, printed silk under pinnings, matching stole, late 1960s, **$65**; blue velvet and silver brocade, sequins on collar, blue feather trim at hem, up one side and on back drape, label "Edthye, Original Designs by Mr. Ben," early 1960s, **$95**; full black Chantilly lace skirt over black taffeta, late 1940s, **$45**; blush silk chiffon blouse with black lace appliqué and black silk chiffon with pin tucks, late 1940s, **$40**.

Evening wear and lingerie, left to right: gown, iridescent purple strapless style, ruching from bodice to near hem, purple taffeta lining, cotton floral appliqué, late 1950s, **$65**; evening coat, navy blue silk etched velvet with roses pattern, elbow length sleeves, single button closure, silk satin lining, mid-1950s, **$45**; teddy, pale pink crème, tan fillet lace, silk ribbon appliqué, early 1900s, **$40**.

Gown

Black velvet, full skirt, silk rose detailing, cream organdy collar, labeled "Trains-Norell," c1950 .... **75.00**

Brown lace full-length, brown chenille embroidery on net over brown net, crepe chartreuse velvet sash with brown carved Bakelite buckle, c1930 .... **125.00**

Charcoal gray and green silk velvet, pin tucks and smoking on sleeves, deep V-neckline, c1930 .... **95.00**

Deep aqua silk chiffon, elaborately embroidered with freeform shapes of clear glass beads, blue, rose, and white glass beaded Art Deco motifs, c1920 .... **550.00**

Gold and rust floral printed silk chiffon, cape collar, underpinnings of tan silk crepe, c1930 .... **85.00**

Gray and blue woven silk with cream stripe, pagoda sleeves, ruching on bodice, cream braid on sleeves and bodice, bodice lined with cream linen, c1865 .... **95.00**

Mauve silk chiffon, sleeveless, elaborately embroidered with lilac satin threads, silver glass beads in Art Deco motif, lilac feather trim at hem, underpinnings of ivory silk chiffon, c1920 .... **275.00**

Pale green silk chiffon, trimmed with pale green silk satin, embroidered at scalloped hem with silver and white glass beads, prong-set rhinestones, c1925 ..... **175.00**

Pale lilac silk, sq cut steel buttons, cream lace collar, bubble-effect skirt, draped back, c1900, wear **60.00**

Pumpkin and lilac silk etched velvet, sleeveless, floral design, fur at hem, c1920 .... **275.00**

Sheer cream silk in windowpane weave, overprinted with sepia, rose, and blue floral pattern, silk trim at cuffs, bodice lined with cream muslin, c1820 .. **500.00**

Tan silk, long sleeves, dropped waistline, button detailing, embroidery, c1920 .... **75.00**

Hand bags, beaded, left to right: glass beaded with peacock motif on both sides, royal blue and aqua, burgundy flowers, black and yellow geometric shapes, elaborately embossed frame with chain handle, early 1900s, 7" x 8-1/2" plus fringe, **$350**; glass beaded on both sides in floral design, shades of rose, blue, and green on cream ground, embossed brass frame with chain handle, mauve silk lining, small oval mirror and rosettes, early 1900s, 8" x 11 plus fringe, **$300**.

Handbag

Alligator, brown, brass clasp, brown leather lining, c1945 .... **45.00**

Black silk faille, embroidered with black glass beads, matching fringe, c1900 **95.00**

Floral tapestry, rose, green, and blue on cream ground, black border, brass frame with chain handle, c1940, 8-1/2" x 5-1/2" **30.00**

Hermes, Cabana, large blue leather form, silver tone hardware, two shoulder straps, leather interior with four pockets, 37 cm. **1,765.00**

Hermes, Constance, rigid red alligator form, gold tone hardware, large "H"-shaped magnetic closure, shoulder strap, leather interior with two pockets, 23 cm **3,525.00**

Hermes, Kelly, supple black calfskin form, gold tone hardware, detachable shoulder strap, leather interior with three pockets, 30 cm **2,350.00**

Hermes, Kelly, rigid blue alligator form, gold tone hardware, detachable shoulder strap, leather interior with three pockets, 33 cm, boxed, orig felt protection insert **10,340.00**

Hermes, Kelly, rigid pebbled brown leather form, gold tone hardware, detachable shoulder strap, leather interior with three pockets, 32 cm, boxed, orig felt protection insert **4,820.00**

Mesh, 10k yg, pierced and scalloped top set with four old mine-cut diamonds, approx 1.12 cts., three oval cabochon turquoise, suspended by trace link chain and gold safety pin, 67.0 dwt., stamped No. "6," European hallmark, c1915 .... **1,120.00**

Mesh, 14k yg, Edwardian, designed with a floral and scroll frame, the bypass-style thumb piece set with two sugarloaf sapphires joined by a trace link chain, 132.5 dwt. **1,116.75**

Mesh, 14k yg, Edwardian, pierced, chased, and engraved floral and foliate closure, suspended from a curb link chain, 96./ dwt. **835.00**

Silver and enamel, Birmingham, England, 1938, maker's mark "EJH," oval, lid with lavender basse taille enamel, leather lined interior, silver link chain, monogrammed, 6-1/4" l, 3-7/8" d **250.00**

Hat, lady's fashion type

Aqua silk pillbox, aqua veil, colorful beads embroidery, c1960 .... **50.00**

Black velour, wide brim, black feathers, black and white ostrich plumes, c1910 .. **95.00**

Hat, child's, straw, red, velvet streamers, red, white, and blue cotton flowers, late 1940s, **$45**.

Top hat, black silk, **$175**, and paisley shawl, **$195**.

Photo courtesy of Dotta Auction Co., Inc.

Wide-brimmed black velvet, under brim of blue velvet, blue ostrich plume, silver stamped on the black silk lining "Dives Pomeroy & Stewart," c1910 .... **150.00**
Wide-brimmed natural straw, gold grosgrain ribbon, white cotton daisies, labeled "Jean Allen," c1945 .... **35.00**

Hat, man's, top hat, orig box **85.00**

Jacket
Battenburg cream lace, long sleeves, gathering at shoulders, c1890 .... **350.00**
Lace, cream Irish crochet, borders of elaborate Irish crochet with shamrock motif, V-neckline, four tan crocheted buttons, c1910 .... **325.00**
Silk velvet, purple, lined with purple silk, fabric covered buttons, patch pockets, c1890 .... **120.00**
Wool flannel, black, bolero, black taffeta lining, black fur tri, c1955 .... **65.00**

Lingerie dress
White batiste, embroidery and lace insertion on bodice, and skirt, ruching below waistline, c1910 .... **45.00**

White eyelet lace, white lawn, detailed bodice with pin tucks, lace yoke and collar, scalloped hem, c1900 .. **65.00**
White lawn, eyelet lace, lace insertion, ruffles at hem, c1790 .... **375.00**

Nightgown
Pale pink satin, diminutive roses pattern, cut on bias, c1940 .... **35.00**
White cotton, embroidered yoke, buttons up front, c1910 .... **35.00**
White cotton, lace cutwork yoke, embroidered, matching lace cuffs, c1910 .... **55.00**

Pajamas, leopard print flannel, Dora Lee, c1950, unworn **35.00**

Pants suit, charcoal gray wool flannel, long sleeved tunic top, high collar, straight legged pants, entirely set with prong-set rhinestones, fully lined, labeled "Made In The British Crown Colony of Hong Kong, Best & Co., Fifth Ave, New York," c1960, several rhinestones loose **70.00**

Petticoat
Cream organdy, pin tucks, lace, ruffles at hem, train, c1890 .... **35.00**
White cotton, scalloped eyelet lace hem, front tucked panel, c1880 .... **40.00**

Robe, printed green, tan, gray, yellow, and ivory silk, swirls, floral, and feather shapes, c1945 .... **60.00**

Scarf, Hermes, silk
Cosmos, blue and white horse-drawn chariots riding upon clouds on light blue and purple background **250.00**
Fetes Venitiennes, harlequins and guests at masquerade ball on background of brown, orange and purple...... **200.00**

Shoes, left: black silk pumps, steel buckles, c1910, **$45**; right: brown suede pumps with perforations on uppers, brown silk ties, early 1920s, **$35**.

Shawl
Cream silk, floral cream satin embroidery, knotted fringe, braided dec, back tassel, c1890 .... **150.00**
Ivory silk, floral ivory satin embroidery, knotted satin fringe, Spanish, c1900, 44" sq **75.00**
Woven silk taffeta, light gray plaid, rose and green satin flowers, long knotted silk fringe, c1900, 70" sq .. **125.00**

Slip, ivory silk, net darning trim in floral design, camisole top lace straps, ivory satin embroidery, c1910 .... **65.00**

Skirt, lace alternating with voile, black, train, underpinnings of cream silk taffeta, pinking and ruffles, c1870, some minor damage on tulle and lining **150.00**

Smoking jacket, man's, silver and black floral design brocade, black silk faille lapels, black silk lining, c1950 .... **25.00**

Suit, gray wool tweed, fabric cov buttons, button detailing on jacket pockets, lined with pale gray crepe, flared skirt with gores, "Freiss Orig" label, c1945 .... **110.00**

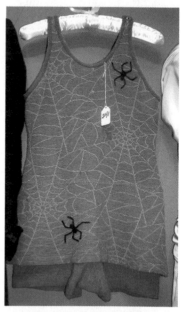

Swimsuit, aqua blue wool, orange-yellow spider-web motif, appliqué of large black spiders, labeled "Bradley, U.S.A.," early 1920s, size M, **$125**.

Photo courtesy of Alderfer Auction Co.

Back left: painted wood stick fan with blue paper, painted with blue flowers, gold, and coral lines, early 1940s, 9" l, **$5**; right: brown wood with silk, hand painted in floral design with butterflies in rose, white, gold, and green on rust-brown ground, late 1800s, 15" l, opens to 27", **$80**; front left: actual tortoiseshell brise fan with brown silk tassel, silk monogram, Austria or German, late 1880s, 9-1/2" w, ribbon holding sticks broken, **$150**; folding set of glasses, faux tortoise celluloid handle pierced work, no lens, 1" l, late 1800s, **$50**; glass beaded reticule, floral design in mustard, green, blue, burgundy, rose, gray and brown, drawstring top, brown cotton lining, late 1800s, 6" x 10", **$90**.

Photo courtesy of Alderfer Auction Co.

COCA-COLA ITEMS

History: The originator of Coca-Cola was John Pemberton, a pharmacist from Atlanta, Georgia. In 1886, Dr. Pemberton introduced a patent medicine to relieve headaches, stomach disorders, and other minor maladies. Unfortunately, his failing health and meager finances forced him to sell his interest.

In 1888, Asa G. Candler became the sole owner of Coca-Cola. Candler improved the formula, increased the advertising budget, and widened the distribution. A "patient" was accidentally given a dose of the syrup mixed with carbonated water instead of still water. The result was a tastier, more refreshing drink.

As sales increased in the 1890s, Candler recognized that the product was more suitable for the soft-drink market and began advertising it as such. From these beginnings, a myriad of advertising items have been issued to invite all to "Drink Coca-Cola."

Notes: Dates of interest: "Coke" was first used in advertising in 1941. The distinctively shaped bottle was registered as a trademark on April 12, 1960.

Sweater
Beige cashmere, double lining of beige lace and nylon, long sleeves, rhinestone buttons, rhinestone clasp at waistline, tan mink snap-on collar, c1955, some rhinestones missing from clasp **40.00**
Black cashmere, labeled "Made in Scotland for Liberty of London" **35.00**

Umbrella
Black silk, silver handle formed as looped snake, Continental, English import hallmarks for London, 1904, 7-1/8" l handle, 36" l overall **150.00**
Gold, brown, orange, and yellow paisley ruffle, unused, orig gold and black hang tag for "Made in U.S.A., 100% Nylon," orig Strawbridge & Clothier box, c1955 ...... **45.00**
Round tapered handle with stamped and engraved vertical bands of leafy scrolls and flowerheads, mother-of-pearl central band, 7-5/8" l handle, 31" l overall **230.00**

Vest, white cotton, mother-of-

pearl buttons, c1910 .... **65.00**

Visiting dress
Dark blue silk, dark blue, bodice and sleeves with light gray silk satin in geometric designs, elaborate embroidery on skirt, underpinnings of lace-trimmed cream silk, embroidered organdy collar, labeled "Rendel, Paris, London, New York," c1900 .... **100.00**
Pale pink silk, two-pc, pink tucks, lace appliqué, lace cuffs, c1890 .... **65.00**
Purple linen, elaborate fabric-covered button detailing, purple silk net trim at neckline and cuffs, c1910, minor damage to net **40.00**

Waistcoat, gentleman's, silk, embroidered with floral vines and sprigs, two covered pockets, applied cherub-printed roundels below, England or France, late 18th C, restorations **250.00**

Walking suit, wool, silk faille, chestnut brown, brown silk velvet trim, pleats at hem, fabric-covered buttons, lace collar **325.00**

Sign, metal, flange, hand holding Pepsi bottle cap over "Gents" sign, c1945, 17" x 15" **700.00**

Sign, metal, red, yellow, and black, "Bigger and Better Pepsi-Cola Worth a Dime, Costs a Nickel," 1936 .... **1,700.00**

Syrup dispenser, ceramic, made by Avon Faience Pottery Co., Tiltonsville, OH, c1904, glazed in two shades of blue, squeeze-bag dec of rose trees and tiny rabbits, in the style of Frederick Rhead, lid with additional squeeze-bag dec also includes medical virtues, such as "Cures Indigestion, Relieves Exhaustion," one of four known, slight repairs **27,000.00**

Utility cooler, labeled "Ice Cold Pepsi-Cola Sold Here 5¢," bottle opener, brass spigot, restored **800.00**

Grading Condition. The following numbers represent the standard grading system used by dealers, collectors, and auctioneers:

C.10 = Mint
C. 9 = Near mint
C.8.5 = Outstanding
C.8 = Excellent
C.7.5 = Fine +
C.7 = Fine
C. 6.5 = Fine – (good)
C. 6 = Poor

Bingo cards, diecut, lot of three, each 8-1/2" x 9" cardboard card printed on front in red and black, each has 25 diecut windows which reveal different numbers for use in calling Bingo game, text across bottom "Compliments Coca-Cola Bottling Co," issued by Kemper-Thomas, Cincinnati, OH. Some surface dust soil, bit of light wear around edges, right side of bottom of each has original owner's initials in blue ballpoint pen, 1940s, **$25**.

Photo courtesy of Hake's Americana & Collectibles.

Binder, 13" x 15-1/2", rigid cardboard, red oilcloth cover, four-ring metal binder to hold advertising sales sheets, c1950, no contents **48.00**

Bookmark, Romance of Coca-Cola, 1916 .... **30.00**

Bottle
Amber, marked "Lewisburg" **30.00**
Christmas, Williamstown, WV **15.00**
Commemorative, Nascar Series, Bill Elliott, Dale Earnhardt, or Bobby Labonte **5.00**

Bowl, 10" w, Vernon Ware, green, artificial ice, 1930s, C-9.8 .... **600.00**

Calendar, 1913, 13-1/2" x 22-1/2", Hamilton King illus **900.00**

Ceiling globe, 14" d, milk glass, four logos, 1930s, C-9.5 . **990.00**

Clock, 18" octagonal, neon, silhouette girl, 1939, C-8.5 .... **1,800.00**

Cooler, Victor, triple-door, attached counter, mounted jukebox, brass foot rail, three floor-mounted bar stools, restored **5,775.00**

Cut-out, 1926, girl under umbrella **3,995.00**

Door kick plate, litho tin, 11-1/2" x 35", scrolling logo
Drink Coca-Cola, 1942 couple on right, C-9.9 .... **2,600.00**
Drink Coca-Cola, 1923 bottle on left, C-9.9 .... **1,765.00**

Door pull, 8" h, plastic and metal, bottle shape, orig instructions and screws, C-9.3-9.5 .... **275.00**

Dry-server, unused **5.00**

Coca Cola advertising cooler, **$700**.
Photo courtesy of Joy Luke Auctions.

Game board, 11-1/4" x 26-1/2", Steps to Health, prepared and distributed by Coca-Cola Co. of Canada, Ltd., copyright 1938, orig unmarked brown paper envelope **60.00**

Mileage meter, 10" x 7", originating in Statesville, NC, C-8.4 .... **1,675.00**

Pin, Hi-Fi Club, gold luster finish, detailed plastic, short metal stickpin, miniature Coke bottle about name in red lettering, phonograph record background inscribed "Sponsored By Your Coca-Cola Bottler," Australian issue, c1950 .... **40.00**

Plate, Vienna Art, topless woman **1,610.00**

Pocket mirror, 1-3/4" w, 2-3/4" h oval, celluloid, 1914, pretty girl, dark green ground, white and red lettering..................... **400.00**

Poster, 1943, two farm girls taking a break, caption "Work Refreshed" **2,750.00**

Prize chance card, 4-1/4" x 5-1/4", printed in red and black on white, c1940, unused .. **12.00**

Toy, delivery truck, Buddy L, pressed steel, yellow body, red, white, and black decals, no bottles, **$45**.
Photo courtesy of Dotta Auction Co., Inc.

Calendar, 1909, paper, original metal strip at top, "Drink Coca-Cola, Delicious And Refreshing," pad begins with April, few areas of restoration, con. 8.5-8.75+, 20-1/2" h, 11" w, **$14,300**.

Photos courtesy of Gary Metz, Muddy River Trading Co.

Calendar, 1912, paper, ""Drink Coca-Cola, Delicious And Refreshing," pad begins with June, museum mounted/framed, light stains/wrinkling, cond. 8-8.25, 31" h, 12" w, **$7,150**.

Display, cardboard hanger, die cut, 3-D, 1944, "Have A Coke," Sprite Boy with Coca-Cola hat, original easel back, cond. 8.75-9, 18" h, 14", **$4,730**.

Signs, tin, die-cut: (left) 1958, 6-pack with "Regular Size" dot on carton, cond. 9.5-9.75, 11" h, 13" w, **$2,970**; (right) 1950, six-pack, "6 for 25¢," shows wire handle, edge nicks, cond. 9.5, 11" h, 13" w, **$1,760**.

Sign, cardboard, 1906, Lillian Nordica, "Coca-Cola, At Soda Fountains, 5¢," few light stains/small tears, period frame, cond. 7.5-8, 46" h, 26" w, **$15,400**.

Radio
Bottle shape, 24" h, 1930s, C-8.2 .... **8,500.00**
Cooler shape, red, 1950s **2,250.00**
Salesman's sample, cooler, Glasscock **10,450.00**
Sandwich plate, 7-1/4" d, white ground, script slogan, bottle and glass in center, Knowles, C-9.8 .... **750.00**

Sign, porcelain
6" x 18", diecut, two-color, script, orig box, attaching instructions, screws, C-10 .... **1,100.00**
23" x 26", porcelain, diagonal slash, fountain service, 1934, C-9.7 .... **4,700.00**
24" d, porcelain, single bottle in center, no slogan, 1950, C-9.2 .... **1,800.00**
60" x 42", porcelain, curb-side service, two-sided, green, red, and white, 1933, C-9.6 .... **3,000.00**

Sign, tin
Drink Coca-Cola, emb tin litho, vertical, c1931, 12-1/4" x 4-1/2", C.8.5 .... **625.00**
Drink Coca-Cola, Ice Cold, Gas To-Day, tin, 1936 .... **2,700.00**
Man and woman, 1941 .... **550.00**
Sign, wood, 11-3/8" x 9", Drink Coca-Cola, fancy metal filigree at top, orig Kay Display label on back, c1930, C.8+ **775.00**
String holder, two-sided, showing six-lace and logo "Take Home in Cartons," 1940s, C-9.5 .... **4,000.00**
Thermometer, 12" d, c1950, round, red and white **180.00**
Tip tray, 1913 .... **395.00**
Toy, van, Corgi, 5" l diecast metal and plastic replica, copyright 1978, 2-3/4" x 6" x 3-1/2" color box with display window **35.00**

Tray
1926, oval, girl handing coke to viewer, 13" x 19", C-10 .... **15,250.00**
1930, bathing beauty, C-8 .... **195.00**
1935, Madge Evans, C-7.5 .... **165.00**
1942, girl in convertible being waited on by another girl, C-9.5 .... **450.00**
Vending machine, 23-5/8" x 21-5/8" x 64" h, Select-O-Matic, Westinghouse, six dial selector, bottle opener set into front, c1960 .... **3,200.00**

Tray, Springboard Girl, 1939, American Art Works, Coshocton, OH, 13-1/2" x 10-1/2", **$425**.
Photo courtesy of Joy Luke Auctions.

Tray, Roadster, 1942, American Art Works, Coshocton, OH, some wear and scratches, 13-1/4" x 10-1/2", **$88**
Photo courtesy of Joy Luke Auctions.

COFFEE MILLS

History: Coffee mills or grinders are utilitarian objects designed to grind fresh coffee beans. Before the advent of stay-fresh packaging, coffee mills were a necessity.

The first home-size coffee grinders were introduced about 1890. The large commercial grinders designed for use in stores, restaurants, and hotels often bear an earlier patent date.

Wood, single drawer, cast iron grinder and handle, **$125**.
Photo courtesy of Dotta Auction Co., Inc.

Wood, Golden Rule, Columbus, Ohio, cast iron grinder and handle, **$185**.
Photo courtesy of Dotta Auction Co., Inc.

Wood, single drawer, cast iron grinder and handle, partial original label "Colonial Coffee Grinder, Wrightsville Hardware Co.," **$75**.

Arcade, 17" h, wall type, crystal jar, emb design, marked "Crystal" and "Arcade" orig lid rusted.............................. **185.00**
Crown Coffee Mill, cast iron, mounted on wood base, decal "Crown Coffee Mill Made By Landers, Frary, & Clark, New Britain, Conn, U.S.A.," number 11 emb on top lid............ **525.00**
Enterprise
#00, 12-1/2" x 7-1/2" x 8-3/4", two wheels, store type, orig paint, orig decals, C8+ **1,450.00**
#9, orig dec and decals, bright orange/red paint, blue on top of base and edges of wheels, gold detailed lettering, drawer in base stenciled "No. 9," eagle finial, white porcelain knob,

minor wear, restored break on lid, 28-1/2" h...... **1,200.00**

Cast iron, remnants of decorative decals at top, base embossed "Enterprise Mfg Co., Philadelphia, PA," **$500**.

Pine, fingered joints, one drawer, iron pull, iron top cup and handle, wooden knob, c1880, 5-3/4" sq, 6" h **95.00**
Tin, tole dec of tulip and stars, 12" h **250.00**
Woodruff Edwards, Elgin, IL, 66" h, store type, 28" d wheels, eagle finial, repainted .. **1,800.00**

COIN-OPERATED ITEMS

History: Coin-operated items include amusement games, pinball machines, jukeboxes, slot machines, vending machines, cash registers, and other items operated by coins.

The first jukebox was developed about 1934 and played 78-RPM records. Jukeboxes were important to teen-agers before the advent of portable radios and television.

The first pinball machine was introduced in 1931 by Gottlieb. Pinball machines continued to be popular until the advent of solid-state games in 1977 and advanced electronic video games after that.

The first three-reel slot machine, the Liberty Bell, was invented in 1905 by Charles Fey in San Francisco. In 1910, Mills Novelty Company copyrighted the classic fruit symbols. Improvements and advancements have led to the sophisticated machines of today.

Vending machines for candy, gum, and peanuts were popular from 1910 until 1940 and can be found in a wide range of sizes and shapes.

Additional Listings: See *Warman's Americana & Collectibles* for separate categories for Jukeboxes, Pinball Machines, Slot Machines, and Vending Machines.

Adviser: Bob Levy.

Notes: Because of the heavy usage these coin-operated items received, many are restored or, at the very least, have been repainted by either the operator or manufacturer. Using reproduced mechanisms to restore pieces is acceptable in many cases, especially when the restored piece will then perform as originally intended.

Cash register, National, 1914, brass, Model 317, **$1,300**.

Arcade
Bag Puncher, Mills Novelty, 1926 .... **4,500.00**
Big Bronco, Exhibit Supply, 1951 .... **1,300.00**
Bowling League, Genco, 1949 .... **800.00**
Hunter, Silver King, 1949 **500.00**

Gum
Big Top, Advance, capsule, 1969 .... **300.00**
Cebco Hot Nut, two globes, 1930 .... **400.00**

E-Z, Ad-Lee Novelty, gumballs, 1908 .... **1,500.00**
Master Novelty, Atlas, 1951 .... **150.00**

Slot machine, Mills, 1934, 5 cents, Chevron QT, **$2,200**.

Slot machine, Callie, 1930, 10 cents, Superior Jackpot, **$2,500**.

Jukeboxes
AMI, G200, 1950 .... **700.00**
Rockola, Deluxe 20, 1939 .... **1,700.00**
Seeburg, M100B, 1955 **2,000.00**
Wurlitzer, 700, 1940 .... **4,500.00**

Slot machines
Caille, Cadet, 1934 .... **900.00**
Groetchen, Deluxe Columbia, 1938 .... **900.00**
Jennings
　Bronze Chief, 1940 .. **1,600.00**
　Sun Chief, 1948 .... **2,900.00**
　Today Vender, 1928 . **2,000.00**

Slot machine, Jennings, 1933, one cent, Little Duke, **$2,800**.

Slot machine, Mills, 1938, 25 cents, Bursting Cherry, **$2,300**.

Slot machine, Pace, 1936, 5 cents, All Star Comet, **$2,300**.

Mills
Diamond Front, 1939
.... **1,600.00**
Token Bell Hightop, 1948
.... **1,800.00**
Torch Front, 1928..... **1,400.00**
War Eagle, 1931 ...... **2,200.00**

Pace
Bantam, 1930 .... **1,800.00**
Deluxe Comet, 1939 **1,400.00**
Whatling
Bird of Paradise, Rolatop, 1935........................ **5,500.00**
Treasury, 1939 .... **3,000.00**

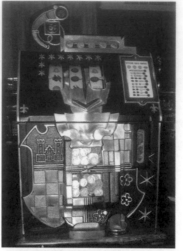

Slot machine, Mills, 1938, 5 cents, Castle, Gold Award, **$3,000**.

Jennings slot machine, Bronze Chief, **$2,800**.

Miscellaneous
American Scale, 1937 ... **200.00**
Jergens Lotion, lotion dispenser, 1937 .... **350.00**
Keen Kut Razor Blades, 1940 .... **200.00**
Kitco Towels, Kirch, 1936 .... **125.00**
National Postage, Northwestern, 1950 .... **125.00**

Watling Horoscope Scale, 1957 .... **350.00**

COINS

History: Coin collecting has long been one of the most respected and honored aspects of the collecting world. Today it still holds its fascination as new collectors come onto the scene every day. And just like the old-time collectors, they should be ready to spend time reading and learning more about this fascinating hobby. The States Quarter Series has spurred many of us to save quarters again and that has encouraged all types of coin collecting.

After the Declaration of Independence, America realized it needed its own coinage. Before that time, foreign coins were used in addition to paper currency. The first real coin of the young America was a copper coin, known as the Fugio Cent. Many of the early states created their own coins until the federal mint was constructed in Philadelphia after 1792. By 1837, the purity of silver was increased from 89.24 to 90 percent with minor adjustments to this weight occurring until 1873. Early dominations included a silver 3-cent piece, a gold $3 piece (1854) $1 and $20 (1849). The coinage law of 1857 eliminated the half-cent, changed the size of some coins, and forbid the use of foreign coins as legal tender. By the time of the Civil War, the two-cent and nickel three-cent pieces and the five-cent nickel were created. The phrase "In God We Trust" was added at this time. From the late 1870s, coins were plentiful. From 1873 to 1918, several laws were passed to force the government to buy silver and strike an abundance of silver dollars. President Theodore Roosevelt is credited with having the Mercury dime, the Walking Liberty half-dollar and the St. Gaudens double eagle, and the buffalo nickel created. Commemorative coins were also becoming very popular at this time. Designs on coins continue to change to reflect events, such as the Bicentennial.

It would be impossible to list values for all types of coins in a general price guide such as *Warman's,* so the following is included to give a general idea of coins. More information about specific coins is available in the various publications, including the *2003 Standard Catalog of World Coins,* published by Krause Publications.

Grading: The value placed on a coin is highly dependent on its "grade" or condition. The general accepted grades are as follows:

Uncirculated (Unc) (Mint State)(Ms) is known as "Very Good." These coins will show no wear at all, and should appear as though they just came from the mint.

Almost Uncirculated (AU) is known as "Good." An *Almost Uncirculated* coin describes coins with slight signs of wear.

Extremely Fine (EX) (Extra Fine) (XF) is known as "Fair." Extremely Fine coins exhibit wear that is readily seen, but still has clear details.

Very Fine (VF) is known as "Poor." A "Very Fine" coin will show obvious signs of wear, but still be clear of defects.

Fine (F) is the lowest grade most people would consider collectible. In this grade, about half the design details will show. The wear should be so slight that the viewer requires a magnifying glass to see it. There are several sub-categories in all these grades.

Very Good (VG). Coins graded at this level will show heavy wear, outlines will be clear.

Good (G). Coins at this grade are considered uncollectible except for novelty purposes.

About Good (AG) and *Fair (Fr).* These grades are for coins with much wear, often the rims are worn down and the outlines of the design are disappearing.

Poor (Pr) is the lowest grade possible; sometimes the coin will barely be identifiable.

Proof (PF) refers not to a grade, but rather a special way of making coins, usually as presentation pieces. A *Proof* will usually be double struck with highly polished coins on polished blanks.

Reproduction Alert: Counterfeit coins of all denominations exist.

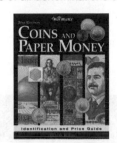

For more information, see *Warman's Coins and Paper Money,* 3rd edition.

$2-1/2, gold
1836	**365.00**
1925	**215.00**
1929	**200.00**

$10, 1879, gold **320.00**
$20, 1927, gold **520.00**

Barber Half Dollar, 1892-1915, designed by Charles E. Barber.
1892, VG	**23.00**
1897S, VF	**400.00**
1905, VG	**19.00**
1913, VG	**25.00**
1915, VF	**190.00**

Buffalo Nickel, 1913 to 1938
1913, mound, Unc.	**32.00**
1918S, VG	**32.50**
1936D, VG	**25.00**

American in Space, proof set, first edition, sterling silver, **$15.**

Coin photos courtesy of Dotta Auction Co., Inc

Double Eagle $20 gold piece, 1924, modeled by St. Gaudens, walking Liberty verso, eagle in flight with motto recto, 1-5/16" d . **470.00**

Eisenhower Dollar, 1971-1978
1791D, PF	**3.00**
1973S, silver, Ms	**8.00**
1976S, silver, block letters, PF	**12.00**

1978D, PR	**3.50**
1836, gold	**325.00**
1899, gold, half eagle.	**200.00**

Franklin Half Dollar, 1948 to 1963
1948, Ms	**13.75**
1950, XF	**6.00**
1952, XF	**3.00**
1961, Ms	**4.25**

Half Cent; production ended in 1859.
Braided hair, proof, 1849	**3,200.00**
Classic head type, 1810, VG	**140.00**
Draped bust type, 1804, spiked chin version, VG	**45.00**
Liberty cap type, 1793, VG	**2,000.00**

$10 gold coin, 1915 Indian head, **$275.**

Kennedy Half Dollar, 1964-2001. Obverse designed by Gilroy Roberts.
1964, XF	**2.00**
1965, silver clad, BU	**1.35**
1965-70, XF	**1.00**
1970S, Proof	**7.75**
1971-date	**.50**
1976, Bicentennial reverse, BU	**1.25**
1979, filled "S," Proof	**2.50**
1981S, Proof	**2.00**
1989D, BU	**1.50**
1996P, BU	**2.00**

Indian Head, Liberty, 1911, gold, **$125.**

Indian Head Cent, 1859-1909
1860, copper-nickel allow, F	**37.00**
1867, bronze, XF	**155.00**
1909S, F	**300.00**

Jefferson Nickel, 1938 to present
1938, VG	**.05**
1942-1945, silver, VG	**.50**
1971S, proof	**1.60**

Large Cents
Classic head type, 1808-
1814, 1810, VG............. **600.00**
Coronet type, 1816-1857
1817, 13 stars, VG........ **15.00**
1838, VG..................... **14.00**
1847, VG..................... **19.50**
Draped bust type, 1796 to
1807
1800, VG..................... **350.00**
1804, restrike, Unc **450.00**
Flowing hair type, 1793,
wreath, VG................ **1,200.00**
Liberty cap type, 1793-1796,
1794, VG..................... **250.00**

Liberty Nickel, 1883 to 1913
1883, no cents, G **3.75**
1883-1913, Ms.............. **60.00**

Liberty, 1836, gold, **$95.**

Lincoln Cent, 1909-present
1909 to 1958, VG.............. **.05**
1943, VG........................... **.15**
1959-82, Ms..................... **.15**
1982-present .... **.011**

Mercury Dime, 1916-1945,
designed by Adolph Weinman.
1916, VF......................... **6.00**
1929, D, Ms **25.00**
1940, VG......................... **1.10**
1944D, Ms **5.50**

Liberty, 1836, gold, worn, **$115.**

Morgan Dollar, 1878-1921,
designed by George T. Morgan.
1878, 8 tail feathers, VG **20.00**
1881S, VG..................... **15.00**
1887, Ms....................... **24.00**
1889CC, VF **500.00**
1899, Ms..................... **100.00**
1921S, Ms..................... **26.00**

Roosevelt Dime, 1946-2001,
designed by John R. Sinnock.
1946, BU...................... **1.05**
1950S, XF..................... **1.25**
1953S, XF........................ **.65**
1964D, BU........................ **.90**
1970S, proof .... **.80**
1980P, BU........................ **.40**
1995D, BU........................ **.35**

Liberty, 1879, gold, **$100.**

Seated Liberty Dime, 1837-
1891
1837-1838, no stars, G. **30.00**
1838-1860, Ms............ **250.00**
1860-1891, G................. **8.75**

Seated Liberty Dollar, 1840-
1873
1840, G **100.00**
1846, F........................ **175.00**
1853, EF **575.00**
1866, G **100.00**

Seated Liberty Half Dollar,
1839-1891, designed by
Christian Gobrecht, several
variations.
1839-1886, G................ **16.00**
1840, small reverse letters,
VG................................ **60.00**
1853, arrows and rays, G
.... **16.50**
1854-55, arrows, G....... **16.00**
1857, arrows removed, VF
.... **45.00**
1873-74, arrows, G....... **16.50**
1866-1891, G................ **15.00**

Liberty, 1900, gold, **$75.**

Seated Liberty Quarter, 1838-
1891, designed by Christian
Gobrecht, several variations.
1840O, VG.................. **25.00**
1852, VG..................... **145.00**
1853, arrows at date, VG
.... **20.00**
1856, arrows removed, VG
.... **20.00**
1860S, arrows removed, VG
.... **50.00**
1866, motto above eagle, VG
.... **450.00**
1873, arrows at date, VG
.... **23.00**
1876, arrows removed, VG
.... **17.00**

Silver Three Cent
1851-1853, G................ **18.50**
1854-1858, Ms............ **240.00**
1859-1873, G................ **17.50**

Walking Liberty Half Dollar,
1916-1947. Designed by Adolph
Weinman.
1918, F......................... **12.00**
1935, XF **6.00**
1939, XF **10.00**

Washington Quarter, 1932-
1998. Designed by John
Flanagan.
1932, VG......................... **7.50**
1941, VG......................... **1.75**
1946, BU......................... **3.75**
1957D, BU....................... **2.50**
1972, BU........................... **.75**

COMIC BOOKS

History: Shortly after comics first
appeared in newspapers of the
1890s, they were reprinted in book
format and often used as
promotional giveaways by
manufacturers, movie theaters,
and candy and stationery stores.
The first modern-format comic was
issued in 1933.

The magic date in comic
collecting is June 1938, when DC
issued Action Comics No. 1,
marking the first appearance of
Superman. Thus began the
Golden Age of comics, which
lasted until the mid-1950s and
witnessed the birth of the major
comic-book publishers, titles, and
characters.

In 1954, Fredric Wertham
authored *Seduction of the
Innocent*, a book that pointed a
guilt-laden finger at the comics
industry for corrupting youth,

causing juvenile delinquency, and undermining American values. Many publishers were forced out of business, while others established a "comics code" to assure parents that their comics were compliant with morality and decency standards upheld by the code authority.

The silver age of comics, mid-1950s through the end of the 1960s, witnessed the revival of many of the characters from the Golden Age in new comic formats. The era began with Showcase No. 4 in October 1956, which marked the origin and first appearance of the Silver-Age Flash.

While comics survived into the 1970s, it was a low point for the genre; but in the early 1980s, a revival occurred. In 1983, comic-book publishers, other than Marvel and DC, issued more titles than had existed in total during the previous 40 years. The mid- and late-1980s were a boom time, a trend that appears to be continuing.

Reproduction Alert: Publishers frequently reprint popular stories, even complete books, so the buyer must pay strict attention to the title, not just the portion printed in oversized letters on the front cover. If there is any doubt, look inside at the fine print on the bottom of the inside cover or first page. The correct title will be printed there in capital letters.

Also pay attention to the dimensions of the comic book. Reprints often differ in size from the original.

Warman's
Comic Book
FIELD GUIDE

John Jackson Miller and Maggie Thompson
Values and Identification

For more information, see *Warman's Comic Book Field Guide.*

Note: The comics listed here are in near-mint condition, meaning they have a flat, clean, shiny cover that has no wear other than tiny corner creases; no subscription creases, writing, yellowing at margins, or tape repairs; staples are straight and rust free; pages are supple and like new; generally just-off-the-shelf quality.

Abbott and Costello, St. John, #21	**50.00**
Ace Comics, #16	**200.00**
Adventures of Mighty Mouse, St. John, #15	**35.00**
Adventures of Rex the Wonder Dog, #29	**7.00**
Alien Legion, Vol. 2, #6	**1.50**
All American Comics, #36	**900.00**
Amazing Detective Cases, #3	**85.00**
Amazing Mystery Funnies, #2	**1,150.00**
Amazing Spider-Man, #4	**1,900.00**
American Splendor, #14	**12.00**
Andy Panda, Gold Key, #10	**2.00**
Avengers, #24	**200.00**
Babe Ruth Sports Comics, #6	**120.00**
Baffling Mysteries, #2	**150.00**

Lois Lane, Superman DC Comics, No. 83, **$3**.

Batman, #18	**1,500.00**
Beetle Bailey, #13	**12.00**
Blue Ribbon Comics, M.L.J., #3	**600.00**
Captain America, #130	**7.50**
Chip 'n' Dale, Dell, #15	**22.00**
Classics Illustrated	
#16, *Gulliver's Travels*	**185.00**
#54, *Man in the Iron Mask*	**40.00**
#128, *Macbeth*	**10.00**
Combat, #3	**25.00**
Crime Does Not Pay, #43	**100.00**
Dagwood Comics, #7	**25.00**

Daredevil, #9	**340.00**
DC Super Spectacular, #20	**84.00**
Dennis the Menace, #32	**20.00**
Dick Tracy Comics Monthly, Harvey, #38	**85.00**
Exciting Comics, Nedor, #11	**450.00**

Fantastic Four, Marvel, November 56, *Klaw the Murderous Master of Sound*, **$65**.

Fantastic Four, #20	**200.00**
Fightin' Texan, St. John, #16	**50.00**
Flame, #5	**400.00**
Flash Gordon Comics, Harvey, #4	**110.00**
Flat Top, Harvey, #3	**10.00**
Forbidden Love, #2	**325.00**
Forbidden Worlds, #8	**450.00**
Gene Autry and Champion, Dell, #112	**20.00**
Generation X, Marvel, #5	**2.00**
GI Joe I Battle, #1	**64.00**
Girls' Love Stories, DC, #18	**75.00**
Green Lantern, #27	**125.00**
Hercules, Marvel, #3	**1.50**
Hopalong Cassidy, DC, #87	**75.00**
House of Secrets, #4	**300.00**
Incredible Science Fiction, E.C., #31	**250.00**
Invaders, The, Marvel, #10	**4.00**
Josie & The Pussycats, Archie, #77	**4.00**
Justice League of America, #14	**150.00**
Kid Eternity, #10	**135.00**
Kobra, #2	**3.00**
Legion of Super-Heroes, The, DC, 2nd series, #272	**1.75**
Leave It To Beaver, #1285	**310.00**
Little Lulu, #14	**125.00**
Little Orphan Annie, #1	**90.00**
Love Letters, #18	**15.00**

Jace Pearson's Tales of the Texas Rangers, Dell, Sept-November, **$40**.

Marvel Preview, #1 .... **2.00**
Millie the Model Comics, Marvel, #3 .... **100.00**
Modern Comics, #98 ...... **200.00**
More Fun Comics, DC, #27 .... **1,775.00**
Mystery in Space, #66 .... **410.00**
Nickel Comics, Fawcett, #5 .... **600.00**
Orion, #1 .... **2.95**
Our Army At War, #21 ..... **135.00**
Panic, E. C., #1 .... **210.00**
Police Comics, #50 .... **250.00**
Rawhide Kid, #49............ **100.00**
Red Seal Comics, Harry A. Chester, #16 .... **315.00**
Sad Sack World, Harvey, #1 .... **45.00**
Sea Devils, #54 .... **125.00**
Secrets of Haunted House, DC, #10 .... **3.00**
Six Gun Heroes, #81 .... **12.00**
Smash Comics, #38 .... **425.00**
Strange Tales, #57 .... **265.00**
Superman, #109 .... **420.00**
Tarzan, Lord of the Jungle, 1995 .... **35.00**
Teen Titans, The, #1 .... **130.00**
Tip Top Comics, 1938 ..... **150.00**
Transmetropolitan, #1 .... **8.00**
Uncanny Tales, Marvel, #11 .... **200.00**
Uncle Scrooge, Disney, #244 .... **4.00**
Voodoo, Farrell, #1 .... **350.00**
X-Men-14, #18 .... **560.00**
X-Men-24, #60 .... **75.00**
War Heroes, Charlton, #1.. **25.00**
Weird War Tales, DC, #1 . **125.00**
Whiz Comics, Fawcett, #60 .... **200.00**

Walt Disney Comics, *Donald and Nephews, Happy New Year*, January 1948, Vol. 8, No. 4, No. 88, **$75**.

X-Men, *If Iceman Should Fail*, 18 March, Marvel, **$45**.

Young All-Stars, #8............. **1.50**
Young Justice, #3............... **3.00**
Zane Grey Stories of the West **10.00**
Zero Zero, #2 .... **4.00**
Zoo Funnies, 1946 .... **48.00**
Zorro, Gold Key, #1........... **70.00**

COMPACTS

History: In the first quarter of the 20th century, attitudes regarding cosmetics changed drastically. The use of make-up during the day was no longer looked upon with disdain. As women became "liberated," and as more and more of them entered the business world, the use of cosmetics became a routine and necessary part of a woman's grooming. Portable containers for cosmetics became a necessity.

Compacts were made in myriad shapes, styles, combinations and motifs, all reflecting the mood of the times. Every conceivable natural or man-made material was used in the manufacture of compacts. Commemorative, premium, souvenir, patriotic, figural, Art Deco, and enamel compacts are a few examples of the types of compacts that were made in the United States and abroad. Compacts combined with other forms, such as cigarette cases, music boxes, watches, hatpins, canes, and lighters, also were very popular.

Compacts were made and used until the late 1950s, when women opted for the "au naturel" look. The term "vintage" is used to describe the compacts from the first half of the 20th century as distinguished from contemporary examples.

Additional Listings: See *Warman's Americana & Collectibles* for more examples.

Adviser: Roselyn Gerson.

Compact, Austrian, for Houbigant, c1924, 14k yellow gold, channel edged rectangular form, overall flower and scroll chased pattern, interior fitted with pair of rouge pots, mirror and lipstick case, marked "Houbigant," hallmarks and maker mark for F. Mesmer, 1-1/2" x 3", **$635**.

Photo courtesy of David Rago Auctions, Inc.

Art Deco, 14k yg, linear engine turned design, black onyx edge dec, mirror and powder puff, matching lipstick case, European hallmarks **1,000.00**

Cartier, 1-7/8" x 2-5/8", 9k yg, rect form, ribbed case with diamond-set thumbpiece, powder compact with fitted mirror, 61.5 dwt (including mirror), English hallmarks, sgd "Cartier London" **420.00**

Celluloid, unknown maker
3" d, orange compact studded with floral rhinestone motif **45.00**
5" celluloid diamond shaped purse, 2" tassel and silk cord, mottled cream, green and brown with oval cameo attached to center top, mirror, powder puff and chrome scent vial **275.00**

Coty, #405, envelope box. **65.00**

Djer Kiss, with fairy **95.00**

European, 14k gold compact, rect, linear, engine-turned design, channel-set red stone thumbpiece, European hallmarks **500.00**

Evans, goldtone, heart shape, black twisted carrying cord, lipstick concealed in black tassel suspended from bottom.. **250.00**

Fifth Avenue, vanity case "Cosmetist," aquamarine enamel, powder, rouge, lipstick, cleansing cream, and mascara, England **175.00**

Foster & Bailey, Providence, vanity case, sterling silver and enamel, 3-1/2" x 2", rect, canted corners, lid enameled in center over diamond-shaped starburst ground, vase of roses on white ground, bordered by turquoise enamel cornered by roses, green cabochon thumb piece open to hinged mirror, off-center hinged double compartment each with cabochon thumb piece, braided wrist chain, c1880 .... **800.00**

Italian, hand-mirror shape, sterling silver, stylized floral engraving, lipstick concealed in handle, coral cabochon thumb piece **325.00**

Jensen, Georg, sterling silver, polished oval case accented with pine cone and leaf motif, hinged cover opens to reveal fitted mirror and powder compact, sgd "Georg Jensen, Inc." **165.00**

Kigu, lady swinging **45.00**

Max Factor, 2-1/4" d, solid perfume, round faux jade pendant, gold-tone twisted braided wire disk, orig Khara fragrance **35.00**

Norida, emb lady, silver tone **75.00**

Rex Fifth Avenue, vanity-pochette, navy blue, gold polka dots, taffeta drawstring, mirror on outside base **90.00**

Sterling silver, 2-18" d round compact with lid enameled to center with 18th C lady, white basse taille surrounded with black border, opening to mirror and makeup compartment, strung with white chord suspending 2 1/8" l white basse taille lipstick case, American, 20th C **175.00**

Tiffany & Co., Art Deco, sterling silver, gold, and sapphire, sq engraved lineal design, surmounted by gold and sapphire crescent, mirror and powder compartment, sgd **450.00**

Unknown maker, compact
Castanets shape, ebony wood, metal Paris insignia centered on lid, orange tasseled carrying cord **220.00**
Sterling, 2" x 3", enamel panel on one side with landscape and palm trees, rect engraved sterling silver case, chain handle, int. fitted for make-up with mirror, marked "Sterling," minor wear **215.00**
Telephone-dial shape, red, white, and blue, slogan "I Like Ike" imprinted on lid, red map of USA on lid center ... **225.00**

Goldtone, rectangular, monogrammed, **$40**

Photo courtesy of Dotta Auction Co., Inc.

Unknown maker, compact, English, Birmingham, sterling silver and enamel
2-1/2" sq, canted corners, green enamel over "L"-shaped engine-turning, scalloped sunray issuing from scrolls, c1940 .... **225.00**
2-7/8" sq, canted corners, blue enamel over spiraling engine-turning, central nautical flag with crown **250.00**

Unknown maker, compact, Europe, early 20th C, silver, 800 silver, 2-3/8" l, 1-1/2" w, oval, enameled violet on lid, int. mounted with mirrors, losses to int. **290.00**

Unknown maker, vanity bag, SS mesh, hallmarked, octagonal, goldtone int. and finger ring carrying chain **500.00**

Van Cleef & Arpels, 2-3/4" x 3-1/2", Retro, silver gilt, rect form, thumbpiece set with single-cut diamonds and calibre-cut sapphires in stylized bow motif, fitted mirror, two powder compartments, and lipstick holder inscribed with name and NY address, brown leather Van Cleef & Arpels slip case . **750.00**

CONSOLIDATED GLASS COMPANY

History: The Consolidated Lamp and Glass Company was formed as a result of the 1893 merger of the Wallace and McAfee Company, glass and lamp jobbers of Pittsburgh, and the Fostoria Shade & Lamp Company of Fostoria, Ohio. When the Fostoria, Ohio, plant burned down in 1895, Corapolis, Pennsylvania, donated a seven-acre tract of land near the center of town for a new factory. In 1911, the company was the largest lamp, globe, and shade works in the United States, employing more than 400 workers.

In 1925, Reuben Haley, owner of an independent design firm, convinced John Lewis, president of Consolidated, to enter the giftware field utilizing a series of designs inspired by the 1925 Paris Exposition (l'Exposition Internationale des Arts Décoratifs et Industriels Modernes) and the work of René Lalique. Initially, the glass was marketed by Howard Selden through his showroom at 225 Fifth Avenue in New York City. The first two lines were Catalonian and Martele.

Additional patterns were added in the late 1920s: Florentine (January 1927), Chintz (January 1927), Ruba Rombic (January 1928), and Line 700 (January 1929). On April 2, 1932, Consolidated closed it doors. Kenneth Harley moved about 40 molds to Phoenix. In March 1936, Consolidated reopened under new management, and the "Harley" molds were returned. During this period, the famous Dancing Nymph line, based on an eight-inch salad plate in the 1926 Martele series, was introduced.

In August 1962, Consolidated was sold to Dietz Brothers. A major fire damaged the plant during a 1963 labor dispute and in 1964, the company permanently closed its doors.

For more information, see *Warman's Glass*, 4th edition.

Butter dish, Coreaposis pattern, opaque white ground, pink flowers, yellow centers, green leaves, blue shadows, green band on cover, **$75**.

Bonbon, cov, 8" d, Ruba Rhombic, faceted, smoky topaz, catalog #832, c1931 .... **325.00**
Bowl, 5-1/2" d, Coronation, Martelé, flared, blue **75.00**
Box, cov, 7" l, 5" w, Martelé line, Fruit and Leaf pattern, scalloped edge................................ **85.00**
Butter dish, cov, 6" h, Cosmos, white custard glass, blue, pink, and yellow daisies **250.00**
Candlesticks, pr, Hummingbird, Martelé line, oval body, jade green, 6-3/4" h................ **248.00**

Cocktail, Dancing Nymph, French Crystal.................. **90.00**
Cookie jar, 6-1/2" h, Regent Line, #3758, Florette, rose pink over white opal casing.... **370.00**
Cup and saucer, Dancing Nymph, ruby flashed **265.00**
Dinner service, Five Fruits, service for six, goblet, plate, sherbet, one large serving plate, purple wash, mold imperfections, wear **375.00**
Goblet, Dancing Nymph, French Crystal.............................. **90.00**
Humidor, Florette, pink satin **225.00**
Jar, cov, Con-Cora, #3758-9, pine cone dec, irid.......... **165.00**
Lamp
  Cockatoo, 13" h, figural, orange and blue, black beak, brown stump, black base **450.00**
  Flower basket, 8" h, bouquet of roses and poppies, yellows, pinks, green leaves, brown basketweave, black glass base........................... **300.00**
Mayonnaise comport, Martelé Iris, green wash **55.00**
Miniature lamp, 10" h, opalescent blue **380.00**
Night light, Santa Maria, block base **450.00**
Old-fashioned tumbler, 3-7/8" h, Catalonian, yellow **20.00**
Perfume bottle, 5-1/2" h, Ruba Rombic, gray frosted body, nick on stopper................... **1,420.00**
Plate
  8-1/4" d, Bird of Paradise, amber wash................ **40.00**
  10-1/4" d, Catalonian, yellow **45.00**
  12" d, Martelé, Orchid, pink, birds and flowers **115.00**
Puff box, cov, Lovebirds, blue **95.00**
Salt and pepper shakers, pr
  Cone, pink **75.00**
  Cosmos **115.00**
  Guttate, green............. **85.00**
Sauce dish, Criss-Cross, cranberry opalescent........ **55.00**
Sherbet, ftd, Catalonian, green **20.00**
Snack set, Martelé Fruits, pink **45.00**
Sugar bowl, cov, Guttate, cased pink **120.00**
Sugar shaker, 3-1/2" d, puff quilted body, pink, brass lid **150.00**
Sundae, Martelé Russet Yellow Fruits **35.00**

Syrup, Cone, squatty, pink **295.00**
Toothpick holder, Florette, cased pink **75.00**
Tumbler
  Catalonian, ftd, green, 5-1/4" h **30.00**
  Guttate, pink satin **65.00**
  Katydid, clambroth **165.00**
  Ruba Rhombic, faceted, ftd, silver gray, 6" h **210.00**
Umbrella vase, Blackberry **550.00**

Vase, Lovebirds, opaque white body, turquoise overlay, **$95**.

Vase
  6" h, Regent Line, #3758, cased blue stretch over white opal, pinched **175.00**
  6-1/2" h, sea foam green, lavender, and tan, floral pattern **150.00**
  8-1/2" h, Katydid, blue wash, fan-shaped top **300.00**
Whiskey glass, 2-5/8" h, Ruba Rhombic, faceted, transparent jungle green, catalog #823 .... **265.00**

CONTINENTAL CHINA AND PORCELAIN (GENERAL)

History: By 1700, porcelain factories existed in large numbers throughout Europe. In the mid-18th century, the German factories at Meissen and Nymphenburg were dominant. As the century ended, French potteries assumed the leadership role. The 1740s to the 1840s were the golden age of Continental china and porcelains.

Americans living in the last half of the 19th century eagerly sought the masterpieces of the European porcelain factories. In the early 20th century, this style of china and porcelain was considered "blue chip" by antiques collectors.

Additional Listings: French— Haviland, Limoges, Sarreguemines, and Sevres; German—Austrian Ware, Bavarian China, Dresden/Meissen, Rosenthal, Royal Bayreuth, Royal Bonn, Royal Rudolstadt, Royal Vienna, Schlegelmilch, and Villeroy and Boch; Italian—Capo-di-Monte.

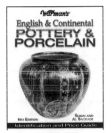

For more information, see *Warman's English & Continental Pottery & Porcelain*, 4th edition.

French

Choisy, plate, 8-1/4" d, earthenware transfer printed and hand enameled, each with different numbered scene relating to story of soldier's courtship and military life, naïve enamel accenting, mid-19th C, price for set of 12 .... **500.00**

Creil
Jug, 5-1/4" h, transfer printed, canary ground, imp "CREIL" **300.00**
Pitcher, 10-3/4" h, glazed pottery, ewer-form, central beige band dec with trees, cream ground, imp "CREIL" **420.00**

Faience
Bulb pot, 3-1/8" d, sq, molded acanthus-capped scroll feet, conforming handles, front with scene of courting couple, verso landscape, each side with floral sprays, sq form insert, gilt highlights, attributed to Marseilles, last quarter 18th C, pr **900.00**

Inkstand, 13-1/2" l, figural, cartouche-shaped base molded with scrolls, front painted with harbor scene flanked by tower and knight-shaped inkpots, back sections support large figure of lion with raised paw resting on shield with armorial **650.00**
Plate, 9" d, blue and white floral dec, foliate border **115.00**
Sugar caster, 8-1/2" h, brightly polychrome scene of courting couple in landscape, floral sprays borders, dec band of fleur-de-lis border, pierced cov with conforming dec, early 19th C **450.00**

French, Paris, urns, pair with scene of Arabian figures and ruins on green ground with gold highlights, c1850, 8-1/2" h, sold together with smaller example with sailing ship, **$500**

Photo courtesy of Pook & Pook.

H.A. Balleroy Bros., attributed to, late 19th C, charger, 22-1/4" d, painted with scene of gentlemen studying drawings at trestle table, inscribed lower left "Le Portrait de L'Hote faience d'apres Brillouin par Pascault," gilt rim, mounted in 34" sq Aesthetic Movement gilt and copper frame with round inner surround....................... **1,100.00**
Lessore, Emile, platter, 14-1/4" l, oval, earthenware, polychrome figural landscape with putti, artist signed, printed factory mark for Hautin and Boulenger, France, c1855, rim chip **450.00**
Paris
Cache pot, 6" h, ovoid, apple-green ground, floral roundels in leaf surround, two gilt lion's head masks on sides, narrow undertray, late 19th C . **115.00**
Candlesticks, pr, 9" h, everted sconce, column-form standard, shaped base with man and woman among rocaille leaves............. **200.00**

Dessert plate, 9-1/8" d, hand painted, four with flower centers, two with fruit centers, all with peach borders, gilt scrolls, maroon band at molded rim, late 19th C **750.00**
Lamp base, 10-3/4" h, egg-shaped bodies, enamel dec multicolored floral sprays and gilt vines on lavender ground, drilled and electrified, late 19th C, price for pr **250.00**
Urn
10" h, gilding, hand-painted scene, panel with winter lake and wooden buildings, floral garlands on pale yellow ground on reverse, well molded men's faces on handles, wear, lid missing **350.00**
10-5/8" h, gilding, hand-painted scene, two oval reserves, one with church near lake, other with courting couple, double handles with faintly molded heads, wear, lid missing **375.00**
Vase garniture, 8" h, 8 1/4" h, 9-1/2" h, three vases, each with aqua ground, floral bouquet roundels in gilt surrounds, short scroll handles, domed foot molded with scallop shells, late 19th C **500.00**
Veilleuse, 4-1/2" h pot, 9" h overall, hand painted, small pot with black and pink bands, over enameled with gilt scrolls, short gilt spout, angular handle, octagonal pagoda-form stand hp with scenes titled "acqueduque de Buc," showing elevated aqueduct, and "a Bonnebose (Calvados)," showing village, 20th C, base missing.. **475.00**
Samson & Co.
Character figure, 6-3/8" to 7-5/8" h, three figures in masks and caps, two wielding swords, other dagger, bearded figure with guitar, each by vine-covered tree trunk, rect base, guilloche borders, 20th C, price for four-pc set.......................... **450.00**
Figure, 12-1/4" h, Neptune, upraised hands standing on scallop shell, dolphin at feet, rocaille base encrusted with shells and seaweed, gilt accents, late 19th C ... **230.00**

Perfume bottle, 2-7/8" l, figural, boy with vessel seated on dolphin, enamel detailing, boy's head as stopper, late 19th C **230.00**

Unknown maker

Plate, 10" d, centers painted with pastoral scenes, tooled gilt border, white ground, pink rim with three scenes within gilt cartouches, mid-19th C, price for pr **815.00**

Tray, 12-3/4" x 18-1/2", painted in Oriental manner to resemble cloisonné, parrot and fish on turquoise ground gold geometric design, cast bronze frame with bamboo and scroll Oriental designs with trace of gilding, some areas of verdigris, unmarked **575.00**

Longwy pottery, vase, flattened circular form, narrow flared neck, beaded necklace form decoration around base of neck, descending on front and back as female face with curly hair, scrollwork band around neck, decorated in turquoise glaze on grayish-white ground, crackle finish, stamped "Atelier Primavera, Longwy," 11-1/2" h, **$500**.

Photo courtesy of Alderfer Auction Co.

Germany

Böttger, tea cup and saucer, 3-1/8" h, 5-7/8" d saucer, red stoneware, black lacquered ground, stylized auricular handles, c1715 .... **31,070.00**

Herend, dinner service, partial, Indian Basket pattern, puce dec

on white ground, 10 dinner plates, six salad plates, five bread and butter plates, six bone dishes, five soup bowls, four serving trays of various size and form, gravy boat, four cups and six saucers, early 20th C **1,450.00**

Hutschenreuther

Plaque, 5-1/8" x 6-7/8", oval, Madonna and Child, giltwood frame, late 19th C **600.00**

Service plate, 10-7/8" d, central dec, summer flowers within heavily gilt cavetto, rim worked with scrolling acanthus, textured ground, under-glaze green factory marks, minor rubbing, 12-pc set **1,600.00**

Mehlem, vase, 13-1/2" h, detailed painted birds, irises, and foliage, bronze patinated handles and base, imp marks, "Franz Anton Mehlem Bonn," c1900, price for pr ... **1,380.00**

Paris china, two-tier serving dish, salmon border bands, gold trim, ornate porcelain standards and ring handle, **$150**.

Photo courtesy of Wiederseim Associates, Inc.

Nymphenburg

Dinner service, each hand painted in enamels and trimmed in gilt with cartouches of landscapes in blue bead pattern, titles on reverse, 12 10" d dinner plates; 11 8-1/4" d plates; 8-1/4" d cov soup tureen with undertray; two coffee cups and saucers; 12 tea cups; 16 saucers; 7-1/2" h cov water pitcher; 2-5/8" h cream jug; 3-5/8" h cov sugar bowl; 18-1/2"

l oval tea tray; two 6-5/8" d cov vegetable dishes; two 7" h fruit coolers with inserts; 8-7/8" square serving dish; 10-3/4" l triangular serving dish; two 9-1/2" d serving dishes; printed marks, mid-10th C **28,200.00**

Vase, 10-1/2" d, wide baluster form, enamel dec, continuous landscape scene, titled on underside "Vorfrohling in Oberbayorn," signed "R. Sieck," 20th C **750.00**

Unknown maker

Cup and saucer, bucket-shaped 3-5/8" h cup, cerulean blue band over horizontal gilt beaded band above landscape scene, short gilt acanthus scroll handle, three gilt paw feet, similarly beaded and gilded saucer ... **1,035.00**

Plaque, 5" l, girl with candle, titled "Guten Nahct," oval, reeded giltwood frame, late 19th/early 20th C **1,035.00**

Budapest, Fischer, pitcher, pink flowers, green leaves, blue butterflies, 14" h, chip under base, **$125**.

Photo courtesy of Joy Luke Auctions.

Italian

Pattarino, mask, 11-1/2" h, Bacchus, finely molded, polychrome glaze, sprigged hair adjorned with applied grape clusters and vines, inscribed "Prof. E. Pattarino, Italy" **2,645.00**

COOKIE JARS

History: Cookie jars, colorful and often whimsical, are popular with collectors. They were made by almost every manufacturer, in all types of materials. Figural character cookie jars are the most popular with collectors.

Cookie jars often were redesigned to reflect newer tastes. Hence, the same jar may be found in several different variations and these variations can affect the price.

Marks: Many cookie-jar shapes were manufactured by more than one company and, as a result, can be found with different marks. This often happened because of mergers or separations, e.g., Brush-McCoy, which became Nelson McCoy. Molds also were traded and sold among companies.

For more information, see *Warman's Cookie Jars*.

Abingdon Pottery
Bo Peep, No. 694D, 12" h
.... **425.00**
Choo Choo, No. 561D,
7-1/2" h............................ **120.00**
Daisy, No. 677, 8" h **50.00**
Pumpkin, No. 674D, 8" h
.... **550.00**
Three Bears, No. 696D,
8-3/4" h............................ **245.00**
Windmill, No. 678,
10-1/2" h.......................... **500.00**

Brayton Laguna Pottery
Partridges, Model No. V-12,
7-1/4" h............................ **200.00**
Provincial Lady, high-gloss white apron and scarf, red, green, and yellow flowers and hearts, marked "Brayton Laguna Calif. K-27," 13" h
.... **455.00**
Swedish Maid, 1941, incised mark, 11" h.................. **600.00**

Old Woman in a Shoe, **$70**.

Hull Pottery
Barefoot Boy **320.00**
Duck **60.00**
Gingerbread Boy, blue and white trim **400.00**
Gingerbread Man, 12" h
.... **550.00**
Little Red Riding Hood, open basket, gold stars on apron
.... **375.00**

Gingerbread Man, brown glaze with white drip trim, **$35**.

Metlox Pottery
Bear, blue sweater **100.00**
Chef Pierre.................. **100.00**
Pine Cone, gray squirrel finial, Model No. 509, 11" h .. **115.00**
Rex Dinosaur, white **120.00**
Tulip, yellow and green
.... **425.00**

Red Wing Pottery
French Chef, blue glaze
.... **250.00**
Grapes, yellow, marked "Red Wing USA," 10" h........ **125.00**
Rooster, green glaze .. **165.00**

Clown, yellow body, remnants of blue trim, unmarked, **$65**.

Cookie Bucket, McCoy **$75**.

Shawnee Pottery
Cinderella, unmarked . **125.00**
Dutch Boy, striped pants, marked "USA," 11" h .. **190.00**
Dutch Girl, marked "USA," 11-1/2" h **175.00**
Great Northern Boy, marked "Great Northern USA 1025," 9-3/4" h **425.00**
Jo-Jo the Clown, marked "Shawnee USA, 12," 9" h
.... **300.00**
Little Chef **95.00**
Muggsy Dog, blue bow, gold trim and decals, marked "Patented Muggsy U.S.A.," 11-3/4" h **850.00**
Owl, eyes repainted **95.00**
Smiley Pig, clover blossom dec, marked "Patented Smiley USA," 11 1/2" h........... **550.00**
Winnie Pig, clover blossom dec, marked "Patented Winnie USA," 12" h **575.00**
Stoneware, cobalt blue dec, unknown maker
Basketweave and Morning Glory, marked "Put Your Fist In," 7-1/2" h................. **625.00**
Flying Bird, 9" h **1,250.00**

Watt Pottery, Apple design, **$400**.

Watt Pottery
Apple, No. 21, 7-1/2" h **400.00**

Cookie Barrel, wood grain,
10-1/2" h......................... **50.00**
Goodies, No. 76, 6-1/2" h
.... **150.00**
Happy/Sad Face, No. 34,
wooden lid **165.00**
Starflower, No. 503, 8" h
.... **350.00**

COPELAND AND SPODE

History: In
1749,
Josiah
Spode was
apprenticed
to Thomas

Whieldon and in 1754 worked for
William Banks in Stoke-on-Trent. In
the early 1760s, Spode started his
own pottery, making cream-
colored earthenware and blue-
printed whiteware. In 1770, he
returned to Banks' factory as
master, purchasing it in 1776.

Spode pioneered the use of
steam-powered pottery-making
machinery and mastered the art of
transfer printing from copper
plates. Spode opened a London
shop in 1778 and sent William
Copeland there about 1784. A
number of larger London locations
followed. At the turn of the
century, Spode introduced bone china. In
1805, Josiah Spode II and William
Copeland entered into a
partnership for the London
business. A series of partnerships
between Josiah Spode II, Josiah
Spode III, and William Taylor
Copeland resulted.

In 1833, Copeland acquired
Spode's London operations and
seven years later, the Stoke plants.
William Taylor Copeland managed
the business until his death in
1868. The firm remained in the
hands of Copeland heirs. In 1923,
the plant was electrified; other
modernization followed.

In 1976, Spode merged with
Worcester Royal Porcelain to
become Royal Worcester Spode,
Ltd.

Bust, 11-1/2" h, Una, by John
Hancock, traces of printed verse
on back, short socle, late 19th C
.... **300.00**

Dinnerware, New Stone pattern, 42 pieces, tan ground, orange Oriental motif, **$195**.

Cabinet plate, 9-1/2" d, artist
sgd "Samuel Alcock," 1-3/4"
jeweled border, intricate gold,
beading, pearl and turquoise
jeweling, c1889.............. **750.00**
Coffee cup and saucer, 2-1/4" h
cylindrical cup with allover
maroon and gilt scrolled dec,
5" d saucer, retained by Tiffany &
Co., late 19th C, price for set of
12.................................... **325.00**
Dinner service
Indian Tree, service for 10,
serving pcs, 46 pcs.... **500.00**
Maritime Rose pattern,
service for 12, serving pieces,
some repairs............ **1,100.00**

Dinner plate, red rose center, blue
border with white floral decoration,
gold rim, **$20**.

Figure, parian
16-1/2" h, Ophelia, standing
female figure modeled
clenching flowers in her cloak,
impressed W. Calder Marshall
RA, publishing date and
manufacture, England, c1863,
missing a leaf of one floret
.... **500.00**
25" h, Chastity, standing
female figure modeled
holding some lilies, impressed
"J. Durham, sc," title and
manufacturer, England, c1865
.... **1,530.00**
Fish plate, 9-3/4" d, artist sgd
"H. C. Lea," four-part gold-
swirled design, hp fly in each
section, c1891 .... **175.00**

Jug, orange, teal green, and
gold dec, matte cream ground,
ornate handle with two
mythological characters, c1847
.... **450.00**
Plate, 9-1/2" d, blue and white,
hunting scenes **225.00**
Platter, 18" x 23-1/4" d, Blue
Willow pattern, oval, deep,
shaped edge, marked
"Copeland & Garrett/Late
Spode" **375.00**

Two plates with historical views, 10" d,
each $65, also shown is flow blue cup
and saucer, **$40**.

Photo courtesy of Joy Luke.

Service plate, 10-1/4" d,
Brompton pattern, floral border,
central design of birds and
foliage, retailed by Wright,
Tyndale & Van Roden, Inc.,
Philadelphia, marked "Rd. No.
608584," price for set of 10
.... **335.00**
Spill vase, 4-3/4" h, flared rim,
pale lilac, gilt octagonal panels
with portrait of bearded man,
band of pearls on rims and
bases, Spode, c1920 ..... **425.00**
Tea set, Blue Willow, retailed by
Tiffany & Co., pattern registered
January 1879, printed at rim with
quotation from Robert Burns
"Auld Lang Syne," 5" h cov
hexagonal teapot, creamer, cov
sugar, seven cups, six saucers,
20-3/4" d round tray with
scalloped gilt rim, gilt handles,
gilt foo dog lid finials, price for
17-pc set........................ **950.00**

Tray, 8-1/2" l, black transfer, passion flowers, grape vines border, emb grapes, vines, and leaves on tab handles, c1900 .... **200.00**

Tureen, cov, 13" w, 11" h, white, gold and blue accents, marked "Spode New Stone" **1,470.00**

Urn, cov, 15" h, Louis XVI style, cobalt blue ground, medallions on each side with bouquet of roses, majolica, repair to one handle, nick to one lid, pr **900.00**

Water pitcher, 8-1/4" h, bulbous, tan acanthus leaf handle and spout, green field dec with white relief classical figures of dancing women, white relief banded floral garland dec at neck, marked "Rd. No. 180288" **250.00**

COPPER

History: Copper objects, such as kettles, teakettles, warming pans, and measures, played an important part in the 19th-century household. Outdoors, the apple-butter kettle and still were the two principal copper items. Copper culinary objects were lined with a thin protective coating of tin to prevent poisoning. They were relined as needed.

Reproduction Alert: Many modern reproductions exist.

Additional Listings: Arts and Crafts Movement and Roycroft.

Notes: Collectors place great emphasis on signed pieces, especially those by American craftsmen. Since copper objects were made abroad as well, it is hard to identify unsigned examples.

Pot, pouring spout, handle, **$85**.

Breadbox, 12" l, 7-1/2" w, 11" h, chamfered oblong rect form, hinged cov, paneled domical form, brass finial raising from lozenge-shaped plaque over brass ring handles, brass bottom, Neoclassical, possibly Dutch, c1800 .... **165.00**

Carpenter's pot, 11" l, 8" h, globular, dovetailed body, raised on three plain strap work iron legs, conforming handle ... **70.00**

Censer, 13" d, lobed, carved and pierced lid set with white jade, China, 19th C **1,300.00**

Charger, 29-1/2" d, hand hammered, emb high relief of owl on branch, naturally forming patina, Liberty paper label **3,110.00**

Desk set, hammered blotter, letter holder, bookends, stamp box, each with bone carved cabochon, branch and berry motif, Potter Studio, fine orig patina, die-stamp mark ... **750.00**

Tea kettles, back left. 12-1/2" h tea kettle, dovetailed construction, cast brass handle support, copper grip, gooseneck spout, brass finial, some denting, **$100**; right: 9-1/2" h tea kettle with 3-1/2" brass stand, dovetail construction, cast brass handle supports, copper grip, brass finial and rim, **$120**; front: 9-3/4" h tea kettle, dovetailed construction, cooper swing handle with brass attachments, modified gooseneck spout, pierced lid with raised floriform decoration, denting, loss to finish, repairs, **$125**.

Photo courtesy of Alderfer Auction Co.

Fish poacher, cov, 20-1/2" l, oval, rolled rim, iron swing ball handle, 19th C **350.00**

Inglenook hood, 30" w, 8" d, 34-1/2" h, hammered, emb Glasgow roses, English, small tear at bottom **1,610.00**

Panel, 6-3/8" h, 2-7/8" w, repoussè of Bodhisattva seated on lotus seat, high relief figure, chased detail, traces of red pigment and gilding, Southeast Asia, 18th C, slight bends **500.00**

Pot, cov, 19-1/2" l, 12" w, 16" h, twin handles, oval, raised on four strap work legs, fitted with

tubular end handles, shallow domed cov stamped with shield design, center stationary handle, English, 19th C **215.00**

Screen, 24" w, 38-1/4" h, Arts & Crafts, ruffled edges, repousse design of oak tree, acorns, sun behind it, iron supports with copper coils wrapped around on front **495.00**

Tea kettles, front. 12" h, dovetailed construction, cast brass handle support, copper grips, gooseneck spout, brass acorn finial, impressed "J" on underside; back: 13" h, dovetailed construction, cast brass handle support, copper grips, gooseneck spout, brass acorn finial, impressed "O" on underside, price for pair, **$150**.

Photo courtesy of Alderfer Auction Co.

Tea kettle, 12" h, gooseneck, dovetailed construction, swivel handle, brass finial, stamped "W. Wolfe" **3,520.00**

Tray, 13-1/2" d, Stickley Brothers, hammered copper, loped rim emb with dots, stamped "36" no patina **800.00**

Umbrella stand, 25" h, hand hammered, flared rim, cylindrical body, two-strap work-loop handles, repoussé medallion, riveted flared foot, c1910 .. **650.00**

Umbrella stand, brass band trim, **$120**.

Photo courtesy of Dotta Auction Co., Inc.

Vase, 5-1/2" d, 7" h, hammered, ovoid, Dirk Van Erp, fine orig mottled patina, D'Arcy Gaw box mark, small shallow dent on rim **8,100.00**

Vessel, 4" d, 3-1/4" h, hammered, ovoid, closed-in rim, orig dark patina, Dirk Van Erp closed box mark **2,300.00**

Wall sconce, 4-1/2" w, 11" h, hammered, flame head, riveted Arts & Crafts details, attributed to Dirk Van Erp, cleaned patina **425.00**

Water urn, 14" h, copper body, int. with capped warming tube, applied brass ram's head handles, urn finial, brass spout, sq base with four ball feet, unmarked, repairs to lid .. **125.00**

CRANBERRY GLASS

History: Cranberry glass is transparent and named for its color, achieved by adding powdered gold to a molten batch of amber glass and reheating at a low temperature to develop the cranberry or ruby color. The glass color first appeared in the last half of the 17th century, but was not made in American glass factories until the last half of the 19th century.

Cranberry glass was blown, mold blown, or pressed. Examples often are decorated with gold or enamel. Less-expensive cranberry glass, made by substituting copper for gold, can be identified by its bluish-purple tint.

For more information, see *Warman's Glass*, 4th edition.

Reproduction Alert:
Reproductions abound. These pieces are heavier, off-color, and lack the quality of older examples.

Basket, 7" h, 5" w, ruffled edge, petticoat shape, crystal loop handle, c1890 .... **250.00**

Bride's basket, 5" h, 3-1/2" d bowl, German silver-filigree frame, plain cranberry bowl **115.00**

Centerpiece, 19-1/2" h, central trumpet-form vase, shallow dish, pedestal foot, gilt Greek-key dec, Victorian **300.00**

Cologne bottle, 7" h, faceted, finely cut faceted stopper **175.00**

Condiment dish, underplate, 6-1/2" h, scrolling vines and grapes dec, Continental . **175.00**

Creamer, 5" h, 2-3/4" d, Optic pattern, fluted to, applied clear handle **95.00**

Cruet, 9" h, optic ribbed body, trifold rim, applied clear handled **100.00**

Decanter, 10-1/2" h, craquelle, bulbous stick form, pinch-sided, crystal collar, oval stopper .. **150.00**

Dresser box, 5" d, blown out melon ribs, enameled scrolling on bronze feet, French, late 19th C **175.00**

Epergne, central trumpet form vase and two side vases, all having applied colorless glass decoration, two colorless glass swirled inserts, ruffled edge base, 21" h, **$550**.

Photo courtesy of Alderfer Auction Co.

Epergne, 19" h, 11" d, five pcs, large ruffled bowl, tall center lily, three jack-in-the-pulpit vases **1,200.00**

Finger bowl, Inverted Thumbprint pattern, deep color **200.00**

Garniture, 14" d bowl, pr 11" h candlesticks, cranberry overlay cut to clear, faceted cut dec, Continental...................... **450.00**

Goblet, 6" h, acanthus scrolling, clear banded cut stem with

polychrome scrolling, foot dec with band of peacock eyes, mkd Royal Baron," Meyrs Neff crown, Lobmeyer...................... **550.00**

Lamp, fluid, 8" h, deep cranberry font connected to sq black base, later electric socket base soldered over early brass collar, brass connector, 1860-75 .... **880.00**

Nappy, 5-1/2" d, heart shape, tooled crystal feet and handle, English **100.00**

Pipe, 18" l, hand blown, tapering-bent neck, bulbous bowl, three bulbs at base, white-enamel dec at outer rim of bowl **250.00**

Pitcher
6-1/2" h, 4-1/8" d, Ripple and Thumbprint pattern, bulbous, round mouth, applied clear handle...................... **175.00**
10" h, 5" d, bulbous, ice bladder int., applied clear handle...................... **250.00**

Salt, master, ftd, enameled floral dec................................. **200.00**

Sherbet
4-1/4" h, ftd, polychrome and acanthus scrolling, various colored dotted peacock eyes, Lobmeyer **400.00**
4-1/2" h, translucent cranberry, dec with purple, red, yellow, green, and white scrolling flowers on horizontal gilt bands, beaded highlights, Moser........................... **500.00**

Sugar shaker, 4-1/2" h, molded fern pattern **150.00**

Sugar shaker, paneled body, gold washed pierced top, **$95**.

Tankard water pitcher, 11" h, acanthus scrollwork in shades of purple, red, green, and blue, gilt peacock eyes with various color dots, applied clear handle, Lobmeyer **1,100.00**

Tumble-up, Inverted Thumbprint pattern............................ **195.00**

Tumbler, Inverted Thumbprint pattern.............................. **65.00**

Vase

5-3/4" h, ribbed body, heavy application of colorless leaves, collar, and scrolled feet, berry pontil, attributed to Harrach, c1890 .... **100.00**

8-7/8" h, bulbous, white-enameled lilies of the valley dec, cylindrical neck .. **150.00**

9" h, bulbous stick, flaring rim, cranberry, banded gold and silver collar, polychrome scrolling, dots, and florals, Moser **300.00**

Watch stand, 7" h figural gilt bronze base with stork, hook for suspending pocket watch, cranberry glass posy vase set in reticulated scroll holder, Austrian or French, c1870 .... **700.00**

CRUETS

History: Cruets are small glass bottles used on the table holding condiments such as oil, vinegar, and wine. The pinnacle of cruet use occurred during the Victorian era, when a myriad of glass manufacturers made cruets in a wide assortment of patterns, colors, and sizes. All cruets had stoppers; most had handles.

Aventurine, 6-1/2" h, applied clear reeded handle, cut faceted stopper........................... **375.00**

Bluerina, 7-1/4" h, deep royal blue neck fades to clear at shoulder, optic inverted thumbprint design in body, applied clear glass handle, teardrop-shaped airtrap stopper, in-the-making thin elongated bubble in neck **500.00**

Bohemian, amber cut to clear, floral arrangement intaglio carved on ruby flashed ground of three oval panels with carved frames of floral swags, five cut-to-clear panels at neck, three embellished with gold scrolls, all edged in brilliant gold, 16 decorative panels edged in gold, base and stopper both sgd "4" **750.00**

Burmese, 7" h, Mt. Washington, shiny finish, butter-yellow ribbed, body, applied handle, and mushroom stopper....... **1,250.00**

Cut and etched, glass, cut flowers motif, pressed oval stoppers (possibly replaced), pair, **$65**.

Chocolate, opaque, Greentown Cactus, no stopper **125.00**

Leaf Bracket, orig stopper **295.00**

Cranberry, 9" h, optic ribbed body, trifold rim, applied clear handled.......................... **100.00**

Custard glass, Wild Bouquet pattern, fired-on dec **500.00**

Moser, 6" h, eight raised cabochon-like ruby gems, deep cut edges of burnished gold, mounted on colorless body, eight alternating panels of brilliant gold squiggles and stylized leaves, handle cut in three sharp edges, six gold dec panels on stopper, each set with ruby cabochon, inside of mouth and base of stopper sgd "4," some loss to gold squiggles **585.00**

Pattern glass, orig stopper

Amazon, bar-in-hand stopper, 8-1/2" h **185.00**

Beveled Star, green **225.00**

Croesus, large, green, gold trim............................. **395.00**

Daisy and Button with Crossbars **75.00**

Delaware, cranberry, gold trim **295.00**

Esther, green, gold trim.. **465.00**

Fluted Scrolls, blue dec . **265.00**

Millard, amber stain **350.00**

Riverside's Ransom, vaseline **225.00**

Tiny Optic, green, dec **150.00**

Peachblow, New England, shiny finish, Wild Rose, pink-white handle, orig white stopper **1,500.00**

Rubina Verde, 7" h, Hobbs, Brockunier & Co., Polka Dot No. 308, flashed ruby red trefoil spout and upper half, intense vaseline base, handle, and stopper, slight flake at tip of stopper **585.00**

Sapphire blue

7-1/4" h, Hobnail, faceted stopper, applied blue handle, damage to three hobs .. **385.00**

7-1/2" h, 3-1/4" d, enameled pink, yellow, and blue flowers, green leaves, applied clear handle and foot, cut clear stopper **165.00**

Satin, 7-1/2" h, blue Raindrop MOP, clear frosted reeded handle, clear cut faceted stopper, flake **385.00**

Spatterware, 8" h, red, white, and yellow mottled body, yellow int., gold painted leafy dec, applied clear handle........ **150.00**

CUSTARD GLASS

History: Custard glass was developed in England in the early 1880s. Harry Northwood made the first American custard glass at his Indiana, Pennsylvania, factory in 1898.

From 1898 until 1915, many manufacturers produced custard-glass patterns, e.g., Dugan Glass, Fenton, A. H. Heisey Glass Co., Jefferson Glass, Northwood, Tarentum Glass, and U.S. Glass. Cambridge and McKee continued the production of custard glass into the Depression.

The ivory or creamy yellow-custard color is achieved by adding uranium salts to the molten hot glass. The chemical content makes the glass glow when held under a black light. The more uranium, the more luminous the color. Northwood's custard glass has the smallest amount of uranium, creating an ivory color; Heisey used more, creating a deep yellow color.

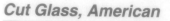

Custard glass was made in patterned tableware pieces. It also was made as souvenir items and novelty pieces. Souvenir pieces include a place name or hand-painted decorations, e.g., flowers. Patterns of custard glass often were highlighted in gold, enameled colors, and stains.

For more information, see *Warman's Glass,* 4th edition.

Reproduction Alert: L. G. Wright Glass Co. has reproduced pieces in the Argonaut Shell and Grape and Cable patterns. It also introduced new patterns, such as Floral and Grape and Vintage Band. Mosser reproduced toothpicks in Argonaut Shell, Chrysanthemum Sprig, and Inverted Fan & Feather.

Left: Berry bowl, Argonaut shell, **$195;** Right: Butter dish, Louis IV, **$300.**

Banana stand, Grape and Cable, Northwood, nutmeg stain **315.00**
Berry bowl, individual size, Chrysanthemum Sprig, 5" l x 3-3/4" w, 2-5/8" h, blue, slight loss to gold, sgd "Northwood" **165.00**
Berry bowl, master
  Beaded Circle, 8-5/8" d, 5" h, scalloped top, Northwood **485.00**
  Chrysanthemum Sprig, 10-1/2" l x 8" w, 4-7/8" h, blue, slight loss to gold, sgd "Northwood" **385.00**
Bonbon, Fruits and Flowers, Northwood, nutmeg stain **225.00**

Bowl, Grape and Cable, Northwood, 7-1/2" d, basketweave ext., nutmeg stain **70.00**
Butter dish, cov
  Everglades **375.00**
  Grape and Cable, Northwood, nutmeg stain.............. **450.00**
  Tiny Thumbprint, Tarentum, dec **300.00**
  Victoria....................... **300.00**

Berry bowl, master, Geneva, fired-on green decoration on shell, gold highlights and scalloped edge, 11" l, $265.

Compote, Geneva............ **65.00**
Creamer, Heart with Thumbprint **85.00**
Cruet, Argonaut Shell, 6-1/2" h, orig stopper, minimal loss to gold dec.................................. **985.00**
Goblet, Grape and Gothic Arches, nutmeg stain........ **80.00**
Hair receiver, Winged Scroll **125.00**
Jelly compote, 5" h, Argonaut Shell, gold edge, raised green leaves, gold seashells **235.00**
Nappy, Northwood Grape. **60.00**
Pitcher, Argonaut Shell... **325.00**
Plate, Grape and Cable, Northwood **45.00**
Punch cup
  Diamond with Peg **40.00**
  Louis XV....................... **35.00**

Berry bowl, master and two matching individual berry bowls, Chrysanthemum Sprig, blue custard, gold trim, $350.

Photo courtesy of Joy Luke.

Salt and pepper shakers, pr, Chrysanthemum Sprig.... **165.00**
Spooner
  Beaded Circle, 4-1/4" h, Northwood, wear to gold **195.00**

  Wild Bouquet, 4-1/2" h, Northwood, good floral dec, wear to gold.............. **285.00**
Sugar, cov
  Diamond with Peg **175.00**
  Georgia Gem, pink floral dec **185.00**
  Tiny Thumbprint, rose dec **185.00**
Table set, Inverted Fan and Feather, cov butter, creamer, spooner, cov sugar, Northwood, gold dec **500.00**
Tankard pitcher, Diamond with Peg **275.00**
Toothpick holder
  Chrysanthemum Sprig, 2-3/4" h, blue, gold leaves and blossoms, sgd "Northwood," tiny inside edge base flake **545.00**
  Chrysanthemum Sprig, 2-3/4" h, custard, gold dec, script sgd "Northwood" **100.00**
  Louis XV...................... **200.00**
Tumbler
  Beaded Circle, 4" h, each circle with one blue blossom, and six pink blossoms and two green leaves, Northwood, worn gold rim trim....... **165.00**
  Chrysanthemum Sprig, 3-3/4" h, blue, slight loss to gold dec **185.00**
  Wild Bouquet, 3-3/4" h, Northwood................. **285.00**

CUT GLASS, AMERICAN

History:
Glass is cut by grinding decorations into the glass by means of abrasive-carrying metal or stone wheels. A very ancient craft, it was revived in 1600 by Bohemians and spread through Europe to Great Britain and America.

American cut glass came of age at the Centennial Exposition in 1876 and the World Columbian

Exposition in 1893. The American public recognized American cut glass to be exceptional in quality and workmanship. America's most significant output of this high-quality glass occurred from 1880 to 1917, a period now known as the Brilliant Period.

Marks: Around 1890, some companies began adding an acid-etched "signature" to their glass. This signature may be the actual company name, its logo, or a chosen symbol. Today, signed pieces command a premium over unsigned pieces since the signature clearly establishes the origin. However, signatures should be carefully verified for authenticity since objects with forged signatures have been in existence for some time. One way to check is to run a fingertip or fingernail lightly over the signature area. As a general rule, a genuine signature cannot be felt, a forged signature has a raised surface.

Many companies never used the acid-etched signature on their glass and may or may not have affixed paper labels to the items originally. Dorflinger Glass and the Meriden Glass Co. made cut glass of the highest quality, yet never used an acid etched signature. Furthermore, cut glass made before the 1890s was not signed. Many of these wood-polished items, cut on blown blanks, were of excellent quality and often won awards at exhibitions.

For more information, see *Warman's Glass*, 4th edition.

Banana bowl, 11" d, 6-1/2" d, Harvard pattern, hobstar bottom **220.00**

Basket
7-1/2" h, 8-1/2" d, four large hobstars, two fans applied

crystal rope-twisted handle **350.00**
9-1/2" h, 11-1/2" d, five large hobstars, fancy emb floral silver handle and rim .. **225.00**
Bonbon, 8" d, 2" h, Broadway pattern, Huntly, minor flakes **135.00**
Bowl, cov, 17-1/2" h, steeple form finial, flared scalloped rim, ftd, flute, oval, punty and vesica cuts, eastern United States, c1840, several edge nicks, repairs **215.00**
Bowl, open
8" d, 1-1/2" h, rayed base, diamond point border, sgd "Libbey" in circle **150.00**
8" d, 2" h, brilliant cut, cross bars and flowers, scalloped rim, sgd "Libbey" in circle, some grinding to edge **175.00**
8" d, 4" h, three brilliant cut thistles surround bowl, flower in center, scalloped edge, etched "Libbey" label, price for pr **400.00**
9" d, 4" h, Hartford, stars with button border, scalloped edge, minor edge flakes **125.00**
10" d, deep-cut buttons, stars, and fans **220.00**
12" d, 4-1/2" h, rolled-down edge, cut and engraved flowers, leaves, and center thistle, notched-serrated edge **275.00**
Box, cov, 5" d, 2-3/4" h, cut-paneled base, cover cut with large eight-pointed star with hobstar center surrounded by fans, C. F. Monroe **275.00**
Bread tray, 8" x 12", Anita, Libbey in circle mark **535.00**

Butter dish, covered, large flower with feathered foliage, strawberry diamond and other motifs, **$175**.

Butter dish, cov, Hobstar **250.00**
Candlesticks, pr
10" h, faceted cut knobs, large teardrop stems, ray base **425.00**
12" h, Adelaide pattern, amber, Pairpoint **250.00**
Celery dish, sgd "J. Hoare" **350.00**
Centerpiece, 10-3/4" d, wheel cut and etched, molded, fruiting foliage, chips **490.00**
Champagne, Kalana Lily, pattern, Dorflinger............ **75.00**
Champagne bucket, 7" h, 7" d, sgd "Hoare" **400.00**
Champagne pitcher, 11" h, Prism pattern, triple notch handle, monogram sterling silver top........................ **425.00**
Cheese dish, cov, 6" h dome, 9" d, plate, cobalt blue cut to clear, bull's eye and panel, large miter splints on bottom of plate **250.00**
Cider pitcher, 7" h, hobstars, zippers, fine diamonds, honeycomb-cut handle, 7" h **225.00**
Cologne bottle
6" h, Hob and Lace pattern, green cased to clear, pattern-cut stopper, Dorflinger **625.00**
7-1/2" h, Holland pattern, faceted-cut stopper.... **275.00**
Compote
6-3/4" d, 5-1/2" h, deep bowl with trefoil, curved edge, three hobstars, and panels with diamond point, fan, and zipper patterns, short pedestal, round base, etched maple leaf mark of T. B. Clark & Co., Honesdale, PA, minor grinding to sawtooth edge **395.00**
7" d, 4-1/4" h, strawberry and chain pattern, serrated edge, low pedestal base, minor roughness and grinding **95.00**
8-1/4" d, 8-3/4" h, Russian cut, scalloped rim and foot, zipper cut faceted stem teardrop center, minor pinpoints and grinding **500.00**
9-1/8" d, 6-1/4" h, hobstars on scalloped edge bowl, straight paneled stem with zipper cut edges, minor flakes.... **400.00**
Creamer and sugar, pr
3-1/4" h, 3-3/4" h, hobstar designs, handles with oval cutting, minor roughness on spout........................... **250.00**

4-1/2" h, pedestal, geometric cuttings, zippered handles, teardrop full length of handle, sgd "Hawkes" **750.00**

5-1/2" h, pedestal, Carolyn variation, notched handles **895.00**

Cruet, 6-7/8" h, round, stars on body, paneled neck with zipper cut edges, scallop cut handle, rayed base, faceted stopper, handle sgd "Tuthill" **250.00**

Decanter, orig stopper

7-7/8" h, pineapple and zipper cut designs, paneled neck with zipper cut designs, diamond pattern on base, faint label of "J. Hoare & Co. Corning 1853" **350.00**

10-1/2" h, quart, triple ring, strawberry diamonds and fans separated by rayed vesicas, flute-cut shoulder and base, polished pontil mark, non-matching cut hollow stopper, Pittsburgh, second quarter 19th C, very minor rim flake **220.00**

11" h, Russian pattern, pr **600.00**

11-1/2" h, stars, arches, fans, cut neck, star cut mushroom stopper **125.00**

Dish

5" d, hobstar, pineapple, palm leaf **45.00**

8" d, scalloped edge, allover hobstar medallions and hobs **175.00**

Dresser box, cov, 7" h, 7" w, Harvard pattern variation, three-ftd, silver-plated fittings, orig beveled mirror on swivel hinge under lid, cut by Bergen Glass Co., couple of minute flakes **750.00**

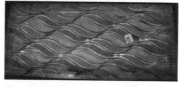

Dresser tray, cut Art Deco wave like decoration, rectangular, **$125**.

Fern dish, 3-3/4" h, 8" w, round, silver-plate rim, C. F. Monroe, minor roughness to cut pattern, normal wear on base, no liner **200.00**

Flower center

5" h, 6" d, hobstars, flashed fans, hobstar chain and base **325.00**

7-3/4" h, 12" d, etched and wheel cut motif, honeycomb flared neck, some wear **500.00**

Goblet

7" h, Buzzstar, pineapple, marked "B & B" **40.00**

8-1/2" h, intaglio vintage cut, 8-1/2" h, sgd "Sinclaire" **80.00**

Humidor, cov

7-1/2" d, Middlesex, hollow stopper, sponge holder in lid, Dorflinger................... **490.00**

9" h, hobstars, beaded split vesicas, hobstar base, matching cut glass lid with hollow for sponge **575.00**

Ice bucket

6-5/8" h, colorless, body cut with vertical flutes, beaded silver-mounted rim with sterling silver swing handle marked for Wilcox Silver Plate Co., early 20th C......... **320.00**

7" h, hobstars and notched prisms, 8" d underplate, double handles........... **940.00**

Ice cream tray, Empress pattern variation, 10" x 17-1/2", sgd "Libbey" **1,000.00**

Jar, cov, 10" h, diamond cut finial on stepped lid, ftd ovoid vessel, four Oriental influenced cut medallions, cane and star-cut ground, 20th C, several nicks **260.00**

Knife rest, 4" l................... **95.00**

Lamp, Gone with the Wind style, cut shade and base, stars, whirls, hobstars, original burner, flakes, **$125**.

Lamp

23" h, hobstars, cross-cut diamonds, flashed star cuttings, triangular shaped hanging prisms........ **1,300.00**

24" h, cut glass rounded shade with pointed top, inverted trumpet form base, both with etched rose dec, wide borders of geometric design, ring of cut glass prisms...................... **525.00**

Loving cup, three handles, sterling top **350.00**

Nappy, two handles

6" d, hobstar center, intaglio floral, strawberry diamond button border, 6" d........ **45.00**

9" d, deep-cut arches, pointed sunbursts and medallions **135.00**

Nappy, divided into four sections, cut and pressed decoration, cane center and border, floral decoration, two ring handles, **$85**.

Nappy, three handles, divided, whirled stars, ring handle, **$125**.

Orange bowl, 9-3/4" x 6-3/4" x 3-3/4" h, hobstars and strawberry diamond........ **200.00**

Perfume bottle

3-1/2" l, cranberry overlay, shaped sides, notched cuts, S. Mordan & Co., silver-mounted cap **325.00**

6-1/2" h, bulbous, allover cutting, orig stopper ... **220.00**

Perfume flask, 4-3/4" l, pistol-form, etched silver-gilt mounts, short chain, spring-action trigger opens lid set with maker's medallion, French, late 19th/early 20th C **1,380.00**

Pickle tray, 7" x 3", checkerboard, hobstar **45.00**

Pitcher
8-7/8" h, baluster form body, upper section vertically ribbed and cut, lower section with stylized flowerheads, facet cut handle, silver-plated rim mount with beaded edging, monogrammed, marked "Wilcox Silver Plate Co." **750.00**
12-1/2" h, tapered body with quatrefoil flowers, tiny diamond point surface, surrounded by fans and hobstars, paneled neck with zipper cuts, spout with diamonds, cut ridges on applied handle, spout has been reworked on underside **475.00**
14-1/8" h, baluster, vertical flutes with bead and lozenge cuts, crosshatched and diamond-cut diamonds at base, mounted with sterling bead-edged spout, monogrammed **250.00**

Plate, large, hobstars, whirls, criss cross designs, serrated edge, **$90.**

Plate, large, central daisy motif, radiating foliage, additional etched rounds, hobstar border, serrated edge, 12" d, **$125.**

Plate
10" d, Carolyn pattern, J. Hoare **525.00**
12" d, alternating hobstar and pinwheel **100.00**

Potpourri jar, 6" h, baluster shaped cut glass base, silver lid with portrait medallion and floral banding **200.00**

Punch bowl
11" h, 10" w, two pcs, Elgin pattern, Quaker City ... **600.00**
13-3/4" d, 15-1/4" h, Rajah pattern, sgd "Pitkin and Brooks" **2,750.00**
14-3/8" d, 13-1/4" h, round, set into base, cut rim, miter star cut pattern, acid-etched maker's mark for T. G. Hawkes & Co., Corning, NY, on base **1,880.00**

Punch ladle, 11-1/2" l, silver plated emb shell bowl, cut and notched prism handle **165.00**

Relish
8" l, two handles, divided, Jupiter pattern, Meriden **120.00**
13" l, leaf shape, Clear Button Russian pattern **375.00**

Salad bowl, Russian pattern **90.00**

Salt, open, Russian pattern, master size **45.00**

Salt shaker, prism columns **30.00**

Serving dish, 11" d, two layers, apple and pear branches, grape vine dec, Gravic **395.00**

Tankard pitcher
10-1/4" h, Harvard cut sides, pinwheel top, mini hobnails, thumbprint notched handle **200.00**
11" h, hobstar, strawberry diamond, notched prism and fan, flared base with bull's eye, double thumbprint handle **275.00**

Tobacco humidor, 7" h, Flute pattern, ornate Whiting sterling lid with sponge holder **650.00**

Tray
12" d, hobstars, caning, and notched prisms inside vesicas arranged around center star, sgd "Libbey" twice .. **2,000.00**
12" d, round, Monarch, sgd "Hoare" **975.00**
14" x 7-1/2", Sillsbee pattern, Pairpoint **335.00**

Tumbler
Band of strawberry diamonds and fans, plain base edge, polished pontil, Pittsburgh-type, first half 19th C, 3-1/4" h, 3-1/8" d **150.00**
Harvard, rayed base **45.00**
Hobstars **40.00**

Urn, cov, Russian pattern **175.00**

Vase
8" h, 11" d, squatty body, short flaring neck, scalloped rim **550.00**
11" h, fan, amber, engraved grape leaves and vines, round disk base, acid-etched Hawkes mark, small chip on base............................ **300.00**
12-1/2" h, 6-1/2" d, floral and diamond point engraving, sgd "Hawkes" **250.00**
14" h, ruffled edge, cut iris dec, Gravic **295.00**
16" h, corset shape, well-cut hobstar, strawberry diamond, prism, flashed star and fan **300.00**
19-1/2" h, lobed rim, alternating vertical cut patterns, star-cut disk base, 20th C **750.00**
23-1/4" h, two pcs, trumpet shape, hobstars and paneled ring design, base and top joined with metal post covered with diamond faceted ball.............. **1,350.00**
24-1/2" h, Monarch pattern, sgd "J. Hoare" **3,750.00**

Tall vase, ruffled top, green cut to clear floral decoration, English, **$2,600.**

Water carafe
Harvard pattern **185.00**
Hobstars and notched prisms
.... **125.00**
Pinwheel and Fan cutting,
notched neck, 8" h, 4" w
.... **125.00**

Water pitcher
9-1/2" h, Harvard
patternpanels and intaglio cut
sprays of flowers and foliage
.... **300.00**
10" h, Keystone Rose pattern
.... **190.00**

Water set, Daisy & Button
pattern, 10" h pitcher, eleven
water tumblers **250.00**
Whiskey jug, 6-1/4" h, bulbous,
thistle and grape cutting, orig
stopper, sgd "Sinclaire" .. **295.00**
Wine, 4" h, flint, cut panels,
strawberry diamonds, and fans,
Pittsburgh **60.00**
Wine cooler, Russian pattern
.... **145.00**

DECOYS

History: During the past several
years, carved wooden decoys,
used to lure ducks and geese to
the hunter, have become widely
recognized as an indigenous
American folk-art form. Many
decoys are from 1880 to 1930,
when commercial gunners
commonly hunted and used rigs of
several hundred decoys. Many
fine carvers also worked through
the 1930s and 1940s. Individuals
and commercial decoy makers
also carved fish decoys.

Because decoys were both
hand made and machine made,
and many examples exist, firm
pricing is difficult to establish. The
skill of the carver, rarity, type of
bird, and age all affect the value.

Reproduction Alert.

Notes: A decoy's value is based
on several factors: (1) fame of the
carver, (2) quality of the carving,
(3) species of wild fowl—the most
desirable are herons, swans,
mergansers, and shorebirds—and
(4) condition of the original paint.

The inexperienced collector
should be aware of several facts.
The age of a decoy, per se, is
usually of no importance in
determining value. However, age

does have some influence when it
comes to a rare or important
example. Since very few decoys
were ever signed, it is quite
difficult to attribute most decoys to
known carvers. Anyone who has
not examined a known carver's
work will be hard pressed to
determine if the paint on one of his
decoys is indeed original.
Repainting severely decreases a
decoy's value. In addition, there
are many fakes and reproductions
on the market and even
experienced collectors are
occasionally fooled. Decoys
represent a subject where dealing
with a reputable dealer or auction
house is important, especially
those who offer a guarantee as to
authenticity.

Decoys listed here are of
average wear, unless otherwise
noted.

Atlantic Brant, Mason,
Challenge grade, c1910, from
the famous Barron rig (Virginia),
nearly mint condition, age
shrinkage neck crack repair,
tight filled factory back crack
.... **4,500.00**
Baldgate Wigeon Drake,
miniature, A. Elmer, Crowell, East
Harwich, MA, identified in ink,
rect stamp on base, 2-1/2" x 4"
.... **635.00**
Black Bellied Bustard,
miniature, H. Gills, initialed "H.
G. 1957," identified in pencil,
natural wood base, 3-1/2" x 4"
.... **230.00**
Black Bellied Plover, unknown
American 20th C maker, orig
paint, glass eyes, mounted on
stick on lead base
12-1/2" h, minor paint loss,
small chips to beak . **2,530.00**
13-1/2" h, minor paint loss,
beak repair **1,725.00**
Black Breasted Plover, Harry C.
Shourds, orig paint **2,650.00**
Black Duck
A. Elmer Crowell, East
Harwich, MA, orig paint, glass
eyes, stamped mark in oval
on base, sleeping, wear,
crack, 5-1/4" h **525.00**
Ira Hudson, preening, raised
wings, outstretched neck,
scratch feather paint **8,500.00**
Mason, Challenge, c1910,
hollow, fine orig paint, some
neck filler replaced .. **3,500.00**

Mason, Premier, c1905,
Atlantic Coast, oversized,
solid-bodied special order,
most desirable snaky head,
excellent orig condition, some
professional restoration, filled
in-the-making back crack, tail
chip on one side of crack,
neck filler replacement
.... **4,500.00**
Mason, Standard, c1910,
painted eye, dry original
paint, all of its original neck
filler, invisible professional dry
rot repair in the base .. **750.00**
Unknown maker, carved balsa
body, wood head, glass eyes,
orig pant, 15-1/2" l **150.00**
Wildfowler, CT, inlet head,
glass eyes, worn orig paint,
green overpaint on bottom on
sides, 13" l, c1900 ...... **220.00**

Three ducks, some wear, each **$75-$125.**
Photo courtesy of Wiederseim Associates, Inc.

Black Drake, miniature
A. Elmer Crowell, East
Harwich, MA, identified in ink,
rect stamp on base, break at
neck, reglued, minor paint
loss, 3-1/2" x 4-3/4" **635.00**
James Lapham, Dennisport,
MA, identified in black ink,
oval stamp, minor
imperfections, 2-1/2" x 4"
.... **290.00**
Bluebill Drake, carved by
Robert Elliston, painted by wife
Catherine Elliston, 19th C, Illinois
River **6,700.00**
Bluebill Hen, Mason Challenge,
c1910, hollow, orig paint
.... **3,450.00**
**Blue-Winged Teal Drake and
Hen Pair**, Davey W. Nichol,
Smiths Falls, Ontario, Canada,
1960, matched pair, raised
wings, scratch feather patterns,
sgd on bottom **1,650.00**

Brant, old black, white, and gray paint, glass eyes, age splits on base, minor chips to gesso on back, 14-1/2" l **115.00**

Broadbill Drake and Hen Pair, Mason, c1910, painted eyes, rare gunning rigmates, untouched original condition, neck filler missing, some shot evidence, hen has small, superficial chip on one side **1,450.00**

Pair of carved and painted duck decoys attributed to Wendell Smith, Chicago, $900

Photo courtesy of Joy Luke.

Bufflehead Drake
Bob Kerr, carved detail, glass eyes, orig paint, scratch carved signature, 10-1/2" l, c1980 .... **250.00**
James Lagham, Dennisport, MA, identified in ink, oval stamp on base, 3" x 4-1/2" **345.00**
Harry M. Shrouds, carved, hollow body, painted eyes **1,800.00**

Canadian Goose
Hurley Conklin, carved, hollow body, swimming position, branded "H. Conklin" on bottom **600.00**
Unsigned, carved wood, shaped tin, canvas covering on body, later gray, brown, white, and black paint, glass eyes, restored splits in neck, 22 1/2" l **100.00**
Unsigned, gray, black, and white paint, incised carved initials "P.C." on base, carved open bill, relief detail on wings and tail feathers, glass eyes, iron legs, glued break at neck, 27" l, 26-5/8" h **300.00**

Canvasback
Chesapeake Bay, carved and painted, glass eyes, metal ring, 12" l, 7-1/2" w, 10-3/4" h **1,650.00**

Unknown carver, pine, paint dec, lead weight, metal ring, 8-3/4" l, 6" w, 5" h **1,210.00**

Canvasback drake, $275.
Photo courtesy of Wiederseim Associates, Inc.

Curlew
Dan Leeds, Pleasantville, NJ, 1880-1900, carved and painted brown, stand, 13" l **2,415.00**
Harry V. Shrouds, orig paint **2,000.00**

Curlew Oyster Eater, Samuel Jester, Tennessee, c1920, carved and painted, slight paint wear, age crack in body, stand, 16" l, 9" h **1,035.00**

Elder Duck, 17-3/4" l, old black and white paint, green stripe around head, yellow bill, Maine, unsigned **250.00**

Flying Duck, glass-bead eyes, old natural surface, carved pine, attributed to Maine, c1930, 16" l, 11" h **2,300.00**

Goldeneye, drake, unknown Maine carver, c1900, oversized, classic Maine inletted neck and raised shoulders, worn orig paint with clear patterns, branded "Gigerrish" or "G.I. Gerrish," 13" l **1,850.00**

Great Northern Pike, attributed to Menominee Indian, WI, c1900, painted green, glass eyes, ribbed sheet metal fin, tall stand, 36" l, 9" h **3,450.00**

Green Wing Teal Duck, miniature, A. Elmer Crowell, East Harwich, MA, identified in ink, rect stamp on base, 2-1/2" x 4" **865.00**

Heron, unknown maker, carved wig and tail, wrought iron legs **900.00**

Herring Gull, attributed to Gus Wilson, c1910-20, used as weathervane, traces of old paint, metal feet, weathered and worn, 18-3/4" l **3,110.00**

Hooded Merganser Drake, William Clarke, Oakville, Ontario, Canada, c1900, transitional plumage, excellent orig condition, minor in-use wear **2,450.00**

Loon, carved and painted, wooden rudder, America, 19th C, stand, paint wear, 27" l. **9,200.00**

Mallard Drake
Ben Schmidt, Detroit, relief carved, feather stamping, glass eyes, orig paint, orig keep, marked "Mallard drake Benj Schmidt, Detroit 1960," 15-1/4" l **450.00**

Four ducks, some wear to factory paint, each **$75-$125**.
Photo courtesy of Wiederseim Associates, Inc.

Bert Graves, carved, hollow body, orig weighted bottom, branded "E. I. Rogers" and "Cleary" **900.00**
James Lapham, Dennisport, MA, sgd and identified in ink on bottom, 4" x 5"........ **435.00**
Mason, Challenge, c1910, rare hollow model with elaborate Mason Premier style paint patterns, no tail chip, professional repair to some splintering on end of bill, tight neck crack on left side, some shot evidence on right side **3,500.00**
Mason, Premier, c1900, hollow snakey head, orig condition **6,500.00**
Robert Elliston, carver, painted by wife Catherine Elliston, 19th C, Illinois River **6,200.00**

Carved and painted duck decoy attributed to Bill Shaw, Lacon, Illinois, $850.

Photo courtesy of Joy Luke.

Mallard Drake and Hen Pair, Mason, c1905, glass eyes, gunning rigmates, excellent orig condition, some neck filler replaced, drake has filled factory crack on side **1,750.00**
Mallard Hen
Robert Elliston, carved, hollow body, orig paint........ **1,800.00**
Mason Premier, c1905, hollow, excellent orig paint, rich red breast, professional tail chip repair and neck putty restoration............... **3,900.00**
Merganser Drake, Mason Challenge, Detroit, MI, c1910, strong orig paint with no cracks, some shot holes have been filled on one side, branded "C. Simpson"..................... **7,500.00**
Owl, carved wood, glass eyes, orig polychrome paint, 20" h **1,700.00**
Perch, Heddon, ice-type **800.00**
Pintail Duck
Drake, Paw Paw Bait Co., c1932-36, stenciled company name on bottom.......... **800.00**

Drake and hen, John H. Baker, Bristol, PA, 20th C, painted in naturalistic tones, glass eyes, sgd, imp maker's signature, lead ingot affixed to bases stamped "John Baker Bristol, PA," paint flakes on hen.......................... **1,100.00**
Plover, Joe Lincoln, winter plumage, feather painting, orig paint...................... **800.00**
Red Breasted Merganser Drake
George Boyd, NH, carved, orig paint **8,000.00**
Amos Wallace, ME, inlet neck, carved crest, detailed feathered paint **2,000.00**
Redhead Drake, Dan Bartlett, Prince Edward County, Ontario, Canada, c1920, hollow, fine orig paint............................... **950.00**
Robin Snipe, Obediah Verity, carved wings and eyes, orig paint **4,400.00**
Ruddy Duck, miniature, maker unknown, identified in ink on base, paint loss to bill, 2" x 2-3/4" **690.00**
Ruddy Duck Drake, Len Carmeghi, Mt. Clemens, MI, hollow body, glass eyes, orig paint, sgd and dated, 10-3/4" l **250.00**
Ruffled Grouse, miniature, A. Elmer Crowell, East Harwich, MA, rect stamp, mounted on natural wood base, 3-1/2" x 4-1/2" **865.00**
Sea Gull, 14" l, weathered surface, used as weathervane, attributed to WI, late 19th/early 20th C **1,840.00**

Shore bird, tin, two-piece hollow form, some paint remaining, 11" l x 6" h, mounted on pewter chamberstick, minor loss of tail, rust on surface, $80.

Photo courtesy of Alderfer Auction Co.

Shorebird, carved and painted, mounted on wooden stand, minor wear, America, early 20th C, 6-3/4" l, 9-1/2" h **775.00**
Swan, unknown Chesapeake Bay, MD, maker, carved wood, braced neck, white paint, 30" l **900.00**
Widgeon, matted pair, Charlie Joiner, MD, sgd on bottom **800.00**

Wood Duck, drake, D. W. Nichol, Smiths Falls, Ontario, 1950s, slightly turned head........ **2,450.00**
Yellowlegs, carved and painted, New Jersey, c1890, stand, 11" l **2,185.00**

DEDHAM POTTERY

History:
Alexander W. Robertson established a pottery in Chelsea, Massachusetts, about 1866. After his brother, Hugh Cornwall Robertson, joined him in 1868, the firm was called A. W. & H. C. Robertson. Their father, James Robertson, joined his sons in 1872, and the name Chelsea Keramic Art Works Robertson and Sons was used.

The pottery's initial products were simple flower and bean pots, but the firm quickly expanded its output to include a wide variety of artistic pottery. It produced a very fine redware body used in classical forms, some with black backgrounds imitating ancient Greek and Apulian works. It experimented with underglaze slip decoration on vases. The Chelsea Keramic Art Works Pottery also produced high-glazed vases, pitchers, and plaques with a buff clay body, with either sculpted or molded applied decoration.

James Robertson died in 1880 and Alexander moved to California in 1884, leaving Hugh C. Robertson alone in Chelsea, where his tireless experiments eventually yielded a stunning imitation of the prized Chinese Ming-era blood-red glaze. Hugh's vases with that glaze were marked with an impressed "CKAW." Creating these red-glazed vases was very expensive, and even though they received great critical acclaim, the company declared bankruptcy in 1889.

Recapitalized by a circle of Boston art patrons in 1891, Hugh started the Chelsea Pottery U.S., which produced gray crackle-glazed dinnerware with cobalt-blue decorations, the rabbit pattern being the most popular.

The business moved to new facilities in Dedham, Massachusetts, and began production in 1896 under the name Dedham Pottery. Hugh's son and grandson operated the business until it closed in 1943, by which time between 50 and 80 patterns had been produced, some very briefly.

Marks: The following marks help determine the approximate age of items:

- "Chelsea Keramic Art Works Robertson and Sons," impressed, 1874-1880
- "CKAW," impressed, 1875-1889
- "CPUS," impressed in a cloverleaf, 1891-1895
- Foreshortened rabbit only, impressed, 1894-1896
- Conventional rabbit with "Dedham Pottery" in square blue stamped mark along with one impressed foreshortened rabbit, 1896-1928
- Blue rabbit stamped mark with "registered" beneath, along with two impressed foreshortened rabbit marks, 1929-1943

Reproduction Alert: Two companies make Dedham-like reproductions primarily utilizing the rabbit pattern, but always mark their work very differently from the original.

Butter pat, Rabbit pattern, **$125.**

Bowl, 8-1/2" sq
Rabbit pattern, reg. stamp **600.00**
Swan pattern, reg. stamp **725.00**
Bowl, 9-3/8" d, 3-3/4" h, Poppy pattern, cut edge rim, Oriental-type, sloping poppies, registered blue ink stamp, "D" in red, minor glaze miss near base edge **1,035.00**

Breakfast plate, 8-3/4" d
Crab pattern, blue ink stamp, glaze imperfections **375.00**
Rabbit pattern, assembled set, marks include blue registered stamp, imp foreshortened rabbit, and 1931 stamp, set of six, one with rim chip **635.00**
Butter plate, 4-3/8" d, Swan pattern, registered blue ink stamp **260.00**
Candlesticks, pr
Elephant pattern, reg. blue stamp........................ **525.00**
Rabbit pattern, reg. blue stamp........................ **325.00**
Creamer and sugar, 3-1/4" and 4", Rabbit pattern, blue stamp and "1931" on creamer, blue registered stamp on sugar **350.00**
Cup and saucer, Rabbit pattern, 3-7/8" d cup, 6" d saucers with rabbit borders, blue registered stamps, set of six **700.00**
Knife rest, Rabbit form, blue reg. stamp..................... **575.00**
Paperweight, Rabbit form, blue reg. stamp..................... **495.00**
Pickle dish, 10-1/2" l, Elephant pattern, blue reg. stamp . **750.00**
Pitcher
3-1/4" h, Rabbit pattern **175.00**
5-1/8" h, Chickens pattern, blue stamp............... **2,300.00**
7" h, Turkey pattern, blue stamp......................... **585.00**
9" h, Rabbit pattern, blue stamp **700.00**
Style of 1850, blue reg. stamp **975.00**

Paperweight, frog, signed "Dedham Pottery," artist's initials "C. D.," nick to web, 2-1/8" l, **$715.**
Photo courtesy of Skinner, Inc.

Plate, 6" d
Clover pattern, reg. stamp **625.00**
Iris pattern, blue stamp, Maude Davenport's "O" rebus **280.00**

Rabbit pattern, registered blue ink stamp, set of four, foot chips on two **290.00**
Plate, 6-1/8" d
Horse Chestnut pattern, one impressed rabbit mark **150.00**
Magnolia pattern, blue ink stamp mark................ **115.00**
Plate, 7-1/2" d, Lobster pattern, registered blue ink stamp, two imp rabbits...................... **290.00**
Plate, 8-1/4" d, Rabbit pattern, glaze burst...................... **125.00**
Plate, 8-1/2" d
Crab pattern, blue stamp **550.00**
Elephant pattern, blue reg. stamp......................... **650.00**
Oriental Poppy, single rabbit and blue ink stamp mark, in-the-making glaze bursts **265.00**
Rabbit pattern, blue stamp **175.00**
Rabbit pattern, blue stamp, Maude Davenport's "O" rebus **235.00**
Snow Tree pattern, blue stamp........................ **210.00**
Upside down dolphin, CPUS **900.00**

Plate, Horse Chestnut pattern, blue ink stamp, early 20th C, 8-1/2" d, **$150.**
Photo courtesy of Skinner, Inc.

Plate, 10" d
Dolphin pattern, blue reg. stamp........................ **875.00**
Elephant pattern, blue reg. stamp........................ **900.00**
Pine Apple pattern, CPUS **775.00**
Turkey pattern, blue stamp, Maude Davenport's "O" rebus **475.00**
Plate, 10-1/4" d, Rabbit pattern, registered blue ink stamp, one imp rabbit...................... **150.00**
Platter, 9-7/8" l, 6-3/8" w, Rabbit pattern, rect, blue ink stamp, two imp rabbits...................... **260.00**
Salt and pepper shakers, pr, Rabbit pattern, 3-1/2" h, glaze miss **200.00**
Sherbet, two handles, Rabbit pattern, blue stamp **350.00**

Tea cup and saucer

Azalea pattern, reg. stamp
.... **130.00**
Butterfly pattern, blue stamp
.... **345.00**
Duck pattern, reg. stamp
.... **190.00**
Turtle pattern, reg. stamp
.... **680.00**
Water Lily pattern, reg. stamp
.... **130.00**
Teapot, 6-1/8" h, Rabbit pattern, blue stamp **875.00**
Tea set, 8-1/2" h teapot, creamer, cov sugar, five 4" d cups, five saucers, waste bowl, small plate, Rabbit pattern, ink stamps on base, glaze voids and bubble bursts **1,000.00**
Tea tile, 6-1/4" d, Rabbit, round form with projections at ears and feet, white crackle glaze with outline of long-eared rabbit in blue, glaze missing to depict eyes against a blue-green ground, white clay body, base chip **390.00**

Vase, volcanic, bulbous, frothy chocolate, indigo, and green glaze, incised "Dedham BW Pottery/ DP32A 048646751P," 3-3/4" d, 7" h, 1/2" rim bruise to rim, minor grinding chips, and base lines, **$920**.
Photo courtesy of David Rago Auctions, Inc.

Vase

6-1/2" h, 4-1/2" d, experimental, by Hugh Robertson, thick glossy emerald green glaze dripping over indigo, pink, brown, and green volcanic base, incised "Dedham Pottery HCR"
.... **4,500.00**
9-1/8" h, ovoid, mottled green glossy glaze, incised "Dedham Pottery" with Hugh Robertson's initials, c1900
.... **2,500.00**

Vase, experimental, by Hugh Robertson, covered in thick glossy celadon green and purple frothy glaze, marked "BW/Dedham Pottery/HCR/ B.T.," 10" h, 5" d, **$1,200**.
Photo courtesy of David Rago Auctions, Inc.

9-1/4" h, bulbous body, long neck, mottled green glossy glaze, incised "Dedham Pottery", William Robertson's initials, c1900 .... **2,650.00**

DELFTWARE

History: Delftware is pottery with a soft, red-clay body and tin-enamel glaze. The white, dense, opaque color came from adding tin ash to lead glaze. The first examples had blue designs on a white ground. Polychrome examples followed.

The name originally applied to pottery made in the region around Delft, Holland, beginning in the 16th century and ending in the late 18th century. The tin used came from the Cornish mines in England. By the 17th and 18th centuries, English potters in London, Bristol, and Liverpool were copying the glaze and designs. Some designs unique to English potters also developed.

In Germany and France, the ware is known as Faience, and in Italy as Majolica.

Reproduction Alert: Since the late 19th century, much Delft-type souvenir material has been produced to appeal to the foreign traveler. Don't confuse these modern pieces with the older examples.

Bowl, 9" d, 3-3/4" h, interior and exterior painted with polychrome orange, yellow, and blue flowers, late 18th C, hairline **900.00**
Charger
13" d, floral design, building scene, manganese and blue, edge chips **615.00**
13-1/8" d, blue and white, foliate devices, Dutch, 19th C, chips, glaze wear **410.00**
13-5/8" d, blue and white, foliate devices, 19th C, chips, glass wear, restoration **320.00**
16 1/2" d, center branch with fruiting blossoms, two birds, conforming florals on wide rim, sgd "G. A. Kleynoven," c1655 .... **2,250.00**
Dish
8-1/4" d, molded rim, blue and white, stylized landscape and floral design, edge chips
.... **315.00**
12-3/8" l, fluted oval, blue and white floral design, attributed to Lambeth, chips **440.00**
Flower brick, 4-5/8" l, 2-1/2" h, blue and white, Chinese figures in landscape, Dutch, 18th C, chips, cracks **375.00**
Garniture, three bulbous 17-1/4" h cov urns, two octagonal tapered 12-3/4" h vases, polychrome dec foliage surrounding central blue figural panels, Dutch, late 18th/early 19th C **8,625.00**
Inkwell, 4-1/2" h, heart shape, blue and white floral dec, wear and edge chips **495.00**

Tile, blue and white Christmas scene with gent in rocking chair in front of fireplace, titled "Kerstmis 1969," back marked "V. K. Delft, Gda, Made in Holland, Merry Christmas, 1969," hanger on back, **$40**.

Jar, 5" h, blue and white, chips, pr **715.00**

Lamp base, octagonal bottle form with continuous blue and white Oriental figural landscape design, England, 18th C, foot rim chips, drilled **690.00**

Model, 17-1/2" h, tall case clock, blue dec white ground, panels of figural and architectural landscapes between scrolled foliate borders, 19th C, slight glaze wear **320.00**

Mug, 6-3/8" h, blue and white, armorial surrounded by exotic landscape, palm trees, marked on base, Dutch, 19th C, minor chips, glaze wear **490.00**

Plate
  7-7/8" d, tin glazed earthenware, central blue rosette, England, 18th C, chips **125.00**
  8-1/2" d, painted in polychrome manganese, blue, green, and red with stylized flowers, late 18th C, few glaze chips around rims **950.00**
  8-7/8" d, tin glazed earthenware, flowers, bird in birdbath in center, minor damage **150.00**
  9" d, tin glazed earthenware, Oriental fence and chrysanthemum dec, yellow rim, axe and "X" mark, minor damage **150.00**
  9-1/8" d, white tin glazed earthenware, two-tone blue flowers, wavy border, "6" mark, edge flakes, old repairs **115.00**
  9-1/4" d, tin glazed earthenware, blue Chinoiserie motifs, manganese purple cracked-ice pattern border, England, 18th C, chips **295.00**

Plate, Dutch, scallop edge, central circular panel featuring crested bird amid flowers, surrounded by concentric bands of floral motifs, concentric blue lines on back of rim, bottom marked with blue under-glaze "hatchet," mark used c1759, 10" d, rim chips, **$350**.

Photo courtesy of Alderfer Auction Co.

Posset pot, 4-3/4" h, blue and white, birds among foliage, England, 19th C, minor chips and cracks **920.00**

Sauce boat, 8-1/4" l, applied scrolled handles, fluted flaring lip, blue and white Oriental design, edge chips and hairline, later added yellow enamel rim **440.00**

Saucer, 8-3/4" d, table ring, blue, iron-red, yellow, and manganese bowl of flowers dec **825.00**

Strainer bowl, 9-1/8" d, blue and white floral design, three short feet, chips **520.00**

Tankard, 9" h, tin glazed earthenware, pewter mounts, polychrome floral sprays, "IK 1793," indistinct signature inscribed on pewter top, England, 18th C, cracks . **400.00**

Tea caddy, 5-7/8" h, blue and white floral dec, scalloped bottom edge, marked "MVS 1750," cork closure, wear, edge flakes, old filled in chip on lid **550.00**

Tile, 5" sq, Fazackerly, polychrome dec of floral bouquets, c1760, price for pr, one with edge nicks, other with edge flaking and chips ... **350.00**

Tobacco jar, 10" h, blue and white, Indians and "Siville," older brass stepped lid, chips **1,870.00**

Vase, 18" h, urn shape, ftd, cherub framed with applied fruit wreath, two figure centaurs on each side, mkd with hand painted rooster and "22". **350.00**

Vase, cov, 23" h, Delft blue and white, oval paneled sides with Chinese style dec alternating with female figures in courtyard setting, flowers, and fence design, hexagonal form rim, foot, and cov, cat finial, unidentified mark, Holland, 18th C, rim damage, footrim chips, chips to cat's ears, typical edge flaking of tin glaze **815.00**

Vase, bulbous, blue and gray floral motif, 7" h, crazing, rim and bottom chips, **$850**.

Photo courtesy of Alderfer Auction Co.

Wall plaque, 23-1/2" l, cartouche shape, blue enamel dec, windmill shoreline scene, Dutch, early 20th C **530.00**

Wall pocket, 6-1/4" w, 4-1/2" d, 7" h, vasiform, ogee backplate, pierced grillwork, blue and white scenes of figures at harbor, scrollwork borders, applied flower buds on sides, 20th C, price for pr **350.00**

DEPRESSION GLASS

For more information, see *Warman's Depression Glass*, 3rd edition; *Warman's Depression Glass Field Guide*; and *Warman's Glass*, 4th edition.

History: Depression glass was made from 1920 to 1940. It was an inexpensive machine-made glass and produced by several companies in various patterns and colors. The number of forms made in different patterns also varied.

Depression glass was sold through variety stores, given away as premiums, or packaged with certain products. Movie houses gave it away from 1935 until well into the 1940s.

Like pattern glass, knowing the proper name of a pattern is the key to collecting. Collectors should be prepared to do research.

Reproduction Alert: The number of Depression glass patterns that have been reproduced continues to grow. Reproductions exist in many patterns, forms, and colors. Beware of colors and forms that were not made in the original production of the pattern. Carefully examine every piece that seems questionable and look for loss of details, poor impressions, and slight differences in sizes.

American Sweetheart

Manufactured by MacBeth-Evans
Glass Company, Charleroi,
Pennsylvania, from 1930 to1936.
Made in blue, Monax, pink, and
red. There was limited production
in Cremax and color-trimmed
Monax.

American Sweetheart, dinner plate,
monax, **$25**.

Item	Blue	Cremax	Monax	Monax w/color trim	Pink	Red
Berry bowl, 3-1/4" d, flat	-	-	-	-	80.00	-
Berry bowl, 9" d	-	50.00	75.00	200.00	65.00	-
Cereal bowl, 6" d	-	19.50	20.00	50.00	24.00	-
Chop plate, 11" d	-	-	24.00	-	-	-
Console bowl, 18" d	1,400.00	-	475.00	-	-	1,100.00
Cream soup, 4-1/2" d	-	-	135.00	-	85.00	-
Creamer, ftd	195.00	-	11.50	110.00	18.00	175.00
Cup	160.00	-	15.00	100.00	20.00	95.00
Lamp shade	-	450.00	500.00	-	-	-
Pitcher, 60 oz, 7-1/2" h	-	-	-	-	995.00	-
Pitcher, 80 oz, 8" h	-	-	-	-	795.00	-
Plate, 6" d, bread & butter	-	-	7.50	24.00	8.00	-
Plate, 8" d, salad	125.00	-	10.00	30.00	12.00	125.00
Plate, 9" d, luncheon	-	-	14.00	45.00	-	-
Plate, 9-3/4" d, dinner	-	-	25.00	90.00	42.00	-
Plate, 10-1/4" d, dinner	-	-	30.00	-	45.00	-
Platter, 13" l, oval	-	-	85.00	225.00	70.00	-
Salt & pepper shakers, pr, ftd	-	-	395.00	-	500.00	-
Salver plate, 12" d	275.00	-	30.00	-	30.00	200.00
Saucer	25.00	-	7.00	18.00	5.75	45.00
Serving plate, 15-1/2" d	450.00	-	250.00	-	-	350.00
Sherbet, 3-3/4" h, ftd	-	-	25.00	-	25.00	-
Sherbet, 4-1/4" h, ftd	-	-	25.00	110.00	25.00	-
Soup bowl, flat, 9-1/2" d	-	-	95.00	170.00	85.00	-
Sugar lid	-	-	300.00	-	-	-
Sugar, open, ftd	195.00	-	15.00	110.00	15.00	175.00
Tidbit, two-tier	350.00	-	95.00	-	-	250.00
Tidbit, three-ier	750.00	-	275.00	-	-	600.00
Tumbler, 5 oz, 3-1/2" h	-	-	-	-	110.00	-
Tumbler, 9 oz, 4-1/4" h	-	-	-	-	85.00	-
Tumbler, 10 oz, 4-3/4" h	-	-	-	-	185.00	-
Vegetable bowl, 11"	-	-	90.00	-	80.00	-

Aurora

Manufactured by Hazel Atlas
Glass Company, Clarksburg, West
Virginia, and Zanesville, Ohio, in
the late 1930s. Made in cobalt
(Ritz) blue, crystal, green, and
pink.

Aurora, plate, 6-1/2" d, cobalt blue, a
good buy at **$5**.

Item	Cobalt Blue	Crystal	Green	Pink
Bowl, 4-1/2" d	60.00	-	-	60.00
Breakfast set, 24 pcs, service for 4	500.00	-	-	-
Cereal bowl, 5-3/8" d	20.00	12.00	9.50	15.00
Cup	20.000	6.00	10.00	15.00
Milk pitcher	27.50	-	-	25.00
Plate, 6-1/2" d	12.50	-	-	12.50
Saucer	6.00	2.00	3.00	6.00
Tumbler, 10 oz, 4-3/4" h	27.50	-	-	27.50

Beaded Block

Manufactured by Imperial Glass
Company, Bellaire, Ohio, from
1927 to the 1930s. Made in amber,
crystal, green, ice blue, iridescent,
milk white (1950s), opalescent,
pink, red (extremely rare), and
vaseline. Some pieces are still
being made in pink and are
embossed with the "IG"
trademark.

Item	Amber	Crystal	Green	Ice Blue	Irid.	Opal	Pink	Vaseline
Bowl, 4-1/2" d, lily	20.00	15.00	22.00	24.00	18.00	30.00	18.00	24.00
Bowl, 4-1/2" d, two handles	18.00	10.00	22.00	28.00	20.00	30.00	12.00	28.00
Bowl, 5-1/2" sq	18.00	8.00	20.00	12.00	10.00	15.00	10.00	12.00
Bowl, 5-1/2" d, one handle	18.00	8.00	20.00	12.00	10.00	15.00	20.00	12.00
Bowl, 6" deep	24.00	12.00	24.00	15.00	12.00	24.00	18.00	15.00
Bowl, 6-1/4" d	24.00	8.50	20.00	12.00	12.00	18.00	10.00	12.00
Bowl, 6-1/2" d, two handles	24.00	8.50	20.00	12.00	12.00	18.00	28.00	12.00
Bowl, 6-3/4" d	28.00	12.00	28.00	14.00	15.00	20.00	14.00	14.00

Item	Amber	Crystal	Green	Ice Blue	Irid.	Opal	Pink	Vaseline
Bowl, 7-1/4" d, flared	30.00	12.00	28.00	14.00	15.00	20.00	14.00	14.00
Bowl, 7-1/2" d, fluted	30.00	22.00	30.00	24.00	20.00	24.00	24.00	24.00
Bowl, 7-1/2" plain	30.00	20.00	30.00	22.00	24.00	24.00	20.00	22.00
Candy dish, cov, pear shaped	-	-	395.00	-	-	-	-	650.00
Celery, 8-1/4" d	35.00	18.00	35.00	18.00	18.00	30.00	16.50	18.00
Creamer, ftd	25.00	25.00	25.00	24.00	24.00	50.00	30.00	24.00
Jelly, 4-1/2" h, stemmed	20.00	10.00	20.00	12.00	12.00	15.00	12.00	12.00
Jelly, 4-1/2" h, stemmed, flared lid	24.00	20.00	24.00	30.00	15.00	24.00	15.00	12.00
Pitcher, one pt, 5-1/4" h	95.00	115.00	125.00	115.00	115.00	125.00	195.00	115.00
Plate, 7-3/4" sq	20.00	7.50	20.00	10.00	10.00	15.00	8.00	10.00
Plate, 8-3/4"	20.00	24.00	30.00	30.00	20.00	24.00	20.00	20.00
Sugar, ftd	25.00	24.00	30.00	30.00	20.00	60.00	30.00	20.00
Syrup	-	-	-	-	-	-	-	165.00
Vase, 6" h, ftd	215.00	20.00	35.00	35.00	25.00	110.00	36.00	30.00

Cloverleaf

Manufactured by Hazel Atlas Glass Company, Clarksburg, West Virginia, and Zanesville, Ohio, from 1930 to 1936. Made in black, crystal, green, pink, and yellow. Collector interest in crystal is minimal, prices would be about 50 percent of those listed for green.

Cloverleaf, green saucer, **$6**; pink plate, **$12**; pink cup, **$8**.

Item	Black	Green	Pink	Yellow
Ashtray, match holder in center, 4" d	65.00	-	-	-
Ashtray, match holder in center, 5-3/4" d	90.00	-	-	-
Bowl, 8" d	-	95.00	-	-
Candy dish, cov	-	65.00	-	130.00
Cereal bowl, 5" d	-	50.00	-	55.00
Creamer, 3-5/8" h, ftd	25.00	12.00	-	24.00
Cup	18.50	9.00	8.00	12.00
Dessert bowl, 4" d	-	30.00	30.00	35.00
Plate, 6" d, sherbet	40.00	6.50	-	10.00
Plate, 8" d, luncheon	16.00	9.00	12.00	18.00
Plate, 10-1/4" d, grill	-	25.00	-	40.00
Salad bowl, 7" d	-	60.00	-	65.00
Salt & pepper shakers, pr	100.00	40.00	-	14.00
Saucer	7.00	6.00	6.00	5.00
Sherbet, 3" h, ftd	22.00	15.00	10.00	12.00
Sugar, 3-5/8" h, ftd	25.00	12.00	-	24.00
Tumbler, 9 oz, 4" h, flat	-	65.00	26.50	35.00
Tumbler, 10 oz, 3-3/4" h, flat	-	50.00	30.00	-
Tumbler, 10 oz, 5-3/4" h, ftd	-	30.00	-	42.00

Colonial Fluted

Rope
   Manufactured by Federal Glass Company, Columbus, Ohio, from 1928 to 1933. Made in crystal and green.

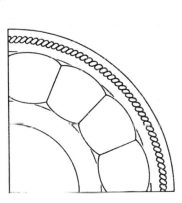

Colonial Fluted sugar, open, green, **$25**; creamer, green, **$14.**

Item	Crystal	Green
Berry bowl, 4" d	11.00	12.00
Berry bowl, 7-1/2" d	16.00	18.00
Cereal bowl, 6" d	15.00	18.00
Creamer, ftd	12.00	14.00
Cup	5.00	7.50
Plate, 6" d, sherbet	2.50	4.00
Plate, 8" d, luncheon	5.00	10.00
Salad bowl, 6-1/2" d, 2-1/2" deep	22.00	35.00
Saucer	2.50	4.00
Sherbet	6.00	8.50
Sugar, cov	21.00	25.00
Sugar, open	8.00	10.00

Della Robbia, #1058

Manufactured by Westmoreland Glass Company, Grapeville, Pennsylvania, from late 1920s to 1940s. Made in crystal with applied luster colors and milk glass.

Della Robbia plate, dinner, crystal, **$95.**

Della Robbia, compote 13" d, luster trim, **$145.**

Item	Crystal	Item	Crystal
Basket, 9"	210.00	Cake salver, 14" d, ftd	120.00
Basket, 12"	300.00	Candlesticks, pr, 4" h	65.00
Bowl, 8" d, bell, handle	48.00	Candlesticks, pr, 4" h, two-lite	160.00
Bowl, 8" d, heart shape, handle	95.00	Candy jar, cov, scalloped edge	85.00
Bowl, 12" d, ftd	12.00	Champagne, 6 oz.	25.00
Bowl, 13" d, rolled edge	115.00	Chocolate candy, round, flat	75.00
Bowl, 14" d, oval, flange	155.00	Cocktail, 3-1/4 oz.	15.00
Bowl, 15" d, bell	175.00	Comport, 12" d, ftd, bell	115.00

Item	Crystal
Comport, 13" d, flanged	125.00
Creamer, ftd	18.00
Cup, coffee	18.50
Finger bowl, 5" d	30.00
Ginger ale tumbler, 5 oz	25.00
Goblet, 8 oz., 6" h	28.00
Iced tea tumbler 11 oz., ftd	35.00
Iced tea tumbler 12 oz., 5-3/16" h, straight	40.00
Iced tea tumbler 12 oz., bell	32.00
Iced tea tumbler, 12 oz., bell, ftd	32.00
Mint comport, 6-1/2" d, 3-5/8" h, ftd	45.00
Nappy, 7-1/2" d	42.00
Nappy, 8" d, bell	45.00
Nappy, 4-1/2" d	30.00
Nappy, 6" d, bell	35.00
Nappy, 6-1/2" d, one handle	32.00
Nappy, 9" d	60.00
Pitcher, 32 oz.	200.00
Plate, 6" d, finger bowl liner	12.00

Item	Crystal
Plate, 6-1/8" d, bread and butter	14.00
Plate, 7-1/4" d, salad	22.00
Plate, 9" d, luncheon	35.00
Plate, 10-1/2" d, dinner	95.00
Plate, 18" d	195.00
Platter, 14" l, oval	195.00
Punch bowl, 14" d	225.00
Punch bowl liner, 18" d plate, upturned edge	200.00
Punch cup	15.00
Salt and pepper shakers, pr	55.00
Saucer	10.00
Sherbet, 5 oz, low foot	22.00
Sherbet, 5 oz, 4-3/4" h, ftd	24.00
Sugar, ftd	27.50
Sweetmeat comport, 8" d	115.00
Torte plate, 14" d	125.00
Tumbler, 8 oz., ftd	30.00
Wine, 3 oz	25.00

Doric and Pansy

Manufactured by Jeannette Glass Company, Jeannette, PA, from 1937 to 1938. Made in ultramarine with limited production in pink and crystal.

Doric and Pansy, child's sugar, open, ultramarine, **$50;** child's creamer, ultramarine, **$50.**

Item	Crystal	Pink	Ultramarine
Berry bowl, 4-1/2" d	12.00	12.00	24.00
Berry bowl, 8" d	-	24.00	75.00
Bowl, 9" d, handle	15.00	20.00	35.00
Butter dish, cov	-	-	600.00
Candy, cov, three-part	-	-	22.50
Cup	12.00	14.00	20.00
Creamer	72.00	90.00	145.00
Plate, 6" d, sherbet	8.00	12.00	14.50
Plate, 7" d, salad	-	-	40.00
Plate, 9" d, dinner	7.50	8.00	30.00
Salt shaker, orig top	-	-	325.00
Saucer	4.50	4.50	5.50
Sugar, open	80.00	85.00	145.00
Tray, 10" l, handles	45.00	-	25.00
Tumbler, 9 oz, 4-1/2" h	-	-	500.00

Children's

Item	Pink	Ultramarine
Creamer	35.00	50.00
Cup	35.00	48.00
Plate	12.00	12.50
Saucer	7.00	8.50
Sugar	35.00	50.00
14-pc set, orig box	400.00	425.00

Floragold

Louisa

Manufactured by Jeannette Glass Company, Jeannette, Pennsylvania, 1950s. Made in iridescent. Some large comports were later made in ice blue, crystal, red-yellow, and shell pink.

Flora gold, dinner plate, iridescent, **$40**; bowl, 5-1/4" ruffled, iridescent, **$16**.

Item	Iridescent
Ashtray, 4" d	10.00
Bowl, 4-1/2" sq	6.50
Bowl, 5-1/4" d, ruffled	16.00
Bowl, 8-1/2" d, sq	22.00
Bowl, 8-1/2" d, ruffled	14.00
Butter dish, cov, 1/4-pound, oblong	30.00
Butter dish, cov, round, 5-1/2" w sq base	800.00
Butter dish, cov, round, 6-1/4" w sq base	55.00
Candlesticks, pr, double branch	60.00
Candy dish, one handle	16.50
Candy or cheese dish, cov, 6-3/4" d	130.00
Candy, 5-3/4" l, four feet	12.00
Celery vase	420.00
Cereal bowl, 5-1/2" d, round	40.00
Coaster, 4" d	10.00
Comport, 5-1/4", plain top	795.00
Comport, 5-1/4", ruffled top	895.00
Creamer	21.00
Cup	8.00
Fruit bowl, 5-1/2" d, ruffled	8.50

Item	Iridescent
Fruit bowl, 12" d, ruffled, large	15.00
Nappy, 5" d, one handle	12.00
Pitcher, 64 oz	45.00
Plate, 5-1/4" d, sherbet	15.00
Plate, 8-1/2" d, dinner	40.00
Platter, 11-1/4" d	30.00
Salad bowl, 9-1/2" d, deep	42.50
Salt & pepper shakers, pr, plastic tops	60.00
Saucer, 5-1/4" d	12.00
Sherbet, low, ftd	16.00
Sugar	22.00
Sugar lid	15.00
Tidbit, wooden post	35.00
Tray, 13-1/2" d	75.00
Tray, 13-1/2" d, with indent	65.00
Tumbler, 11 oz, ftd	20.00
Tumbler, 10 oz, ftd	20.00
Tumbler, 15 oz, ftd	110.00
Vase	420.00

Florentine No. 2

Poppy No. 2

Manufactured by Hazel Atlas Glass Company, Clarksburg, West Virginia, and Zanesville, Ohio, from 1932 to 1935. Made in amber, cobalt blue, crystal, green, ice blue, pink, and yellow. Ice blue production is limited to 7-1/2" h pitcher, valued at $525. Amber production is limited to 9- and 12-oz tumblers, both currently valued at $80; cup and saucer, valued at $75, and sherbet, valued at $45. Cobalt blue production is limited to 3-1/2" comport, valued at $60 and 9-oz tumbler, valued at $80.

Reproductions: † 7-1/2" h cone-shaped pitcher and 4" h

Florentine No. 2, cup, yellow, **$85**.

footed tumbler. Reproductions found in amber, cobalt blue, crystal, deep green, and pink.

Item	Crystal	Green	Pink	Yellow
Ashtray, 3-1/2" d	18.50	18.50	-	25.00
Ashtray, 5-1/2" d	20.00	25.00	-	35.00
Berry bowl, 4-1/2" d	14.50	16.50	17.50	22.50
Berry bowl, 8" d	24.00	26.00	30.00	35.00

Item	Crystal	Green	Pink	Yellow
Bowl, 5-1/2" d	32.00	35.00	-	42.00
Bowl, 7-1/2" d, shallow	-	-	-	85.00
Bowl, 9" d, flat	27.50	27.50	-	-
Butter dish, cov	115.00	125.00	-	165.00
Candlesticks, pr, 2-3/4" h	45.00	48.00	-	70.00
Candy dish, cov	110.00	100.00	150.00	165.00
Cereal bowl, 6" d	28.00	28.00	-	40.00
Coaster, 3-1/4" d	-	-	-	25.00
Coaster, 3-3/4" d	18.50	18.50	-	25.00
Coaster, 5-1/2" d	20.00	25.00	-	35.00
Cocktail, 3-1/4" h, ftd	-	-	-	14.50
Comport, 3-1/2" d, ruffled	25.00	25.00	25.00	-
Condiment tray, round	-	-	-	65.00
Cream soup, 4-3/4" d, two handles	16.50	16.00	18.50	20.00
Creamer	8.00	12.00	-	14.50
Cup	7.50	8.00	-	12.00
Custard cup	60.00	60.00	-	85.00
Gravy boat	-	-	-	65.00
Gravy boat underplate, 11-1/2" l	-	-	-	115.00
Iced tea tumbler, 12 oz, 5" h	35.00	35.00	-	45.00
Juice tumbler, 5 oz, 3-1/8" h, flat	14.50	14.50	14.50	22.00
Juice tumbler, 5 oz, 3-1/8" h, ftd	13.00	15.00	-	21.00
Parfait, 6" h	30.00	32.00	-	65.00
Pitcher, 24 oz, cone, ftd, 6-1/4" h	-	-	-	35.00
Pitcher, 28 oz, cone ftd, 7-1/2" h †	60.00	40.00	-	50.00
Pitcher, 48 oz, 7-1/2" h	60.00	70.00	120.00	32.00
Pitcher, 76 oz, 8-1/4" h	90.00	95.00	225.00	400.00
Plate, 6" d, sherbet	6.00	6.00	-	7.50
Plate, 6-1/2" d, indent	16.00	17.50	-	30.00
Plate, 8-1/2" d, salad	8.50	9.50	9.00	10.00
Plate, 10" d, dinner	16.50	16.00	-	19.00
Plate, 10-1/4" d, grill	15.00	15.00	-	14.50
Plate, 10-1/4" d, grill, cream soup ring	35.00	35.00	-	-
Platter, 11" oval	15.00	16.00	18.50	24.00
Relish, 10" d, divided, three-part	22.50	24.00	26.00	32.00
Relish, 10" d, plain	22.50	24.00	26.00	32.00
Salt & pepper shakers, pr	48.00	48.00	-	65.00
Saucer	5.00	4.00	-	3.50
Sherbet, ftd	10.00	12.50	-	14.50
Sugar, cov	8.50	9.00	-	38.00
Tumbler, 5 oz, 3-1/4" h, ftd	18.00	15.00	15.00	-
Tumbler, 5 oz, 4" h, ftd †	15.00	15.00	18.00	20.00
Tumbler, 5 oz, 3-5/16" h, blown	18.50	18.50	-	-
Tumbler, 6 oz, 3-9/16" h, blown	16.00	18.50	-	-
Tumbler, 9 oz, 4" h	14.50	18.50	16.00	22.50
Tumbler, 9 oz, 4-1/2" h, ftd	25.00	25.00	-	38.00
Tumbler, 10 oz, 4-11/16, blown	19.00	19.00	-	-
Tumbler, 12 oz, 5" h, blown	20.00	20.00	-	20.00
Vase, 6" h	30.00	32.00	-	65.00
Vegetable bowl, cov, 9" l, oval	55.00	60.00	-	85.00

Holiday

Button and Bows

Manufactured by Jeannette Glass
Company, Jeannette,
Pennsylvania, from 1947 to the
1950s. Made in crystal, iridescent,
pink, and shell pink.

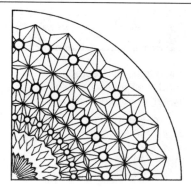

Holiday, water pitcher, pink, **$45.**

Item	Crystal	Iridescent	Pink
Berry bowl, 5-1/8" d	-	-	16.00
Berry bowl, 8-1/2" d	-	-	55.00
Butter dish, cov	-	-	60.00
Cake plate, 10-1/2" d, three legs	-	-	220.00
Candlesticks, pr, 3" h	-	-	125.00
Chop plate, 13-3/4" d	-	-	140.00
Console bowl, 10-1/4" d	-	-	225.00
Creamer, ftd	-	-	20.00
Cup, plain	-	-	15.00
Cup, rayed bottom, 2" d base	-	-	12.00
Cup, rayed bottom, 2-3/8" d base	-	-	16.00
Juice tumbler, 5 oz, 4" h, ftd	-	-	60.00
Pitcher, 16 oz, 4-3/4" h	17.50	35.00	85.00
Pitcher, 52 oz, 6-3/4" h	-	-	45.00
Plate, 6" d, sherbet	-	-	8.50
Plate, 9" d, dinner	-	-	25.00
Platter, 11-3/8" l, oval	-	17.50	30.00
Sandwich tray, 10-1/2" l	-	20.00	28.00
Saucer, plain center	-	-	5.00
Saucer, rayed center, 2-1/8" d ring	-	-	7.50
Saucer, rayed center, 2-1/2" d ring	-	-	7.50
Sherbet	-	-	12.00
Soup bowl, 7-3/4" d	-	-	82.00
Sugar, cov	-	-	30.00
Sugar lid	-	-	20.00
Tumbler, 5 oz, 4" h, ftd	-	15.00	35.00
Tumbler, 5-1/4 oz, 4-1/4" h, ftd	8.00	-	45.00
Tumbler, 6" h, ftd	-	-	195.00
Tumbler, 9 oz, 4" h, ftd	-	-	55.00
Tumbler, 10 oz, 4" h, flat	-	-	28.00
Vegetable bowl, 9-1/2" l, oval	-	-	36.00

Mt. Pleasant
Double Shield
Manufactured by L. E. Smith, Mt. Pleasant, Pennsylvania, from the 1920s to 1934. Made in: amethyst, black, cobalt blue, crystal, green, pink, and white.

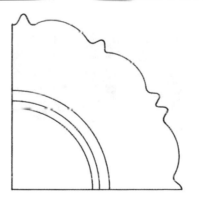

Mt. Pleasant, left: creamer, black, **$20;** back: sugar, black, **$20;** right: bowl, 8" d, black, **$35;** front: cup, black, **$15.**

Item	Amethyst	Black	Cobalt Blue	Green	Pink
Bonbon, 7" d, rolled edge	24.00	24.50	24.00	16.00	16.00
Bowl, 6" d, three legs	-	25.00	-	-	-
Bowl, 6" w, sq, two handles	27.50	18.00	24.00	15.00	15.00
Bowl, 7" d, three ftd, rolled out edge	18.50	24.50	18.50	17.50	17.50
Bowl, 8" d, scalloped, two handles	37.50	35.00	37.50	20.00	20.00
Bowl, 9" d, scalloped, ftd	28.00	32.00	30.00	-	-
Bowl, 10" d, two handles	30.00	34.00	32.00	-	-
Cake plate, 10-1/2" d, ftd	45.00	47.00	40.00	-	-
Cake plate, 10-1/2" d, two handles	26.00	40.00	28.00	17.50	17.50
Candlesticks, pr, single lite	28.00	42.50	30.00	24.00	28.00
Candlesticks, pr, two lite	48.00	55.00	50.00	30.00	32.00
Creamer	21.00	20.00	22.50	20.00	24.00

Item	Amethyst	Black	Cobalt Blue	Green	Pink
Cup	15.00	15.00	14.00	12.50	12.50
Fruit bowl, 4-7/8" sq	16.00	20.00	18.00	12.00	12.50
Fruit bowl, 9-1/4" sq	30.00	50.00	35.00	20.00	20.00
Fruit bowl, 10" d, scalloped	40.00	40.00	40.00	-	-
Leaf, 8" l	12.50	17.50	16.00	-	-
Leaf, 11-1/4" l	25.00	30.00	28.00	-	-
Mayonnaise, 5-1/2" h, three ftd	25.00	28.00	25.00	17.50	17.50
Mint, 6" d, center handle	25.00	26.50	25.00	16.00	16.00
Plate, 7" h, two handles, scalloped	15.00	16.00	16.50	12.50	12.50
Plate, 8" d, scalloped	16.00	15.00	16.00	12.50	12.50
Plate, 8" d, scalloped, three ftd	17.50	27.00	17.50	12.50	12.50
Plate, 8" w, sq	17.50	25.00	17.50	12.50	12.50
Plate, 8-1/4" w, indent for cup	17.50	19.00	17.50	-	-
Plate, 9" d, grill	20.00	20.00	20.00	-	-
Plate, 12" d, two handles	35.00	35.00	35.00	20.00	20.00
Rose Bowl, 4" d	25.00	30.00	27.50	20.00	20.00
Salt and pepper shakers, pr	50.00	50.00	45.00	25.00	25.00
Sandwich server, center handle	40.00	37.50	40.00	-	-
Saucer	5.00	5.00	5.00	3.50	3.50
Sherbet	15.00	16.50	16.50	12.50	12.50
Sugar	9.00	20.00	15.00	20.00	20.00
Tumbler, ftd	25.00	27.50	27.50	-	-
Vase, 7-1/4" h	30.00	35.00	40.00	-	35.00

Normandie

Bouquet and Lattice

Manufactured by Federal Glass Company, Columbus, Ohio, from 1933 to 1940. Made in amber, crystal, iridescent, and pink.

Normandie, plate, dinner, iridescent, $10.

Item	Amber	Crystal	Iridescent	Pink
Berry bowl, 5" d	9.50	6.00	6.50	12.00
Berry bowl, 8-1/2" d	35.00	24.00	30.00	80.00
Cereal bowl, 6-1/2" d	30.00	20.00	10.00	35.00
Creamer, ftd	20.00	10.00	8.00	18.00
Cup	8.00	4.00	6.00	9.50
Iced tea tumbler, 12 oz, 5" h	40.00	-	-	-
Juice tumbler, 5 oz, 4" h	38.00	-	-	-
Pitcher, 80 oz, 8" h	115.00	-	-	245.00
Plate, 6" d, sherbet	4.50	2.00	3.50	5.00
Plate, 7-3/4" d, salad	10.00	5.00	55.00	14.00
Plate, 9-1/4" d, luncheon	12.50	6.00	16.50	100.00
Plate, 11" d, dinner	32.00	15.00	10.00	18.00
Plate, 11" d, grill	15.00	8.00	10.00	25.00
Platter, 11-3/4" l	24.00	10.00	12.00	80.00
Salt and pepper shakers, pr	50.00	20.00	-	4.00
Saucer	4.00	1.50	3.50	10.00
Sherbet	7.50	6.50	9.00	9.00
Sugar	8.00	6.00	7.00	12.00
Tumbler, 9 oz, 4-1/4" h	25.00	10.00	-	50.00
Vegetable bowl, 10" l, oval	27.50	12.00	25.00	45.00

Old Colony
Lace Edge, Open Lace
Manufactured by Hocking Glass Company, Lancaster, Ohio, from 1935 to 1938. Made in crystal and pink. Crystal Old Colony pieces are valued at about 50 percent of pink, as are frosted or satin finish prices. Many other companies made a look-alike to Old Colony, so care must be exercised.

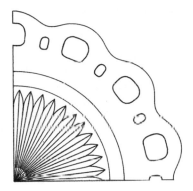

Old Colony, candlestick, pink frosted finish, hand applied floral decoration, **$125.**

Item	Pink	Item	Pink
Bonbon, cov	65.00	Plate, 10-1/2" d, dinner	36.00
Bowl, 9-1/2" d, plain	40.00	Plate, 10-1/2" d, grill	28.00
Bowl, 9-1/2" d, ribbed	35.00	Plate, 13" d, four-part, solid lace	65.00
Butter dish, cov	70.00	Plate, 13" d, solid lace	65.00
Candlesticks, pr	350.00	Platter, 12-3/4" l	42.00
Candy jar, cov, ribbed	65.00	Platter, 12-3/4" l, five-part	40.00
Cereal bowl, 6-3/8" d	24.00	Relish dish, 7-1/2" d, three-part, deep	60.00
Comport, 7" d, cov	60.00	Relish plate, 10-1/2" d, three-part	25.00
Comport, 9" d	950.00	Salad bowl, 7-3/4" d, ribbed	60.00
Console bowl, 10-1/2" d, three legs	250.00	Saucer	15.00
Cookie jar, cov	75.00	Sherbet, ftd	112.00
Creamer	25.00	Sugar	25.00
Cup	24.00	Tumbler, 5 oz, 3-1/2" h, flat	120.00
Flower bowl, crystal frog	30.00	Tumbler, 9 oz, 4-1/2" h, flat	22.00
Plate, 7-1/4" d, salad	27.50	Tumbler, 10-1/2 oz, 5" h, ftd	95.00
Plate, 8-1/4" d, luncheon	32.00	Vase, 7" h	650.00

Parrot
Sylvan
Manufactured by Federal Glass Company, Columbus, Ohio, from 1931 to 1932. Made in amber and green with limited production in blue and crystal.

Parrot, berry bowl, green, 8" d, **$75**; plate, salad, green, 7-1/2" d, **$40**.

Item	Amber	Green	Item	Amber	Green
Berry bowl, 5" d	22.50	30.00	Hot plate, 5" d, pointed	875.00	900.00
Berry bowl, 8" d	75.00	80.00	Hot plate, round	-	950.00
Butter dish, cov	1,250.00	475.00	Jam dish, 7" d	35.00	-
Creamer, ftd	65.00	55.00	Plate, 5-3/4" d, sherbet	24.00	35.00
Cup	35.00	35.00	Plate, 7-1/2" d, salad	-	40.00

Item	Amber	Green	Item	Amber	Green
Plate, 9" d, dinner	50.00	50.00	Soup bowl, 7" d	35.00	45.00
Plate, 10-1/2" d, grill, round	35.00	-	Sugar, cov	450.00	175.00
Plate, 10-1/2" d, grill, square	-	30.00	Tumbler, 10 oz, 4-1/4" h	100.00	130.00
Platter, 11-1/4" l, oblong	65.00	70.00	Tumbler, 12 oz, 5-1/2" h	115.00	160.00
Salt and pepper shakers, pr	-	270.00	Tumbler, 5-3/4" h, ftd, heavy	100.00	120.00
Saucer	18.00	18.00	Vegetable bowl, 10" l, oval	75.00	65.00
Sherbet, ftd, cone	30.00	27.50			

S-Pattern

Stippled Rose Band

Manufactured by MacBeth-Evans Glass Company, Charleroi, Pennsylvania, from 1930 to 1933. Made in amber, crystal, crystal with amber, blue, green, pink, or silver trims, fired-on red, green, light yellow, and Monax.

Item	Amber with trim	Crystal colors	Crystal	Fired-On	Yellow
Berry bowl, 8-1/2" d	8.50	12.00	-	-	8.50
Cake plate, 11-3/4" d	50.00	48.00	55.00	-	50.00
Cake plate, 13" d	80.00	65.00	75.00	-	75.00
Cereal bowl, 5-1/2" d	6.00	4.00	6.00	12.00	6.00
Creamer, thick	7.50	6.50	8.00	15.00	7.50
Creamer, thin	7.50	6.50	8.00	15.00	7.50
Cup, thick	5.00	4.00	5.50	10.00	5.00
Cup, thin	5.00	4.00	5.50	10.00	5.00
Pitcher, 80 oz	-	75.00	-	-	-
Plate, 6" d, sherbet	3.50	3.00	4.00	-	3.50
Plate, 8-1/4" d, luncheon	7.00	7.00	9.50	-	5.00
Plate, 9-1/4" d, dinner	9.50	-	12.50	-	9.50
Plate, grill	8.50	6.50	9.00	-	8.50
Saucer	4.00	3.00	4.00	-	4.00
Sherbet, low, ftd	8.00	5.50	8.50	-	8.00
Sugar, thick	7.50	6.50	8.00	15.00	7.50
Sugar, thin	7.50	6.50	8.00	15.00	7.50
Tumbler, 5 oz, 3-1/2" h	6.50	5.00	6.50	-	6.50
Tumbler, 10 oz, 4-3/4" h	8.50	9.00	7.50	-	8.50
Tumbler, 12 oz, 5" h	15.00	10.00	17.50	-	15.00

Strawberry

Manufactured by U. S. Glass Company, Pittsburgh, Pennsylvania, early 1930s. Made in crystal, green, pink, and some iridescent.

Strawberry, plate, salad, pink, **$15.**

Item	Crystal	Green	Iridescent	Pink
Berry bowl, 4" d	7.50	12.00	7.50	12.00
Berry bowl, 7-1/2" d	16.00	20.00	16.00	20.00
Bowl, 6-1/4" d, 2" deep	40.00	60.00	40.00	60.00
Butter dish, cov	125.00	185.00	135.00	195.00

Item	Crystal	Green	Iridescent	Pink
Comport, 5-3/4" d	55.00	60.00	55.00	60.00
Creamer, large, 4-5/8" h	24.00	35.00	24.00	35.00
Creamer, small	12.00	18.50	12.00	18.50
Olive dish, 5" l, one handle	8.50	14.00	8.50	14.00
Pickle dish, 8-1/4" l, oval	8.00	14.00	8.00	14.00
Pitcher, 7-3/4" h	150.00	185.00	150.00	195.00
Plate, 6" d, sherbet	5.00	13.50	5.00	8.00
Plate, 7-1/2" d, salad	10.00	14.00	10.00	15.00
Salad bowl, 6-1/2" d	15.00	20.00	15.00	20.00
Sherbet	6.00	13.50	6.00	13.50
Sugar, large, cov	60.00	85.00	60.00	85.00
Sugar, small, open	12.00	32.00	12.00	32.00
Tumbler, 8 oz, 3-5/8" h	20.00	32.00	20.00	38.00

Thumbprint

Manufactured by Federal Glass Company, Columbus, Ohio, from 1927 to 1930. Made in green.

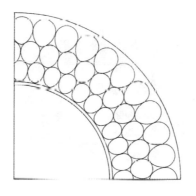

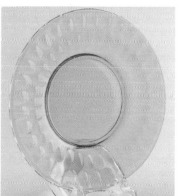

Thumprint, luncheon plate, 8" d, green, **$7**.

Item	Green	Item	Green
Berry bowl, 4-3/4" d	10.00	Plate, 9-1/4" d, dinner	24.00
Berry bowl, 8" d	25.00	Salt and pepper shakers, pr	65.00
Cereal bowl, 5" d	10.00	Saucer	4.00
Creamer, ftd	12.00	Sherbet	9.00
Cup	8.00	Sugar, ftd	12.00
Fruit bowl, 5" d	10.00	Tumbler, 5" h	8.00
Juice tumbler, 4" h	6.00	Tumbler, 5-1/2" h	10.00
Plate, 6" d, sherbet	4.50	Whiskey, 2-1/4" h	6.50
Plate, 8" d, luncheon	7.00		

Yorktown

Manufactured by Federal Glass Company, in the mid 1950s. Made in crystal, iridescent, smoke, white, and yellow. Values for all the colors are about the same.

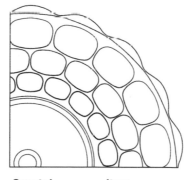

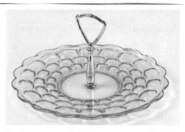

Yorktown, sandwich server, crystal, gold colored metal handle, **$15**.

Item	Crystal	Item	Crystal
Berry bowl, 5-1/2" d	4.50	Celery tray, 10" l	10.00
Berry bowl, 9-1/2" d	10.00	Creamer	5.00

Items	Crystal	Items	Crystal
Cup	3.50	Punch cup	2.50
Fruit bowl, 10" d, ftd	18.00	Saucer	1.00
Iced tea tumbler, 5-1/4" h, 13 oz	7.50	Sherbet, 7 oz	3.50
Juice tumbler, 3-7/8" h, 6 oz	4.50	Snack cup	2.50
Mug	15.00	Snack plate with indent	3.50
Plate, 8-1/4" d	4.50	Sugar	5.00
Plates, 11-1/2" d	8.50	Tumbler, 4-3/4" h, 10 oz	6.00
Punch bowl set	40.00	Vase, 8" h	15.00

DISNEYANA

History: Walt Disney and the creations of the famous Disney Studios hold a place of fondness and enchantment in the hearts of people throughout the world. The 1928 release of "Steamboat Willie," featuring Mickey Mouse, heralded an entertainment empire.

Walt and his brother, Roy, were shrewd businessmen. From the beginning, they licensed the reproduction of Disney characters on products ranging from wristwatches to clothing.

In 1984, Donald Duck celebrated his 50th birthday, and collectors took a renewed interest in material related to him.

Additional Listings: See _Warman's Americana & Collectibles_ for more examples.

Adviser: Theodore L. Hake.

Book, _Mickey Never Fails,_ School Days in Disneyville, **$75**.

Bambi

Charm bracelet, 6" l gold luster metal link bracelet, five figural gold luster charms of red/brown Bambi and Faline, blue Thumper, black and white Flower, yellow/green Friend Owl, 1950s......... **20.00**

Figure, 4" x 6" x 7-1/2" h, painted and glazed ceramic,

by American Pottery Co., Bambi with head tilted upward, 1940s............. **65.00**

Studio fan card, 7" x 9", stiff buff paper, brown design, Walt Disney facsimile signature, small copyright, 1940s........................... **35.00**

Serigraph, Cinderella and Prince Charming, color laser background of castle, acetate sheet with 8" x 8" image, blue 16" x 20" mat, attached certificate of authenticity noting series of 9500, Disney Co. seal on one corner of serigraph, bottom margin also signed in black by Marc Davis, **$150**.

Photo courtesy of Hake's Americana & Collectibles.

Cinderella

Costume, 8-1/4" x 11" x 2-3/4" orig box, two pcs, Ben Copper, copyright Walt Disney Productions, late 1960s, box illus include Spider-Man, Hulk, Thor, and Wonder Woman, wear to box, costume bright **30.00**

Puzzle, 9" x 12", frame tray, Jaymar, c1960 .... **8.00**

Soaky, 10-1/2" h, soft plastic body, hard plastic head, blue dress, movable arms **20.00**

Disneyland

Book, _A Visit to Disneyland,_ Whitman Big Tell-A-Tale, copyright 1965, 6" x 8-1/2", 28 pgs, color photos **20.00**

Coloring book, 8" x 11", Whitman #1050, copyright 1965, covers of Mickey and Minnie beckoning viewer toward castle in Disneyland,

Matterhorn in background, some pages neatly colored **8.00**

Game, Disneyland Riverboat Game, 8" x 16" x 1-3/4" deep box, Parker Bros, copyright 1960, 14-3/4" sq board, 6-3/4" full-color cardboard movable tack, four different colored metal boat playing pcs. **50.00**

Poster, 19" x 26-1/2", Disneyland Haunted Mansion, full color, glossy, copyright 1982, mansion at twilight, inset photo of mother and child being scared by ghost, tightly rolled **25.00**

Disneyland ferris wheel, tin litho, J. Chein & Co., **$550**.

Photo courtesy of Dotta Auction Co., Inc.

Disney Studios, Christmas card, 7-1/4" x 9-1/4", copyright 1936, orig mailing envelope, Los Angeles Dec. 22, 1936 postmark, front illus of Mickey, Minnie, Donald, and Pluto in snowstorm, small copyright text on back............................. **300.00**

Disney World

Convention badge, 4" d, black printing, gold background, "110 Club '79/Disney World" **10.00**

Flicker, I Like Walt Disney World, red metal case, text on reverse including "Vari-Vue" and Walt Disney World logo, black, white, and red image of Mickey wearing blue bow tie, changes to slogan in white on red background **15.00**

Donald Duck ink blotter, Sunoco Oil, Nu-Blue Sunoco, unused, 1940s, 4" x 7", **$60**.

Photo courtesy of Dotta Auction Co., Inc.

Donald Duck with drum, toy, litho tin windup, Linemar, **$250**.

Photo courtesy of Dotta Auction Co., Inc.

Donald Duck

Bank, 3" x 4" x 7-1/2" h, hard vinyl, standing against red wall, Play Pal Plastics ... **15.00**

Costume, 8-1/4" x 11" x 3-1/2" orig box, thin molded plastic mask, one pc costume, Ben Cooper, copyright 1974 **15.00**

Egg cup, 2-1/4" x 4" x 3-1/2" h, color image of Donald pushing wheelbarrow, brown/iridescent tan, unmarked, 1950s **145.00**

Figure, 4-1/2" x 5" x 9", jointed, soft plastic, few flakes to paint **30.00**

Glass, 4-5/8" h, Donald Duck Beverages, blue, white, and yellow wrap-around design, Donald and three nephews, each holding glass with their name on it and word "More!" repeated three times, 1950s **65.00**

Christmas card, 1943, white card stock, illustration of newborn duck holding card that reads "1944," interior with monthly calendar for 1944 surrounded by choice color illustrations of Disney characters depicting events and holidays, including Mickey, Minnie, Pluto, Goofy, the Three Pigs, Donald and his nephews, Joe Carioca and Panchito, small text "A Hallmark Card" on back, 7-3/4" x 10", 3" l vertical crease line, **$95**.

Photo courtesy of Hake's Americana & Collectibles.

Napkin, 6 1/2" sq, textured white paper, pair of scalloped edges, front with large color image of Donald holding glass in one hand and milk bottle in other, 1950s **15.00**

Night light, 3-1/4" x 5-1/2", pink, purple, and white display card, 2-1/2" hard plastic figural night light, General Electric, blue, white, and yellow Donald head, red plug-in base, purple text for Mickey Mouse Club membership **25.00**

Orig art

Model sheet, 9 3/4" x 11", tan paper cov by lead pencil art and text by Frank Follmer, sgd at bottom margin, 12 different images of Donald, accompanied by document regarding Follmer **200.00**

Pencil drawing, from Lonesome Ghosts, 10" x 12" sheet of animation paper, 3" x 3-1/2" image in lead pencil, red pencil outline under Donald, 1937, #153 from numbered sequence, full figure Donald walking, angry expression **250.00**

Pencil sharpener, 2" x 3" x 4-1/2" h hard plastic, Donald on top of red base with double pencil sharpener unit, c1960 .... **38.00**

Child's book, *Donald's Penguin*, hardcover, Garden City Publishing Co. Inc., copyright 1940, based on 1939 short of same name, 24 pages, art on every page, either black and white illustrations or choice full-color film scenes, end papers have same design in black with green featuring illustrations of Donald and penguin, color cover features different penguin illus on front and back, 8-1/2" x 9-1/2", some penciling to inside front cover, moderate scattered wear, surface paper rubs along all edges, front and back covers have small surface paper rubs and scratches, **$65**.

Photo courtesy of Hake's Americana & Collectibles.

Dumbo

Planter, 4-1/4" x 7-1/2" x 6-1/2" h painted light gray glazed china, Dumbo next to water barrel, high relief figure of Timothy holding feather, Leeds Co., 1949 .... **40.00**

Premium button, 1-1/4" d, black, white, red, and gray, "D-X" printed on platform, reverse Kay Kamen back paper includes small image of running Mickey, 1942 ... **24.00**

Toothbrush holder, 3-1/2" x 5-1/2" x 3-3/4", painted ceramic, matte finish, three openings for toothbrushes, incised 1942 copyright **150.00**

Elmer Elephant, book, *Elmer Elephant*, David McKay Co., copyright 1936, hardcover, 48 pgs with color illus, full color Donald Duck bookplate **95.00**

Fantasia

Plate, 9-1/2" d, Flower Ballet, Vernon Kilns, dark maroon, yellow, green, and blue, copyright 1940 .... **75.00**

Souvenir movie program, 9-1/2" x 12-1/2", softcover, from orig 1940 release, Western Printing Co., black and white photos of Walt Disney and other contributors, full color plates of scenes from film **50.00**

Match covers, each flattened, matches neatly removed, red, white, and blue, Pepsi logo plus insignia design on front of each, reverse includes same Pepsi text on each in red, insignia designs feature animal characters as well as Disney characters including Dumbo, Donald Duck, Baby Pegasus, Thumper, Little Hiawatha, Centaurette, etc., #1, 2, 7-29, 32-37, 39, 40, 42 from numbered set of 48, 1940s, 1-1/2" x 4-1/4", scattered general light wear, **$165**.

Photo courtesy of Hake's Americana & Collectibles.

Flip the Frog

Ashtray, 2-1/2" x 5" x 3-1/4" h, china, marked "Made in Japan," early 1930s, image of Flip seated on edge of basket, surrounded by grapes and leaves, holding bass fiddle, small piece of fiddle missing **175.00**

Coloring book, 10-1/2" x 15", 28 pgs, Saalfield, copyright 1932, black and white illus, full color sample pictures, one page colored, slight wear to covers, 6" split at spine. **90.00**

Goofy

Blotter, 4" x 7", Sunoco Oil, Goofy and angry polar bear, broken-down car, copyright 1939, unused **40.00**

Booklet, 4" x 9", eight pgs, Copyright Protection For Disney Works **12.00**

Cel, 10-1/2" x 12-1/2" acetate sheet, 4" x 5-1/2" cel image of Sport Goofy, color laser background of stadium, #A-76 from numbered sequence, from 1980s Disney TV show **150.00**

Glass, 4-1/4" h, Goofy and Wilbur 1939 Walt Disney All Star Parade, green wrap-around design, black title, Goofy in boat with Wilbur the grasshopper and fish ... **60.00**

Mickey Mouse, doll, Knickerbocker, swivel head, felt ears, cloth body, composition shoes, replaced pants, 16" h, **$550**.

Photo courtesy of Dotta Auction Co., Inc.

Mickey Mouse

Ashtray, 3-1/2" x 4" x 3-1/4" h, china, marked "Made in Japan," 1930s, Mickey and Minnie seated on back edge **250.00**

Bank, 3-14" x 3-1/2" x 6", movable head, painted composition, Crown Toy Mfg Co., 1938, standing next to chest with coin slot on front, orig trap, key missing . **175.00**

Better Little Book, *Mickey Mouse and the Dude Ranch Bandit,* Whitman #1471, copyright 1943, 352 pgs **45.00**

Big Little Book, *Mickey Mouse Sails for Treasure Island,* Whitman, copyright 1935, premium imprint for Kolynos Dental Cream on back cover, very fine **85.00**

Book

Mickey Mouse Movie Stories Book 2, by David McKay, copyright 1934, hardcover, 200 pgs, black and white art, scattered wear and aging to cover, 2-1/2" splint in spine **145.00**

Mickey Mouse Presents Santa's Workshop, 7-1/4" x 10", Collins, England, late 1930s, hardover, 80 pgs, black and white and color illus, full color cover art

repeated on dust jacket **175.00**

Mickey Mouse Storybook, 6-1/4" x 8-1/2", softcover, by David McKay, 64 pgs, 1931, black and white illus from early cartoons, wear **65.00**

Child's umbrella, 23" l, 33" d, black metal frame, shaft with fabric covering, plaid design, mostly red, black, white, blue, green, and yellow accent stripes, 3-1/4" h 3-D pained composition figure of Mickey as handle, back of head "Mickey Mouse, copyright," 1930s **100.00**

Compact, 1-1/2" x 1-3/4" x 3/8" h, chromed metal, red, black, and yellow enamel paint design of Mickey standing next to Minnie on lid, from series by Cohn & Rosenberger, c1934 ..... **90.00**

Fan, folding, 5-1/2" l, opens to 8-1/2", white had plastic, center tree and birds with Mickey, metal loop, mkd "Made in Hong Kong," aging to tassel **30.00**

Figure, 8-1/2" h, 2-3/4" sq base, bisque, marked "Made in Japan," 1930s, two movable arms, name incised on front edge of base, string tail missing **850.00**

Magazine, *Mickey Mouse Magazine,* Vol. 1, #2, December 1933 issue, 16 pgs, red and green Christmas cover, green and white contents, imprint for Highland Dairy, near mint, 5-1/4" x 7-1/4" **250.00**

Napkin ring, 1" x 1-1/4" x 5-1/4" hollow celluloid figure attached to 2" d x 1" w celluloid napkin ring, 1930s, mkd "Made in England" **95.00**

Orig art panel, 6-1/4" x 6-3/4", Mickey Mouse and the Bat Bandit, by Floyd Gottfredson, single panel trimmed from 1934 daily strip, pen and ink, blue pencil accents, thin art board, penciled by Gottfredson, inked by Ted Thwaites, scene of Mickey and bandit on horseback running across cliff, exchanging gunfire, word balloon "Step On It, Steamboat! We Gotta Head 'im Off!" **650.00**

Pencil box, 5-5/8" x 5" x 1-1/4" h, painted composition, figural, with high relief details on each side, Dixon #2770, 1930s, excellent.......... **600.00**

Salt and pepper shakers, pr, 4-3/4" h, ceramic, red shirt, yellow pants, brown shoes, green base with name on front in black, red and gold foil sticker "Original Dan Brechner Exclusive," early 1960s............................. **35.00**

Sand pail, 5-3/4" h, 5-3/4" d at top, tin litho, attached carrying handle, Ohio Art, copyright 1938, golf theme, wrap-around illus with Mickey, Donald, Goofy, and black cat, play wear **300.00**

Toy, 9" h, diecut cardboard toy, 5" x 9-1/2" x 2-1/4" h orig box, Dolly Toy Co., 1930s, graphics on box with Mickey climbing rope to meet Minnie, castle background, figural toy, wire tail, attached 36" l string which Mickey climbs when tension is applied, very fine
.... **600.00**

Transfer, 6-1/4" x 8" orig envelope, five of eight 5-1/2" x 7-1/4" tissue paper "Indelible Transfer Decorations, McCall Kaumagraph, 1930s, different designs of Mickey and Minnie, orig instruction sheet
.... **40.00**

Wristwatch, Ingersoll, 1-1/4" d chromed metal case, dial with large black, white, and yellow Mickey, hands point to numerals, second wheel with three tiny Mickey images, vintage replacement strap, 1933, working order and clean dial **325.00**

Minnie Mouse

Bottle, 9" h, heavy glass, Rochester Healthful Beverages, 2" x 2-1/2" black and white silk screened label on front, 1930s............ **135.00**

Figure, 3-1/2" h, bisque, blue dress, yellow shoes, green hat, yellow/gold mandolin, mkd "Made in Japan, C 69," few paint flakes............. **55.00**

Salt and pepper shakers, 2" x 2" x 5-1/4" h, painted and glazed ceramic, 1950s, Dan Brechner Exclusive foil sticker, ink stamp copyright, WD-52, standing on top of wood crates which house noisemakers, names on front of base, orig stoppers .. **75.00**

Pinocchio

Book, *Pinocchio Linen-Like, #1061,* Whitman, copyright 1940, 7" x 7-3/4", 12 pgs, full color art on each page . **45.00**

Candy bar wrapper, 3-1/4" x 8-1/4", Schutter Candy Co., copyright 1940, black, white, yellow, and red image of Jiminy and premium "Official Conscience Medal" **60.00**

Game, 10" x 15" x 1-3/4" h, Pinocchio Race Game, Chad Valley, c1940, scene of Pinocchio and Jiminy Cricket encountering Foulfellow and Gideon leaving Geppetto's workshop on box lid, some fading to box, 14-1/2" sq board, game pcs........ **140.00**

Planter, 3" x 5-1/2" x 4-1/2", painted and glazed ceramic, Figaro dipping paw into aquarium planter, raised image of fish on front, c1940
.... **35.00**

Record, Little Toot, 7" sq, 45 rpm, Capitol label, copyright 1948........................... **18.00**

Silly Symphonies

Book, *Mickey Mouse Presents His Silly Symphonies Babies in the Woods, King Neptune,* 48 stiff paper pages, four full-color pop-ups, full-color art on front and back hardcovers, tape repairs **165.00**

Record, 78 rpm, 7" d, RCA Victor label, from 1934 set of three black and white picture disks, #226, Lullaby Land of Nowhere/Dance of the Bogey Man, art on each side, very fine.................... **300.00**

Snow White

Autographed photo, Adriana Caselotti, 8" x 10" glossy black and white publicity photo, voice of Snow White, vintage image of her next to film scene, boldly inscribed and sgd in blue.................... **45.00**

Birthday card, 4-1/4" x 5-1/2", White & Wyckoff, copyright 1938, black, white, red, blue, and green design, front with Doc and Sleepy in front of doorway, opens to Snow White dancing with Doc as others play instruments **30.00**

Book, *Masks of the Seven Dwarfs and Snow White,* Whitman, copyright 1938, 10-1/2" x 10-3/4", eight stiff paper sheets with punch-out masks, near mint, unpunched
.... **400.00**

Pencil drawing, Sneezy from Snow White, #157 of numbered sequence, 2-1/2" x 4-3/4" image in lead pencil, full figure image of him about to sneeze, on 10" x 12" sheet of animation paper, 1937, **$100**.

Photo courtesy of Hake's Americana & Collectibles.

Candy box, "Walt Disney's Seven Dwarfs," 3" x 6" x 1" cardboard box, seven orig rolls of candy drops by Curtis, c1938, each with different flavor and Dwarf wrapper, diecut image of Doc on box lid, illus to "Made Your Own Dwarf Cut-Outs" using wrappers **275.00**

Comic book, *Walt Disney Comics Digest, The Washed Up Witch,* #7, 1969....... **10.00**

Figure, 1-1/2" x 2-1/4" x 4-1/2", celluloid with plaster filling, marked "Foreign" on back, "Celluloid" on underside, c1938, some pulling at seams
.... **75.00**

Glass, 3-1/4" h, brown Dopey image, text "Dopey/Snow White & the Seven Dwarfs," back marked "Bosco Glass," 1938.............................. **45.00**

Orig art, pencil drawing of Happy, 10" x 12" sheet of animation paper, 2-3/4" x 4" centered image in lead pencil, 1937, #54 of numbered sequence.................... **100.00**

Song folio, *Snow White and the Seven Dwarfs,* 9" x 12", 52 pgs, Bourne Inc. Music Publishers, copyright 1938, 1950s printing.............. **25.00**

Three Pigs

Ashtray, 3-1/4" x 5" x 3-1/4" h, china, marked "Made in Japan" with copyright, 1930s, iridescent blue base, cream inside, black details, three pigs seated on back... **140.00**

Figure set, 3-1/2" Big Bad Wolf, three pigs and Red Riding Hood 3" to 3-1/8" h, bisque, color accents, some paint loss **350.00**
Postcard set, set of 12 numbered 3-1/2" x 5-1/5" cards, marked "Paris," French text, backs also marked "Disney," each with full-color art telling story, sent by soldier to daughter in US, each with typed or handwritten note, sent on consecutive days in April 1945 .... **150.00**
Tin, 6" d, 2" d tin litho, marked "By Arrangement with Walt Disney-Mickey Mouse Ltd.," scene of Wolf hiding behind tree, spying on pigs, wrap-around design on side in red and bright gold luster, English **175.00**
Walt Disney, postcard, 5" x 7", glossy stiff paper, full color portrait of Walt in center, surrounded by character images of Mickey, Donald, Ludwig, Pluto, Goofy, and Tinker Bell, blue background, unused, 1960s **20.00**
Zorro
Costume, 16" x 37", unused, attached to orig diecut cardboard hanger display, Lindsay, late 1950s, black diecut leatherette mask, black fabric cloak/sash, silver image of Zorro on rearing Toronado, 3-1/4" d Member Lindsay Ranch Club badge **50.00**
Figure, 3" x 4" x 7" h, painted and glazed ceramic, Enesco, orig foil sticker, copyright, "WDE.140," attached foil-covered cardboard string tag, replaced metal sword ... **125.00**
Game, 8" x 15-1/2" x 1-1/2" deep box, Whitman, copyright 1965, 15-1/2" sq board, complete set of picture letter cards, one generic plastic marker missing **75.00**
Pencil by Number Coloring Set, 9-1/4" x 12-1/4" x 1" deep color box, Transogram, late 1950s, 11 of 12 orig black and white pictures to color, wear to box............................. **40.00**

DOLLHOUSES

History: Dollhouses date from the 18th century to modern times. Early dollhouses often were handmade, sometimes with only one room. The most common type was made for a young girl to fill with replicas of furniture scaled especially to fit into a dollhouse. Specially sized dolls also were made for dollhouses. All types of accessories in all types of styles were available, and dollhouses could portray any historical period.

Colonial style three-story house, white clapboards, blue shutters, red roof and clear plastic windows, electrified, as-found with contents including wooden furniture, accessories, rugs, 1970s, 36" w, 18" d, 24" h, **$45.**

Photo courtesy of Alderfer Auction Co.

Interior of the Colonial three-story house pictured above.

Photo courtesy of Alderfer Auction Co.

American

21" w, 43" h, ivory-painted gable and center hallway, five large rooms and attic bedroom, attached garage, separate blue shutters and window boxes, most furnishings from same period as house, approx. 40 items, made by John Leonard Plock, NY architect, c1932.... **250.00**
21-1/4" l, 28-3/4" h, Victorian, last quarter 19th C, two-story house, modified Federal style, mansard roof with widow's walk, fenced-in front garden, simulated grass and fountains, polychrome details **400.00**

28-1/4"-w, 17-1/4" d, 32-1/2" h, gambrel roof, painted off-white, red paste board scalloped shingles, front opening half doors, six rooms, original paper wall and floor coverings, hinged door in rear roof, front steps, orig furniture, bisque dolls, accessories, and rugs, some paint and paper wear **920.00**

Unknown American Maker, hand crafted, Colonial style, white clapboards, copper gutters, wall papered interior walls, detailed trim, two floors, two-story side porch, hand-cut shingles, **$400.**

Photo courtesy of Dotta Auction Co., Inc.

Bliss, chromolithograph paper on wood
12-1/2" h, two-story, two single windows down, one double window up, remnants of windows and curtains, small porch and balcony on front, marked "R. Bliss" on front door, soiling to paper, cardboard front warped **525.00**
14" h, two-story, blue litho paper on roof, blue wood on back, red wood chimney and base, two open lower windows and two upper windows, house opens in front, litho wall and floor coverings inside, marked "R. Bliss" on door, some wear, one wall slightly warped........ **575.00**
16-1/2" h, two-story, front porch with turned columns, working front door, overhanging roof with lattice-work balcony, blue-gray roof with dormer windows, hinged front, int. with two rooms, printed carpeting and wallpaper, celluloid windows with later lace curtains, electric lights, two scratch-built chairs **1,725.00**

Unknown American maker, hand crafted, 1950s style, two floors, red hearts on white shutters, one-piece tin litho roof, white porch posts and railing, **$125**.

DOLLS

History: Dolls have been children's play toys for centuries. Dolls also have served other functions. From the 14th through 18th centuries, doll making was centered in Europe, mainly in Germany and France. The French dolls produced in this era were representations of adults and dressed in the latest couturier designs. They were not children's toys.

During the mid-19th century, child and baby dolls, made in wax, cloth, bisque, and porcelain, were introduced. Facial features were hand painted, wigs were made of mohair and human hair, and the dolls were dressed in the current fashions for babies or children.

Doll making in the United States began to flourish in the 1900s with companies such as Effanbee, Madame Alexander, and Ideal.

For more information, see Warman's Dolls: Antique to Modern.

Marks: Marks of the various manufacturers are found on the back of the head or neck or on the doll's back. These marks are very important in identifying a doll and its date of manufacture.

Additional Listings: See *Warman's Americana & Collectibles* for more examples.

Elastolin, Germany, 29" w, farmyard, house, barn, fencing, trees, and various figures **1,150.00**

German, 35" w, 11-1/4" d, 17" h, Nuremberg Kitchen, dark yellow walls with deep red trim, red and black checkerboard floor, cream stove hood, green furniture, tin stove, tin and copper pots, set of scales, wash boiler, baking pans, utensils, pottery, porcelain, and pewter tableware, late 19th C, some paint wear and imperfections **2,300.00**

McLoughlin, 12" x 17" x 16", folding house, two rooms, dec int., orig box **950.00**

Keystone, Fire Department, litho tin, white, green, and gold, **$050**.

Schoenhut, 20" x 26" x 30", mansion, two-story, eight rooms, attic, tan brick design, red roof, large dormer, 20 glass windows, orig decal, 1923 .... **1,750.00**

Tootsietoy, 21" w, 10-1/8" d, 16" h, house, furniture, and accessories, printed Masonite, half-timbered style, two rooms down, two up, removable roof, open back, orchid and pink bedroom sets, orchid bathroom, brown dining room set, flocked sofa and chairs, green and white kitchen pcs, piano, bench, lamps, telephone, cane-back sofa, rocker, some damage and wear to 3/4 scale furniture **525.00**

Alt, Beck & Gottschalk, 23" h, bisque shoulder head, blue paperweight eyes, multi-stroke brows, painted upper and lower lashes, closed mouth, molded blond hair, kid body with pin joints at hips and knees, bisque lower arms, antique white dressing gown, blue coat, new underclothing, marked "998 No. 10" at back bottom of shoulder plate **950.00**

Victorian type two-story house, wrap-a-round front porch on two sides, dormers, several pieces of window trim missing and glass replaced, electrified, early 20th C, 24" w, 25" d, 24" h, **$350**.

Photo courtesy of Alderfer Auction Co.

Alt, Beck & Gottschalk, baby character, bisque head, molded hair, blue sleep eyes, open mouth, cloth body, composition arms and legs, 14" h, marked "A.B. & G. 1528-36," marked "A.B. & G. 1528-36," **$185**.

Photo courtesy of Joy Luke Auctions.

Amberg

12-1/2" h, Bottle Babe Twins, solid-dome bisque heads, light blue sleep eyes, softly blues brows, painted upper and lower lashes, open mouths, molded tongues, lightly molded and painted hair, cloth bodies with non-working criers, composition arms, right arms molded to hold celluloid bottles, orig white lace-trimmed baby dresses, slips, crocheted bonnets, diapers, and socks, hold orig celluloid baby bottle, blue and white celluloid rattle, marked "A.M./Germany/341/3" on back of heads, "Amberg's/Bottle Babe/Pat. Pending/Amberg Dolls/The World Standard" on dress, both dolls have light rubs on cheeks or hair, cloth bodies are aged, some flaking on arms, paint flaked off right arm of one, price for pr **500.00**

15" h, New Born Babe, solid dome bisque head, blue sleep eyes, softly blushed brown, painted upper and lower lashes, closed mouth, lightly molded and painted hair, cloth body with composition hands, white lace-trimmed antique baby dress, slip and diaper, light dust in bisque, tiny run on upper lip, left side seam split near bottom of torso ... **315.00**

Armand Marseille

6-1/2" h, Googly, bisque socket head, large slide glancing blue sleep eyes,

single strike brows, closed smiling mouth, dark mohair wig, crude composition five-pc toddler body, lace-trimmed organdy baby dress, matching bonnet, slip, diaper, stockings, crocheted booties, marked "G. 253 B Germany A. 11/0 M" on back of head, repainted body **675.00**

10" l, 9" d head circumference, Dream Baby, brown bisque socket head, brown sleep eyes, closed mouth, black painted hair, brown bent limb composition baby body, fine lawn christening gown with tucks, ruffles, and lace trim, c1920 .... **300.00**

23" h, 990 baby, bisque socket head, brown sleep eyes, feathered brows, painted upper and lower lashes, open mouth, well-accented lips, two upper teeth, antique human hair wig, composition bent-limb baby body, antique baby dress, slip, diaper, new crocheted sweater, cap and booties, marked "Armand Marseille/Germany/990/A 12 M" on back of head, heavy French-style body, arms repainted

and have rough finish, right big toe missing, other toes repaired and repainted, normal wear at joints .. **275.00**

Arranbee

17" h, Nancy Lee, composition head, brown sleep eyes with real lashes, painted lower lashes, single stroke brows, closed mouth, orig human-hair wig in orig set, five-pc composition body, orig brown-flannel belted dress, white ruffle trim, orig underwear combination, orig socks and brown-suede shoes with fringe tongue, marked "R & B" on back of head, unplayed with condition **300.00**

21" h, Nanette, hard plastic head, blue sleep eyes with real lashes, single-stroke brows, painted lower lashes, closed mouth, saran wig, five-pc hard-plastic walking body, orig red and white striped dress with red organdy sleeves and apron, blue vinyl wide belt with charms attached, wrist tag, curlers on card, comb, marked "R & B" on head, "Nanette/An R & B Quality Doll/R & B Dolly Company New York 3, NY" on

Left: A. M. bisque, replaced wig, blue sleep eyes, open mouth, leather pin jointed body, cloth lower legs, bisque lower arms, redressed, crier mechanism, marked "A. 2-1/2 M.," 19" h, **$150**; center: Walkure, bisque, original brown curly mohair wig, brown slip eyes, open mouth, pierced ears, papier-mâché ball-jointed body, original clothing, marked "7-1/2 Walkure Germany," 19-1/2" h, **$475**; right: Handwerck, bisque, original blond curly mohair wig, blue sleep eyes, open mouth, pierced ears, papier-mâché ball-jointed body stamped "Handwerck," redressed in antique dress, marked "Handwerck 2-1/2," 20" h, **$465**.

Photo courtesy of Alderfer Auction Co.

label on end of box, "R & B/ Nanette/Walks/Sits/Stands/ Turns Her Head/R & B Doll Company New York City" on wrist tag, near mint in aged box, lid damaged and repaired **700.00**

Averill, Georgene
20" h, Bonnie Babe, solid dome bisque flange head, brown sleep eyes, softly brushed brows, painted upper and lower lashes, open mouth, two lower teeth, molded tongue, cloth mama doll body, composition lower arms and legs, antique long baby dress, marked "Copr by Georgene Averill 1005 3652 4 Germany" on back of head, body recovered **475.00**

17" h, solid dome bisque flange head, blue sleep eyes, softly blushed brows, painted upper and lower lashes, open laughing mouth, two lower teeth, molded tongue, deeply molded dimples, lightly molded and painted curly hair, cloth mama-doll body, composition arms and lower legs, non-working crier, dressed in possibly orig white lace-trimmed baby dress, slip, underwear, socks, and knit booties, silk and lace bonnet, marked "Copr by Georgene Averill 1005 3652 3 Germany" on back of head, cloth body aged and lightly soiled **600.00**

Bahr & Proschild, 19" h, 300, bisque socket head on bisque shoulder plate, blue set threaded paperweight eyes, feathered brows, painted upper and lower lashes, open mouth, four upper teeth, pierced tongue, orig human hair wig, kid body with cloth torso, bisque lower arms, gussets at elbows, hips, and knees, antique white dress with lace trim, antique underclothing, orig blue velvet hat with flower trim, marked "300/10" on back of head, inherent red firing line at rim in back, minor wig pulls, tiny rub on right cheek, body aged and discolored **300.00**

Barrois, E., 17-1/2" h, Poupee, pale bisque swivel head on shoulder plate, set blue eyes with threaded detail, fine multi-stroke brows, painted upper and lower lashes, closed mouth with

accented lips, orig blond mohair wig with orig tortoiseshell comb, kid body with kid over wood upper arms, mortise-and-tenon type knee joints, white dotted Swiss dress, possibly orig underclothing, socks, and shoes, marked "E 4 B," at rear edge of bisque shoulder plate, lower bisque arms replaced **1,200.00**

Bisque
4-1/2" h, Oriental pair, olive-tone bisque socket heads, dark brown pupil-less set eyes, single stroke brows, painted upper and lower lashes, closed mouth, orig black mohair wigs, male with orig queue, five-pc olive-tone bisque bodies jointed at shoulders and hips, Oriental embroidered silk clothing, unmarked, price for pr . **825.00**

10" h, Just Me, painted bisque socket head, blue side-glancing sleep eyes, single stroke brows, closed mouth, orig mohair wig, five-pc composition body jointed at shoulders and hips, orig white dress with orange and green felt trim, orig white cotton socks and white paper shoes with buckles, marked "Just Me/Registered/Germany/A 310/6/0 M" on back of head, needs to be restrung .. **900.00**

18" h, Miss Liberty, bisque shoulder head, painted blue eyes with molded lids, multi-stroke brows, tiny painted upper and lower lashes, closed mouth, molded earrings, molded and painted blond hair with copper molded earrings, molded and painted blond hair with copper tiara, two black ribbons across top of head and lay against left side of neck, molded bun with waterfall effect, cloth body, leather lower arms, red leather boots as part of lower leg, antique ecru wool dress with lace trim, antique underclothing, small holes in dress **1,650.00**

Bru Jne, 22" h, bisque socket head, bulbous blue paperweight eyes, heavy feathered brows, painted upper and lower lashes, closed mouth, pierced ears, hand tied mohair wig, kid body with scalloped kid attaching body to shoulder plate, kid over wood

upper arms, bisque lower arms, wooden lower legs, dressed in outfit made from antique ecru fabric and trims, beige and blue French style hat, French shoes marked "9," marked "Bru Jne/10" on back of head, "Bru" visible above kid on left rear shoulder, "No. 8" visible above kid on right rear shoulder, "Bebo Bru Bte S.G.D.G./Tout Contrefacteur sera saisi et poursuivi conformement a la Loi" on paper label on chest, 1" firing flaw on right forehead at crown, left little finger replaced **7,300.00**

Century Doll Co., 18" h, bisque shoulder plate, blue sleep eyes, feathered brows, painted lashes, open mouth, four upper teeth, molded and painted hair, kid body pin jointed at hips and knees, jointed wood and composition arms, composition lower legs, redressed, marked "Made in Germany/Century Doll" on back of shoulder plate **325.00**

Chase, Martha, black cloth, dark brown painted on eyes, soft brick red painted mouth **11,165.00**

China, unmarked
16" h, Frozen Charlie, pink tint, painted blue eyes, feathered brows, closed mouth, accent line between lips, painted blond hair with brush strokes around face, un-jointed body with arms held in front, hands in fists, finger nails and toe nails outlined, antique pink crocheted long dress and matching bonnet **675.00**

18" h, open mouth, low brow, china shoulder head with turned head, painted blue eyes, red accent line, single-stroke brows, open mouth, molded teeth, molded and painted wavy hair, cloth body, china lower arms and lower legs, painted garters, molded and painted brown shoes with heels, possibly orig beige print dress, underclothing **850.00**

Cloth, 21" h, Philadelphia Baby, painted head and shoulders, heavily lidded brown painted eyes, deeply modeled mouth, brown hair, cloth body, painted lower limbs, gray and white striped cotton shift, white undergarments, c1900, overall wear, paint rubs and loss **1,100.00**

Quality antique dolls from many manufacturers awaited collectors at Dawn's Dolls and Collectibles, at the March 2004 Atlantique City show.

Cochran, Dewees, 15" h, Cindy, latex socket head, painted blue eyes, multi-stroke brows, painted upper lashes, closed mouth, human hair wig, five-pc latex body jointed at shoulders and hips, faded peach taffeta dress with tan collar and hem, purple velvet trim, marked "Dewees Cochran/Dolls" on torso under left arm **325.00**

Cuno & Otto Dressel
14" h, bisque head, blue sleep eyes with lashes, open mouth, two upper teeth, replaced auburn mohair wig, fully articulated composition body, blue dress, imp "Cuno & Otto Dressel," early 20th C, some repair to body **200.00**
15-1/2" h, girl, painted bisque socket head, blue sleep eyes with real lashes, feathered brows, shading around eyes, open mouth, four upper teeth, orig human hair wig, jointed wood and composition teen-age body with high knee joints, orig clothing, short dress, slip, teddy, socks, and leather shoes, marked "Cuno & Otto Dressel/Germany" on back of head............... **450.00**

Demalcol, 9-1/2" h, Googlie, bisque socket head, blue eyes set to side, single-stroke brows, painted upper and lower lashes, closed smiling mouth, human-hair wig, new jointed-composition body, blue and white flowered dress, matching bonnet, new underclothing, socks and shoes, marked "Demalcol/5/0/Germany" on back of head................... **525.00**

Eden Bebe, 16-1/2" h, bisque socket head, blue paperweight eyes, feathered brows, painted upper and lower lashes, open mouth, six upper teeth, pierced ears, replaced mohair wig, jointed wood and composition French body, redressed, pale blue and ecru outfit, blue and beige jacket, antique underclothing, new stockings, and old shoes, marked "Eden Bebe/Paris/7/Depose" on back of neck, "7" on front of neck, light kiln dust on left cheek, flaking at neck socket of body and on both lower legs, normal wear at joints and on hands............... **1,200.00**

Effanbee
11" h, Grumpy Cowboy, composition shoulder head, painted blue eyes to side, single-stroke brows, closed pouty mouth, molded and painted hair, cloth body, composition arms and feet, cowboy outfit with plaid shirt, gold pants, green bandanna, imitation-leather chaps, holster with gun, replaced felt hat, marked "Effanbee/Dolls/Walk Talk Sleep" on back of shoulder plate, light crazing, light wear back of head, few flakes off shoulder plate, wear on edges of feet **475.00**
17" h, American Child Boy, composition head, painted blue eyes, multi-stroke brows, tiny painted upper and lower lashes, closed smiling mouth, orig human-hair wig, five-pc composition child body, orig blue wool two-pc suit, jacket and shorts, white shirt, multicolored tie, orig socks and black leatherette shoes, unmarked, light facial crazing, few light lines of crazing on legs.......................... **1,050.00**
19-1/2" h, American Child, composition head, blue sleep eyes with real lashes, multi-stroke brows, painted lower lashes, closed mouth, orig human hair wig with orig curlers, five-pc composition child body, orig blue and white striped zippered dress, nylon panties, orig white socks with blue trim, blue leatherette tie shoes, marked "Effanbee/American Children" on back of head, "Effanbee/Anne-Shirley" on back, unplayed with condition
.... **1,500.00**

Gaultier, Francois
10-1/2" h, Poupee, bisque socket head, bisque shoulder plate, light blue paperweight eyes, feathered browns, painted upper and lower lashes, closed mouth, pierced ears, orig mohair wig, cloth body with kid arms, individually stitched fingers, dressed in probably orig blue and white two-pc outfit with train, marked "2/0" on back of head, "F. G." on right shoulder, illegible mark on left shoulder, some age discoloration to body, one left finger missing **1,250.00**
21" h, Bebe, bisque socket head, large blue paperweight eyes, feathered brows, painted upper and lower lashes, full-closed mouth, molded tongue, pierced ears, replaced mohair wig, jointed wood and composition body with straight wrists, new blue silk dress with matching bonnet, new underclothing, socks and lace-up boots, marked "F. G. (in scroll)/8" on back of head, fingers touched up, minor repairs **2,200.00**

Halbig, Simon
7" h, Oriental, bisque, medium skin tone, dark pupil-less stationary eyes, closed mouth orig black mohair Oriental-style wig, swivel neck, kid-lined neck socket and legs, long black stockings, brick red one-strap shoes, imp "852 3," late 19th C, some mottling/soil to bisque **920.00**

Left: Heinrich Handwerck, bisque, replaced wig, blue sleep eyes, open mouth, pierced ears, papier-mâché ball jointed body, redressed, red stamp "Heinrich Handwerck Germany," 24" h, **$295**; center: Armand Marseille, bisque head, replaced wig, stationary brown eyes, open mouth, leather pin jointed body, lower bisque arms, left hand repaired, redressed, marked "370 AM-5 DEP," 24", **$125**; right: German, bisque, mold imperfection on forehead, brown human hair wig, stationary blue eyes, open mouth, plaster pate, repainted papier-mâché body, redressed in antique dress, marked "K Made in Germany 14-1/2" "Germany 164," 24-1/2" h, **$185**.

Photo courtesy of Alderfer Auction Co.

8" h, bisque head, blue sleep eyes, open mouth, four molded teeth, pierced ears, blond mohair wig, chunky straight wrist articulated composition body, orig finish and stringing, new red faille dress, imp "1079 DEP," c1900, tiny chip to right ear hole **550.00**
21" h, C M Bergmann bisque head, brown sleep eyes with lashes, open mouth, synthetic auburn wig, jointed composition body, period white lawn dress with lace insertion, sprinkling of pepper spots primarily to the right cheek, early 20th C..... **260.00**
Hamburger & Co., 22-1/2" h, Viola, bisque socket head, blue sleep eyes, feathered brows, painted upper and lower lashes, open mouth, four upper teeth, synthetic wig, jointed wood and composition body, antique dress with lace trim, underclothing, new socks and leather shoes, marked "Made in/Germany/Viola/H & Co./ 7" on back of head, several wig pulls on right side of forehead, light rub on nose, small inherent cut on H in back of head, repairs at neck socket of body, bottom of torso and left upper arm, normal wear at joints, finish of legs slightly different color than rest of body **300.00**
Hand sewn
15" h, Amish, OH, lavender dress, white apron, purple bonnet, arms and legs made from corn cobs, staining **345.00**

16" h, Amish, PA, green dress, black cape and bonnet **690.00**
17-1/2" h, Mennonite, PA, red and black checkered dress, black bonnet, fading, holes to cloth............................ **965.00**
Handwerck, 16" h, bisque head, blue sleep eyes, open mouth, pierced ears, orig blond mohair wig, fully articulated composition body, Alice in Wonderland blue dress and white pinafore, dark brown shoes, imp "109-6 Germany Handwerck" **460.00**

Handwerck, Heinrich
28" h, bisque socket head, blue set eyes with real lashes, fur brows, painted lower lashes, open mouth, four upper teeth, pierced ears, antique human hair wig, jointed wood and composition Handwerck body, new flowered dress, marked "Germany/Heinrich/ Handwerck/Simon & Halbig/5" on back of head, "Heinrich Handwerch/5" stamped in red, rub on right cheek, minor flake at earring hole, eyes, lashes, and brows replaced **300.00**
32-1/2" h, bisque socket head, blue sleep eyes, molded and feathered brows, painted upper and lower lashes, open mouth, accented lips, four upper teeth, pierced ears, orig human-hair wig, jointed wood and composition Handwerck body with orig finish, antique white child's dress, antique underclothing, cotton socks, black patent leather shoes, marked "Germany/Handwerck/Simon & Halbig/7" on back of head, "Heinrich Handwerck/ Germany/7" stamped in red on lower back, finish flaking on lower left arm and knees, left knee ball replaced **1,025.00**
Handwerck, Max, 21" h, bisque head, blue sleep eyes, open mouth, inset teeth, pierced ears, jointed-composition body, orig finish, newly made pink linen dress and hat, imp "421 10 Germany M HANDWERCK 2-1/2", bisque speckling, small chin pit **320.00**

Harmann, Kurt, 26" h, bisque head, brown sleep eyes, open mouth, replaced blond mohair wig, fully articulated composition body, new blue satin and lace dress, worn period blue leather shoes, imp mark "30 5 K (over script H) 4," early 20th C, white scratch line each cheek.. **230.00**

Hertel, Schwab & Co.
9" l, 7" d head circumference, twin character babies, blue sleep eyes, open mouths, two upper teeth, wispy blond tufts of hair, composition bent-limb bodies, matching period long white baby gown, one with pink, one blue ribbon trim, imp marks "152/2/0," early 20th C, price for pair... **635.00**
15" h, 140 character, bisque socket head, painted brown eyes, red accent line, feathered brows, closed mouth, accented lips, mohair wig, jointed wood and composition body, straight wrists, white factory chemise, dark green pants, matching cap, cotton socks, and new leather shoes, marked "140/4" on back of head, light rub on right cheek, minor repair at neck socket of body, light flaking on right upper leg
.... **4,200.00**
20" h, bisque socket head, blue paperweight eyes, feathered brows, painted upper and lower lashes, open mouth with accented lips and six upper teeth, pierced ears, replaced human-hair wig, jointed composition body with straight wrists, separate balls at shoulders, elbows, hips and knees, nicely redressed in pale pink French-style dress, new underclothing, socks and shoes, marks "8/0" on back of head and "Jumeau Medaille d'Or Paris" stamped in blue on lower back, replaced antique paperweight eyes, tiny flake at each earring hole, tiny fleck on upper rim at inside corner of right eye, body has good orig finish with wear at all joints, on toes and heels **1,100.00**

Heubach, Ernest
12-1/2" h, 399 baby, solid dome painted bisque socket head, brown sleep eyes, single stroke brows, painted upper and lower lashes, closed mouth, lightly molded and painted hair, composition bent-limb baby body, orig multicolored "grass" skirt, marked "Heubach *Koppelsdorf/399*9/0/ Germany" on back of head
.... **350.00**
21" h, 300 baby, bisque socket head, set brown eyes, feathered brows, painted upper and lower lashes, open mouth, accented lips, four upper teeth, replaced wig, composition bent-limb baby body, antique white long baby dress, lace-trimmed antique baby bonnet, underclothing, diaper, and booties, marked "Heubach * Koppelsdorf/300 * 6/Germany" on back of head, arms and legs repainted, cracks in finish under repaint, neck socket touched up, repair on right arm joint and right wrist **275.00**

Heubach, Gebruder, 22" h character, bisque shoulder head, blue intaglio eyes, two tone single stroke brows, closed mouth with shaded lips, molded and painted hair, tan oil cloth body with bisque lower arms, pin joints at hips and knees, cloth lower legs, new light blue velvet suit, white lace trimmed shirt, new socks and shoes, marked "8/Germany" on back of head..................... **350.00**

Heubach, Koppelsdorf
10-1/2" h, Screamer, bisque head, painted hair, painted blue intaglio eyes, open-closed screaming mouth, furrowed brow, straight-limb composition toddler body, maroon velvet short overalls, white shirt, imp "7684," sunburst mark............. **690.00**

Left: German, bisque, brown human hair wig, brown sleep eyes, open mouth, papier-mâché jointed body, fingers broken, replaced legs, marked with H symbol and "K" over "4," 25" h, **$195**; center: Fulper, bisque shoulder head, brown mohair wig, blue sleep eyes, open mouth, later leather pin jointed body, two bisque lower left arms, one cloth arm replaced, cloth lower legs, redressed, marked "CMU" in diamond symbol, "S-10, Made in U.S.A.," 23" h, **$75**; right: C. M. Bergmann, bisque, replaced wig, stationary blue eyes, open mouth with broken tooth, papier-mâché ball jointed body, paint worn on fingers, redressed, marked "C. M. Bergmann Simon & Halbig S & H 3," 25" h, **$275**.
Photo courtesy of Alderfer Auction Co.

24" h, bisque head, blue sleep eyes with lashes, open mouth, brown human-hair wig, fully jointed wood and composition body, period underwear, new print cotton dress, imp mark "312," early 20th C, rub on cheek **220.00**

Horsman, 15" h, toddler, composition socket head, brown sleep eyes, single stroke brows, painted upper and lower lashes, mohair wig, jointed composition toddler body, straight wrists, diagonal hip joints, old white organdy dress with lace trim, underclothing, socks, high button boots, marked "E.I.H./Co." on back **650.00**

Ideal

13" h, Shirley Temple, composition head, hazel sleep eyes with real lashes, painted lower lashes, feathered brows, open mouth, six upper teeth, orig mohair wig in orig set, five-pc composition body, orig plaid "Bright Eyes" dress, underwear combination, replaced socks, orig shoes, marked "13/Shirley Temple" on head, "Shirley Temple/13" on back **700.00**

20" h, Shirley Temple, composition head, hazel sleep eyes, real lashes, painted lower lashes, feathered brows, open mouth, six upper teeth, molded tongue, orig mohair wig in orig set, five-pc composition child body, orig dotted organdy dress with pleats from "Curly Top" movie, orig underwear, combination socks and shoes, marks: "20/Shirley Temple/Co Ideal/N & T Co." on back of head, "Shirley Temple/20*" on back, and "Genuine/Shirley Temple/registered U.S. Pat. Off/Ideal Nov & Toy Co./ Made in U.S.A." on dress tag ... **500.00**

28" h, Lori Martin, vinyl socket head, blue sleep eyes with real lashes, painted lower lashes, feathered brows, closed smiling mouth, rooted hair vinyl body jointed at waist, shoulders, hips, and ankles, orig tagged clothing, plaid shirt, jeans, vinyl boots with horses, marked "© Metro Goldwyn Mayer Inc./Mfg by/

Ideal Toy Corp/80" on back of head, "© Ideal Toy Corp./6-30-5" on back, "National Velvet's/Lori Martin/© Metro Goldwyn Mayer, Inc./All Rights Reserved" on shirt tag **550.00**

Jumeau

9" h, Great Ladies series, bisque socket head, blue paperweight eyes, single stroke brows, painted upper and lower lashes, closed mouth, orig mohair wig, five-pc composition body, painted flat black shoes, orig white brocade gown with gold "diamond" jewelry, orig underclothing, marked "22 1/3/0" on back of head, "fabrication/Jumeau/Paris/Made in France" on front of paper tag, "Marie-Louise/2, Femme de/Napoleon Ier/Epoque 1810" hand written on back of paper tag **475.00**

14" h, bisque socket head, paperweight eyes, multi-stroke brows, painted upper and lower lashes, open mouth, four upper teeth, pierced ears, orig mohair wig, orig pate, jointed wood and composition late French bodies, boy and girl doll dressed in orig ethnic costumes of Finistere Department of Brittany, France, marked "4" on back of heads, price for pr **2,000.00**

16" h, Poupee Peau, bisque socket head on bisque shoulder plate, cobalt blue set eyes, multi-stroke brows, painted upper and lower lashes, closed mouth, pierced ears, orig mohair wig in orig curls, kid lady body with gussets at elbows, hips, and knees, individually stitched fingers, possibly orig clothing, factory chemise as blouse, ecru silk skirt with purple flowers, lavender and white striped under skirt, half slip, pants, socks, and boots with elastic inserts in sides, unmarked, one boot heel missing **3,750.00**

20" h, Bebe, bisque head, brown paperweight eyes, mauve eye shadow, closed mouth, pierced applied ears, orig red Jumeau earrings, imp

DEPOSE E.9J, cork pate, orig blond mohair wig, jointed straight wrist, eight-ball composition body marked "Jumeau Medaille d'Or," vintage commercial dress of aqua satin and ecru silk faille, brown leather shoes, marked "E.J., France," c1885, tiny red age line side of nose . **5,475.00**

23" h Jumeau, Bebe Soleil box, bisque socket head, blue paperweight eyes, feathered brows, painted upper and lower lashes, open mouth, accented lips, six upper teeth, human-hair wig, jointed wood and composition French body, dressed in factory chemise pants, "Tete Jumeau" stamped in red, "9" incised on back of head, "Bebe due Bon Marche" partial paper label on lower back, "10700" written upside down on upper back, "S.F.B. J. Paris Bebe Soleil Yeux Mobiles Formes Naturelles Entierement Articule" on label on end of box, 2" hairline on right side of forehead, body finish flaking or loose in places, wear on edges of feet, at joints and on hands, box bottom repaired, lid missing **1,400.00**

35" h, bisque socket head, brown paperweight eyes, heavy feathered brows, painted upper and lower lashes, open mouth, six upper teeth, pierced ears, human hair wig over rock pate, jointed wood and composition French body with jointed wrists, working mama/papa pull strings, old white child's dress, underclothing, socks, black child's shoes, marked "14" on back of head **1,400.00**

Jutta, 26" h, 1914 baby, bisque socket head, brown sleep eyes, feathered brows, painted upper and lower lashes, open mouth, two upper teeth, spring tongue, replaced human hair wig, composition baby body, navy blue sailor top, hat, shorts, red and white striped socks, leather baby shoes, marked "Jutta/1914/14 J" on back of head, cracks on both hands, left little finger missing **800.00**

Left: German bisque, blond mohair wig, blue sleep eye, open mouth, repainted papier-mâché ball jointed body, one finger broken, redressed, marked "Made in Germany C∫ DEP 7-1/2 160," 16" h, **$195**; center: unmarked bisque socket head, bisque shoulder plate, brown human hair wig, brown paperweight eyes, closed mouth, leather gusseted body, bisque lower arms, redressed, 18" h, **$685**; right: A. M., bisque, replaced synthetic wig, stationary blue eyes, open mouth, papier-mâché ball-jointed body, redressed, mold/kiln imperfections, marked "A. M. 6. DEP," 18-1/2" h, **$150**.

Photo courtesy of Alderfer Auction Co.

Kamkins, 19" h, girl, cloth, molded face with painted features, blue eyes, orig brown mohair wig, cloth body and limbs, blue cotton dress, orig undergarments, purple Kamkins stamp mark on back of head, early 20th C, some soil and wear on face **1,150.00**

Kammer & Reinhardt

10" h, 115A baby, bisque socket head, blue sleep eyes, feathered brows, painted upper and lower lashes, closed mouth, orig mohair wig, five-pc composition baby body, antique-style white baby dress, slip, lace-trimmed panties, eyelet bonnet, marked "1/K*R/Simon & Halbig/115A/30" on back of head, wear to orig finish, arms mostly repainted, touch-up around neck socket, on toes, and feet.................... **1,300.00**

14" h, 100 baby, solid dome bisque socket head, painted blue eyes, single-stroke brows, open/closed mouth, molded and brush-stroked hair, bent limb composition baby body, possibly orig long baby dress, full slip half slip, diaper, undershirt, knit

booties, long fleece coat, matching hat, marked "36/K*R/100" on back of head, head perfect, orig body finish worn............................ **275.00**

19" h, 115/A character toddler, bisque head, brown sleep eyes, closed pouty mouth, reddish-blond caracul wig, side-jointed composition toddler body, red and green plush jester's costume, also orig pink gingham outfit, imp "K*R Simon & Halbig 115/A, 48," c1910 .... **4,320.00**

Kestner

6" h, 208, all bisque, stiff neck, brown sleep eyes, single-stroke brows, painted upper and lower lashes, open/closed mouth, orig mohair wig, all bisque body jointed at shoulders and hips, mold and painted white shirred socks and black one-strap shoes, marked "208/3" on back of head and on arms and legs at joints, "Made in Germany" round red stamp on back, "Baby Rose Germany" on round red label on tummy, orig box **300.00**

11" h, 257 baby, bisque socket head, brown sleep

eyes, feathered brows, painted upper and lower lashes, open mouth, two upper teeth, antique mohair wig on old cardboard pate, composition baby body, new sailor romper, marked "Made in Germany/J.D.K./257/28" on back of head **350.00**

16", 237, Hilda, bisque socket head, blue sleep eyes, feathered brows, painted upper and lower lashes, open mouth, two upper porcelain teeth, orig blond skin wig, composition Kestner baby body, white organdy baby dress, matching bonnet, marked "J Made in Germany 13/JD.K./237 ges gesch/N 1070" on back of head **2,000.00**

20-1/2" h, 161, bisque socket head, brown sleep eyes, feathered brows, painted upper and lower lashes, open mouth, four upper teeth, replaced human hair wig, orig plaster pate, jointed wood and composition Kestner body, ecru dress with red cross stitch trim, marked "F∫ Made in Germany 10 1/2/161" on back of head, "Germany 3" stamped in red on right rear hip............................... **475.00**

32" h, 164, bisque socket head, blue sleep eyes, molded and feathered brows, painted upper and lower lashes, open mouth, shapely accented lips, four upper teeth, skin wig, jointed wood and composition Kestner body, faded dark blue velvet sailor suit, white shirt, old socks and shoes, marked "M1/2 made in Germany 16 1/2/164" on back of head, "Excelsior/Germany/7" stamped in red on right lower back, body has orig finish with light wear, normal wear at joints, right finger repaired **1,200.00**

Kley & Hahn, 11-1/2" h, 525Baby, solid dome bisque socket head, blue sleep eyes, feathered brows, painted upper and lower lashes, open-closed mouth, lightly molded and brush stroked hair, composition baby body, antique baby dress, marked "4/Germany/K&H (in banner)/525" on back of head, repainted......................... **275.00**

Left: Kammer & Reinhardt, bisque head, blond mohair wig, blue sleep eyes, open mouth, five-piece papier-mâché bent limb baby body, restoration to hand, redressed, marked "K*R Simon Halbig 126 26," 10-1/2" l, **$120**; center: A. M., marked "A. M. Germany 351, 12K," 11" l, bisque dome head, blue sleep eyes, open mouth, repainted five-piece papier-mâché bent limb baby body, restoration to foot, redressed, **$120**; right: 233, bisque, short brown human hair wig, stationary brown eyes, open mouth, cloth "frog" body, celluloid hands, redressed, hairline crack at bridge of nose, marked "233 7/0," 8-1/2" l, **$40**.

Photo courtesy of Alderfer Auction Co.

Knickerbocker, 11" h, Mickey Mouse, cloth swivel head, white facial, black oilcloth pie eyes, large black nose, painted open/closed smiling mouth with accent lines, black felt ears, unjointed black cloth body, orange hands with three fingers and a thumb, red oversized composition feet, black rubber tail, orig shorts with two buttons on front and back, some fading **650.00**

Konig & Wernicke, Germany, early 20th C
17" h, character toddler, bisque head, brown sleep eyes, open mouth, two upper teeth, tongue, orig dark brown mohair wig, fully articulated side hip-joint composition toddler body marked "Made in Germany," period cotton sailor outfit, blue pants, white overblouse, white fabric shoes, imp "Made in Germany 99/7," some wear to finish of limbs, repaint to hands **750.00**
27" l, 16-1/2" d head circumference, character baby, bisque head, early 20th century, blue sleep eyes, open mouth, two upper teeth, wobble tongue, orig brown mohair wig, bent limb composition baby body, red

circle stamp "K & W," minor wear **815.00**

Kruse, Kathe
13" h, Schlenkerchen, all-stockinette, pressed and oil-painted double-seam head, painted features, brown hair, shaded brown painted eyes with eyeliner, light upper lashes, closed mouth in smiling expression, cloth neck ring, stockinette covered, padded armature frame body, mitten hands, rounded feet, unlaundered off-white undergarments, soles stamped "Kathe Kruse, Germany," c1922, paint rub tip of nose, soil **5,475.00**
21" h, Sand Baby, hand painted head, painted blue eyes, single stroke brows, closed mouth, painted hair, stockinette covered body jointed at shoulders, loose joints at hips, formed navel, "Kathe Kruse" stamped on bottom of left foot, incomplete number stamped on bottom of right foot **550.00**

Kuhnlenz, Gebruder, 22" h, 38 Girl, bisque shoulder head, blue threaded paperweight eyes, feathered brows, painted upper and lower lashes, closed mouth, human hair, cloth Goldsmith body,

red corset, brown leather lower arms, red lower legs with red kid boots, silver two-pc outfit made from antique fabrics, marked "G.K." on back of head, "38-27.5" at bottom of shoulder plate **250.00**

Madame Alexander, First Ladies Series, Billie Taylor Bliss, vinyl, 1976-78, 13" h, **$75**.

Photo courtesy of Alderfer Auction Co.

Lenci
8" h, Mascotte, pressed felt swivel head, painted brown "surprise" eyes to side, single-stroke brows, painted upper lashes, open-closed two tone mouth, orig red mohair wig in braids, cloth body with felt arms and legs, orig blue and white polka dot nylon dress, white felt collar, red felt belt, orig one-pc underwear, red felt sandals, light display soil, front of dress faded **150.00**

12" h, girl, pressed felt swivel head, painted brown side-glancing eyes, painted upper lashes, closed mouth with two-tone lips, orig mohair wig, cloth torso, felt limbs, orig pink felt dress with blue trim, blue felt coat with matching hat, orig underclothing, socks, blue felt shoes, marked "2" on bottom of right foot, "Lenci/ Made in Italy" on cloth label inside coat **400.00**

28" h, lady, "Mary Pickford" felt face, light gray-blue painted eyes to right, long nose, closed mouth, long bare felt arms, classic Lenci fingers, white and green organdy summer frock, felt wide-brimmed bonnet, all trimmed with felt flowers and ruffles, silk stockings, pale green felt shoes with felt flowers, orig Lenci tag sewn to dress, c1930, small stain back of skirt **1,840.00**

Limbach, 23" h, character, bisque socket head, blue sleep eyes with real lashes, painted upper and lower lashes, open mouth, accented lips, six upper teeth, human-hair wig, jointed wood and composition body, new white lacy dress, underclothing, new socks and shoes, marked "W/crown/17 72 in shamrock/Limbach" on back of head, two right fingers and three left fingers repaired, finish flaking around neck socket of body, cracks in finish on side seams of torso, wear at all sockets on torso............. **625.00**

Madame Alexander, First Ladies Series III, Jane Pierce, 1982-84, vinyl, 12" l, NRFB, **$75**.

Photo courtesy of Alderfer Auction Co.

Madame Alexander

14" h, Marme from the Little Women Series, hard plastic head and body, gray sleep eyes, closed mouth, dark brown wig in snood, gray and pink print dress with orig tags, organdy shawl, shoes and socks, c1955 .... **200.00**

18" h, Sweet Violet, hard plastic head, blue sleep eyes with real lashes, painted lower lashes, feathered brows, closed mouth, orig synthetic wig, hard plastic body jointed at shoulders, elbows, wrists, hips, and knees, walking mechanism, orig tagged blue cotton dress, underclothing, flowered bonnet, white gloves, black side-snap shoes, carrying orig pink Alexander hat box, marked "Alexander" on back of head, "Madame Alexander/All Rights Reserved/New York, U.S.A.," c1954, unplayed-with condition comb and curlers missing **1,700.00**

23" h, Special Girl, composition head, composition shoulder plate, blue sleep eyes with real lashes, painted lower lashes, feathered brows, closed mouth, orig human-hair wig in orig set, cloth torso with composition arms and legs, orig pale blue taffeta dress with lace and ribbon trim, attached blue panties, orig socks and center snap shoes, "Madame/Alexander/New York U.S.A." on dress tag **750.00**

Menjou, Adolph, 32" h, composition shoulder head, painted brown eyes with accent line, molded monocle on right eye, feathered brows, molded and painted mustache, open-closed mouth, seven upper teeth, molded white shirt collar with hole, presumably for a tie, molded and painted hair, excelsior-stuffed cloth body with long limbs, composition white hands as gloves, composition lower legs as socks and shoes, orig black two-pc suit with satin lapels **725.00**

Motschmann-style, 14-1/2" h, china, flange swivel head, painted blue eyes, single strike brows, closed mouth molded and painted hair in "Alice" hairstyle, molded hair band, Taufling body, papier-mâché shoulder plate and hip section, china lower arms and legs, molded and painted boots, six painted side buttons, possibly orig homemade white dress, short chemise, leg covers **2,500.00**

Madame Alexander, Beth, #412, hard plastic, straight legs, original Little Women booklet, 8" h, NRFB, **$125**.

Photo courtesy of Alderfer Auction Co.

Parian, 24" h, untinted bisque shoulder head, painted blue eyes with red accent line, single stroke brows, closed mouth, pierced ears, molded and painted café au lait hair, molded blue tiara trimmed with gold, molded braid across top, on lower sides, and down middle of back of head, old cloth body with red leather boots as part of leg, new arms by Emma Clear, white dotted Swiss and lace dress, antique underclothing, unmarked, old repair to tiara, body aged **1,900.00**

Petzold, Dora, 16-1/2" h, composition head, painted blue eyes with eye shadow, single-stroke brows, accented nostrils, closed mouth, orig mohair wig, stockinette body stitch-jointed at shoulders and hips, mitten-type hands with stitched fingers, possibly orig white velvet dress with embroidery and lace trim, white teddy, orig socks and marked shoes, marked with girl in circle, "D P/7/7/0" on back of head, girl in circle with "D P" on bottom of shoes **275.00**

Poupee Bois, 17-1/2" h, bisque socket head, bisque shoulder plate, pale blue threaded paperweight eyes, feathered brows, painted upper and lower lashes, closed mouth, pierced ears, orig human hair wig, wooden fashion body articulated at shoulders, elbows, wrists, hips, and knees, swivel joint on upper arms and upper legs, nicely redressed with antique fabric and lace, possibly orig stockings and high button boots, marked "4" on back of head **4,400.00**

Poupee Raynal, 19" h, pressed felt swivel head, painted blue eyes, single-stroke brows, painted upper lashes, closed mouth with three-tone lips, orig mohair wig in orig set, five-pc cloth body with stitched fingers, orig light blue organdy dress with pink flower appliqués, matching hat, orig teddy, blue organdy slip, socks, white leather shoes, "Paris" typed on piece of paper pinned to back, unplayed with condition .. **725.00**

German, bisque socket head, original wig, sleep eyes, painted feathers, redressed, large hat with plume, **$200.**

Putnam, Grace

8" h, Bye-Lo Baby, solid dome bisque swivel head, tiny blue sleep eyes, softly blushed brows, painted upper and lower lashes, closed mouth, lightly molded and painted hair, all bisque baby body jointed at shoulders and hips, orig knit pink and white two-pc baby outfit with matching cap, marked "Bye-Lo Baby/©/Germany/G.S. Putnam" on label on chest, "6-20/Copr. By/Grace S. Putnam/Germany" incised on back, "6-20" on hips and right arms, "20" on left arm, chip on right back of neck edge of head, minor firing line behind left ear **525.00**

11" h, 10" d head circumference Bye-Lo Baby, solid dome bisque flange head, blue sleep eyes, softly blushed brows, painted upper and lower lashes, closed mouth, lightly molded and painted hair, cloth body with celluloid hands and "frog" legs, Bye-Lo baby gown, slip, orig flannel undershirt and diaper, cotton stockings, marked "Copr. by/Grace S. Putnam/Made in Germany" on back of head, "Bye-Lo Baby/Pat Appl'd For/Copy/by/Grace/Storey/Putnman" stamped on front of body **200.00**

20" h, 16 1/2" d head circumference, Bye-Lo Baby, solid dome bisque flange head, blue sleep eyes, softly blushed brows, painted upper and lower lashes, closed mouth, lightly molded and painted hair, cloth body with "frog" legs, celluloid hands, antique baby christening dress, long slip, underskirt, socks and booties, marked "Copr. By/Grace S. Putnam/Made in Germany" on back of head, partial Bye-Lo Baby stamp on front of torso, body aged and soiled, right hand missing two fingers **250.00**

Recknagel, 9" h, character, bisque socket head, tiny painted blue squinty eyes, single-stroke brows, open-closed mouth, five painted upper teeth, four lower teeth, molded tongue, molded and painted short hair with molded pink bow, five-pc chubby composition body, crude unpainted torso, molded and painted socks and shoes, redressed in pink lace-trimmed dress, matching hair ribbon, lace pants, marked "R 5/A/8/0" on back of head, light dust in bisque, light wear on orig body finish **675.00**

Redmond, Kathy

13" h, Eleanor Roosevelt, bisque shoulder head, well modeled pained features, molded and painted hair and necklace, cloth body, bisque arms and lower legs with molded black shoes, orig purple two-pc suit, marked "Eleanor Roosevelt R (in cat)" on back of shoulder plate ... **300.00**

14" h, Mary Todd Lincoln, bisque shoulder head, painted blue eyes, painted brows, closed mouth, molded brown hair, molded white roses and green leaves, molded white snood with gold highlights, molded necklace and earrings, molded white bisque ruffle with single rose on shoulder plate, cloth body, bisque lower arms and legs, black silk dress with blue accents, orig underclothing, marked "Mary Lincoln/R (in cat) 17" on back of shoulder plate **175.00**

S & Q, 28" h, 201 baby, bisque socket head, set brown eyes, feathered brows, painted upper and lower lashes, open mouth, two upper teeth, molded tongue, mohair wig, composition baby body, navy blue velvet boy's shorts, jacket, and matching hat, white shirt, stockings, white baby shoes, marked "+ 201 SQ" (superimposed) "Germany 14" on back of head.............. **700.00**

Schmidt, Bruno, 22" h, 2042, solid dome bisque socket head, painted brown eyes, two-tone single-stroke brows, open-closed mouth, accented lips, brush-stroked hair, jointed composition body, redressed in maroon velour two-pc suit, ecru satin shirt with lace trim, black cotton socks, new black shoes, marked "5/B.S.W. in heart/2042" on back of head, "Handwerck" stamped in red in middle of lower back **1,500.00**

Schmidt, Franz, 15" h, 1285 baby, solid dome bisque socket head, blue sleep eyes, softly blushed brows, painted upper and lower lashes, closed mouth, molded and painted hair, composition baby body, smocked baby dress, marked "1285/32/F S & C/Made in Germany" on back of head **575.00**

Schoenau & Hoffmeister, 13-1/2" h, Masquerade set, bisque socket head, set brown eyes, single stroke brows, painted upper and lower lashes, open mouth, four upper teeth, antique mohair wig, five pc composition body, walking mechanism, orig pastel dress with pale green ribbon trim, orig gauze-type underclothing, socks, leather shoes with black pompons, marked "4000 5/0/S PB (in star) H 10" on back of head, "F" on back of legs, "Germany" stamped on bottom of shoes, tied in red cardboard box with two lace-trimmed compartments, blue pierrot costume brimmed with black, white, and ruffled collar, matching cone-shaped hat, black face mask with lace trim, light rub on nose **525.00**

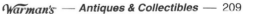

Madame Alexander, Scarlet, Gone with the Wind, white dress, original box, 12" h, minor stains on dress, **$60**.

Photo courtesy of Joy Luke Auctions.

Schoenhut

11" h, toddler, wood socket head, painted blue eyes, single-stroke brows, closed mouth, orig mohair wig, wooden body jointed at shoulders, elbows, wrists, hips, knees, and ankles, redressed, marked "Schoenhut/Doll/Pat Jan 17th 1911/USA" on oval label on back, "H. C. Schoenhut/©/ (illegible)" on round label on back of head, light wear on finish of face, rub on nose, wear on toes **425.00**

19" h, 19/308 girl, wooden socket head, brown intaglio eyes, feathered brow, closed mouth with excellent modeling, orig mohair wig, spring-jointed wooden body jointed at shoulders, elbows, wrists, hips, knees, and ankles, white dress with red dots in Schoenhut style, slip, knit union suit, replaced cotton socks and red flocked shoes, marked "Schoenhut Doll/Pat. Jan 17th 1911/ U.S.A." on oval label on back, very light touch up on left cheek, nose, edge of lips, craze lines on front of lower neck, light crazing on right cheek and outer corner of left eye, body has "suntan" color with normal wear at joints and light overall soil, few flakes off ankles **450.00**

Schoenhut & Hoffmeister,

20" h, 13-1/2" d head circumference, character baby, bisque head, blue sleep eyes with lashes, hint of smile, open mouth, two upper teeth, pointy chin, orig dark brown mohair wig, bent-limb composition baby

body, white cotton slip, imp "SHPB" in a star, "5, Germany," early 20th C, white spot back of head at rim **325.00**

S.F.B.J.

11" h, 301, bisque socket head, blue sleep eyes with real lashes, open mouth, four painted upper teeth, pierced ears, human-hair wig, jointed wood and composition body, jointed wrists, antique white lace dress and bonnet, marked "S.F.B.J./301/Paris/1" on back of head, "2" incised between shoulders, "2" on bottom of feet, good original body finish **600.00**

18" h, 236 toddler, bisque socket head, blue sleep eyes, feathered brows, painted lower lashes, open/closed mouth, two upper teeth, orig mohair hair, jointed wood and composition toddler body, antique dark purple satin two pc outfit, matching cap, replaced socks and shoes, marked "S.F.B.J./ 236/Paris/8" on back of head, cracks in wood on lower half right arm **550.00**

Simon & Halbig

12-1/2" h, 1428, bisque socket head, blue sleep eyes, single stroke brows, tiny painted upper lashes, open/closed mouth, replaced synthetic wig, jointed wood and composition body, new red velvet two pc boy's outfit, socks, new brown boots, marked "1428/4" on back of head, lower leg repainted **1,000.00**

18" h, 1039, bisque socket head, bisque shoulder plate, blue flirty eyes, real lashes, feathered brow, painted lower lashes, open mouth with outlined lips, four upper teeth, pierced ears, orig mohair wig, orig white glass beads at neck joint, kid body, bisque lower arms, gussets at elbows, hips, and knees, cloth lower legs, pink silk two-pc outfit made from old fabric, antique underclothing, new socks and shoes, marked "S.H. 1038/DEP/6/Germany" on back of head, inherent firing line behind right ear, head loose on shoulder plate, normal aging and light soil to body **375.00**

22" h, 1039, bisque socket heat, blue flirty eyes, real lashes, molded and feathered brows, painted upper and lower lashes, open mouth with accented lips, four upper teeth, pierced ears, human hair wig, jointed wood and composition French type body, torso cut for working crier, both arms with kiss throwing mechanism, knees jointed, both legs with walking mechanism, rose French-style new dress, antique underclothing, replaced socks and shoes, marked "1039/German/Simon & Halbig/S & H/10-1/2" on back of head **500.00**

Terri Lee

12" h, Buddy Lee, hard plastic head with stiff neck, eyes painted to side, single-stroke brows, painted upper lashes, closed mouth, molded and painted hair, hard plastic body jointed at shoulders only, molded and painted black boots, orig Phillips 66 suit with labeled shirt and pants, black imitation-leather belt, marked "Buddy Lee" on back, "Union Made/Lee/ Sanforized" on label on back of pants, "Phillips/66" on label on front of shirt **215.00**

16" h, Terri Lee, hard plastic head, oversized painted brown eyes, single-stroke brows, long painted upper and lower lashes, closed mouth, synthetic wig, five-pc hard plastic body jointed at shoulders and hips, orig yellow Evening Formal, #3570D orig socks and shoes, long white coat, #3690A, matching hat, 1954, marked "Terri Lee" on back, Terri Lee tag on coat... **475.00**

18" Connie Lynn, hard plastic head, blue sleep eyes with real lashes, single-stroke brows, painted lower lashes at corners of eyes, closed mouth, orig skin wig, hard plastic baby body, orig two-pc pink baby outfit, plastic panties, orig socks and white baby shoes, Terri Lee Nursery Registration Form and three Admission Cards to Terri Lee Hospital, Connie Lynn tag on clothing, orig box, unplayed with condition **625.00**

Unis France, 9-1/2" h, 60, bisque socket head, light blue sleep eyes, single stroke brows, open mouth with 4 upper teeth, orig mohair wig, crude five-pc composition body, dressed in orig ethnic costume of Pont-l'Abbe in Brittany, France, marked "Unis/France/71 60 140/11/0" on back of head.......... **175.00**

Simon & Halbig, Matthes Berlin, 156/2-1/2, bisque, blue sleep eyes, open mouth, jointed composition body, 9" h, **$365.**

Photo courtesy of Joy Luke Auctions

Vogue

7-1/2" h, Toddles Hansel and Gretel, composition heads, painted blue eyes looking to the right, single stroke brows, painted upper lashes, closed mouths, orig mohair wigs, five pc composition body, orig Tyrolean outfits, marked "Vogue" on back of head, orig clothing labels, orig boxes, price for pr.................. **500.00**

7-1/2" h, Toddles, Nurse, composition, painted blue eyes looking to right, single stroke brows, painted upper lashes, closed mouth, orig mohair wig, body jointed at shoulders and hips, orig white nurse's outfit and hat, oil cloth snap shoes, marked "Vogue" on head "Doll Co." on back, orig gold label on dress **475.00**

Wax, unmarked, 18" h, reinforced poured-wax shoulder head, set blue glass eyes, multi-stroke brows, painted upper and lower lashes, closed smiling mouth, pierced ears, orig mohair wig, cloth body, wax-over composition lower arms and lower legs, antique red/white gingham dress, orig underclothing, socks and leather

shoes, color worn on lips, eyelashes and brows, minor crack in wax on right front of shoulder plate, cracks on right leg, body is aged, soiled, and repaired........................... **475.00**

Wislizenus, Adolph, 18" h, girl, bisque socket head, brown sleep eyes, feathered brows, painted upper and lower lashes, open mouth, accented lips, pierced ears, replaced human-hair wig, jointed composition body with orig finish, possibly orig clothing, white low waisted dress, antique underclothing, socks and shoes marked "8," blue velvet coat and matching hat with ribbon trim, marked "8/ A.W./Germany/6" on back of head, "46" stamped in red on bottom of feet.................. **550.00**

DOORSTOPS

History: Doorstops became popular in the late 19th century. They are either flat or three-dimensional and were made out of a variety of different materials, such as cast iron, bronze, or wood. Hubley, a leading toy manufacturer, made many examples.

All prices listed are for excellent original paint unless otherwise noted. Original paint and condition greatly influence the price of a doorstop. To get top money, the original paint on a piece must be close to mint condition. Chipping of paint, paint loss, and wear reduce the value. Repainting severely reduces value and eliminates a good deal of the piece's market value, thereby reducing its value. A broken piece has little value to none.

Reproduction Alert:
Reproductions are proliferating as prices on genuine doorstops continue to rise. A reproduced piece generally is slightly smaller than the original unless an original mold is used. The overall casting of reproductions is not as smooth as on the originals. Reproductions also lack the detail apparent in originals, including the appearance of the painted areas. Any bright orange rusting is

strongly indicative of a new piece. Beware. If it looks too good to be true, it usually is.

Notes: Pieces described contain at least 80 percent or more of the original paint and are in very good condition. Repainting drastically reduces price and desirability. Poor original paint is preferred over repaint.

All listings are cast-iron and flat-back castings unless otherwise noted.

Doorstops marked with an asterisk are currently being reproduced.

Basket of fruit, paint worn, **$95.**

Bear, 15" h, holding and looking at honey pot, brown fur, black highlights **1,500.00**

Bellhop, 8-7/8" h, blue uniform, with orange markings, brown base, hands at side **300.00**

Bowl, 7" x 7", green-blue, natural colored fruit, sgd "Hubley 456" **125.00**

Boy, 10-5/8" h, wearing diapers, directing traffic, police hat, red scarf, brown dog at side. **665.00**

Caddie, 8" h, carrying brown and tan bag, white, brown, knickers, red jacket*...................... **725.00**

Cat

8" h, black, red ribbon and bow around neck, on pillow* **155.00**

10-3/4" h, licking paw, white cat with black markings, marked "Sculpture Metal Studios" **425.00**

13-5/8" h, reaching, full figure, two-piece hollow casting, green eyes, off-white body **675.00**

Child, 17" h, reaching, naked, short brown curly hair, flesh color **1,375.00**

Clipper ship, 5-1/4" h, full sails, American flag on top mast, wave base, two rubber stoppers, sgd "CJO" **65.00**

Cosmos Flower Basket, 17-3/4" h, blue and pink flowers, white vase, black base, Hubley **1,350.00**

Cottage, 8-5/8" l, 5-3/4" h, Cape type, blue roof, flowers, fenced garden, bath, sgd "Eastern Specialty Mfg Co. 14" **150.00**

Dancer, 8-7/8" h, Art Deco couple doing Charleston, pink dress, black tux, red and black base, "FISH" on front, sgd "Hubley 270" **1,475.00**

Scottie, black, **$350**.

Dog

7" h, three puppies in basket, natural colors, sgd "Copyright 1932 M. Rosenstein, Lancaster, PA, USA" ... **350.00**

8" x 7-1/2", Beagle pup, full figure, cream with darker markings **685.00**

9" h, Boston Bull, full figure, facing left, black, tan markings **175.00**

10-1/2" x 3-1/2", St. Bernard, lying down, full figure, cream with brown markings, Hubley **775.00**

14" x 9", Sealyham, full figure, Hubley, cream and tan dog, red collar..................... **675.00**

Dolly, 9-1/2" h, pink bow in blond hair, holding doll in blue dress, white apron, yellow dress, Hubley........................... **365.00**

Doorman in Livery, 12" h, twin men, worn orig paint, marked "Fish," Hubley **1,760.00**

Drum major, 12-5/8" h, full figure, ivory pants, red hat with feather, yellow baton in right hand, left hand on waist, sq base **225.00**

Basket of flowers, pink roses, green leaves, blue flowers with yellow centers, white basket, **$175**.

Duck, 7-1/2" h, white, green bush and grass.............. **335.00**

Elephant, 14" h, palm trees, early 20th C, very minor paint wear **335.00**

Fisherman, 6-1/4" h, standing at wheel, hand over eyes, rain gear **185.00**

Frog, 3" h, full figure, sitting, yellow and green **50.00**

Giraffe, 20-1/4" h, tan, brown spots, squared off lines to casting **2,850.00**

Golfer, 8-3/8" h, 7" w, cast iron, flat-backed figure, putting position, plaid snap-brim hat, belted jacket and knickers, orig paint with tan clothing accented with brown and green, green foliage, America, late 19th/early 20th C, small areas of paint loss **470.00**

Golfer, 10" h, overhand swing, hat and ball on ground, Hubley* **475.00**

Halloween Girl, 13-3/4" h, 9-3/4" l, white hat, flowing cape, holding orange jack-o-lantern with red cutout eyes, nose, and mouth*......................... **2,000.00**

Indian chief, 9-3/4" h, orange and tan headdress, yellow pants, and blue stripes, red patches at ankles, green grass, sgd "A. A. Richardson," copyright 1928............... **295.00**

Lighthouse, 14" h, green rocks, black path, white lighthouse, red window and door trim **385.00**

Mammy

8-1/2" h, full figure, Hubley, red dress, white apron, polka-dot bandanna on head **225.00**

Mammy, red, white, and black, 90 percent original paint, **$650**.

10" h, full figure, one piece hollow casting, white scarf and apron, dark blue dress, red kerchief on head*. **325.00**

Monkey

8-1/2" h, 4 5/8" w wrap-around tail, full figure, brown and tan **265.00**

14-3/8" h, hand reaching up, brown, tan, and white . **650.00**

Old Mill, 6-1/4" h, brown log mill, tan roof, white patch, green shrubs............................ **425.00**

Owl, 9-1/2" h, sits on books, sgd "Eastern Spec Co" **285.00**

Cottage, brown roof, white walls, green shutters, red, pink, yellow and green hollyhocks, green grass base, **$165**.

Pan, 7" h, with flute, sitting on mushroom, green outfit, red hat and sleeves, green grass base **165.00**

Peasant woman, 8-3/4" h, blue dress, black hair, fruit basket on head **250.00**
Penguin, 10" h, full figure, facing sideways, black, white chest, top hat and bow tie, yellow feet and beak, unsgd Hubley **435.00**
Policeman, 9-1/2" h, leaning on red fire hydrant, blue uniform and titled hat, comic character face, tan base, "Safety First" on front **725.00**
Prancing horse, 11" h, scrolled and molded base, "Greenlees Glasgow" imp on base, cast iron **175.00**

Parrot, yellow, red, blue, and green, some loss to original paint, **$450**.

Pair of penguins, cream and black paint, **$425**.

Quail, 7-1/4" h, two brown, tan, and yellow birds, green, white, and yellow grass, "Fred Everett" on front, sgd "Hubley 459"*
.... **365.00**
Rabbit, 8-1/8" h, eating carrot, red sweater, brown pants **350.00**
Rooster, 13" h, red comb, black and brown tail **360.00**
Squirrel, 9" h, sitting on stump eating nut, brown and tan
.... **275.00**

Storybook
4-1/2" h, Humpty Dumpty, full figure, sgd "661" **375.00**
7-3/4" h, Little Miss Muffett, sitting on mushroom, blue dress, blond hair **175.00**
9-1/2" h, Little Red Riding Hood, basket at side, red cape, tan dress with blue pattern, blond hair, sgd "Hubley" **150.00**
12-1/2" h, Huckleberry Finn, floppy hat, pail, stick, Littco Products label **475.00**

Basket of red tulips, blue bow, white ruffled base, **$300**.

Peacock, green feathers with yellow and black trim, **$250**.

Sunbonnet Girl, 9" h, pink dress
.... **235.00**
Whistler, 20-1/4" h, boy, hands in tan knickers, yellow striped baggy shirt, sgd "B & H"
.... **2,750.00**
Windmill, 6-3/4" h, ivory, red roof, house at side, green base*
.... **115.00**
Woman, 11" h, flowers and shawl* **285.00**
Zinnias, 11-5/8" h, multicolored flowers, blue and black vase, sgd "B & H" **185.00**

DRESDEN/ MEISSEN

History:
Augustus II, Elector of Saxony and King of Poland, founded the Royal Saxon Porcelain Manufactory in the Albrechtsburg, Meissen, in 1710. Johann Frederick Boettger, an alchemist, and Tschirnhaus, a nobleman, experimented with kaolin from the Dresden area to produce porcelain. By 1720, the factory produced a whiter hard-paste porcelain than that from the Far East. The factory experienced its golden age from the 1730s to the 1750s under the leadership of Samuel Stolzel, kiln master, and Johann Gregor Herold, enameler.

The Meissen factory was destroyed and looted by forces of Frederick the Great during the Seven Years' War (1756-1763). It was reopened, but never achieved its former greatness.

In the 19th century, the factory reissued some of its earlier forms. These later wares are called "Dresden" to differentiate them from the earlier examples. Further, there were several other porcelain factories in the Dresden region and their products also are grouped under the "Dresden" designation.

Marks: Many marks were used by the Meissen factory. The first was a pseudo-Oriental mark in a square. The famous crossed swords mark was adopted in 1724. A small dot between the hilts was used from 1763 to 1774, and a star between the hilts from 1774 to 1814. Two modern marks are swords with a hammer and sickle and swords with a crown.

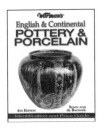

For more information, see *Warman's English & Continental Pottery & Porcelain*, 4th edition.

Dresden, chocolate cups and saucers, matching undertray, white ground, multicolored floral decoration, gilt trim, **$245**.

Photo courtesy of Wiederseim Associates, Inc.

Bowl, floral form, hand-painted floral decoration, hand-painted gilt design on border, impressed "D" mark, 10" d, 4" h, **$135**.

Photo courtesy of Alderfer Auction Co.

Dresden

Cabinet vase, 4-3/4" h, cylindrical, ruby, gold scrolling hand-painted scene of children playing, sgd "Dresden"... **800.00**

Compote, 14-1/4" h, figural, shaped pierced oval bowl with applied florets, support stems mounted with two figures of children, printed marks, late 19th/early 20th C **350.00**

Cup and saucer, hp medallion, marked "GLC Dresden" .. **150.00**

Dessert plate in frame, 8" d printed and tinted plate, scenes of courting couples, insets, and floral sprigs, gilt details, 15-3/4" sq giltwood shadowbox frame, early 20th C, set of four... **175.00**

Dresden, portrait plate, shaped rim, hp portrait of seated young woman with décolleté neckline, flowers in her hair, raised gilt beads in floral motif, gold and white floral sprays on iridescent purple ground, portrait signed "Helm," Dresden mark on back, 10-1/4" d, **$1,150**.

Photo courtesy of Alderfer Auction Co.

Figural group

5-3/4" h, 5-1/2" w, Putti charting the heavens, putto seated at table, peering through telescope, another putto studying celestial globe, ovoid base, late 19th/early 20th C, loss, crazing... **375.00**

11" h, two ladies, modeled as mischievous maidens in 18th C dress, ovoid base, early 20th C **460.00**

Loving cup, 6-1/2" h, three handles, woodland scene with nymph, gold trim............ **475.00**

Plaque, 13-1/2" x 11", molded relief of two partially nude women, flowing gowns, gilt florals, mounted in 22" x 16" glazed shadow box frame, mid 20th C, price for pr.......... **435.00**

Portrait vase, 6" h, front with oval roundel printed with portrait bust of 18th C lady, gilt floral surround, central band of beaded landscape cartouches and foliate scrolls, faux jeweled diapered ground, two short gilt flying-loop handles **635.00**

Urn, cov, 14-1/2" h, domed lid with fruit finial, body with two gilt flying-loop handles, trumpet foot on sq base, rose Pompadour ground, painted scenes of courting couples and floral bouquets, late 19th/early 20th C, price for pr, one damaged.......................... **700.00**

Vase, 13-1/4" h, alternating panels of figures and yellow floral bouquets, Thieme factory, late 19th C....................... **115.00**

Vase, cov, 14" h, alternating panels of lowers and turquoise ground floral bouquets, c1900, minor damage, pr **375.00**

Meissen

Basket, leaf form, entwined branch handle, gilt dec, over flowing polychrome porcelain blossoms, underglaze blue crossed swords mark, incised "Y5," c1847, some losses **1,725.00**

Cabinet plate, 9-5/8" d, enameled center with cupid and female in wooded landscape, gilt dec pink and burgundy border, titled on reverse "Lei Wiedergut" **490.00**

Chandelier, 23" h, baluster-form shaft with hand-painted flower and leaf motifs, similar applied motifs on white ground, six S-scroll arms with conforming applied floral dec, candle cups, suspending tassels with applied floral bouquets............... **900.00**

Clock, 18-3/4" h, Rococo style, clock face surrounded by applied floral dec, four fully molded figures representing four seasons **3,400.00**

Compote, 12" h, stemmed, reticulated two handle basket, raised polychrome flowers, porcelain stem of two semi-nude cherubs, blue cross swords mark under glad, some restoration to flowers....... **775.00**

Cup and saucer, flower-filled basket dec........................ **90.00**

Demitasse cup and saucer set, six cups and saucers with different designs, including oriental dragons, phoenix birds, and assorted flowers, each with blue underglaze blue swords mark, 18-1/4" w, 10-1/4" d, 3-3/4" h faux alligator box with crossed swords mark, box worn and damaged **500.00**

Meissen, left: plate, reticulated rim, central medallion with hand-painted scene of figural group in garden scene, pink ground, gilt accents, blue crossed swords mark, 9-7/8" d, **$1,380**; center: KPM covered cup and saucer, floral decoration with gilt highlights on bright yellow ground, blue scepter mark, 2-1/2" d cup, 4" h, 5-1/4" d saucer, **$200**; right: plate, reticulated rim, central medallion with hand-painted scene of figural group in garden scene, bright yellow ground, gilt accents, blue crossed swords mark, 9-7/8" d, **$1,500**.

Photo courtesy of Alderfer Auction Co.

Dessert service, partial, pink floral dec, gilt trim, five 8" d plates with pierced rims, two 11-1/2" h compotes with figures of boy and girl flower sellers in center of dish, pierced rims, 20th C **1,850.00**
Dinner service, partial, Deutsche Blumen, molded New Dulong border, gilt highlights, two oval serving platters, circular platter, fish platter, 8-1/2" cov tureen with figural finial, two sauce boats with attached underplates, two serving spoons, sq serving dish, two small oval dishes, cov jam pot with attached underplate and spoon, 20 dinner plates, 11 teacups and saucers, nine salad plates, 10 bread plates, 10 soups, 74-pc set **8,500.00**
Dish, cov, 6-5/8" h, female blackamoor, beside covered dish with molded basketweave and rope edge, modeled on freeform oval base with applied florets, incised #328, 20th C **575.00**
Figure
4-1/4" h, seated man holding basket of flowers and rooster, blue cross swords mark **450.00**
4-1/4" h, young girl with basket of flowers, hand painted polychrome, gilt accents, underglaze blue crossed swords mark **675.00**

5" h, Continental woman holding basket of flowers, crossed swords mark . **350.00**
5" h, cupid dressed as blacksmith, heart on anvil, shell base, hand painted polychromo, gilt accents, underglaze blue crossed swords mark **875.00**
5" h to 5-3/4" h, monkey band, all in 18th C dress, figure carrying drums, hag piper, clarinet player, harpsichordist riding another monkey, conductor, ovoid gilt accented bases, late 19th/early 20th C, losses. **5,300.00**
7" h, 5-3/4" d, five children at play with dog and lamb, hand painted polychrome, gilt accents, underglaze blue crossed swords mark, minor edge damage, repairs **1,610.00**
14-1/4" h, cockatoo, perched on tree stump, flower and leaves at base, early 20th C **2,300.00**
Mirror, 9-1/2" l, oval, heavily applied with leaves and flowers, top adorned with two cherubs supporting floral garland, Germany, c1900 .... **1,380.00**
Nodder, 7-1/8" h, Oriental gentleman, seated cross legged, nodding head, moving hands and tongue, white robe patterned with indianische blumen, gilt collar, blue slippers,

underglaze blue crossed swords mark, incised "157," gilt painter's numerals "36," mid/late 19th C **5,750.00**

Meissen, plate, central scene of battle, paneled rim with alternating geometric diapering and floral motifs, blue underglaze mark with pommels, scratches through mark, wear to gilding, 2" rim hairline, 9-5/8" d, **$165**.

Photo courtesy of Alderfer Auction Co.

Plate, wide reticulated border with polychrome decorated flowers, center with hand-painted courting scene on cobalt blue ground, crossed swords Meissen mark, 9-1/2" d, **$1,650**.

Photo courtesy of Alderfer Auction Co.

Plate, 9" d, molded with four cartouches of bunches of fruit, shaped edge with C-scroll and wings, gilt dec, late 19th C, price for pr **250.00**
Stand, 5-1/2" d, 3" h, top painted and encrusted with flowers, pierced apron dec with floral garlands, scrolled legs, underglaze blue crossed swords mark **250.00**
Tea set, partial, brown, pink, green, blue, gray, purple, and orange enameled birds in center, dragons on rim, gilt accents, seven teacups, seven 6" d saucers, nine 7" plates, 23 pcs **700.00**

Tray, 17-3/8" l, oval, enameled floral sprays, gilt trim, 20th C **400.00**

Urn on pedestal, 21" h, figural cartouches, scattered floral dec, two handles in form of pair of entwined snakes, mounted as lamps, pr **4,000.00**

Vase, cov

8-1/4" h, Schnellball, thistle shaped bodies with domed lids, encrusted with small white flowerheads, applied with flowerhead spherules, branches and birds, lid with bird and branch finials, Meissen, 20th C, price for pr **7,100.00**

13-1/2" h, facial form body, plinth of applied scrolled acanthus borders, similar dec domed lid with encrusted floral bouquets, bolted, crossed swords underglaze with star and numeral II, some losses...................... **1,380.00**

Vase, 15-1/2" h, scrolled snake handles, cobalt blue ground, gold and silver floral dec, 19th C, new gold trim to handles **2,300.00**

Wall garniture, 12-5/8" w, 19" l two-light girandole in rococo-style frame topped by putto figure, two figures of children among flowers on sides, brackets for two serpentine candle arms, two 15-1/2" w, 15-3/4" h scenic plaques with center painted scenes of bustling harbor, similar styled frames, sockets for candle arms, two 15-3/4" w, 15-3/4" h rococo-style three-light wall sconces, framed as rocaille scroll with three floral-encrusted serpentine candle arms, 19th C **3,100.00**

Wine cooler, 25" d, 9-1/2" h, exterior boldly painted with sprays of deutsche Blumen, interior with fish, insects, and vegetation, gilt-edged scalloped rim set with two handles, underglaze blue crossed swords mark **10,160.00**

DUNCAN AND MILLER

History: George Duncan, and Harry B. and James B., his sons, and Augustus Heisey, his son-in-law, formed George Duncan & Sons in Pittsburgh, Pennsylvania, in 1865. The factory was located just two blocks from the Monongahela River, providing easy and inexpensive access by barge for materials needed to produce glass. The men, from Pittsburgh's south side, were descendants of generations of skilled glassmakers.

The plant burned to the ground in 1892. James E. Duncan Sr. selected a site for a new factory in Washington, Pennsylvania, where operations began on February 9, 1893. The plant prospered, producing fine glassware and table services for many years.

John E. Miller, one of the stockholders, was responsible for designing many fine patterns, the most famous being Three Face. The firm incorporated and used the name The Duncan and Miller Glass Company until the plant closed in 1955. The company's slogan was, "The Loveliest Glassware in America." The U.S. Glass Co. purchased the molds, equipment, and machinery in 1956.

Additional Listing: Pattern Glass.

For more information, see *Warman's Glass*, 4th edition.

Animal
Heron, crystal **125.00**
Swan, 8" h, Sanibel, blue opalescent.................. **165.00**

Bowl, First Love, crystal, 11" d, scalloped **72.00**

Bud vase, First Love, crystal, 9" h **75.00**

Candlestick, Canterbury, orchid carving, 3" h **68.00**

Candy box, cov, Canterbury, crystal, three parts, 6" d.... **70.00**

Champagne
Cascade, crystal, 4-3/4" h, #17365.......................... **25.00**
Lily of the Valley, crystal **35.00**

Candlestick, Tree of Life pattern, 4" d base, 3-1/2" h, **$20**.

Cocktail
Caribbean, blue, 3-3/4 oz **45.00**
Cascade, crystal, 4-1/2" h, #17365.......................... **55.00**
Lily of the Valley, crystal **32.50**

Compote, Spiral Flutes, amber, 6" d.................................... **20.00**

Console bowl, 11" d, Rose etch, crystal **37.50**

Cordial, Cascade, crystal, #17365 .... **55.00**

Cornucopia, #121, Swirl, blue opalescent, shape #2, upswept tail **75.00**

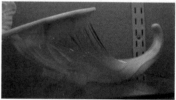

Cornucopia, opalescent white and pale blue, small feet, **$48**.

Creamer and sugar, Passion Flower, crystal **42.00**

Cup, Sandwich, crystal **9.00**

Finger bowl, Astaire, red . **65.00**

Fruit bowl, Sanibel, 6-1/2" l, pink opalescent **40.00**

Goblet, water
Caribbean, crystal **37.00**
Cascade, crystal, 6-1/4" h, #17365.......................... **25.00**
First Love, crystal, 10 oz **35.00**
Lily of the Valley, crystal **30.00**
Plaza, cobalt blue......... **40.00**
Sandwich, crystal **24.00**

Iced tea tumbler, Cascade, crystal, 6" h, #17365..... **25.00**

Juice tumbler
Lily of the Valley, crystal **28.00**
Sandwich, crystal, 3-3/4" h, ftd **12.00**

Mint tray, Sylvan, 7-1/2" l, crystal, ruby handle **35.00**
Nappy, Sandwich, crystal, two parts, divided, handle **14.00**
Oyster cocktail, Lily of the Valley, crystal **30.00**
Plate
  Canterbury, 8" d, crystal . **8.00**
  Cascade, crystal, 7" d .. **22.00**
  First Love, 8-1/2" d **25.00**
  Full Sail, amber, 8-1/2" d
  .... **18.00**
  Spiral Flute, crystal, 10-3/8" d
  .... **15.00**
  Terrace, cobalt blue, 7-1/2" d
  .... **30.00**

Teardrop pattern, relish, two parts, $12.50.

Punch cup, Caribbean, crystal, cobalt blue handle **22.00**
Relish
  First Love, three parts, #115, two handles, 10-1/2" x 1-1/4", minor wear **60.00**
  Language of Flowers, three parts, three handles, #115
  .... **37.50**
  Terrace, four parts, 9" d, crystal **55.00**
  Tear Drop, three parts, applied handle, crystal . **24.00**
Sherbet
  Canterbury, chartreuse . **15.00**
  Sandwich, crystal **20.00**
Sugar
  Caribbean, crystal **12.00**
  Tear Drop, crystal, 8 oz. **10.00**
Sugar shaker, Duncan Block, crystal **42.00**
Tray, Sanibel, 13" l, blue opalescent **125.00**
Tumbler, Chanticleer, 3 oz, crystal satin **45.00**
Vase, American Way, 9" h, flared, crystal, amber and cranberry vine dec **195.00**
Whiskey, sea horse, etch #502, red and crystal **48.00**
Wine
  Cascade, crystal, 5-1/4" h, #17365......................... **25.00**
  Lily of the Valley, crystal
  .... **30.00**
  Sandwich, crystal **24.00**

EARLY AMERICAN GLASS

History: The term "Early American glass" covers glass made in America from the colonial period through the mid-19th century. As such, it includes the early pressed glass and lacy glass made between 1827 and 1840.

Major glass-producing centers prior to 1850 were Massachusetts (New England Glass Company and the Boston and Sandwich Glass Company), South Jersey, Pennsylvania (Stiegel's Manheim factory and many Pittsburgh-area firms), and Ohio (several different companies in Kent, Mantua, and Zanesville).

Early American glass was popular with collectors from 1920 to 1950. It has now regained some of its earlier prominence. Leading auction sources for early American glass include American Bottle Auctions, Garth's, Green Valley Auctions, Heckler & Company, James D. Julia, and Skinner, Inc. A standard reference book used by early collectors as well as collectors today was written by George and Helen McKearin, *American Glass*, Crown Publishers in 1941. Many collectors and dealers refer to the "McKearin" plate numbers when describing early American glass.

Additional Listings: Cup Plates, Flasks; Sandwich Glass; Stiegel-Type Glass.

For more information, see *Warman's Glass*, 4th edition.

Bowl, Pittsburgh, 19th C, colorless, round bowl with outfolded rim, alternating cut diamond with fan and printies with blaze cutting, knopped stem on circular base, 11-1/2" d, 9-1/2" h, **$775.**

Photo courtesy of Skinner, Inc.

Bottle, 9-7/8" h, blown, half post case, colorless, copper wheel engraved flowers on all sides, larger two resembling crosshatched tulips, chipped lip **200.00**
Bowl, free-blown, deep
  5-1/4" d, 2" h, flaring folded rim, light amber, slightly domed base, rough pontil mark, American, first half 19th C **525.00**
  5-7/8" d, 1-3/8" h, concave shoulder, folded rim, amber, slightly domed base, rough pontil mark, American, mid-19th C **1,100.00**
  6" d, 4" h, slightly flaring folded rim, light ruby, domed base, rough pontil mark, American, second half 19th C **440.00**
  6-7/8" d, 3-5/8" h, slightly flaring folded rim, brilliant emerald green, slightly domed base, rough pontil mark, American, mid-19th C **1,870.00**
  7" d, 4-1/4" h, slightly concave sides, delicate folded rim, deep muddy black amber, domed base, rough pontil mark, American, first half 19th C **1,980.00**
  8-1/2" d, 3-3/4" h flaring folded rim, amber, slightly domed base, rough pontil mark, American, first half 19th C **1,650.00**
  13" d, 5" h, wide folded rim, aquamarine, slight kick-up, rough pontil mark, New York state, possibly Cleveland Glass Works, mid-19th C **880.00**
Celery vase, 9-1/4" h, Diamond Thumbprint, flint, scalloped rim, bulbous ribbed stem, round base **175.00**

Compote

4-1/8" h, 4-3/8" d rim, 3-3/8" d foot, free-blown, colorless, applied blue threading around outside of bowl, applied hollow reverse baluster stem, high domed circular foot with folded rim, rough pontil mark, American or European, late 18th/early 19th C **1,155.00**

9" h, 11-1/2" d, pressed, Diamond Thumbprint, flint, scalloped rim, bulbous ribbed stem, round base........ **230.00**

Cordial

Cordial, blown, 4-1/2" h, clear, red, dark green, and cotton twist stem **175.00**

Creamer

Creamer, 4-1/8" h, pressed, Gothic Arch, Palm, and Chain, colorless, lightly scalloped rim, molded handle, circular even scallop foot, Boston & Sandwich and others, 1835-45, chip under spout **135.00**

Cream jug

Cream jug, free-blown, 5" h, 3" d rim, 2-5/8" d foot, deep olive amber with white flecks, crude applied strap-type handle, circular foot, heavy rough pontil mark, possibly Saratoga Glass Works, first half 19th C . **1,100.00**

Decanter

7" h, 3" d base, blown molded, pint, deep olive green, slightly flaring plain lip, rayed base, rough pontil mark, Keene, NH, 1820-40, McKearin GIII-16 .... **825.00**

9-5/8" h, pressed, double Bellflower, ribbed, medium green to olive, second period **175.00**

Curtain tiebacks, amber, floriform, fittings, 3-1/2" d, **$125**.

Photo courtesy of Alderfer Auction Co.

Dish

6-1/4" x 9-1/4" x 1-5/8" h, Gothic Arch and Plume, oval, colorless, center with stippled background, plain table ring, even scallop rim, Midwestern, 1835-45, large shallow rim spall **235.00**

7" d, 1-5/8" h, Eagle, octagonal, colorless, central design of eagle with American shield surrounded by 13 stars, shoulder with three alternating designs of shields, acanthus leaves and five-point star medallions, plain even scallop rim, possibly Boston & Sandwich, 1835-45, loss of scallops, rim chipping **100.00**

Flip

Flip, etched, blown, colorless

3-7/8" h, copper wheel engraved borders of crosshatched ovals, wide fluting **295.00**

4-1/4" h, copper wheel engraved tulip in basket **350.00**

6-1/4" h, copper wheel engraved border with crosshatched ovals, three-quarter ribbing............ **400.00**

6-1/2" h, copper wheel engraved designs of four floral panels **500.00**

Hat

Hat, 2-1/8" h, 2-5/8" d rim, 1-3/4" d base, blown molded, colorless, inward folded rim, rayed base, rough pontil mark, possibly Boston & Sandwich Glass Co., 1825-35, McKearin GII-18 .... **145.00**

Crystal ball on matching stand, **$250**.

Hurricane shades

Hurricane shades, pr, 21-3/4" h, blown, colorless, baluster form, medial frosted band with wheel-etched flowering vine, circular folded foot, America, 19th C **2,235.00**

Hyacinth vase

8" h, amethyst, good color, minor wear.................. **100.00**

8-1/4" h, amethyst, added foot with folded rim, medium color, minor wear.................. **575.00**

Inkwell

Inkwell, 2" h, 2-5/8" d, blown molded, dark olive amber, 14 diamond base, rough pontil mark, Keene, NH, 1820-1840, McKearin GII-18, top and side wear **160.00**

Jar

Jar, 8-1/2" h, blown molded, olive-green, wide rim, ten panels about shoulder, eastern United States, early 19th C, minor scratches **2,115.00**

Milk pan

Milk pan, 7-1/2" d, 2-1/4" h, free-blown, flaring folded rim, deep brilliant teal, slightly domed base, small rough pontil mark, second half 19th C **470.00**

Nappy

Nappy, 6-5/8" d, 1-3/8" h, Paneled Diamond, colorless, each panel topped by fan, point, and five scallop rim, possibly Boston & Sandwich, 1828-1835, light flaking/mold roughness....... **70.00**

Pan

7-5/8" d, 1-3/4" h, free-blown, lily pad dec, flaring folded rim, brilliant light green, slightly domed base, rough pontil mark, New York, probably Redford or Redwood Glass Works, 19th C **11,000.00**

8-7/8" d, 3" h, free-blown, slightly flaring folded rim, brilliant amethyst, nearly flat base, polished pontil mark, second half 19th C **330.00**

Pitcher

Pitcher, free-blown

5" h, ftd, applied reeded handle, cobalt blue, eastern United States, early 19th C **1,200.00**

8" h, 6" d rim, threaded neck, applied strap-type handle, heavy medial rib, aquamarine, kick-up base, rough pontil mark, New York state, possibly Cleveland Glass Works, first half 19th C **3,300.00**

Plate

Plate, 7" d, 1-1/8" d, Anchor and Shield, deep olive green, Midwestern, rim chip **315.00**

Storage jar

Storage jar, 11-3/4" h, blown, olive green, flared rim, minor scratches **95.00**

Sugar bowl

Sugar bowl, cov

4-3/4" h, 4-3/8" d rim, pressed, Colonial variant, hexagonal, emerald green, polished finial, base with high scallop rim, rayed and polished underneath, mid-19th C, under rim chip on cov **660.00**

5-3/4" h, free-blown, cobalt blue, domed cov, galleried rim, ftd, eastern United States, early 19th C **1,500.00**

8-1/4" h, 4-1/4" d, rim, 3-3/4" d foot, translucent blood read bowl and stem, swirled grass green and red foot and cover, bowl slightly compressed bulbous form, galleried rim, wafer attached to hollow knop stem, lower wafer, circular foot with slight red swirls, strongly swirled boldly domed cover with applied mushroom type finial, rough pontil on both base and cov, possibly New England, mid-19th C, rim chip and flake on bowl **660.00**

Toddy plate, 4-1/4" d, Lee-Rose No. 802, fiery opalescent alabaster, 76 even scallops, 1830-45, rim chip **110.00**

Tumbler

2-1/2" h, 2-3/8" d rim, 1-3/4" d base, blown molded, taper, colorless, rayed base, rough pontil mark, probably Boston & Sandwich Glass Co., 1825-35, McKearin GII-19 ... **165.00**

3-3/8" h, 2-7/8" d, blown molded, cylindrical, colorless, rayed base, rough pontil mark, probably Boston & Sandwich Glass Co., 1825-35, McKearin GV-4 .... **275.00**

3-1/2" h, 3-3/8" d rim, nine-panel, brilliant teal, panels arched at top, American, probably New England, mid-19th C **615.00**

4-1/2" h, eight panel, ftd, translucent light starch blue, alabaster surface, third quarter 19th C **80.00**

Twine holder, 4-1/4" h, 4" d, Punty, deep red overlay cut to clear, orig metal reinforcement ring, probably New England, c1875 .... **150.00**

Vase, free-blown

7-1/2" h, 3-3/4" d rim, 2-3/4" foot, bright grass green, opal loopings, Marbrie, baluster, applied circular foot, rough pontil mark, South Jersey, second half 19th C **550.00**

11" h, 4" d rim, 4-1/4" d foot, colorless body, opal loopings, Marbrie, rolled over rim, applied triple shoulder ring, colorless applied solid stem, circular foot, rough pontil mark, Pittsburgh or New Jersey, mid-19th C... **1,155.00**

11-1/2" h, 5" d rim, 3-3/4" d foot, medium amethyst, trumpet, applied waist ring, solid plain stem, circular foot, faint pontil mark, second half 19th C **220.00**

Two vaseline glass candlesticks, 8" h, **$200**.

Photo courtesy of Joy Luke.

Water jug, 8-1/4" h, 5" d rim, 4" d base, blown molded, colorless, applied hollow handle, light horizontal rings, rayed base, rough pontil mark, Boston & Sandwich Glass Co., 1825-35, McKearin GV-17 .... **3,100.00**

Window pane, 4-7/8" x 6-7/8", Gothic Arch, colorless, six individual arches, scrolls, and rosettes above, faintly sgd "Bakewell" on revere, Pittsburgh Flint Glass Manufactory of Benjamin Bakewell, 1830-45, broken into two pcs, several edge chips **1,100.00**

Wine glass, blown molded, 3-1/4" h, 2" d, colorless, button stem, rough pontil mark, possibly Boston & Sandwich Glass Co., 1820-40, McKearin GII-19, small flake **210.00**

Wine glass, free-blown

5-3/4" h, colorless, blown ogee bowl with basal molding, fine enamel twist stem with single white opaque enamel ribbon central twist column, wide conical foot, rough pontil mark, third quarter 18th C **475.00**

6" h, colorless, plain pointed bowl with shoulder, angular knop stem, conical foot with faint pontil mark, mid-18th C **420.00**

6-3/4" h, colorless, blown twisted bowl, multiple spiral air twist stem, wide conical foot, rough pontil mark, mid-18th C **500.00**

Witch ball and stand, 4-3/4" d ball, 7-1/2" h, 4-7/8" d stand, free-blown, aquamarine, trumpet vase form stand with applied threading, circular foot with four point rough pontil mark, ball with rough open pontil mark, mid-19th C **450.00**

ENGLISH CHINA AND PORCELAIN (GENERAL)

History: By the 19th century, more than 1,000 china and porcelain manufacturers were scattered throughout England, with the majority of the factories located in the Staffordshire district.

By the 19th century, English china and porcelain had achieved a worldwide reputation for excellence. American stores imported large quantities for their customers. The special-production English pieces of the 18th and early 19th centuries held a position of great importance among early American antiques collectors.

For more information, see *Warman's Glass*, 4th edition.

Bow

Bowl, 4-1/2" d, blue trailing vine, white ground, c1770 .... **175.00**

Candlesticks, pr, two birds on flowering branches, dog and sheep on grassy base, wood stand, c1755 .... **1,200.00**

Egg cup, 2-1/2" h, two half-flower panels, powder blue ground, pseudo Oriental mark, c1760 .... **900.00**

Plate, 9" d, Turk's Cap Lily, dragonfly and moths, c1755 .... **850.00**

Adams, milk pitcher, The Farmers Arms, $85.

Bradley Pottery

Jug, 15-3/4" h, stoneware, applied in high relief with fruiting grapevine band above individually applied designs including windmill, cottage, manor house, farming implements, wheelbarrow, and wagon, all surrounding central British coat of arms, impressed to one side of shoulder "MRS. ROBERTS" and "BARRELL INN" on other side, "BAGWORTH 1849" impressed below coat of arms, inscribed under the base "Made By John Bacon At Bradley Pottery 1849" inscribed under base, hairlines, rim chip **1,300.00**

English soft paste, cups and saucers, handleless, Strawberry pattern, pink luster strawberries, green leaves, copper luster vines, set of five, **$650**.
Photo courtesy of Alderfer Auction Co.

Chelsea

Candlesticks, pr, 7-1/2" h, figural, draped putti, sitting on tree stump holding flower, scroll-molded base, encircled in puce, gilt, wax pan **850.00**
Cup and saucer, multicolored exotic birds, white ground, gold anchor mark, c1765 .... **750.00**
Plate, 8-1/2" d, multicolored floral design, scalloped rim, gold anchor mark **475.00**

Davenport

Cup plate, Teaberry pattern, pink luster **40.00**
Jug, 5-1/2" h, Jardiniere pattern, blue, orange, green, peach, and gold, peach luster rim, c1805-20 .... **450.00**
Plate, 8-1/4" d, Oriental style design similar to Gaudy Welsh Grapes pattern, orange, blue, fuchsia, green, and gilt, transfer labels on back, minor wear, set of four **350.00**
Serving bowl, cov, 7" w, 9-3/4" l, Chinoiserie Bridgeless pattern, internal bowl with steam holes, c1810 .... **700.00**
Tea service, Imari pattern, 18" l tray, teapot, creamer, cov sugar, four cups and saucers **850.00**

Allerton, milk pitcher, bulbous, white ground, dark blue transfer decoration, blue floral rim border, marked, **$175**.

Derby

Beaker, 3-1/8" h, two short shell-shaped handles, two painted landscape roundels in gilt borders, scenes titled "Near Spondon" and "Near Breadshall," both Derbyshire scenes, pale yellow ground, late 18th/early 19th C **1,265.00**
Dessert dishes, two 9-3/4" l heart-shaped dishes; 11-1/4" l navette-shaped dish; underglaze blue and iron red dec of trees and flowering vines, gilt enamel accenting, mid-19th C **400.00**

Figure, 8" h, 8-1/2" h, pastoral, boy resting against tree stump playing bagpipe, black hat, bleu-do-roi jacket, gilt trim, yellow breeches, girl with green hat, bleu-du-roi bodice, pink skirt, white apron with iron-red flowerheads, gilt centers, leaves, scroll molded mound base, crown and incised iron-red D mark, pr **2,200.00**
Jar, cov, 22" h, octagonal, iron-red, bottle green and leaf green, alternating cobalt blue and white grounds, gilding, grotesque sea-serpent handles, now fitted as lamp with carved base, 19th C, pr **10,000.00**
Plate, 10-1/8" d, enamel dec, stylized Imari-type designs of birds in three, shaped molded rim, Bloor mark, second quarter 19th C, price for set of seven **300.00**

Devon Art Pottery

Jug, 8-1/4" h, pottery, slip dec, brown and yellow glazed sgraffito designs, late 19th C **1,530.00**

Earthenware

Stirrup mug, fox head, polychrome, early 19th C, small losses to ear tips, 5" l **715.00**

Flight, Barr & Barr

Crocus pot, 9" w, 4" d, 6-1/4" h, D-form, molded columns and architrave, peach-ground panels, ruined abbey landscape reserve, gilding **2,400.00**
Pastille burner, 3-1/2" h, cottage, four open chimneys, marked, c1815 .... **425.00**
Tea service, gilt foliate, orange ground banded border, 9-1/2" h cov teapot (finial restoration), 7" l teapot stand, 4-3/4" h creamer, 4-1/2" h sugar bowl, 6-5/8" d waste bowl, two 8" deep dishes, 10 coffee cans, 11 teacups, 11 saucers, minor chips to cups and saucers, incised "B" mark, c1792-1804, light wear to gilt at rim throughout.............. **1,320.00**

Grainger

Punch bowl, 13-5/8" d, ext. enamel dec with large floral bouquets on either side of clipper ship titled above "City of Poonah," gilt inscription

"Presented by Captain James Wilson to John Carr Esq. 1839," int. with central crest of stag, floral and foliate border in green, buff and gold, c1839, int. glaze stains........................... **3,525.00**

Herculaneum

Jug, 10" h, creamware, black transfer printed, obverse "Washington," oval design with medallion portrait on monument surmounted by wreath, birth, and death dates below, flanked by eagle and grieving woman, upper ribbon inscribed "Washington in Glory," lower ribbon "America In Tears," reverse transfer of American sailing vessel, American eagle beneath spout, inscription "Herculaneum Pottery Liverpool," incised mark on base, imperfections **1,100.00**

Caughley, jug, molded cabbage leaves, mask spout, transfer-printed blue floral decoration, underglaze blue crescent mark, c1785, 8-1/2" h, **$800.**

Photo courtesy of Sloans & Kenyon Auctions.

Jackfield

Cheese dish, dome cover, black glaze, white, yellow, pink, and blue flowers, gilding, 7-1/2" h **125.00**
Creamer, 4-1/4" h, bulbous, emb grapes design, leaves, and tendrils, gilt highlights, three pr paw feet, ear-shape handle **185.00**
Pitcher, 6-1/2" h, applied handle, black, traces of enameling, bird, initials and "1763," wear, small flakes............................... **125.00**
Sugar bowl, cov, 4-1/2" h, 3-3/4" d, scalloped SS rims, SS-mounted cov and ornate pierced finial................................. **250.00**

Lowestoft

Teapot, cov, 5-1/4" h, fluted globular body, polychrome enamel dec Chinese figural courtyard scenes, 18th C, cover with small chips, hairline to interior collar **4,150.00**

Masons

Creamer, 4" h, Oriental style shape, marked "Mason's Patent Ironstone".......................... **85.00**
Jug, 8" h, octagonal, Hydra pattern, waisted straight neck, green-enameled handle, lion-head terminal, underglaze blue and iron-red flowers and vase, two imp marks and printed rounded crown mark, c1810-30 .... **320.00**
Platter, 13-1/2" x 10-3/4", Double-Landscape pattern, Oriental motif, deep green and brick red, c1883.............. **265.00**
Potpourri vase, cov, 25-1/4" h, hexagonal body, cobalt blue, large gold stylized peony blossom, chrysanthemums, prunus, and butterflies, gold and blue dragon handles, and knobs, trellis diaper-rim border, c1820-25 .... **1,750.00**

New Hall

Bowl, 5" d, Pattern 425, Window pattern, over-glaze polychrome enamels, late 18th C **350.00**
Coffeepot, cov, 9-5/8" h, Pattern 425, Window pattern, pear shape, over-glaze polychrome enamels, late 18th C **1,950.00**
Dessert dishes, set of six, each with wide pale blue ground, floral and vine relief, gilt trim, polychrome enamel dec centers, 9-1/8" l oval with basket of fruit; five 9-1/4" l ovals with landscapes; four 7-7/8" strawberry shaped, c1825, each with gilt rim wear **940.00**
Dinner service, partial, landscape transfer dec, six shaped dishes, six plates, cup, two saucers, cov sauce tureen with ladle...................... **1,100.00**
Miniature, tea set, Pattern 2720, over-glaze enamel floral bands, consisting of a 3-3/4" h cov teapot; 3-1/4" h cov sugar bowl; 2-3/8" h cream jug; four tea cups with 2-3/4" d saucers, 19th C **1,000.00**
Punch bowl, 11-1/8" d, Pattern 425, Window pattern, overglaze polychrome enamel dec, late 18th C **1,800.00**

Teapot, cov, 5-1/4" h, Pattern 425, Window pattern, oval shape, overglaze polychrome enamels, late 18th C.... **1,750.00**
Teapot stand, 6-5/8" l, Pattern 425, Window pattern, overglaze polychrome enamels, late 18th C **750.00**
Tea service, partial
    Pattern 264, gilt decorated with foliage, 6-1/2" h oval shaped cov teapot and cover; 6-3/4" l oval teapot stand; 5-5/8" h oval shaped cov sugar bowl; 4" h cream jug; 4-3/4" cov tea canister; 7-7/8" d serving dish; 8-3/8" serving dish; eight 3-1/4" d tea bowls; 10 coffee cups; seven 5" d saucers, hairlines, late 18th C **1,775.00**
    Pattern 1064, polychrome enamel dec, two 5-3/4" h cov teapots; two 7-1/2" l teapot stands; two 3-5/8" h cream jugs; 4-1/2" h rect cov sugar bowl; 5" h oval cov sugar bowl, three 6-1/2" d bowls; three 7-7/8" d shallow bowls; nine coffee cups, three tea bowls, 17 assorted teacups, 29 assorted saucers, early 19th C, chips, hairlines on many pcs................ **1,410.00**

E. Walley, plate, Scroll pattern, green, gold, pink, and dark red decoration, marked "Scroll," E. Walley printed and impressed mark, **$90.**

Rockingham

Tea set, rococo-style, each with central pale buff band, enamel decorated landscape cartouche, gilt scrolled foliate trim, 10-1/2" l cov teapot with scrolled foliate handle and serpent-form spout, rim hairline, light gilt wear to spout and handle; 4-3/8" h creamer, slight chip to side of handle; 6" h cov sugar bowl; 7-1/8" d waste bowl, c1820 .... **220.00**

Swansea

Tea set, floral pattern, underglaze blue, black transfer, gilt trim, 12 8" d plates; 11 each teacups, coffee cups, saucers; teapot; creamer; three trays; 7-1/2" d bowl, some professional repair, worn gilt, several pcs with chips and hairlines.......... **590.00**

Brownfield & Son, fish platter, center farm scene with pheasant and other game birds flying above, shaped floral border, marked "Brownfield & Son, Trademark, Woodland," registry diamond reads "Rd. No. 14058," **$125**.

Ralph Wood

Figure, pearlware

9-1/8" h shepherd and 8-3/4" h shepherdess, 18th C, mounted to lamp bases, restoration, losses.... **1,000.00**

11-1/2" h, seated herding couple, man playing pipe, lamb, goat, and dog at their feet, mounted to a lamp base, 18th C, losses, restoration **235.00**

Woods

Cup and saucer, handleless, Woods Rose...................... **65.00**

Dish, 8" l, 6" w, dark blue transfer of castle, imp "Wood" **165.00**

Jug, 5-3/4" h, ovoid, cameos of Queen Caroline, pink luster ground, beaded edge, molded and painted floral border, c1820 .... **425.00**

Plate, 9" d, Woods Rose, scalloped edge............... **125.00**

Stirrup cup, 5-1/2" l, modeled hound's head, translucent shades of brown, c1760 .... **2,200.00**

Whistle, 3-7/8" h, modeled as seated sphinx, blue accents, oval green base, c1770 .. **600.00**

Myott, platter, square, two small handles, multicolored floral decoration with gilt centers, red borders, marked "Myott Staffordshire England 2446," **$20**.

Kent, plate, transfer decoration of "Cheap" shop, red border, verse: Buy what thou hast no need of, and ere long thou wilt sell thy necessaries, At a great pennyworth pause awhile, Many are ruined by buying bargains," **$45**.

Worcester, Chamberlain's, armorial

Sauce tureen, cov, stand, pr, 15" l, 10-1/2" h, finial in form of bull's head and crown, modeled on the crest of the Marquis of Abergavenny, painted Japan pattern of flowering Oriental plants, reserves painted with arms of Admiral Lord Nevill, Marquis of Abergavenny above the motto Ne Vile Velis; red script mark, c1813................. **8,365.00**

Soup tureen, cov, stand, 15" l, 10-1/2" h, finial in form of bull's head and crown, modeled on the crest of the Marquis of Abergavenny, painted Japan pattern of flowering Oriental plants, reserves painted with arms of Admiral Lord Nevill, Marquis of Abergavenny above the motto Ne Vile Velis; red script mark, c1813............... **11,355.00**

Worcester, Dr. Wall

Cup and saucer, Oriental design, flowers, mythical animals, oriental mark in underglaze blue.............. **950.00**

Plate, 7-1/2" d, scalloped edge, Oriental design, flowers, mythical animals, oriental mark in underglaze blue.......... **850.00**

Plate, center cobalt blue flower, copper luster trim, green and pink accents, 8-1/2" d, **$65**.

ENGLISH SOFT PASTE

History: Between 1820 and 1860, a large number of potteries in England's Staffordshire district produced decorative wares with a soft earthenware (creamware) base and a plain white or yellow glazed ground.

Design or "stick" spatterware was created by a cut sponge (stamp), hand painting, or transfers. Blue was the predominant color. The earliest patterns were carefully arranged geometrics that generally covered the entire piece. Later pieces had a decorative border with a central motif, usually a tulip. In the 1850s, Elsmore and Foster developed the Holly Leaf pattern

King's Rose features a large, cabbage-type rose in red, pale red, or pink. The pink rose often is called "Queen's Rose." Secondary colors are pastels—yellow, pink, and, occasionally, green. The borders vary: a solid band, vined, lined, or sectional. The King's Rose exists in an oyster motif.

Strawberry Chinaware comes in three types: strawberries and strawberry leaves (often called strawberry luster), green featherlike leaves with pink flowers (often called cut-strawberry, primrose, or old strawberry), and relief decoration. The first two types are characterized by rust-red moldings. Most pieces have a cream ground. Davenport was only one of the many potteries that made this ware.

Yellow-glazed earthenware (canary luster) has a canary yellow ground, a transfer design that is usually in black, and occasional luster decoration. The earliest pieces date from the 1780s and have a fine creamware base. A few hand painted pieces are known. Not every piece has luster decoration.

Because the base material is soft paste, the ware is subject to cracking and chipping. Enamel colors and other types of decoration do not hold well. It is not unusual to see a piece with the decoration worn off.

Marks: Marked pieces are uncommon.

Additional Listings: Gaudy Dutch, Salopian Ware, Staffordshire Items.

Creamware

Basket, 7-1/2" x 6-1/2", 9-1/2" x 7-1/2" undertray, green trim, open sides, woven bottom, undertray with conforming pattern, reticulated border, green trim, hairline on basket side, wear on sides of underplate **950.00**
Coffeepot, cov, 10" h, pear shape, polychrome dec black transfer of Tea Party and Shepherd prints, leaf-molded spout, chips, restoration to body, attributed to Wedgwood, c1775 .... **350.00**
Jug, 5-1/8" h, reeded lapped handle, emb floral applications, sides dec with red and green floral sprays, 19th C, glaze wear, small rim nicks **260.00**
Mug, 3 1/3" h, Orange Institution, red transfer printed symbols with verse above "Holiness to the Lord" and verse below "May the Orange Institution stand as firm as the Oak and the Enemies fall off like the leaves in October," England, early 19th C **300.00**

Pitcher, 6-1/4" h, two oval reserves with black transfer printed scenes of naval engagements, "The Wasp Boarding the Frolic," sgd "Bentley, Wear, and Bourne Engravers and Printers Shelton, Staffordshire," reverse depicting "The Constitution taking the Cyane and Livant," light green ground, luster embellishments, imperfections **2,760.00**
Plate, 9-1/2" d, shaped edge, cutout floral design, unmarked, flakes on rim, price for pr **715.00**
Platter, 18" l, 14-1/2" w, oval, scallop dec rim, chips, restorations **300.00**
Sugar bowl, 5-1/8" d, 2-3/4" h, int. with red and green enamel floral dec, purple luster and underglaze blue, ext. marked "Be Canny with the Sugar" flanked by small flowers . **385.00**
Teapot
4-3/4" h, molded acanthus spout, ribbed handle, small flakes **385.00**
6-1/2" h, flower knop, floral dec entwined reeded handle with touches of gilt, rim chip, restored spout, gilt loss, 19th C **230.00**

Cup, handleless, King's Rose, pink interior band, **$75**.

King's Rose

Bowl, 7-3/4" d, Rose, broken solid border, flakes............ **55.00**
Cup and saucer, handleless
Oyster pattern, hairline cracks **40.00**
Rose, vine border **150.00**
Plate
5-5/8" d, pink border, wear **55.00**
7-3/8" d, some flaking... **90.00**
8-1/4" d, vine border, three pcs.............................. **255.00**
9-3/4" d, scalloped border, four pcs **220.00**

Pitcher, 5-5/8" h, dark red rose, blue and yellow flowers, green leaves, some wear.......... **220.00**
Soup plate, 9-1/2" d, broken solid border, scalloped edges, some flakes, three pcs.... **360.00**
Teapot, 5-3/4" h, broken solid border, some flakes **140.00**

Pearlware

Bowl
4-3/4" d, black and brown slip-filled rouletted band at rim, field of rust with blue, black, and white scroddled dots, early 19th C, repaired **940.00**
8-1/2" d, cream top band, rust, dark brown, and buff marbling, repaired...... **825.00**
Coffeepot, cov, 13" h, baluster form, dome lid, ochre, green, brown, and blue floral dec, early 19th C, imperfections ... **200.00**
Creamer, cup shape, straight sides, applied handle, light brown stripes, yellow band, gilt and light brown foliage band, slight bubbles to yellow, minor spout rim flake **125.00**
Cup and saucer, handleless, 3-1/2" d cup, 5" d saucer, black transfer scene of horse-drawn chariot, flying putti set of six **525.00**
Figure
3" l, sheep, brown, blue, and yellow ochre sponging, small edge flakes................. **275.00**
3-1/4" h, squirrel, nut and collar with ring, polychrome, orange coat, attributed to Derby, minor wear and small flakes on base **635.00**

Pearlware, figure, crying boy in white smock, square base, late 18th/early 19th C, 8" h, chips, restoration to hands, **$350**.

Photo courtesy of Sloans & Kenyon Auctions.

Jar, 12" h, cobalt blue underglaze design of wave formed by diamonds and scrolls, animal form handles, hp red and green flowers **250.00**

Jug, 4-3/4" h, barrel-form, orange, blue, green, white, medium brown, and dark brown marble slip dec, extruded handle, early 19th C, repaired **1,175.00**

Mug, 5" h, hp floral bunches, bands of brown and yellow, craquelure, hairline, chip **200.00**

Pitcher, 6-3/4" h, black transfer printed with polychrome enamel and luster dec, oval reserve depicting "a West View of the Cast Iron Bridge over the River Wear built by R. Burdon Esq.," Sailor's Farewell on reserve, sailor's verse beneath spout, rim dec with floral border, minor rim chips, staining................. **550.00**

Plate, 6-1/2" d, early depiction of Seal of US, central whimsical eagle in blue, gold, and brown, two brown rim lines **1,410.00**

Punch bowl, 9-5/8" d, 4-3/8" h, stylized floral bands on int., floral bands and central medallion on ext., polychrome enamel dec, late 19th C..................... **1,265.00**

Salt, open, 2-3/4" d, rounded form, dark brown banding, dark brown dendritic dec on rust field, narrow green glazed reeded band, early 19th C, cracked, rim chip **590.00**

Teapot, 5-3/4" h, octagonal, molded designs, swan finial, Oriental transfer, polychrome enamel, attributed to T. Harley, some edge flakes and professional repair **425.00**

Vase, 7" h, five-finger type, underglaze blue, enameled birds and foliage, yellow ochre, brown, and green, silver-luster highlights, chips and crazing, pr **500.00**

Wall plaque, 8-1/2" w, 12-1/4" l, oval, molded, polychrome dec, female Harvest figure, late 18th C, minor chip **435.00**

Queen's Rose

Cream pitcher and sugar, cov, vine border, some flakes. **250.00**

Cup and saucer, handleless, broken solid border......... **495.00**

Plate
6-1/2" d, broken solid border **50.00**

Mug, transfer decoration with Masonic theme, pink luster banding, quote: "The world's a city with many a crooked street. And death's a market place were all men meet. If life was merchandise which men could buy, the rich would live, the poor alone would die," 3-3/4" d, 4" h, wear, **$220**.

Photo courtesy of Alderfer Auction Co.

8-1/4" d, vine border, scalloped edge **85.00**
10" d, vine border **110.00**

Teapot, 5-1/2" h, pink rose, green leaves, small chips on spout and lid **150.00**

Strawberry China

Bowl, 4" d **165.00**

Cup and saucer, pink border, scalloped edge............... **225.00**

Plate **145.00**

Platter, large.................. **450.00**

Soup bowl, 8-1/4" d, red, green, pink, and yellow flower and strawberry border, basket of strawberries and roses in center **880.00**

Sugar bowl, cov, raised strawberries, strawberry knob **175.00**

Tea bowl and saucer, vine border **250.00**

Yellow Glazed

Child's mug
2-1/8" h, silver rest, foliate banding, hairline......... **175.00**
2-5/8" h, black banding with black and gray earthworm dec on green field, extruded handle with foliate terminals, impressed partial maker's mark on bottom, England, early 19th C, chips to base edge, glaze wear to rim **2,990.00**

Pitcher, 4-3/4" h, transfer dec of foliate devices, reserve of shepherd with milk maid, hand-painted dec, c1850 .... **635.00**

Sugar bowl, cov, 5-1/2" h, printed transfer of The Tea Party, fishing scene, iron-red painted rims **1,250.00**

Tea bowl and saucer, iron-red print of two cupids, marked "Sewell"...................... **250.00**

Teapot, 5-1/2" h, printed transfer of The Party, iron-red painted rims, minor hairline, spout damage **850.00**

FAIRY LAMPS

History: Fairy lamps, which originated in England in the 1840s, are candle-burning night lamps. They were used in nurseries, hallways, and dim corners of the home.

Two leading candle manufacturers, the Price Candle Company and the Samuel Clarke Company, promoted fairy lamps as a means to sell candles. Both contracted with glass, porcelain, and metal manufacturers to produce the needed shades and cups. For example, Clarke used Worcester Royal Porcelain Company, Stuart & Sons, and Red House Glass Works in England, plus firms in France and Germany.

Fittings were produced in a wide variety of styles. Shades ranged from pressed to cut glass, from Burmese to Nailsea. Cups are found in glass, porcelain, brass, nickel, and silver plate.

American firms selling fairy lamps included Diamond Candle Company of Brooklyn, Blue Cross Safety Candle Co., and Hobbs-Brockunier of Wheeling, West Virginia.

Two-piece (cup and shade) and three-piece (cup with matching shade and saucer) fairy lamps can be found. Married pieces are common.

Marks: Clarke's trademark was a small fairy with a wand surrounded by the words "Clarke Fairy Pyramid, Trade Mark."

Reproduction Alert: Reproductions abound.

Left: Fireglow, blue glass, decorated with flower, clear candle cup with ruffled rim, nick on base, **$80**; right: lighthouse, blue opaque glass, hexagonal, **$95**.

Photo courtesy of Joy Luke

3-1/2", bisque, tri-face baby girl **70.00**
3 3/4", blue satin mother-of-pearl shade, clear Clarke Fairy pyramid insert **225.00**
4", Burmese, dec shade, clear Clark's Cricklite base **900.00**
4", yellow satin swirl shade, clear S. Clark's Fairy pyramid base **150.00**
4" d, 4-1/2" h, ruby red, white loopings, matching piecrust crimped base, inclusion on shade **585.00**
4" h, ruby red Criklite, white loopings, satin dome shaped shade, clear cup mkd "S. Clarke's Patent Trade Mark" **335.00**
4-1/2", clear molded flame shade, controlled bubbles, clear S. Clarke's Fairy pyramid base **60.00**
4-1/2", figural green glass shade in shape of monk, set on frosted shoulders base **110.00**
4-1/2", metal, colored inset jewels, reticulated shade with bird designs **185.00**
5", blue satin swirl shade, matching base, ruffled top and edge **325.00**
5-1/2", green Nailsea shade, porcelain Doulton Lamplih dec base, sgd "S. Clarke's Fairy" in center **1,300.00**
5-1/2", lavender and frosted white shade, matching ruffled base, zigzag design **150.00**
5-3/4", ruby red, profuse white loopings, bowl shaped base with eight turned up scallops, clear glass candle cup holder marked "S. Clarke Patent Trade Mark Fairy" **1,250.00**
6", blue and white frosted ribbon glass dome top shade, ruffled base, clear marked "S. Clarke" insert, flakes on shade... **490.00**

6" h, white and yellow striped shade, clear S. Clarke Fairy insert, nestled on matching white and yellow ruffled base... **500.00**
6-1/4", yellow satin shade, matching ftd base, clear sgd "S. Clarke Fairy" insert **650.00**

Porcelain, hp Christmas tree decoration, clear Clarke base, Austrian, **$60**.

Photo courtesy of Joy Luke.

6-1/2", Webb, blue shade dec with bird and branch, clear Clarke's Cricklite insert, sq blue satin base **1,500.00**
7" d, 6" h, ruby red Criklite, white loopings, dome shaped shade, bowl shaped base with 26 pleats, clear glass candle cup sgd "S. Clarke Patent Trade Mark Fairy", ... **975.00**
7-1/2" d, 5-1/2" h, Burmese Criklite, dome shaped shade, pleated bowl shaped base, clear glass candle cup sgd "Clarke's Criklite Trade Mark" **1,350.00**
8" Burmese, egg-shaped shade, crystal insert, colorful porcelain bowl, stamped S. Clark's patent trademark, English trademark backstamp **1,380.00**
8-1/2" Clarke Pyramid, light, holder, and white porcelain mug, frosted shade set on finger loop base, sgd "Clarke Food Warmer," adv slogans on mug **125.00**
8-3/4", green opaque shade, gold and blue enamel dec, clear pressed glass pedestal base **275.00**

FAMILLE ROSE

History: Famille Rose is Chinese export enameled porcelain on which the pink color predominates. It was made primarily in the 18th and 19th centuries. Other porcelains in the same group are Famille Jaune

(yellow), Famille Noire (black), and Famille Verte (green).

Decorations include courtyard and home scenes, birds, and insects. Secondary colors are yellow, green, blue, aubergine, and black.

Rose Canton, Rose Mandarin, and Rose Medallion are mid- to late-19th century Chinese-export wares, which are similar to Famille Rose.

Famille Rose decoration, brush pot, quails perched on rock among flowers, China, early 20th C, Qianlong four-character mark on base, 4-3/4" d, 5-1/4" h, **$975**.

Bowl, 8" d, shallow, polychrome birds and butterflies, pink flowers, fruit, and vegetables, gilt rims, few rim chips, price for set of six **395.00**
Brush washer, 2-7/8" h, 3-5/8" d, sprays of peonies, cicada, and grass hopper on side, chi dragon in iron red and gold slithering around rim and peering into well, four-character mark in iron red on recessed base, "Jerentang Zhi," China, early 20th C **1,035.00**
Cache pot, stand, 11" l, 7-1/4" w, 6" h, clusters of flowers on plain ground, 10-1/2" l, 7-1/2" w, 1-1/2" h stand, repaired, reglued foot **1,100.00**
Charger, 12" d, central figural dec, brocade border **265.00**
Dish, cov, 11" d, figural dec, Qing dynasty **200.00**
Figure
  13" h, peacocks, pr **275.00**
  16" h, cockerels, pr..... **550.00**
Garden set, 18-1/2" h, hexagonal, pictorial double panels, flanked and bordered by floral devices, blue ground, 19th C, minor glaze loss **1,100.00**

Famille Verte decoration, covered jar, painted with Kilin within round medallions, framed by band of ruyi, overall floral decoration, round pommel lid, China, 18th C, 10" d, chips on lid rim, **$1,250**.

Urns, pair, Famille Verte, cartouches of coastal scenes, Chinese Export, c1900, 17" h urn, 35" h overall, converted to electric lamps, **$615**.

Photo courtesy of Pook & Pook.

Jar, cov, 19" h, baluster form, domed lid, ovoid finial, birds on rocky outcrop, flowering branches dec, early 20th C, price for pr **500.00**
Jardinierè, 9-3/4" h, flowering branches dec, Jiaqing **700.00**
Lamp base, 12-1/2" h, made from ginger jar, pink, orange, and purple roses and other flowers, green foliage, on base, electrified **320.00**

Mug, 5" h, Mandarin palette, Qianlong, 1790 .... **425.00**
Plate, 10" d, floral dec, ribbed body, Tongzhi mark, pr ... **275.00**
Platter, 19" l, ogee form, export, China, 18th C **1,100.00**
Pot, cov, 4-1/2" h, iron-red and gilt "JHS," cross, three swords in scalloped cartouche, "Jesus Hominum Salvator," phoenix standing on pierced rock among flowers and ducks, blue key fret base border, ruyi band on shoulder, iron-red seal on base, six-character mark, "Daoguang," China, c1821-50, minor scratches, carved wooden lid, wear to gilding **700.00**
Tray, 8" l, oval, multicolored center armorial crest, underglaze blue diaper and trefoil borders, reticulated rim, late 18th C........................ **550.00**
Tureen, 15-1/2" l, 10-1/2" h, pink roses, polychrome butterflies, birds, fruits, and gourds in shades of orange, blue, green, yellow, foliage finial, twig handles, gilt accents, orange peel glaze, minor wear to gilt, hairline in base............... **815.00**

Famille Rose, plaque, lobed, enameled cicada perched on yellow flower, China, early 20th C, 9-1/8" l, 8" w, **$125**.

Vase
  5-1/4" h, flat pear shape with pointed sides, two raised panels outlined in iron-red and gold, molded horizontal lines on body, iron-red four-character mark on base, "Shen de Tang Zhi," China, 19th C **200.00**
  9" h, underglaze blue with enameled landscape, early 20th C **1,000.00**
  9-1/4" h, pair, flowering peony and butterflies, mkd on base in square "Hongxian Nian Zhi," Chinese, early 20th C, pr **1,750.00**
  9-7/8" h, baluster, pr ... **450.00**

Famille Rose, vase, two vignettes with noble men and women, background of flowers and turquoise enamel, straight neck, China, 19th C, 13-1/4" h, dimple on one side of neck, fritting on rim, **$550**.

  10-1/2" h, diamond shape with flanged edges, landscapes and flowers, six-character Ch'ien Lung mark in red on the base, China, 19th C **1,120.00**
  23-1/2" h, birds and flowers dec, 19th C................ **450.00**
Vase, cov, 26" h, shouldered ovoid, large cartouches with scenes of warriors on horseback, dignitaries holding court, molded fu-dog handles, conforming cartouches on lid, fu-dog finial, c1850-70, pr **2,400.00**
Water dropper, 7-1/8" l, pr, molded as lotus flowers, stem forming spout, inscribed in stems with commemorative inscriptions, Guangxu, China **3,150.00**

Famille Verte

Bottle, 7-3/4" h, porcelain, enameled flowering peonies and birds, Chinese, 19th C, replaced wooden lids, price for pr **1,495.00**
Figure, 17" h, pair of cockerels, China, 19th C **1,880.00**
Ginger jar, cov, 10-1/2" h, ovoid, foo dog beside sea reserve, floral and butterfly patterned ground, Kangxi **420.00**

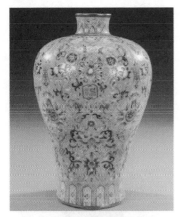

Famille Rose decoration, Meiping, painted peaches, flowers, scrolling foliage, and calligraphy, yellow ground, Chinese Jiaqing mark, Republic period, 9-1/2" h, **$3,500.**

Photo courtesy of Sloans & Kenyon Auctions.

Vase
9-1/8" h, 4-7/8" d, high relief dec, warrior on horseback riding under pine tree in mountainous landscape, base with incised Qianlong four-character mark in sq reserve, China, 18th or 19th C.. **425.00**
17-1/4" h, dec with magpies flying among prunus trees, black ground, Rouleau, China, pr **1,920.00**

FENTON GLASS

History: The Fenton Art Glass Company began as a cutting shop in Martins Ferry, Ohio, in 1905. In 1906, Frank L. Fenton started to build a plant in Williamstown, West Virginia, and produced the first piece of glass there in 1907. Early production included carnival, chocolate, custard, and pressed glass, plus mold-blown opalescent glass. In the 1920s, stretch glass, Fenton dolphins, jade green, ruby, and art glass were added.

In the 1930s, boudoir lamps, Dancing Ladies, and slag glass in various colors were produced. The 1940s saw crests of different colors being added to each piece by hand. Hobnail, opalescent, and two-color overlay pieces were popular items. Handles were added to different shapes, making the baskets they created as popular then as they are today.

Through the years, Fenton has beautified its glass by decorating it with hand painting, acid etching, and copper-wheel cutting.

Marks: Several different paper labels have been used. In 1970, an oval-raised trademark also was adopted.

Additional Listing: Carnival Glass.

For more information, see *Warman's Fenton Glass* and *Warman's Glass*, 4th edition.

Basket
Hobnail, cranberry...... **295.00**
Swirl, blue opalescent, 8-1/2", 1978............................ **125.00**
Vasa Murrhina, 8-1/2", #64327M..................... **175.00**
Bell, milk glass, #3667MI . **20.00**
Bonbon
#3937MI, milk glass, handle **17.50**
#8250 Rosalene Butterfly, two handles........................ **35.00**
Bowl
#846 Pekin Blue, cupped **40.00**
#1562 Satin etched Silvertone, oblong bowl **55.00**
#7423 Milk glass bowl, hp yellow roses.................. **65.00**
#8222 Rosalene, basketweave **30.00**
Bride's basket, Cranberry Opalescent Hobnail, 10-1/2" d bowl, 11-1/2" h SP frame. **300.00**
Bud vase, #3950MI, milk glass, 10" h **22.50**
Candlestick, single
#318 Pekin Blue, 3" h.... **40.00**
#951 Silvercrest Cornucopia **37.50**
Candy box, cov
#1980CG Daisy and Button **45.00**
#7380 Custard hp pink daffodils, Louise Piper, dated March 1975.................. **160.00**
Compote, #8422 Waterlily ftd, Rosalene **30.00**
Cocktail shaker, #6120 Plymouth, crystal.............. **55.00**

Green opaque bonbons, rear with butterflies, fruits on front, original foil labels, **$40.**

Loving cup, white carnival, two scrolling handles original label, **$65.**

Creamer
#1502 Diamond Optic, black **35.00**
#6464 RG Aventurine Green w/Pink, Vasa Murrhina ,, **45.00**
Creatures (animals and birds)
#5174 Springtime green iridized blown rabbit..... **45.00**
5193 RE Rosalene fish, paperweight **25.00**
#5197 Happiness Bird, cardinals in winter **32.50**
Cruet, #7701 QJ, 7" Burmese, Petite Floral **175.00**
Cup and saucer, #7208 Aqua Crest **35.00**
Egg, on stand
Amethyst, iridized......... **65.00**
Brown, hp roses **48.00**
Custard...................... **25.00**
Custard, hp roses......... **48.00**
Holly, milk glass, hp...... **48.00**
Epergne
#3902 Petite Blue Opal, 4" h **125.00**
#3902 Petite French Opal, 4" h **40.00**

Epergne, Diamond Lace, vaseline, **$220**.

Fairy light
#1167 RV Rose Magnolia Hobnail three pcs, Persian Pearl Crest, sgd "Shelly Fenton" **80.00**
#3380 CR Hobnail, three pcs, Cranberry Opal............. **75.00**
#8406 WT Heart, Wisteria **65.00**
#8408 VR Persian Medallion, three pcs, Velva Rose-75th Anniv. **75.00**

Ginger jar, Blue Roses, hp, blue satin **175.00**

Goblet, #1942 Flower Windows Blue **55.00**

Hat
Butterfly and Berry, green, cobalt blue rim, 3" **65.00**
Crystal Crest, milk glass, crimped rim, 4" **85.00**

Hurricane lamp, ruby, hp **125.00**

Jack in the pulpit hat
Cranberry opalescent, 4-1/2" h...................... **175.00**
Peach Crest, crimped rim, 5-1/2" h **95.00**

Jug, #6068 Cased Lilac, handled, 6-1/2"................. **50.00**

Liquor set, #1934 Flower Stopper, floral silver overlay, eight-pc set.................... **250.00**

Logo
Burmese **125.00**
Custard, hp, rect.......... **85.00**
Vaseline, FAGCA, 1980 **75.00**
Velva Rose, FAGCA, 1980 .... **75.00**

Lotus bowl, #849 Red...... **25.00**
Nappy, heart, White Crest, ruby and white **75.00**
Nut bowl, Sailboats, marigold carnival **50.00**

Pitcher
Amber Crest **115.00**
Plum Opal, Hobnail, water, 80 oz. **190.00**

Powder box, #6080, Wave Crest, blue overlay............ **85.00**

Plate
Lafayette & Washington, light blue iridized, sample **60.00**
#107 Ming Rose, 8" **30.00**
#1621 dolphin handled, Fenton Rose, 6" **25.00**

Silvercrest, dessert plates, white, original red and silver foil labels, set of four, **$85**.

Punch bowl set, Silver Crest, 15" d, 7-5/8" h ftd punch bowl, 12 4" d, 2-3/4" h cups, 12-3/4" l handle **650.00**

Rose bowl, #8954TH hanging heart................................. **95.00**

Salt and pepper shakers, pr, #3806 Cranberry Opal, Hobnail, flat **47.50**

Sherbet
#1942 Flower Windows, crystal **35.00**
#4443 Thumbprint, Colonial Blue **20.00**

Spittoon, Peking Blue, 7" d, 4-1/2" h............................ **65.00**

Sugar and creamer, #9103 Fine Cut & Block (OVG).......... **20.00**

Temple jar, #7488 Chocolate Roses on cameo satin **25.00**

Tumbler
#1611 Georgian, Royal Blue, 5-1/2", ftd, 9 oz **18.00**
#3700, Grecian Gold, grape cut............................... **15.00**
#3945MI Hobnail, 5 oz . **10.00**

Tumble-up, Blue Swirl, 8" h, 5-1/2" w, applied handle, c1939 .... **900.00**

Vase
Blue Ridge, bulb shape, milk glass, plain rim, 5" h **85.00**
Hobnail, blue opalescent, 5-1/2" h **80.00**

#3004, bulbous shouldered body, everted rim, two applied cobalt blue irid handles, Karnak Red, hanging heart dec, 9-1/2" h **6,000.00**

Vase, Egyptian Mosaic, shape No. 3024, urn form, blue disk base, inlaid multicolored mosaic pattern, blue threading, original paper label "2024, vase mosaic inlaid," 1925, 8-1/2" h, **$2,000**.

Photo courtesy of Skinner, Inc

Vase, Rose Overlay, #192A, tri-crimp, c1948, 8-1/2" h, **$30**.

#3759 Plum Opal, Hobnail, swung **150.00**

#5858 Wild Rose, wheat **85.00**

#7547 Burmese, hp pink Dogwood, 5-1/2" h........ **75.00**

Water pitcher, 8-1/2" h, custard, hand-painted fall scene with red barn, chickens, rooster, birds flying, sgd "Jan Curtis," applied ribbed handle **395.00**

Water set, Blue Opalescent, 8-1/4" h cannonball-shaped pitcher, six 5" h tumblers. **550.00**

FIESTA

History: The Homer Laughlin China Company introduced Fiesta dinnerware in January 1936 at the Pottery and Glass Show in Pittsburgh, Pennsylvania. Frederick Rhead designed the pattern; Arthur Kraft and Bill Bensford molded it. Dr. A. V. Bleininger and H. W. Thiemecke developed the glazes.

The original five colors were red, dark blue, light green (with a trace of blue), brilliant yellow, and ivory. A vigorous marketing campaign took place between 1939 and 1943. In mid-1937, turquoise was added. Red was removed in 1943 because some of the chemicals used to produce it were essential to the war effort; it did not reappear until 1959. In 1951, light green, dark blue, and ivory were retired and forest green, rose, chartreuse, and gray were added to the line. Other color changes took place in the late 1950s, including the addition of a medium green.

Fiesta ware was redesigned in 1969 and discontinued about 1972. In 1986, Homer Laughlin China Company reintroduced Fiesta. The new china body shrinks more than the old semi-vitreous and ironstone pieces, thus making the new pieces slightly smaller than the earlier pieces. The modern colors are also different in tone or hue, e.g., the cobalt blue is darker than the old blue.

Reproduction Alert.

For more information, see *Warman's Fiesta Ware*, and *Warman's American Pottery & Porcelain*, 2nd edition.

Ashtray
Ivory	55.00
Red	60.00
Turquoise	50.00
Yellow	48.00
Bowl, 5-1/2" d, green	**60.00**
Cake plate, green	**1,950.00**
Candlesticks, pr, bulb	
Cobalt blue	**125.00**

Homer Laughlin has produced some new colors in their popular Fiesta pattern. It's important for collectors to understand when different colors were made.

Color Name	Color palette	Years of Production
Red	Reddish-orange	1936-43 1959-72
Blue	Cobalt blue	1936-51
Ivory	Creamy yellow-white	1936-51
Yellow	Golden yellow	1936-69
Green	Light green	1936-51
Turquoise	Sky blue	1937-69
Rose	Dark dusky rose	1951-59
Chartreuse	Yellow-green	1951-59
Forest green	Dark hunter green	1951-59
Gray	Light gray	1951-59
Medium green	Deep bright green	1959-69
Antique gold	Dark butterscotch	1969-72
Turf green	Olive green	1969-72
Cobalt blue	Very dark blue, almost black	1986-
Rose	Bubblegum pink	1986-
White	Pearly white	1986-
Black	High gloss black	1986-
Apricot	Peach-beige	1986-98
Turquoise	Greenish-blue	1988-
Yellow	Pale yellow	1987-2002
Periwinkle blue	Pastel gray-blue	1989-
Sea mist green	Pastel light green	1991-
Lilac	Pastel violet	1993-95
Persimmon	Coral	1995-
Sapphire (Bloomingdale's exclusive)	Blue	1996-97
Chartreuse	More yellow than green	1997-99
Pearl gray	Similar to vintage gray, more transparent	1999-2001
Juniper green	Dark blue-green	1999-2001
Cinnabar	Brown-maroon	2000-
Sunflower	Bright yellow	2001-
Plum	Rich purple	2002-
Shamrock	Grassy green	2002-
Tangerine	Bright orange	2003-

Ivory	125.00
Red	120.00
Turquoise	110.00

Candlesticks, pr, tripod, yellow
.... 550.00

Carafe

Cobalt blue	495.00
Ivory	385.00

Casserole, cov, two handles, 10" d

Ivory	195.00
Red	200.00
Yellow	160.00

Cereal bowl, orange, **$35.**

Photo courtesy of Sky Hawk Auctions.

Chop plate, 13" d, gray **95.00**

Coffeepot

Cobalt blue	235.00
Ivory	390.00
Red	250.00
Turquoise	250.00
Yellow	185.00

Compote, 12" d, low, ftd

Cobalt blue	175.00
Ivory	165.00
Red	185.00
Turquoise	160.00
Yellow	165.00

Creamer

Cobalt blue	35.00
Ivory	30.00
Red	65.00
Turquoise	24.00
Yellow	30.00

Creamer and sugar, figure-eight server, yellow creamer and sugar, cobalt blue gray ... **315.00**

Cream soup bowl

Cobalt blue	60.00
Ivory	55.00
Red	65.00
Turquoise	48.00
Yellow	45.00

Cup, ring handle

Cobalt blue	35.00
Ivory	30.00
Red	30.00
Turquoise	25.00
Yellow	25.00

Demitasse cup, stick handle

Cobalt blue	75.00

Ivory	80.00
Red	85.00
Turquoise	75.00
Yellow	65.00

Demitasse pot, cov, stick handle

Cobalt blue	650.00
Ivory	535.00
Red	575.00
Turquoise	650.00
Yellow	465.00

Dessert bowl, 6" d

Cobalt blue	50.00
Ivory	45.00
Turquoise	40.00
Yellow	40.00

Dinner plate, ivory, **$15.**

Egg cup

Cobalt blue	75.00
Ivory	72.00
Red	80.00
Turquoise	55.00
Yellow	70.00

Fruit bowl, 5-1/2" d

Ivory	33.00
Turquoise	25.00
Yellow	25.00

Fruit bowl, 11-3/4" d, cobalt blue **485.00**

Gravy boat

Cobalt blue	75.00
Ivory	65.00
Red	85.00
Turquoise	45.00
Yellow	50.00

Juice tumbler

Cobalt blue	40.00
Rose	65.00
Yellow	40.00

Marmalade jar, cov

Cobalt blue	335.00
Ivory	325.00
Red	345.00
Turquoise	325.00
Yellow	250.00

Mixing bowl

#1, 5" d, red	375.00
#2, cobalt blue	195.00
#2, yellow	140.00
#4, green	195.00

Fruit bowls, gray, **$45**; two yellow, **each** **$28**; chartreuse, **$45**, all 5-1/2" d.

#5, ivory	275.00
#7, ivory	580.00

Mixing bowl lid, #1, red
.... **1,100.00**

Mug

Dark green	90.00
Ivory, marked	125.00
Rose	95.00

Mustard, cov

Cobalt blue	325.00
Turquoise	275.00

Nappy, 8-1/2" d

Cobalt blue	55.00
Ivory	55.00
Red	55.00
Turquoise	42.00
Yellow	45.00

Nappy, 9-1/2" d

Cobalt blue	65.00
Ivory	65.00
Red	70.00
Turquoise	55.00
Yellow	60.00

Onion soup, cov, turquoise
.... **8,000.00**

Pitcher, disk

Chartreuse	275.00
Turquoise	110.00

Pitcher, ice lip

Green	135.00
Turquoise	195.00

Plate, deep

Gray	42.00
Rose	42.00

Plate, 6" d

Dark green	15.00
Ivory	7.00
Light green	9.00
Turquoise	8.00
Yellow	5.00

Plate, 7" d

Chartreuse	12.00
Ivory	10.00
Light green	8.50
Medium green	30.00
Rose	14.00
Turquoise	8.50

Plate, 9" d

Cobalt blue	15.00
Ivory	14.00
Medium green	75.00
Red	15.00
Yellow	13.00

Plate, 10" d, dinner
Gray 42.00
Light green 28.00
Medium green 125.00
Red 35.00
Turquoise
.... 30.00
Platter, oval
Gray 35.00
Ivory 25.00
Red 45.00
Yellow 22.00
Relish
Ivory base and center,
turquoise inserts 285.00
Red, base and inserts 425.00
Salad bowl, large, ftd
Cobalt blue 375.00
Red 460.00
Turquoise 335.00
Yellow 400.00
Salt and pepper shakers, pr
Red 24.00
Turquoise 135.00
Saucer
Light green 5.00
Turquoise 5.00

Soup plate, turquoise, $30.

Soup plate
Ivory 36.00
Turquoise 29.00
Sugar bowl, cov
Chartreuse 65.00
Gray 75.00
Rose 75.00
Syrup
Green 450.00
Ivory 600.00
Red 695.00
Sweetmeat compote, high
standard
Cobalt blue 95.00
Ivory 85.00
Red 100.00
Turquoise 125.00
Yellow 400.00
Tea cup, flat bottom, cobalt blue
.... 100.00

Teapot, cov
Cobalt blue, large 335.00
Red, large 245.00
Rose, medium 350.00
Tumbler, cobalt blue 75.00

FINE ARTS

History: Before the invention of cameras and other ways to mechanically capture an image, paintings, known as portraits, served to capture the likeness of an individual. Paintings have been done in a variety of mediums and on varying canvases, boards, etc. Often it was what was available in a particular area or time that influenced the materials. Having one's portrait painted was often a sign of wealth and many artists found themselves in demand once their reputations became established. Today art historians, curators, dealers, and collectors study portraits to determine the age of the painting and often use clues found in the backgrounds or clothing of the sitter to determine age, if no identification is available. Many portraits have a detailed provenance that allows the sitters, and often the artists, to be identified.

In any calendar year, tens, if not hundreds of thousands, of paintings are sold. Prices range from a few dollars to millions. Since each painting is essentially a unique creation, it is difficult to compare prices.

The sampling in this edition concentrates on landscapes.
Boel, John Henry, British, 19th-20th C, Angling Amongst the Lilly Pads, oil on canvas, sgd with intertwinsed "J.H. Boel" lower right, dated 1892, 30" x 20"
.... 2,415.00
Brown, Aimee D., American, July Corn, oil on canvas, sgd lower right, 24" x 20" 350.00
Cone, Marvin, American, 1893-1965, Fall Landscape, 1923, oil on canvas, sgd lower right "Marvin D Cone," dated 1923, 32" x 38" 103,500.00
Dodge, Francis, American, 1878-, Landscape with Stone Wall, sgd lower left "F. Dodge," 20" x 16" 410.00

Charles Chaplin, French, 1825-1891, attributed, seated young lady wearing white dress, pink ribbons, blowing bubbles, oil on canvas, 16" x 12-1/2", **$1,610**.
Photo courtesy of Pook & Pook.

Charles Chase Emerson, American, 1874-1922, portrait of Ludwig Frank, signed "Chase Emerson" lower left, identified on reverse, oil on canvas board, 22" x 16-1/4", framed, varnish inconsistencies, **$360**.
Photo courtesy of Skinner, Inc.

Dzigurski, Alexander, American, 1911-1995, Quiet Waters, oil on canvas, sgd lower right "A. Dzigurski, 1950 Italy," 23-3/4" x 30" 1,725.00
English, Frank F., American 1854-1922
Along the River, watercolor on paper, sgd lower left, 20" x 13"
.... 1,035.00
Farmscape with Sheep, watercolor, sgd lower right, 13" x 20" 1,380.00
Finck, F., American, 19th C, Snowbound, oil on canvas, sgd lower right, dated "93", 18" x 14" 520.00
Fredericks, Ernest T. (F. Swedlun), American, 1877-1950s, Rolling Hills in Autumn, oil on canvas, sgd lower right, 36" x 24" 300.00

Gay, George Howell, American, 1858-1931, Early Spring, watercolor on paper, sgd lower left, 13" x 31" **750.00**

Clarence I. Dreisbach, titled "Jingle Bells," winter scene with horse drawn sleigh, oil on canvas, signed lower left, 20" x 24", **$4,600**.

Photo courtesy of Alderfer Auction Co.

Grimm, Paul, American, 1892-1974, Delightful Region, oil on canvas, sgd lower left, titled on verse, 30" x 24" **5,060.00**

Grose, Daniel Charles, American 1838-1890, Autumn-Hudson River Valley, oil on canvas, sgd lower right "D. C. Grose," dated '87, 12" x 8" **865.00**

Grover, Oliver Dennitt, American, 1861-1927, Grinnel Mountain Lake McDermott, Montana, oil on canvas, sgd lower left, dated 1924, 30" x 24" **3,450.00**

Hare, John Cathbert, American, 1908-1978, Autumn the Connecticut Valley, oil on canvas, sgd lower right, title inscribed on stretcher, 20" x 16" **920.00**

Held, Alma, Amercican, 1898-1988, Early Fall, oil on canvas, sgd lower left, verso with exhibition label, c1924, 18" x 24" **1,100.00**

Kilbert, Robert, American, 1880-1945
  Autumn Landscape, oil on canvas, sgd lower right, 10" x 14"............................... **460.00**
  Forest Interior with Stream, oil on board, sgd lower right, 18" x 22" **1,150.00**

Kinnear, Joseph, British, 1858-1917, Glen Groe, oil on paper laid down on wood panel, sgd lower left, verso inscribed Glen Groe," 10" x 14", unframed **435.00**

Knab, Frederick, American, 1873-1918, Autumn Landscape, oil on canvas, sgd lower right "Fr. Knab," 26" x 20" **460.00**

Kotz, Daniel, American, 1848-1933, The Forest Brook, pastel on board, sgd lower left, 18" x 25"................................... **420.00**

Lamb, Adrian, American, 1901-, Landscape with Scattered Clouds, oil on board, sgd lower right, 13-3/4" x 11-1/2"..... **375.00**

Milleson, Royal H., America, 1849-1926, Fall Landscape with Distant Village, oil on canvas, sgd lower left, 20" x 24" **1,265.00**

Nielson, Arthur, Danish, 1883-1946, The Road in the Farm, oil on canvas, sgd lower right, 20" x 26-1/4" **750.00**

Nisita, Carlo Antonia, American, Wooded Landscape, oil on artist board, sgd lower right, 10" x 14" **460.00**

Podchernikov, Alexis Matthew, American, 1896-1933, Dunes in Blooms, oil on board, sgd lower left, 21" x 17" **3,680.00**

Sartelle, Herbet, American, 1885-1955, California Mountain Glow, oil on canvas, sgd lower right, 24" x 30" **1,610.00**

C. J. White, folk style landscape, foreground with farm buildings, human and animal figures, pond with waterfall, horse and buggy on bridge, oil on masonite, signed lower right, 18" x 24", **$175**.

Photo courtesy of Alderfer Auction Co.

Shepard, Clarence E., American, 1869-1949, Autumn Landscape with Bridge, oil on canvas, sgd lower right, dated 1930, 27" x 22" **635.00**

Steiner, 24" h, 33" w, oil on canvas, Swiss alpine scene of mountain village, restored, rebacked on canvas, 35" h, 45" w frame with gold repaint and minor damage **450.00**

W. R. Waters, portrait of child wearing burgundy velvet dress, lace collar, straw hat, holding riding crop, leaning against St. Bernard type dog, oil on canvas, signed and dated lower right "W. R. Waters, 1851," 34" x 44", relined, minor scratching, paint loss, **$7,475**.

Photo courtesy of Alderfer Auction Co.

FIREARM ACCESSORIES

History: Muzzle-loading weapons of the 18th and early 19th centuries varied in caliber and required the owner to carry a variety of equipment, including a powder horn or flask, patches, flints or percussion caps, bullets, and bullet molds. In addition, military personnel were responsible for bayonets, slings, and miscellaneous cleaning equipment and spare parts.

During the French and Indian War, soldiers began to personalize their powder horns with intricate engraving, in addition to the usual name or initial used for identification. Sometimes professional horn smiths were employed to customize these objects, which have been elevated to a form of folk art by some collectors.

In the mid-19th century, cartridge weapons replaced their black-powder ancestors. Collectors seek anything associated with early ammunition—from the cartridges themselves to advertising material. Handling old ammunition can be extremely dangerous because of decomposition of compounds. Seek advice from an experienced collector before becoming involved in this area.

Reproduction Alert: There are a large number of reproduction and fake powder horns. Be very cautious!

Notes: Military-related firearm accessories generally are worth more than their civilian counterparts.

Calendar, 1918, Marble Arms & Mfg Co., artwork by Philip R. Goodwin, top image of two hunters, one with gun raised at animal across river, bottom image with man by campfire, docked canoe.............. **5,230.00**
Canteen, 7" d, 2-5/8" deep, painted, cheese-box style, dark red paint overall, one side painted gold with a large primitive eagle with shield breast, the top of the shield red with cream lettering "No. 37," other side painted in gold letters,

"Lt. Rufus Cook," pewter nozzle, sq nail construction, strap loops missing....................... **1,650.00**
Cartridge board, 22" x 25", Winchester, New Haven, CT, 1874, showing range of rimfire cartridges, wood frame, some shelf spoiling, corner repair to frame........................ **12,915.00**
Cartridge box
3-7/8" x 2" x 1", Hall and Hubbard, .22 caliber, green and black label "100 No. 1/22-100/Pistol Cartridges," cov with molded cream and black paper, empty, missing about half green side label... **300.00**
4" x 2-1/8" x 1-1/4", Union Metallic Cartridge Co., .32 caliber, cream and black label "Fifth .32 caliber/No. 2/Pistol Cartridges," engraving of Smith & Wesson 1st Model 3rd Issue, checked covering, orange and black side labels, unopened **210.00**

Catalog
Colt's-The Arm of Law and Order, 5-3/4" x 7-3/4", 42 pgs, black and white illus and specifications of 16 models of Colt revolvers and automatic pistols **25.00**
Savage Arms Corp., Chicopee Falls, MA, 1951, 52 pgs, 8-1/2" x 11", No. 51, *Component Parts Price List for Savage, Stevens, Fox Shotguns & Rifles* **35.00**
Winchester Repeating Arms, New Haven, CT, 1918, 215 pgs, 5-1/2" x 8-1/2", Cat No. 81, illus of repeating and single-shot rifles, repeating shotguns, cartridges, shells, primers, percussion caps, shot........................... **250.00**

Flasks, top: gutta percha with brass trim, **$90**; bottom: brass, embossed scrolls, **$125**.

Photo courtesy of Dotta Auction Co., Inc.

Flask, 8" l, brass, dead game, emb, stamped "Am. Flask & Cap Co." **200.00**
Knapsack, 13-5/8" x 13-1/4", painted canvas, flap having American eagle with shield among stars and surrounded by oval cloud border, scrolled banner inscribed "RIFLE CADET," painted in red, white, blue, and gold on black ground, two leather strap and iron buckles, reverse with ink inscription, "Benjamin Pope Bridgewater July 4th 1820," minor paint losses, wooden hanger and twine attached to the back **31,725.00**
Poster, store type, 41-1/2" x 32", Winchester Rifles, Shotguns and Ammunition For Sale Here, two bear dogs in foreground, bloodhounds in back... **6,300.00**
Powder horn, engraved
10-1/2" h, America, c1823, incised animal figures, scallop, and linear borders on butt end, inscribed "M RIFLE COMP'Y 1823/ horne" next to the initials "AM," wood plug with applied wire staple for carrying strap, carved wooden stopper **450.00**
14-1/8" l, Providence, RI, c1858, inscribed "JOB WATERMAN HIS HORN/ CALEB HARRIS/FEB y THE 10 AD 1758/ PROVIDENCE" in four circular or lobed reserves, applied silver plated brass mouthpiece, copper band around butt rim, leather band with woven twill strap sewn to nook **900.00**
16" l, John Goddard, late 18th C, incised dec, borders of wave-like and compass motifs, scene with figure driving horse and carriage with gun overhead and dog, sgd "JOHN GODDARD," indistinct date 1747 or 1777, butt end with extension lobe pierced for carrying strap, pine plug **1,175.00**
16-1/2" l, engraved "Robert Guy's Horn" down side, smaller engraving near spout, dated "1840," domed pine plug, flared end for carrying strap, hole 1" above name **250.00**
18" l, engraved, initialed "Wm M. 1799," also "J. M. 1814," surrounded by series of inscribed circles, flat pine plug **1,200.00**

18" l, engraved, "stil not this horn for fear of shame for hear doth stand the oner name jacob lewis 1785, (sic)" two rows of geometric devices round bottom, carved and incised lines at spout, dome-shaped wooden plug, America, late 18th C, small age crack, wear....... **1,610.00**

Primer, 7" l, engraved, New York scene, primitively engraved men and animals, date "1852" added later, c1800 .... **1,155.00**

Miniature powder horn, silver metal, panels of hp hunting scenes, hinged lid painted with stag in wooded setting, stylized fish finial, fitted with two metal loops, some loss to paint, chain or cord missing, 5-1/2" l, **$980**.

Photo courtesy of Alderfer Auction Co.

Powder horn, marked "Richard John Banister, Ship Cove, His Horn April 1878," depiction of ship, 10" l, **$350**.

Photo courtesy of Alderfer Auction Co.

Product leaflet

Western Silvertip Ammunition, 3-1/2" x 6" closed, glossy paper, color printing, diecut upper corner, one side shows 18 variations of brass cartridges in differing gauges for large game hunting, one panel devoted to three Winchester hunting rifles, 1956............................... **25.00**

Western-Winchester, 3-1/4" x 6-1/2" closed, full color printing, illus and describes western Super-X and Xpert shotgun shells and cartridges, 1957 .... **15.00**

Shotgun box, empty

Austin Cartridge Co., Crack-Shot, 16 gauge, full-color scene of three hunting dogs on front.................... **2,310.00**

Chamberlin Cartridge Co., 12 gauge, Blue Rocks .. **1,100.00**

Clinton Cartridge Co., Pointer Brand, 12 ga, smokeless powder, pointer in center with bird in mouth, light blue top and lettering, gold border, red ground, 4-1/8" x 4-1/8" x 2-1/2" **350.00**

J. F. Schmelzer & Sons Arms Co., 12 gauge carver cartridges, illus of hunter and pointed on front **1,750.00**

Peters Quick Shot, 12 gauge shotgun shells **5,835.00**

Robin Hood Eclipse Cartridge, 12 gauge, near smokeless powder shells **2,550.00**

Sign, 36" x 30", Winchester Guns and Ammo, guns and dead game image by Alexander Pope, tin litho, wood structural backing, dark green background **1,300.00**

Tin, Oriental Smokeless Gunpowder, half pound, four litho labels with full-color ducks **1,810.00**

Tinder box, 4-3/8" d, tin, candle socket, inside damper, flint, and steel **330.00**

Tinder lighter, flintlock
5-1/2" l, rosewood pistol grip, tooled brass fittings **750.00**
6-1/2" l, compartment for extra flint, taper holder **550.00**

Water keg, 9" x 7-1/2" x 9", wooden, American, late 18th/early 19th C, oval, flattened bottom, two Shaker-style wide-tongued wooden straps, large hand-forged nail on each end for carrying cord, orig wood stopper **400.00**

FIREARMS

History: The 15th-century Matchlock Arquebus was the forerunner of the modern firearm. The Germans refined the wheelock firing mechanism during the 16th and 17th centuries. English settlers arrived in America with the smoothbore musket; German settlers had rifled arms. Both used the new flintlock firing mechanism.

A major advance was achieved when Whitney introduced interchangeable parts into the manufacturing of rifles. Refinements in firearms continued in the 19th century. The percussion

ignition system was developed by the 1840s. Minie, a French military officer, produced a viable projectile. By the end of the 19th century, cartridge weapons dominated the field.

Notes: Two factors control the pricing of firearms—condition and rarity. Variations in these factors can cause a wide range in the value of antique firearms. For instance, a Colt 1849 pocket-model revolver with a five-inch barrel can be priced from $100 to $700, depending on whether all the component parts are original, some are missing, how much of the original finish (bluing) remains on the barrel and frame, how much silver plating remains on the brass trigger guard and back strap, and the condition and finish of the walnut grips.

Be careful to note a weapon's negative qualities. A Colt Peterson belt revolver in fair condition will command a much higher price than the Colt pocket model in very fine condition. Know the production run of a firearm before buying it.

Laws regarding the sale of firearms have gotten stricter. Be sure to sell and buy firearms through auction houses and dealers properly licensed to transact business in this highly regulated area.

BB gun, Marx, Marksman Repeater, as found condition, **$150**.

Carbine

Hall-North, Model 1843, percussion, .52 caliber, rifled 21" barrel, bold metal stampings, signature and 1849 on receiver, traces of old brown finish, walnut stock with old split between trigger guard and barrel, small repairs near breech, 40" l.................... **935.00**

Joslyn Model 1862, .52 caliber, 22" round barrel, walnut stock, clear inspector's markings, brass buttplate, trigger guard and barrel band, stamped signatures on lock and breech block, 38-5/8" l **650.00**

C. S. Richmond, .58 caliber, 25" barrel, all-steel hardware, brass nose cap, butt plate stamped "U.S.," Type 3, humpback lock, "C. S. Richmond, 1864" mark, no sling swivels, 43" l **3,300.00**

Sharp's New Model 1863, breech loading, walnut stock and forearm, double inspectors markings, 22" blued barrel, areas of very light case coloring on lock, butt plate, hammer, barrel band, and receiver, clear stampings on lock, 34" l **1,980.00**

Spencer, Civil War Model, .52 caliber rimfire, 22" round barrel, overall brown finish on all metal surfaces, worn walnut stick, faint inspector's mark, forearm with additional coat of varnish, 39" l **2,100.00**

Dueling pistols, percussion, Continental, early 19th C, each with fine carving, engraved hunting dogs and stag on lock mechanism, engraved gilt trigger guard and butt plate, original mahogany case, some patches, some cracking to box, 16" l, **$3,200**.

Photo courtesy of Wiederseim Associates, Inc.

Pistols, box closed, **$3,200**.

Photo courtesy of Wiederseim Associates, Inc.

Dueling pistols, percussion, each with fine carving, engraved locks, gilt lettering "Nouvelle jne a Angouleme," 16-1/2" l, walnut fitted box with tools, **$4,025**.

Photo courtesy of Wiederseim Associates, Inc.

Springfield, Model 1884 Trapdoor, saddle ring, mint bore, Buffington sight, stamped "C. Proper," range with inspector's cartouche......................... **825.00**

Wesson, Frank, 28" octagonal barrel, folding rear peep sight, walnut stock with orig dark finish, rear open sight missing, 43" l overall **275.00**

Dueling pistols,

percussion lock

English, London, second quarter 19th C, dolphin hammer, belt clip, engraved scrollwork on frame, checkered burl-wood grip, barrel engraved "London," 8-1/2" l, price for pr **650.00**

English, Queen-Anne style, London, for J. Wilson, late 18th C, scrolled mask butt, grip set with small monogrammed cartouche, plain stylized dolphin hammer, cannon barrel engraved with cartouches, and maker's mark on underside, 8" l, price for pr **500.00**

Flintlock long arms

Brooks, Cecil, Jager, custom, figured walnut stock with relief carved acanthus leaves on either side of comb, also around cheek piece and entry pipe, metal surfaces finished bright, good amount of engraving, inlaid signature plate on 25-3/4" l octagonal swamped barrel, sliding lid patch box with ivory inlaid panel, scrimshaw hunting scene, large variegated stray inlay on cheek piece, 41-1/2" l **4,600.00**

Buchele, W., Bicentennial, curly maple stock, relief carved bust of George Washington with flag behind cheek piece along with acanthus leaves on either side of comb, brass hardware including engraved patch box with eagle finial, applied Liberty Bell, twelve inlays along with brass and nickel silver floral wire inlay, 58-1/2" l **3,500.00**

Cooper, J, lock sgd "J. Cooper," engraved detail, brass hardware including patch box, curly maple stock with nickel silver escutcheons, thumb piece with faint checkering, 38-1/2" l octagonal barrel turned found for bayonet on last 3" with lug, conversion to flint with pieced repair to forend and other replacements, 54-1/2" l... **950.00**

French, Model 1766 Charlesville Musket, 44-3/4" l orig barrel length, lock plate only partially legible, matching ramrod, top jaw and top screw period replacements **1,250.00**

Golcher, Joseph, Philadelphia, PA, c1800, .54 caliber, octagonal barrel, brass patch box, butt plate, trigger guard, carved and brass-fitted pick compartment, brass and silver inlays along tiger maple stock, lock plate marked, barrel initialed, 54" l, 38-1/2" l **4,750.00**

Flintlock pistol, Continental, 18th C, proof marks, 14-1/2" l, **$1,760**.

Photo courtesy of Wiederseim Associates, Inc.

Kentucky, R. E. Leman, cal. 38, 37-3/8" oct. bbl with small brass front sight and fixed rear sight, top flat in front of chamber area is marked "R.E. LEMAN/ LANCASTER PA/WARRANTED," unmarked flat lock plate, applied grain tiger striped stock, simple brass trigger guard, two-pc patch box with crescent butt plate and dbl. set triggers, ovoid forestock with integral ramrod groove and two small brass guides, dark heavy patina on iron and wood **920.00**

Pennsylvania, attributed to W. Haga, Reading School, 50-1/2" l octagon to round barrel, maple stock, relief carving, incised details, brass hardware with flintlock, some age cracks, glued repair, good patina, replaced patch box lid **1,760.00**

U. S. Model 1819, Hall, breech loading, second-production type, Harpers Ferry Armory, John Hall's patents, .52 caliber, single shot, 32-5/8" round barrel, three barrel bands, breechblock deeply stamped **1,200.00**

Virginia, curly-maple stock with good figure, relief carving, old mellow varnished finish, brass hardware, engraved and pierced patch box, Ketland lock reconverted back to flint, silver thumb piece inlay, 41-1/2" l barrel and fore-end shortened slightly, small pierced repair at breech area, top flat engraved "H. B." **3,300.00**

Flintlock pistols-single shot
English

Blunderbuss, 29-1/2" overall, 14" round iron barrel with Birmingham proofs, fitted with 12-1/2" triangular snap bayonet, walnut full stock with lightly engraved brass furniture, two ramrod pipes, butt plate,

trigger guard, small shield-shaped wrist plate, two lock-plate screw escutcheons, attributed to John Whitehouse, early 19th C, metal parts complete and orig throughout, missing sliver of wood along right side at muzzle ... **1,500.00**

Tower, .60 caliber, 12" round barrel, full-length military stock, brass trigger guard, butt cap and sidelined, lock plate marked "Tower" behind hammer and crown over "GR" forward of hammer, proofed on left side of barrel at breech, crown on tang behind tang screw, good condition, re-browned and cleaned, replaced front sight, working order **700.00**

French, military, 16" overall length, 9" round iron barrel, flat beveled lock plate with faceted pan fitted with flat beveled reinforced hammer, brass furniture, unmarked......... **800.00**

Halsbach & Sons, Baltimore, MD, holster pistol, c1785 to early 1800s, 9" brass part round, part octagon barrel, .65 caliber, lock marked "Halsbach & Sons," large brass butt cap with massive spread wing eagle (primitive) in high relief

surrounded by cluster of 13 stars, large relief shell carving around tang of barrel, full walnut stock, pin-fastened **1,750.00**

Kentucky, T. B. Cherington, 12-1/2" octagonal smoothbore barrel, stamped "T. P. Cherington" on barrel and lock plate, .45 caliber, brightly polished iron parts, walnut stock **2,500.00**

U. S. Model 1805, 10" round iron barrel with iron rib underneath holding ramrod pipe, lockplate marked with spread eagle and shield over "US" and vertically at rear "Harper's Ferry" over "1808," .54 caliber, walnut half stock with brass butt plate and trigger guard, Flayderman 6A-008........ **3,000.00**

Musket

Colt, Model 1861, .58 caliber, 39" barrel, "17th N.Y.V." beneath stock, good signature, date, and stampings on metal, inspector's cartouche on stock, bright gray metal, areas of pitting around bolster and lock **1,375.00**

Enfield, dated 1856, cal 58, unmarked, percussion, 39" bbl, square base front sight/bayonet lug with 800 meter military sight, lock plate has markings of a crown over "VR" and date "1856," right side of butt stock carries cartouche of circle with broad arrow and date "1856," three bbl bands with sling swivels and slotted head ramrod, upper bbl band and sling loop, as well as sling loop on trigger and ramrod, appear to be recent replacements, bbl retains smooth gray-brown patina with heavy pitting over breech end, light refinish to wood, worn and damaged nipple............................. **815.00**

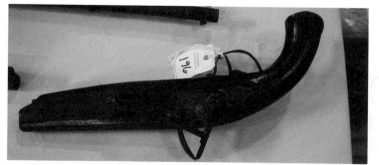

Flintlock pistol, Continental, 19th C, large, lock signed "Ma Nal de Charleville," lacking fling holder, restorations, 15" l, **$450**.

Photo courtesy of Wiederseim Associates, Inc.

Harper's Ferry, Model 1816 Conversion Musket, cal 69, standard 1816 Model, makers' name and date 1837 vertically behind hammer, small eagle over "US" in front of hammer on lock plate, 42" bbl with top bayonet lug and front sight on rear strap of split front band, iron mounted with three bands and tulip head ramrod, left flat has inspector's initials "JAS," conversion accomplished by mounting nipple at breech end of bbl and filling flash pan cut-out with brass, fine condition, iron retains dark smoky patina with light pitting around nipple area, fine hand-rubbed patina, broken away nipple......... **690.00**
Parker Snow & Co., Miller conversion, 40" round barrel, bold stampings include signature, eagle, and 1864 on lock, 56" overall............ **1,375.00**
Springfield, Model 1863 Musket, cal 58. 40" bbl, heavily rusted, deeply pitted except for replacement ramrod, stock is sound, but has some scorching damage, bolster is battered from lack of nipple, lock works **815.00**

Percussion pistol

American, engraved, sgd on lock "P. D. Gwaltney & Co.," Norfolk, Va," conversion from flintlock, checkered walnut stock with steel hardware, pineapple finial on trigger guard, swamped octagonal barrel with thin gold band of inlay at breech, small chip, hairline at lock mortise, end cap missing, 15-3/4" l **850.00**
English
  Folding bayonet, simple engraving on frame, stands of flags and "Lenning," old hairlines in grip, 4" l barrel, 8-1/2" l......................... **250.00**
  Single shot, sgd "W. Parker" on lock, "Maker to His Majesty, London" on barrel, finely checkered bag grip, narrow pierced repair just below lock, 8-1/4" l...... **715.00**
Gibbs, Tiffany & Co., Sturbridge, MA, early 19th C, underhammer percussion pistol, 6" cast steel barrel with engraved flower and vine motifs and imp marks: "202," "E HUTCHINGS & CO AGENTS BALTO," "GIBBS TIFFANY & CO. STURBRIDGE MASS.," eagle motif; rosewood grips with geometric mother-of-pearl inlay,

silver back strap engraved "Dr. C.A. Cheever;" mahogany hinged case with engraved silver plaque on top "From Eusebius Hutchings of Baltimore, Md. to Charles A. Cheever Portsmouth, New Hampshire," interior contour lined with black velvet, fitted with accessories including copper powder flask, brass bullet mold with mahogany handles marked "202," cleaning rod, ramrod, five small leather ammunition pouches, loss on underhammer, 9-7/8" l pistol, 12-5/8" x 5-5/8" x 2-1/4" case, descended from Cheever family **3,200.00**
Remington, 1858, New Model, bold inspector's stamp on grips, sub inspector's initials on various other parts, old brown finish with some bluing remaining on cylinder, elevated front sight appears to be early addition **980.00**
Target, figured walnut buttstock, brass buttplate, steel trigger guard, 22-3/4" octagonal barrel stamped 340L at muzzle, single hammer mounted on breech/frame, ramrod missing, narrow pieced repair to stock, 38-1/2" l **300.00**
U. S. Springfield, lock stamped with signature and 1856, eagle on Maynard primer door, 12" barrel dated 1855, brass hardware with iron back strap, walnut shoulder stock, brass hardware, few hairlines, pierced repair on hammer, 28-1/2" l **1,750.00**
Waters, 8-1/2" round barrel, bright metal, stamped address and "1838" on lock, double inspector markings on stock, 14" l **660.00**

Pistol

Colt Model 1911 Army, .45 caliber auto, orig blued finish, checkered walnut grips, good signature and other stampings, 8-1/2" l............................ **825.00**
Sharp's Pepperbox, four shot, .22 caliber, 3" barrels, traces of orig bluing, stamped signature, patent information around hammer screw, gutta percha grips with checkered design, 5-1/2" l............................ **220.00**
Volcanic Lever Action, Navy, .38 caliber, 8" barrel, signature "The Volcanic Repeating Arms Co." on top, walnut grips, brass

frame with old patina, minor pitting on one side, tab for magazine tube broken, spring missing, 14-1/2" l **9,900.00**

Revolver

Baby Dragoon, cal. 31, standard 5" oct. bbl without rammer, cylinder has round stop holes, brass grip frame with one-pc wood grips, top flat of bbl is devoid of orig Colt markings, very faintly visible word "Orleans," presumably stamp of New Orleans retailer, medium gray-brown patina on iron, repaired and refinished grip, shoulder repairs on back strap, accompanied by hand-written letter stating that this revolver was owned and used by Confederate Col. Henry C. Kollogg **1,025.00**
Colt
  Model 1849 Pocket, 4" barrel, .31 caliber, faint New York address, all serial numbers matching, replaced catch **495.00**
  Model 1860 Army, matching serial numbers, butt signature, New York address, overall light brown to gray surface on metal, brass trigger guard, iron grip straps, 8" barrel, 14" overall, old corner chips on grips, period black leather holster with raised "U. S." design and eight or three over stamped "G" on front flap, worn to grain, 13" l................... **675.00**
  Model 1861 Navy, cal. 36, 7 1/2" round bbl, case color frame with silver-plated trigger guard and back strap, Naval battle cylinder scene with one-pc fine old ivory grips, very deep relief Mexican eagle on left side, accompanied by orig Colt casing containing Colt's patent short angle spout flask and iron bullet mold, packet of Johnston & Dow's skin cartridges, Eley cap tin **9,500.00**
Lefaucheux Pin Rimfire, old bright surface on barrel, frame, and cylinder, bold signature and proofmarks, walnut grips finely alligatored varnish, 6-3/8" octagon to round barrel, one Lefaucheux cartridge on mount, 12-1/2" l........................... **450.00**

Remington

Beals, 7-3/4" barrel, 13-1/2" l,
old dark finish **825.00**
Model 1858, .44 caliber, 8"
octagonal barrel, good
signature with faint inspector's
stamp on grips, 14" l... **880.00**
Model 1861 Navy, 7-3/8"
octagon barrel, allover matte
gray finish, signature stamp
.... **990.00**

Warner, pocket, cal. 28., 3-3/4"
round bbl, cased with small flask
and incorrect accessories, gray-
brown patina overall, faint
Warner markings on top of
frame, light surface rust overall,
grips badly chipped at base,
gun does not fit partitions in case
very well **920.00**

Top to bottom: Springfield 1883 conversion rifle, **$675**; percussion long rifle, 18th/19th C, octagonal barrel, brass patch box, conversion, 57" l, **$725**; Kentucky long rifle, maple, percussion lock mechanism, signed "Atkinson Warranted," brass patch box, 58-1/2" l, **$775**; Kentucky flintlock long rifle, 18th C, maple, engraved lock "Warranted," brass patch box and trigger guard, 58" l, **$3,750**.

Photo courtesy of Wiederseim Associates, Inc.

Rifle

Allin Conversion Model 1866,
40" round barrel, worn browned
finish, three bands, "U. S.
Springfield" lock with eagle and
1865 date, walnut stock, in-the-
making file marks, 56" l ... **250.00**

Conestoga Rifle Works, half-
stock Kentucky, cal. 36, bbl cut
to 34-1/4", fixed sights, tiger
striped stock, pewter nose cap,
dbl. set triggers, two-pc patch
box, brass furniture, dark brown
iron, polished brass, fine dark
wood, set trigger won't hold,
hammer won't cock......... **410.00**

Top: Winchester 1883 lever action rifle, 44-40 cal., 46" l, **$1,200**; bottom: flintlock trade musket, 18th C, carved walnut stock, gilt decorated lock, marked "London," trigger guard, 41" l, **$1,550**.

Photo courtesy of Wiederseim Associates, Inc.

Percussion, half stock
Fordney, Melchoir, Lancaster
County, (died 1846), 39-1/4"
octagon barrel, sgd "M.
Fordney," curly maple stock,
old mellow refinishing,
checkered wrist, fine
engraving on brass hardware,
fair border engraving on
barrel, chips around lock
mortise, some age splits

beneath forearm, small putty
repair on one side of tang,
front portion of triggerguard
replaced, 55" l.......... **1,150.00**
McComas, Alexander, 1843-
75, stamped "A. McComas,
Baltimore" on top of barrel,
checkered walnut stock with
steel hardware, small cap
box, beavertail cheekpiece,
34" l octagon barrel, restored
stock split behind lock, chip
off cap box, 49-1/2" l.... **420.00**
Partial stamped signatures on
lock and barrel for J. Henry &
Son, 36-3/8" octagon barrel
with browned surface, walnut
stock, stepped beaver tail,
steel butt plate, brass trigger
guard, nickel silver inlays,
small "U. S." stamp just below
trigger guard, 52-1/2" l, orig
8-1/2" l powder horn ... **950.00**

Remington, rolling block
Military, approx .45 caliber, full
stock, three barrel bands, 35"
tapered round barrel with
adjustable rear sight, clear
signature on tag, ramrod
missing, 50-1/2" l **220.00**
Remington signature and
address on tang, crown
proofs, "G" stamp on
buttstock, old dark finish,
brass handle bayonet, dents,
one band spring mission, 50" l
.... **330.00**

Springfield, Model 1873
Trapdoor, 45-70 caliber, cadet
model, 29-1/2" round blued
barrel, three click tumbler, eagle
mark and signature on lock with
eagle's head and "V. P." on
breech area, minor dents on
stock, ramrod, 48-3/4" l... **450.00**

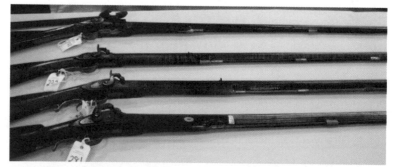

Top to bottom: Flintlock fowling piece, signed on lock "Ketland and Co.," smooth bore barrel, 61-1/2" l, **$1,450**; percussion long rifle, maple, brass patch box, signed "R. Ashmore & Son" on lock, octagonal barrel signed "G.C. and G.R.," conversion, 53" l, **$1,210**; percussion long rifle, maple, octagonal barrel, set trigger, lock signed "Lancaster, PA, Leman," carved stock, damage to stock, 48-1/2" l, **$1,320**: US Springfield 1861 percussion rifle, brass patch box, 55-1/2" l, **$675**.

Photo courtesy of Wiederseim Associates, Inc.

Winchester, Model 1873 Special Order, cal. 44 WCF, standard grade, 24" oct. bbl, half-nickel front sight, slot blank in rear dovetail, early Lyman tang sight, button magazine with uncheckered wood, straight stock and crescent steel butt plate with trap **1,610.00**

Shotgun

European, double barrel, 12 gauge, 30-1/2" Damascus barrels, silver band overlay, sgd "R. Baumgarter in Bernburg" on barrel, engraved stag on tang, "I lubertus Gewehor," figured walnut stock, horn trigger guard, 47" l **275.00**

Fox Sterlingworth, 16 gauge, double barrel, 26" barrel, top lever break-open, hammerless, double trigger, blued, checkered walnut pistol grip stock and forearm.......................... **400.00**

Parker Brothers, double barrel, "D" grade, Damacus steel barrels, figured walnut stock with checkering, finely engraved #2 frame with skeleton butt plate, 14" pull, extra barrel with own forearm, same serial number on both........................... **1,495.00**

San Marco Magnum, Wildfowler, goose gun, 10 gauge, 32" over and under full choke barrels, never fired, Dunn's leather and canvas case **700.00**

Stevens, Model 970, 12 gauge, single shot, 32" l round barrel with octagonal breech, top lever break-open, hammerless, automatic shell ejector, automatic safety, blued, case hardened frame, checkered walnut pistol grip stock and forearm........................... **95.00**

FIREHOUSE COLLECTIBLES

History: The volunteer fire company has played a vital role in the protection and social growth of many towns and rural areas. Paid professional firemen usually are found only in large metropolitan areas. Each fire company prided itself on equipment and uniforms. Conventions and parades gave the fire companies a chance to show off their equipment. These events produced a wealth of firehouse-related memorabilia.

Additional Listings: See *Warman's Americana & Collectibles* for more examples.

Fire extinguishers, left: Phoenix Dry Powder Fire Extinguisher Compound 22, tin litho container, eagle decoration, dated April 25, 1899, original contents, **$95**; right: New Era Chemical Fire Extinguisher, tin litho, Meadville, PA, 22" h, original contents, **$85**.

Photo courtesy of Dotta Auction Co., Inc.

Advertising button

Baldwin II NO 22 May 26, '97, Williamsport, elderly gentleman, Whitehead & Hoag back paper, 1-1/4" d **15.00**
Central NY Volunteer Fireman's Convention, Auspices Seward Tribe Alaska Esquimaus, June 26-28, 1910, Auburn, NY, 1-1/2" d........................... **20.00**
Keystone Fire Co. No. 1 Shillington, PA, Dedication May 31, 1924, real photo, man standing by doorway of two story building, Keystone Badge paper, 1-1/4" d .. **15.00**
Marion Fire Co. Stouchsburg, Pa, real photo, truck with ladders and hose reel parked on street in front of house and tree, men standing at left, 1-1/4" d **15.00**
Pennsylvania State Firemen's Convention, Allentown, 1930, multicolored, fireman in helmet, 1-1/4" d **18.00**
Woodbury Fire Dept, black on gold, center pumper wagon, Friendship No. 1, 1930 event, attached to small red, white, and blue fabric ribbon.. **20.00**

Badge

Columbia PA, 1896, arch reads "Centennial of Columbia Fire Co., pumper **40.00**
Compliments of, diecut fire trumpets and hydrants on hanger, asst chief name, c1890, 2-1/2" h **35.00**
15th Annual Convention National Ass'n Fire Engineers, 1887 .... **45.00**
Mapleton, Iowa, June 7, '06, multicolored scene of two firemen holding hose at left, larger scene of two fireman using tools against fire bursting thru doorway, Whitehead & Hoag back paper, 1-3/4" h **40.00**
Wilmington, DE, 1907, fabric with celluloid pin........... **15.00**
Bell, 11", brass, iron back **125.00**
Belt, red, black, and white, 43" l, marked "I lampden" **85.00**
Box, cov, 17" l, 13-3/4" w, 14" h, oval, wallpaper covering with fire engine scene, blue ground, white and green highlights, inside lined with Der York Democrat 1834 newspaper **13,750.00**

Fire bucket

3" h, 1-7/8" d, miniature, tin, bail handle, orange paint dec, "Fire Bucket" printed on side **615.00**
12-1/2" h, leather, stitched seams, nailed strap handle, old black paint, brown painted int., wear **175.00**
19-1/4" h, leather, leather handle attached with iron rings, old dark green paint over dark red with black painted handle and collar, black lettering "L.TOWER. - 3.," in yellow outlined banner, America, early 19th C, alligatored paint surface **715.00**

21-1/2" h, leather, painted red, black collar, leather handle, gilt lettering "1801. FOUNTAIN NO.2," with black shading, America, c1801, losses, handle wear. **2,280.00**

Fire extinguisher

Babcock, American La France Fire Engine Co., Elmire, NY, grenade, amber glass **500.00**

Hayward's Hand Fire Grenade, yellow, ground mouth, smooth base, 6-1/4" h, c1870............................. **85.00**

Red Comet, red metal canister, red glass bulb **50.00**

Fire mark, painted cast iron, William Penn in oval center, marked "Leader," $225.

Fire mark, cast iron, oval

8" x 11-1/2", relief molded design, pumper framed by "Fire Department Insurance," polychrome paint........ **495.00**

8" x 12", black, gold eagle and banner dec, marked "Eagle Ins. Co. Cin O"............ **950.00**

Helmet

Leather, 9" x 14-1/4" x 11", Anderson + Jones, Broad St., NY, emb and ribbed leather, brass trumpetered holder, painted tin front piece lettered "cataract hose 2 j.g.," manufacturer's stamp on underside of brim, repaint, leather losses.............. **635.00**

Stamped aluminum, black enameling, leather front panel marked "Chopmist, F.D.," interior makers label for Cairns & Brothers, Clifton, N.J." **200.00**

Ink blotter, Fireman's Fund 75th Year, Allendale, CA, fireman with little child, 1938, 4" x 9" **7.50**

Helmet, assistant chief engineer, red and white paint, wear, **$185**.

Ledger marker, Caisse General Fire Insurance, statue of Liberty illus, multicolored, tin litho, 12-1/4" l, 3" w **275.00**

Medal, Jacksonville Fire Co., silvered brass, firefighting symbols circled by "I.A.F.E.-1917-Jaconsville, Fla.," reverse "Compliments of N. Snellenburg & Co. Uniforms, Philadelphia, Pa," looped ring **15.00**

Nozzle, hose, 16" l, brass, double handle, marked "Akron Brass Mfg. Co., Inc."....... **165.00**

Parade hat, 6-1/2" h, painted leather, polychrome dec, green ground, front with eagle and harp, banner above "Hibernia," back inscribed "1752" in gilt, "1" on top, red brim underside, some age cracks, small losses to brim edge **3,335.00**

Print, 22-1/2" x 17-1/4", color lithograph, *Engine of the Red Jacket Veteran Fireman's Association...Champion of the New England League, 1894*, printed for the Brooks Bank Note Company, Boston, folio .. **1,410.00**

Sales sheet, 8-1/2" x 11" glossy paper, Iron Horse Metal Ware Products, Rochester Can Co., NY, pictures five galvanized red fire pails **20.00**

Sign, Philadelphia Underwriters, 14" x 20", heavy porcelain, detailed graphic image in center with fire mark in upper right corner, made in England **600.00**

Stickpin, 7/8" celluloid button on 1-3/4" stickpin, Honor To Our Brave, fireman portrait, red shirt, blue helmet, 1900s **15.00**

Toy

Arcade, fire pumper, 1941 Ford, cast iron, painted red, emb sides, cast fireman, hose reel on bed, rubber tires, repaired fender, 13" l .. **440.00**

Arcade, ladder truck, cast iron, painted red, two cast fireman, rubber tires, bed contains ladder supports, open frame design, 9-1/4" l **440.00**

Hubley, Ahrens Fox fire engine, cast iron, rubber tires, 7-1/2" l......................... **475.00**

Kenton, fire pumper, cast iron, painted red, gold highlights on boiler, and ball, emb sides, disc wheels with spoke centers........................ **615.00**

Kingsbury, horse-drawn ladder wagon, sheet metal, pained red, wire supports, holding yellow wooden ladders, two seated drivers, pulled by two black horses, yellow spoke wheels, bell on frame rings as toy is pulled, 26" l.......................... **2,150.00**

Williams, A. C., fire pumper, cast iron, painted red, gold highlights, cast driver, bell, and boiler, rear platform with railing, rubber tires, 7-1/2" l **315.00**

Puzzle, Milton Bradley Co., American Fire Dept, A Sectional Picture Toy, 1882, one piece missing, original box, **$125**.

Watch fob, presentation, two sided embossed silver medal with crystal bezels, one side with raised female allegorical figure surrounded by 13 stars, other side with inscriptions "NORTHERN LIBERY FIRE CO. No 1./INSTITUTED MAY 1, 1756./ INCORPORATED MAR 18th 1833.," oval frame with scrolled crest engraved "Retired FROM Service SAM'L ALEXANDER Mar, 15, 1871," America, 19th C, solder repair to crest....... **450.00**

FIREPLACE EQUIPMENT

History: In the colonial home, the fireplace was the gathering point for heat, meals, and social interaction. It maintained its dominant position until the introduction of central heating in the mid-19th century.

Because of the continued popularity of the fireplace, accessories still are manufactured, usually in an early-American motif.

Reproduction Alert: Modern blacksmiths are reproducing many old iron implements.

Bellows, wood, leather, and brass, painted black with red and green floral decoration, **$45**.
Photo courtesy of Joseph P. Smalley, Jr.

Andirons, pr, brass, 8-3/4" w, 16" d, 12" h, brass, round ball finials, scrolled spur legs, ball feet **385.00**

Andirons, pr, brass and iron
8" w, 27" d, 14-3/4" h, belted ball tops, baluster ring-turned shaft, sq stepped base, conforming log stops on curved log supports, America, mid-19th C, dents **500.00**
9-1/2" w, 16-1/2" d, 21-1/2" h, America, last quarter 18th C, brass urn-tops over iron knife-blade shaft, lower brass shield, arched legs over penny feet **650.00**
10-5/8" w, 17-3/4" d, 18-1/2" h, J. Davis, Boston, Massachusetts, faceted steeples over belted balls, columnar shafts, spurred cabriole legs with slipper feet, conforming steeple-top log stops, signed "J DAVIS BOSTON" on billet bars. **950.00**
11-1/4" w, 25" d, 16-5/8" h, ball top with concentric ring turnings, shaped columns, cabriole legs, spurred knees, slipper feet, conforming log stops, one imp "BOSTON," c1800, losses and cracks near log stops **600.00**

19" d, 9" h, New York, first quarter 19th C, beaded belts on double lemon finials, round plinths supported on spurred cabriole legs with ball feet, minor wear **775.00**

Andirons, pr, bronze, 31" h, ribbon-wrapped torches tapering to leaftip, reeded stem with husk-accented bifurcate base, Louis XVI-style, 19th C **2,400.00**

Andirons and matching tools, Federal, 24" h brass ring-turned shaft andirons with spurred legs, ball feet, similarly turned fireplace 32" h tongs and 33" h shovel **1,100.00**

Bellows, painted gold fruit, green leaves, red and black decoration, 19th C, front panel detached at nozzle, wear, **$90**.
Photo courtesy of Pook & Pook.

Bellows, 17-3/4" l, 8" w, wood and leather, brass tacks, brass wind spout, white ground paint with some dec on back, floral dec on front and handle, good condition leather **550.00**

Coal grate, 26" w, 9-1/2" d, 16" h, George II, brass-mounted iron, bowed central section of four rails over grate, ash drawer between bow front side panels, applied brass starbursts, surmounted with brass urn finials, English, last quarter 19th C **200.00**

Fireboard, 36" x 44-3/8", wide central raised panel, paint dec to depict seaside village, ships, and houses, surround painted to depict tiles with numerous ships, houses, and trees, America, early 19th C, wear, fading **7,650.00**

Fire dogs, pr
7-1/2" w, 6-1/2" h, brass, central horizontal reeded orb raised on three reeded legs, reeded horizontal bar on top, Aesthetic Movement, English, third quarter 19th C **150.00**
15" h, cast iron, rampant lion bearing twisted horizontal bars, seated on rope twist rounded and octagonal base, late 19th/early 20th C . **700.00**

16-1/4" w, 14" h, gilt bronze, squat urns draped in husks on top, short fluted column with central leaf-scrolled band, large urn opposing berry finial across horizontal cross bar, Louis XVI-style, 19th C **1,300.00**

Fire grate, cast iron and brass, George III, early 19th C, serpentine railed basket above pierced brass frieze centering spread-wing eagle on scrolled supports, vasiform finials, ball feet, 22-1/4" x 21" x 13", **$700**.
Photo courtesy of Sloans & Kenyon Auctions.

Fire fender
51-1/4" w, 18-1/2" d, 12-1/4" h, brass rail on serpentine fender, vertical wirework with swag dec, England or America, late 18th/early 19th C, minor wear to brass rail, loss of one wire **5,600.00**
52" l, 18" d, 12-1/2" h, wire and brass, serpentine, brass ball finials **1,155.00**

Fire screen
26-1/2" w, 44" h, walnut, openwork cresting, revolving screen painted with dec scenes, trestle base, Renaissance Revival, American **300.00**
28-3/4" h, gilt bronze, cartouche-shaped wire firescreen with central floral stem within rocaille borders, Louis XV-style, together with set of brush, shovel, and tongs in 24" h beaded stand; pair of small 10-3/8" h firedogs formed as rocaille acanthus scrolls **600.00**
30-1/4" h, 36-3/8" l, wire and brass rail **770.00**
31" w, 40" h, bamboo, brass mounted, foliate painted panel, turned supports and trestle base, Victorian .. **150.00**

32-3/4" h, leaded glass, tripartite, central square panel and two narrow side panels set with multicolored textured and bull's eye glass pieces, brass surround, griffin-form trestle feet, Renaissance Revival, late 19th/early 20th C **1,100.00**

33" w, 41-1/4" h, tubular frame, ormolu scrolling at top, scrolled feet, center oil on canvas with courting scene, French, sgd "G. Jones" on lower right, early 20th C **700.00**

Rack, iron, wide flat long handle, eight spindles wide, **$45**.

Photo courtesy of Joy Luke.

Fire tools, 30-7/8" and 31-3/8" l, brass and iron, ball finial on belted ball top, shovel and tongs, minor dents, scattered pitting **420.00**

Footman, 18" w, 15" d, 12" h, brass, Georgian-style, rect top, turned side handles, pierced apron, cabriole front legs, straight round rear legs, English **365.00**

Hearth broom, 8-1/4" w, 22" l, hardwood handle, bristle holder, carved and painted face of black man, handle end stamped with rocket, inscribed "Forward Biltmore, NC," wear **445.00**

Hearth toaster, 16-3/8" w, 23" l, America, late 18th C, wrought iron, toast support embellished with scrolled heart motifs, turned wooden handle with remains of green and red paint **825.00**

Fire screen, Victorian, mahogany frame, 17-1/2" w x 21-1/2" h needlepoint picture of Victorian lady in garden setting, mounted on board, mahogany frame with carved stem on base, carved knees, pad feet, 52" h overall, **$500**.

Photo courtesy of Alderfer Auction Co.

Hearth trivet, wrought iron 15-1/2" l, 6-1/4" d, round, flattened handle, hanger hook, three-legged base, rust **220.00**

23-1/2" l, 11-1/2" w, sq, square grilling surface, flattened handle, circular end, four sun-like stamps **250.00**

Kettle shelf, 13" w, 10-1/2" d, 13-1/2" h, brass and wrought iron, "D" shape with cast top with pierced scrolling, floral medallions around skirt, iron cabriole legs ending in large penny feet, one decorative rosette missing from front **460.00**

Kettle stand, 10-3/4" h, brass and wrought iron, tripod base, round column, painted black, circular brass top with pierced designs, scalloped edges **100.00**

Mantelpiece, faux marble painted, attributed to Vermont, early 19th C

60" w, 6-3/4" d, 48-1/4" h, rect shelf above cove molding, flanking rect capitals on pilasters and plinths, orig white paint with gray veining, surface wear **715.00**

61" w, 6-1/2" d, 49-1/4" h, projecting shelf above molding, rect capitals on

pilasters and plinths, orig gray-green paint with white veining, paint wear .. **1,000.00**

Mantle urns, pr, 17-1/2" h, gray marble with white striations, applied ormolu and gilded spelter dec, stamped "P.H. Mourey" around base, minor wear to gilding **500.00**

Fire place screen, brass, English, **$75**.

Photo courtesy of Wiederseim Associates, Inc.

Pole screen

English, candle shield, orig green and mustard paint, table-top **11,500.00**

English, 1760-80, mahogany, pole with shaped top, turned tapering urn-shaped pillar, cabriole leg base ending in arris pad feet on platforms, orig needlework panel, gold and blue floral pattern, brown ground, outlined with applied wood moldings, old surface, imperfections **5,175.00**

Irish, Chippendale, inlaid walnut and fruitwood veneers, oblong panel with scalloped edges, orig silk needlework of a dragon, saber legs with line border inlay graduate into triangular block with three turned supports, tripod base, short turned feet below applied blocks, some stains on fabric, few veneer chips missing, 53-1/2" h **470.00**

Tinder lighter, pistol shape, flintlock striker

5-1/8" l, mahogany, brass tinderbox, lyre-shaped front support, small candle socket with drop pan, etched scrollwork on the side **1,430.00**

8" l, walnut, steel tinder box, candle socket, simple curved support, front end with compartment for tinder/candles, inscribed "Laurent Gille" **935.00**

FISHING COLLECTIBLES

History: Early man caught fish with crude spears and hooks made of bone, horn, or flint. By the mid-1800s, metal lures with attached hooks were produced in New York State. Later, the metal was curved and glass heads added to make them more attractive. Spinners with painted-wood bodies and glass eyes appeared around 1890. Soon after, many different makers were producing wood plugs with glass eyes. Patents, which were issued in large numbers around this time, covered the development of hook hangers, body styles, and devices to add movement to the plug as it was drawn through the water. The wood plug era lasted up to the mid-1930s when plugs constructed of plastic were introduced.

With the development of casting plugs, it became necessary to produce fishing reels capable of accomplishing the task with ease. Reels first appeared as a simple device to hold a fishing line. Improvements included multiplying gears, retrieving line levelers, drags, clicks, and a variety of construction materials. The range of quality in reel manufacture varied considerably. Collectors are mainly interested in reels made with high-quality materials and workmanship, or those exhibiting unusual features.

Early fishing rods, which were made of solid wood, were heavy and prone to breakage. By gluing together tapered strips of split

bamboo, a rod was fashioned which was light in weight and had greatly improved strength. The early split-bamboo rods were round and wrapped with silk to hold them together. As glue improved, fewer wrappings were needed, and rods became slim and lightweight. Rods were built in various lengths and thicknesses, depending upon the type of fishing and bait used. Rod makers' names and models can usually be found on the metal parts of the handle or on the rod near the handle.

Reproduction Alert: Lures and fish decoys.

For more information, see *Warman's Fishing Lures.*

Badge, 1-3/4" d, Fishing, Trapping, Hunting License, NY, 1930 .... **55.00**

Bait bucket, painted blue, stenciled "Falls City-Magic-Minnow Bucket" **1,980.00**

Bait trap, Katch-N-Karry, Glassman Mfg. Co., Jackson, TN, patented 1941, wood, 4" dia wire mesh circle, litho of bluegill and roach **375.00**

Bank, 3-1/2" x 4" x 7" h, painted composition, bobbing head, round fisherman In hat and sunglasses, mermaid by side, coin slot in back, 1960s, felt covering over base **30.00**

Bobber, hand painted

5" l, panfish float, black, red, and white stripes **12.00**

12" l, pike float, yellow, green, and red stripes **24.00**

Book

Complete Book of Fresh Water Fishing, P. Allen Parsons, 1965, 332 pgs, illus **15.00**

Lures: The Guide to Sport Fishing, Keith C. Schuyler, Stackpole Co., 1955, dj.. **20.00**

The Complete Angler: or Contemplative Man's Recreation: A Discourse on Rivers, Fish-Ponds, Fish & Fishing in 2 Parts, Issac Walton and Charles Cotton, supplementary and explanatory Sir John Hawkins **125.00**

Calendar print, 12" x 13", Bristol, 1905, young couple and their guide getting ready for fishing excursion, cut down and laid down on old style mat board, old frame with wood backing **330.00**

Canoe, Old Town Sponson, 16' **1,430.00**

Catalog

Creek Chub Bait Co., Garrett, IN, 1934 .... **330.00**

Evinrude Motors, Milwaukee, WI, 1961, Catalog of Outboard Motors **32.00**

Garcia Fishing Equipment & Supplies, Garcia Corp., Teaneck, NY, c1955, accordion fold large 11-1/4" x 30" sheet **20.00**

Hardy Brothers, 1910 . **495.00**

Montague Rod & Reel Co., Montague City, MA, c1949, Catalog No. 49-M **55.00**

Orvis, c1900 .... **330.00**

Penn Fishing Tackle Mfg., Philadelphia, PA, 1952, Catalog No. 17 of Penn Reels **32.00**

Shakespeare Co., Kalamazoo, Catalog No. 27, 1927, some pages uncut **175.00**

Wallsten Tackle Co., Chicago, IL, 1940s, Fishing Tips, Courtesy of Cisco Kid Lures **21.00**

Weber Lifelike Fly Co., Stevens Point, WI, 1941, Catalog No. 22, Flies & Fly Tackle **70.00**

White, E. M. & Co., Old Town, ME, c1922, E. M. White Builders of White Canoes **40.00**

Child's kit, 4-1/2" x 1-1/2" x 7-1/2", Mickey Mouse Fishing Kit, copyrighted "Walt Disney Enterprises," tin litho, 1920s, C.8+ **500.00**

Cigarette card, King of England deep-sea fishing, New Zealand, 1937 .... **12.00**

Clock, mechanical, fish punching hole in side of boat with moving hammer, Hero Clock Co., wind-up, marked "Made in China" **40.00**

Creel, bamboo and leather, **$85**.

Photo courtesy of Alderfer Auction Co.

Creel

5" x 9" x 9" h, split, reinforced rim on lid, off center hole, orig split splint hinges, wire and loop lid latch, heavy fabric support attached to shoulder strap **2,200.00**

5-1/2" x 13" x 7" h, leather trimmed turtle, bulbous shape, split reed and cord reinforcing on bottom, orig twisted reed hinges and harness loops, sliding figural turtle lid latch, wood rule on lid, dec cross hatch weaving on front, old leather harness **1,210.00**

6" x 15" x 7" h, turtle, tight rattan weave, bulbous shape, orig twisted reed hinges and harness loops, split reed and cord reinforcing on bottom, figural turtle latch, wood rule on lid, dec cross hatch weaving on front, leather and web harness **1,650.00**

7" x 17", turtle, bulbous shape, tight rattan weave, full length leather hinge, emb 98" rule, leather worker's stamp "ILHAN New Boulder Colo," leather harness, small mahogany priest attached with leather thong **5,500.00**

Decoy, fish, wood

6-1/2" l, Leroy Howell, gray body, black metal fins. **115.00**

7" l, Ice King, perch, painted, Bear Creek Co. **75.00**

31-1/2" l, wood, paint dec, America, early 20th C, minor paint wear and losses **1,495.00**

Display, salesman's sample, Pequea, Strasburg, PA

9" x 13", oilcloth cov box, two panels, lures **1,870.00**

9" x 15", oilcloth cov box, 19 round bodied cork floats **1,100.00**

9-1/2" x 13", oilcloth cov box, eight lures, 18 assorted feathered trebles, large weedless example **330.00**

9-1/2" x 13", two-sided, lures and pearl spoons **1,650.00**

18" x 29-1/2" d, two panels, assortment of 58 floats **18,700.00**

21" x 21", display case, 33 different colorful winders with bobbers **3,410.00**

Fishing license, for resident use

Connecticut, 1935, yellow, black, and white **65.00**

Pennsylvania, 1945, blue and white, black serial number **18.00**

Flask, pewter, emb on both sides, one side with fisherman landing trout, other side with fisherman netting catch, marked "Alchemy Pewter, Sheffield, England" **175.00**

Float, Ideal **200.00**

Fly, Carrie Stevens.......... **440.00**

Fly fishing display

c1910, C. J. Frost, Stevens Point, WI, 9' l **3,080.00**

c1911, painted wood trout replica, fly fishing reel, flies, net, wood case, 39-3/4" l, 3-3/4" d, 13-1/4" h **195.00**

Folk art, 25" h, 40-1/4" l, wood carving, titled "Two Fish and a Frog," sgd "L. A. Plummer, 1904" in lower right, polychrome dec, minor cracks **17,250.00**

Ink blotter, 3-1/2" x 6-1/4", Flies and Casts, J. C. Arsenault, New Brunswick, Canada.......... **55.00**

Knife, Marbles Woodcraft **385.00**

License holder, paper envelope, Florida Game and Fresh Water Commission, stamped with County Judge's name **22.00**

Lure

Al Foss Dixie Wiggler, #13, 1928, metal box, extra hook, pocket catalog, 3-1/2" l **100.00**

Allen, Vamp, stripy finish **550.00**

Blee, Charles, submarine bait, all metal **2,000.00**

Case Bait Co., rotary marvel, c1910........................ **360.00**

Creek Chubb Bait Co.

Giant Pike, 12-1/2" x 2-3/4" orig box **195.00**

Glitter beetle, red and white **615.00**

Jigger 4100, red side . **140.00**

Mouse........................ **470.00**

Pikie minnow, early orig box **440.00**

Plunking dinger, all black **100.00**

Red beetle **315.00**

Sarasota, #3317, c1927-31, luminous yellow head . **800.00**

Detroit Glass, minnow tube, fish form, four treble hooks, orig box, c1914 .... **3,500.00**

DeWitt, Bil, minnow, orig box with papers **90.00**

Dunk's Double Header, black plug, c1931 .... **125.00**

Four Brothers, Neverfail Minnow, orig box **615.00**

Garland Bros., Plant City, FL, cork head minnow **315.00**

Harkauf fly rod lure, 1-1/8" l, wood body, **$550**.

Hanson

GE pull-me-slow, two hooks **90.00**

Muskegon spoon jack minnow, green back, five-hook **275.00**

H. Comstock, 1883, Flying Helgramite **4,400.00**

Heddon

#175, heavy casting minnow, worn leaping bass box **420.00**

#300, Dowagiac surface minnow **275.00**

#300, husky minnow, orig box **660.00**

#400, bucktail surface minnow **615.00**

#450, killer **175.00**

#1500, dummy double, unmarked box, orig paper **360.00**

Henning, glass minnow tube **440.00**

J. A. Holzapfe, Jackson, MI, mushroom, bass, orig box **660.00**

Jamison, wig-wag......... **95.00**

K & K, animated minnow **160.00**

Like Live Bait Co., Jacksonville, FL, mechanical, patent no. 1,7658,160, orig box........................ **13, 200.00**

Manhattan Casting Bait, No. 2, White, orig box........ **495.00**
Moonlight Bay #1, c1904, 4" shallow cup................. **400.00**

Musky

Crazy crawler 2510 mouse **250.00**
Giant vamp 7350, jointed, natural scales, c1930 . **130.00**
Surfasser 300, two hooks, rainbow....................... **150.00**
Paw-Paw, sucker, perch finish, tack eyes **30.00**
Pfleuger All-in-One................... **470.00**
Floating monarch minnow, c1906........................... **90.00**
Never Fail Minnow, three hooks **300.00**
Surprise minnow **185.00**
Sam-Bo, 4" l, bass, pike, pickerel, orig box **215.00**
Shakespeare Mouse white and red, thin body, glass eyes, 3-5/8" l **30.00**
Underwater minnow, five-hook, c1907 .... **150.00**
South Bend Tackle Co. Panatellia, green crackle-back finish, glass eyes, boxed **50.00**
Truck-Oreno, red and white wood **2,970.00**
Vacuum Bait, red and white dec........................... **100.00**
Souvenir, Lucky Lure, Souv of Indian Lake, OH, 3-1/2" l, nude black female, MOC **130.00**
Strike-It-Lure, green, yellow, and red spots, glass eyes **40.00**
W. D. Chapman, Theresa, NY, metal minnow and propeller **2,200.00**
Winchester, 9011, three-hook **500.00**
Winchester, green plug, repainted by Dale Roberts **130.00**

Minnow bucket, green collapsible canvas, wire bail, orig black painted wooden handle, stamped "No. 08 Mfg for the Planet Co. Patent" **155.00**
Net, boat, 32" handle, wood **90.00**
Net, trout
Brodin, name branded on wood handle, unused ... **50.00**
English, folding, triangular, alloy and brass construction, 30" handle, rubber grip, belt

clip, mkd "Made in Great Britain," unused **85.00**
Hardy, collapsible, alloy construction, 24" handle, belt clip............................... **27.50**

Painting

14-1/2" x 19-3/4", The Start, A. Von Beust, sgd "AVB" in lower left corner, young Victorian couple with guide getting ready for fishing excursion, used as orig for illus by Bristol Rod Co., 1905, tempera, 19-1/2" x 25" frame with thin mat........................ **15,400.00**
17" x 24", oil on canvas, Waiting for the Party, 19th C angler sitting in Windsor chair with his equipment, orig gold frame, unsigned **470.00**
Patch, 3-3/4" x 5", Atlantic City Surf Fishing Tournament ... **12.00**
Pinback button, Johnsburg Fish & Game Club, red and white, forest safety theme, 1930s **10.00**
Poacher's gig, hand forged five pronged rake-type device, long worn wooden handle, from Eastern Shore, MD or VA, 63" l **145.00**
Pond boat, 30" h, 28" l, 10" w sailer, rudder.................. **200.00**
Poster
13-1/2" x 18", Bristol Fishing Rod Co., colorful scene of young Victorian couple enjoying picnic while lad lifts edge of her dress with rod and line, gold frame, cloth liner......................... **4,400.00**
17" x 24", Kingfisher, They Can't Get Away From Kingfisher Lines, E. J. Martin's Sons Kingfisher Brand, Braided Silk Lines, Rockville, Conn, girl ice fishing, matted, 24" x 32" frame......... **8,360.00**

Reel

ABU Ambassador 5000, bait casting, red finish, leather case with spare parts . **125.00**
A.L. Walker, Y, German silver Model 100, 4/0, salmon **1,650.00**
Model 200, 4/0, salmon **1,870.00**
Anson Hatch, side mount C-1866, mkd "Hatch's Patent June 19, 1866" **5,500.00**
Army and Navy, English alloy, trout, 2-1/8" d **220.00**
Arthur Kovalovsky, No. 64, made for Zane Grey, patented 2,022,204, front plate mkd "Arthur Kovalovsky Hand Made Patented 1,958,919-Hollywood Cal," big game, 8 1/2" d, 6-1/2" w spool, 17 lbs **20,900.00**
B. C. Milam, Frankford, KY, #2, casting............... **1,760.00**
B. F. Meek & Sons #2, casting.................. **935.00**
#8, mkd "Hand Made," German silver, bait casting **6,160.00**
#33 Bluegrass **85.00**
#44, trout, German silver **5,280.00**
Bogdan, Model 200, salmon, right hand wind......... **825.00**
Charles M. Clinton, Ithaca, NY, German Silver, c1900 .... **6,820.00**
DAM, quick casting, black finish, red agate line guide, orig box **85.00**
Dr. Allonzo H. Fowler, Ithaca, NY, hard rubber, Fowler's Improved Gem Fly Reel **6,600.00**
Edward R. Hewitt, custom made, initials "M.S.I.," aluminum, raised pillars, trout fly, orig leather case........ **13,750.00**

Reel, Lenard Atwood, Farmington Mills, Maine, 1907 patent, original box, **$1,400**.
Photo Courtesy of Lang's Sporting Collectables, Inc.

Hardy

Cascepedia, salmon, 2/0 size
.... **12,375.00**
Princess, trout, German silver
reversible line guide ... **200.00**
Uniqua, trout, 3-1/8", flat
telephone latch **275.00**
Hendryx Safety Reel, trout
.... **995.00**
H. L. Leonard
Model 50B, wide spool, fly
.... **1,760.00**
Patent 1877, upright trout
.... **3,080.00**

Horton Mfg.

#3, suede bag **425.00**
#7 Blueglass **880.00**
#33 Bluegrass Simplex,
suede bag **425.00**

Pocket reel oiler and screwdriver, B. F.
Meek & Sons, Louisville, KY, c1910, **$825**.

*Photo Courtesy of Lang's Sporting Collectables,
Inc.*

Edw. Vom Hofe

German silver, c1870, tiny
upright trout **7,810.00**
Perfection, Model 360, size 2,
German silver and hard
rubber, trout **8,820.00**
Peerless, Model 355, size 3,
German silver and hard
rubber, trout **5,280.00**
Model 621, size 4/0 .... **250.00**
Salmon, Cascapedia **4,290.00**

Julius Vom Hofe

Fly, plain, early size 3 . **880.00**
Freshwater, casting, Pat. Nov.
17, 85, Oct. 8, 1887, torn bag
.... **165.00**
Ocean, 3/0B **300.00**

Meisselbach, #260,
featherlight, skeleton, fly,
vertical box **330.00**
Morgan James, side mount,
pillbox style, brass, c1860
.... **9,350.00**
Niangua, casting **660.00**

Orvis, presentation

EXR1, trout, right hand wind
.... **110.00**
EXR111, trout, spare spool,
right hand wind **110.00**
Otto Zwarg, Model 400,
multiplying, salmon, 2/0 size
.... **1,710.00**

Pflueger

Atlapac, 9/0 size, 5" d. **330.00**
Hawkeye, bulldog logo, trout,
German silver and hard
rubber **350.00**
Philbrook & Paine, hand
made, raised pillar, trout, mkd
"Pat Apld For" **9,625.00**

Restigouche

1896 patent **1,540.00**
1897 patent **1,320.00**
1902 patent **1,540.00**

Trout reel, Morgan James (1815-78),
Utica, NY, c1860 brass pillbox style
side mount reel, **$9,350**.

*Photo Courtesy of Lang's Sporting
Collectables, Inc.*

Seamaster

Duel mode, anti-reverse,
saltwater fly, all black.. **990.00**
Mark III, duel mode, anti-
reverse, saltwater fly, gold
and black **880.00**

Shakespeare

Standard **150.00**
Standard, professional **150.00**
Tournament **110.00**
South Bend, #1131A, casting,
shiny finish, orig box **18.00**

Stan Bogdan, hand made, baby trout

2-3/4" d, 3/4" w spool, hard
leather case **1,485.00**
2-3/4" d, 3/4" w, left hand
wind, orig pouch, unused
.... **1,732.00**
Talbot Star **385.00**

Thos. J. Conroy, NY, Wells
model, c1889, trout . **3,300.00**
Union Hardware Co., raised
pillar type, nickel and brass
.... **25.00**
Unmarked, wood, brass
fittings, c1880-1920, 6" d
.... **85.00**
Walker, TR-4, fly **1,210.00**
Waltonian, Square Stamping
Co., Barneveld, NY, casting
.... **660.00**

Winchester

Model #2844, raised pillar
bay, 3" d, 1-7/8" w spool rest,
nickel plated **275.00**
Model #2944, raised pillar
light saltwater, 3-1/4" d, 1-7/8"
w spool, nickel plated. **250.00**
Wm. H. Talbot Eli, casting
.... **880.00**

Rod

C. W. Jenkins, CO, Model GA
70-39, trout, 7', two-pc, two
tips, for 4 wt line, orig bag and
tube **935.00**
Dickerson, trout, Model
861711, Special 1937, 8-1/2',
three-pc, two tips, orig bag
and tube **2,100.00**

E. C. Powell

Heavy trout or light salmon,
Marysville, 8-1/2', two-pc, two
tips, patent numbers denoting
hollow built configuration, orig
bag, later tube **910.00**
Trout, "A" taper, 8-1/2', two-pc,
two tips, (one replaced),
hollow built, orig bag and tube
.... **770.00**
Trout, B-9, 9', two-pcs, two
tips, for 6 wt line, hollow built,
professionally restored, orig
bag and tube **825.00**
Trout, "C" taper, 8-1/2', two-
pc, two tips, hollow built, orig
bag and tube **990.00**
F. E. Thomas, Bangor, ME
Salmon, two handed, 12',
three-pc, two tips, canvas
sack, tip tube, several wraps
need replacing **220.00**
Trout, Dirigo, 8', three-pc, two
tips, orig bag, later tube
.... **580.00**
Trout, Dirigo, 9', three-pc, two
tips, orig bag, later tube,
varnish roughness **165.00**
Trout, Special, 8-1/2', three-
pc, two tips, orig bag and
tube, restored **385.00**
Trout, Special, 9', three-pc,
two tips, cork spacer on reel
seat, orig bag, hanging tag,
and tube **440.00**

Gary Howells, trout, 7-1/2', two-pc, two tips, for 5 wt line, possibly unused, orig bag and tube ... **2,750.00**
George Halstead, Danbury, CT, split bamboo, 7-1/2', trout **3,410.00**
Gillum, trout, 7-1/2', two- pc, two-tip, light line, orig bag and tube, missing four guides, needs refinishing **3,850.00**
Goodwin Granger, split bamboo, 7' **1,100.00**

Hardy
Centenary set, commemorative, reproduction of 1890s 8' Gold Medal split bamboo rod, blued Houghton Perfect 2-5/8" reel, both numbered "64," of 100 sets made in 1992, rosewood chest with brass plaque **2,915.00**
Salmon Deluxe Rod, extra tip, aluminum case, 9' **175.00**
Split bamboo fly, 7' 2", one tip **200.00**
Harold Gillum, Ridgefield, CT, split bamboo, 6-1/2' and 7-1/2', sold as pr **7,700.00**
H. L. Leonard
Fly, 6-1/2' **1,450.00**
Fly, Leonard Tournament, extra tip, metal case, 9' **300.00**
Red wrap, 7-1/2' **1,925.00**
Split bamboo, model 50DF, 8' **880.00**
#37ACM-6' **3,025.00**
#37-6' **1,925.00**
Horrocks & Illotson, 9' 3", two tips, split-bamboo fly, maroon wraps **50.00**
Montaque, bamboo, two tips, orig case **135.00**
Omar Needham, Rangeley, ME, Needham's Special, light salmon, 9', two-pc, two tips, impregnated, screw down-locking reel seat, orig condition, orig bag and tube **220.00**

Orvis
Battenkill, 8-1/2', two-pc, two tips, orig bag and tube **425.00**
Light Spinning, 7', two-pc, one tip, orig bag and tube **220.00**
Model 1882, trout, 9-1/2', three-pc, two tip, modern guide replacements, orig bag **110.00**
Salmon, 9-1/2', two-pc, two tips, orig bag and tube. **360.00**
Spinning, 6-1/2', two-pc, one tip, superlight, orig bag and tube **250.00**
Paul H. Young, Perfectionist, trout, 7-1/2', two-pc, two tips, 1978, orig bag and tube **2,570.00**

Payne
Light trout, 4'4", two-pc, three tips, 1-5/8 oz, orig bag, hanging tag, and tube **7,975.00**
Salmon, 10-1/2', three-pc, two tips, removable 6" butt extension, orig canvas sack, tip tube, and ferrule plugs **450.00**
Salmon, dry fly, Model 430, 9', two-pc, two tips, removable 6-3/4" butt extension, 6-1/8 oz, unused, orig bag, tube, and tube cover **2,100.00**
Trolling, 9', three-pc, two tips, roctorod butt and tip section, orig bag and tube **410.00**
Trout, Model 96, 6-1/2', two-pc, two tips, orig bag and tube **3,300.00**
Trout, Model 98, 7', two-pc, two tips, extra tip, orig bag and tube **3,850.00**
Trout, Model 200, 8', three-pc, two tips, spare unfinished tip, five guides, orig bag and tube **3,080.00**
Trout, Model 204, 8-1/2', three-pcs, two tips, screw-up locking over walnut reel seat, poor varnish, Abercrombie &

Fitch & Fitch Co. stamp, orig bag and tube **1,870.00**
Trout, 9', three pcs, two tips, screw up-locking reel seat, orig bag and tube.... **1,760.00**
R. L. Winston, San Francisco, trout, 8-1/2', two-pc, one tip, for 7 wt line, hollow built, orig bag and tube.............. **525.00**

Sam Carlson
Light salmon, Four Quad, 8-1/2', two-pc, two tips, 3" removable butt extension, orig bag and tube **1,870.00**
Trout, Four, 7-1/2', two pc, two tips, orig bag and tube **2,530.00**
Trout, Thomas Special, 7', two-pc, two tips, orig bag and tube **1,540.00**
Shakespeare, Premier Model, 9', three-pc, two tips, split-bamboo fly, red silk wrappings, cloth bag, metal tube **75.00**
Shakespeare Springbrook, fly fishing, orig bag **100.00**
S. J. Small, split bamboo, three-rod set **2,640.00**
Superlight, 5' spinning rod **660.00**
Thomas & Thomas, Caenis, 7-1/2', light trout, blued hardware and ferrules, two-pc, two tips, orig bag and tube **1,760.00**
Union Hardware Co., 7-1/2', Kingfisher, saltwater boat rod, split-bamboo fly, dark brown wraps **35.00**

Walt Carpenter
Trout, Browntone, Model No. 91276, 7-1/2', two-pc, two tips, for 4-wt line, unused, orig bag, tube, and tube bag **2,750.00**
Trout, Browntone Special, 8'3", three-pc, two tips, dark flamed cane, cap, and ring reel seat, mahogany spacer, blue hardware, wrapper on handle, orig bag and tube **3,300.00**
Trout, 7'9", two-pc, two tips, for 5-wt line, blued hardware and ferrules, orig bag and tube **2,530.00**
Trout, 8', three-pc, two tips, for 5-wt line, light cane, screw up-locking reel seat, unused, orig bag and tube.... **2,200.00**
Walton Powell, trout, 9', two-pc, two tips, extra mid section, professionally restored **220.00**

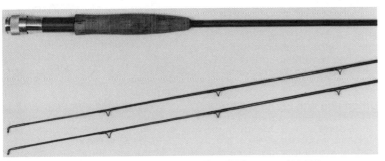

Trout rod, Harold "Pinky" Gillum, Ridgefield, CT, 6-1/2 feet, cane, **$13,200.**

Salesman's sample, cutaway model of Shakespeare Sea Wonder No. 280 Model FB spinning reel **50.00**

Scale, brass, "Chamllons Improved, New York, Pat. Dec 10 1967"................................. **30.00**

Tackle box, leather **450.00**

Vise, fly tying
7" l, 2-1/2" w, steel and brass, bolts to table **210.00**
7-1/2" l, 6" h, cast iron and steel, can be used free standing or bolted down **240.00**

Wallet, 5-1/2" x 12", opens to 12" x 19", H.L. Leonard, 30 plastic pockets displaying 30 different kinds of poly blend, orig contents **40.00**

FLASKS

History: A flask, which usually has a narrow neck, is a container for liquids. Early American glass companies frequently formed them in molds that left a relief design on the front and/or back. Historical flasks with a portrait, building, scene, or name are the most desirable.

A chestnut is hand-blown, small, and has a flattened bulbous body. The pitkin has a blown globular body with a spiral rib overlay on vertical ribs. Teardrop flasks are generally fiddle shaped and have a scroll or geometric design.

Notes: Dimensions can differ for the same flask because of variations in the molding process. Color is important in determining value—aqua and amber are the most common colors; scarcer colors demand more money. Bottles with "sickness," an opalescent scaling that eliminates clarity, are worth much less.

For more information, see *Warman's Glass,* 4th edition.

Historical

Baltimore monument, , amber upper and lower sections shading to brown center, emb "Corn for The World" and "Baltimore," applied collared lip with ring, slightly domed base, Baltimore Glass Works, mid-19th C, quart, 8-1/2" h, McKearin GVI-4, lip chip **310.00**

Columbia and eagle B & W, open pontil, pint, McKearin GI-121, slight interior stain keeps **425.00**

Columbia, Liberty cap, eagle, Kensington and Union on reverse, pale aqua, bubbles **800.00**

Eagle-Cornucopia, early Pittsburgh district, 1820-40, light greenish-aquamarine, sheared mouth, pontil scar, pint, McKearin GII-6 ... **475.00**

Eagle-Willington/Glass Co., Willington glass Works, West Willington, CT, 1860-72, bright medium yellowish-olive, applied double-collared mouth, smooth base, half pint, McKearin GII-63 .... **210.00**

For Pike's Peak Prospector-Hunter Shooting Deer, attributed to Ravenna Glass Works, Ravenna, OH, 1860-80, aquamarine, applied mouth with ring, smooth base, quart, McKearin GXI-47, 1/4" shallow flake **325.00**

Masonic, pale yellow green, emb "Franklin," plain lip, faint rough pontil mark, Monongahela and early Pittsburgh district, 1825-50, pint, 6-3/4" h..... **440.00**

Masonic-Eagle, Zanesville, emb "Zanesville, J. Sheppard & Co.," golden amber, pint, McKearin GIV-32 ..... **2,975.00**

Railroad and eagle
Olive green, no inscriptions, pint, 6-5/8" h, McKearin GV-9 .... **450.00**
Olive green, open pontil, pint, McKearin GV-9 .... **375.00**

Railroad, medium blue green, emb "Success to the Railroad" on both side, plain lip, rough pontil mark with straight seam, Lancaster Glass Works, pint, 6-3/4" h, McKearin GV-1, 1825-75 .... **90.00**

Union and Wm Frank & Sons, Pitts on one side, cannon on other, aqua, pint, 7-1/2" h, McKearin GXII-39, interior blisters, minor residue, flake on base **100.00**

Pattern molded

4-5/8" l, Midwest, 1800-30, 24 ribs swirled to the right, golden amber, sheared mouth, pontil scar.................................. **190.00**

7-3/8" l, Emil Larson, NJ, c1930, swirled to the right, amethyst, sheared mouth, pontil scar, some exterior high point wear **250.00**

Pictorial

Cornucopia and urn of fruit
Aqua green, pint, 7-1/4" h, McKearin GIII-4, minor int. residue, small pot stone. **250.00**
Dark olive, pint, 6-1/2" h, McKearin GIII-4 .... **125.00**
Golden amber, half pint, 5-1/2" h, McKearin GIII-10, minor surface wear **220.00**

Cornucopia/urn, emerald green, pint, pontil, McKearin GIII-17, **$450**.

Photo courtesy of American Bottle Auctions.

Cornucopia, light green, emb "Lancaster Glass Works, NY," plain lip, iron pontil mark, 1825-50, pint, 6-1/2" h, McKearin GIII-16...................................... **420.00**

Double eagle, olive amber, pint, 7-1/2" h, McKearin GII-85, roughness inside neck.... **250.00**

Duck, aquamarine, emb "Will You Take A Drink? Will A (duck figure) Swim?" broad flat lip with ring below, smooth base with indented corner, possibly Lockport Glass Works, mid- to late-19th C, pint, 7-3/4" h, McKearin GXIII-29 .... **235.00**

Eagle
Deep golden amber, plain lip, rough pontil mark, possibly Coffin & Hay, Hammonton, NJ, 1825-50, half pint, 5-5/8" h, McKearin GII-56, section of lip restored **235.00**

Deep olive green, plain lip, rough pontil mark, probably Keene-Marlboro-Street, 1825-50, pint, 6-3/4" h, McKearin GII-73/74, high spot wear **135.00**

Flora Temple, deep amber, emb "Floral Temple, Harnes Trot 2.19 3/4," applied plain lip with ring below, plain base, possibly Whitney Glass Works, Glassboro, NJ, mid- to late-19th C, pint, 8-1/2" h, McKearin GXIII-22 .... **315.00**

Shield and clasped hands, aquamarine, emb "Waterford," applied double collared lip, rough iron pontil mark, probably Waterford Glass Works, NJ, mid-to late-19th C, quart, 9" h, McKearin GXII-2, flake **80.00**

Soldier on horse, yellow, strong olive green overtones, applied double collared lip, rough pontil mark, mid- to late-19th C, quart, 8-1/2" h, McKearin GXIII-16 .... **880.00**

Horse putting cart/eagle, olive green, pint, pontil, McKearin GV-7a, **$700**.
Photo courtesy of American Bottle Auctions.

Pitkin type

Midwest, 1800-30, 6-1/4" l, ribbed and swirled to the right, 16 ribs, olive green with yellow tone, sheared mouth, pontil scar, some int. stain **300.00**

New England, 1783-30, sheared mouth, pontil scar, 5-1/4" l, ribbed and swirled to the left, 36 ribs, light olive yellow **375.00**

Pattern molded, flattened ovoid, medium olive amber, 36 rib broken swirl to right, short neck, plain lip, kick-up base, rough pontil mark, probably New England, early 19th C, pint, 6-3/4" h **360.00**

Hunter-fisher, attributed to Whitney Glass Works, NJ, aqua, 9-1/2" h; aqua glass flask with tree of life and sheaf of wheat designs, 9-1/4" h; aqua ribbed jug form flask, 8-3/4" h, **$415**.
Photo courtesy of Pook & Pook.

Portrait

Adams-Jefferson, New England, 1830-50, yellow amber, sheared mouth, pontil scar, half pint, McKearin GI-114 .... **325.00**

General Jackson, Pittsburgh district, 1820-40, bluish-aquamarine, sheared mouth, pontil scar, pint, McKearin GI-68 .... **1,500.00**

General Taylor, pale greenish aquamarine, emb "Genl Taylor Never Surrenders" and "A Little More Grape Capt Bragg," plain lip, rough pontil mark, probably Baltimore Glass Works, 1825-75, pint, 7-1/8" h, McKearin GS-4 .... **160.00**

Jenny Lind, Fislerville Glass Works, aqua, calabash, 9-1/4" h, McKearin GI-107, several int. blisters **115.00**

Lafayette-DeWitt Clinton, Coventry Glass Works, Coventry, CT, 1824-25, yellowish-olive, sheared mouth, pontil scar, half pint, 1/2" vertical crack, weakened impression, McKearin GI-82 .... **2,100.00**

Rough and Ready Taylor-Eagle, Midwest, 1830-40, aquamarine, sheared mouth, pontil scar, pint, McKearin GI-77 .... **1,200.00**

Washington
Deep blue green, plain lip, rough pontil mark, probably Lockport Glass Works, 1825-50, quart, 8" h, McKearin GI-61 .... **2,860.00**
Medium blue green, emb "The Father of His Country," applied rounded lip with bevel below, rough pontil mark, possibly Dyottville Glass Works, Philadelphia, 1825-50,

quart, 8-1/4" h, McKearin GI-47 .... **450.00**
Sapphire blue, violet overtones, emb "The Father of His Country, Dyottville Glass Works Philada, Gen Taylor Never Surrenders," plain lip, rough pontil mark, 1825-75, quart, 8-1/4" h, McKearin GI-37 .... **3,850.00**

Pittsburgh or Zanesville, swirled, light green, c1835, 6-3/4" h, **$460**.
Photo courtesy of Pook & Pook.

Washington and Jackson, light to medium amber, open pontil, pint **230.00**

Washington and Taylor
Olive green, pint, 6-1/2" h, McKearin GI-31, some surface wear and minor int. blisters **260.00**
Sapphire blue, soda style applied top, open pontil, quart, McKearin GI-54 .... **2,600.00**

Majolica, 4-1/2" h, polychrome dec bulldog, landscape, and crest design, Italy, 19th C **200.00**

Pewter, 14" h, Pilgrim, shaped figural handles, moon-shaped body, molded foliage, pierced base, losses, 16th C **345.00**

Pottery

Pig shape, brown Albany glaze, incised "Brachmann & Moosard, Importers and Dealers in Wines & Liquors, 81 West Third Street, Cincinnati," Anna Pottery, 7" l **13,500.00**

Scroll

Aquamarine, flat ring below plain lip, faint large iron pontil mark, quart, 8-1/2" h, McKearin GIX-4, 1825-50 .... **110.00**

Greenish aquamarine, plain lip, rough pontil mark, 8-7/8" h, quart, McKearin GIX-2, 1825-50 .... **90.00**

Honey amber, pint, 7" h, minor surface wear **350.00**

Medium blue green, plain lip, rough pontil mark, quart, 8-3/4" h, McKearin GIX-1, 1825-50 .... **190.00**

Swirled ribbed body, green, half pint, American early 18th C, 5" h, green glass quart flask, c1830, 9" h, rim chip, **$350**.

Photo courtesy of Pook & Pook.

Sunburst

Geep blue green, tooled lip, rough pontil mark, 1825-75, three-quarter pint, 7" h, McKearin GVIII-29 .... **220.00**

Medium green, plain lip, rough pontil mark, New England, early to mid-19th C, pint, 8" h, McKearin GVIII-2 .... **440.00**

Medium yellow olive, plain lip, rough pontil mark, Coventry, CT, early to mid-19th C, pint, 7-1/2" h, McKearin GVIII-3.............. **615.00**

FLOW BLUE

History: Flow blue, or flown blue, is the name applied to china of cobalt blue and white, whose color, when fired in a kiln, produced a flowing or blurred effect. The blue varies from dark royal cobalt blue to navy or steel blue. The flow may be very slight to a heavy blur, where the pattern cannot be easily recognized. The blue color does not permeate through the body of the china. The amount of flow on the back of a piece is determined by the position of the item in the sagger during firing.

Known patterns of flow blue were first produced around 1830 in the Staffordshire area of England. Credit is generally given to Josiah Wedgwood, who worked in that area. Many other potters followed, including Alcock, Davenport, Grindley, Johnson Brothers, Meakin, Meigh, and New Wharf. They were attempting to imitate the blue and white wares brought back by the ship captains of the tea trade. Early flow blue, 1830s to 1870s, was usually of the pearl ware or ironstone variety. The later patterns, 1880s to 1900s, and the modern patterns after 1910, were of the more delicate semi-porcelains. Most flow blue was made in England but it was made in many other countries as well. Germany, Holland, France, Spain, Wales, and Scotland are also known locations. Many patterns

Educational Alert: The Flow Blue International Collectors' Club, Inc. has been studying and discussing new versus reproduction flow blue and mulberry. There are still areas of personal judgment as yet undetermined. The general rule accepted has been *"new"* indicates recent or contemporary manufacture and *"reproduction"* is a copy of an older pattern. Problems arise when either of these fields is sold at *"old"* flow blue prices.

In an effort to help educate its membership, the club continues to inform of all known changes through its conventions, newsletters, and the Web site: www.flowblue.com.

Warman's is working to those ends also. The following is a listing of *"new"* flow blue, produced since the 1960s.

Blossom: Ashworth Bros., Hanley, 1962. Wash bowl and pitcher made for many years now, in several items.

Vinranka: Upsala-Ekeby, Sweden, 1967-1968. Now discontinued and highly collectible, a full dinnerware set.

Romantic Flow Blue: Blakeney Pottery, 1970s. Resembles Watteau, but not exact. The old patterns never had the words "flow blue" written on them.

Victoria Ware: mark is of lion and uniform, but has paper label "Made in China," 1990s. Made in various patterns and design, but the give-away is the roughness on the bottoms, and much of it has a pea green background. Some of this line is also being made in Mulberry.

Floral pitchers (jugs) and teapots bearing a copied "T. Rathbone England" swan mark.

Williams-Sonoma and Cracker Barrel are also each releasing a vivid blue and white line. Both are made in China. One line is a simplified dahlia flower on white; the other has summer bouquets. Both are well made and readily available, just not old. The reproductions are more of a threat to collectors.

Waldorf: by New Wharf cups and saucers are out, but missing "England" from their mark and are made in China.

Iris: by Dunn, Bennett, Burslem, has been reproduced in a full chamber set.

Touraine: by Stanley, by far the most prolific reproduction made recently, in 2002. Again, the "England" is missing from the mark, and it is made in China. Nearly the entire dinnerware set has been made and is being sold on the market.

In all cases, regarding new pieces and reproductions, be aware of unglazed areas on the bottoms. The footpads are rough and just too white. The reproductions, particularly the Touraine, are heavier in weight, having a distinctive thick feel. The embossing isn't as crisp and the pieces are frequently slightly smaller in overall size than the originals.

Check the Flow Blue International Collectors' Club, Inc., Web site and also www.repronews.com. Join the club, study the books available, and always, always, KNOW your dealer! Good dealers guarantee their merchandise and protect their customers.

were made in the United States by several companies, Mercer, Warwick, Sterling, and the Wheeling Pottery to name a few.

Adviser: Ellen G. King.

Acme, Hancock
    Chocolate pot, cov **450.00**
    Teapot, cov **285.00**

Albany, Grindley
    Fish platter **475.00**
    Soap dish, cov, drainer
    .... **220.00**
    Soup tureen, cov, four pcs
    .... **550.00**

Alma, Adderly, spittoon .. **425.00**

Alexandra, Hancock, sauce
    tureen, cov **250.00**

Amoy, Davenport
    Butter dish, three pcs . **350.00**
    Cake plate, square, tab
    handle **450.00**
    Child's creamer, restoration to
    spout **550.00**
    Child's cup and saucer,
    restoration to cup **500.00**
    Child's plate **500.00**
    Child's punch bowl, rim chip
    restored **795.00**
    Child's sugar bowl, small chip
    inside **1,100.00**
    Child's teapot, restoration to
    rim **3,000.00**
    Compote, low foot **375.00**
    Honey dish **185.00**
    Plate, 10-1/2" d **175.00**
    Platter, 13" d, restoration
    .... **225.00**
    Platter, 18" l **550.00**
    Soup bowl, 10-1/2" d .. **150.00**
    Sugar bowl, cover, restoration
    to cover **300.00**
    Teapot, cov **650.00**
    Waste bowl, large **400.00**

Arabesque, Mayer
    Platter, 17-1/2" l, under rim
    chip **350.00**
    Teacup and saucer **195.00**
    Teapot, restoration to spout
    .... **350.00**
    Vegetable dish, merchant
    mark **100.00**

Arcadia, Wilkenson
    Creamer and sugar, cov
    .... **195.00**
    Platter, 14" l **400.00**

Argyle, Grindley
    Butter dish, cov **550.00**
    Creamer **275.00**
    Platter, 17" l **385.00**
    Teapot, cov, restoration to
    spout **500.00**

Asiatic Pheasant, Hughes,
    vegetable tureen, cov. **225.00**

Athens, Adams, punch cup
    .... **200.00**

Atlas, Grindley, slop pail, cov
    .... **850.00**

Azalia, Longton, syrup pitcher,
    small spider **300.00**

Beaufort, Grindley
    Platter, 14" l **275.00**
    Vegetable tureen, cov. **300.00**

Beauties of China, Mellor &
    Venables, creamer **250.00**

Bleeding Heart with Ribbon,
unknown maker
    Plate, 7-1/2" d **175.00**
    Plate, 10-1/2" d **200.00**

Bluebell, Dillwyn-Swansea, syrup pitcher, **$450**.

All flow blue photos courtesy of Ellen King.

Bluebell, Dillwyn-Swansea
    Cake plate, tab handles
    .... **325.00**
    Creamer, 5-1/4" **375.00**
    Cream pot, cov **400.00**
    Hot water pitcher **350.00**

Blue Danube, Johnson Bros,
    platter, 14" l **295.00**

Bombay Japan, Minton, loving
    cup, large, handles **275.00**

Boston, Possil Pottery, Scotland,
    bowl, 10" d, handles **275.00**

Brushstroke, unknown maker, pitcher, luster rim, **$425**.

Brushstroke, Allertons, pitcher,
    7", luster **250.00**

Brushstroke, unknown maker
    Bowl, 8" d **150.00**
    Creamer **225.00**
    Cup and saucer **155.00**
    Platter, 16" l **375.00**
    Salt, master **150.00**
    Sugar bowl, cov **255.00**

Buccleuch, Ridgway
    Butter dish, cov, polychromed
    .... **425.00**
    Cup plate **110.00**

Burton, Mayer, jardinière, large
    .... **450.00**

Byzanthium, BWM, child's cup
    and saucer **50.00**

California, Wedgwood, butter
    dish base **100.00**

Candia, Cauldon, soup, rimmed,
    9" d **75.00**

Carlton, Alcock
    Compote, handles **375.00**
    Plate, 9" d **65.00**
    Salt, master **150.00**

Cashmere, Ridgway, Morley
    Bowl, oval, 8-1/2" l **200.00**
    Cake plate, pedestal **2,500.00**
    Ewer bowl, restored.... **375.00**
    Pitcher **700.00**
    Plate, 6-1/4" d **100.00**
    Plate, 9" d **225.00**
    Plate, 10-1/2" d **250.00**
    Platter, 10-1/2" l **400.00**
    Platter, 15-1/2" l **775.00**
    Sauce dish **100.00**
    Soup bowl **145.00**
    Soup tureen, cov, undertray
    .... **3,200.00**
    Teacup and saucer **200.00**
    Teapot, cov **850.00**
    Toddy plate, 5" d **375.00**
    Undertray, reticulated . **275.00**
    Vegetable tureen, cov **975.00**
    Warming plate, stopper
    missing **1,250.00**

Cassino, Davenport, child's
    sugar bowl, cov **275.00**

Cavendish, Keeling
    Cheese dish, cov **250.00**
    Vase, 13" h **150.00**

Chapoo, Wedgwood
    Pitcher, 6-1/2" h **300.00**
    Plate, 9-1/2" d **150.00**
    Platter, 12-1/2" l, one under
    rim chip **250.00**
    Platter, 18" l **550.00**
    Sugar bowl, cov, restored
    .... **375.00**
    Teacup and saucer **150.00**
    Teapot, cov, restored spout
    .... **750.00**
    Vegetable tureen, cov, hairline
    in base **350.00**

Chen-Si, Maddock
    Milk pitcher **325.00**
    Sugar bowl, cov **255.00**

Chen-Si, Meir
Cup and saucer, handleless
.... **120.00**
Soup bowl, 10-1/2" d .. **110.00**
Waste bowl **100.00**
Chinese, Dimmock
Potpourri jar, cov, restored
.... **1,800.00**
Vase, large **1,600.00**
Chinese Bells, Meigh, teacup
and saucer, handleless ... **250.00**
Chusan, Clementson
Platter, 13" l **325.00**
Razor box, cov **255.00**
Relish, mitten shape ... **275.00**
Sugar bowl, cov **250.00**
Teapot, cov, finial restored
.... **400.00**
Vegetable tureen, cov,
hexagonal, ftd **325.00**

Claremont, Johnson Bros, plate, 9" d, **$75**.

Claremont, Johnson Bros, plate,
9" d **75.00**
Clarence, Grindley
Bone dish **85.00**
Teacup and saucer **125.00**
Clayton, Johnson Bros
Bone dish **55.00**
Plate, 10" d **95.00**
Clytie, Wedgwood
Platter, 16" l **450.00**
Platter, 18" l **800.00**
Colburg, Edwards
Oyster bowl **100.00**
Soup tureen, cov **725.00**
Colonial, Meakin
Gravy boat, undertray **125.00**
Platter, 16" d **255.00**
Teacup and saucer **95.00**
Conway, New Wharf
Bone dish **65.00**
Plate, 10" d **135.00**
Platter, 14" x 10" **220.00**
Countess, Grindley
Creamer **150.00**
Sugar bowl, cov **250.00**
Teapot, cov **350.00**

Country Scenes, unknown
maker
Gravy, underplate **125.00**
Plate, 9" d **60.00**
Cracked Ice, Warwick
Chocolate cup and saucer
.... **155.00**
Ferner, restoration **175.00**
Lamp, converted to electric
.... **900.00**
Relish, leaf shape **175.00**
Daffodil, unknown English
maker, chocolate pot, cov
.... **350.00**
Dainty, Maddock
Sauce/dessert bowl,
individual size **45.00**
Vegetable tureen, cov. **285.00**
Delft, Minton, pitcher, 5-1/2"
.... **115.00**

Devon, Brownsfields, syrup pitcher, pewter lid, **$325**.

Devon, Brownfields, syrup
pitcher, pewter lid **325.00**
Dundee, Ridgways
Sauce/dessert bowl, round,
individual size **40.00**
Plate, 8" d **50.00**
Vegetable tureen, cov. **255.00**
Excelsior, Fell
Soup tureen, cov **550.00**
Waste bowl **120.00**
Fairy Villas, Adams, vegetable
bowl, open, round, 10" d. **225.00**
Figural, unknown maker, relief
jug, figural handles, large
.... **1,850.00**
Floral, Cauldon
Lavabo, paper holder,
hairlines **700.00**
Umbrella holder, hairlines
.... **450.00**
Florida, Ford, plate, 9-1/2" d
.... **65.00**

Formosa, Mayer
Plate, 9-3/4" d **110.00**
Teapot, cov **575.00**
Galleons, Doulton, milk pitcher
.... **325.00**
Gironde, Grindley
Bone dish **55.00**
Platter, 21-3/4" l **495.00**
Glorie De Duci, Doulton
Biscuit jar, cov **325.00**
Sponge dish, drainer .. **275.00**
Gothic, Furnivals, plate,
10-1/2" d **85.00**
Grace, Grindley
Butter pat **55.00**
Gravy boat, undertray **225.00**
Platter, 14" l **350.00**
Platter, 18" l **450.00**
Vegetable tureen, cov **350.00**
Harley, Grindley
Shaving mug **150.00**
Toothbrush holder **175.00**
Harvest, Hancock, chamber pot
.... **250.00**
Hindustan, Wood & Brownsfield
Soup tureen ladle **450.00**
Soup tureen, cov **500.00**
Wash basin and pitcher
.... **850.00**

Hong Kong, Meigh, syrup pitcher, 7" h, **$450**.

Hong Kong, Meigh
Child's creamer **300.00**
Child's toddy plate **125.00**
Plate, 7" d **85.00**
Plate, 10" d **150.00**
Platter, 16" l **450.00**
Platter, 20" l, well and tree
.... **695.00**
Sugar bowl, cov **100.00**
Teapot, cov, restoration to pot
edge **475.00**
Vegetable tureen, cov **450.00**

Hopberry, Meigh
Child's cup and saucer
.... **125.00**
Child's gravy boat....... **165.00**
Child's teapot, cov **200.00**
India, Bishop & Stonier
Jardiniere.................... **400.00**
Vase, 6" h, price for pr **250.00**
India, Villeroy & Boch, plate,
pierced **100.00**
Indian, Pratt
Creamer, large........... **350.00**
Soup bowl, 10-1/2" d .. **100.00**
Soup tureen, cov **600.00**
Indian Jar, Furnival
Plate, 9-1/2" d **80.00**
Soap dish, cov, drainer
.... **275.00**
Janette, Grindley, soup tureen,
cov **375.00**
Jeddo, Adams, soap dish, cov,
insert **285.00**
Kezle, Grindley, gravy boat,
undertray........................ **200.00**
Kin Shan, Challinor
Fernery bowl, 10" d..... **225.00**
Plate, 10-1/2" d **175.00**
Knox, New Wharf
Butter pat..................... **45.00**
Platter, 11-1/2" l........... **150.00**

La Belle, Wheeling, pitcher, ice lip,
$1,200.

La Belle, Wheeling
Bowl, 10" x 8-1/4" **200.00**
Bread tray.................. **150.00**
Cake plate **175.00**
Celery dish **280.00**
Charger, 11" d............. **275.00**
Child's creamer........... **450.00**
Chocolate cup and saucer
.... **550.00**
Punch cup **225.00**
Spittoon...................... **850.00**
Sugar bowl, cov.......... **250.00**
Teacup and saucer..... **175.00**
Teapot, cov **1,500.00**
Turkey serving set, platter,
twelve 10" d plates... **1,400.00**

Vegetable bowl, round, open
.... **285.00**
Wall plaque, lovely lady, 15"
.... **450.00**
Lahore, Phillips, teapot, cov,
inverted heart **375.00**
Lazuli, Swansea, foot bath
.... **600.00**
Lily, Kaolin Ware, platter, green
polychrome, 12" l **275.00**
Lorne, Grindley
Platter, 14" l **225.00**
Vegetable tureen, cov. **350.00**
Lugano, Ridgways
Bowl, 9-1/2" d **150.00**
Platter, 11-1/2" l **250.00**
Luzerne, Mercer
Platter, 13-1/4" l.......... **395.00**
Relish dish, 12" **175.00**
Soup tureen, cov **455.00**
Madras, Doulton
Candle sconces, pr **350.00**
Teapot, cov, individual size
.... **225.00**
Madras, Upper Hanley
Child's teapot, cov **225.00**
Vegetable tureen, cov, oval
.... **275.00**
Manilla, Podmore Walker
Platter, 13-1/4" l.......... **425.00**
Sugar bowl, cov.......... **265.00**
Syllabub cup **150.00**
Margot, Grindley, mug.... **200.00**
Marguerite, Grindley
Bone dish **60.00**
Butter dish, three pcs . **350.00**
Melbourne, Grindley, sugar
bowl, cov...................... **225.00**
Mongolia, Johnson Brothers
Plate, 8" d **65.00**
Platter, 16-1/2" l........... **450.00**
Teacup and saucer..... **125.00**
Morning Glory, Ridgway
Platter, 12" l **275.00**
Teacup and saucer..... **135.00**
Nankin, Fell, platter, 11" l **100.00**
Nautilus Shell, Pinder, Bourne &
Co., spoon warmer, 7-1/2"
.... **850.00**
Neoplitan, Johnson Brothers
Soup tureen, cov, ladle, and
tray.............................. **650.00**
Vegetable tureen, cov. **245.00**
Ning Po, Hall
Cake plate, tab handles
.... **265.00**
Creamer...................... **250.00**
Pitcher, 8".................... **220.00**
Plate, 10-1/2" d **125.00**
Sugar bowl, cov.......... **285.00**

Norbury, Doulton, toothbrush holder,
$350.

Normandy, Johnson Brothers
Platter, 16" l................. **285.00**
Platter, 17" l................. **325.00**
Punch cup, ftd, saucer **275.00**
Soup tureen, cov, undertray
.... **1,250.00**
Vegetable bowl, 10" oval
.... **150.00**
Oregon, Mayer
Creamer...................... **250.00**
Plate, 8" d **100.00**
Teacup and saucer..... **150.00**
Vegetable tureen, cov **385.00**
Wash basin and pitcher
.... **950.00**
Oriental, Alcock
Dessert set, 14 pcs, red
polychromed **1,400.00**
Plate, 10" d, polychromed
.... **200.00**
Platter, 13" x 9", polychromed
.... **385.00**
Platter, 21", well and tree
.... **950.00**
Teacup and saucer..... **125.00**
Wash basin and pitcher
.... **1,100.00**
Osaka, Kent, biscuit jar, cov
.... **250.00**
Pansy, Warwick
Bean pot, cov **550.00**
Cake plate, 11" **150.00**
Celery **125.00**
Chocolate pot, cov **550.00**
Gravy boat.................. **225.00**
Plate, 9" d, scalloped.. **100.00**
Trivet, 6-1/2" **125.00**
Pelew, Challinor
Creamer, 5-1/4" h........ **275.00**
Cup and saucer, handleless
.... **175.00**
Plate, 10-1/2" d **275.00**

Polychrome pattern, unknown maker, fruit compote, stemmed, handles, **$575**.

Polychrome patterns, unknown makers
  Barber bottle, oranges, reds
  .... **325.00**
  Biscuit jar, cov, turquoise
  .... **450.00**
  Milk pitcher, florals, pinks,
  7-1/2" h........................ **175.00**
  Tazza, ftd, handle, green and
  pinks **375.00**
  Tea caddy, cov **450.00**
Poppy, unknown maker
  Dresser set, tray, ring tree,
  and two lidded boxes . **450.00**
  Teapot, cov, removable
  strainer........................ **365.00**
Regalia, Hughes, vegetable
tureen, cov **175.00**
Rose, Wheeling Pottery, biscuit
jar, cov............................. **300.00**
Roseville, Maddock
  Gravy boat, undertray **165.00**
  Vegetable tureen, cov. **250.00**
Scinde, Alcock
  Chamber pot, cov....... **550.00**
  Child's cup and saucer
  .... **275.00**
  Child's tea bowl **800.00**
  Child's teapot, cov **475.00**
  Creamer, gothic shape **450.00**
  Plate, 9-1/2" d **125.00**
  Plate, 10-1/2" d **225.00**
  Platter, 10" l................ **355.00**
  Platter, 16" l................ **585.00**
  Platter, 20" l................ **850.00**
  Relish dish **275.00**
  Soap dish, three pcs .. **775.00**
  Sugar bowl, cov.......... **350.00**
  Teacup and saucer, pumpkin
  shape........................... **225.00**
  Teapot, cov **650.00**
  Vegetable tureen, cov, ftd
  .... **550.00**
  Wash pitcher.............. **500.00**
  Waste bowl **250.00**
  Water pitcher, 12-1/2" . **850.00**
Shanghai, Grindley
  Creamer...................... **195.00**

Gravy boat, attached
undertray **200.00**
Plate, 10" d **100.00**
Platter, 12" l................ **250.00**
Platter, 14" l................ **325.00**
Sugar bowl, cov.......... **225.00**
Vegetable tureen, cov. **350.00**

Sloe Blossom, unknown maker, mug, large, **$425**.

Sloe Blossom, Unknown maker
  Child's cup and saucer
  .... **250.00**
  Mustard pot, pewter lid
  .... **295.00**
  Plate, 10" d **375.00**
  Platter, 20" l................ **850.00**
Sobraon, Alcock
  Chamber pot **250.00**
  Punch cup **150.00**
  Shaving mug **225.00**
  Sugar bowl, cov, pumpkin
  shape........................... **350.00**
Syria, Grindley, chamber set:
wash bowl, pitcher, toothbrush
holder, hot water pitcher, shaving
mug, sponge dish, soap dish
.... **2,200.00**
Temple, Podmore Walker
  Plate, 9-3/4" d **120.00**
  Platter, 20" l................ **395.00**
  Teacup and saucer,
  handleless **125.00**
Tonquin, Adams
  Gravy boat.................. **150.00**
  Plate, 10-1/4" d, paneled
  .... **145.00**
  Platter, 16" l................ **450.00**
  Teacup and saucer..... **135.00**
  Teapot, cov, restoration to
  finial **500.00**
Tonquin, Heath
  Creamer...................... **375.00**
  Plate, 10-3/4" d **150.00**
Touraine, Alcock
  Bone dish **125.00**
  Butter dish, cov **295.00**
  Butter pat................... **125.00**
  Plate, 8-3/4" d **75.00**
  Plate, 10" d **125.00**
  Teacup and saucer....... **95.00**
  Teapot, cov **675.00**
  Toothbrush holder....... **275.00**

Vegetable dish, individual,
oval **135.00**
Vegetable tureen, cov **350.00**
Trellis, Ford & Sons, milk pitcher,
8-1/2" **250.00**
Virginia, Maddock, butter dish,
cov **225.00**
Waldorf, New Wharf
  Creamer...................... **220.00**
  Plate, 9" d **80.00**
  Plate, 10" d **100.00**
  Platter, 11" x 9" **150.00**
  Sugar bowl, cov.......... **165.00**
  Teacup and saucer..... **110.00**
  Vegetable tureen, cov **350.00**
  Waste bowl, 5-1/2"...... **100.00**
Watteau, Doulton
  Charger, 13" d............ **250.00**
  Drainer, oval, small **225.00**
  Soup bowl, 10" d **55.00**
Waverly, Maddock
  Butter dish, cov **275.00**
  Teacup and saucer..... **120.00**
Whampoa, Mellor & Venables
  Butter tub, cov, drainer
  .... **315.00**
  Mustard pot, cov **275.00**
  Teapot, cov **425.00**
Wild Rose, Warwick
  Cake plate, handle, 12"
  .... **195.00**
  Chocolate cup and saucer
  .... **165.00**
  Chocolate pot, cov **550.00**
  Nut dish **175.00**
  Pitcher, 7" h................ **250.00**
Willow, Doulton
  Cheese dish, cov, slant top
  .... **375.00**
  Creamer...................... **225.00**
  Pitcher, 5-1/2" **200.00**
  Vegetable bowl, open, round,
  8" d **130.00**
Windmill, Warwick, egg cup
.... **165.00**
York, unknown maker, dresser
jar, cov **175.00**

FOLK ART

History: Exactly what constitutes folk art is a question still being vigorously debated among collectors, dealers, museum curators, and scholars. Some want to confine folk art to non-academic, handmade objects. Others are willing to include manufactured material. The term is used to cover objects ranging from crude drawings by obviously untalented children to academically trained artists' paintings of "common" people and scenery. Some record setting prices for folk art were achieved during the auction of the collection of Eugene and Dorothy Elgin, at Conestoga Auction Company, Inc., in April of 2004.

Scherenschnitte, valentine for Amy DuBois, circular form originally folded into eight sections, each with different handwritten verse, cutwork design accented with watercolor, 19th C, 10" d, foxing, loss to edges, **$550**.

Photo courtesy of Alderfer Auction Co.

Bald eagle, 26-3/8" h, carved and painted wood, stylized, glass eyes, stippled surface, Ohio, attributed to early 20th C, mounted on carved pine base, minor age cracks **5,000.00**

Billfold, beadwork eagle with shield, two stars, crossed American flags, old label. "This pocketbook was made by a Mrs. Davis in the Virginia Colony AD 1758, was found in her son's HB Davis's pocket at the surrender of Lord Cornwallis from George Davis," 7-1/2" l, some deterioration to fabric, some losses **950.00**

Bird tree, 20" h, 21" w, carved and polychromed, seven stylized birds on wire legs, base made from surface root, PA, c1890-1910 .... **17,050.00**

Birth record, 9" x 7", watercolor and ink on paper, Mary Hoyt, born May 6, 1807, two cream, beige, and light brown birds in ovals, flanked by patterned outline and column-like lines, reverse sgd "Henniker May 7, 1829 by Moses Connor," unframed, minor staining **8,225.00**

Box, cov, 6" w, 3-1/2" d, 4-1/2" h, carved oak, America, late 19th/early 20th C, figure of man wearing cap with visor, sitting cross-legged on large dog, both have tails, border of turned

finials joined by spiral rails, dovetailed box, leaf-carved drawer, paneled sides, old variegated varnish finish **1,265.00**

Bust, 6" h, attributed to Albert Abelt, Cumberland County, PA, titled "My Favorite Teacher," carved and painted wood, fabric flowers on hat, soulful eyes, blue dress, ex-Elgin **24,200.00**

Candle stand, 16" w, 15-1/2" d, 30-1/4" h, laminated hardwoods, sq top with egg and dart molding, four ladies legs shaped supports with turned drop, old mellow finish, repairs **375.00**

Carving

Angel

28" l, 17" h, relief carved angel holding star of Bethlehem and scroll, faded inscription begins "Glory to God in the...," right arm with old iron work repair, American, 19th C **1,100.00**

41" l, 9" h, pine plank naively carved with face of angel, outstretched wings, radiating layered feathers, remnants of orig polychrome dec, light weathering to gray patina, possibly PA, 19th C **900.00**

Bulls heads, life-size, real horns, glass eyes, old weathered paint, carved by Noah Weiss (1842-1907, Northampton County, PA), dated 1870, price for pr **38,500.00**

Theorem, blue and white striped bowl filled with colorful flowers, painted on white velvet, signed "French" for Garnet B. French, sponge painted frame, discoloration, 5-1/4" x 19-1/4", **$400**.

Photo courtesy of Alderfer Auction Co.

Drawing, pencil, 13-7/8" x 17-1/4", farm scene, detailed two-story house, smaller barns, picket fence, hills and trees in background, stains and foxing, 16-1/2" x 20-3/4" gilt frame **980.00**

Drawing, watercolor

c1840, girl in red dressed flanked by stylized tulip columns, inscribed "Ann Potter's profile drawn by Ruby Devol," verse "Can love for me inspire your tender heart. Dare I to hope and with that hope be blessed. Pursed we shall to us will him virtuous paths and find for time prove more," orig red painted frame **20,000.00**

1841, man and woman on either side of two handled urn of flowering roses, tulips, and other flowers, inscribed "A Walk in the Garden, Constructed by Michael Palmer, June 14, AD 1838-This is to certify that wife, Sarah B. Abrise, is superior in reciting first class this evening. May 21, 1841," 14" x 17" **28,000.00**

19th C, American School, two girls standing, each holding red book, wearing applied gold foil brooch, lace collars accented with pinprick designs, framed, 9" x 7", tear lower left, repaired tears on edges **1,410.00**

Family record, 16-3/4" x 20-7/8", Elijah and Mary Ann (Blew) Smalley, "Executed by E.S. Van Glove," attributed to Indiana, c1866, pen and ink on paper, recording vital statistics of them and their 11 children, decorated with four columns and foliage, imperfections **300.00**

Figure, carved and painted wood

5" h, man with drum, Alabama, late 19th/early 20th C, stand **360.00**

6-1/2" h, woman, standing, applied extended arms, metal tack eyes and buttons, alligatored surface, America, late 19th C, stand **600.00**

7-1/2" h, 6-1/2" l, 4-1/2" h, bird on pedestal, pegged articulated head, wings, and body, paper label on base "Done by Stanley Nick Gustwick, Coudersport, Pa" **880.00**

20" h, 22" l, 7-1/2" w, crane, carved wood body, neck, and legs, tin tail and wings, tack eyes, painted gray, green and red, aged patina, legs made from turned spindles of old chair, made by Emanuel Myers, York County, PA, broom maker **9,350.00**

25-1/2" l, snake, old dark red paint, yellow polka dots, black, white, and blue eyes, early 20th C, old chip on tail **575.00**

30" l, airplane, four engines, tin tail, 44" w wooden wings, propellers, orig red and white paint, some flaking and touch up **250.00**

Grotesque face jug, stoneware, 5-1/2" h, brown-speckled glaze, found in Ohio, 19th C, imperfections **14,950.00**

Hammer, 13" l, oak and iron, figural, handle surmounted by carved man's head and upper torso, found in PA, 19th C **1,955.00**

Theorem, basket of fruit, blue grapes, green leaves, wheat, red cherries, 16" x 20", **$150**.

Photo courtesy of Wiederseim Associates, Inc.

Memorial, 31" x 23" x 6-1/2", incised gilt and ebonized deep recessed shadow box frame, white painted cast iron profile of Lincoln surrounded by wreath of wire stemmed wax silk flowers, grouped with ribbon tied and waxed silk roses and calla lilies, surmounted by white dove with wings spread in flight, c1875 .... **700.00**

Model, 29" l, 11-1/4" d, 8" h, Chinese style side-wheel paddle boat, small horse-drawn cart, two horses powering wheels, carved man, minor breaks **115.00**

Picture frame, 12-5/8" w, 15-3/4" h, painted and incised wood, meandering vine and dot border, corner bosses, one corner boss missing **920.00**

Plaque, 14" d, sun face, carved polychrome, molded edge, America, early 19th C, minor imperfections, stand .. **16,100.00**

Scherenschnitte, 11-1/2" x 14-1/2", birth certificate, dated

Sept. 5, 1780, for Anna Elizabeth Lauerin, Berks County, PA, Tolpehaden Tow ship, cut-work and painted dec border of flowers, tulips, and hearts attached with vine-work, black ink text, glued down, staining, loss **925.00**

Sculpture, 34-1/2" h, seagull, wood and tin, orig paint, wooden ice fishing decoy in beak, standing on pylon surrounded by fishing related items including netting, lures, eel spear, bobbers, lead sinkers, wear **450.00**

Still life, watercolor on paper, American School, 19th C, framed

10-3/4" x 9-1/2", fruit and foliage in gray bowl, shades of red, green, and blue, pinprick dec, general toning, tiny scattered stains. **1,150.00**

15" x 13", *Bouquet of Spring Flowers in a Vase,* sgd "Frances Thompson, 1841," tulips, narcissus, and other spring flowers, white handled urn-form vase dec with sea shells, very minor toning **2,715.00**

Theorem, rooster, David Y. Ellinger, (American, 1913-2003), oil on velvet, signed lower left "D. Ellinger," 13" x 12-3/4", **$2,875**.

Photo courtesy of Pook & Pook.

Theorem

12-1/4" w, 15-1/2" h, Lady Liberty feeding eagle, basket of flowers, trees, and flag, on velvet, gilt frame, c1790, fading, discoloration to textile **3,190.00**

12-3/8" x 15", basket of flowers, oil and watercolor, sgd "Julia P. Paine," c1840, ... **12,000.00**

16-1/2" w, 13-1/2" h, basket of fruit still life, watercolor on velvet, unsigned, American School, 19th C, molded giltwood frame, toning **4,150.00**

22-1/4" l, 17" h, Canton porcelain bowl of fruit, strawberries, pear, blueberries, bird nested in center, sgd "D. Ellinger," orig grain painted frame . **4,950.00**

Tinsel picture, 22" x 17", flower arrangement, reverse-painted glass backed with foil and paper, American School, late 19th C, Victorian frame, repaired **180.00**

Trivet, 11-1/2" l, 4" w, 1-3/4" h, heart form, single pc carved chestnut, serrated edges, applied legs, wrought iron tacks on top **2,100.00**

Valentine, 12-1/2" h, 8-1/4" w, pinprick and watercolor on paper, woven, pink paper ribbon border, German verse, woman in pink carrying bottle, soldier in blue uniform on horseback, separated by medallion "Treue Liebe," (True Love,) glued down to another pc of paper, some damage, translation included **500.00**

Wall hanging, 19-1/2" w, 19" h, attributed to Noah Weiss, Northampton, Lehigh County, PA, relief carved pine, two hunting dogs and two quail, painted white, black, and brown dogs, green grass, mottled white sky, painted black frame, aged patina, ex-Elgin **8,250.00**

FOSTORIA GLASS

History: Fostoria Glass Co. began operations at Fostoria, Ohio, in 1887, and moved to Moundsville, West Virginia, its present location, in 1891. By 1925, Fostoria had five furnaces and a variety of special shops. In 1924, a line of colored tableware was introduced. Fostoria was purchased by Lancaster Colony in 1983.

For more information, see *Warman's Glass*, 4th edition.

Ashtray

American, 2-7/8" sq **7.50**
Coin, crystal................... **30.00**
June, blue **75.00**
Baker, June, topaz, oval, 9"
.... **195.00**
Bell, Chintz, orig label **130.00**
Berry bowl, June, blue, 5" d
.... **50.00**
Bonbon, Bridal Wreath, #2630
Century, cut 833, three toes
.... **75.00**
Bouillon, Versailles, topaz **30.00**

Bowl

American, oval, 10" l **30.00**
Baroque, blue, 4" sq, one
handle........................... **22.00**
Corsage, flared, 12" d. **110.00**
Grape Leaf, green, 12" d
.... **175.00**
June, 12" d, blue **125.00**
Bread and butter plate, Trojan,
topaz, 6" d...................... **10.00**

Cake salver

Century, crystal............. **60.00**
Coin, crystal.................. **98.00**
Corsage, 10-1/2" d........ **32.00**
Navarre, crystal, handles,
10" d.............................. **60.00**

Candleholders, pr

Baroque, 4" h, one-lite, silver
deposit Vintage dec on base,
#2496............................. **75.00**
Baroque, 8-1/2" h, 10" w, two-
lite, removable bobeche and
prisms, #2484 .... **375.00**
Buttercup, 5-1/2" h, #2594,
etch 340 .... **250.00**
Coin, red, tall **150.00**
Meadow Rose............. **185.00**
Trojan, topaz, 2", #2394, etch
280............................... **145.00**
Trindle, #2594, three-lite,
Buttercup etch, 8" h, 6-1/2" w
.... **250.00**

Bud vase, **$45**; jug, **$65**; tall covered urn, **$65**; Coin pattern, olive green.

Candy dish, cov

Baroque, crystal **40.00**
June, yellow................ **370.00**
Navarro, three parts.... **175.00**
Versailles, blue, three parts
.... **345.00**
Card tray, Brocaded Daffodil,
two handles, pink, gold trim
.... **40.00**
Celery tray, Trojan, topaz **100.00**
Cereal bowl, June, rose, 6" d
.... **85.00**

Champagne

Bridal Wreath, #6051, cut 833
.... **35.00**
Buttercup, #6030, etch 340
.... **32.00**
Corsage, #6014, etch 325
.... **32.00**
Dolly Madison.............. **18.00**
June, saucer, petal stem
.... **27.00**
Versailles, pink **40.00**

Cheese and cracker

Chintz **70.00**
Colony **55.00**

Cigarette box, cov

Morning Glory etching.. **65.00**
Oriental **170.00**
Cigarette set, Baroque, azure,
#2496, five pcs **450.00**

Claret

Bridal Wreath, #6051, cut 833
.... **38.00**
Camelia **30.00**
June, pink **175.00**
Navarre **80.00**
Trojan, yellow, 6" h **100.00**

Cocktail

Baroque, yellow............ **15.00**
Vesper, amber **30.00**

Compote

Baroque, crystal, 6" **18.00**
Corsage, #2496 Baroque,
etch 325........................ **75.00**

Trojan, topaz, #2400, etch 280
.... **85.00**
Condiment set, American, pr
salt and pepper shakers, pr,
cloverleaf tray, pr cruets . **200.00**
Console set, Baroque, azure,
#2496, 10-1/2" d bowl, pr
candlesticks................... **300.00**
Cordial, Dolly Madison..... **30.00**
Cosmetic box, cov, American,
2-1/2" d, flake on bottom. **900.00**
Courting lamp, Coin, amber
.... **150.00**
Creamer, individual size
Bridal Wreath, #2630 Century,
cut 833........................... **30.00**
Century **9.00**
Raleigh **8.00**

Console set, low console bowl with gold edge trim, matching candlesticks, Oakwood pattern, iridescent finish, **$225**.

Creamer, table size
Baroque, azure, #2496. **55.00**
Chintz **20.00**
Raleigh **10.00**
Trojan, topaz................. **22.00**
Creamer, sugar, tray, individual
size
Camelia **45.00**
Century......................... **30.00**
Cream soup
Colony **95.00**
Versailles, pink............. **65.00**
Vesper, amber **30.00**
Cruet, June, yellow......... **700.00**
Crushed fruit jar, cov, America,
c1915-25, 5-7/8" d, 6" h **1,600.00**
Cup and saucer
Baroque, blue............... **35.00**
Buttercup...................... **34.00**
Camelia **20.00**
June, azure................... **45.00**
Minuet, green **55.00**
Trojan, topaz, #2375 Fairfax,
etch 280......................... **40.00**
Decanter, orig stopper,
Hermitage, amber, #2449
.... **125.00**
Dinner plate
Versailles, pink, slight use
.... **75.00**
Vesper, amber **30.00**
Figure
Deer, standing, crystal,
4-1/2" h **45.00**

Lute and Lotus, ebony, gold highlights, 12-1/2" h, price for pr **975.00**
Mermaid, crystal, 10-3/8" h **225.00**
Fruit cocktail, Hermitage, topaz, #2449 .... **22.00**
Goblet, water
Baroque, azure, #2496 . **45.00**
Bouquet, crystal, #6033, etch 342 .... **35.00**
Buttercup, #6030, etch 340 .... **40.00**
Dolly Madison **20.00**
Golden Lace, gold trim. **24.00**
Meadow Rose.............. **30.00**
Navarre **40.00**
Trojan, topaz **75.00**

Creamer and sugar, Horizon pattern, Spruce green, original foil labels, **$35**.

Grapefruit, Coronet **9.00**
Gravy boat, liner, Kasmir, blue **180.00**
Ice bucket, Versailles, pink **155.00**
Iced-tea tumbler
Bouquet, crystal, #6033, etch 342 .... **35.00**
Navarre, pink **75.00**
Jelly, cov
Coin, amber **30.00**
Meadow Rose, 7-1/2" d **90.00**
Jug
Hermitage, green, #2449, three pints.................. **145.00**
Manor, #4020, wisteria foot **1,500.00**
Trojan, topaz, #5000, etch 280 .... **600.00**
Juice tumbler, June, topaz, ftd **30.00**
Lily pond, Buttercup, 12" d **55.00**
Marmalade, cov, American **125.00**
Mayonnaise
Baroque, azure, #2496 . **95.00**
Bouquet, #2360 Century, etch 342................................ **110.00**
Buttercup **90.00**
Navarre **90.00**

Milk pitcher, Century........ **60.00**
Mint, Baroque, azure, #2496, handle, 4" d **48.00**
Nappy, handle
Baroque, azure, #2496 . **48.00**
Coin, blue, 5-3/8" d **30.00**
Nut cup, Fairfax, amber ... **15.00**
Oil cruet, Versailles, yellow **550.00**
Old-fashioned tumbler, Hermitage, azure **35.00**
Olive, Hermitage, amber, #2449 .... **32.00**
Oyster cocktail, Hermitage, amber, #2449 .... **18.00**
Parfait, June, pink **180.00**
Pickle castor, American, ornate silver plated frame, 11" h **900.00**
Pickle tray, Century, 8-3/4" **15.00**
Pitcher, Lido, ftd **225.00**
Plate
Baroque, green, 7-1/2" d **28.00**
Century, 9-1/2" d **30.00**
Corsage, 8" d, etch 325 **22.00**
Rose, 9" d **15.00**
Platter
June, topaz, 12" l, oval **145.00**
Trojan, topaz, 12" l, oval **80.00**
Punch bowl, ftd, Baroque, crystal, orig label **425.00**
Relish dish, cov, Brocaded Summer Gardens, three sections, white **75.00**
Relish dish, open
Corsage, three parts, #2496, Baroque, etch 325 .... **75.00**
June, topaz, two parts, 8-1/4" l **40.00**
Ring holder, American, 4-1/2" l, 3" h **800.00**
Rose bowl, American, small **18.00**
Salad plate, Buttercup **12.00**
Salt and pepper shakers, pr
Bridal Wreath, #2630 Century, cut 833, chrome tops.... **95.00**
Coin, red **60.00**
Coronet **15.00**
Versailles, topaz, ftd ... **200.00**
Sauce boat, Versailles, pink, matching liner **300.00**
Server, center handle, Trojan, topaz, etch 280 .... **135.00**
Sherbet
Baroque, azure, #2496 . **45.00**
Buttercup, #6030, etch 340 .... **32.00**
Hermitage, green, #2449 .... **22.00**
June, azure **40.00**
Trojan, topaz, #5099, etch 280 .... **48.00**
Snack plate, Century, 8" d . **25.00**

Sugar, individual size, Baroque, blue................................. **4.00**
Sugar, cov, table size, Trojan, topaz **22.00**
Syrup, American, Bakelite handle............................ **200.00**
Sweetmeat, Baroque, azure, #2496.......................... **58.00**
Torte plate
Baroque, azure, #2496, 14" d **125.00**
Colony, 15" d **80.00**
Heather, 13" d **45.00**
Tray, Navarre, 8" l **100.00**
Tumbler, water
Hermitage, topaz, #2449 .... **30.00**
June, ftd **55.00**
Trojan, topaz, 5 oz, 4-1/2" l **30.00**
Urn, cov, Coin, amber, 12-3/4" h **68.00**
Vase
Baroque, azure, #2496, 8" h **225.00**
Flying Fish, teal, 7" h..... **65.00**
Hermitage, topaz, #2449, 6" h **45.00**
Oak Leaf Brocade, c1929-31, 8" h............................ **240.00**
Versailles, yellow, 8" h, flip **395.00**
Whipped-cream pail, Versailles, blue **270.00**
Whiskey, Hermitage, topaz, #2449............................... **20.00**
Wine
Buttercup, #6030, etch 340 .... **45.00**
Chintz **40.00**
Coin, red **90.00**
Corsage, #6014, etch 325 .... **45.00**
Hermitage, amber, #2449 .... **20.00**

FRAKTUR

History: Fraktur, the calligraphy associated with the Pennsylvania Germans, is named for the elaborate first letter found in many of the hand-drawn examples. Throughout its history, printed, partially printed/partially hand-drawn, and fully hand-drawn works existed side by side. Schoolteachers or ministers living in rural areas of Pennsylvania, Maryland, and Virginia often made frakturs. Many artists are unknown.

Fraktur exists in several forms—geburts and taufschein (birth and baptismal certificates), vorschrift (writing examples, often with alphabet), haus sagen (house blessings), bookplates and bookmarks, rewards of merit, illuminated religious texts, valentines, and drawings. Although collected for decoration, the key element in fraktur is the text.

Notes: Fraktur prices rise and fall along with the American folk-art market. The key marketplaces are Pennsylvania and the Middle Atlantic states.

Alphabet, 9-3/4" w, 12" h, upper and lower case written in fraktur schrift, orange and black ink, old inlaid frame, minor discoloration and tears **250.00**

Birth certificate, Geburts and Taufschein

6-7/8" w, 9" h, hand drawn, attributed to Samuel Bentz, Lancaster County, PA, for Susanna Hacker, born 1828, spherical, geometric, and stylized floral and finial dec, old frame, some staining **4,950.00**

8" w, 11" h, Henry Young, watercolor, man in blue frock coat holding glass of wine, inscribed between two red, yellow, and blue eight-point stars, for "Mr. Michael Snyder- A Son of Andrew Snyder and his wife Catherine, born Seysel May 25 AD 1820 in Derry Township Columbia County State of Pennsylvania" **19,000.00**

9-1/2" h, 15" h, printed, Daniel May, York, PA, for William Brennemann, 1847, Codorus Township, York County, PA, hand illuminated in blue, green, pink, and yellow, filled by decorator, contemporary marbleized paint dec frame, tears, minor discoloration **180.00**

10-3/8" w, 17-3/4" h, hand drawn, attributed to Ehre Vater artist, for Margaretha Mayerin, Sept. 28, 1800, Cumberland County, PA, two columns, centralized heart and two birds, tulip and floral dec, illuminated in red, yellow, green, and blue, painted frame, minor folds, tears, small restoration to corner **8,250.00**

12-1/2" w, 7-1/2" h, printed and hand drawn, printed text for Johann Valentine Schuller, hand drawn potted flowers and text attributed to J. Schuller, for Marigreth Schneider, 1789, Pinecreek, Berks County, PA, illuminated in red, yellow, and green, black painted frame **3,025.00**

14-1/2" w, 12-1/2" h, printed by J. Hartman, 1818, Lebanon County, PA, for Joseph Rudy, 1818, Dauphin County, PA, illuminated in brown and yellows, filled in and signed by Charles Overfield, Hannover, Germany, 1847, framed **600.00**

15" w, 12-3/4" h, hand drawn, attributed to Johseph Lochbaum, for Johannes Schlichter, 1792, ink, illuminated in red, yellow, and green, floral motifs and hearts, two flying eagles, religious text in hearts, black painted frame **4,675.00**

Bookplate

6-1/2" w, 8-1/4" h, watercolor on laid paper, tulips and other flowers, bright red, yellow, and green, yellow and black birds, worn gilt frame, PA origin........................ **2,990.00**

6-3/4" l, 4" h, hand written, "Jacob Witmeyer's Book, born in 1835," York County, PA, illuminated in yellow, red, green, and blue ink, red ochre painted frame **385.00**

Child's Book of Moral Instruction (Metamorphis), watercolor, pen and ink on paper

5-3/4" x 7-1/2", dec on both sides of four leaves, each with upper and lower flaps showing different versus and color illus, unknown illustrator **345.00**

6" x 7", printed form on paper, hand colored elements, The Great American Metamorphosis, Philadelphia, printed by Benjamin Sands, 1805-06, printed on both sides of four leaves, each with upper and lower flaps, engraved collar illus by Poupard...................... **420.00**

6-1/4" x 7", dec on both sides of four leaves, when folded reveals different versus and full-page color illus, executed by Sarah Ann Siger, Nazareth, PA, orig string hinges . **575.00**

Birth and baptismal certificate for Margaretha Sussamans, born Oct. 6, 1796, Marlborough Township, Montgomery County, PA, polychrome decoration in border along with two poems in heart outlines, signed by artist Martin Brechall, 13" x 16", folding, tearing, edge chipping, **$1,725.**

Photo courtesy of Alderfer Auction Co.

Christmas card, 6-1/2" w, 4" h, German text, greeting inside stylized oval, circular border, framed............................ **825.00**

Confirmation certificate, 6" x 7-3/4", watercolor, pen and ink on paper, David Schumacher, paired tulips and hearts, for Maria Magdalena Spengler, dated 1780................... **4,600.00**

Copybook, Vorschrift, 8" w, 5-5/8" h, pen and ink, red watercolor, laid paper, German text with ornate Gothic letters in heading, blocked cut area in lower left unfinished, minor edge damage, 11-3/8" w, 9-1/2" h yellow and red leather covered frame.............................. **250.00**

Gebruts and Tauf-schein, uncolored, dated 1822, German text, nicely added information, minor edge wear, **$275**.

Drawing
4-1/4" w, 5-3/4" h, hand drawn, blue bird within two black snakes climbing poles to arch, decorative name "S. A. Kline," handwritten "A. C. Martin, April 22, 1823," orig frame........................ **1,980.00**

8-1/4" w, 10-3/8" h, hand drawn, Snow Hill Cloister, Franklin County, PA, potted flowers with compass wheels, tulips, and parrots, decorative border, drawn in red ink, colored in yellow, blue, and green, old painted frame **6,600.00**

9-7/8" l, 5-1/8" h, hand drawn and colored, house and barn, farm life, cows, horses, rabbit, and snake, buggy and Conestoga wagon, sun with face, pen and green, orange, yellow and brown, dated 1856 in lower right corner, framed **7,975.00**

Ein brief, 11-1/2" w, 15" h, printed and hand illuminated, printed by King und Baird,

Philadelphia, purple, orange, and yellow, ein brief to guard against fired, old frame... **315.00**

Family register, 19-3/4" w, 16" h, hand drawn, blue-green and red border with stars and flowers in corners, hearts, cherubs, and cross hatch work at center, German names, written in old brown ink, dates from 1814 to 1870, heart and hand medallion with inscription "Orphans Home and Ft. Wayne Hospital, Allen Co., Ind," sgd "John Cornelius Martin," old taped tear near top margin, small piece of corner missing......................... **1,100.00**

Himmelsbrief, 9-3/4" w, 7-1/2" h, printed, attributed to Stettinius and Leper, text, Hanover, York County, PA, wood blocks of vases and flowers, hand illuminated in red, yellow, and green, old tiger maple frame, water stained **100.00**

Framed manuscript, musical score, tulips decoration, **$215**.

Photo courtesy of Wiederseim Associates, Inc.

House blessing (Haus Segen) 7-1/2" h, 12" w, block printed and hand drawn, printed text, dated 1787, hand dec attributed to Arnold Hovelmann, tulip and flowers, border dec, illuminated in red, yellow, green, and brown, old painted frame **10,450.00**

15-1/2" h, 11-3/4" w, printed by Johann Ritter, Reading, hand colored, orange, green, blue, yellow, brown, and black, professionally repaired and rebacked on cloth, 18-1/4" h, 14-3/8" w old stenciled dec frame.... **500.00**

Marriage certificate, 8" x 12-1/2", watercolor, pen and ink

on paper, Daniel Schumacher, paired red, yellow and green birds flanking an arch with crown, for Johannes Haber and Elisabeth Stimmess, Windsor Township, Berks County, PA, dated 1777 .... **1,035.00**

Reward of merit, 3-1/4" w, 4-7/8" h, hand drawn, cut-work, attributed to Jacob Botz, Lancaster, PA, floral motif, two birds perched on tulips, cut-work to floral motif, name Salome Schmidin below, red, blue, and green........................... **3,740.00**

FRATERNAL ORGANIZATIONS

History: Benevolent and secret societies played an important part in America from the late 18th to the mid-20th centuries. Initially, the societies were organized to aid members and their families in times of distress. They evolved from this purpose into important social clubs by the late 19th century.

In the 1950s, with the arrival of the civil rights movement, an attack occurred on the secretiveness and often-discriminatory practices of these societies. Membership in fraternal organizations, with the exception of the Masonic group, dropped significantly. Many local chapters closed and sold their lodge halls. This resulted in the appearance of many fraternal items in the antiques market.

Benevolent & Protective Order of the Elks, (BPOE)

Book, *National Memorial*, 1931, color illus........................... **35.00**

Bookends, pr, bronzed cast iron, elk in high relief......... **75.00**

Pinback button, orange, lavender, and green, white accents, gold rim, brown elk symbol, tiny inscription "Souvenir Elks Convention Los Angeles 1909" **25.00**

Shaving mug, pink and white, gold elk head, crossed American flags and floral dec, marked "Germany" on bottom **90.00**

Tip tray, Philadelphia, 21st Annual Reunion, July 1907, rect, 4-7/8" x 3-1/4" **135.00**

Eastern Star, dresser tray, glass top, metal fittings, enameled emblem with gold trim in center, dried flowers under glass top, two handles, **$25**.

Eastern Star

Demitasse cup and saucer, porcelain **25.00**
Pendant, SP, rhinestones and rubies **45.00**
Ring, gold, Past Matron, star-shape stone with diamond in center **150.00**

Independent Order of Odd Fellows (I.O.O.F)

Ceremonial staff, 3" w, 1-1/2" d, 64" h, polychrome carved wood, reverse tapering staff surmounted by carved open hand in cuffed sleeve holding heart in palm, old red, gold, and black painted surface, mounted on iron base, minor surface imperfections **2,300.00**
Gameboard, reverse painted black and gold metallic squares bordered by "I.O.O.F" chain links and other symbols, areas of flaking, 20-1/2" x 20-1/2" black oak frame **350.00**
Vignette, 7-3/4" x 14-1/2", oil on board, hand beneath three links holding heart and card bearing archery scene, molded gilt gesso frame, flaking, subtle surface grime.................. **920.00**
Wall hanging, 75" l, 47-1/2" h, painted canvas, from Odd Fellows Lodge #4 in Whitehall, NY, 19th C, several symbols reflecting high ideals, imperfections **2,990.00**
Watch fob, 94th Anniversary, April 12, 1913.................... **30.00**

Knights Templar

Business card, Reynolds, J. P., Columbia Commandery No. 18 (K of P) Sturgis, MI, color logo, c1890 .... **6.00**

Knights Templar, pin tray, Alleghany Commandery, Alleghany, Penna, tan ground, red and gold highlights, **$20**.

Loving cup, china, three handles, green and white, gold tracery, Knights Templer insignia and Pittsburgh, 1907, marked "American China Co." **75.00**
Magazine, *The Magazine for York Rite Masons*, 12 issues from 1982-83............................. **18.00**
Shot glass, bowl supported by three golden swords, dated 1903, Pittsburgh................ **25.00**
Tumbler, emb Indian head, dated 1903, Pittsburgh **45.00**

Knights Templar, plate, 51st Annual Conclave, Knights Templar, Penna, Gethsemane Commandry, No. 75, York, PA, 1904, blue transfer print, **$65**.

Masonic

Advertising button, Illinois Masonic Hospital, black and white litho, c1920 .... **10.00**
Apron, 14" x 12", leather, white, blue silk trim, white embroidery, silver fringe **35.00**
Book, *An Inquiry In The Nature & Tendency of Speculative Freemasonry*, John Stearns, 1829, 210 pgs.................. **65.00**
Bookends, pr, patinated metal, "appl'd for" on back **200.00**
Box, cov, 5" x 16-1/4" x 12-1/2", Chinese Export black lacquer, molded top with mother-of-pearl and lacquer Masonic devices,
sides with floral dec, top loose, lock mechanism missing, minor lacquer loss **920.00**
Ceremonial cane, 33-1/2" l, carved lizards, rounded top knop with emblem and eagle, metal top, several age cracks **350.00**
Fob, silvered brass, June 14-15, 1927 event, Inscription for "Grand Lodge, F & A.M. Wisconson," blank reverse **18.00**
Goblet, St. Paul, 1908 ...... **70.00**
Jug, 5-5/8" h, lusterware, transfer printed and painted polychrome enamels, horseman, inscribed "James Hardman 1823," Masonic dec, royal coat of arms, minor wear **410.00**

Lions International, sign, round, metal and enamel, 30" d, **$50**.
Photo courtesy of Joy Luke Auctions.

Match holder, 11" h, wall type, walnut, pierce carved symbols **75.00**
Painting, 23-1/4" h, 20" w, oil on canvas, "Our Motto," framed, retouched, craquelure . **2,645.00**
Pendant, 10k yg, designed as double-headed eagle, set with old European and single-cut diamonds, approx. total wt. 0.78 cts, opening to reveal various enameled emblems, 13.3 dwt, missing two stones **500.00**
Pocket watch, Hiram Watch Inc., 14k yg, open face, blue dial with raised gold tone Masonic symbol indicators, case with engraved Masonic scenes and symbols, Hallmark 15 jewel movement, winding stem topped with blue stone cabochon **2,115.00**
Ring, 14k rose gold, enameled cross on one side, enameled 32 degrees on other, double eagle head set with 10-point diamond, hand engraved 1900-20 . **175.00**

Sign, 28-3/4" w, 34" h, shield shape, polychrome wood, several applied wood Masonic symbols, including All-Seeing Eye, sun, moon, stars, large central "G," pillars, etc., gilt highlights, blue field, red and white stripes below, molded gilt frame, wear and losses **3,055.00**

Tobacco jar, 4-7/8" l, 3-7/8" w, 7-1/4" h, cast iron, brass, and lead, oval brass finial on domed octagonal cover, fitted onto conforming container plated with lead, sides decorated with various engraved designs: "Daniel Hall" over a foliage-filled pitcher flanked by tobacco pipes and goblets, shield with Masonic symbols encircled with "FRIENDSHIP LOVE AND TRUTH," ship at sea and anchor; the lid and base painted dark red with black, green, and yellow highlights, wear........... **1,175.00**

Shriners, fez, Arabia Shrine Temple, Houston, 7-1/8", **$35.**

Shriner

Cup and saucer, Los Angeles, 1906 .... **70.00**
Dinnerware, Rajah, partial set, various marks, 52 pcs..... **150.00**
Goblet, St. Paul, 1908, ruby stained, pedestal foot **70.00**
Ice-cream mold, 4-1/4" d, pewter, crescent with Egyptian head, marked "E & Co., NY" **30.00**
Mug, Syria Temple, Pittsburgh, 1895, gold figures **125.00**
Shot glass, cranberry and clear, symbols and officers' names, St. Louis, 1909 .... **300.00**

FRUIT JARS

History: Fruit jars are canning jars used to preserve food. Thomas W. Dyott, one of Philadelphia's earliest

and most innovative glassmakers, was promoting his glass canning jars in 1829. John Landis Mason patented his screw-type canning jar on November 30, 1858. This date refers to the patent date, not the age of the jar. There are thousands of different jars and a variety of colors, types of closures, sizes, and embossings.

Collectors refer to fruit jars by the numbering system "RB," which was established by Douglas M. Leybourne, Jr. in his book, *The Collector's Guide to Old Fruit Jars, Red Book 9.*

A. & D. H. Chambers Union, quart, yellow, olive green tint, applied groove ring wax sealer, tin lid mkd "A. & D. H. Chambers Pittsburgh, Pa (five-point star in center), wire yoke, 7-5/8" h, 3-3/4" d base, RB 582..... **990.00**

A. Stone & Co. (arched) Philada Manufactured by Cunningham & Co. Pittsburgh PA" (on fivelines), half gallon, aqua, high kick up, bare iron pontil mark, applied lip groove ring wax sealer, 9-3/4" h, 4-1/2" d base, RB 2752 **1,320.00**

All Right
Half gallon, aqua, reverse mkd "Patd Jan. 28th 1868," base mkd "Pat Nov 26 1867," ground lip, unmarked metal dome shaped lid, wire clamp, 7-1/4" h, 4-1/2" d base, RB 61-3, two rim chips **90.00**
Quart, aqua, reverse mkd "Patd Jan 26th 1868," base mkd "PAT Nov 26 1867" and "12" in center, ground lip, unmarked metal dome shaped lid, wire clamp, 7-3/4" h, 3-3/4" d base, RB 59 .... **110.00**

Almy (arched), quart, aqua, base mkd "Patented Dec 25, 1877 (star)" and "B," lid mkd "C," ground lip, Mason shoulder seal, glass screw-on lid, 7-1/8" h, 3-7/8" d base, RB 63, chips on lid **100.00**

Banner (encircled by) Patd Feby 9th 1864 Reisd Jan 22D 1867," quart, aqua, ground lip, press-down glass lid, neck indentation in rear, 7-1/2" h, 3-3/4" d base, RB 403, several rim flakes **135.00**

Beaver, facing right, chewing log, over word "Beaver," midget pint, Ball blue, base mkd "3," unmarked glass insert and screw band, stippled tail, 5-5/8" h, 3-1/4" d base **385.00**

Bloeser Jar, quart, aqua, ground rim, glass lid mkd "Pat Sept 27, 1887," orig wire and metal clamp with neck tie wire, 8" h, 3-3/4" d, RB 468, rim chip **90.00**
Cohansey Glass Mf'g Co., Pat Mar 20. 77" (on base), half gallon, aqua, barrel shape, base also mkd "3," glass lid mkd "Cohansey Glass Mfg Co., Philada. PA," and "Y" in center, groove ring wax sealer, 9-1/8" h, 4" d base, RB 633-1, roughness, bruise on lid rim **70.00**
Cunningham & Co., Pittsburgh (on base), half gallon, deep aqua, bottom push up, bare iron pontil mark, applied lip to receive cork stopper, 9-3/4" h, 4-5/8" d base, RB 721..... **310.00**

Eagle
Half gallon, aqua, unmarked glass lid, iron yoke clamp with six-pointed star-shape thumbscrew, applied lip, 10" h, 4-1/2" d base, RB 872 .... **110.00**
Quart, aqua, applied smooth lip, fabricated closure, 7-5/8" h, 3-7/8" d base, RB 871............................... **90.00**

Flaccus Bros., steer's head, amber, matching reproduction lid, RB 1014, **$220.**
Photo courtesy of American Bottle Auctions.

F & J Bodine Manufacturers, Philadelphia PA, quart, aqua, unmarked tin lid, soldered wire clamp, 7-1/8" h, 3-7/8" d base, RB 374, small open bubble under base edge **70.00**

Fahnestock Albree & Co., quart, dark aqua, pushed up bottom, pontil mark, Willoughby stopple mkd "J. O. Willoughby Patented, January 4, 1859," 8-1/2" h, 3-3/4" d base, RB 970, replaced wing nut, surface wear........................ **360.00**

Gem, three gallon, aqua, reverse mkd "Manufactured by The Hero Glass Works, Philadelphia PA," ground lip, glass insert mkd "Pat. Feb 12. 56. Dec 17.61. Nov 4.62. Dec 6.94, June 9.68. Sept 1.68. Sep 8.68. Dec.22.68. Jan 9 69," screw band, 17-5/8" h, 8-3/8" d base, RB 1058 ... **3,575.00**

Glass Pail, one-half pint, teal, base mkd "Glass Pail Pat. Boston Mass June 24. 84," unmarked metal two pc lid with bail handle, 4-1/2" h overall, 3" d base, RB 20 .... **525.00**

Globe, quart, red amber, base mkd "65," ground lip, red amber glass lid mkd "Patented May 15 1886," iron clamp and metal band around neck, 8-1/8" h, 3-3/4" d base, RB 1123.... **135.00**

Griffen's, Patent Oct 7 1862 (on lid), quart, amber, ground lip, glass lid with cage like clamp, 7" h, 3-3/4" d base, RB 1154, rim chip and flake **70.00**

Hansee's, (PH monogram) Palace Home Jar, quart, clear, base mkd "Pat. Dec 19 1899," ground lip, monogrammed glass lid, wire clamp and neck tire wire, 7-1/2" h, 3-3/4" d base, RB 1206, edge chips and flakes **50.00**

Johnson & Johnson, New York (vertically), quart, cobalt blue, ground lip, cobalt lid, screw band, 7-1/8" h, 3-3/8" sq base, RB 1344 .... **360.00**

Joshua Wright Philada, half gallon, aqua, barrel shape, applied lip, 10-1/2" h, 3-3/4" d base, RB 3036 variant **180.00**

Lafayette (in script, underlined), quart, aqua, base mkd "2," stopper neck finish three-pc glass and metal stopper, mkd "Patented Sept 2 1884 Aug 4 1885," 8-1/2" h, 3-5/8" d, RB 1452 .... **110.00**

Mansfield
Pint, clear, base mkd "Mansfield Knowlton May '03 Pat. Glass W'K'S," and "2" in circle, glass lid, metal screw cap, lid mkd "Mansfield Glass W'ks Knowlton Pat. May .03," 5-1/8" h, 3-1/8" d base, RB 1619, light 1/4" crack.... **15.00**
Quart, clear with light aqua tint, base mkd "Mansfield Knowlton May '03 Pat. Glass W'K'S," glass lid, metal screw cap, lid mkd "Mansfield Glass W'ks Knowlton Pat. May .03," 7" h, 3-5/8" d base, RB 1619, rim flake **80.00**

Mansfield Improved Mason, quart, lavender tint, glass insert, screw band, 7" h, B 1621 variant, rim flake **60.00**

Mason's (cross) Patent Nov. 30th 1858, (erased The Pearl), gallon, dark aqua, ground lip, Mason shoulder seal, plain zinc lid, 12" h, 5-7/8" d base, RB 1943, rim flakes............ **1,100.00**

Mason's CFJCO Improved, half gallon, amber, base mkd "H43," ground lip, amber insert mkd "P," screw band illegibly mkd, 9-1/8" h, 4-1/2" d base, RB 1711, rim chip and flake **190.00**

Mason's CFJCO Improved Patent Nov. 30th, 1858, gallon, aqua, base mkd "F122," ground lip, Mason's shoulder seal, metal lid mkd "Trademark Boyd's Porcelain Lined Patd Mar.30.58. June 9.63.Mar.30.69 Extd. Mar.30.72," 12" h, 6" d, base, RB 1920, partially open bubble, rim wear, lid cleaned.......... **2,310.00**

Mason's Patent Nov. 30th, 1858, half gallon, green, amber swirls, smooth lip, metal "Ball" lid with milk glass insert mkd "Boyd's Genuine Porcelain Lined Cap 18V," 8-3/4" h, 4-3/8" d base, RB 1787 .... **360.00**

Mason's Patent Nov. 30th 1858, quart, teal, RB 1787, rough ground lip, $275.

Photo courtesy of American Bottle Auctions.

Mason's Patent Nov. 30th, 1858, quart, Ball blue, reverse mkd with Tudor rose emblem, base mkd "A 83," ground lip, disk immerser lid, ext. mkd "TradeMark The Mason Disk Protector Cap Patd. Nov 30 1880," and Tudor rose emblem in center, bottom of disk mkd "Pat. Nov 23.75. Sept 12.76. Nov 30.80, July 20. 1886," 7-1/4" h, 3-3/4" d base, RB 1875... **125.00**

Millville Atmospheric Fruit Jar, 56 oz, aqua, reverse mkd "Whitall's Patent June 18th 1861," glass lid, squared iron yoke

clamp with thumbscrew, 9" h, 4-3/8" d base, RB 2181 ...... **45.00**

Moore's Patent Dec 3D 1861, quart, aqua, correct but slightly ill-fitting lid, rounded iron yoke clamp with thumbscrew, 8-1/8" h, 3-5/8" d base, RB 2204, edge flakes on lid, flakes on interior jar flange.................................. **55.00**

Owl, pint, milk glass, glass insert emb with daisy rosette, serrated screw band, 6-1/8" h, 2-1/2" d base, RB 3085 .... **100.00**

Pansy (superimposed over erased Best), quart, amber, 20 vertical panels, ground lip, glass insert, screw band, 5-1/4" h, 4 1/2" d base, RB 2287, rim flaking **220.00**

Patented Oct. 19, 1858 (on lid), quart, aqua, ground lip, glass lid with internal lugs, lugs on neck of jar, 7" h, 3-7/8" d base, RB 1212.............................. **45.00**

PET, half gallon, aqua, correct glass lid, spring wire clamp, lid mkd "Patented Aug 21st 1869. T.G. Otterson," 9-7/8" h, 4-3/8" d base, RB 2359 .... **200.00**

Potter & Bodine Airtight Fruit Jar Philada, half gallon, reverse mkd "Patented April 13th 1858," groove ring wax sealer, 8-1/4" h, 4-1/4" d base, RB 2383, patched hole on edge of base, 2-1/4" h crack **70.00**

Safety Valve Patd May 21, 1895 HC, over triangle on base, half gallon, dark aqua, Greek Key design around shoulder and base, glass lid mkd "1," ground lip, metal band clamp with bail handle, 8" h, 5-1/8" d base, RB 2539................................... **55.00**

Safety Valve Patd May 21, 1895 HC, over triangle on base, pint, emerald green, partially ground lip, emerald green glass lid, metal band clamp, stamped "Safety Valve Patd May 21, 1895," 5 3/4" h, 3" d base, RB 2538................................. **210.00**

Smalley Full Measure AGS (monogram), quart, amber, base mkd "Patented Dec 13 1892 April 7 1896, Dec 1, 1896," 7-1/4" h, 3-5/8" sq base, RB 2648 .... **90.00**

Standard (arched), quart, light cobalt blue, reverse heel mkd "W. McC & Co," applied groove ring wax sealer, four-point star under base, tin lid mkd "W. McCully & Co. Glass Pittsburg," 7-1/2" h, 3-3/4" d base, RB 2701-variant, 1/2" wide chip on outer rim................................... **880.00**

Star, emblem encircled by fruit, quart, aqua, ground lip, neck slopes inward to opening, zinc insert and screw band, 7-3/4" h, 3-3/4" d base, RB 2724... **150.00**

Sun (in circle with radiating lines) Trade Mark, quart, aqua, base mkd "J. P. Barstow," and "4," ground lip, unmarked glass lid, metal yoke clamp, mkd "Monier's Pat April 1 90 Mar 12 95," 7-3/4" h, 3-7/8" d base, RB 2761 .... **100.00**

Star and crescent, self-sealing jar, embossed star and crescent moon, pint, ground lip, **$450**.

Photo courtesy of American Bottle Auctions.

The Empire, quart, aqua, base mkd "Pat Feb 13 1866," ground rim, glass lid, 8-1/2" h, 3-3/4" d base, RB 927, chipping, bruise to ground rim..................... **80.00**

The Gem, gallon, aqua, base mkd "H. Brooke Mould Maker NY Pat'd Nov 26th 1868. Patd Dec 17th 1861 Reis' Sept 1st 1868," ground lip, glass insert mkd "Mason's Improved May 10 1870," screw band, 12-3/8" h, 5-7/8" d base, RB 1071, loss of lip flange **880.00**

The Hero, half gallon, deep aqua, base mkd "Patd Nov 26 1867" and "5" in center, ground lip, glass insert with "WHA" monogram on interior center, series of patent dates on exterior, screw band, 9" h, 4-1/2" d base, RB 1242, two rim chips **15.00**

The Hero, quart, aqua, base mkd "Patd Nov 26 1867. Pat'd Dec 17 '61 Nov 4 '62 Dec 14 '69 Reis's Sept 1 '68 June 9' 69," and "87" in center, ground lip, glass insert with "WHA," monogram on interior center, series of patent dates on exterior, screw band, 7-1/8" h overall, 3-3/4" d base, RB 1244, rim roughness **25.00**

The Hero, quart, honey amber, base mkd "Pat Nov 26 1867," and "6 (reversed) 7" in center, ground lip, metal lid with partially legible patent dates from 1862 through 1869 including Dec. 22, 1868 and Dec. 14, 1869," 7-1/2" h, 3-3/4" d base, RB 1242 .... **6,600.00**

The Heroine, pint, aqua base mkd "22," ground lip, glass inset mkd "Pat. Feb 12.59 Dec. 17.61. Nov 4. 62.Dec 6.64. June 9.68. Jan 1.68. Sep 1.68. Sep 8.68 Dec 22.68," screw band, 6-5/8" h, 3-1/4" d base, RB 1248, rim chip with flakes **125.00**

The King, Pat Nov .2, 1869, quart, aqua, base mkd "3," ground lip, glass lid and iron yoke clamp, 7-1/2" h, 3-3/4" d base, RB 1418, one half of rim broken out........................ **125.00**

The Valve Jar Co., Philadelphia, quart, aqua, base mkd "Patd Mar 1-th 1868," ground lip, glass lid, wire coil clamp, 7-1/2" h, 4" d base, RB 2873, open bubble on edge of base.................... **385.00**

The Van Vliet Jar of 1881, half gallon, aqua, base mkd "6," ground lip, glass lid mkd "Pt May 3d 1881," metal yoke clamp with unmarked thumbscrew, attached wire extending vertically around entire jar, 9-1/4" h, 4-1/2" d base, RB 2878, bruises **525.00**

Trade Marks Mason's CFJCO Improved, midget pint, aqua, base mkd "C178," ground lip, glass insert mkd "Trade Mark Mason's Improved Registered May 23d 1871 (CFJCo monogram in center) screw band stamped "Consolidated Fruit Jar Co. New York. Trade Mark Mason's Improved Registered May 23 1871," 6" h, 3-1/4" d base, RB 1722..... **25.00**

W. Chrysler, Pat. Nov. 21, 1865, quart, aqua, applied lip, 7-3/4" h, 3-3/4" d base, RB 597-1, three annealing lines............ **1,210.00**

FULPER POTTERY

History: The Fulper Pottery Company of Flemington, New Jersey, made stoneware pottery and utilitarian ware

beginning in the early 1800s. It switched to the production of art pottery in 1909 and continued until about 1935.

The company's earliest artware was called the Vasekraft line (1910-1915), featuring intense glazine and rectilinear, Germanic forms. Its middle period (1915-1925) included some of the earlier shapes, but they also incorporated Oriental forms. Their glazing at this time was less consistent but more diverse. The last period (1925-1935) was characterized by watered-down Art-Deco forms with relatively weak glazing.

Pieces were almost always molded, though careful hand glazing distinguished this pottery as one of the premier semi-commercial producers. Pieces from all periods are almost always marked.

Marks: A rectangular mark, FULPER, in a rectangle is known as the "ink mark" and dates from 1910-1915. The second mark, as shown, dates from 1915-1925; it was incised or in black ink. The final mark, FULPER, die-stamped, dates from about 1925 to 1935.

Adviser: David Rago.

For more information, see Warman's American Pottery & Porcelain, 2nd edition.

Bowl, 8" d, 5" h, flower holder, blue-green crystalline glaze, rect ink mark **110.00**

Bud vase, 9" h, baluster, Butterscotch flambé glaze, ink racetrack mark................ **275.00**

Chinese urn, 9" h, 9" d, two handles, Mirrored Black glaze, vertical mark, few short scratches **1,400.00**

Doorstop, 8" x 10", figural bulldog, amber, blue, purple crystalline glaze, unmarked, restoration to tip of ear and one toe............................ **600.00**

Low bowl, collar rim, covered in fine, frothy blue mirror glaze dripping over Famille Rose ground, vertical mark, 3-3/4" x 10", **$490**.

Effigy bowl
10-1/4" d, 7-1/4" h, Copperdust Crystalline glaze int., Mirrored Black glaze ext. vertical mark **1,400.00**
10-1/2" d, 7-1/2" h, mahogany and amber glaze int., indigo and matte beige ext., vertical mark **700.00**

Ibis bowl, 10-1/2" d, 5-1/2" h, green and blue flambé over Copperdust Crystalline, ink racetrack mark **815.00**

Jug, 11-3/4" h, 7-3/4" d, tall handle, Copperdust Crystalline glaze, vertical mark **1,600.00**

Jug, tall handle, Copperdust Crystalline glaze, vertical mark, 11-3/4" h, 7-3/4" d, **$1,600**.

Lamp, table
15-1/4" d, 18-1/2" h, mushroom-shaped lamp shade, covered in strong Leopard Skin Crystalline glaze, inset with leaded slag glass pieces, two orig sockets, rect ink mark on both pcs, hairline between two inset pcs **5,750.00**
17" d, 21-1/2" h, mushroom-shaped shade covered in

brown, celadon and blue glaze, inset with green and amber slag glass, on Cucumber Green matte base, rect ink mark on both, possibly married piece **1,610.00**

Place card vases, 2-1/4" h, covered in matte turquoise to gunmetal green flambé glaze, orig cardboard box which reads "For a dinner most select/These place card vases are quit correct/I know you like all things that's new/Hence I'm sending these to you, Fulper Co., Flemington, NJ, set of twelve **1,600.00**

Urn
7-1/2" d, 12" h, two handles, fine Mirrored Green, Mahogany, and Ivory flambé glazes, rect ink mark...................... **1,200.00**
11-3/4" d, 11-3/4" h, hammered, frothy indigo and light bleu glaze, incised racetrack mark, stilt-pull bruise......................... **865.00**

Urn, embossed upright handles, covered in frothy blue-green mirrored glaze, vertical mark, 11-1/2" x 9", **$2,530**.

Fulper photos courtesy of David Rago Auctions, Inc.

Vase
4-3/4" d, 7" h, bullet, frothy Leopard Skin Crystalline glaze, ink racetrack mark, two small opposing bursts at rim, grinding chips on base **520.00**
6-1/4" h, 5-3/4" w, pillow, Cat's Eye flambé glaze, ink racetrack mark **175.00**
6-3/4" h, 7" d, bulbous, two handles, mottled gray and amber flambé glaze, vertical mark........................... **475.00**

Vase, bulbous, banded neck, covered in frothy Moss-to-Rose flambé glaze, vertical mark, small glaze neck, **$400**.

Vase, flat shoulder, covered in fine Leopard Skin Crystalline glaze, vertical mark, 7-1/4" x 8", **$1,150**.

7-1/2" h, 6-1/4" d, squatty, two buttressed handle, frothy Moss-to-Rose flambé glaze, vertical mark............... **400.00**
8" h, 5-1/4" d, ovoid, light green crystalline glaze, vertical mark............... **460.00**
9" h, 8-3/4" d, bulbous, double ribbon handles, textured surface, Mission Verde matte green glaze, vertical mark **1,100.00**
11-1/2" h, 7-3/4" d, Cattail, covered in Leopard Skin crystalline glaze, rect ink mark, rim minor burst bubble **2,300.00**
11-1/2" h, 9" d, bulbous floriform, emb panels, covered in exceptional mirrored Cat's Eye flambé glaze, raised racetrack mark **2,990.00**

12" h, 11-1/2" d, bulbous, hammered texture, Mirrored Black, cobalt and blue crystalline flambé glaze, vertical mark, grinding chip **2,200.00**
13" h, 7-1/2" d, tear shape, gunmetal to Copperdust Crystalline flambé glaze, vertical mark, restoration to flat chip on foot ring. **1,900.00**
16-1/2" h, 9" d baluster, Cat's Eye flambé glaze, vertical mark......................... **1,600.00**

Vessel
6" d, 5" h, squatty, two angular handles, frothy blue flambé glaze, ink racetrack mark, restoration to one handle **195.00**
6" d, 6-1/2" h, bulbous, three horn-shaped handles, ivory, blue, and Mirror Black flambé glaze, vertical ink mark **860.00**
7-1/2" d, 6-1/4" h, spherical, two buttressed handles, mirrored Cat's Eye flambé glaze, ink racetrack mark **435.00**
11-1/2" d, 13-1/4" h, bulbous, four short handles, covered in Leopard Skin Crystalline glaze, incised racetrack mark, restoration to drill hole in bottom...................... **2,990.00**

FURNITURE

History: Two major currents dominate the American furniture marketplace—furniture made in Great Britain and furniture made in the United States. American buyers continue to show a strong prejudice for objects manufactured in the United States. They will pay a premium for such pieces and accept them above technically superior and more aesthetically appealing English examples.

Until the last half of the 19th century, English examples and design books dictated formal American styles. Regional furniture, such as the Hudson River Valley (Dutch) and the Pennsylvania German styles, did develop. Less-formal furniture, often designated as "country" or vernacular style, developed throughout the 19th and early 20th

centuries. These country pieces deviated from the accepted formal styles and have a charm that many collectors find irresistible.

America did contribute a number of unique decorative elements to English styles. The American Federal period is a reaction to the English Hepplewhite period. American designers created furniture that influenced, rather than reacted to, world taste in the Gothic-Revival style and Arts and Crafts, Art Deco, and Modern International movements.

Furniture styles

Furniture styles can be determined by careful study and remembering what design elements each one embraces. To help understand what defines each period, here are some of the major design elements for each period.

William and Mary, 1690-1730: The style is named for the English King William of Orange and his consort, Mary. New colonists in America brought their English furniture traditions with them and tried to translate these styles using native woods. Their furniture was practical and sturdy. Lines of this furniture style tend to be crisp, while facades might be decorated with bold grains of walnut or maple veneers, framed by inlaid bands. Moldings and turnings are exaggerated in size. Turnings are baluster-shaped and the use of C-scrolls was quite common, giving some look of moment to a piece of furniture. Feet found in this period generally are round or oval. One exception to this is known as the Spanish foot, which flares to a scroll. Woods tend to be maple, walnut, white pine, or Southern yellow pine. One type of decoration that begins in the William and Mary period and extends through to Queen Anne and Chippendale styles is known as japanning, referring to an imitation lacquering process.

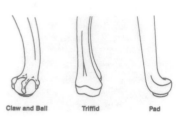

Claw and Ball   Triffid   Pad

Queen Anne, 1720-1760: Evolution of this design style is from Queen Anne's court, 1702 to 1714, and lasted until the Revolution. This style of furniture is much more delicate than its predecessor. It was one way for the young Colonists to show their own unique style, with each regional area initiating special design elements. Forms tend to be attenuated in New England. Chair rails were more often mortised through the back legs when made in Philadelphia. New England furniture makers preferred pad feet, while the makers in Philadelphia used triffid feet. Makers in Connecticut and New York often preferred slipper and claw and ball feet. The most popular woods were walnut, poplar, cherry, and maple. Japanned decoration tends to be in red, green and gilt, often on a blue-green field. A new furniture form of this period was the tilting tea table.

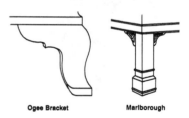

Ogee Bracket   Marlborough

Chippendale, 1755-1790: This period is named for the famous English cabinetmaker, Thomas Chippendale, who wrote a book of furniture designs, *Gentlemen and Cabinet-Makers Director*, published in 1754, 1755, and 1762. This book gave cabinetmakers real direction and they soon eagerly copied the styles presented. Chippendale was influenced by ancient cultures, such as the Romans, and Gothic influences. Look for Gothic arches, Chinese fretwork, columns, capitals, C-scrolls, S-scrolls, ribbons, flowers, leaves, scallop shells, gadrooning, and acanthus. The most popular wood used in this period was mahogany, with walnut, maple, and cherry also present. Legs become straight and regional differences still exist in design elements, such as feet. Claw and ball feet become even larger and more decorative. Pennsylvania cabinetmakers used Marlborough foot, while other regions favored ogee bracket feet. The center of furniture manufacturing gradually shifts from New England and Mid-Atlantic city centers to Charleston. One of the most popular form of this period was a card table that sported five legs instead of the four of Queen Anne designs.

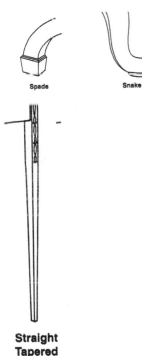

Spade   Snake

**Straight
Tapered**

Federal (Hepplewhite), 1790-1815:
This period reflects the growing patriotism felt in the young American states. Their desire to develop their own distinctive furniture style was apparent. Stylistically it also reflects the architectural style known as Federal, where balance and symmetry were extremely important. Woods used during this period were

first and foremost mahogany and mahogany veneer, but other native woods, such as maple, birch, or satinwood, were used. Reflecting the architectural ornamentation of the period, inlays were popular, as was carving, and even painted highlights. The motifs used for inlay included bellflowers, urns, festoons, acanthus leaves, and pilasters to name but a few. Inlaid bands and lines were also popular and often used in combination with other inlay. Legs of this period tend to be straight or tapered to the foot. The foot might be a simple extension of the leg or bulbous, or spade shaped. Two new furniture forms were created in this period. They are the sideboard and the worktable, reflecting forms that came into favor as they served a very functional use. Expect to find a little more comfort in chairs and sofas, but not very thick cushions or seats.

When a piece of furniture is made in England, or styled after an English example, it may be known as Hepplewhite. The time frame is the same. Robert Adam is credited with creating the style known as Hepplewhite during the 1760s and leading the form. Another English book heavily influenced the designers of the day. This one was by Alice Hepplewhite, and titled *The Cabinet Maker and Upholsterer's Guide,* with publisher dates of 1788, 1789, and 1794.

Sideboard, Hepplewhite, Pennsylvania, c1810, cherry, bowfront top over frieze drawer flanked by two short drawers above two cupboard doors flanked by bottle doors, all with line inlaid edges, square tapering legs with bellflower inlay and banded cuffs, 67" w, 41" h, **$7,475**.

Photo courtesy of Pook & Pook.

Sheraton, 1790-1810:
The style known as Sheraton closely resembles Federal. The lines are somewhat straighter and the

designs plainer than Federal. Sheraton pieces are more closely associated with rural cabinetmakers. Woods would include mahogany, mahogany veneer, maple, and pine, as well as other native woods. This period was heavily influenced by the work of Thomas Sheraton and his series of books, *The Cabinet Maker and Upholster's Drawing Book*, from 1791-1794, and his *The Cabinet Directory*, 1803, and *The Cabinet-Maker, Upholsterer, and General Artist's Encyclopedia* of 1804.

Dining table, Sheraton, Pennsylvania, c1815, tiger maple and cherry, two parts, top with rounded corners, conforming skirt supported by turned and reeded legs, 76" l, 40-1/2" w, 29" h, **$5,300**.

Photo courtesy of Pook & Pook.

Empire (Classical), 1805-1830:
By the beginning of the 19th Century, a new design style was emerging. Known as Empire, it had an emphasis on the classical world of Greece, Egypt, and other ancient European influences. The American craftsmen began to incorporate more flowing patriotic motifs, such as eagles with spread wings. The basic wood used in the Empire period was mahogany. However, during this period, dark woods were so favored that often mahogany was painted black. Inlays were popular when made of ebony or maple veneer. The dark woods offset gilt highlights, as were the brass ormolu mountings often found in this period. The legs of this period are substantial and more flowing than those found in the Federal or Sheraton periods. Feet can be highly ornamental as when they are carved to look like lion feet, or plain when they extend to the floor with a swept leg.

Regional differences in this style are very apparent, with New York City being the center of the design style as it was also the center of fashion at the time.

New furniture forms of this period include a bed known as a sleigh bed, with the headboard and footboard forming a graceful arch, similar to that found on a sleigh, hence the name. Several new forms of tables also came into being, especially the sofa table. Because the architectural style of the Empire period used big open rooms, the sofa was now allowed to be in the center of the room, with a table behind it. Former architectural periods found most furniture placed against the outside perimeter of the walls and brought forward to be used.

Victorian, 1830-1890: The Victorian period as it relates to furniture styles can be divided into several distinct styles. However, not every piece of furniture can be dated or definitely identified, so the generic term "Victorian" will apply to those pieces. Queen Victoria's reign affected the design styles of furniture, clothing, and all sorts of items used in daily living. Her love of ornate styles is well known. When thinking of the general term, Victorian, it is best to think of a cluttered environment, full of heavy furniture, and surrounded by plants, heavy fabrics, and lots of china and glassware.

Bookcases, stacking, Victorian, glass fronts, **$425**.

Photo courtesy of Dotta Auction Co., Inc.

French Restauration, 1830-1850: This is the first sub-category of the Victoria era. This style is best simplified as the plainest of the Victorian styles. Lines tend to be sweeping, undulating curves. It is named for the style that was popular in France as the Bourbons tried to restore their claim to the French throne, from 1814 to 1848. The Empire (Classical) period influence is felt, but French Restauration lacks some of the ornamentation and fussiness of that period. Design motifs continue to reflect an interest in the classics of Greece and Egypt. Chair backs are styled with curved and concave crest rails, making them a little more comfortable than earlier straight back chairs. The use of bolster pillows and more upholstery is starting to emerge. The style was only popular in clusters, but did entice makers from larger metropolitan areas, such as Boston, and New Orleans, to embrace the style.

Chair, side, Gothic Revival, attributed to New York, c1840, stained maple, each with shaped crest above four turned spindles, cane seat, serpentine front seat rails on sabre legs connected by concave stretcher, price for pair, **$750**.

Photo courtesy of Sloans & Kenyon Auctions.

The Gothic Revival period, 1840-1860: This is one relatively easy to identify for collectors. It is one of the few styles that celebrates elements found in the corresponding architectural style: turrets, pointed arches, and quatrefoils—things found in 12th and 16th centuries that were adapted to this interesting mid-century furniture style. The furniture shelving form known as an étagère is born in this period, allowing Victorians to have more room to display their treasured collections.

Furniture that had mechanical parts also was embraced by the Victorians of this era. The woods preferred by makers of this period were walnut and oak, with some use of mahogany and rosewood. The scale used ranged from large and grand to small and petite. Carved details gave dimension and interest.

Rococo Revival, 1845-1870: This design style features the use of scrolls, either in a "C" shape or the more fluid "S" shape. Carved decoration in the form of scallop shells, leaves, and flowers, particularly roses, and acanthus further add to the ornamentation of this style of furniture. Legs and feet of this form are cabriole or scrolling. Other than what might be needed structurally, it is often difficult to find a straight element in Rococo Revival furniture. The use of marble for tabletops was quite popular, but expect to find the corners shaped to conform to the overall scrolling form. To accomplish all this carving, walnut, rosewood, and mahogany were common choices. When lesser woods were used, they were often painted to reflect these more expensive woods. Some cast iron elements can be found on furniture from this period, especially if it was cast as scrolls. The style began in France and England, but eventually migrated to America where it evolved into two other furniture styles, Naturalistic and Renaissance Revival.

Elizabethan, 1850-1915: This sub-category of the Victorian era is probably the most feminine-influenced style. It also makes use of the new machine turned spools and spiral turnings that were fast becoming popular with furniture makers. New technology advancements allowed more machined parts to be generated. By adding flowers, either carved, or painted, the furniture pieces of this era had a softness to them that made them highly suitable. Chair backs tend to be high and narrow, having a slight back tilt. Legs vary from straight to baluster turned types to spindle turned. This period of furniture design saw more usage of needlework upholstery and decoratively painted surfaces.

Louis XVI, 1850-1914: One period of the Victorian era that flies away with straight lines is Louis XVI. However, this furniture style is not austere; it is adorned with ovals, arches, applied medallions, wreaths, garlands, urns, and other Victorian flourishes. As the period aged, more ornamentation became present on the finished furniture styles. Furniture of this time was made from more expensive woods, such as ebonized woods or rosewood. Walnut was popular around the 1890s. Other dark woods were featured, often to contrast the lighter ornaments. Expect to find straight legs or fluted and slightly tapered legs.

Naturalistic, 1850-1914: This furniture period takes the scrolling effects of the Rococo Revival designs and adds more flowers and fruits to the styles. More detail is spent on the leaves—so much that one can tell if they are to represent grape, rose, or oak leaves. Technology advances enhanced this design style as manufacturers developed a way of laminating woods together. This layered effect was achieved by gluing thin layers together, with the grains running at right angles on each new layer. The thick panels created were then steamed in molds to create the illusion of carving. The woods used as a basis for the heavy ornamentation were mahogany, walnut, and some rosewood. Upholstery of this period is often tufted, eliminating any large flat surface, as the tufting creates curved peaks and valleys. The name of John Henry Belter is often connected with this period, for it was when he did some of this best design work. John and Joseph W. Meeks also enjoyed success with laminated furniture. Original labels bearing these names are sometimes found on furniture pieces from this period, giving further provenance.

Renaissance Revival, 1850-1880: Furniture made in this style period reflects how cabinetmakers interpreted 16th and 17th century French designs. Their designs range from curvilinear and florid early in the period to angular and almost severe by the end of the period. Dark woods, such as mahogany and walnut, were primary with some use

of rosewood and ebony. Walnut veneer panels were a real favorite in the 1870s designs. Upholstery, usually of a more generous nature, was also often incorporated into this design style. Ornamentation and high relief carving included flowers, fruits, game, classical busts, acanthus scrolls, strapwork, tassels, and masks. Architectural motifs, such as pilasters, columns, pediments, balusters, and brackets are another prominent design feature. Legs are usually cabriole or pretty substantial turned legs.

Mirror, Renaissance Revival, late 19th C, ebonized and parcel gilt, walnut, molded frame with incised geometric and scrolling decoration, each corner with ebony roundel, gilt framed rect mirror plate, 34" x 30-1/4", **$800**.
Photo courtesy of Sloans & Kenyon Auctions.

Néo-Greek, 1855-1885: This design style easily merges with both the Louis XVI and Renaissance Revival styles. It is characterized by elements reminiscent of Greek architecture, such as pilasters, flutes, column, acanthus, foliate scrolls, Greek key motifs, and anthemion high relief carving. This style originated with the French, but was embraced by American furniture manufacturers. Woods are dark and often ebonized. Ornamentation may be gilded or bronzed. Legs tend to be curved to scrolled or cloven hoof feet.

Eastlake, 1870-1890: This design style is named for Charles Locke Eastlake who wrote a very popular book in 1872 called *Hints on Household Taste*. It was originally published in London. One of his principles was the relationship between function, form, and craftsmanship. Shapes of furniture from this style tend to be more

rectangular. Ornamentation was created through the use of brackets, grooves, chamfers, and geometric designs. American furniture manufacturers were enthusiastic about this style since it was so easy to adapt for mass production. Woods used were again dark, but more native woods, such as maple and pine were incorporated. Legs and chair backs are straighter, often with incised decoration.

Magazine stand, Eastlake, c1880, ebonized and parcel gilt, two adjustable hinged racks, turned supports, shaped legs, folding easel support, 19" w, 45" h, **$850**.
Photo courtesy of Skinner, Inc.

Art Furniture, 1880-1914: This design period represents furniture designs gone mad, almost an "anything goes" school of thought. The style embraces both straight and angular with some pieces that are much more fluid, reflecting several earlier design periods. This period sees the wide usage of turned moldings and dark woods, but this time stained to imitate ebony and lacquer. The growing Oriental influence is seen in furniture from this period, including the use of bamboo, which was imported and included in the designs. Legs tend to be straight; feet tend to be small.

Arts and Crafts, 1895-1915: The Arts and Crafts period furniture represents one of the strongest periods for current collectors. Quality period Arts and Crafts furniture is available through most of the major auction houses. And, for those desiring the look, good quality modern furniture is also made in this style. The Arts and Crafts period furniture is generally rectilinear and a definite correlation is seen between form and function. The primary designers of this period were George Stickley, Leopold Stickley, J. George Stickley, George Niedeken, Elbert Hubbard, Frank Lloyd Wright, and the Englishman William Morris. Their furniture designs often overlapped into architectural and interior design including rugs, textiles, and other accessories. Woods used for Arts and Crafts furniture is primarily oak. Finishes were natural, fumed, or painted. Upholstery is leather or of a fabric design also created by the same hand. Hardware was often made in copper. Legs are straight and feet are small, if present at all, as they were often a simple extension of the leg. Some inlay of natural materials was used, such as silver, copper, and abalone shells.

Chest of drawers, Arts & Crafts, Gustav Stickley, designed by Harvey Ellis, gallery top, nine drawers, tapered trapezoidal legs, mushroom pulls, arched apron, original finish, red decal inside top right drawer, 36" w, 20" d, 50-1/2" h, **$8,100**.

Photo courtesy of David Rago Auctions, Inc.

Art Nouveau, 1896-1914: Just as the Art Nouveau period is known for women with long hair, flowers, and curves, so is Art Nouveau furniture. The Paris Exposition of 1900 introduced furniture styles reflecting what was happening in the rest of the design world, such as jewelry and silver. This style of furniture was not warmly embraced, as the sweeping lines were not very conducive to mass production. The few manufacturers that did interpret it for their factories found interest to be slight in America. The French held it in higher esteem. Woods used were dark, stylized lilies, poppies, and other more fluid designs were included. Legs tend to be sweeping or cabriole. Upholstery becomes slimmer.

Desk, Art Nouveau, made for Boys Lyman St. School, Westborough, MA, mahogany, cast iron mounts, drop front, fitted interior, open shelves, weighted pulleys working sliding panel which opens to reveal drawers and shelves, three drawers, open shelf, paw feet, 33-1/2" w, 17" d, 83-1/2" h, **$3,525**.

Photo courtesy of Skinner, Inc.

Art Deco, 1920-1945: Furniture of the Art Deco period reflects the general feel of the period. The Paris *"I Exposition International des Arts Décorative et Industriels Modernes"* became the mantra for designs of everything in this period. Lines are crisp, with some use of controlled curves. The Chrysler Building in New York City remains the finest example of Art Deco architecture and those same straight lines and gentle curves are found in furniture. Furniture makers used expensive materials, such as veneers, lacquered woods, glass, and steel. The cocktail table first enters the furniture scene during this period. Upholstery can be vinyl or smooth fabrics. Legs are straight or slightly tapered; chair backs tend to be either low or extremely high.

Bedside tables, Art Deco style, ebonized supports and plinth bases, pair, 14-1/2" w, 24" d, 24" h, **$750**.

Photo courtesy of Sloans & Kenyon Auctions.

International Movement, 1940-present: Furniture designed and produced during this period is distinctive as it represents the usage of some new materials, like plastic, aluminum, and molded laminates. The Bauhaus and also the Museum of Modern Art heavily influenced some designers. In 1940, the museum organized competitions for domestic furnishings. Designers Eero Saarien and Charles Eames won first prize for their designs. A new chair design combined the back, seat, and arms together as one unit. Tables were designed that incorporated the top, pedestal, and base as one. Shelf units were also designed in this manner. These styles could easily be mass-produced in plastic, plywood, or metal.

Chairs, arm, International Movement, pair of Norman Cherner for Plycraft, molded plywood, walnut veneer, bentwood legs, one has Plycraft label, 24-1/4" w, 17" d, 30-3/4" h, **$1,150**.

Photo courtesy of David Rago Auctions, Inc.

Reproduction Alert: Beware of the large number of reproductions. During the 25 years following the American Centennial of 1876, there was a great revival in copying furniture styles and manufacturing techniques of earlier eras. These centennial pieces now are more than 100 years old. They confuse many dealers, as well as collectors.

Different types of feet found on furniture

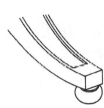

Ball

Hairy Paw

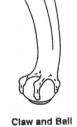

Claw and Ball

Triffid

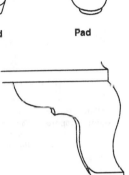

Pad

Cut-out

French

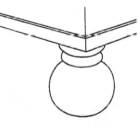

Bracket

Ogee Bracket

Marlborough

Spanish

Turned Ball

Spider

Spade

Snake

Different types of legs and hardware found on furniture

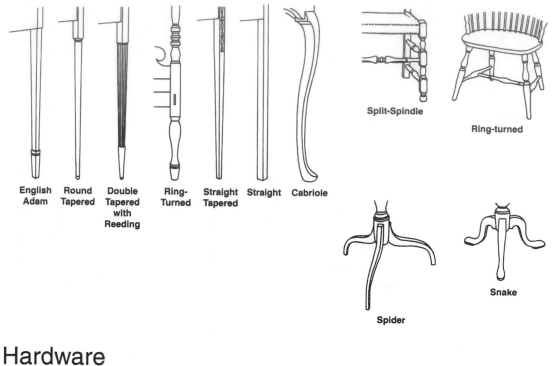

English Adam — Round Tapered — Double Tapered with Reeding — Ring-Turned — Straight Tapered — Straight — Cabriole — Split-Spindle — Ring-turned — Spider — Snake

Hardware

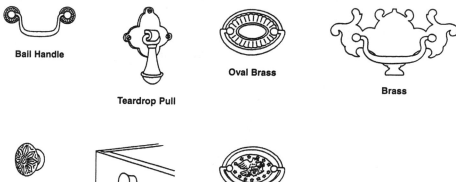

Bail Handle — Teardrop Pull — Oval Brass — Brass

Pressed Glass

Wooden Knob — Eagle Brass

Construction Details

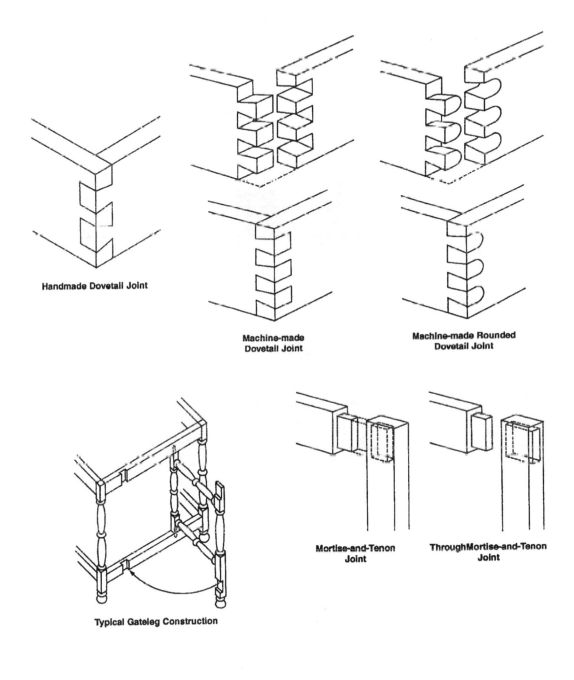

Handmade Dovetail Joint

Machine-made
Dovetail Joint

Machine-made Rounded
Dovetail Joint

Typical Gateleg Construction

Mortise-and-Tenon
Joint

ThroughMortise-and-Tenon
Joint

Great examples of Southern furniture are rising as collectors look for pieces with form, decoration, and provenance. Because of factors such as climate, insect, and the Civil War, well-crafted Southern furniture tends to be in shorter supply than some other types of American furniture. Awareness of what constitutes Southern-style furniture has been heightened by the efforts of the Museum of Early Southern Decorative Arts, Winston-Salem, NC (www.mesda.org). The museum has conducted groundbreaking research on the topic, including a three-volume book by Bradford Rauschenberg and John Bivins, *Furniture of Charleston,* to name but one of their well-done titles.

Some furniture terms unique to Southern styles include: beaten biscuit board; bottle case; huntboard; sugar chest. A beaten biscuit board is a marble or stone top on four legs. The style of a bottle case is not unique to Southern furniture; it is known as a cellaret or case in other styles. A huntboard might be called a side board or buffet in a different geographical region. A sugar chest is typically a square or rectangular box on four tapered or turned legs, sometimes with the interior of the case divided.

Sample prices of Southern furniture: Lazy Susan table, sold with four ladderback chairs, $3,350; Pembroke table, Charleston-made, $266,500, sold at Skinner, Bolton, MA.

Additional Listings: Arts and Craft Movement, Art Deco, Art Nouveau, Children's Nursery Items, Orientalia, and Shaker Items.

Notes: Furniture is one of the types of antiques for which regional preferences are a factor in pricing. Victorian furniture is popular in New Orleans and unpopular in New England. Oak is in demand in the Northwest, but not as much so in the middle Atlantic states.

Prices vary considerably on furniture. Shop around. Furniture is plentiful unless you are after a truly rare example. Examine all pieces thoroughly—avoid buying on impulse. Turn items upside down; take them apart. Price is heavily influenced by the amount of repairs and restoration. Make certain you know if any such work has been done to a piece before buying it.

The prices listed here are "average" prices. They are only a guide. High and low prices are given to show market range.

For more information, see *Warman's American Furniture* and *Warman's Arts & Crafts Furniture.*

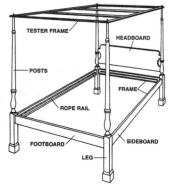

Typical Parts of a Bed

Beds

Art Deco, France, c1930, single curvilinear bed frame with hanging shelf compartments, price for pr, 82" l **1,410.00**

Art Nouveau, Emile Galle, French, c1890, satin wood and marquetry inlay, mirrored armoire, single size bed, bed stand, floral inlays of iris in walnut, kingwood, and tulipwood, mother-of-pearl accents, headboard sgd in marquetry "Galle" **3,800.00**

Arts and Crafts
Limbert, #651, daybed, angled headrest with spade cut-out, orig finish, recovered cushions, branded, numbered, 74" w, 25" d, 23" h **650.00**
Stickley Bros, attributed to, headboard with narrow vertical slats and panels, tapered feet, orig side rails, orig finish, minor scratches, stenciled "9001-1/2," 80-1/2" l, 56-1/2" w, 30" h **1,355.00**
Stickley, Gustav, single size, pyramidal posts, nine spindles to the head and footboard, complete with side rails, branded mark, 79-1/2" l, 43-3/4" w, 49-1/4" h .. **8,575.00**

Baroque, Italian, simulated marble high scrolling headboard dec in patiglia with vacant cartouches and foliage, carved scrolling feet, painted, green and blue marbleized dec, losses to paint and gilt, pr, 45-3/4" w, 84" h **3,750.00**

Belle Epoque, French, c1910, walnut, each pc mounted with bronze floral wreaths, hardware, and claw feet, three-door armoire, two twin beds, four drawer dresser, two dressing chairs, wall unit with chests, mounted with 20" x 12" bronze plaque of mother and child **4,200.00**

Biedermeier, figured mahogany veneer, octagonal posts, turned feet and finials, paneled head and footboards, orig rails, some veneer damage, 38" w, 72" l, 45" h, pr **750.00**

Chippendale, tall post, curly maple, turned posts, scrolled headboard with poplar panel, orig side rails, old mellow refinishing, minor repairs to posts, 60" w, 72" l, 80" h **3,000.00**

Classical
Massachusetts, c1825-35, carved mahogany, tall post, scrolled mahogany headboard flanked by reeded, carved, and ring-turned posts, acanthus leaf, beading, gothic arches, and foliage carving, reeded and turned feet, orig rails later fitted for angle irons and bed bolts, orig surface, central finial missing, 59" w, 81" d, 98" h **6,900.00**

Middle Atlantic States, 1835-45, carved mahogany veneer, low post, scrolled and paneled headboard, leaf-carved finials flanked by posts with pineapple finials, acanthus leaves above spiral carved and ring-turned posts, orig rails, bed bolts, and covers, refinished, imperfections, 58-1/2" w, 78" d, 56-1/2" h **1,100.00**

New England, c1820, painted, turned tall post, turned and tapering head posts flanking shaped headboard, spiral-carved foot post joined by rails fitted for roping, accompanying tester, old red paint, restored, 54" w, 79" l, 60-1/2" h **1,400.00**

Country, American, rope, high post, curly maple, areas of light curl, evidence of old red wash, turned and tapered legs, boldly turned posts taper toward the top, paneled headboard with scrolled crest, turned top finial, 53-1/2" w, 70" l rails with orig bolts, pierced restorations **1,890.00**

Country, American, day bed, birch, old red paint, tapered supports on head and footboards, tapered legs, raised turned feet, casters, contemporary blue and white upholstery, 74" l, 25-1/2" d, 27-1/4" h **400.00**

Country, American, trundle, southwestern PA, walnut, mortised joints, turned posts, and finials, shaped corners along top edge of head, foot, and sideboards, refinished, 71-1/2" l, 44" d **125.00**

Edwardian, A. H. Davenport, early 20th C, painted maple, bed, two door side cabinet, two chairs, dressing table .. **5,450.00**

Empire, American

Single, fitted as daybed or sofa, mahogany and mahogany figured veneer, turned and acanthus carved posts, upholstered cushion, 31-1/2" x 80" x 43-3/4" h **825.00**

Tall post, curly maple posts, poplar scrolled headboard with old soft finish, turned detail, acorn finials, rails and headboard replaced, 57-1/4" w, 72-1/2" l rails, 89" h **1,650.00**

Empire-style, sleigh, red painted, scrolled ends, bronze mounted foliate and mask mounts, 20th C, price for pr **1,650.00**

Federal

American, first half 19th C, cherry, tester, three-quarter, rect headboard with concave side edges, footboard lower, baluster-turned posts continuing to turned legs, rails with rope pegs, 81-1/2" l, 53-1/2" w, 78-1/4" h **500.00**

Massachusetts, attributed to Abner Toppan, Newburyport, 1810, canopy, cherry, vase and ring-turned, reeded, and swelled foot posts joined to chamfered tapering head posts and arched headboard by an arched canopy frame, old red stained surface, 72" l, 49" w, 83" h; accompanied by chamber stand with sq pierced top on beaded sq legs joined by cutout skirt and medial shelf with incised beaded drawer, refinished, remnants of red stain, also accompanied by orig receipt, 12" top, 31" h **9,400.00**

New England, c1815, maple, arched canopy above vase and ring-turned reeded and swelled foot posts, vase and ring-turned legs joined to ring-turned tapering head posts and arched headboard, old red-stained surface, minor imperfections, 51" w, 70" l, 80" h **5,000.00**

New England, c1810, tester, maple, vase and ring-turned foot posts continuing to tapering sq legs and molded spade feet joined to sq tapering head posts continuing to sq legs, arched headboard, later arched canopy, refinished, 51" w, 83-3/4" h **815.00**

New England, c1810-15, mahogany, turned and carved, tall post tester, arched canopy frame on vase and ring-turned spiral carved fluted tapering foot posts, joined to the turned tapering head posts with shaped headboard, ring-turned tapering feet, 45-1/2" w, 72" d, 61" h **1,775.00**

Salem, MA, c1810, mahogany, tall post, vase and ring-turned swelled fluted foot post with leaf carving on fluted plinths

continuing to vase and ring-turned legs joined to ring-turned tapering head posts, shaped headboard, old surface, 51" w, 71" d, 650" h **3,175.00**

Bed, Sheraton, tester, maple, carved fluted posts, shaped headboard, **$500**.
Photo courtesy of Wiederseim Associates, Inc.

George III, four poster, carved walnut, brass mounted, circular tapered head posts, shaped mahogany headboard, reeded and acanthus-carved foot posts, ring-turned feet, casters, 9-1/2" h **10,000.00**

Gothic Revival, American, c1850, carved mahogany, tall headboard with three Gothic arch panels, leaf-carved crest rail, flanked by heavy round ribbed posts topped by ring-turned finials, arched and paneled footboard flanked by lower foot posts, heavy bun feet **4,750.00**

Hepplewhite-style, Philadelphia, c1943, mahogany, four tall posts each with reeded slender vasiform section over short vasiform turned carved with continuous swag designs, upholstered tester, 82" l, 62" w, 93" h **1,550.00**

International Movement, George Nelson for Howard Miller, Thin Edge, caned headboard, 34" x 76" x 35" **1,610.00**

International Movement, day bed

Tugendhat-style, after design by Mies van der Rohe, rect black leather cushion with head rest, webbed wood frame, four cylindrical legs, 77" l, 38" w, 15-1/2" h **2,350.00**

Hans Wegner, Denmark, retailed by Georg Jensen Inc., New York, c196 teak, natural woven backrest, lifts and folds to create upholstered day bed, retail label on base, 78" l, 33-3/4" d, 28-3/4" h .. **2,710.00**

Queen Anne, Pennsylvania, early 19th C, low poster, turned and painted pine, head and footposts with flattened ball finials, shaped head and footboards, tapered feet, orig rope rails, orig green paint, 48-1/2" w, 74-3/4" h **3,600.00**

Renaissance Revival, walnut, double, high headboard topped by rounded pediment, pointed finial............................. **1,700.00**

Rope
Country, curly maple and cherry, old mellow finish, urn shaped finials, scrolled headboard, large turned foot rail, 68-1/2" l orig rails, 51-1/2" w, 47" h **200.00**
Country, pine and poplar, old dark red over orig lighter red paint, short turned finials and feet, 69" l orig rails, 51" w, 31" h headboard **250.00**
Pennsylvania, summer/winter, softwood, painted blue, removable turned posts, arched headboard, replacement canopy support, 50-1/2" w, 77" l, 80-1/2" h **2,200.00**

Sheraton, canopy
Carved mahogany, headboard posts simple turned with ring and block turnings, simple headboard, heavily carved footboard posts with spiral turnings and acanthus leaf bell, sq tester with curtains, 58" w, 73-1/2" l, 88" without finials **3,200.00**
Painted, headboard with D-type cut outs on side, footboard with reeded and turned posts, canopy frame, painted red, 52" w, 76" l, 68" h **750.00**

Sheraton, country, day, pine, old brown finish, ring turned and tapered legs, ball feet, pegged construction, adjustable back, large dovetails at corners, contemporary cushions, 20" d, 70-1/2" l **900.00**

Victorian, high headboard
Brass, c1900, four capped corner posts, fine applied brass scroll on headboard and footboard, 57" w, 78" l, 69" h........................ **1,850.00**

Bench, settle, Arts & Crafts, J. M. Young, drop-arm, slats all around, corbels and quatri-linear posts, drop-in spring seat, paper label, original finish, 72" l, 31-1/2" d, 34-1/2" h, **$1,800**.

Photo courtesy of David Rago Auctions, Inc.

Brass, c1900, straight top rail, curved corners, ring-shaped capitals, cast iron side rails, 55" w, 61" h **1,200.00**
Walnut, plain, 52" w, 50" h **250.00**
Walnut and burlwood, ornately carved crest, 56" w, 90" h........................ **1,150.00**

Benches

Arts & Crafts, settle
Stickley Bros, cube, vertical slats, orig drop-in seat covered in new green leather, excellent orig finish, stenciled number, 50" l, 22-1/2" d, 33" h **2,530.00**
Stickley, Gustav, No. 208, even arm, vertical slats all around, top rail mortised through legs, drop-in spring seat covered in new green leather, red Gustav decal, 76-1/2" l, 32" d, 29-1/4" h, light standing, some color added to orig finish **6,900.00**
Stickley, Gustav, No. 222, tapering posts, tightly spaced canted slats to back and sides, leather upholstered drop-in seat, fine orig finish, red decal, minor veneer chips, 36" x 80" x 32" **11,500.00**
Stickley, Gustav, No. 225, single board horizontal back panel, vertical side slats, recovered brown leather drop-in seat, over-coated orig finish, unmarked, 59-3/4" l, 31" d, 29-1/4" h **7,475.00**

Stickley, L. & J. G., cube, border vertical panels on back and under each arm, brown leather cushion, orig condition and finish, orig upholstery, "The Work of L. and J. G. Stickley" label, 72" l, 27" w, 28" h **3,450.00**
Stickley, L. & J. G., open arm, cloud lift top rail, horizontal backslat and corbels, new tan leather upholstered seat cushion, new finish, The Work of L & J. G. Stickley label, 53" l, 26" w, 36" h, some looseness **1,650.00**
Young, J. M., cube, capped top rail, vertical slats all around, fabric cov drop-in spring seat, refinished, unmarked, 78" l, 29-1/2" h, 34" h........... **2,870.00**

Bucket
Country, walnut, sq nail construction, shaped ends, four mortised shelves, old dry brown finish, age splits, one shelf notched out in back, 39-1/2" w, 12-1/2" d, 44" h **1,700.00**
Pennsylvania, softwood, mortised construction, shaped cut-out legs, blue-green over earlier red surface, 80" l, 18" d, 29-1/2" h.................... **2,750.00**
Pennsylvania, softwood, beaded sides and shelves, stepped lower shelf with shaped cut-out feet, dovetailed, mortised, and nailed construction, old red painted surface, two shelves, 34-1/2" w, 14" d, 47-1/2" h **5,225.00**

Classical, window
Boston, 1835-45, carved
mahogany veneer,
upholstered seat, veneered
rail, leaf-carved cyma curved
ends, joined by ring-turned
medial stretcher, 48" w,
16-1/4" d, 17-1/2" h .. **2,185.00**
New York, 1815-25, mahogany
veneer, curving upholstered
seat flanked by scrolled ends,
scrolled base, old refinish,
some veneer cracking and
loss, 20th C olive green velvet
upholstery, 39-1/2" w, 14" d,
23-5/8" h.................... **3,500.00**
Classical Revival, mahogany,
carved paw feet and lion's
heads, maroon velvet cushion,
old finish, 16-1/2" l, 29-1/4" w,
23" h **600.00**
Country
Pennsylvania, softwood,
mortised leg, double skirt,
shaped cut-out legs, old
orange painted surface, 36" l,
13-1/2" d, 15-1/2" h .. **3,520.00**
Pennsylvania, softwood,
mortised leg, shaped cut-out
legs, double molded skirt and
towel bars, old blue-gray
painted base, 38" l, 12" d,
20" h.......................... **6,600.00**
Pennsylvania, softwood,
mortised leg, shaped cut-out
legs, reinforcing slats, old red
painted surface, 53" l,
11-1/2" d, 17-3/4" h ... **1,430.00**
Pine, old worn and weathered
green repaint, one board top
with rounded front corners,
beaded edge apron, cut-out
feet mortised through top, age
crack in one end of top, 104" l,
13-1/2" w **325.00**
Decorated, orig dark green with
reddish brown paint, yellow line
dec, mortised construction,
some sq nails, arched end
panels, replaced shoe feet,
some later nails added, 33" w,
14" d, 23-1/4" h................ **275.00**

Bar stool, Thonet, black suede
upholstery, ebonized frame with
circular stretchers, two have Thonet
factory tags, 14-1/4" d, 30-1/4" h, **$525**.
Photo courtesy of David Rago Auctions, Inc.

Federal
New England, c1810, window,
mahogany, upholstered seat
and rolled arms, sq tapering
legs, H-form stretchers,
refinished, minor repair to one
leg, 39-1/2" l, 16" d, 29" h
.... **900.00**
New York, c1825, window,
figured mahogany, each end
with rect crotch-figured crest
centering removable slip seat,
matching seat rail, saber legs,
40-1/2" l.................... **3,500.00**
George III, English, mid-18th C,
window, mahogany, rect seat,
scrolling arms, later velvet cov,
straight legs, blind fret craved,
H form stretcher, pr, 38" l
.... **4,750.00**
Gothic Revival, American,
c1820-40, carved mahogany,
angled over-upholstered seat,
carved seat rails centering
quatrefoil, facet lancet-carved
legs, molded faceted feet, 65" l,
20" d, 15-1/2" h............. **1,750.00**
Kneeling, Pennsylvania, walnut,
mortised, turned splayed legs,
oval cut top, 36" l, 10" d, 9" h
.... **250.00**
Louis XVI-style, window, carved
cherry, overstuffed seat,
channeled rails, flanked by
molded, overscroll arms carved
with be-ribboned foliate sprays,
turned, tapered, and leaf-
capped legs.................... **200.00**
Meeting hall, pine and
butternut, old sun bleached
finish, tapered pencil post legs
mortised through single board
seat, narrow crest rail and
supports, from Amana Colonies,
93" w, 19" d, 35" h **600.00**
Piano, Arts & Crafts, Gustav
Stickley, cut-out handles on
plank sides, plank top, broad up-
ended cross-stretcher, orig
finish, red decal, 36" l, 12-3/4" w,
22" h **4,600.00**
Victorian-style, chaise lounge,
Chesterfield, early 20th C, tufted
brown leather, adjustable
backrest, casters, 62" l **3,000.00**
Wagon seat, New England, late
18th C, painted, two pairs of
arched slats joining three turned
stiles, double rush seat flanked
by turned arms ending in turned
hand-holds, tapering legs, old
brown paint over earlier gray,
15" h seat, 30" h **1,200.00**
Wicker, painted white, hooped
crest rail flanked by rows of dec

curlicues, spiral wrapped posts
and 6 spindles, pressed-in oval
seat, dec curlicue apron,
wrapped cabriole legs, X-form
stretcher, 35" w, 31" h...... **500.00**
Windsor, settle, 20th C green
paint, yellow in turnings, 29
spindles with bamboo turnings
across back with turned arms,
well-shaped seat with incised
rain gutter around back, eight
splayed legs joined by cross
stretchers, splits in seat, old iron
braces added underneath for
support, 77-1/2" w, 22" d,
36-3/4" h...................... **2,100.00**

Bentwood

In 1850, Michael Thonet of Vienna
perfected the process of bending
wood using steam. Shortly
afterward, Bentwood furniture
became popular. Other
manufacturers of Bentwood
furniture were Jacob and Joseph
Kohn, Philip Strobel and Son,
Sheboygan Chair Co., and Tidoute
Chair Co. Bentwood furniture is
still being produced today by the
Thonet firm and others.

Bentwood, child's chair, **$125**.
Photo courtesy of Dotta Auction Co., Inc.
Box
5" d, circular, c1780, blue and
white open and closed tulips
dec on dry salmon ground,
.... **10,000.00**
12" l, 6" h, oval, laced seams
on lid and base, old dark
green paint on ext., dark red
on int., dark red "AKHD Anno
1804" on lid, wear, splits
.... **300.00**

13" d, continuous scene of man, woman, two dogs, tulips, rose trees, bulging crack, no lid **16,000.00**
17-3/4" w, 9-3/4" d, 7-3/8" h, oval, dark green paint, laced seams, replaced lacing, glued edge splits........ **150.00**
22" l, 13" d, 8-1/4" h, oval, laced seams, orig blue paint, black and red foliage around borders, initials "F.G.S.B. 1836," sq nails around base, edge damage, age splits **700.00**

Chair, Austrian, Vienna Secession-style, c1910, side, back splat with three circular perforations, three slender spindles, painted black, set of eight **5,500.00**

Bench, International Movement, George Nelson for Herman Miller, two blond wood slatted benches on ebonized round edged legs, early, unmarked, some finish wear, 48-1/4" l, 18-3/4" w, 14" h, **$1,400**.
Photo courtesy of David Rago Auctions, Inc.

Bentwood, child's desk, one piece, **$350**.
Photo courtesy of Dotta Auction Co., Inc.

Cradle, 41" l, 39" h, ivory fittings **440.00**
Hall tree, Thonet, c1910, bentwood frame, contrasting striped wood inlay, coat hooks with central beveled mirror above one door, metal drip pan, orig label, 57" w, 13" d, 76" h **2,750.00**
Plant stand, Thonet, Austria, late 19th C, round top with black printed classical urn and flower motif, bentwood tripod base, imp "Thonet," paper label, wear, couple of breaks on feet, 18-5/8" d, 30-5/8" h **210.00**

Rocker, Thonet, arched twined top rail, cut-velvet fabric fitted back, armrests, and seat, elaborate scrolling frame, curved runners, 53" l **750.00**

Side table, Austria, late 19th C., circular top in black stain, three curvilinear bentwood legs joined to center ring, crack to ring, 19-1/4" d, 31-1/2" h, **$200**.

Stool, Thonet, attributed to Marcel Kammerer, Austria, 1901, beech, sq seat, four legs, U-shaped braces forming spandrels, shaped bronze sabot feet, 14-1/4" sq, 18-1/2" h **1,500.00**
Table, Josef Hoffman, c1905, circular top, wooden spheres dec below rim, 21-1/4" h **500.00**

Blanket chests

Chippendale
Country, attributed to southwest PA, cherry, chestnut secondary wood, dovetailed case, cov interior till, dovetailed drawers, molded base, shaped bracket feet with

scalloped returns, wrought iron strap hinges, old refinishing, replaced brass pulls, restorations and replacements to feet and lid, 22-3/4" d, 28-1/2" h **1,050.00**
Pennsylvania, 1785, figured walnut, molded rect hinged top opens to interior with lidded till, dovetailed case inlaid with "17 MM 85" with panel bordered by geometric banding, horizontal applied molding below, two thumb molded half drawers, bracket feet, two orig escutcheons, old surface, minor imperfections, 47" w, 22" d, 47" h **14,100.00**

Decorated
American, poplar, orig black over red sponge dec, one board top, molded top, arched cut-outs on end aprons, scalloped front apron, int. fitted with covered till, dovetailed drawer, cast iron hinges, minor touch-up, later coat of varnish, 43-1/4" w, 17" d, 21-1/4" h **495.00**
New York, Schohaire County, early 19th C, 6 board, painted blue, molded top, dovetailed constructed base with painted diamond and draped frieze with Chinese export punchbowl and ladle, dotted, banded, vine, and diamond border flanked by enamel Stiegel flip glasses with circular borders, minor imperfections, 37" w, 17" d, 15" h **6,900.00**

Blanket chest, English, oak, chip carved paneled lid and front, early iron hardware, 50-1/2" w, 19" d, 21" h, losses, early hinge replacements, **$600**.
Photo courtesy of Alderfer Auction Co.

Ohio, c1820-40, pine and poplar, six-board construction, eagle dec, cover with considerable paint wear, restoration, 49-1/2" w, 21" d, 23-3/4" h **2,300.00**

Ohio, attributed to Knox County, dovetailed poplar, orig sponged circles and meandering borders, two board top with molding, scalloped base painted black, beveled aprons, fitted int. with covered till, early iron casters, 39" w, 29-1/2" d **825.00**

Pennsylvania, Dauphin County, made for Madlen Nafrez, 1808, three blue panels on front, center one with name and date, other two panels with six pointed stars **35,000.00**

Pennsylvania, softwood, front panel dec with six arched top panels, potted floral and foliate motif in style of Heinrich Otto, side panels dec with eight-point stars, molded lid and base, wrought iron strap hinges, interior till, 51" w, 23" d, 22-1/2" h **11,000.00**

Pennsylvania, c1780, three tombstone shaped panels with stylized flowers, unicorns in center, reddish brown ground, loss to paint on lid **9,500.00**

Blanket chest, Lehigh Valley, Pennsylvania, painted poplar, dower chest, dated 1786, lift lid over case, cartouche inscribed "Elisabeth Schonlisi 1786" above three panels with potted flowers, sides with similar panels over mid molding above two short drawers, straight bracket feet, 47" w, 27-1/2" h, **$4,000.**

Photo courtesy of Pook & Pook.

Dowry, Mahantango Valley, Pennsylvania, "Samuel Grebiel 1799," orig paint dec, red, blue, mustard, black, and white, two shaped polygons painted in blue grain painting, identical

polygons on each side, two in front with banner above with name and date, int. lidded till, black painted dovetailed bracket base, off-set strap hinges, orig lock, 48-1/2" w, 21" d, 23-1/2" h **3,000.00**

Federal, PA, early 18th C, pine and cherry, molded lift top, well with till, case with two thumb-molded graduated drawers, dovetailed bracket feet, old refinish, minor imperfections, 40" w, 20-1/2" d, 43" h **1,880.00**

Grain painted, New York state, c1830, molded hinged lift top, lidded till, molded bracket black painted base, orig fanciful ochre and raw umber graining, 48" w, 22" d, 29" h **1,265.00**

Jacobean, oak, paneled construction with relief carving, drawer and feet replaced, repairs to lid and molding, old dark finish, 44-1/2" w, 19-1/2" d, 31-3/4" h **825.00**

Dower chest, Pennsylvania German, attributed to Lehigh County, PA, paint decorated, two stippled decorated panels above date and name "17 VAL-LEN-DIN" with centered tulip and flower decoration "HU-BER 85" over two drawers, original straight bracket feet, 48" w, 27" h, **$2,600.**

Photo courtesy of Wiederseim Associates, Inc.

Blanket chest, Pennsylvania, possibly Montgomery County, painted, poplar, blue-green stippled painted finish, red details, three drawers, original Sandwich glass knobs, original feet, cast iron hinges, painted panel on front "Johannes Hoffert 1837," 51" l, 22" d, 28" h, old hinge replacement, missing glue blocks, lid of glove box, and crab lock, **$12,650.**

Photo courtesy of Alderfer Auction Co.

Miniature, England, early 19th C, mahogany, molded lift-top

with wire hinges, dovetail constructed box base, mid molding trim, heavy molded bracket base, worm holes, wear, 14-1/4" l, 6-3/4" h **1,035.00**

Mule, America, pine, thumb-molded top, two overlapping dovetailed drawers, bracket feet, old dark finishing, int. lined with 1875 Boston newspaper, pierced repairs to feet and drawer fronts, 40" w, 18" d, 34-3/4" h **700.00**

Painted

Massachusetts, first quarter 19th C, molded hinged top, case of two drawers, tall cut-out feet with valanced skirt, orig red brown grain paint with contrasting beige grained drawers, orig pulls, 36-3/4" w, 17-1/4" d, 37-3/4" h **11,750.00**

New England, early 19th C, hinged top, well with till, case with singe drawer, cut-out base, orig mustard-brown graining resembling wood, minor imperfections, 39-1/4" w, 18-1/4" d, 40" h **850.00**

New England, early 19th C, six-board, rect top, case with two drawer, cut-out feet joined by straight skirt, all-over orig reddish brown and yellow grain paint resembling exotic wood, old brass pulls, minor imperfections, minor paint wear, 41-1/4" w, 18-1/2" d, 32-1/4" h **2,115.00**

Ohio, wide poplar boards, orig red paint, traces of silvery white star designs on lid and front, dovetailed case, molded top edge, bracket feet, small scalloped returns, molded base, int. till with lid, hinges and narrow hinge rail old replacements, minor edge wear, 49-1/4" w, 21" d, 26" h **650.00**

Pennsylvania, Bucks County, dated 1770, red moldings and base, mottled reddish-brown ground, large triple banded hearts on front and sides, corners with half-hearts, over lozenges with names and date, two lower drawers, molded skirt with central drop, cut-out bracket feet, int. till, secret drawers, orig paint, minor losses, one side foot and back braces replaced, 49" l, 24" d, 29-1/2" h **18,750.00**

Blanket chest, Lancaster, Pennsylvania, painted dower chest by Embroidery Artist, dated 1788, molded lift lid decorated with central cartouche in black, red, and white with tulip and geometric border, stylized stars in corners, over case with central heart inscribed "Maria Stohlern 1788," flanked by tombstone panels with tulips and stars, over midmolding above two short drawers with stars, straight bracket feet, blue ground, illus in *The Pennsylvania –German Decorated Chest* by Fabian, 52" l, 23" d, 27" h, **$55,200**.

Photo courtesy of Pook & Pook.

Queen Anne, New England, c1750, marriage chest, pine, hinged rect lift lid, upper half faced with faux drawer fronts, brown paint, 35" **4,000.00**
Sheraton, country, pine and poplar, orig red paint, molded edge top, paneled front and ends, sq corner posts, mortised and pinned frame, scalloped apron, turned feet, 44" w, 19-1/2" d, 25-1/2" h **900.00**
William and Mary, New England, c1700, oak and yellow pine, joined, drawer base, old finish, minor imperfections, 48-1/2" w, 22" d, 32-3/4" h **4,500.00**

Bookcases

Arts & Crafts
English, double door, corbelled overhanging top, inlaid pewter, ebony, and fruitwood tulips, leaded glass panels with green tear-shaped inserts, curvilinear backsplash, emb strap handles, orig finish, unmarked, some corbels loose, 46" w, 12-1/2" d, 52-1/2" h.................. **2,615.00**
Limbert, Grand Rapids, MI, early 20th C, oak, two elongated glass panels on each of two doors, three adjustable shelves on each side, round copper pulls,

medium brown finish, branded mark on reverse, imperfections, 40-1/2" l, 14" d, 57-1/2" h **2,775.00**
Stickley Bros, quarter-sawn oak, double door, slatted gallery top, single panes of glass, orig medium finish, brass tag, 35-1/2" w, 12" d, 50" h.......................... **4,875.00**
Stickley, Gustav, quarter sawn oak, double door, eight glass panes to each door, gallery top, hammered copper V-pulls, three int. shelves, top and bottom mortised thru sides, red decal and paper Craftsman label, refinished, 42-3/4" w, 13" d, 56-1/4" h **5,175.00**
Stickley, Gustav, quarter sawn oak, double door, 12 panes per door, gallery top, brass V-pulls, mortised top, paper label, 54" w, 13" d, 55" h, refinished, warp in right door, stripped hardware ... **5,175.00**
Stickley, L. & J. G., Fayetteville, New York, c1912, oak, no. 641, gallery top with through tenons, Handcraft decal, some stains, door missing, 30" w, 55" h **1,300.00**
Biedermeier-style, inlaid cherry, outset molded cornice with ebonized bead, front with two recessed glazed doors, four shelves, outset molded base

raised on black feet, burr poplar panels, ebonized stringing, 53-1/2" w, 21" d, 72" h **700.00**
Chippendale
English, two pcs, mahogany, oak and pine secondary woods, top with two doors with geometric mullions and old glass, four adjustable shelves, two dovetailed drawers with beaded edges, short bracket feet, molded base, old replaced oval brasses, old refinishing, restorations to cornice and feet, later backboards, 32-3/8" w, 14" d, 83-1/4" h **2,300.00**
New England, southern, late 18th C, mahogany and maple, scroll top, top section with molded scrolled cresting, carved pinwheel terminals centering carved fan and bordered with punchwork flanked by flame urn-turned finials, two thumb-molded recessed panel doors opening to compartmented shelved int., lower section with fall front desk opening to stepped multi-drawer compartmented int. above case of four graduated scratchbeaded drawers, bracket feet, replaced brasses, refinished, imperfections, 39" w, 21" d, 84-3/4" h **7,100.00**

Arts & Crafts type, three doors, leaded glass, **$450**.

Chippendale-style, New England, mahogany, broken arch pedestal over two arched-paneled doors, fitted secretary int. with pigeonholes, six small drawers, lower section with fall front, stepped fitted int., straight front, two small and two wide drawers, brass bail handle, escutcheons, lock plates, straight bracket feet, 42" w, 24" d, 93-3/4" h **3,200.00**

Classical, Boston, 1830s, carved mahogany veneer, cove molded cornice above two glazed doors flanked by columns with leaf carved tops and turned bases, fold-out felt lined writing surface, sectioned for writing implements, two small cock-beaded drawers over two long drawers, flanked by similar columns with carved tops, four reeded and carved bulbous feet, glazed doors open to bird's eye maple veneered int. with two adjustable shelves, valanced open compartments, five small drawers, brasses and wooden pulls appear to be orig, old refinish, imperfections, 44-3/4" w, 22-1/4" d, 88" h **11,500.00**

Eastlake
America, c1785, ebonized, three glazed doors flanked by turned carved columns, incised and gilt dec, three drawer base, 58" w, 14" d, 74-1/2" h.................. **1,850.00**
America, c1880, cherry, rect top, flaring bead trimmed cornice, pair of single pan glazed cupboard doors, carved oval paterae and scrolls across top, adjustable shelved int., stepped base with line-incised drawers, bail handles, 47-1/2" w, 15-1/4" d, 69-1/4" h **1,200.00**

Empire, crotch mahogany veneers, top section: large architectural type cornice, two large glass doors with cathedral top muttons, three adjustable shelves; base: 11 drawers, oval brass knobs, applied base molding, two panes of glass cracked, 66" w, 83" h ... **5,500.00**

Empire style, French, 19th C, ormolu mounted mahogany, fitted with four tall grill-inset and paneled doors, shelved interior, corners mounted with herm-form pilasters, wreath and paw feet, 108" w, 12" d, 84-1/2" h **5,900.00**

Federal
Boston or Salem, MA, c1815-1820, carved mahogany and mahogany veneer, top section with shaped gallery joining square plinths above flat cornice molding, two hinged glazed doors with beaded Gothic arches, four adjustable shelves, projecting base of four cockbeaded short drawers, corners carved with acanthus leaves and fluting, punch-work above vase and ring-turned reeded tapering legs, old refinish, imperfections, 50" w, 18-1/2" d, 87-1/2" h **9,900.00**
Southern States, attributed to, 1790-1810, mahogany, veneered pediment embellished with inlaid floral vines and leaves above mullioned glazed doors, int. adjustable beaded shelves, lower case as hinged butler's desk with int. of valanced compartments and small drawers outlined with stringing, case of three graduated string inlaid drawers, skirt with inlaid vines and leaves, French feet, old refinish, replaced brasses, restored, 40-1/2" w, 21-1/2" d, 93-1/2" h **4,700.00**

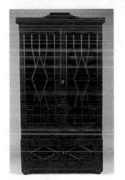

Bookcase, George III, third quarter 18th C, mahogany, upper section with pair of mullioned glass doors opening to shelves, slant lid enclosing interior of pigeonholes and drawers; lower section with four long, graduated drawers flanked by engaged quarter-columns, ogee bracket feet, 41" w, 21" d, 82" h, $4,120.

Photo courtesy of Skinner, Inc.

George III, third quarter 18th C, inlaid mahogany, dentil-molded cornice above two paneled doors, shelved interior, two candle slides, slant front enclosing fitted interior, two short and three graduated drawers, bracket feet, 37" w, 22" d, 85-1/2" h........................ **4,600.00**

George III-style, with 18th century elements, mahogany, later swan's neck cresting above pair of paneled doors opening to shelves, fitted with candle roots, lower section with slant lid enclosing a fitted int., all above three long drawers, ogee bracket feet, 35" w, 20" d, 95" h **2,650.00**

George III style/Edwardian, early 20th C, painted satinwood, breakfront, upper section with four glazed doors, lower section fitted with five drawers on each end, projecting center section with secretaire drawer over pair of cabinet doors, polychrome dec, 75" w, 18" d, 88" h............ **11,750.00**

Georgian, early 18th C
Inlaid walnut, bureau bookcase, rect cornice, two paneled doors opening to shelves, fitted slant-lid desk, two short over two long drawers, bracket feet, inlaid allover with scrolling vines, 44" w, 22" d, 89" h **10,575.00**
Mahogany, shaped octagonal cornice over glazed doors, above two cabinet doors, bracket feet **2,900.00**

International Movement
Delineator Series, designed by Paul McCobb, manufactured by The Lane Co., retailed by Angelus Furniture Showroom, Los Angeles and San Francisco, mid-20th C, walnut, upper cabinet fitted with open shelf over six cubby holes and two drawers, open shelf over pull-out writing surface, lower cabinet fitted with median shelves, one round pull missing, 36-3/8" w, 15" d, 78" h.......................... **600.00**
Unknown maker, c1960, teak, three fully finished modular sections in metal framework, with panel to create right angle, each 35-1/4" w, 17" d, 68-1/2" h, accompanied by magazine illus of unit **2,350.00**

Louis XV-style, block front, ormolu mounts, floral marquetry, banded inlay, top surface worn, scratches, 56" w, 16" d, 55" h **2,500.00**

Box, decorated, original red paint, eagle and banner, and "Hannah Miller" on lid, front with pheasants with cornucopia, ends with birds kissing on one end, apart on other, yellow, green, gold, and black, interior lined with work orange paper, small areas of touch-up, found in Vermont, 9" w, 4-5/8" d, 4-3/4" h, **$12,100**.

Box photos courtesy of Garth's Auctions, Inc.

Box, decorated, sliding lid, gold, black, red, and yellow decoration on deep blue ground, small area of touch-up on rim, minor age crack, attributed to PA, 7-1/4" w, 4-1/4" d, 3-1/2" h, **$8,250**.

Box, decorated, poplar, dome top, grained repaint, yellow and red lined borders, painted fans in corners, gold initials "A.H." on lid, fitted lock, minor age cracks, 10-1/2" w, 6-1/2" d, 5" h, **$715**.

Box, candle, attributed to, poplar, original brown and green decoration, dovetailed, molded edge on rim, raised panel on sliding lid, minor edge damage, 10-1/2" w, 6" d, 4" h, **$5,775**.

Box, decorated, pine, dome top, original black paint, blue edge striping, stenciled decoration in red and silver, freehand red and yellow flowers on lid, brass bale handle and lock with hasp, minor edge wear, New England, possibly MA, 10" w, 6-1/2" d, 5" h, **$5,225**.

Box, sewing, MA, pine, original stencil decoration, green borders, silver and gold stars, red lines, smoke ground, sliding lid with flower and leaf design, brass pull, pencil inscription, "Mary Houghton Stowe who was born in Hubbardstone, Mass. In 1808," ball feet, minor wear, 9" w, 6" d, 4-1/4" h, **$5,225**.

Regency, late, early 19th C, mahogany, bookcase/breakfront, concave fronted cornice, frieze carved with anthemion, upper section fitted with four arched and glazed doors; lower section fitted with fall front writing surface and fitted int., all above two pedestals fitted with shelves and drawers, 84" w, 26" d, 93" h **7,475.00**

Renaissance Revival, American, late 19th C

Carved mahogany, two glass doors, shelved interior, case carved with central portrait bust and scrolling foliage, two columns, gadrooned ball feet, 61" w, 18" d, 64" h **2,115.00**

Walnut, rect case carved with foliage and angular flowerheads, two doors, two base drawers, 54" w, 16" d, 57" h **1,550.00**

Walnut, rect top, three shaped, foliate, and corbel carved doors, shelved interior, plinth base, 73" w, 13" d, 49" h **2,350.00**

Walnut, three tall glazed doors, shelved interior, projecting base with three drawers, 74" w, 20-1/2" d, 90" h **3,850.00**

Revolving, American, second half 19th C, oak, molded rect top, five compartmentalized shelves with slatted ends, quadruped base with casters, stamped "Danners Revolving Book Case...Ohio," 24" w, 24" d, 68-1/4" h **1,200.00**

Rococo-style, Italian, late 19th C, serpentine front with three shelves, cabriole legs, dec with Chinoiserie scenes, green ground, 38" w, 14" d, 49" h **600.00**

Victorian, Globe-Wernicke, barrister type, stacking, three sections, oak, glass fronted drawers, drawer in base, metal bands, orig finish **900.00**

Boxes

Artist's, PA, 1850-70, fancy inlay, tiger maple, bird's eye maple, and walnut **950.00**

Ballot, walnut, eight slide lid compartments, names of election officials and writing under lid, 19th C voting forms from East Berlin, PA, last used in 1892, 32-1/2" l, 8-1/4" w, 4-1/4" h **2,200.00**

Band, oval

Bucher-type paint dec, black ground, house and trees on center of lid, red/orange, white, and green floral tulip on top and sides, yellow highlights, 9-1/4" l, 6-1/8" w, 4-1/2" h, provenance: Eugene and Dorothy Elgin collection, Conestoga Auction Co., April 3, 2004 .... **15,950.00**

Unknown artist, nailed construction, painted light blue with patina turning blue to gray, pencil sgd "Elisha Whipple" under lid, 6-3/4" l, 5" w, 4" h **2,530.00**

Box, lap desk, painted black exterior with polychrome floral decoration, gold trim, unfolds to writing surface, **$95**.

Photo courtesy of Dotta Auction Co., Inc.

Bible, chestnut, some curl in lid, molded edges, front panel with punched design, initials and date "L. T. 1705," int. with cov till and single drawer, wrought-iron lock, old dark patina, hasp missing, some edge damage, pulls added to drawer, 27" l **650.00**

Book, PA, c1860, ftd, drawer, top painted with arabesque design, spine with geometric devices in red and gilt, black ground, red borders, mottled mustard painted edges, minor paint war, 6-3/8" w, 5-1/8" d, 2-5/8" h **250.00**

Bride's, oval, bentwood, overlapping laced scenes, orig painted dec, couple in colonial dress, white, red, brown, and black on brown stained ground, German inscription and 1796 in white, edge damage, 15-7/8" l, 10" w, 6-1/2" h **495.00**

Candle, hanging

Poplar, orig dry red paint, peaked back two-board back, base board extends beyond lower front and includes six cut-outs for spoons, reeded sides, wire nail construction, small chip on front, 12" w, 7" d, 6" h **285.00**

Walnut, poplar secondary wood, dovetailed case, hinged lid, good figure on front and lid, arched backboard, one drawer in lower front with orig turned walnut pull, mellow old finish, minor glued split, 14" w, 7-14" d, 8-3/4" h **600.00**

Cheese, 6-1/2" h, 12-1/8" d, pine, circular, incised "E. Temple" on lid, painted blue, America, 19th C, cracks, paint wear, minor losses **175.00**

Collar, 13" l, 5" h, wallpaper covering, oval, marked "E. Stone no. 116 1/2 William Street, New York" **575.00**

Cutlery, walnut, dovetailed, int. divided into two compartments, pierced handle, later tapered leg stretcher base, dark finish, 15-5/8" w, 10-1/2" d, 23" h **300.00**

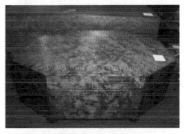

Bird's eye maple, eight-sided, divided interior, small bun feet, **$195**.

Decorated, dovetailed, pine, orig grain painting, rect, dovetailed, conforming hinged lid, ochre ground paint with red putty or vinegar painted seaweed-like designs, orig lock, wallpaper lined int., New England, 1820s, missing top bail handle, later waxing of surface, 14-5/8" w, 7-1/8" d, 6-3/4" h **690.00**

Document

Grain painted and gilt stenciled, America, c1825, pine, rect, hinged lid, grain painted exterior simulating rosewood with gilt stenciled designs of fruit and foliage on top, gilt stenciled floral designs with green highlights on front and sides, leaf and pendant pinecone motifs on black borders with ovolo corners, minor paint losses, 18-5/8" w, 8-1/8" d, 6-3/4" h **2,350.00**

Grain painted, pine, old brown wavy dec over mustard ground, dovetailed, orig internal lock, old padlock on outside, insect damage, 17-1/4" w, 11-3/4" d, 11-1/2" h **250.00**

Pine, gilt stenciled, New York State or New England, c1825, hinged dovetail constructed, rect, brass swing handle, top with gilt-stenciled flowers in footed bowl, sides with fruit and flowers, geometric borders, black ground, crack, minor paint wear, 14-3/4" w, 9-3/8" d, 5-1/4" h **1,000.00**

Pine, painted, rect, hinged lid, carved and scribed compass stars and rosettes, incised checkerboard, foliate, and heart motifs, painted in shades of red, black, and mustard, wallpaper-lined interior with till, name "Peter Glawson, August 11th, 1863" inscribed on the back, small corner losses, minor paint wear, 13" w, 7-1/8" d, 5-3/4" h **5,590.00**

Federal, America, early 19th C, inlaid mahogany, rect dovetail construction, hinged lid, bracket feet, inlaid oval paterae on top, circular paterae on front, top and sides bordered by string inlay, kite-shaped escutcheon, 11" w, 7-1/2" d, 7" h **825.00**

Paint decorated, America, c1830, pine, rect, hinged lid, iron latch, vinegar painted graining with dark brown over pinkish-brown base color, 15" w, 8-1/2" d, 5-5/8" h **600.00**

Dresser box, inlaid, Geometric designs in mixed woods on sarcophagus form box, fitted interior, 14" w, 7" d, 5-1/2" h, **$250**.

Photo courtesy of Alderfer Auction Co.

Dome-top, paint decorated

America, poplar, dovetailed, orig stenciled black and bittersweet colored vining on front, worn red and black on top, yellow brown ground on ends, some areas of green remain on side, orig iron lock and hasp, age splits, 24" l, 14" d, 12-3/4" h **980.00**

Schoharie, New York, early 19th C, pine, painted blue, hinged top with iron latch, decorated with letters "RM" in rectangle and linear borders in black, white, red, yellow, and green, front with flowers and floral border in similar colors, wear, cracks, 27" w, 12-1/4" d, 11" h **1,880.00**

Worcester County, MA, early 19th C, paint dec, rect. wire hinged lid, painted black, foliate, swag, and linear embellishments in shades of yellow and red, iron latch and handles, paint wear, crack, 20-1/4" w, 10" d, 7-3/4" h **2,235.00**

Dec by Bucher, white ground, red houses and tulips on top and all sides, borders picked out in blue, early 19th C, 9" l **13,500.00**

Dough, pine and poplar, rect removable top, tapering well, splayed ring-turned legs, ball feet, Pennsylvania, 19th C, 38" w, 19-3/4" w, 29-1/2" h **500.00**

Grain painted, America, early 19th C, rect, carved from one piece of pine, sliding lid, incised compass, chip-carved dec on top and sides, brass escutcheon on side, old green surface, wear, age crack, 8-3/4" l, 5" w, 1-7/8" h **2,000.00**

Knife box, covered, slots for knives, **$125**.

Photo courtesy of Dotta Auction Co., Inc.

Knife

9" w, 10" d, 15-3/4" h, English, inlaid flame mahogany veneer over pine, bow front, scalloped corners with banded inlay, brass handles on both sides, star inlay on int. of lid, old refinish, contemporary, dovetailed int. lifts out, slotted for letters, hidden compartment below, some sections of inlay missing, age splits in veneer **550.00**

14-1/2" h, mahogany veneer with inlay, edge veneer damage, int. incomplete, inlaid oval on inside of lid **225.00**

16" h, 9-3/4" w, 14-1/2" d, Federal, flamed grained mahogany, serpentine and block front, reeded front columns, fitted int., orig keys, pr **2,500.00**

Letter box, Victorian, English, satinwood veneer, mahogany secondary wood, ebonized moldings, recesses for pens, drop front with divided letter compartments, old finish, two polished glass inkwells, 12-1/2" w, 8-1/2" d, 11-1/4" h **920.00**

Pantry, America, 19th C, pine top and bottom, oval, lapped maple sides fastened with copper tacks, painted blue, 4-1/4" d, 1-1/2" h **950.00**

Pencil box, child's, slide-lid, carved from single pc of cherry, carved heart shaped handle, compass wheel dec, 10" l, 2-1/2" h **1,045.00**

Pipe box, hanging, New England, c1800, lollipop top, poplar and pine **6,250.00**

Presentation, walnut, simulated inlay, carved spread wing eagle on lid, presented to Gen George McClellan by Rauch Club, Milwaukee, Nov. 8, 1864 .... **6,800.00**

Razor, sailor's, carved cherry, rect, heart-shaped handle, chip carved borders, incised sailing vessel on swivel top, 19th C, 10-3/4" l, 1-3/4" w, 1-1/2" h ... **325.00**

Salt, hanging, walnut, sq nail construction, base molding, heart shaped wall mounted, hinged lid, paint dec, tan ground, brown highlighted graining, 8-1/2" l, 8-3/4" w, 13-1/8" h **1,320.00**

Sewing

America, 19th C, mahogany inlaid, hinged lid, center inlaid oval reserve with shell motif, ext. with inlaid borders and corners, int. lid centered with diamond motif, lift-out tray with several compartments, minor imperfections, 12-1/4" w, 7-1/4" d, 5-5/8" h **1,000.00**

Chinese Export, 19th C, lacquered, Chinoiserie dec, scenic panels surrounded by mosaic patterns, Greek key border, brass bail handles on each end, int. with mirrored lid and fitted compartments, single fitted drawer, containing various sewing implements, minor wear and crackling, 17-1/4" w, 11-1/2" d, 5-3/4" h **475.00**

Slide lid

America, decorated, pine, bittersweet and white scrolling, initials "A.H.D. 1826" on blue ground, dovetailed corners, reeded lid, mix of orig rose head and later nails in bottom, age splits in base, some rim damage, replaced int. runner, 24-1/2" l, 15-1/2" d, 8-1/2" h **420.00**

America, oak, lid with unusual reeded diamond design, dovetailed corners, old dark refinishing, pieced restorations to edges, 19-1/2" w, 12-1/4" d, 10-1/2" h **250.00**

America, pine and poplar, orig reddish brown surface, sq cut nails on base, small lock with key inlet in one end, 16" l, 10" d, 10" h **175.00**

America, walnut, dovetailed joints, pegged base, paneled lid with gouge caved finger pull, four interior compartments, orig finish, 10-1/4" l, 4-3/4" w, 3" h **770.00**

European, pine, dovetailed, comb graining around sides, floral dec and molded edge on lid, European inscription on base with "1815," pieced restorations and touch up to ends, 10-3/4" w, 7-3/8" d, 5-5/8" h **230.00**

Pennsylvania, John Drissel, Bucks County, attributed to, c1790, pine, pegged construction, gouge-carved edge and finger pull, painted red ground with red, blue, white, and green PA German

compass, floral and tulip designs, name on lid "Peter Nehs," German text "I came to a country where I read on the wall be God fearing and don't break what doesn't belong to you," 11" l, 6-3/4" w, 4-1/4" h, provenance: Eugene and Dorothy Elgin collection, Conestoga Auction Co., April 3, 2004 .... **82,500.00**

Spice box

America, pine and poplar, eight drawer, dovetailed, molding at top and base, brass pulls, orig red-brown finish, pencil drawing of man and horse with illegible name on one drawer side, 13-1/4" l, 10-1/2" w, 12-1/8" h .. **1,100.00**

Pennsylvania, attributed to Mahantongo Valley, c1780, slide lid, dovetailed, dusty blue ground, white, salmon, green and yellow tulip dec on four sides and top, 9" x 5" **33,000.00**

Storage

8-1/2" l, 6-1/2" w, 3-1/2" h, America, late 19th C, pine, painted red, floral and linear dec, int. paper lined ... **635.00**

18-7/8" l, 8-3/4" h, Massachusetts, early 19th C, ochre-painted pine, six board, dovetailed, thumb molded lid dec with flags, shield, and banner inscribed "Mass. Militia 2nd Regt. 1st B. 2nd D," partial paper tag tacked to lid inscribed " K Rogers Boston," minor imperfections **1,150.00**

Sugar box

Amish, pyramid shaped lid, brass knob, black and salmon painted sides, five-point yellow and black star on front, 7" sq **11,500.00**

Country, fruitwood, single base drawer with holes drilled in interior, wrought iron cane cutter mounted at middle, brass pull on lid, old mellow refinishing, 14" w, 9-3/4" d, 9" h **250.00**

Tea bin, 24-1/8" h, 17-1/2" w, 25" d, dec of gentleman toasting lady, dec by Ralph Cahoon, oil on wood, with certificate of authenticity from Cahoon Museum of American Art **2,530.00**

Box, tantalus, rosewood, c1840, black lacquer with gold decoration, 15 crystal glasses, four decanter, one glass missing, minor chips, **$700**.

Photo courtesy of Wiederseim Associates, Inc.

Utensil box, poplar, dovetailed, sq nail construction, scrolled sides and handle dividers, worn salmon painted finish, 11-1/2" l, 9" w, 5" h **1,100.00**

Vegetable shredding, hanging, orig dry red paint, chestnut and pine, c1850 .... **3,500.00**

Wall

America, pine, one drawer, dovetailed, sq nail construction drawer with four-part divider, brass pull, wood hinges, old leather repair, 10-3/4" l, 10" d, 17-3/4" h **1,045.00**

America, poplar, early round head nail construction, paint dec, eight drawers, green ground, sponged and fanned graining, yellow and black highlights, green trim around drawers, red base, porcelain drawer pulls, 8-1/8" l, 4" w, 14" h **19,800.00**

Pennsylvania, attributed to Henry Lapp, Lancaster County, PA, sq and early round head nail construction, eight drawers, red ground with comb graining, yellow drawers, porcelain pulls, one drawer repaired, 8-1/2" l, 3-3/4" d, 14-1/2" h **9,075.00**

Wallpaper covered, paper and wood construction

Eight-sides, blue, orange, and yellow foliage, 22-3/4" l, 18-1/2" w, 16-1/2" h .. **4,675.00**

Oval, blue ground wallpaper with orange highlights, geometric ad floral dec, int. lined with German and English text newspaper, paper label mkd "Laura May, Jack's Box, Dec 29, 1890," 8" l, 5-1/4" w, 3-3/4" h .. **910.00**

Oval, eagle, yellow ground, green and pink highlights, int. lined with German text newspaper, 5-1/2" l, 3-3/4" h, 3" h............................. **580.00**

Oval, green ground, yellow and red highlights, lid lined with Lancaster German text newspaper, mkd "Dr. C. Weaver," 6-1/4" l, 4-1/2" w, 3-1/2" h.................... **1,540.00**

Oval, light green ground, maroon, green, and black highlights, bird and floral dec, int. lined with English text PA newspaper, 8-1/4" l, 5-1/8" w, 4-1/8" h....................... **420.00**

Rectangular, pink ground, red and white floral dec, int. lined with German text newspaper, 4-1/4" l, 3" w, 1-1/2" h .. **715.00**

Round, pink ground, red and white floral highlights, int. lined with German and English text newspaper, 3" d, 1-7/8" h.................... **1,650.00**

Slide lid, pine, nailed construction, red base, green, white, and black wallpaper, minor usage wear, 7" l, 4-1/4" w, 3-1/4" h......... **880.00**

Work, 12" w, 10-1/2" d, 7-1/4" h, European, marquetry inlaid mahogany veneer, pine secondary wood, slant top lid with pincushion covered in old burgundy velvet, paper lined int., till with lid, engraved strap hinges, old finish, repairs **275.00**

Writing, English, 20th C

Mahogany, dovetailed case and two drawers, red velvet liners, compartment with lift lid on top, ivory pulls on top drawer, replaced wooden pulls on lower drawer . **230.00**

Mahogany, old ebonized finish, dovetailed drawer in base with divided interior, open compartment behind roll top, two small int. drawers within top with ivory pulls, sgd under drawer "Sawlish, Sunday, 27th of February, 1820, J. H. Jacob," and religious verse, 14-1/2" w, 10-1/2" d, 6-1/2" h **200.00**

Cabinet, six drawers, labels, **$145**.
Photo courtesy of Dotta Auction Co., Inc.

Cabinets

Apothecary, pine, yellow grain dec, 29 drawers over two open shelves, cut-out base and sides, bracket feet, open back, 62" l, 12" d, 54" h.................. **1,550.00**

Bar, Art Deco, walnut, sarcophagus form, two doors, sq top with drop-front cabinet on left, mirrored bar, small drawer on right between two open bays, 48" w, 21" d, 54-1/2" d **600.00**

Cellaret, George III, mahogany, serpentine, top enclosing a green baize interior, brass handles at sides, square-section tapering legs, 18" w, 18" d, 25" h **1,675.00**

China

Art Moderne, mahogany, double doors, floral-carved relief panels, int. shelves, two drawers below, 45" w, 17" d, 62" h......................... **2,000.00**

Arts & Crafts, Limbert, #428, trapezoidal form, two doors, each with four windows at top over one large window, orig copper pulls, sides with two windows over one, refinished, branded, 40" w, 19" d, 63" h **4,250.00**

Edwardian-style, curved glass sides, single flat glazed door, illuminated int., mirrored back, 42" w, 16" d, 64" h, pr **1,675.00**

International Movement, Gilbert Rhode, manufactured by Herman Miller, glass-sided china cabinet top over two doors with burled fronts, brushed steel pulls, refinished, glass doors and shelves missing, 36" w, 17" d, 58" h.......................... **800.00**

Victorian, American, c1900, oak, ornate, crest with carved wind god, leaves, and scrolls, curved glass door and side panels, four glass shelves, mirrored back, column supports, claw feet, 51" w, 19" d, 77" h **2,650.00**

Cabinet, law blanks, brass plaque reads "John B. Clark & Sons, Phila," oak, two long drawers over two banks of smaller drawers, **$350**.

Corner, Victorian, late 19th C, walnut, three graduated shelves supported on openwork scrolls, accented with split spindles, base with central cupboard door set with carved fruit, enclosing drawer, short bracket feet, 75-1/2" h, **$1,175**.
Photo courtesy of Skinner, Inc.

Chinoiserie, two drawers, double doors, two adjustable int. shelves, walnut veneer with inlay and black lacquer, gilded detail, attached base with turned legs, 20th C, 43" w, 15-1/2" d, 63" h **625.00**

Corner

George III style, 20th C, inlaid mahogany, molded swan's neck cresting, pair of mullioned glass doors, shelved interior, two lower paneled doors, bracket feet, inlaid with fans, 45" w, 22" d, 91" h.......................... **1,110.00**
Georgian, early, 18th C, japanned, two part, molded cornice and outset corners above two pairs of doors flanked by solid pilasters, shaped plinth base, decorated overall with Chinoiserie scenes on black ground, 35" w, 19" d, 90" h **7,650.00**
Renaissance Revival, American, walnut, hanging, spindle-inset cornice, two glazed doors and reeded pilasters **400.00**

Curio, French

Bombé-shaped base, ornate, old gold repaint, carved rococo dec and gesso, beveled glass front, glass side panels, high scrolled feet, scalloped base aprons, 35" w, 15" d, 71-1/2" h **950.00**

Serpentine front, flowers around case, courting scene on lower case and door, metallic gold ground, ormolu dec around edges and arched crest, two removable glass shelves, worn red velvet covering bottom shelf, mirrored back, 33-1/2" w, 17" d, 74" h **850.00**

Cabinet, display, Ladies Gloves, 72 drawers, glass enclosed display areas with blue backgrounds, **$3,600**.

Display, Aesthetic Movement, America, late 19th C, carved mahogany, pair of glass doors, two drawers fitted in plinth base, 61" w, 23" d, 72" h, **$2,850**.

Photo courtesy of Skinner, Inc.

Display

Biedermeier-style, poplar and burr-poplar, single door, outset molded cornice, three-pane glazed door flanked by similar stiles and sides, three mirror-backed shelves supporting shaped half shelves, block feet, 41" w, 16" d, 68" h **800.00**
Edwardian, late 19th C, rosewood, dentil molded cornice, two glazed doors and projecting lower section fitted with three drawers, sq tapered legs joined by shelf stretcher, 25" w, 15" d, 56" h **2,415.00**
Empire-style, gilt metal mounted mahogany, rect case fitted with arched glass door, stemmed bun feet, foliate cast mounts, 33" w, 16" d, 68" h......................... **1,975.00**
Queen Anne style, green japanned, pair of shaped and mullioned glass doors, shelved int., cabriole legs, Spanish feet, multicolored chinoiserie scenes, 38" w, 15-1/2" d, 80-1/2" h .. **1,530.00**
Renaissance Revival, late 19th/early 20th C, oak, foliate and fruit carved borders, shaped feet, glass front and sides **6,500.00**

Dressing, Art Deco, France, c1925, rect curvilinear top, centered mirror over four drawers flanked on each side by full-length curvilinear cabinets, shaped foot skirt, 68 1/2" w, 19-1/2" d, 66-7/8" h **1,100.00**

Fall front, Renaissance Revival, American, ebonized and parcel gilt, angular cresting, fall front enclosing plain interior, trestle base, curved legs, 26" w, 45" h **900.00**

Cabinet, display, designed to hold canes, curved oak and glass, round, **$4,200**.

Secretary, modern Chippendale-style reproduction, walnut with inlaid stars, 40" w, 94-1/2" h. Did not meet auction reserve and was not sold.

Secretary, Chippendale, Pennsylvania, cherry, two piece, upper: broken arch pediment, boldly carved floral rosettes, turned and carved finials, double doors each with seven panes of glass in geometric arrangement, fluted quarter columns, applied reeded detail, base: slant top lid with fully developed fitted interior of eight dovetailed drawers with serpentine fronts, center door with blocking and carved fan with five graduated drawers with serpentine fronts, eight pigeonholes each with hidden drawers and fan carving, two letter drawers with fluted columns and reeding, four overlapping dovetailed drawers, fluted quarter columns, ogee foot, original eagle brasses, H-hinges, and latches, original finish, minor repairs to feet and some replaced glue blocks, 38-1/4" w, 20-3/4" d, 90" h, **$88,000**.

Photo courtesy of Garth's Auctions Inc.

Highboy, Queen Anne, New England, c1740-60, cherry, flat top, step molded overhanging cornice four wide graduated drawers, base with one wide drawer over three small drawers, center fan carved, scalloped skirt with two pendant drops, cabriole legs, pad feet, later butterfly brasses, one drawer front chipped, two repaired, 40" w, 20-1/8" d, 70-1/2" h, **$16,800**.

Photo courtesy of Samuel T. Freeman & Co., Philadelphia, PA.

Filing, Arts & Crafts
American, c1910, golden oak, plain vertical stack, five drawers, orig brass nameplates and pulls . **650.00**
Stickley, L. & J. G., Manlius, NY, re-issue, two-drawer, rect, hammered copper hardware, branded "Stickley," round yellow and red decal in int drawer, wear to top finish, 21-3/8" w, 28" l, 31" h .. **360.00**

Cabinet, William and Mary style, walnut veneer, double arched top section over three drawers, scrolled carved cabriole legs, doors missing, interior painted, **$675**.

Hanging
Middle Eastern, inlaid mother-of-pearl, lancet molded cornice, turned shelf supports, spindle inset door above three small open shelves, 20" w, 7-1/2" d, 20" h **425.00**
Renaissance Revival, American, walnut, spindle-inset gallery, floral incised door and shelved interior, shaped and angular pendant, 26" w, 8" d, 26" h **765.00**
Ledger, American, 19th C, walnut and mixed hardwoods, poplar secondary wood, dovetailed case, single paneled door, int. with divided compartments, later salmon paint, pr, 15-1/2" w, 12" d, 24" h.................................... **600.00**
Sheet music, first half 20th C
Mahogany, rect top over door, opening to 21 doors of

Cabinet, spice, painted, French, **$195**.
Photo courtesy of Dotta Auction Co., Inc.

graduated sizes, 20" w, 14-1/2" d, 34" h **325.00**
Mahogany, one door, back rail with beveled mirror, drawer, 18" w, 47" h **225.00**
Side
Aesthetic Movement, American, ebonized and parcel gilt, upper section with spindle galleries and mirrored back, lower section with central door with angular foliate designs, flanked by open shelves, angular gilt foliage throughout, 43" w, 14" d, 66" h **3,410.00**
Arts & Crafts, oak, single door, orig sq copper pull, notched toe-board, refinished, 22" w, 22" d, 38" h **700.00**
Baroque, Dutch, oak, rect case fitted with three paneled doors, borders carved in shallow relief with scrolling tulip vines, stemmed bun feet, 82" w, 20" d, 53" h **1,380.00**
Biedermeier, late 19th C, fruitwood parquetry, rect top, canted corners, pr of cabinet doors enclosing shelves, bracket feet, 55-1/4" w, 24-3/4" d, 40-1/2" h .. **1,725.00**
Empire-style, late 19th/early 20th C, gilt bronze mounted mahogany, rect marble top, conforming case fitted with cabinet door, pull-out shelves, plinth base, 20-3/4" w, 16-1/4" d, 52-1/4" h **750.00**
Gothic-style, late 19th/early 20th C, oak, rect case fitted with two doors, upper door carved with gothic tracery, lower with linenfold paneling, sides with linenfold paneling, block feet, 22" w, 19" d, 52" h **450.00**
Louis XVI, Provincial, late 18th/early 19th C, oak, paneled door carved with urns, 41" w, 18-1/2" d, 73" h **1,380.00**

Napoleon III, c1850-70, brass and mother-of-pearl inlaid, ormolu mounts, white serpentine marble top, conforming case, fitted with door, bracket feet, 35-1/2" w, 16" d, 41" h **2,645.00**
Regency, early 19th C, rosewood, shelf with gallery above mirrored back over single drawer above grilled door flanked by columns with maiden terms on squared plinth base, 24-1/2" w, 17-1/2" d, 45-1/2" h, price for pr **14,160.00**
Renaissance Revival, attributed to New York, c1865-75, ebonized, marquetry, and parcel-gilt, central elevated cupboard flanked by two similar cupboards, 75" w, 15" d, 64" h **4,900.00**

Cabinet, Victorian, late 19th C, mahogany, two parts, dentil molded cornice above central winged figure over glass doors, and central paneled door, lower section with multiple drawers, 56" w, 96" h, **$4,000-$6,000**.
Photo courtesy of Wiederseim Associates, Inc.

Spice

Counter-type, poplar, old brown sponge dec, vertical stack with four sq nailed drawers with beveled edges, turned wooden pulls, chamfered side moldings, tongue and groove boards on sides of case, one drawer front split, 8-3/8" w, 17-1/2" d, 19-5/8" h **495.00**

Hanging, second half 20th C, rope twist top molding over geometric border flanking eight drawers, inlaid star and heart dec, porcelain knobs, inlaid with ivory and mixed woods, minor losses, 15" w, 8" d, 18" h **475.00**

Vitrine

Biedermeier, first half 19th C, part ebonized, triangular pediment and dentilled cornice above two mullioned glazed doors flanked by two columns, block feet, 47" w, 21" d, 67" h **4,600.00**

Biedermeier-style, peaked crest over two glazed doors flanked by ebonized columns, square block feet, price for pr, 45-1/4" w, 18-1/2" d, 73" h **5,350.00**

George III-style, early 20th C, mahogany, open swan's neck cresting, glazed doors, lower section with glass top shelf, sq legs joined by stretchers, 22" w, 18-1/2" d, 68" h **1,495.00**

Louis XVI-style, c1850, giltwood, outset molded rect top, frieze with beribboned floral garlands, front with glazed door with inset corners, flanked by fluted stiles, opening to two shelves, glazed sides, paneled skirt with swags, turned, tapered, and fluted legs with paterae, 27-1/4" w, 16" d, 61-1/2" h **1,200.00**

Candlestands

Adjustable

American, c1780, central cherry shaft, turned double adjustable candle arm, ring turned burl base, orig patination, 29" h **9,000.00**

American, c1790, maple, screw-post, traces of orig salmon paint **4,500.00**

Chippendale, probably Massachusetts, late 18th C, carved mahogany, tilt-top square molded diagonally hinged top in tapering vase and ring post, tripod cabriole leg base ending in elongated claw and ball feet, refinished, minor imperfections, 17-3/4" l, 17-1/4" w, 27-1/2" h, **$1,650**.

Photo courtesy of Skinner, Inc.

Chippendale

America, mahogany, round single board top, vase shaped column, cabriole legs, padded snake feet, old finish, well executed repair to one leg, reduced in size, 17-1/2" d, 28-1/4" h **875.00**

Boston or Salem, MA, late 18th C, mahogany, carved oval tilt top, vase and ring-turned post, tripod cabriole leg base ending in arris pad feet on platforms, refinished, one leg repaired, 16-1/2" w, 22-3/4" d, 27-1/2" h .. **1,535.00**

Massachusetts, late 18th C, mahogany, serpentine molded tilt top, vase and ring-turned post on tripod cabriole leg base, arris pad feet on platforms, old finish, very minor imperfections, 28" w, 27-3/4" d, 28-3/4" h .. **4,200.00**

New England, late 18th C, tilt-top, walnut, circular molded top, vase and ring-turned post and tripod cabriole leg base, arris pad feet, old refinish, imperfections, minor repair, 17" d, 28" h **2,500.00**

New Hampshire, attributed to Lt. Samuel Dunlap, old refinish, birch, painted red, imperfections, 16-1/2" w, 16-1/8" d, 26-1/2" h .. **2,950.00**

Pennsylvania, Chester County, Octorora, walnut, tilt top, molded edge burl top, bird cage support, ball turned pedestal, cabriole legs, well executed carved feet, 6" age crack in top, 24" d top, 29-1/2" h **4,400.00**

Candle stand, 18th C, mahogany, oval burled tilt top, spade feet, 24" x 16-3/4" top, 27-1/2" h, **$750**.

Photo courtesy of Alderfer Auction Co.

Candlestand, Chippendale style, mahogany, dish top, inlaid center rosette, **$195**.

Photo courtesy of Wiederseim Associates, Inc.

Chippendale-style, America, early 20th C, inlaid mahogany, round tilt top with small raised edge, circular inlaid center fan, reeded urn shaped column, tripod base, well carved claw and ball feet, orig dark finish, 23-3/4" d top, 28-1/2" h ... **225.00**

Country, cherry and maple, southeastern New England, late 18th C, circular top, vase and ring turned post and tripod base, three tapering legs, remnants of old dark green paint, imperfections, 12" d, 25" h **1,150.00**

Federal

Connecticut, attributed to, c1790, cherry inlaid, rect top with string inlaid border, vase and ring-turned chip carved post, tripod base of arris cabriole legs, imperfections, 15" l, 13-3/4" w, 26-3/4" h **1,120.00**

Connecticut River Valley, c1790, cherry, shaped top with serpentine sides and ovolo corners, vase and ring-turned post, tripod cabriole leg base, arris pad feet, refinished, minor restoration, 17-3/4" l, 18" w, 26" h **3,000.00**

Dunlap School, Antrim, New Hampshire area, late 18th century, painted, octagonal top with shaped underside, turned tapering pedestal ending in turned cap flanked by cabriole leg base ending in pad feet, Victorian polychrome dec with gilt highlight, minor imperfections, 13-5/8" x 13-1/2" top, 26-1/2" h **25,850.00**

Massachusetts, c1820, inlaid birch and maple, scroll-shaped tilt top contoring inlaid oval wavy birch panel, vase and ring turned and reeded post, tripod shaped tapering legs, refinished, 15-1/8" w, 21-3/4" d, 29" h **5,760.00**

Massachusetts, late 18th C, cherry, sq top with serpentine sides and rounded corners, vase and ring-turned post, tripod cabriole legs, arris feet, refinished, imperfections, note taped to underside of top reads "candlestand Starr-Allen family of Deerfield," 14-3/8" w, 15" d, 26-1/4" h **950.00**

Massachusetts, late 18th C, mahogany, oval tilt top, vase and ring-turned post, tripod base with cabriole legs, arris pointed pad feet on platforms, old surface, very minor imperfections, 23-1/4" w, 17-1/4" d, 27" h **8,850.00**

New England, c1790, cherry, serpentine top, vase and ring-turned post, tripod cabriole leg base, pad feet, old refinish, imperfections, 15-1/2" l, 16" w, 24-3/4" h...................... **775.00**

Candlestand, Federal, New England, c1820, maple top, tiger maple spider leg base, turned pedestal, refinished, original reddish color, 21-2/3" l, 17" w, 28-3/4" h, **$450**.

Photo courtesy of Alderfer Auction Co.

New England, c1800, painted, circular top, vase and ring-turned post and tripod cabriole leg base, old black paint over earlier red stain, polychrome floral cluster dec and pin striping, 16-1/4" d, 26" h...................... **2,115.00**

New England, late 18th/early 19th C, cherry, rect octagonal top with applied cockbeaded edge, swelled ring-turned post, tripod base of arched, shaped, tapering legs ending in plain feet, refinished, imperfections, 20-1/2" w, 16-3/4" d, 28-1/4" h **825.00**

New Hampshire, early 19th C, birch, painted, sq top with rounded corners, urn shaped turned pedestal, high arched cabriole tripod base, pad feet, old red paint, imperfections, 13-3/4" w, 13-1/4" d, 26-1/4" h **7,475.00**

Rhode Island, late 18th century, cherry, circular top with scratch-beaded edge, ring-turned tapering column, tripod cabriole leg base ending in arris pad feet, old finish, minor imperfections, 17-1/2" d, 27-3/4" h .. **1,100.00**

Hepplewhite, country, birch and maple, old dark brown surface, round single board top, vase turned column, three serpentine tapered legs, old shims, 18" d, 27-1/2" h...................... **1,050.00**

George II, c1750, mahogany, circular tilt top, birdcage support, baluster standard, cabriole legs, pad feet, 26-1/2" d, 27-1/2" h, **$800**.

Photo courtesy of Pook & Pook.

Painted and decorated,

Connecticut, late 19th C, cherry, octagonal top with molded edge, turned pedestal with urn shaping over high-arched cabriole leg base ending in pad feet, early black paint with 19th C yellow striping on pedestal and legs, minor imperfections, 15-1/4" w, 15-3/4" d, 29-1/2" h........ **4,025.00**

Primitive, 40" h, wooden, adjustable candle arm, dark brown patina, early 19th C **715.00**

Queen Anne

New England, mid-18th C, butternut and maple, octagonal, applied molded edge, baluster turned support, tripod cabriole leg base, old refinish, traces of red paint, imperfections, 17-1/2" l, 17" w, 29" h **1,530.00**

New England, late 18th C/ early 19th C, cherry, round top, single double-sided candle drawer below, tapering and ring-turned post, tripod cabriole base, pad feet, old dark stain, alterations and repairs, 16-1/2" d, 26-1/4" h **850.00**

Southern New England, late 18th C, cherry, tilt top with molded edge, swelled ring-turned pedestal, cabriole legs, pad feet, refinished, repairs, alterations, 18" w, 18-1/4" d, 27-1/4" h .. **1,410.00**

Regency, English, mahogany, tilt-top, scalloped one board top, boldly turned column, tripod base, saber legs with beaded edges, old refinish, repairs and restoration to top, label underneath "From the summer home (1890-1929) Goshen, NY of Charlotte Beardsley (1852-1914) and George Van Riper (1845-1925), 24" w, 17-1/2" d, 28" h **595.00**

Windsor, walnut and curly maple, octagonal top, turned column, octagonal platform base, three turned legs, pegged and wedged construction, old brown finish, 12" w, 11-1/4" d, 24-3/4" h **980.00**

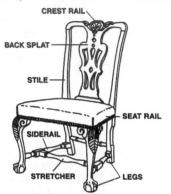

CREST RAIL

BACK SPLAT

STILE

SEAT RAIL

SIDERAIL

STRETCHER   LEGS

Typical Parts of a Chair

Chair, arm, carved backsplat with armorial type crest, scrolled arm rests, cabriole legs, paw feet, "H" stretcher, **$200**.

Chairs
Arm

Adirondack-style, rustic twig construction, including small

arms, green paint, roped seat, c1910 .... **2,300.00**

Aesthetic Movement, after Philip Webb's Sussex chair for Morris & Co., c1885, new natural rush seat, turned spindles, orig black paint, unmarked, 21-1/4" w, 19" d, 36-1/4" h **1,045.00**

Art Deco, France, c1925, giltwood, sloping U-form back rail ending in gently swollen reeded arm supports, D-shaped seat upholstered seat cushion, pr **15,750.00**

Art Nouveau, L. Majorelle, France, c1900, carved mahogany, horseshoe-shaped back rail, upholstered back, front of arm supports carved with pine cones and needles, continuing to form molded front legs with similar carving, dark green leather upholstery **7,000.00**

Chair, arm, Arts & Crafts, even-arms, broad horizontal back and side rails, mortised and keyed lower stretcher, unsigned, refinished, replaced leather cushion, 27" w, 22-1/2" d, 32" h, **$500**.

Photo courtesy of David Rago Auctions, Inc.

Chair, arm, Arts & Crafts, Gustav Stickley, No.340, designed by Harvey Ellis, arched aprons, three vertical back slats, red decals, refinished, replaced leather, edge wear, price for pr, 24-1/2" w, 21" d, 40" h, **$1,300**.

Photo courtesy of David Rago Auctions, Inc.

Arts & Crafts

Indiana Hickory, twig construction, orig hickory splint seat, weathered finish, branded signature, 26" w, 17" d, 37" h **50.00**

Olbrich, Joseph Marie, Jugendstil, mahogany, small back panel inlaid with fruitwood floral pattern, inset upholstered seat, unmarked, good old refinish, 23-1/2" w, 19" d, 41-1/2" h **1,840.00**

Stickley, Charles, four back slats, recovered spring cushion seat, orig finish, remnant of decal, 26" w, 22" d, 41" h **230.00**

Stickley, Gustav, Model no. 2604, oak, arched crest rail over three horizontal back slats, shaped flat open arms, prominent front leg posts, offset front, back, and side stretchers, dark brown finish, red decal under arm, c1902, wear, 26-3/4" w, 26" d, 37" h
.... **1,840.00**

Stickley, Gustav, Thornden, two horizontal back slats, narrow arms, 1902-04 red decal, replaced seat, orig finish, minor edge wear, 37" x 21" x 21-1/2" **3,105.00**

Stickley, Gustav, V-back, vertical back slats, replaced leather seat, orig faceted tacks, good orig finish, red decal, 27" w, 20-1/2" d, 37" h
.... **1,045.00**

Stickley, L. & J. G., fixed back, drop arm, slats to seat, corbels, replaced drop-in green leather spring seat and back cushion, waxed finish, L & J. G. Stickley Handcraft label, 32-1/2" w, 33" d, 41" h
.... **5,750.00**

Stickley, L. & J. G., spindled back, open arms, corbels, seat recovered in leather, refinished, unmarked, 24-1/2" w, 21" d, 38-1/2" h **690.00**

Banister-back, New England, mid-18th C, turned maple, yoked crest rail above four molded banisters joining vase and ring-turned stiles, shaped scrolled arms on vase and ring-turned supports continuing to legs, turned feet joined by double sausage-turned stretchers, early splint seat, old refinish, imperfections, 14-1/2" h seat, 43" h **1,175.00**

Centennial, Colonial Revival, Queen-Anne Style, wing back, hardwood cabriole legs, turned stretcher, upholstery removed, old dark finish, 46" h **900.00**

Chippendale, English or Irish, walnut, pierced Gothic back splat, scrolled handholds, slip seat cov in cream colored silk upholstery, sq legs, small scalloped returns on front apron, refinished, one foot ended out, 19" h seat, 37" h back **400.00**

Chippendale-style, walnut, light green leather upholstery, brass tack borders, shaped arms, sq molded legs, stretcher bases, wear, some splits in leather seats, 18-3/4" h seat, 38-1/4" h, price for six-pc set **1,200.00**

Egyptian Revival, American, c1865, ebonized and parcel-gilt, upholstered scrolling back and seat, matching upholstered arm pads, sphinx head arm supports, claw feet, 39-1/2" h **8,050.00**

Empire-style, mahogany, rect padded back, padded arms, ormolu-mounted classical busts, bowed padded seat, sq tapering legs with brass caps, white striped upholstery **850.00**

George III, mahogany, shaped top rail, three pc vertical splat, upholstered seat, tapering sq section legs **475.00**

Gothic Revival, America, walnut, old finish, reupholstered in damask, age cracks, 52-1/2" h **200.00**

Hepplewhite, birch, pegged construction, eight vertical posts across back, slip seat, tapered legs with broadly shaped stretchers, relief arched fans on front and sides, old mellow refinishing, originally potty seat, base reworked, arms repegged, age splits, 18-1/2" h seat, 37" h back **450.00**

Louis XIV, early 18th C, fauteuil, giltwood, serpentine cresting, scrolled and reeded arms, over upholstered seat, scrolled legs joined by stretchers **2,990.00**

Louis XIV-style, Baroque, late 19th C, walnut, rect backrest, foliate carved arms and legs, X-form stretcher, price for pr **2,650.00**

Neoclassical, Italian, late 18th/ early 19th C, walnut, urn and wheat carved splat, downswept arms, raised sq tapering legs, 34-1/4" h **1,100.00**

Chair, arm, New England, c1740, banister back, carved yoke crest, **$575**.
Photo courtesy of Pook & Pook.

Queen Anne
Middle Atlantic states, last half 18th C, arched crest with square corners, raked stiles, scrolled arms on vasiform supports, trapezoidal seat, frontal cabriole legs ending in pad feet, raked rear legs, imperfections, 16-1/2" h seat, 49" h **21,150.00**
New Hampshire, hardwood with old black repaint, molded and curved back posts with vase splat and carved crest, turned posts support molded and scrolled arms, turned legs, Spanish feet, turned rungs with bulbous front stretcher, old rush seat, some loss to feet, 15-3/8" seat, 41" h **4,125.00**

Regency
Mahogany, octagonal crest rail over shaped horizontal splat, open arms, shaped padded seat, sq tapering legs **600.00**
Mahogany, rect top rail above horizontal spiral-turned splat and reeded scrolling arms, upholstered seat, ring turned front legs, rear saber legs **600.00**

Regency-style, mahogany, bent reeded crest rail over shaped splat, upholstered seat, tapering turned legs **200.00**

Renaissance Revival, attributed to Pottier & Stymus, New York, 1865, walnut, scrolled arms, upholstered back and seed, spherules on seat rail, 38" h **1,100.00**

Rococo Revival, John H. Belter, rosewood, Rosalie pattern, laminated, solid back, crest carved with large rose, fruit, and grape clusters, yellow silk upholstery, tufted back, 42-1/2" h **3,500.00**

Rococo-style, Italian, late 19th/ early 20th C, grotto, scallop shell seat, dolphin-shaped arms, rusticated legs **1,725.00**

Savonarola-style, mahogany, Old Man of the North carved in crest rail **230.00**

Shaker, attributed to Canterbury, NH, c1835, birch and pine, concave rect back rail, turned stiles, four spindles, shaped seat, splayed turned tapering legs joined by stretchers, old refinish, traces of red stain, minor imperfections, 17" h seat, 24-1/2" h.......................... **600.00**

Victorian, George Huntzinger, NY, patent March 30, 1869, walnut, pierce carved crest, rect upholstered back panel flanked by turned and curved slats and stiles, low upholstered barrel-back, arm frame carved with classical heads, upholstered seat, pierced and scroll-carved front drop under seat connected to turned rung joining carved and turned front legs, ball feet, front leg stamped......... **2,100.00**

Windsor
Bow-back, Pennsylvania, scrolled arms, bamboo turned spindles and legs, later tan and brown swirl paint dec seat, black frame, 16" h seat, 35" h.......................... **470.00**
Brace-back, continuous arm, B. Green, CT, late 18th C, bowed crest rail continuing to shaped arms above six spindles, vase and ring-turned arm supports, shaped saddle seat, splayed vase and ring-turned legs joined by swelled stretchers, repairs, 16" h seat, 37" h.......... **950.00**
Comb-back, attributed to Philadelphia, PA, mixed woods, areas of old dark green paint, arched top with finely scrolled ears, nine back spindles, bentwood arm rain

ending in shaped hand rests, D-shaped seat with incised line borders around edges, baluster and ring turned legs, blunt arrow feet, stretcher base, old pegged restoration on arm rail, 23-1/2" w, 17-1/2" h seat, 42" h **11,275.00**
Comb-back, old worn red paint over yellow, evidence of earlier paint history, seven spindle back with well shaped crest, bowed arm rain with turned supports, oval seat with incised detailing around spindles, splayed baluster and ring turned legs, "H" stretcher, 17-5/8" h seat, 41-1/4" h back........ **20,700.00**
Continuous arm, New England, c1815, nine-spindle back, saddle seat, stamped "J Ash," 36" h **1,100.00**
Continuous arm, Pennsylvania, early 19th C, nine-spindle back, bamboo turnings, 38" h............. **275.00**
Double bow-back, New England, c1800-15, maple, ash, and pine, incised crest rail above seven spindles, applied scrolled arm, writing surface to right, both with bamboo-turned supports on shaped seat, centering drawer mounted on underside, splayed bamboo-turned feet joined by stretchers, orig red-brown stained surface, imperfections, 16" h, 45-1/2" h **3,525.00**
Sack-back, Lancaster County, PA, carved knuckles, D-shaped seat, bulbous "H" stretcher, turned splayed legs, blunt arrow feet, worn green-black paint, 16" h seat, 36" h........................ **3,025.00**
Sack-back, Rhode Island, 1790-1800, painted maple and ash, arched crest above tapering spindles through crest which continues to shaped handholds above turned arm supports on incised plank seat with pommel on swelled and ring-turned splayed legs joined by swelled stretchers, old black paint, worn surface, imperfections, 16" h seat, 39-3/4" h........................ **2,250.00**
Slough-back, English, George III, late 18th C, yew and elm,

back with turned spindles, center vasiform splat framed by pair of flattened stoles surmounting serpentine crest rail, shaped arm rail on plain spindles, saddle shaped seat, cabriole legs, pad feet, repairs, refinished, 29" w, 15-1/2" d, 46" h **500.00**

Corner

Aesthetic Movement, American, possibly by Tisch, rosewood, cushioned and spindle-inset arms, lappet and scroll carved sq tapering legs. **1,650.00**

Chippendale, walnut, rolled back rest with stepped detail, pierced harp shape splats, serpentine arm supports, scrolled handholds, molded seal frame, slip seat covered in worn upholstery, scalloped aprons, cabriole legs with relief carved shells on knees, claw and ball feet, old dark surface, restorations and replacements **1,870.00**

Chippendale-style, 20th C, mahogany, shaped arms, openwork splats, rush slip seat raised on cabriole legs, claw and ball feet **575.00**

Country, New England, late 18th/early 19th C, maple, arms with scrolled terminals, shaped crest, scrolled horizontal splats attached to swelled and turned baluster forms continuing to turned legs, joined to similar stretchers, old surface, replaced rush seat, minor imperfections, 16-3/8" h seat, 30-1/2" h back **1,610.00**

Queen Anne, country, old black and gold paint, shaped crest rail with medallion handholds, rose head nails, replaced paper rush seat, turned legs and supports, 16" h seat, 28-1/4" h back **520.00**

William and Mary, New England, 18th C, shaped backrest and chamfered crest, scrolled handholds, three vase and ring-turned stiles continuing to turned legs, joined to front leg by turned double stretchers, old dark brown paint, replaced wood seat, 30" h **1,380.00**

Chairs, dining, set of four, original paint decoration, yellow grand, red and black flowers and bands, 13-1/2" w, 18" h seat, 32-1/2" h, **$2,000**.
Photo courtesy of Alderfer Auction Co.

Dining

Arts & Crafts

Stickley, Gustav, ladder-back, four slats, cloud-lift aprons, drop-in seats recovered in leather, 37" h, overcoat finish, roughness to edges, some with red Gustav decal, set of eight........................ **6,300.00**

Stickley, L. & J. G., arched vertical back slats, drop-in spring seat, covered in new green leather, good new finish, orig labels, 37-1/2" h, 17" w, price for set of four **3,335.00**

Assembled set, English, c1800-60, turned ash and alder, open spindle back with two or three tiers of short turnings between flattened stiles, rush seat, tapered round legs, pad feet, bulbous turned front stretcher, plain turned side and rear stretchers, two-arm chairs, 10-side chairs, some with feet ended out, 19" w, 16" d, 38" h, price for set of 12......... **1,875.00**

Biedermeier, fruitwood and part ebonized, black faux-leather upholstery, 36" h, restorations, set of four **2,500.00**

Centennial, Colonial Revival, Sheraton-style, mahogany, two arms, eight sides, shield back, reeded front legs, corner posts with carving of urns, needlepoint slip seats, 19-1/2" w, 17-1/4" d, 37-1/2" h....................... **3,000.00**

Chippendale-style, Baker, CT, black lacquer, saber-leg, c1960, set of eight **2,100.00**

Chairs, dining, Chippendale style, mahogany, two arm chairs, four side chairs, pierced splats, straight molded legs, cream upholstered seats, **$1,320**; one shown with red, green, and natural coverlet, **$125**.

Photo courtesy of Wiederseim Associates, Inc.

Classical, New England, c1830-40, figured maple, concave crests above vasiform splats and rails, scrolled and raked stiles, caned seats with serpentine fronts, saber legs joined by stretchers, old refinish, 17-1/4" h seat, 32" h, set of six **950.00**

Eastlake, American, c1870, mahogany, one armchair, six side chairs, fan-carved crest rail, reeded stiles and stretchers, block-carved front legs, 35" h, minor damage, set of seven **850.00**

Federal, Rhode Island or Salem, MA, c1795, mahogany carved, set of four side and matching arm chair, shield back with molded crest and stiles above carved kylix with festoons draped from flanking carved rosettes, pierced splat terminating in carved lunette at base above molded rear seat rail, seat with serpentine front rail, sq tapering legs joined by stretchers, over-upholstered seats covered in old black horsehair with scalloped trim, old surface, 16-1/2" h seat, 37-3/4" h **23,000.00**

George III, mahogany, squared inlaid crest, reeded stiles, pierced and inlaid splat, upholstered seat, square tapering legs joined by an H-form stretcher, set of six **2,600.00**

George III-style
Mahogany, foliate carved openwork baluster splat, trapezoidal slip-seat, sq legs joined by stretchers, price for set of 12, two armchairs and 10 side chairs **9,400.00**
Mahogany, 20th C, comprising two armchairs and 10 side chairs, serpentine cresting, pierced vasiform splat, and drop seat, sq legs, price for set of 10 .... **3,525.00**

International Movement, manufactured by Oda, similar to design by Neils O. Moller, Denmark, c1960, two armchairs and four side chairs, teak, new upholstery over original, 31" h, price for set of six **1,530.00**

Louis XVI-style beechwood, incorporating antique elements, comprising two armchairs and 10 side chairs, solid baluster splat, green leather drop-seat, circular fluted and tapered legs, price for set of 12......... **2,505.00**

Regency-style, late 19th/early 20th C, mahogany and inlay, two armchairs, six side chairs, curved inlaid crest rail, dec horizontal splats, pale blue silk upholstery, Greek key design, 33-3/4" h **10,350.00**

Renaissance Revival, America, c1870, oak, two arm and eight side chairs, each with foliate and beast carved cresting, paneled seat rail and turned legs, set of 10 .... **3,105.00**

Sheraton, one armchair, five side chairs, walnut and mahogany, mahogany flame veneer panels, rect crests with brass line inlay, rope twist carving on back crosspieces, reeded serpentine rear stiles, ring turned front legs, old refinishing, contemporary burgundy upholstered seats, restorations, 17" h seats, 31" h backs **1,150.00**

William IV, second quarter 19th C, mahogany, shaped carved crest rail above horizontal splat, trapezoid slip seat, circular fluted tapering legs, set of six: one arm chair, five side chairs **3,600.00**

Easy (Wing, Great chair)

Boston, MA, 1710-1725, maple, crest continues to shaped wings above outwardly scrolling arms, serpentine shirt joins block and ring-turned front legs connected to sq raking rear legs by similar side stretchers, ring-turned swelled and blocked medial stretcher, old black paint, 20th C cotton show cover, restoration, 19" h, 49" h **15,275.00**

Connecticut, attributed to, mid-18th C, turned and painted, yoked crest rail above vasiform splat joining turned stiles with canted vase and ring-turned arms ending in knob handholds on vase and ring-turned supports continuing to button feet joined by double bulbous front stretchers and planed side stretchers, painted red/brown over earlier paint, minor imperfections, 16-1/2" h seat, 48" h **6,500.00**

Federal, New England, early 19th C, birch, serpentine crest continues to shaped wings, out scrolled arms, tight seat over sq tapering front legs joined by sq stretchers to rear sq raking legs, floral upholstery, minor imperfections, 14-1/2" h seat, 47-1/4" h **3,110.00**

Fauteuil

Louis XV style, beechwood, frames carved with foliage, price for pr **2,710.00**

Louis XV style, painted, typical form with foliate carved frames, price for pr **1,300.00**

Louis XVI-style, painted, floral and foliate carved top rail, upholstered back and seat, carved apron, cabriole legs, price for pr **2,600.00**

Neoclassical, Continental, possibly Italian, early 19th C and later, painted green, carved floral crest and oval back, out scrolling arms, fluted tapering legs, painted throughout with flowers, price for pr **4,780.00**

Neoclassical, Continental, possibly Italian, early 19th C and later, painted, chapeau de gendarme crest rail above out scrolling arms, fluted tapering legs, blue and gray floral tapestry, price for pr **4,100.00**

Side chairs, left: Chippendale, America c1750-80, mahogany, carved crest rail, pierced and carved splat, beading on rails and straight front legs, old repairs to splat and left stretcher, 21-1/2" w, 19" d, 38" h, **$1,910**. Right: Queen Anne to Chippendale transitional, Pennsylvania, Philadelphia, c1740-70, mahogany, incised crest with carved shell, bold ears, pierced vasiform splat, inverted carved shell on skirt, cabriole legs with shell-carved knees ending in pad feet with unusual turnings, rear legs have chamfered corners, seat rail incised "IIII," 23" w, 21" d, 40" h, **$5,100**.

Photo courtesy of Samuel T. Freeman & Co., Philadelphia, PA.

Dining table and chairs, Modernism-era, T.H. Robsjohn-Gibbings, radiating walnut veneer-topped table with dowel legs, three leaves, label, 48" d, 29" h, **$2,310**; set of six chairs, two arm chairs, four side chairs, curved slat backs, original orange upholstery, curved legs, 23" w, 20" d, 35" h, **$1,650**.

Photo courtesy of Treadway Gallery, Inc.

Side chair, Queen Anne to Chippendale Transitional, Pennsylvania, Philadelphia, c1750-60, walnut, shell-carved crest rail with double-scrolled volutes, continuing to carved rounded stiles, vasiform splat, balloon fitted slip seat supported by two shell-carved cabriole legs with two volutes, ending in claw and ball feet, square back legs, rear to splat lock reglued, front seat rail inscribed with two strokes, balloon seat frame inscribed "IIII," indicating the chair was part of a set, back seat rail contains letters "SM" in white chalk, letters similar to others found on chairs belonging to Samuel Morris, 19" w, 16-3/4" d, 41" h, **$336,000**.

Photo courtesy of Samuel T. Freeman & Co., Philadelphia, PA.

Sheraton-style, English, early to mid-20th C, mahogany, green faux leather upholstery, scrolled and molded arms, balloon shaped seat, turned and reeded legs, matching arm supports, brass tack trim, 17" h seat, 34" h back **450.00**

Folding

Austrian, Thonet, late 19th C, bentwood, oval backrest and seat, scrolling arms and legs **600.00**

Hall

William IV, octagonal scrolled backrest, center painted crest, shaped seat, turned tapering legs ending in peg feet ... **475.00**

High chair, oak, pressed back, **$125**.
Photo courtesy of Dotta Auction Co., Inc.

High chair, Louis XV, c1800, fruitwood, crest rail with flower carved cartouche, pierced splat with potted flower, square tapering legs with H stretcher, **$300**.
Photo courtesy of Pook & Pook.

Highchair, child's

New England, late 18th C, attributed to, turned maple and birch, turned tapering stiles with finials joining three arched slats, shaped arms on vase and ring-turned supports, splayed legs joined by double stretchers, old refinish, 20" h seat, 40" h .. **1,100.00**
Shaker-style, ladder back, woven splint seat, turned finials, foot rest, mustard paint, 24" h seat, 38" h back **880.00**
Windsor, New England, 1825-40, rect crest above three spindles and outward flaring stiles, turned hand-holds on shaped seat, splayed turned tapering legs joined by stretchers, vestiges of stippled red and black paint, "M.H. Spencer, N.Y." in script on bottom of seat, 22-1/2" h seat, 31-1/2" h **775.00**

Ladderback

Child's, woven splint seat, turned finials, red finish, 6-1/2" h seat, 3" h back **250.00**
Connecticut, mixed hardwoods, old deep brown finish, bowed arms, turned supports continue down to medallions on top run of base, back with four arched slats, high finials, replaced woven splint seat, turned posts and stretchers, 14-1/2" h seat, 42" h back **375.00**
Pennsylvania, woven splint seat, turned finials, painted red, 13" h seat, 42" h back **150.00**

Library

George III, c1800, mahogany and caned, pink upholstered loose cushion, 33-1/2" h **2,070.00**

Lolling, Federal

Massachusetts, 1790-1800, mahogany, serpentine crest above half serpentine molded shaped arms, concave supports, over-upholstered serpentine seat on sq tapering frontal legs, raked rear legs, casters missing, minor imperfections, 16-1/2" h seat, 42" h **4,700.00**
New England, c1790, mahogany, reverse serpentine crest over upholstered back joining shaped arms and molded concave supports on four

tapering sq legs, joined by sq stretchers, old refinish, imperfections, 17" h seat, 43-1/4" h **6,900.00**

Lounge, International Movement

Charles and Ray Eames, MI, purchased c1949, molded plywood mahogany seat and legs, 22" w, 26" h **1,880.00**
George Nakashima, New Hope, PA, c1975, walnut conoid lounge chair, 31" w, 33-1/3" d, 30-1/2" h chair, 24" w, 24" d, 10-1/4" h ottoman **4,700.00**
Hans Wegner, Denmark, c1960, teak, reclining upholstered cushion seat, 29-1/4" w, 48" d, 34-1/2" h chair, 29-1/2" w, 23-1/2" d, 13-1/2" h ottoman **4,700.00**

Morris chair, Gustav Stickley No. 369, drop arm, five slats under each arm, decal inside back right leg, original finish, broken back pivot leg, 32-3/4" x 37-1/2" x 37" h, **$7,000**.
Photo courtesy of David Rago Auctions, Inc.

Morris chair, Arts & Crafts

Stickley, Gustav, no. 332, slats to the floor under flat arms, orig brown leather cushions, orig finish, red decal, arms re-pegged and re-glued, 31-1/2" w, 36" d, 37" h **6,275.00**
Stickley, L. & J. G., Fayetteville, NY, c1915, chair model no. 411, matching model no. 397 footstool, four carved slats on adjustable back, flat open arms with through tenon leg posts and four corbel supports with upholstered spring cushion seat and back, light brown finish, 29-1/4" w, 35" d, 40-1/4" h; footstool with, spring cushion, 20" w, 14" d, 16-1/2" h, both with red and yellow decal "The Work of L. & J. G. Stickley" **1,725.00**

Provenance adds value

Low-back side chair, Essex County, MA, 1665-95, red oak, ash, and maple, square back joins square stiles which continue to floor, joined to front block and ring turned legs and turned feet by similar square stretchers, boldly turned front medial stretcher, old 19th C leather, imperfections, 15-3/8" h, 36" h **34,075.00**

Provenance: This chair, which descended in the consignor's family, came from the home of Deacon Nathaniel Whipple on the Main Road, Hamilton, MA. "Deacon Nathaniel Whipple, b. October 1721, Ipswich, Essex, MA, married 1744 and died December 1809 in Hamilton, Essex, MA." The "skin" or leather was bought by another ancestor Willis H. Ropes (1855-1946), Ropes Street, South Salem, and put on the old oak frame at Salem Fraternity by Herber Farwell according to an accompanying note. A family genealogy accompanies this lot, which was sold by Skinner, Inc.

Wainscot, Pennsylvania, 18th C, walnut, pegged construction, shaped crest, raised paneled back, shaped arms, turned legs, stretcher base, 24-1/4" w, 19-1/2" d, 17-1/2" h seat, 42" h back **7,150.00**

Chair, side, Hepplewhite, Maryland, c1790, mahogany, three-part open work back splat, upholstered seat, 18" w, 17-1/2" h seat, 35-1/2" h, **$250**.
Photo courtesy of Alderfer Auction Co.

Chairs, side, Arts & Crafts, L. & J. G. Stickley, ladder-back, saddle seats, original decal, some wear to original finish, price for set of four, 17-3/4" x 16-1/2" x 36", **$950**.
Photo courtesy of David Rago Auctions, Inc.

Arrowback, 19th C mustard paint, tan, brown, red, and black dec of cornucopias on crest, leaves on back and front stretcher, incising around seat, brushed detain between, evidence of earlier green, bamboo turned base, 15-3/4" h, 32" h **935.00**

Art Deco, Europe, wooden gondola backs, ivory sabots on front legs, cream striped fabric upholstery, pr, 25" h **2,000.00**

Arts & Crafts
Stickley, Gustav, H-back, drop-in seat recovered in burgundy leather, red decal, over-coated orig dark finish, roughness to leg edges, 17" w, 16" d, 40" h **690.00**
Stickley, L. & J. G., Fayetteville, New York, c1916, oak, model no. 940, three vertical slats below crest rail, slip seat, double side stretcher, branded mark, price for set of six, 35-3/4" h **2,235.00**

Banister back
New England, last half 18th C, paint dec, shaped crest above four split balusters joining vase and ring-turned stiles, trapezoidal rush seat, vase and ring-turned legs joined to rear legs by turned double stretchers, old surface painted dark brown with gilt stencil and polychrome floral designs, 17-1/2" h seat, 44" h **1,100.00**

New Hampshire, coastal, mid to late 18th C, painted black, flaring fishtail carved crest over three split banisters flanked by vase and ring-turned stiles with ball finials, trapezoidal rush seat over ring-turned frontal legs joined by double turned stretchers, rear legs with old piecing, 17" h seat, 43" h **1,425.00**

Biedermeier, curved crest rail, central horizontal splat joined by three vertical splats, upholstered seat, squared tapering legs, set of four **1,675.00**

Chair, side, mahogany, wide shaped back splat over narrow slatted back with applied trim, upholstered seat, shaped skirt, double stretchers, **$65**.
Photo courtesy of Dotta Auction Co., Inc.

Centennial, Queen Anne style, European, walnut, pierced and scrolled back splat, serpentine real stiles, balloon shaped slip seat, cabriole legs, scrolled knees, pad feet, old mellow finish, price for pr, 18-1/2" h seat, 41-1/2" h back **600.00**

Chippendale
America, mahogany, arched crests, interlaced double scroll back splat with piercing, old slip seat cov in black faux leather, sq legs with beaded edges, stretcher base, old dark finish, restorations, price for pr, 19-1/2" h seat, 38" h back **1,785.00**
America, mahogany, serpentine crest with beaded edges, pierced vase shaped back splat, tapered rear stiles, replacement slip seat, sq legs with chamfered backs and beaded corners, stretcher base, old finish, rockers added at one time, now with pieced restorations as it was converted back to chair, 17" h seat, 35-3/4" h **450.00**
Boston or Salem, Massachusetts area, 1755-85, carved mahogany, serpentine crests end in raked molded ears, center carved shells above owl-shaped splats with carved volutes above slip seats, Marlborough front legs with beaded outer edges, joined by similar sq stretchers to rear raking legs, old refinish, minor imperfections, price for pr, 16-5/8" h seat, 38" h **4,200.00**
Connecticut River Valley, tiger maple, serpentine crest with raked molded terminals above pierced splat, old rush seat, block and vase turned front legs joined by turned stretcher, old refinish, 17-1/4" h seat, 39" h **900.00**
Country, maple with some curl, pierced spat and shaped crest with carved ears, sq legs, mortised and pinned stretchers, old mellow refinishing, damage to paper rush seat because of breaks in front seal rail, 39" h . **110.00**
Massachusetts, late 18th C, cherry, shaped crest rail above pierced splat and raked stiles, upholstered slip seat, sq chamfered legs

joined to raking rear legs by sq stretchers, refinished, repairs, 17-1/2" h, 38" h **600.00**
Massachusetts, late 18th C, mahogany, shaped crest rail above pierced scroll and diamond splat flanked by raked stiles, trapezoidal upholstered slip seat, beaded straight legs joined to raking rear legs by sq stretchers, imperfections, 18" h seat, 37-1/2" h **500.00**
New London, CT, 1760-95, carved cherry, serpentine crest rails, pierced splats with C-scrolls and beaded edges, molded ohooo, flanked by stiles and rounded backs, molded seat frames and straight legs with beaded edges, pierced brackets joined by sq stretchers, old refinish, set of five, 17" h seat, 39" h **10,350.00**
New York, 1755-65, carved mahogany, carved crest ending in raked molded terminals above pierced splat with C-scrolls, slip seat, molded seat frame, front carved cabriole legs ending in ball and claw foot, rear raked legs, old surface, imperfections, 18" h seat, 39-1/2" h **2,990.00**
Pennsylvania, attributed to, late 18th C, carved mahogany, serpentine crest rail with cockbeaded edge and scrolled terminals above pierced shaped splat, molded raking stiles, trapezoidal slip seat, beaded Marlborough front legs joined to raking rear legs by sq stretchers, restored, 17" h, 36-1/2" h **1,775.00**
Rhode Island, c1765-95, mahogany, shaped and carved crest rail, pierced splat, raked stiles, trapezoidal slip seat, molded front legs joined to raked rear legs by sq stretchers, old finish, imperfections, 18" h seat, 38" h **1,100.00**
Chippendale-style, country, late 19th or early 20th C, mixed hardwoods, dark reddish-brown finish, pierced heart and scroll back splat, tapered real stiles, paper rush seat, turned legs and stretchers, Spanish feet, 18-1/2" h seat, 40" h back **435.00**

Classical
Baltimore, painted and dec, scrolled crest above inverted vase-shaped splat, cane seat, dec front legs joined by medial stretcher, stencil dec, orig gilt classical motifs on black ground, 34-1/2" h **750.00**
Boston, MA, attributed to, c1835, mahogany veneer, curving crest with the continuous stile and rail construction, shaped splats, bowed veneered front seat rails, frontal curving legs, rear raking legs, price for set of six, minor imperfections, 17" h seat, 31" h................ **4,350.00**
New England, c1825, carved and turned tiger maple, baluster turned cresting above acanthus carved, pierced splat joining raked stiles above trapezoidal rush seat, vase and ring-turned outward flaring frontal legs and turned stretchers, refinished, imperfections, price for set of six, 18" h seat, 34-1/2" h **1,765.00**
New York, 1810-20, carved mahogany veneer, scroll back, beaded edges, horizontal splats carved with leafage and other classical motifs, slip seat, curving legs, old surface, 16-1/2" h, 32" h, set of six **5,200.00**
Country, Ohio, painted mustard, black, and gold fruit and leaves, red painted surface in the manner of J. Huey, Zanesville, OH, c1840 .... **7,500.00**
Decorated, attributed to Carlisle, PA, plank seat, orig black over red dec, floral panels surrounded by gold stencils, bordered with salmon and yellow line border dec, carefully cleaned, applied coat of protective varnish, professionally executed slight touch-up, 17" h seat, 31" h, price for set of six.................... **3,650.00**
Federal
Boston, MA, or Portsmouth, New Hampshire, c1800, mahogany, square back with scratch beading enclose three pierced splats above trapezoidal shaped over upholstered seats, sq tapering front legs outlined in stringing and joined by sq stretchers to raked rear legs, refinished, one chair with a pierced rear stile, price for set of four, 18" h seat, 35-1/2" h **1,175.00**

Massachusetts or Rhode Island, c1780, mahogany inlaid, shield back, arched molded crest above 5 molded spindles and inlaid quarter fan, over-upholstered seats with serpentine fronts, molded tapering legs joined by stretchers, 17-1/2" h seat, 37" h, pr **5,475.00**
New England, attributed to, maple, rush seat, dec with polychrome flowers on yellow ground, 18" w, 16" d, 35" h, price for pr **500.00**
New Hampshire, Portsmouth, attributed to Langley Boardman, 1774-1833, mahogany, sq back, reeded on rest rail, stiles, and stay rail, over upholstered serpentine seat, molded sq tapering front legs, sq stretchers and rakes rear legs, refinish, minor imperfections, 18" h seat, 36" h **1,035.00**
George III, late 18th C, mahogany, yoke shaped crest rail, pierced splat carved with wheat sheaves, slip-in padded seat, squared molded legs, price for pr **650.00**
Gothic Revival, New York City, 1850s, mahogany veneer, trefoil pierced splats, curved stay rails, veneered seal rails, curving rococo legs, old refinish, 20th C upholstery, 16-1/2" h seat, 33-1/2" h, set of eight ... **6,900.00**
Hepplewhite, American, mahogany, shield back, rush seat **325.00**
Hitchcock, Hitchcocksville, CT, 1825-32, rosewood grained surface, orig gilt dec, urn centering cornucopia splat, old rush seats, ring-turned legs, orig surface, 35-1/2" h, price for set of four **1,265.00**
International Movement
Designed by Mies van der Rohe, manufactured by Knoll Associates, NY, cantilevered tubular steel frame, green leather padded and upholstered seat, price for pr, 33-1/2" h.................... **6,450.00**
Mies van der Rohe Barcelona chairs, attributed to Knoll Associates, NY, black leather cushions on flat bar base, price for pr, 29-1/2" w, 29-1/2" d, 29-1/2" h....................... **5,590.00**
Warren McArthur Corporation, machined and tubular anodized aluminum with

original upholstery, green decal labels. Height 32 inches **2,150.00**
Ladderback
Pennsylvania, rush seat, ball turned finials, turned front stretcher, old mustard paint, wear to feet, 14-1/2" h seat, 41" h back................... **385.00**
Pennsylvania, woven splint seat, turned finials, boldly turned front stretcher, turned legs, old brown paint, 14" h seat, 38-1/2" h back.... **525.00**
Pennsylvania, woven splint seat, turned finials, boldly turned front stretcher, reddish-brown finish, 16" h seat, 40" h back............................. **330.00**
Pennsylvania, woven splint seat, turned finials, boldly turned front stretcher, old green-black paint, 17" h seat, 40" h back................... **385.00**
Pennsylvania, woven splint seat, turned finials and front stretcher, reddish-brown finish, 16-1/2" h seat, 39-1/2" h back............................. **360.00**
Neoclassical, Boston, MA, 1815-20, mahogany, curving carved crests flanked by gadrooning above similarly curved horizontal splats enclosing carved elements flanked by reeded curving stiles that continue to half way on front legs and also elaborate front seat rails, curving rear legs and slip seats, upholstered in 20th C green watered moiré fabric, price for pair, 17-1/4" h seat, 33-1/2" h back.............. **1,175.00**
Plank seat, Pennsylvania, orig paint dec, fruit with green leaves on crest, yellow and white line borders on reddish brown ground, wear, old touch up, set of six, 18-1/2" h seat, 33-1/4" h back............................. **700.00**
Queen Anne
American, early 18th C, burl walnut, shaped cresting, serpentine slat, slip-seat raised on shell carved cabriole legs, hoof feet, price for pr **1,650.00**
Country, finely alligatored black paint, double arched crest, pierced vase shaped back splat, tapered rear stiles, replaced paper rush seat, pad feet, boldly turned front stretcher, small glued splits on crest, 17" h seat, 38-1/2" h back............................. **375.00**

Chair, side, Queen Anne, English, c1760, walnut and mahogany, shaped crest and splat, pad feet, H-stretcher, replaced seat frame, 18" h seat, 38-1/2" h back, $425.

Photo courtesy of Alderfer Auction Co.

English, mahogany, scalloped and scrolled real splat, serpentine rear stiles, later red velvet covering on balloon seat, cabriole legs, relief carved shells on knees, pad feet, old refinishing, two returns replaced, 17" h seat, 39-1/2" back **1,610.00**
New England, mid-18th C, painted, carved and spooned crest rail above vasiform splat and raking stiles, trapezoidal slip seat, blocked vase and ring-turned legs, carved Spanish feet joined by bulbous turned front stretcher and straight side stretchers, old black paint over earlier paint, imperfections, 16-1/2" h seat, 41" h back.......... **600.00**
Newport, RI, 1750-75, black walnut, curving crest above vase-shaped pierced splat, compass seat, front and side rail shaping, cabriole front legs joined to rear sq tapering legs by block and vase-swelled side stretchers, swelled and turned medial stretchers, rear feet without chamfering, old refinish, minor repairs, affixed brass plaque reads "Ebenezer Storer 1730-1807," 17" h seat, 38-1/4" h **2,990.00**

Regency-style, walnut, five brass robs as back splats, balloon seats with old replaced upholstery, applied ormolu mounts, tapered and fluted legs and rear stiles, old finish, set of four, 17-1/2" h seat, 32" h back **450.00**

Rococo Revival, John H. Belter, rosewood, Rosalie without the Grapes pattern, laminated, solid back, crest carved with large rose and fruit, red silk upholstery, casters, pr, 37-1/2" h **2,550.00**

Sheraton, walnut, raised medallion crest, rope twist detail on back slats, ring turned and reeded front legs, rear saber legs, serpentine stiles, old finish, contemporary upholstered seats, restorations, one crest pieced, set of six, 19" h seat, 33" h back **750.00**

Slat back, Delaware River Valley, late 18th C, turned maple, five reverse graduated concave arched slats joining turned stiles with bulbous finials, rush seat, vase and ring-turned frontal legs joined by bulbous turned front stretcher and side stretchers, old surface, 17" h seat, 45-1/2" h **4,120.00**

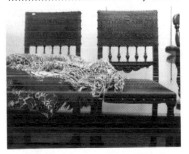

Chairs, side, Victorian, pressed leather backs and seats, set of three, **$175**.

Photo courtesy of Dotta Auction Co., Inc.

Victorian, ebonized, lacquered, Wedgwood mounts, openwork backrest, caned seat, turned legs, price for pr **1,410.00**

William IV, England, carved rosewood, foliate carved backrest with central diamond-shaped upholstered panel, slip seat, leaf carved circular legs, c1835, price for pr **700.00**

Windsor
Bamboo turned, Pennsylvania, grain dec, red, green, and yellow floral, bud, and foliate dec crest rail, 18" h seat, 34" h back **935.00**

Birdcage, New England, c1810, two horizontal spindles and seven vertical spindles joining bamboo-turned slightly swelled stiles, shaped seats, splayed swelled bamboo-turned legs and stretchers, old worn black paint, price for set of five, 18" h seat, 35-1/2" h **3,300.00**

Bow-back, New England, c1810, bowed crest rail above seven spindles and shaped saddle seat, splayed swelled bamboo-turned legs and stretchers, some paint loss to black paint, 17-1/2" h seat, 39" h............................ **650.00**

Bow-back, New England, late 18th C, black painted, molded bowed crest rails above seven spindles and shaped saddle seat on splayed vase and ring-turned legs and swelled stretchers, price for pr, imperfections, 17-1/4" seat, 38-1/4" h.......... **2,820.00**

Brace-back, nine spindles bow back, well shaped seat with incised detail around spindles, vase and ring turned legs, turned "H" stretcher, old mellow refinish, restorations, 17-1/2" h, seat, 36-3/4" h **385.00**

Butterfly, Pennsylvania, seven-spindle back, bamboo turnings, poplar seats, hickory legs and spindles, refinished, price for pr, one with crack in top rail.......................... **285.00**

Clerk's, attributed to New England, c1790, ash, shaped concave crest above seven spindles, vase and ring-turned stiles, shaped saddle seat, splayed vase and ring-turned legs joined by turned, swelled stretchers, old refinish, imperfections, 26" h, 41-1/2" h **1,430.00**

Comb-back, mixed woods, arched crest with flared ears, seven-spindle back, turned arms, bentwood arm rail, shield shaped seat, vase and ring turned legs, stretcher base, light refinish, 17" h seat, 38-1/4" h **800.00**

Fan-back, Massachusetts, attributed to, late 18th C, shaped crest rail with scroll carved terminals above seven spindles, vase and ring

turned stiles and shaped saddle seat, splayed vase and ring turned legs joined by swelled stretchers, old black paint, 18" h seat, 36-1/2" h **715.00**

Fan-back, New England, late 18th C, red stained, shaped crest rail above seven spindles, vase and ring-turned stiles, shaped saddle seat, splayed vase and ring-turned legs joined by swelled stretchers, imperfections, 17" h seat, 36" h.......... **775.00**

Fan-back, New England, late 18th C, shaped crest rail above seven spindles and vase and ring-turned stiles, shaped saddle seat and splayed vase and ring-turned legs joined by swelled stretchers, old brown paint, 17" h seat, 37" h.......... **600.00**

Fan-back, New England, late 18th C, shaped crest rail with scroll-carved terminals above seven spindles and vase and ring-turned stiles, shaped saddle seat and splayed vase and ring-turned legs and swelled stretchers, old black/brown paint over earlier green and red paints, 17" h seat, 36" h........................ **7,675.00**

Spindle-back, plank seat, H-stretcher, painted tan, wear, 18" h seat, 36-1/2" h back **50.00**

Chair, wing, Chippendale-style, molded legs connected by H-stretcher, cream trellis-pattern upholstery, **$750**.

Photo courtesy of Sloans & Kenyon Auctions.

Slipper

Aesthetic Movement, American, walnut, V-shaped cresting, openwork floral and disc carved frieze, angular floral carved legs **500.00**

Arts & Crafts, Gustav Stickley, spindled back, drop-in spring seat recovered in brown leather, orig finish, black decal, 17-3/4" w, 16" d, 37" h **1,150.00**

Victorian, c1875, rosewood, angular foliate carved backrest with urn form splat, over upholstered seat and circular turned legs **300.00**

Victorian, late, c1880, ebonized and bobbin turned needlepoint upholstery, foliate dec seat **175.00**

Chests of drawers

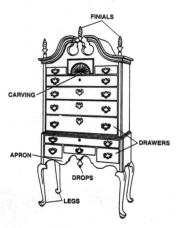

Typical Parts of a Highboy

Art Deco, Quigley, France, c1925, parchment covered, rect top, three tapering drawers, pyramid mirrored stiles, bracket feet, back branded, 44-1/2" x 35" **2,750.00**

Arts & Crafts, English, dresser, orig pivoting mirror with chamberstick shelves, glove boxes, copper repoussé panels, two drawers over one long drawer, orig medium-dark finish, unmarked, split to side, 42-3/4" w, 21-1/2" d, 64" h **1,725.00**

Biedermeier, c1820, maple, rect case fitted with two drawers, splayed sq legs, 36" w, 19" d, 31" h **1,725.00**

Chest of drawers, Chippendale, walnut, four graduated cockbeaded drawers, reeded corner columns, losses, 41-1/2" w, 22" d, 34" h, **$2,000**.

Photo courtesy of Alderfer Auction Co.

Chippendale

Baltimore, Maryland, mahogany, line inlaid, two split upper drawers, three lower full width graduated cock beaded dovetailed drawers, molded base, ogee bracket feet, 35-1/4" w, 19-1/2" d, 33-1/2" h .. **6,050.00**

Boston, MA area, 1770-80, carved mahogany, reverse serpentine, shaped mahogany top with veneered edge overhangs case of conforming veneered drawers, cockbeaded drawer separators, molded base, ball and claw feet, old refinish, veneer losses, 38-1/4" w, 20-3/4" d, 34-1/4" h... **3,525.00**

Connecticut, late 18th C, carved cherry, rect top with molded edge, cockbeaded case of four graduated drawers, gadrooned carved ogee bracket base, replaced brasses, refinished, imperfections, 36-1/2" w, 17" d, 37-1/2" h **4,450.00**

English, mahogany, oak secondary wood, molded top with pull-out writing surface, four dovetailed graduated drawers with molded edges, old brass pulls, ogee feet, molded base, old refinishing, old restorations, backboards renailed, 34" w, 18" d, 33-1/4" h **2,875.00**

Massachusetts, c1780, maple, rect overhanging top, four thumb-molded graduated drawers, ogee bracket feet, replaced brass pulls, old refinish, imperfections, losses, 32-1/2" w, 17" d, 33" h **4,700.00**

Massachusetts, attributed to, last half 18th C, maple, flat molded cornice, case of two thumb-molded short drawers and six graduated long drawers, bracket feet, brasses appear to be orig, old red stained surface, minor imperfections, 36" w, 18-1/2" d, 57" h **8,820.00**

New England, late 18th C, cherry, rect overhanging top, case of five graduated thumb-molded drawers, base with ogee feet, replaced brass, refinished, restored, 36-3/4" w, 17-3/4" d, 34-3/4" h .. **2,350.00**

New England, late 18th C, maple, flat molded cornice, case of two thumb molded short drawers and four graduated long drawers, ogee bracket feet, brasses appear to be original, refinished, minor restoration, 36" w, 18" d, 42" h **4,200.00**

New England, late 18th C, maple, molded cornice overhangs case of five thumb-molded graduated drawers, molded bracket base, original brass, refinished, imperfections, 35-1/2" w, 18-1/8" d, 47" h **3,100.00**

Pennsylvania, c1780, walnut, five drawers, reeded quarter columns, ogee bracket feet, orig varnish............. **12,000.00**

Rhode Island, late 18th C, carved tiger maple, tall, cornice with dentil molding, case of seven graduated thumb-molded drawers, molded tall bracket base with central drop, top drawer with fan-carving, orig brasses, early surface, 38" w, 18-3/4" d, 63-3/4" h **27,600.00**

Southern, walnut, yellow pine secondary wood, orig two-board top with variegated fan inlays in corners, double star in middle, chamfered corners on case, with small urns and line inlay, five dovetailed drawers with banded inlay borders, ogee feet with scalloped returns, molded base, refinished, old replaced brasses, small areas of veneer damage, inlay restorations, minor insect damage, feet are old well-executed replacements, 39" w, 21-1/4" d, 38-1/8" h **2,645.00**

Modern pieces with an antique look

Furniture makers have long copied each other's styles, and the 20th century furniture makers are continuing that practice. Collectors should be aware that some of today's well-made replica furniture may sell for. Here are some examples:

Breakfront secretary, Hendredon, Georgian-style, mahogany, shaped cornice over four glazed doors above secretary drawer, over two cabinet doors, flanked on each side by five graduated drawers, 26-1/2" w, 17-1/2" d, 87-1/2" h **1,770.00**

Chest of drawers, Hendredon, dark brown, gold sponge dec finish simulating tortoise shell, four drawers, short block feet, flush mounted brass handles on drawers and sides of cases, branded signature inside drawers, 28" w, 12-1/2" d, 28-1/4" h, price for pr..... **500.00**

Chest on chest, Virginia Crafters, walnut, oak and poplar secondary woods, urn and flame finials, broken arch top with carved rosettes, reeded columns, 11 drawers with carved shell on top drawer, ogee feet with scalloped returns, batwing brasses, branded signature on back, 40-1/4" w, 22-1/4" d, 90 1/2" h **1,610.00**

Credenza, Chippendale-style, Kittinger, mahogany and mahogany veneer, oak secondary wood, four dovetailed drawers down left, smaller center drawer with cabinet below, longer drawer over open compartment flanking on right with adjustable shelf, molded edge and base trip, branded label, emb metallic emblem in drawer, 81-1/2" l, 19-1/2" d, 30" h **900.00**

Reproduction furniture: desk, Drexel, mahogany, letter rack at each side on top of desk, leather insert, central drawer, three small drawers at each side, fluted tapered legs, 50" w, 25" d, 33" h, **$500**.

Photo courtesy of Joy Luke.

Reproduction: desk, Chippendale-style, Goddard Townsend School, by Franklin Heirloom Furniture, 1977, slant top, block front, fully fitted interior, 42" w, 42" h, **$2,900**.

Photo courtesy of Wiederseim Associates, Inc.

Desk, Chippendale-style, Kittinger, mahogany and mahogany veneers, oak secondary wood, four dovetailed drawers on both sides, center drawer, thing applied moldings create decorative panels on sides and front, shaped bracket feet, molding around bases, emb metallic label, 72" w, 36-1/4" d, 30 1/2" h **1,695.00**

Dining chairs, Baker, Regency-style, four side and two arm chairs **4,250.00**

Dining table, Regency-style, Baker, 20th C, satinwood crossbanded mahogany, rect top, three leaves, double reeded pedestals, downswept legs, casters, 132" l extended, 48" w, 30" h.................. **2,585.00**

Settee, Windsor, continuous arm, by Steve, painted by Peter Deen, cherry, scrolled arms, spindle back, turned legs, stretchers, distressed green paint, 56-1/2" l, 17-1/2" d, 17-1/2" h seat, 29" h back **2,475.00**

Sugar chest, Sheraton-style, country, cherry, poplar secondary wood, hand made, two hinged lids, two dovetailed drawers, high turned feet, turned cherry pulls, interior divided into four compartments, small pieced repairs, 47-1/2" w, 20-1/4" d, 34-3/4" h **900.00**

Table, lamp, Kittinger, mahogany, concave shaped top, one drawer, shelf in base, branded and metal labels inside dovetailed drawer, tapered logo, casters, 19" w, 18" d, 26" h **250.00**

Windsor side chairs, set of six, painted red-brown, sgd "R. D. L." (Drew Lausch), painted by Peter Deen, 17-1/2" h seat, 37" h back **4,675.00**

Chippendale to Hepplewhite, transitional, cherry, pine secondary wood, dovetailed case with reeded quarter columns, cove molded cornice, eight dovetailed graduated drawers, French feet with scalloped returns, molding around base, orig oval brasses, old mellow refinishing, 42-1/2" w, 23" d, 63-3/4" h............. **5,300.00**

Chippendale-style, America, late 19th/early 20th C, black walnut, mahogany, pine secondary wood, two board top, five finely dovetailed drawers with beaded edges, two drawers with divided interiors, bracket base with thin molded edge, brass bale pulls, wire nails, 42" w, 20" d, 41-1/2" h **900.00**

Classical

New England, 1825-30, bird's eye maple, rect top, case with projecting cock-beaded bird's-eye maple veneered drawers, above three graduated drawers with flanking engaged vase and ring-turned spiral carved columns continuing to turned feet, opalescent pattern glass pulls, refinished, 41" w, 20" d, 47-1/2" h **1,530.00**

Ohio, attributed to, 1830s, tiger and bird's-eye maple, backsplash above overhanging top, case with recessed panel sides, cock-beaded graduated drawers flanked by spiral carved columns and colonettes above dies, turned tapering legs and feet, shaped skirt, refinished, replaced glass pulls, imperfections, 46" w, 19-3/4" d, 57-1/4" h **2,000.00**

Chest of drawers, Chippendale, middle-Atlantic states, attributed to Charleston, c1790, mahogany, rect top with thumb molded serpentine front and sides, conforming case with four serpentine drawers flanked by chamfered satinwood inlaid stiles, straight bracket feet with line inlays, brasses appear to be original, 46" w, 36-3/4" h, **$23,000**.

Photo courtesy of Pook & Pook.

Chest of drawers, cottage style, painted pale green, original painted flowers and foliage on each drawer, arched scrolled back with rectangular mirror, pair of candle shelves, and handkerchief boxes, four drawers, **$295**.

Photo courtesy of Dotta Auction Co., Inc.

Eastlake, American
   Curly walnut, burl veneer, carved detail, scrolled crest, four dovetailed drawers, two handkerchief drawers, well detailed molded panel fronts, refinished, 39" w, 17-1/2" d, 46" h............................ **750.00**
   Mahogany, five full drawers, two half drawers, carved leaf and branch dec, 38" w, 55" h **300.00**

Empire
   America, c1830, cherry, orig dark red flame graining over salmon ground on façade, worn orig red on sides, maple and poplar secondary woods, two-board top with old chip along back edge, serpentine pilasters on either side of four dovetailed drawers, old clear glass pulls, inset panels on ends, turned feet, age splits in top, 43" w, 22-5/8" d, 46-3/5" h **500.00**
   America, c1830, tiger maple, rect top, protruding frieze section fitted with single wide drawer over three drawers between applied half-round turnings, vase and ball turned feet, period round brass pulls, 42-1/2" w, 21-1/2" d, 44-1/2" h **2,750.00**
   Maine, attributed to, cherry, mahogany veneer, pine secondary wood, two-board top with shaped back splash, four dovetailed drawers with orig brass pulls and key escutcheons, high crisply turned feet, refinished, veneer repairs, pulls cleaned with minor dents, 41-1/4" w, 20" d, 41-1/2" h **1,100.00**

Federal
   America, bowfront, mahogany, flame mahogany veneer, pine secondary wood, old replaced top with biscuit corners, four dovetailed drawers with applied beading, replaced brass pulls, rope twist carvings on front pilasters, high boldly turned feet, refinished, pierced restorations, one rear foot replaced, 40-1/2" w, 19" d, 36-3/4" h **770.00**
   Baltimore, MD, c1810, mahogany veneered and inlaid, serpentine, top with veneered edge overhangs conforming case of four graduated drawers outlined in narrow banding and stringing with ovolo corners, shaped skirt, flaring French feet connected to shaped sides, replaced brasses, old refinish, imperfections, 45-3/4" w, 22-1/4" d, 38" h **5,585.00**
   Connecticut, attributed to, c1790-1810, cherry, rect overhanging top with string inlaid edge, case with four scratch-beaded graduated drawers, bracket base,

replaced brasses, refinished, minor imperfections, 37-3/4" w, 19-1/2" d, 35" h **4,415.00**
   Maryland, attributed to, 1810-20, cherry and poplar inlaid, rect top with string inlaid edge, case of four graduated drawers with cockbeaded surrounds flanked by quarter-engaged columns, base with scalloped front skirt and flaring feet, refinished, replaced brass, repairs, 40-1/4" w, 18-5/8" d, 35-1/2" h **2,115.00**
   Maryland, attributed to, early 19th C, mahogany inlaid, mahogany veneered top with inlaid edge, case of cockbeaded drawers with oval stringing, serpentine veneered skirt flanked by tapering French feet, refinished, old replaced brass, some restoration, 44-1/2" w, 20-1/8" d, 43" h **1,880.00**
   Massachusetts, early 19th C, cherry, rect top with cross banded edge overhangs conforming case of four graduated scratch beaded drawers, cut-out bracket base, replaced brass, refinished, 40-1/4" w, 20-5/8" d, 35-1/2" h **2,750.00**
   Massachusetts, early 19th C, mahogany veneer, bowed top with cross-banded veneered overhanging edge, conforming case of cockbeaded veneered drawers, molded base with shaped feet, original brass, old refinish, 41-1/4" w, 23-1/2" d, 35" h **4,125.00**
   Middle Atlantic states, 1815-25, mahogany, mahogany veneer, and cherry, rect, top above case of four graduated, cockbeaded drawers, upper drawer with cross banded mahogany inlay, shaped veneered skirt, slightly flaring French feet, refinished, replaced brasses, restored, 44-1/4" w, 19-7/8" d, 45-1/2" h **2,115.00**
   New England, early 19th C, inlaid cherry, bow front top with string-inlaid edge overhangs conforming case of inlaid drawers, stringing in outline, quarter fans, and central paterae above shaped skirt flanked by flaring French feet, replaced brass, old refinish, repairs, 42-3/4" w, 21" d, 36-3/4" h **3,100.00**

New Hampshire, possibly by the Dunlaps, early 19th C, carved and inlaid wavy birch, rect top with inlaid edge overhangs case of four drawers with stringing in ovolo outline; flanked by quarter-engaged columns wrapped with vine- like stringing, diminutive fan carving above and below columns, molded base with carved geometric shapes, sharply spurred bracket feet, mostly original brass, old refinish, imperfections, 38-1/2" w, 19-1/4" d, 38-1/2" h **11,200.00**

Portsmouth or Greenland, New Hampshire, 1810-14, bow front, mahogany and flame birch veneer, bow front mahogany top with inlaid edge overhanging conforming case, four cock-beaded three-paneled drawers, divisions outlined with mahogany cross banded veneer and stringing above skirt, central veneered rect drop panel, high bracket feet joined by shaped side skirts, similar rear feet, turned pulls appear to be orig, old refinish, minor repairs, 40-1/4" w, 21-1/4" d, 39" h **28,750.00**

Rhode Island, c1800-10, maple, rect top, molded edge, case of four thumb-molded graduated drawers, valanced skirt joining shaped French feet, orig oval brasses, old refinish, imperfections, 42" w, 18-1/4" d, 38-3/4" h .. **1,765.00**

George III, bachelor's, mahogany, rect top over two short and three long drawers, bracket feet, 24-1/2" w, 18-1/2" d, 34" h **2,600.00**

George III-style, 19th C, mahogany, serpentine-front, thumb-molded top above four graduated and cock-beaded drawers, channel-carved bracket feet, 43" w, 24" d, 43" h **4,415.00**

Grain painted, attributed to ME or New Hampshire, late 18th C, carved pine, central fan-carved drawer flanked by four small drawers above four long drawers, base with front and side shaping, restoration, 41-1/2" w, 18-3/4" d, 49-1/4" h **4,410.00**

Chest of drawers, Hepplewhite, inlay, round brasses, escutcheons, **$500**.

Photo courtesy of Wiederseim Associates, Inc.

Hepplewhite

America, c1800, mahogany, straight front, four cock beaded drawers, eagle punched brasses, plain plank sides, bracket feet, shaped interiors, replaced top band, repairs to feet, lightly refinished, 42-1/2" w, 21" d, 37" h **1,550.00**

America, c1810, mahogany, poplar secondary wood, two-board top, four dovetailed drawers with beaded edges, older replaced emb brasses, scalloped fan inlay on lower apron, banding around lower case, French feet, refinished, restorations, replacements, 39" w, 19-3/4" d, 42-5/8" h **1,475.00**

American, 19th C, bow front, cherry, shaped top, four graduated drawers, flared feet, 38-3/4" w, 22" d, 40" h **3,600.00**

Country, refinished pine, red stain, solid bird's eye maple drawer fronts with natural finish, 4 dovetailed drawers, cut out feet and apron, old brass knobs, age cracks in front feet, 37-3/4" w, 35-3/4" h **1,100.00**

Louis Philippe, second quarter 19th C, walnut, later rect top, conforming case fitted with three drawers, shaped bracket feet, 47" w, 20" d, 31" h **425.00**

Queen Anne, Southeastern New England, c1700, painted oak, cedar, and yellow pine, rect top with applied edge, case of four drawers each with molded fronts, chamfered mitered borders, separated by applied horizontal moldings, sides with two

recessed vertical molded panels above single horizontal panel, base with applied molding, four turned ball feet, old red paint, minor imperfections, 37-3/4" w, 20-1/2" w, 35" h **26,450.00**

Renaissance, Italian, walnut, composed of antique elements, fitted with three long drawers, foliate and shield shaped carved drawer pulls, paw feet, 36" w, 17" d, 37" h **2,450.00**

Chest of drawers, Sheraton, country, cherry, four drawers with edge beading, flanked by columns, shaped skirt, glass knobs, **$225**.

Photo courtesy of Dotta Auction Co., Inc.

Chest of drawers, Sheraton, c1820, cherry, two deep drawers over three long drawers, **$650**.

Photo courtesy of Wiederseim Associates, Inc.

Sheraton

Cherry, two-board top with step down and molded edge, case with reeded pilasters and inset side panels, four dovetailed and beaded drawers, turned legs, ball feet, old refinishing, old replaced brass pulls, traces of red wash on front, 41-3/4" w, 21-3/4" d, 40-1/2" h **990.00**

Cherry, walnut secondary wood, six dovetailed drawers, small variegated sq inlays at upper corners, turned legs with reeding on front two, similar reeding up front posts, paneled ends, refinished, replaced eagle brasses, top reset with small bow tie shaped splice added below, minor edge restoration to drawers, 42-3/4" w, 18-3/4" w, 44-1/2" h **1,500.00**

Transitional, New England, late 18th or early 19th C, cherry, overhanging rect top, conforming case, four graduated drawers with cockbeaded surrounds, serpentine skirt flanked by flaring veneered French feet, period brasses, refinished, 45-3/4" w, 20-3/4" d, 36-1/2" h.......... **1,410.00**

Chest of drawers, Victorian, mahogany, five drawers, top one with curved front, carved pilasters, animal foot, **$750**.
Photo courtesy of Dotta Auction Co., Inc.

Victorian

American, oak, rect mirror, pair of handkerchief boxes, two small drawers over three graduated long drawers, emb design creates circular decoration on top three drawers, orig brass hardware, 40" w, 68" h **375.00**

American, poplar, mahogany veneer facade, serpentine top drawer, two serpentine stepback drawers, five dovetailed drawers, applied beading, worn finish, 40" w, 19-3/4" d, 47" h **330.00**

American, walnut, white marble top, 3 drawers, one hidden drawer in base, carved fruit and nut pulls, 39" w, 32" h **700.00**

William and Mary

American, burl veneer, bachelor's, five dovetailed drawers, pull-out shelf, worn finish, veneer damage, replaced base molding, turned feet, and backboards, orig brasses, 30" w, 19" d, 35" h........................ **1,980.00**

Southern Massachusetts or Rhode Island, tiger maple, graduated drawer construction, two over four drawers, applied moldings to top and bottom, turned turnip feet, old grunge finish, three escutcheon plates present, rest of hardware missing, some repair, 36-1/4" w, 18-1/4" d, 48" h **2,950.00**

Chest of drawers, other, stationary, English, 19th C, mahogany, six small drawers, each lined with green baize, side hinged locking panel, burl, **$325**.
Photo courtesy of Dotta Auction Co., Inc.

Chests of drawers, other

Apothecary, painted blue, 32 drawers, 96" l **2,900.00**

Bureau a Cylindre, Louis XV-style, gilt-bronze mounted rosewood and marquetry, rect top with pierced gallery above roll-top enclosing fitted interior, above single drawer, cabriole legs, allover dec with flowers and scrolling foliage, 29-1/2" w, 21" d, 42" h................... **1,420.00**

Campaign, mahogany, pine secondary wood, brass trim, dovetailed case, int. with lift-out tray, one dovetailed drawer, some shrinkage to lid, 30-3/4" w, 18-1/4" d, 19" h................ **385.00**

Chamber, Federal, attributed to the Seymour Workshop, Boston, c1915, mahogany inlaid, rect top with inlaid edge overhangs case with single tripartite drawer

above six smaller drawers flanking central cabinet on arched inlaid skirt, four turned reeded and tapering legs, similar arched side skirts, upper drawer with oval central stringing reserve, all drawers are outlined in ebonized inlay, missing dressing mirror from int. drawer, minor imperfections, 44-3/4" w, 19-1/2" d, 34-1/4" h **42,550.00**

Chest on chest

Biedermeier, walnut and ebonized, molded plinth cornice, five upper drawers, lower section with two drawers, bun feet, 41" w, 22" d, 64" h **2,300.00**

Chippendale, RI, 1750-1796, carved tiger maple, scrolled molded top with flame carved side finials, raised paneled faux drawers and six thumb-molded working drawers, lower case of four similar graduated drawers on molded base with ogee feet, some dark mahogany stain, some original brass, central finial is later addition, feet repairs, other imperfections, 38-1/2" w, 18-7/8" d, 87" h **23,500.00**

George III
Mahogany, rect cornice with molding and dentil trim, three short drawers over three graduated drawers, lower section with three graduated drawers, bracket feet, 31-1/2" w, 17-1/2" d, 59-1/2" h . **4,720.00**

Mahogany, rect molded and dentillated cornice above three short drawers, over three graduated drawers, lower section with three graduated drawers supported by bracket feet, 31-1/2" w, 17-1/2" d, 59-1/2" h.. **4,720.00**

Queen Anne
Salem, MA, attributed to, c1740-60, tiger maple, upper case with molded cornice, five graduated thumb-molded drawers, lower case with one long drawer with two drawer façade, and one long drawer with three short drawer façade, centrally caved fan, four arris cabriole legs with high pad feet on platforms, joined by cyma-curved skirt centering scrolled drops, possibly old brasses, old refinish, minor imperfections, 38-3/4" w, 19-1/2" d, 73-3/4" h **16,450.00**

Southern NH, late 19th C, maple, upper case with cove molded cornice, five graduated thumb-molded drawers, lower case with three graduated drawers, valanced frame joining four short cabriole legs on high pad on platform feet, old refinish, replaced braces, drawers with chalk and pencil inscriptions, vestiges of old red paint, minor imperfections, 40-1/2" w, 20" d, 80" h............ **11,750.00**

Chest on frame

Queen Anne, Connecticut, 1740-70, painted, flaring cornice with cove molding, case of thumb-molded drawers, arranged in two over four graduating pattern, frame with vigorously scrolling front and side skirts joined to cabriole legs with arris knees, arris disc feet, old red repaint, imperfections, 40" w, 23-1/4" d, 63-1/2" h **9,200.00**

Chest, other, silver chest, American, c1870, English walnut, poplar secondary wood, dovetailed case, hinged lid, fitted compartment for hollow ware, dovetailed flatware drawer, brass swing handles, shoe feet with casters, copy of label inside lid, William Wilson & Son Manufacturers of Silver Ware, southwest corner of Fifth & Cherry St., Philadelphia, 25-1/2" w, 19" d, 24" h, **$500.**

Photo courtesy of Alderfer Auction Co.

Queen Anne-style, English, walnut and burl veneer, mahogany secondary wood, case with four dovetailed

drawers, brass teardrop pulls, cabriole legs, duck feet, 20th C, 19-1/4" x 33-1/2" base, 38-1/2" h **825.00**

Chest over drawers

Chippendale, New England, 18th C, painted, molded lift-top above double arch molded case of two graduated false drawers and two working drawers, turned wooden pulls, high bracket feet centering cut-out pendant, orig red painted surface, 37-3/4" w, 18" d, 45-1/2" h............. **8,900.00**

Grain painted, Northern New England, early 19th C, pine, hinged top opens to storage cavity above two thumb-molded drawers, vigorously shaped front and side skirts, faux bois done with ochre and burnt umber, old brasses, minor imperfections, 39-3/4" w, 18-7/8" d, 39-7/8" h **2,350.00**

William and Mary, New Jersey, cherry, poplar secondary wood, molded lift-lid, cotter-pin hinges, two faux upper drawer fronts, two full width dovetailed lower drawers, molded base, cut-out feet, incised brass Chinese drop pulls, shaped key escutcheons, replaced hardware, 42-1/2" w, 17-1/4" d, 44-1/2" h **2,750.00**

Commode

Baroque, North Italian, early 18th C and later, walnut, molded rect top above frieze drawer and three long drawers, sides with fielded panels, bracket feet, 48" w, 23" d, 35-1/2" h........................ **5,100.00**

Biedermeier, birch and ebonized wood, rect top above four drawers flanked by columns, shaped skirt, bracket feet, price for pr, 34-3/4" w, 16-1/2" d, 35-1/2" h **2,950.00**

Louis XV, mid-18th C, tulipwood and kingwood parquetry inlaid, serpentine front, two short over three long serpentine drawers, flared feet, foliate cast mounts, 50" w, 24" d, 32" h **4,700.00**

Louis XV, Provincial, third quarter 18th C, walnut, serpentine top, case fitted with two short and two long drawers, each carved with rocaille and channel dec, 51" w, 24" d, 31" h **4,700.00**

Louis XV-style

Tulipwood and marquetry, gray shaped rect marble top over three graduated drawers, slightly splayed feet ending in gilt metal sabots, 44" d, 19-1/2" d, 34-1/4" h **2,850.00**

Tulipwood and marquetry, tan and caramel rect mottled marble top above an apron of intertwined gilt-metal laurel garlands above two drawers, tapering legs ending in floral sabots, price for pr, 40-3/8" w, 18-7/8" d, 33-3/4" h **21,240.00**

Louis XV/XVI-style transitional

c1770, parquetry inlaid, reverse breakfronted marble top, conforming case fitted with three drawers, short angular cabriole feet, checkered crossbanding throughout, 47" w, 20" d, 34" h **2,530.00**

20th C, ormolu mounted marquetry, inlaid tulipwood, serpentine marble top, conforming case, two drawers and angular legs, floral inlay, 36" w, 20" d, 36" h.... **1,410.00**

Neoclassical, petit, mahogany and marquetry, molded rect top above three drawers decorated with griffins, sphinxes, and rinceaux, tapering square-section feet, 29" w, 18-1/2" d, 33-1/2" h........................ **2,600.00**

Regency, French, 18th C

Bronze and brass mounted kingwood parquetry, marble top, three drawers flanked by brass inset and fluted stiles, shaped feet, 30" w, 18" d, 30-1/2" h **4,600.00**

Serpentine marble top, conforming kingwood case, brass fluting, two drawers, cabriole legs, 29" w, 19" d, 30" h......................... **4,700.00**

Gentleman's dressing chest

Regency, English, c1820, mahogany, bow-fronted case fitted with hinged top enclosing mirror, lower case fitted with two long drawers, flared feet, 36" w, 24" d, 35" h.................... **1,880.00**

Chests, other, high chest, Pennsylvania, c1780-1810, walnut, dovetailed case, dentil molding, reeded quarter columns, three over two over five drawers, ogee bracket feet, some replaced drawer bottoms and drawers, replaced hardware and feet, losses to dentil molding, refinished, 39-1/2" w, 21-1/2" d, 64" h, **$1,650.**

Photo courtesy of Alderfer Auction Co.

Highboy

Chippendale, associated with John Goddard and Job Townsend, Newport, RI, 1760-80, carved mahogany, enclosed scrolled pediment centering fluted plinth surrounded by urns and flame finials above two applied plaques over two short and three long graduated thumb molded drawers, set into lower case of one long and three short drawers above cyma curved skirt, centered carved shell, frontal cabriole legs ending in ball and claw feet, similar rear legs ending in pad feet, old replaced brasses, refinished, repairs, 39" w, 20-1/2" d, 84" h **36,550.00**

Chippendale-style, America, late 19th/early 20th C, mahogany, broken arch pediment, flame finials, reeded quarter columns at corners, inset panels on either end of top, eight dovetailed drawers with brass pulls, gadrooning around base and edges of base and lower section, cabriole legs with scrolled returns, raised acanthus leaf carvings, claw and ball feet, old reddish brown finish, 48-1/2" w, 24-1/4" d, 81" h **1,200.00**

Queen Anne

America, cherry, poplar and pine secondary wood, top dovetailed case, circular fan at top, replaced molded cornice, seven graduated drawers on top, four drawers on base, base with pegged construction, molded trim on dovetailed drawers, carved fan at lower center, scalloped aprons, shaped returns, well shaped cabriole legs, pad feet, mellow refinish, replaced bat wing brasses, pierced restorations to some drawer fronts, replaced returns and waist molding, 35" w top, 40" w base, 22" d, 71-1/2" h **6,200.00**

Connecticut, attributed to, c1760-80, cherry and maple, broken arch pediment with three flame finials on fluted plinths, upper case with fan carved thumb-molded short drawer flanked by two shaped short drawers, four graduated long drawers, lower case with long drawer over two short drawers flanking fan carved drawer, carved scrolling skirt joining four cabriole legs, pad feet, replaced brasses and finials, old refinish, repairs and imperfections, 38-1/4" w, 19" d, 86" h **24,675.00**

Dunlap School, NH, c1770-80, carved maple, cove-molded cornice over upper case of five graduated long drawers, lower case of three graduated thumb-molded long drawers, upper and lowermost drawers each fan carved, cyma-curved skirt centering scrolling drops, joining four cabriole legs with shaped returns, pad feet on platforms, dark stained surface, possibly orig brasses, minor imperfections, chalk inscriptions on drawer backs, 39-1/4" w, 21-1/2" d, 78-3/4" h **14,100.00**

Massachusetts or southern New Hampshire, 1760-80, tiger maple, flaring cornice above four thumb-molded drawers on lower case of one long drawer and three small drawers, the central one with fan carving above three flat-headed arches, cabriole legs, high pad feet, replaced brasses, refinished, minor imperfections, 37-3/4" w at

mid molding, 19-5/8" d at mid molding, 72" h **16,450.00**

North Shore, MA, 18th C, maple, flaring cove-molded cornice with concealed drawer above four thumb-molded graduated drawers in upper case over mid-molding, two long drawers, lower case visually divided into three drawers centering by carved fan over cyma-curved side skirts, cabriole legs and high pad feet, old surface, old brasses, imperfections, 35-1/2" w, 17-5/8" d, 71" h **31,050.00**

Rhode Island, c1730-60, attributed to Abram Utter, tiger maple and cherry, top section with flat molded cornice, case of two thumb-molded short drawers, three long drawers, lower section with projecting molding above case of central thumb-molded short drawer flanked by deeper drawers, four arris cabriole legs, pad feet, all joined to deeply valanced skirt with applied cock beading and two turned drop pendants, replaced brasses, old refinish, minor imperfections, 37" w, 19-1/4" d, 63-3/4" h **29,375.00**

William and Mary-style, 18th C, cross banded walnut, upper section with two short over three long drawers, base with three drawers on trumpet turned legs, 40" w, 21" d, 69" h **1,850.00**

Chest of drawers, other, high chest, Chippendale, Pennsylvania, c1775, ogee cornice above Greek key molding, nine drawers flanked by fluted quarter columns, spurred ogee bracket feet, 39" w, 63-3/4" h, **$12,650.**

Photo courtesy of Pook & Pook.

Linen chest

Georgian, shaped rect cornice over two doors opening to drawersabove two short and two long drawers, splayed feet, 48" w, 21" d, 84" h **3,100.00**

Hepplewhite, English, two pcs, mahogany and mahogany flame veneer, oak secondary wood, two door to with flame veneer panels, divided int. with five drawers on right side, brass bar and hooks on other, three dovetailed drawers in base with mahogany border inlay with beaded edges, shaped apron, French feet, refinished, old replaced brass pulls, fitted int. top drawer with four small drawers and eleven pigeon holes, pieced restorations, 49" w, 23" d, 83 1/2" h.............. **1,200.00**

Liquor chest

Early 19th century, mahogany veneer, chest with brass swing handles opens to reveal compartmented int., 12 blown molded wine and spirit bottles, each with inscribed paper labels and dec with gilt flowers, bowknots, and borders about the neck and shoulders, lift out tray fitted with tumblers, funnel and stemware with similar gilt decoration, one tumbler cracked, some veneer loss, 17" w, 12-1/2" d, 11-1/2" h **1,410.00**

Lowboy

Queen Anne, Rhode Island, maple, pine secondary wood, case dovetailed at rear, pegged at sides, old replaced two-board curly maple top, four dovetailed drawers with beaded edges, batwing brasses, scalloped aprons, cabriole legs, slipper feet, refinished, small insect holes, restorations with some alterations, 32-1/2" w, 22-1/2" d, 30-1/4" h **1,760.00**

William and Mary style, early 20th C, red japanned, serpentine black marble top, conforming case fitted with five small drawers, shaped kneehole, cabriole legs, pad feet, price for pr, 28-1/2" w, 17" d, 29-1/2" h **3,400.00**

Mule chest

New England, poplar, old dark red wash, rect lid, single board ends, two dovetailed drawers in base, well shaped serpentine bracket feet, orig wood pulls, glued split in lid, replaced hinges, added supports, 45-3/4" l, 20-3/4" d, 44" h **850.00**

Chests, other, tall chest, Queen Anne, Chester County, PA, c1740, Octorara, walnut, molded cornice, three over two over four lipped drawer configuration, original brasses, high removable Spanish feet, 37" w, 60" h, **$19,800**.

Photo courtesy of Wiederseim Associates, Inc.

Spice

Ohio, attributed to, walnut, poplar secondary wood, mortised and paneled front door, small brass pull, three drawers with orig turned walnut pulls, turned feet, 14-1/2" w, 12-1/4" d, 18-3/4" h **2,400.00**

Pennsylvania, 1780-1800, walnut, dovetailed, cove-molded cornice, raised panel hinged door, opens to int. of 11 small drawers, brass pulls, molded base, old surface, 15-1/2" w, 11" d, 18-1/4" h **14,950.00**

Sugar chest

Middle Atlantic states, attributed to, early 19th C, inlaid cherry, hinged lid with molded edge, interior cavity with single (missing) divider over facade with stringing in outline, oval inlaid central reserve and quarter corner inlays, restoration, 32-1/4" w, 16-1/2" d, 34-3/4" h **12,925.00**

Tall

Federal, New England, late 18th C, tiger maple, cove molded top, case with six thumb-molded drawers, central fan carved drop pendant flanked by high bracket feet, orig brasses, old refinish, repairs, 41" w, 54-5/8" h **8,625.00**

Cradles

Chippendale-style, birch, canted sides, scalloped headboard, turned posts and rails, refinished, 37-1/2" l **400.00**

Country

America, Tiger maple, dovetailed, heart cut-outs, large rockers, 36" l, 26" w, 16" h.......................... **675.00**

New England, 18th C, painted pine, arched hood continuing to shaped and carved dovetailed sides, rockers, old light green paint, old repairs, 40" l **300.00**

Pennsylvania, late 18th C, dovetailed, refinished curly maple, cut-out hearts, age cracks and shrinkage, 41" l **550.00**

Eastlake, 1875, walnut, paneled headboard, footboard, and sides, scrolling crest above short turned spindles, platform support, orig finish, dated **495.00**

Rustic, twig construction, rocker base, unsigned, 33" l, 22" d, 22" h **120.00**

Windsor, New England, c1800-20, bamboo turned spindles, worn finish... **850.00**

Cradle, Victorian, stained pine, 30" x 41" x 20", **$175**.

Photo courtesy of David Rago Auctions, Inc.

Victorian, 19th C, painted wrought wire and cast iron, scrolled trestle base, later int. inset rect marble plaque, 40" l, 37" h **940.00**

Typical Parts of a Cupboard

Cupboard, corner, Pennsylvania, c1840, two pieces, cherry, 12 light single door over two paneled doors, ogee molding on top and waist, interior with plate grooves, 30" corner, 87" h, replaced hardware, **$4,320**.

Photo courtesy of Alderfer Auction Co.

Cupboards

Armoire

Art Deco, France, c1928, sycamore and fruitwood, interior fitted with top shelf over divided compartment, hardware fitted for wardrobe, flanked by two shelves, lollipop-shaped key, 51-1/4" w, 19" d, 71" h **1,650.00**

Arts & Crafts, English, single-door, overhanging top supported by corbels, mirror, emb copper panels of stylized flowers, unmarked, refinished, new back and shelves, one corbel missing, 40" w, 18" d, 75" h **1,050.00**

Classical, New York, c1835, mahogany, bold projecting molded Roman arch cornice, two paneled doors flanked by tapered veneered columns, ogee bracket feet, 74" w, 31" d, 94" h **3,200.00**

Empire-style, Continental, early 19th C, mahogany, shaped cornice above two paneled doors opening to shelves, ribbed lunette-shaped feet, 42" w, 17" d, 74" h **1,610.00**

Louis XV/XVI-style, transitional, 19th C, kingwood and parquetry, molded marble top with serpentine sides, pair of doors, each with two shaped and quarter-veneered flush panels, serpentine sides, coated stiles with gilt-brass chutes, sq-section cabriole legs joined by shaped skirt, stamped "Dubreuil," 44" w, 18-1/2" d, 59" h **950.00**

Cupboards, armoire, Sheraton, country, two doors, long drawer, painted white, **$250**.

Photo courtesy of Dotta Auction Co., Inc.

Restoration, New York, c1830, mahogany, flat top with cornice molding, two doors, birds' eye maple lined int., concealed drawer below, ribbed blocked feet, 56" w, 19-1/2" d, 90" h **2,800.00**

Victorian, American, c1840, walnut, bold double ogee molded cornice, two arched paneled doors, shelved int., plinth base, ogee bracket feet, 62" w, 24" d, 89" h **1,400.00**

Bee keeper's hutch, Canadian, pine, orig red and black painted top panel, paneled door on lower front, door on either end, drop front covers interior workshelf, hinged lid, pegged construction, lid marked "Patent Union, Bee Hive, W. Phelps Pat." 47" w, 19" d, 43-1/4" h **750.00**

Chifforobe, Art Deco, 1935, herringbone design waterfall veneer, arched center mirror, dropped center section, four deep drawers flanked by tall cupboard doors, shaped apron......... **450.00**

Chimney, country, pine, old blue-gray paint, picture frame molding around front of case, single door, beaded panel, brass pull, four int. shelves, age splits, 29" w, 12-1/2" d, 55-1/4" h **575.00**

Cupboard, corner cupboard, Lancaster County, PA, c1830-50, one piece, yellow grain painted finish, two paneled upper doors over two paneled lower doors, bracket feet, cast iron hinges, original finish, 34" corner, 85" h, scuffs to finish, **$2,000**.

Photo courtesy of Alderfer Auction Co.

Cupboard, corner, Baroque-style, c1940, carved oak, single glass door, egg and dart molding, foliate carved twisted full columns, ball and claw feet, lion's head centered on skirt, four butterfly shelves, 30" corner, 69" h, chips on toes, **$700**.

Photo courtesy of Alderfer Auction Co.

Cupboard, corner, hanging, blind, pine, **$250**.

Photo courtesy of Wiederseim Associates, Inc.

Corner

Blind paneled doors, Kentucky, walnut, bracket feet **3,000.00**

One piece, Chippendale, Southern states, 1760s, pine, heavy projecting cornice molding above arched molded surround, flanking similarly shaped raised panel doors opening to two shelves above two additional fielded panel doors, flanked by fluted pilasters, opening to single serpentine shelf, refinished, hardware replaced, repairs, 64" w, 30" d, 93-3/4" h **7,475.00**

One piece, paneled pine, New England, 19th C, flat ogee molded cornice, arched opening flanks three painted scalloped shelves, two fielded panel cupboard doors, single int. shelf, old refinish on ext., old red color on shelves, 50" w, 20" d, 88" h **4,255.00**

Two pieces, cherry, two doors, orig six wavy glass panes over two doors with four tin panels punch dec with cornflower motif, replacement wooden knobs, repairs, restoration, refinished **1,425.00**

Two pieces, Pennsylvania, softwood, molded cornice, reeded stiles, arched top glazed door, serpentine shelves with spoon notches, two dovetailed drawers, two lower paneled doors, molded bracket base, dry blue painted surface, white door, black painted interior, 49" w, 30" d, 89-1/2" h, ex-Elgin **29,700.00**

Cupboard, corner, PA, c1820-35, walnut, single arched glazed door over two paneled doors, H-hinges, bracket feet, dovetailed case, butterfly shelves, 31" corner, 82" h, replaced feet, some replaced glass, **$2,400**.

Photo courtesy of Alderfer Auction Co.

Cupboard, corner, Victorian, cherry, three piece, top section with heavy molded cornice, carved squared capitals at corners, single door with carved arches in corners, brass trim, four-shelf interior, mid section with mirrored back, base with pair of cupboard doors with matching arch and brass trim, **$950**.

Photo courtesy of Dotta Auction Co., Inc.

Cupboard, corner, mahogany veneer, two-piece, broken arch cornice above arched glass door, lower section with two doors, scalloped base, restorations, 44" w, 92-1/4" h, **$1,650**.

Photo courtesy of Wiederseim Associates, Inc.

Court, European, oak, two-pc, mortised construction, top section with two doors and central panel

Incised diamonds and pinwheels, free standing turned pilasters on either side, scrollwork with date "16MIVI" below cornice, two doors with three inset panels each on lower case doors and ends separated by molded T-shaped cross pieces, well executed replaced scrolled wrought iron butterfly hinges, old dark finish, restorations, old alterations, age splits, 63" w, 19-1/4" d, 62-1/2" h...................... **2,950.00**
Relief flowers, scrolled vining, matching vining below cornice, leaf and arch carvings across center, three inset panels each on lower case doors and ends separated by molded T-shaped cross pieces, well executed replaced scrolled wrought iron butterfly hinges, old dark finish, restorations, old alterations, 49-1/2" w, 20-1/8" d, 67" h **1,200.00**

Desk top, New England, pine, old grain painted dec, two solid doors with relief carved vertical panels, brass hinges, moldings at top and bottom, shaped feet are extensions of case, 10 cubby holes in int., orig green paint on ext. and int., 29" w, 12" d, 27-1/4" h **1,750.00**

Dresser, Provincial, English, 18th C, oak, plate rack with four shelves flanked by architectural uprights, two paneled doors centered by three drawers, bracket feet, 83" w, 19" d, 71" h **4,720.00**

Hanging
Carlisle, Cumberland, County, Pennsylvania, poplar, molded cornice, raised paneled door, int. shelf, lip molded dovetailed drawer, bold scalloped cut-outs, stained to resemble walnut, restoration to cornice, 27" w, 11-1/2" d, 35" h, ex-Elgin.......... **7,975.00**
Country, decorated, dovetailed case, painted green, brick red, brown, and white dec on sponged ground, initialed and dated "F.P.S. 1855," molded cornice and base, two dovetailed drawers below two doors, two int. shelves, pierced restorations, areas of insect damage, 28-3/4" w, 10-3/4" d, 29-3/4" h...................... **750.00**

Cupboard, country, early 19th C, blind, two pieces, poplar, arched paneled doors, scalloped shelved interior, doors with original paint, doors were removed years ago and stored, feet replaced, 88" h, **$2,400.**

Photo courtesy of Wiederseim Associates, Inc.

English, Chippendale, corner, oak, pine secondary wood, cove molded cornice, dovetailed case, single door with beaded edges, geometric mullions with old wavy glass, molded base, three int. shelves, old brown finish, old repairs, 30-1/4" w, 16-1/2" d, 43" h **2,530.00**
Pennsylvania, softwood, painted red, molded cornice, raised carved circular trim, serpentine molded door, interior shelf, lip molded dovetailed drawer, molded base, restoration to door, 27-1/2" w, 14" d, 31-1/4" h **3,025.00**

Jelly, country, central Pennsylvania, poplar, old salmon paint, sq nail construction, gallery top, two paneled doors, well-shaped apron, bracket feet, three shelved int., wear, 43-3/4" w, 18-1/2" d, 54" h **1,380.00**
Kas, Long Island, NY, c1730-80, cherry, pine, and polar, architectural cornice molding, two raised panel thumb-molded doors flanked by reeded pilasters, applied moldings, single drawer, painted detachable disc and stretcher feet, replaced hardware, refinished, restored, 65-1/2" w, 26-1/4" d, 77-1/4" h.......... **4,500.00**

Cupboard, open, two pieces, pine, three shelves over lower section with four small drawers flanked by two drawers and doors, straight bracket feet, 57" w, 93" h, **$2,000.**
Photo courtesy of Wiederseim Associates, Inc.

Kitchen, orig blue paint, six center drawers with porcelain pulls, two side bins, one bin lid sgd "Ezra Woodside Montare, April 20, 1905," cutting board, continuous scalloped face board covering lower front and feet, back shaped like picket fence, 72" l, 21" d, 54" h **7,200.00**

Linen press, Federal, Boston, 1820-25, mahogany veneer, three parts, veneered entablature with central rect outlined in stringing above veneered frieze, pair of recessed panel doors which open to five pull-out drawers with shaped sides, lower case with molding and three cock-beaded drawers, flaring high bracket feet, inlaid escutcheons, orig brasses, feet restored, surface imperfections, 48" w, 22-1/4" h, 83-1/2" h **6,900.00**

Milk, Pennsylvania, primitive, softwood, molded edge, vertical beaded board door, wrought iron strap hinges with penny ends, cut-out block feet, three interior shelves, red painted surface, 38 1/2" w, 15" d, 58" h .. **1,100.00**

Pewter
Country, one pc, cherry and walnut, beveled cornice with flat top, four shelves flanked by tapered sideboards, notched aprons on ends, two doors in base, old refinishing, originally built-in, edge wear, repairs, 36" w, 16" d, 81-1/2" h **920.00**
New England, two part, dark maple and cherry, cornice molding above molded sides and plate rails, stepped out surface, three drawers above recessed panel cupboard doors, single shelved interiors, sq feet, straight skirt, turned wooden pulls, restored, 58-3/4" w, 17-1/2" d, 79" h **4,500.00**
Pennsylvania, c1780, walnut, scalloped cornice, three open shelves, lollipop one board side, two cupboard doors with batwing hinges, worn and scrubbed patina **40,000.00**

Pie safe
Georgia, pine and cherry, six tin panels, punched sunflower and heart motifs, double door cupboard base **4,800.00**
Kentucky, orig red grain paint, pegged construction, six

punched tins, punched circular motif, as found condition **1,200.00**
Southeastern United States, early 19th C, walnut, rect top above along drawer, two hinged cupboard doors each with two pierced tin panels with designs of hearts and initials "J.B." flanked by leafy branches, ends with three conforming decorated panels, sq tapering legs, refinished, minor imperfections, 39-1/2" w, 17" d, 49-1/2" h **5,300.00**
Tennessee, cherry, twelve tin panels, punched fylfots **4,250.00**

Schrank, PA, poplar, decorated, orig paint, sponged brown, salmon, green, and blue, two panels dec with maker's name and date, "Philip-Man, 1796-28 Mey (sic), dentil cornice, reeded quarter columns, ogee feet, 62" w, 70" h, ex-Clark Garrett **300,000.00**

Cupboard, corner, two pieces, cherry, architectural domed door with 15 original panes, burled mahogany panels on lower doors, Sandwich glass knobs, ivory inlay, **$8,500**.
Photo courtesy of Dotta Auction Co., Inc.

Slant back, New England, late 18th C, pine, flat molded cornice above beaded canted front flanking shelves, projecting base with single raised panel door, old refinish, doors missing from top, imperfections, 37-1/2" w, 18" d, 73" h **2,300.00**

Spice, northern Europe, last half 18th C, wall-type, painted, flat molded cornice, hinged cupboard door, molded recessed panel opening, compartmentalized int., molded base, old dark green paint bordered by red, int. drawers missing, imperfections, 16" w, 8" d, 17" h **1,500.00**

Step-back, wall
America, Empire, c1830, mahogany and mahogany veneer, molded cornice top, three eight-light doors, adjustable shelves, cabinet base with three cupboard doors, sliding center doors in top and base, 79-1/2" w, 21" d, 93" h **11,100.00**
Pennsylvania, attributed to, one piece, curly maple, mellow golden color, two mortised and paneled doors on top, one int. shelf, two board top with high pie shelf, five dovetailed drawers in base in three-over-two configuration, turned legs with excellent figure, replaced brass pulls, one glued break on the lower corner of door, 44-1/2" w, 19-1/2" d, 60-1/4" h **8,525.00**
Pennsylvania or Ohio, attributed to, 1830-40, painted cherry, flaring cornice molding above fluted frieze, pair of glazed doors open to two-shelf int., flanked by fluting above stepped out surface, two drawers over two recessed panel doors opening to single shelf int., recessed panel sides, four short turned legs, all over red paint, brass pulls, imperfections, 50" w, 21-1/2" d, 88" h **18,400.00**

Storage, Montgomery County, PA, poplar, dovetailed case, molded top, two paneled doors, French bracket feet, int. shelves, scraped finish down to red, replaced back boards, moldings, 49" w, 18" d, 72" h **1,100.00**

Wall
America, two pieces, pine and walnut, old mustard paint and faint brown grain dec, traces of earlier red in some areas, brown sponging to three curved front drawers and on raised panels of lower doors, cove molded cornice, two-

door top with six panes of glass in each door, vertical central panel with three panels, all top panes are tombstone shaped, chamfered corners, turned feet with applied half turned pilasters, blue painted int. with cut-outs for spoons, 61" w, 21" d, 85-3/4" h.................. **5,500.00**

Cupboard, wall, New England, c1830-50, mahogany, secretary top with adjustable shelves, two top doors over base with two drawers over two lower doors, replaced hardware, missing return molding on base, 54" w, 18" d, 93-1/2" h, **$1,000**.

Photo courtesy of Alderfer Auction Co.

Canadian, Hepplewhite, two pieces, pine, beveled and cove molded cornice, two doors in top section with two panes of glass each, two int. shelves with red and white paint, molded waist, five drawers in base with incised beading, turned wooden pulls, well scalloped base, high bracket feet, refinished, evidence of earlier red paint, edge chips, couple of glued splits to feet, 48" w, 23-1/2" d, 78-1/2" h..................... **935.00**
Federal, New England, second quarter 19th C, painted, two parts, paneled, cornice molding, chamfered front corners, stepped-out surface with three scratch beaded drawers above two paneled doors, single shelved int., molded base,

bracket feet, orig red surface, turned wood pulls probably original, repairs, 57-1/2" w, 23-1/4" d, 85" h............. **6,500.00**

Cupboard, wall, early 19th C, two-piece, poplar, original red paint, white porcelain knobs, raised paneled upper door, scalloped shelved interior, two drawers and single paneled door in base, feet replaced, 88" h, **$2,350**.

Photo courtesy of Wiederseim Associates, Inc.

Jacobean, oak and part painted, two parts, upper section with pegs and shelves, projecting lower section with two doors, each with geometric and floral carving, 64" w, 20" d, 80" h **3,000.00**
New England, possibly Vermont, hooded, lollipop one board sides, three open shelves on top, single paneled cupboard door in base, dark green paint............... **11,500.00**
New York, upstate, early 19th C, painted, flat cornice, case with two hinged doors each with two recessed vertical panels, shelved int., old gray paint, imperfections, 43" w, 18" d, 78" h **1,000.00**
Wardrobe
Chippendale, English, mahogany, pine secondary wood, cove molded cornice, two-door front with three raised

panels each, three inset panels on each side, scalloped bracket feet, molded base, brass lock escutcheons, refinished, formerly fitted with shelves and rod, restorations, replacements, 53-3/4" w, 24" d, 78" h........................... **1,500.00**

Wardrobe, mahogany, signed "Lejambre," Philadelphia, griffin and floral carved frieze, two mirrored doors, base with two carved drawers, 75" w, 25" d, 102" h, **$4,675**.

Photo courtesy of Wiederseim Associates, Inc.

French, late 19th C, walnut, walnut veneer applied in herringbone pattern on ends, open pediment crest, double door mirrors with pillars on each side, 50" w, 98-1/2" h **1,000.00**

Desk, Arts & Crafts, Gustav Stickley, postcard desk, letterholder backsplash, two drawers, paneled back and sides, recessed bookshelf below, original finish, early red decal, 39-1/2" l, 22" d, 36" h, **$1,610**.

Photo courtesy of David Rago Auctions, Inc.

Desk, Biedermeier style, matched veneers, fall front over pair of doors, detailed interior, **$950.**

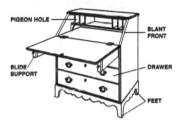

Typical Parts of a Desk

Desks

Aesthetic Movement, Herter Brothers, Washburn Commission, mahogany, fall front, top section: shelf with gallery top supported by turned and blocked posts, back panel with dec gold threaded material; middle section: slant lid, two supporting pull-out arms, central panel of marquetry inlaid with garland of flowers ending in bows, int. with two drawers, five cubbyholes, supported by two turned front legs, two bottom section with shelf and paneled back, missing orig writing surface, raised panel back, needs restoration, commissioned by Hon. William Drew Washburn for MN Greek Revival house, copy of orig bill of sale, 30" w, 20" w, 53-1/2" h **9,000.00**

Art Deco, Leopold Corp, Burlington, IA, walnut veneered, semi-oval top over center drawer flanked by pull-out writing surface and two drawers, bronze handles, light brown finish, "Charles S. Nathan Office

Equipment New York" distributor's metal tag in drawer, veneer loss, wear, 66-1/8" l, 36-1/8" d, 29" h................ **900.00**

Arts & Crafts, Stickley, Gustav, Syracuse, NY, lady's, c1912, model no. 720, cabinet with four vertical shelves, two small drawers, three horizontal shelves, rect top, two short drawers, paper Craftsman label, 38" w, 23" d, 37" h **1,725.00**

Desk, Arts & Crafts, Lifetime, postcard style, divided letter holder, single drawer, round copper pulls, maker's decal in drawer, original finish, 34" w, 20" d, 34" h, **$850.**

Photo courtesy of David Rago Auctions, Inc.

Desk, Chippendale, mahogany, fall front, fitted interior with central door, six letter slots, six drawers, four graduated drawers, bracket feet, replaced hardware, splits to veneer, **$1,100.**

Photo courtesy of Alderfer Auction Co.

Chippendale

Connecticut, late 18th C, mahogany, block front, slant front lid, fitted tiered int. with nine dovetailed drawers, pigeonholes, two pull-out letter drawers with fluted columns, flame-carved finials and door with blocking and fan carving, dovetailed case, four dovetailed drawers,

conforming apron, bracket feet, replaced brasses, old refinishing, feet replaced, repairs to case, 41-3/4" w, 21-1/2" d, 42-3/4" h ... **3,850.00**

Massachusetts, c1770-80, slant lid, mahogany, lid opens to int. of central fan, concave caved drawer, two conforming drawers flanked by document drawers with half-baluster fronts, four valanced compartments, two drawers, cock-beaded case of four graduated drawers, ogee bracket feet, center drop pendant, old brass bail pulls, refinished, imperfections, 40" w, 20" d, 43" h **9,400.00**

New England, late 18th C, cherry, slant lid opens to an interior of open valanced compartments above small blocked drawers flanking central open compartment, thumb-molded graduated drawers, molded bracket base with central pendant, replaced brass, old refinish, repairs, 38" w, 19-3/4" d, 40-3/4" h **2,500.00**

New England, late 18th C, maple, pine secondary wood, old dark brown surface, slant lid, interior with nine pigeon holes over five small drawers, dovetailed case, four dovetailed graduated drawers with beaded edges, molded base, bracket feet, old replaced batwing brasses, old repairs, 36" w, 17-1/2" d, 41-1/4" h **4,900.00**

North Shore, Massachusetts, late 18th C, mahogany carved oxbow serpentine slant lid, int. of blocked fan-carved prospect door, conformingly curved three-door interior flanked by four valanced compartments and three drawers, cockbeaded case of four graduated drawers, carved cabriole legs, claw and ball feet centering shell and scroll carved pendant, replaced brasses, refinished, imperfections, 41" w, 23" d, 44" h........................ **5,875.00**

Rhode Island, late 18th C, cherry, slant front, stepped int. of small drawers, central one with shaping, case of beaded graduated drawers, ogee bracket feet, orig brasses, old refinish, restoration, 39" w, 20" d, 43" h **3,800.00**

Virginia, attributed to, late 18th C, carved walnut, slant lid opens to stepped interior of six valanced small compartments flanked by pinwheel carved end-drawers above small drawers, case of graduated drawers with cockbeaded surrounds, molded bracket base, brasses appear early, refinished, repairs, 40" h, 19" d, 41-3/4" h **3,820.00**

Desk, Chippendale, c1780, walnut, slant front, document drawer, pigeon holed interior, 36" w, 41" h, **$2,500**.

Photo courtesy of Wiederseim Associates, Inc.

Drop-front, Philadelphia, 1830, tiger maple, mahoganized finish **6,000.00**

Eastlake, lady's, walnut, two parts, top section sits on pegs, top: mirror with two columns supported shelves, fancy carving, pressed dec; base section: double hinged writing surface with dec floral carving, writing surface with two panels of green felt, lifts to reveal compartment desk int. with two drawers, one side fitted with two long drawers, gallery shelf in base, dec applied pieces, shoe foot base, metal asters, 31-1/2" w, 19" d, 57" h **1,150.00**

Edwardian, c1900, kneehole, mahogany, rect cross banded top with central oval medallion, front canted corners, long frieze drawer, two banks of three drawers, center cupboard door, foliate marquetry dec, 37-1/2" w, 31" h **600.00**

Edwardian-style, 20th C, marquetry inlaid mahogany, U-shaped superstructure fitted with drawers and doors, serpentine case fitted with drawers, sq tapered legs, 35" w, 24" d, 37" h **2,645.00**

Empire, butler's, cherry and curly maple, poplar secondary wood, scrolled crest with turned

rosettes, pull-out desk drawer with arched pigeon holes and three dovetailed drawers, three dovetailed drawers with applied edge beading, turned and carved pilasters, paneled ends, paw feet, old finish, some edge damage, 44-1/2" w, 23" d, 57-3/4" h **1,925.00**

Federal

America, butler's, mahogany and mahogany veneer, rect top, case of three cock-beaded short drawers, pull-out desk with cock-beaded drawer façade flanked by wide drawers opening to prospect door over short drawer flanked by document drawer, two short drawers, two compartments, one long drawer, allover pull-out shelf, three graduated cock-beaded long drawers, cut-out feet joined by shaped skirt, old refinish, 47" w, 19" d, 45-1/2" h **1,300.00**

Massachusetts, eastern, c1800-10, tambour, mahogany and mahogany veneer inlaid, upper section with tambour doors flanked by pilasters with chevron inlay enclosing two short drawers over three valanced compartments centering prospect door with inlaid stringing enclosing two short drawers over double valanced compartments, lower section with folding lid over case of two cock-beaded string inlaid long drawers, legs inlaid with bellflowers and stringing tapering to inlaid cuffs, old replaced brasses, old refinish, blue painted int., repairs and imperfections, 38" w, 19-1/4" d, 34-1/2" h **11,750.00**

Massachusetts, possibly Worcester County, c1800, inlaid mahogany and cherry, slant thumb molded lid centering inlaid satinwood diamond panel bordered by rosewood crossbanding and stringing, fitted int. of eight drawers and seven valanced compartments, swelled case of four graduated cockbeaded drawers bordered by crossbanding on inlaid base, flaring French feet, replaced brasses, old refinish, minor imperfections, chalk inscriptions, 38-3/4" w, 21" d, 44" h **4,450.00**

New England, early 19th C, mahogany and mahogany veneer inlaid, top section shaped gallery above flat molded cornice, two glazed doors enclosing compartments and drawer, flanking door and small drawer; projecting base with fold-out writing surface, two cock-beaded short drawers, two graduated long drawers, four sq tapering legs, inlaid cross-banding, old refinish, some restoration, inscribed "22 Geo. L. Deblois Sept. 12th 1810," 37-1/8" w, 20" d, 51-1/2" **3,000.00**

New Hampshire, early 19th C, slant lid, wavy birch, lid opens to two-stepped int. case of drawers with four cock-beaded surrounds, serpentine skirt, tall arched feet, orig brasses, old refinish, repairs, 37-1/2" w, 18-1/4" d, 45" h **2,760.00**

New York State, early 19th C, mahogany veneer inlaid, slant lid and three graduated drawers outlined in stringing with ovolo corners, int. of veneer and outline stringing on drawers, valanced compartments, prospect door opening to inner compartments and drawers, flanking document drawers, orig brasses, old surface, veneer cracking loss and patching, other surface imperfections, 41-1/2" w, 21-1/2" d, 44" h **2,550.00**

Pennsylvania, early 19th C, walnut inlaid, slant front, lid and cock-beaded drawers outlined in stringing, base with band of contrasting veneers, int. of small drawers above valanced compartments, scrolled dividers flanking prospect door which opens to two small drawers, three drawers, old refinish, repairs, 40" w, 20" d, 44-1/2" h **3,550.00**

George III, English

Mahogany, oak secondary wood, kneehole, molded top, single cabinet door in center, single long drawer with divided interior over two banks of three dovetailed drawers with beaded edges and old brasses, bracket feet, molded base, old refinishing, some splits, restoration to veneer, 40-1/4" w, 20-1/2" d, 33" h **2,650.00**

Mahogany, rect top with partial gallery above a long drawer, kneehole flanked by two short drawers, ring-turned legs, brass casters, 34" w, 20" d, 31" h **700.00**

George III-style, pedestal, walnut, gilt-tooled brown leather top, central frieze drawer, two pedestals fitted on both sides with drawers and paneled doors, 65-1/2" w, 35" d, 30" h **2,585.00**

Hepplewhite, oxbow slant front, maple and birch, pine secondary wood, int. with ten small drawers with brass knobs, seven pigeon holes, four graduated dovetailed drawers with beaded edges, old replaced oval brasses, high French feet, scalloped returns, band of inlay around base, refinished, restorations to scalloped valances and lid supports, 39-1/2" w, 18" d, 47" h **2,100.00**

Louis XV, tulipwood and gilt bronze mounted, top having central writing stand, flanked by two hinged doors opening to storage, central frieze drawer; lower section: black lacquered shaped rect top with Chinoiserie scene, central faux drawer, sides each having single drawer raised on cabriole legs with gilt bronze mounts ending in sabots, stamped "Durand," 25" w, 15-1/2" d, 31-3/8" h **11,800.00**

Louis XV-style, parquetry, shaped rect top with inset red leather top, single drawer, cabriole legs, gilt bronze sabots, 23-1/2" w, 20" d, 27-5/8" h **3,800.00**

Provincial, English, early 19th C, rect top, central drawer, shaped octagonal standards, H-form stretcher, octagonal block feet **1,660.00**

Queen Anne

America, early 18th C, crossbanded walnut, slant-lid, rect top, fitted interior of stepped pigeonholes and drawers, split lower case fitted with two short over three long graduated drawers, bracket feet, 35-3/4" w, 23" d, 39-1/2" h **5,885.00**

Desk, Plantation, American, 19th C, fold-down front, molded cornice, large ledger shelf, fitted interior with four pigeonholes over larger valanced section, four vertical dividers, single drawer, turned legs, **$750**.

Photo courtesy of Dotta Auction Co., Inc.

Northern Maine, 19th C, maple, slant front, int. with valanced compartments above small drawers, end drawers separated by scrolled dividers, case of three thumb-molded drawers, molded bracket base with central drop pendant, old darkened surface, 35-1/2" w, 17-1/2" d, 40-1/4" h .. **5,175.00**

Vermont, c1750, tiger maple and cherry, slant front, int. with central fan-carved drawer, two valanced compartments flanked by molded document drawers, four valanced compartments, three drawers, case with four thumb-molded graduated drawers, bracket feet, replaced brasses, old refinish, imperfections, and repairs, 36" w, 18" d, 41-1/2" h **3,220.00**

Regency, English, c1850, lady's, cylinder, mahogany, tambour top, fitted int., slide-out writing surface, over two drawers, lyre base, 30" h writing surface, 35-1/2" w, 20" d, 38" h .. **3,000.00**

Renaissance Revival, American, fall front, turned spindle cresting, paneled fall front and fitted interior, angular trestle base, 26-1/2" w, 16" d, 53" h **850.00**

Queen Anne, two pieces, bombe slant front, burlwood veneer, pine and oak secondary woods, four-drawer compartment interior, leather writing surface, four-drawer base, arched skirt, Queen Ann legs, early 19th C, labels affixed "Westing, Evans & Egmore, Cabinetmakers, Upholsterers, Philadelphia, 24-1/2" w, 15-1/4" d, 28" writing height, 37" h, veneer splitting and chipping, **$2,875**.

Photo courtesy of Alderfer Auction Co.

Rococo-style, Italian, painted, slant-lid, fitted interior, serpentine case fitted with three conforming drawers, flared bracket feet, 35" w, 17" d, 40-1/2" h **4,465.00**

School master's, Pennsylvania, early 19th C, walnut, interior drawers and compartments, molded lid, dovetailed skirt drawer, tapered legs, 34-1/2" w, 24" d, 37-1/2" h **4,400.00**

Sheraton

American, stand-up, walnut, slant front, four graduated drawers, turned feet, ivory escutcheons, Sandwich glass pulls, flanked by paint dec columns, simply fitted int. with secret drawers, one pull replaced, repair to lid, hinges replaced, int. refitted, 35" h writing surface, 35" w, 43" h **1,200.00**

Country, slant lid, cherry, pine and poplar secondary wood, two dovetailed drawers behind slant lid, two large compartments, three dovetailed drawers in base, turned feet, orig oval brasses with emb pineapple in basket design, refinished, alternations, restored break on one back leg, 37" w, 19-1/4" d, 38-1/2" h **990.00**

Victorian

Bamboo, lacquered rect top with leather inset over long drawer and four vertical drawers, 35" w, 20" d, 29" h **720.00**

Walnut, hinged rect top, fitted int., single frieze drawer, turned legs, 28" w, 20-1/4" d, 33" h **400.00**

William and Mary, attributed to CT, early 18th C, tulipwood and oak, fall-front lid with raised panel, int. of four compartments, three drawers, well with sliding closure, double arched molded front, base with long drawer, four turned legs, joined by valanced skirt, shaped flat cross stretchers, turned feet, replaced brasses, old refinish, minor imperfections, 24-3/4" w, 15" d, 42-1/2" h **17,250.00**

William and Mary-style, American, 20th C, oak, seven dovetailed drawers, applied moldings, molded edge top, brass tear drop pulls, old finish, turned legs and stretchers, one piece of molding missing from drawer, 27-3/4" x 59" x 31" h **500.00**

Dry sink, PA, c1840, dovetailed well, single door, continuous sides form feet, 47" w, 20" d, 34-1/2" h, refinished, $750.

Photo courtesy of Alderfer Auction Co.

Dry sinks

Curly maple, rect well, work surface on right with small drawer, two poplar wood cupboard doors, short bracket feet, hardwood edge stripes, minor repairs, refinished, 55" w, 34-1/2" h **2,400.00**

Grain painted, New England, rect well with tin lining, rounded splashboard, two small drawers, two cupboard doors, shelf int., bracket feet, brown and yellow pine graining, 49" w, 38" h **900.00**

Dry sink, Pennsylvania, painted, mixed woods, full length hinged lid, two drawers over two scrolled cupboard doors, white porcelain knobs, original cast iron latches, lid raised, **$375**.

Photo courtesy of Dotta Auction Co., Inc.

Painted, attributed to PA, early 19th C, rect overhanging top, well, cut-out ends with exposed tenons, joined by medial shield fitted with later copper insert, painted red, 44-3/4" w, 18-1/2" d, 32" h **2,645.00**

Pine, three drawers on high back, sink with back-curved sides, paneled doors opening to self, stile feet, c1900, 43" w, 18-1/2" d, 33-1/2" h **900.00**

Pine and poplar, galleried well, one small dovetailed drawer, two paneled doors, cut-out feet, 46" w, 18-1/4" d, 37-3/4" h **600.00**

Poplar, painted, rect well above pair of paneled cupboard doors, scroll-cut apron continuing to low bracket feet, cast iron thumb latch replaced, layers of old worn green paint, 39-1/2" w, 16-13/4" d, 33" h **650.00**

Hall trees and hat racks

Bench

Gothic Revival, oak, composed of some antique elements, tall backrest inset with foliate and figural panels, lift seat and foliate carved lower panels, 34" w, 73" h **690.00**

Gothic-style, late 19th C, oak, tall backrest fitted with three figural, foliate, and seraph carved panels, lift seat, chip-carved sq legs, 60" w, 66-1/2" h **1,855.00**

Dry sink, Country, 19th C, pine, dovetailed well top, two drawers over pair of cupboard doors, straight bracket feet, **$775**.

Photo courtesy of Wiederseim Associates, Inc.

Chair

Arts & Crafts, Limbert, #79, hall chair, unique "bicycle" shape, orig leather back and shaped seat over slab leg with keyed construction, orig finish, branded and numbered, orig leather has been reinforced, 19" w, 20" d, 42" h **1,100.00**

Cast iron, Union Army motif, patch boxes on base, belt with buckle carved for cane holder, swords and rifles forming back, topped with Union shield, piece found in PA GAR hall **10,500.00**

William IV, octagonal scroll worked backrest, center painted crest, shaped seat, turned tapering legs, peg feet **475.00**

Hall rack

Art Nouveau, France, early 20th C, mahogany, flaring mahogany panel, five brass curved coat hooks centered by mirror, umbrella stand below, 47" w, 85" h... **1,200.00**

Arts & Crafts, attributed to Charles Rohls, early 20th C, oak, tall sq shaft, two tiers of four wooden hooks, each near the top, half buttresses running up from the cross base on all four sides, sq wafer feet, 64" h **1,100.00**

Bavarian, late 19th/early 20th C, figural carved wood, mountain goat standing before tree branches, base carved with ferns and flowerheads, ovoid umbrella well **2,250.00**

Colonial Revival, Baroque-style, American, 1910, cherry, shell carved crest over cartouche and griffin carved panel back, lift seat, high arms, mask carved base, paw feet, 39-1/2" w, 21-1/2" d, 51" h **700.00**

Reformed Gothic, American, mahogany, angular superstructure with mirror and pegs, cane well, circular legs, 25" w, 13" d, 84" h **750.00**

Renaissance Revival, American, walnut and part ebonized, upper section with arched cornice, rect mirror plate, turned hat pegs; lower section with marble top, curved cane supports, medial drawer, circular fluted legs, base fitted with shell-form cast iron pans, 51" w, 16" d, 89" h **3,200.00**

Victorian, American, burl walnut, ball finials above paneled and shaped cornice, rect mirror flanked by turned garment holders, marble top drawer supported by turned legs, shaped base, painted metal plant holders, 29" w, 14" d, 93" h **1,400.00**

Hat rack

Arts & Crafts, wrought steel, hat and coat style, our sided, double hooks and spindles, unmarked, 21" w, 21" d, 75" h **865.00**

International Movement, Charles Eames, "Hang-It-All," manufactured by Tigrett Enterprises, c1953, white enameled metal frame, multicolored wooden balls, 20" w, 6" d, 16" h **800.00**

Windsor, American, pine, bamboo turned, six knob-like hooks, orig yellow varnish, black striping, 33-3/4" w **200.00**

Stand, Arts & Crafts, coat and umbrella type, wrought steel, cut-out apron, spindles, brass hooks, unmarked, 27" w, 10-1/2" d, 73" h **850.00**

Umbrella stand, Black Forest, Germany, early 20th C, carved walnut, figural bear, fierce expression, loose chain around neck, holding tray in raised paw, porcelain base liner, 48" h **5,750.00**

Mirror, round, beveled, design, **$150**.
Photo courtesy of Dotta Auction Co., Inc.

Mirrors

Adams-style, 20th C, oval frame, relief molded gesso, urn and feather crest, scrolled foliage and sways, restored split on crest, few chips, 23-1/2" w, 42" h **460.00**

Aesthetic Movement, America, c1880, overmantel, gilt, central cornice supported by two small columns over frieze dec with scene of snake attacking bird in tree, mirror plate highly dec with leaves, orig label of L. Utler, 47 Royal St., New Orleans, 64" w, 6" d, 84" h **3,600.00**

Art Deco, France, 1930, octagonal mirror in wrought iron frame, rose and leaf dec, 36" w, 24" h **250.00**

Arts & Crafts

Boston Society of Arts and Crafts, 1910, carved wood, rect, carved and gilded frame, ink mark, initials, orig paper label, 11-1/4" w, 18-1/2" h **700.00**

Limbert, oak, frame with geometric inlaid design over rect cane panel shoe-foot base, recoated orig frame, orig glass, 20" w, 8" d, 22" h **600.00**

Baroque, Continental, second quarter 18th C, giltwood, fruit filled cartouche form resting, mirrored borders with grapevines and scrolls, foliate carved pendant, 63" h . **5,750.00**

Biedermeier, c1830, walnut, ogee molded cresting, paneled sides, 26" w, 37" h **350.00**

Centennial, Chippendale-style, mahogany and mahogany veneer, pine secondary wood, broken arch crest with gilt eagle, gesso liners with orig gilding and rosettes, leaf vining down each side, refinished, restoration and touch up to eagle and areas of gilding, 26-1/4" w, 56-1/2" h **950.00**

Mirror, circular convex, gilt gesso frame, scrolling decorations, topped with spread wing eagle clutching arrows, c1920, 26" w, 40" h, **$650**.
Photo courtesy of Alderfer Auction Co.

Cheval, German, ebonized, swivel rect mirror, rounded ends, low sq mount, artist sgd, 70" h **425.00**

Chippendale

America, late 18th C, mahogany and gilt gesso, scrolled frame, molded gilt incised liner enclosing glass, old surface, 21-3/4" w, 44" h **3,100.00**

England or America, late 18th C, mahogany and parcel gilt, scrolled frame, molded and gilt incised liner, old refinish, replaced glass, 20-1/2" w, 36" h **500.00**

England, mid-18th C, walnut and parcel-gilt, gilt-gessoed carved phoenix on leafy branch above scrolled frame with applied gilt leafy floral and fruit devices, gilt incised liner framing beveled glass, restoration, 20-1/2" w, 44" h **6,465.00**

New England, late 18th C, mahogany and gilt gesso, scrolled frame centering gilt gesso eagle in crest above gilt incised molded liner, imperfections, 18-1/2" w, 40" h **500.00**

Pennsylvania, mahogany and gilt gesso, labeled John Elliot & Son, Philadelphia, 1804-1810, scrolled frame with pierced cresting centering phoenix above molded gilt incised liner, label affixed to backboard is last one used by the firm, imperfections, repairs, 19-1/2" w, 34" h **950.00**

Mirror, Centennial-style, mahogany, rectangular frame, beaded edge, curved top with applied ribbon tied foliage, **$115**.

Photo courtesy of Dotta Auction Co., Inc.

Chippendale-style

Cheval, late 19th C, carved mahogany, oval plate, four-legged base carved with foliage, claw and ball feet, 75" h............................ **635.00**

Table top, mid-18th C, carved wood, black lacquer, and polychrome florals, central top figure of Oriental man with umbrella, hinged prop on verso, suspension loop, 20" w, 29" h.......................... **1,150.00**

Classical

Dressing, America or England, 1810-20, carved mahogany and mahogany veneer, cylinder top opens to reveal four drawers, centering one door, ivory pulls, above single divided long drawer, restoration, 19" w, 10-5/8" d, 32" h........................ **1,610.00**

Girandole, America or England, 1810-20 gilt gesso, crest with eagle flanked by acanthus leaves, convex glass, ebonized molded liner with affixed candle branches, foliate and floral pendant, imperfections, 23" w, 35" h **5,175.00**

Overmantel, New England, c1820-40, painted and giltwood, rect mirror frame with sq corner blocks, applied floral bosses joined by vase and ring turned split baluster columns, molded black liner, old gilt surface, replaced mirror glass, surface imperfections, 46" w, 23" h **920.00**

Wall, New York, 1830s, carved and eglomise, entablature overhangs veneered frieze, reverse painted land and waterscape flanked by leaf carved split balusters, orig eglomise and mirror glass, old refinish, minor losses and crazing, 38" h.............. **460.00**

Courting, wooden frame, reverse painted glass inserts and crest with bird and flowers, orig mirror glass with worn silvering, penciled inscription on back with "restored 1914," touch-up to reverse painting, brass back corner braces, 10-7/8" w, 16-1/2" h **935.00**

Eastlake, walnut, carved crest, 29" w, 63" h..................... **575.00**

Edwardian, late 19th C, overmantel, boxwood marquetry inlaid, arched cresting inlaid with musical still life and scrolling vines, shaped mirror plate flanked by cross banded stiles, 60" w, 68" h...................... **900.00**

Empire, flame mahogany veneer over pine, scalloped crest with scrolled ends, inset oval panel at top, applied half turned pilasters, ogee base, worn silvering, glue repairs at ends of crest, old alligatored varnish finish, 21" w, 51" h **770.00**

Mirror, Federal, walnut and mahogany, brass rosettes, turned columns, two glasses, 15" w, 32" h, top glass replaced, **$250**.

Photo courtesy of Alderfer Auction Co.

Federal

America, two parts, orig gilding, black painted on applied half turnings, raised floral corner blocks, orig reverse painting with lady and child on recamier, repainted floral borders, touch up on panel, minor wear, 18-3/4" w, 39-3/4" h **550.00**

Architectural, two parts, pine, old alligatored white paint over orig gilding, stepped cornice with applied ball dec, molded pilasters on sides, applied corner blocks at bottom, reverse dec with ribbons, silver, and black leaves on white ground, edge damage, 15-1/4" w, 24-1/4" h **450.00**

Massachusetts, c1820, gilt gesso and wood, molded cornice with applied spheres above reverse painted tablet showing sea battle, glass below flanked by rope twist molded pilasters, imperfections, 19" w, 32-1/2" **1,300.00**

Massachusetts, c1875-20, gilt gesso and wood, molded cornice with applied spheres above reverse painted and stenciled tablet showing a cottage and bridge arching a brook, glass flanked by rope twist molded pilasters, minor imperfections, 17" w, 28-1/4" h **600.00**

Massachusetts, early 19th C, giltwood and eglomise, turned engaged columns enclose reverse-painted tablet showing woman seated on red and gold neoclassical stool, holding parrot, flanked by red and gold drapery above a mirrored glass, old regilding, replaced mirror glass, 15-3/4" w, 32" h **500.00**

New England, c1800, mahogany, scrolled frame, rect mitered liner with inlaid contrasting stringing, refinished, 20-3/4" w, 38" h **1,000.00**

New England, c1820-25, mahogany and mahogany veneer, molded cornice above sq and reeded capitals, half engraved vase and ring-turned, acanthus leaf, diamond faceted columns on sq plinths, refinished, replaced glass, imperfections, 18-1/2" w, 40-1/2" h **355.00**

New York City, c1780-1800, mahogany, swan's neck crest, carved urn, bouquet-type finial with carved florets on wires, veneered frame flanked by wire-bound wood vine work pendants, scrolled apron, heavily reworked, refinished, gold paint, 21-1/2" w, 53" h **675.00**

Tabernacle, attributed to New York or Albany, 1795-1810, gilt gesso, molded cornice with pendant spherules over frieze with applied sunflower and wheat sheaf device, flanked by checkered panels over two-part looking glass, flanked by applied double half columns, gilt surface, replaced glass tablet, 14" w, 30-1/2" h..................... **865.00**

Wall, giltwood, labeled "Parker and Clover Looking Glass and Picture Frame Makers 180 Fulton St. New York," molded cornice with applied spherules above eglomise table of girl in pasture landscape holding dove, mirror flanked by spiral carved pilasters, 13-3/4" w, 29-1/8" h................... **2,875.00**

Federal, late, attributed to New England, c1820-30, gilt gesso, molded cornice with acorn form drops over frieze centering carved leaf motif flanked by vine and leaf applied devices, two-part mirror glass with grape and leaf designs, flanked by vase, ring, and spiral turned split balusters, old gilt surface, minor imperfections, including replaced mirror glass, 19" w, 37" h............................... **700.00**

Hall, mirror, commemorative, embossed tin, Our Boys of '98, The Maine, Dewey and Schley, hat hooks and mirror, **$295**.

Photo courtesy of Dotta Auction Co., Inc.

Federal-style, late 19th or early 20th C, convex, eagle crest, worn gilding, ebonized liner, eagle with small chain, ball in beak, restorations to wings, 16-1/2" w, 24-1/2" h......... **700.00**

Folk Art, America, 1902, possibly prisoner made, pine, carved hearts, stars, and various numerals and patterns, year

Mirror, overmantel, gilt frame with central urn, three panels, each with floral and swag cutting, and brass rosettes, **$175**.

Photo courtesy of Dotta Auction Co., Inc.

"1902," minor wear, 29-1/2" x 29-7/8"......................... **1,410.00**

George II-style, English, 19th C, carved gesso and giltwood, C-scroll and shell carved arched crest, serpentine and rect mirror plate, scrolled foliate corner pendants, C-scroll, shell, and acanthus carved shaped apron, 29" w, 65-1/2" h **1,800.00**

Mirror, George III, England, late 18th C, hall, giltwood and verre eglomise, bearing paper label for "J. & W. Vokins, Looking Glass and Picture Frame Manufacturers," London, rectangular mirror plate flanked by fluted columns, topped by row of spherules, peaked pediment topped by pineapple finial hung with pair of spherules on chains, centered by verre eglomise panel of musical instrument vignette on green ground, losses, 45" h, **$1,175**.

Photo courtesy of Skinner, Inc.

George III, late 18th C, giltwood, crest centered by hoho bird over C-scrolls, flanked by swag-draped urns, frame sides with further C-scrolls, 26-1/2" w, 52" h..... **3,100.00**

Hepplewhite, shaving, mahogany, inlay, two dovetailed drawers, feet, posts, and mirror are old replacements, 17-3/4" h **225.00**

Louis XV-style, pier, 19th C, carved giltwood, large rect mirror topped by crest carved with leafy scrolls and rocaille, marble-topped ovolo 19-1/4" h shelf, flat leaf edge, gilt metal brackets, reeded scrolls with anthemion and female mask terminals, 33" w, 73" h **1,725.00**

Neoclassical, Continental 19th C, Trumeau, painted gray, parcel gilt, top with gilt molding over gilt gesso figure of reclining goddess flanked by urns, over rect two-part mirror plate in gilt floral and leaftip surround, 40" x 98" **3,820.00**

Neoclassical-style, 20th C, pier, gilt wood, crest with roundel with urn issuing foliage flanked by cornucopias, beveled rect plate within surround decorated with garlands of flowers, corners with Greek key motif, 35" w, 68" h **1,200.00**

Painted, attributed to the work of Nehemiah Partridge, eastern Massachusetts, first quarter 18th C, rect molded frame painted red, intersecting linear designs in black, wear, 7-7/8" w, 9-1/4" h **4,700.00**

Queen Anne
American, walnut and pine, old reddish brown paint, beveled glass, orig hand planed backboard, scrolled crest with replacements and veneer, 12-1/4" w, 23" h **650.00**

Scroll, mahogany, old finish, molded frame, detailed scrolled crest, minor split in bottom edge of frame, 9" w, 16-1/4" h **550.00**
Walnut, scrolled crest above molded rect frame enclosing beveled mirror glass, backboard inscribed "Capt S Cobb," refinished, glass resilvered, 10-1/2" w, 22-1/2" h **1,175.00**

Mirror, Queen Anne style, early 20th C, black painted Chinoiserie decoration, domed crest painted with two figures, foliates, pagoda, and pair of hoho birds, similarly painted raised frame, hinged backing, 34" h, **$825**.

Photo courtesy of Skinner, Inc.

Renaissance Revival, American
Hall, parcel gilt walnut, openwork lappet and floral cresting, shaped plate, frame carved with leaftips, pegs and incised lines, 35" w, 75" h **950.00**
Over mantel, parcel gilt walnut, arched mirror plate, carved in high relief with lappets, roundels and architectural motifs, 62" w, 60" h........................... **750.00**
Pier, walnut and parcel gilt, molded cornice carved with sawtooth and paterae, long mirror plate flanked by columns, low marble top, turned legs, 27" w, 12" d, 100" h......................... **500.00**
Wall, walnut and parcel gilt, sawtooth and spindle cresting, shaped plate and fluted pilasters, 45" w, 31" h **425.00**

Rococo
Continental, third quarter 18th C, giltwood, shaped mirror plate, arched top, frame carved with foliage and C-scrolls, 28" w, 54" h .. **4,025.00**

Northern Europe, late 18th C, walnut and gilt gesso, shaped molded cresting with foliate devices enclosing reverse painted tablet showing man in powdered wig above rect molded walnut veneered gilt-lined frame on shaped pierced bracket, imperfections, 14" w, 31" h **950.00**
Rococo-style, c19th C, gilt wood, cartouche form, surround carved with scrolls hung with icicles, plate replaced, possibly re-gilt, 47" h **1,315.00**
Sheraton, mahogany, spiral turned split columns and bottom rail, inlaid panels of mahogany, rosewood, and cherry, architectural top cornice, split mirror, 24-1/2" w, 47" h **300.00**
Victorian, Rococo Revival, 19th C, giltwood, shaped mirror plate, frame with foliate canopy cresting and mirrored borders, elaborately carved allover in high relief with birds, icicles, columns, and foliage, 35" w, 64" h **1,900.00**

Rocker, Heywood Wakefield, wicker, original certificate, **$350**.

Photo courtesy of Dotta Auction Co., Inc.

Rockers

Art Nouveau, American, c1900, oak, fumed finish, carved arms, saddle seat, three splats with floral-type capitals **400.00**
Arts & Crafts
American, oak, four vertical back slats, corbel supports under arms, recovered orig spring cushion, orig finish, 29" w, 34" d, 36" h **200.00**
Limbert, #580, oak, T-back design, orig recovered drop-

in cushion, recent finish, branded, 24" w, 29" d, 34" h **150.00**
Plail, oak, slatted barrel back, D-shaped recovered seat, refinished, unsigned, 26" w, 28" d, 31" h **2,500.00**
Stickley Brothers, oak, six vertical back slats, recovered orig spring cushion, worn orig finish, branded, 25" w, 27" d, 35" h........................... **220.00**
Bentwood, rustic, hickory and pine, old finish, repairs, 15-3/4" h seat, 37-1/2" h back........ **225.00**
Boston, American, 19th C, maple, spindle back **200.00**
Colonial Revival, Windsor-style, Colonial Furniture Co., Grand Rapids, MI, comb back, birch, mahogany finish, turned legs, 21" w, 17" d, 27-1/2" h **200.00**

Rocker, Eastlake style, platform type, reupholstered padded backrest, seat, and head rest, turned spindles, **$250**.

Photo courtesy of Joseph P. Smalley, Jr.

Rocker, International Movement, Charles Eames for Zenith, yellow fiberglass, rope edge, black wire cat's cradle base, birch runners, Zenith label, one re-glued shock mount, some staining to seat, 27-1/4" x 25" x 27", **$865**.

Photo courtesy of David Rago Auctions, Inc.

Decorated

America, orig black over red dec, gold stenciled urn of fruit and flowers on crest, shaped seal, scrolled arms, well turned legs, repaired damage to arms, 15" h seat, 40" h **220.00**

Pennsylvania, dark green, gold foliate on crest, slats, and seat, traces of red border with yellow line detail, turned legs, shaped medallion stretcher, scrolled arms, repaired break in one arm, 17" h seat, 42" h **220.00**

International Movement,

Charles Eames, manufactured by Herman Miller, salmon fiberglass zenith shell, rope edge, black wire struts, birch runners, c1950, 25" w, 27" d, 27" h **1,400.00**

Ladderback,

Pennsylvania, orig rush seat, turned finials, block and turned arm supports, painted green, 15" h seat, 39-1/2" h back **315.00**

Rocker, Victorian, carved mahogany frame with scrolls and foliage, rose motif needlepoint with maroon background, padded arms, matching footrest, **$350**.

Photo courtesy of Joseph P. Smalley, Jr.

Rocker, Victorian, carved face on curved back crest rail, shaped back splat, turned spindles, arms, and stretchers, **$135**.

Photo courtesy of Dotta Auction Co., Inc.

Wicker, painted white, sq back, basket weave pattern over openwork back, rect armrests with wrapped braces, openwork sides, braided edge on basketweave seat and skirt, X-form stretcher, 32" w, 33" h **200.00**

Windsor

American, c1850, grain painted, stencil dec, scrolled crest, tail spindle back, shaped seat, bamboo turned legs, box stretcher **450.00**
New England, early 19th C, rect splat stencil dec with grapevines highlighted in freehand yellow fancy work above the raked spindles and stiles, scrolled arms, shaped seat, bamboo-turned legs on rockers, all-over burnt-sienna and black dec, 15" h seat, 43" h........................ **1,300.00**
Pennsylvania, bamboo turnings, cheese cutter rockers, yellow ground paint with smoke dec, red highlights, floral and strawberry dec crest, 17" h seat, 30-1/2" h.......... **3,300.00**

Secretaries

Biedermeier-style, inlaid walnut, molded rect top, four drawers, top drawer with fall front, fitted int. with ebonized writing-surface, molded block feet, 50-1/4" w, 23-3/4" d, 35-1/2" h........................ **1,000.00**
Centennial, inlay mahogany, two parts: top with four drawers over six cubbyholes center, line inlay door opening to reveal two cubbyholes and large drawer,

sliding tambour doors flanked by inlay panels with simulated columns; lower: fold-over line inlay lid, two drawers with line inlay, diamond inlay on legs, some lifting to veneer, replaced cloth writing surface, 37-1/4" w, 19-3/4" d, 46" h **800.00**

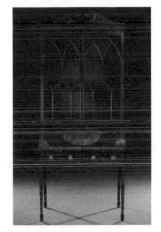

Secretary, Edwardian, two sections, upper section: fan-pierced broken pediment above ribbon-tied foliate spray, two glazed doors with gothic arch mullions, adjustable shelved interior; base with cylinder front, fitted interior of small drawers and pigeon holes, adjustable tooled-leather writing slope, cylinder front inlaid with tassel-and-bead draped urn suspended from ribbon-tied chain within satinwood inlaid oval reserve flanked by foliate-inlaid spandrels, two small drawers inlaid with laurel swags, lion's head circular pulls, square tapering bellflower inlay base, **$7,500**.

Photo courtesy of Sloans & Kenyon Auctions.

Chippendale

Connecticut, two pcs, maple and curly maple, pr of panel doors over fall front, fitted int., four drawers, orig pierced brass drop bail hardware **45,000.00**
Maryland, attributed to, late 18th C, inlaid walnut, top with molded and pierced swan's-neck cresting with inlaid terminals centering a plinth with cross banded border and urn finial above cross banded frieze, two glazed doors enclosing adjustable shelves, candle slides below on base with fall front opening, central prospect door flanked by string-inlaid document boxes, three drawers and four valanced compartments, case of four cockbeaded graduated drawers, ogee bracket feet,

replaced brasses, refinished, restoration, 40" w, 22" d, 95" h **7,700.00**

Massachusetts, c1770-90, carved mahogany, scrolled and molded pediment above tympanum with projecting shell and arched raised panel doors flanked by fluted pilasters, candle slides, raised panel slant lid with blocked facade, molded conforming base, bracket feet, int. of upper bookcase divided into open compartments above four small drawers, int. of lower case with two fan-carved blocked drawers, similar prospect door, small blocked and plain drawers, scrolled compartment dividers, replaced brasses, old finish, restored, 39" w, 22" d, 93-1/2" h **19,550.00**

New England, late 18th C, block front, two pieces, upper section: flame finial, two blind doors, cyma-carved panels, various-sized open compartments on int., lower section with fur front drawers, plain slant front, fitted int., some later replacements, 91" h **38,180.00**

Rhode Island, Providence area, 1765-85, carved cherry, scrolled molded pediment flanks central plinth and finial above applied shell carving atop central fluted and stop-fluted column flanked by raised panel doors, shelved int. enclosed by quarter-engaged fluted and stop-fluted columns, lower case of two stepped int, of serpentine end-blocked drawers with serpentine dividers, valanced compartments, central document drawers with applied columns, above four graduated thumb-molded drawers flanked by fluted and stop-fluted engaged quarter-columns, shaped bracket feet ending in platforms, old surface, some original brasses, presumed owners' names scratched on underside of case: "Abner Lampson, 1743-1797 and Ward Lampson, 1773-1850, Washington N.H." imperfections, 38-1/4" w, 21" d, 80" h **55,815.00**

Classical, Boston, 1820-25, secretaire a'abattant, carved mahogany and mahogany veneer, marble top above cove molding, mahogany veneer facade flanked by veneered columns topped by Corinthian capitals, terminating in ebonized ball feet, recessed panel sides, fall front opens to desk int. over two cupboard doors, old refinish, 35" w, 17-1/2" d, 57-1/2" h **16,100.00**

Colonial Revival, Colonial Desk Co., Rockford, IL, c1930, mahogany, broken arch pediment, center finial, two glazed mullioned doors, fluted columns, center prospect with acanthus carving flanked by columns, four graduated drawers, brass eagle, carved claw and ball feet, 41" w, 21" d, 87" h **1,000.00**

Eastlake, American, burl walnut and mahogany, shaped cornice, pair of glazed cabinet doors, cylinder front, writing surface, two doors in base, shaped apron, 27" w, 22" d, 66" h **1,500.00**

Empire, America, c1840, mahogany veneer, fall-front, dovetailed construction, two sections, top with two four-light cathedral glass doors, base with fall-front deck, five-drawer int., over three drawers flanked by curved columns, turned feet, 41-1/2" w, 20" d, 7' 4" h **1,425.00**

Empire-style, late 19th C, gilt bronze mounted mahogany, rect top, fall front with fitted int., over pr of recessed cupboard doors, flanked by columns, paw feet, 44-1/4" w, 23-1/2" d, 49-1/4" h **1,955.00**

Federal
Massachusetts, Boston or North Shore, early 19th, mahogany inlaid, top section: central panel of bird's eye maple with cross banded mahogany veneer border and stringing joined to the plinths by a curving gallery above flat molded cornice, glazed beaded doors with Gothic arches and bird's eye maple panels and mahogany cross-banding and stringing enclosing shelves, compartments, and drawers; lower: projecting section with fold-out surface inlaid with oval bird's eye maple panel set in mitered rect with cross

banded border and cock-beaded case, two drawers veneered with bird's eye maple panels bordered by mahogany cross-banding and stringing, flanked by inlaid panels continuing to sq double tapered legs, lower edge of case and leg cuffs with lunette inlaid banding, old finish, replaced brasses, imperfections, 41" w, 21-3/4" d, 74-1/2" h .. **9,775.00**

Massachusetts, coastal southern, c1816, inscribed "Wood" in chalk, mahogany, three pcs, molded cornice with inlaid dentiling above diamond inlaid frieze over two paneled cupboard doors with quarter-fan inlays opening to eight-compartment int., center case with tambour doors centering oval veneered prospect door, flanked by inlaid and reeded applied pilasters, valanced compartments, prospect door opens to single valanced compartment with drawer below, lower case with string inlaid fold-out writing surface, similarly inlaid drawers flanked by stiles, panel inlays, skirt, inlaid dentiling above legs with inlaid bellflowers, line inlay and inlaid cuffs, early surface, replaced pulls, minor veneer loss, 40" w, 20-1/2" d, 81-3/4" h **34,500.00**

New Hampshire, paint decoration, two pieces, pine, old alligatored reddish-brown and yellow dec over earlier red, chamfered corners on dovetailed cases, molded cove cornice, tree dec on two paneled doors, slant front with tree dec, int. with 13 dovetailed drawers with central prospect door, four dovetailed drawers in base with applied beading, slightly shaped bracket feet with applied base molding, replaced wooden pulls, replaced H hinges, touch-up to top doors **7,425.00**

George III, last quarter 18th C Mahogany, molded cornice, two glazed doors, fitted interior with three shelves, rect molded base with pull out secretary drawer, two short and two long graduated drawers, 48" w, 18" d, 98" h **9,440.00**

Mahogany, upper section with two mullioned and glazed doors; lower section fitted with secretary drawer over three long drawers, bracket feet
.... **1,645.00**

Secretary, Louis XVI style, Provincial, slant front, arched ogee cornice above paneled cupboard doors, fitted interior, two cupboard doors, short scroll legs, 44" w, 19" d, 103-1/2" h, **$3,200**.
Photo courtesy of Sloans & Kenyon Auctions.

George III/Early Federal, America, third quarter 18th C, mahogany, two sections, upper: shaped architectural pediment with gilt-metal ball and spike finials, cavetto cornice over cross banded frieze, chequer-banding, front with pair of 13-pane astragal doors, two adjustable shelves, base: outset fall-front opening, fitted int., four graduated cock-beaded oxbow-fronted drawers, conforming molded plinth base, molded and spurred bracket feet, 44-1/4" w, 24-1/4" d, 93-1/2" h **17,000.00**
Hepplewhite, North Shore, MA, mahogany, bookcase upper section, slant front desk
.... **6,250.00**
International Movement, Gilbert Rhode, manufactured by Herman Miller, upper bookcase with drop front desk over four doors, carved wooden pulls in burl and paldio veneers, refinished, c1940, 66" w, 15" d, 72" h **2,600.00**
Louis XV-style, rosewood, bombe form, inset shaped white marble top, fall front, fitted interior, above four aligned

Settee, PA, c1830, pine and poplar, half spindle, two board seat, eight legs, green painted finish with floral decoration, 72" l, 21" d, 15-1/2" h seat, 32" h, repainted, redecorated, **$400**; child's rocker on top with bird and berry motif paint decoration on black ground, red arms, 12" w, 22-1/2" h, repainted, **$150**.

drawers, cabriole legs with gilt metal paw feet, 37" w, 19" d, 66-3/4" h **2,125.00**
Renaissance Revival, American, c1865, walnut, two sections, upper: bookcase section, S-curved pediment with center applied grapes and foliage carving, two arched and molded glazed doors, shelved int., three small drawers with applied grapes and foliage carved pulls; lower: fold-out writing surface, two short drawers over two long drawers with oval molding and applied grapes and foliage carved pulls, matching ornamentation on skirt, 48" w, 21" d, 95" h **5,000.00**
Sheraton, New England, mahogany and mahogany flame veneer, cove molded cornice, three drawers across top with oval brasses, two paneled doors in top with fine flame veneer, three interior drawers, four pigeon holes with adjustable shelf, three dovetailed drawers with applied beading, figured book page veneer, reeded legs with ring turnings and molded surround at base of case, refinished, few repaired veneer splits, pierced repairs, stains in bottom, replaced brasses, 42" w, 20" d, 50-1/2" h............. **1,760.00**
Victorian, two pieces, walnut, top: crown molding cornice, two glazed doors with burl and walnut buttons; base: burl cylinder roll with two-drawer walnut int., pigeon holes, slide-out writing surface, base: three long drawers with burl dec,

tear drop pulls, refinished, 40" w, 23" d, 86" h.......................... **1,850.00**
William III, English, c1700-10, burl walnut veneer, two sections, recessed upper with double-domical crest, pair of domically crested doors mounted with beveled glass mirror panels of conforming upper outline, plain int. of three adjustable wood shelves above pr of candle slides; lower section with canted front, hinged fall-front writing board, shaped desk int. with valanced central cubby hole between two pairs of valanced narrow cubby holes over two shaped drawers each, horizontal sliding door, flanked by two-tier side units with single drawer bases, straight front of two graduated narrow drawers over two graduated wide drawers, highly figured burl on drawers match writing board and doors, engraved period brasses, later short straight bracket feet, minor veneer damage, 40" w, 23-1/2" d, 84" h **18,750.00**

Settees

Art Deco, attributed to Warren McArthur, c1930, tubular aluminum frame, sheet aluminum seat and back supports, removable vinyl cushions, 68" l.............. **5,750.00**
Arts & Crafts
   Limbert, #939, oak, 11 back slats, corbels under arm, recovered orig drop-in cushion, branded, refinished, 75" w, 27" d, 40" h...... **800.00**

Stickley, Gustav, No. 222, tapering posts, tightly spaced canted slats to back and sides, leather upholstered drop-in seat, fine orig finish, red decal, minor veneer chips, 36" x 80" x 32"
.... **11,500.00**

Stickley, L. & J. G., oak, drop-arm form, 12 vertical slats to back and drop-in orig spring cushion, recovered in brown leather, refinished, unsigned, 65" w, 25" d, 36" h **1,800.00**

Unknown America maker, 20th C, even arm, oak, crest rail over nine wide vertical slats, three on each side, joined by sq vertical posts, medium brown finish, replaced seat, joint separation, 65" w, 25-3/4" d, 32" h **2,650.00**

Biedermeier-style, beechwood, curved open back, three vasiform splats, out-curved arms, caned seat raised on six sq-section sabre legs **650.00**

Classical, American, c1850, mahogany, serpentine front, carved crest, transitional rococo design elements, 82" l..... **600.00**

Colonial Revival, William and Mary style, American, c1930, loose cushions, turned baluster legs and stretcher, 48" l .. **750.00**

Settee, Federal style, carved mahogany, downcurving reeded arms, reeded tapering legs ending in peg feet, 60-1/2" l, **$850+**.

Photo courtesy of Sloans & Kenyon Auctions.

Eastlake-style, Confidant, walnut, upholstered scrolling backs with horizontal pierced splats, upholstered seats, tapering square-section legs, 26" w, 26" d, 46" h **600.00**

Empire-style, late 19th/early 20th C

Gilt bronze mounted mahogany, settee, pair of side chairs, each with foliate and figural mounts, 80" l settee,

price for three pieces
.... **1,725.00**

Mahogany, two seats, curved backs, each armrest ending on ram's head, hoof-foot feet
.... **2,100.00**

Settee, Federal, Baltimore, c1800, attributed to Renshaw, triple chairback, downward sloping arms with urn turned supports, bowfront seat supported by turned legs, original overall gilt decoration on black painted ground, 48" l, 18-1/2" w, 34" h, **$5,750**.

Photo courtesy of Pook & Pook.

French Restauration, New York City, c1840, rosewood, arched upholstered back, scrolled arms outlined in satinwood terminating in volutes, rect seat frame with similar inlay, bracket feet, 80" l, 27" d, 33-1/2" h............. **1,200.00**

George II, mahogany, serpentine crest over upholstered back and seat, round reeded, tapering legs
.... **1,500.00**

George III, early 19th C, black lacquer and faux bamboo, settee, pair of arm chairs, price for three pieces............ **1,265.00**

Gothic Revival, American, c1850, carved walnut, shaped crest rail surmounted by center carved finial, stiles with arched recessed panel and similarly carved finials, upholstered back and seat, open arms with padded armrests and scrolled handholds, carved seat rail, ring turned legs, ball feet, 67-1/2" w, 23-1/2" d, 49-3/4" h **800.00**

Louis XVI-style, third quarter 19th C, gilt bronze mounted ebonized maple, Leon Marcotte, New York City, c1860, 55-1/2" l, 25" d, 41-1/2" h............. **2,185.00**

Queen Anne-style, inlaid back flanked by shepherd's crook arms, cabriole legs **2,250.00**

Renaissance Revival, America, c1875, carved walnut, triple back, each having carved crest and ebonized plaque inlaid with

musical instruments, red floral damask upholstery **1,200.00**

Rococo Revival

Attributed to John Henry Belter, c1885, 65" l settee, pair of lady's chairs, pair of side chairs, each with laminated rose and foliate carved cresting, grapevine openwork sides, cabriole legs, price for three pieces.......... **14,375.00**

Attributed to J. & J. Meeks, rosewood, laminated curved backs, Stanton Hall pattern, rose crest in scrolled foliage and vintage, tufted gold velvet brocade reupholstery, age cracks and some edge damage, 65-1/2" l **5,500.00**

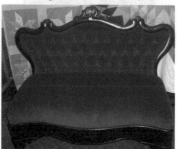

Settee, Victorian, c1880, shell carved crest at back and skirt, tufted back, serpentine front, bracket feet, reupholstered in red velvet, 48" w, 20" d, 15" h seat, 34" h, **$450**.

Photo courtesy of Alderfer Auction Co.

Victorian, carved rosewood, c1870, shaped and padded back, two arched end sections joined by dipped section, each with pierced foliate crest, over upholstered serpentine front seat, flanked by scroll arms, conforming rail continue to cabriole legs, frame leaf carved........................ **850.00**

Wicker, tightly woven rect back, inverted triangle-dec, tightly woven arms, rect seat with woven diamond herringbone pattern, continuous braided edging from crest to front legs, turned spindle apron, 43" w, 36" h................................ **500.00**

Windsor, New England, early 19th C, birdcage, maple, ash, and hickory, bamboo turned birdcage crest over 27 turned spindles flanked by stiles joining bamboo-turned arms and supports over bench seat, eight bamboo-turned legs joined by stretchers, old refinish, imperfections, 72" l, 14-1/2" h seat, 31-1/2" h............. **2,415.00**

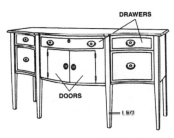

Typical Parts of a Sideboard

Sideboards

Art Deco, France, c1928, walnut and burl book-matched veneer, Bakelite cabinet doors and drawer pulls, 76" l, 19-1/2" d, 50-5/8" h **900.00**

Art Nouveau, Louis Majorelle, 1900, oak and mahogany, rect, bowed front, inset marble top, tow long drawers, undulating brass pulls cast with sheaves of wheat, tow cupboard doors with large applied brass sheaves of wheat and undulating leaves, molded apron, four lug feet, 65" w, 39-1/8" h **6,000.00**

Sideboard, Arts & Crafts, Gustav Stickley, No. 814, plate rack, two cabinet doors with strap hardware, three small drawers over linen drawer, red decal inside drawer, paper label on back, refinished, 56" l, 22" d, 48" h, **$3,750**.

Photo courtesy of David Rago Auctions, Inc.

Arts & Crafts

English, attributed to, with two "V" backsplashes, two drawers with ring pulls, bottom shelf, casters, orig finish, marked "S79FUM90," 42" l, 20" d, 45-1/4" h **1,150.00**

Limbert, Charles P., Grand Rapids, MI, c1910, oak, oblong top, mirrored back above case, three short drawers flanked by paneled cupboard doors over long drawer, cooper pulls and strap hinges, sq legs,

chamfered tenons, branded mark, 49-1/2" w, 53-1/2" h **900.00**

Stickley Brothers, backsplash, single drawer with hammered brass hardware, lower shelf, good orig finish, branded "Stickley Brothers," stenciled "B735," light edge wear, 36" l, 19" d, 37" h **2,185.00**

Stickley Brothers, paneled plate rack, four drawers, three panel doors with hammered brass hardware, good orig finish, branded "Stickley Brothers," stenciled "8833," wear to copper patina on iron hardware **4,025.00**

Stickley, Gustav, model no. 967, gallery top over two short drawers and long drawer, two cupboard doors below, iron strap hinges and door pulls, red decal, 1902, imperfections, 59-3/4" w, 23-3/4" w, 43-3/4" h **32,300.00**

Stickley, L. & J.G., Fayetteville, New York, c1916, oak, plate rail on rect top, three central drawers flanked by two cabinet doors, over single long drawer, branded mark, 47" w, 19-3/4" d, 44" h **5,300.00**

Centennial, Chippendale-style, America, late 19th C, mahogany, block front with shell carving, four drawers, front cabinet doors, gadrooned apron, cabriole legs, claw and ball feet, 68" w, 24" d, 40" h **950.00**

Classical

Mid Atlantic States, 1840-45, carved mahogany and cherry veneer, rect top over mahogany veneered drawer, two recessed panel doors opening to one shelf int., flanked by veneered scrolled supports, veneered base, old refinish, hardware changes, splashboard missing, 40" w, 18-3/4" d, 40-1/8" h .. **2,550.00**

New York, 1830s, carved mahogany veneer, splashboard with molded edge and four spiral carved and turned columns, topped by urn-shaped finials, rect top overhands recessed paneled case, cock-beaded drawers and cupboards outlined with crass banded mahogany veneer, two top drawers with dividers above short drawers, bottle drawers flanked by end

recessed panel doors, left one with single shelf int., right one with two-shelf int., flanked by columnar leaf carved supports over frontal carved paw feet, rear feet are heavily turned and tapering, old refinish, imperfections, 60-1/4" w, 23-5/8" d, 56-3/4" h **2,760.00**

Empire

American, carved mahogany and figured veneers, break front, three drawers, four doors across base with inset gothic panels of figured veneer, well carved paw feet, orig brass hardware, old dark finish, 73-1/2" l, 23" d, 42" h **1,650.00**

French, late 19th C, gilt bronze mounted mahogany, shaped mottled green marble top above three frieze drawers decorated with palmettes, three cupboard doors decorated with mask in laurel surround and winged maidens, flanked by pilasters with sphinx head capitals, shaped base, gilt bronze feet; top bearing old paper label "BEDEL & CIE/LE GARDE MEUBLE PUBLIC," 71" w, 23" d, 40" h **8,400.00**

French, late 19th/early 20th C, gilt bronze-mounted mahogany, shaped mottled green marble top above three frieze drawers decorated with scrollwork and palmettes, three cupboard doors decorated with portrait medallion, cornucopias, and torches, flanked by pilasters with sphinx head capitals, shaped base, 78" w, 25" d, 40" h......................... **6,000.00**

Federal

Baltimore, Maryland, 1790-1810, mahogany inlaid, veneered top with ovolo corners and string inlay in outline, case of central drawer and four cupboard doors all embellished with veneered ovals outlined in banding and interspersed with maple veneered rectangles, sq tapering legs with stringing in outline and forming five graduated loops above cuff inlays, case with old surface, replaced brass, imperfections, 75-1/8" w, 25-1/2" d, 39-3/4" h **14,100.00**

Massachusetts, Boston, 1810-20, mahogany, maple, and rosewood veneer, two-tiered case, demilune superstructure, maple inlaid panels surrounded by cross banded rosewood veneer above cock-beaded end drawers, small central drawer flanked by end cupboards, six ring turned tapering legs, case with concentric turnings, reeding, cock beading, and scenic landscape jointed on underside of arched opening, old surface, replaced pulls, replaced leg, veneer loss, later landscape painting, 74-1/2" l, 24-1/2" d, 44-3/4" h **9,200.00**

Massachusetts or Rhode Island, early 19th C, mahogany, crossbanded, rect top with ovolo corners and reeded edge overhangs case of cockbeaded drawers and central cupboards flanked by turned columns continuing to reeding above ring-turned swelled legs, turned feet, refinished, restored, replaced legs, 42-3/4" w, 21-1/2" d, 41-1/4" h.................... **8,820.00**

Middle Atlantic States, c1790, attributed to, mahogany and cherry inlaid, overhanging top with canted corners and serpentine front, central cock-beaded door inlaid with cherry panel with quarter fan inlays and mahogany mitered border, cock-beaded wine drawer with three-drawer facade at one end, three cock-beaded graduated drawers on other, ends with cherry veneered panels, four sq inlaid tapering legs ending in molded spade feet, lower edge of case with molding, old finish, minor imperfections, 48-1/2" w, 21-5/8" d, 37" h **19,950.00**

New England, c1790, mahogany and mahogany veneer, overhanging top with shaped front, conforming case, central pullout surface, bowed cock-beaded drawers, two cupboard doors flanked by concave drawers and cupboard doors, six sq tapering legs, replaced brasses, old refinish, imperfections, 64" w, 20-1/8" d, 37-1/2" h **5,500.00**

Southern States, attributed to Francis Marion Kay 1816-87, cherry and other hardwoods, yellow pine secondary wood, replaced rest, three drawers over two doors, another drawer over prospect door at center, lower doors divided by half turned pilasters, six turned legs, one door is restored, hinges replaced, 60-1/4" w, 21-1/4" d, 49" h **3,410.00**

Virginia, 1790-1810, walnut and yellow pine, molded rect top, cock-beaded case with end drawers, right drawer visually divided into two drawers, left with two working drawers, central cupboard cock-beaded door, four square tapering legs, old brass pulls, old refinish, repairs, inscription on drawer reads "Virginia Hunt Board, early 19th cent. from family of Admiral Todd, Naval Commander prior to and during the Civil War, Virginia," 56" w, 22" d, 39" h **5,520.00**

Federal-style, Southern States, huntboard, yellow pine, overhanging rect top, case with three drawers, skirt with central shaping, four sq tapering legs, orig brasses, refinished, 21" w, 19-1/2" h **1,840.00**

George III, c1790, inlaid mahogany, crossbanded and bowfronted top, case fitted with four drawers, sq tapered legs, inlaid throughout with stringing and quarter fans, 79" w, 24" d, 34-1/2" h........................ **5,875.00**

George III-style, late 19th C Mahogany, bow front, shaped top, single drawer flanked by doors, sq tapering legs, spade feet, 54" w, 26-1/2" d, 36" h........................ **2,000.00**

Mahogany, inlaid, satinwood crossbanding, serpentine top, conforming case fitted with five drawers and two doors, sq tapered legs, 64" w, 22" d, 38-1/4" h **1,175.00**

George III/Hepplewhite, mahogany, flame grain mahogany, satinwood, and oak, paterae and shell inlay, 36" h **11,160.00**

Gothic, Kimbel & Cabus, New York, c1875, design no. 377, walnut, galleried top over two cupboard doors over open self over slant front over central drawer over open well flanked by twocupboard doors, galleried base shelf, bracket feet, 39-1/4" w, 17-3/4" d, 73" h **9,775.00**

Hepplewhite, mahogany and mahogany veneer with inlay, bowed center section with conforming doors and dovetailed drawer, two flat side doors, sq tapered legs, banding and stringing with bell flowers on legs, corner fans on doors and drawers, reworked, repairs, replaced brasses, 58-1/4" w, 18-1/2" d, 37-3/4" h **2,200.00**

Sideboard, Georgian-style, serpentine front, cross banding, inlay detail, center drawer flanked by cupboards, **$2,750**.

Photo courtesy of Wiederseim Associates, Inc.

Sideboard, Hepplewhite, 19th C, mahogany, shaped top, above conforming drawers and doors, square tapered legs with inlay, some losses, **$600**; bentwood box on top, **$125**.

Photo courtesy of Wiederseim Associates, Inc.

Sideboard, International Movement, Heywood-Wakefield, champagne finish, drawers over three cabinet doors, two interior drawers and single shelf, branded mark, 59-3/4" l, 19" d, 32-1/2" h, **$500**.

Photo courtesy of David Rago Auctions, Inc

Louis XV, Provincial, oak, rect top and case, fluted frieze, three paneled doors enclosing re-fitted interior of drawers, short cabriole legs, 85" w, 19" d, 40" h **3,525.00**

Neoclassical, Boston, 1820-25, mahogany veneer, corner style, paneled and scrolled splashboard over top with veneered molded edge, curving front which overhangs conforming case of three veneered drawers over two recessed paneled doors, single shelved int., similar recessed panel sides above flattened ball feet with brass banding, replaced brass pulls, old surface with some imperfections, 60" w, 35" d, 42" h **55,200.00**

Queen Anne, converted from highboy base, walnut, pine secondary wood, pegged construction, two dovetailed drawers, one with relief carved shell, scalloped aprons, cabriole legs, pad feet, old dark surface, age splits, replaced returns, 38-1/2" w, 20-1/2" d, 35" h **1,150.00**

Regency-style, 20th C, inlaid mahogany, serpentine top, conforming case fitted with three central long drawers, drawer and door at each side, inlaid with quarter fans and checkering, 65" w, 21-1/2" d, 40" h ... **2,000.00**

Renaissance Revival, America, cherry, curled mahogany drawer fronts, burled arched panel doors **900.00**

Second Empire, French, c1870, ebonized wood, scrolled crest with pierte dure florals with in gilt metal cartouche, three section mirrored back divided by ebonized brackets, three drawers, center cupboard door flanked by two glazed cupboard doors, shelved int., figural gilt metal mounts, pietre dura floral and bird dec within gilt bronze cartouche, 67" w, 18" d, 77" h **4,600.00**

Sheraton, country, walnut and curly maple, beaded edge top, four dovetailed drawers, scalloped aprons, turned legs, line inlay around apron and drawer fronts, old varnish finish, replaced glass pulls, wear and edge damage, one heart inlay missing, large water stain on top, 69-1/2" w, 21-1/2" d, 43-1/2" h **5,500.00**

Southern, Kentucky, c1850, walnut and cherry, gallery on three sides of rect top, four drawers over four cupboard doors with punched tin panels dec with quarter fans and fylfots, 66" l **17,500.00**

Victorian, American, late 19th C, pine, serpentine crest, rect top, four small drawers over two banks of four drawers, center cupboard, 65" w, 19" d, 51-1/2" h **750.00**

Sofa, International Movement, Charles Eames for Herman Miller, upholstered in original orange and red Alexander Girard fabric, chromed and black enameled flat steel frame, unmarked, 72-1/4" l, 28-1/2" d, 35-3/4" h, **$1,400**.

Photo courtesy of David Rago Auctions, Inc.

Sofas

Aesthetic Movement, American, walnut, shaped backrest, scrolled end above arcaded apron, circular turned legs, matching bolt of orig fabric, 70" l **1,200.00**

Art Nouveau, Carlo Bugatti, 1900, ebonized wood, rect back, mechanical seat, slightly scrolling rect arms, parchment upholstery, painted swallows and leafy branches, hammered brass trim, four block form feet, 68-3/8" l **1,900.00**

Centennial, Chippendale-style, American, late 19th C, mahogany, shaped back, rolled arms, yellow velvet upholstered seat, gadrooned apron, cabriole legs with carved knees, claw and ball feet, 62" l **1,500.00**

Chippendale, country, step down back with step down arms, bowed front with large down filled cushions, eight molded carved legs, cup caster feet, reupholstered, 76" w, 32" d, 36" h **3,000.00**

Classical
Mid Atlantic States, 1805-20, carved mahogany and bird's eye-maple veneer, Grecian style, scrolled and reeded arm and foot, punctuated with brass rosettes, continuing to similar reeded seat rail with inlaid dies, reeded saber legs flanked by brass flowerettes, brass paw feet on casters, old surface, 75" l, 14-1/2" h seat, 35" h **3,680.00**

Marshmallow sofa, Modernism-Era, George Nelson, manufactured by Herman Miller, 1957, circular cushions in original Alexander Girard fabrics, sample version, made to illustrate range of fabrics available, 18 cushions each in a different fabric, satin chrome and black enamel frame, 51" w, 32" d, 30" h, **$15,400**.

Photo courtesy of Treadway Gallery Inc.

Chests of drawers, Federal, New Hampshire, Portsmouth, c1805-15, mahogany and flame birch, edge of birch top outlined with patterned inlay, case of four cock-beaded drawers, each visually divided into three panels by flame birch veneer outlined in stringing and banded mahogany veneer, flame birch veneer drop lane pendant centering veneered skirt, elongated French foot, original brasses, old refinish, 40-1/4" w, 21-1/8" d, 36" h, **$83,900**.

Photo courtesy of Skinner Auctioneers and Appraisers of Antiques and Fine Art Boston and Bolton, MA.

New England, 1820-40, carved mahogany veneer, cylindrical crest ends, leaf carved volutes, upholstered seat and rolled veneer seat rail, leaf carved supports, carved paw feet, 92" w, 16-1/2" h seat, 34-3/4" h **1,650.00**

Sofa, Eastlake, c1880, walnut and mahogany, cameo back, padded scrolled arms, front reeded legs with bulbous turnings, matching straight chair not shown, 66" l, 16" h seat height, 49" h, later ivory upholstery, **$500**.

Photo courtesy of Alderfer Auction Co.

Edwardian-style, Chesterfield, tufted brown leather, flattened bun feet, 81" l **5,000.00**
Empire, mahogany and figured mahogany veneer frame, well-detailed carving with sea serpent front legs, turned back legs, lyre arms with relief carved flowers and cornucopia, rope turned crest rail, refinished, reupholstered in floral tapestry

on ivory ground, bolster pillows, 107" l **3,850.00**
Federal
America, carved mahogany, mahogany veer paneled top crest with scrolled sides, front carved with rosette and leaf dec, carved paw feet with front stylized wings, red flower dec upholstery, 96" w, 19-1/2" d, 32" h **1,000.00**
Massachusetts or New Hampshire, early 19th C, mahogany veneer paneled crest topped with reeding that continues on top of arms to reeded arm supports, bird's-eye maple inlaid dies on front swelled and reeded legs, turned feet with sq raked rear legs, old refinish, feet repairs, 32-1/4" h **2,820.00**
New Hampshire, c1815, carved mahogany, upholstered, straight crest continuing to shaped sides with carved arms on vase and ring reeded and swelled posts and cock-beaded panels, bowed seat rail, vase and ring-turned legs with cock-beaded rect inlaid dies, old finish, minor imperfections, 78" w, 24" d, 17" h seat, 34" h back **2,415.00**
George III-style, English, carved oak, double arched upholstered high backrest, scrolled arms, loose cushion seat, acanthus carved legs, claw and ball feet, 58" l **1,200.00**

Louis XV style, recamier Mahogany, tied ribbon and wheat-sheaf carved backrest, scrolled end, foliate carved terminals on gadrooned feet, casters, 91" l **1,410.00**
Walnut, high scrolled backrest, carved foliate on armrests and cabriole legs, 90" l **650.00**
Neoclassical, Baltic, c1825, carved mahogany, paneled cresting, padded arms with lions heads and anthemia, upholstered seat and back, shaped feet, 68" l **2,185.00**
Regency-style, heavily carved, acanthus leaves and claw feet, 80" l, 31 1/2" h **260.00**

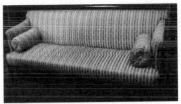

Sofa, Sheraton, mahogany, scrolled crest, down turned arms, four turned tapered legs, upholstered in yellow, ivory, and blue striped silk, 78" l, 25" d, 17" h seat, 36-1/2" h, loss to rear legs, braced, chips on arms, **$750**.

Photo courtesy of Alderfer Auction Co.

Sofa, Sheraton, walnut, carved legs, casters, floral upholstery, **$600**.

Photo courtesy of Wiederseim Associates, Inc.

Sofa, loveseat, Victorian, c1880, rose-colored tufted upholstery, provenance: University of Pennsylvania president's residence, **$250**.

Photo courtesy of Wiederseim Associates, Inc

Sofa, Victorian, mahogany, mahogany inlay beneath back crest roll, leaf relief carvings on front rolled arms, claw front legs, pineapple carved real legs, reupholstered, 72" l, 26" d, 20" h seat, 36" h, legs loose, some veneer chips, **$650**.

Photo courtesy of Alderfer Auction Co.

Renaissance Revival, American, carved walnut, 72" l settee, five armchairs in two sizes, angular carved frames **2,350.00**

Rococo Revival, John B. Belter, carved rosewood, triple back, carved central rose and fruit on sides, scroll band underneath, carved segmented scroll, tufted back red silk upholstery, brass caster feet, old restoration to central crest, worn seat fabric, 62" w, 42" h................. **4,500.00**

Sheraton to Empire, transitional, carved mahogany, scrolled arms with molded detail, applied rosettes, relief carved leaf supports, brass caps on turned front legs, relief twist carvings, applied moldings on front panels, casters on base, dark refinish, glued break in one scroll, reupholstered, 70" w, 17-1/2" h seat, 34-1/2" h back **550.00**

Victorian, late, American, c1890, camel back, reupholstered, turned legs, 60" l **750.00**

Stands

Baker, wrought iron, 48" h, 14-1/2" d, 84" h.............. **500.00**

Basin, Federal, New England, early 19th C, mahogany veneer, scalloped backsplash above basin cut outs, shaped skirt over medial shelf with one working and one faux cockbeaded drawer outlined in cross banded veneer, four reeded legs, turned feet, old surface, replaced brass, minor imperfections, 24" w, 16-1/4" d, 43-1/2" h........ **1,300.00**

Bird cage, wicker, painted white, tightly woven quarter moon-shaped cage holder, wrapped pole standard, tightly woven conical base, 74" h **225.00**

Book, Arts & Crafts, oak, four open shelves with cutout sides and through tenons, 45-3/4" h **500.00**

Canterbury, Regency, early 19th C, mahogany, drawer with paper label for "G. Ibison Furniture Broker & Appraiser, Cumberland Place, Near the Elephant & Castle," restoration, 19-1/4" l, 14" d, 22-1/2" h............ **1,380.00**

Card, Aesthetic Movement, American

Marquetry inlaid and parcel gilt, circular top inlaid with floral marquetry, fluted and turned pedestal with turned rod decoration, splayed legs, 17-1/2" d, 33-1/2" h **450.00**

Polychrome and part gilded walnut, circular top, turned and fluted stem, four turned and splayed legs, 12-1/2" d, 33" h.......................... **530.00**

Cellarette

Arts & Crafts

Stickley, Gustav, flush top, pull-out copper shelf, single drawer, cabinet door, copper pulls, orig finish, large red decal, veneer lifting on sides and back, 22" w, 16" d, 39-1/2" h **4,315.00**

Stickley, L. & J. G., arched backsplash, pull-out copper shelf, two-door cabinet, hammered copper strap hinges, ring pulls, top refinished, orig finish on base, "The Work of ..." decal, 35-1/2" x 32" x 16".. **13,800.00**

Federal, attributed to Middle Atlantic states, c1790-1800, mahogany inlaid, octagonal top, conforming case, both inlaid with contrasting stringing, interior well with removable lead liner, four sq tapering legs inlaid with bellflowers and stringing, brasses appear to be orig, old refinish, sun faded top, imperfections, 22-1/4" w, 17-1/4" w, 25-1/4" h **28,200.00**

George III, English, mid-19th C, mahogany, lozenge form, brass bands, twin loop carry handles, racked chamfered tapering legs, 24" w, 17-1/2" d, 27-1/2" h **7,500.00**

Chamber, Federal

New England, early 19th C, painted and dec, dec splashboard above wash stand top with round cut-out for basin, medial shelf with drawer below, orig yellow paint with green and gold stenciling and striping, paint wear, imperfections, 18-1/4" h, 1" d, 39-1/4" h **350.00**

North Shore, MA, c1815-25, carved mahogany, shaped splashboard, veneered cabinet door flanked by ovolu corners, carved columns of leaves and grapes on punchwork ground, ring

turned tapering legs, brass casters, old replaced brasses, old refinish, minor restoration, 21-1/2" w, 16" d, 35-5/8" h **2,300.00**

Portsmouth, NH, c1800, mahogany inlaid, shaped splashboard with center quarter round shelf, pierced top with bow front, square string inlaid supports continue to outward flaring legs with patterned inlays, medial shelf, satinwood skirt, small center drawer with patterned inlaid lower edge, shaped stretchers with inlaid paterae, old finish, minor imperfections, 23" w, 16-1/2" d, 41" h **5,750.00**

Demilune, Hepplewhite, country, c1800, pine, salmon paint, dark red finger-line dec **10,000.00**

Dumbwaiter

Georgian, three tiered, mahogany, each graduated dished tier raised on turned standard, three down swept legs, 22-1/2" d largest tier, 38-1/2" h **600.00**

Queen-Anne style, walnut, three circular shelves, splayed legs, pad feet, 21" d, 39" h.......................... **300.00**

Easel

Aesthetic Movement, 19th C, ash, cresting with stylized scroll, rod and ball design, straight legs and spindle-inset supports, 64" h **275.00**

Louis XVI-style, mahogany and parcel-gilt, picture support hung with berried laurel swags, trestle-end frame carved with acanthus, imbrications, and dolphins, 25" w, 23-1/2" d, 82" h. **950.00**

Étagère

Classical, New England, 1860s, mahogany and mahogany veneer, spool turned gallery, ball finials, three shelves with similar supports, two recessed panel cupboard doors, single shelf int., ball turned feet, old refinish, imperfections, 35-1/4" w, 15-3/4" d, 66" h **990.00**

Regency, late, English, early 19th C, six tiers, corner, columnar supports, basal drawer, brass casters, 18" w, 14" d, 62" h **3,000.00**

Victorian, three rect tiers raised by turned columns over two cabinet doors, ball feet, casters, 20-1/2" w, 16" d, 51-1/2" h **1,180.00**

Folding, Chippendale New York State or Pennsylvania, 1755-775, cherry, dished top rotates and titles, birdcage support, swelled and turned pedestal, cabriole tripod base, pad feet, old refinish, imperfections, 17-1/2" d, 26" h **3,220.00**

Pennsylvania, 1760-80, walnut, molded dish top, inscribed edge tilts, tapering pedestal with suppressed ball, cabriole legs ending in pad feet, imperfections, 22" d, 29" h **4,600.00**

Magazine stand, Arts & Crafts, Roycroft, pedestal, canted sides, overhanging top, keyed through-tenons, orb and cross mark on each side, dry original finish, staining, wear, seam separation, chips, 22-1/2" x 18" x 64" h, $6,000.

Photo courtesy of David Rago Auctions, Inc.

Magazine
Arts & Crafts
Stickley, Gustav, Tree of Life, carved sides, four shelves, orig finish and tacks, unmarked, minor edge wear, 14" sq, 43-1/2" h **1,610.00**

Magazine stand, Arts & Crafts, Gustav Stickley, No. 514, oak, tongue-and-groove paneled sides, square posts, leather strips tacked to shelf ends original finish, early red decal under top shelf, wear to top, 35-1/2" x 14-1/4" x 14-1/2", $8,100.

Photo courtesy of David Rago Auctions, Inc.

Stickley, L. & J. G., single broad slat on either side, arched toe board, new finish, "The Work of L. & J. G. Stickley" decal, 36" w, 12" d, 30" h **2,990.00**

Eastlake, carved maple, walnut, and bird's eye maple veneer, finely turned posts with ball finials on top corners, turned legs, dovetailed drawer, drop pulls, old finish, old gold paint in carving and turnings, one corner restored, 22" w, 14-1/2" d **230.00**

Regency-style, late 19th C, mahogany, four divisions, dipped dividers, frieze drawer, turned legs on casters, 23" w, 16" d, 24" h **1,775.00**

Renaissance Revival, third quarter 19th C, mahogany, walnut, parcel-gilt, and ebonized gilt-metal, hanging, back plate with acanthus crest flanked by fleur-de-lis and bellflowers, uprights mounted on top with gilt-metal bust roundels, central hinged magazine folio set with gilt composition oval bust of Mercury, gilt incised detailing, 19-3/4" w, 21-1/2" h **300.00**

Victorian, late 19th or early 20th C, mahogany, burled walnut veneer, turned corner posts and finials with scrolled and pierced panels, short boxed stops which conform to ends, dovetailed drawer with

carved pull and applied fretwork, four trumpet turned legs, brass casters, 28-1/2" w, 16" d, 21" h **1,150.00**

Night, Art Deco, attributed to Maurice Defrene, France, c1925, amboyna wood inlaid with stylized flowers in various fruitwoods and mother-of-pearl, price for pr, 15" w, 18" d, 29-1/2" h **2,235.00**

Pedestal
Aesthetic Movement, American
Ebonized, rect top, turned stem, angular supports, four curved legs, 17" w, 14" d, 35-1/2" h **500.00**

Gilded and velvet mounted walnut, sq top, gilded lappet corners, sq base, 12" sq, 37-1/2" h **750.00**

Renaissance Revival, American, ebonized walnut, sawtooth frieze, turned supports, four-footed circular base, 18" w, 12-1/2" d, 34" h **450.00**

Plant
Arts & Crafts
Limbert, ebon oak lino, overhanging top, four caned panels on each side, recent finish, branded signature, 14" w, 14" d, 34" h **2,100.00**

Stickley, Gustav, sq top flush with cloud-lift apron, narrow board mortised through corseted stretchers with tenon and key, orig finish, 1902-04 red decal, crack in one stretcher, 14" sq, 27" h **3,450.00**

French-style, 20th C, black lacquered finish, turtle-shaped top with open well, ormolu wreath and quiver designs, acanthus leaves, hoof-shaped caps on feet, 19 1/4" w, 14-1/2" d, 30" h **275.00**

Folk Art, carved and painted root, America, polychrome painted animal heads radiating from entwined root base, inscribed "MAS 1897," 23" w, 38-1/2" h **1,725.00**

Victorian, walnut and pine, three tiers, two top round, larger one octagonal, turned legs, scalloped aprons, old finish, 31" d, 37-1/2" h. **420.00**

Portfolio, William IV, English, c1830, carved rosewood, folding mechanism **3,500.00**

Quilt rack, Renaissance Revival, American, walnut, faceted turned rods on trestle base, 27" w, 35" h...................... **200.00**

Reading, Federal, Albany, NY, early 19th C, mahogany, reading stand above ring-turned tapering post on rect shaped canterbury, turned tapering spindles, casters, 22-1/4" w, 14" d, 47-1/2" h............. **3,200.00**

Stand, sewing, Hepplewhite style, inlaid mahogany, **$250.**

Photo courtesy of Wiederseim Associates, Inc.

Sewing, Sheraton, country, black walnut, poplar secondary wood, lift top, fitted int. compartment with four int. dovetailed drawers and pigeon holes, single dovetailed drawer with figured front and incised beading, well-turned legs with ring turnings, replaced brass pull, pegged construction, lock missing, one leg with well-executed repair, 20" w, 19-1/2" d, 29" h **1,155.00**

Sheet music stand, Aesthetic Movement, American, rosewood, hinged sides, pedestal, four downswept legs, 18" w, 5" d, 36" h **500.00**

Single drawer

Country, mahogany and fruitwood, incised monogram on left apron "SC" in script, two board top with gallery, small dovetailed drawer in apron, turned legs and supports, base shelf, old mellow refinishing, insect damage, 16-1/2" w, 16-1/4" d, 28" h........................... **450.00**

English, 19th C, rosewood veneer, mahogany secondary wood, small urn-shaped finials on top, dovetailed center drawer, wooden pulls, three shelves, turned legs, old refinishing, minor edge chips, filled splits, 19-1/4" w, 14-1/2" d, 39-1/2" h... **1,050.00**

Hepplewhite, cherry, pine and poplar secondary wood, two-board top, dovetailed drawer with brass pull, slender legs taper to feet, refinished, old tin patch over knot hole in drawer bottom, 17-3/4" w, 18" d, 27-1/2" h **500.00**

Pennsylvania, early, softwood, one molded drawer, deeply beaded skirt, splayed tapered legs, scrubbed top, old tan over red painted base, 21-3/4" w, 21-1/2" d, 30" h............. **1,650.00**

Sheraton, country, curly maple and walnut, poplar secondary wood, two board top, dovetailed drawer, turned legs, old replaced brass pull, old finish, chip on foot ring, 18" w, 17-1/4" d, 28-3/8" h **700.00**

Sheraton, country, decorated, orig brown sponged dec over bittersweet colored ground, old dry varnish, pine, two board top, sq nail construction in drawer, splayed ring turned legs, ball feet, minor wear, 21" w, 20-3/4" d, 31" h **3,335.00**

Sheraton, country, walnut and cherry, poplar secondary wood, single board top, well turned legs with raised panels that flank dovetailed beveled edge drawer, orig glass pull, dark refinishing, old repairs, 20-1/2" w, 18" d, 28-3/4" h **500.00**

Tabouret, Regency-style, carved oak, cushioned top above frame carved with elaborate floral sprays, raised and scrolled toes, 23" w, 19" h **500.00**

Tier

Classical Revival, late 19th C, sq onyx top, two tiers, scrolled metal skirt, legs with central leaf tip band, second medial shelf, outward scrolled feet, 31-3/4" h **360.00**

English, mahogany, small gallery on top, four shelves, ring-turned columns, half

turned moldings resemble bamboo, brass casters, refinished, few trim pcs replaced, putty restorations under shelves, 16" sq, 44-3/4" h **350.00**

Stand, tea, folding tray, later needlepoint with English storefronts, **$150.**

Photo courtesy of Dotta Auction Co., Inc.

Federal, New England, late 18th/early 19th C, mahogany, three trays of diminishing size, molded edges, each rotates on turned urn-shaped shaft, cabriole leg tripod base, arris pad feet, old refinish, minor imperfections, largest tier 23-1/4" d, 43-1/4" h.. **7,650.00**

Two drawers, Hepplewhite, cherry, pine secondary wood, single board top, two dovetailed and beaded drawers with orig brass pulls, high tapered legs, old mellow finish, 14-3/8" w, 17" d, 28-7/8" h **1,050.00**

Umbrella, Arts & Crafts, early 20th C, oak, sq form, four posts, top and bottom stretchers with mortise and tenon joinery, one dark brown finish, other medium brown finish, marked "Cedric S. Sweeter Jan 23, 1920," 12" w, one 28-3/4" h, other 29" h, price for pr **230.00**

Vitrine, Mahogany, line border inlay, satinwood panels, top with drop front, molded edges, tapered sq legs, brass casters, joined by stretcher base, 21-1/2" w, 16-1/2" d, 28" h **600.00**

Wash

Eastlake, walnut and burlwood, three drawers, replaced white marble top, 29" w, 38" h **265.00**

Empire, figured mahogany veneer, poplar secondary wood, dovetailed gallery fitted with narrow shelf, bowed top with cut-outs for wash bowl and two jars, serpentine front supports, turned rear posts, dovetailed drawer in base with brass pulls, high well turned legs, refinished, edge chips, 18" w, 16" d, 37-3/4" h **385.00**

Federal

American, mahogany and figured mahogany veneer, bow front with two small drawers, cutout for bowl, cutout sides, single dovetailed drawer in base, turned legs, worn finish, some water damage, replaced top and two small drawers, 20-1/4" w, 17-1/4" d, 30-1/4" h **275.00**

Rhode Island, c1790, mahogany veneer, top with four shaped corners, canted corners, engaged ring-turned columns ending in reeded legs flanking cock-beaded drawers outlined in cross banded veneer, top two drawers with sections, replaced brasses, old refinish, imperfections, 20-3/4" w, 15-1/2" d, 28-1/2" h .. **4,025.00**

Hepplewhite, bow front, mahogany and figured veneer, pine and poplar secondary woods, dovetailed gallery, top with cutout for bowl and two cup inserts, dovetailed beaded drawer below door with brass pull, tapered legs with beaded panels on front, restoration to center leg, 24" w, 17" d, 40" h **600.00**

Victorian, walnut, white marble top, one drawer, pr lower cupboard doors, carved fruit and nut pulls, 30" w, 30" h **300.00**

Whatnot, Corner, Victorian, late 19th C, Chinoiserie bamboo and lacquer, frame set with two diamond-shaped mirrors and shelves, 22" w, 13" d, 56" h **250.00**

Stand, wash, cottage style, painted pale green, original painted flowers and foliage on long drawer and pair of cupboard doors, scrolled backsplash, carved foliate pulls, extra painted panel shown on top, **$200**.

Photo courtesy of Dotta Auction Co., Inc

Work

Classical, early 19th C, carved maple and rosewood veneer, top outlined with rosewood veneer banding above sectional veneered drawer, lower drawer flanked by short columns, tapering pedestal joining four leaf carved legs ending in carved hairy paw feet on castors, old refinish, 20-3/4" w, 18-1/2" d, 28-3/4" h **500.00**

Federal

Middle Atlantic region, 1815-25, bird's eye maple and oak veneer, top with hinged leaves, two working and two faux string inlaid drawers, top one fitted, ring-turned swelled legs joined by similar double stretchers, curving legs, scrolled feet, old refinish, imperfections, 17-1/4" w, 18" d, 28-1/4" h **2,750.00**

New England, early 19th C, cherry, rect top with rounded corners, turned and swelled pedestal, outwardly curving legs, refinished, imperfections, 21-3/4" w, 15-7/8" d, 29-1/2" h **500.00**

New England, early 19th C, mahogany, rect top, single drawer, turned and reeded legs, old refinish, imperfections, 22" w, 16-3/4" d, 28-1/2" h **750.00**

Hepplewhite, New England, c1810, cherry inlaid, sq top, outline stringing and quarter fan inlays on ovolo corners, line inlaid drawer and skirt, line inlaid sq tapering legs, cross banded cuffs, brass drawer pull, refinished, 19" w, 19" d, 27" h **2,650.00**

Renaissance Revival, American, c1860, lift top opening to real satinwood interior fitted with compartments, narrow drawer above semi-circular bag drawer, pair of stylized lyre form ends jointed by arched stretcher surmounted by turned finial **875.00**

Sheraton, New England, 1805-15, mahogany, veneered, outset rounded corners, shaped top, pull-out suspended fabric bag below single drawer, ring-turned and reeded round tapering legs ending in ring-turned tapering vasiform feet, old refinish, 16-1/2" w, 18-1/2" d, 28-1/4" h **3,500.00**

Steps

Bed, New England, early 19th C, pine and tulipwood, two steps, thumb-molded drawer below bottom one, flanked by shaped sides, demilune base, old color, repaired, 15-1/2" w, 10" d, 17-1/2" h.......................... **575.00**

Circus, America, early 20th C, painted white stringers, red, yellow, and blue treads, 25" w, 90" d, 27" h **435.00**

Library

George III, English, late 18th C, mahogany, rect molded hinged top, eight steps, 40 1/2" w, 53-1/2" h.. **2,500.00**

Regency, English, early 19th C, mahogany, three steps, inset green leather treads, scrolling banister, sq balusters, feet with brass casters, 46" w, 27" w, 56" h.......................... **2,400.00**

Stools

Cricket, Arts & Crafts, Limbert, #205-1/2", rect top covered with new leather, splayed sides, inverted heart cut-out, single stretcher with through-tenon, replaced keys, orig finish, branded, 20" w, 15" d, 18" h **950.00**

Stool, foot, oval top with floral needlepoint top, **$175**.
Photo courtesy of Joy Luke.

Foot

Arts & Crafts, oak

Barber Brothers, oak, nicely replaced leather seat, some color added to orig finish, paper label, 13" w, 13" d, 11" h **110.00**

Limbert, cricket, #205-1/2, rect orig leather top and tacks, splayed sides with inverted heart cut-out having single stretcher with through-tenon construction, orig finish, branded and numbered, 20" w, 15" d, 19" h **2,000.00**

Painted, attributed to York County, PA, pine, paint dec, man eating oysters in center of top, red ground, scalloped border, inscription "By D. J. Rash for C. F. Rash," stylized leaves on sides and feet, 15-5/8" l, 9-3/4" w, 10-3/4" h **18,700.00**

Queen Anne, 18th C, walnut, rect frieze, 4 cabriole legs each with shell carving on knees, pad feet, slip seat, 22-1/2" w, 17" d, 17" h **1,950.00**

Sheraton, curly and bird's eye maple, old finish, cane top, minor damage to top, 7-3/4" w, 13" l, 6-1/2" h **440.00**

Victorian, late 19th C, carved walnut, short cabriole legs carved at knees with shells, shaped skirting carved with acanthus, velveteen upholstery, 12-3/4" w, 16" l, 11" h **175.00**

Windsor, attributed to Maine, early 19th C, rect top, four swelled legs joined by X-form stretchers, orig dark brown grain paint which resembles exotic wood, yellow line accents, paint imperfections, 12" 2, 8" d, 7" h **625.00**

Stool, hand painted, green ground, country scene with windmill on top, **$125**.
Photo courtesy of Dotta Auction Co., Inc.

Stool, hand made, round top, four shaped legs, painted white, **$35**.
Photo courtesy of Joseph P. Smalley, Jr.

Joint

Early, oak, old finish, wear and age cracks, 11" w, 16-1/2" l, 17-3/4" h **990.00**

Jacobean-style, oak, rect plank top, shaped skirt, block and ring-turned legs joined by box stretcher, 18" w, 11-1/4" d, 21" h **700.00**

Milking stool, well turned round wooden seat, splayed bamboo legs and stretchers, old red and yellow graining over cream ground, wear, 10" d, 6-1/4" h **180.00**

Ottoman, Empire, c1830, figured mahogany, serpentine form, shaped supports, wooden casters, green and gold velvet upholstery, 17" w, 13" h, **$480**.
Photo courtesy of Sloans & Kenyon Auctions.

Ottoman, Classical, attributed to Boston, MA, c1830, mahogany veneer, overstuffed cushions rest inside mitred frame atop molded base, ogee bracket feet, wooden casters, refinished, minor imperfections, 20" w, 18" d, 17-1/2" h, price for pr ... **2,235.00**

Piano

Louis XVI-style, late 19th C, carved beech, circular, adjustable, close-nailed over stuffed top, petal-carved frieze, leaf-capped turned, tapered, and fluted legs, wavy cross-stretcher **850.00**

Renaissance Revival, American, telescopic, X-form, turned wooden screws adjust height, 20" h **325.00**

Victorian, early 19th, mahogany, upholstered, revolving, 20" h **200.00**

Stool, piano, four legs, adjustable, glass feet, Victorian, **$185**.
Photo courtesy of Dotta Auction Co., Inc.

Seat-type

Country, folk art, attributed to Fredericksburg, PA, late 19th/ early 20th C, painted and dec, octagonal seat, chamfered edge, trimmed with border band of carved hearts, tall splayed and chamfered legs also trimmed with carved hearts and joined by slender rungs, overall polychrome **1,850.00**

George III, late 19th C, mahogany, gold floral satin upholstered rest seat, sq tapering supports, molded H-form stretchers, pr, 19-1/2" l, 17" h **1,650.00**

International Movement

Eames, Charles, manufactured by Herman Miller, Time-Life, walnut, concave seat, 13" d, 15" h
.... **1,000.00**
Platner, Warren, manufactured by Knoll, bronze wire base, peach fabric upholstered seat, 17" d, 21" h........ **325.00**
Renaissance Revival, American, walnut, cushioned and hinged seat opening to well, trestle base with angular supports, 23-1/2" w, 11" d, 19" h........................... **265.00**
Windsor, American, 19th C, oblong plant seat raised on three tall, turned and slightly swelled legs joined by T-stretcher, traces of old green paint, 15" w, 24-1/2" h .. **200.00**

Typical Parts of a Table

Tables

Architect's, George III, English, late 19th C, mahogany, hinged tooled leather work surface above opposing hinged work surface, turned pedestal on three splayed legs, pad feet, some reconstruction, 29" w, 19-1/4" d, 29-1/2" h **2,300.00**
Bank, Neoclassical-style, brass and metal, rect glass-inset top above frieze pierced with putti and scrolling foliage, trestle end supports cast as sphinxes, joined by stretcher, black marble block supports, removed from Hyde Park Bank of Chicago, 62" w, 39" d, 40" h **800.00**

Breakfast

Chippendale to Hepplewhite, transitional, walnut, one board top, beaded edge apron, sq legs with slight taper, molded corner, and inside chamfer, H stretcher, old finish, stains on top, 19" w, 29-1/4" l, 28-1/4" h
.... **8,250.00**

Table, banquet, Hepplewhite, c1790, inlaid mahogany, "D"-shaped ends, four extra leaves, patch on top, cracks, losses, lacking casters, 25" h, **$250**.
Photo courtesy of Wiederseim Associates, Inc.

Classical, New York, 1820-30, carved mahogany inlaid, top with brass inlay in outline, stamped brass on edge of shaped leaves, one working and one faux drawers, flanked by drop pendants, four pillar curved platform support, leafage carved legs, carved paw feet, casters, replaced pulls, old finish, repairs, losses, 39" w, 24" d, 28" h **2,450.00**

Federal

Massachusetts, central, c1810, inlaid cherry, rect hinged top with ovolo corners, base with straight skirt, edged with lunette inlay, flanked by sq tapering legs outlined in stringing, topped with icicle inlay, old refinish, 36" w, 17" d, 29" h **1,150.00**
Massachusetts or New England, 1815, mahogany oval top, hinged leaves, flanking two drawers, one working, one faux, both outlined in stringing and have central panel of figured mahogany veneer above chevron-style inlaid banding, reeded, turned, tapering legs, turned feet, old refinish, surface imperfections, 35-3/8" w, 20-1/4" d, 29-3/4" h
.... **8,225.00**
New York City, c1815, carved mahogany veneer, rect top, shaped leaves, one working and one faux end drawers, cross banded mahogany veneer, turned acanthus leaf carved pedestal, four

acanthus leaf carved legs, brass hairy paw feet, old refinish, repairs, 25" w closed, 38-1/2" l, 30-1/4" h ... **1,725.00**

Card
Classical

Attributed to firm of Isaac Vine and Isaac Vine Jr., Boston, 1819-24, carved mahogany and mahogany veneer, rect top with beaded edges, skirt with recessed panel, C-scrolls and carved volutes over tapering pedestal accented by carved leafage above serpentine veneered platform with carved and scrolled feet on casters, old refinish, imperfections, 37" w, 17-1/2" d, 28-1/2" h...... **1,840.00**
Attributed to Thomas Astens, New York City, 1822, carved mahogany and satinwood, rect swivel top with rounded ends, outlined in cross banded mahogany veneer, satinwood veneered skirt, faceted pineapple-like carving above acanthus leaf carving on pedestal, shaped legs, carved paw feet on casters, old refinish, imperfections, 36" w, 18-1/4" d, 28" h.......... **3,335.00**
New York, 1820-30, carved mahogany, mahogany veneer rect swivel top with rounded front carved corners, leaf carved and shaped shaft, curving platform which joins 4 scrolling leaf caved legs ending in carved paw feet, refinished, minor imperfections, 36" w, 17-1/2" d, 30" h **1,495.00**

Federal

Boston or Charlestown, MA, c1800, mahogany inlaid, demilune top with inlaid top edge above undercut lower edge, three-paneled conforming skirt with outline stringing, interspersed with inlaid dies, string inlaid legs, refinished, top detached, other imperfections, 35-3/4" w, 17-1/2" d, 30" h **2,500.00**

Boston or Charlestown, MA, early 19th C, mahogany and figured maple inlaid, rect top with ovolo corners and inlaid top edge above undercut lower edge, skirt with figured maple rect panel and inlaid rect dies, sq double tapering legs ending in cuff inlays, old refinish, imperfections, 35-3/4" w, 17" d, 29-1/2" h...................... **2,235.00**

North Shore, MA, c1815, mahogany veneer carved, serpentine facade with ovolo front corners, ring-turned leaf and spiral carved legs, turned feet, old refinish, imperfections, 37-1/2" w, 17-5/8" d, 30-1/4" h **900.00**

Philadelphia, c1800, mahogany and satinwood veneer, serpentine top, string inlaid skirt flanking rect satinwood center, sq tapering legs outlined in stringing with diamond-shaped die, terminating in cuff inlays, refinished, imperfections, 36" w, 18-3/8" d, 29-3/4" h..... **5,600.00**

Sheraton

American, pine, old brown flame graining, top with later black paint, finely turned legs with raised acanthus leaf bands below serpentine apron, large raised relief leaf carvings at corners, ball feet, 34-1/2" w, 17-1/2" d, 30" h 1,**725.00**

English, mahogany, mahogany flame veneer, banded inlay around top, old red felt insert on interior surfaces, inlaid panels and diamonds on aprons, turned legs, relief ring detail, tapered to applied ormolu paw feet, old finish, pieced repair at one hinge, minor edge damage, 36" w, 16-7/8" d, 29-3/4" h **2,100.00**

Victorian, rosewood, rounded rect top with red baize surface, quadripartite base, scrolling feet, 36" w, 36" d, 29-1/2" h **950.00**

Center

Aesthetic Movement, American

John Jeliff, attributed to, inset white marble top and turret-form corners, paneled frieze with angular pendants, boldly scrolled and faceted trumpet legs joined by and H-form stretcher, delicately carved elongated leaftips, 46-1/2" w, 30-1/2" d, 30-1/2" h .. **4,000.00**

Walnut, white marble top, paneled frieze, four angular legs on scrolled base, 36" w, 24" d, 30" h **1,650.00**

Baroque-style, late 19th C, painted, parcel gilt, octagonal marble veined rose colored top above plain frieze, acanthus carved, shaped and tapered legs, 44-1/2" w, 30" h **2,820.00**

Biedermeier, inlaid walnut, shaped rect top, molded frieze with drawer, canted, sq-section cabriole legs, 25" w, 37" l, 27-3/4" h.......... **1,100.00**

Classical

Boston, attributed to, c1825, carved mahogany and mahogany veneer, circular top with inset leather surface, cross banded border, conforming base with four drawers, gilt brass lion's head ring pulls, vase and ring-turned spiral carved center support, gadrooned circular platform, four scrolled reeded and paneled legs, gilt brass hairy paw feet and casters, refinished, minor imperfections, 27-3/4" d, 28" h **12,925.00**

Philadelphia, c1827, carved mahogany veneer, rect top with molded edge, cock-beaded frieze with single central working drawer flanked by faux drawers, turned and carved pedestal ending in gadrooning above stepped, curved pedestal, 4 belted ball feet, old surface, minor imperfections, carving similar to work of Anthony G. Quervelle (1789-1856), Philadelphia, 45-1/4" w, 20" d, 34-3/4" h **2,550.00**

Gothic Revival, attributed to New York State, 1935-45, mahogany veneer, hexagonal top with molded edge overhangs shaped frieze, three faceted columns atop flat base with concave sides on scrolled feet, old refinish, restored, 34-1/4" d, 31" h............ **1,120.00**

International Movement, Wienerwerkstatte, c1930, mahogany and brass, circular top with cross banded edge, conforming frieze, sq-section support flanked by four further cylindrical supports, raised on truncated pyramidal base, 25-1/4" d, 30-1/2" h **550.00**

Louis XV-style, 19th C, mahogany inlaid, ormolu mounted walnut, shaped rect top, one short drawer, opposite faux drawer, cabriole legs, cast sabots, 35" w, 22" d, 28" h **600.00**

Napoleon III, top inset with porcelain plaque depicting Figuros Dining, surrounded by portrait plaques depicting interior scenes, circular carved base mounted with gilt bronze flowers and rams heads, three-sided concave plinth, 35-1/2" d, 34" h.......................... **20,100.00**

Renaissance Revival, inlaid profile portrait of George Washington, eagle, American flags, images of farming, industry, sailing, and travel, c1876..................... **20,900.00**

Victorian, bamboo, lacquer octagonal top, four legs joined by a stretcher with medial shelves, 28" w, 20" d, 28" h **600.00**

Coffee table, International Movement, Paul Evans, 1970, sculpted bronze base comprised of multi-level vertical panels, rectangular glass top with beveled edge, base marked "PE/70," 72" l, 36" w, 16-1/4" h, **$860**.

Photo courtesy of David Rago Auctions, Inc.

Chair

American, late 18th C, cherry, three-board top, hinged seat lid, scalloped edge sides, apron, shoe feet, black paint on underside of top, old refinishing on base, minor repairs, 45-1/2" d top, 28-1/2" h................ **9,350.00**

New England, late 18th C, pine and birch, top tilts above plant seat flanked by sq tapering arm supports which continue to chamfered legs, four sq stretchers, old refinish, 40-1/2" w, 42" d, 28-3/4" h **1,100.00**

New England, early 19th C, pine, maple, and walnut, three-board top tilts above plank seat, walnut arms with turned tapering supports, similar legs terminate in ball and pad feet, old stained red brown surface, repairs, 48-1/4" w, 46-3/4" d, 27-3/4" h **3,300.00**

Coach, Georgian, split leather writing surface closing to box form, S-curve legs joined by stretchers, 24-1/4" w, 24-1/4" d, 31 1/4" h **1,180.00**

Conference table, International Movement, Florence Knoll for Knoll, elliptical rosewood veneer top, chrome-plated steel pedestal base, Knoll Associates label, 96" l, 54" w, 28-1/2" h, provenance: from office of John Wanamaker, Philadelphia, PA, **$2,300**.

Photo courtesy of David Rago Auctions, Inc.

Console table, Arts & Crafts, Limbert, trestle legs, three central slats over one long stretcher, branded under top, refinished, 72" l, 22" d, 29" h, **$5,200**.

Photo courtesy of David Rago Auctions, Inc.

Console table, Victorian, Gothic Revival, c1850, carved mahogany, rectangular, Gothic apron and faceted posts joined by turned stretcher, 39" x 40" x 18-1/2", **$535**.

Photo courtesy of David Rago Auctions, Inc.

Console

Empire, American, mid 19th C, rect white marble top over single drawer, down swept legs joined by medial shelf, 28-3/4" w, 17" d, 28-1/2" h **1,800.00**

George III, mahogany, rect banded top over two drawers, square tapering legs, 51-1/2" w, 23-1/2" d, 34" h **1,400.00**

Neoclassical, attributed to Italy, first half 19th C and later, parcel gilt and painted, inset marble top above frieze painted with rinceaux and scrolling foliage, centered by carved portrait medallion, stop fluted tapering legs, 38" w, 19-1/2" d, 33" h **3,350.00**

Neoclassical-style, 20th C, green painted, parcel gilt, brown marble top above frieze decorated with scrolling foliage, fluted tapering legs, price for pr, 31" w, 14-1/2" d, 35" h **2,400.00**

Rococo-style, polychrome painted and parcel gilt, veneered green marble top, heavily carved scrolling legs joined by stretcher surmounted by shell, 45" w, 23" d, 34" h **4,600.00**

Table, dressing, French, shaped black marble top, single drawer, carved wood and double cane backsplash supporting oval mirror with carved crest, carved acanthus leaf and garland cabriole legs with stretcher base, conforming bench, 52" l, 12" d, 33" h, damage to one leg of bench, **$700**.

Photo courtesy of Alderfer Auction Co.

Table, console, Hepplewhite, English, early 19th C, demilune, paint decorated with garlands of roses and classical scenes, **$1,210**.

Photo courtesy of Wiederseim Associates, Inc.

Card table, Arts & Crafts, Gustav Stickley, New York, c1902, No. 447, two side drawers with faceted wooden pulls, stretchers mortised through legs, keyed through-tenon center stretcher, original finish, early red box decal, minor stains on top, 30" w, 18" d, 28-3/4" h, **$20,000**.

Photo courtesy of David Rago Auctions.

Tea table, Queen Anne, Massachusetts, coastal northern, or New Hampshire, c1730-60, mahogany, molded tray top overhangs straight molded frieze, scrolled skirt, cabriole legs, scrolled knee returns, pad feet on platforms, old refinish, imperfections, 30" w, 19-1/2" d, 27-1/2" h, **$41,400**.

Photo courtesy of Skinner Inc.

Tea table, Chippendale, New England, 18th C, apple wood, tilt-top, serpentine top, cabriole leg base, pad feet, refinished, one foot pierced, 35" w, 34" d, 27-1/4" h, **$460**.

Left: drop-front desk, Arts & Crafts, Limbert, Grand Rapids and Holland, Michigan, slant-front, gallery top, fitted interior, single drawer with square hammered copper pulls, original finish, branded mark, ring stain on top, 33" w, 18-1/4" d, 34-1/2" h, **$1,100**. Right: library table, Arts & Crafts, Limbert, Grand Rapids and Holland, Michigan, rectangular overhanging top, single drawer with square hammered copper pulls, arched apron, original finish, branded mark, 48" w, 28" d, 29" h, **$1,400**. Arts & Crafts lamp also shown.

Photo courtesy of David Rago Auctions.

Dining
Arts & Crafts

Limbert, #403, cut-corner top over intricate base, slab supports with three spindles in an oval cut-out keyed stretchers connecting to a center leg, one leaf, orig finish, numbered, 50" w, 50" d, 30" h........................ **2,500.00**

Stickley, Gustav, c1920, variant of model 634, oak, oval top, six leaves, sq leg posts with mortise and tenon joinery, 46" w, 54-3/4" to 120-3/4" d, 30" h........................ **11,500.00**

Unknown maker, possibly California, c1912, oak, rect board on board top, lower median shelf with through tenons, cutout sides, shoe foot base, deep brown restored finish, 83 1/2" w, 35-1/4" d, 29" h........ **3,200.00**

Empire, carved figure mahogany, mahogany veneer, pine secondary wood, two board top, two 14-3/4" d scalloped leaves, pineapple carved column, short turned drops on corners, brass line inlay along aprons, finely carved paw feet and relief hair on legs, refinished, splits in column, repairs, 30" w, 23 1/4" d, 27-3/4" h........................ **1,560.00**

Federal

Massachusetts, late 18th C, mahogany, rect top with similar drop leaves, straight skirts, molded tapering legs ending in casters, refinished, repairs, provenance: according to family verbal history, this table belonged to General Benjamin Lincoln, who served in Washington's Army during the American Revolution, and accepted the sword of Cornwallis when the British surrendered, 46-3/4" w, 47-3/4" extended, 28-3/4" h **1,550.00**

New England, c1820-25, cherry and bird's eye maple, two parts, two rect ends each with hinged drop-leaf, ring-turned tapering legs ending in ball feet, orig surface, minor surface mars, 82" w, 44-1/2" d, 28-3/4" h.................. **1,725.00**

Federal-style, 19th C, mahogany, three part drop leaf sections, turned,

octagonal legs with casters, 162" l, 48" d, 29" h.... **6,375.00**

George III, late 19th C Mahogany, drop leaf, gate leg, 55-1/4" w, 18-1/2" d, 29-1/4" h **1,770.00**

Mahogany, rect top with rounded corners and reeded edge, double turned pedestals on paneled and reeded downswept legs, brass cap casters, two leaves, 48" w, 115" l with leaves, 28-3/4" h **9,990.00**

George III-style

Crossbanded mahogany, wide inlaid borders, three turned pedestals, downswept feet, brass cap casters, two leaves, 13' l extended, 53" w, 29" h..................... **5,875.00**

Mahogany, D-shaped top with rounded corners and reeded edge, twin pedestal bases of column raised on tripod base, downswept legs, brass toe caps and casters, 120" l, 44" w, 29-1/4" h **2,100.00**

Mahogany, rect top, rounded corners, reeded edge, triple turned pedestals, reeded downswept legs, brass cap casters, two additional leaves, 12'6" l extended, 53-1/2" w, 29-1/2" h **7,100.00**

Georgian-style, painted green, rect top, gadrooned edge, plain frieze, shell carved cabriole legs, claw and ball feet, 53" w, 39" d, 28" h........................... **900.00**

International Movement, Hans Wegner, c1960, teak, circular top fitted on cross stretcher frame with metal mounts set into four tapered circular legs, 61" d **1,880.00**

Louis XVI-style, walnut, circular top splitting to accommodate eight leaves, plain frieze, circular tapered legs, 54-1/2" w, 30-1/2" h..................... **1,175.00**

Queen Anne

Boston area, c1740-50, inlaid figured walnut, top heavy thumb-molded edge outlined in stringing, hinged leaves flank serpentine shaped skirts above the cabriole legs, pad feet, old surface, imperfections, 42" w, 14-1/4" d, 40-3/4" d extended, 28" h **11,200.00**

Virginia or North Carolina, 1760-70, walnut, top with

molded edge, hinged demilune leaves flank straight skirts above block and swelled turned straight legs, pad feet, old refinish, imperfections, 50-1/2" w, 18-3/4" d, 57-3/4" extended, 29-1/2" h **5,600.00**

Regency, late, early 19th C, inlaid mahogany, three parts, D-shaped ends, rect center section, all cross banded in satinwood, checker cross banded frieze and sq tapered legs ending in spade feet, four leaves, 155" l, 54" w, 29" h **5,175.00**

Regency-style, late 19th C, mahogany, rect top, reeded edge, rounded corners, three ring-turned pedestals, molded cabriole legs, casters, two leaves, 48" w, 177" l, 29" h **17,250.00**

Display, Edwardian, inlaid mahogany, shaped rect glazed top on sq tapering legs joined by X-form stretcher **600.00**

Dressing

Chippendale, attributed to Pennsylvania, c1760-80, carved mahogany, rect molded top, case of two cockbeaded graduated drawers flanked by reeded stop-fluted lambrequin corners, cabriole legs, pad feet on platforms, all joined by shaped apron, old brasses, refinished, restored, 31" w, 18" d, 29-1/2" h **5,875.00**

Classical, New England, c1820-40, grain painted and dec, scrolling crest over two short drawers, projecting top with rounded corners on conforming base, single drawer, ring-turned and incised tapering legs, allover grain paint resembling rosewood, highlighted by stencils of fruit bowls and scrolling leaves and flowers, gold, green, and black line dec, minor imperfections, 30" w, 15-1/4" d, 39" h . **1,550.00**

Empire, mahogany, small case top with drawer, dovetailed drawer in center, thin molding around lower apron, figured mahogany veneer over pine, high ring turned legs with relief rope twist carvings, small pieced restorations, 35-1/2" w, 17-3/4" d, 36-1/2" h **1,650.00**

Federal, New York state, c1825, carved mahogany and mahogany veneer, brass inlaid, cock-beaded rect mirror, scrolled acanthus leaf carved supports with brass emb rosettes above three short drawers, projecting case of two short drawers, one long drawer joining four vase and ring-turned acanthus carved legs, casters, refinished, repaired, 36-1/4" w, 21-1/2" d, 55" h **1,725.00**

George I/II, English, c1725, walnut veneer, banded rect top with rounded front corners overhanging shallow straight front fitted with five shallow drawers of banded treatment, plain cabriole legs, pad feet, veneer losses, worm damage, 32" w, 17" d, 30" h **1,875.00**

Drop leaf

Chippendale

New England, southern, c1760-80, cherry, oval overhanging drop leaf top, cut-out apron, scrolled returns, four cabriole legs ending in claw and ball feet, imperfections, 44-1/2" l open, 15-1/2" w, 27" h **4,410.00**

Pennsylvania, late 18th C, walnut, shaped skirt, molded Marlborough legs, old surface, minor imperfections, 15-1/2" w, 46-3/4" l, 29" h **550.00**

Rhode Island, c1780, carved mahogany, rect drop leaf top, four sq molded stop fluted legs joined by cut-out apron, repairs, 47-3/4" w, 38-1/4" d, 29" h **2,100.00**

Classical, attributed to NY, c1820, carved mahogany and mahogany veneer, rect top, overhanging shaped leaves, conforming base with single drawer, beaded skirt, suspending four circular drops on leaf carved pedestal, four curved scrolling acanthus leaf carved and molded legs, brass paw feet on casters, possibly orig glass drawer pull, old refinish, very minor imperfections.............. **1,650.00**

Federal, New England, 1795-1810, mahogany, rect overhanging top, straight skirt, four sq tapering legs, old

Table, game, Centennial, Hepplewhite-style, mahogany veneer with inlay, gate leg, D-shape front with cockbeading above tapered legs, 35-1/2" w, 17" d closed, 34" d open, 28" h, reinforced with angle brackets, crack on one side of top, **$950**.

Photo courtesy of Alderfer Auction Co.

refinish, imperfections, 14-1/2" w, 28" l extended, 26-1/2" h **1,300.00**

Georgian, oak, shaped rect top opening to round surface, six round tapering legs ending in pad feet two legs swing out to support raised leaves, 42-1/2" w, 47" w open, 29" h............................ **900.00**

Hepplewhite, American Birch, old reddish brown surface, two board top, single board leaves, tapered legs, old split in top, 48" w, 19" d, 29-1/2" h **750.00**

Cherry, pegged joints, single board top, scalloped leaves, dovetailed corners on aprons, tapered legs, old mellow finish, old replaced hinges, iron braces added beneath top, 52" l, 19-1/2" d, 18-1/2" leaves, 29" h **575.00**

Queen Anne, early 18th C, mahogany, D-shaped leaves, shaped apron, circular tapering legs, pad feet, 54" w, 49-1/2" h, 28" h **1,765.00**

Regency, mahogany, oak secondary wood, figured veneer on top and D-shaped leaves with banding, single dovetailed drawer on one side with line inlay on front, false

drawer on opposite end, urn shaped column with raised rings, tapered saber legs with inlaid ebony dec, brass caps and casters, old refinishing, old restorations, black staining on underside, 13-1/2" w, 18" d, 27" h **1,035.00**

Sheraton, figured birch, single board top, warped single board leaves, one dovetailed beaded edged drawer, well turned legs, band inlay below end aprons, old finish, replaced brass pull, wear, some replaced supports, 41-3/4" w, 18-1/4" d..... **700.00**

Game

Arts & Crafts, Miller Furniture Co., removable circular top, four plank legs inlaid with stylized floral design, paper label, felted gaming surface missing, overcoated top, 36" d, 31" h **1,150.00**

Empire, tilt-top, mahogany and mahogany flame veneer, top with ogee aprons on sides, turned drops, carved pineapple column, platform base with scrolled leaf returns to carved paw feet, one drawer on side, old dark finish, 40-1/2" w, 20" d, 30" h **450.00**

George III, English, c1790, cross banded mahogany, D-shaped, plain frieze, sq tapered and molded legs, 35" w, 17" d, 28" h **1,150.00**

Hepplewhite, American, 19th C, inlaid cherry, hinged demilune to, conforming apron, sq tapering legs **400.00**

Phyfe, Duncan, c1820, mahogany, top with band of line inlay on edge, urn pedestal, saber legs, top loose, minor veneer loss, 39" w top open, 29" h **1,875.00**

Queen Anne, English, mahogany, hinged two-board top with molded edge, dovetailed drawer, shaped returns, relief carved detail at knees, well shaped cabriole legs, pad feet, rear swing legs, old dark finish, old replaced brass pulls, minor restoration, side returns missing, old splits in top, 35-1/2" w, 16" d, 28-3/4" h **1,550.00**

Renaissance Revival, A. Cutler & Son, Buffalo, NY, c1874, ebonized and parcel-gilt, drop leaf, orig paper label, wear to baise surface, 36" w, 13-3/4" d, 28-3/4" h **700.00**

Sheraton, mahogany, shaped top, cookie corners, shaped frieze, turned reeded legs, replaced supports under top, 36" w, 30-1/2" h **1,225.00**

Victorian, late 19th C, mahogany, rect top, felt playing surface, frieze drawer, Wedgwood mounts, sq tapered legs, 25" w, 15-3/4" d, 30" h.......................... **5,000.00**

William and Mary-style, with antique elements, seaweed marquetry inlaid walnut, D-shaped top with concave front, frieze similar shaped, frieze drawer, turned legs joined by stretchers, 32" w, 14" d, 30" h............... **2,875.00**

Library
Arts & Crafts

English, overhanging top, arched apron, legs carved with stylized tulips, unmarked, refinished, seam separation to top, minor nicks and edge roughness at feet, 46" w, 27" d, 30" h.............. **1,955.00**

Games table, International Movement, Edward Wormley for Dunbar, top inset with green-tooled leather panel, circular recesses in each corner, dark stained wood frame. Green Dunbar tag, some scratches to top, small nicks along edges, 36" square, 28" h, **$750**

Photo courtesy of David Rago Auctions, Inc.

Library table, Chippendale, English, 19th C, oak, rectangular molded top, three drawers, scalloped skirt, square lets, 33-1/4" w, 29" h, **$675**.

Photo courtesy of Wiederseim Associates, Inc.

Robertson Co., H. P., Jamestown, NJ, early 20th C, oak, oval top over single drawer, flanked by side shelves, lower median shelf, imperfections, 48" w, 29-1/4" d, 29-1/4" h **950.00**

Stickley, Gustav, three drawers, hammered copper pulls, sq posts, broad lower shelf, red decal, refinished, 66" l, 36" w, 30-1/2" h **3,775.00**

Stickley, L. & J. G., Fayetteville, NY, similar to model no. 520, oak, rect top, single drawer, corbel supports, low median shelf with through tenons, red and yellow decal "The Work of L. & J. G. Stickley" on int. drawer, imperfections, 42" w, 28-1/8" d, 29-1/4" h .. **1,265.00**

Classical, attributed to Boston, c1825-35, carved mahogany and mahogany veneer, rect top with rounded corners, conforming skirt with two working drawers and four faux drawers, carved shaped supports with scrolled brackets and applied bosses on platforms, scrolled feet joined by medial vase and ring-turned stretcher, old refinish, minor imperfections, 54-1/2" w, 26-1/2" d, 29-3/4" h **4,410.00**

Table, library, Louis XVI style, ormolu mounts, tooled green leather top, single drawer, **$1,000**.

Photo courtesy of Wiederseim Associates, Inc.

Georgian-style, Morris and Co., late 19th/early 20th C, mahogany, tooled red leather top and gadrooned edge, two end drawers, boldly carved cabriole legs, claw and ball feet, 90" l, 53" d, 30" h. **3,450.00**
Renaissance Revival, third quarter 19th C, carved oak, rect top, two frieze drawers with mask form pulls, griffin form legs, shaped plinth, 54" w, 28" d, 30" h **3,910.00**

Low table, International Movement, mid-20th C, triangular glass top with rounded corners, conforming geometric base, 26-3/4" w, 19-1/4" h **360.00**

Night, Louis XV/XVI style, 19th C, inlaid marquetry, oval, sliding cup rest at side, fitted with three drawers, cabriole legs joined by medial shelf, inlaid allover with flower filled vases, pitchers and table articles, price for pr, 12" w, 9-1/2" d, 26-1/2" h **940.00**

Occasional

Aesthetic Movement, American, two circular mahogany veneer tiers on stylized tree branch-form legs, 12-1/2" w, 33" h .. **500.00**
Arts & Crafts, Gustav Stickley, circular overhanging top, faceted finial over arched cross-stretchers, very good orig finish, red decal, 24" d, 29" h........................ **2,185.00**
Biedermeier, early 19th C, birchwood, solid gallery top, inset petit point needlework panel, plain frieze, turned legs joined by stretchers, casters, inscription underneath reading "J. J. Werner, Paris," 21-1/2" w, 18-1/2" d, 29-3/4" h **2,760.00**
International Movement, Mies van der Rohe design, Knoll Associates, NY, circular smoked glass top, tubular metal base, 27-3/8" d, 19-1/2" h...................... **765.00**
Refectory, late 19th or early 20th C, oak, 1-1/2" thick three-board top, two large turned and carved supports, stretcher base, shoe feet, old dark finish, 71-1/2" l, 27-1/2" d, 30-1/2" h.................. **1,550.00**
Sawbuck, primitive, pine, sq nail construction, two board top, sq legs with chamfered outer corners, old refinishing, old repairs, 48-1/2" l, 34-3/4" w, 28" h **900.00**

Serving

Federal, New England, c1800, inlaid mahogany, band inlay around top and leaves, large satinwood oval on top, single dovetailed drawer with satinwood band inlay, bow-front top with end-blocking and serpentine sides with string-inlaid edge above conforming base, single drawer outlined in veneer banding flanked by rect dies above similar banding and string inlaid legs, brasses appear original, old refinish, imperfections, 34-1/2" w, 17" d, 32" h.............. **16,450.00**
George III, c1800 Mahogany, slightly bowed top, pair of drawers, sq tapering legs **1,725.00**
Satinwood and marquetry, demilune, later fitted with spring action drawers, restoration, 62-1/4" w, 23-1/2" d, 32-3/4" h **19,550.00**

Sewing table, mahogany, drop leaf, two drawers, bulbous pedestal, curled foot, 27-1/2" h, **$175**.

Photo courtesy of Joy Luke Auctions.

Sewing

Federal

Boston, MA, c1805, mahogany veneer, mahogany top with outset corners above two veneered cock-beaded drawers, sliding bag frame, flanked by legs with colonettes above reeding, ending in turned tapering feet, old brass, old finish, 20-3/4" w, 15-3/4" d, 28-1/4" h **1,610.00**
New England, mahogany veneer, mahogany top with hinged drop leaves, reeded edge, flanking three veneered drawers, top fitted for writing, bottom with sliding sewing bag frame, ring-turned and spiral carved legs, casters, old refinish, replaced brasses, 18-1/2" w, 18-1/8" d, 29-1/4" h **1,150.00**

French-style, early 20th C, inlaid mahogany, hinged scalloped top finely inlaid with flowers and scrolled leaves, scalloped aprons, delicate cabriole legs with beaded edging, applied ormolu on apron, knees, and feet, shallow int. compartment, old refinish, some alterations, 25" w, 18-1/2" d, 30-1/2" h **600.00**

Sheraton, mahogany, drop leaf, two drawers over one drawer, ring and spiral turned legs, brass cup and caster feet, 20-1/2" closed, 27-3/4" open, 18" d, 28-1/2" h........... **1,200.00**

Table, side, traditional Victorian-Eastlake, c1860, marble top, mahogany, rectangular top with cut-away corners, white marble top, fretwork base, 35" l, 25" d, 29" h, **$1,295**, shown with Satsuma vase on top.

Photo courtesy of Alderfer Auction Co.

Close-up of detailed carved cherubs and claw feet found on side table with square oak top, inset white veined marble, acanthus carving on skirt and pedestal base, **$250**.

Photo courtesy of Dotta Auction Co., Inc.

Side

Baroque, Continental, 17th C and later, walnut, rect top, tapered frieze, scalework and scrolling vine carved legs joined by X-form stretcher, 49-1/2" w, 23-1/2" d, 31" h **600.00**

Classical, New York, 1835-45, mahogany, rect marble top with rounded corners, conforming ogee molded skirt, pierced and scrolled supports, pillar and scroll bases, applied ripple molding joining scrolled medial shelf, casters, old finish, minor imperfections, 31" w, 18-1/2" d, 31" h **3,750.00**

Federal, attributed to southern New England, c1800-10, mahogany and tiger maple veneer inlay, serpentine top with elliptic ends, conforming base, frieze drawer, inlaid tiger maple veneer panels outlined with crossbanding and stringing, four sq tapering legs with conforming inlay continuing to inlaid cuffs, restored, 23-1/4" w, 17" d, 28-1/4" h **10,575.00**

Louis XV, third quarter 18th C, beechwood, demilune, gray and white marble top, plain frieze, sq cabriole legs, 42-1/2" w, 22" d, 27" h **1,530.00**

Louis XV-style

Marquetry inlaid mahogany, kidney-shaped top above lower shelf, cabriole legs **830.00**

Parquetry inlaid, kidney shaped marble top, three-quarter gallery, sq tapered legs, three drawers, 18" w, 11" d, 30 1/2" h **060.00**

Tulipwood, parquetry inlaid, oval marble top, three drawers, sq tapered legs, 18-1/2" w, 12" d, 30-1/2" h **1,100.00**

Neoclassical, Italian, c1800, fruitwood, inlaid walnut, rect case, two drawers, sq tapered legs, inlaid with leafy vines, 20-1/2" w, 13" d, 29-1/2" h, price for pr **3,525.00**

Regency-style, shaped top inset with needlework, turned standard, tripartite base **250.00**

Renaissance Revival, American, walnut, marble top, thumb

Table, tavern, Pennsylvania, 18th C, walnut, two board pinned top, battens dovetailed through it, two lipped drawers, outside stretcher, turned legs, 60" l, 34" d, 30" h, drawer boxes and feet replaced, provenance: purchased by consignor at Oct 1953 auction of estate of George S. Kaufman, auction catalog accompanies table, **$1,000**. Child's Windsor arm chair on top, signed by I. Pugh, Chester County, Pennsylvania, c1810, bamboo turned legs and spindles, 12" w, 8-1/2" h seat, 20-1/2" h overall, **$250**.

Photo courtesy of Alderfer Auction Co.

molded edge, shaped corners, four angular legs with central turned post, mounted with roundels, casters, 28-1/2" w, 20" d, 29" h **750.00**

Rococo, Italian, 19th C, walnut, serpentine top and case, foliate carved apron, two drawers, cabriole legs, 36" w, 18" d, 34" h **1,765.00**

Rococo-style, 19th C, crossbanded fruitwood, serpentine top and case, three drawers, 13" w, 10-1/2" d, 29" h **450.00**

Victorian

Bamboo, octagonal lacquer top over four drop leaves, four legs joined by stretcher with medial shelf, 22" w, 22" d, 28" h **600.00**

Mahogany, sq top, frieze with applied branch form carvings, branch form legs, 27" d, 25-3/4" d, 29-3/4" h **250.00**

Silver, George III, c1765, carved mahogany, galleried tray top, low relief carved everted lip, repeating border of C-scrolls and foliage, swirling scroll bordered apron, molded sq cabriole supports with trailing

acanthus carving at knees, Spanish feet, alternations to top, repairs, 31-3/4" l 28-3/4" h **2,000.00**

Sofa

Edwardian, c1895, painted satinwood, rounded drop leaves, two frieze drawers, trestle supports ending in brass paw casters, 36" w closed, 26-1/2" d, 28-1/2" h **8,100.00**

Regency, c1820, crossbanded mahogany, wide rect top, drop leaves with canted corners, frieze drawers to both sides, turned trestle bases, inlaid with boxwood and ebony, 52" w, 36" d, 28-1/2" h **3,525.00**

Tavern

Country, Pennsylvania, softwood, circular top, stretcher base, beaded skirt, legs with old orange painted surface, most orig wrought brass and iron tacks, many with remnants of probably orig muslin-like fabric underneath tack head, 28" d, 25-1/2" h **4,950.00**

Moravian, Pennsylvania, 18th C, walnut, pegged construction, pin top, three board thumb molded top, dovetailed drawer, boldly turned legs, horizontal stretchers, turned feet, restoration to feet, 61" w, 34" d, 30" h.............. **6,050.00**

Tea

Art Deco, France, c1928, walnut, rect top opens and swivels on U-shaped base, 44" l open, 22" closed, 35-1/4" w, 28-1/4" h... **1,880.00**

Chippendale

America, possibly Philadelphia, piecrust tilt top, figured mahogany one-piece circular top, ogee and crescent form carving, birdcage support, fluted column, compressed ball knop, three legs with plain knees, ball and claw feet, 28-1/2" h................. **10,575.00**

Connecticut, late 18th C, cherry, round top tilts and revolves above birdcage mechanism, tapering shaft with suppressed ball and ring turnings, tripod cabriole leg base, pad feet, refinished, imperfections, 36-1/2" d, 28-3/4" h.................... **3,100.00**

Country, mahogany, two board dish top and key old replacements, urn shaped column with birdcage, cabriole legs, padded snake feet, old refinishing, shims added, 29-1/4" d, 26-3/4" h........ **850.00**

Chippendale-style, America, mahogany, round tilt-top, well turned column, cabriole legs, snake feet, orig dark finish, minor edge wear, block needs stabilization, 32" d top, 27-1/2" h...................... **500.00**

George III, mahogany, circular tilt top, ring turned standard, tripod legs, pad feet, 32-1/4" d, 28-1/2" h .. **1,100.00**

Hepplewhite, tilt top, poplar one board top with cut corners, birch tripod base with spider legs, turned column, old refinishing with painted foliage border designs in shades of gold and black, top replaced, repairs, 15-1/2" w, 23-1/2" l, 28-3/4" h **440.00**

Queen Anne

Massachusetts, 1740-60, maple, oval overhanging drop-leaf top, cabriole legs, pad feet on platforms joined by cutout apron, old refinish, repairs, 31" w, 32-1/2" d, 27" h **30,550.00**

New England, c1760-80, cherry, circular tilt top, vase and ring-turned post and tripod cabriole leg base, pad feet, refinished, minor imperfections, 34-1/4" d, 27-1/2" h **1,175.00**

Victorian, papier-mâché, gilt and mother-of-pearl inlaid, shaped round tilt top, dec with urn of flowers, turned standard, tripartite base, 22" w, 22" d, 29" h **885.00**

Tilt-Top

Federal, New England, mahogany inlaid, octagonal top with string inlay in outline, urn shaped pedestal, cabriole legs, arris pad feet on platforms, orig surface, very minor imperfections, 22" w, 14-3/4" d, 29-1/2" h **3,750.00**

Georgian, late 18th C, mahogany, plain circular top over turned baluster standard, three cabriole legs ending in shaped pad feet, 32" d, 27-3/8" h **1,100.00**

Tray, Edwardian, c1900, satinwood and inlay, two oval tiers, removable wood and glass tray, slightly splayed sq tapering legs joined by stretcher, 36" w, 20-1/4" d, 32" h............ **1,150.00**

Trestle

Country, Pennsylvania, removable sliding scrubbed top, shaped cut-out legs, mortise and tenon stretcher, old green painted surface, 66" l, 16" d, 28-1/2" h **3,575.00**

William IV, parquetry inlaid specimen wood, c1835, rect top, pendant applied frieze, trestle with turned ends and stretcher, cabriole legs, 33-1/4" w, 17-1/2" d, 29-1/2" h **2,000.00**

Tripod

George III-style, mahogany, tilt-top, piecrust edge, acanthus carved stem and tripod base, slipper feet, 22-1/2" d, 28" h **825.00**

Georgian-style, 20th C, mahogany, silver plated

mounts, serpentine reticulated gallery, turned stem, cabriole legs, price for pr, 15" d, 22" h **450.00**

Work

Biedermeier, walnut and mahogany, rect top with line inlay around center panel, dovetailed drawer with divided interior, beaded aprons, exaggerated serpentine legs, central stretcher, stamped signature "A. Gastaldi" on back of drawer, old refinishing, restorations, 24-1/2" w, 16-3/4" d, 31-1/4" h **665.00**

Classical, Boston, 1830, mahogany veneer, solid top, hinged rounded drop leaves with beaded edges, flank two convex veneered drawers, top one fitted for writing, lower with replaced fabric sewing fabric bag, turned tapering legs which flank shaped veneered platform, ebonized bun feet, orig stamped brass pulls, imperfections, minor warp in leaf, 19" w, 19" d, 28-3/4" h **980.00**

Federal

Massachusetts, early 19th C, mahogany veneer, sq top with molded edge, hinged leaves flank two working drawers and bag frame, spiral carved legs, turned feet, casters, original brass, old refinish, 18-1/4" w, 17-1/4" d, 29-7/8" h **1,645.00**

New England, c1825, butternut, birch, and bird's eye maple, overhanging rect top, two drawers, straight skirt, vase and ring-turned legs, old brass pulls, refinished, minor imperfections, 20" w, 18-3/4" d, 29" h **1,175.00**

Federal, late, New York State, c1820, tiger maple, shaped hinged top lifts above two drawer facade, upper faux one, lower working one with divided interior, turned pedestal, four incurvate legs ending in tiny ball feet, brasses replaced, refinished, 22-1/2" w, 15-7/8" d, 32" h **2,820.00**

George III, early 19th C, mahogany, rect top, canted corners, fitted int., sq tapered and slightly splayed legs joined by stretchers . **2,380.00**

Hepplewhite, country, walnut and pine, wooden peg construction, one board top, tapered and splayed legs, later blue paint, thin coat of varnish, minor hairlines, split, minor insect damage on legs, 25" x 33" top, 29-1/2" h **650.00**

Queen Anne

Country, walnut, yellow pine and poplar secondary woods, pegged construction, three board top, beaded aprons with two dovetailed drawers, tapered legs, pad feet, orig brass pulls, old finish, 48" w, 31" d, 29" h **1,200.00**

New England, late 18th C, maple and pine, scrubbed top, straight skirt with beaded edge, turned tapering legs ending in turned button feet, old surface, remnants of red on base, 28" w, 28-1/2" l, 27" h **2,530.00**

Pennsylvania, c1760-1800, black walnut and pine, painted, removable blank three-board pine top, supported by cleats and four dowels, two thumb-molded drawers, straight skirt with beaded edge above straight cabriole legs ending in pad feet, orig apple green paint, old replaced wooden pulls, surface imperfections, cracked foot, 48-1/2" w, 32" d, 27" h **2,500.00**

Sheraton, mahogany and mahogany veneer, three dovetailed drawers, turned legs with ring turned detail, orig gilded lion head brasses, old finish, top drawer is fitted with tilt-up writing surface, age cracks in sides, some veneer damage to writing tablet, 16" w, 18" l, 27-3/4" h **1,430.00**

William and Mary-style, walnut, ebonized trim, two-board top, one dovetailed drawer, turned stretchers and legs, repairs and old replacements, 22-3/4" w, 34" d, 27-1/4" h **935.00**

Writing, Aesthetic Movement, American, walnut, felt top, two frieze drawers, angular foliate carved trestle base, casters, 36-1/2" w, 22" d, 29" h **400.00**

GAME BOARDS

History: Wooden game boards have a long history and were some of the first toys early Americans enjoyed. Games such as checkers, chess, and others were easy to play and required only simple markers or playing pieces. Most were handmade, but some machine-made examples exist.

Game boards can be found in interesting color combinations. Some include small drawers to hold the playing pieces. Others have an interesting molding or frame. Look for signs of use from long hours of enjoyment.

Today, game boards are popular with game collectors, folk art collectors, and decorators because of their interesting forms.

Reproduction Alert.

Checkerboard, America, 19th C, inlaid wood, rectangle, alternating light and dark wood inlaid squares, contrasting rayed corners and borders, ebony pegged frame with inlaid triangle decoration, age crack, 18-1/2" x 24", **$300.**

Photo courtesy of Skinner, Inc.

Checkerboard

10-1/2" w, 19-1/2" h, painted green and yellow, late 19th C, paint imperfections **1,955.00**
12-1/2" w, 12-3/4" h, painted black and white, tan colored ground, sgd "F. Smith," PA, c1870 .... **1,955.00**
13-7/8" w, 13-3/4" h, painted hunter green and iron red, black frame, yellow grain paint on reverse, America, 19th C, minor paint war **1,380.00**
14" w, 20-1/4" h, oak and mahogany squares, galleried edge with two reserves on sides with sliding lid compartments to hold checkers, two sets of

checkers, one round, one square, minor wear, light alligatoring to old black paint on lids and gallery **330.00**
15-1/4" sq, painted black and salmon, New England, 19th C **2,300.00**
16" sq, blue and white, yellowed varnish, New England, 19th C **3,335.00**
16" w, 17-1/2" h, painted red and white checkerboard, orig cherry frame, Newburyport, MA, c1850 .... **980.00**
17" w, 16" h, painted green and white, unfinished, inscribed on reverse, late 19th/early 20th C **460.00**
17-1/2" x 24", pine, breadboard ends, additional strip on one side, old red and black checkerboard slightly off center, varnished, age split, minor edge wear **200.00**
18" w, 21" h, painted red and black, yellow dec, Michigan, c1880 .... **2,415.00**
18-1/2" sq, painted yellow and black, green detailing, c1880 .... **5,465.00**
19-1/2" sq, painted slate, incised geometric design, hand painted to resemble hardstones, shades of marbleized green and red, solid dark red checks, shaded yellow ground, mottled black border, New England, late 19th C, minor paint wear at margins **1,645.00**
20" w, 18-3/4" h, painted and gilt dec, molded edge, reverse marked "Saco Lodge No. 2," Saco, Maine, 19th C **5,175.00**
21-1/2" x 17-1/2", incised checkerboard under glass, red, lime green, yellow, and black, reverse painted in red, white, and blue, framed, America, 20th C, minor paint wear **650.00**
25" x 15", poplar, old dry paint with gold and black blocks surrounded by red borders, black ground, red roundels with gold stars in each corner, reverse side painted red, breadboard ends with wire nails **825.00**

Double-sided

7-1/4" w, 7" h, painted pine, brown and black checkerboard on one side, painted brown Old Mill game inscribed on reverse, two sliding panel compartments, New York State, early 19th C **1,150.00**

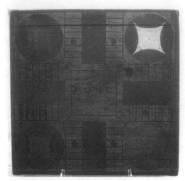

Double sided, one side with checkerboard design, other with Parcheesi, wood, hand-painted wood, minor loss and wear, 20" square, **$535.**

Photo courtesy of Alderfer Auction Co.

12-1/4" w, 12" h, painted apple green, brown, and black, obverse with checkerboard, reverse with snake-motif game, America, mid-19th C .. **36,800.00**
14" sq, mustard and black **975.00**
14-1/4" sq, painted black and red, obverse with checkerboard, reverse with Old Mill, applied molded edge, New England, c1850-70 .... **4,890.00**
14-7/8" w, 15-7/8" h, painted deep blue-green, red and black, checkerboard on obverse, backgammon on reverse, America, 19th C **2,530.00**
15" w, 16" h, painted mustard, red, and green, checkerboard on obverse, backgammon on reverse, America, 19th C **3,335.00**
17" sq, obverse with Parcheesi, painted red, teal, orange, and green, checkerboard on reverse with orange, black, and yellow paint, c1900, paint wear to obverse at edges **2,530.00**
18-1/2" sq, painted, one side with Parcheesi game and primitive scene of hunter returning home in center, checkerboard on other side, small plated feet at corners, age split **4,485.00**
20-1/8" x 20-1/2", painted wood, sq board with applied frame, one side checkerboard painted yellow, black, green, and red, other side backgammon game in the same colors, America, 19th C, wear...................... **1,645.00**
21-1/4" x 21-1/2", painted, applied molding, red and black checkerboard outlined in yellow

on one side, Ouija board with black stenciled lettering and symbols on reverse, America, late 19th C...................... **470.00**
23" w, 17-1/4" h, painted apple green, black, and red, checkerboard on obverse, backgammon on reverse, game piece compartments, America, c1870-80 .... **3,750.00**

Folding

12-1/2" w, 31" h, painted avocado green, colorful raised segmented tracks, opens for storage, mid-20th C, wear **575.00**

Parcheesi, rectangular, white, red, black, and green polychrome decoration, **$595.**

Parcheesi

18" w, 17-3/4" h, folding, patriotic red, white, and blue stars and dec, New England, late 19th C **4,350.00**
18-1/2" sq, folding, painted American flag and spade, heart, diamond, and club motifs, MA, c1870, minor paint imperfections **46,000.00**
19-1/2" sq, folding, painted green, white, black, and yellow, varied geometric designs on game corners, America, 19th C **2,875.00**
25" w, 24-1/2" h, painted, center rosette, bull's eye corners, attributed to Maine, 19th C, wear **4,600.00**
27-1/2" w, 27" h, painted red, yellow, and green, New England, 1870-80......................... **5,750.00**

GAME PLATES

History: Game plates, popular between 1870 and 1915, are specially decorated plates used to serve fish and game. Sets originally included a platter, serving plates, and a sauce or gravy boat. Many sets have been divided. Today, individual plates are often used as wall hangings.

Birds

Plate
8" sq, each hand painted with gold trim, light and dark gray corners, center with game birds, gold outlines, mauve circular mark "Carlsbad Mark & Gutherz," price for 11-pc set............................... **700.00**
9-1/4" d, hp, set of 12 with different center scene of shore birds in natural setting, apple green edge, printed gold scrolled rim dec, artist sgd "B. Albert," Theodore Haviland & Co., France, early 20th C **865.00**
9-1/2" d, duck, pastel pink, blue, and cream ground, duck flying up from water, yellow flowers and grasses, sgd "Laury," marked "Limoges," not pierced for hanging...... **120.00**
13-1/4" d, game bird and pheasant, heavy gold, scalloped emb rococo border, marked "Coronet Limoges, Bussilion".................. **250.00**
Platter
16" l, two handles, quail, hp gold trim, Limoges...... **150.00**
18" d, flying grouse, scrolled gilt rim, hp, artist sgd "A. Brousselton," mkd "Limoges/Crown/Coronet/France" . **615.00**
Set
Seven pcs, wild game birds, pastoral scene, molded edges, shell dec, Fazent Meheim, Bonn, Germany............. **250.00**
Twelve pcs, 10-1/2" d plates, game birds in natural habitat, sgd "I. Bubedi" **3,500.00**
Fourteen pcs, 20-3/4" platter with strutting tom turkey, 9" gravy boat, twelve 10" d plates with different turkey designs, hp, artist sgd "Gasri," green "LDBC Hambeau Limoges" mark **700.00**

Deer

Plate, 9" d, buck and doe, forest scene **60.00**
Set, 13 pcs, platter, 12 plates, deer, bear, and game birds, yellow ground, scalloped border, "Haviland China," sgd "MC Haywood" **3,200.00**

Fish

Plate
8" d, bass, scalloped edge, gray-green trim, fern on side of fish, Limoges **65.00**
8-1/2" d, colorful fish swimming on green shaded ground, scalloped border, gold trim, sgd "Lancy," "Bairritz, W. S. or S. W. Co. Limoges, France," pierced for hanging....................... **50.00**
Platter
14" l, bass on lure, sgd "RK Beck" **125.00**
23" l, hp, Charoone, Haviland **200.00**
Set
Seven pcs, platter, six serving plates, each with different fish dec, white ground, gold trim, Italian **125.00**
Eight pcs, four plates, 24" l, platter, sauce boat with attached plate, cov tureen, Rosenthal.................. **425.00**
Eleven pcs, 10 plates, serving platter, sgd "Limoges" **360.00**
Fifteen pcs, 12 9" plates, 24" platter, sauce boat with attached plate, cov tureen, hp, raised gold design edge, artist sgd, Limoges **800.00**

GAMES

History: Board games have been commercially produced in this country since at least 1822, and card games since the 1780s. However, it was not until the 1840s that large numbers of games were produced that survive to this day. The W. & S. B. Ives Company produced many board and card games in the 1840s and 1950s. Milton Bradley and McLoughlin Brothers became major producers of games starting in the 1860s, followed by Parker Brothers in the 1880s. Other major producers of games in this period were Bliss, Chaffee and Selchow, Selchow and Righter, and Singer.

Today, most games from the 19th century are rare and highly collectible, primarily because of their spectacular lithography. McLoughlin and Bliss command a premium because of the rarity, quality of materials, and the extraordinary art that was created to grace the covers and boards of their games.

In the 20th century, Milton Bradley, Selchow and Righter, and Parker Brothers became the primary manufacturers of boxed games. They have all now been absorbed by toy giant Hasbro Corporation. Other noteworthy producers were All-Fair, Pressman, and Transogram, all of which are no longer in business. Today, the hottest part of the game collecting market is in rare character games from the 1960s. Parker Brothers and All-Fair games from the 1920s to 1940s also have some excellent lithography and are highly collectible.

Additional Listings: See *Warman's Americana & Collectibles.*

Notes: While people collect games for many reasons, it is strong graphic images that bring the highest prices. Games collected because they are fun to play or for nostalgic reasons are still collectible, but will not bring high prices. Also, game collectors are not interested in common and "public domain" games such as checkers, tiddlywinks, Authors, Anagrams, Jackstraws, Rook, Pit, Flinch, and Peter Coodles. The game market today is characterized by fairly stable prices for ordinary items, increasing discrimination for grades of condition, and continually rising prices for rare material in excellent condition. Whether you are a dealer or collector, be careful to buy games in good condition. Avoid games with taped or split corners or other box damage. Games made after about 1950 are difficult to sell unless they are complete and in excellent condition. As games get older, there is a forgiveness factor for condition and completeness that increases with age.

These listings are for games that are complete and in excellent condition. Be sure the game you're looking to price is the same as the one described in the listing. The 19th century makers routinely published the same title on several different versions of the game, varying in size and graphics. Dimensions listed here are rounded to the nearest half inch.

A Christmas Dinner game, Parker Brothers, 1897, **$1,000**.

Bull in a China Shop, Milton Bradley, 1937 .... **100.00**
Chiromagia Game, McLoughlin, three answer sheets, two question discs, lid missing **100.00**
Clue, Parker Brothers, c1949, separate board and pieces box **25.00**
Dixie Pollyana, Parker Brothers, c1952, 8" x 18", all wooden pcs, four orig dice and diceaups **100.00**
Elsie and Her Family, Selchow & Righter Co., 1941, 12-1/2" x 14-1/2" x 1-1/2" **200.00**

Elsie and Her Family, Selchow & Righter, N.Y. #204, copyright 1941, 12-1/2" x 14" x 1-1/2" deep colorful red box with Elsie, Elmer and Beulah on lid, **$65**.
Photo courtesy of Hake's Americana & Collectibles.

Fish Pond, McLoughlin Bros., c1898, 8" x 18", children on cover **125.00**

Flying the United States Air Mail Game, Parker Bros, 1929 copyright, 17" x 27-1/2" playing board, orig playing pcs, deck of cards, 1-1/2" x 14-1/2" x 18" box **55.00**

Game of Billy Possum, c1910, 8" x 15" **600.00**

Game of Bo Peep, J. H. Singer, 8-1/2" x 14" **275.00**

Game of Snow White and the Seven Dwarfs, The, Milton Bradley, Walt Disney Enterprises, 1937 .... **100.00**

Game of the Wizard of Oz, The, Whitman, c1939, 7" x 13-1/2" **300.00**

Hi Ho Silhouette Game, 1932 .... **30.00**

Junior Combination Board, Milton Bradley, c1905, 16-1/2" sq **85.00**

Limited Mail and Express Game, The, Parker Brothers, c1894, 14" x 21", metal train playing pieces **250.00**

Lone Ranger Hi Yo Silver Game, Parker Brothers, 1938 .... **200.00**

Mansion of Happiness, The, W. & S. B. Ives, c1843.... **950.00**

Mickey Mantle's Big League Baseball Game, Gardner Games **195.00**

Lindy The Flying Game, Parker Bros., "Improved Edition," original box, **$225**.

Monopoly, Parker Brothers, c1935, white box edition #9, metal playing pieces and embossed hotels **150.00**

Monopoly, Parker Brothers, 1946 Popular Edition, separate board and pieces box....... **25.00**

Motorcycle Game, Milton Bradley, c1905, 9" x 9" **250.00**

New Board Game of the American Revolution, Lorenzo Borge, 1844, colored scenes and events, 18-1/2" w opened **690.00**

One Two, Button Your Shoe, Master Toy Company, 11" x 12" **145.00**

Peter Coddles Trip to New York, Milton Bradley, orig instruction sheet, 6" x 8-1/2" **65.00**

Radio Amateur Hour Game, 10" x 13" **145.00**

Strange Game of Forbidden Fruit, Parker Brothers, c1900, 4" x 5-1/2" **35.00**

Tiddledy Winks Game, stork motif, **$15**.

Truth or Consequences, Gabriel, c1955, 14" x 19-1/2" **75.00**

Uncle Sam's Mail, Milton Bradley, c1910, 16-1/4" x 15" x 1-1/4" **115.00**

Young America Target, Parker Bros................................... **75.00**

GAUDY DUTCH

History: Gaudy Dutch is an opaque, soft-paste ware made between 1790 and 1825 in England's Staffordshire district.

The wares first were hand decorated in an underglaze blue and fired; then additional decorations were added over the glaze. The over-glaze decoration is extensively worn on many of the antique pieces. Gaudy Dutch found a ready market in the Pennsylvania German community because it was inexpensive and extremely colorful. It had little appeal in England.

> **Reproduction Alert:** Cup plates, bearing the impressed mark "CYBRIS," have been reproduced and are collectible in their own right. The Henry Ford Museum has issued pieces in the Single Rose pattern, although they are porcelain rather than soft paste.

Marks: Marks of various potters, including the impressed marks of Riley and Wood, have been found on some pieces, although most are unmarked.

Adviser: John D. Querry.

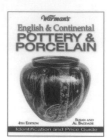

For more information, see *Warman's English & Continental Pottery & Porcelain*, 4th edition.

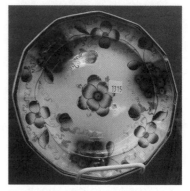

Plate, floral and strawberry pattern, grape clusters highlighted in cobalt blue, pink, blue, and green, marked "T. Walker" on back, **$90**.

Butterfly
Coffeepot, 11" h....... **9,500.00**
Cup and saucer, handleless, minor enamel flakes, chips on table ring **950.00**
Plate, 7-1/4" d **645.00**
Sugar bowl, cov......... **900.00**
Teapot, 5" h, squat baluster form **2,400.00**

Carnation
Bowl, 6-1/4" d **925.00**
Creamer, 4-3/4" h....... **700.00**
Pitcher, 6" h............... **675.00**
Plate, 9-3/4" d **1,265.00**
Saucer, cobalt blue, orange, green, and yellow, stains, hairline, minor flake on table ring, 5-1/2" d **115.00**
Teapot, cov **2,200.00**
Waste bowl **675.00**

Dahlia
Bowl, 6-1/4" d **1,800.00**
Plate, 8" d **2,800.00**
Tea bowl and saucer... **8,000.00**

Plate, cobalt blue flowers and leaves, copper luster trim, **$115**.

Double Rose
Bowl, 0-1/4" d.............. **545.00**
Creamer...................... **650.00**
Gravy boat.................. **950.00**
Plate, 8-1/4" d **675.00**
Sugar bowl, cov.......... **750.00**
Tea bowl and saucer .. **675.00**
Toddy plate, 4-1/2" d... **675.00**
Waste bowl, 6-1/2" d, 3" h
.... **850.00**

Dove
Creamer...................... **675.00**
Plate, 8-1/8" d, very worn, scratches, stains......... **245.00**
Plate, 8-1/2" d **770.00**
Tea bowl and saucer .. **500.00**
Waste bowl **650.00**

Flower Basket, plate, 6-1/2" d
.... **375.00**

Grape
Bowl, 6-1/2" d, lustered rim
.... **475.00**
Plate, 8-1/4" d, cobalt blue, orange, green, and yellow, minor stains **450.00**
Sugar bowl, cov.......... **675.00**
Tea bowl and saucer .. **475.00**
Toddy plate, 5" d........ **475.00**

Leaf, bowl, 11-1/2" d, shallow
.... **4,800.00**

Plate, Morning Glory motif, cobalt blue flowers, two-toned green leaves, pink highlights, chips, **$25**.

Plate, Morning Glory motif, cobalt blue flowers and leaves, chip, **$35**.

No Name
Plate, 8-3/4" d **17,000.00**
Teapot, cov **16,000.00**

Oyster
Bowl, 5-1/2" d **675.00**
Coffeepot, cov, 12" h
.... **10,000.00**
Plate, 10" d **1,550.00**
Soup plate, 8-1/2" d.... **550.00**
Tea bowl and saucer **1,275.00**
Toddy plate, 5-1/2" d .. **475.00**

Single Rose
Coffeepot, cov **8,500.00**
Cup and saucer, handleless, minor wear and stains **330.00**
Plate, 7-1/4" d **550.00**
Plate, 10" d **975.00**
Quill holder, cov....... **2,500.00**
Sugar bowl, cov......... **700.00**
Teapot, cov **1,200.00**
Toddy plate, 5-1/4" d .. **250.00**

Sunflower
Bowl, 6-1/2" d **900.00**
Coffeepot, cov, 9-1/2" h
.... **6,500.00**
Cup and saucer, handleless, wear, chips **575.00**
Plate, 9-3/4" d **825.00**

Plate, Urn pattern, c1810, some loss to glaze, 9-7/8" d, **$920**.

Photo courtesy of Pook & Pook.

Urn
Creamer...................... **475.00**
Cup and saucer, handleless
.... **550.00**
Plate, 8-1/4" d **910.00**
Plate, 9-7/8" d, very worn, scratches, stains, rim, chips
.... **225.00**
Sugar bowl, cov, 6-1/2" h, round, tip and base restored
.... **295.00**
Teapot...................... **895.00**

Cup and saucer, War Bonnet pattern, **$520**.

Photo courtesy of Pook & Pook.

War Bonnet
Bowl, cov **225.00**
Coffeepot, cov **9,500.00**
Plate, 8-1/8" d, pinpoint rim flake, minor wear **880.00**
Teapot, cov **4,400.00**
Toddy plate, 4-1/2" d . **975.00**

Zinna, soup plate, 10" d, Impressed "Riley" **4,875.00**

GAUDY IRONSTONE

History: Gaudy Ironstone was made in England around 1850. Ironstone is an opaque, heavy-bodied earthenware which contains large proportions of flint and slag. Gaudy Ironstone is decorated in patterns and colors similar to those of Gaudy Welsh.

Marks: Most pieces are impressed "Ironstone" and bear a registry mark.

Biscuit jar, 7-1/2" h, Rococo molded body, polychrome floral, Flow Blue accents, backstamp monogram for "F. J. Emery," Burslem, England, c1890 **195.00**

Bread plate, 10-1/4" l, 5-1/4" w, marked "Tunstall, England, by Enoch Wedgwood" **65.00**

Charger
10-7/8" d, blue star design, orange-red flowers, blue green detail, wear....... **150.00**

Dinner service, Strawberry pattern, 95 pieces, flow blue underglaze decoration, red, green and gilt overglaze decoration, three octagonal platters, 10-3/4" l, 13-3/4" l, 15-3/4" l; 9-1/2" octagonal serving dish; two shell form 8-3/4" l relish dishes; 11" h coffeepot, 9-1/2" h teapot, 8-1/2" h covered sugar, three 6" h creamers, 14 handle-less 3-3/4" d cups, 12 6" d saucers, 18 9-1/2" d plates, 14 8-5/8" d plates; 10 7-7/8" d plates, two 6-5/8" d plates, 10 2-3/4" d bowls, two 10-3/4" d bowls, 5-1/2" d waste bowl, scattered chips, crazing, repairs, **$9,200**.

Photo courtesy of Alderfer Auction Co.

Plates, flow blue underglaze decoration, red, green, and gilt floral decoration painted over glaze, copper luster rims, two 9-1/4" d octagonal plates, six 8-1/2" d round plates, scattered edge chips, **$300**.

Photo courtesy of Alderfer Auction Co.

Soup plate, 9-7/8" d, Blackberry pattern, underglaze blue, yellow, and orange enamel and luster, one imp "Elsmore & Forster, Tunstall," price for set of three
.... **650.00**

Platter, octagonal, Morning Glory pattern, deep cobalt blue, green, pink, **$500**.

Photo courtesy of Joseph P. Smalley, Jr., Auctioneer.

11-3/8" d, stylized urn, large cobalt blue and orange-red flowers, small green leaves, copper luster highlights, price for pr **435.00**
12-1/8" d, center yellow daisy-shaped flower surrounded by orange-red flowers, tornado shaped blossoms, cobalt blue leaves, copper luster detail, imp "Emberton" on back, minor scratches **350.00**
14-1/8" d, 2-5/8" h, red Adams type roses, green leaves, blue feathers, red and yellow border, partial imp label, wear **250.00**
Coffeepot, cov, 10" h, Strawberry pattern **650.00**
Creamer and sugar, 6-3/4" h, fruit finial, Blackberry pattern, underglaze blue, yellow, and orange enamel and luster, wear, small flakes, int. chip on sugar **990.00**
Cup and saucer, handleless Blackberry pattern, underglaze blue, yellow, and orange enamel and luster, imp label or registry mark with "E. Walley," price for set of 10 .... **1,375.00**
Deep blue and orange flowers, pink and copper luster leaves................ **225.00**
Jug, 7-1/2" h, yellow, red, white, and blue tulips on sides, light blue pebble ground, luster trim, rim outlined **350.00**
Pitcher, 11" h, six-color floral dec, blue, green, burgundy, mauve, black, and yellow,

molded serpent handle, dec has been enhanced, then reglazed, spider.............................. **320.00**

Pitcher, large red rose, blue cornflowers, green leaves, embossed scrolls around top and handle, **$225**.

Plate
6-1/4" d, Morning Glories and Strawberries pattern, underglaze blue, polychrome enamel and luster trim .. **80.00**
9-1/2" d, Blackberry pattern, underglaze blue, yellow, and orange enamel and luster, some wear, set of seven **1,320.00**
Platter, 18" x 14-1/2", recessed tree and well, cobalt blue floral dec, over glaze tomato red detail, imp "Mason's Patent Ironstone," wear, some flowers simply outlined **250.00**

Strawberry pattern, left: covered sugar bowl with paneled sides, applied acanthus leaf handles, 8-1/2" h, small interior rim chip, **$575**; right: pitcher, paneled sides, 8-1/2" h, cracking in handle, discoloration on rim, small chip, **$850**.

Photo courtesy of Alderfer Auction Co.

Sugar bowl, cov, 8-1/2" h, Strawberry pattern **425.00**

Teapot, 9-3/4" h, domed cov, floral finial, paneled body, blue flower, red and green strawberries, gilt highlights, c1850 .... **2,300.00**

Wash basin and pitcher, 14" d bowl, 13" h pitcher, hexagonal, blue morning glories and leaves, copper accents, hp red, green, and yellow berries, hairlines **1,225.00**

GAUDY WELSH

History: Gaudy Welsh is a translucent porcelain that was originally made in the Swansea area of England from 1830 to 1845. Although the designs resemble Gaudy Dutch, the body texture and weight differ. One of the characteristics is the gold luster on top of the glaze. In 1890, Allerton made a similar ware from heavier opaque porcelain.

Marks: Allerton pieces usually bear an export mark.

For more information, see *Warman's English & Continental Pottery & Porcelain*, 4th edition.

Bethesda, pitcher, 6-3/8" h, paneled form, scalloped rims, figural dragon handles, imp "Ironstone, China," some wear, price for pr **300.00**

Chinoiserie, teapot, c1830-40 .... **750.00**

Columbine
Bowl, 10" d, 5-1/2" h, ftd, underglaze blue and polychrome enamel floral dec **400.00**
Plate, 5-1/2" d **65.00**
Tea set, c1810, 17-pc set **625.00**

Conwys, jug, 9" h **750.00**

Pitcher, green mark "Allertons, Est. 1831, Made in England," **$125**.

Photo courtesy of Potts Auction Co., Inc.

Daisy and Chain
Creamer **175.00**
Cup and saucer **95.00**
Sugar, cov **195.00**
Teapot, cov **225.00**

Flower Basket
Bowl, 10-1/2" d **190.00**
Mug, 4" h **90.00**
Plate............................ **65.00**
Sugar, cov, luster trim . **195.00**

Grape
Bowl, 5-1/4" d **50.00**
Cup and saucer............ **75.00**
Mug, 2-1/2" h **65.00**
Plate, 5-1/4" d **65.00**

Plate, underglaze cobalt blue floral design, **$75**.

Grapevine Variant, miniature pitcher and bowl, 4-1/4" h pitcher, 4-1/2" d bowl, cobalt blue, orange, green, and luster, scalloped edges **250.00**

Oyster
Bowl, 6" d..................... **80.00**
Creamer, 3" h **100.00**
Jug, 5-3/4" h, c1820 ..... **85.00**
Soup plate, 10" d, flange rim **85.00**

Primrose, plate 8-1/4" d . **350.00**

Server, three bowls, each with brick red, cobalt blue, green leaves, and gold decoration on white ground, shaped silver base with scrolling handle, leaf decoration, **$295**.

Photo courtesy of Wiederseim Associates, Inc.

Strawberry
Cup and saucer............ **75.00**
Mug, 4-1/8" h **125.00**
Plate, 8-1/4" d **150.00**

Tulip
Bowl, 6 1/4" d **50.00**
Cake plate, 10" d, molded handles...................... **120.00**
Creamer, 5-1/4" h........ **125.00**
Plate, tea size **95.00**
Tea cup and saucer, slight crazing in cup............ **115.00**
Teapot, 7-1/4" h.......... **225.00**

Syrup pitcher, pewter lid, underglaze blue and red floral decoration, gilt highlights, **$325**.

Wagon Wheel
Cup and saucer............ **75.00**
Mug, 2-1/2" h **95.00**
Pitcher, 8-1/2" h **195.00**
Plate, 8-3/4" d **85.00**
Platter **125.00**

GIRANDOLE AND MANTEL LUSTRES

History: A girandole is a very elaborate branched candleholder, often featuring cut glass prisms surrounding the mountings. A mantel lustre is a glass vase with attached cut glass prisms.

Girandoles and mantel lustres usually are found in pairs. It is not uncommon for girandoles to be part of a large garniture set. Girandoles and mantel lustres achieved their greatest popularity in the last half of the 19th century both in the United States and Europe.

One of pair of colorless glass mantle lusters with hurricane shades, prisms, ribs and rims with gold trim, white floral decoration, price for pair, **$300**.

Photo courtesy of Joy Luke.

Girandoles

9-7/8" w, 17" h, Longwy, Aesthetic Movement, third quarter 19th C, two-light, rect, central beveled mirror plate, surrounded by Islamic-inspired tiles in brass frame, scrolled candle arm with two acorn-shaped nozzles, removable bobeches **750.00**
12" h pr candlesticks, center 15-1/4" h three-light candelabra, emerald green cut glass prisms, turned and tapered brass columns, white marble bases, worn gilding **575.00**
15" h, cast brass, east Indian man dressed in feathered turban, fancy robes, scimitar hanging from chain, white marble base, faceted prisms

with cut stars and flowers, minor edge flakes, roughness to prisms, price for pr **115.00**
17-1/4" w, 16-1/2" w, brass, three songbirds on flowering vine, three socket top, cut glass prisms, white alabaster base, worn gilding, old patina, few flakes **115.00**
18" h, 15" w, cast brass, high relief rococo scrolling and vintage detail, applied flowers on base, columns shaped like large leaves about to burst into blossom, three sockets each with clear cut glass prisms, orig gilding and bobeches, soldered restorations on branches, price for pr **990.00**

Mantel garnitures

10-1/4" h, urn form, two short scroll handles, incised on side with Japonesque florals in silver and gold coloration, trumpet foot further dec with Japonesque patterning and insects, sq section marble base, inset to front with mixed metal-style patinated plaque depicting drummer and dancer, Aesthetic Movement, third quarter 19th C, price for pr **690.00**
14" h, 12" h, three cov baluster jars and two vases, Hundred Antiques dec, in famille rosé enamels, China, 19th C, price for five-pc set **2,185.00**
20-5/8" h, bronze and crystal, three-light candelabra, stylized lyre form garniture hung with cut and pressed glass prisms, above three scrolled candle arms, trefoil base, price for pr **980.00**

Mantel lusters, pink cased glass, hand-painted floral panel, gilt accents, large hanging prisms, gilt wear, flakes on rim, 14-1/4" h, **$650**.

Photo courtesy of Alderfer Auction Co.

Mantel lustres

9" h, overlay glass, white cut to pink, enamel flowers, gilt accents, cut glass prisms, Bohemian, price for pr **425.00**
10" h, cranberry glass, white enamel foliage dec rims, gilt trim, vining floral dec, cut faceted prisms, flakes and roughness to prisms, price for pr **615.00**
10-3/4" h, 5-3/8" d rim, blown translucent clambroth glass, gauffered rim, rough pontil, seven prisms, late 19th C, price for pr **150.00**
12" h, ruby glass, overlay and enameled plaques, fluted, heavy gilt, cut glass prisms, France, 19th C, price for pr **2,645.00**

GOOFUS GLASS

History: Goofus glass, also known as Mexican ware, hooligan glass, and pickle glass, is a pressed glass with relief designs that were painted either on the back or front. The designs are usually in red and green with a metallic gold ground. It was popular from 1890 to 1920 and was used as a premium at carnivals.

It was produced by several companies: Crescent Glass Company, Wellsburg, West Virginia; Imperial Glass Corporation, Bellaire, Ohio; LaBelle Glass Works, Bridgeport, Ohio; and Northwood Glass Co., Indiana, Pennsylvania, Wheeling, West Virginia, and Bridgeport, Ohio.

Goofus glass lost its popularity when people found that the paint tarnished or scaled off after repeated washings and wear. No record of its manufacture has been found after 1920.

Marks: Goofus glass made by Northwood includes one of the following marks: "N," "N" in one circle, "N" in two circles, or one or two circles without the "N."

Ashtray, red rose dec, emb adv **18.00**
Basket, 5" h, strawberry dec **50.00**
Bonbon, 4" d, Strawberry pattern, gold, red, and green dec **40.00**

Bread tray, red rose buds, gold leaves, embossed trim, two small handles, **$65**.

Bowl, gold and red pears and apples decoration, **$35**.

Bowl, Leaf and Beads, Northwood, c1906-08, opalescent ruffled ring around center design of leafs, center cold painted gold and red, N mark, 9" d, **$55**.

Bowl
6-1/2" d, Grape and Lattice pattern, red grapes, gold ground, ruffled rim **45.00**
10-1/2" d, 2-1/2" h, Cherries, gold leaves, red cherries **35.00**
Bread plate, 7" w, 11" l, Last Supper pattern, rod and gold, grapes and foliage border **65.00**
Candy dish, 8-1/2" d, figure-eight design, serrated rim, dome foot **60.00**
Charger, grape and leaves center **125.00**
Coaster, 3" d, red floral dec, gold ground **12.00**
Compote
4" d, Grape and Cable pattern **35.00**
6" d, Strawberry pattern, red and green strawberries and foliage, ruffled **40.00**
6-1/2" d, Poppy pattern, red flowers, gold foliage, green ground, sgd "Northwood" **40.00**
Decanter, orig stopper, La Belle Rose **50.00**
Dresser tray, 6" l, Cabbage Rose pattern, red roses dec, gold foliage, clear ground **35.00**

Jewel box, 4" d, 2" h, basketweave, rose dec **50.00**
Mug, Cabbage Rose pattern, gold ground **35.00**
Nappy, 6-1/2" d, Cherries pattern, red cherries, gold foliage, clear ground **35.00**

Nappy, triangular, red and gold strawberries, gold leaves, ring handle, **$40**.

Perfume bottle, 3-1/2" h, pink tulips dec **20.00**
Pickle jar, aqua, molded, gold, blue, and red painted floral design **50.00**
Pin dish, 6-1/2" l, oval, red and black florals **20.00**

Plate, gold ground, two bright red roses in center, border with diamond quilting and acanthus scrolling, **$45**.

Plate
6" d, Sunflower pattern, red dec center, relief molded **20.00**

7-3/4" d, Carnations pattern, red carnations, gold ground **20.00**
11" d, Cherries, some paint worn off **35.00**
Platter, 18" l, red rose dec, gold ground **65.00**
Powder jar, cov, 3" d, puffy, rose dec, red and gold **40.00**
Salt and pepper shakers, pr, Grape and Leaf pattern **45.00**
Syrup, relief molded, red roses dec, lattice work ground, orig top **85.00**
Toothpick holder, rod rose and foliage dec, gold ground .. **40.00**
Tray, 8-1/4" d, 11" d, red chrysanthemum dec, gold ground **45.00**
Tumbler, 6" h, red rose dec, gold ground **35.00**
Vase
6" h, Cabbage Rose pattern, red dec, gold ground ... **45.00**
9" h, Poppies pattern, blue and red dec, gold ground **45.00**

GOUDA POTTERY

History: Gouda and the surrounding areas of Holland have been principal Dutch pottery centers for centuries. Originally, the potteries produced a simple utilitarian tin-glazed Delft-type earthenware and the famous clay smoker's pipes.

When pipe making declined in the early 1900s, the Gouda potteries turned to art pottery. Influenced by the Art Nouveau and Art Deco movements, artists expressed themselves with free-form and stylized designs in bold colors.

Reproduction Alert: With the Art Nouveau and Art Deco revivals of recent years, modern reproductions of Gouda pottery currently are on the market. They are difficult to distinguish from the originals.

Bowl
7" h, Art Nouveau scrolled floral and foliage dec, shades of green, brown, and blue, cracked white semi-matte glazed ground, black rooster mark on base, Arnhem factory, c1910, repairs to rim.... **100.00**

10-1/4" d, 2-1/2" h, dec with three clusters of flowers in symmetrical pattern, matte glaze, shades of orange, yellow, and blue, black ground, blue painted maker's mark, c1927 .... **225.00**

11-3/4" d, 2-3/4" h, stylized floral design, matte glaze, yellow, orange, green, and blue, black ground, black painted Regina marks, c1927, rim repair **185.00**

Candlesticks and vase set, pr 9-1/2" h candlesticks, 10-3/4" h vase, Art Nouveau style dec, matte glaze blue, orange, turquoise, brown, and yellow, painted "Westland (house) Gouda Holland," date and artist's initials **400.00**

Candlesticks, pr, 18" h, bulbed cup, ruffled rim drop pan, tall ribbed flared standard, Art Nouveau-style motif, high glaze, shades of blue, green, yellow, and black, underglaze mark "Gouda Blauw (house)," date mark, artist's initials, and "Made in Holland, 872, 893," dec attributed to Franciscus Ijsselstein, c1926, base chip on one **435.00**

Clock garniture, 20-1/2" h clock, 16-3/4" h pr candlesticks, circular clock mouth with painted ceramic face supported by four ceramic arms on baluster-shaped body and flared base, candlesticks of similar form, all dec with Art Nouveau-style flowers, glossy glaze pink, purple, blue, green, and tan, sgd "Zuid Holland" and imp house and "R" on base, repairs to candlesticks **2,875.00**

Charger, 12" d, multicolored flowers, rope border, black trim **150.00**

Compote, 7-5/8", black ground, geometric design, multicolored scroll int. **175.00**

Ewer

7" h, handle, floral and foliage design, high glaze, shades of purple, mauve, green, blue, and taupe, base painted "Made in Zuid Holland (house)", and artist's initials **325.00**

7-5/8" h, handle, stylized floral and foliage design, high glazes, shades of green, pink, and purple on tan and brown

ground, painted "Made in Zuid, Holland" **350.00**

Incense burner, 8" h, Roba, flowers and geometric designs, green ground **120.00**

Jug, 5-3/4" d, Rosalie, cream ground, green handle, turquoise interior, marked "Rosalie, #5155," and "Zuid-Holland, Gouda," c1930 .... **195.00**

Lamp base, 11-3/4" h, flared rim, tapered oval form, butterfly design, matte glaze, shades of green, blue, gold, red and cream, base painted "380 Butterfly (tree, house) AJK Holland," c1920 .... **290.00**

Miniature, vase, 2-1/4" h, floral and foliate design, high glaze, shades of green, purple, red, brown, and black **125.00**

Tray, scalloped, painted yellow flowers and cobalt blue medallions, stamped "Fanny Gouda," 10" x 13", **$195**.

Photo courtesy of David Rago Auctions, Inc.

Pitcher, 8-1/4" h Henley, stylized designs in shades of green, blue, rust and gold on black ground matte glaze, all with maker's marks, crazing, 1923 .... **275.00**

Plate, 8-1/4" d, Unique Metallique, scalloped edge, deep blue-green ground, irid copper luster dec **350.00**

Shoe, 4-7/8" h, floral and foliate design, high glaze, shades of green, purple, red, brown, and black **125.00**

Urn, 8-1/8" h Gotton, stylized designs in shades of green, blue, rust and gold on black ground matte glaze, all with maker's marks, crazing, 1923 .... **275.00**

Vase

4-1/2" h, raised rim, squatty form, flower blossoms dec, semi-matte glaze, yellow, brown, blue, and cream,

black ground, painted and paper labels **200.00**

6" h, Art Nouveau style, elongated neck, squat form, stylized flowers and leaves, high glaze, white, green, and rust, taupe ground, painted "Holland Utrecht" on base **200.00**

7-1/4" h, two handles, ftd, bulbous, brown, blue, and green butterflies dec, crackled white matte ground, black stamped rooster mark on base, Arnhem factory, c1910.......................... **150.00**

7-3/4" h, two handles, bulbed neck flanked by arched handles on squatty body, tulip and foliate designs, high glaze gray, green, yellow, and brown tones, painted "Distel," Distel factory, early 20th C **520.00**

9-3/4" h Breetvelt double handles, all with stylized designs in shades of green, blue, rust and gold on black ground matte glaze, all with maker's marks, crazing **295.00**

10" h, two handles, ovoid, ftd, floral and foliage design, high glaze, shades of purple, mauve, green, blue, and taupe, base painted "Made in Zuid Holland (house)", and artist's initials **350.00**

10-1/2" h, tapered oval, flowers and leaves, semi-matte glaze, gold, brown, turquoise, cream, and black, painted maker's marks **200.00**

10-3/4" h, flared rim, ovoid form, stylized flowers and foliage, matte glaze, shades of yellow, green, blue, orange, and brown, painted mark "Del Breetvelt (house) Zuid Holland Gouda".......... **420.00**

13-1/4" h, elongated neck on bulbous body, Art Nouveau stylized lilies, foliage, high glaze purple, green, yellow, and black, base painted with wooden shoe "NB Faience du (illegible) Holland 504 Dec A" **865.00**

20-1/4" h, flared, stylized lily dec, high glaze, purple, brown, green, dark blue, yellow, and cream, painted mark "Made in Holland (house)," c1898, price for pr **575.00**

GRANITEWARE

History: Graniteware is the name commonly given to enamel-coated iron or steel kitchenware.

The first graniteware was made in Germany in the 1830s. Graniteware was not produced in the United States until the 1860s. At the start of World War I, when European companies turned to manufacturing war weapons, American producers took over the market.

Gray and white were the most common graniteware colors, although each company made its own special color in shades of blue, green, brown, violet, cream, or red.

Older graniteware is heavier than the new. Pieces with cast-iron handles date between 1870 to 1890; wood handles between 1900 to 1910. Other dating clues are seams, wooden knobs, and tin lids.

Reproduction Alert: Graniteware still is manufactured in many of the traditional forms and colors.

Additional Listings: See *Warman's Americana & Collectibles* for more examples.

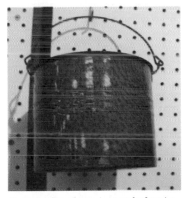

Berry bucket, three rings on body, wire handle, gray and white speckle, medium size, **$90.**

Berry pail, cov, 7" d, 4-3/4" h, cobalt blue and white mottled **65.00**
Bowl, 11-3/4" d, 3-3/4" h, green and white **50.00**
Cake pan, 7-1/2" d, robin's egg blue and white marbleized **45.00**
Candlestick, gray, finger hold **115.00**

Coffee boiler, **$95,** on top of inverted large dish pan, **$35,** both turquoise and white spatter.

Dinner plate, dark blue and white spatter, **$30.**

Coffeepot, 10" h, gray, tin handle, spout, and lid **525.00**
Colander, 12" d, light blue, pedestal base **45.00**
Cookie sheet, mottled blue and white **225.00**
Cup, 2-3/4" h, blue and white medium swirl, black trim and handle **50.00**
Frying pan, 10-1/4" d, blue and white mottled, white int. .. **135.00**
Funnel, cobalt blue and white marbleized, large **50.00**
Grater, medium blue **115.00**
Kettle, cov, 9" h, 11-1/2" d, gray mottled **50.00**
Measure, one cup, gray ... **45.00**
Mixing bowls, red and white, nested set of four, 1930s. **155.00**
Muffin pan, blue and white mottled, eight cups **250.00**
Pie pan, 6" d, cobalt blue and white marbleized.............. **25.00**

Assorted blue spatter pieces, ranging form light blue to cobalt blue, from left: lid, two serving spoons, **$15 each**; small open berry pail, white interior, wooden bail handle, **$75**; small mixing bowl, **$20**; coffee boiler, **$85**; inverted dish pan, **$35**; medium size colander, **$65**; inverted rectangular roaster with self handle, **$30**; inverted medium size dish pan, **$25**; inverted shallow pan, **$25**.

Roaster, three pieces, oval, green and white spatter, **$45.**

Wash basin, aqua and white speckle, stamp mark "Elite Austria Reg. No. (illegible) 26," chip, **$45.**

Pitcher, 11" h, gray, ice lip **110.00**
Roaster, emerald green swirl, large **250.00**
Skimmer, 10" l, gray mottled **25.00**
Teapot, 9-1/2" w, 5" h, enameled dec, small chips **525.00**
Tube pan, octagonal, gray mottled **45.00**

Wash bowl and pitcher set, aqua and white, cobalt blue rims, $115.

Utensil rack, 14-1/2" w, 22" h, shaded orange, gray bowls, matching ladle, skimmer, and tasting spoon **400.00**
Wash basin, 11-3/4" d, blue and white swirl, Blue Diamond Ware **150.00**

GREENTOWN GLASS

History: The Indiana Tumbler and Goblet Co., Greentown, Indiana, produced its first clear, pressed glass table and bar wares in late 1894. Initial success led to a doubling of the plant size in 1895 and other subsequent expansions, one in 1897 to allow for the manufacture of colored glass. In 1899, the firm joined the combine known as the National Glass Company.

In 1900, just before arriving in Greentown, Jacob Rosenthal developed an opaque brown glass, called "chocolate," which ranged in color from a dark, rich chocolate to a lighter coffee-with-cream hue. Production of chocolate glass saved the financially pressed Indiana Tumbler and Goblet Works. The Cactus and Leaf Bracket patterns were made almost exclusively in chocolate glass. Other popular chocolate patterns include Austrian, Dewey, Shuttle, and Teardrop and Tassel. In 1902, National Glass Company bought Rosenthal's chocolate glass formula so other plants in the combine could use the color.

In 1902, Rosenthal developed the Golden Agate and Rose Agate colors. All work ceased on June 13, 1903, when a fire of suspicious origin destroyed the Indiana Tumbler and Goblet Company Works.

After the fire, other companies, e.g., McKee and Brothers, produced chocolate glass in the same pattern designs used by Greentown. Later reproductions also have been made, with Cactus among the most heavily copied patterns.

Reproduction Alert.

Cat in hamper covered dish, chocolate glass, $225.

Animal-covered dish
    Dolphin, chocolate **225.00**
    Rabbit, dome top, amber **250.00**
Bowl, 7-1/4" d, Herringbone Buttress, green................ **135.00**
Butter, cov, Cupid, chocolate **575.00**
Celery vase, Beaded Panel, clear **100.00**
Compote, Teardrop and Tassel, clear, 5-1/4" d, 5-1/8" h...... **50.00**
Creamer
    Cactus, chocolate **85.00**
    Indian Head, opaque white **450.00**
Goblet
    Overall Lattice **40.00**
    Shuttle, chocolate **500.00**

Mug, indoor drinking scene, chocolate, 6" w, 8" h........ **400.00**
Mustard, cov, Daisy, opaque white **75.00**
Paperweight, Buffalo, Nile green **575.00**
Pitcher, cov, Dewey, chocolate, 5-1/4" h........................... **115.00**
Plate, Serenade, chocolate **65.00**
Relish, Leaf Bracket, 8" l, oval, chocolate **75.00**
Salt and pepper shakers, pr, Cactus, chocolate.......... **130.00**
Sugar, cov, Dewey, cobalt blue **125.00**
Syrup, Cord Drapery, chocolate, plated lid, 6-3/4" h.......... **295.00**
Toothpick holder, Hobnail and Shell, chocolate **185.00**
Tumbler
    Cactus, chocolate **60.00**
    Dewey, canary.............. **65.00**
Vase, 8" h, Austrian........... **55.00**

GRUEBY POTTERY

History: William Grueby was active in the ceramic industry for several years before he developed his own method of producing matte-glazed pottery and founded the Grueby Faience Company in Boston, Massachusetts, in 1897.

The art pottery was hand thrown in natural shapes, hand molded, and hand tooled. A variety of colored glazes, singly or in combinations, was produced, but green was the most popular. In 1908, the firm was divided into the Grueby Pottery Company and the Grueby Faience and Tile Co. The Grueby Faience and Tile Company made art tile until 1917, although its pottery production was phased out about 1910.

Minor damage is acceptable to most collectors of Grueby Pottery.

Adviser: David Rago.

Bowl, 9" d, 5-1/2" h, flaring, broad molded leaves, cucumber matte green ground, dec by Ruth Erickson, imp circular mark, incised "ER," two very short and shallow opposing lines.. **1,900.00**

Humidor, cylindrical, decorated by Wilhemina Post, band of ivory and yellow five-petaled tobacco blossoms, thick curdled matte green ground, stamped pottery mark, WP, paper label, three hairlines from rim, restoration to lid, 4-1/2" d, 7-1/2" h, **$4,600**.

Photo courtesy of David Rago Auctions, Inc.

Jardinière, 7-1/2" x 9", two-color three rows of curled leaves below nine light blue five-petaled flowers, oatmeal matte green glaze, stamped "Grueby Faience/174" and "EG," couple of minor flecks.................. **575.00**

Miniature vase, 3" h, green-gray glaze, sgd "GRUEBY POTTERY BOSTON USA," in mold, 1899
.... **600.00**

Paperweight, 3" l, scarab, blue-gray glaze, sgd "GRUEBY FAIENCE Co. BOSTON. U.S.A.," c1905 .... **650.00**

Planter, 4-1/2" h, 12" l, flaring, by Edith R. Felton, modeled leaves, closed-in rim, rich cucumber matte green glaze, circular Faience mark, ERF, three short tight lines at top, use scratches on interior **1,100.00**

Tile, cuenca dec
   6" sq, large oak tree against blue sky, puffy white clouds, #28 on reverse......... **1,150.00**
   6" sq, "The Pines," polychrome cuenca, marked "FH" **1,485.00**
   6-1/4" sq, yellow tulip on matte green ground, mounted in sterling silver trivet base by Karl Leinonen (Boston League of Arts & Crafts), tile unmarked, mount stamped "Sterling" and "L," very light abrasion to surface.. **2,990.00**

Vase
   3-1/2" h, 3" d, flat shoulder, tooled and applied rows of leaves, matte green glaze, shaved off mark **2,600.00**

Vase, Kendrick, full height tooled and applied leaves reticulated below row of shorter flat leaves, feathered matte green glaze, by Wilhemina Post, circular Faience stamp and "W.P./3/4," 12" h, 8" d, few minor touch-ups to leaf edges, **$27,500**.

Photo courtesy of David Rago Auctions, Inc.

Vase, bulbous, rolled rim, alternating rows of tight yellow buds and broad leaves, rich medium to dark matte green ground, circular mark, 4" h, 4-1/4" d, **$2,900**.

Photo courtesy of David Rago Auctions, Inc.

   4" h, 4-1/4" d, bulbous, rolled rim, alternating rows of tight yellow buds and broad leaves, rich medium to dark matte green ground, circular mark........................ **2,900.00**
   7-1/4" h, 4-1/2" d, tapering, crisply modeled with broad flat leaves, flowing ochre matte glaze, circular die-stamp mark, several small flakes to leaf edges **4,500.00**
   7-1/4" h, 5-1/2" d, ovoid, carved stylized leaves, medium matte green ground, imp circular mark, incised "MEJ" **1,500.00**

Vase, five-sided neck, full height tooled and applied leaves alternating with ivory buds, leathery matte brown glaze, by Wilhemina Post, Grueby Pottery stamp mark and "WP/4/10," 11-1/4" h, 5-1/2" d, minute old bruise to one corner, **$8,500**.

Photo courtesy of David Rago Auctions, Inc.

   7-3/4" h, 7-3/4" d, flaring rim, squat base, tooled and applied blossoms alternating with rounded, curled leaves, leathery matte green glaze, circular pottery stamp 187, 2" bruise to rim............ **2,200.00**
   9-1/2" h, 6" d, cylindrical neck, bulbous bottom, base dec with overlapping modeled leaves, medium green matte glaze, circular mark . **2,300.00**
   11-1/4" h, 5-1/2" d, five-sided neck, full height tooled and applied leaves alternating with ivory buds, leathery matte brown glaze, by Wilhemina Post, Grueby Pottery stamp mark and "WP/4/10," minute old bruise to one corner **8,500.00**
   11-1/2" h, 5-3/4" d, ovoid, by Marie Seaman, green buds alternating with spade-shaped leaves, rich cucumber matte glaze, die-stamped faience mark, 28 MS, nicks to leaf edges **3,500.00**

11-1/2" h, 9-1/2" d, large swollen cylindrical body, narrow rim, modeled broad leaves alternating with blades, matte green glaze, imp pottery and artist's marks on base, Ruth Erickson (1899-1910), Boston, c1905, rim chips and edge nicks **3,525.00**

12" h, 8" d, Kendrick, full height tooled and applied leaves reticulated below row of shorter flat leaves, feathered matte green glaze, by Wilhemina Post, circular Faience stamp and "W.P./3/4," few minor touch-ups to leaf edges...................... **27,500.00**

13" h, 9-1/2" d, alternating rows of yellow buds and modeled green leaves, fine two-tone cucumber matte green glaze, by Marie Seaman, circular mark, incised "MS," nicks to leaf edges, small drilled hole through center of base **6,000.00**

21" h, 8-1/2" d, full height leaves alternating with yellow buds, cucumber matte glaze, early circular mark, some dark streaking to glaze, bruise with minor clay loss at rim **4,500.00**

Vessel, spherical vessel, broad leaves, covered in leathery matte green glaze, stamped pottery mark, initials "ERF," partial paper label, few minor edge nicks to edges, 4-3/4" d, 4" h, **$5,750**.

Photo courtesy of David Rago Auctions, Inc.

Vessel

4-1/2" d, 4-1/4" h, spherical, crisply dec, tooled and applied pointed leaves, dark green matte glaze, remnant of paper label **4,600.00**

9-1/2" d, 4-1/4" h, three-color, tooled and applied yellow and green waterlilies and lilypads,

leathery dark green ground, circular pottery mark "JE/1-14," 1914, very short tight rim bruise.................... **53,500.00**

HALL CHINA COMPANY

History: Robert Hall founded the Hall China Company in 1903 in East Liverpool, Ohio. He died in 1904 and was succeeded by his son, Robert Taggart Hall. After years of experimentation, Robert T. Hall developed a leadless glaze in 1911, opening the way for production of glazed household products.

The Hall China Company made many types of kitchenware, refrigerator sets, and dinnerware in a wide variety of patterns. Some patterns were made exclusively for a particular retailer, such as Heather Rose for Sears.

One of the most popular patterns was Autumn Leaf, a premium designed by Arden Richards in 1933 for the exclusive use by the Jewel Tea Company. Still a Jewel Tea property, Autumn Leaf has not been listed in catalogs since 1978, has been produced on a replacement basis with the date stamped on the back.

Additional Listings: See *Warman's Americana & Collectibles* for more examples.

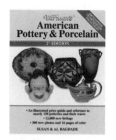

For more information, see *Warman's American Pottery & Porcelain*, 2nd edition.

Cookie jar, cov

Autumn Leaf, Tootsie **265.00**
Blue Blossom, Five-Band shape **275.00**
Chinese Red, Five-Band shape **150.00**

Gold Dot, Zeisel **95.00**
Meadow Flower, Five-Band shape **230.00**
Owl, brown glaze............. **90.00**
Red Poppy **50.00**

Casserole, self handles, Autumn Leaf, **$120**.

Kitchen ware and advertising

Bean pot, New England, #1, Orange Poppy **80.00**
Casserole, cov, Chinese Red, Sundial, #4, 8" w **65.00**
Coffeepot, percolator, ducks and partridge dec........... **100.00**
Cuspidor, 7-1/4" d, 4-1/4" h, green and white............... **90.00**
Drip jar, 4-1/2" h, 5" w, Little Red Riding Hood................. **3,300.00**
Jug, Primrose, rayed **20.00**
Mixing bowl, nested set of three, 6" d, 7-1/2" d, 8-1/2" d, pink, basketweave and floral dec, gold trim.................... **85.00**
Mug, 4" h, 2" d, Braniff International Airlines **18.00**
Refrigerator bowl, Addison Gray and Daffodil, ink stamped "GE Refrigerators, Hall
Ovenware China, Made for General Electric," c1938... **12.00**
Sauce boat, 10" l, Quartermasters logo emb near handle on both sides, c1940 .... **25.00**

Patterns

Autumn Leaf
   Bowl, 5-1/2" d **7.50**
   Coffeepot, electric **300.00**
   Cup and saucer............ **18.00**
   Juice reamer.............. **250.00**
   Pepper shaker, 4-1/4" h, gold trim.............................. **20.00**
   Pie bird, 5" h **40.00**
   Plate, 8" d **15.00**
   Teapot, cov, automobile shape, 1993............... **465.00**
   Tidbit tray, three tiers .. **125.00**
   Tumbler, 5-5/8" h, 2-3/4" d, frosted **45.00**
   Utensil holder, 7-1/4" h, marked "Utensils"....... **275.00**

Dripolator, light blue base and lid with gold leaf decoration, marked, **$75**.

Blue Bouquet
Bowl, 7" d, 3" h	**30.00**
Creamer, Boston	**25.00**
Cup and saucer	**28.00**
French baker, round	**35.00**
Platter, 13" l	**35.00**
Soup, flat	**30.00**
Spoon	**100.00**
Teapot, Aladdin infuser	**165.00**

Cameo Rose
Bowl, 5-1/4" d	**3.00**
Butter dish, 3/4 lb.	**30.00**
Casserole	**25.00**
Creamer and sugar	**10.00**
Cream soup, 6" d	**7.00**
Cup and saucer	**9.00**
Plate, 8" d	**2.50**
Teapot, cov, six cup	**35.00**
Tidbit, three tier	**40.00**

Gamebirds
Percolator, electric	**140.00**
Teapot, cov, two-cup size, ducks and pheasant	**200.00**

Pitcher, ball shape, Autumn Leaf, **$70**.

Mount Vernon
Coffeepot	**125.00**
Creamer	**12.00**
Cup	**10.00**
Fruit bowl	**8.00**

Gravy boat	**20.00**
Saucer	**4.00**
Soup bowl, 8" d, flat	**16.50**
Vegetable bowl, 9-1/4" l, oval	**20.00**

Red Poppy
Bowl, 5-1/2" d	**5.00**
Cake plate	**17.50**
Casserole, cov	**25.00**
Coffeepot, cov	**12.00**
Creamer and sugar	**15.00**
Cup and saucer	**8.00**
French baker, fluted	**15.00**
Jug, Daniel, Radiance	**28.00**
Plate, 9" d	**6.50**
Salad bowl, 9" d	**14.00**
Teapot, New York	**90.00**

Silhouette
Bean pot	**50.00**
Bowl, 7-7/8" d	**50.00**
Coffeepot, cov	**30.00**
Mug	**35.00**
Pretzel jar	**75.00**
Trivet	**125.00**

Front: batter pitcher, "ear handle," **$90**; rear ball-shaped pitcher, both Autumn Leaf pattern, gold trim, **$70**.

Tulip
Bowl, 10-1/4" l, oval	**36.00**
Coffee maker, drip, Kadota, all china	**115.00**
Condiment jar	**165.00**
Fruit bowl, 5-1/2" d	**10.00**
Mixing bowl, 6" d	**27.00**
Plate, 9" d, luncheon	**16.00**
Platter, 13-1/4" l, oval	**42.00**
Shakers, bulge-type, price for pr	**110.00**
Sugar, cov	**25.00**

Teapots
Camellia, gold roses, windshield, gold trim on handle, spout, rim, and finial, mkd "Hall 0698 6 cup made in USA" **100.00**
Chinese Red, donut, 9-1/2" w, 7-1/2" h **500.00**

Cleveland, turquoise and gold **165.00**
Lipton Tea, off white stoneware, aluminum cozy, 9-1/2" l, 7-1/2" h **30.00**
Radiance & Wheat **360.00**

HALLOWEEN

History: There are differing schools of thought as to how the origin of our Halloween celebrations came to be. There are those who believe that it got its beginning thousands of years ago from the beliefs of the Celts as well as those of their religious leaders, the Druids. The Celts were simple people with simplistic convictions. Spirits, whether good or bad, ruled their world and affected the way they lived or died and these convictions even went as far as forecasting the weather and the outcome of crops. The harvest signaled the end of their year while the New Year began with the arrival of winter. This end-of-year celebration was a time of family togetherness and feasting which would include fortune telling and the foretelling of matrimonial prospects. At these family gatherings, the spirits of the "dead" relatives were also welcome for the mortal blood relations believed that these said spirits returned home for the festival of the harvest. The "Veil," which was considered the separation between life and death, was at its thinnest which allowed the ghosts to cross over and join the living, albeit for a short visit. These seasonal rituals would eventually evolve into the Halloween festivities that were celebrated in the early part of the 20th Century.

Contrary to popular belief, Halloween celebrations of the 1910s, 20s and even into the early part of the 1930s were, for the most part, not geared to children but young adults. Trick-or-Treating, as we know it, did not come to the fore until the late 1920s so until then, house parties were the norm. The lucky hostess was one who purchased a Halloween Bogie Book from the Dennison Company and utilized the numerous party topics that included themes, decorating, games, menus and even costumes. As in days of yore, fortune telling once again featured heavily in our All Hallow's Eve celebrations as can be attested by the proliferation of fortune-telling games manufactured by the Beistle Company.

As the years passed, Halloween's popularity grew and with it came an artistic outpouring of seasonal items from the hands of some very talented artists, both here and abroad. Die cuts, lanterns, invitations, place cards, games, noisemakers, paper goods (tablecloths, napkins, table borders, etc.) were just some of the pieces that were fabricated from material such as papier mâché, tin, wood, plastic and the like.

Currently, the pieces that are bringing the highest dividend are those dating from the early 1900s and are of German make. The charm, and, at times, the grotesqueness of these collectibles is evident from the time and genius that was put into each piece. The fact that these German artisans captured the essence of the Halloween holiday is quite extraordinary since Germany, along with most European countries, did not celebrate Halloween.

Many collectors of vintage Halloween pieces wax nostalgic about the 1980s and early 1990s when it was possible to buy up these collectibles at embarrassingly low prices. Many a stellar collection has been started for mere pennies on the dollar. Not so today. With the advent of the Internet, collectors now have the opportunity to peruse hundreds of items that pertain to their collecting category and utilize on-line auction venues. Auction houses throughout the country have realized this growing popularity and have accordingly increased their sales by offering "live auction" options. Now you can bid on your items of interest at an auction house in Minneapolis while you're sitting at your home computer. There is a downside:

where once you had the chance of acquiring a choice item and just had the locals to contend with, you now have the world sitting in. However, there are hidden treasures out there waiting to be discovered.

Adviser: Claire M. Lavin.

Jack-o-Lantern candy container, "egg crate" or pulp, late 1940s/early 1950s, bottom marked "ATCO Co." (Animal Trap Co.), 5" d, 4-1/2" h, **$65**.

Bogie book, Dennison
1915............................ **335.00**
1928, slight wear **305.00**
Candy container
3-1/4" h, champagne bucket shape, bottom slides out to place candy inside bucket, German, some wear ... **850.00**
5" h, witch, glass, wire bail handle, 95% of orig paint
.... **810.00**
6-1/2" h, 6" w, Jol man, sack candy container, Fibro Toy, cardboard, c1940....... **245.00**
Costume, Grandpa Munster, c1964, wear **1,510.00**
Cymbals, 5-1/2" d, tin litho, 1920s, some dings, minor scratches, price for set ... **600.00**
Diecut
Cat in candle, Dennison, 6-1/4" h, 5-3/4" w, c1920
.... **230.00**
Figurines, German, 3-1/4" h, boxed set of eight, orig box
.... **1,530.00**
Flying witch, Dennison, few creases, minor surface wear
.... **165.00**
Lightning Wampus, aka The Halloween Devil, Beistle, c1931, 30" h............. **525.00**
Moon with arms around black cats, Beistle, 6" h, small tape marks on back............ **170.00**

Tiara, 5" h, 9-1/2" w, 1920s, German...................... **800.00**
Witch, bat-winged, 18" x 18-1/2" open, Beistle, c1925, some creases...................... **245.00**
Figure, celluloid
Black cat on Jol, owl on top of moon, c1930, pr **785.00**
Squirrel eating acorn while sitting atop pumpkin, c1930, 3" h, tiny dents in bottom **65.00**
Game, Katzy Party, Selchow, 1920s **105.00**
Halloween apron, 22" h, crepe paper, dec with witches, bats, jack-o-lanterns, and black cats, c1918, small holes and tears
.... **120.00**
Halloween party book, Beistle, c1925 .... **635.00**
Jack-o-lantern
Pulp, F. N. Burt, 1950s **420.00**
Tin, horn nose, bail handle missing, some minor scratches................... **120.00**

Lantern, layered papier-mâché pumpkin with compo wash, original paper inserts, German, 1908-12, 4-1/2" d, 4" h, **$5,000**.

Halloween photos courtesy of Claire Lavin.

Teapot, 3-1/2" d, 4-1/2" h, **$675**; 2-1/4" d waste bowl, **$500**, from 1910-20s tea set, both marked "Germany."

Lantern
8" d, printed on cardboard, transparent eye, nose and mouth with honeycomb tissue folding sides, Beistle, c1929, fitted for electric or candle light, some wear **800.00**

11" x 11-1/4", Tommy Whiskers, Beistle, c1938 .... **350.00**
Nodder, 8-1/2" h, papier-mache, German, c1920, slightly soiled **1,700.00**
Parade jack-o-lantern, 7" d, tin, c1908 .... **1,575.00**
Pennant
 15-1/2" l, cat head diecut, German, c1920, some minor rubbing **415.00**
 15-1/2" l, jack-o-lantern head diecut, German, c1920 .... **950.00**
Roly poly, 3-1/2" h, witch and broom, celluloid, c1930 .. **775.00**
Sugar bowl, cov, 2-1/2" h, German, c1920 .... **265.00**
Tambourine, 7" d, witch on goose flying over city, Chein, c1920, light scuff marks, few scratches, dents **255.00**
Teapot, 4" h, German, c1920 .... **500.00**

HAMPSHIRE POTTERY

History: In 1871, James S. Taft founded the Hampshire Pottery Company in Keene, New Hampshire. Production began with redwares and stonewares, followed by majolica in 1879. A semi-porcelain, with the recognizable matte glazes plus the Royal Worcester glaze, was introduced in 1883.

Until World War I, the factory made an extensive line of utilitarian and art wares including souvenir items. After the war, the firm resumed operations, but made only hotel dinnerware and tiles. The company was dissolved in 1923.

For more information, see *Warman's American Pottery & Porcelain*, 2nd edition.

Lamp base, embossed with full height leaves alternating with blossoms under smooth matte green glaze, two-socket electrified oil font, unmarked, pot 15" x 9", rim shaved to accommodate font, **$1,700**.

Photo courtesy of David Rago Auctions, Inc.

Lamp base, squatty, embossed tulips, matte green glaze, stamped "HAMPSHIRE POTTERY," 11-1/2" d, 6" h, **$1,100**.

Photo courtesy of David Rago Auctions, Inc.

Bowl, 5-1/2" d, 2-1/2" h, matte green glaze over foliate-forms, imp "Hampshire, M.O." ... **320.00**
Chocolate pot, 9-1/2" h, cream, holly dec **275.00**
Compote, 13-1/4" d, ftd, two handles, Ivory pattern, light

green highlights, cream ground, red decal mark................ **175.00**
Inkwell, 4-1/8" d, 2-3/4" h, round, large center well, three pen holes **125.00**
Oil lamp, 3-1/2" x 7", matte green glaze, price for pr, one handle restored............... **485.00**
Stein, 7" h, 1/2 liter, transfer printed scene of Pine Grove Springs resort **110.00**
Tankard, 7" h, band of stylized dec, green matte glaze, imp "Hampshire".................... **100.00**

Vase, blue-green and pink mottled matte glaze, stamped and paper label "Hampshire Ware, ???71," 7-1/2" h, **$400**.

Photo courtesy of David Rago Auctions, Inc.

Vase
 4" h, 5-1/2" d, thick matte green glaze, incised detail at rim, imp pottery mark, cipher, and number "76," c1908, spider hairline at base, possibly in-the-making **325.00**
 6" h, 5-1/4" d, barrel shape, emb dandelions, feathered matte cobalt blue glaze, Hampshire Pottery 4 64 .... **950.00**
 6-3/4" h, soft matte blue-green glaze, modeled leaf blades centered by buds and trailing stems, imp pottery mark and "M" cipher, numbered "33" c1908........................ **765.00**

7" h, 4-1/2" d, ovoid, full height leaves, frothy matte blue-green glaze, cobalt blue and apricot shoulder, Hampshire Pottery 98 .... **700.00**

8-1/4" h, wide mouth, glossy blue glaze, broad overlapping leaf dec, incised pottery mark and "M" cipher, Keene, New Hampshire, c1908 ...... **600.00**

8-3/4" h, mottled drip glaze, soft clay and blue-green colors on slate blue ground, repeating leaf dec, incised pottery mark, "M" cipher, c1908 .... **765.00**

9-1/4" h, 6-1/2" d, bottle shape, imp leaves, feathered green glaze, blue-gray ground, Hampshire Pottery 124 .... **1,000.00**

HATPINS AND HATPIN HOLDERS

History: When oversized hats were in vogue, around 1850, hatpins became popular. Designers used a variety of materials to decorate the pin ends, including china, crystal, enamel, gem stones, precious metals, and shells. Decorative subjects ranged from commemorative designs to insects.

Hatpin holders, generally placed on a dresser, are porcelain containers that were designed specifically to hold these pins. The holders were produced by major manufacturers, among which were Meissen, Nippon, R. S. Germany, R. S. Prussia, and Wedgwood.

Tray lot of hairpins and large comb, two smaller decorative combs, **$75**.

Hatpin

Brass

1-1/4" d, 9" l pin, Victorian Lady, cameo type profile, round, Victorian, orig finish **110.00**

1-1/2" x 1-3/4", 9" l pin, child with flowing hair, flanked by sunflowers, Victorian, orig finish **125.00**

2" d, 9-1/2" l pin, military button **125.00**

2-1/4" l, oxidized, four citrine-colored stones in each of four panels, citrine-colored stones on 1/2" bezel **315.00**

Enamel, 5-1/2" l, 14k yg, hinged American flag **275.00**

Hand-painted china, violets, gold trim **35.00**

Glass, 2" l faceted amber glass bead, 13-1/4" l japanned shaft **125.00**

Ivory, ball shape, carved design **65.00**

Jet, 1-1/4" elongated oval knobby bead, 8" l pin **200.00**

Metal, 9-1/4" l, round disk, Art-Nouveau style lady with flowing hair **125.00**

Satsuma, Geisha Girl dec **245.00**

Sterling silver

1-1/4" d, 11" l pin, Arts & Crafts motif of ivy leaf in circle, Charles Horner, hallmarks for Chester, England, 1911 .... **195.00**

6-1/2" l, elongated tear shape, marked "Horner" **95.00**

Hatpin holder, carnival glass, Grape & Cable pattern, marigold, **$200**.

Hatpin holder

Belleek, 5-1/4" h, relief pink and maroon floral dec, green leaves, gold top, marked "Willets Belleek," dated 1911 ...... **125.00**

Limoges, grapes, pink roses, matte finish, artist sgd **60.00**

Nippon, 4-7/8" d, hp blue daisy flowers, marked "E. O. China" **185.00**

Royal Bayreuth, tapestry, portrait of lady wearing hat, blue mark **575.00**

R. S. Germany, 4-1/2" d, pink roses, green foliage, pink luster trim **315.00**

R. S. Prussia, 7" h, 3" d, peach flowers, green foliage **180.00**

HAVILAND CHINA

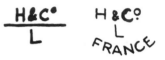

History: In 1842, American china importer David Haviland moved to Limoges, France, where he began manufacturing and decorating china specifically for the U.S. market. Haviland is synonymous with fine, white, translucent porcelain, although early hand-painted patterns were generally larger and darker colored on heavier whiteware blanks than were later ones.

David revolutionized French china factories by both manufacturing the whiteware blank and decorating it at the same site. In addition, Haviland and Company pioneered the use of decals in decorating china.

David's sons, Charles Edward and Theodore, split the company in 1892. In 1936, Theodore opened an American division, which still operates today. In 1941, Theodore bought out Charles Edward's heirs and recombined both companies under the original name of H. and Co. The Haviland family sold the firm in 1981.

Charles Field Haviland, cousin of Charles Edward and Theodore, worked for and then, after his marriage in 1857, ran the Casseaux Works until 1882. Items continued to carry his name as decorator until 1941.

Thousands of Haviland patterns were made, but not consistently named until after 1926. The similarities in many of the patterns makes identification difficult. Numbers assigned by Arlene Schleiger and illustrated in her books have become the identification standard.

For more information, see *Warman's American Pottery & Porcelain*, 2nd edition.

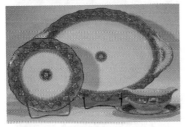

Dinner plate, 21" l platter, gravy, pink flowers on green gilded border, marked "Theodore Haviland," plate, **$20**; platter, **$45**; gravy, **$40**.

Photo courtesy of Joy Luke Auctions

Bone dish, 8-1/4" l, hp
  Crab dec....................... **60.00**
  Turtle dec.................... **65.00**
Bouillon cup and saucer, hp bluebirds, luster ground, gold rims, artist sgd "Poirer," green marks, price for set of 12 **100.00**
Bowl, 8" d, hp, yellow roses **35.00**
Butter dish, cov, Gold Band, marked "Theo Haviland" ... **45.00**
Butter pat, sq, rounded corners, gold trim.......................... **12.00**
Cake plate, 10" d, gold handles and border **35.00**
Celery dish, scalloped edge, green flowers, pale pink scroll **45.00**
Chocolate pot, cov, 10-1/2" l, Countess pattern, green mark, c1893............................. **475.00**
Cream soup, underplate, cranberry and blue scroll border **30.00**

Creamer and sugar, small pink flowers, scalloped, gold trim **65.00**
Cup and saucer, Etoile... **470.00**
Dinner set
  Forever Spring, service for five **165.00**
  Pink roses, 69 pcs **500.00**
  Violets, gold trim, service for 12, plus serving pcs **1,295.00**

Dinner service, white, delicate pink florals, green leaves, gold trim, 86 pieces, marked "Theodore Haviland, Limoges China," **$200**.

Photo courtesy of Dotta Auction Co., Inc.

Game plate, 9-1/4" d, hp, center scene of shore birds in natural setting, apple green edge, printed gold scrolled rim dec, artist sgd "B. Albert," Theodore Haviland & Co. blanks, early 20th C, price for set of 12 **865.00**
Gravy boat, attached underplate
  Chantilly..................... **270.00**
  Monteray..................... **315.00**
  Schleiger #57............. **250.00**
Milk pitcher, 8" h, 4-3/4" d, pink flowers, green branches, underglaze green Haviland mark, red "Haviland & Co., Limoges for PDG, Indianapolis, Ind." **450.00**

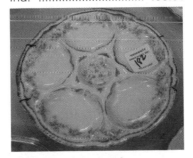

Oyster plate, delicate pink roses, green foliage, gilt trim, five shaped oyster depressions and center round well, marked "Theodore Haviland Limoges, France," **$275**.

Photo courtesy of Wiederseim Associates, Inc.

Oyster plate, scattered green florals, gilt trim, five shaped oyster depressions and center round well, marked "Theodore Haviland Limoges, France, Patent Applied For," **$275**.

Photo courtesy of Wiederseim Associates, Inc.

Oyster plate, five wells
  Rose dec, bright red roses, blue forget-me-nots, hp muscle scars, importer's mark "Warren & Wood, Providence, RI".......................... **700.00**
  Seascape, shellfish, aquatic plants, under glaze mark, CFH/GDM mark......... **845.00**
  Seaweed, raised dec, underglaze green mark, importer's mark "J. E. Caldwell Co., Philadelphia,PA," 8-3/4" d **600.00**
  Wave design, multicolored metallic dec, gold highlights and brushed rim, CFH/GDM mark.......................... **725.00**
Oyster plate, six wells
  Floral transfers, hp muscle marks, gold trim, c1881-90, price for set of six.... **1,650.00**
  Hand brushed gold dec, white ground, five oyster wells, center sauce well, underglaze green mark, price for set of four **760.00**
  Rose pattern, violet rim trim, c1877, price for set of six **1,350.00**
Pitcher, 7-1/2" h, Rosalinde **280.00**
Plate, dinner
  Crowning Fashion, tan.... **8.00**
  Golden Quail **275.00**
Platter
  Chantilly..................... **275.00**
  Golden Quail **350.00**
Relish dish, blue and pink flowers **25.00**
Sandwich plate, 11-1/2" d, Drop Rose pattern **275.00**
Sugar bowl, Haviland Limogens **75.00**

Plate, multicolored phoenix in center, floral rim border with medallions with phoenix motif, gold trim, marked "Theodore Haviland Limoges France, Rajah," $45.

Teacup and saucer, small blue flowers, green leaves **30.00**
Teapot, Portland **250.00**
Tea set, 8-1/2" d, 8" h teapot, rope and anchor pattern, transfer-printed, hand tinted blossoms, stamped "Haviland-Limoges" mark, restoration to lids, price for three-pc set
.... **200.00**
Tureen, cov, pink roses, green ivy, 12" l, 6-1/2" h **360.00**
Vase, 5-1/2" h, 3-5/8" d, tan, brown, pink, and rose, two oval scenes of lady in large hat, baskets and flower garlands, Charles Field Haviland and GDA Limoges mark **275.00**
Vegetable dish, open, Golden Quail, 9-1/2" x 7-1/2" **435.00**

HEISEY GLASS

History: The A. H. Heisey Glass Co. began producing glasswares in April 1896, in Newark, Ohio. Heisey, the firm's founder, was not a newcomer to the field, having been associated with the craft since his youth.

1900–58

Many blown and molded patterns were produced in crystal, colored, milk (opalescent), and Ivorina Verde (custard) glass. Decorative techniques of cutting, etching, and silver deposit were employed. Glass figurines were

introduced in 1933 and continued in production until 1957 when the factory closed. All Heisey glass is notable for its clarity.

Marks: Not all pieces have the familiar H-within-a-diamond mark.

For more information, see *Warman's Glass*, 4th edition.

Reproduction Alert: Some Heisey molds were sold to Imperial Glass of Bellaire, Ohio, and certain items were reissued. These pieces may be mistaken for the original Heisey. Some of the reproductions were produced in colors never made by Heisey and have become collectible in their own right. Examples include: the Colt family in Crystal, Caramel Slag, Ultra Blue, and Horizon Blue; the mallard with wings up in Caramel Slag; Whirlpool (Provincial) in crystal and colors; and Waverly, a 7-inch, oval, footed compote in Caramel Slag.

Animal
Gazelle **1,450.00**
Plug horse, Oscar....... **115.00**
Pony, kicking.............. **175.00**
Sealyham terrier **145.00**
Sparrow **150.00**
Ashtray
Old Sandwich, #1404, moongleam, individual size
.... **67.50**
Ridgeleigh, #1469, club shape........................... **10.00**
Bitters bottle, #5003, tube
.... **165.00**
Bowl
Plantation Ivy, crystal, 10" d
.... **65.00**
Queen Anne, 8" d, light use
.... **25.00**
Buffet plate, Lariat, #1540, 21"
.... **70.00**
Butter dish, cov, Rose ... **200.00**
Cake plate, Rose, 15" d, pedestal **325.00**
Camellia bowl, Lariat, #1540, 9-1/2" d.............................. **40.00**

Candelabra, crystal, 10" w, 16-1/2" h, price for pr **695.00**
Candlesticks, pr
Flamingo, #112 .... **150.00**
Mercury, #122 .... **70.00**
New Era, #3877 .... **90.00**
Orchid, Trident, two-lite
.... **155.00**
Pinwheel, #121 .... **90.00**
Regency, two-lite, #1504
.... **98.00**
Thumbprint and Panel, #1433
.... **140.00**
Trophy, #126, flamingo **275.00**
Windsor, #22, 7-1/2" h **140.00**
Caramel, cov, Lariat, #1540, 7"
.... **75.00**

Celery tray, Colonial-type pattern, marked, $85.

Celery, Empress, Sahara, 10" l
.... **45.00**
Centerpiece bowl, Ridgeleigh, #1469, 11" d.................... **225.00**
Champagne, Duquesne, tangerine, saucer........... **235.00**
Cheese dish, cov, Lariat, #1540, ftd...................................... **40.00**
Cheese plate, Twist, #1252, Kraft, moongleam **62.50**
Cigarette holder, Crystolite
.... **25.00**
Claret
Carassone, Sahara, 4 oz
.... **68.00**
Orchid, Tyrolean line, 4-1/2 oz
.... **150.00**
Coaster
Colonial........................ **10.00**
Plantation..................... **50.00**
Cocktail
Lariat, #1540, moonglo cut
.... **12.00**

New Era pattern, sugar and creamer, "H" in diamond mark, **$65**.

Rose Etch **32.50**
Seahorse, crystal **145.00**
Cocktail shaker
Cobel, #4225, quart...... **55.00**
Orchid Etch, sterling foot
.... **200.00**
Console set, Twist, moongleam,
12" oval ftd bowl, pr 2" candles,
Cattail cutting **295.00**
Cordial
Carcassone, #390, Sahara
.... **115.00**
Minuet, crystal **150.00**
Peerless, crystal **28.00**

Greek Key pattern, creamer in front,
$45; nappy in back, **$30**.

Creamer and sugar
Twist, #1252, oval, Sahara
.... **165.00**
Waverly, #1519, orchid etch
.... **75.00**
Cream soup, Queen Anne,
etching **20.00**
Cruet, Greek Key, crystal **145.00**

Cup and saucer
Empress, Sahara yellow,
round **40.00**
Twist, #1252, flamingo .. **55.00**
Custard cup, Queen Anne
.... **15.00**
Floral bowl, Orchid, Waverly,
crimped, 12" d, 4" h, some
scratches **55.00**
Gardenia bowl, Orchid, Waverly,
13" d **90.00**
Goblet
Galaxy, #8005 .... **25.00**
Moonglo, crystal **35.00**
Narrow Flute, #393 .... **28.50**
Plantation Ivy, crystal.... **36.00**
Provincial, #1506 .... **15.00**
Spanish, #3404, cobalt blue
.... **155.00**
Tudor............................ **12.00**
Honey, Plantation, #1567, ivy
etch, 6-1/2" **80.00**
Hurricane lamp base, Lariat,
#1540, pr.......................... **85.00**
Iced-tea tumbler, Moonglo,
crystal **35.00**
Jug, Old Sandwich, #1404,
Sahara, half gallon **225.00**
Luster, Ipswich, crystal .. **465.00**
Mayonnaise bowl, Orchid, two-
part, Queen Anne **65.00**
Mayonnaise ladle, #6,
Alexandrite...................... **245.00**
Muffin plate, Octagon #1229,
12" d, moongleam............. **47.50**
Nut dish
Empress, #1401, individual,
Alexandrite **175.00**
Narrow Flute, #393,
moongleam................... **15.00**
Oyster cocktail, Pied Piper
.... **15.00**
Paperweight, rabbit **225.00**

Parfait glass, Orchid, 5-1/2" h,
2-7/8" d, price for set of eight
.... **480.00**
Pitcher, Orchid, tankard . **625.00**
Plate
Colonial, 4-3/4" d **4.75**
Empress, Moongleam, 7" d
.... **25.00**
Minuet, 8" d.................. **19.75**
Orchid, Waverly, 8" d ... **40.00**
Ridgeleigh, #1469, 8" d **10.00**
Punch bowl set, Crystolite,
punch bowl, 12 cups, ladle
.... **400.00**
Relish
Normandie etch, star, #1466
.... **95.00**
Orchid, three-part, three
handles, 7-1/4" d **55.00**
Provincial, #1506, 12" ... **35.00**
Twist, #1252, flamingo, 13" l
.... **40.00**
Waverly, two-part.......... **25.00**
Rose bowl, Plateau, #3369,
flamingo **65.00**
Salt shaker, Old Sandwich,
#1404 .... **30.00**
Sandwich plate, Rose.... **220.00**
Serving tray, center handle,
Orchid Etch...................... **150.00**
Sherbet, Moonglo, crystal **35.00**
Soda
Coronation, #4054, 10 oz **9.50**
Duquesne, #3389, 12 oz, ftd,
tangerine **210.00**
Newton, #2351, 8 oz,
Fronetnac etch **20.00**
Strawberry dip plate, Narrow
Flute, #393, with rim........ **195.00**
Sugar, Crystolite, individual
.... **17.50**
Tankard, Orchid, ice lip, 9-1/2" h,
7" w **480.00**
Toothpick holder, Fancy Loop,
emerald, small base flake, wear
to gold trim...................... **120.00**
Tumbler, Carassone, Sahara,
ftd, 2 oz **72.00**
Vase
Prison Stripe, #357, cupped,
5"................................ **55.00**
Ridgeleigh, #1469, Sahara,
cylinder, 8" h **245.00**
Water bottle, Banded Flute,
#150................................ **125.00**
Wine
Creole, Alexandrite, 5-1/2" h
.... **175.00**
Minuet, crystal, 6" h **85.00**

HOLT-HOWARD COLLECTIBLES

History: Three young entrepreneurs, Grant Holt and brothers John and Robert Howard, started Holt-Howard from their apartment in Manhattan, in 1949. All three of the partners were great salesman, but Robert handled product development, while John managed sales; Grant was in charge of financial affairs and office management. By 1955, operations were large enough to move the company to Connecticut, but it still maintained its New York showroom and later added its final showroom in Los Angeles. Production facilities eventually expanded to Holt-Howard Canada; Holt-Howard West, Holt-Howard International.

The company's first successful product was the Angel-Abra, followed closely by its Christmas line. This early success spurred the partners to expand their wares. Their line of Christmas and kitchen-related giftware was popular with 1950s consumers. Probably the most famous line was Pixieware, which began production in 1958. Production of these whimsical pieces continued until 1962. Other lines, such as Cozy Kittens and Merry Mouse, brought even more smiles as they invaded homes in many forms. Three things that remained constant with all Holt-Howard products were a high quality of materials and workmanship, innovation, and good design.

The founders of this unique company sold their interests to General Housewares Corp. in 1968, where it became part of the giftware group. By 1974, the three original partners had left the firm. By 1990, what remained of Holt-Howard was sold to Kay Dee Designs of Rhode Island.

Holt-Howard pieces were marked with an ink-stamp. Many were also copyright dated. Some pieces were marked only with a foil sticker, especially the small pieces, where a stamp mark was too difficult. Four types of foil stickers have been identified.

Adviser: Walter Dworkin.

Pixieware, Jam n' Jelly, blond haired girl, pink flowers with yellow centers, **$125**.

All Holt Howard photographs courtesy of Walter Dworkin.

Christmas

Air freshener, Girl Christmas Tree **65.00**
Ashtray, Snow Baby **35.00**
Ashtray/cigarette holder, Starry-eyed Santa **45.00**
Bells, Elf Girls, pr............. **55.00**
Bottle opener, wooden
    Santa **28.00**
    Snowman **28.00**
Candle climbers, Ole Snowy, snowman, set................... **48.00**
Candleholders
    Camels **38.00**
    Carolers trio **30.00**
    Elf Girls, NOEL, set of four **38.00**
    Ermine Angels with snowflake rings, set...................... **48.00**
    Green Holly Elf, pr **35.00**
    Madonna and Child...... **25.00**
    Naughty Choir Boy, set of two **30.00**
    Reindeer, pr **38.00**
    Santa driving car candleholders, traffic light candle rings, pr **55.00**
    Santa riding stage coach, pr **38.00**
    Santas, NOEL, set of four **90.00**
    Snow Babies, igloo, set of two **55.00**
    Three Choir Boy **60.00**
    Three Snowmen........... **50.00**
    Totem Pole, Santa........ **25.00**
    Wee Three Kings, set of three **60.00**

Cigarette holder with ashtrays, Santa King, stackable .. **70.00**
Coffee mug, Green Holly Elf **23.00**
Cookie jar, pop-up, Santa **150.00**
Cookie jar/candy jar combination, Santa **155.00**
Creamer and sugar
    Reindeer..................... **48.00**
    Winking Santas........... **55.00**
Decanter and glasses, Santa King **100.00**
Dish, divided, Green Holly Elf **50.00**
Floral ring, Green Holly Elf **48.00**
Head vase, My Fair Lady . **75.00**
Letter and pen holder, Santa **55.00**
Napkin holder, Santa, 4".. **25.00**
Nutmeg shaker, Winking Santa **55.00**
Pitcher and mug set, Winking Santa................................. **75.00**
Place card holders, Green Holly Elf, set of four.................... **40.00**
Planter
    Camel **40.00**
    Elf Girl in Sleigh **58.00**
    Ermine Angel.............. **38.00**
    Green Holly Elf, pr **75.00**
Punch bowl set, punch bowl and eight mugs, Santa ... **145.00**
Salt and pepper shakers, pr
    Cloud Santa................. **38.00**
    Holly Girls, pr.............. **23.00**
    Rock' N' Roll Santas, on springs......................... **75.00**
    Santa and Rudolph sleeping in bed **105.00**
    Santa and snowman in NOEL candleholder **95.00**
    Snow Babies................ **35.00**
Server, divided tray, Santa King **60.00**
Wall pocket
    Green Holly Elf.............. **65.00**
    Santa ornament **58.00**

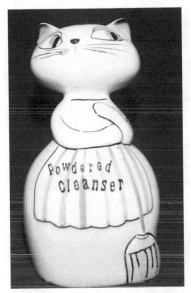

Cozy Kittens, powdered cleanser,
6-3/4" h, **$70**.

Cozy Kittens

Ashtray, with match holder
.... **55.00**
Bud vase, pr.................... **105.00**
Butter dish, cov **105.00**
Condiment jar, Cat
   Instant Coffee **190.00**
   Jam 'n Jelly **180.00**
   Ketchup **180.00**
   Mustard **180.00**
Cookie jar, pop up **250.00**
Cottage cheese crock **60.00**
Creamer and sugar **200.00**
Kitty catch clip **38.00**
Letter holder/caddy **58.00**
Match dandy **75.00**
Memo minder **90.00**
Meow milk pitcher **110.00**
Meow mug **35.00**
Meow oil and vinegar **175.00**
Salt and pepper shakers, pr
.... **20.00**
Sewing kit, Merry Measure
.... **70.00**
Spice set of four, with rack
.... **110.00**
String holder **45.00**
Sugar pour **85.00**
Totem pole stacking seasons
.... **65.00**

Cows

Creamer and sugar **75.00**
Milk glass, moo cow **32.00**
Salt and pepper shakers, pr
   Heads **40.00**
   Moveable tongues **50.00**

Easter

Candelabra, three rabbits **58.00**
Candle climbers, four-pc set
   Feathered Chicks, cracked
   egg floral frog bases **78.00**
   Honey Bunnies, floral frog
   bases **78.00**
Candleholder
   Totem pole, chicks........ **38.00**
   Totem pole, rabbits....... **38.00**
Egg cups, Slick Chick, pr of egg
cups with Chick salt and pepper
shaker, four-pc set **50.00**
**Salt and pepper shakers with
napkin holder**, Winking
Wabbbits...................... **60.00**
Salt and pepper shakers, pr
   Bunnies in baskets **28.00**
   Rabbit, pink and yellow **25.00**

Jeeves, three pieces, left: olives, **$135**,
liquor decanter, **$165**, cherries; **$135**.

Jeeves, butler

Ashtray............................ **70.00**
Chip dish......................... **80.00**
Liquor decanter............. **165.00**
Martini shaker set **195.00**
Olives, condiment jar **135.00**

Merry Mouse

Cocktail kibitzers, mice, set of
six................................. **120.00**
Coaster, ashtray, corner ... **55.00**
Crock, "Stinky Cheese" **50.00**
Desk pen pal **85.00**
Match mouse **70.00**
Salt and pepper shakers, pr
.... **35.00**

Minnie & Moby
Mermaids

Ashtray, Moby................. **55.00**
Cotton ball dispenser, Minnie
.... **75.00**
Matchbox holder, Moby.. **65.00**
Pill box, Minnie & Moby .. **50.00**

Planter, seahorse, Minnie &
Moby, pr **85.00**
Powder jar, Minnie & Moby
.... **50.00**

Pelican Pete, tape dispenser, 8-3/4" l
copyrighted 1958, **$68**.

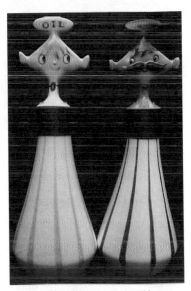

Sam n' Sally salad cruet set, 9" h, one
for oil, other for vinegar, copyrighted
1958, **each $185**.

Miscellaneous

Ashtray
   Golfer Image............... **110.00**
   Li'l Old Lace **50.00**
Bank, bobbing, Dandy Lion
.... **135.00**
Bud vase, Daisy Dorable . **70.00**
Candelabra, Li'l Old Lace, spiral
.... **50.00**
Candle climbers, Honey
Bunnies, with bases, set... **85.00**
Candle holder, Market Piggy
.... **28.00**
Candle rings, Ballerina, with
bases, set **58.00**
Cookie jar, pop-up, Clown
.... **225.00**
Desk organizer, Market Piggy
.... **78.00**
Letter holder, Pheasant ... **60.00**
Memo holder, Pheasant ... **60.00**

Holt-Howard Collectibles

Napkin doll, Sunbonnet Miss
.... **75.00**
Planter, Doe & Fawn......... **35.00**
Salt and pepper shakers, with
napkin holder, Winking Wabbits
.... **60.00**
Salt and pepper shakers, pr
  Bell Bottom Gobs (sailors)
.... **50.00**
  Chattercoons, Peppy and
  Salty.............................. **38.00**
  Daisy Dorables, ponytail girls
.... **35.00**
  Goose 'N' Golden Egg.. **35.00**
  Pink cat, white poodle .. **65.00**
  Rock 'N' Doll Kids, on springs
.... **75.00**
Peepin' Tom & Tweetie Birds
  Butter dish, cov........... **65.00**
  Candle holder/floral holder
.... **38.00**
  Candle food-warmer set,
  three pcs..................... **65.00**
  Creamer, sugar, and
  saccharin holder, 4-1/2" **75.00**
  Egg cups, thermal salt and
  pepper tops, 4" h......... **60.00**
  Salt and pepper shakers, set
.... **35.00**
  Stackable condiment bowls,
  set of three.................. **40.00**
Pencil holder and sharpener,
  two-pc set
  Chickadee **65.00**
  Cock-A-Doodle............. **60.00**
  Professor Perch **65.00**
Tape dispenser
  Chickadee **50.00**
  Pelican Pete................. **68.00**
Tea maker, Tea Time Tillie **38.00**

Pixiewares, sundae servers, copyrighted 1959, 5" w: Berries, **$695**; Goo, **$1,000**; Nuts, **$600**.

Pixiewares, 1958

Bottle bracelets
  Bourbon...................... **100.00**
  Gin **100.00**
  Scotch........................ **100.00**
  Whiskey **100.00**
Child's Pixie spoon
  Carrot nose, flesh-colored
  Pixie **135.00**

Pixiewares, condiment jars, 5-1/2" h, mustard, ketchup, jam 'n jelly, each **$75**.

Pixiewares, condiment jars, cocktail olives, **$130**; cherries, **$120**; onions, **$145**.

Green head Pixie........ **135.00**
Orange head Pixie...... **135.00**
Yellow chicken beak Pixie
.... **135.00**
Condiment jar
  Cherries **120.00**
  Cocktail Cherries **135.00**
  Cocktail Olives **130.00**
  Cocktail Onions **155.00**
  Instant Coffee **255.00**
  Jam 'N' Jelly **75.00**
  Ketchup **75.00**
  Mustard....................... **75.00**
  Olives......................... **100.00**
  Onions........................ **145.00**
L'il sugar and cream crock
.... **155.00**
Liquor decanter
  "Devil Brew".............. **580.00**
  "300 Proof"................. **580.00**
  "Whisky" **580.00**
Oil cruet, Sally.............. **185.00**
Oil cruet, Sam **185.00**
Stacking seasons, shakers, set
of four.............................. **85.00**

Pixiewares, 1959

Ashtray Pixie
  Blue stripe **160.00**

Green stripe............... **160.00**
Pink stripe **160.00**
Red stripe **160.00**

Pixiewares, liquor decanters, 10-1/2" h, 300 Proof, Whiskey, solid color base, copyrighted 1958, **each $580**.

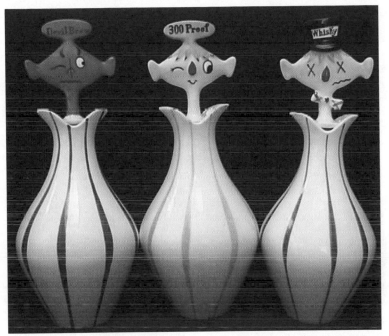

Pixiewares, liquor decanters, striped bodies, 10-1/2" h, Devil Brew, 300 Proof, Whiskey, copyrighted 1958, **each $580**.

Pixiewares, stacking seasons, wooden holder, copyrighted 1958, **$85**; Salty & Peppy shakers, 4-1/2" h, copyrighted 1959, **$350**.

Pixiewares, set of four spoons, 6-1/2" l, copyrighted 1958, each **$135**

Pixiewares, instant coffee, 5-1/2" h, **$255**; creamer, 2-3/4" h, sugar, 5" copyrighted 1958, **set $155**.

Pixiewares, salad dressing bottles, 7" h, flat heads, Russian, Italian, French, copyrighted 1959, **each $140**.

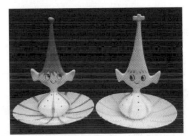

Party Pixies, hors d'oeurve dishes, 7-1/2" h, 5-3/4" d, each **$200**.

Condiment jar
Chili Sauce................... 365.00
Honey 725.00
Mayonnaise 185.00
Relish 225.00
Hanging planter, rare..... 450.00
Party Pixies hors d'oeuvre dish
Green stripe boy pixie **200.00**
Orange stripe girl pixie, Australian.................... **475.00**
Pink stripe girl pixie **200.00**
Salad dressing jar
Flat head, French Pixie
.... 140.00
Flat head, Italian Pixie. 140.00
Flat head, Russian Pixie
.... 140.00
Round head, French Pixie
.... 125.00

Round head, Italian Pixie
.... 125.00
Round head, Russian Pixie
.... 125.00
Salty & Peppy shakers.. 350.00
Snack Pixie bowl
Berries 685.00
Goo........................... 1,000.00
Ketchup Katie............. 675.00
Mustard Max............... 675.00
Nuts 600.00
Onion Annie................ 685.00
Oscar Olives............... 575.00
Peanut Butter Pat........ 675.00
Pickle Pete.................. 675.00
Tartar Tom.................. 850.00
Teapot candleholder hurricane vase, complete with glass globe
Blue stripe boy 285.00
Pink stripe girl............. 285.00

Towel hook
Brother........................ 150.00
Dad............................ 150.00
Mom........................... 150.00
Sister.......................... 150.00

Red Rooster, "Coq Rouge"
Butter dish, cov 65.00
Candleholders, pr........... 30.00
Coffee mug 14.00
Coffee server, 36 oz 65.00
Cookie jar 100.00
Creamer and sugar 55.00
Dinner plate 18.00
Electric coffee pot, six cups
.... 70.00
Mustard condiment jar ... 55.00
Pitcher
12 oz........................... 45.00
32 oz........................... 60.00
48 oz........................... 75.00

Salt and pepper shakers, pr,
4-1/2" **25.00**
Snack tray **18.00**
Spoon rest **25.00**
Wooden
 Canister set, four pcs ... **85.00**
 Cigarette carton holder. **45.00**
 Recipe box **70.00**
 Salt & pepper shakers, pr
 .... **23.00**

Tigers

Child's cup **15.00**
Cookie jar **40.00**
Napkin holder **20.00**
Salt and pepper shakers, pr
.... **23.00**

HORN

History: For centuries, horns from animals have been used for various items, e.g., drinking cups, spoons, powder horns, and small dishes. Some pieces of horn have designs scratched in them. Around 1880, furniture made from the horns of Texas longhorn steers was popular in Texas and the southwestern United States.

Ale set, silver plate-mounted cov 9-3/4" h jug, two 5-1/2" h beakers, fitted 17-3/4" l x 15" h plated frame with twisted gallery and upright handle, tripartite circular base with Greek Key border, raised on stepped block feet, English, early 20th C
.... **850.00**
Arm chair, steer horn, leather upholstered seat, four pairs of matched horns form base, American, 20th C **575.00**
Cane
 33-3/4" l, 4" w x 5-1/4" h staghorn "L"-shaped handle, high relief carved hunting scene, detailed family crest on top round portion, scene spirals around handle starting at bottom continuing to top, medieval hunt with dogs, men with spears and lances pursing two bears, thin coin silver spacer, Malacca shaft with round silver eyelets, 2-1/4" polished staghorn ferrule, attributed to Germany, c1880
 .... **2,800.00**
 34-1/8" l, 7-1/2" l wild boar's tusk handle, pointed silver

cap with leaf dec, marked "sterling" on one end, other end with sq cap inscribed "Judge Henry Bank Jr. from KeoKuK Bar Feb. 15, 1919," 1-1/8" dec silver collar, dark briarwood shaft, 1-1/4" white metal and iron ferrule
.... **1,100.00**
 35" l, 1-3/4" w, 4" h dark horn handle, carved as perched eagle, clear and black glass eyes, lighter horn beak, 2/3" woven silver thread collar, blond Malacca shaft, 1-1/2" horn ferrule, Continental, c1895...................... **490.00**
Case, 6-1/8" l, 2-3/4" h, two part, both sides with tiger underneath pine tree, top with ideogram within circle, written characters on inside flange, cord attached to lower part passes through hole in cover, Korea, 19th C, cracking and some lifting of horn
.... **150.00**
Cup, 5" h, rhinoceros, carved as magnolia flower, base of branch and leaves, carved wood stand, 18th C or earlier, losses **1,100.00**
Furniture suite, American, late 19th C, 48" w x 25" d x 44" h loveseat, one 38" w x 24" d x 44" h chair, one 32" w x 28" d x 35" h chair, each upholstered, mounted with animal horns, wooden legs, brass casters, from William Wrigley residence, Chicago, IL **6,375.00**

Snuff box, rectangular, hinged lid and oval sides, held together with white metal straps and brass nails, marked "L'Auvergnate; Marque Deposee, R.L.," French, late 19th C, 3-1/2" x 1-7/8" x 7/8", **$175**.

Photo courtesy of Gamal Amer.

Plaque, wall mounted, water buffalo horns, brass caps on ends, engraved dec, 33" l
.... **275.00**
Seal, 2" h, 1-1/4" d, stupa form, carved scene of cranes and flora

atop stylized waves, Chinese or Korean, 19th C **100.00**
Snuff box, 2" l, 2-3/4" w, 3/4" h, rect, carved PA motifs, floral dec, red paint on hinged lid, birds carved on sides, star on bottom
.... **450.00**
Tea caddy, cov, 14-1/2" w, 9" d, 7-1/2" h, Ango-Indian, Vishapatnam, early 19th C, antler veneer, steer horn, ivory, int. cov compartments, etched scrolling vines, restorations
.... **1,850.00**
Tumbler, 4-3/8" h, silver trim and shield **195.00**
Vinaigrette, Victorian, late 19th C, staghorn, 2-1/2" l rough-textured horn mounted with thistle-cast lid, quatrefoil neck band, horn with guilloche strapping, short link chain
.... **350.00**

HULL POTTERY

History: In 1905, Addis E. Hull purchased the Acme Pottery Company, Crooksville, Ohio. In 1917, the A. E. Hull Pottery Company began making art pottery, novelties, stoneware, and kitchenware, later including the famous Little Red Riding Hood line. Most items had a matte finish, with shades of pink and blue or brown predominating.

After a disastrous flood and fire in 1950, J. Brandon Hull reopened the factory in 1952 as the Hull Pottery Company. New, more-modern-style pieces, mostly with glossy finish, were produced. The company added dinnerware patterns, and glossy finished pottery. The company closed its doors in 1986.

Marks: Hull pottery molds and patterns are easily identified. Pre-1950 vases are marked "Hull USA" or "Hull Art USA" on the bottom. Many also retain their paper labels. Post-1950 pieces are marked "Hull" in large script or "HULL" in block letters.

Each pattern has a distinctive letter or number, e.g., Wildflower has a "W" and a number; Waterlily, "L" and number; Poppy, numbers in the 600s; Orchid, in the 300s. Early stoneware pieces are marked with an "H."

For more information about these marks and Hull Pottery patterns and history, consult Joan Hull's book, *Hull, The Heavenly Pottery,* 7th ed., 2000, and, *Hull, The Heavenly Pottery Shirt Pocket Price List,* 4th ed., 1999.

Additional Listings: See *Warman's Americana & Collectibles* for more examples.

Adviser: Joan Hull.

Bandana Duck, green and yellow, black beak, marked "Hull Art," **$35**.

Pre-1950 Matte

Bowknot
B-4 6-1/2" h vase **250.00**
B-7 cornucopia **325.00**
B-12, 10-1/2" h basket **750.00**
B-17 candleholders, pr **225.00**

Calla Lily
500-32 bowl **200.00**
520-33, 8" h vase **150.00**

Dogwood (Wild Rose)
501, 8-1/2" h basket.... **300.00**
508 10-1/2" window box **195.00**
513, 6-1/2" h vase **125.00**

Little Red Riding Hood
Creamer and sugar, side pour **400.00**
Dresser or cracker jar . **800.00**
Lamp........................ **2,500.00**
Salt and pepper shakers, pr, small **120.00**
Teapot, cov **395.00**

Magnolia
3 8-1/2" h vase **125.00**
9 10-1/2" h vase **200.00**
14 4-3/4" h pitcher **75.00**
20 15" floor vase **500.00**

Open Rose/Camellia
106 13-1/2" h pitcher .. **650.00**
119 8-1/2" h vase **175.00**
127 4-3/4" h vase **75.00**

Magnolia, pink glossy, No. 18, **$75**.

Orchid
302 6" h vase **175.00**
304 10-1/2" h vase **350.00**
310 9-1/2" jardinière.... **450.00**

Poppy
601 9" h basket **800.00**
610 13" pitcher **900.00**
613 6-1/2" h vase **200.00**

Rosella
R-2 5" h vase **35.00**
R-6 6-1/2" h vase **45.00**
R-15 8-1/2" h vase **75.00**

Tulip
101-33 9" h vase **245.00**
107-33 6" h vase **125.00**
109-33-8" pitcher **235.00**

Waterlily
L-14, 10-1/2" basket ... **350.00**
L-16, 12-1/2" vase....... **395.00**

Wild Flower, No. Series
53 8-1/2" h vase **295.00**
61 6-1/2" h vase **175.00**
66 10-1/4" h basket.. **2,000.00**
71 12" h vase **450.00**

Woodland
W9 8-3/4" h basket **245.00**
W11 5-1/2" flower pot and saucer.......................... **175.00**
W13 7-1/2" l wall pocket, shell **195.00**
W14 10-1/2" window box **200.00**

Post 1950

Blossom Flite
T4 8-1/2" h basket....... **125.00**
T13 12-1/2" h pitcher .. **150.00**

Butterfly
B9 9" h vase.................. **55.00**
B13 8" h basket **150.00**
B15 13-1/2" h pitcher .. **200.00**

Continental
C29 12" h vase **95.00**
C55 12-1/2" basket **150.00**
C62 8-1/4" candy dish . **45.00**

Woodland, post, glossy basket, No. 22 12-1/2, **$250**.

Ebb Tide
E-1 7" h bud vase **75.00**
E-8 ashtray with mermaid **225.00**
E-10 13" h pitcher **275.00**

Parchment and Pine
S-3 6" h basket **95.00**
S-11 and S-12 tea set. **250.00**
S-15 8" h coffeepot **175.00**

Serenade
S1 6" h vase.................. **55.00**
S-15 11-1/2" d fruit bowl, ftd **125.00**
S17 teapot, creamer and sugar **275.00**

Sunglow
53 grease jar **60.00**
82 wall pocket, whisk broom **75.00**
85 8-3/4" h vase, bird .. **60.00**

Tokay/Tuscany
3 8" h pitcher **95.00**
8 10" h vase **150.00**
10 11" l cornucopia **65.00**

Tropicana
T53 8-1/2" h vase........ **550.00**
T55, 12-3/4" h basket.. **750.00**

Woodland, post, glossy vases, No. 4 6-1/2", **$65**.

Woodland (glossy)
W1 5-1/2" h vase........... **45.00**
W15 8-1/2" h vase, double
.... **75.00**
W19 14" d console bowl
.... **100.00**

HUMMEL ITEMS

History:
Hummel items are the original creations of Berta Hummel, who was born in 1909 in Massing, Bavaria, Germany. At age 18, she was enrolled in the Academy of Fine Arts in Munich to further her mastery of drawing and the palette. Berta entered the Convent of Siessen and became Sister Maria Innocentia in 1934. In this Franciscan cloister, she continued drawing and painting images of her childhood friends.

In 1935, W. Goebel Co. in Rodental, Germany, began producing Sister Maria Innocentia's sketches as three-dimensional bisque figurines. The Schmid Brothers of Randolph, Massachusetts, introduced the figurines to America and became Goebel's U.S. distributor.

In 1967, Goebel began distributing Hummel items in the U.S. A controversy developed between the two companies, the Hummel family, and the convent. Law suits and counter-suits ensued. The German courts finally effected a compromise: the convent held legal rights to all works produced by Sister Maria Innocentia from 1934 until her death in 1946 and licensed Goebel to reproduce these works; Schmid was to deal directly with the Hummel family for permission to reproduce any pre-convent art.

Marks:
All authentic Hummel pieces bear both the signature "M. I. Hummel" and a Goebel trademark. Various trademarks were used to identify the year of production:

Crown Mark (trademark 1): 1935-1949
Full Bee (trademark 2): 1950-1959
Stylized Bee (trademark 3): 1957-1972
Three Line Mark (trademark 4): 1964-1972
Last Bee Mark (trademark 5): 1972-1979
Missing Bee Mark (trademark 6): 1979-1990
Current Mark or New Crown Mark (trademark 7): 1991 to the present

Additional Listings: See *Warman's Americana & Collectibles* for more examples.

For more information, see *Warman's Hummel Field Guide.*

Collector plate, 1979, Singing Lesson, Hummel #272, boy playing horn, **$45**.
Photo courtesy of Dotta Auction Co., Inc.

Dolls, porcelain, Gretel on left, Hansel on right, Goebel, both MIB, **each $125**.
Photo courtesy of Dotta Auction Co., Inc.

Angel, Festival Harmony, #172/II, with mandolin, **$140**.
Photo courtesy of Dotta Auction Co., Inc.

Candleholder, Angel Lights, plate, original beeswax candles, #241, mark 5, **$150**.
Photo courtesy of Dotta Auction Co., Inc.

Bookends, pr, Chick Girl, #618, full bee, trademark-2....... **320.00**
Candleholder, Watchful angel, #194, trademark 2 .... **400.00**
Candy box, cov, Happy Pastime, #III/169, trademark 4
.... **125.00**
Clock, 11-1/8" h, Chapel Time, 1986, orig box and instructions **700.00**
Figure
Apple Tree Boy, #142V
.... **1,200.00**
Band Leader, #129, trademark 5 .... **120.00**
Congratulations, #17/0, trademark 1, 5-3/4" h.. **750.00**
Daily News, #184, 5" h **400.00**
For Father, #87, trademark 2, 5-7/8" h **600.00**

Just Resting, #112/13/0, trademark 4 .... **90.00**

Little Fiddler, #2/III, trademark 6 .... **775.00**

Merry Wanderer, #11/0, trademark 3 .... **600.00**

Pleasant Journey, 1987 .... **1,500.00**

Puppy Love, #73, trademark 1, 5-1/4" h **600.00**

School Girls, #177/III, #5, 9-1/2" h **1,400.00**

Strolling Along, #5, trademark 2, 5-3/4" h **550.00**

Umbrella Girl, 7-1/2" h. **1,400.00**

Valentine Gift, #387, trademark 5, 1977, Goebel Collectors Club edition **650.00**

Font

Child Jesus, #26/0, MK 4 **35.00**

Holy Family, #246, trademark 2 .... **85.00**

Seated Angel, #10/1, trademark 3 .... **420.00**

Figure, little girl holding up flowers, **$100**.

Figure, boy, cello on back, large size, trademark 2, incised 89/2, **$400**.

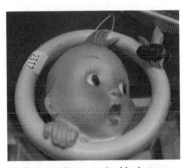

Wall plaque, boy surprised by bee on edge of ring, trademark 2, incised "M J. Hummel, #50/0 A," stamped "Western Germany," **$90**.

Font, one angel, dressed in blue, singing, other angel, dressed in green, playing mandolin, bee in large V mark, impressed marks, **each $45**.

Lamp, table, Culprits, #44, 9-1/2" h, c1930 .... **475.00**

Madonna, pale blue and tangerine, open book on lap, bird perched on one side, child in emerald dress, holding blue flower, white raised dot pattern clock, mkd "Goebel W Germany" **795.00**

Plate, 1971, first edition, Christmas series **600.00**

IMARI

History: Imari derives its name from a Japanese port city. Although Imari ware was manufactured in the 17th century, the pieces most commonly encountered are those made between 1770 and 1900.

Early Imari was decorated simply, quite unlike the later heavily decorated brocade pattern commonly associated with Imari. Most of the decorative patterns are an underglaze blue and overglaze "seal wax" red complimented by turquoise and yellow.

The Chinese copied Imari ware. The Japanese examples can be identified by grayer clay, thicker glaze, runny and darker blue, and deep red opaque hues.

The pattern and colors of Imari inspired many English and European potteries, such as Derby and Meissen, to adopt a similar style of decoration for their wares.

Reproduction Alert: Reproductions abound, and many manufacturers continue to produce pieces in the traditional style.

Bottle vases, 11" h, lobated form, underglaze blue with red, green, aubergine enamels and gilt, Japan, late 19th C, price for pr **775.00**

Bowl

6" d, designs of dragons and auspicious emblems, 19th C, set of 12 .... **400.00**

9" w, sq form with ribs, design of various flowers, Wan Li six-character mark on base, 19th C **120.00**

13-3/4" d, gilt floral scrolling, heraldic emblems surrounding central dragon, six-character mark on base, 19th C **560.00**

Charger

14-1/2" d, underglaze blue and enamel dec, central reserve of planter with flowers, grape and brocade borders, Japan, late 19th/early 20th C **250.00**

20-1/4" d, 4-3/4" h, hp, cinnabar red, underglaze dark blue, green, and gilt, dragons in clouds circle border, leaves and clouds below, two phoenixes in center, ext. cov with blossoming vines, center base with cinnabar and gilt flower, glued repair to edge, gilt imperfections **715.00**

Imari

22" d, fans with warriors and dragons dec, sgd "Koransha," late 19th C **1,645.00**

Creamer and sugar, 5-1/2" h creamer, 5-7/8" cov sugar, ovoid, dragon form handles, gilt and bright enamels, shaped reserves, dragon-like beasts, stylized animal medallions, brocade ground, high dome lid, knob, cipher mark of Mount Fuji, Fukagama Studio marks, Meiji period............................ **500.00**

Dish, octagonal, large, blue underglaze decoration, red and green overglaze decoration, **$275**.

Photo courtesy of Wiederseim Associates, Inc.

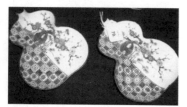

Dishes, gourd shape, Imari flowering tree with checkered design in foreground, brown rim glaze, underside with underglazed blue tendrils, Fuku mark on base, Japanese, 18th C, 6-3/4" l, one with small neck rim chip, price for pair, **$1,650**.

Dish

6-3/4" l, gourd shape, flowering tree with checkered design in foreground, brown glaze on rim, underside with underglaze blue tendrils, Fuku mark on base, Japanese, 18th C, pr, one with rim chip **1,650.00**

8-3/8" d, central scene with fence and flowering tree dec, shaped cartouches enclosing flowers and hares on crackle blue ground at rim, gilt highlights, Meiji period, price for pr **650.00**

Food box, 6" h, three section, ext. and lid with phoenix and floral design, underglaze blue, iron-red, and gilt enamels, 19th C **400.00**

Jar, cov, 26" h, ribbed forms with shishi finials, Japan, late 19th C, price for pr **2,000.00**

Jardinière, 10" h, hexagonal, bulbous, short flared foot, alternating bijin figures and immortal symbols, stylized ground **250.00**

Luncheon set, partial, 12 8" d plates, four 10-1/4" oblong serving dishes, two boat-shaped serving dishes, sq serving dish, coffee van, Spode, 19th C, 20 pcs **2,820.00**

Planter and stand, 17" d, 43" h, lobed form, floral dec, brocade patterns, Japan, late 19th C **460.00**

Pair of lidded jars, all over orange and blue design, 10" h, **$250**.

Photo courtesy of Joy Luke.

Plate

8-1/2" d, reserves of dragons and flowers arranged around phoenix roundel, Japan, 19th C, set of nine **470.00**

9" d, brocade pattern, 19th C, set of nine **470.00**

17-1/4" sq, scalloped edge, central design of basket of flowers, 19th C......... **1,765.00**

Platter, 18" d, alternating panels of figures and foliage, trellis work ground, Japanese, late 19th C **475.00**

Punch bowl, 12" d, rubbed, c1870 .... **1,650.00**

Teabowl and saucer, 5" d, floriform, floral spray dec, gilt highlights on saucer **200.00**

Tea set, 6-1/8" h teapot; teapot stand; creamer; cov sugar; 8-1/4" d serving plate; two 7-3/4" d serving plates; two 6" d bowls; 16 5-3/8" d saucers; 11 coffee cans, 12 teacups, English, early 19th C, 48 pcs............... **2,235.00**

Plate, center with butterfly swooping over large peony, rich border with dragon and geometric patterns, back border with Buddhistic emblems, underside marked with Koranska Fukagama mark, Japan, late 19th C, 12-1/8" d, slight wear to gilding, **$550**.

Umbrella stand, blue underglaze decoration, overglaze decoration of Imari reds, wide central band with panels of floral motifs, top and bottom having wide cobalt blue bands with red floral decoration, mid-19th C, 10" d, 24" h, **$425**.

Photo courtesy of Alderfer Auction Co.

Umbrella stand, 25" h, allover hexagonal panels with gold pheasants and orange drawings, flowers, and plant, orange, tomato red, yellow, green, and cobalt blue, old shield shaped "U.S. Customs" label underneath............. **550.00**

Urn, 36-1/2" h, tomato red, light green, mauve, and cobalt blue, dark gold details, floral panels on sides with pheasants and cranes, geometric band of dec around base, minor roughness around rim.................... **2,100.00**
Vase, 14-1/2" h, baluster, late Meiji period, c1900 .... **775.00**

IMPERIAL GLASS

History: Imperial Glass Co., Bellaire, Ohio, was organized in 1901. Its primary product was pattern (pressed) glass. Soon other lines were added, including carnival glass, Nuart, Nucut, and Near Cut. In 1916, the company introduced Free-Hand, a lustered art glass line, and Imperial Jewels, an iridescent stretch glass that carried the Imperial cross trademark. In the 1930s, the company was reorganized into the Imperial Glass Corporation. The firm was sold to Lenox, in 1976, and ceased all operations by 1984.

Imperial acquired the molds and equipment of several other glass companies—Central, Cambridge, and Heisey. Many of the retired molds of these companies are once again in use for a short period of time before Imperial closed.

Marks: The Imperial reissues are marked to distinguish them from the originals.

For more information, see *Warman's Glass*, 4th edition.

Bowl, Leaf pattern, purple, carnival glass, 9" d, **$30**.

Engraved or hand cut

Bowl, 6-1/2" d, flower and leaf, molded star base............. **25.00**
Candlesticks, pr, 7" h, Amelia **35.00**
Celery vase, three-side stars, cut star base................... **25.00**
Pitcher, tankard, Design No. 110, flowers, foliage, and butterfly cutting................. **60.00**
Plate, 5-1/2" d, Design No. 12 .... **15.00**

Jewels

Bowl, 6-1/2" d, purple Pearl Green luster, marked **75.00**
Console set, Golden Green, 10-1/2" d bowl, pr 9-1/2" h candlesticks, 1920s....... **350.00**
Rose bowl, amethyst, green irid **75.00**
Vase
6-1/2" h, bulbous, mustard yellow, orange irid int., shape #1690......................... **100.00**
8-1/2" h, cylindrical bud, emerald green, orange irid int. **100.00**
11" h, cylindrical, irid marigold, wear at collar **75.00**

Pressed, cake plate, pedestal base, amber, original figural paper red, white and blue label, **$30**.

Lustered (freehand)

Candlestick, 10" h, slender baluster, cushion foot, clear, white heart and vine dec, tall cylindrical irid dark blue socket, orig paper label **440.00**

Hat, 9" w, ruffled rim, cobalt blue, embedded irid white vines and leaves **120.00**
Ivy ball, 4" h, Spun, red, crystal foot.................................. **90.00**
Vase
6-1/2" h, bulbous shouldered, irid marigold, price for pr **300.00**
10" h, bulbous, strong marigold irid, random blue heart and vine dec **550.00**
10" h, corset shape, irid green, white heart and vine dec, orange int. **550.00**

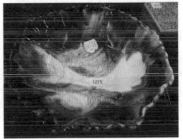
Bowl, slag glass, marbleized white and red, rose motif, original paper label, three feet, **$65**.

Nuart

Ashtray **20.00**
Lamp shade, marigold.... **50.00**
Vase, 7" h, bulbous, irid green **125.00**

Nucut

Berry bowl, 4-1/2" d, handles **15.00**
Celery tray, 11" l............. **18.00**
Creamer **20.00**
Fern dish, 8" l, brass lining, ftd **30.00**
Orange bowl, 12" d, Rose Marie **48.00**

Pressed, cake plates, pedestal base, avocado green, original labels, price for pair, **$65**.

Pressed

Bar bottle, Cape Cod..... **150.00**
Basket, Cape Cod, No. 160/73/0 .... **350.00**

Bowl, Molly, amber, gold embossed borders, footed bowl, pair of closely related candleholders, sold as set, **$125.**

Birthday cake plate, Cape Cod
.... **325.00**
Bowl
  Cape Cod, 11" l, oval.... **90.00**
  Windmill, amethyst, fluted,
  8" d, 3" h........................ **45.00**
Bread and butter plate, Cape
Cod **7.00**
Canapé plate, matching
tumbler, #400/36 .... **36.00**
Center bowl, Cape Cod, No.
160/751, ruffled edge........ **65.00**
Champagne, Cape Cod, azalea
.... **22.00**
Coaster, Cape Cod, No. 160/76
.... **10.00**
Creamer, #400/30.............. **9.00**
Cruet, orig stopper, Cape Cod,
No. 160/119, amber **28.00**
Decanter, orig stopper, Cape
Cod, No. 160/163.............. **75.00**
Dish, covered
  Dog, caramel slag, ALIG 1982
  .... **165.00**
  Dove, satin crystal, IG mark
  .... **75.00**
  Lion, amber, from Heisey
  mold mkd "CG".......... **125.00**
  Pie wagon, caramel slag,
  ALIG 1982................... **225.00**
Figure
  Chipmunk, Ultra Blue, ALIG
  mark........................... **195.00**
  Clydesdale, Ultra Blue, ALIG
  mark........................... **250.00**
  Wood Duck, Ultra Blue, IG
  mark........................... **225.00**

Goblet
  Cape Cod, No. 1602, Verde
  green **20.00**
  Traditional **15.00**
Jar, cov
  Cathay, Verde Green .. **135.00**
  Owl, green and white slag, IG
  mark............................ **85.00**
Nappy, Quilted Diamond,
marigold, ring handle........ **35.00**
Pitcher, Cape Cod, No. 160/19,
ice lip **85.00**
Plate, Windmill, caramel slag, IG
mark.................................. **75.00**
Relish
  Candlewick, two-part, 6-1/2"
  .... **25.00**
  Cape Cod, three-part ... **35.00**
Rose bowl, Molly, black, silver
deposit floral dec, 5" h...... **45.00**
Salad plate, 8" d, Cape Cod,
use scratches **11.00**
Sherbet
  Cape Cod **10.00**
  Traditional **10.00**
Sugar, #400/30 .... **9.00**
Tea cup, #400/35............... **8.00**
Toothpick holder, 2-1/2" h,
carnival or milk white, IG mark
.... **30.00**
Tumbler, Georgian, red ... **18.00**
Whiskey set, Cape Cod, No.
160/280, metal rack, clear
bottles, raised letters Bourbon,
Rye, and Scotch **650.00**

INDIAN ARTIFACTS, AMERICAN

History: During the historic period, there were approximately 350 Indian tribes grouped into the following regions: Eskimo, Northeast and Woodland, Northwest Coast, Plains, and West and Southwest.

American Indian artifacts are quite popular. Currently, the market is stable following a rapid increase in prices during the 1970s.

For more information, see *Warman's Native American Collectibles.*

Basket, covered, jar form, green and red decoration of birds alternating with masks, Navajo, c1900, 11" d, 7-1/2" h, some exterior fading, **$200.**

Photo courtesy of Alderfer Auction Co.

Anthropological records, *The 1870 Ghost Dance,* by Cora DuBois, Univ of California Press, Berkley, CA, 1939, paperback, black cloth tape binding. **150.00**
Awl case, beaded
  7" l, Mescalero Apache, late 19th C, chevron beaded, sliding cover, transparent ruby red, green, yellow, navy and white beads, large "white heart" red beads on top leather thongs beaded leather fringe with tin cone tinklers, tassels **575.00**

9-1/2" l, attributed to Apache, chevron and scallop, beaded in ruby red, Ute blue, white seed beads, gold, and green, finely beaded leather tassel drops, tassels **1,150.00**

10-1/2" l, Plains, either Central or Southern, Morning Star design, translucent green, greasy orange (pumpkin), blue, and white beads, tassels, wooden needle inside **920.00**

Bag

11-1/2" l, beaded cloth and hide, Plateau, pictorial beading, eagle, US flag, red, white, and blue banner, shield on orange bead background, eagle with carnival glass body, fringe................ **420.00**

27" l, 7" w, Sioux, beaded graphic flags on one side, geometric design on reverse, sinew sewn beading in rosy red "white hearts," cut metallic, navy, white, medium green, and translucent green, medium blue, and rare pumpkin, beaded throat with quill wrapped dangle and beaded dangle with tin cone feather tassels, fringe, wear at top.................. **2,645.00**

Basket, flat tray form, bands and blocks in dark brown and mustard color, coil formed, dark brown and beige wrapping on edge, loop for hanging, attributed to Papago or Hopi Third Mesa, 10" d, **$75**.

Photo courtesy of Alderfer Auction Co.

Basket

3-3/4" d, California, Pomo, late 19th C, gift, coiled, small compressed form, tightly woven with geometric devices, very fine feather tufts **1,265.00**

Basket, coiled basket, diamond design, 8-3/4" d, 4" h, **$275**.

Photo courtesy of Alderfer Auction Co.

7" l, Northwest Coast, Tlingit, twined polychrome rattle top, lidded jar form, woven with bold false embroidered geometric devices using five colors **2,415.00**

12" d, coiled, flaring sides **400.00**

Belt, 40" l, Plateau, beaded butterflies, flowers, and leaves, vining stems, light and dark blue, yellow, light and dark green, orange red and dark red beads on white beaded ground, navy blue stitched cloth border **150.00**

Basketry tray, 16" l, Salishan, circular, central imbricated star surrounded by border of diamonds, shaped handles, wear **200.00**

Birdstone, quartz **450.00**

Bonnet, child's, 5-1/2" h, Sioux, c1890, cap style, sinew sewn beading, lined with early acid dye calico, geometric bead design in red "white heart," cut metallic and green on white ground, edge beading old yellow and deep blue alternating squares, red silk ribbon lining around face, tie worn and faded pink **2,100.00**

Bowie knife, 12" l, semi-clip point blade, brass ferrule, stag horn handle.................... **230.00**

Bowl, basketry

8" d, 4" h, stepped band design in martynia around upper circumference, California Mission, c1910, patina......................... **420.00**

10-1/4" d, 2-3/8" h, Western Apache, finely patinated Morning Star design radiating from center, willow and martynia, one rim stitch missing **500.00**

15-1/4" d, Apache, pictorial, human figures, animals, and geometric devices ... **3,500.00**

Bowl, pottery

8" d, 4" h, Acoma Pueblo, polychrome, white slip, avian and curvilinear design around circumference, "Acoma NM" painted in slip on bottom, penciled 3.00 price, c1930-40 .... **150.00**

9-1/4" d, 2-1/2" h, Hopi, possibly Nampeyo, c1900, rim has extra clay coil forming inner rim, thin and thicker framing band, opposing geometric design elements painted outside, inside faded figural animal with feather, orangish slip, small crack with chip at rim, wear, patina **1,495.00**

Blanket, Southwest, light gray, black, red, turquoise, and white geometric motifs, white stripes and fringe, **$600**.

Case, 36" h, 12" w, Northern Plains, possibly Metis/Sioux or possibly Cree, c1890-1900, finely beaded on buckskin, floral and constellations, faceted silver metallic, opalescent green, rose red, and other colors ... **2,300.00**

Cradleboard, child size

21" h, 8" w, Ute, Great Basin, girl's, c1890, yellow stained ochre leather, wooden base loop, traditional Ute wicker frame, deep sky blue with green, black, and pearly white in floral effect, orig lace inside, hood missing, few loose beads............. **1,150.00**

Cradle, Plains, Cheyenne, 1880s, beaded hide and cloth, buffalo hide form, continuous red stripe bisecting stepped triangles, floating forked diamond devices, rawhide and canvas backing, bead colors: white center red, medium green, yellow, light blue, and translucent dark blue on white ground, fragments of hide ties to secure missing boards, some stiffness to hide, 26-1/2" l, **$8,850.**

Photo courtesy of Skinner, Inc.

31-1/4" l, Ute, girl's, c1880-1895, yellow ochre staining, two loom beaded ornaments contain initials "M.E.," piece overlapped and sewn shut, beaded flap with clear, red "white hearts," green edged with blue and old yellow, beaded hood and board ornamentation with Ute blue, ruby, yellow, dark blue, and white, tab trim stained/painted, long leather fringe on back, some bead loss, minor wear **4,600.00**

39" l, Ute, Transmontane style, c1875-1890, rare flag motifs around curvature of top, stained yellow for a girl, finger-like rows on flap covering laces done on early red and blue strouding with red "white hearts," navy black unstable beads, greasy yellow, and white beads, red stroud trade cloth beaded in black and white at hood edge, cross flap at top of opening geometrically beaded with later cut metallic, orangey red "white hearts" and translucent blue and green beads, attached umbilical fetish bead wrapped in white heart reds and blue with brass bead drops, weasel claw amulet for safety in travel and strength,

miniature brass show sole, small Victorian key, fringe at back, replaced laces, provenance: linked to Col. Eugene C. Haynes (1844-1922), Centerville, IA, who gifted cradleboard to C. J. Wilson, further documented by typewritten note .. **6,900.00**

Cradleboard, doll size 11-5/8" l, Apache, c1910, slatted hood, top hoop, muslin baby wrap and hood beaded in green, gold, black, and white, blue and white edging at sides, with doll **500.00**

14" l, 6" w, Chippewa, c1860, formed wooden back with heart cutout, curved bow and heart pierced dec on backboard, painted muted green, beaded cradle wrap finely beaded with floral design in realistic bluebells and wild anemones, faded velvet backing, glued break along middle of board **1,450.00**

20" l, Plateau, possibly Nez Perce, late 19th C, various shades of blue, dark blue, red "white heart" and yellow beads, leather fringe on back, muslin doll with trade cloth hood **2,875.00**

20-7/8" l, Northern Plains/Plateau, Blackfoot or Umatilla, c1890, geometric beading to head of cradle, ceremonial cloth design with circles of red and green on yellow ochre background, wooden carved doll........................... **1,955.00**

Cuffs, pr, 6" h, Yakima, Pendleton Roundup, c1900, pictorial beading, cowboy on one, cowgirl on other, American flags on sides with multicolor bead fringe flowing downward, yellow, black, white, sky blue, and clear rose beads **750.00**

Cuff gauntlets, pr, 8-1/2" l, Plateau, for wear at Pendleton Roundup, floral beading, graphic roses in blues and red/orange, long flowing fringe, slight bead loss............... **230.00**

Dispatch bag, 17-7/8" l, 9-3/4" w, 6" twisted fringe, Arapaho, c1890, flat, beaded simple geometric design with Southern Cross motifs, commercial leather, attachment handle, green, rose "white heart," white, and black seed beads, cut metallic beads **3,450.00**

Dress, child's, 27" l, Southern Plains, Southern Arapaho or Kiowa, c1875-85, supple skin, beaded with seed beads around bottom in scallops of red and white, details in deep sky blue and yellow, yellow ochre stained below scallops, one neck band similar to scallops, other band of deep rose beads with blue, white, and yellow, late blue and red clear heart trade beads on decorative tassels, fringed with sq double tab side flaps **6,620.00**

Fiddle, 14-1/8" l, Apache, one horsehair string, made from century plant flower stalk, incised green and yellow design, patina............................. **350.00**

Frog jar, 7-1/2" d, 6" h, Zuni Pueblo, c1880-1900, painted red ochre and black, typical white slip with relief figures of frogs and swirling flower design..... **6,900.00**

Gauntlets, pr, 13-1/2" l, 8-1/2" w, Plateau, Umatilla, Nez Perce or Yakima, 19th C, early Pendleton Roundup type wear, cotton homespun cloth interior, tiny seed beads in many shades form lance shaped finger strips, patriotic flags and shields on hands, bright floral display on cuffs, worn binding, slight insect damage, patch at right thumb **1,495.00**

Jar, Blackware
4" d, 3" h, San Ildefonso, Marie and Santana, c1943-56, mountain and stepped cloud design around circumference, matte black on black style, highly polished body, sgd "Marie & Santana," slight abrasion, slight haze points **865.00**

6" d, 6-1/2" h, Santa Clara Pueblo, Mary Cain Santa Clara, carved blackware, avanyu and arrow design around upper body, sgd "Mary Cain Santa Clara" (aka Blue Rain), minor roughness **700.00**

Jar, pottery
3-1/2" d, 2-7/8" h, Zia Pueblo, polychrome, geometric design and bird, pale slip ground **200.00**

7" d, 6-1/2" h, Pueblo, Acoma or possibly Laguna, polychrome, bottle bottom, lower orange areas heavily smoke smudged, scalloped rim, repaint areas at edge with possible chip repair.... **815.00**

Knife sheath

3-3/4" l, 3" dangle, Sioux, blue and yellow beads on white bead background, blue bead edging, red quill wrapped tin cone dangle at tip, tin cones with feather fluff on body **300.00**

4-1/4" l, Northern Plains, sinew sewn, Morning Star design, blue, green, and pink with yellow bead ground, orange quilled, tin cone tipped, 6" dangle......................... **435.00**

4-1/2" l, Plains, Sioux, red, yellow, green beading on white, tin cone and horsehair dangles at tip.............. **200.00**

5-3/4" l, Northern Plains, possibly Blackfoot, sinew sewn, faceted navy, green, red "white hearts," faceted red, and seed white beads **615.00**

Miniature, Parfleche case, 5-1/2" l, 3-1/2" w, folded, made as toy or model in style of Northern Plains or Plateau **420.00**

Navajo rug, geometric pattern, red, pale brown, chocolate brown, and ivory, some stains and repairs, 8'2" x 5'4", **$1,000**.

Photo courtesy of David Rago Auctions, Inc.

Moccasins, pr

2" l, Sioux, miniature, red "white heart," white, blue, and cut metallic beads, aged stamping on bottom "Ralph Velich Taxidermist, Omaha, Neb"........................... **520.00**

3-7/8" l, Plains, doll, overall beading in clear green with opalescent white beads, red "white heart" and white beads around top edge **420.00**

4" l, Sioux, child's, beaded in translucent gold, check design in green and white, side and central red bands **460.00**

4-5/8" l, child's, blue stripe on vamp, lower areas multicolored................ **420.00**

5" l, Plateau (Blackfoot or Crow), child's, yellow, pink, and navy floral dec on bright bleu ground, one sole worn much harder **320.00**

5" l, Sioux, ceremonial, child size, beaded soles with two shades of blue, white, and red "white heart" accents, uppers with green, gold, old yellow, blue, and white beading, sinew sewn **900.00**

6" l, Cheyene, child's, sinew sewn, split back, birds on vamps, orangish red "white hearts," sky blue, bluish white, navy beads, some faceted beads **520.00**

7" l, Southern Plains, sinew sewn on buffalo, heel fringe and seam, very tiny red "white hearts," green, old yellow, break to one tie........... **720.00**

9" l, Southern Plains, Cheyenne, late 19th C, yellow ochre stained hide, heel tassel remnant, line of blue beads up heel seam, varied sky blue, navy, greasy yellow, and red on white beads, some damage to beads **460.00**

9" l, 16" h, Western Apache, White River area, high style, turned up "noses" dec with metal conchos, loom beaded strips, diagonal red, blue, and white design across vamp **575.00**

Model cradleboard, with doll, 21-3/4" h, Apache, Sunshade hood stained orange, leather cradle stained yellow ochre, beaded in rows of blue, white, and black beads, muslin doll with thread features and stained yellow ochre beaded Western Apache moccasins, two bead rows missing................ **2,100.00**

Moose call, 20" l, Northeast, late 19th C, conical bark, ask ring, binding at horn and mouthpiece, sewn, spring scraped bark with negative figures of moose, birds, and horses, scalloped around horn **250.00**

Parfleche bonnet case, child's, 15-1/8" l, rawhide, buffalo hook mark, simple line design at ends **2,415.00**

Parfleche case, 26" l, 12" w, Crow, green, blue, and red geometric design, old tag reads "Indian suitcase, May 1891," remnant tie, staining **2,100.00**

Olla, pottery, Southwest, Acoma, c1900, high rounded sides, tapering neck, concave base, black geometric and floral devices, cream colored ground, red painted bottom and inner rim, broken and reassembled lid, 12-1/2" d, 10-1/2" h, **$940**.

Photo courtesy of Skinner, Inc.

Photo, 13 3/8" l, 10 3/8" h, silver print with sepia tones, by Edward S Curtis, shows Indians riding horses in single file, signature and "L.A." lower right, glued down to thin card backing, 14" x 17" orig brown and black frame, sold with book *Portraits from North American Indian Life*, by Coleman and McLuhan **1,150.00**

Pipe, 4" x 3", Eastern Woodlands, 1830s, carved from natural burl, freeform bowl, carved figure of man at right angle below, some old patinated damage **300.00**

Pipe stem, 31" l, Eastern or Dakota Sioux, spaled maple, tack dec along length, tacks alternate circles with figures of buffalo, turtle, man, and deer or elk, tacks date to 1870 .... **2,300.00**

Pocket book, 11-1/2" x 11-1/2", Plateau, c1920-35, German silver purse frame, front and back beaded in differing geometric designs, red, yellow, green, dark blue, and sky blue, white bead background, shell bead handle, two bead fringe loops missing.................. **300.00**

Pouch

3" l, 2" w, Southern Plains, beaded in yellow and black on white ground, bordered by transparent, rose, and navy, booth leather, rare lavender rose beads, damaged brass beaded handle, two tabs edged in yellow, white, and navy, center in translucent green and rose, tassels, flap damage, bead loss . **1,050.00**

4-3/4" l, 4" w, Apache, rect, graphic design of outlined "Gaan" on front, blue, black and white bead details, surrounded by border of black and white diagonal beading, bottom border rose "white hearts" with green edging, flap with beaded cross, blue, white, old yellow, and navy, stained yellow ochre, flap covers top of gaan when closed **1,050.00**
5" l, 5-1/4" w, Iroquois, Niagara Falls, 1919, crossed American flags on one side, branch of holly with berries on other, large white bead edging, fringe loops ... **250.00**

Pipe bowl, Great Lakes, Ojibwa, 19th C, black pipestone form, slightly flared round bowl, square shaft, red pipestone, round-topped tapered prow, lead inlay, bold checkered and linear devices, 7-1/4" l, **$1,175**.

Photo courtesy of Skinner, Inc.

Rug, Navajo
26" x 41", Two Gray Hills style, intricate intertwining hook design in black and white, gray carded ground ... **350.00**
48-1/2" x 75", Ganado style, central stepped pattern in red, black and neutral tan, white and dark brown hand-spun wool, natural gray ground, tan, red and brown border, normal edge wear **1,725.00**
52" x 79", Ganado or Klagetoh area, c1930, central elongated diamond design, hand carded natural, black, and gray wool, double dye red border design, stains, wear **1,380.00**
83-1/2" x 51", Crystal style, two central stepped diamonds, arrows, and interlocking rectangles in red and natural white, dark brown, and tan hand-spun wool, natural gray ground, red and natural dark brown stepped border, normal edge wear **1,850.00**
Shaman basket, cov, 5-1/2" d, round, pocket in lid **3,600.00**

Spoon, 7" l, Sioux, shaped horn, beaded leather handle wrap in dark translucent green, rose "white heart," greasy yellow beads with feather tipped tin dangles **320.00**
Strike A Light bag, 5-3/4" l, 3-1/2" w, Southern Plains, c1910, beaded base, stepped diamond design, medium blue, maraschino red "white hearts," dark navy with white beads, bottom fringe, flap with beaded edging and metal concho with fringe around perimeter, two hairpipe beads, large blue trade beads on twisted handle, boot leather base **650.00**
Tail bag, beaded, 19" l, Apache, Ute form and style, late 19th C, rose "white heart," red "white heart," black, white, and blue, old yellow, fringe below dangles missing.......................... **1,380.00**
Tapestry weaving, 25" x 24", Navaho Yeibechi, finely woven male dancers lead by Talking God, blue, brown, russet, white and black wool, gray wool ground **460.00**
Tipi bag, 12" w, 8" h, Crow, early 19th C, beaded buffalo hide, white, green, red "white hearts," blue and navy design strips, diagonal design alternates with block colors, stroud edged in pony type beads on each side, flap, ties at top **2,300.00**

Tobacco bag, 10" l, woman's, c1910, beaded star or cross, rose, greens, Crow pink, yellow, navy, and white, letter of authenticity included **700.00**
Tomahawk, 27" l, plain brass, handle shows evidence of dec around stem, bead wrapped ornamentation at end with long fringe........................... **2,530.00**
Trade ax peace pipe, 19th C
Brass head, notched design on handle................. **4,000.00**
Iron forged, tiger maple handle................... **36,000.00**
War club, 24" l, last quarter 19th C, carved and painted wood, brass tacks, antler **1,150.00**
War club head, 4-5/8" h, possibly Northern Plains, c1880, stone, ram's head, sculptured and colored, tack eyes, beaded strip holds stone, wooden handle broken off, yellow ochre and blue oxide stain **420.00**

INKWELLS

History: Most of the commonly found inkwells were produced in the United States or Europe between the early 1800s and the 1930s. The most popular materials were glass and pottery because these substances resisted the corrosive effects of ink.

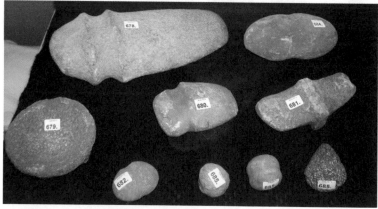

Stone implements: back, left to right: celt (axe head without grooves), attributed to eastern US, post 1500 A.D., 3-1/2" l, **$320**; axe head, full groove, attributed to Ohio or Mid-West, believed to be pre-1500, 7" l, incomplete, **$175**; center row: mortar, volcanic stone, three feet, Columbia River region, 1,500 to 2,500 years old, 4" d, 2-1/2" h, **$100**; axe head, archaic, full groove, pecked hard stone, New England, pre-Columbian, 5" l, **$100**; axe head, probably ceremonial, eastern US, pre-Columbian, 5-3/4" l, **$100**; front row: axe head, full grove, Mid-West, 2000 to 2500 B.C., **$250**; pestle or seed grinder, Mid-West, 2-7/8" h, **$90**; miniature mortar, 2-1/4" d, **$65**; full groove axe head, eastern US, probably New York, pre-historic, 1-3/4" l, **$125**.

Photo courtesy of Alderfer Auction Co.

Inkwells were a sign of the office or wealth of an individual. The common man tended to dip his ink directly from the bottle. The years between 1870 and 1920 represent the golden age of inkwells when elaborate designs were produced.

Bronze, ornate embossed back and base, two glass inkwells with original lids, **$175**.

Ceramic, French, pelican standing on rectangular base, green crystalline glaze on yellow ground, painted "8115/56/ FRANCE," base glaze chip, 7-1/2" h, **$500**.

Photo courtesy of Skinner, Inc.

Brass, 9-1/4" l, 5-7/8" h, engraved peaked cornice-form backplate cut with central trefoil and flowers, cabochon bloodstone surrounded by four cabochon red stones, rect base with engraved border, central cut glass well flanked by turned pen supports, Gothic Revival style, England, third quarter 19th C **250.00**

Bronze
7-1/4" l, oval bronze tray, enameled in ivory and jewel dec, pen rest with urn-shaped inkwell, Viennese-style, mid-19th C **700.00**
8" d, 5-1/2" h, central lidded baluster form inkwell, round dish raised on quadripartite leaf-form bronze base, dark green enamel ground, stylized foliate bands with gilt accents, faux jewelling, French, late 19th C **435.00**

12" l, cast, Victorian, figural, greyhound dog changed to fencepost, two orig glass wells with covers **815.00**
Cast metal, 12" l, 8-1/2" h, figural, young girl and large dog, bronzed finish, Victorian, c1906.......................... **750.00**
Copper, 3" d, repoussé, inlays of men, woman, and monkeys, further engraving and gilt, Japan, Meiji period (1868-1911) **420.00**
Glass, crystal, square, four molded rococo feet, 3-1/4" w, 3-1/2" h.......................... **175.00**
Gilt metal, 14" l, bronze, French, rococo style, lion's head supporting pen rest above tray with two cov wells, dolphin feet **460.00**
Paperweight, 6 1/4" h, 4 1/2" d, multicolored concentric millefiori, base with 1848 date canes, Whitefriars **175.00**
Pearlware, 5-1/2" h, gilt highlights, imp "By F. Bridges, Phrenologist," and "EM" on base, England, 19th C, very minor chips, gilt wear...... **520.00**
Porcelain, 5" h, formed as three crested birds, magenta, gilding, white band painted with polychrome flowers, insert and lid, underglaze blue crossed arrows, French **200.00**
Sterling silver, two bottles, matching pen tray, center sander, Victorian, hallmarked **1,800.00**

Pottery, George Ohr, donkey, gunmetal semi-matte glaze, stamped "GEO. E. OHR, BILOXI, MISS," firing line through back, 5-1/4" l, 2-1/2" h, **$1,485**.

Photo courtesy of David Rago Auctions, Inc.

Stoneware
Brushed cobalt blue on top, imp "C. Crolius. Manhattan-Wells, New York," 3-1/8" d, 1-5/8" h, few chips on base **3,200.00**

Incised oval stamp "C. Crolius Stone Ware Manufacturer Manhatten Wells, New York," flat cylindrical form, incised edges, upper one enhanced with cobalt blue slip, center well surrounded by three pen holders, 3-1/2" d, 1-1/4" h, three lower edge chips **2,990.00**
Wood, Matthew Bolton, Birmingham, c1795, rect, emb silver mounts, gadroon and shell edge, two silver mounted cut glass inkwells in gardrooned holders, four scroll legs, paw feet, 14" l, 10" w **1,725.00**

IRONS

History: Ironing devices have been used for many centuries, with the earliest references dating from 1100. Irons from the medieval, Renaissance, and early industrial eras can be found in Europe, but are rare. Fine engraved brass irons and hand-wrought irons predominated prior to 1850. After 1850, the iron underwent a series of rapid evolutionary changes.

Between 1850 and 1910, irons were heated in four ways: 1) a hot metal slug was inserted into the body, 2) a burning solid, e.g., coal or charcoal, was placed in the body, 3) a liquid or gas, e.g., alcohol, gasoline, or natural gas, was fed from an external tank and burned in the body, or 4) conduction heat, usually drawing heat from a stove top.

Electric irons are just beginning to find favor among iron collectors.

Additional Listings: See *Warman's Americana & Collectibles* for more examples.

Advisers: David and Sue Irons.

Reproduction Alert: The highly detailed German charcoal iron known as "dragon chimney" is currently being reproduced in Europe.

Charcoal
Acme Carbon Iron, 1910 .... **125.00**
Cummings & Bless, tall chimney, 1852................. **110.00**

Charcoal, German 3, Muster Schutz, griffin latch, late 1800, IBI 60(R) 8-1/2" l, **$250**.

All iron photographs courtesy of Adviser Dave Irons.

Cutwork sides, wrought, French **350.00**
Dragon chimney, highly detailed, German **450.00**
Improved Progress Iron, 1913 .... **250.00**

Children's

Brass, ox tongue slug, 4" **180.00**
Cap, oval, French, 3-1/2", "WP" **60.00**
Charcoal, tall chimney, 3-1/2" **250.00**
Dover Sad Iron, No. 812, 4" **45.00**
Swan, all cast, 2" **125.00**
The Pearl, 3-3/4" **75.00**
Tri-bump handle, all cast, 2-3/8" **40.00**
Wapak 2, cast, 4" **50.00**

Flat iron

Czechoslovakia, green, detachable handle **125.00**
Enterprise, boxed set of three, detachable handles, wooden box **350.00**
Enterprise, "Star Iron," holes in handle **70.00**
IXL, cast **20.00**
LeGaulois, cast, French ... **50.00**
Ober, #6, patent 1912 .... **50.00**
Round back, "L" handle, Belgium **90.00**
Sensible, detachable handle, No. 3 .... **75.00**
Weida's Patent 1870, fold-back cold handle **350.00**

Fluter, combination type

Hewitt, revolving, clamp-on side fluter plate **350.00**

Little Giant, fluter at angle **350.00**
Street's Magic, 1876, three pcs **450.00**

Fluter, machine type

English, box frame, fine flutes **275.00**
H. B. Adams, clamp-on .. **325.00**
Manville, cone shape **400.00**
The Knox Imperial, good paint **350.00**

Fluter, rocker type

Geneva Improved, brass plates **300.00**
Howell's Wav Fluter, 1866 .... **450.00**
The Boss **300.00**

Fluter, roller type

American Machine **90.00**
Clarks, holes in handle... **180.00**
Sundry Mfg. Co. **250.00**

Goffering irons

Clamp-on, single barrel, all wrought **350.00**
Double barrel, cast base **500.00**
Single, brass, ornate "S," oval base **250.00**
"S" wire, single barrel, oval base **75.00**

Charcoal, Dutch brass, mid-1800, IBI 65, 8" l, **$425**.

Liquid fuel, gasoline, or kerosene

Coleman 4A, blue **125.00**
Diamond Akron Lamp Co. **70.00**
Ellison Bros., revolving, tank in handle **900.00**
Montgomery Ward, gasoline iron **75.00**
Perfection **200.00**

Liquid fuel, natural gas

Clarks, Fairy Prince, blue, English **150.00**
Humphrey **125.00**
Nu-Styl, La Rue Gas Iron, removable 2# weight **500.00**
Vulcan Gas Iron **75.00**

Mangle board

Horse handle, geometric carving, orig paint **1,000.00**
Turned handle, no carving **100.00**

Miscellaneous

Give-away, Lent Tailor Supplies **600.00**
Iron sole plate to attach bottom of iron **30.00**
Laundry stove, holds eight irons **450.00**

Slug irons

Austrian, ox tongue, brass, L handle **250.00**
Bless-Drake, salamander box iron, top lifts off **250.00**
Denmark, brass, vine engraving, dated 1810 ... **450.00**
French, hand made, decorative posts, lift gate, c1800 ..... **700.00**
Majestic, combination, revolving **750.00**

Polisher, MAB COOKS, patented Dec. 5, 1848, IBI 271(M), 5" l, **$135**.

Special purpose

Billiard table iron, London **300.00**
Egg iron, hand held **80.00**
Glove form, steam heated, brass **200.00**
Hat
    Shackle, adjustable curved edge **140.00**
    Tolliker, two crescent shaped grooves...................... **125.00**
    Tolliker, wood, brass base **150.00**

Polisher
  French, CF, raised pattern on bottom......................... **200.00**
  Hood's, patent 1867, soapstone body.......... **400.00**
  Star polisher................ **150.00**
Sleeve iron
  Grand Union Tea Co. **60.00**
  Hub **50.00**
  Pluto, electric **200.00**

IRONWARE

History: Iron, a metallic element that occurs abundantly in combined forms, has been known for centuries. Items made from iron range from the utilitarian to the decorative. Early hand-forged ironwares are of considerable interest to Americana collectors.

Reproduction Alert: Use the following checklist to determine if a metal object is a period piece or modern reproduction. This checklist applies to all cast-metal items, from mechanical banks to trivets.

  Period cast-iron pieces feature well-defined details, carefully fitted pieces, and carefully finished and smooth castings. Reproductions, especially those produced by making a new mold from a period piece, often lack detail in the casting (lines not well defined, surface details blurred) and parts have gaps at the seams and a rough surface. Reproductions from period pieces tend to be slightly smaller in size than the period piece from which they were copied.

  Period paint mellows, i.e., softens in tone. Colors look flat. Beware of any cast-iron object whose paint is bright and fresh. Painted period pieces should show wear. Make certain the wear is in places it is supposed to be.

  Period cast-iron pieces develop a surface patina that prevents rust. When rust is encountered on a period piece, it generally has a greasy feel and is dark in color. The rust on artificially aged reproductions is flaky and orange.

Additional Listings: Banks, Doorstops, Fireplace Equipment, Molds, Irons, Kitchen Collectibles, Lamps, and Tools.

Andirons, pr, 20" h, cast, faceted ball finials, knife blade, arched bases, penny feet, rusted surface................ **325.00**
Apple roaster, 34-1/4" l, wrought, hinged apple support, pierced heat end on slightly twisted projecting handle, late 18th C **1,650.00**
Baker's lamp, 4-1/4" h, 8-1/2" l, cast iron, attached pan, hinged lid, bottom marked "No. 2 B. L.," pitted.............................. **250.00**
Bill holder, Atlantic Coast Line, cast, c1915, 4" h **50.00**
Boot scraper, 11-1/2" l, 18-1/2" h, cast, Scottie Dog, figural side profile, America, early 20th C, minor surface rust............ **590.00**

Boot scraper, lyre center, scalloped base, **$85**.

Calipers, pr, wrought
  18-1/2" l, double, two arms meeting at "Y"-shaped central piece, ring handle with old split **125.00**
  18-1/2" l, ending in delicate ladies legs, stamped "WTI 1863" **115.00**
Candlestick, 9-3/4" h, wrought, spiral iron stem, curled finger loop and tab, wooden push up, old, cone shaped wooden base with dark patina **160.00**
Carriage fenders, cast, shaped like horse leg, sgd "Fiske, New York," c1880, price for pr **4,800.00**
Cleaver, 11-1/2" l, 4-1/2" h, figural-shaped blade with eagle's head, handle terminating in brass boot, 20th C, stand, minor surface corrosion .. **490.00**
Compote, 10" w, 7" h, cast, flower form bowl, shaped and

molded star base, America, late 19th C, old rust surface .. **200.00**
Cookie mold, 5-1/4" l, oval, bird on branch, cast iron........ **335.00**
Door knocker, 5-1/2" l, cast, fox head, ring hangs from mouth **85.00**
Embossing wheel, 4" l, 1-3/4" w, 9-1/4" h, cast iron and bronze, scrolled foliate motif on wheel edge, imp maker's marks for M. W. Baldwin, Philadelphia, handle missing **460.00**
Figure, 24-1/4" w, 39" h, cast, Lady Liberty, Mott Foundry, New York, c1850, holding goblet and torch with octagonal marble base, later white wood plinth **7,425.00**

Doorknocker, wrought iron serpent form, 19th C, 11" l, **$460**.
Photo courtesy of Pook & Pook.

Fireback, 21-1/2" w, 33" h, cast, late Regency-style, arch top flanked by dolphins, central polychrome scene of shepherd with his flock by fountain, beaded surround, scrolling leaf border **300.00**
Herb grinder, 16-1/2" l, 4-1/2" w, 4" h, cast, footed trough form, 6" d round disk-shaped crusher with wooden handle through center, late 18th/early 19th C **980.00**
Hitching post, 31" h, cast, jockey, yellow, red, green, black, and white painted detail, wired for lantern......................... **275.00**
Jousting helmet, 18" h, wrought, 12th C style, 19th C, cylindrical, tapering vertically at front, narrow eye slits, pierced circular and cruciform breaths **1,495.00**
Kitchen utensils, 16" l, 9" h hanging rack, wrought, step down crest with scrolled heart, cut out cross bar, three spatulas, two dippers, with tooling and initials **675.00**
Knife, folding, 8-1/4" l closed, 15-1/2" l open, hand-forged blade with a trigger locking mechanism pivots into iron sheath bound with carved wood handle, held with two iron bands and six pins, blade illegibly marked, late 18th/early 19th C, wear **150.00**

Lamp, floor, arrow-shaped finial on shaft, two sockets, scrolled wrought iron tripod feet, woven striped paneled shades, scattered corrosion, price for pr **815.00**
Letter sealer, 1" d, coat of arms, European, late 18th/early 19th C **40.00**
Mirror, 22" h, cast, gilt, rococo scrolled acanthus frame, oval beveled mirror, Victorian ... **75.00**
Mold, 7-1/4" w, 8" d, 8" h, figural pumpkin, smiling man face, invented by John Czeszczicki, Ohio, 1930, used to grow pumpkins in human forms, surface corrosion, later stand **635.00**

Nutcracker, cast iron, repainted, $75.
Photo courtesy of Joy Luke Auctions.

Toy, horse and buggy, cast iron, some original paint, 11" l, $250.
Photo courtesy of Joy Luke Auctions.

Mortar and pestle, 10-1/2" d, 8-1/4" h, urn shape, cast iron, pitted **50.00**
Pipe tongs, 17-1/4" l, wrought iron, 18th C **1,150.00**
Rush light holder, 15-3/4" h, wrought, twisted detail on stem and arm of counterweight, high tripod feet riveted to disk, traces of black paint **330.00**
Shelf brackets, pr, 5-1/2" h, swivel **20.00**
Spittoon, cast iron, top hat, Standard Manuf Co., Pittsburgh, PA, painted black, glazed porcelain int. **415.00**
Sugar nippers, 10" l, tooled flower at pivot points **600.00**
Trivet, 7-3/4" d, round, marked "The Griswold Mfg. Co., Eire, PA, USA/8/Trivet/206" **35.00**
Umbrella stand, 30-3/4" h, cast, backplate formed as figure of Admiral Nelson, titled at base, stepped base with double shell-form removable drip pan ... **750.00**

Utensil rack, 10-3/4" l, wrought iron, scrolled crest, five hooks with acorn terminals, minor brazed repair **770.00**
Wafer iron, 5-1/4" d, 24" l, imp with seal of U.S., c1800, minor imperfections **550.00**
Wall frame, 8-1/2" h, 6" d, cast iron, gilt eagle crest, elaborately dec frame, C-scrolls and foliate devices, 19th C.............. **575.00**

IVORY

History: Ivory, a yellowish white organic material, comes from the teeth or tusks of animals and lends itself to carving. Many cultures have used it for centuries to make artistic and utilitarian items.

A cross section of elephant ivory will have a reticulated crisscross pattern. Hippopotamus teeth, walrus tusks, whale teeth, narwhal tusks, and boar tusks also are forms of ivory. Vegetable ivory, bone, stag horn, and plastic are ivory substitutes, which often confuse collectors. Vegetable ivory is a term used to describe the nut of a South American palm, which is often carved. Look for a grain that is circular and dull in this softer-than-bone material.

Note: Dealers and collectors should be familiar with The Endangered Species Act of 1973, amended in 1978, which limits the importation and sale of antique ivory and tortoiseshell items.

Ball, high relief carved flowers, stained details, carved wood stand, Japan, 19th C, 2-1/2" d ball, 4-1/2" h with stand, $375.

Ball, carved, 2" d, three boys forming circle, clothes with traces of paint, China, 19th C, 3-3/4" with base, age cracks **115.00**
Box, cov, 4-1/2" h, cylindrical, carved scene of figures in landscape, screw-on lid, China, 19th C **220.00**
Bridge, 12" l, carved from hippopotamus tusk, various figures in palace setting . **175.00**
Brush pot
3-1/8" h, 2" d, incised and stained dec, mountainous landscape with people in foreground, wooden base, China, 19th C, age cracks **450.00**
3-5/16" h, 1-7/8" d, incised and stained dec, mountainous landscape with people in foreground, ivory base, inscriptions around foot, China, 19th C, age cracks **495.00**
3-7/8" h, 1-7/8" d, shaped panels carved with people in landscape, base with openwork dec, China, 19th C, crack on side of base . **320.00**
6" h, relief carving of figures and landscapes, China......... **500.00**
Chess set
2-1/2" to 5" h, 16 crimson stained pieces, 15 natural pieces, detailed Chinese figures, lacquered case, gilt dec scenes and mother-of-pearl inlay, Oriental, 20th C **1,100.00**
3" to 7" h natural and tea-stained pieces, each carved with Oriental figures standing on mystery ball bases, inlaid box with brass clasp .. **700.00**
3-1/2" to 7" h, each piece carved in form of Chinese figures, 16 natural color, 16 tea stained, fitted wood case with playing field, Oriental, 20th C **920.00**
Cup, cov, foliate finial, oval body, carved frieze of putti with hound, mask and acanthus baluster stem, round foot, Continental, early 18th C **1,200.00**
Doctor model, carved, Chinese, 20th C
10-3/4" l, wooden stand, age crack........................... **650.00**
13" l, embellish with coral and turquoise necklace and bracelets, holding fan, wooden stand, age crack **850.00**

Fan, 11" l, carved, painted figures amidst courtyard setting, inlaid with painted ivory faces, black lacquer and parcel gilt can, base inscribed in gilt "E. Cardinal's Canton," Chinese export, 19th C **1,195.00**

Figure, female warrior, standing, holding sword, Chinese, late Qing dynasty, early Republic period, 12" h **$1,775**.

Photo courtesy of Sloans & Kenyon Auctions.

Figure, man with monkey on leash, man smoking pipe, wearing mask fitted to top of head, carrying bag, colored carved detail on clothing and features of man and monkey, red inlaid signature cartouche on bottom, 6-1/2" h, **$550**.

Photo courtesy of Alderfer Auction Co.

Figure, carved
1" h, 1-7/8" l, ox, recumbent, head turned to right, halter attached to ring through nose, crossing over and resting on blanketed back, inlaid eyes, himotoshi and sgd "Gyokuzan" on base, lightly stained details, Japan, 19th C **300.00**

Figure, two men carrying third in litter, signature on inlaid carnelian rectangle on bottom, 2" w, 1-1/2" h, **$650**.

Photo courtesy of Alderfer Auction Co.

3-1/8" h, ascetic in kneeling position, arms raised, body leaning forward in bowing motion, inlaid eyes, traces of red pigment on skirt, mounted on wooden base, China, 18th or 19th C, right foot replaced **260.00**
5-1/2" h, lady, body leaning to right, double gourd bottle on ribbon dangling from her waist, string of beads in her right hand, branch in her left, branch curving and resting behind head, stained details, carved wooden stand, China, 19th C, age cracks in hand and left arm **1,035.00**
5-3/4" h, immortal, frog on left shoulder, black colored hair and shoes, China, 19th C **850.00**
7-1/4" h, Quanyin holding scroll in her left hand, standing on lotus pedestal, stained details, China, 18th C, age cracks, ivory separated at mouth and reglued, age cracks **460.00**
7-1/2" h, Vishnu and his consort, Indian **300.00**
8-3/8" h, woman in western attire, carrying purse and umbrella, China **300.00**
11-3/4" h, God of longevity, China **600.00**
12-3/16" h, guardian, right hand resting on sword with dragon entwined around it, two curved ribbons framing head, wooden stand with cloud designs, well carved and stained detail, China, 19th C, slight age cracks, missing right dragon whisker **1,150.00**
12-3/8" h, lady, holding wine pot, side with sages under pine trees, cov with foo dog, left hand holding handle, long flowing scarf with several joints, elaborate hair

contained in phoenix headdress, China, 18th or 19th C, wear to painted surface, age cracks and filled in areas **1,265.00**
12-1/2" h, woman holding a basket and flowers, China **600.00**
13" h, Bodhistiva, standing, elaborate dress, two lotus pods flanking head, sinuous tendrils held in each hand, mounted on carved wooden stand, China, 19th C . **1,265.00**
20" h, gentleman and woman, both carrying peony blossom spray and basket, following natural curve of tusk, painted details, China, 20th C, pr **1,675.00**
Jagging wheel, 19th C
5-3/4" l, pierced carved, whalebone, minute losses **2,875.00**
7-1/8" l, figural, unicorn, inlaid eyes and nostrils, minor losses **4,600.00**
Letter opener, 9-3/4" l, oblong blade carved to end with writhing dragon, Chinese, early 20th C **115.00**
Mask, 8-3/4" l, 4-3/8" w, 2" d, Jomen carved from one piece of ivory, old man, wrinkled face, deep sinuous curves, raised furrowed brow, locks of hair brought up form side and tied in bow, long beard, back side carved in narrow grooves, ears pierced with hold for hanging wire, unsigned, Japan, Meiji period, minor nick at tip of beard **2,875.00**
Okimono
2" d, 2" h, seven gods of good fortune, faces emerging form basket, well carved details, lightly stained, sgd on base, Japan, Meiji period, age cracks **300.00**
2-1/8" h, figure of young boy and dog, sgd on bottom, Japan, Meiji period, crack on boy's face **200.00**
3" l, man sitting with his left arm resting on small chest, wood grain finely carved and stained, handles of dark horn, sake cup resting on top, holding pipe case in right hand, robes with geometric designs and medallions, part of robe overlapping underside of chest, sgd on base in sq seal, Japan, 19thj C............ **1,000.00**

Four carved Okimono, left: Daikoku and Ebisu, one sitting on bag with abacus on his knee, other standing and pulling rice grains from large sack, Japan, Meiji period, 3" h, crack on back, **$120**; seven gods of good fortune on the Kakarabune with child sharing top of sail with Daikoku, signed, Japan, early 20th C, 6-5/8" h, **$300**; center: Sambaso dancer, tongue exposed, raised left arm enveloped by sleeve of his robe, cluster of bells in his right, bowl beneath his raised right foot, robes with pine branch design, stained, Japan, Meiji period, 4-3/4" h, crack thru upper body, **$250**; right: Ashinaga with grimacing expression as crab bites his right leg, Tenaga perched on his shoulders, pulling crab with long arms, applied shibayama decoration, signed on red tablet, Japan, Meiji period, 5-1/8" h, some loss to inlay, crack on back of Tenaga and base, **$550**.

3-1/8" l, 1-5/8" h, young boy playing with toy model of horse, right hand gripping ribbon attached to horse's mouth, left hand passing under horse, holding drum, sgd on rect reserve, Japan, Meiji period, crack on base **250.00**

4-1/2" l, Takarabune, seven gods of good future, stained detail, sgd on base, Japan, Meiji period **375.00**

5-1/2" h, man spilling from his hat cucumbers attached to vine, frog resting on top, details slightly stained, red signature tablet on base, Japan, 19th C **700.00**

6" h, Samuari holding double gourd sake bottle in his left hand, open fan in right, garment draped over large sword attached to cord over his right shoulder, man keeling beside him holding sake cap in his left hand, gift box wrapped by cord and a bucket lie on foreground, signature on underside of box, Japan, Meiji period, damage to sticks of fan **1,035.00**

9-1/4" h, sectional, marine ivory, man and young boy standing on tree stumps, man playing samisen, small chest with fan on top hangs from his shoulder, child holding fan in left hand, right hand with upside down book with written pages, lightly stained details, sgd on bases, Japan, c1900, missing pc from fan, traces of glue **250.00**

Page turner, Shibiyama, 17" l, thin blade dec sparrows in flowering tree, gold and pewter colored paint, inlaid with nacre and coral, carved handle with sparrows being chased by rodent, Japanese, one inlay missing **520.00**

Parasol handle, carved
8-3/8" l, monkeys and butterflies feasting on fruit, details partially colored and stained, Japan, c1900, crack on side **165.00**

13" l, tapering form with dragons, phoenix, and other birds, blank cartouche with metal divider and tip, stained horn finial on end, China, 19th C **200.00**

Pickwick, 3-1/4" h, carved, 19th C, minor losses, repair.... **210.00**

Plaque, carved
3-7/8" d, General (Mad Anthony) Wayne, America, late 18th/early 19th C, round, relief carved three-quarter view bust length portrait, banner below inscribed with name, houses and foliage in background, age crack, conforming molded wood frame **500.00**

4-7/8" l, 3" w, low relief carving of figures in garden landscape, letters ARDS on bottom, Chinese, 18th or 19th C, slight staining and age cracks **575.00**

7-5/8" l, 4-1/8" w, one side with plants emerging from rock, other side with figures in interior and pine trees in background, stylized wave border, Chinese, 18th C, slightly curved, age cracks **650.00**

Puzzle ball, nine interior balls, outer ball with deep carving of dragons amidst clouds, interior balls with geometric patterns, standard with fountain form emerging from open mouth of dragon on base with stylized wave motif, Chinese, 20th C, 4" d ball, 13-1/2" h overall, **$1,550**.

Puzzle ball, 4" d ball, 13-1/2" h with stand, nine interior balls, outer ball with deep carving of dragons amidst clouds, interior balls with geometric patterns, fountain form stand with open mouth of dragon on base, stylized wave motif, Chinese, 20th C **1,450.00**

Seal, 3-7/8" l, intaglio, handle, 19th C, cracks................. **400.00**

Sphere, okimono, surface entirely carved with mice, sgd "Masamitsu," Japan, Meiji period (1868-1911) **1,100.00**

Square, 10" l, whalebone and ivory inlaid walnut, diamond motif inlay, 19th C, cracks to ivory **1,095.00**

Stand, 7" h, pierced relief, pink and cream flowers, peony and lotus flowers, green stones **425.00**

Temple container, 23-1/2" h, pieced construction, overall carving, Greek key bands, relief carved dragons in six arched panels around body, in medallions at neck and foot, green jadite rings handing from mouths of mythical beasts as handles, each lid with armored warrior with horse, one woman with spear and bow case, other bearded man with spear and sword, round inset blue, green, red, and orange "gems," sgd, age cracks, minor edge damage, price for pr.... **2,400.00**

Tusk, 18-1/4" l, carved marine tusk, line of eight buffalo in diminishing size, carved wooden stand, China, early 20th C, age cracks **200.00**

Vase

3-1/4" h, chased and stained dec of phoenix amidst paulownia, flattened spherical body with Shibayama roundels, Japanese, 19th C, very tight hairline **650.00**

5-3/4" h, oval, carved sages among pine trees, China, 19th C, minute loss, small tight age crack in neck **350.00**

17-1/2" h, tusk section, Shibayama dec of cart and flowers in horn, wood, mother-of-pearl, and coral, Japan, 19th C **1,410.00**

Walking stick, 34-1/4" l, 1-1/3" d x 4-3/4" h elephant ivory handle, raised 2/3" basket-weave carving halfway down length, 1/3" plain silver collar, cherry-wood shaft, 1-1/3" white metal and iron ferrule, American, c1880 .... **400.00**

Wrist rest, 10-1/4" h, carved in high relief with numerous figures in palace garden, China, 19th C **1,265.00**

JADE

History: Jade is the generic name for two distinct minerals: nephrite and jadeite. Nephrite, an amphibole mineral from Central Asia that was used in pre-18th-century pieces, has a waxy surface and hues that range from white to an almost-black green. Jadeite, a pyroxene mineral found in Burma and used from 1700 to the present, has a glassy appearance and comes in various shades of white, green, yellow-brown, and violet.

Jade cannot be carved because of its hardness. Sawing and grinding with wet abrasives such as quartz, crushed garnets, and carborundum achieve shapes.

Prior to 1800, few items were signed or dated. Stylistic considerations are used to date pieces. The Ch'ien Lung period (1736-1795) is considered the golden age of jade.

Bowl, lobed form, sides carved with lotus, two raised handles with carved rings, four scrolled feet, wooden base carved with openwork cash design, China, 19th or 20th C, 11-1/2" l x 7-1/4" x 4-1/2" h bowl. **$650.**

Boulder, 13" h, finely carved interior of Guanyin figure, light green tones, polished amber colored ext., Oriental, 20th C **815.00**

Box, 3-3/8" l, rect, silver mounted, early 20th C **320.00**

Bowl, carved

2-11/16" d, 2-1/4" h, two angular handles, carved studs and designs, China, 18th C or earlier.......... **290.00**

3-1/4" d, 2" h, russet inclusions, China, 19th C, internal fissures on base, rim fissure **435.00**

Bracelet, 3-3/8" d, Archaic carved black jade, white inclusions, outside carved with Zhuanshu script, mounted with silver colored metal, internal band with eight straps of different designs, four ending with ruyi heads, China, four old breaks and regluing........ **200.00**

Brush washer, carved

2-1/2" l, 1-3/8" h, gray color with russet inclusions on base, carved bat and leafy branch, China, 18th C **350.00**

3-5/8" l, 2-1/4" w, 1-1/8" h, hollowed out peach form, animal head handle, apple green inclusions, China, 18th C or earlier, filled-in fissure, minor fritting............... **200.00**

Candlesticks, pr, 12-7/8" h, dark green, carved low relief goose with out-spread wings, stands on tortoise, head supports three tiered pricket, tripod bowl with int. carving, reticulated wood base with carved key scroll motifs and floral scrolls ... **550.00**

Carving

4" x 2-1/2", double gourd and foliage, pale green color stone, China, 18th/19th C, fitted stand............... **2,250.00**

5" l, reclining hound, highly translucent green stone **710.00**

6-1/4" h, figural woman, pale lavender stone with green and tan accents, China **360.00**

7" l, horse, nephrite of celadon color with brown striations, China, 19th/20th C...... **450.00**

7" l, pair of birds on nests, long tails, forest green color stone, China, early 20th C **710.00**

13" h, pair of phoenixes, pale lavender stone with areas of apple green and russet, fitted, carved hardwood stands, repair to one crest ... **1,000.00**

Ceremonial knife, 9-3/8" l, carved, archaic style designs, traces of red pigment, China, 18th C or earlier **90.00**

Dish, 5-3/4" d, brownish-celadon, carved in Mughal style, open chrysanthemum flower, China, 19th C **475.00**

Figure, carved

2-1/8" l, 2" w, 3/4" h, turtle, celadon colored flat carapace and head, russet colored lower body and four feet, China, 18th C.............. **175.00**

Figure, duck holding flowering branch in beak, feet tucked underneath, russet and dark brown inclusions, China, 18th C, 5" l, 3" h, chip to tip of leaf, **$5,750**.

2-5/8" h, white, man with frog resting on his head, Chinese, 19th C **750.00**

5-5/8" h, mottled, maiden with crane and sacred fungus, China, 19th C, stand partially rebuilt with plaster **625.00**

3-1/4" h, 4-1/4" l, pale green jade with gray and russet inclusions, two ducks facing opposite directions, each holding lotus sprig in beak, carved fitted wood stand, China, 19th or 20th C, small chip to edge of one leaf
.... **325.00**

4-1/8" h, 6" l, off-white, mottled celadon, and gray-green color stone, mythical fierce beast with vase on its back, carved fitted wood stand with wire inlay, China, 19th or 20th C, teeth broken **100.00**

4-3/8" h, 4-1/2" l, white, apple green inclusions, dark green underfoot, carved duck with fish in its beak, wings carved with tips pointed outwards, China, 19th C, neck restored, over-painted................ **260.00**

4-3/4" h, 10-1/2" l, lotus leaf forming elongated oval bowl with lobed edges, raised from bunch of branches, duck resting on lotus pod, carved and fitted wood stand with lotus design, China, 18th or 19th C, small loss to stand, natural fissure conforming to design, small chips..... **650.00**

5-3/4" h, green, dark gray inclusion running vertically, maiden holding flowering branch in right hand and resting on her left shoulder, China, 20th C, glued to wooden stand............. **135.00**

6" h, white, apple green, russet, and gray inclusions, maiden holding vase, hair combed with large chignon, standing, glued to carved quartz base with flowers on side, hole pierced in base, China, 19th or 20th C, base chipped **135.00**

7-1/8" h, 4-1/2" w, mottled gray and black, Guandi in sitting position, long hair cascading down lower back, hold carved thru right clenched hand, carved wooden base, China, 19th C, chips to right foot, glued to stand **1,035.00**

7-1/4" to 9-1/4" h, carved yellow-green, dark gray inclusions, four birds perched on tree trunk, carved fitted wood stand, China, 20th C, one foot missing from stand **375.00**

9-5/8" h, mottled gray and black, lady holding teapot flanked by phoenix and attendant with fan, carved wood base, China, 20th C, small chips, base glued on **435.00**

10-1/2" h, celadon, woman, whisk in her right hand, leafy branch in left, branch curving behind her neck and resting on left shoulder, hair styled with large chignon on top of head, russet inclusions on flower and part of garment, China, 19th or 20th C, small fissure at back of head
.... **200.00**

Flute, 22" l, light and dark colored cylinders of celadon green tone, wooden frame, India, early 20th C............. **75.00**

Inkstone, 3-5/8" l, oval, depression to one side, black and white mottling, incised rim band................................ **200.00**

Letter opener, 10-3/4" l, carved interlocking C scrolls between keyfret bands handle, SS knife **250.00**

Libation cup, 5" l, celadon jade, incised dec, dragon head handles, Chinese, Qing dynasty, price for pr **425.00**

Palace figure, 76" h, carved herons, more than 200 pieces of dark green mottled jadeite feathers applied over wooden form, mahogany stained wooden plinth, 20th C, minor losses, price for pr **1,150.00**

Pendant, carved
Axe shape, white stone, China, 18th C.............. **215.00**

Chi dragon, pale mottled green, dark inclusions at base, openwork chi dragon on crescent, China, 18th or 19th C, 1-3/4" l, 2-1/4" d, 1-1/4" h, small rim chips............. **200.00**

Duck and lotus plants, highly translucent brown color stone, China, 18th C.............. **300.00**

Ducks and lotuses, white stone, China, 18th C **1,000.00**

Gourd shape, leafy branch, Chinese, 19th C, 1-3/4" l **200.00**

Plaque, pale lavender, bright green spots, China, 18th C
.... **200.00**

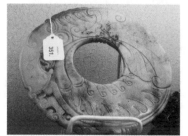

Ritual Pi disk, coiled fish nose to nose with chi dragon, stylized waves and ruyi designs, fitted stand carved with bats among clouds, pale green with russet inclusions, China, 18th C or earlier, 8-3/8" d, 5-1/6" thick, 14-11/16" h with stand, areas of pitting, small crack, old break to stand, **$3,600**.

Pi disk, carved
2-1/2" d, 3/4" thick, brown and russet inclusions, deep groove carved on one side near edge, China, 18th C
.... **100.00**

8-3/8" d, 5/16" thick, pale green with russet inclusions, coiled fish nose to nose with chi dragon, stylized waves, ruyi designs, fitted stand carved with bats among clouds, areas of pitting, China, 18th C or earlier, small crack on inner circle, old break to stand, small chips.......................... **3,600.00**

Plaque, carved
3-3/8" w, 3-7/8" l, 5-3/8" h, complex design of cranes with entwined lotus plants and tendrils, raised curved shape, back edge with carved holes for attachment, mounted with three silver colored metals on wood base, China, 18th C, small fissure................ **435.00**

4-3/4" h, 3-1/2" w, 1/8" thick, oval, openwork dec, central figure holding flag surrounded by flowers, center with carved quartz cabochon secured with metal pin, China, 20th C **150.00**

Saucer, 6" d, low relief carving of five bats around central longevity emblem, pale green color stone, late 19th/early 20th C, price for pr **650.00**

Seal, carved
1-1/8" h, crouching boy, Chinese, 19th C **265.00**
1-1/8" h, recumbent foo dog, dark green spinach jade, Chinese, 19th or early 20th C **275.00**
1-1/2" h, foo dog, Chinese, 19th C **245.00**

Snuff bottle, Grayish-white, mottled russet skin on one side, rose quartz stopper **550.00**

Ruyi scepter, jade and wood, each plaque carved to depict a dragon chasing the flaming pearl of wisdom, Chinese, late Qing dynasty-early Republic period, 21-1/2" l, **$1,000**.

Photo courtesy of Sloans & Kenyon Auctions.

Tablet, 3-3/4" l, 1" h, spinach, plain rect shape, carved and recessed wood stand, China, 19th C **520.00**

Urn, cov, 11" h, Buddhist figure, open work foliage, lavender and green jadeite, polished finish, Oriental, 20th C **1,100.00**

Vase, carved
6-5/8" h, celadon, well carved figure riding dragon and chasing flaming pearl, phoenix with figure on back carved on shoulder, rocks emerging around base, well hollowed interior, China, 18th or 19th C, natural fissure **2,875.00**
7" h, Hu form, stone of celadon color with white striations and brown markings, China, 19th C **1,300.00**

Vase, cov, carved, 9-3/4" h, spinach, flattened oval form, body carved with archaistic designs, stepped shoulder and plain neck, cov with large oval finial terminating with raised nipple, China, 18th or 19th C **220.00**

Water coupe, 5" x 4", Mughal-style carving of peach and foliage, pale green color stone **3,000.00**

Water dropper, 2-1/2" h, celadon, carved wine pot, rat forming handle, leaf and tendril on side, lid and spout of silver metal with pearl and traces of enamel on carved round foot, China, 18th or 19th C, small chip to foot **290.00**

JEWELRY

History: Jewelry has been a part of every culture. It is a way of displaying wealth, power, or love of beauty. In the current antiques marketplace, it is easiest to find jewelry dating after 1830.

Jewelry items were treasured and handed down as heirlooms from generation to generation. In the United States, antique jewelry is any jewelry at least 100 years old, a definition linked to U.S. Customs law. Pieces that do not meet the antique criteria but are at least 25 years old are called "period" or "heirloom/estate" jewelry.

The names of historical periods are commonly used when describing jewelry. Styles found in antique jewelry reflect several different design styles. These styles usually mirror what is found in the same period in other mediums, whether it is fine art, furniture, clothing, or silver. Each style has some distinctive characteristics that help to determine that what style it is. However, it is also important to remember that design styles may overlap as popular designs were copied and/or modified slightly from one designer and decade to another. Fashions often dictated what kind of jewelry was worn.

Georgian, 1714-1830. Fine jewelry from this period is very desirable, but few very good quality pieces have found their way to auction in the last few years. More frequently found are memorial pieces and sentimental jewelry. Memorial pieces were made or worn to commemorate a loved one. Sentimental jewelry was often worn to express emotions that were not proper to express during those times. Often these sentimental jewelry pieces had flowers and other items, with each flower having a different sentiment attached to it. Diamonds were set open backed. Colored gemstones were set with closed back settings lined with colored foil that enhanced their natural color. A popular motif was the bow, along with floral sprays and feathers. These designs tend to be rather stylized and flat. Paste (a high lead content glass) stones were popular and when set with foil backs they sparkled. Sadly, much jewelry from this period has been lost, as it was melted down to fund war efforts. During this time period, many folks would not wear expensive looking jewelry, as it was not wise to show one's wealth in such a manner. Gold was in short supply, so other metals were used to make fittings and chains.

Bracelet, Victorian, 14k, yellow gold, flexible design centering oval locket compartment with engraved floral and blue enamel cover, hinged to nine decorated links, **$450**.

Photo courtesy of Sloans & Kenyon Auctions.

Victorian, 1837-1901. The life of Queen Victoria set this whole period of design style. While Prince Albert lived, romantic themes in jewelry prevailed. One design element identified from the early part of the Victorian period is the snake, then thought of as a symbol of eternity or everlasting love. Victoria's engagement ring was a snake with a tail in its mouth. Snake necklaces, bracelets, and rings were also very popular. Floral designs of this period become more three-dimensional and truer in form to nature. The term "en tremblant," where the piece is designed to move with the motion of the wearer, reflects on the design as well as the French influence. Another popular symbol is a hand. Again, symbolic means were taken from whether the hand was clasped or open, holding flowers, or gemstones. Hair jewelry made from a loved one's hair was often given as a token of love.

The fashion of long-sleeved bodices with high necks caused throat pins to be popular. The practice of wearing ribbons around the neck and pinned with a brooch was also popular when necklines were lower. Earrings were not very popular in the early Victorian period because of the popular hairstyles. Bracelets were usually worn in multiples and on both arms. When Prince Albert suddenly died in 1861, the gayety of English life subsided. Add to this the many widows created by the Civil War and one can understand why black mourning jewelry became such a fashion statement. Entirely black jewelry was popular, as was jewelry with black trim or backgrounds, such as black onyx. Positive influences of this period included interest in revivals of ancient cultures, such as Egypt. By this period, manufacturers were learning how to mass-produce jewelry.

By the end of the Victorian period, smaller and lighter pieces of jewelry became fashionable. Gold was still in short supply, but the newly developed electro-plating techniques allowed more gold colored jewelry to be made. Seed pearls were plentiful. Cameos and mosaics also became popular. Diamonds move from closed and foil settings to open-backed settings during this period. New cuttings shaped diamonds and other gemstones in ways that allowed more facets. The discovery of diamonds in South Africa helped lower prices in the 1880s, but they were always expensive. Other gemstones, like garnets, are found as both facet cut and cabochon. Natural stones like turquoise and agates were popular, too.

Brooch, Edwardian, platinum, bead and prong-set throughout with 76 rose, single, and full-cut diamonds, approx. total weight 1.70 cts, French hallmark, **$2,350**.
Photo courtesy of Skinner, Inc.

Edwardian, 1890-1920. The Edwardian period also takes its name from an English Monarch, King Edward VII. This style emphasized the use of diamonds, pearls, and platinum in more monochromatic designs. The development of platinum led to strong, but lacy looking, filigree designs. Up until the Edwardian period, platinum used in jewelry making was usually plated with other metals as it was considered a lesser material. Diamond-cutting techniques continued to improve and new cuttings, such as marquise, baguette, and emerald cuts, became popular. Gemstones such as amethysts and peridots, blue sapphires, demantoid garnets, alexandrites, and rubies are also cut in these styles. Turquoise and opals are used as highlights. Jewelry for men was very popular in this period. The style is also known as Belle Époque.

Brooch, Arts & Crafts, Clarence Crafters, Chicago, early 20th C, sterling silver, mirrored abstract design with two cabochon corals inset, imp "CC" mark and "STERLING," 1-3/8" l, **$650**.
Photo courtesy of Skinner, Inc.

Arts and Crafts, 1890-1920. This period of jewelry is dominated by hand-made creations, often inspired by medieval and renaissance designs. Known for the high level of craftsmanship evident in metals, jewelry reflected the natural elements so loved in this period. Guilds of artisans banded together. Some jewelry was mass-produced, but the most highly prized examples of this period are hand made and signed by their makers. The materials used reflect what was being used in other crafts: silver, copper, and some gold. Enamel highlights added colors. Cabochons, leaves, and naturally shaped pearls predominate the style.

Brooch, Art Nouveau, Chinese, enamel, grapevine motif with carnelians, vermeil, some enamel loss, 2-1/2" x 3-1/2", **$375**.
Photo courtesy of David Rago Auctions, Inc.

Art Nouveau, 1895-1910. The free-flowing designs associated with the Art Nouveau period are what are found in jewelry from that time. Borders and backgrounds undulate and often include vines, flowers, and leaves. Enamel decoration is one of the more distinctive elements of this style. Gemstones also enhanced the wide palette of colors available. Jewelry from this period is again mass-produced, but quickly went the way of fashion when clothing styles changed with the onset of the Art Deco period.

Art Deco, 1920-1935. The flappers and their love of straight lines dominate this period. When examining Art Deco jewelry, look for a skyscraper or fireworks motif, as both symbolize this striking period. French designers were the most influential. Many pieces from this period are large and were used as accents to the new lighter clothing styles. In 1924, Coco Chanel declared, "It does not matter if they are real, as long as they look like junk," setting the stage for an explosion of costume jewelry. Rhinestones, pastes, and cut glass became important parts of molded designs of silver or pot metal.

Bracelet, Retro, platinum, 18k yellow gold, stylized design of ruby circular links, platinum and diamond spacers, gold modified V-shaped links, approx 0.80 cts, 7-1/2" l, 26.8 dwt, **$1,950.**

Photo courtesy of Sloans & Kenyon Auctions.

Retro Modern, 1935-1945. A resurgence of romanticism overtook the design world at the start of this period. Colored gemstones were back, along with the now popular costume jewelry. The style embraces some aspects of former periods, such as the streamlined look of the 1920s, but also the softness and natural aspects of the Victorian period. Color spilled over to settings with bi-color, rose, and yellow gold being popular. Machine-made pieces incorporate bold designs and colors with most motifs rather massive.

Bracelet, cuff, Modern, Georg Jensen, Denmark, c1940, sterling silver, cuff, marked "55," original box, **$875.**

Photo courtesy of David Rago Auctions, Inc.

Post-War Modern, 1945-1965. Designer jewelry is the most collected of this jewelry period. Names such as Harry Bertoia, Sam Kramer, and Ed Wiener are just a few of the top designers from this period. These designs were executed in various mediums, including brass, silver, Lucite, and plastics, as well as traditional materials. To be collectible, jewelry from this period should be signed or somehow identifiable. Designs tend to be sleek and innovative.

For more information, see *Warman's Jewelry, 3rd edition;* and *Warman's Jewelry Field Guide.*

Notes: The value of a piece of old jewelry is derived from several criteria, including craftsmanship, scarcity, and the current value of precious metals and gemstones. Note that antique and period pieces should be set with stones that were cut in the manner in use at the time the piece was made. Antique jewelry is not comparable to contemporary pieces set with modern-cut stones and should not be appraised with the same standards. Nor should old-mine, old-European, or rose-cut stones be replaced with modern brilliant cuts.

The pieces listed here are antique or period and represent fine jewelry (i.e., made from gemstones and/or precious metals). The list contains no new reproduction pieces. Inexpensive and mass-produced costume jewelry is covered in *Warman's Americana & Collectibles.*

Bar pin

Art Deco
Platinum and diamond, bezel and bead-set with old European and single-cut diamonds, approx. total wt. 2.74 cts **1,650.00**
Platinum and diamond, center old European-cut diamond weighing approx. 0.75 cts, further bead and bezel-set with fourteen old European-cut diamonds, millegrain accents, gold pin **1,000.00**
Platinum, center old mine-cut diamond measuring approx. 0.66cts, further set with 23 old European and circular-cut diamonds in filigree and millegrain mount, 2-1/2" l. **765.00**
Sapphires and pearls, A.J. Hedges &Co., alternately set with nine square sapphires and two rows of seed pearls,

14k yg mount, hallmark, 2-1/2" l **300.00**
Edwardian, center line of bezel-set oval rubies, surrounded by 42 old European and full-cut diamonds, approx. total wt. 2.28 cts, platinum topped 14k gold mount, hallmark "AF K," Austrian guarantee mark **3,525.00**
Etruscan Revival, 14k gold, rose gold arched terminals, applied bead and wirework dec **260.00**
Victorian, 14k yg, center carnelian intaglio of three cherubs within wirework frame, applied floral, bead, and ropetwist motifs **420.00**

Beads

Post-War Modern, Guillemette L'Hoir Paris, c1970, comprising lavender round, tubular, and graduating fitted shaped plastic beads, sgd, 16-1/2" l **450.00**

Bracelet

Art Deco
Articulated geometric links bead and bezel-set throughout with 318 old European, square, and single-cut diamonds, approx. total wt. 11.79 cts, millegrain accents and open platinum gallery, French guarantee stamps, 7-3/8" l **18,800.00**
Articulated links composed of 96 old European-cut and full-cut diamonds, approx. total wt 5.76 cts, channel-set onyx border, millegrain accents, platinum mount, sgd "Tiffany & Co.," 7-1/8" l, one onyx missing **16,450.00**
Bead and bezel-set throughout with 165 old European, transitional, single, and marquise-cut diamonds, total approx. wt. 8.30 cts, millegrain accents, open platinum gallery, stamped "SO," 7-1/8" l **10,575.00**
Central links with bead-set old European and single-cut diamonds, approx. total wt. 1.46 cts, alternating with channel-set rect step-cut sapphires, platinum mount, sgd "Tiffany & Co.," 7" l **6,200.00**
Flexible links set with 191 full- and baguette-cut diamonds weighing approx. 5.53 cts, platinum mount, 7" l, missing one small diamond .. **8,820.00**

Line of 40 prong-set old European-cut diamonds, framed by lines of channel-set square-cut emeralds, approx. total diamond wt. 3.98 cts, platinum mount with 18k white gold clasp, engraved gallery, 7-1/4" l, one emerald missing **5,400.00**
Set throughout with old European, single, baguette, and marquise-cut diamonds, platinum mount, approx. total wt. 1.86 cts, 7" l........ **3,000.00**
Seven center old mine and European-cut diamonds, approx. total wt. 1.75 cts, flanked by rect pierced links, 14k white gold, 7" l... **1,410.00**
Seven rect step-cut sapphires alternating with flexible honeycomb of bead-set old European and single-cut diamonds, approx. total wt. 4.64 cts, platinum mount, stamped "MD," French platinum guarantee stamps, 7-1/8" l................... **16,450.00**

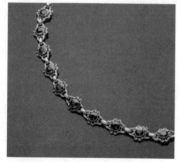

Bracelet, Art Nouveau, 14k yellow gold, 10 undulated scroll links, each with collet-set circular 7mm amethyst joined by reeded links, 7-1/2" l, **$1,850**.

Art Nouveau, 14k yg, 10 openwork plaques in floral and scroll motif each centering collet-set sapphire, hallmark for Riker Bros., 7" l............. **4,350.00**
Arts & Crafts, five bezel-set cushion-cut sapphires alternating with five old European-cut diamonds, approx. total diamond wt. 2.00 cts, joined by oval links, millegrain accents, c1915, 7-3/4" l............. **3,645.00**
Coin, 14k yg, heavy curb link chain suspending 1892 U.S. five dollar coin in a wirework frame, 27.1 dwt., 6" l **325.00**
Edwardian
Bangle, 14k yg, five bezel-set circular-cut sapphires within openwork design, 7" int. circumference............. **400.00**
Link, center old mine, European, and rose-cut diamonds in pierced and millegrain mount, flanked by knife-edge bar links, platinum-topped 18k gold, 6-1/2" l **1,120.00**
Etruscan Revival, 18k yg, hinged bypass bangle terminating in two ram's heads, applied bead and wirework dec, 22.5 dwt, 6-1/2" int. circumference, hallmark "P," evidence of solder **2,585.00**
Jade, SS, four oval jade plaques pierced and carved with floral motifs, joined by woven foxtail chain bracelet, 7-1/4" l.... **175.00**
Post-War Modern
Hermes, sterling silver, heavy flattened anchor links, sgd, 7-3/4" l...................... **1,100.00**
Van Gogh, hinged bangle, 14k yg, overlapping textured gold leaves highlighted by prong-set circular-cut ruby, emerald, and sapphire accents, 13.8 dwt, sgd "Van Gogh," c1950 .... **530.00**

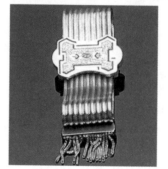

Bracelet, Victorian, 18k yellow gold, garter, fine 22 mm wide mesh ribbon, adjustable ogee slide, refined taille d'epargne tracery, foxtail fringe with losses, **$635**.

Photo courtesy of David Rago Auctions, Inc.

Retro Modern, double "tubogas"-style bracelet surmounted by bezel and bead-set old European-cut diamonds set in silver flowerheads, stems incorporating initials "H & L," 14k yg, French hallmarks **425.00**
Victorian
Bangle, 14k yg, seed pearl buckle motif, black and brown enamel accents, 6-1/4" d interior circumference, small dents........................... **550.00**
Bangle with locket, center medallion dec with gold floral and swag design on cobalt blue enamel ground set with pearls, center opens to reveal glass locket compartment, bracelet decorated with applied black tracery enamel motifs, 14k yg, 45.5 dwt., locket probably not original, but is of the period .. **1,120.00**
Slide, 18k yg, mesh design with adjustable oval slide engraved with scroll and fleur-de-lis motifs, edged with palmettes dec with black tracery enamel, foxtail fringe terminals, 137.8 dwt **1,200.00**

Brooch

Art Deco, diamond and platinum
Carved jade plaque depicting scrolling vines and gourds, corners accented by 22 single-cut diamonds, platinum frame, French guarantee stamps and hallmark..................... **2,585.00**
Center old European-cut diamond weighing approx. 1.29 cts, frame of 78 French, baguette, and circular-cut diamonds, millegrain accents, platinum frame, sgd "Raymond Yard" **5,650.00**
Center prong-set emerald-cut synthetic emerald, surrounded by an openwork geometric platinum frame set throughout with old European, baguette, and single-cut diamonds, approx. total wt. 1.52 cts, gold pin stem..................... **2,000.00**
Elongated oval form bead and bezel-set with sixty-six old European-cut diamonds, approx. total wt. 7.51 cts, millegrain accents, open platinum gallery, sgd "Tiffany & Co." **11,200.00**
Open geometric form, center bezel-set oval sapphire measuring 8.40 x 6.90 x 4.30mm, surrounded by 140 bezel and bead-set single and old European-cut diamonds, approx. total wt. 4.61 cts, millegrain accents, engraved gallery, platinum frame **4,700.00**
Open navette form bead and bezel-set throughout with old European-cut diamonds, approx. total wt. 2.33 cts, millegrain accents, gold pin **1,530.00**

Overlapping circles bead-set with old European-cut and single-cut diamonds, approx. total wt. 1.50 cts, center bezel-set rect step-cut emerald, millegrain accents, platinum frame, missing one diamond..................... **940.00**

Two circular cut diamonds each weighing approx. 0.69 cts, 162 bead and collet-set old European-cut and single-cut diamonds, highlighted by eight straight baguette-cut diamonds, approx. total wt. 10.44 cts, platinum frame, c1930...................... **4,700.00**

Art Nouveau

Floral spray, white-cream translucent enamel lilies centered by cultured pearls, green enamel leaves, joined by gold coiled cord, 14k polished gold stems .. **750.00**

Krementz & Co., light green enamel scrolling leaves centering heart-shape peridot, three old European-cut diamond accents, hallmark **1,150.00**

Orchid, light greenish-yellow and purple openwork leaves, baroque pearl and old European-cut diamond highlights, retractable bail, 14k gold................... **1,265.00**

Pansy, yellow shading to purple enamel leaves edged by seed pearls, center old-European-cut diamond, retractable bail......... **1,495.00**

Trout, basse-taille greenish-blue fading to pinkish-white iridescent translucent enamel **850.00**

Woman with flowing hair and dolphin with demantoid garnet eye amid waves within chased and engraved scallop shell, old mine-cut diamond moon, 14k yg mount ... **385.00**

Arts & Crafts, Josephine Hartwell Shaw, 14k yg, center bezel-set oval amethyst surrounded by grapevine motif, sgd............................ **3,410.00**

Edwardian

Bezel-set cushion shape faceted sapphire measuring approx. 12.25 x 9.80 x 7.29 mm, framed by rose-cut diamond Greek key devices, silver-topped 18k gold mount,

partial French hallmarks and guarantee stamp **5,640.00**

Heart-shape form set throughout with seed pearls, highlighted by two bezel-set peridots, English 9k stamp, 10k gold paper clip chain, 16-3/4" l...................... **500.00**

Navette-form openwork brooch set with fancy-cut aquamarine and rose-cut diamonds.................... **600.00**

Sword and scabbard, 14k yg, connected by trace link chain, seed pearls, four prong-set old European-cut diamond accents **235.00**

Quatrefoil design centered by clipped corner amethyst measuring 16 x 14 mm within pierced frame bead and bezel-set throughout with old mine, single, and old European-cut diamonds, approx. total wt. 8.00 cts, platinum and 18k gold mount, fitted box mkd "Jays of London," missing brooch attachment............... **5,400.00**

Jugendstil, SS, shaped pendant set with two oval green agate, reverse stamped "MiG, TF, 900, depose" for Max Joseph Gradl, Theodor Fahrner **885.00**

Post-War Modern

Robert Altman, 14k yg, seated poodle, prong-set with ruby, emerald, and sapphire highlights, 11.7 dwt, sgd **470.00**

Richard Fishman, 24k yg, hand formed open work abstract circular brooch, sgd "Richard Fishman 1979" **940.00**

Renaissance Revival, T.B. Starr, 18k yg, scrolling form, black and white enamel, seven cultured pearl accents, hair compartment en verso, sgd **1,645.00**

Retro Modern

Bow bead-set throughout with old European, full, and single-cut diamonds, approx. total wt. 1.20 cts, accented by channel-set French-cut rubies and sapphires, gold pin, c1940, missing one stone **2,470.00**

Bow, pink and yellow gold, 14k, sgd "Tiffany & Co.," 5.4 dwt............................. **360.00**

Swirl, star and prong-set with full-cut diamond and ruby melee, flexible snake-chain

terminals, 14k, 30.8 dwt. **825.00**

Victorian

14k yg, boss framed by rope motifs terminating in double tassels star-set with rose-cut diamond melee........... **300.00**

14k yg, scrolled form bezel-set with turquoise cabochons, chain suspending gold drop with turquoise accents (drop may be later addition) **300.00**

White gold, amethyst and cultured pearl, single oval amethyst with carved top of lady in profile, faceted bottom, white gold, 22 carats, surrounded by small pearls, 5.80 dwts **800.00**

Brooch, Victorian, gold, Rococo relief centering an emerald-cut citrine, approximately 18 cts, old marks for 800 gold, possibly Portuguese, **$810**.

Photo courtesy of David Rago Auctions, Inc.

Buckle

Art Nouveau, sterling silver, two repoussé plaques of female faces with flowing hair and flower blossoms, hallmark for William B. Kerr & Co. **300.00**

Edwardian, rect openwork buckle edged with demantoid garnets spaced by old European-cut diamonds, silver-topped gold mount **1,380.00**

Cameo, pendant/brooch, Art Deco, shell, 14k white gold octagonal filigree frame, oval cameo of woman with flowing hair, one diamond earring, **$200**.

Photo courtesy of David Rago Auctions, Inc.

Cameo, Victorian

Brooch, 14k gold, shell, young lady with floral corsage, filigree frame with leaf motifs **235.00**
Pendant/brooch, 14k gold, shell cameo habille bead-set with an old European-cut diamond set within frame, retractable bail, solder to neckchain on reverse **180.00**
Pendant necklace, Victorian, 14k gold, hardstone, carnelian agate cameo within oval frame with applied foliate motifs and flexible fringe, suspended from 18" l chain, pendant bail missing suspended element **450.00**

Circle pin

Art Deco
Platinum, bead-set with 44 single and full-cut diamond melee, channel-set with square step-cut sapphire accents **1,100.00**
Platinum, alternating bead-set old European-cut diamonds with French-cut emeralds, approx. total wt. 0.40 cts, gold pin stem **1,300.00**

Cigarette case

Art Deco, 14k yg
Engraved horizontal bands, monogram, stamped "14kt," 2-7/8" l **550.00**
Raised vine border, 89.3 dwt, stamped "Austria" **390.00**

Clasp

Art Deco, platinum and diamond
Barrel-shaped, prong-set old European and single-cut diamonds **425.00**
Oval with open work, prong-set single-cut diamonds highlighted by two bezel-set old European-cut diamonds, millegrain accents **465.00**

Clip

Art Deco, Platinum and diamond, two old European-cut diamonds, 35 old European-cut diamonds **2,100.00**
Retro, pave and circular-cut diamond set caps surmounted by similarly set swag, suspending spray of 18 square-cut rubies and eight tapered baguette-cut ribbons, Austrian import assay marks, hallmark **4,715.00**

Cross

Antique, 18k yg, bezel-set with circular-cut amethysts, emeralds, and pearls, applied bead and wirework accents **2,950.00**
Opal, six bezel-set oval opals within 14k yg ropetwist and bead frame, suspended from fine trace link chain, 16-1/2" l. **650.00**

Cufflinks, pair, Art Nouveau, 18k yellow gold, edges with leaf motifs, diamond emerald and ruby accents, French guarantee stamps, **$215**.

Photo courtesy of Skinner, Inc.

Cufflinks, pair, Retro, 14k yellow gold, 18mm disks with radial-cut detail surmounted by a bright green jade "wheel of life" centered by a prong-set diamond, Tiffany & Co., **$575**.

Photo courtesy of David Rago Auctions, Inc.

Cuff links, pair

Platinum and diamond, geometric design, ten 0.10 carat round brilliant cut diamonds, 14.40 dwts **490.00**
Platinum, ruby, and blue sapphire, two fine 0.40 carat rubies, two fine oval 0.40 carat blue sapphires, 12.40 dwts **490.00**

Dress clips, pair

Dress clips, pair, Art Deco, bead-set with 72 full and single-cut diamonds, channel-set square step and calibre-cut sapphire highlights, millegrain accents, platinum mount, with brooch conversion, **$3,200**.

Photo courtesy of Skinner, Inc.

Art Deco

Platinum, two marquise shaped 1.20 carats diamonds, eighteen baguette cut 1.60 carats total diamonds, two 0.20 carat marquise shape diamonds, numerous small transitional round brilliant cut diamonds (2.50 carats total), 13.60 dwts **5,260.00**
18k yg, WM Wise & Son, 18kt yg, shield form, bead and bezel-set with old European-cut and single-cut diamonds, approx. total wt. 0.88 cts, millegrain accents, sgd **1,880.00**

Earrings

Art Deco, pendant-type, each with jadeite cabochon and bead-set single-cut diamonds suspending jadeite drop, platinum mount, later silver screw-back findings, missing one diamond **1,765.00**
Etruscan Revival, 14k yg, pendant-type, coach cover, applied bead and wirework accents, later findings . **1,530.00**
Post-War Modern
Cartier Paris, clips, 18k yg, centering sapphire cabochon, full-cut diamond frame, approx. total wt. 1.20 cts, sgd, boxed **4,120.00**
Kanaris, 18k yg, dogwood blossoms, sgd "Kanaris," 14.3 dwt............................. **460.00**
Tiffany & Co., 18 k yg, aventurine quartz, carved knot, sgd................. **1,000.00**
Retro Modern, clips, 14k yg, abstracted floral form with circular-cut sapphires and cultured pearls, sgd "Tiffany & Co." **450.00**
Victorian, pendant-type, gold, engraved foliate tops suspending two gold balls **920.00**

Jabot

Art Deco
Cartier, platinum, 18k yg, diminutive arrow bead-set with old European and single-cut diamonds, millegrain accents, no.5749, French guarantee stamp, sgd **1,300.00**

Platinum, each end with oval coral cabochon surrounded by bezel and bead-set old European-cut diamonds, approx. total wt. 0.88 cts **1,530.00**

Edwardian, 18k yg, each flared end with pave-set diamond melee framing golden and ivory tone cultured pearl, possibly natural **3,900.00**

Lavaliere, Art Deco, 14k white gold, filigree link, rectangular stamped links with three octagonal frosted crystal panels, each set with diamond suspending similar rectangular panel with filigree decoration and diamond, 15" l chain, 2-3/4" l pendant, **$750.**

Photo courtesy of David Rago Auctions, Inc.

Lavaliere

Edwardian

Amethyst, 14k gold, centered by oval amethyst within openwork scrolled frame surmounted by seed pearl trefoil, suspending similar drop, joined by trace link chain, 15" l **450.00**
Platinum, bow and foliate wreath set throughout with old mine, old European, rose, and single-cut diamonds, suspending two knife-edge bar pendants with old mine-cut diamond terminals weighing approx. 1.17 cts. and 1.00 cts. respectively, surmounted on 18k yellow gold diamond motif with remains of blue and green guilloche enamel, major loss to enamel **4,600.00**
Platinum, heart-shape aquamarine suspends two collet-set old European-cut diamonds with pear-shape aquamarine terminal, three

pearl accents, fine 14k white gold ropetwist chain **1,410.00**

Egyptian Revival, 14k gold, centered by amethyst intaglio scarab within shaped lotus flower mount, baroque pearl drop terminal, stylized floral links, amethyst intaglio scarabs set at intervals, 16-1/2" l **1,380.00**

Locket, Victorian, designed as micromosaic Roman temple set in malachite ground, surrounded by decorated leaves, beadwork, and wire-twist frame, attached to 15k yellow gold Victorian chain, **$715.**

Photo courtesy of Sloans & Kenyon Auctions.

Locket

Art Deco, 15k gold, sq black enamel locket unfolding to reveal six pages suspended from black enamel baton and fancy link chain, 28" l **650.00**

Art Nouveau, 14k yg, helmeted Roman warrior in center, old European-cut diamond highlight, 4.4 dwt. **150.00**

Edwardian

Carrington & Co., circular white enamel and green guilloche enamel locket accented by an old European-cut diamond, platinum trace link chain alternating with green and white enamel baton links, hallmark, 20" l, some enamel loss to locket
.... **1,590.00**
French, 18k yg locket with pale blue guilloche enamel, rose and old European-cut diamond surmount, suspended from platinum chain with blue enamel baton links and seed pearls, 20" l,

French guarantee stamp on locket **2,700.00**

Victorian, 14k yg

Oval, turquoise enamel and five stars with old mine-cut diamond accents, reverse with hair compartment, pendant hook, later trace link chain, evidence of solder **325.00**

Pale yellow gold engraved disc surrounded by deeper gold, heavily engraved frame, rose and white gold curb-link chain, 24.7 dwt **360.00**

Lorgnette, Art Deco, platinum, set with 39 full and single-cut diamonds, two calibre-cut onyx cabochons, millegrain accents, suspended from added sterling silver paper clip chain with black enamel baton links, 24-1/2" l, **$1,650.**

Photo courtesy of Skinner, Inc.

Lorgnette

Art Deco, Tiffany & Co., platinum, bail bead and bezel-set with old European and single-cut diamonds, approx. total wt. 0.44 cts, opens to reveal lenses with octagonal frames
.... **1,175.00**

Art Nouveau, 14k gold, repoussé iris handle, collet-set diamond highlight, verso monogrammed **990.00**

Edwardian, 18k gold, engraved dec handle and eye piece, handle set with three bands of rose-cut diamonds, French assay marks **750.00**

Victorian, pale blue, ivory, pink and green enamel in floral design with old European-cut diamond highlight, 18k yg
.... **1,410.00**

Money clip

Post-War Modern, paper clip motif, 14k yg, Tiffany & Co., 16.30 dwts **275.00**

Necklace

Six strands of seed pearls alternated with openwork coral beads, center carved pierced floral motif coral pendant, 14k yg, c1930, 16-1/4" l **470.00**

Necklace, cascade style, composed of 12 strands of silk, faceted emerald beads graduate from 3.5mm to 6mm, 380ct, gold and lame adjustable slide clasp, strands range from 13" to 20" in length, 84 grams, **$1,265.**

Photo courtesy of Alderfer Auction Co.

Fringe necklace, Edwardian, 18k yellow gold, composed of ruby and seed pearl florets joined by seed pearl links suspending graduating circular and square-cut ruby fringe from knife edge bars, center pendant hook, 16" l, **$1,765.**

Photo courtesy of Skinner, Inc.

Seventy-nine ivory pearls graduating in size from 4.30 to 8.81 mm, platinum box clasp set with cushion-cut diamond weighing approx. 1.22 cts framed by calibre-cut rubies, 23-1/2" l **3,175.00**

Ninety-two transitional, old European, baguette, and rect step-cut diamonds, approx. total wt. 7.21 cts, platinum, 14-3/4" l **17,650.00**

Art Nouveau

Butterfly with bezel-set amethysts, seed pearl border, old European-cut diamond highlight, later amethyst drop, suspended later 14k gold and amethyst bead necklace, 16-1/2" l **1,120.00**

Citrine, center faceted citrine within 14k yg foliate links accented by collet-set diamonds, European hallmark, 30.7 dwt, 16" l **5,300.00**

Necklace, Art Nouveau style, sterling silver, floral motif around green and black scarab beetle, link chain, back imp "BRANDT/STERLING," 12-1/2" l, **$470.**

Photo courtesy of Skinner, Inc.

Three center shaped cartouches designed with florettes and scrolls, joined by baton-shaped fancy links, 18k yg, French guarantee stamp, 6.5 dwt, 16" l **1,000.00**

Arts and Crafts, elliptical-shaped jade within conforming enamel scrolled links joined by trace link chains, similarly set pendant suspending three jade drops, 18k gold, 18" l, sgd "Tiffany & Co.," some enamel loss............................. **31,050.00**

Edwardian

Center articulated seed pearl and old European-cut diamond scrolling floral vine, joined by ropetwist chain, 15k gold, 15" l **940.00**

Festoon, 9k gold, amethyst, graduating collet-set oval, round, and pear-shape amethysts joined by double trace link chain, 17" l.. **1,495.00**

Fringe, 18k yg, designed with wiretwist flowerhead links set with old European-cut diamonds and demantoid

garnets, edged by freshwater pearls, bottom swag suspending 17 teardrop-shape citrine drops in millegrained bezels, 14-1/4" l **6,500.00**

Turquoise cabochons joined by delicate trace link chain, 10k gold mount, 15" l, fringe loss to central tassel... **450.00**

Etruscan Revival, Ivy leaf and berry motif, barrel clasp, 18kt yg, 15-3/8" l.................. **2,850.00**

Jugendstil, SS, shaped pendant centered by oval green agate, suspended from silver paper clip chain, pendant stamped on reverse "TF" for Theodor Fahrner, 935, Depose, 21" l **1,530.00**

Retro Modern, 14k yg, each link designed as leaf surmounting a ring, convertible to two bracelets, 72.8 dwt, 17" l **1,120.00**

Victorian

14k gold and garnet, three floral engraved medallions surmounted by emerald-cut garnets set in ropetwist frames, reverse with plaited hair locket, suspended from 16-1/2" l snake chain .. **420.00**

18k yg, 18 concave disks centering coral bead within gold wirework frames, joined by oval-shaped links, some replaced beads and links **1,650.00**

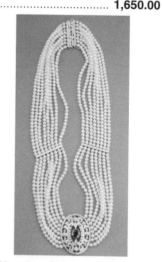

Necklace, dog collar, composed of eight rows of cultured pearls centering sapphire and diamond plaque of open-work filigree design, further accented with diamond set bars, approx 1.00 cts, **$4,150.**

Photo courtesy of Sloans & Kenyon Auctions.

Negligee

Edwardian

Floral and foliate elements, old European and old mine-cut diamond, seed pearl accents, platinum mounts, later 19-1/2" l 14k white gold fancy link chain, one melee missing **3,055.00**

Two rose-cut diamond flower terminals framed by calibre-cut rubies suspended from knife-edge bar links highlighted by bezel-set full and rose-cut diamonds, millegrain accents, 20" l fancy link chain, platinum and 18k gold mount, orig fitted Parisian jeweler's box **4,935.00**

Opera glasses

Lefils, Paris, late 19th C, blue enamel dec with pink and gold floral sprays, mother of pearl eyepieces, engraved name, 4" w **360.00**

Pearls

Bracelet

Caged freshwater pearls interspersed with 18k gold beads with applied wirework, 8" l, convertible to necklace with 14k gold rope chain **425.00**

Seventy two white cultured pearls with rose overtones, measuring approx. 5.90 to 6.0 mm, 14k white gold bar spacers and clasp with 11 full-cut diamond highlights, 7-1/4" l **715.00**

Brooch, Mikimoto, 14k yg, designed as abstract leaf with clusters of cultured pearl flowers, sgd **420.00**

Earclips, pr

Button pearl suspending chain link button pearl and diamond set cap terminating in teardrop shape pearl, set in 18k white gold, probably natural pearls **3,300.00**

Elizabeth Locke, center gray pearl within 18k gold frame, hallmark **1,880.00**

Necklace

Baroque, 31 South Sea Baroque pearls graduating in size from 10.70mm to 16.20mm, 14k white gold boule with diamond melee, 19-1/2" l **4,700.00**

Cultured, David Webb, 31 graduating pearls measuring approx. 9.08 to 12.78 mm, invisible pearl and 14k white gold clasp, 16" l **1,530.00**

Cultured, David Webb, 35 graduated pearls measuring approx. 11.02 to 13.12 mm, invisible pearl and 14k white gold clasp, 17" l, together with 3-3/4" l extension **2,115.00**

Cultured, one hundred twenty-nine pearls ranging in size from 6.7 to 7.5 mm, 14k gold gem-set clasp, 14-1/2" l **420.00**

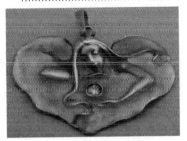

Pendant, Art Nouveau, 14k yellow gold, enameled, designed as undulating heart with woman's face, flowing hair in shaded pink and white enamel, accented with old European-cut diamond, **$695**.

Photo courtesy of Sloans & Kenyon Auctions.

Pendant

Art Deco

Platinum, numerous small old European cut diamonds (3.70 carats total), 18k white gold chain, 10.90 dwts **4,185.00**

Sterling silver, coral and black enamel, Theodore Fahrner, offset by two rect faceted black stone panels (probably onyx), gilt chain mkd "935," pendant stamped "TF (linked) 935" **1,880.00**

Yellow and white gold, Buddha, red coral, diamonds, lapis lazuli, turquoise, pearls, and black enamel, three pear shaped rose cut diamonds (0.80 carat total), 35 rose-cut diamonds (0.75 carat total), six 2.20 and 3.30 mm pearls, removable clip on bale **6,575.00**

Art Nouveau

Collet-set sapphires and diamonds set within trefoil open wirework form, accented by rose-cut diamond points, joined by later festoons of fine trace link chain terminating in rose

and circular-cut diamonds within triangular frames, later clasp, 18-1/2" l **1,410.00**

Plique-a-jour enamel, lavender and green irid enamel flowers, green, pink, and white plique-a-jour enamel leaves, rose-cut diamonds and pearl accents, 18k gold mount with later faux pearl chain.............. **1,265.00**

Cartier, designed as cross composed of eleven rect-cut aquamarines, 18k yg, sgd, provenance: from estate of Reverend Thomas Mary O'Leary (1875-1949), Bishop of Springfield.................... **1,410.00**

Edwardian

Platinum top, 18k yg, four 3.00 mm pearls, one old European cut diamond, 24 rose-cut diamonds (0.34 carat total,) 4.70 dwts **1,100.00**

Platinum top, 18k yg, one old European 0.60 carat diamond, 59 rose-cut diamonds (0.70 carat total,) suspended from 14k white gold chain, 3.40 dwts **1,920.00**

Post-War Modern, Picasso, illustrated in *Jewelry as Sculpture as Jewelry* by Institute of Contemporary Art, Boston, 1973

Ovale, 1972, 23k yg, numbered 1/20, oval with raised figures, orig fitted wooden box............. **8,460.00**

Poisson, 1972, 22k yg, numbered 17/20, abstract fish within angular frame, orig fitted wooden box.... **9,400.00**

Renaissance Revival, shield form with Renaissance motifs, rose-cut diamonds, rubies, pearls and emerald, cobalt blue enamel highlights, silver-topped 18k gold mount............... **885.00**

Victorian

Circular pendant edged by gold beads and decorated with black tracery enamel, suspending gold bead pendants, fancy double trace link chain, 14k yg, 14.1 dwt., 23-1/2" l....................... **385.00**

Pietra dura, rose branch, one open flower, two buds, inlaid in shades of pink, varying shades of green as leaves, 14k rose gold bezel and bale **400.00**

Pendant/brooch

Art Deco, platinum, navette set with five old mine and European-cut diamonds weighing approx. 5.33 cts, further surrounded by 142 bead-set old mine and European-cut diamonds weighing approx. 13.32 cts, approx. total wt. for all diamonds, 18.65 cts, provenance: accompanied by orig sketch by designer, Edmond Frisch, 336 Park Ave., New York **9,900.00**

Art Nouveau, 14k yg, circular-shaped, profile of classical woman accented by chased gold hair, enameled earring and face **1,000.00**

Edwardian, 14k yg, scrolling form set throughout with rose-cut diamonds and pearls, three freshwater pearl and diamond drops............................... **715.00**

Victorian, 14k yg
Enameled inverted horseshoe framing three rounded forms, engraved accents, seed pearl highlights, 15.6 dwt, fitted box from Savage & Lyman Jewellers, Montreal..... **600.00**
Openwork scrolling form bezel-set with three oval amethysts, suspending drop with pear-shape amethyst, chain festoons, 18.5 dwt, boxed...................... **1,000.00**

Pendant watch

Edwardian, Black, Starr & Bros, watch in light blue guilloche enamel with floral diamond surmount and frame, accompanied by platinum and diamond chain with American hallmark, 21" l............... **3,300.00**

Pin

Art Nouveau
Buckle, 14k yg, low relief sinuous vine motifs, inscribed "Sara Getty," sgd "Drosten" **560.00**
Dogwood blossom, center old European-cut diamond weighing approx. 0.50 cts, black enamel, 14k yg, American hallmark...... **775.00**
Lady in profile, 18k yg, rose-cut diamond accent, French guarantee stamps, sgd "TW"
Dogwood blossom, center old European-cut diamond

weighing approx. 0.50 cts, black enamel, 14k yg, American hallmark..... **775.00**
Lady in profile, 18k yg, rose-cut diamond accent, French guarantee stamps, sgd "TW" **325.00**

Edwardian, starburst, center 10.32 x 6.18 mm greenish-brown oval tourmaline, surrounded by sixteen old European-cut diamonds mounted on 14k gold rays, evidence of solder, possibly color change tourmaline, color changes to golden-olive color **1,175.00**

Post-War Modern, duckling, 14k gold, freshwater pearl wings, red stone eye, sgd "Ruser" ... **390.00**

Victorian, 18k, tapering silver-topped baton with graduated bead-set rose-cut diamonds, entwined with engraved yellow gold form completed by pearl, French guarantee stamp **350.00**

Portrait brooch

Antique, 14k gold
Portrait of mother and child holding grapes, mother-of-pearl reverse, engraved gold frame, backing loose.. **325.00**
Portrait of young gentleman executed in watercolor on ivory, engine-turned verso with locket compartment inscribed "W.E. Hearsey," c1840...................... **1,765.00**

Religious pendant

Art Deco, 18k yg, rounded form, blue stone cabochon cross at base which releases leather covered doors, revealing figure of St. Christopher, inscribed "T.M. O'L. 1925," French hallmarks, from estate of Reverend Thomas Mary O'Leary (1875-1949), Bishop of Springfield.................... **1,100.00**

Ring, gentleman's

Cameo
Black, white, and brown agate, carved Jesus profile, yellow gold setting, late 19th C, 4.80 dwts **215.00**
Coral, red, Socrates portrait, 14k yg, mid-19th C, 6.30 dwts **400.00**
Medium blue-green beryl, bearded soldier in high relief

profile, vg, Victorian, 5.80 dwts.......................... **575.00**

Enamel, multicolored, black onyx, portrait of North African gentleman with red and green stripes, yg, Victorian, 5.00 dwts **250.00**

Intaglio
Carnelian, Hermes with staff, 14k yg, 8.80 dwts **275.00**
Rhodolite garnet, Romulous and Remus in profile, yg, 5.10 dwts **300.00**

Seal, black and white agate intaglio, coat of arms, 14k yg, 6.30 dwts **120.00**

Ring, nugget style, 14k yellow gold, one 15mm x 11mm oval center amethyst, approx 9 ct, surrounded by six diamonds, 21.3 grams, size 8-1/2, **$2,000**.
Photo courtesy of Alderfer Auction Co.

Ring, lady's

Art Deco, platinum and diamond
Bezel-set with an old European-cut diamond weighing approx. 0.80 cts, framed by 18 single-cut diamonds and French-cut emeralds, single-cut diamond-set split shoulders, openwork gallery and engraved shank, two emeralds chipped ... **3,820.00**
Bypass, prong-set old European-cut diamond weighing approx. 0.75 cts offset by cultured pearl, shank with bead-set diamond melee bordered by channel-set sapphires, platinum mount, sgd "Marcus & Co.".. **2,585.00**
Center bezel-set old European-cut diamond weighing approx. 1.00 cts, within onyx navette, further bead-set with old European and single-cut highlights, platinum................... **3,650.00**
Center bezel-set old European-cut diamond within stepped frame bead-set with single-cut diamonds, approx.

total wt. 0.91 cts, split shank
.... **2,115.00**
Center cushion cut blue 2.00 carat sapphire, 36 transitional round brilliant cut diamonds (1.70 carats) **3,150.00**
Center emerald-cut sapphire measuring 6.55 x 4.60 x 3.80mm, flanked by old European-cut diamonds, approx. total wt. 1.25 cts, pierced mount with single-cut diamond highlights.. **4,230.00**
Center rect step-cut emerald framed by eight full-cut diamond melee, millegrain accents, open gallery and foliate engraved shoulders
.... **940.00**
Nine old European-cut diamonds navette set, approx. total wt. 0.70 cts, pierced and millegrain mount
.... **650.00**
Rounded form centering bezel-set old European-cut diamond flanked by lines of channel-set sapphires, set throughout with bead-set old European-cut diamonds, approx. total wt. 0.98 cts, millegrain accents ... **1,175.00**
Row of four bezel-set old European-cut diamonds framed by 16 bezel-set old European-cut diamonds, approx. total wt. 1.24 cts, millegrain accents ... **1,880.00**
Thirteen old European-cut diamonds, approx. total wt. 0.61 cts, millegrain and engraved pierced mount
.... **765.00**
Two center old European-cut diamonds, approx. total wt. 1.00 cts, further set with 22 single and old European-cut diamonds, millegrain and pierced mount, French guarantee stamp **1,880.00**

Ring, Art Deco, platinum, approx. 1 ct mine-cut and Holland-cut diamonds, calibre-cut sapphires, **$635.**

Photo courtesy of David Rago Auctions, Inc.

Art Deco, 14k white gold, center bead-set transitional-cut diamond within raised octagonal-shaped mount, openwork gallery with millegrain accents, approx. diamond wt. 0.87 cts **2,350.00**

Ring, Art Nouveau, Egyptian style, 14k yellow gold, designed as bypass of two scarabs with collet-set star sapphires, **$435.**

Photo courtesy of David Rago Auctions, Inc.

Art Nouveau, 18k yg, shaped rectangular plaque etched with initials "HP" flanked by stylized flowers within open and ribbed shank, inscribed "Vitaline a Hubert, 2 Janv. 1910," size 7-1/2 ..... **355.00**
Arts & Crafts, 14k yg, three circular-cut pink sapphires, white pearl set among swirling leaves and vines continuing to shoulders, sized **1,175.00**
Edwardian
Bead and bezel-set with 11 old European and old mine-cut diamonds, approx. total wt. 1.80 cts, platinum topped 14k gold mount........ **1,645.00**
Bezel-set fancy-cut aquamarine flanked by single rose-cut diamonds, silver-topped 18k gold mounts
.... **575.00**
Center oval sapphire measuring 6.15 x 5.35 x 3.20mm, surrounded by 10 old European-cut diamonds, 14k yg mount, Bigelow Kennard Co box **1,100.00**
Intaglio, orange and white carnelian, winged dragon with flower in mouth, 18k yg, 7.20 dwts **160.00**
Retro Modern, Birks, platinum, pave-set single-cut diamond buckle motif, channel-set with graduating line of sq step-cut sapphires **2,000.00**
Victorian, snake, tri-color gold engraved body, (approx total 0.45 cts) old European-cut diamond, stones missing from eyes **400.00**

Ring

Diamond solitaire

Center bezel-set brilliant-cut diamond weighing 0.74 cts, framed by full-cut diamonds, engraved shank, size 6, accompanied by report stating stone is F color, SI2 clarity **4,700.00**
Center prong-set emerald-cut diamond weighing approx. 2.45 cts, flanked by tapering diamond baguettes, platinum mount, size 7-1/2 ..... **8,225.00**
Center prong-set full-cut diamond weighing approx. 2.98 cts, 14k gold mount, along with 18kt gold band, size 5-1/2 and 6-1/4 respectively **11,750.00**
Center prong-set transitional-cut diamond weighing approx. 2.37 cts, flanked by tapering diamond baguettes, platinum mount, size 6-1/4
.... **13,550.00**
Center rect-cut diamond weighing 5.89 cts, flanked by tapering diamond baguettes, platinum mount, size 7
.... **16,500.00**
Center rect step-cut diamond flanked by tapered emerald baguettes, platinum mount, approx. diamond wt. 2.60cts, size 5 .... **5,400.00**

Rosary beads

Crucifix, 18k gold and platinum crucifix, Sloan & Co., black hardstone beads suspending two sided medal, yellow gold crucifix with platinum Christ, 43.1 dwt, hallmark, missing one bead, chain detached, provenance: from estate of Reverend Thomas Mary O'Leary (1875-1949), Bishop of Springfield **360.00**

Stickpin, Art Nouveau, 18k yellow gold, designed as an open-mouthed green man framed by foliage, ruby eyes, French hallmarks, **$535.**

Photo courtesy of Skinner, Inc.

Stickpin

Art Deco, platinum
Cartier, Y-shaped form, two
cultured pearls, bead-set
diamond melee, no. 2608,
French maker's mark, sgd
.... **765.00**
Channel set rubies with
diamond melee.......... **475.00**
Sugarloaf sapphire cabochon
with diamond melee and ruby
accents...................... **425.00**
Art Nouveau
Bulldog with collar, red stone
eyes, gold................... **225.00**
Crescent moon, 14k yg **95.00**
Enameled pansy, 14k yg,
American hallmark...... **100.00**
Enameled woman, hallmark
for Alling & Co., gold .. **400.00**
Highwheeler bicycle, gold
.... **325.00**
Edwardian, nine bead-set old
European-cut diamonds, set in
platinum, centered by cultured
pearl in floret design, 14k gold
shank **775.00**
Egyptian Revival, enameled
asps framing turquoise
cabochon, 14k yg **115.00**
Victorian, flowerhead design
centering a round opal framed
by 11 old mine-cut diamonds,
14k yg setting **360.00**

Suite, gentleman's

Cufflinks, pr, tie bar, 13 straight
baguette cut rubies, 2.50 carats,
14k yg, 17.10 dwts.......... **350.00**
Cufflinks, pr, and tie tac, 9.00
mm black cultured pearls, three
black 7.50 mm cultured pearls,
18kt yg, stamped
"Schlumberger Tiffany 18k," 9.40
dwts **1,000.00**
Cufflinks, pr, and tie tac, bombe
knot form, hammered surface,
18k yg, Henry Dunay, stamped
"Dunay 18K c 750," 21.20 dwts
.... **510.00**
Tuxedo stud set, pr cufflinks,
gentleman's, each pc set with
round red coral cabochon with
center old European cut 0.14
carat diamond, 18k yg, marker's
mark and stamped "BTE
S.G.D.G. PARIS R & G," French
hallmarks, 6.90 dwts **1,560.00**

Suite, lady's

Revival-style, bracelet and ring,
14k, hinged flexible braided
bangle centering three
contiguous balls with wirework
and applied bead decoration,

ring ensuite, 14.4 dwt, bangle
slightly misshapen **470.00**
Retro Modern, necklace and
brooch, 18-1/2" l necklace of
expandable links forming loose
knot at front with attachment for
removable 18kt gold and
platinum brooch with circular-cut
rubies and bead-set old
European-cut and full-cut
diamonds, 62.1 dwt. **3,820.00**
Victorian, demi-parure
Bracelet and earrings, 7-3/4" l
bracelet composed of 15k
gold florets with turquoise
cabochons; pr earrings each
with two 14k gold circles with
turquoise cabochons
suspending three small drops
.... **1,765.00**
Brooch and ear pendants
Coral, agate chalcedony,
brooch with center coral bead
within engraved reserve
framed by milky agate
chalcedony, ear pendants
ensuite **650.00**
Coral, each with carved coral
rose blossoms and foliage on
14k gold stems, boxed
.... **235.00**
14k yg, each lyre form with
drops, black tracery enamel
accents, boxed, provenance:
set was given to Elizabeth
Statham Morris in 1872 by her
husband Judge Page Morris,
Minnesota congressman and
vice-presidential candidate in
the 1870s................. **2,475.00**
Pendant/brooch and earclips,
all with circular-cut amethysts
and foxtail fringe, 14k yg,
brooch sgd "W. & S.B.,"
boxed, earrings with later
screw-back findings,
evidence of solder... **1,175.00**

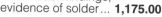

Watch chains, Victorian, left: heavy link
chain with abalone and onyx fob, **$95;**
right: heavy gold-filled rope chain with
fob and watch key with micro mosaic
scene, **$150.**

Photo courtesy of Joy Luke Auctions.

Watch chain and slide

Victorian, 14k yg, fancy round
link chain supporting engraved
slide set with lozenge-shape
cabochon amethyst, reverse with
worn engraving, possibly "C.L.
Hunter," 16.6 dwt, 24-1/2" l
.... **500.00**

Watch fob

Art Nouveau
Carter Howe & Co., 14k yg,
triple link chain composed of
lotus buds and flowers joined
by trace links suspending
double griffin-head seal,
hallmark...................... **940.00**
Whiteside & Blank, 14k yg,
heart-shaped leaves and
sinuous vine motifs joined by
grosgrain strap, hallmark
.... **400.00**

Watch fob chain

Victorian, gentleman's, yg, gold
filled locket with black and white
onyx cameo of soldier in
neoclassical design, chain 12.90
dwts **180.00**

Watch pin

Art Nouveau
Dragon clutching an arrow,
14k yg, partially obliterated
American hallmark...... **940.00**
Four leaf clover, seed pearl
and enamel dec, diamond
highlights, 14k yg mount
.... **750.00**
Profile of young woman with
flowing hair, encircled by
enameled buds, foliage, and
emerald-set blossom, 14k yg
mount...................... **1,765.00**

JUDAICA

History: Throughout history, Jews
have expressed themselves
artistically in both the religious and
secular spheres. Most Jewish art
objects were created as part of the
concept of Hiddur Mitzva, i.e.,
adornment of implements used in
performing rituals both in the
synagogue and home.

For almost 2,000 years, since
the destruction of the Jerusalem
Temple in 70 A.D., Jews have lived
in many lands. The widely differing
environments gave traditional
Jewish life and art a multifaceted
character. Unlike Greek, Byzantine,

or Roman art, which has definite territorial and historical boundaries, Jewish art is found throughout Europe, the Middle East, North Africa, and other areas.

Ceremonial objects incorporated not only liturgical appurtenances, but also ethnographic artifacts such as amulets and ritual costumes. The style of each ceremonial object responded to the artistic and cultural milieu in which it was created. Although diverse stylistically, ceremonial objects, whether for Sabbath, holidays, or the life cycle, still possess a unity of purpose.

Notes: Judaica has been crafted in all media, though silver is the most collectible.

Astrolabe, 5-1/4" h, bronze, finely chased lettering, symbols and foliage, 19th C **200.00**
Award of merit badge, 2-1/2" h, silver, Temple Ahawath Chesed Religious School, 1892, awarded to Walter R. Herschman..... **265.00**
Bible, Leviticus, Paris, Robert Estienne, 1544-1546, 16 mo, vellum boards, printed in square Hebrew type with vowel points, surrounding Latin commentary in small and neat hand, fifty bound-in pages of theological treatise **900.00**
Box, cov, 4" l, silver, dec with the Binding of Isaac, hinged lid, Dutch, 18th/19th C **1,650.00**
Bridal necklace, silver, rows of rect plaques applied with granulation and hung with filigree pendants, Yeminite **470.00**
Broadside, Warning to the Inhabitants of the City of Jerusalem, Palestine, 19 October 1938, sgd R.N. O'Connor, major general, commanding seventh division, text in English, Arabic and Hebrew............................ **210.00**
Carpet, 19-3/4" x 43", Bezalel wool, design of Rachel's Tomb, flanked by seven-branch menorahs, stylized Zion lettering, cranberry, gray, green, and blue, sgd "Marvadia, Jerusalem," early 20th C............................ **3,820.00**
Charger, 12-1/4" d, majolica, depicting Joseph and his brothers, Italian, 19th C imperfections **890.00**
Figure, 9" h, old Jewish man, Gardiner, Russia, late 19th C **940.00**

Flagon, 8" h, stoneware, with incised and blue glazed "Star of David," pewter lid, German, late 19th C **150.00**
Floor screen, 72" h, three-panel, sgd G.D. Felice, 1940, polychrome dec, ceremonial scenes and fruit and foliage **1,530.00**
Folk art, 11-1/2" x 17 1/4", Wedding Feast, carved and painted wood and plaster, sgd J.J. Stark **275.00**
Haftorah scroll, 22-1/2" h scroll, square hand-lettered ink on vellum, cherry wood rollers, probably Germany, late 18th C **4,120.00**
Hanukah lamp
  5-1/2" h, brass, backplate with lions, menorah, and "these lights are holy" in Hebrew, over candleholders, servant lamp to side, Bezalel, Jerusalem, early 20th C **715.00**
Havdalah compendium, 7" h, candleholder with egg and dart and foliate designs, drawer for spices, base formed as full-figured bird, circular base, Czechoslovakian, mark for Prague, c1814-1866 .... **3,055.00**
Havdalah plate, 8-1/2" d, porcelain, hand painted and transfer dec, M.L. Schwab, Frankfurt a Main, Germany, late 19th C **235.00**
Kiddush cup
  2" h, silver, beaker-form, rim with Hebrew inscription, wide band of foliage and scroll-work, mkd "12," Polish, 19th C **325.00**
  2-1/2" h, sterling silver, engraved "presented by Cong. Ahavath Achim, Revere, E. Kassoy," Russian-style **250.00**

2-3/4" h, silver and parcel gilt, beaker form with finely chased scrollwork and cartouche, mkd "800M," Continental, late 19th C **590.00**
3-1/2" h, silver, flared rim over plain tapered body, Hebrew inscription pertaining to circumcision, Dutch, date letter for 1927, .833 fine **775.00**
3-3/4" h, silver, tapered form, slightly flared foot, intricate acid etched vintage design, palm trees, appropriate Hebrew text, Bezalel, Jerusalem, second quarter 20th C **940.00**
4-3/4" h, silver and silver filigree, applied filigree decoration and three medallions, Bezalel, Jerusalem, early 20th C **890.00**
5-1/2" h, silver, flared cup with engine-turned detail, slender stem, square foot, Germany or Poland, first half 19th C **600.00**
9-1/2" h, German silver, neoclassical motif, hand-hammered leaf and berry band at rim, reeded stem, circular foot, German presentation inscription from "Israelitischen kultus-Gemeinde," mkd "800," Gorman, early 20th C.. **1,530.00**
Laver, 7" h, copper, heavily cast foliate motifs, appropriate Hebrew inscription, Continental **1,120.00**
Lulav (palm branch) holder, 28-1/4" h, enameled brass, cylindrical form, Hebrew text "Joseph is a fruitful bough...," probably Egyptian, 19th C **1,530.00**
Marriage box, 4-1/4" d, pewter, circular, scene of couple, inscribed "Mazel Tov," 19th C **250.00**

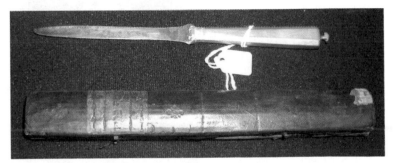

Circumcision knife, silver, original case, **$300.**

Menorah, cast iron, **$1,750**.

Matzoh bag, 15" d, embroidered silk, cream ground, colorful lion, crown, and foliage, Europe, early 20th C **200.00**

Matzoh plate, 10" d, Tepper blue transfer dec, vignettes of the Seder, identified in Hebrew and English, Ridgways, early 20th C **180.00**

Menorah/Candelabra, 19" h, brass, Modernist design, movable candle arms, domed circular base with Hebrew inscription, 1920s............ **470.00**

Mezuzzah

6-3/8" h, silver gilt and enamel, foliate motifs, mounted on wooden backing, Russian-style **325.00**

6-1/2" h, carved ivory front with lions, crown, and columns, silver rect backplate with scroll-work and cabochon coral, Polish style **325.00**

New Year's card, 6-3/4" h, lithographed diecut pop-up, Sukkot, Germany, c1890-1910 .... **150.00**

Paper cut, 9" x 7-1/2", rect format, delicate cut work deer and birds amidst foliage, text pertaining to protecting against evil eye, 9" x 7-1/2", matted, late 19th/early 20th C.......... **1,000.00**

Painting, framed

5-3/4" x 7-3/4", *Rabbi in His Study*, Hans Winter, sgd lower right, identified on reverse, oil on board **2,350.00**

7-1/2" x 9-1/2", *Still Life with Pomegranates*, Reuven Rubin, sgd "Rubin" in Hebrew and English lower left, oil on canvas board........... **9,990.00**

11-3/4" x 9", *Pondering Rabbi*, Josef Johann Suss, sgd lower right, oil on canvas **1,100.00**

23-1/4" x 19", *Rabbi with Torah*, Maria Szanthos, sgd lower right, oil on canvas **1,000.00**

Pillow, red velvet, silver embroidery and bead decoration, **$45**.

Plaque, 6-3/8" h, bronze, mother and child placing money in Tzdaka box, Boris Schatz insignia upper right, Bezalel, Jerusalem, early 20th C.................................. **825.00**

Plate, 6-1/2" d, white molded ground with brown transfer depicting "Sacred History of Joseph and his Bretheren....," English, early 19th C, chips **130.00**

Pocket watch, Waltham, gilt, Hebrew numerals, subsidiary seconds dial, removable nickel silver case...................... **600.00**

Postcard album

113 cards, various Jewish personalities, late 19th/early 20th C **825.00**

124 cards, New Year and holiday cards........... **1,650.00**

Presentation bowl, 9" d, sterling silver, shaped rim and foliate motifs, inscribed "presented by the Petoefi Sick & Benevolent Society," Theodore B. Starr, NY, c1910............................ **360.00**

Purim noisemaker, 11-3/4" h, silver and silver-gilt, applied turquoise, carnelian and paste stones, filigree work, appropriate Hebrew text, Turkmenistan **1,530.00**

Sabbath candlestick

10-3/4" h, bronze, cast with fox hunt motifs, base with menorah's, Star of David and blessing for candles, France or America, c1875 ...... **235.00**

12" h, repoussè silver, tulip-form candleholder over foliate cast baluster stem, plain square foot, Abraham Reiner, Warsaw, c1862-68, bobeches replaced, price for pr.................. **1,300.00**

12-3/4" h, silver plated, cast neoclassical motifs, leaf and scroll form feet, removable bobeches, Warsaw, late 19th C, price for pr **650.00**

Seder dish, 16" d, bone china, plate and small dishes for implements of the Seder, illustrations by Eric Tunstall, RI, Royal Cauldon, England, 20th C **300.00**

Seder plate, 9-1/2" d, porcelain, transfer dec, center with order of the Seder in tones of rose, yellow and brown, shaped aqua rim with floral sprays, German, late 19th/early 20th C **590.00**

Shabbat knife, 5-1/2" l, metal and mother-of-pearl, inscribed in Hebrew "Shabbat Kadosh," Czechoslovakian, early 20th C **180.00**

Shabbat wine carafe, 10-3/4" h, pottery, white ground, hand-decorated in blue, gold, black and green polychrome, lions, grape clusters, and vines, appropriate Hebrew text, pottery stopper, Holland, 20th C, minor chip to base **450.00**

Shiviti plaque, 15-1/2" x 19-1/2", ink and gouache, Star of David within architectural surround, late 19th/early 20th C, framed **1,175.00**

Spice box, 2-1/2" l, silver, rect form, lid with fruit form finial, three-part divided spice compartment, ball feet, German, indistinctly marked, 18th/19th C **1,175.00**

Spice container

7" h, silver and silver filigree, pendant flag over knop and tapered spire, central filigree compartment for spice, plain stem, circular foot, engine-turned details throughout, Berlin, second half 19th C **1,650.00**

10" l, silver, articulated fish, hinged compartment to hold spices, red eyes **600.00**

10-3/4" h, silver, pendant flag over tapered spire, bell and birds, baluster compartment for spice, baluster support, circular foot on cast leaf and berry feet, mkd "833," Polish, late 19th C **825.00**

11" h, silver and silver filigree, pendant flag over knop and tapered spire, birds and bell, filigree compartment for spice, hung with bells, turned support, domed circular base with cast leaf and berry feet, mkd "84" and "I.P." for I. Pearlman, Russian... **2,000.00**

12" h, silver and silver filigree, Berlin, late 19th C, damage **560.00**

Table cloth, 60" x 84", printed cotton, cream ground, overall floral and paisley pattern and Hebrew lettering, Persian, 1930s **225.00**

Table cover, Sabbath and festival, 15-1/2" x 20", silk, magenta ground with printed scenes after Jakob B. Brandeis, late 19th/early 20th C **180.00**

Tallis bag, 15-3/4" h, embroidered velvet, rect black field, scene of Jerusalem and appropriate text, verso with owners name "Nathan

Trachtenberg" within foliate motif, Germany, early 20th C **500.00**

Tankard, 5" h, silver, Hebrew inscription, George III, London, 1763-1764, maker possibly W & R Peaston, plain form with leaf-molded scrolled handle, monogrammed and inscribed 6th Nisan, 1810 in Hebrew and A.M. 10 April 5570 in English **1,120.00**

Tin container, 4-3/4" h, Rokeach's Pure Cocoa, lithographed tin, dark blue with white and orange, Brooklyn, NY, early 20th C **90.00**

Torah binder (Wimpel)

Embroidered linen, typical benedictions of Torah, Hupah and Good Deeds, also mentioning proximity of child's birth to Hanukah, German, dated 25 Kislev, 1839. **450.00**

Painted linen, brightly decorated with typical benedictions for Torah, Hupah and Good Deeds, made for Wilhelm Dollag, born May 21, 1895, probably Alsace-Lorraine **180.00**

Torah curtain, embroidered, rust-brown velvet, finely worked lion, foliate motifs and Hebrew lettering in gilt-metal thread, probably Europe, 19th C **1,765.00**

Torah ornaments, sterling silver, 14" h breast plate with crown and lions, columns flaking ark above festival plaques, inscribed 1920; 16" h pair of finials with crowns over baluster bodies suspending bells, tapered shaft, velvet covers, K. Paston, New York, early 20th C **1,000.00**

Vase, 6-1/2" h, patinated brass, tapered hexagonal form, stylized acid etched motif, Bezalel, Jerusalem, early 20th C .. **600.00**

KPM

History: The "KPM" mark has been used separately and in conjunction with other symbols by many German porcelain manufacturers, among which are the Königliche Porzellan Manufactur in Meissen, 1720s; Königliche Porzellan Manufactur in Berlin, 1832-1847; and Krister Porzellan Manufactur in

Waldenburg, mid-19th century.

Collectors now use the term KPM to refer to the high-quality porcelain produced in the Berlin area in the 18th and 19th centuries.

Cheese board, rose and leaf garland border, pierce for hanging, marked **48.00**

Cup and saucer, hunting scene, filigree, 19th C **65.00**

Dinner service, partial, basketweave molded rim, enamel painted sepia-toned floral sprays, 10 6-3/4" d side plates, nine 9-1/2" d dinner plates, eight 8-3/8" d salad plates, 12" l oval platter, 13-5/8" l oval platter, 8" oblong dish, late 19th/early 20th C, price for 30-pc set **520.00**

Figure, 8-1/2" h, 3-1/2" d, young man with cocked hat, long coat, trousers, and boots, young lady in Empire-style dress, fancy hat and fan, white ground, brown details, gold trim, round base, blue underglaze KPM mark, price for pr **350.00**

Perfume bottle, 3-5/8" l, rococo-cartouche form, sepia enamel dec of cherub in flight, floral bouquet, gilt detailing, gilt-metal and coral mounted stopper, late 19th C **230.00**

Plaque

5" x 7", young beauty facing right, sgd "Grenier" lower left, verso imp "K.P.M" with scepter, c1900, ornate 14-1/2" frame **2,300.00**

Plaque, depicting condemnation of Christians to the tigers, "Langhamer" signed in lower right corner, impressed "KPM" on verse, scepter mark, gilt gesso frame with acanthus leaf decoration and Greek Key design, 9-1/2" x 6-1/2" plaque, 17" x 13-1/2" frame, **$4,320.**

Photo courtesy of Alderfer Auction Co.

Plaque, 10-1/4" x 8-1/2" oval, two boys with loaf of bread and glasses of wine, with their faithful canine companion, impressed KPM mark, Berlin, late 19th C, 13-3/4" x 11-7/8" giltwood frame with Tilden Thurber label, **$2,720**.

Photo courtesy of Skinner, Inc.

7-1/2" w, 10" h, First Snowfall, grandfather with two grandchildren standing in doorway, snowy foreground, 21" w, 18" h elaborate carved wood frame of scrolling acanthus, imp scepter mark and "KPM," artist sgd lower right "F. X. Thallmaier Munchen" **4,370.00**
9-1/2" x 6-1/2", monk tasting wine, c1900, ornate frame, imp on verso KPM and specter mark............ **1,840.00**
10" w, 12" h, Sistine Madonna, after Raphael, finely dec, period gilt frame, verso imp with scepter mark and "KPM" **1,955.00**
12-3/4" l, 7-7/8" w, Ruth, after painting by Bouguereau, late 19th C **2,300.00**
13-3/4" d, titled "Entflohen," two young beauties seated in windswept wood, diaphanous gowns, floral headbands, anthemion and quatrefoil border, irid teal ground, 22-1/4" d giltwood and gesso frame...................... **10,925.00**

Punch bowl, cov, 12" d, 14-1/2" h, domed lid, Dionysian putto figural finial, enamel dec on one side with 18th C wigged gentleman at a drunken meeting of punch society, similar scene of gentleman at table to one side, vignette of couple outside village on other, floral bouquets and sprigs, imp basketweave rim, gilt edging, underglaze blue mark, late 19th C **2,775.00**
Teapot, 6" h, oval, medallion with floral dec, gilt ground........ **95.00**
Vase, 8-1/2" h, baluster, two handles, hp multicolored florals, celery green ground **200.00**

Tea bottle, ovoid, molded and gilt enamel decoration with rocaille vines, domed lid with gilt flower finial, late 19th C, 4-1/4" h, **$150**.

Photo courtesy of Skinner, Inc.

KITCHEN COLLECTIBLES

History: The kitchen was the focal point in a family's environment until the 1960s. Many early kitchen utensils were handmade and prized by their owners. Next came a period of utilitarian products made of tin and other metals. When the housewife no longer wished to work in a sterile environment, enamel and plastic products added color, and their unique design served both aesthetic and functional purposes.

The advent of home electricity changed the type and style of kitchen products. Fads affected many items. High technology already has made inroads into the kitchen, and another revolution seems at hand.

For more information, see *Warman's Americana and Collectibles*, 11th edition.

Additional Listings: Baskets, Brass, Butter Prints, Copper, Fruit Jars, Graniteware, Ironware, Molds, Tinware, and Woodenware. See *Warman's Americana & Collectibles* for more examples, including electrical appliances. See *Warman's Flea Market Price Guide* also.

Cake set, porcelain cake plate and matching server, cream ground, multicolored orchids, blue forget-me-nots, green foliage, gold trim, marked "Germany," **$45**.

Bean pot, cov, 6-1/2" h, Bristol glaze, handle, c1900 .... **25.00**
Broom holder, Little Polly Brooms, tin litho, image of little girl sweeping floor, 2-1/2" w, 6-1/4" h........................... **425.00**
Butter churn, 49" h, old blue paint, America, 19th C, minor imperfections **345.00**
Butter paddle
6-1/4" l, maple, unusual carved handle resembling bird with open beak, small rim chip............................. **125.00**
9-3/4" l, burl, dark patina, simple hooked handle **165.00**
Cheese sieve, 10" d, 7" h, plus handle, hand-molded yellow clay, Albany glaze........... **320.00**
Colander, 13" h, stoneware, brown Albany glaze, handled, attributed to Midwest, c1870 .... **75.00**
Cookbook
Mastering the Art of French Cooking, Julia Child, volumes one and two, Knopf, 1971-76, dj................................. **27.50**
The Good Housekeeping Illustrated Book of Desserts, Step-by-Step Photographs, Hearst Books, 1991, 5th printing, dj **12.00**
Cookie mold
23-1/2" l, 5-1/4" w, people and rooster on one side, four animals and two birds on other, minor edge wear **125.00**
28" l, 3-3/8" w, carved woman at well, man and woman near potted plant, few worm holes **250.00**
Cutting board, 13-3/4" w, 27-1/4" l, rect, hardwood, scrolled top edge and handle, minor splits...................... **615.00**

Left: coffeepot, white enameled body, pewter scalloped top, spout, handle, and base, **$175**; right: syrup, white enameled body, autumnal decoration, silvered metal spout, handle, and base, **$250**.

Dough box, pine and turned poplar, PA, 19th C, rect removable top, tapering well, splayed ring-turned legs, ball feet, 38" w, 19-1/4" d, 29-1/2" h **425.00**

Egg beater, 10-1/2" l, Jacquette Scissor, marked "Jacquette, Phila, PA, Patented No. 3" **550.00**

Firkin, cov, 15" d, 14-1/2" h, wood, painted green, bentwood handle, wooden banding, splits on top **990.00**

Flour sifter, 14" h, 12" w, Tilden's Universal, wood, partial intact paper label....................... **335.00**

Food chopper, 7" w, wrought iron, scalloped edge blade, turned wood handle **270.00**

Fork
   6-1/2" l, two prongs, bone handle........................... **65.00**
   21" l, two prongs, wrought iron, flattened handle, heart shaped hanger **550.00**

Grater
   4-3/4" h, 2-1/2" w, pierced tin, hanging ring **50.00**
   10-1/4" l, 4" w, wooden, metal blade, hanger hole **85.00**

Griddle, cast iron, Griswold, No. 10 .... **70.00**

Ice bucket, Frigidaire, frosted green glass **35.00**

Kettle, cast iron, Griswold No. 4 .... **85.00**

Ladle, 20" l, 5-3/8" d, brass bowl, wrought iron handle with decorative heart hanger . **880.00**

Lemon squeezer, iron, glass insert, marked "Williams" .. **50.00**

Left: griddle, Griswold, #9, Erie, PA, cast iron, **$35**; right: camp-type shovel, metal, soldered, loop hanging handle, **$15**.

Knife sharpener, Kent, Patentee & Manufacturer, 199 High Hilborn, London, original decal with instructions, **$200**.

Knives and forks, red Bakelite handles, some other miscellaneous utensils, wooden holder, **$65**.

Meat tenderizer, 9-1/2" h, stoneware, orig wood handle, marked "Pat'd Dec. 25, 1877" in relief on bottom, diamond point extensions with some use wear **90.00**

Nutmeg grater, 7" l, Champion, brass and wood **635.00**

Pantry box, cov, 11-1/2" d, 6-1/2" h, oak, bail handle **175.00**

Pastry board, wood, three sided **32.00**

Pie crimper, 7" l, carved bone, unicorn with carved fish tail, ball-shaped hooves, front let glued, late replacement crimper, medium brown stain **220.00**

Pie lifter, 18" l, wrought iron, turned wood handle.......... **95.00**

Pie safe, hanging, 31" w, 19" d, 31" h, mortised pine case, old thin red wash, door, sides, and back with punched tins with geometric circles and stars, white porcelain door pull, two int. shelves, edge damage... **990.00**

Potato masher, 9" l, turned maple................................. **40.00**

Pot scraper, Sharples Tubular Separator, tin litho, graphic advertising on both sides, 3-1/8" x 2-1/4"............................. **275.00**

Rack, 20" l, rect backplate with arched top, red and white enameled checkerboard pattern, narrow well, single rod suspending two strainer spoons **250.00**

Mixing bowls, nested set, Kitchen Kraft Oven Serve, floral and silver trim, set of three, **$45**.

Popcorn popper, embossed "Wilson Mfg Co.'s Family Corn Popper, Miles, O," some discoloration and rust, **$30**.

Reamer
Grapefruit, green, US Glass, cone chips **575.00**
Orange, pink, Hazel Atlas **195.00**
Orange, Sunkist, blocked pattern, white milk glass, Walker #331b **125.00**

Rolling pin
16-1/2" l, curly maple, dark color, good patina **275.00**
22" l, milk glass, cylindrical, turned wood handles, marked "Imperial Mfg., Co. July 25, 1921" **95.00**
23-1/2" l, 4-1/2" w, wooden, turned handle, peg mortised joint **1,320.00**

Sausage stuffer, 17-1/2" l, turned wood plunger **30.00**

Scoop, 5-1/2" w, 12-3/4" l, rect, carved poplar, round handle **55.00**

Sieve, 18-1/2" l, 5-1/2" d, brass, wrought iron scrolled handle with rattail hanging hook **330.00**

Skillet, cast iron, Griswold, No. 14 .... **165.00**

Slaw board
5-3/4" w, 21-1/4" h, walnut, cut-out heart design, shaped neck on back, semi-circular base........................... **500.00**
6" w, 11" l, tombstone shape **220.00**
7" w, 16-1/2" h, walnut, top with stylized heart cut-out, outlined by field of small carved dots, crowned by three six-pointed Germanic carved stars in field of impressed snowflakes, lower edge gouge carved, molded and dated siderails, hand wrought nut, bottom edge sgd "S.O.A. 1887," York County, PA **2,100.00**
7" w, 19" h, walnut, two metal blades, carved star dec, scalloped edges and borders, initialed "F.N." **220.00**
13" l, 7" d, 7-1/4" h, two-tier, hickory or ash, old brown surface, pierced detail on either side, steel blade, brass fittings, age splits, one scallop missing **100.00**

Soap cutting board, 9" l, 6-1/2" w, 1-1/8" h, wooden, molded sections, use wear . **55.00**

Spatula, 10" l, iron, D-shape, baluster like turnings on handle **200.00**

Spice set, Griffiths, set of 16 glass jars with yellow tops, each with spice name, orig rack **160.00**

Plate warmer, Manning Bowman, white ironstone plate with green trim, **$75.**

Salt box, white graniteware body, wooden lid, black lettering, wear and chips, **$45.**

Stove, cast iron, chrome, nickel, colorful ceramic tile back **6,000.00**

Sugar shaker, Dutch boy and girl, Tipp City **22.00**

Syrup jug, 8" h, adv, clay inscribed "W. D. Streeter, Richland, NY," Albany glaze, c1890, tight hairline on side **35.00**

Taster, 7" l, brass and wrought iron, polished **150.00**

Utensil, tin, two graters, crimper, and cookie cutters all in one cylindrical form, 2-3/4" d, 4-1/2" h, **$315.**

Photo courtesy of Alderfer Auction Co.

Tin
Donovan's Baking Powder, Mt. Morris, NY, 1 lb, paper label, 5-1/4" h, 3" d **475.00**
Egg-O Brand Baking Powder, paper label, 2-3/4" h, 1-1/4" d **110.00**
Kavanaugh's Tea, 1 lb, little girl on porch in dress, talking to doll, mother sipping tea in window, cardboard sides, tin top and bottom, 6" h, 4-1/2" w, 4-1/2" d **500.00**
Miller's Gold Medal Breakfast Cocoa, red and black, c1890, 2" h, 1-5/8" w, 1-1/8" d .. **250.00**
Opal Powdered Sugar, Hewitt & Sons, Des Moines, 8" h, 4-1/2" w, 3-1/4" d........ **180.00**
Parrot and Monkey Baking Powder, 4 oz, full, 3-1/4" h, 2-1/8" d **375.00**
Sunshine-Oxford Fruit Cake, early 1900s, sq corners **20.00**
Towle's Log Cabin Brand Maple Syrup, cabin shaped, woman and girl in doorway, 4" h, 3-3/4" l, 2-1/2" d .. **110.00**

Trivet, 12" l, lyre form, wrought iron frame and turned handle, brass top, replaced foot, stamped maker's mark **45.00**

Wafer iron, cast iron, octagonal, church with steeple and trees dec on one side, pinwheel with plants and star flowers on reverse, wrought iron handles **400.00**

KUTANI

History: Kutani originated in the mid-1600s in the Kaga province of Japan. Kutani comes in a variety of color patterns, one of the most popular being Ao Kutani, a green glaze with colors such as green, yellow, and purple enclosed in a black outline. Export wares made since the 1870s are enameled in a wide variety of colors and styles.

Beaker, 4-1/2" h, hp flowers and birds, red, orange, and gold, white ground, marked "Ao-Kutani" **95.00**

Bottle, 8-3/4" h, 3-3/8" w, sq form, each rect panel profusely dec with underglaze enamels, one panel with inscription, base with signature in rect panel, Japanese, 18th C, very tight hairline running through base on bottom of signature......... **425.00**

Bottle, square form, each rectangular panel profusely decorated with underglaze enamels, one panel with inscription, signature in rectangular panel on base, Japanese, 18th C, 3-3/8" w, 8-3/4" h, very tight hairline, **$425.**

Bowl, 6-3/8" d, gilt and bright enamel design, figural, animal, and floral reserves, kinrande ground, base inscribed "Kutani-sei," set of 10 .... **400.00**

Censer

6" x 5-1/2", modeled as shishi, purple, yellow, and green glaze, mounted as lamp, gilt metal fittings, Japan, 19th C **385.00**

7" h, sq, lid decorated with Daikoku's hammer, Japan, early 20th C **300.00**

Charger, painted overall with many figures on gold ground, red and gold geometric border, impressed and painted marks on underside, Japanese, Meiji period, 16" d, **$500.**

Photo courtesy of Alderfer Auction Co.

Charger, 18-3/8" d, pomegranate tree, chrysanthemums, and two birds on int., birds and flowers between scrolling foliate bands,

irregular floral and brocade border, 11-character inscription **600.00**

Chawan (tea bowl), 5" d, 3" h, sunflower design, orange and green, imp mark "RIJU" .. **100.00**

Chocolate pot, white ground, hp scenes of lake, three white cranes on shore, Mt. Fiji in distance, hills with wildflowers, white and pink chrysanthemums, two white cranes with black tails, lid painted with wild flowers on cliff, crane, gold bamboo branch, gold knob, cream colored handle, wear to knob **95.00**

Creamer and sugar, summer scene, two court ladies, red, blue, gray, and gold, red handle, spout, and feet with gold overlay, c1910 .... **95.00**

Dessert service, country life dec, gold cloud borders, eight plates, two compotes, 20th C **435.00**

Figure

7" l, duck, gilt figure, purple, blue, green, and yellow feathers, Japan, late 19th C **1,100.00**

14" h, geisha with kitten, green, yellow, and brick red enamels, Japan, late 19th/early 20th C **600.00**

Jar, cov, 20-1/2" h, ovoid, fan shaped reserves of warriors, molded ribbon tied tasseled ring handles, shippo-tsunagi ground, multicolored brocade patterned dome lid, pr **1,400.00**

Plate, deep, red and gold Kutani decoration, painted sages under pine tree, round and geometric medallions, back border with flowers in white reserved, marked "Kutani," Japan, Meiji period, 14-1/2" d, **$450.**

Sake cup, 2-3/16" h, 1-1/8" w, crane in red center, gold lacquer trim **35.00**

Sake cup washer, 6" d, 4-1/2" h, red Kutani geometric patterns, Japanese, 19th C **125.00**

Tea caddy, 6" h, bulbous, hexagonal, Nishikide diapering, figural raised gold reserves of children, red script mark. **195.00**

Teapot, cov, 8" h, white, trees and flowers, gold trim, marked "Hand Painted Craftsman China, Kutani 391 Japan" **45.00**

Tray, 14" l, polychrome and gilt dec, figural scene, red, orange, and gold border............. **350.00**

Vase

7-1/4" h, classic shape, white emb chrysanthemums on white ground, marked "Trade Mark Fujita Kutani, Made in Japan" **95.00**

10" h, double-gourd, red and gold roundels of auspicious animals on flowered ground, Japan, 19th C **300.00**

12-1/2" h, globular form with trumpet mouth, design of flowers on yellow ground **235.00**

LALIQUE

LALIQUE

History: René Lalique (1860-1945) first gained prominence as a jewelry designer. Around 1900, he began experimenting with molded-glass brooches and pendants, often embellishing them with semiprecious stones. By 1905, he was devoting himself exclusively to the manufacture of glass articles.

In 1908, Lalique began designing packaging for the French cosmetic houses. He also produced many objects, especially vases, bowls, and figurines, in the Art Nouveau and Art Deco styles. The full scope of Lalique's genius was seen at the 1925 Paris l'Exposition Internationale des Arts Décorative et Industriels Modernes.

For more information, see *Warman's Glass*, 4th edition; and *Warman's Lalique*.

Marks: The mark "R. LALIQUE FRANCE" in block letters is found on pressed articles, tableware, vases, paperweights, and automobile mascots. The script signature, with or without "France," is found on hand-blown objects. Occasionally, a design number is included. The word "France" in any form indicates a piece made after 1926.

The post-1945 mark is generally "Lalique France" without the "R," but there are exceptions.

Reproduction Alert: The Lalique signature has often been forged; the most common fake includes an "R" with the post-1945 mark.

Automobile hood ornament, Hirondelle, clear and frosted, c1928, molded "R. LALIQUE FRANCE," **$1,955**.

Photo courtesy of David Rago Auctions, Inc.

Ashtray

3-3/4" d, Irene, bright green, white patina, stenciled "R. Lalique France," c1931, Marcilhac pg 276, no. 304 .... **1,100.00**
4-1/2" d, Simone, clear and frosted, sepia patina, stenciled "R. Lalique France," c1929, Marcilhac pg 275, no. 300 .... **300.00**

5-1/2" d, Jamaique, clear and frosted, sepia patina, engraved "R. Lalique France," Marcilhac pg 274, no. 296 .... **225.00**

Bookends, pr
6-1/4" h, Hirondelles, sgd "Lalique, France" **500.00**

Bowl
8-5/8" d, Acacia No. 2, opalescent, stenciled "R. LALIQUE FRANCE," c128, Marchilhac pg 755, no. 3249 .... **300.00**
9" d, 6-1/4" h, Doves, frosted doves with spread wings, oval, etched "Lalique (r in circle) France" in small script **400.00**
11-7/8" d, Cremieu, opalescent, molded "R. LALIQUE FRANCE," engraved No. 400, c1928, Marchilhac pg 297, no. 400 .... **550.00**
14-1/2" d, 2-3/4" h, Daisy, deep rim relief dec with band of overlapping daisies, colorless body fluted, brown patina accents, acid-etched mark "Lalique Cristal France," post WWII **425.00**

Box, cov
3-1/4" d, Pommier du Japon, black, whitish patina, molded "R. LALIQUE," c1919, Marcilhac pg 227, no. 26 .... **1,200.00**
3-1/4" d, Quatre Scarabees, black, whitish patina, molded "R. LALIQUE," c1911, Marcilhac pg 225, no. 15 .... **1,600.00**
3-1/4" d, Veronique, black, whitish patina, molded "R. LALIQUE," c1919, Marcilhac pg 227, no. 25 .... **1,700.00**

Cane handle
3-3/8" l, clear and frosted, sepia patina, c1905, Marcilhac pg 141 .... **900.00**

Car mascot
No. 1124, Faucon, molded signature "R.Lalique" and etched "France," orig Breves Galleries metal mount, 6-1/4" h **2,100.00**
No. 1138, Tete D'Aigle, later example, molded signature "R. LALIQUE" and engraved "Lalique France," 4-1/2" h **300.00**

Coupe
8-1/4", Graines d'Asperges No. 2, opalescent, molded DVA mark, Marcilhac pg 751, no. 3221 .... **350.00**

Figure, female nude figure, 5-1/2" h, **$950**.

Photo courtesy of Joy Luke Auctions.

Figure
Bamara, lion, 8" h, designed by Marie Claude Lalique, introduced 1987, MIB.. **1,200.00**
Black panther, 14-3/8" l, 4-3/8" h, designed by Marie Claude Lalique, introduced 1989, MIB **1,300.00**
Cat, 4" h, crouching, frosted, designed by Rene Lalique, 1932 .... **1,200.00**
Cheetah, 10" h, 8-1/4" l, designed by Marie Claude Lalique, MIB **2,600.00**

Hat pin
7-3/4" l shaft, 10" l overall, clear and frosted, sepia patina over gilt metal foil, orig silvered metal mounting and shaft, c1912
Feuilles, Marchilhac pg 566, no. 1558 .... **2,800.00**
Scarabees, Marchilhac pg 566, no. 1559 .... **1,800.00**

Inkwell
2" x 6-1/4", Mures, clear and frosted, blue patina, engraved "R. Lalique France, No. 431," c1920, Marchilhac pg 316, no. 421 .... **8,500.00**
3-1/2" x 4", Cernay, clear and frosted, green patina, molded "R. LALIQUE," c1924, Marchilhac pg 318, no. 437 .... **5,000.00**
6" sq base, Biches, clear and frosted, gray patina, engraved "R. Lalique," c1912, Marchilhac pg 315, no. 427 .... **2,700.00**

Jewelry
Bracelet, Cerisier, peacock blue, 12 1-1/8" h elements, engraved "Lalique," c1928, Marchilhac pg 532, no. 1329, small chips, one element reglued **2,000.00**
Brooch, 1-1/4" d, Trois Anges, clear, sepia patina, gold reflecting foil, gilt metal backing, stamped "Lalique poincon," c1912, Marcilhac pg 545, no. 1373 .... **800.00**

Brooch, 2-1/8" d, Chauve-Souris, electric blue, white patina, silver reflecting foil, gilt metal mount, stamped "Lalique poincon," c1912, Marcilhac pg 538, no. G.L. **6,000.00**
Pendant, 2-1/8" d, Cigognes, clear and frosted, gray patina, molded "LALIQUE," c1919, Marcilhac pg 581, no. 1663 .... **250.00**

Letter seal, Tete D'Aigle, black, whitish patina, c1911, engraved "Lalique," **$1,725.**
Photo courtesy of David Rago Auctions, Inc.

Menu plaques, pair, Raisin Muscat, clear and frosted, c1924, engraved "R. Lalique France no. 3475," **$815**
Photo courtesy of David Rago Auctions, Inc.

Letter seal, R. Lalique
1-5/8" h, Sauterelle, electric blue, c1913, molded "LALIQUE," Marcilhac pg 249, no. 183 .... **650.00**
2" h, Rapace, blue, c1931, engraved "R. Lalique," Marcilhac pg 257, no. 234 .... **1,700.00**
2-1/2" h, Statuette Drapee, clear and frosted glass with green patina, c1913, early engraved signature, Marcilhac pg 249, no. 181 .... **3,000.00**

3-1/8" h, Tete D'Aigle, dark amber, engraved "R. Lalique France," c1911, Marcilhac pg 248, no. 175 .... **1,700.00**
Paperweight
3-1/2", Toby, clear and frosted, stenciled "R. Lalique France," c1929, Marcilhac pg 391, no. 1192 **1,200.00**
4-1/2", bird, Ailes Fermees, clear and frosted, engraved "R. Lalique France," Marcilhac pg 386, no. 1156 .... **375.00**

Perfume bottle
2-3/8" h, Camille, electric blue, white patina, molded "R. LALIQUE FRANCE," engraved "R. Lalique France," c1927, Marcilhac pg 335, no. 516 .... **3,000.00**
3-7/8" h, Bouquet de Faunes, for Guerlain, clear and frosted, gray patina, orig black leather presentation case, unmarked, orig retailer labels on base, c1925, Marcilhac pg 940, no. 1 .... **1,300.00**
3-7/8" h, Narkiss, for Roger et Gallet, clear and frosted patina, black enamel, modeled "R.L. FRANCE," Marcilhac pg 947, no. 1 .... **2,700.00**
5-7/8" h, 3-3/4" w, heart shape, Coeur-Joie, Nina Ricci **825.00**

Vase, Perles, opalescent, c1925, molded "R. LALIQUE," **$1,045.**
Photo courtesy of David Rago Auctions, Inc.

Vase
4-7/8" h, Dahlias, clear and frosted, sepia patina, black enamel, molded "R LALIQUE," c1925, Marcilhac pg 425, no., 938 ...... **2,300.00**

Perfume, atomizer, Epines, clear and frosted, metal mount, c1920, stenciled "R. LALIQUE FRANCE," **$230**
Photo courtesy of David Rago Auctions, Inc.

5" h, frosted colorless bulbous body, repeating open-petal dahlias with black centers, etched mark "R. Lalique France," Marcilhac no. 3938, model created in 1923 .... **1,410.00**
5" h, Rampillon, opalescent, stenciled "R. LALIQUE FRANCE," c1927, two shallow chips, Marcilhac pg 437, no. 991 .... **1,100.00**
5-3/8" h, Dauphins, opalescent, blue patina, stenciled "R. LALIQUE," engraved "France," Marcilhac pg 464, no. 10-900 .. **2,200.00**
6-1/2" h, Nivernais, bright green, engraved "R. Lalique France, No. 1005," c1927, Marcilhac pg 440, no. 1005 .... **3,500.00**
6-1/2" h, Soudan Art, design created in 1928, ovoid body, relief dec with three bands of running stags and flowers, sgd "R. Lalique France" on base, Marcilhac no. 1016 .... **1,120.00**
6-7/8" h, Espalion, electric blue, engraved "R. Lalique, France No. 996," c1927, Marcilhac pg 438, no. 996 .... **1,300.00**
7-1/4" h, Amiens, topaz, whitish patina, stenciled "R. LALIQUE," c1929, Marcilhac pg 443, no. 1023, some int. staining, int. flaw in one handle...................... **1,200.00**
7-1/4" h, Coquillles, clear and frosted, blue patina, molded "R. LALIQUE," c1920, Marcilhac pg 424, no. 932 .... **1,100.00**
11-1/4" h, Tourterelles, opalescent, blue patina, engraved "R Lalique," c1925, Marcilhac pg 431, no. 963 .... **14,000.00**

11-3/8" h, Douze Figurines Avec Bouchon, clear and frosted, engraved "R. Lalique France," c1920, Marcilhac pg 420, no. 914, small bruise to base of stopper barrel **7,000.00**

LAMP SHADES

History: Lamp shades were made to diffuse the harsh light produced by early gas lighting fixtures. These early shades were made by popular Art Nouveau manufacturers including Durand, Quezal, Steuben, and Tiffany. Many shades are not marked.

For more information, see *Warman's Glass*, 4th edition.

Leaded glass shade, muted slag glass panels, red cherries, purple grapes, shaded apples and pears, green leaves, crown like top, **$250**.

Photo courtesy of Dotta Auction Co., Inc.

Aladdin
Cased, green............. **870.00**
Satin, white, dogwood dec **65.00**

Cameo, 6-1/2" h, gold satin glass cut to clear in acorn and leaves pattern, price for pr **225.00**

Fostoria
4-1/2" h, gold, 24 ribs ... **85.00**
4-3/4" h, iridescent gold, 24 ribs.............................. **90.00**
4-3/4" h, opal, ribbed, gold interior........................ **100.00**

Lustre Art, 5" h, opal, gold ribbon dec **100.00**
Palme-Koenig, 6-3/4" h, opaline, pink drag loops.............. **110.00**

Quezal
4" h, opal, green and gold pulled feather design . **375.00**
4-1/2" h, egg shape, green and gold pulled feather design........................ **200.00**
4-3/4" h, gold snakeskin design........................ **170.00**
4-3/4" h, green and gold leaf design, gold threading **150.00**
5" h, chartreuse gold and dark green reverse drape pattern, ribbed **575.00**
5" h, irid opal, gold pulled feather design, fitter rim chips **75.00**
5" h, opal ground, irid blue pulled feather dec, tipped in gold **300.00**
5-1/4" h, irid gold, white scaled pattern graduating to irid green rim, sgd "Quezal" **225.00**
5-1/2" h, irid, bell shaped, gold zipper pattern..... **145.00**
5-1/2" h, irid gold, pulled feathers...................... **270.00**
6" h, cylindrical, vertical ribbing, irid calcite, inscribed "Quezal" **150.00**
6-1/2" h, trumpet shape, dark gold, ribbed............... **115.00**

Steuben, shape #985, opal, straight rim, decorated with green and gold drag loops, 3-1/2" h, **$250**.

Photo courtesy of Early Auction Co.

Slag glass dome, 24" d, caramel slag, curved **200.00**

Steuben
3-1/2" h, shape #985, opal, green and gold drag loops, straight rim.................. **250.00**
4" h, shape #64, gold Aurene, scalloped rim, fleur-de-lis mark, price for matched set of four **525.00**

4-1/8" h, shape #853, verre-de-soie, engraved festoon pattern, ruffled rim **200.00**
4-1/4" h, Aurene, gold, ribbed, fleur-de-lis mark......... **125.00**
4-1/4" h, shape #938A, gold, inverted urn form, ribbed **160.00**
4-1/4" h, shape #2268, verre-de-soie, ribbed............. **75.00**
4-1/2" h, bell shape, alabaster body, irid green and gold hooked feather, fleur-de-lis mark, price for pr..... **1,200.00**
4-1/2" h, shape #2533, calcite, acid etched Warwick pattern **95.00**
4-3/4" h, shape #823-1/2, verre-de-soie, engraved hanging flower pattern **175.00**
4-3/4" h, shape #2533, calcite, acid etched oak leaf and acorn pattern............... **90.00**
4-3/4" h, shape #7198, opal, Marbellite.................... **50.00**
5" h, acid etched calcite, scrolling pattern, fleur-de-lis mark, price for set of three **300.00**
5" h, shape #672, verre-de-soie, trumpet shape, ribbed, price for pr........... **125.00**
5" h, shape #799, tulip shape, green and gold pulled feathers, 1" re-glued chip **65.00**
5" h, shape #819S, green and gold drag loop design, ruffled rim................... **225.00**
5" h, tulip shape, gold Aurene, fleur-de-lis mark, price for matched pr................. **225.00**
5" w, mushroom shape, gold Aurene hooked pulled feather on opal ground, additional zipper dec **350.00**
5-1/4" h, tulip shape, gold Aurene, unmarked, price for matched pr................. **175.00**
5-1/2" h, shape #2327, calcite, acid etched ivy pattern, price for three **500.00**
5-1/2" h, shape #2354, calcite, acid etched Lumene pattern **70.00**

Tiffany
3" h, irid gold, internally dec in coin spot pattern, scalloped rim, price for matched set of four, one with minute fitter rim chip............................ **500.00**
5-1/4" h, ribbed, conical, Favrile, irid, price for matched set of five, two with very minor fitter rim chips......... **1,200.00**

Lampshades, left: opal ribbed shade, gold interior, **$115**; right: iridescent gold, 24 ribs, 4-3/4" h, **$85**.

Photo courtesy of Early Auction Co.

Unidentified American maker

4" h, irid gold, bell shaped
.... **80.00**
4-1/4" h, irid gold, bell shaped
.... **90.00**
4-1/4" h, irid gold, ribbed
body.............................. **85.00**
5" h, bulbous, Calcite, price
for pr **100.00**
5-1/2" h, irid, opal green
pulled feather.............. **100.00**
5-1/2" h, irid, gold and white
pulled feather.............. **125.00**

LAMPS AND LIGHTING

History: Lighting devices have evolved from simple stone-age oil lamps to the popular electrified models of today. Aime Argand patented the first oil lamp in 1784. Around 1850, kerosene became a popular lamp-burning fluid, replacing whale oil and other fluids. In 1879, Thomas A. Edison invented the electric light, causing fluid lamps to lose favor and creating a new field for lamp manufacturers. Companies like Tiffany and Handel became skillful at manufacturing electric lamps, and their decorators produced beautiful bases and shades.

Reproduction Alert.

Astral

11" h globe, 26" h overall, Cornelius & Co., gilt brass weighted base with Gothic detailing, applied prism ring with ovoid frosted etched glass globe with Greek key and floral designs, patent 1897, electrified, flakes on rim................... **775.00**
22-1/2" h, sq white marble base, ribbed then turned brass column, cut glass prisms, frosted shade with etched

Salesman's sample, Aladdin lamp kit, original case with Aladdin lamp, two shades, mantles, chimney, and advertisements, **$250**.

Photo courtesy of Dotta Auction Co., Inc.

flowers and vintage dec, electrified **250.00**
24-5/8" h, grapevine etched colorless glass shade, gilt metal font, glass prisms, standard with Rococo bronze fittings, flared, ribbed, blue glass shaft with gilt highlights, white marble base, electrified, imperfections, America, 19th C **920.00**

Banquet

Classical Revival, 21-3/8" h, Goldsmiths Co., English, early 20th C, silver plate and cut glass, bowl form cut glass oil font, fluted Corinthian column, tapered sq section loaded base with flower filled urns connected by swags, electrified...... **800.00**
Victorian, 30-1/2" h, cranberry shading to pink satin glass shade, set with amber, red, and green jewels, pink shaded cased glass font, column fitted on enameled iron base, burner mkd "Kosmos Brenner," c1880
.... **980.00**

Boudoir

Aladdin, 14-1/2" h, 8" d, reverse painted bell shade, pine border, floral molded polychromed metal base **225.00**
Handel, 14" h, 7" d, gilt-finished spelter base, reverse painted etched glass shade with umber harbor scene, orange sky, shade stamped "Handel 6450," Handel Lamps cloth tag on base, chips to patina **1,150.00**

Boudoir lamp, Art Deco style skyscraper shape, light blue glass, original wiring, **$300**.

Heintz Art Metal Shop, Buffalo, NY, 9-1/4" h, 8-1/2" d, bronze shade with cut-out Art Nouveau style flowers and foliage, in three sections, similar dec in silver overlay on round bronze base, paper label, two dents . **1,265.00**

Obverse painted scenic, 13-1/2" h, closed top mushroom-cap glass shade with textured surface mounted on gilt metal handled lamp base, weighted foot, hand-painted silhouetted forested landscape scenes, rim marked "Patented April 29th, 1913" **1,150.00**

Pittsburgh Lamp, Brass & Co., 14" h, 7" d shade, reverse painted ribbed shade, winter landscape of black barren trees on snowy ground, blue shading to yellow and orange ground, metal base with raised foliage dec, raised "P.I.B. & Co." 2080" on base **635.00**

Van Erp, Dirk, 12" x 10-1/2", hammered copper and mica, four panel shade, single socket, small beanpot base, orig patina, open box mark **9,000.00**

Chandelier, cobalt blue, bell shaped globe, matching smoke shade, original metal fixtures, **$395**.

Photo courtesy of Wiederseim Associates, Inc.

Chandelier, Victorian, basket form, gilt metal basket weave, crystals in interstices, large glass finial rising from center of basket, eight scrolling arms with acanthus leaf terminations, crystal swirl glass bobeches, four ascending scrolls ending in acanthus leaves and berries, crystal drops throughout, 24" h, 27" d, **$1,955**.

Photo courtesy of Alderfer Auction Co.

Chandelier

Arts & Crafts

18" h, 14-1/2" d, hammered bronze frame with pierced designs, suspending hammered bronze socket holders with four gold Aurene glass shades, c1910 **1,380.00**

27" h, 32" d, six panels, red brass, replaced mica panels, three-light cluster, orig dark patina, period chain and ceiling cap **2,300.00**

AVEM, 27-1/2" d, mold blown art glass, six arms terminating in candle lights, alternating with scrolls, silvered metal mounts, c1935, wiring restored **600.00**

Degue, 30" h, 19" d, colorless mold-blown and etched glass shade with stylized flowers and leaves, wrought iron frame with vine ornamentation, sgd "Degue 534," France, c1930 .... **600.00**

Empire-style, 31" l, 20th C, gilt metal and cut glass, six light, top with six outscrolled flat leaves hung with crystals, slender reeded standard with central cut glass orb, flat leaf ring supporting six short serpentine scrolled candle arms offset by pierced ribbon-tied laurel wreaths, strung throughout with crystal strands, end of standard with further crystals **1,100.00**

Morreau, 20" h, 20" d, gilt and emb iron frame suspending four leaded-glass domed shades, central matching spherical shade, frame emb "The Morreau Co." **1,100.00**

Muller Freres, France, 31" h, 17-1/2" d, five triangular-etched glass shades with geometric designs, wrought iron frame, signed "Muller Freres Luneville, c1930 .... **1,060.00**

Desk

Handel, 18-1/2" h, 10-1/2" d, lobed harp base, swiveling single socket, leaded green slag glass geometric shade, orig dark bronzed patina, base and shade stamped "Handel" **2,200.00**

Steuben, 20" h, 7" d, bronze, adjustable, irid hammered glass shade, orig patina, shade sgd "Steuben" **860.00**

Student, 23-1/2" h, brass frame and adjustable arm, white glass shade, early 20th C **260.00**

Tiffany, 13-1/2" h, 7" d swirl dec irid green ribbed dome Damascene shade cased to white, marked "L.C.T" on rim, swivel-socket bronze harp frame, rubbed cushion platform, five ball feet, imp "Tiffany Studios New York 419" **3,740.00**

Unknown maker

20-1/4" h, brass, ribbed gold irid bell-form shade, unsgd **300.00**

25" h, 4" d frosted blue satin shade with tadpole dec, adjustable brass arm and dome base **200.00**

Desk, orange and white marbleized turtle shaped top panel, blue and white marbleized slag side panels, trophies on sides, acorn on pull chain, **$295**.

Photo courtesy of Dotta Auction Co., Inc.

Early American

Betty lamp, 10" h, tin, saucer base, weighted column, attached handle, some damage to wick support **150.00**

Cage lamp, 6" d, wrought iron, spherical, self righting gyroscope font, two repaired spout burners **500.00**

Candle holder, 19" h, wrought iron, hanging type, primitive twisted arms and conical socket **385.00**

Candle stand, 57-1/4" h, 24-1/2" w, wrought iron, double arms, brass candleholders and drip pans, attributed to PA, 18th C, pitting, losses to drip pans **8,100.00**

Fluid

3-1/2" h, blown glass, colorless, conical font, applied foot, applied angular handle with thumb rest and medial channel, rough pontil mark, 1820-40 .... **250.00**

5" h, blanc de chine, figural, small boy with heart-shaped medallions around necks, each holds small bowl on his head for lamp oil and small wick, minor rim flakes, price for pr **250.00**

5-1/4" h, blown glass, colorless, ball font, wafer attached to pressed base with extended round corners, possibly Boston & Sandwich Glass Co., Sandwich, MA, 1840-60, minor base chips at low points................... **70.00**

6" h, blown glass, colorless, flattened font, solid stem, round base, pewter collar **150.00**

6-1/2" h, blown glass, colorless, blown font attached with wafers to pressed lacy base, drop burner, some roughness, edge flakes **265.00**

6-3/4" h, blown glass, colorless, blown font with etched swag and tassel design, pressed stepped base, fluid burner, edge flakes **150.00**

6-3/4" h, blown glass, colorless, conical font, ringed wafer attached to pressed stepped base, possibly Boston & Sandwich Glass Co., Sandwich, MA, 1840-60, base chips **70.00**

7-1/2" h, blown glass, colorless, urn shaped font, disk wafers, pressed sq stepped base with vertical ribbing between extended round corners, pewter collar, correct pewter and tin whale burner, rough pontil mark, possibly Boston & Sandwich Glass Co., Sandwich, MA, 1830-45, chips and flakes to base............................ **145.00**

7-1/2" h, blown threaded glass, light cranberry with opposing white spiraling threads, font attached to reeded brass stem, single marble base, early #2 brass collar, probably Joseph Walter & Co. Flint Glass Works or Boston & Sandwich Glass Co., 1860-75, some manuf bubbles at base of font interior causing minor thread distortion.................. **1,980.00**

9-3/4" h, blown glass, colorless, bulbous font, ringed wafer attached to pressed

base, early pewter collar with correct whale oil burner, possibly Boston & Sandwich Glass Co., Sandwich, MA, 1830-45, minor base chips, slight lean to font **200.00**

10-1/2" h, blown glass, colorless, bulbous font, bladed wafer, pressed paw-foot base, early pewter collar, possibly Boston & Sandwich Glass Co., Sandwich, MA, 1830-45 .... **880.00**

10-1/2" h, blown glass, colorless, urn shaped font, ringed and disk water construction, large blown and hollow ball shaped knop, pressed stepped base, early brass collar, double tube fluid burner with caps and chain, possibly Boston & Sandwich Glass Co., Sandwich, MA, 1830-45, normal flakes under base........................... **660.00**

11-1/4" h, pressed glass, colorless, Loop font, paneled hexagonal base, pewter collar and cap, minor roughness, price for pr.................. **200.00**

13-3/4" h, white cut to cranberry glass font, brass collar, marble and brass base with lime green glass stem insert........................... **650.00**

14-1/2" h, cut overlay, star and quatrefoil, opaque white cut to colorless font, connected to white alabaster/clambroth Baroque base, early #2 brass collar and connector, probably Boston & Sandwich Glass Co., 1860-80, overlay abrasions.................. **990.00**

Grease, 6-1/2" h, tin, brass labels "S.N. & H.C. Ufford, Boston," saucer base with concentric rings, one missing shade brackets and ring carrier, soldered repairs, price for pr **1,250.00**

Hanging, 22-1/2" l, 4-3/4" d, wrought iron, "U"-shaped swing hanger with long hook, wick holder with chicken finial **175.00**

Lace maker's, 7-3/4" h, colorless, round blown font attached to blown base, hollow stem **375.00**

Loom light, 14-3/4" h, wrought iron, candle socket, trammel **500.00**

Miner's lamp, 7-3/8" h, cast and wrought iron, chicken finial, replaced hanger **110.00**

Peg, 2" d, 4-1/2" l, overlay glass, pink cut to white cut to clear, frosted peg attached with clear wafer, brass collar........... **450.00**

Petticoat, 9" h, tin, round pan base, large ring handle applied to one side of column, small pick and chain attached to handle **260.00**

Rush light holder, 9-1/2" h, wrought iron, candle socket counter weight, tripod base, penny feet, tooled brass disk at base of stem, simple tooling **470.00**

Skater's lamp, 6-3/4" h, brass, clear glass globe marked "Perko Wonder Junior," polished, small splint in top of brass cap **160.00**

Student, 19" w, 7-1/4" h, brass, embossed "MILES PATENT" on whale oil font, adjustable candle holder and pierced shade, removable tin snuffer, brass ring finial, weighted dish base, traces of black paint, England, late 18th/early 19th C, candle holder loose from drip pan...... **1,650.00**

Taper jack, 5" h, Sheffield silver on copper, old repairs **195.00**

Floor lamp, Handel, single socket harp, chipped glass hemispherical shade reverse painted with moonlit tropical scene with tall ship, shade marked "Handel 65-749," cloth label on base, original bronze patina, 56-1/2" h, 14" d, **$7,000**.

Photo courtesy of David Rago Auctions, Inc

Floor, Gustav Stickley, mahogany, silk-lined wicker shade, wrought iron hardware, buttressed base, original finish, branded on bottom, drilled hole on side, some breaks in shade, socket shaft broken, 58" h, **$2,990**.

Photo courtesy of David Rago Auctions, Inc.

Floor

Bradley and Hubbard, 56" h, 7" d, small domed leaded glass shade, green slag glass, gold key border, open framework adjustable standard, domed circular foot **400.00**

Faries Mfg. Co., Decatur, IL, 65-1/4" h, 12" d, bright chrome torchere, flaring trumpet shade, diecast mark **150.00**

Handel

56-1/2" h, 14" d, chipped glass hemispherical reverse painted shade, moonlit tropical scene with tall ship, orig bronze patina, single socket harp, shade mkd "Handel 65-749," cloth label on base.................... **7,000.00**

64" h, 24" d yellow and amber opalescent bent glass paneled shade with faux lead came, green diamond details, five-light, patinated copper columnar base, scrolling feet, marked "HANDEL" on base **9,780.00**

Sarfatti, Gino, manufactured by Arteluce, Italy, 74-1/4" h, c1950, three arm, adjustable, steel, wood, and leather, c1950 .... **3,750.00**

Tiffany/Aladdin, 50" h, 10" d spun bronze shade, reflective white int., marked "Tiffany Studios New York," adjustable bridge lamp base with Arabian

Nights motif, orig dark bronze patina, elaborate platform base, stamped "Tiffany Studios New York 576" **2,990.00**

Unknown maker, 57-1/4" h, black and gold painted metal, topped by three acanthus scrolls, tripartite base with pad feet, Baroque style, electrified **765.00**

Yellin, Samuel, 61-1/2" h, 17-1/2" d, wrought iron, twisted tripod base, conical finial, two socket frame, mkd "Samuel Yellin Phila PA" **4,000.00**

Hanging lamp, white glass shade with hand painted leaves and flowers, clear glass oil font, brass fixtures, electrified, **$350**.

Photo courtesy of Dotta Auction Co., Inc.

Hanging lamp, glass, blue shading to cream, red flowers with yellow centers, green leaves, original hanging chain, **$350**.

Hanging lamp, tin conical shade, embossed brass base, electrified, **$250**.

Hanging

American, 19th C, 18" h, patinated metal and cut glass, hall type, candle socket, Gothic arches, diamonds and flowerheads dec **1,380.00**

Arts and Crafts

17" drop, 22-1/2" d, four massive iron cross bars, hand hammered and bronzed surface, support chocolate slag glass shades with brass fleur-de-lis guards, electrified **950.00**

30" drop, 20-1/2" d brass and slag glass shade, linked metal chain suspending shade composed of eight panels of green, caramel, and white bent slag glass panels, dropped apron with emb and cut-out brass border overlay with Dutch windmills, trees, and cottages over band of multicolored slag glass, prisms below **920.00**

Handel, Meriden, CT, early 20th C, 11" d, reverse painted, model number 6997, mushroom-shaped glass shade decorated on exterior and interior with exotic blue and gold birds, burgundy and green floral branches and leaves, bronzed metal fittings, stamped "Handel," shade sgd and numbered **3,290.00**

Morgan, John, and Sons, NY, attributed to, 39-1/2" h drop, 25-1/4" d, 11-1/2" h leaded shade, verdigris bronze leaves surrounding ceiling hook suspending four chains supporting six-socket domed shade, similar bronze leaf dec, dropped apron, shade with striated green, amber, and white slag glass segments, round transparent purple "jewels" form grape-type clusters, few cracked segments **6,325.00**

Perzel, 40-1/4" d, chrome, metal, and glass **1,225.00**

Tiffany, 18" l, 15" d, attributed to Tiffany Glass and Decorating Co., late 19th C, square green and opalescent diamond-shaped glass jewels arranged as central pendant chandelier drop, twisted wire frame **2,990.00**

Unknown maker, 32" h, two 6-1/2" h amber etched shades, brass, slender hanging stem, repaired wiring **375.00**

Piano

Handel, 17" l, gilt leaded lavender and opalescent yellow leaded shade suspended from bronze base, scrolled arm, unmarked, attributed to, c1915 .... **750.00**

Tiffany, 6-3/4" h, 19" l tripartite gold amber glass turtleback shade, framed in bronze, three center gold irid turtleback tiles, single-socket swiveling "dog leg" shaft, shade and weighted base imp "Tiffany Studios New York" **4,025.00**

Table

American, early 20th C

19-1/4" h, 15-1/2" d, 20 radiating caramel and white slag glass panels on domed shade, medial geometric green glass border, alternating green and caramel slag glass border, undulating dropped apron, two-socket fixture, ribbed trefoil base with brown/green patina, minor corrosion, some cracked segments **920.00**

24-3/4" h, 18" d reverse painted shade, hemispherical frosted glass shade, int. painted with trees and foliage silhouetted against yellow-orange shaded sky and water, two-socket bronze patinated cast metal base, raised scroll, foliate, and flower motif, base marked "A & R Co.," minor wear **920.00**

Table lamp, Gone With the Wind style, hand painted red, white, and pink morning glories, red beaded fringe trim, electrified, **$200**.

Photo courtesy of Dotta Auction Co., Inc.

Table lamp, four sided metal shade with pink slag glass inserts and pierced work gallery, wick adjuster marked "Made in US of America," square font with pierced floral decoration, waisted pedestal with square base supported on four paw feet, electrified, 22-1/2" h, **$300**.

Photo courtesy of Alderfer Auction Co.

Baccarat, attributed to, 36" h, blown molded glass, deep emerald green columns and fonts with relief twist designs, black marble bases, brass and brass plated fittings, harp and finial, fittings replaced, pr **1,380.00**

Table, Bigelow and Kennard, leaded glass shade, gothic geometric pattern in white and light green slag glass, three-socket bronze-patinated base, unmarked, 21-1/2" h, 16" d, **$4,025**.

Photo courtesy of David Rago Auctions, Inc.

Bigelow Kennard, Boston, 26" h, 18" d domed leaded shade, opalescent white segments in geometric progression border, brilliant green leaf forms repeating motif, edge imp "Bigelow Kennard Boston/Bigelow Studios," three socket over Oriental-style bronze base cast with foo dog handles, Japonesque devices ... **2,875.00**

Boston Glass Works, early 20th C, 22" h, 18-1/2" d bent panel slag glass shade, floral and foliate overlay, bronze patina over six radiating striated caramel and white bent slag glass panels, two-socket fixture with similar illuminated base, minor patina wear, few dents **750.00**

Bradley and Hubbard, Meriden, CT, early 20th C

18" h, frosted domed shade with stylized floral dec in burgundy, brown, and green, sgd urn form base **750.00**

22" h, 15-3/4" d reverse-painted shade with eight lilies in gold and earthtones, shade decorated on exterior with textured brown blades, patinated brown metal strapwork base, maker's stamp on standard, one socket needs repair. **2,710.00**

Duffner and Kimberly, New York, 26" h, 24-1/2" d dome leaded glass shade with tuck-under irregular rim, multicolored blossoms with yellow centers, green leaves, long stemmed flowers extending to top on segmented white background, three socket bronze lobed shaft with quatraform shaped base **7,435.00**

Table lamp, Handel, reverse painted textured shade with wooded landscape, shade marked "Handel 6159, JB" with three slash marks below, bronze base stamped "Handel," cloth tag sewn to felt on underside, 23" h, **$8,000**.

Photo courtesy of Alderfer Auction Co.

Table lamp, Handel, chipped glass shade reverse painted by John Bailey, moonlight tropical scene with tall ship, shade marked "Handel 6391, John Bailey," unmarked three socket bronze base with clefs, original cap, some verdigris on base, 24" h, 18" d, **$8,100**.

Photo courtesy of David Rago Auctions, Inc.

Handel, Meriden, CT 22-1/2" h, 17-1/2" d reverse painted domical glass shade, band of black eyed susans with orange petals, brown centers, and green leaves against yellow ground, outlined on textured exterior in black, sgd "Handel 6956 BD," three sockets with acorn pulls, bronzed metal vasiform base **3,290.00**
23" h, 18" d chipped reverse pained shade, pink and green bouquets of wild roses and butterflies, two socket base, orig pierced cap, some verdigris to bronze patina, shade mkd "Handel 6688," base unsigned......... **9,000.00**
23-1/4" h, 15" d ribbed glass reverse painted shade, tall ships on sea, classical acanthus leaf three-socket base, some verdigris to bronze patina, orig cap, Handel 5887R, base unsigned, small chips to edge of shade................... **5,500.00**
23-1/2" h, 18" d conical shade with light green ground and blue gray lower border, segmented by band of pink apple blossoms on branches, stamped "Handel Lamps Pat'd No. 979664," sgd "Handel 6742," three sockets on bronze metal standard, some spotting.......... **3,820.00**
24" h, 18" d chipped glass reverse painted shade, moonlit tropical scene with tall chip painted by John Bailey, three socket bronze base with clefs, orig cap, shade mkd "Handel 6391 John Bailey," base unmarked **8,000.00**
25" h, 18" d chipped glass reverse painted shade, moonlight forest scene with brook, three socket, four footed Arts & Crafts base with some verdigris to bronze patina, orig cap, Handel 6324 .... **6,000.00**
Heintz, 15" h, 13" d, sterling on bronze, single socket, mushroom shaped shade and flaring base overlaid with delicate sprig pattern, bronze patina, few short scratches **1,600.00**
Jefferson, 17" h, 12" d, reverse painted scenic shade with winter scene on textured satin shade, brass candlestick base, unsigned, c1915 .... **460.00**

La Verre Francais, 19" h, cased glass, frosted ext. over swirled orange, yellow, and cobalt blue, sgd on both shade and base, electrified, replaced shade holder........................... **1,350.00**
MB Co., 20-1/2" h, paneled shade, conical base, openwork silver-plate grape vine designs, five panels of green and white slag glass, cast leaf finial, engraved leaves on base, base marked "Made and Guaranteed by the MB Co. USA," electrified, five sockets.................. **1,200.00**
Muller Fres, 20" h, frosted domed shade with mottled dec, inscribed "Mueller Fres Luneville," brass tri-support stylized fleur-de-lis base **1,000.00**
Pairpoint, 20-1/2" h, 11-1/2" d domed closed top mushroom-cap glass shade, Vienna, coralene yellow int., painted stylized olive green leaves and red berries, gold outline on ext., ball-decorated ring supported by four arms, quatraform base molded with foliate devices, imp "Pairpoint Mfg Co., 3052" **2,070.00**

Table, Pittsburgh Lamp Co., Pittsburgh, PA, 1890-1930, large domical reverse-painted "Call of the Wild" shade with partial paper label, unsigned owl base, 22" h, 18" d, **$2,820**.

Photo courtesy of Skinner, Inc.

Pittsburgh Lamp, Brass and Glass Co., Pittsburgh, c1920, model no. 1595, 27" h, 17-3/4" d domed frosted and textured glass shade, interior painted with mountainous landscape, exterior painted with pine trees, paper manufacturer's label affixed to interior, three-socket patinated metal ribbed standard set into weighted metal base, scroll, shield, floral, and foliate motifs in relief, wear to patina **1,955.00**
Steuben, attributed to, 23" h, jade green long neck vasiform glass standard with white threading spiraling on neck, double socket, leaf-form bronzed metal mounts **420.00**

Table lamp, Seuss, leaded glass shade with red and white blossoms, green foliage, four-socket tree trunk base, unmarked, original bronze patina, one replaced socket, 23" x 23", **$11,000.**

Photo courtesy of David Rago Auctions, Inc.

Suess Ornamental Glass Co., Chicago, 23" h, 22" d leaded glass shade with stylized yellow, orange, green, and white slag flowers and leaves, brass-washed base, unmarked **5,350.00**

Tiffany Studios, 22-1/2" h, 16" d dome shade, layered and striated leaded glass segments designed as tulip blossoms and leaves, red, orange, amber, blue, and green, metal rim tag imp "Tiffany Studios New York 1456," three-socket bronze base with three pronged crutch supporting oval shaft, sq base with mottled brown and green patina, round disk on base imp "Tiffany Studios New York 444" **32,220.00**

Unidentified maker, 52-1/2" h, alabaster, fluted gourd-shaped body with flared top, black marble base, brass paw feet and fittings, tall brass stem, double electric sockets **300.00**

Van Erp, Dirk, 17-1/2" h, 13" d, hammered copper classical base, four paneled mica shade with vented cap, single socket, fine orig patina and mica, open box mark/San Francisco **9,200.00**

Williamson, Richard, & Co., Chicago, 25" h, 20" d peaked leaded glass dome, amber slag bordered by red tulips, pink and lavender-blue spring blossoms, green leaf stems, carved glass, mounted on four-socket integrated shaft with stylized tulip blossoms above leafy platform, imp "R. Williamson & Co./Washington & Jefferson Sts./Chicago, Ill," restored cap at top rim **3,220.00**

LANTERNS

History: A lantern is an enclosed, portable light source, hand carried or attached to a bracket or pole to illuminate an area. Many lanterns have a protected flame and can be used both indoors and outdoors. Light-producing materials used in early lanterns included candles, kerosene, whale oil, and coal oil, and, later, gasoline, natural gas, and batteries.

Coach, E. Miller & Co., America, late 19th/20th C, kerosene, hourglass-shaped beveled glass walls, black painted sheet iron components with nickel-plated brass trim, maker's mark on burner, wear, 22-3/4" h, **$450.**

Photo courtesy of Skinner, Inc.

Barn, 5 1/4" w, 5-3/4" d, 8-3/4" h, mortised wood frame, four panes of glass, bentwood handle, tin cover over top vent, twisted wire latch, old patina, discolored glass in door, minor damage, make-do repaired split on top **825.00**

Candle
9-3/8" h, tin, double folding door covering orig glass panel, folding handle in back, brass candle socket with spring loaded push-up in base, traces of black paint, door hinges glued, lid possible replacement . **230.00**

11-1/4" h, tin, octagonal paneled glass globe, punched tin top, ring handle, and font, globe surrounded by wire guards, replaced tin font with candle socket, war, minor damage, traces of japanning on top **300.00**

12" h, wood frame, beveled base and top, pegged construction, arched tin deflector on top, wire bale carrier, old refinishing, old pieced restoration on top, one pane cracked, minor insect damage **250.00**

Dark room, 17" h, orig black paint, white striping, tin kerosene font and burner "Carbutt's Dry Plate lantern, PA April 25th 1882" label **75.00**

Folding, 10" h, tin, glass sides, emb "Stonebridge 1908" .. **75.00**

Globe, 17-1/2" h, fixed pear-shaped globe, pierced tin frame, ring handle, traces of black paint, America, mid-19th C **215.00**

Dietz, Acme Inspector Lamp, embossed handle, L.V.R.R., **$395.**

Photo courtesy of Dotta Auction Co., Inc.

Hall, 26" h, glass and polychrome, gold painted flat leaf top suspending cut glass drops, joined by curved scrolls, suspending ovoid shade formed by five curved colorless glass panels in metal framework topped by ribbon tied laurel branches, accented with faceted bead trim, bead and glass prism trefoils, Italian, late 19th C **2,100.00**

Dietz, loop handle, large round clear lens, **$225**.

Photo courtesy of Dotta Auction Co., Inc.

Japanese, Patterson Bros., Lansing, MI, adv, panes with General U. S. Grant, puppies, young girl, and wilderness scene **195.00**

Jeweled, 11-1/2" h, sheet brass, punched designs radiating out from faceted blue, red, green, and pale gold glass jewels, bottom marked "NH Car Trimming Co. New Haven, Conn," ring hanger **250.00**

Miner, 9-3/4" h, heavy duty iron and brass, threaded brass font and hasp, iron top with brass label "Thomas & Williams, Cambria Type...Aberdare," minor dents **115.00**

Nautical, 23" h, 11" d, masthead, copper and brass, oil fired, orig burner, label reads "Ellerman, Wilson Line, Hull," mid-19th C **265.00**

Painted tin, 15-3/4" l, 12" d, 19-3/4" h, triangular black painted tin frame with glass panels, int. mirror paneled reflector, small tin kerosene lamp, glass chimney, America, late 19th C, seam separations **175.00**

Paul Revere Type, 16" h, punched tin, circular punching on door and body, cone top, round handle, light overall pitting **275.00**

Railroad, Pennsylvania Railroad, 5" h red globe, marked "Keystone Lantern Co., Philadelphia," wire ring base **445.00**

Hanging, Bradley and Hubbard, Meriden, CT, c1910, pagoda style, octagonal paneled metal roof over eight caramel slag glass panels with metal overlay, B&H mark, 8" d, 18" l lantern, drop including ceiling plate 30" l, **$1,300**.

Photo courtesy of Skinner, Inc.

Tin, punched decorated with flower motif, leaded glass panels and hinged door, scalloped back plate, single candle holder, **$85**.

Skater
7" h, brass, grass green globe **550.00**
7" h, brass, peacock blue globe, slip in to with short crack in glass **175.00**
7" h, tin, amethyst globe, top mkd "Jewel," rust........ **835.00**
7" h, tin, cobalt blue globe, two scratches, rust **520.00**
7" h, tin, deep amethyst globe, top and globe both mkd "Jewel," rust............. **1,100.00**

Tin
12" h, tin, four panes of glass, hinged door, wire guards, wire bale handle, old worn gold paint, wear.................. **115.00**

12" h, tin, tin base and top with pierced stars and diamonds, molded glass globe with wire guards, ring handle, removable tin font, brass burner, traces of black paint............................. **200.00**

12-1/2" h, pear-shaped mold blown glass globe, pierced tin top and base, ring handle, tin oil font with two spring clips, burner missing, soldered repairs, black repaint.. **300.00**

15" h, brass base and top with hinged, fluted peak, onion-shaped blown glass globe, wire guards, two wire bale handles, removable tin font held by two wires, burner missing, minor dents .. **230.00**

16-1/2" h, tin, old black paint, clear brown glass insert, applied rings top and bottom, pierced diamonds and stars, make-do candle socket is old glass inkwell, New England, edge dents on base ... **250.00**

LEEDS CHINA

History: The Leeds Pottery in Yorkshire, England, began production about 1758. Among its products was creamware that was competitive with that of Wedgwood. The original factory closed in 1820, but various subsequent owners continued until 1880. They made exceptional cream-colored wares, either plain, salt glazed, or painted with colored enamels, and glazed and unglazed redware.

Marks: Early wares are unmarked. Later pieces are marked "Leeds Pottery," sometimes followed by "Hartley-Green and Co." or the letters "LP."

Reproduction Alert:
Reproductions have the same marks as the antique pieces.

Creamer, creamware, hand-painted floral sprays on body, garland on neck, applied loop handle, inscription beneath spout "Stir the wet 1797," 5-5/8" h, rim repair, flaking to spout and foot ring, **$728.**

Photo courtesy of Alderfer Auction Co.

Bowl, 8" d, pearlware, shallow, molded basketwork, pierced loop, rim edged in cobalt blue, 18th C **225.00**

Charger, 14-3/8" d, yellow urn with double handles and brown swag design holds cobalt blue, brown, and yellow flowers, green foliage, blue line detail surrounding dec, scalloped blue father edge, in-the-making separation along inner edge, minor glaze flakes **1,870.00**

Chop plate, 11-1/4" d, blue and yellow brown polychrome flowers, green foliage, white ground, blue scalloped feather edge, wear, old chip beneath rim **825.00**

Creamer, yellow, brown, and green tulip, umber and green sprig design on sides, dark brown stripe on rim and applied handle, flakes on table ring **800.00**

Cup and saucer, handleless
Blue, yellow, green, and goldenrod floral design, underglaze blue brushed crescent mark **220.00**
Brown rim stripes, blue, green, shades of gold, and yellow floral swag, flakes, chips on saucer table ring, stains on cup **150.00**

Cup plate
4" d, round, green feathered edge **150.00**

4-1/4" d, octagonal, green feathered edge **200.00**
Dish, 5-3/4" l, leaf form, green feathered edge, imp "Rogers" **225.00**
Egg cup, 2-3/4", creamware, reticulated **150.00**
Medallion, 1-3/4" x 2-5/8" d, set of 12, black basalt, assorted subjects, shapes and sizes, impressed marks, England, late 19th C **530.00**

Pitcher, trailing orange, blue and green floral vines, 5-1/4" h, **$1,035.**
Photo courtesy of Pook & Pook.

Miniature
Creamer and sugar, blue flower, green and brown buds, tooled handle on 2-3/4" h creamer, minor flake on 2-1/2" h sugar **350.00**
Cup and saucer, handleless, pearlware, gold flower, green and brown leaves **275.00**
Teapot, cov, 4" h, yellow bands with green, orange, blue, and brown sprigs, flakes **450.00**
Mug, 5" h, multicolored polychrome floral dec **250.00**
Mustard pot, cov, 3 3/8" h, pearlware, cobalt blue bands, 18th C, minor rim chips ... **425.00**
Pepper pot, 4-1/2" h, green feathered edge, roughness, loss on rim and near holes **200.00**
Plate
8" d, green feathered edge, patterned design **225.00**
8-1/2" d, green feathered edge, imp border design of acanthus leaves, imp "Riley" **200.00**
10" d, pearlware, central floral spray surrounded by trailing vine, brown, ochre, green, and blue, feathered blue scalloped edge, 18th C **275.00**

Plate, green scalloped edge, blue and yellow flowers, brown and green leaves, 8-3/4" d, **$575.**
Photo courtesy of Pook & Pook.

Platter
17-1/4" x 14", oval, blue feathered edge **1,600.00**
19" x 14-1/4", elongated octagonal form, green-feathered edge, rim wear **525.00**
Sauce boat, underplate, 7-1/2" l, 3-3/4" h sauce boat, 6-1/2" x 5-1/4" underplate, green feathered edge, small crack on base, minor edge roughness **335.00**
Teapot, cov, creamware, 4-3/4" h, intertwined ribbed handle, molded floral ends and flower finial, polychrome enameled rose **3,025.00**
Tureen, cov, 8-1/2" h, cov with pierced rim, melon finial, enamel dec, feather band trim, floral sprays and wreaths, urn designs, late 18th C, slight edge nicks and enamel flaking **980.00**
Waste bowl, 4-1/4" d, 3" h, blue band, green, gold, mustard, and black leaves, minor flakes on table ring **110.00**

LENOX CHINA

History: In 1889, Jonathan Cox and Walter Scott Lenox established The Ceramic Art Co. at Trenton, New Jersey. By 1906, Lenox formed his own company, Lenox, Inc. Using potters lured from Belleek, Lenox began making an American version of the famous Irish ware. The firm is still in business.

Marks: Older Lenox china has one of two marks: a green wreath or a palette. The palette mark appears on blanks supplied to amateurs who hand painted china as a hobby. The Lenox company currently uses a gold stamped mark.

Bouillon cup and saucer, Detroit Yacht Club, palette mark **85.00**

Candlesticks, pr, Holiday, 7-1/2" h, pillar **140.00**

Chocolate set, cov chocolate pot, six cups and saucers, Golden Wheat pattern, cobalt blue ground, 13-pc set ... **275.00**

Coffeepot, Lenox Legend **170.00**

Cream soup, Tuxedo, green mark **40.00**

Cup and saucer, Alden.... **25.00**

Dinner plate, Montclair, two platinum bands, set of four **195.00**

Dinner service
   Golden Wreath, service for 20, serving pcs, 138 pcs .. **650.00**
   Imperial pattern, 12 each dinner plates, salad plates, bread plates, cups, saucers, one platter.................. **275.00**

Gravy boat and underplate
   Biltmore Hotel, New York City, Gorham silver plated lid, base mkd "2047 Lexon 12 oz," lid mkd "The Biltmore 1917 Gorham 02702 Electroplate," 7-1/4" d, 4-3/4" h **165.00**
   Tuscany, bird and scroll dec, gold rim....................... **260.00**

Pitcher, imitation of Tucker China, multicolored floral decoration, gold trim, **$250**.

Photo courtesy of Dotta Auction Co., Inc.

Honey pot, 5" h, 6-1/4" d underplate, ivory beehive, gold bee and trim..................... **85.00**

Jug, 4" h, hp, grapes and leaves, shaded brown ground, sgd "G. Morley" **250.00**

Perfume lamp, 9" h, figural, Marie Antoinette, bisque finish, dated 1929..................... **650.00**

Platter
   Castle Garden, coupe shape, gold trim, small **200.00**
   Plum Blossoms, medium **240.00**

Salt, 3" d, creamy ivory ground, molded seashells and coral, green wreath mark........... **35.00**

Server, Holiday, 16" x 11", oval **155.00**

Shoe, white, bow trim..... **190.00**

Vase, modern production, **$45**.

Tankard set, 14-1/2" h tankard, four 5-1/2" h steins, hp by W. Clayton, tippling Monk draining vintage bottle on tankard, different monk posed on each stein, ornate handles, shaded green grounds, wear to gilt at rim interiors **995.00**

Teapot, Weatherly, coupe shape, platinum trim **215.00**

Vase, 11-3/4" h, 4-1/2" d, corset shape, pink orchids dec by William Morley, green stamp mark, artist sgd **850.00**

Vegetable dish, cov, Lenox Legend............................ **260.00**

LIBBEY GLASS

1896–1906

History: Edward Libbey established the Libbey Glass Company in Toledo, Ohio, in 1888 after the New England Glass Works of W. L. Libbey and Son closed in East Cambridge, Massachusetts. The new Libbey company produced quality cut glass, which today is considered to belong to the brilliant period.

In 1930, Libbey's interest in art-glass production was renewed, and A. Douglas Nash was employed as a designer in 1931.

For more information, see *Warman's Glass*, 4th edition.

Center bowl, shape #3019, amberina, pedestal base, pontil signed with trademark, c1917, 12" d, 5-3/4" h, ex-Maude Feld, **$6,250**.

Photo courtesy of Early Auction Co.

Art glass

Bowl, 5-1/8" h, amberina, crimson shading to amber, Diamond Quilted pattern, applied amber peaked overlay extends mid-length, orig Libbey paper label, ex-Maude Feld **2,100.00**

Bud vase, 9" h, shape #3008, amberina, slender neck, wafer base, c1917 .... **1,250.00**

Center bowl, 12" d, 5-3/4" h, shape #3019, amberina, pedestal base, pontil sgd with trademark, c1917, ex-Maude Feld **6,250.00**

Cologne bottle, 8-3/4" h, catalog #3041, amberina, ribbed elongated body shading from fuchsia to amber, raised disk base, blown stopper-dauber with fuchsia amber shading, pontil sgd with trademark **1,100.00**

Compote, 7-1/4" d, 8-3/8" h, catalog #3017, amberina, Libbey acid stamp mark, partial paper label, ex-Maude Feld **4,000.00**

Creamer and sugar, 5-3/8" h creamer, 3-1/2" h, 4-3/4" d sugar, crystal, blue-green opaque dot trim, dark blue-green glass feet, polished pontil **475.00**

Miniature, vase, 3-1/4" h, amberina, flattened oval neck extend to flaring circular body, fuchsia shading to amber, applied rigaree collar, raised dec, ex-Maude Feld **850.00**

Sugar bowl, open, 4-1/2" w, 2-3/4" h, opaque blue, satin finish, two handles, c1893 .... **550.00**

Cocktail set, ice bucket, stemware, tumblers, Silver Foliage pattern, frosted ground, silver leaves, **$125.**

Toothpick holder

2-1/4" h, amberina, crimped bulbous body, deep red to amber, Inverted Baby Thumbprint pattern, ex-Maude Feld **600.00**

2-1/2" h, amberina, Diamond Quilted pattern, barrel shape **250.00**

Underplate, 6-1/4" d, amberina, Swirl pattern, scalloped rim **150.00**

Vase

2-7/8" h, tapering ovoid, circular neck, amberina, shades from very deep ruby to amber, raised and imp dec, orig "Libbey Amberina" label, ex-Maude Feld **750.00**

Compote, catalog #3017, amberina, Libbey acid stamp mark, partial paper label, 7-1/4" d, 8-3/8" h, ex-Maude Feld, **$4,000.**

Photo courtesy of Early Auction Co.

4-3/4" h, sq mouth, deep crimson extending to graduated double circular body, raised ovals, inverted circular dec, four applied amber shells, ex-Maude Feld **2,100.00**

7-1/2" d, mushroom shape, clear ribbed glass, allover yellow finish **120.00**

8" h, ftd, amberina, Optic Ribbed pattern, acid stamped "Libbey Amberina" **500.00**

Rose bowl, Maize pattern, cased, yellow exterior, creamy white interior, **$195.**

Photo courtesy of Alderfer Auction Co.

Cut glass

Banana boat, 13" x 7" x 7", scalloped pedestal base, 24-point hobstar, hobstar, cane, vesica, and fan motifs, sgd **1,500.00**

Bowl, 8" d, 4" h, three brilliant cut thistles surround bowl, flower in center, scalloped edge, etched

"Libbey" label, price for pr **400.00**

Charger, 14" d, hobstar, cane, and wreath motifs, sgd ... **300.00**

Miniature lamp, 2" sq base, 10-3/8" h, pinwheel design, sgd **425.00**

Tumble-up, star burst, hobstar, fern, and fan motifs, minor handle check **725.00**

Vase, 18" h, No. 982, Senora pattern, cut glass, ftd, hexed vesicas, deep miter cuts, three 24-point hobstars at top between crossed miter cuts, small stars and trellises, clear knob and stem, scalloped foot cut with extended single star, Libbey over saber mark, c1896-1906, some flaws **2,500.00**

LIMOGES

History: Limoges porcelain has been produced in Limoges, France, for more than a century by numerous factories, in addition to the famed Haviland.

Marks: One of the most frequently encountered marks is "T. & V. Limoges," on the wares made by Tressman and Vought. Other identifiable Limoges marks are "A. L." (A. Lanternier), "J. P. L." (J. Pouyat, Limoges), "M. R." (M. Reddon), "Elite," and "Coronet."

Plate, hand painted, yellow roses, gold lattice trim, green mark, and signed in gold on back "Mary Barber, Feb. 17, 1903, from Hasseltine Moore," 8" d, **$65.**

Bowl, 4-1/2" h, ftd, hp, wild roses and leaves, sgd "J. E. Dodge, 1892" **85.00**

Box, cov, 4-1/4" sq, cobalt blue and white ground, cupids on lid, pate-sur-pate dec **195.00**

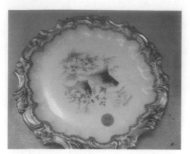

Fish plate, hand painted, two fish and aquatic plants, gold scrolling border, marked "Souvenir Limoges, T & V France," **$60**.

Photo courtesy of Dotta Auction Co., Inc.

Cache pot, 7-1/2" w, 9" h, male and female pheasants on front, mountain scene on obverse, gold handles and four ball feet **225.00**
Cake plate, 11-1/2" d, ivory ground, brushed gold scalloped rim, gold medallion, marked "Limoges T & V" **75.00**
Candy dish, 6-1/2" d, ftd, two handles, silver overlay, white ground, c1920 .... **95.00**
Chocolate pot, 13" h, purple violets and green leaves, cream-colored ground, gold handle, spout, and base, sgd "Kelly JPL/France" **350.00**
Creamer and sugar, cov, 3-1/4" h, purple flowers, white ground, gold handle and trim **100.00**
Cup and saucer, hp, roses, gold trim, artist sgd **75.00**
Dessert plates, 8-1/4" d, Laviolette, gilt scalloped rim, printed green husk trim, center violet and grape sprays, retailed by Lewis Straus & Sons, New York, late 19th/early 20th C, price for 12-pc set **220.00**
Dresser set, pink flowers, pastel blue, green, and yellow ground, large tray, cov powder, cov rouge, pin tray, talc jar, pr candlesticks, seven-pc set **425.00**
Figure, 25" h, 13" w, three girls, arms entwined, holding basket of flowers, books, and purse, marked "C & V" and "L & L" **460.00**
Fish service, 22-3/4" platter, ten 9-1/4" plates, sgd "A. R. Bullock 1894" **1,555.00**
Hair receiver, blue flowers and white butterflies, ivory ground, gold trim, marked "JPL" **80.00**

Lemonade pitcher, matching tray, water lily dec, sgd "Vignard Limoges" **350.00**
Nappy, 6" d, curved gold handle, gold scalloped edges, soft pink blossoms, blue-green ground **35.00**

Oyster plate, five oyster-shaped wells, white ground, pink and white roses, green leaves, blue forget-me-not borders, gold trim, signed "GDA France" in black, green wreath mark, **$250**.

Photo courtesy of Wiederseim Associates, Inc.

Oyster plate, five oyster-shaped wells, round center well, white ground, multicolored florals, gold trim, marked "G. D. & Co., Limoges France" in green, "1205" in red, **$195**.

Oyster plate, five deep oyster wells, white ground, green fern decoration, gold trim, marked "T & V France," **$150**.

Photo courtesy of Wiederseim Associates, Inc.

Oyster plate, 9-1/4" d, molded, scalloped edge, gilt rim, enamel dec of poppy sprays, raised gilt detailing, marked "A. Lanternier & Co., Limoges," early 20th C, price for set of eight..... **1,500.00**
Panel, 4-1/2" x 3-3/8", enameled, Christ with crown of thorns, framed **250.00**
Pitcher, 6" h, 5-1/8" d, platinum handle, platinum mistletoe berries and leaves, gray and pink ground, Art Deco style, marked "J. P. Limoges, Pouyat" **155.00**
Plaque, 7-5/8" x 4-1/2", enameled, cavalier, after Meissonier, multicolored garb and banner, late 19th C .. **460.00**

Punch bowl, grapes and leaves decoration, separate stand with four lion paw feet, 14-3/4" d, 9-3/4" h, **$700**.

Photo courtesy of Joy Luke Auctions.

Plate
  8" d, transfer scene of peacocks and flowers, hp border.......................... **290.00**
  9-1/2" d, Cavalier smoking pipe, marked "Coronet" **90.00**
Punch bowl, 14" d, hand pained grapes, marked "T& V Limoges France Depose," minor repairs **320.00**
Snuff box, cov, hp, wildflowers and gold tracery, pink ground, artist sgd, dated 1800 .... **200.00**
Tankard set, 14" h tankard, four mugs, hp, grape dec, gold and green ground, five-pc set. **450.00**

Trinket box, white rabbit on lid, green base with orange carrot, figural rabbit closure, **$90**.

Photo courtesy of Joy Luke Auctions.

Tea set, 9-1/2" h cov teapot, two 3" h cups, two 4-1/2" d saucers, 15" d tray, cream ground, floral dec, gold trim, red stamp "L. S. & S. Limoges France," green stamp "Limoges France" on two saucers, slight wear **500.00**
Vase, 15" h, hand painted, sgd "Florence Sladnick" **350.00**

LITHOPHANES

History: Lithophanes are highly translucent porcelain panels with impressed designs. The designs result from differences in the thickness of the plaque; thin parts transmit an abundance of light, while thicker parts represent shadows.

Lithophanes were first made by the Royal Berlin Porcelain Works in 1828. Other factories in Germany, France, and England later produced them. The majority of lithophanes on the market today were made between 1850 and 1900.

Candle shield, 9" h, panel with scene of two country boys playing with goat, castle in background **275.00**
Fairy lamp, 9" h, three panels, lady leaning out of tower, rural romantic scenes **1,250.00**
Lamp, 20-3/4" h, colored umbrella style shade, four panels of outdoor Victorian scenes, bronze and slate standard, German **675.00**
Night lamp, 5-1/4" h, sq, four scenes, irid green porcelain base, gold trim, electrified
.... **650.00**
Panel
   PPM, 3-1/4" x 5-1/4", view of Paterson Falls **190.00**
   PR Sickle, 4-1/4" x 5", scene of two women in doorway, dog, and two pigeons, sgd, #1320
   .... **100.00**
   Unmarked, 6" x 7-1/2", Madonna and Child **175.00**
Pitcher, puzzle type, Victorian scene, nude on bottom ... **175.00**
Stein, regimental, half liter
.... **200.00**
Tea warmer, 5-7/8" h, one-pc cylindrical panel, four seasonal landscapes with children, copper frame, finger grip and molded base **250.00**

LIVERPOOL CHINA

History:
Liverpool is the name given to products made at several potteries in Liverpool, England, between 1750 and 1840. Seth and James Pennington and Richard Chaffers were among the early potters who made tin-enameled earthenware.

By the 1780s, tin-glazed earthenware gave way to cream-colored wares decorated with cobalt blue, enameled colors, and blue or black transfers.

Bubbles and frequent clouding under the foot rims characterize the Liverpool glaze. By 1800, about 80 potteries were working in the town producing not only creamware, but soft paste, soapstone, and bone porcelain.

Reproduction Alert:
Reproduction Liverpool pieces were documented as early as 1942. One example is a black transfer-decorated jug made in the 1930s. The jugs vary in height from 8-1/2 to 11 inches. On one side is "The Shipwright's Arms"; on the other, the ship Caroline flying the American flag; and under the spout, a wreath with the words "James Leech."

A transfer of the Caroline also was used on a Sunderland bowl about 1936 and reproduction mugs were made bearing the name "James Leech" and an eagle.

The reproduction pieces have a crackled glaze and often age cracks have been artificially produced. When compared to genuine pieces, reproductions are thicker and heavier and have weaker transfers, grayish color (not as crisp and black), ecru or gray body color instead of cream, and crazing that does not spiral upward.
Bowl, creamware
   10-7/8" d, black transfer printed and polychrome enamel dec, int. with British sailing ship, red, white, blue, gold, and green enamels above inscription "James and

Sarah Venn Bridgewater, 1796," rim dec with military devices, outside with vignettes of "Poor Jack," and "Billy's Farewell," sea creatures and mermaids, imperfections **560.00**
   11-3/8" d, black transfer printed, polychrome enamel dec, int. with American sailing vessel Apollo, border of military devices, ext. with nautical themes, coat of arms, vignette of lovers holding heart, above inscription "J. & S. Appleton," green, yellow, red, white, and blue enamels, imperfections **5,875.00**
Cup and saucer, handleless, black transfer, bust of Washington and other gentleman on cup, "Washington, His Country's Father" on saucer, hairline in cup **330.00**

Jug, black transfer printed creamware, "THE UNION OF THE TWO GREAT REPUBLICS" on a banner under French and American flags, Liberty cap, wreath, weapons, and flowers, reverse with profile bust portrait of George Washington over banner with "Long Live the President of the United States," flanked by Liberty saying "My Favorite Son," Justice saying "Deafness to the Ear that will patiently hear & Dumbness to the Tongue that will utter a Calumny against the immortal Washington," early 19th C, crack, loss, spout chips, 6-5/8" h, **$2,500.**

Photo courtesy of Skinner, Inc.

Jug, creamware
   7-1/4" h, 3-1/2" d, transfer printed, obverse with compass and verse, reverse with The Sailors Adieu, minor imperfections **750.00**
   8" h, 4" d, transfer printed, obverse with The Sailor's Return, reverse with courting couple above verse "A Sailor's life's a pleasant life…" on other, motto reserve below spout "From Rocks & Sands and every ill…" imperfections
   .... **550.00**

8-3/4" h, black transfer printed and polychrome dec, obverse American Militia, oval scenic reserve with militiaman with flag, ships, and armament, surrounded by inscription, reverse with American sailing vessel above banner inscribed "Success to Trade," American eagle with Jefferson quote, dated 1802 under spout, red, blue, green, and yellow enamels, yellow highlight around rim, minor imperfections **3,525.00**

8-3/4" h, black transfer printed, "L. Insurgent and Constellation, Feb 10, 1799," depicting naval battle with American frigate on left, French frigate on right, inscription beneath each, reverse "Shipbuilding," oval wreath inscribed "Success to the Wooden Walls of America" beneath spout, imperfections **1,650.00**

9" h, 4-3/4" d, transfer printed, obverse with Washington, Liberty, and Franklin viewing map of early 19th C US, reverse with three-masted ship painted with polychrome enamels, eagle and shield, standing figure of Hope below spout, imperfections ... **990.00**

9-1/8" h, 5" d, transfer printed, obverse with Commodore Preble, reverse with Commodore Prebles Squadron Attacking the City of Tripoli Aug. 3, 1804, imperfections **2,185.00**

9-1/4" h, 4-5/8" d, transfer printed and painted with polychrome enamels, obverse with Hope, reverse with three-masted ship flying American flag, American eagle below spout with Jefferson quote, dated 1804, imperfections **3,740.00**

9-1/2" h, 4-1/2" d, transfer printed and painted with polychrome enamels, obverse with Boston Fusilier, reverse with "United We Stand, Divided We Fall," eagle and shield below spout, imperfections **17,250.00**

10" h, 5" d, transfer printed and painted with polychrome enamels, obverse with Proscribed Patriots, reverse with "Success to America

whose Militia…," eagle and shield with Jefferson quote dated 1802 below spout, repaired **3,220.00**

10-1/4" h, 4-7/8" d, transfer printed, obverse with Salem Shipyard and verse, revere with transfer printed with polychrome enamels of Boston Frigate, transfer "LW" in cartouche above eagle and shield, imperfections . **4,890.00**

10-1/2" h, black transfer printed, obverse with mortally wounded officer surrounded by his aides, successful sharpshooter waves his cap from background, reverse with British Man-of-War, beneath spout and rim dec with floral devices, imperfections **1,650.00**

11-1/2" h, 5-3/4" d, transfer printed, obverse with three-masted ship, reverse with The Joiners Arms, eagle and shield below spout, repaired **865.00**

11-3/4" h, 6-5/8" d, transfer printed, obverse with ship *Massachusetts*, reverse with map of Newburyport Harbor with "Success to the Commerce of Newburyport" on other, gilt embellishments, circular reserve of Columbia, minor imperfections **14,950.00**

Jug, pearlware, 6-1/4" h, black transfer printed, obverse with American eagle with ribbon in its beak, inscribed "E. Pluribus Unum," 15 scattered stars above it's head, reverse with vignette of embracing couple, fleet of sailing vessels below spout, rim dec with scattered blossoms, black enamel highlights on rim, shoulder, and handle edges, minor imperfections **1,120.00**

Plate, 10" d, black transfer printed, ten are dec with sailing vessels, one inscribed "Returning Hopes" with lady waiting for return of her lover's ship, minor imperfections, price for 11 pc set................. **1,570.00**

Sauce boat, 5-3/4" l, oval, paneled sides, underglaze blue floral dec, attributed to Pennington & Part, c1780 .... **460.00**

Tureen, cov, 12-1/4" d, 9-1/2" h, domed cov with oval handle, round base, black transfer dec

on lid, int., and ext. depicting figure flanked by two coat-of-arm shields, two monograms "TF" and "BW" within oval, imperfections **1,100.00**

LLARDÓ PORCELAINS

History: Brothers Vicente, Jose, and Juan Llardó opened a workshop in Almácera, Spain, in 1953. Through the talents and artistry of these brothers, the workshop has grown into an international company known for its fine porcelains. The first retail outlet for Llardó porcelains was opened in 1955 in Valcenia. The factory has now expanded to employ over 2,500 artisans at the City of Porcelain. Through the years, some of the figures have been retired. In 1988, Llardó opened a museum in New York City.

The second generation of the Llardó family has gradually prepared themselves to take on responsibilities of managing an international company. In 1984, three of the children of the founders, one for each brother, joined the Board of Administration. Gradually, other members of the second generation have also joined the company. Since September 2003, two children of each of the founding brothers are now on the Board of Administration: David and Juan Vicente for Vicente, Mamen and Maria Jose for Jose, and Rosa and Maria Angeles for Juan. The board is presided by Juan Vicente Llardó. The goal of the current board is to keep the flame of its artistic ancestors alive through high quality porcelains.

Mother pig and two piglets, **$65.**

As with many collectibles, the value of the porcelain figure can be enhanced by having the original box, packing materials, etc. Some members of the Llardó family travel to retail outlets and sign pieces, adding extra value to the sculpture.

Angel
Angelic Harmony **600.00**
Angel's wish **95.00**
Angel with baby **115.00**
Angel with clarinet **350.00**
Heavenly cellist **200.00**
Little angel with tambourine
.... **100.00**
Winter angel **300.00**

Carousel horse, original box, **$185.**

Bird with cactus in flower, #130, original box, **$265.**

Animal
Donkey in love **300.00**
Elephant family **800.00**
Elk **900.00**
Sleeping bunny **100.00**
Spike Dinosaur **100.00**
Ballerina
Act II, 1979 .... **900.00**

Ballerina waiting backstage, 1969 .... **400.00**
Dressing for the ballet **350.00**
En Pointe, 1998 .... **415.00**

Child with bear, original box, **$165.**

Cat
Cat and mouse **80.00**
Kitty Care **200.00**
Kitty Patrol.................. **185.00**
Nao Cat, playing with ball of string, c1981 .... **65.00**
Dog
Beagle puppy, lying.... **250.00**
Dalmatian, begging.... **300.00**
German Shepard with pup
.... **400.00**
Playful Poodle **150.00**
People
At the Ball **600.00**
Breezy Afternoon **180.00**
Dancer **185.00**
Don Juan **650.00**
King's Guard, 1990 ..... **900.00**
Mother and daughter, dressed in nightgowns, mkd "Paul Sebastian, 1990," 7-1/2" h **185.00**

Three figures, left: girl and cat seated on ottoman, **$95**; center: baseball player, **$95**; right: Victorian girl, pink jacket, long blue skirt, **$75.**

Three figures, left: girl tending to sick dog, **$95**; center: boy reading as puppy jumps over back, **$85**; young couple, girl attempting to give a kiss, **$65.**

Spanish dancer, original box, **$195.**

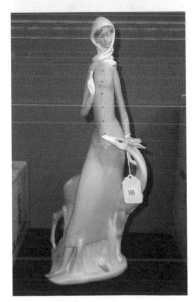
Woman with deer, **$180.**

LOETZ

History: Loetz is a type of iridescent art glass that was made in Austria by J. Loetz Witwe in the late 1890s. The Loetz factory at Klostermule produced items with fine cameos on cased glass, good quality glassware for others to decorate, as well as the iridescent glasswares more commonly associated with the Loetz name.

For more information, see *Warman's Glass*, 4th edition.

Marks: Some pieces are signed "Loetz," "Loetz, Austria," or "Austria."

Vase, taupe ground with some brown inclusions, applied iridescent amethyst loopings, 6" h, **$195.**

Atomizer, 7" h, cameo, lemon yellow ground overlaid in blue, cameo cut leafy stemmed cockle shell flowers, sgd "Loetz" in cameo, c1910, no stopper **435.00**

Bowl
 5" h, squatty, everted quadrafold rim, irid green, three applied tadpoles **175.00**

5-1/2" h, ovoid body, quadrafold pinched rim, irid amber green, undulating irid blue horizontal dec, sgd "Loetz Austria" **1,900.00**
7" d, 8-1/2" d, opalescent, pinched rim, columnar support, triangular foot, engraved with artist cipher for Maria Kirschner **3,585.00**
13" d, Schaumglas, green and white mottled body **125.00**
13-1/2" d, 7-1/2" h, ruffled rim, wide body with dimpled shoulder, irid red, gold linear dec, polished pontil, unsigned **825.00**

Bud vase, 8-1/2" h, figural flower form, irid, ruffled, crystallized leafy foot, irid gold entwining leafy branch **1,000.00**

Cabinet vase, 3" h, bulbous, tricorn rim, green, overall blue finish.................................... **130.00**

Candlestick, 15-1/2" h, irid finish, base chip.............. **115.00**

Cup, 3-3/4" d, round bowl, gold and polychrome irid, applied handle, incised "Loetz Austria" **290.00**

Decanter, 11-1/4" h, Orpheus pattern, irid green, turquoise medallions, controlled threading, slight loss to threading at top **175.00**

Low bowl, 8-1/2" d, 3" h, fold down rim, int. with bluish-gold irid, ext with detailed irid oil spot dec, slight rim roughness **250.00**

Mantel lamp, 11" h, Federzeichnung, satin, cased in blue, airtrapped dec, overall gold tracery, enameled dec rim **1,100.00**

Rose bowl, 6-1/2" d, ruffled purple irid raindrop dec.. **265.00**

Sweetmeat jar, cov, 5" h, irid silver spider web dec, green ground, sgd **450.00**

Urn, 9-1/4" h, ovoid, irid, blue oil spot dec, inscribed "Loetz, Austria" **1,600.00**

Vase
 4" h, shouldered, irid green textured body, blue thumbprints, undulating lines **1,000.00**
 4-1/4" h, corset shape, irid gold body cased in pink, sterling silver overlay **1,000.00**
 4-3/4" h, squatty stick, irid blue.............................. **200.00**

Vase, baluster, flared ruffled rim, iridescent brown and yellow mottled glaze, floral silver overlay, bright green interior, wear to silver at rim, 11" h, **$225.**

Photo courtesy of Alderfer Auction Co.

 5" h, melon ribbed, everted rim, irid green, blue coin spots, vertical lines..... **500.00**
 5" h, Titania, shading from deep ruby to emerald, overall silver irid **2,200.00**
 5-1/4" h, olive green, wavy silver blue irid stripes, "Loetz Austria" inscribed on pontil **1,150.00**
 5-1/2" h, Feerzeichnung, flattened bulbous body extends to cylindrical neck, ruffled rim, shading from green to opal, gilt highlights, floral leaf and vine dec **900.00**
 6" h, ovoid shouldered, bright lemon yellow, irid blue undulating lines, sgd "Loetz Austria" **1,200.00**
 6-1/2" h, Schaumglas, red and white mottled bulbous body **315.00**
 7" h, figural, fish, gold body, irid Papillion finish, applied green fin feet **700.00**
 7" h, gold colored, irid finish, c1900......................... **250.00**
 7" h, Marmorierte Glas, tapered polished marble ground, enameled dec at shoulder and fluted rim, pastel interior, c1890-1910.................. **500.00**

7-1/4" h, emerald green, diamond quilted mother of pearl pattern, overlaid sterling silver florals, trailing vines, inscribed "L" and "Sterling," c1890 .... **1,850.00**

8" h, cylindrical, irid opal, applied branch dec, losses **110.00**

8" h, ovoid, quadrafold pinched rim, irid green graduating to cinnamon, blue oil spots and wavy lines dec **1,200.00**

8" h, Schaumglas, green and white mottled body, orig paper label **250.00**

8-1/2" h, bulbous stick, deep irid amber, irid blue pulled work dec, gold highlights **1,300.00**

9-1/2" h, Rusticana, waisted cylindrical, irid blue on green body **250.00**

12-3/4" h, deep red, silver blue irid "Rubin Phanomen" finish, c1890 .... **3,450.00**

Luster Ware

History: Lustering on a piece of pottery creates a metallic, sometimes iridescent, appearance. Josiah Wedgwood experimented with the technique in the 1790s. Between 1805 and 1840, lustered earthenware pieces were created in England by makers such as Adams, Bailey and Batkin, Copeland and Garrett, Wedgwood, and Enoch Wood.

Luster decorations often were used in conjunction with enamels and transfers. Transfers used for luster decoration covered a wide range of public and domestic subjects. They frequently were accompanied by pious or sentimental doggerel, as well as phrases that reflected on the humors of everyday life.

Copper luster was created by the addition of a copper compound to the glaze. It was very popular in America during the 19th century, and collecting it became a fad from the 1920s to the 1950s. Today it has a limited market.

Using a gold mixture made pink luster. Silver luster pieces were first covered completely with a thin coating of a "steel luster" mixture, containing a small quantity of platinum oxide. An additional coating of platinum, worked in water, was then applied before firing.

Sunderland is a coarse type of cream-colored earthenware with a marbled or spotted pink luster decoration, which shades from pink to purple. A solution of gold compound applied to the white body developed the many shades of pink.

The development of electroplating in 1840 created a sharp decline in the demands for metal-surfaced earthenware.

> **Reproduction Alert:** The market for copper luster has been softened by reproductions, especially creamers and the "polka" jug, which fool many new buyers. Reproductions are heavier in appearance and weight than the earlier pieces.

Creamer, copper luster, wide cream colored band, two panels of rust transfer depicting woman listening to musician, band of magenta and rust leaf garland decoration on cream ground, 6-1/4" w spout to handle, 5-1/2" h, small spout flake, **$80**.

Photo courtesy of Alderfer Auction Co

Canary

Child's mug, 1-3/4" h, "A Present for Charles," pink luster trim, minor wear **625.00**

Miniature, creamer, 2-3/4" h, red and green flowers, pink luster accents and rim, pinpoint flake **850.00**

Pitcher, 6-1/4" l, 6" h, baluster form, low neck and spout, sides printed with scenes titled "Attempt before the guard...," On Guard, Single Stick, Staffordshire, c1810 .... **220.00**

Copper

Goblet, 3" d, 3-3/4" h, mauve and green colored band with floral dec around mid section, c1850 .... **85.00**

Pitcher, 4" h, blue band with molded flower dec on both sides, copper luster bulbous base **50.00**

Tea cup and saucer, turquoise blue background, copper luster floral band **65.00**

Vase, 7-1/4" w, 6-1/2" h, two handles, stag scene **70.00**

Two copper luster pitchers, left: applied blue and white swirled decoration, ornate scrolled handle, **$95**; right: plain, **$75**.

Sugar bowl, covered, copper luster, blue band with enameled decoration, **$120**.

Photo courtesy of Wiederseim Associates, Inc.

Pink

Child's mug, 2" h, pink luster band, reddish hunter and dogs transfer, green highlighted foliate transfer **85.00**

Creamer, 4-3/8" h, stylized flower band, pink luster highlights and rim, ftd **75.00**

Cup and saucer, magenta transfers, Faith, Hope, and Charity, applied green enamel highlights, pink luster line borders **60.00**

Figure, 4-1/2" h, dogs, white, luster gilt collar, cobalt blue base with gilt trim, Staffordshire, pr **620.00**

Pitcher, 5-3/4" h, emb ribs, eagle, and flowers in pink and purple luster **150.00**

Maastricht Ware

Plate, 7-3/4" d, green transfer of "Employ time well," emb floral border with polychrome enamel and luster trim **75.00**

Plaque, 9-3/8" l, 8-3/8" h, rect, "The Great Eastern Steam Ship," black transfer with polychrome, pink luster shaped border **450.00**

Posset cup and saucer, tray, 5" h, wide luster bands flanked by two red bands, 19th C **295.00**

Punch bowl, 10" d, black transfer print, "The Shipwright's Arms" on int., pink luster borders on ext., imperfections **120.00**

Teapot, 12" h, House pattern, Queen-Anne style, repaired finial on lid **285.00**

Toddy plate, 5-1/16" d, pink luster House pattern, emb floral sprigs border **45.00**

Waste bowl, 6" d, House pattern **125.00**

Silver

Coffee service, 7-3/8" h cov coffeepot, cov sugar bowl, six coffee cans and saucers, silver luster grape and leaves, rust enamel accents, yellow ground **450.00**

Creamer, 4" h, 5" w, ribbed loop base, incised band near top, shaped handle **85.00**

Cup and saucer, handleless, overall floral band on cup, scattered florals on saucer **45.00**

Goblet, 4-3/8" h, silver luster grapes and vines, white ground, lustered foot **220.00**

Jug, 5-1/2" h, blue printed hunting scene, border of flowers and leaves, luster ground, Staffordshire, c1815 .... **975.00**

Pitcher, 5-1/2" h, squatty body, wide lip, overall silver luster, 19th C **95.00**

Spill vase, 4-1/8" h, gray marbleized applied vines and fruits, silver luster accents, white int., pr **95.00**

Sunderland

Bowl, 8-1/4" d, polychrome highlighted black transfers of ship and verse, pink marble luster, mid-18th C **265.00**

Creamer, 5" h, "The Sailor's Tear," outlined in florals, verse with sailing ship and "May Peace and Plenty…," luster trim **275.00**

Tea set, covered teapot, creamer and sugar, silver luster on white ground, England, **$125**.

Jug, pearlware
7" h, two oval reserves with black transfer printed portraits, "Captain Hull of the Constitution" and "Pike-be always ready to die for your country," imperfections **5,750.00**
8-3/4" h, God Speed the Plow, black and white printed transfer of farmer's coat of arms flanked by farmer and wife, surrounded by various symbols in agricultural setting, hand colored with polychrome enamels, reverse with inspirational verse, oval reserve beneath spout sgd "Mary Hayward Farmer Sandhurft Kent," embellished with pink luster and floral dec, imperfections **1,150.00**
9-3/8" h, black transfer printed, pink luster and polychrome enamel dec, obverse British ship under full sail, verse in cartouche "May Peace and Plenty On our Nation Smile and Trade with Commerce Bless the British Isle," reveres with verse in floral wreath "The Sailor's Tear," Mariner's Compass flanked by British ships under spout, imperfections... **650.00**

Mug, 5" h, black transfer of compass on front, "The Sailor's Farewell" on reverse **160.00**

Mustard pot, 4" h, loop handle **150.00**

Pitcher, 7-1/8" h, hex panels, black transfers of John Wesley on one side, verse on other, pink marble luster, c1850 .... **150.00**

Plaque, 8-1/2" l, 7-1/2" w, "Thou God Seeist Me," luster trim, Dixon mark..................... **175.00**

Plate, 10" d, center transfer print of Pike and "Be always Ready to Die for your Country," pink luster

and yellow banded border, c1820......................... **2,650.00**
Salt, master, Cloud pattern, ftd **50.00**

MAASTRICHT WARE

History: Petrus Regout founded the De Sphinx Pottery in 1836 in Maastricht, Holland. The firm specialized in transfer-printed earthenwares. Other factories also were established in the area, many employing English workmen and adopting their techniques. Maastricht china was exported to the United States in competition with English products.

Bowl, Timor pattern, 10" d, **$290**.

Bowl, 5-3/4" d, red, green, and blue agate pattern, "Petrous Regout, Maastricht" and lion mark................................. **35.00**

Cup and saucer, Oriental pattern, 3-1/4" d, 2" h cup, c1929 .... **25.00**

Pitcher, 5" h, rooster with iris and leaves, red transfer, marked "Regout & Co. Haan" **75.00**

Plate
7-1/2" d, rusty brown border, pink and yellow roses in center, Royal Sphinx mark, c1891.......................... **50.00**
8-1/4" d, Timor pattern.. **30.00**
8-1/2" d, Canton pattern, Geisha girls and man on walkway, marked "Canton, P. Regout Maastricht," c1836 .... **40.00**
10" d, Delft, blue and white windmill scene, Royal Sphinx mark............................. **50.00**

Platter, 11-1/2" d, gaudy polychrome florals, red, yellow, and green white ground ... **70.00**

1111111111111111111

MAJOLICA

History: Majolica, an opaque, tin glazed pottery, has been produced in many countries for centuries. It was named after the Spanish Island of Majorca, where figuline—a potter's clay—is found. Today, however, the term "majolica" denotes a type of pottery was made during the last half of the 19th century in Europe and America.

Majolica frequently depicts elements of nature: leaves, flowers, birds, and fish. Designs were painted on the soft-clay body using vitreous colors and fired under a clear lead glaze to impart the rich color and brilliance characteristic of majolica.

Victorian decorative art philosophy dictated that the primary function of design was to attract the eye; usefulness was secondary. Majolica was a welcome and colorful change from the familiar blue and white wares, creamwares, and white ironstone of the day.

Marks: Wedgwood, George Jones, Holdcraft, and Minton were a few of the English majolica manufacturers who marked their wares. Most of their pieces can be identified through the English Registry mark and/or the potter-designer's mark. Sarreguemines in France and Villeroy and Boch in Baden, Germany, produced majolica that compared favorably with the finer English majolica. Most Continental pieces had an incised number on the base.

Although 600-plus American potteries produced majolica between 1850 and 1900, only a handful chose to identify their wares. Among these manufacturers were George Morely, Edwin Bennett, the Chesapeake Pottery Company, the New Milford-Wannoppee Pottery Company, and the firm of Griffen, Smith, and Hill. The others hoped their unmarked pieces would be taken for English examples.

Reproduction Alert: Majolica-style pieces are a favorite of today's interior decorators. Many exact copies of period pieces are being manufactured. In addition, fantasy pieces incorporating late Victorian-era design motifs have entered the market and confused many novice collectors.

Modern majolica reproductions differ from period pieces in these ways: (1) modern reproductions tend to be lighter in weight than their Victorian ancestors; (2) the glaze on newer pieces may not be as rich or deeply colored as on period pieces; (3) new pieces usually have a plain white bottom, period pieces almost always have colored or mottled bases; (4) a bisque finish either inside or on the bottom generally means the piece is new; and (5) if the design prevents the piece from being functional—e.g., a lip of a pitcher that does not allow proper pouring—it is a new piece made primarily for decorative purposes.

Some reproductions bear old marks. Period marks found on modern pieces include (a) "Etruscan Majolica" (the mark of Griffen, Smith and Hill) and (b) a British registry mark.

Adviser: Mary D. Harris.

Note: Prices listed here are for pieces with good color and in mint condition. For less-than-perfect pieces, decrease value proportionally according to the degree of damage or restoration.

For more information, see *Warman's American Pottery & Porcelain*, 2nd edition; and *Warman's English & Continental Pottery & Porcelain*, 4th edition.

Basket
Bird on branch, pink ribbon on handle, 10" x 6-1/2" **250.00**

Yellow, angel faces on each side, 8" **200.00**

Bread tray
Floral, butterflies, pastel colors, "Waste Not Want Not" **250.00**

Bowl, footed, scallop shell and seaweed, Phoenixville, PA, 8" d, **$110**.
Photo courtesy of Wiederseim Associates, Inc.

Geranium and basketweave, "Eat thy bread with thankfulness," 12-3/4" **300.00**

Bud vase, Minton, yellow, green ribbon, triple holes, 6". **450.00**

Butter pat
Cobalt blue, sunflower **140.00**
Holdcroft, fan shape, bird in flight **175.00**
Wedgwood, chrysanthemum **150.00**

Cake stand
Etruscan, morning glory, 8-1/4" **175.00**
George Jones, leaf on napkin, white ground, 9" w, 6" h **450.00**
Wedgwood, green leaf, green ground, 8" d, 2-1/2" h .. **125.00**

Candlestick, figural
Palmer Cox Brownie, 8-1/2" h **250.00**
Wardle, water lily form, all green **125.00**

Cheese keeper, cov
Bird on branch, yellow ground, ribbon and bow accents **375.00**
George Jones, apple blossom and basketweave, 10" d **1,900.00**
Mottled brown and green, wedge shape, florals, 12" l **250.00**
Turquoise, blackberry and cow, 11-1/2" h **700.00**

Compote, Wedgwood, double dolphin, nautilus shell top, 16" **800.00**

Compote, pedestal base, decorated with pink and yellow daisies, 9" d, 5" h, **$220**.
Photo courtesy of Joy Luke.

Pair of cups and saucers decorated with pink flowers on deep blue ground, George Jones, **$1,200**.

Photo courtesy of Joy Luke.

Cup and saucer

Banks and Thorley, Basketweave and Bamboo, butterfly handle........... **275.00**

Etruscan, bamboo **125.00**

Lovebirds on branch, green and tan.......................... **75.00**

Shell shape, pink, yellow, and brown.......................... **175.00**

Humidor, cov, figural

Clown head, yellow hat and collar, 6" h **75.00**

Man, night cape and pipe, 4-1/2" h.......................... **75.00**

Oriental lady, hat, 5" h... **75.00**

Policeman, pot bellied, 10-1/2" h...................... **150.00**

Sailor, hat and beard, 5".. **50.00**

Flower pot and saucer, Morning Glory design, pink flower, green leaves, green and brown mottled ground, wear to rim, **$65**.

Fruit basket, center portrait, wire work basket, **$350**.

Jardinière and pedestal, paneled, raised floral decoration, cobalt blue decoration, pedestal with Asian figures on cobalt blue ground, green and white base, 22" d, 32" h, chipping, cracking, **$300**.

Photo courtesy of Alderfer Auction Co.

Jardinière, Wardle, Bamboo and Fern, 8"................... **550.00**

Match striker, Continental

Happy Hooligan, hat .. **100.00**

Lady with tambourine, 10-1/2" **100.00**

Man with violin, 12" **125.00**

Monk, stein and brick barrels, 8".................................... **100.00**

Monkey, cobalt blue cape, 5-1/2" **125.00**

Mug

Etruscan, Water Lily.... **250.00**

Samuel Lear, classical urn **100.00**

Wedgwood, grape and vine **150.00**

Mustache cup and saucer, Wild Rose and Rope........... **250.00**

Oyster plate

French Orchies, blue and beige, 10" d **150.00**

Minton, pink wells, 9" d **450.00**

Russian, Imperial eagle, 9-1/2" d **500.00**

Seaweed and Shell, cobalt blue center, 10" d........ **375.00**

Pitcher

Bird and bird nest, 9" h **225.00**

Gnarled tree truck and florals, 8" h............................. **150.00**

Robin, mottled, 9-1/4" h **100.00**

Stork in marsh, 11" h... **225.00**

Water lily, green and yellow, 8" h.............................. **175.00**

Plate

Bellflowers, cobalt blue, 8-3/4" d **225.00**

Bird and Fan, pebbles, cobalt blue, 9" d **150.00**

Bird in flight, fern and cattail, white ground, 8-1/2" d.. **125.00**

Blackberry and basketweave, brown, 9" d **125.00**

Platter

Dragon fly and leaf, pink border, 11-1/2" l **200.00**

Eureka, bird and fan, diamond shaped, 15-1/2" l **250.00**

Leaves and ferns, oval, greens and brown, 12" **250.00**

Plate, Shell and Seaweed, Etruscan, 7" d **$70**.

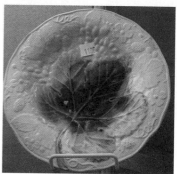

Plate, green, yellow, and pink maple leaf center, embossed white ground with strawberries, blossoms, and leaves, 8" d, **$95**.

Plate, leaf center, green, yellow, and white, **$60**.

Plate, leaf center, **$50**.

Sardine box, cov
English, green and brown
mottled **250.00**
Fielding, Fan and Scroll,
attached underplate, blue and
yellow.......................... **500.00**
Wedgwood, boat shaped
anchor finial **550.00**
Server, Holdcroft, duble leaf,
squirrel handle, 13" **675.00**
Spittoon, Etruscan, Pineapple,
yellow and green............. **500.00**
Syrup, pewter top
Holdcroft, Pond Lily,
turquoise, 3-3/4".......... **300.00**
Wedgwood, Caterer jug,
turquoise and brown, 7-1/2"
.... **250.00**
Wedgwood, Doric, mottled
cobalt blue and brown,
7-1/2" h........................ **125.00**
Teapot, cov
Basketweave and floral, pink
and turquoise, pewter lid,
6-3/4" h....................... **275.00**
Bird and Bird's Nest, figural,
brown and green, 9" ... **225.00**
Fielding, Fan and Scroll,
insect, pebble ground, cream
and purple, 7" **275.00**

Teapot, covered, seaweed and colorful
shells, pink interior, shell finial, branch
form handle and spout, embossed
bottom mark indicates manufacture by
Griffen, Smith & Hill between 1878
and 1889, impressed mark, "E24,"
9-1/2" w from handle to spout, 6-1/2" h,
small flakes on rim and spout, hairline
crack on inside lip of lid, **$400**.

Photo courtesy of Alderfer Auction Co.

Left: wall pocket, naturalistic bunch of
white radishes, unmarked, **$175**; right:
pitcher, green lily-of-the-valley
decoration on brown tree bark ground,
pink interior, **$195**.

Pyramid shape, brown, yellow,
and green, 8-1/2" **250.00**
Wild Rose, yellow pebble
ground, white flowers, 5-1/2"
.... **225.00**
Tray, Minton, bird, oak leaf
shape, 8" **500.00**
Tureen, George Jones,
mackerel on bed of ferns, 19"
.... **4,250.00**

MAPS

History: Maps provide one of the
best ways to study the growth of a
country or region. From the 16th to
the early 20th century, maps were
both informative and decorative.
Engravers provided ornamental
detailing, such as ornate
calligraphy and scrolling,
especially on bird's-eye views and
city maps.

Maps generally were published
as plates in books. Many of the
maps available today are simply
single sheets from cut-apart books.

In the last quarter of the 19th
century, representatives from firms
in Philadelphia, Chicago, and
elsewhere traveled the United
States preparing county atlases,
often with a sheet for each township
and each major city or town.
A Map of North America,
Edward Wells, London, 1700,
double page, engraved, wide
margins, 355 x 480 mm .. **635.00**
**A Map of the British Empire in
America**, from the Head of
Hudson's Bay to the Southern
bounds of Georgia, London,
c1750, engraved, folding, hand
colored and in outline, wide
margins, 265 x 325 mm
.... **260.00**

Amsterdam, French legend, matted,
framed, **$125**.

Americae Nova Tabula, Willem
Blaeu, Amsterdam, 1633, double
page, engraved, wide margins,
365 x 465 mm **2,990.00**
**A New and Accurate Map of
the World**, John Overton,
London, 1670, engraved,
folding, double-hemispheric,
margins trimmed, 390 x 515 mm
.... **8,625.00**
A New Map of Nova Scotia,
Thomas Jeffreys, London, 1750,
double page, engraved, very
wide margins, all edges tissue-
backed on verso, 325 x 415 mm
.... **220.00**
**A Plan of the Town and Chart of
the Harbour of Boston**, London,
February 1775, engraved,
folding, extracted from 1775
issue of *Gentleman's Magazine*,
290 x 350 mm.................. **220.00**
Atlas Map of Fulton County,
Illinois, 1871 .... **290.00**
Asia, Giovanni Botero, Rome,
c1595, small double page,
engraved, trimmed margins, 205
x 245 mm **300.00**
British Dominions in America
agreeable to the Treaty of 1763,
Thomas Kitchin, Dury, London,
1777, double page, engraved,
hand colored in outline, wide
margins, 445 x 540 mm .. **6,440.00**
Canada et Louisiane, George
Louis Le Rouge, Paris, 1755,
double page, engraved, wide
margins, hand colored in
outlined, 625 x 510 mm .. **375.00**
Capt. James Lane Property,
Bedford, MA, 1773, watercolor
and ink on paper, shows
distances, boundaries, and 223
acres, divided between sons
James and Samuel in
accordance with last will and
testament, "Surveyed and
divided by Stephen Davis,
Surveyor of Lands," 12-3/4" x
30-1/2", laid down on muslin,
creases and separations, tears,
fading, staining **150.00**

Haycock Township, removed from 1870s, Bucks County atlas, hand colored, **$120**.

Cruchley's New Plan of London, George Frederick Cruchley, London, 1836, engraved, 30-section map, hand colored, linen backed, orig board cover with publisher's label, 460 x 855 mm overall **175.00**
Dutch, 7-3/8" x 12-1/4", black on white engraving by O. Lindeman, red, green, brown, and yellow hand coloring showing hemispheres, contemporary 13-1/2" x 17-1/2" frame and matting, 2" tear repaired from back **250.00**
Haemisphaerium Stellatum Astrale Antiquum, Andres Cellarius, Amsterdam, 1660, double page, engraved celestial map, hand colored, wide margins, clear tear at vertical fold at lower margin just extending into image, 440 x 515 mm **2,530.00**
Jamaica, John Thomson, Edinburgh, 1817, double page, engraved, two insets showing harbors of Bluefields and Kingston, wide margins, hand colored in outline, 440 x 630 mm **320.00**
Land Survey Map of Boston Cabinet Maker Stephen Badlam, by Matthew Withington, 1786, pen and ink on paper showing parcel of land in Dorchester, Massachusetts, written description and compass star directional highlighted with watercolor, 20" x 11-1/2", creases, small edge losses, repaired tears, stains **650.00**

Philadelphia, hand colored, engraved vignettes, matted, framed, light water damage, **$350**.

Map of Oregon and Upper California, John Charles Fremont, Washington, 1848, folding, lithographed, hand colored in outline, overall browning, 905 x 755 mm **2,185.00**
Minnesota & All of Unsettled Dakota Territory, Colton, 1855, hand colored, 17" x 14"..... **95.00**
Northern America, including Russian Alaska, entire British Possessions & Danish Iceland, Colton, 1857, hand colored, 17" x 14" **95.00**
Ohio, A J. Johnson, New York, with view of capitol building in corner, from "*New Illustrated Family Atlas of the World 1864*," printed, hand colored, matted, unframed, 23" h, 29" w **75.00**

Puzzle, W. Peacock, London, Superior Dissected Maps, complete, original box, **$195**.

Philadelphia, and Liberties section, set of three, published by John Reed, engraved by James Smithers, vignettes of Pennsylvania Hospital, House of Employment, State house, each 31-1/2" x 24", provenance

descended from Gen George Meade family, late 18th C, each with some chipping, tears, foxing **9,750.00**
United States of America, W. and D. Lizars, London, c1810, engraved, folding, hand colored, margins trimmed, several folds closed at lower edge with archival tape, 395 x 460 mm **260.00**

MARBLEHEAD POTTERY

History: This hand-thrown pottery was first made in 1905 as part of a therapeutic program introduced

by Dr. J. Hall for the patients confined to a sanitarium located in Marblehead, Massachusetts. In 1916, production was removed from the hospital to another site. The factory continued under the directorship of Arthur E. Baggs until it closed in 1936.

Most pieces found today are glazed with a smooth, porous, even finish in a single color. The most desirable pieces have a conventional design in one or more subordinate colors.
Centerpiece bowl, 3-3/4" h, 8-1/4" d, flaring, incised lotus leaf design on ext., dark blue matte glaze, imp sip mark **425.00**
Chamberstick, 4" h, 4-1/2" d, bright yellow matte glaze, imp ship mark **275.00**
Flower pot, 5" d, terra cotta glaze, imp ship mark **195.00**
Humidor, 5" h, 4-1/4" d, lightly modeled stylized dark blue flora, speckled sandy ground, rare large paper label, Arthur Baggs, marked "AEB and MHC/$5.00" **4,100.00**
Tile, 6" sq, cuerda seca, polychrome trees and house, matte gray ground, mounted in period frame, ship mark, remnant of paper label, restoration to Y-shaped crack **1,725.00**

Tile frieze, two 7-1/2" sq tiles, incised lake scene, matte yellow, browns, and greens, imp mark, paper label, orig price tag on each, orig frame retaining sticker marked "o. 2-64 tiles Poplars with Reflections, Dec by A. E. Baggs, Price $10.00," minor edge nicks, kiln pops, from estate of Dr. Hall, founder of Marblehead Pottery ... **21,850.00**

Trivet, 6" sq, stylized flowers, matte blue, green, yellow, and red, imp mark, paper label, remnant of price label, from estate of Dr. Hall, founder of Marblehead Pottery **865.00**

Vase, barrel shape, painted by Hannah Tutt, yellow blossoms, green leaves, blue stems, smooth gray speckled ground, stamped ship mark and "HT," 4" h, 4-1/4" d, **$3,250.**

Photo courtesy of David Rago Auctions, Inc.

Vase, ovoid, by Arthur Baggs, incised decoration of stylized green leaves, speckled dark blue matte ground, ship mark and "M," 6-3/4" h, 4" d, **$1,500.**

Photo courtesy of David Rago Auctions, Inc.

Vase
2-3/4" d, 4-1/4" h, cabinet, tapering, designed by Arthur Baggs, dec by Hannah Tutt, incised chevron pattern, two-tone mottled matte green glaze, imp ship mark, artist's cipher **5,350.00**
3-3/4" h, bulbous, smooth indigo matte glaze, imp ship mark.......................... **475.00**
4-1/4" d, 6-1/4" h, geometric, lightly tooled, stylized light brown trees, matte speckled sand-colored ground, imp ship mark **4,750.00**
5" d, 6" h, beaker shape, brown gooseberry leaves, indigo branches, dark blue ground, imp ship mark **1,955.00**
6" h, curved rim, widening at base, mottled lavendor semi-matte glaze, imp mark, c1915-36 .... **650.00**
6" d, 6-1/4" h, barrel shape, blue and gray band of flying geese, speckled gray ground, remnant of imp ship mark, drilled bottom **4,025.00**
8" d, 6-1/4" h, fan shape, matte blue glaze, imp mark, paper label **320.00**

Vessel, 2-1/4" h, 4-1/2" d, squatty, incised and painted stylized pattern in dark green on lighter green ground, ship mark, incised "MT" .. **3,750.00**

Wall pocket, 5-1/4" w, 5" h, speckled gray ext., robin's egg blue int., unmarked **295.00**

MATCH HOLDERS

History: The friction match achieved popularity after 1850. The early matches were packaged and sold in sliding cardboard boxes. To facilitate storage and to eliminate the clumsiness of using the box, match holders were developed.

The first match holders were cast iron or tin, the latter often displaying advertisements. A patent for a wall-hanging match holder was issued in 1849. By 1880, match holders also were being made from glass and china. Match holders began to lose their popularity in the late 1930s, with the advent of gas and electric heat and ranges.

Grading Condition. The following numbers represent the standard grading system used by dealers, collectors, and auctioneers:

    C.10 = Mint
    C. 9 = Near mint
    C.8.5 = Outstanding
    C.8 = Excellent
    C.7.5 = Fine +
    C.7 – Fine
    C. 6.5 = Fine – (good)
    C. 6 = Poor

Hanging type, cast iron, scrolled decoration, **$35.**

Advertising
Ballard Flour, 6-5/8" x 1-7/8", tin litho, figural obelisk shape, Egyptian hieroglyphics, C.8- **925.00**
Buster Brown Bread, 6-7/8" x 2-1/8", tin litho, baker serving bread to Buster Brown and friends, wear to match basket, C.8-............................ **475.00**
Ceresota Prize Bread Flour, 5-3/8" x 2-1/2", figural, diecut, tin litho, boy slicing bread, C.8+ **300.00**
Moxie Nerve Food, 7-1/8" x 2-5/8", diecut tin litho, C.8++ **600.00**
Vulcan Plow Co., 7-7/8" x 2-3/4", diecut, C.8+ **825.00**
Wrigley's Juicy Fruit Gum, 4-7/8" x 3-3/8", tin litho, red, white, and black, C.8.. **400.00**

Bisque, 4" h, 3-5/8" d, natural-colored rooster with beige basket, two compartments, round base with pink band **135.00**

Desk type, upright brass holder with foliate border, square striated marble base with recessed center, felt pads, **$45**.

Brass, 3" h, bear chained to post, cast, orig gilt trim .. **225.00**
Bronze, 3" h, shoe, mouse in toe
.... **125.00**
Cast iron, figural, high-button shoe, 5-1/2" h, black paint, c1890 .... **50.00**
Glass, 3" h, 3-1/4" d, shaded rose to pink overlay satin, ball-shape, glossy off-white lining, ground pontil.................. **155.00**
Majolica
  Bull dog, striker, large. **440.00**
  Happy Hooligan with suitcase, striker, rim nick to hat.............................. **110.00**
  Monk, striker, hairline in base
  .... **140.00**
Papier-mâché, 2-3/4" h, black lacquer, Oriental dec **25.00**
Porcelain, seated girl, feeding dog on table, sgd "Elbogen"
.... **125.00**

Hanging type, tin, places for matches in back, "Burnt Matches" in front, **$15**.

Hanging type, cream painted metal, black silhouette of girl with parasol in garden, **$35**.

Sterling silver, 1-3/4" x 2-1/2", hinged lid, diecut striking area, cigar cutter on one corner, lid inscription "H. R." and diamond, inside lid inscribed "Made for Tiffany & Co./Pat 12, 09/Sterling"
.... **95.00**
Tin, 2-3/8" h, top hat, hinged lid, orig green paint, black band
.... **65.00**
Torquay pottery, 2" h, 3-1/8" d, ship scene, reads "A match for any Man, Shankin" **85.00**

MATCH SAFES

History: Pocket match safes are small containers used to safely carry matches in one's pocket. They were first used around the 1840s. Match safes can be found in various sizes and shapes, and were made from numerous materials such as sterling, nickel-plated brass, gold, brass, ivory, and vulcanite. Some of the most interesting and sought after ones are figurals in the shapes of people, animals, and anything else imaginable. Match safes were also a very popular advertising means from 1895-1910, and were used by both large and small businesses.

Reproduction Alert:
Reproduction, copycat, and fantasy match safes abound. Reproductions include Art Nouveau styles, figural/novelty shapes, nudes, and many others. Fantasy and fakes include Jack Daniel's and Coca-Cola.

A number of sterling reproduction match safes are marked "925" or "Sterling 925." Any match safe so marked requires careful inspection. Many period, American match safes have maker's marks, catalog numbers, 925/1000, or other markings. Period English safes have hallmarks. Beware of English reproduction match safes bearing the "DAB" marking. Always verify the date mark on English safes.

Check enameled safes closely. Today's technology allows for the economic faking of enamel motifs on old match safes. Carefully check condition of enameling for telltale clues.

Note: While not all match safes have a striking surface, this is one test, besides size, to distinguish a match safe from a calling card case or other small period boxes. Values are based on match safes being in excellent condition.

Bowling motif, man smoking cigarette, holding bowling ball, German silver, 2-1/2" x 1-5/8", **$375**.

All match safe photos courtesy of George Sparacio.

Adolphe Thiers, French statesman, figural bust, nickel plated, 2" x 1-3/8"........... **400.00**
Advance Traction Engine, celluloid wrapped, multicolored graphics, 2-3/4" x 1-1/2" . **300.00**
Anheuser Busch, engine and coal tender, falling lid type, by C. J. Hauck, nickel-plated brass, patent Aug. 14, 1883, 3" x 1-5/8"
.... **250.00**

Baby face in tapered shirt, figural, brass, 2-3/8" x 1-1/8" **200.00**

Bat woman motif, by Wm. Kerr Co., cat. #1197, sterling silver, gold wash inside, 2-3/8" x 1-1/2" **800.00**

Book shaped, double ender, ivory, sterling initials, 1-3/4" x 1" **35.00**

Bowling motif, man smoking cigarette, holding bowling ball, German silver, 2-1/2" x 1-5/8" **375.00**

BPOE, elk, clock between antlers, by Webster Co., sterling silver, gold wash inside, 2-3/4" x 1-3/4" **220.00**

Brass, open design over glass, rect, 2" x 1-3/8" **155.00**

Buffalo Steam Rollers, adv, by Whitehead & Hoag Co., celluloid wrapped, black and white graphics, 3" x 1-1/2" **235.00**

Bulldog motif, by Gorham Mfg. Co., cat. # B2202, sterling silver, 2-1/2" x 1-1/2" **400.00**

Cameron Pumps, adv, by Whitehead & Hoag Co., celluloid wrapped, black and white graphics, 2" x 1-1/2" **110.00**

Candle matches, image of young lady, Roche & Cie, Grand Prix Paris 1900, complete with matches, 3-1/8" x 1-5/8" **30.00**

Champagne bottle, figural, adv Veruve Cliquot, cigar cutter, nickel plated brass, 2-3/4" x 1" **125.00**

Chariot race motif, sterling silver, gold wash inside, 2-3/8" x 1-3/4" **385.00**

Cherub, sealed design, by Gorham Mfg. Co., cat. #1305, sterling silver, 2-1/2" x 1-1/2" **515.00**

Cherub and wishbone motif, by Wm. Kerr Co., cat. #6, sterling silver, 2-5/8" x 1-1/2" **135.00**

Chicago World's Fair, 1893, image "USA Man of War" on top, litho tin, multicolored graphics, mkd "Bryant & May Wax Vestas," 1-1/4" x 1-7/8" **115.00**

Cigar, figural, by Tiffany & Co., sterling silver, 4" x 3/4" **415.00**

Clover motif, by Whiting Mfg., cat. #419, sterling silver, 2-5/8" x 1-3/8" **95.00**

Cobra, ruby eye, by Gorham Mfg. Co., cat #605, sterling silver, 2-1/2" x 1-3/8" **2,000.00**

Cobra motif, sterling silver, Gorham Mfg Co., cat. #605, 2-1/2" x 1-3/8", **$2,000.**

Comic man, smiling/frowning, cigar cutter on end, by J.E. Mergott Co., celluloid wrapped, multicolored graphics, 3" x 1-1/2" **185.00**

Compass, pocket watch shape, swivel ring at top, brass, 2" d **195.00**

Dangerfield's self-igniting, nickel silver, by Harvey Blakeslee, patent June 22, 1880, 1-3/4" x 3-1/4" **95.00**

Diamond Match, bee and flower dec, by Ginna & Co., multicolored litho tin, 1-1/2" x 2-1/2" **55.00**

Door, hinge design, by Webster Co., sterling silver, gold wash inside, 2-3/4" x 1-5/8" **195.00**

Dragon on rampage, nickel plated brass, 2-5/8" x 1-3/8" **95.00**

Drunks outside saloon, by Gorham Mfg. Co., cat. #605, sterling silver, 2-3/4" x 1-3/4" **395.00**

Farmer's Friend, adv, by J.E. Mergott Co., celluloid wrapped, multicolored graphics, 2-3/4" x 1-1/2" **245.00**

Filigree, floral designs, silver, 2-1/2" x 1-1/2" **125.00**

Frog, webbed feet, figural, 2-3/4" x 1-3/8" **225.00**

Fish swimming motif, by R. Blackinton, cat. #376, sterling silver, gold wash inside, 2-1/4" x 1-3/4" **615.00**

Fish motif, by Gorham Mfg. Co., cat. #340, sterling silver, 2-5/8" x 1-5/8" **495.00**

Fleur-de-lis motif, by Dorst Co., sterling silver, inset garnets, 2-3/4" x 1-3/8" **335.00**

Gambling, two counters on one side, hand holding four aces and king on other, silver, soldered, by R. Wallace Co., cat. #051, 2-3/4" x 1-1/2", **$375.**

Gambling, two counters on one side, hand holding four aces and king on other, by R. Wallace Co., cat. #051, silver, soldered, 2-3/4" x 1-1/2" **375.00**

GAR, Sept. 10-15, 1894 National Encampment, by Heern Bros., brass, 2-3/4" x 1-1/2" **225.00**

Gauntlet, figural, brass, striker inside lid, 2-3/4" x 1-1/4" . **315.00**

Gold, brilliant set diamond on one side, 14k, 2-1/4" x 1-3/8" **375.00**

Gold Metal Flour, adv, celluloid wrapped, multicolored graphics, 2-3/4" x 1-1/2" **245.00**

Goldstone, rect, rounded end, brass trim, 3" x 1-1/8" **135.00**

Harvard University, sculling motif, sterling silver, gold wash inside, 2-1/4" x 1-3/4" **395.00**

Horseshoe, mkd "Good Luck," enamel applied to nickel plated brass safe, 1-7/8" x 1-3/8". **45.00**

Horseshoe, raised design, rider on horseback, figural, vulcanite, 1-7/8" x 1-1/2" **65.00**

Indian, Winnabago motif, by Whitehead & Hoag Co., nickel plated brass, 2-3/4" x 1-1/2" **115.00**

Irish symbols, Iberian harp, shamrock, etc., book shaped, bog oak, 2" x 1-1/2" **95.00**

Knight, in armor, holding lance, castle background, sterling silver, 2-3/4" x 1-3/8" **185.00**

Lady seated on potty, brass, 2-3/8" x 1", **$350**.

Lady, seated on potty, figural, brass, 2-3/8" x 1" **350.00**

Life preserver, figural, image of sailor in center, brass, 1-3/4" d **275.00**

Lily pad motif, by Wm. Kerr Co., cat. #966, sterling silver, gold wash inside, 2-1/2" x 1-1/2" **325.00**

Lion's head, by Carter, Howe & Co., sterling silver, gold wash inside, 2-1/2" x 1-1/2" **695.00**

Lisk Co., adv, by Whitehead & Hoag Co., multicolored celluloid inserts, nickel-plated brass, 2-3/4" x 1-1/2" **250.00**

Louisiana Purchase, 1803-1903, copyrighted by I.G.K., brass, 2-3/8" x 1-1/4" **125.00**

Marble, cylindrical, fluted sides, striker on side bar, by Marble Mfg. Co., patent June 5, 1900, 2-5/8" x 7/8" **45.00**

Mauchline, trick psycho box, black transfer, double lid, wood, 3" x 1-1/4" x 3/4" **85.00**

McKinley for President, nickel plated brass, 2-7/8" x 1-1/2" **235.00**

Mythical figure, half man-half bird, by Carter, Howe & Co., sterling silver, 2-1/4" x 1-1/4" **195.00**

Never-slip horseshoes, by Whitehead & Hoag Co., celluloid wrapped, multicolor graphics, 2-3/4" x 1-1/2" **150.00**

Noh, theatrical mask, figural, Japanese, brass, 2" x 1-1/2" **650.00**

Obelisk, figural, nickel-plated brass, 2-1/4" x 7/8" **285.00**

Order of Odd Fellows motif, insert type, nickel plated brass, 2-3/4" x 1-1/2" **65.00**

Overalls, figural, pewter, 2-7/8" x 1-1/4" **125.00**

Pabst Brewing Co., logo, nickel plated brass, push button lid release, 3" x 1-1/4" **55.00**

Padlock, figural, by Millar Wilkinson, English hallmarks for Birmingham, 1880, sterling silver, 1-1/4" x 1" **525.00**

President Harrison, figural, portrait type, brass, mkd "Pat. Oct. 8, 1888," 2-3/4" x 1-3/4" **275.00**

Rattle snakes, bold intertwined design, by Wm. Kerr Co., sterling silver, 2-3/4" x 1-5/8" **795.00**

Reliable Gas Ranges, The Scheidner Trenkanp Co., adv, vulcanite, 1-7/8" x 1-1/4" ... **35.00**

Roulette wheel, enamel on sterling silver, 2-1/4" x 1-1/2" **650.00**

Royal Arcanum motif, insert type, by Aug. Goertz Co., nickel-plated brass, 2-3/4" x 1-1/2" **65.00**

Saddle and polo mallet motif, quasi-figural, silver plate, 2-1/2" x 1-1/2" **185.00**

Scientific American newspaper, figural, by Enos Richardson & Co., sterling silver, enameled stamp, 2-3/8" x 1-1/8" **595.00**

Scottish thistle, figural, brass, 2" x 1-1/2" **115.00**

Seahorse, figural, brass, glass eyes, 2" x 1-1/8" **195.00**

Serpent and rococo motif, by F.S. Gilbert, sterling silver, gold wash inside, 2-1/2" x 1-3/8". **95.00**

Shoe, figural, hobnailed type, 800 silver, 1-3/8" x 2-1/8". **295.00**

Skin-like motif, by Pairpoint Mfg. Co., silver plated, 2-1/2" x 1-1/2" **70.00**

Skull, snakes coming out of eyes, ears, and nose, figural, sterling silver, 2-1/2" x 1-3/4" **1,500.00**

Snake, coiled around oval shaped safe, brass, 2" x 1-1/4" **65.00**

Tadcaster Ale, bottles of ale, by Whitehead & Hoag Co., celluloid wrapped, multicolored graphics, 2-3/4" x 1-1/2" **115.00**

Tartan Ware, McBeth design, cylindrical, vesta socket on top, 2-3/4" x 7/8" **115.00**

Teddy bears, dancing, adv, insert type, by August Goertz Co, nickel plated brass, 2-3/4" x 1-1/2" **195.00**

Teddy Roosevelt, Vice President 1901, by Gorham Mfg. Co., sterling silver, gold wash inside, catalog #ALU, 2-3/8" x 1-7/8" **2,000.00**

Tiger clawing rabbit, figural, Japanese, patinated brass, 2-3/4" x 1-5/8" **1,250.00**

Tiger clawing rabbit, Japanese, patinated brass, 2-3/4" x 1-5/8", **$1,250**.

Tiger lady, by Gorham Mfg. Co., #B3612, sterling silver, 2-3/4" x 1-1/2" **625.00**

Tunbridge Ware, octagon shaped, vesta socket on top, screw lid, concentric striker on bottom, 1-7/8" x 1-1/8" **135.00**

Unity patented cigar cutter, by Horton Allday, sterling silver, 2" x 1-3/8" **150.00**

U.S. Injector, by Whitehead & Hoag Co., celluloid wrapped, multicolored graphics, 2-3/4" x 1-1/2" **135.00**

Venus Rising, German silver, 2-5/8" x 1-5/8" **65.00**

Washington/Hotel Men's Mutual Benevolent Association, by Gorham Mfg. Co., #MDS, sterling silver, 2-1/2" x 1-5/8" **265.00**

Three drunks, Gorham Mfg. Co., cat. #605, 2-3/4" x 1-3/4", **$395.**

Whistle, applied hunting motif, cylindrical, brass, 2-1/2" x 3/4" **225.00**

White Mountain Refrigerators, logo, figural, nickel plated brass, 2-3/4" x 1-5/8" **135.00**

Yachting pennant, enameled on sterling silver, English hallmarks, 2-1/4" x 1-3/8" **350.00**

McCoy POTTERY

History:

The J. W. McCoy Pottery Co. was established in Roseville, Ohio, in September 1899. The early McCoy company produced both stoneware and some art pottery lines, including Rosewood. In October 1911, three potteries merged, creating the Brush-McCoy Pottery Co. This firm continued to produce the original McCoy lines and added several new art lines. Much of the early pottery is not marked.

In 1910, Nelson McCoy and his father, J. W. McCoy, founded the Nelson McCoy Sanitary Stoneware Co. In 1925, the McCoy family sold their interest in the Brush-McCoy Pottery Co. and started to expand and improve the Nelson McCoy Co. The new company produced stoneware, earthenware specialties, and artware.

Marks: The Nelson McCoy Co made Most of the pottery marked "McCoy."

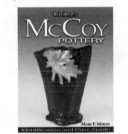

For more information, see *Warman's McCoy Pottery.*

Reproduction Alert:
Unfortunately, Nelson McCoy never registered his McCoy trademark, a fact discovered by Roger Jensen of Tennessee. As a result, Jensen began using the McCoy mark on a series of ceramic reproductions made in the early 1990s. While the marks on these recently made pieces copy the original, Jensen made objects that were never produced by the Nelson McCoy Co. The best-known example is the Red Riding Hood cookie jar, originally designed by Hull, and also made by Regal China.

The McCoy fakes are a perfect example of how a mark on a piece can be deceptive. A mark alone is not proof that a piece is period or old. Knowing the proper marks and what was made in respect to forms, shapes, and decorative motifs is critical in authenticating a pattern.

Additional Listings: See *Warman's Americana & Collectibles* for more examples.

Flower pots, pair, green and white basketweave-type decoration, **$40.**

Bean pot, cov, Suburbia Ware, brown, blue lid **48.00**

Cookie jar, cov
Aunt Jemima **275.00**

Jardinière, arches with block motif, mottled brown glaze, marked, **$95.**

Bobby Baker **95.00**
Bugs Bunny, cylinder, 1971-72 .... **185.00**
Chef, "Cookies" on hat band **85.00**
Clown, bust, c1943 ...... **95.00**
Clown in Barrel, marked "McCoy USA," c1953-56, overall crazing **145.00**
Davy Crocket, 10" h, c1956 .... **325.00**
Engine, black **175.00**
Kangaroo with Joey, 12" h **525.00**
Little Red Riding Hood, 10-1/2" h **650.00**
Panda, upside down, Avon label in heart logo on paw **150.00**
Rooster, shades of brown, light tan head, green highlights **225.00**
Strawberry **125.00**
Touring Car, 6-1/2" h, marked "McCoy USA," c1962-64 .... **155.00**
Creamer and sugar, Sunburst **120.00**
Decanter set, Jupiter 60 Train, Central Pacific locomotive, c1969 .... **350.00**
Flower pot, saucer, hobnail and leaf **40.00**
Hanging basket, Pine Cone Rustic **45.00**
Jardinière, 5-3/4" d, 5-1/4" d, green, brown and gold, emb lion's heads and columns . **45.00**
Jardinière pedestal, 16-1/4" h, Onyx glaze, sgd "Cusick," c1909 .... **400.00**
Lamp base, 14" h, cowboy boots, c1956 .... **150.00**
Low bowl, 9" d, 2-3/4" h, turtle flower frog, polychrome squeezebag dec, swastikas on bowl **500.00**

Planters, pair, Pine Cone, **$45**.

Pitcher, ice lip, embossed floral on sides, deep pink glaze, marked "McCoy, Made in USA," **$75**.

Planter
7-1/2" l, 4-1/2" w, 3" h, brown, white drip dec............... **20.00**
8" h, three large pink chrysanthemums, marked "McCoy"..................... **155.00**
12" l, Hunting Dog, No Fishing on sign........................ **275.00**
Spoon rest, 8" l, yellow, foliage, 1940s, overall crazing..... **145.00**
Strawberry jar, 12" h, stoneware **150.00**
Tankard pitcher, 8-1/2" h, Buccaneer, green **135.00**
Tea set, cov teapot, open creamer and sugar, Pinecone, c1946 .... **350.00**

Umbrella stand, 11" d, 22" h, maroon, rose, and yellow glaze, c1915 .... **795.00**
Valet, eagle...................... **75.00**
Vase
7-1/4" h, cornucopia, green **125.00**
8-3/4" h, bulbous, flaring rim, jeweled, pastel squeezebag dec, green base, mkd "042" **575.00**
9-1/2" h, swan, white, gold trim............................. **250.00**
Wall pocket
Bellows **60.00**
Cuckoo Clock, brown, green, white, yellow bird **225.00**

Tea set, Ivy pattern, 8-1/4" h teapot, creamer, and sugar, all marked, **$100**.
Photo courtesy of David Rago Auctions, Inc.

Vase, two handles, embossed stylized leaves and berries, white semi-matte glaze, marked "USA," attributed to Nelson McCoy, very short tight rim line, 8-1/2" d, 14-1/4" h, **$230**.
Photo courtesy of David Rago Auctions, Inc.

Fan, blue..................... **65.00**
Post Box, green **70.00**
Sunflower, blue **80.00**
Window box, Pine Cone Rustic
.... **40.00**

Wash bowl and pitcher, white, pitcher marked "McCoy," **$90**.

McKee Glass

c1852–1950   1904–30s

History: The McKee Glass Co. was established in 1843 in Pittsburgh, Pennsylvania. In 1852, it opened a factory to produce pattern glass. In 1888, the factory was relocated to Jeannette, Pennsylvania, and began to produce many types of glass kitchenwares, including several patterns of Depression glass. The factory continued until 1951, when it was sold to the Thatcher Manufacturing Co.

McKee named its colors Chalaine Blue, Custard, Seville Yellow, and Skokie Green. McKee glass may also be found with painted patterns, e.g., dots and ships. A few items were decaled. Many of the canisters and shakers were lettered in black to show the purpose for which they were intended.

For more information, see *Warman's Glass*, 4th edition.

Berry set, Hobnail with Fan pattern, blue, master berry and eight sauce dishes......... **170.00**
Candleholder, 6-3/4" w, 5-1/2" h, Rock Crystal, clear, double light **65.00**
Candy dish, cov, Rock Crystal, red, 4-1/2" w, 10-1/2" h... **400.00**
Canister, cov, 10 oz, custard **75.00**
Cereal canister, cov, custard, 48 oz **145.00**
Child's, butter dish, opaque blue, 5" w base, 3-3/4" h **55.00**
Creamer, Aztec, purple carnival **125.00**
Egg beater bowl, spout, Ships, black dec on white............ **70.00**
Flour shaker, Seville Yellow 65.00
Grill plate, custard, marked "McK"................................. **25.00**
Kitchen bowl, 7" d, spout, Skokie Green...................... **75.00**
Measuring cup, four-cup, Seville Yellow.................... **185.00**
Mixing bowls, nested set, Ships, red dec on white, 6", 7", 8", 9"................................. **185.00**
Pepper shaker, Roman Arch, black, "P"........................ **40.00**
Pitcher, 8" h, Wild Rose and Bowknot, frosted, gilt dec. **65.00**
Reamer, pointed top, Skokie Green **45.00**
Refrigerator dish, cov, Custard, 4" x 9"............................. **35.00**
Ring box, cov, Seville Yellow **20.00**

Clock, Daisy and Button pattern, vaseline, **$395**.

Server, center handle, Rock Crystal, red **140.00**
Sugar bowl, Aztec, purple carnival **125.00**
Sugar shaker, 2-3/8" sq, 5" h, Skokie Green, orig label and top **115.00**
Tea canister, custard, 48 oz **145.00**
Tom and Jerry punch bowl set, 11-1/2" d, 5" h punch bowl, eight 3-1/2" h mugs, white, black lettering and trim.............. **95.00**

Tray, 13-1/2" l, 6-1/2" w, 2-1/2" h, Rock Crystal, red, rolled rim **120.00**
Tumbler, Bottoms Up, caramel, 3-1/8" h, 2-3/4" d **90.00**
Water cooler, 21" h, spigot, vaseline, two pcs **325.00**

MEDICAL AND PHARMACEUTICAL ITEMS

History: Modern medicine and medical instruments are well documented. Some instruments are virtually unchanged since their invention; others have changed drastically.

The concept of sterilization phased out decorative handles. Handles on early instruments, which were often carved, were made of materials such as mother-of-pearl, ebony, and ivory. Today's sleek instruments are not as desirable to collectors.

Pharmaceutical items include those things commonly found in a drugstore and used to store or prepare medications.

Advertising
Button, Cloverine Salve Authorized Agent, celluloid, product described in detail, tiny white clover buds on green stems, blue, red, or white rim inscriptions.... **45.00**
Diecut, 8-1/8" x 14-1/8", Johnson & Johnson talcum powder, cardboard litho, baby on back playing with talc container, string hanger, C-7.5 .... **575.00**
Trade card, 13" x 7 1/2", Kidd's Cough Syrup, diecut cardboard, Victorian woman and product advertising **110.00**
Amputation knife, Civil War era **135.00**

Apothecary chest
16-1/2" w, 18" d, 26-1/2" h, Chinese, old black paint, mortised case, shaped aprons with inset panels on sides, six dovetailed drawers with old painted red character labels, ring pulls, and removable dividers **250.00**

Apothecary chest, table-top type, old blue painted surface, Pennsylvania, late 19th C, 20-3/4" w, 11-1/4" h, **$3,450**.
Photo courtesy of Pook & Pook.

33" w, 17" d, 46" h, Oriental, old reddish brown finish, mortised case, 45 detailed drawers, some with divided interiors, ring pulls, red and yellow painted labels on front, sq legs, shaped base aprons, restorations................ **815.00**
Apothecary jar, cov, 10 3/8" h, lip dec in burgundy and gold, black lettering on white ground, stenciled signatures on bases "Pouchet Deroche, Paris," acorn shaped finials, French, wear to gold............................... **320.00**

Apothecary jar, amber glass, white enameled "R" on front, **$400**.

Bifocal spectacles, by McAllister, Philadelphia, silver frame, horseshoe-shaped lenses, sliding temples ... **375.00**
Blood pressure kit, orig manual, 1917 .... **55.00**

Book

The Dental Art in Ancient Times, lecture at A.M.A. Meeting, Atlantic City, 1914, map of Atlantic City, NJ, and boardwalk layout, cuts of ancient artificial teeth and tools, Burroughs Welcome & Co., London, 1914, 216 pgs, 4" x 6-3/4" **34.00**

The People's Common Sense Medical Adviser in Plain English, or Medicine Simplified, Pierce, 1889, illus, 100 pgs **19.95**

Broadside

Dr Harding's Vegetable Medicines, top text reads "Dr. Harding's Vegetable Medicines; A Cure For Constipation, and Those Diseases…," text details various medicines, mid-19th C, some folds, light foxing, minor edge chipping, ink notation on bottom border, 18" x 9-3/4" **150.00**

Drs White & Oatman, top text reads "Stuttering or Stammering Permanently and Easily Cured!" text details accomplishments and details of cure, some folds, mid-19th C, 18" x 8-3/4" **150.00**

Bottles, brown, original labels, left: L. M. Brechbill, Pharmacist, Souderton, PA, "Linseed Oil," right: Oil of Turpentine, **each $15.**

Cabinet, emb tin insert front, wood cabinet

24" x 18" x 7", Munyon's Homeopathic Remedies, 41 orig dovetailed product drawers on back, most labeled **1,750.00**

27" x 20-3/4" x 6-3/4", Dr. LeSure's Famous Remedies **5,700.00**

28-5/8" x 21-1/2" x 7-3/4", Dr. Daniels Warranted Veterinary Medicines, orig finish, C.7.5 .... **2,900.00**

30" x 17-1/4" x 7", Pratts Veterinary Remedies, orig finish, stenciling **2,200.00**

Dental cabinet, 55-3/4" h, 34" w, 12-1/8" h, mahogany, flat top surmounted at rear with long drop-front cabinet raised on stepped base, streamlined main cabinet fitted with tree banks of five stacked short drawers over two banks of two stacked short drawers, over three banks of assorted short drawers above central kneehole franked by two deep short drawers, molded colorless glass drawer pulls, some drawers with porcelain and white glass receptacles and liners, four sq tapering legs, old medium finish, America, early 20th C **1,035.00**

Dispenser, 14-5/8" x 5", Alka-Seltzer, blue and white, tin litho adv sign on front, chrome base, orig cobalt blue tumbler, C.8.5 .... **400.00**

Electro-medical induction coil, 10" h, T. Hall, Boston, silvered coil and switches, mahogany base, pair of later handles **1,150.00**

Field surgeon's set, 10-1/2" w, Lentz & Sons, Philadelphia, all metal instruments, including Rust's pattern bone saw, Liston knife, trephine, bone forceps, etc., metal case with canvas cover case, both marked "2nd Reg. N.G.P." **350.00**

Fleam

Two-blade, tortoiseshell on case **60.00**

Three-blade **45.00**

Forceps tooth key, 7-1/2" l, removable bolster/claw, hatched handles, W & H Hutchinson, Sheffield, England, mid-19th C, restorations **690.00**

Hour glass, 9-1/2" h, Tartanware, McDuff pattern, half hour **175.00**

Jar, orig stopper, 10-1/2" h, Duff's Colic & Diarrhea Remedy, cylindrical glass, recessed reverse painted on glass label, ground stopper matches pattern at base, some minor staining **250.00**

Magic lantern slides, set of 195, c1915 .... **200.00**

Druggist's cabinet, oak, mirrored back, small fitted drawers, cabinet door, **$3,650.**

Medical case, Civil War era **130.00**

Optician's trial set, 21" w, Brown, Philadelphia, retailer's label, oak case, partial set **175.00**

Optometrist's sample case, 20" w, mahogany, containing three trays of 20 spectacles each, chart in lid **690.00**

Photograph

Medical training type, students with skeletons **80.00**

Medical training type, human skull **250.00**

Unidentified doctor's office interior............................ **30.00**

Unidentified doctor with bag **20.00**

Phrenological bust, 9-1/2" h, plaster, Fowler, Wells & Co., Boston, labeled cranium, label on back, damaged **80.00**

Plugger, 8" l, Goodman & Shurtler's Patent, mechanical gold foil, sprung, hinged mallet on ebonite body, interchangeable head..... **460.00**

Scarificator, brass, 16 blades, sgd "Kolb," European, early 19th C **215.00**

Sign

Blackleg Veterinary Medicines, Parke, Davis & Co., diecut cardboard, two cowboys giving shot to calf, 17-1/2" x 11-1/8", C.8++ **775.00**

C. F. Hussey Optometrist, zinc, double sided, polychrome and gilt dec, figural eyeglasses, name, and title in banner at base, late 19th C, 41" l, 12-1/2" h, imperfections.......... **2,550.00**

Lamp, Vapo-Cresolene, original box, used for whooping cough, **$50**.
Photo courtesy of Dotta Auction Co., Inc.

Spatula/knife, pearl handle, Remington...................... **200.00**
Surgical knife, 5" l, from Civil War hospital **40.00**
Surgeon's kit, ebony handles, velvet lined case, Civil War era **1,420.00**
Tin
   Blue Ribbon Brand, American Hygienic Co., Baltimore, MD, yellow, white, and red litho with German Shepherd in center, 1-7/8" x 2-1/4" x 5/16", C.8+............................. **925.00**
   Cadette Tooth Powder, figural tin litho soldier, green cap and coat, full, 7-3/8" x 2-1/4" x 1-1/4", C.8 .... **525.00**
   F. W. Cough Drops, Geo Miller & Co., Phila, "Cured My Cough," detailed graphics, 8" x 5-1/8" x 5-1/8", C.9 .... **1,400.00**
   Patent Superior Liquid Latex, yellow and red, 1-1/2" x 2" x 7/16", C.8.5+ **425.00**
   Town and Country, Nelson Products, NY, 1-5/8" x 2-1/8" x 5/16", C.8++ **1,750.00**
Tooth extractor, 6-3/4" l, W. R. Goulding, New York, marked "Baker & Riley patented 1845," removable claw/bolster, cross-hatched handles **1,380.00**
Tooth key
   5" l, turned horn handle, cranked shaft, adjustable claw **150.00**

Microscope, Spencer, original carrying case, 13" h, **$150**.
Photo courtesy of Joy Luke Auctions.

   5-3/4" l, wrought-iron handle, cranked and curved octagonal shaft, circular bolster, 10 interchangeable claws, possibly French, 19th C **635.00**
   6-1/2" l, turned and hatched removable rosewood handle, turned cranked shaft, adjustable circular bolster and claw, early 19th C **215.00**
Trepan, 10-1/4" l, burnished steel, sgd "Sir Henry a Paris," 18th C, arrowhead perforator, ivory pivot, ebony handle, five elevators **1,725.00**

MERCURY GLASS

History: Mercury glass is a light-bodied, double-walled glass that was "silvered" by applying a solution of silver nitrate to the inside of the object through a hole in its base.

   F. Hale Thomas of London patented the method in 1849. In 1855, the New England Glass Co. filed a patent for the same type of process. Other American glassmakers soon followed. The glass reached the height of its popularity in the early 20th century.

For more information, see *Warman's Glass*, 4th edition.

Compote, white enameled floral decoration, **$195**.
Photo courtesy of Dotta Auction Co., Inc.

Bowl, 8" d, small plug in bottom, some wear **120.00**
Cake stand, 8" d, pedestal base, emb floral dec......... **80.00**
Candlestick, 10-1/2" h.... **110.00**
Cologne bottle, 4-1/4" x 7-1/2", bulbous, flashed amber panel, cut neck, etched grapes and leaves, corked metal stopper, c1840.............................. **160.00**
Creamer, 6-1/2" h, etched ferns, applied clear handle, attributed to Sandwich **140.00**
Curtain tiebacks, 3-1/8" d, 4-1/2" l, etched grape design, price for pr **140.00**

Gazing ball, mercury glass base, **$250**.
Photo courtesy of Dotta Auction Co., Inc.

Vases, pair, cobalt blue, 8-1/2" h, **$145**.

Door knob set, 2-1/4" d .. **80.00**
Goblet, 5" d, gold, white lily of
the valley dec.................. **40.00**
Pitcher, 5-1/2" x 9-3/4" h,
bulbous, panel cut neck,
engraved lacy florals and leaves,
applied clear handle, c1840
.... **225.00**
Salt, master, 2-1/4" h, 2-3/4" d,
circular, ftd, orig base cork,
possibly Boston & Sandwich
Glass Co., 1860-87 .... **50.00**
Sugar bowl, cov, 4-1/4" x 6-1/4",
low foot, enameled white foliage
dec, knob finial **65.00**
Vase, 9-3/4" h, cylindrical, raised
circular foot, everted rim, bright
enameled yellow, orange, and
blue floral sprays and insects, pr
.... **225.00**

METTLACH

History: In
1809, Jean
Francis Boch
established a
pottery at
Mettlach in
Germany's
Moselle
Valley. His
father had started a pottery at
Septfontaines in 1767. Nicholas
Villeroy began his pottery career at
Wallerfanger in 1789.

In 1841, these three factories
merged. They pioneered
underglaze printing on
earthenware, using transfers from

copper plates, and also were
among the first companies to use
coal-fired kilns. Other factories
were developed at Dresden,
Wadgassen, and Danischburg.
Mettlach decorations include relief
and etched designs, prints under
the glaze, and cameos.

Marks: The castle and Mercury
emblems are the two chief marks,
although secondary marks are
known. The base of each piece
also displays a shape mark and
usually a decorator's mark.

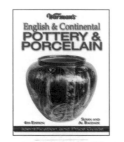

For more information, see *Warman's
English & Continental Pottery &
Porcelain*, 4th edition.

Additional Listings: Villeroy &
Boch.

Note: Prices in this listing are for
print-under-glaze pieces, unless
otherwise specified.

Coaster, 4-7/8" d, PUG, drinking
scene, marked "Mettlach,
Villeroy & Boch" **150.00**

Stein, #2382, stoneware, *Der Durstige
Ritter,* castle tower with peaked lid, lion
herm handle topped by pewter
thumbpiece formed as huntsman, body
molded with scenes of "The Thirsty
Knight" stealing a cask, center shield
signed "H. Schlitt," early 20th C,
11-1/4" h, **$775**.

Photo courtesy of Skinner, Inc.

Jardinière, 16" w, 12" h, #2427,
expanded bulbous body, fish
and flower dec, imp castle mark
and number **1,100.00**
Loving cup, 7-3/8" w, 6-3/4" h,
three handles, musicians dec
.... **185.00**
Plaque
  #1044-1067, water wheel on
  side of building, sgd "F.
  Reiss," PUG, gold wear on
  edge, 17" d **495.00**
  #1168, Cavalier, threading
  and glaze, sgd "Warth," chip
  on rear hanging rim, 16-1/2" d
  .... **465.00**

Left: stein, #485, one liter size, cameo relief with musicians and dancers, inlaid lid,
9-5/8" h, **$365**; center: jardinière, 16" w, 12" h, #2427, expanded bulbous body, fish and
flower decoration, imp castle mark and number, **$1,100**; left: stein, #171, one quarter
liter size, cameo relief with musicians, 6" h, **$110**.

Photo courtesy of Early Auction Co.

#2196, Stolzensels Castle on the Rhein, 17" d **1,100.00**
#2442, classical scene of Trojan warriors in ship, cameo, white high relief, blue-gray ground, artist sgd "J. Stahl," 18-1/4" d, some professional restoration **1,200.00**

Stein, #3878, stoneware, 1/2 litre, stoneware lid with pewter rim and thumb rest, **$60.**

Photo courtesy of Joy Luke Auctions.

Vase, stoneware cameo, #7018, ovoid, teal blue ground, white decoration of classical ladies and cherub with doves verso, classical ladies and man recto, one with incised signature "Stahl," scenes offset with large depictions of daisies and vines, base with leaf tip, early 20th C, drilled, 13-1/2" h, **$390.**

Photo courtesy of Skinner, Inc.

Stein

#485, one liter, cameo relief with musicians and dancers, inlaid lid, 9-5/8" h........ **365.00**
#1526, transfer and enameled, Student Society, Amico Pectus Hosti Frontem, dated 1902, roster on either side of crest, pewter lid, slight discoloration to int **465.00**
#1896, 1/4 liter, maiden on one side, cherub face on other, grape dec, pewter lift handle........................ **350.00**

#2028, 1/2 liter, etched, men in Gasthaus, inlaid lid . **550.00**
#2057, 1/2 liter, etched, festive dancing scene, inlaid lid **325.00**
#2093, 1/2 liter, etched and glazed, suit of cards, inlaid lid **700.00**
#2204, 1/2 liter, etched and relief, Prussian eagle, inlaid lid **780.00**
#2580, 1/2 liter, etched, Die Kannenburg, conical inlay lid, knight in castle **695.00**
#5001, 4.6 liter, faience type, coat of arms, pewter lld.. **850.00**

MILITARIA

History: Wars have occurred throughout recorded history. Until the mid-19th century, soldiers often had to provide for their own needs, including supplying their own weapons. Even in the 20th century, a soldier's uniform and some of his gear are viewed as his personal property, even though issued by a military agency.

Conquering armed forces made a habit of acquiring souvenirs from their vanquished foes. They also brought their own uniforms and accessories home as badges of triumph and service.

Saving militaria may be one of the oldest collecting traditions. Militaria collectors tend to have their own special shows and view themselves outside the normal antiques channels. However, they haunt small indoor shows and flea markets in hopes of finding additional materials.

Reproduction Alert: Pay careful attention to Civil War and Nazi material.

Flag fetches almost $50,000

A Confederate flag discovered in a trunk in the attic of a Tennessee farmhouse sold to a private American phone bidder for $48,000 at Sotheby's on Jan. 16, 2004. The flag was found by Lavinia Skinner and Thelma Rawlins, the Dancyville home's owner, in 1979. The two were rummaging through a trunk filled with family mementos when they found the silk flag, according to an Associated Press report. Skinner told AP she believes Rawlins did not realize the importance of the find as she simply put the piece back into the trunk. By the time of Rawlins' death in 1981, Skinner and her husband, William, a second cousin to Rawlins, had bought the home and its contents.

The flag was loaned to the Haywood County (Tennessee) Museum for three years, according to the AP article. A note pinned to the flag states it was hand sewn by Martha Douglass McFarland. The missive goes on to cite ownership of the flag over the next three generations. It is thought the fabric for the flag came from ladies' garments because wool bunting and cotton were in short supply at the time of its construction.

Sewn into the flag's blue field and surrounded by the 12 stars is "Dancyville Grays," the common name of Company A, the regiment that carried the flag in battle. On the hoist of the flag is the legend "Presented By The Ladies." The "ladies" would have been the wives, sisters, mothers and sweethearts of the soldiers in the regiment. The three stripes in the flag's design have been shortened. According to Sotheby's description, the shortening may have resulted from soldiers taking a swatch of the flag as a souvenir of their time in service—a common practice at the time.

The flag is a first national design, also called the Stars and Bars. It was adopted by the Confederacy in 1861. During battle, however, the flag was sometimes confused with the Union's Star and Stripes. The second national flag, a flag with fewer similarities to the Union flag, was adopted by the Confederacy in 1863.

For more information, see *Warman's Civil War Collectibles* and *Warman's Civil War Field Guide.*

Revolutionary War

Account book, for the Privateer Ship *Chandler*, c1779-84, sailing from Salem, MA, seventy manuscript pages, names 23 different brigs, sloops, schooners and ships that were supplied during the course Revolutionary war, several named individuals, original calf, scattered foxing and toning **7,100.00**

Autograph, document sgd, promotion of First Lieutenant, by Benjamin Harrison, 1783, paper seal, 6" x 8" **650.00**

Book
 Anthony Haswell, Printer, Patriot, Ballader, J. Spargo, 1925, 35 plates, 293 pgs **30.00**
 Yale and Her Honor Roll in the American Revolution, H. P. Johnston, 1888, privately printed, rebound, 357 pgs **40.00**

Broadsheet
 13" x 8-1/2", Oct. 8th, 1779, raising troops, requiring all towns to provide full accounting of supplies, bounties and gratuities given any soldier as part of state's proportion of Continental Army, signed by John Hancock in type, originally sent to Tosfield, CT .. **2,585.00**
 18" x 11-1/2", addressed to the Governor of MA, February 1, 1773, published in the Boston Evening Post, single folio sheet, double-sided, regarding disturbances in the Colonies, minor restorations **1,880.00**

Inaugural button, George Washington, c1789, copper, orig shank attached, American eagle with surrounding date and text design, Albert WI-1-A. . **2,000.00**

Map, Seat of War in New York, contained in Nathaniel Low's Almanack, 1777, printed by J. Gill, Boston, twenty-four pages, in original wrappers, shows positions of Washington and other troops **2,650.00**

Newspaper, 18" x 11", *Thomas's MA Spy: or Worcester Gazette*, May 13th, 1784, volume 14, no. 681, folio, printed by Isaiah Thomas, masthead engraved by Paul Revere, four pages, some mentions of the events of the war **550.00**

Ordnance report, sent by William Perkins to Samuel Adams as Lt. Governor of MA, cover letter and ledger sheets describing condition of heavy cannon carriages and platforms in Boston Harbor **600.00**

Plaque, 3-7/8" d, General (Mad Anthony) Wayne, America, late 18th/early 19th C, carved ivory, round, relief carved three-quarter view bust length portrait, banner below inscribed with name, houses and foliage in background, age crack, conforming molded wood frame **500.00**

Print
 Perry's Victory on Lake Erie, Perry in rowboat, eight sailors in midst of battle, steel engraving from painting by Thomas Birch, engraved by A. Lawson, published by William Smith, Philadelphia, Eastlake frame, 24" x 31" **295.00**
 Washington's Dream, litho by Currier and Ives, NY, 1857, Washington, in uniform, sleeping in camp cabin, vignette dream of three women representing Liberty, Plenty, and Justice standing over America, stepping on crown of tyranny, framed, 25" x 19" **775.00**

Snuff box, cov, 2-7/8" d, gutta percha, round, relief scene of battle, ships, coastline, buildings, French inscription "Prise d'Yorck 1781 (Taking of Yorktown or Battle of Yorktown)" **750.00**

French and Indian War

Marching order, letter addressed to Captain Josiah Thatcher, Yarmouth, his Majesty's Service, Boston, June 24, 1761, ordering Thatcher to

march troops to Springfield to be mustered, sgd by J. Hoar, some fold weakness, 8" x 6-1/4" **185.00**

Uniform button mold, 9" l, brass, American, 18th C, casts six round buttons with central raised letter "I" for infantry, one 25 mm, one 18 mm, four 14.5 mm, each with eyelet, wooden handles missing.............. **625.00**

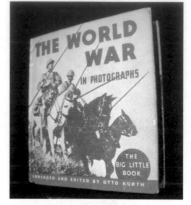

Big Little Book, *The World War in Photographs*, Otto Kurth, red, black, and white cover, $35.

War of 1812

Broadside, Aug. 18, 1814, printed calvary orders for the 2nd Brigade 1st Visis, and 7th Reg 2nd Brig 1st Divis, Edmund Fitzgerland Lt. Col. 7th Reg & Cavalry, one sheet **375.00**

Cartridge box, leather, white cloth strap, very worn, missing plate................................. **70.00**

Flag, 60-1/2" x 110", 13 stars, Naval, hand sewn **1,100.00**

Military drum, large eagle painted on sides, red, and blue stripes, one drum head, 22" h, 17" d.............................. **750.00**

Ship document, British, articles pertaining to private armed ship *Dart* and four carriage guns, six nine-pounders, four swivel guns lying in St. John, New Brunswick, designed to cruise against Americas, details prize division, chain of command, other shipboard administration, dated July 1813, right section includes signatures and ratings of 44 seamen and officers as crew, some staining, edge chipping, foxing, and fold splitting, Whatman 1808 watermark, 21" x 29" **500.00**

Civil War

Autograph

Davis, Jefferson, partly printed check, Union & Planters Bank, Memphis July 22, 1872, cancelled, 2-1/2" x 8-1/4" **1,100.00**

Sherman, William T., ALS, to General Hawley, letter of condolence after death of Hawley's wife, St. Louis, March 10, 1886 .... **460.00**

Belt and plate, black leather belt, brass loops, two piece brass VA state plate, minor wear and splits **2,350.00**

Book set, *The Soldier in Our Civil War,* volumes I and II, copyright 1890, both illustrated, **$200.**

Photo courtesy of Joy Luke Auctions.

Book

Confederate General Robt. E. Lee & His Campaigns in Virginia, 1906, 300 pgs, fold-out maps **45.00**

Harper's Pictorial History of the Civil War, 1896, four volumes **230.00**

Life of Lincoln, Herndon/Welk, c1889, 500 pgs **19.95**

Personal Memoir of General Sheridan, 1889, limited edition, 2 volumes, faux leather, fold-out maps ... **45.00**

Personal Memoir of General Wm Tecumseh Sherman, 1876, limited edition, 2 volumes, faux leather, 800 pgs **45.00**

The Gettysburg Campaign and the Campaigns of 1864 & 1965 in Virginia by A Lieutenant in Confederate Artillery, Stribling, 1905, illus, 308 pgs **45.00**

Broadside

6" x 8-1/2", Union, Against Morgan's Raiders, issued by Office of Provost Marshall, Lexington, Kentucky, July 15th, 1862, calling upon all citizens to be associated with "Home Guards" against Morgan's Raiders..... **2,000.00**

8" x 10", Abraham Lincoln funeral, dated April 17th, 1865, from Governor Joseph Gilmore of New Hampshire, giving profound and moving instructions to people of New Hampshire to observe and participate in day of mourning, "all of the churches within their jurisdiction to be tolled, and minute guns to be fired...drape their stores and dwelling houses with the appropriate emblems of that grief..." **950.00**

12-1/4" x 9-1/2", Union, recruiting, dated September 12, 1861, Saccarappa, ME, "Attention Volunteers Seventy five Men Must be enrolled At Once....," these troops attributed to served in Company C of the 12th ME Volunteers................ **1,175.00**

13-1/2" x 6", Union, recruiting, dated April 1st, 1862, for M'Call's Division, Reading (Pennsylvania), printed with globe form masthead with "our country" and U.S. flag **1,175.00**

17-1/2" x 11-1/2", Union, Condemning U.S. Grant for Battle of Shiloh, c1862, large folio, sold by Applegate & Co., Cincinnati, Ohio, recounting events leading up to battle and Grant's action during conflict............. **750.00**

18-1/2" x 12", Union Draft, dated 1864, proclaiming "War Meeting!," Hingham, MA, black printed on salmon colored paper, light wear **1,000.00**

Cane, 35-3/4" l, carved wood, 1-1/2" w x 3" h oval wood knob, relief carved and polychromed shaft with American flag, 24 Union army corps badges, worn red, white, blue, and green polychrome, 1-3/4" brass ferrule, made for veteran, c1880. **350.00**

Canteen, 7-5/8" d, bull's eye, orig woven cloth strap, pewter spout sgd "Hadden, Porter & Booth, Phila" **325.00**

Cartridge box, cross belt and eagle plate, "Calhoune New York" maker's stamp on inner flap, tin liners, oval U.S. plate **900.00**

Confederate notes, group of $500, $10, and $5, from Richmond, matted and framed, 21-1/2" x 17" **275.00**

Coat, Confederate Officer's, double breasted, blue-gray wool, low collar, blue piping along front, 12 large VA and NC buttons marked "Scovill Mfg. Waterbury," three small buttons with same markings, two have black velvet coverings, Captain's bars on collar, buttons and insignia removed for previous cleaning, minor moth damage to ext. **39,600.00**

Fife, 17-1/2" l, rosewood, nickel silver ends, eight bands, orig dark finish, faint signature "W. Crosby, Boston" **125.00**

Kepi, 13th Infantry soldier's **850.00**

Newspaper, *Cincinnati Gazette,* for year of 1863, fold lines and minor damage, group of 19 newspapers **150.00**

Framed proof sheet engraving related to American Civil War by Bureau of Engraving & Printing, seven images including eagle with outstretched wings, Lincoln, and Cabinet during Emancipation Proclamation reading, portraits of Generals Meade, Grant, McClellan, and Sherman, each sheet measures 4" x 6", provenance: G.F.C. Smillie family, Superintendent of Picture Engraving Dept, US Bureau of Engraving and Printing, 1918-22, **$300.**

Photo courtesy of Alderfer Auction Co.

Photograph, tintype, cased Cavalryman, wearing shell jacket with gilt detail on collar and buttons, lightly tinted blue pants, holding cavalry saber, Colt pistol in belt, forage cap with "D2," sixth plate .. **770.00**

Confederate, checked shirt, butternut colored coat, CDV mount........................ **110.00**

Infantryman, waist-up portrait, holding Hardee hat with feather, "K," and bugle insignia, wearing epaulettes, cartridge box, holding musket with bayonet, ninth plate **550.00**
Soldiers in front of tent, very worn quarter plate tintype, gutta-percha case with relief scene of officers standing at table, scrolled border, minor edge chips................ **470.00**
Pinback button
  Battle of Gettysburg 1913 Anniversary, multicolored, blue lettering................. **25.00**
  Col. W. C. Johnson, G.A.R., black and white photo, orange ground, black lettering for sponsor "Snellenburg Stores, Philadelphia, Pa.," and "G.A.R. Encampment 1899" **20.00**
Shaving mug, 3-3/4" x 3-1/2", hp, US Civil War soldier holding American flag, name Jos. Davis in gold **1,500.00**
Spurs, pr, 4" h, brass, Confederate, Leech & Rigdon style.................................. **115.00**
Sword, belt rig, non-commissioned officer, NCO sword by Ames Mfg, Chicopee MA, marked on blade, also marked "US, GWC, 1864," marked "GKC" on guard, leather scabbard, NCO sword belt ring, eagle buckle, plated wreath, frog for NCO sword and hangers, some leather deterioration to belt and scabbard **900.00**
Textile, 10-1/4" x 10-1/2", printed in black on off-white cloth, "Union-Liberty & Life Without Freedom," poems and images of earlier patriots, New England Chemical Print Company, mid 19th C, framed **450.00**
Walking stick, 36-1/4" h, carved wood, dog's head finial with silver collar inscribed "Thos. Thompson Co. H 106 Reg. Pa. Vols. Evacuation of York Town 1862," natural branch carved with dog, squirrel, leafy vine, and reeded and geometric devices, wear **775.00**

Indian War

Bayonet, Model 1873, 3-1/2" w blade.............................. **80.00**
Belt buckle, Naval officer, brass, stamped "Horstman, Phila" **120.00**

Calendar plate, 1920, The Great World War, 1914-1919, flags and globe in center, coats of arms of countries and calendar pages around border, gold lettering "Compliments of Luther Schoch, Ackermanville, PA," **$35**.
Photo courtesy of Dotta Auction Co., Inc.

Broadside, Ohio massacre, No. 4, 1791, printed in Boston, 1792, foxed, water stained, modern frame............................... **900.00**

Spanish American War

Hat badge, infantry, brass, crossed krag rifles, 2" l **55.00**
Cartridge box, U.S. Army **125.00**
Pinback button, "Remember the *Maine*," battleship scene, patent 1896 .... **25.00**
Spy glass, pocket, brass, Naval, round holder, brown leather grip, 16" l **110.00**

Print showing three images of German and Russian military figures, framed, minor foxing, **$35**.

World War I

American flag, 6-1/4" x 10-1/4" sight, cloth, eight stars and five

stripes, made by Prisoner of War, "Arlon Belgium Dec 11th, 1918" written on mat, framed, some losses, discoloration **350.00**
Bayonet, British, MK II, No. 4, spike, scabbard.............. **20.00**
Book, *The Priceless Gift, The Love Letters of Woodrow Wilson and Ellen Axson Wilson*, 1962, sgd by Henry Steele Commager **13.00**
Buckle, U.S. Balloon Corps, emb hot air balloon **75.00**
Flare pistol, Model 1918, French............................. **100.00**
Gun sling, soft leather, 1917, for 03 Springfield **17.50**
Helmet, German, Pattern, 1916, painted gray/green **80.00**
Overcoat, U.S. Army officers, Melton, olive drab, wool, double breasted, 10 bone buttons **65.00**
Trench flashlight and note pad, German, black tin container, orig pad and pencil **65.00**
Tunic and trousers, gabardine, pinback, Air Corps and U.S. discs **75.00**
Watch fob, Federal Seal, U.S. officer.............................. **15.00**

Toy, World War I, tin horse-drawn ambulance wagon with two horses, four composition soldiers on horseback, 15 composition figures, **$490**.
Photo courtesy of Joy Luke Auctions.

Timepiece, wall, British Royal Airforce, second half 20th C, single fusee movement by Elliot Ltd., round dial with standard and military time, accented with orange, blue, and yellow triangles, RAF embossed lem above the hands, mahogany case, 18-1/2" d, **$450**.
Photo courtesy of Skinner, Inc.

World War II

Armband, Japan, military police, red lettering, white cotton... **48.00**

Book

Baa Baa Black Sheep, Pappy Boyington, Marine Corps Pilot Ace with Flying Tigers, 1958, 400 pgs......................... **38.00**
Blood and Banquets, Fromm, 1942, 350 pgs, photos.. **30.00**
Bunker's War, The World War II Diary of Colonel Paul D Bunker, 320 pgs **38.00**
December 7th, 1941-The Day The Japanese Attacked Pearl Harbor, Prange, 1988, 509 pgs, 34 photo plates..... **38.00**
From Hell to Heaven-Memoirs From Patton's Third Army in WWII, McHugh, 1970, 1st ed **30.00**
Semper Fi, Mac-Living Memories of the US Marines in WWII, Berry, 403 pgs, photos............................ **40.00**
Cane, 30-3/4" l, Civilian Conservation Corps, fully carved, U-shaped horse-head handle, one piece, carved low relief of trees, bathing beauty, alligator, name of carver's friends, "Middle Creek Camp F34 Co. 997," 1933, finish removed around later added date **125.00**
Flag, New Zealand PT boat, printed on blue cotton...... **55.00**
Flyers goggles, Japanese, boxed, gray fur lined cups, yellow lenses..................... **35.00**
Gas mask, German, canister style, rubber mask, canvas straps, carrying container. **80.00**
Helmet, Italian, steel, leather chip strap **100.00**
ID tag, U.S. Army, oval pattern, instruction envelope, chain . **25.00**
Manual, 6-1/4" x 10", War Department, FM30-30, Military Intelligence, *Aircraft Recognition Pictorial Manual,* Bureau of Aeronautics, Washington, DC, 1943, 179 pgs, illus of US, Great Britain, German, Japanese, Italian, Russian, etc. plans **40.00**
Telescope, 14" l, Australian, MK 1, heavy leather case and carrying straps.................. **45.00**

MILK GLASS

History: Opaque white glass attained its greatest popularity at the end of the 19th century. American glass manufacturers made opaque white tablewares as a substitute for costly European china and glass. Other opaque colors, e.g., blue and green, also were made. Production of milk-glass novelties came in with the Edwardian era.

The surge of popularity in milk glass subsided after World War I. However, milk glass continues to be made in the 20th century. Some modern products are reissues and reproductions of earlier forms. This presents a significant problem for collectors, although it is partially obviated by patent dates or company markings on the originals and by the telltale signs of age.

Collectors favor milk glass from the pre-World War I era, especially animal-covered dishes. The most prolific manufacturers of these animal covers were Atterbury, Challinor-Taylor, Flaccus, and McKee.

For more information, see *Warman's Glass,* 4th edition.

Notes: There are many so-called "McKee" animal-covered dishes. Caution must be exercised in evaluating pieces because some authentic covers were not signed. Furthermore, many factories have made split-rib bases with McKee-like animal covers or with different animal covers.

Animal covered dish, lion, white, patent date Aug. 6, 1889, 7" l, 5-1/2" h, **$40**.

Photo courtesy of Joy Luke.

Animal dish, cov
Cat on drum................ **195.00**
Cat on hamper, green, V mark **115.00**
Chick on sleigh, white **115.00**
Dolphin **145.00**
Kitten, ribbed base, Westmoreland, white .. **130.00**
Lion, reclining, white, criss-cross base.................. **135.00**
Robin on nest, med blue **165.00**
Setter dog, blue.......... **265.00**
Swan, closed neck, white **120.00**
Turkey, amethyst head, white body **220.00**
Turkey, white head, dark amethyst body............ **170.00**

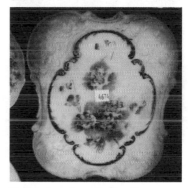

Cake plate, square top, pedestal base, **$55**.

Dresser tray, shaped rectangle, embossed chrysanthemums, hand-painted violets and leaves in center, embossed gold border, wear to painted trim, **$65**.

Bowl, 8-1/4" d, Daisy, allover leaves and flower design, open scalloped edge................ **85.00**
Bust, 5-1/2" h, Admiral Dewey **300.00**
Butter dish, cov, 4-7/8" l, Roman Cross pattern, sq, ftd base curves outward toward top, cube-shape finial **75.00**
Calling card receiver, bird, wings extended over fanned tail, head resting on leaf, detailed feather pattern **150.00**

Compote, Atlas, lacy edge, blue **185.00**
Creamer and sugar, Trumpet Vine, fire painted dec, sgd "SV" **130.00**
Egg cup, cov, 4-1/4" h, bird, round, fluted, Atterbury ... **135.00**
Hat, Stars and Stripes, black rim **235.00**
Lamp, 11" h, Goddess of Liberty, bust, three stepped hexagonal bases, clear and frosted font, brass screw connector, patent date, Atterbury **300.00**
Milk pitcher, 8-3/4" h, Wild Iris, gilt trim, c1825 .... **125.00**
Mug, 3-1/4", Medallion, c1870 .... **50.00**
Plate
    Donkey......................... **50.00**
    Easter, bunny, basket of eggs **35.00**
    Fort Necessity, Indian chief, some orig paint, edge chip **30.00**
    Indian Chief, no paint ... **70.00**
    Rabbit center, horseshoe and clover border **145.00**
    Three dogs and squirrel **65.00**

Plate, flag at top, fleur-de-lis and eagle border, stars embossed on interior border, **$45**.

Spooner/vase, Westmoreland, Charlton decoration, **$35**.

Syrup, Acorn, opaque white with pink swirls, applied glass handle, silver-plated spout, **$48**.

Spooner, 5-1/8" h, monkey, scalloped top **95.00**
Sugar shaker, Forget-me-not, green, orig top **50.00**
Syrup, plain, hp red flowers, damage to pewter top **65.00**
Tumbler, Royal Oak, orig fired paint, green band **50.00**
Vanity box, cov, 7" l, 2" w, 2" h, hand painted enamel floral dec, gold trim, imp "16" on both lid and base........................ **250.00**

MILLEFIORI

History: Millefiori (thousand flowers) is an ornamental glass composed of bundles of colored glass rods fused together into canes. The canes were pulled to the desired length while still ductile, sliced, arranged in a pattern, and fused together again. The Egyptians developed this technique in the first century B.C. It was revived in the 1880s.

Reproduction Alert: Many modern companies are making Millefiori items, such as paperweights, cruets, and toothpicks.

Barber bottle, orig top, red, white dec **350.00**
Beads, 16" l, multicolored millefiori beads, blue glass bead spacers **55.00**
Bowl, 8" d, tricorn, scalloped, folded sides, amethyst and silver deposit **125.00**

From left: teapot-shaped paperweight, 4" h, **$85**; rose bowl, 6" d, **$195**; shoe, 6" l, **$65**.

Photo courtesy of Joy Luke.

Candy dish, 11-1/2" l, 9" w, light blue, various sized multicolored millefiori flowers, swirled shape, Murano, c1950................ **85.00**
Creamer, 3" x 4-1/2", white and cobalt blue canes, yellow centers, satin finish......... **110.00**
Cruet, bulbous, multicolored canes, applied camphor handle, matching stopper **120.00**
Decanter, 12" h, deep black ground, allover multicolored flux and canes, including peachblow, and opal, enamel dec, Gundersen........... **1,450.00**
Demittase cup and saucer, red and white millefiori, angular applied pink handle, broken pontil scars, Italian.......... **275.00**
Door knob, 2-1/2" d, paperweight, center cane dated 1852, New England Glass Co. **395.00**
Goblet, 7-1/2" h, multicolored canes, clear stem and base **150.00**
Lamp, 16-1/2" h, two-pcs, baluster stem, tall mushroom shape shade dec with large and small colorful canes........ **850.00**
Pitcher, 6-1/2" h, multicolored canes, applied candy cane handle............................. **195.00**
Slipper, 5" l, camphor ruffle and heel **125.00**
Sugar bowl, cov, 4" x 4-1/2", white canes, yellow centers, satin finish....................... **125.00**
Sugar shaker, bulbous, reds and yellows, orig top **275.00**
Syrup, pewter top, dark green, browns, blues, applied colorless handle............................. **295.00**
Vase
    4-1/2" h, ftd urn shape, small cane dec **150.00**
    6" h, ftd urn shape, small cane dec **100.00**
    8" h, ftd baluster, large cane dec **150.00**

Bell, 4-1/2" h, **$40**, swan, 6" h, **$50**, rose bowl, 3" h, **$65**; and vase, 8" h, **$45**.
Photo courtesy of Joy Luke.

MINIATURE PAINTINGS

History: Prior to the advent of the photograph, miniature portraits and silhouettes were the principal way of preserving a person's image. Miniaturists were plentiful, and they often made more than one copy of a drawing. The extras were distributed to family and friends.

Miniaturists worked in watercolors and oil and on surfaces such as paper, vellum, porcelain, and ivory. The miniature paintings were often inserted into jewelry or mounted inside or on the lids of snuff boxes. The artists often supplemented commission work by painting popular figures of the times and copying important works of art.

After careful study, miniature paintings have been divided into schools, and numerous artists are now being researched. Many fine examples may be found in today's antiques marketplace.

Miniature painting on porcelain, woman with short dark brown hair, white blouse, hoop earring and locket, unsigned, gilt metal easel frame, 2-1/4" w, 2-3/4" h, **$260**.
Photo courtesy of Alderfer Auction Co.

1-7/8" x 1-3/4", watercolor on ivory, bust length portrait of Elizabeth Freeman (1786-1815), gold brooch frame with seed pearl border, accompanied by three small notes: one note written in 1888 by her daughter Elizabeth Freeman Duren, concerning birthday gift of brooch to her daughter, another written by great-granddaughter stating it was painted about 1812, last written by friend of the family who mentions the brooch was given to her after she bought a portrait from the great-granddaughter, Bangor, Maine, c1812 .... **1,650.00**

1-7/8" x 2-1/4", on ivory, Julia Clarke Brewster (1796-1826), attributed to John Brewster Jr., painted in the Columbia or Hampton, CT area, c1820, orig oval gilded copper locket case within orig red leather hinged case **4,600.00**

2" x 1-3/8", watercolor on ivory, gentleman, Anglo/American School, late 18th C, engraved gold pendant frame, reverse centered with en grisaille dec ivory oval medallion depicting dove with ribbon and two hearts suspended in it's beak above curved panel inscribed "one mind," surrounded by woven hair, glass cracked **650.00**

2-1/8" d, watercolor on ivory double-sided locket, lady with white lace bonnet, black dress with black lace-edged collar, wearing locket; gentleman wearing patterned yellow striped vest, frilled white shirt, mulberry patterned stock, and black jacket, unsigned, American School, 19th C, round gold plated frame **950.00**

2-1/8" d, watercolor on ivory, James L. Small, Camden, Maine, unsigned, American School, 19th C, mounted in oval metal locket case, cobalt blue and white enameled border, pen and ink inscriptions appear on paper backing including "1818," "TL 20 LWV," conjoined V and W and "1850," conjoined V and W and "1850" also incised into the interior of the frame **1,650.00**

Gentleman, hand painted on ivory, man wearing powdered wig, white high-collared shirt, yellow vest, brown jacket, signed "Von der Tachlen," 2-1/4" d, **$330**.
Photo courtesy of Alderfer Auction Co.

Miniature portrait on ivory, oval, young woman, brown curly hair swept up into jeweled tiara and headband, rose colored dress, white sleeves, jewels at shoulders and cleavage, black belt, signed "H. P.," rectangular frame of pieced ivory, inscription verso "from Vienna 1922," 2-3/8" w, 3-1/8" h painting, 5-1/8" h frame, **$350**.
Photo courtesy of Alderfer Auction Co.

2-5/8" d, watercolor, graphite and ink on paper, bust-length profile portrait of young woman, Mary L. Amidon, Dudley, Massachusetts, indistinctly signed "Ten—s" on lower sleeve, sitter identified by ink inscription on reverse, mounted in embossed brass mat in poly-resin case, creases, small tear **775.00**

2-3/4" h, watercolor on ivory, nobleman in powdered wig, blue sash, medal, holding sheet of paper, oval brass frame .. **325.00**

2-3/4" x 2-1/4", watercolor in ivory, military officer wearing a navy blue coat with crimson collar, white braid, and cross belt, silver breast plate, epaulettes, and buttons, unsigned, American School, oval format, ebonized wood frame **1,100.00**

2-3/4" x 2-1/4" l, watercolor on ivory, young boy, sgd "Jared Sparks Handerson, Baltimore" in pencil on reverse, American School, 19th C, oval format........................... **620.00**

2-3/4" x 2-1/4", watercolor on ivory, young gentleman, black great coat, white waist coat, pleated shirt with stickpin and black neck cloth, unsigned, Anglo/American School, 19th C, gilt-metal frame, aperture containing lock of braided hair, fitted leather case **950.00**

3" x 2-1/2", watercolor on ivory, attributed to Frederick Buck, late 18th/early 19th C, young woman with curled hair, wearing coral necklace, oval format...... **825.00**

3" x 2-1/2", watercolor on ivory, Gustavis Tuckerman Jr., sgd and dated "Sacro Fratelli 1847" lower right, inscribed on paper within opening on reverse "Gustavis Tuckerman (Jr.,) Born Edgbaston, England, May 15th 1824, Died New York, February 12, 1897," painted in Palermo, Italy, 1847 by Sacro Fratelli, oval engine-turned gilt-metal frame within rect papier-mâché frame inlaid with abalone floral dec **450.00**

3" x 2-3/4", watercolor on ivory, woman with hair in braided ringlets, beaded cap, floral dress, laced bodice, cast brass frame with ram's head corners **325.00**

3-1/8" x 4-1/4" h, young brunette seated in lush interior, hair dressed with pearls, lace-trimmed gown and blue wrap, signed to left "J. Isabey," Continental, late 19th C, 6" x 4-7/8" gilt-metal frame .. **1,725.00**

3-1/4" x 2-1/2", watercolor on ivory, Napoleonic portrait, tortoiseshell and brass frame, oval format, signature obscured **725.00**

3-3/8" w, 4-1/2" h, watercolor on ivory, young blond military officer, green and red uniform with epaulettes, sgd "Haberle," oval brass frame with horn, small pc missing **320.00**

3-1/2" x 2-3/4", watercolor on ivory, gentleman wearing spectacles, sgd "M. B. Katze," brass framed, fitted in leatherette case **200.00**

3-1/2" x 2-3/4", watercolor on ivory, identified as Elizabeth Maderia, 1934, sgd "E. B. Taylor," reverse with locket of hair, engraved name and date, oval brass frame, fitted in leatherette case **225.00**

Mme. De St. Marc, hand painted on ivory, woman wearing powdered wig, large bonnet with white veil, blue dress with pink bow decoration, signed "Saintet," 3" x 2-1/4", **$315**.

Photo courtesy of Alderfer Auction Co.

3-1/2" x 2-3/4", watercolor on ivory, lady in burgundy, wearing lace bonnet, sgd "G. Harvey" lower right, hinged red leather case with ormolu mat...... **725.00**

3-5/8" x 2-3/4", watercolor and gouache on ivory, two brown-haired, rosy-cheeked children, one wearing a pink dress and holding a tabby kitten in her lap, the other in a purple printed dress, holding a blue ribbon attached to the kitten, unsigned by attributed to Mrs. Moses B. Russell (American, 1809-54), molded giltwood frame, small areas of paint loss on clothing **4,120.00**

3-7/8" x 3-1/2", watercolor on ivory, Richard Wagner, illegible artist's signature, ivory frame, brass liner, nacre inlay **250.00**

4" x 3-1/4", watercolor and pencil on paper, lady in black, hair comb, reverse inscribed "painted May 12th 1834 by J Sears," oval eglomise mat, framed, scattered small abrasions, toning **470.00**

4-1/8" x 3-1/2", watercolor on paper, lady in blue dress, white cap, brown ribbon, attributed to Edwin Plummer, Boston, c1841-46, oval eglomise mat, framed, laid down, small tear, minor toning, losses, repaint to mat **765.00**

4-3/8" h, watercolor on porcelain, woman with classical profile, wearing scarf with pearl and gold brooch, brass frame **200.00**

4-1/2" d, watercolor on paper, gentleman, oval aperture, unsigned, American School, 19th C, framed, crease, minor foxing **890.00**

4-3/4" x 3-5/8", watercolor on paper, woman wearing tortoiseshell comb, sitter identified on reverse as "Mrs. A. Saunders age 18 years," oval eglomise format, molded gilt frame, American School, c1840, toning, gilt loss on mat. **2,585.00**

5" x 3-1/2", watercolor and pencil on paper, Miss Stevens, Andover, MA, area, half-length profile likeness, precise outlines with delicate drawing, bright blue dress with lace offset, dark upswept hair with tortoiseshell comb, background of blue and orange flanked by black spandrels at corners, unsigned, attributed to Edwin Plummer, (MA and ME, 1802-1880), back inscribed in pencil "Stevens, lace, purple," and outline of woman's profile, later black and gilt frame, minor foxing, color loss, some pinpoints, later black and gilt frame............. **21,150.00**

5" x 3-7/8", watercolor on ivory, semi-nude slave girl with two cajoling men, unsigned, Continental, late 19th C, giltwood frame................................ **750.00**

5" w, 7-1/8" h, watercolor on paper, believed to be Commodore Perry, brown curly hair and sideburns, dark blue naval officer's uniform, gold epaulettes, oval ground glued to blue backing, matted with old reeded frame with black paint, some flaking to gold, dark blue alligatored **420.00**

5-1/2" x 4-3/8", watercolor on paper, gentleman wearing black jacket, white vest and stock, seated before window on red upholstered chair before red drapery, penciled inscription "Herbert Lynesey squire Wier," on reverse, unsigned, Anglo/American, 19th C, gilt gesso frame, minor foxing......... **360.00**

Pair framed miniature portraits on wooden panels, boy and girl with flowers, 5-1/2" x 4-3/4", **$800**.
Photo courtesy of Joy Luke.

5-3/4" x 4-3/4", pencil and watercolor on paper, Brigadier General James Miller, Peterboro, NH, American School, early 19th C, oval frame, toning, sold with accompanying note giving brief history of General's career
.... **1,880.00**

5-3/4" x 4-3/4", watercolor on paper, gentleman, reverse identified as "1825, Eleazar Graves, father of Laura Graves Lincoln," unsigned, attributed to Rufus Porter, America, c1792-1884, grain painted frame, laid down, staining in margins, minor toning **445.00**

5-3/4" w, 6" h, watercolor on ivory, double portrait of mother and child, dressed in white, blue trim, pearl tiara on mother, child playing with pocket watch, old German typed label on back identifies woman as "Marquise d'Huret-Gonzenbach," 1803, ebonized frame **600.00**

6" x 7-1/2", watercolor on ivory, young lady, attributed to Jacob Maentel, oval blue ground, lady in blue and white dress, orange ribbon on head covering, orig frame **3,025.00**

6-1/4" w, 7-1/2" h, watercolor and pencil on paper, young man, brown coat, red vest, red paint, bevel edge pine frame.... **350.00**

MINIATURES

History: There are three sizes of miniatures: dollhouse scale (ranging from 1/2 to 1 inch), sample size, and child's size. Since most early material is in museums or extremely expensive, the most common examples in the marketplace today are from the 20th century.

Many mediums were used for miniatures: silver, copper, tin, wood, glass, and ivory. Even books were printed in miniature. Price ranges are broad, influenced by scarcity and quality of workmanship.

The collecting of miniatures dates back to the 18th century. It remains one of the world's leading hobbies.

Buffet with shelf, walnut, two half drawers, two lower cupboards, bracket feet, 13" w, 18" h, **$450**.
Photo courtesy of Joy Luke.

Blanket chest, pine, dovetailed, **$250**.
Photo courtesy of Wiederseim Associates, Inc.

Child or doll size

Bed, 28-5/8" l, 16" w, 15-3/4" h, Arts & Crafts, rect headboard with two cartoon-like images of baby dolls, footboard with two sq-form cut-outs, imperfections
.... **230.00**

Blanket chest, six-board
9-3/4" l, 4-1/2" w, 6-3/4" h, America, early 19th C, pine, wire hinged top, dovetail and mortise and tenon constructed box, cavity with two compartments, natural surface..................... **3,650.00**

11" l, 6" w, 7-1/2" h, America, early 19th C, poplar, dovetailed, sq nail construction, molded lid and base, turned feet, brass hinges, orig red covered by old mustard paint..... **4,400.00**

15-3/4" l, 7-1/2" w, 7-3/4" h, poplar, dovetailed, old thin red wash, applied moldings around lid and base with worn black paint, dated on back "Mar 6, 1827," restorations to hinge rail, feet missing
.... **460.00**

16 3/4" l, 11" w, 12 1/2" h, Lancaster County, PA, dovetailed, bracket feet, molding at lid and bottom, till, red paint dec, old splits in lid
.... **1,760.00**

20-3/4" l, 10-3/8" w, 9-5/8" h, New England, early 19th C, blue painted pine, rect hinged top with applied molded edge, dovetailed case, molded bracket base, wear
.... **550.00**

Bookcase, hp, scalloped cornice over four open shelves, base with three drawers, Peter Hunt dec **1,650.00**

Box on frame, America, early 19th C, grain painted, pine dome-top box with wire hinges, frame with vase and ring-turned legs, int. lined with floral patterned wallpaper, 7" w, 4" d, 5-3/4" h....................... **2,720.00**

Chairs, doll sized, cane seats, saber legs, price for pair, **$100**.
Photo courtesy of Wiederseim Associates, Inc.

Bucket, cov, 4-1/2" d, 3-7/8" h, turned wood, two drilled handles, turned lid, orig yellow paint on outside, orange on inside, white, red, black, and blue designs, some wear and varnish flaking................ **150.00**

Buffet, 9" w, 4-3/4" d, 13-3/4" h, carved wood, dark stained finish, two spindled shelves, lower section with two chip carved front doors, carved and stippled stylized floral dec on sides, Normandy, early 20th C
.... **235.00**

Chair, arm, 7" w, 5-3/4" d, 13-1/2" h, New England, mid-19th C, carved maple, ball, vase, and ring turnings on banister back, stiles ending in ball finials, finely turned arms, legs, and stretchers, orig upholstered seat **470.00**

Chair, side, 10-3/4" seat, 22" h, worn orig light green paint, black striping, gold stenciling, polychrome floral dec, pr .. **625.00**

Chest of drawers, two handkerchief boxes on top, three drawers, pine, scalloped base, dovetailed, mirror missing, **$225**. (Shown with lapped finger storage boxes on top.)

Chest of drawers, long drawer over pair of cupboard doors, simulated bamboo turned decoration with small shelves, **$240**.

Chest of drawers, oak and chestnut, three long drawers, shaped back with crest, candle shelves, and mirror, simulated bamboo turnings, **$295**.

Chest of drawers, Chippendale style, four drawers, bird's eye maple drawer fronts, mahogany case, brass knobs, bun feet, **$350**.

Chest of drawers
10" l, 5-1/2" d, 11-1/2" h, Carlisle, Cumberland County, PA, softwood, paint dec, four drawers, sq nail construction, scrolled ribbon dec on front, wooden pulls, light brown grain paint dec, dark brown highlights to imitate burled walnut **990.00**
14" w, 7-1/2" d, 10-1/4" h, Biedermeier-style, fruitwood

veneer, wire nail construction, three drawers, applied half turned pilasters painted black, capped with ormolu trim, tapered sq legs, old refinishing, green velvet lining in drawers, small brass pulls **550.00**

Cupboard, step-back
24" w, 11" d, 37-1/4" h, middle Atlantic States, mid-19th C, cherry, flat-molded cornice above cock-beaded case, two cupboard doors with raised panels, two shelves int., arched opening over projecting case with two short drawers with applied molding, two raised-panel cupboard doors, old red-stained surface **1,725.00**
24-1/2" w, 8-1/8" d, 33" h, New England, early 19th C, stained, molded top overhangs case of two drawers opening to two-shelved int., stepped out board overhangs two drawers on legs, side shaping, orig surface.................... **1,265.00**

Rocker, Empire style, mahogany, vase-shaped splat, rush seat, scrolled arms, 22" h **225.00**

Settee, 7-5/8" l, 7-5/8" w, 4-1/4" h, carved wood, dark stained finish, serpentine back, openwork spindled flowerheads and chip-carved and stippled stylized floral dec, hinged lid, Normandy, early 20th C **145.00**

Settle bench, 24" l, 6-1/2" w, 6-1/2" h seat, PA, orig gold, copper, and silver fruit dec along crest and back slats, mustard yellow ground with areas of wear and touch-up, scrolled arms, plank seat with incised borders, eight turned legs, restoration **825.00**

Spiral staircase, 17-5/8" w, 8-5/8" d, 22-1/8" h, mahogany, dark rosewood grained finials, rect base with demilune cut out in center, late 19th C **1,500.00**

Stool
7-1/2" l, 4-3/4" w, 4-1/2" h, foot, pine, sq nail construction, D-shape cut-out legs, side skirt, orig natural wood finish with folky diamond and line inlaid wood on top, label "Stool belongs to Hannah C. Raymond" **935.00**

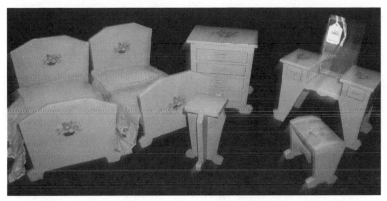

Bedroom suite, cottage style, painted green, pink floral decoration, doll size, **$65**.
Photo courtesy of Alderfer Auction Co.

Table and chairs, Arts & Crafts type style, hand made, doll size, played with condition, **$45**.
Photo courtesy of Alderfer Auction Co.

8-5/8" d, 5-1/2" h, dec pine, round top, shaped legs, painted red with yellow and blue star, circular stenciled dec, America, 19th C, repair **560.00**
Table, drop leaf, Sheraton, walnut, pine secondary wood, leaves with decoratively cut corners, one dovetailed drawer, turned legs, old finish, minor edge damage, hinges replaced, age crack on top, 23-1/2" l, 12-1/2" w, 10-3/4" l leaves, 19" h **1,100.00**

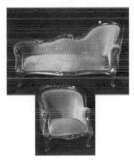

Parlor suite, Victorian, doll sized, mahogany, rose velvet upholstery, 34" l x 18" h sofa with carved backrail, 15" w x 18" h armchair, **$150**.
Photo courtesy of Joy Luke Auctions.

Dollhouse accessories

Bird cage, brass, bird, stand, 7" h **65.00**
Carpet sweeper, gilt, Victorian **65.00**
Christmas tree, decorated **50.00**
Coffeepot, brass **25.00**
Cup and saucer, china, flower design, c1940 .... **10.00**

Decanter, two matching tumblers, Venetian, c1920 **35.00**
Fireplace, tin, Britannia metal tretwork, draped mantel, carved grate **85.00**
Radio, Strombecker, c1930 .... **35.00**
Refrigerator, Petite Princess **75.00**
Silhouettes, Tynietoy, c1930, pr **25.00**
Telephone, wall, oak, speaker and bell, German, c1890 .. **40.00**
Towel stand, golden oak, turned post **45.00**
Umbrella stand, brass, ormolu, sq, emb palm fronds **60.00**

Welsh dresser, burlwood, two shelves, three small drawers, cabriole legs, 13-1/2" w, 17" h, **$575**.
Photo courtesy of Joy Luke.

Dollhouse furniture

Armoire, tin litho, purple and black **35.00**
Bathroom, wood, painted white, Strombecker **40.00**
Buffet set, stenciled, three shelves, column supports, Biedermeier, 6" h............. **400.00**
Chair, ormolu, ornate, 3" h, c1900, pr......................... **75.00**

Cradle, cast iron, painted green, 2" l **40.00**
Desk, Chippendale style, slant front................................... **60.00**
Dining room, Edwardian style, dark red stain, extension table, chairs, marble top cupboard, grandfather clock, chandelier, candelabra, 5" h bisque shoulder head maid doll, table service for six, Gebruder Schneerass, Waltershausen, Thuringa, c1915........... **1,400.00**
Kitchen set, litho tin, Modern Kitchen, all parts and pieces, animals, and related items, orig box, Louis Marx **250.00**
Living room, Empire style, sofa, fainting couch, two side chairs, upholstered tapestry, matching drapery **350.00**
Piano, grand, wood, eight keys, 5" h..................................... **35.00**
Sewing table, golden oak, drawer, c1880................ **100.00**
Table, tin, painted brown, white top, floral design, 1-1/2" x 3/4" h, ornate............................. **30.00**
Tea cart, Petite Princess .. **25.00**
Vanity, Biedermeier **90.00**

MINTON CHINA

History: In 1793, Thomas Minton joined other men to form a partnership and build a small pottery at Stoke-on-Trent, Staffordshire, England. Production began in 1798 with blueprinted earthenware, mostly in the Willow pattern. In 1798, cream-colored earthenware and bone china were introduced.

A wide range of styles and wares was produced. Minton introduced porcelain figures in 1826, Parian wares in 1846, encaustic tiles in the late 1840s, and Majolica wares in 1850. Many famous designers and artists in the English pottery industry worked for Minton.

In 1883, the modern company was formed and called Mintons Limited. The "s" was dropped in 1968. Minton still produces bone-china tablewares and some ornamental pieces.

Marks: Many early pieces are unmarked or have a Sevres-type marking. The "ermine" mark was used in the early 19th century. Date codes can be found on tableware and majolica. The mark used between 1873 and 1911 was a small globe with a crown on top and the word "Minton."

Pilgrim flask, designed by Christopher Dresser, butterflies within Oriental border, sky blue ground, stamped "Minton's" with crown, 6" x 5-1/2", **$2,990**.

Photo courtesy of David Rago Auctions, Inc.

Bud vase and stand, 6-7/8" h, majolica, amphora shape, double handled vase seated in tripod stand, molded ram's heads and hoof feet, impressed mark on base, England, 1863, glaze crazing **1,175.00**
Centerpiece, 16" l, elongated parian vessel, molded scroll handles and feet, pierced rim, two brown reserves, white pate-sur-pate amorini, gilding, dec, attributed to Lawrence Birks, marked "Minton," retailer's marks

of Thomas Goode & Co., Ltd., London, c1889 .... **1,400.00**
Compote, 10-1/2" l, majolica, figural, lobed oval dish and plinth, brown glaze on agate body, dish supported on backs of two cherubs holding laurel wreaths, center lovebirds, impressed mark, c1863 **2,415.00**
Dinner service, partial, Florentine pattern, 12 10-1/2" d dinner plates; 12 9" d luncheon plates; 12 2-3/8" h teacups; 11 saucers; 10 10-1/2" d soup plates; eight 8" d dessert plates; seven 2-5/8" h coffee cups; six 7" d side plates; five 4-5/8" bowls; three 13", 15", 17" l graduated serving platters; two 10-1/2" l cov serving dishes; two small oval dishes; two pickle dishes; two 5-5/8" d side plates; a sq cov serving dish; cov sugar; creamer; milk jug; sauce boat and undertray; 9-3/4" d serving bowl; open 12" l serving tureen; 15" l cov tureen, 108 pieces total, third quarter 19th C...... **2,185.00**
Figure, 10-1/2" h, putti, yellow basket and grape vine, 1867, professional repair at rim of basket **2,750.00**
Floor urn, 35" h, 18" d, majolica, Neo-Classical, turquoise, massive foliage handles
.... **12,650.00**
Garden set, 17-3/4" h, earthenware, barrel form, central pierced band of entwined rings between blue printed bands of flowers, scrolled vines, imp mark, 19th C, glaze wear, price for pr **1,100.00**
Jardinière, 21" h, majolica, ftd, bowl with swags of fruit terminating at lion masks, base molded with three partially draped male figures between cornucopia of fruits, impressed mark, England, c1868, restored
.... **3,525.00**
Nut dish, 9-3/4" l, majolica, leaf-molded dish with squirrel handle, imp mark, c1869, restored chips to ears .. **1,840.00**
Oyster plate, majolica
   Mottled........................ **935.00**
   Turquoise **495.00**
Oyster server, four tiers, majolica, green and brown, white wells, turquoise finial, rim damage to six wells, mechanical turning mechanism missing
.... **3,575.00**

Plate, enamel decoration, Oriental medallion of peony and prunus, sky blue ground, faint stamp, 1874, light wear to gild on rim, 9" d, **$700**.

Photo courtesy of David Rago Auctions, Inc.

Plaque, 11-1/2" sq, painted scene of Dutch man reading document by row of books, initials "HH" lower right, date mark for 1883, framed **290.00**
Plate, 9" d, hp, polychrome dec, garlands and swags on rims, marked "Mintons/England/Rd. No. 608547/73793/Pat. Apr 1st 1913," price for set of 12 **225.00**
Portrait plate, 9" d, Duchess de Berri Caroline, Princis Lambelle, Madame Mars, Madame Elizabeth, sgd "A.S.I.," names on reverse, price for set of four
.... **350.00**
Sweetmeat dish, 8" d, majolica, blue titmouse on branch, leaf-shaped dish, imp mark, 1888
.... **675.00**
Tower pitcher, 12-1/2" h, majolica, castle molded body with relief of dancing villagers in medieval dress, imp marks, c1873, chips to cov thumb rest, spout rim **1,035.00**
Vase, 6-1/4" h, celadon green ground, five-spout, fan form, applied white floral relief, fish head feet, imp mark, c1855, foot rim chip **215.00**

MOCHA

History: Mocha decoration usually is found on utilitarian creamware and stoneware pieces and was produced through a simple chemical action. A color pigment of brown, blue, green, or black was made acidic by an infusion of tobacco or hops. When the acidic colorant was applied in blobs to an alkaline ground, it reacted by spreading in feathery designs resembling sea plants. This type of decoration usually was supplemented with bands of light-colored slip.

Types of decoration vary greatly, from those done in a combination of motifs, such as Cat's Eye and Earthworm, to a plain pink mug decorated with green ribbed bands. Most forms of mocha are hollow, e.g., mugs, jugs, bowls, and shakers.

English potters made the vast majority of the pieces. Collectors group the wares into three chronological periods: 1780-1820, 1820-1840, and 1840-1880.

Reproduction Alert.

Small bowl with handle, earthworm decoration, **$850**.

Photo courtesy of Alderfer Auction Co.

Large bowl with decoration, seaweed decoration, **$395**.

Photo courtesy of Alderfer Auction Co.

Bowl, white and brown bands, white band with blue seaweed decoration, hairline, 12" d, 5-1/2" h, **$100**.

Photo courtesy of Alderfer Auction Co.

Beaker, pearlware

3" h, dark brown, medium brown, and ochre marble decoration on rust field, thin lines of medium brown at rim and base, England, early 19th C, rim chips and glaze wear **2,475.00**

3" h, rust, dark brown, medium brown, and white combed marble slip, England, early 19th C **2,820.00**

Bowl

6-7/8" d, 3-1/2" h, ochre band, black seaweed, crazing, stains **275.00**

7-1/4" d, 3-1/4" h, aqua band, blue stripes, blue, brown, and white earthworm design, faint imp label, stained, small edge flakes **325.00**

Chamber pot, 8-3/4" d, two-tone blue bands, black stripes, black and white earthworm, leaf handle, some wear and edge flakes.............................. **125.00**

Child's mug

2-1/2" h, pearlware, green glazed rouletted upper and lower bands flanking rust field with dark brown scroddled dots, with bisecting lines cut through slip to white body, applied handle, England, early 19th C, repaired. **825.00**

2-5/8" h, black banding with black and gray earthworm dec on green field, yellow glazed, extruded handle with foliate terminals, impressed partial maker's mark on bottom, England, early 19th C, chips to base edge, glaze wear to rim **2,990.00**

Creamer, 5-1/4" h, black and white checkered band on shoulder medium blue glaze **215.00**

Cup, 2-7/8" h, imp border above brown and white earthworm design, blue ground, 19th C, imperfections **375.00**

Coffeepot, baluster-form, footed, pearlware, dark brown bands on buff body, dark brown "tree" designs, extruded ribbed handle, England, 19th century, rim chips on cover, 10-3/4" h, **$1,100**.

Photo courtesy of Skinner, Inc.

Creamer, band of decoration in blue and brown on yellow body, hairlines, 4-1/2" h, **$120**.

Photo courtesy of Alderfer Auction Co.

Ink sander, 3-1/4" h, pearlware, two rows of dark brown trailed slip "tendrils" on blue field, England, early 19th C, two small chips **1,175.00**

Jug, 7-1/2" h, barrel-form, banded in blue and black, black, white, and blue earthworm dec on ocher field, handles with foliate terminals, England, c1840, 5/8" rim chip, associated crack, 1/2" chip on spout **1,880.00**

Measure, 5", 6", and 6-1/4" h, tankard, blue, black and tan seaweed dec, one with applied white label "Imperial Pint," other with resist label "Quart," minor stains, wear, and crazing, three-pc set **440.00**

Milk pitcher, 4-5/8" h, dark bluish-gray band, black stripes, emb band with green and black seaweed, leaf handle, wear and painted over spout flake . **440.00**

Mug

3" h, brown checkerboard design, 19th C **260.00**

3-1/2" h, 4-1/8" d, ftd, pink, blue, and black marbling, England, 19th C, five small hairlines on rim **300.00**

3-7/8" h, barrel-form, black mocha seaweed dec on ocher field between black and blue bands, extruded handles with foliate terminals, England, c1820, small chip on base edge **1,410.00**

6" h, quart, banded in dark brown and rust, two rows of blue, dark brown, rust, and white earthworm flanked by upper and lower white rouletted bands, extruded handle with foliate terminals, England, early 19th C, circular and spider cracks in the base, three rim chips......... **1,765.00**

Mug, band of blue seaweed on cream band on yellow ground, 3" d, 3" h, **$460**.
Photo courtesy of Alderfer Auction Co.

Mustard pot, cov
2-1/2" h, creamware, blue banded lid with blue reeded band, cylindrical body with matching banding, dark brown, rust, gray, and white earthworm pattern, extruded handle with foliate handles, creamware, England, early 19th C, chips to the lid, small crack to the body, discoloration **1,300.00**
3-1/2" h, pearlware, lid with acorn finial, brown bands with dendritic seaweed on rust field, body decorated in the same manner, extruded handle with foliate terminals, England, early 19th C, finial repair, small rim and base chips **1,645.00**
3-1/2" h, pearlware, lid with ball finial banded in dark brown and rust, matching banding on the body, unusual band of rust and dark brown slip in finely trailed diamond pattern, extruded handle with foliate terminals, England, early 19th C, crack in the handle, minor glaze wear **2,585.00**

Pitcher
Large band of dark brown seaweed and beaded diamonds on ochre ground between bands of dark brown and green stripes, imp chevron bands, 8-1/2" h, some minor glaze loss **1,725.00**
Yellowware, brown bands, black seaweed, glaze flaking, three base chips **5,250.00**
Portrait box, 5" d, transfer and painted dec of Napoleon III and Empress Eugenie **150.00**

Salt, open, 2-3/4" d, 1-3/4" h, chocolate brown band, black seaweed dec, small chip on foot **520.00**
Shaker
4-1/8" h, tan bands, brown stripes, black seaweed dec, chips **220.00**
4-7/8" h, blue band, black stripe, brown, black, and white earthworm dec, blue top, repair **330.00**

Tea canister, rare slip-marbled creamware tea appliqué marbled in dark brown, ochre, white, and gray with green-glazed reeded bands at foot and shoulder, England, c1780, one rim chip and slip/glaze losses to side, lacking cover, 4-3/4" h, **$2,500**.
Photo courtesy of Skinner, Inc.

Tea canister, 4" h, blue, black, and white band on shoulder, white fluted band on bottom, medium blue glaze **125.00**
Teapot, 5-7/8" h, oval shape, medium blue, fluted band on bottom, black and white checkered band on top, acorn finial **500.00**
Waste bowl, 4-3/4" d, amber band, black seaweed dec separated into five segments by squiggly lines, green molded lip band, stains and hairlines **275.00**

MOORCROFT

History:
William Moorcroft was first employed as a potter by James Macintyre & Co., Ltd., of Burslem in 1897. He established the Moorcroft pottery in 1913.

The majority of the art pottery wares were hand thrown, resulting in a great variation among similarly styled pieces. Color and marks are keys to determining age.

Walker, William's son, continued the business upon his father's

death and made wares in the same style.

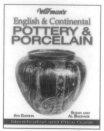

For more information, see *Warman's English & Continental Pottery & Porcelain*, 4th edition.

Marks: The company initially used an impressed mark, "Moorcroft, Burslem"; a signature mark, "W. Moorcroft" followed. Modern pieces are marked simply "Moorcroft," with export pieces also marked "Made in England."

Cabinet vase, orchid design, glossy cobalt blue ground, paper label, 2-1/2" d, 3-3/4" h, **$235**.
Photo courtesy of David Rago Auctions, Inc.

Bowl, 3-5/8" d, pansy dec, pale green ground, imp maker's mark **150.00**
Box, cov, 4-3/4" l, 1-1/2" w, 1-3/4" h, pansy dec on lid, pale green ground, imp maker's mark, crazing **200.00**
Compote, 7-1/4" d, Lily motif, yellow and green ground **150.00**
Ginger jar, cov, 11-1/2" h, pomegranate dec **525.00**
Jar, cov, Cornflower, ivory ground, coat of arms of Kings College, Oxford, c1911 .... **1,450.00**

Lamp base, 6-1/4" d, 11-1/4" h, Anemone.......................... **920.00**
Loving cup, 6" d, 5-1/2" h, Pomegranate pattern, stamped mark, 1914-16, minor rim fleck **1,150.00**
Pitcher, 6-1/4" h, Forget-Me-Not, c1902 .... **1,350.00**
Plate, 7-1/4" d, toadstool, blue ground, imp "Moorcroft Claremont" **600.00**

Plate, Pomegranate and Berry pattern, glossy cobalt blue ground, stamped "Made In England," ink signature, mounted in metal plate hange, small plate ring chip, 8-1/2" d, **$175**.
Photo courtesy of David Rago Auctions, Inc.

Vase, Lily pattern, yellow and red flowers, cobalt blue ground, marked "Moorcroft Made in England," 4-3/4" h, **$225**.

Vase
6-1/2" d, 15" h, Eventide pattern, ovoid, squeezebag green tall trees, cobalt blue ground, stamped "Moorcroft/Made in England" and signature, rim chip, 2" line **1,840.00**
7" h, Leaf & Berry, matte glaze, William's initials in blue **1,150.00**
7-3/8" h, Pomegranate, vasiform, blue ground, red pomegranates, purple seeds, imp factory mark with facsimile signature, printed paper Royal Warrant label, 1928-49...................... **500.00**

12" h, Orchid, flambé, sgd by William in blue, imp "Potter to HM The Queen" **4,350.00**
12-3/8" h, long narrow neck on bulbous base, green poppies, green ground, Moorcroft handmade pottery paper label, painted signature, imp mark, and "made in England," c1918, rim restoration **1,410.00**

MORGANTOWN GLASS WORKS

History: The Morgantown Glass Works, Morgantown, West Virginia, was founded in 1899 and began production in 1901. Reorganized in 1903, it operated as the Economy Tumbler Company for 20 years until, In 1923, the word "Tumbler" was dropped from the corporate title. The firm was then known as The Economy Glass Company until reversion to its original name, Morgantown Glass Works, Inc., in 1929, the name it kept until its first closing in 1937. In 1939, the factory was reopened under the aegis of a guild of glassworkers and operated as the Morgantown Glassware Guild from that time until its final closing. Purchased by Fostoria in 1965, the factory operated as a subsidiary of the Moundsville-based parent company until 1971, when Fostoria opted to terminate production of glass at the Morgantown facility. Today, collectors use the generic term, "Morgantown Glass," to include all periods of production from 1901 to 1971.

Morgantown was a 1920s leader in the manufacture of colorful wares for table and ornamental use in American homes. The company pioneered the processes of iridization on glass, as well as gold and platinum encrustation of patterns. It enhanced Crystal offerings with contrasting handle and foot of India Black, Spanish Red (ruby), and Ritz Blue (cobalt blue), and other intense and pastel colors for which it is are famous. The company conceived the use of contrasting shades of fired enamel to add color to its etchings. It was

the only American company to use a chromatic silk-screen printing process on glass, its two most famous and collectible designs being Queen Louise and Manchester Pheasant.

For more information, see *Warman's Glass*, 4th edition.

The company is also known for ornamental "open stems" produced during the late 1920s. Open stems separate to form an open design midway between the bowl and foot, e.g., an open square, a "Y," or two diamond-shaped designs. Many of these open stems were purchased and decorated by Dorothy C. Thorpe in her California studio, and her signed open stems command high prices from today's collectors. Morgantown also produced figural stems for commercial clients such as Koscherak Brothers and Marks & Rosenfeld. Chanticleer (rooster) and Mai Tai (Polynesian ibis) cocktails are two of the most popular figurals collected today.

Morgantown is best known for the diversity of design in its stemware patterns, as well as for its four patented optics: Festoon, Palm, Peacock, and Pineapple. These optics were used to embellish stems, jugs, bowls, liquor sets, guest sets, salvers, ivy and witch balls, vases, and smoking items.

Most glass collectors recognize two well-known lines of Morgantown Glass today: #758 Sunrise Medallion and #7643 Golf Ball Stem Line. When Economy introduced #758 in 1928, it was originally identified as "Nymph." By 1931, the Morgantown front office had renamed it Sunrise Medallion. Recent publications erred in labeling it "dancing girl." Upon careful study of the medallion, you can see the figure is poised on one tiptoe, musically saluting the dawn with her horn. The second well-known line, #7643 Golf Ball, was patented in 1928; production commenced immediately and continued until the company closed in 1971. More Golf Ball than any other Morgantown product is found on the market today.

Basket
Patrick, #19-4358, Ritz Blue, applied crystal twisted handle, mint leaf prunts, 5" d, 9-3/4" h......................... **750.00**
Quilt, crystal, black/amethyst rope-twist handle, leaf form appliqués where handle joins basket, ground pontil
.... **1,100.00**
Trindle, #4357, amethyst, applied crystal twisted reed handle, c1930, 9"........ **725.00**

Berry jug, Palm Optic, #37, pink, 8-1/2" w, 9-1/8" h **235.00**

Bowl
Fantassia, Bristol Blue, #67, 5-1/2" d **95.00**
Janice, #4355, Ritz Blue, 13" d
.... **475.00**
Woodsfield, Genova Line, 12-1/2" d, #12-1/2 .... **565.00**

Brandy snifter, Golf Ball, #7643, red, crystal base, 4" w, 6-1/4" h
.... **130.00**

Candleholders, pr
Golf Ball, #7643, Torch Candle, single, Ritz Blue, 6" h
.... **300.00**
Hamilton, #87, Evergreen, 5" h
.... **65.00**
Modern, #80, Moss Green, 7-1/2" h......................... **90.00**

Saranac Sunrise, bowl, Gloria Blue, **$85.**
Photo courtesy of Dotta Auction Co., Inc

Candle vase, ruby, 5-1/2" h
.... **55.00**
Candy jar, cov
Mansfield, #200, burgundy matte, 12" h................ **200.00**

Rachael, crystal, Pandora cutting, 6" h................ **395.00**
Champagne
#7617, ruby bowl.......... **48.00**
#7643, Golf Ball, Ritz blue, 5"
.... **55.00**
#7860, Lawton, Azure, Festoon Optic, 5 oz **50.00**
Cocktail
Chanticleer, crystal....... **30.00**
Elizabeth, blue, twisted stem, 5-3/4" h **75.00**
Filament stem, crystal, ruby filament, 4-1/2" h.......... **48.00**
Golf Ball, #7643, crystal, Chateau cutting **25.00**
Ruby bowl, #7617......... **45.00**
Venus, #7577, Anna Rose, Palm Optic, 3 oz **40.00**
Cocktail set, Deco, black, 7-3/4" h pitcher with weighted base, five 3" w, 3" h cocktail glasses............................. **65.00**
Compote, Reverse Twist, #7654, aquamarine, 6-1/2" d, 6-3/4" h
.... **225.00**
Console bowl, El Mexicana, #12933, Seaweed, 10" d. **425.00**
Cordial, 1-1/2 oz
Brilliant, #7617, Spanish Red
.... **140.00**
Golf Ball, #7643, Ritz blue
.... **68.00**
Mikado, crystal **30.00**
Finger bowl, Art Moderne, #7640, Faun etch, crystal and black, 4-1/2" d, ftd........... **150.00**
Goblet
Art Moderne, #7640, Faun etch, crystal and black, 7-3/4" h **125.00**
Golf Ball, #7643, Ritz blue
.... **60.00**
Paragon, #7624, ebony open stem, 10 oz **215.00**
Queen Louise, #7664, 3-1/2" d, 7-1/2" h **400.00**

Old English, cocktails, Ritz Blue, **each $60**.
Photo courtesy of Dotta Auction Co., Inc.

Guest set, Trudy, #23, Bristol Blue, 6-3/8" h **145.00**
Iced tea tumbler, Vision, white on white **45.00**
Ice tub, El Mexicana, #1933, Seaweed, 6" d................ **225.00**
Jug
Kaufmann, #6, Doric star sand blast, 54 oz........ **295.00**
Melon, #20069, Alabaster, Ritz Blue trim **1,450.00**
Measuring cup, 3-1/8" d, 2-7/8" h, adv "Your Credit is Good Pickerings, Furnishings, 10th & Penn, Pittsburgh," clear.. **315.00**
Oyster cup, 2-3/8" d, Sunrise Medallion, blue **190.00**
Pilsner, Floret, etch #796, Lando, 12 oz.................... **65.00**
Plate
Anna Rose, #734 American Beauty etch, 7" d **65.00**
Carlton Madrid, topaz, 6" d
.... **35.00**
Sherbet
Crinkle, #1962, pink, 6 oz
.... **30.00**
Golf Ball, #7643, Ritz blue
.... **50.00**
Sophisticate, #7646, Picardy etch, 5-1/2 oz............... **55.00**

Old English, iced tea goblets, Ritz Blue, **each $65.**
Photo courtesy of Alderfer Auction Co.

Sherry, Golf Ball, #7643, Spanish Red **43.00**
Tumbler, water, Owl
Brown **60.00**
Gold.............................. **65.00**
Urn, #1160, Bristol Blue, ftd, 6-1/2" h........................... **65.000**
Vase
Catherine, #26, Azure, #758 Sunrise Medallion etch, bud, 10" h........................... **265.00**
Gypsy Fire, orig sticker, 4" h
.... **68.00**

Raindrop pattern, red/orange, yellow base, hobnail design on inside graduating in size down to base, 4-1/2" d, 10" h **35.00**

Wine
Empress, #7680-1/2, Spanish Red, 3 oz **90.00**
Filament stem, crystal, cobalt blue filament, 4-1/2" h... **65.00**
Golf Ball, Ritz blue, 4-5/8" h **58.00**
Vision, white on white ... **45.00**
#7617, ruby bowl **65.00**

MOSER GLASS

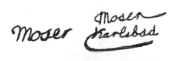

History: Ludwig Moser (1833-1910) founded his polishing and engraving workshop in 1857 in Karlsbad (Karlovy Vary), Czechoslovakia. He employed many famous glass designers, e.g., Johann Hoffmann, Josef Urban, and Rudolf Miller. In 1900, Moser and his sons, Rudolf and Gustav, incorporated Ludwig Moser & Söhne.

For more information, see *Warman's Glass*, 4th edition.

Moser art glass included clear pieces with inserted blobs of colored glass, cut colored glass with classical scenes, cameo glass, and intaglio cut items. Many inexpensive enameled pieces also were made.

In 1922, Leo and Richard Moser bought Meyr's Neffe, their biggest Bohemian art glass rival. Moser executed many pieces for the Wiener Werkstätte in the 1920s.

Basket, 7" h, cranberry, gold encrusted handle, high relief enameled flowers............ **450.00**

Box, cov, 5-1/4" w, amethyst, base dec with band of Amazon warriors, lid with medallion of Spanish galleon, sgd "Moser" **350.00**

Bowl, oblong paneled amber bowl, detailed engraving of bull elk in forest, signed signature on base, 9" l, 3-3/4" h, original lined and fitted box, **$1,000**.

Photo courtesy of Early Auction Co.

Bowl
7" d, enameled scrolled foliate dec, cranberry shaded rim, c1900, matching underplate **1,035.00**
7-1/4" w and 9-1/4" w, horizontal band of cranberry cut to clear, gilt scrolling, pink roses, price for pr **200.00**
9" l, 3-3/4" h, oblong paneled amber bowl, detailed engraving of bull elk in forest, sgd signature on base, orig lined and fitted box.. **1,000.00**
Candy dish, cov, 7-1/2" h, green cut to clear, matching lid, acid stamped "Moser Karlsbad" **150.00**
Cologne bottle, 7-1/2" h, 3-1/2" d, amethyst shaded to clear, deep intaglio cut flowers and leaves, orig stopper, sgd **695.00**

Cordial, 4" h, cranberry bowl, crystal stem, horizontal gilt bands dec with colorful enameled florals and scrolling, price for matched set of six **400.00**
Cream pitcher, 3-1/4" h, translucent body shading to green, gilt medallions, raised green "jewels" **350.00**
Cup and saucer, 4-1/2" w, 2-1/2" h, clear graduating to translucent green, yellow and gold scrolling daffodils, script sgd "Moser" in body, price for matched sets **275.00**
Decanter, 8-3/4" h, flat sided, green translucent glass, gilt collar dec with overall gold floral scrolling **325.00**
Decanter set, 11" h faceted stopper bottle dec with green medallion and fine gold scrolling, six matching 3" h cordials, matching 9-1/2" d tray, chips to stopper finial and cordials **750.00**
Dresser box, cov, hinged 5" d, round, translucent green, autumn oak leaves on brown branches, raised acorn jewels **475.00**
11" l, 4" h, rect, Prussian blue, multicolored fans and foliage dec, small foot chips .. **375.00**
Egg cup, 4-1/4" h, thumbprint patterned translucent colorless ground, red, blue, yellow, and green leaves on brown and yellow vines, chip on foot **230.00**

Punch bowl, covered, 12 matching mugs, deep ruby red, gold and enameled decoration, ring handles, **$950**. Close-up of a mug at top left.

Ewer, 10-3/4" h, cranberry, gilt surface, applied acorns and clear jewels **2,000.00**

Finger bowl, underplate

4-1/2" d bowl, 6" d underplate, translucent amethyst, intaglio cut leafy stemmed flowers, price for set of four **850.00**

6" w, 3" h, cranberry, overall gold scrolling and foliate **250.00**

6" w, 3" h, green, overall gold florals and scrolling **175.00**

7" w, 3-1/2" h, scalloped underplate, clear ground, red, blue, green, and pink acanthus scrollwork, accented with banded peacock eyes, attributed to Lobmeyer.................... **800.00**

7" w, 3-1/2" h, translucent green, gold gilt horizontal bands, pastel scrolling and flowers **600.00**

Goblet

6-1/4" h, shamrock shape, spreading foot, translucent blue body, overall gold flowers and scrolling, gold encrusted stalactite panels with silver scrolling, price for pr **675.00**

6-3/4" h, enameled scrolled foliage, gilt ground, green tinted rim, c1900, price for pr **1,265.00**

7" h, hand painted pastel scrolling flowers on body and foot, gilt bands, rim chip **475.00**

Juice glass, 2-1/2" h, cranberry, blue and pink flowers, gold scrolling over horizontal gilt bands, set of six.............. **200.00**

Pitcher, 6-3/4" h, amberina, IVT, four yellow, red, blue, and green applied glass beaded bunches of grapes, pinched in sides, three-dimensional bird beneath spout, allover enamel and gold leaves, vines, and tendrils **3,200.00**

Portrait vase, 8-1/2" h, woman, gold leaves, light wear.... **450.00**

Rose bowl, 3-1/2" h, cranberry ground, enameled florals and butterfly, applied acorns, c1900 .... **750.00**

Sherbet

4-1/2" h, enameled scrolled foliage, cranberry shaded rim, c1900, price for pr ... **1,100.00**

4-1/2" h, translucent cranberry, dec with purple, red, yellow, green, and white scrolling flowers on horizontal gilt bands, beaded highlights **500.00**

Tumbler, 3-3/4" h, enameled dec, c1910

Pale amber **50.00**

Pale blue...................... **50.00**

Urn, 15-3/4" h, cranberry, two gilt handles, studded with green, blue, clear, and red stones, highly enameled surface, multicolored and gilt Moorish dec.............................. **3,500.00**

Vase, deep amethyst, gold band around top, 12" h, **$285**.

Vase

5-3/4" h, faceted cylindrical, clear graduating to translucent green, four gilt and engraved medallion cartouches, blue accents, script sgd "Moser Karlsbad" **150.00**

9" h, bulbous stick, flaring rim, cranberry, banded gold and silver collar, polychrome scrolling, dots, and florals **300.00**

13" h, marquetry, ribbed, expanded bowl, tapering stem, intaglio cutting, cinnamon-colored marquetry flowers, pontil sgd "Moser Carlsbad" **4,250.00**

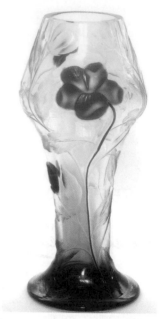

Vase, marquetry, ribbed, expanded bowl, tapering stem, intaglio cutting, cinnamon colored marquetry flowers, pontil signed "Moser Carlsbad," 13" h, **$4,250**.

Photo courtesy of Early Auction Co.

16-1/4" h, trumpet, ftd, optic ribbed, clear shading to pumpkin body, blue and yellow flowers, gray and orange scrolling.......... **500.00**

Wall vase, 10" h, conical, crackle body, enameled raised fish, colorful seaweed..... **900.00**

Water pitcher, 6-3/4" h, alternating gilt and translucent vertical bands dec with white, blue, and amethyst flowers................ **700.00**

Wine

7" h, shamrock shape, trumpet foot, translucent green body, gold scrolling dec, price for pr.......... **125.00**

8" h, elongated gold highlighted faceted stem, overall polychrome enameled scrolling on gold bands **600.00**

MOUNT WASHINGTON GLASS COMPANY

History: In 1837, Deming Jarves, founder of the Boston and Sandwich Glass Company, established for George D. Jarves, his son, the Mount Washington Glass Company in Boston, Massachusetts. In the following years, the leadership and the name of the company changed several times as George Jarves formed different associations.

In the 1800s, the company was owned and operated by Timothy Howe and William L. Libbey. In 1869, Libbey bought a new factory in New Bedford, Massachusetts. The Mount Washington Glass Company began operating again there under its original name. Henry Libbey became associated with the company early in 1871. He resigned in 1874 during the Depression, and the glassworks was closed. William Libbey had resigned in 1872, when he went to work for the New England Glass Company.

The Mount Washington Glass Company opened again in the fall of 1874 under the presidency of A. H. Seabury and the management of Frederick S. Shirley. In 1894, the glassworks became a part of the Pairpoint Manufacturing Company.

Throughout its history, the Mount Washington Glass Company made different types of glass including pressed, blown, art, lava, Napoli, cameo, cut, Albertine, and Verona.

Additional Listings: Burmese, Crown Milano, Peachblow, and Royal Flemish.

For more information, see *Warman's Glass*, 4th edition.

Banquet lamp, 23" h, Colonial Ware (shiny Crown Milano), white ground, sprays of golden roses and single petaled blossoms on globe shaped shade and base, molded-in floral, swag, and geometric dec on base, possibly orig opaque white chimney, burner sgd "Made in United States of America" **2,950.00**
Beverage set, satin, mother-of-pearl, yellow sea weed coralene dec, glossy finish, 9" h, bulbous water pitcher, three spout top, applied reeded shell handle, three matching 4" h tumblers, two blisters on pitcher, three-pc set **750.00**
Bowl, 4-1/2" d, 2-3/4" h, Rose amber, fuchsia, blue swirl bands, bell tone flint **295.00**
Collars and cuffs box, opalware, shaped as two collars with big bow in front, cov dec with orange and pink Oriental poppies, silver poppy-shaped finial with gold trim, base with poppies, white ground, gold trim, bright blue bow, white polka dots, buckle on back, sgd "Patent applied for April 10, 1894," #2390/128............ **950.00**
Compote, 6" d bowl, 9-1/2" h, Napoli, crystal clear ground, ten hp pink full bloom tea roses, green foliage **875.00**
Condiment set, opaque white salt and pepper shakers, cov mustard, hp floral dec, 6-1/2" h silver plated holder sgd "Wilcox Silverplate Co." **235.00**
Cracker jar, 8" h, opal glass, Egyptian motif, several camels at oasis, distant pyramid and mosque, sgd in lid with Pairpoint Diamond P, #3910, corresponding #3910/530 on jar **2,760.00**
Cruet, 7" h, Burmese, shiny finish, butter-yellow body, applied handle, mushroom stopper, each of 30 ribs with hint of pink, color blush intensifies on neck and spout, Mt. Washington **1,250.00**
Dresser box, 4-3/4" d, 3" h, portrait of young girl on cov, indigo blue ground, fancy embellishments at collar and other highlights, opaque white body, orig burgundy colors satin lining, sgd "4622/206" **750.00**
Flower holder, 5-1/4" d, 3-1/2" h, mushroom shape, white ground, blue dot and oak leaf dec **425.00**
Fruit bowl, 10" d, 7-1/2" h, Napoli, solid dark green ground painted on clear glass, outside dec with pale pink and white pond lilies, green and pink leaves and blossoms, int. dec with gold highlight traceries, silver-plated base with pond lily design, two applied loop handles, four buds form feet, base sgd "Pairpoint Mfg. Co. B4704" **2,200.00**
Humidor, 5-1/2" h, 4-1/2" d top, hinged silver-plated metalwork rim and edge, blown-out rococo scroll pattern, brilliant blue Delft windmills, ships, and landscape, Pairpoint........................... **950.00**
Jar, cov, 6" w, 5-1/2" h, peachblow, rim of jar and rim of lid cased in gold metal with raised leaves **400.00**
Jewel box, 4-1/2" d top, 5-1/4" d base, 3-1/4" h, opalware, Monk drinking glass of red wine on lid, solid shaded green background on cover and base, fancy gold-washed, silver-plated rim and hinge, orig satin lining, artist sgd "Schindler" **550.00**

Sugar shaker, raised enamel beaded decoration in floral vine motif, metal shaker fitting, 4-5/8" h, **$250**.

Photo courtesy of Alderfer Auction Co.

Jug, 6" h, 4" w, satin, Polka Dot, deep peachblow pink, white air traps, DQ, unlined, applied frosted loop handle......... **475.00**
Lamp, parlor, four dec glass oval insert panels, orig dec white opalware ball shade with deep red carnations, sgd "Pairpoint" base, c1890................. **1,750.00**
Lamp shade, 4-1/4" h, 5" d across top, 2" d fitter, rose amber, ruffled, fuchsia shading to deep blue, DQ **575.00**
Miniature lamp, 17" h, 4-1/2" d shade, banquet style, milk glass, bright blue Delft dec of houses and trees, orig metal fittings, attributed to Frank Guba.. **795.00**
Mustard pot, 4-1/2" h, ribbed, bright yellow and pink background, painted white and magenta wild roses, orig silver-plated hardware.............. **185.00**

Perfume bottle, 5-1/4" h, 3" d, opalware, dark green and brown glossy ground, red and yellow nasturtiums, green leaves, sprinkler top **375.00**

Pitcher, 6" h, 3" w, satin, DQ, MOP, large frosted camphor shell loop handle............. **325.00**

Plate, 7" d, Colonial Ware (shiny Crown Milano), white ground, pink cabbage rose, sprays of blue forget-me-nots, yellow daisies, purple chrysanthemums, dark red tulips, coral nasturtiums, white apple blossoms, white begonias, five raised gold rococo embellishments, sgd....... **550.00**

Rose bowl, 5" d, satin, blue shading to white base....... **45.00**

Salt and pepper shakers, pr, Four Lobe shape, white ground, colorful violet nosegays, salt top corroded **235.00**

Sugar shaker (muffineer)
3" h, 4" d, melon ribbed, opaque white ground, daffodil yellow orchid blossoms, two-part metal collar with emb butterfly, dragonfly, and blossom **400.00**
4" h, fig shape, bridal white body, daffodil yellow and pink blossoms **1,950.00**
4-1/4" h, egg shape, white shading to blue ground, pink and gold chrysanthemums **385.00**
4-1/2" h, egg shape, satin finish, overall green tint shading to pale green at base, vine laden with green leaves, naturalistically colored violet blossoms **385.00**

Sweet meat, 5-1/2" d, opaque ground, pseudo Burmese enameling, gilt flowers and leaves, accented with jeweled cabochons, emb bail handle, sgd, lid #P4408, one jewel missing............................ **815.00**

Syrup pitcher, Colonial Ware (shiny Crown Milano), white melon ribbed body, 15 sprays of blowers, gold scrollwork, pewter-like collar and lid............. **950.00**

Tumbler, Burmese, shiny finish, thin satin body, soft color blushes from rim to center then shading to pastel yellow base, Mt. Washington **375.00**

Vase
5-3/8" h, 4-1/8" d, Lava, jet black ground, blue, jade green, gray, white, red, and black chips, small in-the-making blister on one color chip......................... **2,500.00**
7-3/4" h, Burmese, satin finish, double gourd shape, finely drawn green and coral leafy tendrils, seven nosegays of blossoms, raised blue enamel forget-me-nots, each with pastel center with five coral dots, Mt. Washington, #147, c1885......................... **985.00**
9" h, Verona, stylized florals outlined in gold and silver, pastel pink background wash, sgd "Verona 918"..... **1,250.00**
10-1/4" h, stick, Burmese, yellow shading to pink, multicolored flowers dec, remnants of orig paper label **1,035.00**
11-1/4" h, gourd shape, 6" l flaring neck, satin, deep brown shading to gold, white lining, allover enameled seaweed design **550.00**

MULBERRY CHINA

History: Mulberry china was made primarily in the Staffordshire district of England between 1830 and 1860. The ware often has a flowing effect similar to flow blue. It is the color of crushed mulberries, a dark purple, sometimes with a gray tinge or bordering almost on black. The potteries that manufactured flow blue also made Mulberry china, and, in fact, frequently made some patterns in both types of wares. To date, there are no known reproductions.

Adviser: Ellen G. King.

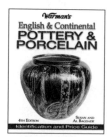

For more information, see *Warman's English & Continental Pottery & Porcelain*, 4th edition.

Educational Alert: The Flow Blue International Collectors' Club, Inc. has been studying and discussing new versus reproduction mulberry and flow blue. There are still areas of personal judgment as yet undetermined. The general rule accepted has been "*new*" indicates recent or contemporary manufacture and "*reproduction*" is a copy of an older pattern. Problems arise when either of these fields is sold at "*old*" flow blue prices.

In an effort to help educate its membership, the club continues to inform of all known changes through its conventions, newsletters, and the Web site: www.flowblue.com.

Warman's is working to those ends also. The following is a listing of "*new*" mulberry, produced since the 1960s.

Victoria Ware: Mark is of a lion and uniform, but has paper label "Made in China," 1990s. Made in various patterns and design, but the give-away is the roughness on the bottoms, and much of it has a pea green background. Some of this line is also being made in flow blue.

Check the Flow Blue International Collectors' Club, Inc., Web site and also www.repronews.com. Join the club, study the books available, and always, always, KNOW your dealer! Good dealers guarantee their merchandise and protect their customers.

Alleghany, Goodfellow, soup tureen, undertray **650.00**

Athens, Adams, posset cup, 12 panels **90.00**

Athens, Meigh
Child's cup and saucer **250.00**
Teapot, cov **400.00**

Beauties of China, Venables
Platter, polychromed, 14" l **325.00**
Teapot, cov **550.00**

Berry, Ridgways, teacup and saucer............................ **155.00**

Bluebell and Fern, unknown maker, plate, 9" d **135.00**

Bouquet, Wedgwood
  Charger, 12-1/2" d **125.00**
  Plate, 9" d.................... **65.00**
  Sauce ladle................ **110.00**
Bryonla, Utzshneider
  Cake plate, stemmed, 14"
  .... **375.00**
  Demitasse cup and saucer
  .... **50.00**
  Dessert dish, 4" **35.00**
  Fruit compote, ftd **220.00**
  Plate, 8" d.................... **45.00**
  Teacup and saucer....... **65.00**
California, Podmore Walker,
plate, 9-3/4" d.................. **80.00**

Corean, Podmore-Walker, creamer,
cockscomb, **$325.**

All mulberry china photos courtesy of Ellen King

Corean, Podmore-Walker, sugar,
covered, cockscomb, **$375.**

Corean, Podmore Walker
  Milk pitcher **195.00**
  Plate, 7-3/4" d **35.00**
  Plate, 8-3/4" d **55.00**
  Plate, 9-3/4" d **85.00**
  Platter, 14" l **225.00**
  Platter, 16" l **275.00**
  Platter, 17" l **350.00**

Corean, Podmore-Walker, teapot,
covered, cockscomb, **$325.**

  Platter, 18" l **425.00**
  Vegetable tureen, cov. **350.00**
Cyprus, Davenport
  Ewer pitcher, 11" h...... **275.00**
  Soap dish, cov............ **250.00**
  Soup tureen, cov **850.00**
Delhi, M. T. & Co.
  Plate, 10-1/4" d **110.00**
  Platter, 14" l **185.00**
Eagle, Podmore Walker, gravy
boat, undertray **125.00**
Flora, Walker
  Creamer, 5-3/4" **150.00**
  Cup and saucer, handleless
  .... **85.00**
  Pitcher, 12" h **200.00**
  Plate, 8" d **75.00**
Genoa, Davenport, platter
13-3/4" **200.00**
Heaths Flower, Heath, plate,
8" d.................................... **90.00**
Hopberry, unknown maker,
child's sugar bowl, cov ... **110.00**
Hyson, Clementson, teapot, cov
.... **355.00**
Jeddo, Adams
  Cup and saucer, handleless
  .... **80.00**
  Platter, 12-1/4" l **225.00**
  Platter, 173/4" l **300.00**
  Sauce tureen, cov, undertray
  .... **275.00**
  Teapot, cov **450.00**
  Vegetable bowl, round, 10" d
  .... **150.00**
Marble, Wedgwood
  Plate, 9" d **65.00**
  Platter, 15-1/2" l **150.00**
  Vegetable bowl, 9-1/2" d
  .... **90.00**
Medina, Furnival, plate, 9" d
  .... **75.00**
Milan, South Wales Pottery,
platter, 14" l **250.00**
Neva, Challinor, soup bowl,
rimmed, 10-1/2" d **135.00**

Jeddo, Adams, wash pitcher, **$300.**

Ning Po, R. Hall
  Cup plate..................... **55.00**
  Gravy boat................... **85.00**
  Plate, 7-1/2" d **60.00**
  Vegetable bowl, oval, 10" l
  .... **100.00**
  Vegetable tureen, cov **200.00**
  Waste bowl **95.00**
Pelew, Challinor
  Teapot, cov **325.00**
  Vegetable bowl, open, round,
  12-1/2" d **250.00**
Ranunculous, Wedgwood,
plate, 9" d......................... **65.00**
Rhone Scenery, Mayer
  Butter dish, cov **175.00**
  Plate, 10" d **65.00**
  Teacup and saucer....... **75.00**
Rose, Challinor
  Plate, 8" d **70.00**
  Plate, 10" d **95.00**
Rose, Walker
  Cup plate................... **110.00**
  Milk pitcher **225.00**
  Waste bowl **70.00**
Rose and Jessamine,
Wedgwood, sauce tureen, two
pcs................................... **165.00**
Royal, Wood & Son
  Plate, 9-3/4" d **85.00**
  Teacup and saucer....... **65.00**
Seaweed, Ridgway
  Teacup and saucer,
  handleless **135.00**
  Plate, 9" d **75.00**
Seville, Wood & Sons, plate,
9-1/4" d **50.00**
The Temple, Podmore Walker
  Bowl, 7" d.................... **125.00**
  Cup plate..................... **95.00**
  Plate, 8-3/4" d **75.00**

Wash basin and pitcher
.... **495.00**
Tiger Lily, Furnival, plate, 10" d
.... **90.00**
Tillenburg, Clementson, plate,
10-1/4" d.......................... **80.00**
Tulip & Fern, unknown maker,
Brushtroke pattern, relish, mitten
shape **155.00**
Vincennes, Alcock
  Platter, 18" l **350.00**
  Relish, mitten shape ... **300.00**
Washington vase, Podmore
Walker
  Plate, 8" d.................... **55.00**
  Platter, 16" l **275.00**
  Platter, 18" l **325.00**
  Sauce tureen, four pcs **550.00**
  Sugar bowl, cov......... **175.00**
Wreath, Furnival, plate, 9-3/4" d
.... **95.00**
Zinna, Bourne & Co., plate, 9" d
.... **95.00**

MUSICAL INSTRUMENTS

History: From the first beat of the prehistoric drum to the very latest in electronic music makers, musical instruments have been popular modes of communication and relaxation.

The most popular antique instruments are violins, flutes, oboes, and other instruments associated with the classical music period of 1650 to 1900. Many of the modern instruments, such as trumpets, guitars, and drums, have value on the "used," rather than antiques market.

Collecting musical instruments is in its infancy. The field is growing very rapidly. Investors and speculators have played a role since the 1930s, especially in early string instruments.

Banjo
  Global, with case........ **225.00**
  Peerless, with case....... **70.00**
Cello, with bow and case
.... **200.00**
Clarinet, with case
  Henry Bouche............. **675.00**
  Selmer........................ **350.00**
Coronet, English, silver plated, stamped "F. Besson, Brevetee...," with case.... **320.00**
Drum set, Gretsch, three pcs, aqua sides **600.00**

Harp, signed "Sebastian Erard," gilt, 66-3/4" h, some losses, **$2,000**.
Photo courtesy of Wiederseim Associates, Inc.

Fife, American, Meacham & Co., Albany, maple, brass fittings, case **320.00**
Flute, American
  Gemeinhardt, with case
  .... **125.00**
  Peloubet, C., five keys, rosewood, round key covers
  .... **550.00**
  Phaff, John, Philadelphia, 19th C, faintly stamped "J. Phaff...," eight keys, rosewood, silver fittings, period case **1,265.00**
Flute, English
  Monzani, London, 19th C, eight keys, head with turned reeding, silver fittings, round covered keys **200.00**
  Rudall Carte & Co., London, silver, multiple stamps, hallmarks, case **750.00**
  Wrede, H., London, c1840, four keys, stained boxwood, ivory fittings, silver round cover keys, case **320.00**

Mandolin, **$350**.
Photo courtesy of Dotta Auction Co., Inc.

Guitar, archtop, D'Angelico, John, Model New York, irregular curl maple two-piece back, medium curl sides, medium grain with cross-bracing top, medium curl neck, bound peghead with inlaid pearl D'Angelico logo, bound ebony fingerboard with split-block pearl inlay, stamped internally "D'Angelico, New York, 1808," 21-7/16" l back, 18-1/2" w bottom bout, 1947 .... **13,800.00**
Guitar, classical
  Bazzolo, Thomas, three-piece rosewood back, similar sides, spruce top of fine grain fully bound, mahogany neck, ebony fingerboard, labeled "Thomas Bazzolo, Luthier #65C24, 1994, Lebanon, Connecticut, USA," and sgd, 18-15/16" l back, 14-1/8" w lower bout, with case.. **750.00**
  Chica, Manuel de la, two-piece Brazilian rosewood back, labeled "Manuel De La Chica, Constructore, De, Violines Y Guitarras, Placeta De La Silleria 8, Granada, Ano De 1966," 19-1/4" l back
  .... **1,725.00**
  Martin, C. F., Style D-35, three-piece Indian rosewood back, similar sides, spruce top of fine to medium grain, mahogany neck with bound ebony fingerboard, inlaid pearl eyes, stamped internally "CF Martin & Co., Nazareth, PA, Made in USA, D-35," 1975
  .... **1,475.00**
Guitar, flat top, Gibson, flat top, orig case........................ **900.00**
Hawaiian guitar, National, New Yorker, with case............. **425.00**
Mandolin, flat back, with case
.... **175.00**

Piano, Steinway and Sons, Style VII, sq grand, carved rosewood, c1879 .... **1,380.00**
Organ
Band, Arthur Bursens, three-section, drums, symbols, and xylophone **16,500.00**
Dance, Arburo, saxophone, accordion, drum, castanets, drums and symbols **17,600.00**
Fairground, Limonaire, built in Germany, 1908, plays folding paper books **24,750.00**
Recorder, Moeck **135.00**
Trumpet, valve type
Buescher **125.00**
Sears & Roebuck **115.00**
Ukulele
Aloha Royal, with case **120.00**
Giamnini, baritone, with case **95.00**
Kkamakall, with case .. **250.00**

Melodeon, Victorian, labeled "C.W. Fisk and Co., Ansonia Conn. Sold by John Marsh, Philadelphia," rosewood, matching stool, **$300**.
Photo courtesy of Pook & Pook.

Vibraphone **950.00**
Viola, no inscription, with orig case, orig bow **475.00**
Violin, German, labeled "Thomas Ranik, Lauten and Geigenmacher in Breslau 1731," one-pc maple back, I spot stamped bow, 19th C fitted rect leather case **1,150.00**
Violin, Hungarian, medium curl two-piece back, similar ribs, medium curl scroll, fine grain top, red color varnish, labeled "Janos Spiegel, Budapest, 1907," 14-1/16" l back, 358 mm, with case **6,620.00**
Violin, Italian
Attributed to Andrea Postacchini, narrow curl one-piece back, irregular curl ribs, faint curl scroll, fine grain top, golden brown color varnish, labeled "Andreas Postacchini Amieie Filius Fecit Firmi Anno

1819, Opus 11?," 14" l back, 356 mm, with case, accompanied by bill of sale **17,250.00**
Bisiach, Leandro, strong medium curl two-piece back, strong narrow curl ribs and scroll, fine grain top, golden brown color varnish, labeled "Leandro Bisiach Da Milano, Fece L'Anno 1942," sgd, 14" l back, 356 mm, with case, undated numbered certificate **18,400.00**
Violin, Mittenwald, Klotz School, medium curl two-piece back, similar ribs and scroll, fine grain top, brown color varnish, unlabeled, c1780, 13-7/8" l back, 353 mm, with case **2,415.00**

Organ, high ornate walnut case, red lining, marked "Dyer & Hughes," **$750**.
Photo courtesy of Joseph P. Smalley, Jr., Auctioneer.

Violin bow, gold mounted
Ouchard, Emile, round stick stamped "Emile Ouchard" at butt, ebony frog with Parisian eye, plain gold adjuster, 63 grams **4,025.00**
Seifert, Lothar, octagonal stick stamped "Lothar Seifert" at butt, ebony frog with Parisian eye, gold and ebony adjuster, 61 grams **1,265.00**
Unstamped, octagonal stick, later frog engraved "A. Vigneron A Paris 1886," 59 grams **1,485.00**
Violin bow, silver mounted
Hill, W. E., round stick stamped "W. E. Hill & Sons" at butt, ebony eye with Parisian eye, plain silver adjuster, 60 grams, baleen wrap **2,530.00**

Morizot, Louis, French, round stick stamped "L. Morizot" at butt, ebony frog with Parisian eye, plain silver adjuster, 60.5 grams **2,300.00**
Nurnberger, Albert, octagonal stick stamped "Albert Nurnberger" at butt, "Saxony" under plain ebony frog, silver and ebony adjuster, 61 grams **1,265.00**
Unstamped, French, Francois-Nicolas Voirin, c1860, round stick, ebony frog with pearl eye, later silver and ebony adjuster, 63 grams **4,890.00**

Saxophone, original case, book, **$300**.
Photo courtesy of Dotta Auction Co., Inc.

Violoncello
America, Settin, Joseph, strong narrow curl two-piece back, similar ribs and scroll, fine to medium grain top, golden brown color varnish, labeled "Joseph Settin Venetus, Fecit Anno Domani 1953," 29-7/16" l back, 748 mm **8,100.00**
Czech, two-piece medium curl back, similar ribs and scroll similar, medium curl top, red color varnish, labeled "CAK Dvorni, A Armadni Dodvatel, Preniceska Tovarna Nastrouju Na Morave, Josetlidil V Brne Zelny Irh 11," 30-3/16" l back, 767 mm **3,795.00**
English, James and Henry Banks, narrow curl two-piece back, medium curl ribs, faint curl scroll, fine to medium grain top, red color varnish, sgd internally on table, "James and Henry Banks, Salisbury," c1800, 28-34" l back, 729 mm **18,400.00**
French, Thibouville-Lamy, Jerome, narrow curl two-piece back, similar ribs, medium curl scroll, medium to wide grain top, orange color

varnish, labeled "Jerome Thibouville-Lamy, 70 Rue Reaumur, Paris, 1938," 29-3/4" l back, 756 mm, with case **3,795.00**

German, irregular narrow curl two-piece back, similar ribs, narrow curl scroll, medium to wide grain top, orange color varnish, labeled "Erich Grunert, Penzberg Anno 1976," 29-3/4" l back, 756 mm, with case.......... 1,150.00

Violoncello bow, nickel plated, round stick stamped "L. Bausch, Leipzig," 81 grams....... **1,840.00**

MUSIC BOXES

History: Music boxes, invented in Switzerland around 1825, encompass a broad array of forms, from small boxes to huge circus calliopes.

A cylinder box consists of a comb with teeth that vibrate when striking a pin in the cylinder. The music these boxes produce ranges from light tunes to opera and overtures.

The first disc music box was invented by Paul Lochmann of Leipzig, Germany, in 1886. It used an interchangeable steel disc with pierced holes bent to a point that hit the star-wheel as the disc revolved, and thus produced the tune. Discs were easily stamped out of metal, allowing a single music box to play an endless variety of tunes. Disc boxes reached the height of their popularity from 1890 to 1910, when the phonograph replaced them.

Music boxes also were incorporated in many items, e.g., clocks, sewing and jewelry boxes, steins, plates, toys, perfume bottles, and furniture.

Bremond, interchangeable cylinder, orchestral music, 12 19" cylinders **82,500.00**

Cellesta, 8-1/4" disc, single-comb ratchet-wind mechanism, walnut case with bone inlaid top and color print in lid, 16 discs **980.00**

Cylinders

Lambert, common, c1900 .... **225.00**

Birds in bird cage, French, working condition, **$495**.

Photo courtesy of Dotta Auction Co., Inc.

Lambert, recording of The Stars & Stripes, pink, 5" d **2,000.00**
Criterion, 15-1/2" disc, matching cabinet **5,200.00**
Lecoulture, D., 17" l, 8-1/4" cylinder, plays four airs, plain case **1,100.00**
Manger, John, large cylinder type **33,000.00**
Match striker, 9" h, gilt cast metal figure of man holding his chamber pot out window, strike-plate activating two-air movement playing "Dixie" and "La Marsille" **635.00**
Mermod Freres, interchangeable cylinder type, three cylinders
Orig finish case **49,500.00**
Restored case **5,500.00**
Olympia, No. 6566, 20-1/2" upright disc, twin-comb mechanism, disengaged coin slide, manual control, two-piece mahogany cabinet, side disc storage, 32 discs, sounding boards replaced, 70" h **6,900.00**
Polychon, No. 27498, 15-1/2" disc, twin comb movement, coin slide, walnut case with bobbin turned corner columns, paneled and inlaid top, monochrome print in lid, disc storage drawer in plinth, 36 zinc disks, 24" w **460.00**

Mira, single comb, mahogany case, 26" w, 20" d, 13" h, and 21 15-1/2" diameter discs, **$3,000**.

Photo courtesy of Joy Luke.

Regina, 15-1/2" disk
Double comb, oak ... **3,520.00**
Style 11 .... **3,000.00**
Style 50 .... **4,000.00**
Singing bird
3-3/4" w, blue enameled case, ivory beak, moving wings and perch, lid with Alpine scene and floral spray........ **2,645.00**
4" w, silver plated, serpentine front and sides, cast with views of country scenes, leather traveling case, bird detached and featherless **815.00**
11" h, brass, moving head, circular base.............. **420.00**

Swiss, six-tune music box, case with inlaid floral motif in lid and painted grain decorated sides, ebonized interior, one cylinder and one 52-tooth comb, three bells with bird strikers, scratch on front of case, 16-3/4" w, **$1,220**.

Photo courtesy of Alderfer Auction Co.

Symphonion
9" disc, offset double combs **1,650.00**
Eroica, tall case clock, plays three disks simultaneously, 25 three-disc sets....... **46,750.00**
Eroica, upright, walnut case, 18 three-disc sets, 81" h **38,500.00**

Swiss, marquetry inlaid music box on stand by Bremond, lid with inlaid mother-of-pearl butterfly, case marked "BAB," 11" cylinder, stand with single fitted drawer containing five additional cylinders, turned, fluted and blocked legs joined by stretcher with central finial, 19th C, 33" h, 26" w, 22-3/4" d, 33" h, **$4,600**.

Photo courtesy of Pook & Pook.

Troll & Baker, six 16" cylinders **38,500.00**

Unknown maker
5-3/8" w, 4" d, 6-5/8" h, morocco covered case formed as upright piano, plays march and air, hinged lid enclosing ivory and ebonized keys with starting latch, mirrored backplate, fitted with two glass perfume bottles, four-piece cut-steel manicure set, Continental, late 19th C **550.00**
8" l, automation, fabric covered cabbage, central white fur covered head of rabbit, glass eyes, plays one air as rabbit emerges from cabbage and moves ears, Continental, late 19th C **550.00**
21-1/2" w, 11" cylinder, six bells, plays eight airs, optional engine turned bells, veneered case **1,380.00**

Unknown Swiss maker
16" l, 10-1/4" d, 8-1/2" h, 6-1/4" cylinder, plays eight airs, drum with five strikers, tune card, rect case inlaid to hinged lid with central cartouche of drum and pipes, line banding throughout, bracket feet, late 19th C **2,425.00**

The Criterion, tabletop, walnut case, litho paper cupid under lid, five discs, **$1,700**.
Photo courtesy of Joy Luke Auctions.

24-5/8" l, 12-3/8" w, 10-1/4" h, 15" cylinder, plays 12 airs, engine-turned bells, tune card, rect case inlaid to hinged lid with central brass and mother-of-pearl cartouche, bracket feet, late 19th C **2,645.00**
Vaucher Fils Paillard, revolver cylinder **27,500.00**

NAPKIN RINGS, FIGURAL

History: Gracious home dining during the Victorian era required a personal napkin ring for each household member. Figural napkin rings were first patented in 1869. During the remainder of the 19th century, most plating companies, including Cromwell, Eureka, Meriden, and Reed and Barton, manufactured figural rings, many copying and only slightly varying the designs of other companies.

Notes: Values are determined by the subject matter of the ring, the quality of the workmanship, and the condition. The following examples are all silver-plated.

Barking dog, 2-1/4" w, 2-3/4" h, unknown maker, barking dog jumping over fence, ring rests on back of dog, ring elaborately engraved with floral and basket weave dec, cartouche form panel incised "Leslie '93," scattered spots of wear or discoloration **185.00**

Combination napkin ring, open salt, pepper shaker, and butter pat, embossed florals, silver plate, marked "Tufts," **$175**.

Begging terrier, 3" w, 2-1/2" h, Hamilton, ring at back, central engraved foliate garland flanked by turned rings and ridged rim on ring, oval base dec with stars and bars, imp "Hamilton & Co., 01541," minor denting to rim of ring.................................. **100.00**
Bird, 3-1/8" w, 3-1/4" h, Reed & Barton, rect platform with tapered sides with raised leaf and scroll dec, reeded ring topped by bird with outspread wings coated on ball, twisted cord and tassel descending from ball on one side of ring, imp "Mf'd. and Plated by Reed & Barton, no. 1310"............ **225.00**
Bird in fruit tree, 2-1/2" w, 3" h, Meriden, bird sitting in branches, ring engraved with birds in branches, circular base with fruit and leaves, imp "Rogers Smith & Co., Meriden, no. 247," minor wear to finish................... **145.00**
Bird on branch, 2-1/2" w, 3-1/2" h, unknown maker, ring having circular base, raised flower and leaf dec, branch rising from base and following curve of ring, bird with wings spread sits atop branch, underside imp "1593," scattered spots of wear to finish..... **375.00**
Birds and bud vase, 2-1/2" w, 5-1/2" h, Wilcox, ring resting on ftd pedestal, two birds with outstretched wings on ring on either side of central bud vase, flared rim, ring with beaded and ridged detail at edges, imp "Wilcox Silver Plate Co., no. 1899," very minor wear to finish **165.00**

Boy with post, 4" w, 3-1/4" h, Meriden, boy holding post, shovel on ground beside him, ring with beaded rim details and central engraved band with foliage attached to one side of base, circular base, imp "Meriden Brittannia Company, no. 30," wear **75.00**

Bud vase, 2-1/2" w, 4-1/2" h, Reed & Barton, circular base with raised fleur-de-lis motif, ring with floral-decorated rims, ewer-form bud vase with flower inside curved handle, imp "Mf'd. & Plated by Reed & Barton, 1337," discoloration of finish at base of ewer **175.00**

Butterfly and two fans, two Japanese style handled fans supporting ring, butterfly underneath ring, central plain band flanked by two raised curved bands with floral garland motif on ring, sq base with raised floral dec, four ball feet, imp "Meriden Brittannia Company, no. 208," minor wear to finish **75.00**

Butterflies and leaf, 2-1/2" w, 2-1/2" h, unknown maker, ring resting on outspread wings of two butterflies resting on leaf, four ball feet, ring with central band and raised rims, floral motif, scattered spots of wear to finish.................................. **225.00**

Chair, 1-3/4" x 4-1/2" h, unknown maker, ring resting on seat of chair, ring with engraved panel and foliate swag, panel incised "M.A. Hall from Ed. V. Louise," scattered wear to finish... **180.00**

Cherub
3" w, 4" h, Rogers, ring resting on hips and legs of cherub, arms and head on top of ring, ring having central plain band flanked by bands, engraved floral dec on ridged ground, circular base, imp "Rogers & Bro., no. 224" **385.00**
3-1/4" w, 1-3/4" h, unknown maker, seated cherub leaning back against ring with floral dec rims, very minor nicking to rims of ring............. **550.00**

Cherub with torch, 3" w, 4" h, Reed & Barton, cherub with fallen drape, one arm outstretched holding torch, leaning on pedestal and ring, ring with reeded rims, chased bird, and floral motif on center band, circular panel

monogrammed "RGM," rect base, imp "Mf'd. & Plated by Reed & Barton, 1285," underside engraved "Aug. 27, 1888," minor loss to finish **525.00**

Cow and tree, 13/4" w, 2-3/4" h, Meriden, oval ring supported by forked branches of tree, cow standing beside, engraved dec of birds on tree branches n ring, circular base, imp "Meriden Brittannia Company, no. 243," wear to finish.................. **100.00**

Crawling child, 2-3/4" w, 1-3/4" h, Rogers, crawling child beside ring, ring with pierced work scrolling dec on edges, imp "Wm. Rogers Mfg. Co., Hartford, Quadruple, 2254" **200.00**

Two putti supporting an engraved napkin ring, engraved base with four ball feet, silverplate, Wilcox Quadruple Plate, #01536, Meriden, Conn., 3-1/4" x 2-1/4", **$225**.

Photo courtesy of Alderfer Auction Co.

Cupid and heart, 2-1/2" w, 2-1/2" h, Rogers, heart-form base with scallop dec at edge, seated cupid with one outstretched arm, arrow resting on base, scalloped dec ring supported by ftd pedestal, engraved "Rudolph, Hearts are Trumps," three ball feet, imp "Rogers & Bro.," no. 435," discolored **160.00**

Cupids in canoe, 4-3/4" w, 3-1/4" h, unknown maker, two cupids in canoe using arrows as oars, central ring with incised concentric rings, supporting bud vase with flared neck, canoe rests on two bracket feet, ring inscribed "Geo," wear to finish **385.00**

Cupid, terrier and hearts, 2-1/4" w, 2-3/4" h, Reed & Barton, ring with turned rims supported on back of terrier, cupid facing outward, leaning on ring, two hearts atop ring, oval base with fern dec, imp "Mf'd. & Plated by Reed & Barton, 1315," minor wear to finish.................. **750.00**

Dancing women, 2-1/2" w, 2-1/4" h, Pelton, central foliate engraved ring flanked by two women dancing with tambourines, cartouche form base, four ball feet, imp "Pelton Bros. Silver Plate Co., no. 17," slight nick to one side of ring **100.00**

Dog and bird, 3" w, 2-1/2" h, Aurora, dog sitting on hind legs, looking at bird with wings raised seated on top of ring, beaded rim, foliate dec, and "Oscar" engraved on ring, imp "Aurora Silver Plate Co., no. 27," wear to finish **95.00**

Dog and bud vase, 3-3/4" w, 2-3/4" h, Tufts, dog standing on hind legs, one front paw resting on scroll-engraved ring, vasiform bud vase at other side of ring, cartouche form base, imp "J.W. Tufts, Boston, no. 1582," minor spots of wear to finish..... **285.00**

Elephant, 3" w, 2" h, unknown maker, ring flanked by elephant with raised trunk, raised dec of elephants on ring, considerable wear to finish................... **130.00**

Eskimo, 2-3/4" w, 2-1/2" h, Meriden, hooded Eskimo holding pole, standing on ice floe, circular base, ring with central plain band flanked by bands of engraved floral dec on ridged ground, imp "Meriden Brittannia Company, no. 220," minor pitting to finish......... **75.00**

Girl jumping rope, 5" w, 4-1/2" h, Wilcox, girl jumping rope, ring behind her resting on pierced scroll and floral motif support, ring with plain center band flanked by flared rims, engraved floral and foliate dec, large circular base with tapered sides, dec with flowers and birds, four feet, imp "Wilcox Silver Plate Co., no. 360," nicks to edges of ring, spots of wear to finish **375.00**

Goat, 2-1/2" w, 1-3/4" h, standing goat figure at one side, ring decorated in engraved floral motif, wear, discoloration to finish **95.00**

Greenaway girl, 3-3/4" w, 7-1/8" h, ring with engraved dec flanked by large Greenaway girl and lily flower, leaves on long upswept stems, one leaf broken off but present, scattered spots of wear to finish.............. **200.00**

Horse, 3-1/2" w, 2-1/2" h, unknown maker, horse rearing up on its hind legs, front hooves resting on scroll dec ring supported by ball, oval pierced scroll work base, wear to finish **135.00**

Central napkin ring supported by two winged figures holding drape, etched decoration, inscribed name "Crane," sterling silver, Gorham anchor mark with #2, 2" h, **$600**.

Photo courtesy of Alderfer Auction Co.

Knights in armor, 2-1/8" w, 1-5/8" h, Simpson, Hall, Miller, central ring engraved with floral swags, flanked by figures of knights in armor, rect base, imp "Simpson, Hall, Miller & Co., no. 110," minor wear to finish .. **215.00**

Lily pad, 3-1/2" w, 2" h, Acme, lily pads and flowers form base, stem forms loop handle and ring support, ring rests on ball, engraved wheat sheaf and sunburst dec on ring, imp "Acme Silver Company, Canada, no. 729," some loss to finish **230.00**

Military band, 3-1/2" w, 3-1/4" h, unknown maker, ring supported by pedestal, flanked by three members of military band and flag bearer, circular base, four pad feet, scattered spots of wear to finish, crack in flag **160.00**

Parrot, 3-1/2" w, 2-1/2" h, Rogers, parrot sitting on branch where ring is resting, ring with raised rings, engraved floral and geometric dec, imp on ring "Rogers & Bro., no. 228," denting to edge of ring ... **185.00**

Peacock, 2-1/4" w, 3-1/2" h, Meriden, peacock standing on ring, engraved floral dec, rect panel inscribed "Charlie," imp "Meriden Brittania Company, no. 151," wear to finish **400.00**

Phoenix birds, 3-1/4" w, 4" h, Simpson, Hall, Miller, ring resting on ftd pedestal, curved handle descending to two phoenix-type birds on either side of ring, ring engraved with scrolling motif forming panel inscribed "Belle," imp "Simpson, Hall, Miller & Co." **200.00**

Putto
3" w, 2" h, Simpson, Hall, Miller, seated putto, ring at his back, ring engraved with owls in tree branches, octagonal base with raised scrolling dec, imp "Simpson, Hall, Miller & Co., no. 211," minor spots of wear to finish. **365.00**

3" w, 2-1/2" h, Webster, putti seated at each end of cartouche form base, ring supported on wings, ring with flared rims and central band with engraved dec, imp "E.G. Webster & Bro., no. 170," denting to one edge of ring **130.00**

3" w, 3" h, unknown maker, standing putto leaning back on ring with faintly engraved foliate dec **420.00**

Putto, bird and wishbone, 3" w, 2" h, unknown maker, ring with engraved foliate spray resting on wishbone, flanked by songbird on one side and putto on other, minor wear to finish **525.00**

Rampant lion, 2-1/2" w, 2" h, unknown maker, rampant lion at one side of ring with raised scrollwork rims **265.00**

Recumbent lion, 2-1/2" w, 2-1/4" h, Meriden, floral dec ring resting on back of lion, rect base, imp on ring "Meriden Britannia Company, no. 152," small base nick **145.00**

Combination napkin ring, posts for salt and pepper shakers, center napkin ring, small vase, floral motif, silver plate, marked "Tufts," shakers missing, **$85**.

Squirrel with nut, 3-1/2" w, 2" h, unknown maker, squirrel alongside ring with scrolling rims, both sitting on branch, ring inscribed "Dudley," imp partially obscured, "143_," spotty wear to finish **300.00**

Terrier, 2" w, 1-1/2" h, unknown maker, terrier at one side, front paws resting on ring with raised scrollwork rims and engraved scroll dec on band, no maker's mark, minor loss to finish **180.00**

Terrier and bird, 3-1/4" w, 2" h, Reed & Barton, terrier barking at bird with outstretched wings atop ring, ring with turned rims with egg and dart type dec, fern dec on oval base, imp "Mf'd. & Plated by Reed & Barton, 1110," minor wear to finish **250.00**

Turtle supporting ring napkin holder, footed rectangular base, small vase with Egyptian motifs, silverplate, Derby Co. Quadruple Plate, #342, 3-1/4" h, **$425**.

Photo courtesy of Alderfer Auction Co.

Turtles, 3-1/2" w, 2" h, unknown maker, plain oval ring resting on two fern leaves, flanked by two turtles, imp "75" **185.00**

Two boys
3" w, 2" h, Middletown, boy leaning on each side of ring engraved with sunburst and scroll dec, imp "Middletown Plate Co., no. 87," wear to finish **100.00**

3" w, 3" h, Meriden, two boys facing outward, supporting sq ring standing on corner in back-stretched hands, sq base with raised scrolling foliate dec, four ball feet, imp "Meriden Brittannia Company, no. 332" **200.00**

Two cherubs, 2-3/4" w, 2-1/4" h, seated cherub on each side of barrel form ring on their backs, imp "Meriden Brittania Company, no. 147," wear to finish **100.00**

Two foxes, 2-1/2" w, 2" h, Meriden, two foxes holding birds on either side of ring with ridged rim, turned rings, and central engraved floral dec, panel engraved "Flora," imp "Meriden Silver Plate Company, no. 217" **120.00**

Two sphinxes, 2-7/8" w, 2-1/4" h, two sphinx-type figures supporting ring on their wings, top of ring dec with incised branches forming diamond motif, imp "Meriden Silver Plate Company, no. 202," minor wear to finish.............................. **75.00**

NASH GLASS

History: Nash glass is a type of art glass attributed to Arthur John Nash and his sons, Leslie H. and A. Douglas. Arthur John Nash, originally employed by Webb in Stourbridge, England, came to America and was employed in 1889 by Tiffany Furnaces at its Corona, Long Island, plant.

While managing the plant for Tiffany, Nash designed and produced iridescent glass. In 1928, A. Douglas Nash purchased the facilities of Tiffany Furnaces. The A. Douglas Nash Corporation remained in operation until 1931.

For more information, see *Warman's Glass*, 4th edition.

Bowl, 7-3/4" x 2-1/2", Jewel pattern, gold phantom luster **285.00**
Candlesticks, pr, 4" h, irid gold, large disc foot and top separated with baluster stem, sgd "650 Nash"............... **350.00**
Compote, 7-1/2" d, 4-1/2" h, Chintz, transparent aquamarine, wide flat rim of red and gray-green controlled stripe dec, base inscribed "Nash RD89" **865.00**
Cordial, 5-1/2" h, Chintz, green and blue......................... **125.00**
Creamer and sugar, 5-3/8" h creamer, 3-1/2" h sugar, blue-green opaque dots, dark blue-green base, creamer with polished pontil, sugar with waffle pontil **475.00**

Goblet, 6-3/4" h, feathered leaf motif, gilt dec, sgd **295.00**
Plate, 8" d, Chintz, green and blue................................. **195.00**
Sherbet, bluish-gold texture, ftd, sgd, #417 .... **275.00**

Vase, iridescent gold, cupped rim tapering to footed base, lower half relief-decorated with stylized flowers on tall leafy stems, base inscribed "Nash 549," 5-3/4" h, **$940**.
Photo courtesy of Skinner, Inc.

Vase

5-1/2" h, Chintz, pastel, transparent oval, internally striped with pastel orange alternating with yellow chintz dec **275.00**
9" h, Polka Dot, deep opaque red oval, molded with prominent 16 ribs, dec by spaced white opal dots, base inscribed "Nash GD154" **1,100.00**

NAUTICAL ITEMS

History: The seas have fascinated man since time began. The artifacts of sailors have been collected and treasured for years. Because of their environment, merchant and naval items, whether factory or handmade, must be of quality construction and long lasting. Many of these items are aesthetically appealing as well.

Account book, *Bark Arab,* showing purchases and sales from October 1853 to December 1856, 96 pgs, folio, New Bedford or Hawaii, label reads "purchased of John Kehew at his Navigation Store in New Bedford," Kehew's label mounted on front paste down, two volumes **1,955.00**
Banner, 26" x 8-1/2", carved and polychrome painted pine, "Don't Give Up The Ship!," American eagle, attributed to John Hales Bellamy **24,150.00**

Diorama, American cruiser, early 20th C, **$250**.
Photo courtesy of Wiederseim Associates, Inc.

Ship's binnacle, Northwest Instrument Co., Seattle, WA, brass stand with two lanterns, plaque with Asian lettering, inscribed "No. 4004," early 20th C, 42" h, break in one lantern, **$395**.
Photo courtesy of Alderfer Auction Co.

Book

Allyn, Captain Gurdon L., *Old Sailor's Story, or a Short Account of the Life, Adventures, and Voyages, The,* Norwich, 1879, 111 pgs, 8vo, orig flexible cloth wrappers......................... **316.00**
Bligh, William, *Dangerous Voyage of Captain Bligh, in an Open Boat, over 1200 Leagues of the Ocean, in the Year 1789,* Dublin, 1818, five full-page woodcut engraved illus, 180 pgs, small 12mo **345.00**
Dexter, Elisha, *Narrative of the Loss of the William and Joseph, of Martha's Vineyard,* Boston, 1842, five wood engraved plates, 54 pgs, 8vo **1,370.00**

Box, cov, 17-3/4" w, 9-1/4" d, 8-5/8" h, sailor made, 19th C, walnut and ivory, rect, dovetail construction, hinged, top and sides with turned and carved pendant ring ivory handles ringed with red and black wax, kite-shaped carved ivory escutcheon, oral history relates that this box came from ship named "Carolus," which operated out of Boston **1,765.00**

Broadside, 415 x 335 mm, issued as circular to mariners at Table Bay, Robben Island, advising of berthing procedures, 1827 .... **345.00**

Cane
32-7/8" l, carved from single piece of tooth, 1-3/4" d x 2" h whale ivory handle, carved sailor's Turks head knot, thin baleen spacer separates whalebone shaft, inlaid at top with four-pointed baleen fingers, white whalebone shaft, tapered with very slight natural bow, American, c1850 .... **2,800.00**

36-1/2" l, 1-3/4" d x 2/3" h flat brass handle, wide all metal black shaft fashioned with metal nubs all along length, when handle pulled off, hollow exposed to reveal watertight compartment to store nautical charts and documents, 3/4" brass ferrule, English, c1890 .... **450.00**

Canoe paddle, 60" l, painted deep red with black crescent moon and star, America, late 19th C, with stand **375.00**

Chronometer, 7-3/4" h, Eggert & Son, New York, early 19th C, mahogany brass bound double lidded case, brass cased movement with engraved silver dial inscribed "Eggert & Son, NEW YORK, No 276," applied ivory plaque inscribed "Eggert & Son 276 New York" **3,200.00**

Clock, 10-1/2" h, brass, Seth Thomas, one-day lever-striking movement, circular case, domed bell mounted below on wooden backboard, late 19th C ... **520.00**

Compass, lifeboat, 8" sq, 7-1/4" h, boxed, 20th C .. **175.00**

Crew list, partly printed, two languages, *Jireh Swift*, lists 13 additional Hawaiian crew members, Lahaina, March 29, 1865 .... **2,000.00**

Diorama, three-mast clipper, side-wheel paddle steamer, and smaller vessel, 17 men in black coats and top hats manning vessels, two painted lighthouses and dwelling in background, green-blue sky with white painted clouds, c1850, 40" l shadowbox **6,500.00**

Figurehead, 30" h, carved, Nantucket Island origin, c1830 .... **12,000.00**

Fishing license, issued to sloop *Kial*, April 23, 1808, for cod fishing, issued in Newport, RI, some edge chipping, fold splitting, 16-1/2" x 10-1/2" **165.00**

Hourglass, 7" h, 19th C .. **550.00**

Inclinometer, 4-1/2" d, brass, cased, bubble type, Kelvin Bottomley & Baird Ltd....... **65.00**

Indenture, document indenturing William McGraa to Isaac Fisher as apprentice mariner for four years, details duties, payment schedule, May 19, 1813, signed by all parties, some foxing, edge chipping, 1810 watermark, 16" x 13-1/2" **100.00**

Jewelry chest, 18 1/4" l, 12-1/2" d, 10-3/8" h, sailor-carved walnut and whalebone, America, 19th C, carved rosette, fan, lapped leaf, pendant, and other designs, front and side drawers, hinged lid opens to mirror which further opens to three oval frames with rope trim, box int. fitted with four compartments with carved lids, carved whalebone drawer and lid handles **2,350.00**

Log book, Ship *Geneva*, George M. Tucker, Master, sailed from Boston, March 4, 1852 towards Richmond, later to San Francisco, then to Calcutta, back to Boston where she docked at Central Wharf on Aug. 13, 1853, worn spine, cover **1,150.00**

Masthead, 16" h, 9-1/2" d, copper and brass, oil fired, complete with burner, 360 degrees, late 19th C **200.00**

Membership certificate, 12-3/8" x 17-1/2", certifying "...That Capt. Green Walden was by a majority of votes regularly admitted a member of the Portland Marine Society at a meeting held the 17th day of September 1839...," certificate dec with reserves depicting various marine scenes, toning, foxing, framed **530.00**

Lamps, table, brass, made from lanterns, impressed mark "Perko, Perkins Marine Lamp Home Corp, Brooklyn, NY, USA," red glass lamps marked "Corning," 36" h, **$1,200**.

Photo courtesy of Alderfer Auction Co.

Ship's lamp, wrought iron ball-form gimbaled, 18th C, 4-1/2" d, **$160**.

Photo courtesy of Pook & Pook.

Model, cased, 23-5/8" l, 12" w, 16-1/4" h, Schooner Yacht *Laura*, carved and painted, fully rigged, painted metal sails, painted figures, metal and wood details, hull painted black, carved wood "water," America, 19th C, imperfections **1,550.00**

Oar, 57-1/2" l, curly maple, well carved, thin broad end, good figure............................... **420.00**

Painting, oil on canvas, framed
17" x 21", two-Masted Schooner *Masconnomet* in Marblehead Harbor, flying American flag, figures on pier in foreground, lighthouse in distance, unsigned, identified beneath image, craquelure, scattered retouch to background sky....... **3,525.00**

21-1/4" x 32", Ships Before the Doges Palace, sgd "Ziller" lower left (Leopold Ziller), framed, strip lined, repaired punctures, retouch, surface grime **3,525.00**

22" x 36", two-masted schooner off Vinalhaven, ME, sgd "Coombs" lower left, repaired tear, retouch to upper right sky **4,250.00**

20" w x 12" h, sailing ship flying American flag, several fishing boats in rough seas, high cliffs in background, sgd "RJ Dawson 1882," 22-3/4" w x 14-3/4" h period gilt frame with wear, small areas of touch-up **1,610.00**
36" x 22", *William,* pictured off Dover with Dover Fort pictured under her bowsprit, sgd "R. B. Spencer" lower left, (Richard Barrett Spencer, c1840-74,) ship identified on bow, scattered retouch, lined **6,450.00**

Quadrant, ebony, cased, marked "D Booth" and "New Zealand" **330.00**

Sail maker's bench, 77" l, 16" w, 15" h, long canvas cov bench, turned splayed legs, one end with compartments and pierced for tools, suspending two canvas pouches, two canvas sacks with sail maker's tools, America, 19th C **1,765.00**

Sailor's razor box, carved cherry, rect, heart-shaped handle, chip carved borders, incised sailing vessel on swivel top, 19th C, 10-3/4" l, 1-3/4" w, 1-1/2" h **325.00**

Sailor's valentine, 9-5/8" octagonal segmented case, various exotic shells, "For My Love," 19th C, very minor losses **750.00**

Sea chest, painted, green, lid painted with flags and pennants centered by Union Jack, name "William Bevan" **2,760.00**

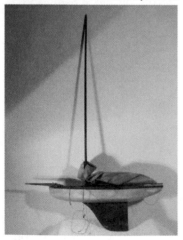

Pond model of sloop, red topsides, original sails, 29" l, **$250.**

Photo courtesy of Wiederseim Associates, Inc.

Puzzle, Parker Bros Pastime Puzzle Youth and Experience, Gloucester Fisherman, original box, 10-3/4" x 14", incomplete, **$45.**

Ship anchor, 54" w, 106" h, cast, iron ring and chain, mounted on later iron brackets, corrosion **825.00**

Ship bell, cast bronze
13" d, 13-1/2" h, weathered surface, raised "J. Warner & Sons, London, 1855" **1,175.00**
14" d, 17" h, raised linear bands **560.00**

Ship billethead, carved wood, 19th C
24" l, 7-1/2" w, scrolled foliate design, painted black, green and gilt highlights, minor loss on scroll, cracks **715.00**
27-1/2" l, 5-1/2" w, and 23" l, 7-1/4" w, scrolled foliate design, weathered cracked surface, pr **4,995.00**

Ship builder's half model, America, 19th C
30" l, 6" h, alternating laminated mahogany and other wood, mounted on walnut panel **1,995.00**
37-1/2" l, 5" h, pine and other woods, mounted on pine panel........................ **1,300.00**
42" l, 10-5/8" h, natural finished pine, black and gilt trim, loose stempost **9,400.00**

Ship license
Issued for ship *Aurora,* 303 tons, armed with 14 guns, two swivel guns, 20 muskets, 20 pistols, 20 cutlasses, 20 pikes, Nov. 4, 1912, minor edge chipping, 12-1/2" x 8" **135.00**

Sailor's urene, America, 19th C, painted, carved pine, ball finial atop graduated sectional frame with five carved spheres, old salmon-colored painted surface, square canted base, minor wear, 18-1/4" h, **$1,530.**

Photo courtesy of Skinner, Inc.

Seaman's scale, wrought iron framework, hooks and needle, brass curved scale with etched numbers, 17-1/2" w, 13" h, **$230.**

Issued to the ship *Nancy* of Newfoundland, two guns weighing 222 tons, issued by High Admiral, April 24, 1812, masthead scene of allegorical figures and chip, scallop cut top, minor soiling, 18" x 11-1/2" **450.00**

Shipping circular, concerning marine papers lost, stolen, or taken by force on various ships, issued to port collector of Bristol, sgd by Clerk of Marine Records of the Treasury Dept, March 31, 1810, federal eagle watermark, some chipping, fold splitting, 15-1/2" x 9-1/2"................. **35.00**

Ship wheel, 48" d, various hardwoods, turned spokes, iron reinforced center hub **350.00**

Stern board, 7-3/4" h, 66" l, Hesperus, New England, 19th C, rect form, rounded ends, chamfered edges, chiseled carved letters flanked by star, painted white on black ground, imperfections **980.00**

Telescope, 32-3/4" l, silver plated, one draw, Troughton & Simms, London, mid-19th C, orig leather casing, inscription reads "Presented by the British Government, Captain Christopher Crowell, Master of the American Ship 'Highland Light' of Boston, in acknowledgment of his humanity and kindness to the Master and the Crew of the Barque 'Queen of Sheba' when he rescued from their waterlogged vessel, on the 16th, December 1861," damage to leather **980.00**

Telescope, brass table top, English, mid-19th C, 35" l, 19" h, **$950**.

Photo courtesy of Pook & Pook.

Watch hutch, Continental Prisoner of War, carved bone, dated "1807," lion, swags, vases of flowers, birds, hearts, etc. on case with single drawer, 6" w, 4" d, 10-1/2" h, with Irish silver pocket watch marked "Geo. Rycroft Dublin," **$2,530**.

Photo courtesy of Pook & Pook.

Trump indicator, brass and copper, ship's wheel, spinning center orb, 4-1/2" x 3-1/2" . **85.00**

Walking stick, 35" l, wood, ivory knop, silver band on shaft engraved "U.S. Frigate Constitution 1797, J.L.S.," brass and iron tip, age cracks on ivory, wear **1,295.00**

Watercolor on paper
9-1/2" h, 11-1/4" l, *Ship Portrait of the U.S.S. Constitution,* unsigned, American School, early 19th C, taken from a ship's log, with Ruse & Turner's watermark .. **1,000.00**
14" h, 20" w, study of steamboat no desolate river during winter, snow topped mountain in background, light shades of brown and blue, sgd "Mc E. Dun 1899," matted with gilt floral frame, minor surface wear **300.00**

NETSUKES

History: The traditional Japanese kimono has no pockets. Daily necessities, such as money and tobacco supplies, were carried in leather pouches, or inros, which hung from a cord with a netsuke toggle. The word netsuke comes from "ne"—to root—and "tsuke"—to fasten.

Netsukes originated in the 14th century and initially were favored by the middle class. By the mid-18th century, all levels of Japanese society used them. Some of the most famous artists, e.g., Shuzan and Yamada Hojitsu, worked in the netsuke form.

Netsukes average from 1 to 2 inches in length and are made from wood, ivory, bone, ceramics, metal, horn, nutshells, etc. The subject matter is broad based, but always portrayed in a lighthearted, humorous manner. A netsuke must have smooth edges and balance in order to hang correctly on the sash.

> **Reproduction Alert:** Recent reproductions are on the market. Many are carved from African ivory.

Notes: Value depends on artist, region, material, and skill of craftsmanship. Western collectors favor katabori, pieces which represent an identifiable object.

Antler, carved
Foreigner or monk holding trumpet pendant from his right hand, facing upward, hair curling on his back, stained details, himotoshi carved on back, unsigned, Japan, 18th or 19th C, 2-1/2" h.... **1,275.00**
Kwanyu holding halberd in right hand, tugging his beard with his left hand, himotoshi on back, stained details, traces of red pigment on face and vestments, legs carved from separate piece and inserted, good patina and wear, Japan, 18th C, 3" h, hole drilled in left foot, small cavity on left leg.................... **500.00**

Corozo nut, carved, basket of flowers, handle at center dividing flowers, small areas of openwork, bottom with attached metal ring himotoshi, Japan, 19th C, 1-1/8" h, crack along top **125.00**

Horn, carved, Hannya mask, sgd on back between himotoshi, stained detail, Japan, 19th C, 2" h, hole at top of head.... **70.00**

Ivory, carved
Bearded man holding pumpkin over his left shoulder, flatly carved figure, good patina, worn details, himotoshi on back, unsigned, Japan, 18th C, 2-7/8" h, age cracks......................... **320.00**
Boy carrying branch laden with precious things, puppy at left foot, sgd "Tomochikia," Japan, 19th C, 1-1/2" l, small crack on shoulder....... **700.00**
Boy holding rooster, stained details, himotoshi carved on back, Japan, c1900, 1-1/2" h **200.00**
Dutchman holding monkey in his arms, details lightly stained, himotoshi spaced wide apart, one hole on back, other carved under his cat, sgd "Takusai" on back, Japan, 18th C, 2-7/8" h **2,600.00**
Foo dog, single hole himotoshi, Japan, 18th or 19th C, 1-5/8" h, age cracks **150.00**
Frog, sitting on rock with splashing water, turning to right, facing upwards, lightly stained details, himotoshi and sgd on base, mounted as ring with braided gold colored metal wire of varying shapes, Japan, 19th C, 2" h **300.00**

Frog, stylized, comical, long thin body, elongated snout, inlaid eyes, himotoshi and signature on base, Japan, 19th or 20th C, 3-1/8" h, age cracks **125.00**
Fukurokuju clipping his toenails, child on left side, stained detail, sgd "Gyokko" on rect on base, Japan, Meiji period, 1-3/4" h, crack in face **460.00**
Goat, standing, head turned sharply to right, front leg slightly raised, arched back with cascading fleece, left horn conforming to curve of neck, lightly stained, himotoshi carved on back, Japan, 18th C, 2-3/16" h, repairs to legs, details slightly worn, good patina, small age cracks **5,200.00**
Horse, grazing, stained detail, himotoshi carved on back, unsigned, Japan, 18th or 19th C **550.00**
Manju, rect, carved frog among persimmons and leaves, carved insect damage on leaves, himotoshi formed by interlacing branches, stained detail, Japan, Meiji period, 1-1/2" l **375.00**
Man and child with basket of fruit, himotoshi and signature carved on base, Japan, c1900, 1-5/8" h............ **200.00**
Octopus crawling out of large pot, himotoshi and signature on back, Gyokuzan, Japan, 19th C, 1-5/8" h **300.00**
Okame, sitting position, stained hair and robe, himotoshi carved at her back, sgd, Japan, early 20th C **200.00**
Oni carrying woman on back, stained detail, Japan, Meiji period, 2" h **375.00**
Oni embracing drum with inlaid studs, inlaid metal eyes, signature on underside of drum, some staining detail, Japan, Meiji period, 1-1/2" l **1,265.00**
Rect, dragon among clouds, large holes forming himotoshi, Japan, 19th C, age cracks **100.00**
Three blind men grappling with each other, himotoshi formed as part of design, slightly stained detail, sgd on base, Japan, Meiji period, 1-1/2" l, normal age cracks **1,495.00**

Three men wrestling snake, unsigned, Japan, 19th C, 2-3/4" l, some losses... **250.00**
Tiger, recumbent, body curled to left, fierce expression, sinuous tail resting on back, inlaid eyes, himotoshi and sgd "Tomotada" on base, Japan, 19th C, 2-1/8" h **400.00**
Turtle carrying young on its back, sgd on bottom, Japan, early 20th C, 2" l, damage to back foot.................... **100.00**
Two figures inside cavern, tengu above, single hole himotoshi, sgd on base, Japan, Meiji period, 1-1/2" h **750.00**
Two happy sages, himotoshi carved on back, unsigned, Japan, 18th or 19th C, 2" h **450.00**
Ivory and wood, carved, man and child, man with toy in left hand, sgd in small red tablet on base, Japan, Meiji period, 1-1/2" h........................... **320.00**
Porcelain, shishimai dancer, child holding lion mask above his head, painted over glaze enamels, himotoshi on back, Japan, possibly Kutani, Meiji period, 2-1/4" h, small chip **125.00**
Staghorn, 2-1/2" d, Manju, carved Kinko sennin on carp, 19th C **200.00**

Wood carving, seated man with bowl over his face, signed, 1" h, **$250**.

Wood, carved
Crouched figure holding basket with peach, homotshi carved on base, good color and patina, Japan, 19th C, 1" h, details slightly worn **200.00**
Foreigner, left arm twisted sharply behind his back, supporting child perched on right shoulder, right hand holding trumpet, himotoshi on back, lacquered, unsigned, Japan, 18th C, 3-1/4" h, areas of wear to lacquer.... **1,400.00**

Fox wearing robe with long sleeves, pulling large laden sack, inlaid horn eyes, tail curling underneath to form himotoshi, sgd on base, stained with even brown patination, Japan, Meiji period, 2" l **920.00**

NEWCOMB POTTERY

History:
The Sophie Newcomb Memorial College, an adjunct of Tulane University in New Orleans, LA, was originated as a school to train local women in the decorative arts. While metalworking, painting, and embroidery were among the classes taught, the production of fine, handcrafted art pottery remains its most popular and collectible pursuit.

Pottery was made by the Newcomb women for nearly 50 years, with earlier work being the rarest and most valuable. This is characterized by shiny finishes and broad, flat-painted and modeled designs. More common, though still quite valuable, are the matte glaze pieces, often depicting bayou scenes and native flora. All bear the impressed NC mark.

Adviser: David Rago.

Charger, painted by Mary Sheerer, medallion of the Newcomb chapel surrounded by trees, border with NEWCOMB COLLEGE N.O., marked "NC/JM/MS/M," c1900, 10-3/4" d, **$18,400**.
Newcomb photos courtesy of David Rago Auctions, Inc.

Bud vase, 9" h, 3-1/4" d, tapered, high glaze, carved yellow jonquils, tall green leaves, blue ground, by Anna Frances Simpson, 1908, marked "NC/Q/FS/CQ52/JM" **6,900.00**
Cabinet vase, 2" d, 4-1/2" h, by Anna F. Simpson, 1926, blue live oak and Spanish moss, gray ground, high glaze, marked "NC/JH/PP56/15/AFS" **3,335.00**
Chocolate set, 10-1/2" h, 6" d chocolate pot, teal blue tall pine trees carved by A. F. Simpson, light blue and green glossy ground, two matching cups, four saucers, mkd "NC/AFS/JM/E112/B," 1911, some damage **5,500.00**
Low bowl, 9-1/4" d, 3-1/4" h, carved pink irises, green leaves, medium blue matte ground, by A. F. Simpson, 1923, marked "NC/NF31/313/JM" and artist's cipher, couple of short, tight lines to rim **1,610.00**
Print, woodblock, 5-1/2" w, 6" h sight, by Mary F. Baker, young girl dec vase, monogrammed "MFB" lower left, matted, framed **2,070.00**
Trivet, 3-3/4" d, swirl of whit blossoms, waxy green ground, by Henrietta Bailey, 1912, marked "NC/HB/JM/FA28/B," orig paper label **1,840.00**
Vase
    3-1/2" h, 3-1/4" d, dec by Aurelia Arbo, band of green and yellow daisies, blue ground, c1937, NC/AA/X23 .... **900.00**
    3-3/4" h, 3-3/4" d, by Sadie Irvine, live oak trees and Spanish moss, pink sky, 1919, NC/SI/JI I/240/KQ75. **2,900.00**
    4-1/2" d, 6-1/2" h, carved matte, by Sadie Irvine, 1924, pink and red loquat fruit and leaves around undulating rim, marked "NC/SK/JM/I47/NP47," small chips to foot ring, short tight line to rim **1,150.00**
    5" d, 9" h, bulbous, by Anna F. Simpson, 1921, carved wreath of pink trumpet vines, green leaves, denim blue ground, marked "NC/JM/LS97/179/A.F.S." **3,220.00**
    5", 11-1/4" h, scenic, ovoid, crisply carved with full moon shining through oak trees and Spanish moss, blue and green matte glazes, by A. F.

Simpson, 1930, marked "NC/SN43/131/JH/AFS," three small flat manuf chips to base **16,100.00**

Vase, bulbous, crisply carved by A.F. Simpson with Spanish moss on live oak trees, full moon in hilly landscape, 1926, marked "NC/AFS/PO81/JM184," 6-1/2" d, 8-1/4" h, **$11,100**.

Vase, transitional, carved by A.F. Simpson, light green crocuses, dark green leaves, indigo ground, 1912, marked "NC/AFS/JM/B/FI30," 3-3/4" d, 8-1/4" h, **$5,350**.

Vase, transitional, carved by Sadie Irvine, Spanish moss on live oak trees with full moon, 1908, marked "NC/CF59/SI/JM/236," 4" d, 7" h, **$4,325**.

Vase, bulbous, decoration by Leona Nicholson, 1909, incised, molded, and surface painted freesia blossoms and stems in white, light blue, yellow, forest green spiked leaves, dark blue ground, blue mark "NC/LN/CW-4/JM/W," 8-1/2" h, 6-1/4" d, **$27,500**.

Vase, bulbous, carved by Henrietta Bailey, pink tea roses on matte cobalt blue ground, 1927, marked "NC/HB/QE81/61," 6-1/2" h, 7" d, **$3,750**.

Vase, carved by A. F. Simpson, moonlit scene with live oaks and Spanish moss, 1930, marked "NC/SN43/131/JH/AFS," three grinding chips to foot ring, 11" h, 5-1/4" d, **$15,000**.

5-1/2" h, 3-1/2" d, bulbous, painted by Sara Levy, bright yellow blossom, green stems, pale ground, c1903, mkd "NC/S.B.L./JM/Q" **6,500.00**

6-1/4" h, 2-1/2" d, corset, band of green scarabs on blue, green, and yellow ground, carved by Leona Nicholson, 1906, orig gunmetal glazed stand, mkd "NC/JM/LN/AZ84" **9,500.00**

6-1/2" h, 3" d, ovoid, by Sadie Irvine, oak trees, Spanish moss, full moon, 1927, NC/SI/326/QL65 .... **2,300.00**

8-1/4" h, 3-1/2" d, narrow, by Sadie Irvine, band of pink and yellow dogwood, blue ground, 1932, NC/SI/92/TW83 .... **1,500.00**

8-1/2" h, 6-1/4" d, bulbous, dec by Leona Nicholson, 1909, incised, molded, and surface painted freesia blossoms and stems in white, light blue, yellow, forest green spiked leaves, dark blue ground, blue mark "NC/LN/CW-4/JM/W" **27,500.00**

Vessel

5-1/4" d, 3-1/4" h, squatty, transitional, by Sadie Irvine, 1914, carved light blue bell flowers, green leaves, dark blue ground, marked "NC/GN47/JM/257/SI" **2,300.00**

6-1/2" d, 4-1/2" h, matte, squatty, by Sadie Irvine, 1922, sharply carved pink Japanese iris, green stems, around undulating top conforming to shape of blossoms, purple and blue ground, marked "NC/SI/JM/213?MV17" **3,220.00**

Vessel, transitional, bulbous, carved by Cynthia Littlejohn, blue and yellow jonquils with green leaves, indigo ground, marked "NC/JM/GI22/ 49/CL," restoration to opposing hairlines, 8-1/2" d, 6-3/4" h, **$5,750.**

Tyge, transitional, by Mazie T. Ryan, 1916, carved jasmine over motto "Drink to Me Only With Thine Eyes and I Will Pledge With Mine," marked "NC/JM/MT Ryan/II2-3," restoration to hairline, 8-1/2" h, 8-1/2" d, **$4,000.**

Photo courtesy of David Rago Auctions, Inc.

7-1/2" d, 6" h, organically shaped, by Marie De Hoa LeBlanc, c1905, three modeled ginkgo leaf handles, semi-matte olive green and gunmetal glaze, marked "NC/Q/JM/MHL," orig price tag **5,175.00**

NILOAK POTTERY, MISSION WARE

History:

Niloak Pottery was made near  Benton, Arkansas. Charles Dean Hyten experimented with native clay, trying to preserve its natural colors. By 1911, he perfected Mission Ware, a marbleized pottery in which the cream and brown colors predominate. The company name is the word "kaolin" spelled backward.

After a devastating fire, the pottery was rebuilt and named Eagle Pottery. This factory included enough space to add a novelty pottery line in 1929. Hyten left the pottery in 1941, and in 1946 operations ceased.

Marks: The early pieces were marked "Niloak." Eagle Pottery products usually were marked "Hywood-Niloak" until 1934, when the "Hywood" was dropped from the mark.

For more information, see *Warman's American Pottery & Porcelain*, 2nd edition.

Additional Listings: See *Warman's Americana & Collectibles* for more examples, especially the novelty pieces.

Note: Prices listed here are for Mission Ware pieces.

Floor urn, Mission Ware, marbleized clay in blue, beige, terra cotta, and gray, stamped "Niloak," factory bubble, 12" d, 23-1/2" h, **$8,050.**

Photo courtesy of David Rago Auctions, Inc.

Bowl, 4-1/2" d, marbleized swirls, blue, tan, and brown **65.00**

Candlesticks, pr, 8" h, marbleized swirls, blue, cream, terra cotta, and brown **250.00**

Flower pot, ruffled rim, green matte glaze, c1930 .... **155.00**

Toothpick holder, marbleized swirls, tan and blue......... **100.00**

Urn, 4-1/2" h, marbleized swirls, brown and blue................. **45.00**

Vase

3-1/4" h, early foil label, c1920-30 .... **95.00**

4-1/2" h, second art mark, c1925............................ **75.00**

4-1/2" h, starved rock mark, c1925............................ **95.00**

6" h, applied twisted handles, Ozark Dawn glaze, c1930 .... **120.00**
8-1/2" h, swirled colors, first art mark, c1910-24 ..... **230.00**
8-3/4" h, Ozark Dawn glaze, c1930 .... **140.00**
10-1/2" h, swollen baluster with broad rim, brown, rose, blue, and cream, second art mark **500.00**

NIPPON CHINA, 1891-1921

History: Nippon, Japanese hand-painted porcelain, was made for export between 1891 and 1921. In 1891, when the McKinley Tariff Act proclaimed that all items of foreign manufacture be stamped with their country of origin, Japan chose to use "Nippon." In 1921, the United States decided the word "Nippon" no longer was acceptable and required all Japanese wares to be marked "Japan," ending the Nippon era.

Marks: There are more than 220 recorded Nippon backstamps or marks; the three most popular are the wreath, maple leaf, and rising sun. Wares with variations of all three marks are being reproduced today. A knowledgeable collector can easily spot the reproductions by the mark variances.

The majority of the marks are found in three different colors: green, blue, or magenta. Colors indicate the quality of the porcelain used: green for first-grade porcelain, blue for second-grade, and magenta for third-grade. Marks were applied by two methods: decal stickers under glaze and imprinting directly on the porcelain.

Basket, handle
7-1/2" h, hp roses, stippled gilt ground, unmarked **90.00**
8-1/2" h, allover moriage dec, unmarked **375.00**
Berry set, 10-1/4" d master bowl, four 5" d individual bowls, azalea dec, enameled and gilt floral borders, green M in wreath mark **90.00**
Bowl
8-1/2" d, hp, sailing ships with palm tree and ruins, three handles, green wreath mark **150.00**

Reproduction Alert
Distinguishing old marks from new:
A common old mark consisted of a central wreath open at the top with the letter M in the center. "Hand Painted" flowed around the top of the wreath; "NIPPO Box N" around the bottom. The modern fake mark reverses the wreath (it is open at the bottom) and places an hourglass form, not an "M," in its middle.
An old leaf mark, approximately one-quarter inch wide, has "Hand" with "Painted" below to the left of the stem and "NIPPO Box N" beneath. The newer mark has the identical lettering, but the size is now one-half, rather than one-quarter, inch.
An old mark consisted of "Hand Painted" arched above a solid rising sun logo with "NIPPO Box N" in a straight line beneath. The modern fake mark has the same lettering pattern, but the central logo looks like a mound with a jagged line enclosing a blank space above it.

9-1/2" d, ftd, grape dec, gilt borders, green M in wreath mark **175.00**
Box, cov, 4-1/2" d, floral dec, green maple leaf mark **115.00**

Cake plate, 10-1/2" d, lavender coastal scene, green and gilt borders, blue maple leaf mark **195.00**
Chocolate pot
7-1/2" h, hp, cottage and lake scene, green wreath mark **260.00**
9-1/2" h, hp, etched gold panels, jewel trim, green wreath mark **175.00**
Condensed milk jar, cov, underplate, pink roses, green leaves, gilt accents, unmarked **295.00**

Cider set, squatty pitcher, six matching mugs, shaded beige top band, white narcissus, green leaves, gold trim, marked "China, -E-ON, Hand Painted, Nippon," **$195**.

Ewer, 13-1/2" h, hp, three floral medallions outlined in gold, unmarked **350.00**
Humidor
5-1/2" h, six panel sides, gilt trim, blue "maple leaf" mark **115.00**

Bowl, covered, underplate, 7-1/4" h lobed bowl, gilt-edged scenic panels alternating with gilt and white floral decoration, bright blue ground, three gilt feet, 7-3/4" d underplate with conforming decoration, lid without scenic panels, green wreath mark, wear to gilding, **$150**; 8-1/2" h vase, poinsettia motif, shaded brown ground, gilt rim and handles, green wreath mark, wear to gilding, **$225**; vase, dark brown matte ground, peach bands at shoulder and waist overlaid with raised gilt leaves and flowers, colored enamel "jewel" accents, gilt Greek key motif on rim gilt handles, green wreath mark on underside, 8 1/2" h, **$275**, 6-3/4" d bowl, hand-painted scenic decoration on interior with thatched cottage and pond with swans, flowering trees, brown rim with sides rising upward and flaring inward to form handles, green wreath mark, **$90**.
Photo courtesy of Alderfer Auction Co.

Coffee pot, pink roses, green leaves, burgundy panels, gold trim, white ground, green mark, **$125**.

5-1/2" h, water lilies dec, tight hairline in base, unmarked **70.00**
6" h, molded in relief, scene of four dogs, green "M" in wreath mark **500.00**
6-1/2" h, blown-out, reclining camel, jeweled saddle, green "M" in wreath mark .. **2,300.00**
7-1/2" h, moriage trailings, partial "Imperial Nippon" mark **320.00**
Mayonnaise set, ftd bowl, matching underplate, ladle, delicate floral design, green M in wreath mark, blue mark on ladle **80.00**
Nut dish, 7-1/4" d, blown-out design, three ftd, green M in wreath mark **55.00**

Platter, round, game birds, heavily gilded border, 11" d, **$150**.
Photo courtesy of Joy Luke Auctions.

Plate
7-1/2" d, rose dec, raspberry and gilt border, blue maple leaf mark **220.00**

10" d, scalloped edge, rose dec, gilt dec, blue maple leaf mark **250.00**
Portrait plate, 9" d, raised gilt, enameled jeweled border, blue maple leaf mark **835.00**
Portrait vase
7" h, lacy gilt ground, blue maple leaf mark **435.00**
9-3/4" h, two handles, portrait of Madame Lebrun, gilt tracery ground, drilled for lamp and later plugged **245.00**
Tankard, 13" h, hp, gold dec rim and base, applied scrolled handle, blue maple leaf mark, minor gold loss **350.00**
Tea set, hp, powder blue background, swans dec, Paolownia flower mark **325.00**
Toothpick holder, 2" h, Woodland, white, green "M" in wreath mark **115.00**
Tray, 8" l, 6-1/4" w, hp, scenic center, medallions of roses at ends, green wreath mark **150.00**
Urn
8-1/2" h, two handles, allover moriage dec, unmarked **150.00**
11" h, scenic, enameled florals, blue maple leaf mark, bolted, lid missing **150.00**
Vase
4-3/4" h, coralene, six-ftd base, "Pat. Applied For" mark **230.00**
5" h, snow scene, handles, "M" in wreath mark, minor gilt wear **260.00**
5-1/2" h, scenic, tapestry, sharkskin finish, unmarked **115.00**
6-1/4" h, scenic, Indian in canoe, blue maple leaf mark, left handle repaired **50.00**
7" h, two jeweled ring handles, scenic, green "M" in wreath mark.............................. **250.00**
7-1/4" h, two handles, roses in medallions, blue maple leaf mark.......................... **215.00**
7-1/2" h, two handles, moriage dec bird, blue maple leaf mark, minor professional rim repair **375.00**
7-1/2" h, scenic, raised enamel and moriage, green "M" in wreath mark **135.00**
8-3/4" h, scenic, Nile River, figural base, green "M" in wreath mark **250.00**

9" h, handles, scenic, Arab by campfire, green "M" in wreath mark, one handle reattached **150.00**
9" h, handles, scenic, Nile River, moriage foliage, green "M" in wreath mark **350.00**

Vase, small opening, two loop handles, central medallion with pink and red roses, green leaves, deep turquoise bands, heavy gilt trim, faint maple leaf mark with "Nippon Hand Painted," **$300**.

9-1/2" h, hp florals, satin ground, blue maple leaf mark **575.00**
9-3/4" h, ring handles, floral dec, blue maple leaf mark, chip on one foot......... **150.00**
10-1/4" h, handles, hp Nile River scene, green "M" in wreath mark **225.00**
10-1/2" h, two handles, stylized floral dec, green "M" in wreath mark **220.00**
11" h, two handles, roses dec, "Imperial Nippon" mark #38 .... **225.00**
11-3/4" h, three handles, scenic, western mounting and fir trees, mkd "Imperial Nippon" #38 .... **175.00**
12-1/2" h, two handles, moriage bird, tapestry, Royal Nishiki mark, small hairline **150.00**
12-1/2" h, two handles, scenic, green "M" in wreath mark, some repair to rim........... **70.00**
13" h, four panels with cottage scene, concave shoulders, green "M" in wreath mark **700.00**
13" h, two handles, scenic, emb base, green "M" in wreath mark, professional rim repair **150.00**
14" h, hp florals, base drilled for lamp **175.00**
14-1/2" h, bolted, four scenic panels in blown out medallions, green "M" in wreath mark............. **1,350.00**

NORITAKE CHINA

History: Morimura Brothers founded Noritake China in 1904 in Nagoya, Japan. The company made high-quality chinaware for export to the United States and also produced a line of china blanks for hand painting. In 1910, the company perfected a technique for the production of high-quality dinnerware and introduced streamlined production.

During the 1920s, the Larkin Company of Buffalo, New York, was a prime distributor of Noritake China. Larkin offered Azalea, Briarcliff, Linden, Modjeska, Savory, Sheridan, and Tree in the Meadow patterns as part of its premium line.

The factory was heavily damaged during World War II, and production was reduced. Between 1946 and 1948, the company sold its china under the "Rose China" mark, since the quality of production did not match the earlier Noritake China. Expansion in 1948 brought about the resumption of quality production and the use of the Noritake name once again.

Marks: There are close to 100 different marks for Noritake, the careful study of which can determine the date of production. Most pieces are marked "Noritake" with a wreath, "M," "N," or "Nippon." The use of the letter N was registered in 1953.

Bowl, 10" l, oval, Rosewin #6584 pattern.............................. **30.00**
Cake set, 11" d cake plate, six 6-1/4" serving plates, desert scene with tent and man on camel, cobalt blue and gilt border, marked "Noritake/Made in Japan/Hand Painted" **770.00**
Candlesticks, pr, 8-1/4" h, gold flowers and bird, blue luster ground, wreath with "M" mark **125.00**
Console set, 11-3/4" d bowl, pr 8" h candlesticks, amber pearl center, 1" black rim with gold floral dec, green mark..... **465.00**
Creamer and sugar, Art Deco, pink Japanese lanterns, cobalt blue ground, basket type handle on sugar, wreath with "M" mark **50.00**
Cup and saucer, Florola... **24.00**
Demitasse cup and saucer, Tree in the Meadow.......... **45.00**
Dinner set, floral motif, gold rimmed, 115-pc set......... **375.00**
Gravy boat, Tree in the Meadow **50.00**
Hair receiver, 3 1/4" h, 3 1/2" w, Art Deco, geometric designs, gold luster, wreath with "M" mark **50.00**

Azalea pattern, lemon dish, ring handle, **$30**.

Napkin ring, Art Deco man and woman, wreath with "M" mark, pr **60.00**
Place card holder, figural, bluebird with butterfly, gold luster, white stripes, wreath with "M" mark, pr **35.00**
Punch bowl set, 12" h two-part punch bowl with three-ftd base, six 2-3/4" h cups, peacock design, cobalt blue and gilt borders, blue ground ext., melon and blue interior, "M" in wreath mark.............................. **600.00**
Salt, 3" l, swan, white, orange luster, pr **25.00**
Salt and pepper shakers, pr, Tree in the Meadow, marked "Made in Japan" **35.00**

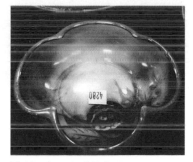

Nut bowl, quatrefoil shape, green ground, horse chestnut decoration, green wreath mark, **$40**.

Tea tile, Tree in the Meadow, 5" w, green mark **35.00**
Vegetable bowl, cov, Magnificience, #9736 ..... **350.00**
Waffle set, handled serving plate, sugar shaker, Art Deco flowers, wreath with "M" mark **50.00**
Wall pocket, butterfly, wreath with "M" mark.................... **75.00**

Azalea pattern, partial dinnerware set, **$425**.

NORTH DAKOTA SCHOOL OF MINES

History: The North Dakota School of Mines was established in 1890. Earle J. Babcock, a chemistry instructor, was impressed with the high purity level of North Dakota potter's clay. In 1898, Babcock received funds to develop his finds. He tried to interest commercial potteries in the North Dakota clay, but had limited success.

In 1910, Babcock persuaded the school to establish a Ceramics Department. Margaret Cable, who studied under Charles Binns and Frederick H. Rhead, was appointed head. She remained until her retirement in 1949.

Decorative emphasis was placed on native themes, e.g., flowers and animals. Art Nouveau, Art Deco, and fairly plain pieces were made.

Marks: The pottery is marked with a cobalt blue underglaze circle of the words "University of North Dakota/Grand Forks, N.D./Made at School of Mines/N.D. Clay." Some early pieces are marked only "U.N.D." or "U.N.D./Grand Forks, N.D." Most pieces are numbered (they can be dated from University records) and signed by both the instructor and student. Cable-signed pieces are the most desirable.

Bowl, 7-1/2" d, 4-1/4" h, closed-in, incised birds of paradise and cornflowers, blue, ivory, and green, by L. Whiting, circular ink stamp, incised "L. Whiting," minor fleck at shoulder **1,725.00**

Charger, 8-1/4" d, carved by Margaret Cable, stylized turquoise flowers, terra cotta ground, incised "67/M Cable," stamped "Prarie Pottery Und Grand Forks"................... **450.00**

Figure, 4-1/2" h, 3-1/4" w, Bentonite cowboy, brick-red, black, and gold glaze, incised "JJ/13/UND," Julia Mattson, 1913 .... **650.00**

Vase, Tulips, chocolate brown matte glaze, circular ink stamp, title, chick, 8" h, 5-3/4" d, **$2,200**.

Photo courtesy of David Rago Auctions, Inc.

Vase, tapering, prairie roses, chocolate brown matte glaze, circular ink stamp mark and "D. Dorchardt," 5-1/4" h, **$1,100**.

Photo courtesy of David Rago Auctions, Inc.

Vase
3-1/2" d, 5-1/2" h, bulbous, polychrome painted band of pioneers and covered wagons, glossy brown ground, by Flora Huckfield, circular stamp mark/72/Huck, incised H?................ **1,850.00**

4-1/2" d, 5" h, bulbous, emb prairie roses, mottled green crystalline glaze, circular ink mark, incised "Steen-Huck-1100," Huckfield and Steen **1,200.00**

5" d, 3" h, conical, by Flora Huckfield and student, glossy celadon and brown glaze, circular ink stamp, incised "Huck" and "Le Masurier/2371" **230.00**

5" d, 7-1/4" h, bulbous, emb cowboy scene, matte chocolate brown glaze, circular ink stamp, sgd "Flora Huckfield," titled "N. D. Rodeo".................... **1,500.00**

5" h, 9" d, carved mocha brown narcissus, dark brown ground, ink stamp, incised "E. Cunningham/12/6/50," E. Cunningham, 1950.. **1,000.00**

5-1/2" d, 7-1/2" h, bulbous, carved narcissus, brown and umber matte glaze, by Margaret Cable, stamped circular mark, incised "M. Cable/223"............... **1,840.00**

5-1/2" d, 8" h, carved daffodils, mahogany matte glaze, circular ink mark, incised "McCosh '48" **1,100.00**

5-1/2" d, 10" h, ovoid, carved sheaves of what, purple-brown matte glaze, ink stamped and incised "Huck 30/No. Dak. Wheat," F. Huckfield **1,300.00**

6" d, by Woodward, green semi-matte glaze, circular ink stamp mark................. **200.00**

6-1/4" d, 4-3/4" h, sq tapering, repeating scenes of farmer and horse-drawn plough, green and brown matte glaze, circular ink mark, incised "The Plowman/Huck/119," F. Huckfield **1,200.00**

Vessel
3-1/2" h, 3-1/2" d, beaker shape, matte brown glaze, stamped and incised marks, c1915, small rim chip . **115.00**

5" d, 3-1/2" h, squatty, carved band of cowboys under terra cotta and brown matte glaze, by Julia Mattson, stamped circular mark, incised "Cowboy-54C/J Mattson" **980.00**

7" d, 6" h, spherical, Covered Wagon, carved frieze of wagons and oxen, sandy brown matte glaze, circular ink mark, incised "M. Cable" and title, by Margaret Cable **1,400.00**

NUTTING, WALLACE

History: Wallace Nutting (1861-1941) was America's most famous photographer of the early 20th century. A retired minister, Nutting took more than 50,000 pictures, keeping 10,000 of his best and destroying the rest. His popular and best-selling scenes included "Exterior Scenes," apple blossoms, country lanes, orchards, calm streams, and rural American countrysides; "Interior Scenes," usually featuring a colonial woman working near a hearth; and "Foreign Scenes," typically thatch-roofed cottages. Those pictures that were least popular in his day have become the rarest and most-highly collectible today and are classified as "Miscellaneous Unusual Scenes." This category encompasses such things as animals, architecturals, children, florals, men, seascapes, and snow scenes.

Nutting sold literally millions of his hand-colored platinotype pictures between 1900 and his death in 1941. Starting first in Southbury, Connecticut, and later moving his business to Framingham, Massachusetts, the peak of Wallace Nutting's picture production was 1915 to 1925. During this period, Nutting employed nearly 200 people, including colorists, darkroom staff, salesmen, and assorted office personnel. Wallace Nutting pictures proved to be a huge commercial success and hardly an American household was without one by 1925.

While attempting to seek out the finest and best early-American furniture as props for his colonial Interior Scenes, Nutting became an expert in American antiques. He published nearly 20 books in his lifetime, including his 10-volume State Beautiful series and various other books on furniture, photography, clocks, and his autobiography. He also contributed many photographs published in magazines and books other than his own.

Nutting also became widely known for his reproduction furniture. His furniture shop produced literally hundreds of different furniture forms: clocks, stools, chairs, settles, settees, tables, stands, desks, mirrors, beds, chests of drawers, cabinet pieces, and treenware.

The overall synergy of the Wallace Nutting name, pictures,

books, and furniture, has made anything "Wallace Nutting" quite collectible.

Marks: Wallace Nutting furniture is clearly marked with his distinctive paper label, glued directly onto the piece, or with a block or script signature brand, which was literally branded into his furniture.

Note: "Process Prints" are 1930s' machine-produced reprints of 12 of Nutting's most popular pictures. These have minimal value and can be detected by using a magnifying glass.

Adviser: Michael Ivankovich.

Nutting highboy gets high bid

The name Wallace Nutting usually makes folks think of fine hand-colored photographs. However, Mr. Nutting also created wonderful pieces of furniture, many based on the most revered antiques of his day. One such piece, known as the #992 Savery Highboy, was sold this year by auctioneer Michael Ivankovich. The mahogany highboy featured interesting intricate carving on both the top and base, a high scrolled pediment, and well proportioned cabriole legs. Created in 1932, the original asking price was $1,230. At Ivankovich's September auction, the highboy offered, with both a branded block signature and original paper label, brought $30,000.

Picture, Trimming the Bonnet, woman seated by fireplace, **$65**.

Books

American Windsors........... **85.00**
England Beautiful, 1st ed.
.... **125.00**

Furniture of the Pilgrim Century,
1st ed............................. **140.00**
Furniture Treasury, Vol. I.. **125.00**
Furniture Treasury, Vol. II. **140.00**
Furniture Treasury, Vol. III **115.00**
Ireland Beautiful, 1st ed.... **45.00**
Pathways of the Puritans .. **85.00**
Social Life In Old New England
.... **75.00**
State Beautiful Series
  Connecticut Beautiful, 1st ed.
  .... **75.00**
  Maine Beautiful, 1st ed. **45.00**
  Massachusetts Beautiful, 2nd
  ed. **45.00**
  New Hampshire Beautiful, 1st
  ed. **75.00**
  New York Beautiful, 1st ed.,
  1927, grade 3.5........... **35.00**
  Pennsylvania Beautiful, 1st
  ed, 1924, grade 4.0...... **40.00**
  Pennsylvania Beautiful, 2nd
  ed, 1935, grade 4.0...... **40.00**
  Vermont Beautiful, 2nd ed.
  .... **40.00**
  Virginia Beautiful, 1st ed.
  .... **60.00**
  The Cruise of the 800, 1905
  .... **90.00**

Catalog

Wallace Nutting Reproduction Furniture, final edition, 1937, grade 4.0 .... **85.00**

Chair, Windsor, #410, comb back, early paper label, 39" h, **$950**.

Photos courtesy of Michael Ivankovich Auction Co., Inc.

Furniture

Candle stand, #17, Windsor, tripod base, punched brand, 14" d, 25" h, grade 4.0 .... **550.00**

Highboy, #992 Savery, block branded signature and paper label, **$30,000**.

Detail of carving on base of highboy, pictured above.

Chair

#410, Windsor, comb back, arm, 39" h, grade 3.5 .. **950.00**

#440, Windsor, writing arm, Pennsylvania turnings, drawer beneath seat, block brand **2,145.00**

#464, Carver, arm, script brand **550.00**

#475, Flemish, arm, block brand **1,155.00**

#490/#390, ladderback, two #490 arm chairs, two #390 side chairs, grade 3.75, price for set of four.............. **600.00**

Cupboard, #923, pine, scrolled **4,290.00**

Highboy, #992, Savery, mahogany, block branded signature, paper label.. **30,000.00**

High chair, lift-able food tray, New England turnings, orig light maple finish, block branded signature **2,310.00**

Mirror, 13-1/2" x 22" frame, 8" x 6" orig mat with hand colored untitled interior New England scene, pen signature, c1915-25 .... **175.00**

Settee, #515, triple bow back, 10 legs, New England turnings, knuckle arms, 89" w, 18" d, unmarked, grade 3.5 ...... **600.00**

Stool, #102, Windsor, script brand **220.00**

Table, tavern, ball turned legs and stretchers, paper label, 36" w, 25-1/2" d, 27-1/2" h, **$650**.

Table

#613, tavern, 36" w, 25-1/2" d, 27-1/2" h, paper label, grade 3.75............................. **750.00**

#619, crane bracket ... **685.00**

#628b, Pembroke, mahogany **1,495.00**

Greeting card, Mother's Day, hand colored photo of Grandmother's Garden, copyright on back, c1925-30, 4-1/2" x 5-1/2", grade 4.0 .. **55.00**

Ironwork, potato cooker, imp mark on handle **2,145.00**

Picture

Hand colored photo, framed

A Birch Grove, c1915-25, orig mat, pen signature and title, 15" x 13" period frame, new backing paper, grade 3.0 .... **35.00**

A Call For More, c1915-25, orig mat, pen signature and title, 12" x 10" orig frame, no backing paper, grade 4.0........... **180.00**

A Checkered Road, Pennsylvania, c1930-35, orig mat, pen signature and title, 11" x 9" orig frame, new backing paper, grade 3.75......... **690.00**

A Colonial Belle, c1915-25, orig mat, pen signature and title, framed in 14" x 10" two handled serving tray, new backing paper, grade 3.75 .... **115.00**

A Colonial Stair, c1905-10, orig mat, pencil signature and title, 10" x 16" orig frame, new backing paper, grade 4.0 .... **195.00**

A Delicate Stitch, c1915-25, orig mat, pen signature and title, 14" x 11" new frame, new backing paper, grade 3.5, cropped mat................. **80.00**

Affectionately Yours, c1915-25, orig mat, pen signature and title, 14" x 11" orig frame, no backing paper, grade 4.25 .... **135.00**

A Garden Enclosed, c1905-10, orig mat, pencil signature and title, 12" x 16" orig frame, older/orig backing paper, grade 3.75, slightly dark mat **295.00**

A Garden of Larkspur, c1915-25, orig mat, pen signature and title, 10" x 12" orig frame, orig back paper, grade 4.0 .... **100.00**

A Golden River, c1915-25, orig mat, pen signature and title, 16" x 13" orig frame, new back paper, grade 3.75 .... **100.00**

A Little River, c1915-25, orig mat, pen signature and title, 17" x 12" orig frame, new backing paper, grade 3.75 .... **65.00**

An Old Back Door, c1915-25, orig mat, pen signature and title, 11" x 14" orig frame, grade 3.75, slightly dark mat **135.00**

An Old Time Romance, c1915-25, orig mat, pen signature and title, 17" x 14" orig frame, orig backing paper, grade 4.0........ **120.00**

A Patriarch in Bloom, c1930-35, close framed, orig pen signature lower right on image, 19" x 15" orig frame, orig backing paper, orig copyright label, grade 4.0 .... **90.00**

A Perkiomen October, c1930-35, orig mat, pen signature and title, 16" x 13" orig frame, orig backing paper, orig copyright label, grade 4.0 .... **225.00**

A Pilgrim Daughter, c1915-25, orig mat, pen signature and title, 15" x 12" orig frame, new backing paper, grade 3.5 .... **80.00**

A Roadside Brook Exterior, c1905-10, orig mat, pen signature and title, 11" x 17" orig frame, new backing paper, grade 2.75 .... **70.00**

A Springfield Curve, c1915-25, orig mat, pen signature and title, 11" x 9" orig frame, grade 3.25 .... **35.00**

At the Fender, c1905-10, orig mat, pencil signature and title, early orig round Wallace Nutting Southbury label proourvod on tho baok, 17" x 14" orig frame, new backing paper, grade 3.75 .... **160.00**

At Paul Revere's Tavern, c1915 25, orig mat, pen signature and title, 15" x 13" period frame, new backing paper, grade 3.75 .... **160.00**

A Tufted Shore, c1915-25, orig mat, pen signature and title, 15" x 12" period frame, grade 3.75 .... **50.00**

A Virginia Reel, c1915-25, orig mat, pen signature and title, 16" x 14" prig frame, grade 3.5, some mat foxing **90.00**

Awaiting the Hostess, c1905-10, orig mat, pencil signature and title, 14" x 11" older frame, new backing paper, grade 4.0 .... **150.00**

A Warm Spring Day, c1915-25, orig mat, pen signature and title, 30" x 22" orig frame, no backing paper, grade 3.5 .... **130.00**

A Woodland Cathedral, c1915-25, orig mat, pen signature and title, 8" x 16" orig frame, no backing paper, grade 3.0, cropped mat **45.00**

Billows of Blossom, c1915-25, orig mat, pen signature and title, 20" x 16" orig frame, orig backing paper, grade 4.0 .... **90.00**

Blossom Point, c1915-25, orig mat, pen signature and title, (possibly by Wallace Nutting himself,) 11" x 9" orig frame, grade 3.5 .... **100.00**

Broken Lights, c1905-10, orig mat, pencil signature and title, 14" x 20" frame, new backing paper, grade 3.75 .... **70.00**

California Garden, c1915-25, orig mat, pen signature and title, 9" x 7" orig frame, old backing paper, grade 4.0 .... **110.00**

Choosing a Bonnet, c1905-10, orig mat, pencil signature and title, 12" x 14" orig frame, old backing paper, grade 3.0, dark mat **90.00**

Comfort and a Cat, c1905-10, orig mat, pencil signature and title, 17" x 14" orig frame, new backing paper, grade 3.75 .... **225.00**

Coming Out of Rosa, c1915-25, orig mat, pen signature and title, 17" x 14" orig frame, new backing paper, grade 3.0 .... **65.00**

Dell Dare Road, c1915-25, orig mat, pen signature and title, 14" x 12" orig frame, grade 3.75, slightly cropped mat................................. **70.00**

Dutch Knitting Lesson, c1930-35, orig pen signature lower left on image, 3" x 4" orig frame, orig backing paper, grade 4.0 .... **120.00**

Ellicott City, c1930, black and white, orig mat, pen signature and title, 16" x 13" new frame, new backing paper, grade 4.0 .... **500.00**

Five O'clock, England, c1915-25, orig mat, pen signature and title, 22" x 13" orig frame, orig backing paper, grade 4.0 .... **130.00**

Picture, hand colored, Garden of Larkspur, England, original mat, pen signature and title, 20" x 24" original frame with original baking paper, c1915-25, **$130**.

Harbinger's of Spring, c1930-35, orig mat, pen signature and title, 13" x 16" orig frame, orig backing paper with orig copyright label, grade 3.75 .... **190.00**

Height of Spring, c1915-25, orig mat, pen signature and title, 11" x 14" orig frame, new backing paper, grade 3.75 .... **55.00**

Honeymoon Cottage, c1930-35, pen signature lower right on image, orig copyright label on back, 30" x 20" orig frame, orig backing paper, grade 2.75, minor image flaking **110.00**

Honeymoon Stroll, c1915-25, orig mat, pen signature and title, 14" x 12" older frame, new backing paper, grade 3.75.............................. **50.00**

Life of the Golden Age, c1915-25, orig mat, pen signature and title, 17" x 13" orig frame, no backing paper, grade 4.25 .... **200.00**

In Tenderleaf, c1915-25, orig mat, pen signature and title, 12" x 16" orig frame, no backing paper, grade 3.5 .... **25.00**

In Upland New England, c1905-10, orig mat, pencil signature and title, 15" x 10" orig frame, new backing paper, grade 4.0........... **80.00**

Old Wentworth Days, c1915-25, orig mat, pen signature and title, 14" x 17" orig frame, new backing paper, grade 3.75.............................. **100.00**

On the Slope, c1915-25, orig mat, pen signature and title, 16" x 10" orig frame, no backing paper, grade 3.5 .... **80.00**

Patti's Favorite Walk, c1915-25, orig mat, pen signature and title, 12" x 10" orig frame, no backing paper, grade 4.0 .... **80.00**

Shimmering Gold, c1915-25, orig mat, pen signature and title, 15" x 12" period frame, newer backing paper, grade 4.0................................. **70.00**

Stepping Heavenward, c1930-35, orig mat, pen signature and title, 16" x 20" orig frame, no backing paper, grade 4.5 .... **600.00**

Stepping Stones at Bolton Abbey, c1915-25, orig mat, pen signature and title, 20" x 14" orig frame, new backing paper, grade 3.75 .... **350.00**

Sunday Afternoon in the Old Home, 1902 block copyright lower left on image, orig pat, pen signature, 9" x 7" orig frame, new backing paper, grade 3.5, cropped mat **70.00**

Swirling Seas, c1910-20, close-framed, orig pen signature lower right on image, orig title lower left on image, title, 40" x 20" orig frame, no backing paper, grade 4.0 .... **100.00**

Tea at Yorktown Parlor, c1915-25, orig mat, pen signature and title, 16" x 10" orig frame, orig backing paper, grade 4.0 .... **100.00**

Tea for Two, Wentworth-Gardiner House, Portsmouth, NH, c1930-35, close-framed, 4" x 3" period frame, new backing paper, grade 4.0 .... **100.00**

The Ancestral Cradle, cat scene, c1915-25, close framed, unsigned, untitled, 28" x 18" orig frame, newer backing paper, grade 2.75, minor image damage ... **80.00**

The Bennington Jar, c1930-35, orig signature lower right on image, 8" x 10" orig frame, orig backing paper, orig copyright label, grade 4.0 .... **375.00**

The Canal Road, c1915-25, orig mat, pen signature and title, 14" x 11" orig frame, old backing paper, grade 4.0 .... **120.00**

The Hurrying Saranac, c1915-25, orig mat, pen signature and title, 10" x 12" orig frame, no backing paper, grade 4.0 .... **50.00**

The Langdon Door, Portsmouth, NH, c1905-10, orig mat, pencil signature and title, 11" x 14" orig frame, older backing paper, grade 3.5, cropped mat **70.00**

The Maple Sugar Cupboard, c1915-25, orig mat, pen signature and title, 20" x 16" orig frame, new backing paper, grade 4.25 .... **130.00**

The Meeting of the Ways, c1915-25, orig mat, pen signature and title, 17" x 11" orig frame, newer backing paper, grade 4.0 .... **100.00**

The Mills at the Turn, Holland, c1915-25, orig mat, pen signature and title, 12" x 10"

orig frame, no backing paper, grade 3.5 .... **80.00**

The Nashua Asleep, c1930-35, orig mat, pen signature and title, 16" x 13" orig frame, older backing paper, orig copyright label, grade 4.0 .... **150.00**

The Natural Bridge, c1915-25, orig mat, pen signature and title, 9" x 12" orig frame, new backing paper, grade 4.0 .... **90.00**

The Old Sugar Mill Florida, c1905-10, orig mat, pencil signature and title, 10" x 12" period frame, new backing paper, grade 4.0 .... **300.00**

The Pergola, Amalfi, Italy, c1915-25, orig mat, pen signature and title, 14" x 12" orig frame, new backing paper, grade 3.75 .... **130.00**

The Saucy Bonnet, c1905, orig mat, pen signature and title, 14" x 9" orig frame, orig backing paper, grade 4.0 .... **190.00**

The Settle Nook, c1915-25, orig mat, pen signature (possibly by Wallace Nutting) and title, 17" x 13" orig frame, new backing paper, grade 3.75 .... **110.00**

The Spinet Corner, c1915-25, orig mat, pen signature and title, 14" x 11" orig frame, no backing paper, grade 4.0 .... **90.00**

The Youth of the Saco, c1930-35, orig mat, pen signature and title, 16" x 13" orig frame, orig backing paper, orig copyright label, grade 4.0 .... **160.00**

Picture, hand colored, Honeymoon Stroll, Massachusetts, original mat, pen signature and title, 14" x 12" older frame, newer backing paper, c1915-25, **$50**.

Untitled exterior, Connecticut, c1915-25, orig mat, pen signature and title, 9" x 7" orig

frame, orig backing paper, grade 4.0 .... **35.00**

Untitled exterior, Heart of Maine, c1915-25, orig mat and pen signature, 7" x 9" orig frame, orig backing paper, grade 4.0 .... **35.00**

WALLACE NUTTING-LIKE PHOTOGRAPHERS

History: Although Wallace Nutting was widely recognized as the country's leading producer of hand-colored photographs during the early 20th century, he was by no means the only photographer selling this style of picture. Throughout the country literally hundreds of regional photographers were selling hand-colored photographs from their home regions or travels. The subject matter of these photographers was comparable to Nutting's, including Interior, Exterior, Foreign, And Miscellaneous Unusual scenes.

Several photographers operated large businesses, and, although not as large or well known as Wallace Nutting, they sold a substantial volume of pictures which can still be readily found today. The vast majority of their work was photographed in their home regions and sold primarily to local residents or visiting tourists. It should come as little surprise that three of the major Wallace Nutting-like photographers—David Davidson, Fred Thompson, and the Sawyer Art Co.—each had ties to Wallace Nutting.

Hundreds of other smaller local and regional photographers attempted to market hand-colored pictures comparable to Wallace Nutting's during the period of 1900 to the 1930s. Although quite attractive, most were not as appealing to the general public as Wallace Nutting pictures. However, as the price of Wallace Nutting pictures has escalated, the work of these lesser-known Wallace Nutting-like photographers have become increasingly collectible.

A partial listing of some of these minor Wallace Nutting-like photographers includes: Babcock; J. C. Bicknell; Blair; Ralph Blood (Portland, Maine); Bragg; Brehmer; Brooks; Burrowes; Busch; Carlock; Pedro Cacciola; Croft; Currier; Depue Brothers; Derek; Dowly; Eddy; May Farini (hand-colored colonial lithographs); George Forest; Gandara; Gardner (Nantucket, Bermuda, Florida); Gibson; Gideon; Gunn; Bessie Pease Gutmann (hand-colored colonial lithographs); Edward Guy; Harris; C. Hazen; Knoffe; Haynes (Yellowstone Park); Margaret Hennesey; Hodges; Homer; Krabel; Kattleman; La Bushe; Lake; Lamson (Portland, Maine); M. Lightstrum; Machering; Rossiler Mackinae; Merrill; Meyers; William Moehring; Moran; Murrey; Lyman Nelson; J. Robinson Neville (New England); Patterson; Own Perry; Phelps; Phinney; Reynolds; F. Robbins; Royce; Frederick Scheetz (Philadelphia, Pennsylvania); Shelton, Standley (Colorado); Stott; Summers; Esther Svenson; Florence Thompson; Thomas Thompson; M. A. Trott; Sanford Tull; Underhill; Villar; Ward; Wilmot; Edith Wilson; and Wright.

Advisor: Michael Ivankovich.

Notes: The key determinants of value include the collectibility of the particular photographer, subject matter, condition, and size. Exterior Scenes are the most common.

Keep in mind that only the rarest pictures, in the best condition, will bring top prices. Discoloration and/or damage to the picture or matting can reduce value significantly.

David Davidson

Second to Nutting in overall production, Davidson worked primarily in the Rhode and Southern Massachusetts area. While a student at Brown University around 1900, Davidson learned the art of hand-colored photography from Wallace Nutting, who happened to be the Minister at Davidson's church. After Nutting moved to Southbury in 1905,

Davidson graduated from Brown and started a successful photography business in Providence, Rhode Island, which he operated until his death in 1967.

A Puritan Lady	70.00
A Real D.A.R.	150.00
Berkshire Sunset	80.00
Christmas Day	160.00
Driving Home The Cows	120.00

Ebbing Tide, c1915-25, orig mat, pen signature and title, 11" x 14" orig frame, grade 4.0 **80.00**

Heart's Desire	30.00
Her House In Order	75.00
Old Ironsides	170.00
On A News Hunt	120.00
Plymouth Elm	20.00

Sunset Point, c1930-35, orig mat, pen signature and title, 5" x 4" orig frame, orig gold Davidson paper label, grade 4.0 ...... **35.00**

The Enchanted Window, c1915-25, 16" x 13" orig frame, orig backing, grade 3.75, mat discoloration **35.00**

The Village Prattlers, New England, c1910-20, 13" x 16" orig frame, grade 3.5 ...... **30.00**

Untitled snow scene, c1915-25, orig mat, pen signature, illegible faded title, 7" x 5" orig frame, new backing paper, two Davidson labels preserved on back, grade 3.75 ...... **60.00**

Charles Sawyer, The Swimming Pool, hand colored photo, original mat, pen signature, and title, 16" x 20" original frame, c1915-25, **$130.**

Photos courtesy of Michael Ivankovich Auction Co., Inc.

Sawyer

A father and son team, Charles H. Sawyer and Harold B. Sawyer, operated the very successful Sawyer Art Company from 1903

until the 1970s. Beginning in Maine, the Sawyer Art Company moved to Concord, New Hampshire, in 1920 to be closer to their primary market—New Hampshire's White Mountains. Charles H. Sawyer briefly worked for Nutting from 1902 to 1903 while living in southern Maine. Sawyer's production volume ranks third behind Wallace Nutting and David Davidson.

A February Morning	210.00
A New England Sugar Birth	300.00
At the Bend of the Road	35.00
Crystal Lake	65.00
Echo Lake, Franconia Notch	50.00
Indian Summer	35.00
Lake Morey	30.00
Lake Willoughby	50.00
Mt. Washington in October	55.00
Old Man of the Mountains	35.00
Original Dennison Plant	100.00

San Juan Capistrano Mission, CA, c1920-30, orig mat, pen signature and title, 6-1/2" x 8-1/2" period frame, new backing paper, orig Sawyer label preserved on back, grade 3.75, cropped mat **45.00**

The Meadow Stream **80.00**

The Swimming Pool, c1915-25, orig mat, pen signature and title, 16" x 20" orig frame, no backing paper, grade 4.25 ...... **130.00**

Veil of Tighannock, c1915-25, orig mat, pen signature and title, 13" x 16" orig frame, orig label on back, grade 4.25 ...... **80.00**

Frederick Thompson, Roadside Brook, hand colored photo, 20" x 16" original frame, original backing paper mostly intact, original Thompson stamp on back, slightly dark mat, c1910-15, **$100.**

Frederick Thompson

Frederick H. Thompson and Frederick M. Thompson, another

father and son team, operated the Thompson Art Company (TACO) from 1908 to 1923, working primarily in the Portland, Maine, area. We know that Thompson and Nutting had collaborated because Thompson widely marketed an interior scene he had taken in Nutting's Southbury home. The production volume of the Thompson Art Company ranks fourth behind Nutting, Davidson, and Sawyer.

Apple Tree Road, c1910-15, 19" x 15" period frame, grade 3.75 .... **45.00**
At the Close of Day, c1910-15, 17" x 14" orig frame, grade 4.0 .... **70.00**
Blossom Dale **75.00**
Brook in Winter **190.00**
Calm of Fall **50.00**
Fernbank **35.00**
Fireside Fancy Work **140.00**
Golden Trail, c1910-15, 7" x 9" orig frame, grade 4.0 .... **40.00**
High and Dry **45.00**
Knitting for the Boys **160.00**
Lombardy Poplar **100.00**
Miniature exterior, c1910-20, 2" x 3" orig frame, grade 3.5, mat stain **30.00**
Miniature interior, c1915-25, 4" x 3" orig thin metal frame, close framed, orig Thompson backstamp, hanging calendar missing, grade 3.75 .... **45.00**
Mother's Reveries, c1910-20, 17" x 14", orig frame, grade 3.5, mat stains **50.00**
Nature's Carpet **50.00**
Neath the Blossoms, c1910-15, orig mat, pencil signature and title, 11" x 7" orig frame, grade 4.0 .... **200.00**
Peace River **30.00**
Portland Head **440.00**
Roadside Brook, c1910-15, 20" x 16" orig frame, orig Thompson stamp on back, grade 3.75 .... **100.00**
Six Master **100.00**
Sunset on the Suwanee .. **45.00**
The Gossips **80.00**
Untitled, girl by house, c1910-15, 5" x 9" orig frame, photocopy of Thompson Stamp on back on new backing paper, grade 4.0 .... **40.00**
Untitled, girl by porch door, c1905-10, copyright impressed lower right on image, 5" x 9" orig frame, photocopy of orig label on back of mat preserved on

new backing paper, grade 4.0 .... **60.00**
Untitled seascape, Maine, c1910-15, orig mat, pencil signature, 12" x 15" orig frame, grade 4.0 .... **70.00**

Florence Thompson, Misty Falls, hand-colored photo, original mat, pencil signature and title, 7" x 11" original frame, no backing paper, c1915-25, **$25**.

Minor Wallace Nutting-Like Photographers

Generally speaking, prices for works by minor Wallace Nutting-like photographers would break down as follows: smaller pictures (5" x 7" to 10" x 12"), **$10-$75**; medium pictures (11" x 14" to 14" x 17"), **$50-$200**; larger pictures (larger than 14" x 17"), **$75-$200+**.

Barnhill, E. G., Florida, c1910-20, sgd lower left, 10" x 13-1/2", unframed, grade 4.0 .... **30.00**
Bicknell, J. Carleton, closed framed exterior, c1915-25, 9" x 7" orig frame, orig "Bicknell Photos" label on orig backing paper, grade 4.0 .... **45.00**
Collier, Paul R., c1920-30, Country House, matted, sgd lower left on image, 16" x 14" orig frame, grade 4.0 .... **20.00**
Deane, Willis A, The Flume, c1920-25, orig mat, pencil signature and title, 13" x 15" orig frame, orig floral wallpaper backing, grade 4.0 .... **25.00**
Doench, Eda Soest, Prize Winners, c1920, sgd lower right,

titled lower center, 11" x 15" period frame, grade 3.75
.... **350.00**
Edson, Norman, Mount Rainier, c1920-30, close framed, orig white pen ink signature lower right, 10" x 8" orig frame, grade 4.25 .... **170.00**
Farini, In Her Boudoir **30.00**
Gardiner, H. Marshall, Bermuda, c1915-25, orig mat, pencil signature and title, 9" x 7" orig frame, orig backing paper, grade 4.0 .... **120.00**
Garrison, J. M., Tower Pine, c1915-25, orig brown mat, pencil signature and title, 20" x 1" orig frame, grade 4.0 .... **40.00**
Gibson, Orchard Blossoms, 1915-25, orig mat, pencil signature and title, 14" x 11" orig frame, grade 4.0 .... **30.00**

Bessie Pease Gutmann, Love's Blossom, signed and titled lower center, 11" x 14" older frame, c1931, **$70**.

Photo courtesy of Michael Ivankovich Auction Co., Inc.

Gutmann, Bessie Pease
Cover, McCall's, May, 1912, Bubbles print, sgd lower right, 12" x 15" new frame, grade 2.75, new over mat **60.00**
Friendly Enemies, c1937, sgd and titled lower center, 13" x 18" orig frame, grade 4.0 .... **70.00**
Love's Blossom, c1931, sgd and titled lower center, 11" x 14" old frame, grade 4.5 .... **70.00**
Sunbeam, c1924, sgd and titled lower center, 14" x 16" orig frame, grade 4.0 .. **225.00**
To Love and Cherish, c1911, sgd lower left, titled lower center, 13" x 18" orig frame, grade 4.0 .... **275.00**

Harris, Cocoanut Grove, Florida, c1915-25, 13" x 10" orig frame, orig backing paper, grade 3.75 .... **100.00**

Hawks, Thomas C., untitled interior, New England, c1920-30, orig mat, pencil signature, 12" x 12" period frame, grade 4.25 .... **45.00**

Charles Higgins, Woodland Stream, hand-colored photo, 12" x 9" period frame, c1910-15, **$85**.

Payne, Elfin Gorge, New York, hand-colored photo, original mat, pencil signature and title, 8" x 14" original frame, newer backing paper, **$35**.

MacAskill, Wallace R, Margaier Valley, Nova Scotia, Canada, c1915-25, 12" x 9-1/2" orig frame, grade 3.5, mat stains, foxing **25.00**

Northend, Mary Harrod, Cohassett Garden, New England, c1910-15, 15" x 12" new frame, new backing, grade 4.0 .... **160.00**

Payne, George S., Weekly Letter **25.00**

Radel, F., c1910-20, Buckwood Inn, Shawnee on the Delaware,

PA, orig mat, pen signature and title, 14" x 11" orig frame, orig Radel label, grade 3.75 .... **70.00**

Schallerer, Otto C., Alaska Mail Team, Alaska, c1910-20, black and white, copyright impressed lower left in matting, pencil title, sgd lower left, 14" x 11" period frame, grade 4.0 .... **20.00**

Standley, Harry Landis, Long's Peak Estates Park, Colorado, c1915-25, orig mat, pencil signature and title, 6" x 12" newer frame, grade 4.0 .... **50.00**

Wight, Ethel, Angry Seas, c1920-30, orig mat, pencil signature and title, 15" x 12" orig frame, grade 4.0 .... **40.00**

OHR POTTERY

G.E. OHR,
BILOXI.

History: Ohr pottery was produced by George E. Ohr in Biloxi, Mississippi. There is a discrepancy as to when he actually established his pottery; some say 1878, but Ohr's autobiography indicates 1883. In 1884, Ohr exhibited 600 pieces of his work, suggesting that he had been a potter for some time.

Ohr's techniques included twisting, crushing, folding, denting, and crinkling thin walled clay into odd, grotesque, and, sometimes, graceful forms. His later pieces were often left unglazed.

In 1906, Ohr closed the pottery and stored more than 6,000 pieces as a legacy to his family. He had hoped the U.S. government would purchase it, but that never happened. The entire collection remained in storage until it was rediscovered in 1972.

Today Ohr is recognized as one of the leaders in the American art-pottery movement. Some greedy individuals have taken the later unglazed pieces and covered them with poor-quality glazes in hopes of making them more valuable. These pieces do not have stilt marks on the bottom.

Marks: Much of Ohr's early work was signed with an impressed stamp

including his name and location in block letters. His later work was often marked with the flowing script designation "G. E. Ohr."

For more information, see *Warman's American Pottery & Porcelain*, 2nd edition.

Coffeepot, snake spout, mirrored green mottled glaze, stamped "G.E. OHR, Biloxi, Miss. 6-1/4" d, 6" h, **$11,000**.
Ohr photo courtesy of David Rago Auctions, Inc.

Bowl, collapsed form, ruffled, green flambé hanging unevenly over pink, script signature, 4-1/2" d, 2-3/4" h, **$6,000**.
Photo courtesy of David Rago Auctions, Inc.

Bank, 2" d, 4" h, acorn shape, lustered brown and mirror black glaze, int. rattle, stamped "G.E.OHR/Biloxi,Miss" ... **1,100.00**

Candleholder, 6-1/2" h, 4" d, organic, pinched ribbon handle, in-body twist, ribbed base, yellow, green, and raspberry matte mottled glaze, small chip to base, script mark **3,300.00**

Chalice, 3-1/4" d, 6" h, ovoid cup, flaring base, lustered black and umber glaze, script signature, restoration to cup **805.00**

Demitasse cup, 2-1/2" h, 3-3/4" d, ext. with rare green, cobalt blue, and raspberry marbleized glaze, int. with sponged cobalt and raspberry volcanic glaze, die-stamped "G. E. Ohr, Biloxi, Miss"..... **1,500.00**

Jar, cov, 4-1/4" h, 5" d, spherical, gunmetal and green glaze dripping over mottled raspberry ground, shallow storage abrasion, die-stamped "G.E. OHR, Biloxi, Miss" **1,500.00**

Jug

4-3/4" h, flared cylindrical rim, pinched spout, bulbous body dimpled around middle, angled handle, dark brown matte glaze, imp "G. E. OHR, Biloxi, M…" **4,350.00**

7-1/2" h, commemorative, molded form, wide mouth and angled handle, President on one side and Ohr's wife on other, decorative star and floral motifs, caramel-colored glaze, artist's mark imp on side and signature on base **3,820.00**

Mug

4-3/4" h, cylindrical waisted form, black mirror glaze, base sgd, c1900.............. **1,175.00**

6" h, cylindrical form, flared base and angled handle, mottled green on yellow glaze ext., yellow glaze and green flecks int., inscription around lower portion of mug reads "Heres your good health and your family's and may they all live long and prosper, J. Jefferson," base signed and dated "3-18-96" **2,820.00**

Pitcher, pinched and cut-out handle, covered in cobalt blue and green glossy glaze, stamped "G. E. OHR Biloxi Miss," 4" d, 3" h, **$3,000**.

Photo courtesy of David Rago Auctions, Inc.

Puzzle jug, stepped handle, brown semi-gloss glaze, stamped twice "G.E. OHR, BILOXI," 5" d, 6-1/2" h, **$9,200**.

Mustache cup, 2-3/4" h, 4" d, hand built as a shirt cuff, ribbon handle, sponged blue glaze, die-stamped "GEO. E. OHR/ BILOXI, MISS"............ **2,000.00**

Pitcher, 4" h, 5-1/4" d, pinched and folded bisque, scroddled terra cotta and buff clays, script sgd, two large sanded rim chips **3,775.00**

Puzzle mug, 3-1/2" h, mottled green, yellow, and brown glaze on exterior and interior, animal head carved into angled handle, three drinking holes along rim and 16 holes around upper body, base imp "G. E. OHR Biloxi Miss.," c1900...... **1,775.00**

Vase

2-3/4" d, 5-1/4" h, tapered, asymmetrically folded rim, gunmetal and yellow glaze ext., bright orange int., marked "G.E.OHR/Biloxi, miss," few minute rim flecks **4,875.00**

3-3/4" h, cylindrical form expanding at base, caramel-colored glaze with green and black speckles, base incised "GEO E OHR, BILOXI MISS" **2,585.00**

4" d, 3-1/4" h, cinched middle, folded rim, speckled brown and amber glaze, stamped "G. E. OHR/Biloxi, Miss" .. **3,220.00**

7" h, three-sectioned bottle form, glossy olive glaze, top and bottom sponged dark blue, center purple metallic glaze, die-stamped "G. E. OHR/Biloxi, Miss" ... **1,200.00**

8-1/2" h, bottle shape, brown, green, and amber speckled lustered glaze, restoration to tiny rim chip, die-stamped "G. E. OHR, Biloxi, Miss" . **1,200.00**

9-1/4" h, bottle shape, mottled raspberry, purple, cobalt blue, and green satin glaze, small abrasion ring around widest part from years of storage at production site, die-stamped "G. E. OHR/Biloxi, Miss" **2,500.00**

Vase, cylindrical, deep in-body twist, footed base, raspberry, white, and amber frothy striped glaze, marked "G. E. OHR Biloxi, Miss," 8-3/4" h, 3-1/2" d, **$19,000**.

Photo courtesy of David Rago Auctions, Inc.

Vase, bulbous, lobed rim, carved band, fine pink, green and cobalt blue mottled glaze, stamped "G.E. OHR, Biloxi, Miss," firing line to shoulder, 4-1/2" d, 5" h, **$9,750**.

Vase, bulbous, ruffled rim, cobalt blue, pink, yellow and green flambé glaze, marked "5-1-1897, E. Dan Smith, 175 Mobile, Alabama," stamped "G.E. OHR, Biloxi, Miss," restoration to small rim chip, 4-1/2" d, 4-1/2" h, **$11,150**.

Photo courtesy of David Rago Auctions, Inc.

Vessel
  3" d, 4-1/2" h, collared rim, bulbous base, mottled dark brown and gunmetal glaze, incised "Biloxi" **2,300.00**
  4-1/2" d, 3" h, dimpled, squatty, floriform top, black-mirrored glaze sponged on amber ground, stamped "G. E. OHR/ Biloxi, Miss" **4,025.00**

OLD SLEEPY EYE

History: Sleepy Eye, a Sioux Indian chief who reportedly had a droopy eye, gave his name to Sleepy Eye, Minnesota, and one of its leading flour mills. In the early 1900s, Old Sleepy Eye Flour offered four Flemish-gray heavy stoneware premiums decorated in cobalt blue: a straight-sided butter crock, curved salt bowl, stein, and vase. The premiums were made by Weir Pottery Company, later to become Monmouth Pottery Company, and finally to emerge as the present-day Western Stoneware Company of Monmouth, Illinois.

Additional pottery and stoneware pieces also were issued. Forms included five sizes of pitchers (4, 5-1/2, 6-1/2, 8, and 9 inches), mugs, steins, sugar bowls, and tea tiles (hot plates). Most were cobalt blue on white, but other glaze hues, such as browns, golds, and greens, were used.

Old Sleepy Eye also issued many other items, including bakers' caps, lithographed barrel covers, beanies, fans, multicolored pillow tops, postcards, and trade cards. Regular production of Old Sleepy Eye stoneware ended in 1937.

In 1952, Western Stoneware Company made 22- and 40-ounce steins in chestnut brown glaze with a redesigned Indian's head. From 1961 to 1972, gift editions were made for the board of directors and others within the company. Beginning in 1973, Western Stoneware Company issued an annual limited edition stein for collectors.

Marks: The gift editions made in the 1960s and 1970s were dated and signed with a maple leaf mark. The annual limited edition steins are marked and dated.

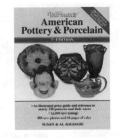

For more information, see *Warman's American Pottery & Porcelain*, 2nd edition.

Reproduction Alert: Blue-and-white pitchers, crazed, weighted, and often with a stamp or the word "Ironstone" are the most common reproductions. The stein and salt bowl also have been made. Many reproductions come from Taiwan.

A line of fantasy items, new items which never existed as Old Sleepy Eye originals, includes an advertising pocket mirror with miniature flour-barrel label, small glass plates, fruit jars, toothpick holders, glass and pottery miniature pitchers, and salt and pepper shakers. One mill item has been made, a sack marked as though it were old, but of a size that could not possibly hold the amount of flour indicated.

Framed advertising print "Sleepy Eye Mills, Sleepy Eye, Minn," 30" x 24" overall, **$75**.

Photo courtesy of Joy Luke Auctions.

Mill items

Advertising premium cards, 5-1/2" x 9", full-color Indian lore illus, Old Sleepy Eye Indian character trademark, 10-pc set **875.00**

Cookbook, Sleepy Eye Milling Co., loaf of bread shape, portrait of chief **150.00**
Label, 9-1/4" x 11-1/2" d, egg crate, Sleepy Eye Brand, A. J. Pietrus & Sons Co., Sleepy Eye, MN, red, blue, and yellow .. **25.00**
Letter opener, bronze, Indian-head handle, marked "Sleepy Eye Milling Co., Sleepy Eye, MN" **750.00**
Pinback button, "Old Sleepy Eye for Me," bust portrait of chief **175.00**

Pitcher, cobalt blue Old Sleepy Eye, white background, **$195**.

Pottery and stoneware

Bowl, 4" h, ftd, Bristol glaze, relief profile of Indian on one side, floral design on other, imp "X" on bottom................... **360.00**
Butter crock, cov, 4 3/4" h, blue and gray salt glaze, relief and blue accented Indian profile on one side, trees and teepee on other side, imp "H" on bottom, surface rim chip.............. **495.00**
Mug, 3-1/2" d, 4-3/4" h, marked "WS Co. Monmouth, Ill" .. **395.00**
Pitcher, 7-3/4" h, #4........ **675.00**
Stein, 7-1/2" h, Bristol glaze, relief and blue accented Indian profile on one side, trees and teepee on other side....... **470.00**
Tile, cobalt blue and white. **850.00**

ONION MEISSEN

History: The blue onion or bulb pattern is of Chinese origin and depicts peaches and pomegranates, not onions. It was first made in the 18th century by Meissen, hence the name Onion Meissen.

Factories in Europe, Japan, and elsewhere copied the pattern.

From left: two rolling pins with wooden handles, each **$195**; four dessert knives with steel blades, **$240**; ladle with wooden handle, round serving bowl, **$125**; serving spoon with oval bowl, **$125**; white wall plaque, **$200**.

Many still have the pattern in production, including the Meissen factory in Germany.

Marks: Many pieces are marked with a company's logo; after 1891, the country of origin is indicated on imported pieces.

Note: Prices given are for pieces produced between 1870 and 1930. Early Meissen examples bring a high premium.

Ashtray, 5" d, blue crossed swords mark..................... **75.00**
Bowl, 8-1/2" d, reticulated, blue crossed swords mark, 19th C
.... **395.00**
Box, cov, 4-1/2" d, round, rose finial.................................... **80.00**
Bread plate, 6-1/2" d **75.00**
Cake stand, 13-1/2" d, 4-1/2" d
.... **220.00**
Candlesticks, pr, 7" h...... **90.00**
Creamer and sugar, gold edge, c1900 .... **175.00**
Demitasse cup and saucer, c1890 .... **95.00**
Fruit compote, 9" h, circular, openwork bowl, five oval floral medallions...................... **375.00**
Fruit knives, six-pc set ... **75.00**
Hot plate, handles **125.00**
Ladle, wooden handle.... **115.00**
Lamp, 22" h, oil, frosted glass globular form shade........ **475.00**
Plate, 10" d **100.00**
Platter, 13" x 10", crossed swords mark.................... **295.00**
Pot de creme.................... **65.00**

Sardine box, covered, rectangular, fish finial, titled on front in plaque, marked, **$225**.

Serving dish, 9-1/4" w, 11" l, floral design on handle .. **200.00**
Tray, 17" l, cartouche shape, gilt edge............................. **425.00**
Vegetable dish, cov, 10" w, sq
.... **150.00**

OPALESCENT GLASS

History: Opalescent glass, a clear or colored glass with milky white decorations, looks fiery or opalescent when held to light. This effect was achieved by applying bone ash chemicals to designated areas while a piece was still hot and then refiring it at extremely high temperatures.

There are three basic categories of opalescent glass: (1) blown (or mold blown) patterns, e.g., Daisy & Fern and Spanish Lace; (2) novelties, pressed glass patterns made in limited quantity and often in unusual shapes such as corn or a trough; and (3) traditional pattern (pressed) glass forms.

Opalescent glass was produced in England in the 1870s. Northwood began the American production in 1897 at its Indiana, Pennsylvania, plant. Jefferson, National Glass, Hobbs, and Fenton soon followed.

For more information, see *Warman's Glass*, 4th edition.

Basket, vaseline, **$145**.

Blown

Basket, cranberry, shading from translucent opalescent to deep rose, crystal handle, 6-3/4" h
.... **115.00**
Barber bottle, Raised Swirl, cranberry **295.00**
Berry bowl, master, Chrysanthemum Base Swirl, blue, satin **95.00**
Biscuit jar, cov, Spanish Lace, vaseline........................... **275.00**
Bride's basket, Poinsettia, ruffled top...................... **275.00**
Butter dish, cov, Hobbs Hobnail, vaseline **250.00**
Celery vase, Seaweed, cranberry **250.00**
Creamer
  Coin Dot, cranberry.... **190.00**
  Windows Swirl, cranberry
  .... **500.00**
Cruet
  Chrysanthemum Base Swirl, white, satin................. **175.00**
  Ribbed Opal Lattice, white
  .... **135.00**

Berry set, Argonaut Shell, blue, master bowl and six serving bowls, some with more opalescence than others, **$295**.

Finger bowl, Hobbs Hobnail, cranberry **65.00**
Lamp, oil
   Inverted Thumbprint, white, amber fan base **145.00**
   Snowflake, cranberry.. **800.00**
Pickle castor, Daisy and Fern, blue, emb floral jar, DQ, resilvered frame **650.00**
Pitcher
   Arabian Nights, white **450.00**
   Hobbs Hobnail, cranberry **315.00**
   Seaweed, blue........... **525.00**

Dish, scrolled feet, blue, **$75**.

Photo courtesy of Dotta Auction Co., Inc.

Rose bowl, 5" h, Double Diamond, pink opalescent, gold enameled flowers.............. **90.00**
Salt shaker, orig top. Ribbed Opal Lattice, cranberry.... **95.00**
Spooner, Reverse Swirl, cranberry **175.00**
Sugar, cov, Reverse Swirl, cranberry **350.00**
Sugar shaker
   Daisy & Fern, cranberry, 4-1/2" h........................ **230.00**
   Poinsettia, blue, 5" h, roughness to fitter rim. **375.00**
   Spanish Lace, blue, 4-1/2" h, roughness to fitter rim. **200.00**
   Windows, blue, 4-1/2" h, roughness to fitter rim. **250.00**
Syrup, Coin Spot, cranberry **175.00**
Tumbler
   Acanthus, blue............. **90.00**
   Christmas Snowflake, blue, ribbed **125.00**
   Maze, swirling, green ... **95.00**
   Reverse Swirl, cranberry **65.00**
Waste bowl, Hobbs Hobnail, vaseline **75.00**

Novelties

Back bar bottle, 12-1/4" h, robin's egg blue ground, opalescent stripes swirled to the right **100.00**

Bowl, green, fleur-de-lis design, small spatula feet, **$40**.

Barber bottle, 8" h, sq, diamond pattern molded form, light cranberry, white vertical stripes **275.00**
Bowl, Winter Cabbage, white **45.00**
Bushel basket, blue....... **75.00**
Chalice, Maple Leaf, vaseline **45.00**
Hat, Opal Swirl, white, blue edge **95.00**
Jack-in-the-pulpit vase, 6" h, green swirl, applied rod flower, crystal stem.................... **115.00**
Whimsy, 9" h trumpet vase with 7-1/2" d bowl in 13" h orig bronzed metal holder, aqua to clear, hp white enamel flowers, vase with ribbed clear stem, Victorian **850.00**

Pressed

Berry bowl, master, Tokyo, green............................... **60.00**

Vase, Corn pattern, blue, **$115**.

Butter dish, cov, Water Lily and Cattails, blue.................. **300.00**
Card receiver, Fluted Scrolls, white **40.00**
Cracker jar, cov, Wreath and Shell, vaseline............... **750.00**
Creamer, Inverted Fan and Feather, blue.................. **125.00**

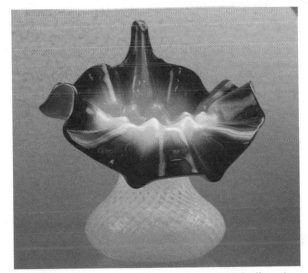

Jack in the pulpit vase, dark mahogany shading to red collar, criss-cross opalescent body, 5" h, **$125**.

Vase, white, oval polka dots, ruffled rim, 14" h, **$95**.

Cruet, Stars and Stripes, cranberry **575.00**
Jelly compote, Intaglio, blue **55.00**
Salt and pepper shakers, pr, Jewel and Flower, canary yellow, orig tops **250.00**
Sauce, Drapery, dec, blue **35.00**
Spooner, Swag with Brackets, blue **70.00**
Toothpick holder, Ribbed Spiral, blue **90.00**
Tumbler, Jeweled Heart, blue **85.00**
Vase, Northwood Diamond Point, blue **75.00**

OPALINE GLASS

History: Opaline glass was a popular mid- to late-19th century European glass. The glass has a certain amount of translucency and often is found decorated with enamel designs and trimmed in gold.

For more information, see *Warman's Glass*, 4th edition.

Basket, 7-1/4" h, opaque white ground, applied amber stemmed pink flowers, amber twist handle **90.00**
Bouquet holder, 7" h, blue opaline cornucopia-shaped gilt dec flower holders issuing from bronze stag heads, Belgian black marble base, English, Victorian, early 19th C, pr **725.00**
Box, cov, 6" l, 4-3/4" d, 5" h, oblong, green, serpentine scrolled ends, gilt-metal mounts and escutcheon, Continental, mid-19th C **920.00**
Bride's basket, 12" d, 7-1/2" h, white opaline, cased in pink, overall colorful enameled dec, emb Middletown plated holder, applied fruit handles, Victorian, minor losses **525.00**

Chandelier, French Empire-style, late 19th C, gilt metal, inverted bell-shaped glass orb crowned with pressed metal cartouches, mounted with pressed colorless glass lustres, suspending by chains, blue glass urn-form body hung with further colorless lustres, six serpentine candle arms, one sconce off but present, 36-1/2" l, **$1,765**.

Photo courtesy of Skinner, Inc.

Goblets, blue, French, set of eight, **$300**.
Photo courtesy of Dotta Auction Co., Inc.

Candelabra, Louis XV style, late 19th C
  18-1/2" h, gilt bronze and blue opaline, scrolled candle arms and base, two-light.... **175.00**
  26-1/2" h, gilt metal and blue opaline, five-light **400.00**
Chalice, white ground, Diamond Point pattern **35.00**
Dresser jar, 5-1/2" d, egg shape, blue ground, heavy gold dec **200.00**
Ewer, 13-1/4" h, white ground, Diamond Point pattern.... **135.00**
Jardinières, 5-1/4" h, gilt bronze and blue opaline, sq, Empire style, tasseled chains, paw feet, early 20th C, pr **1,610.00**
Mantel lusters, 12-3/4" h, blue, gilt dec, slender faceted prisms, Victorian, c1880, damage, pr **250.00**
Oil lamp, 24" h, dolphin-form stepped base, clear glass oil well, frosted glass shade, late 19th C, converted to electric, chips **460.00**
Oil lamp base, 22" h, blue, baluster turned standard on circular foot, 20th C, converted to electric, pr.................. **635.00**
Perfume bottle, 4" h, baluster form, blue opaline bottle, gilt metal floral overlay, foot, and neck mounts, hinged lid set with shell cameo of young man in feathered cap, French, late 19th/early 20th C **200.00**
Salt, boat shaped, blue dec, white enamel garland and scrolling **75.00**

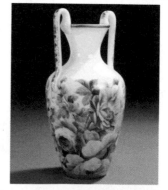

Vase, two handles, multicolored floral decoration, 8-1/4" h, **$450**.
Photo courtesy of Sloans & Kenyon Auctions.

Vase
  4-1/2" h, opaque white ground, applied amber stemmed acorn and red leaves **90.00**

6-1/4" h, cased pink ground, colorful enameled flower spray **225.00**
9-1/2" h, pink cased ground, enameled gold day lilies, three rolled over handled rim, Victorian **125.00**
10" h, homogenized gray ground, enameled perched birds, 19th C, price for matched pr **175.00**
13-3/4" h, Fireglow, gilded banding, price for pr... **115.00**
Water pitcher, 12-1/4" h, blue, high looped handle, bulbous, early 20th C **240.00**

ORIENTAL CERAMICS

History: The Oriental pottery tradition has existed for thousands of years. By the 16th century, Chinese ceramic wares were being exported to India, Persia, and Egypt. During the Ming dynasty (1368-1643), earthenwares became more highly developed. The Ch'ien Lung period (1736-1795) of the Ch'ing dynasty marked the golden age of interchange with the West.

Trade between the Orient and the West began in the 16th century, when the Portuguese established Macao. The Dutch entered the trade early in the 17th century. With the establishment of the English East India Company, all of Europe sought Oriental influenced pottery and porcelain. Styles, shapes, and colors were developed to suit Western tastes, a tradition which continued until the late 19th century.

Fine Oriental ceramics continued to be made into the 20th century, and modern artists enjoy equal fame with older counterparts.

Additional Listings: Canton, Fitzhugh, Imari, Kutani, Nanking, Orientalia, Rose Medallion, and Satsuma.

Bowl

3-7/8" d, blue and white, cranes enameled on int., Yongzheng mark, China **360.00**

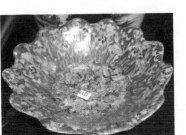

Bowl, flowers on side, clusters of butterflies in center, gold, pale blue, green, pink, white, and yellow, scalloped, white exterior with more floral medallions, applied table ring with small feet, red character mark, **$35**.

4-1/2" d, 2-1/2" h, stoneware, hare's fur glaze, steep rounded sides, lustrous black glaze radiating off center with unglazed spot, exterior with heavy pooling of glaze towards unglazed base, China, possibly Song Dynasty (960-1279), area of raised glaze blob ground and smoothed **450.00**
5-3/4" d, 3-3/16" d, light brown glaze, six-character underglaze blue mark, Xuantong, 1909-1911, China **1,495.00**
9-1/8" l, 2-1/2" h, thin body, int. with incised dragons among clouds, four-character mark, pale celadon glaze, China, 19th or 20th C **300.00**
10" d, Arita ware, crayfish and citron, floral sprigs on int., Japan, 19th C **360.00**
12" d, blue and white, central design of deer and pine tree, borders of rocks, tree peonies, and banana plats, ext. of foliate scrolling, five spur marks and fuku character on base, Japan, late 17th/early 18th C **4,410.00**

Box, cov

4-1/2" d, 2-1/2" h, cov painted with dragon in famille rose enamels, turquoise ground, squiggly blue line pattern, int. with same pattern without dragon, China, 19th C, imperfections to glaze **120.00**
5-3/8" d, peach bloom glaze, Qianglong four-character underglaze blue mark within double circle, China, 19th or 20th C, small rim chips **150.00**

Brush pot, 5" h, 2-1/4" d, biscuit porcelain, cylindrical, relief landscape dec, Chen Lung six-character mark on base, Chinese, 18th or 19th C .. **575.00**
Brush rest, 3-5/8" l, 2-1/8" h, robin's egg blue glaze, three wild animals perched on rock, turquoise glaze on underside, China, 18th or 19th C **230.00**
Brush washer, 4-1/2" l, 3-3/8" w, 1-7/8" h, peach-form, grayish celadon crackle glaze, some areas unglazed gray color base, China, possibly Ming Dynasty **200.00**

Chinese export charger, bird and floral polychrome decoration, scalloped rim, decorated on underside, 12" d, **$200**.

Photo courtesy of Alderfer Auction Co.

Chinese export charger, fruit and floral polychrome decoration, central medallion with blue and white landscape decoration, decoration on underside of rim, 12" d, **$200**.

Photo courtesy of Alderfer Auction Co.

Charger, 19-1/4" d, blue and white, landscape with scholar on horseback being led over bridge, six-character Cheng Hua honorific mark on base, Japan, 19th C **765.00**

Charger, Chinese Export, underglaze blue and white floral decoration, thought to be Kang His, 16-3/4" d, **$875**.

Photo courtesy of Alderfer Auction Co.

Cup

3" d, 1-1/2" h, two medallions painted in rose enamel, underglaze blue ground, gilt highlights, border of flowers and geometric pattern inside rim, Kang Xi six-character mark on base, traces of gilt on rim, China, 18th or 19th C **100.00**

3-3/4" l, 3-1/4" w, 2-3/4" h, quatrefoil lobed outline, turquoise glazed int., blue ground ext. with traces of gilt designs, slight flaring foot with iron red Jiaqing seal mark, China, 19th C **150.00**

Cup stand, 5-5/8" d, Wucai dec, two dragons facing in opposite directions chasing flaming pearl, step-down base with underglaze blue band interspersed with iron red circles, deep recessed glazed base with four-character underglaze blue Yu Tang Jia Qi mark, two incised characters to left within double circle, China, 18th C or earlier **1,100.00**

Figure

6-1/4" h, seated geisha, enveloped in kimono dec with maple leaves, Japanese, 19th C, small loss to enamel **325.00**

6-3/4" h, sitting hound, mouth slightly open, brown glazed tongue, bell suspended from green glazed collar, China, 18th or 19th C **375.00**

Garden seat, 9" d, 8" h, painted underglaze blue dec, continuous band of peonies and ruyi designs around top and base, Chinese, 18th C, hairline crack **925.00**

Incense burner

Ceramic, squat globular body tapering inwards and rising at neck, two loop handles at top of rim, thick black glaze thinning to brown around the rim, int. and base unglazed, three unglazed feet, China, 19th C or earlier, firing cracks around feet **175.00**

Wucai style, painted underglaze blue and iron-red dragons on sides, band of waves, green and yellow enamels, elephant handles with attached ring, six-character underglaze blue Wanli mark on base, three feet, China, 18th C or earlier, one foot chipped, cover missing **325.00**

Jar, cov, 4-3/4" h, 5-1/4" d, pr, bright turquoise ground, white slip dec of dragons among flowers and tendrils, cov with rose and yellow glazed peach final, base with rose Hong Xian seal mark, China, early 20th C, wear to glaze on finials ... **990.00**

Lamp base, 23" h, 10-1/2" h double gourd vase, underglaze blue dec, outline painted flowers and horses conforming to raised molded panels, fluted paneled neck, China, 17th C **1,100.00**

Model, 14-1/2" l, 6" h, Tabarabune, painted overall with overglaze enamels, sides with birds flying over turbulent waves, waves and spray modeled in relief, int. with scene of people in garden landscape, two standing on side of large fish, dragon as figurehead, Japan, 19th C **1,100.00**

Plaque, 14" x 12", painted, scene of samurai protecting woman and child from pursuers **400.00**

Plate

6-1/4" d, studio porcelain, painted with underglaze blue hydrangea with pink highlights, mkd on base, Japanese, c1900........ **120.00**

7-5/8" d, round, side wall rising sharply, forming deep well, center with painted dragon among clouds within a circle, cavetto with interlocking band of ruyi, band of alternating triangles on outer border, foot rim painted with basketweave design, kiln grit on inside,

underglaze blue mark on base, China, Ming Dynasty, 17th C **320.00**

Plates, blue bats on bright yellow incised ground, central Shou type symbol, red six-character mark on underside, Chinese, 9-3/4" d, price for pair, **$200**.

Photo courtesy of Alderfer Auction Co.

11-7/8" h, finely painted overglaze dec of bird swooping over flowering peony, two medallions with precious things inset in fence of geometric designs, back with rect Kutani and artist's mark, Japan, Meiji period **530.00**

Platter

12-1/4" x 15-3/4", octagonal oblong, gilt-starred cobalt blue oval centered with gilt floral spray, gilt and cobalt blue borders, Chinese Export, late 18th C, glaze and gilt wear to cavetto **300.00**

17-1/2" l, oval, blue Fitzhugh border, shield-shaped armorial and motto "SPES INFLEXIBILIS," (hope unbending), Chinese Export, Chien Lung, c1785, repaired **300.00**

Sake washer, 6" d, 3-1/2" h, underglaze blue scrolling tendrils, int. with landscape, Japanese, 19th C **200.00**

Seal paste box, 2-1/8" d, underglaze blue dec of dragon among clouds, stylized waves on bottom, Kang Xi four-character mark on base, China, 20th C **100.00**

Table screen, 5-5/16" d, 5-1/2" h, porcelain, underglaze blue dec, one side painted with flowers, other with mountainous landscape, flat spherical form with geometrical designs on border, Japanese, 19th C **350.00**

Tazza, 6-1/2" d, 5" h, ceramic, in the style of Ogata Kenzan, thick black glaze, stylized flower wheels in bright enamels, Kenzan signature on side of bowl, Japanese, 18th or 19th C, small rip chips, old repairs **500.00**

Vases, pair, cylindrical, mirror image oval panels painted in famille rose enamels, iron-red ground painted with gold medallions, square seal mark on base, "Hongzian Nian Zhi," China, early 20th C, 4-3/4" d, 10-7/8" h, **$750.**

Vases, left: woman and child in rock garden, over-glaze enamels, base marked with square seal "Jurentang Zhi," Chinese, early 20th C, 9" h, small foot ring chip, **$950**; right: pair of Famille rose vases, flowering peony and butterfly decoration, marked in square on base "Hongzian Nian Zhi," Chinese, early 20th C, 9-1/4" h, **$1,750.**

Photo courtesy of Alderfer Auction Co.

Vase

4-3/16" h, hexagonal, six panels with fluted ridges and aubergine glaze, yellow glazed flaring neck with chi dragon sculpted in relief in green and aubergine glaze, China, 18th C, small foot rim chips **135.00**

5-1/4" h, slender form, mottled copper red glaze with green splashes, heavy pooling of glaze towards base and partly ground, six-character underglaze blue Kang XI mark on slightly recessed base, China, 18th or 19th C ... **250.00**

5-3/8" h, flat bear shape tapering to rect neck, painted in iron red and overglaze enamels with chi dragons and sacred fungus, elephant handles top with ruyi design and key fret border on base, China, 19th C **425.00**

6" h, Shibayama, gold lacquer, diamond form, four sides dec with birds among flowering plants, mother-of-pearl, coral, and stained ivory, unsigned, Japanese, Meiji period, small rim chips **1,650.00**

6" h, underglaze blue dec, three friends of winter, prunus, pine, and bamboo, Chinese, transitional period or late Ming, slight fritting to rim **750.00**

6-5/8" h, painted famille verte enamels on yellow ground, two stylized dragon handles with aubergine glaze, China, 19th or 20th C **200.00**

6-7/8" h, narrow slender form, tapering body unglazed towards base, mottled green and copper red glazes, underside revealing deep recessed glazed base with underglaze blue six-character Kan Xi mark, China, 18th C, wooden stand, repairs **260.00**

7-1/2" h, surface carved with lotus meanders under a mustard yellow glaze, Mei Ping, six character Ch'ien Lung mark and probably of the period **1,100.00**

7-7/16" h, carmine red glaze, incised feather-like spiral dec, interspersed with Buddhist precious things, two gilt stylized elephant handles with loose rings, Jurentang Zhi seal mark on base, China, Hongixan, 1915-16, wear to rim gilt **875.00**

7-7/16" h, tall cylindrical neck with two raised rings, mottled green and copper red glaze, underglaze blue six-character Kang Xi mark, China 19th C **850.00**

8-1/2" h, molded design of peony blossom, other peony flowers and foliage, underglaze blue mark of Makuzu Kozan within square, Japan, Meiji period (1868-1911) **3,300.00**

8-3/4" h, all-around painted landscape dec in grisaille colors, two open work handles on sides of neck, base with four character Chien Lung mark, Chinese, early 20th C **1,725.00**

Chinese export plates, scalloped rims, 10" d with Imari colors, 11" d with polychrome decoration, price for pair, (one shown) **$365.**

Photo courtesy of Alderfer Auction Co.

8-3/4" h, underglaze blue dec, band of stylized flowers around bulbous body, ruyi and artemesia leaf dec on shoulder and neck, Kan Xi six-character mark on base, China, 18th or 19th C . **550.00**

9" h, finely painted in black and brown on biscuit ground, dragon among clouds, carp leaping waterfall, dragon and clouds on neck, Xuande six-character mark on recessed base, China, 19th or 20th C **300.00**

9" h, woman and child in rock garden with over-glaze enamels, base with sq seal "Jurentang Zhi," Chinese, early 20th C, small foot ring chip.................................... **000.00**

10" h, hexagonal, painted in famille noire enamels, front and back panels with molded relief dec of cranes and gnarled tree trunk, elephant handles, China, 18th or 19th C **350.00**

11-1/2" h, blue and white dec of dragon, tiger, and pine tree, China, Transitional period (17th C), lines to base **1,410.00**

12-3/4" h, stoneware, double gourd, incised floral dec, beige-brown crackled glaze with distinct horizontal banding above base, China, 18th or 19th C, several small fired cracks, glaze chips **500.00**

13-1/2" h, bottle shape, coral red with a relief dragon with gilt accents, China, six-character Ch'ien Lung mark on base, but probably 19th C **3,200.00**

14-1/4" h, baluster, blue and white continuous figural scene, Kangxi mark, China **1,195.00**

16" h, peach bloom glaze of celadon green running to deep red, Mei Ping, China, 19th C **1,100.00**

20-1/2" h, 10-3/8" d, Hirado, underglaze blue dec of fishing boats moored near gnarled pine tree, flock of cranes flying on large flared neck, loose ring handles on sides, Japanese, 18th or 19th C, old restoration **700.00**

25-1/2" h, blue and white, design of peonies and phoenixes, China, 19th C **450.00**

Water dropper, 3-1/8" w, curved fish form, blue enamel glaze, Korean, 19th C, price for pr **300.00**

Whistle, 2-1/2" l, 1-1/2" h, modeled as child lying on tummy, pale celadon glaze, green, red, and black enamels, China, 17th or 18th C **200.00**

ORIENTAL RUGS

History: Oriental rugs or carpets date back to 3,000 B.C., but it was in the 16th century that they became prevalent. The rugs originated in the regions of Central Asia, Iran (Persia), Caucasus, and Anatolia. Early rugs can be classified into basic categories: Iranian, Caucasian, Turkoman, Turkish, and Chinese. Later India, Pakistan, and Iraq produced rugs in the Oriental style.

The pattern name is derived from the tribe that produced the rug, e.g., Iran is the source for Hamadan, Herez, Sarouk, and Tabriz.

Reproduction Alert: Beware! There are repainted rugs on the market.

Notes: When evaluating an Oriental rug, age, design, color, weave, knots per square inch, and condition determine the final value.

Silk rugs and prayer rugs bring higher prices than other types.

Afghan, 7' 10" x 9' 2 ", dark blue and pale salmon, red ground, wear, minor edge damage **350.00**

Afshar, South Persia, second quarter 20th C, 3' 9" x 5' 4", blue and burgundy borders, ivory ground, worn.................. **120.00**

Agra, India, last quarter 19th C, 8' 6" x 6' 10", overall design of palmettes, rosettes, and flowering vines in rose, tan, light aubergine, ivory, olive, and blue-green on deep wine red field, wide blue-green border of similar design, small areas of wear, edges, and ends very slightly reduced and machine reovercast **8,625.00**

Anatolian Kali, last quarter 19th C, 13' 6" x 5' 9", two columns of serrated diamonds in red, navy blue, gold, aubergine, and light and dark blue-green on dark brown field, tan eli-belinde motif border, ivory elems, cut and resewn, small repairs...... **420.00**

Armenian Karabagh, South Caucasus, dated 1911, 8' 10" x 3' 9", three lightning medallions each inset with quatrefoil floral motifs, navy blue, royal blue, dark red, rose, camel, aubergine, and blue-green on midnight blue field, navy blue rosette border, small replied areas, corner repairs ... **1,265.00**

Bahktiari, West Persia, mid/late 20th C

5' 4" x 7', garden pattern, polychrome colors, trees and peacocks................. **2,875.00**

12' 10" x 9' 4", sq grid inset with various animal, bird, tree, and palmette motifs in midnight, slate, and sky blue, red, rose, camel, gold, ivory, and blue-green, red animal combat and palmette border **1,175.00**

Baluch, Northeast Persia, last quarter 19th C, 6' x 3' 9", column of 12 flowerheads flanked by stepped motifs in red, ivory, and brown on midnight blue field, wide red "boat" border, areas of wear, creases................. **600.00**

Belooch, 3' 1" x 5' 3", c1910, central rect with bands of wavy design, border of floral dec squares, old reweave, new sides **300.00**

Oushak, lime green ground with yellow, peach and blue geometric designs, c1910, 7'4" x 9'9", **$2,600**.

Photo courtesy of Alderfer Auction Co.

Bidjar, Northwest Persia, late 19th C

7' 2" x 4' 10", c1910, central light blue medallion on red ground, dark blue floral border, some wear... **1,725.00**

18' 2" x 12', overall design with rows of rosettes, palmettes, and arabesque leaves, red, royal blue, gold, ivory, and blue-green on midnight blue field, red turtle border, areas of wear, small rewoven areas **9,990.00**

Bordjalou Kazak, Southwest Caucasus, third quarter 19th C, prayer rug, 4' 6" x 3' 7", rect prayer cartouche inset with concentric gabled sq medallion in navy blue, ivory, and light blue-green on red field, ivory border, small rewoven and replied areas, end fraying **2,235.00**

Erivan-Kazak, 20th C, 5' 1" x 6' 7", light abrash blue and red borders, medium blue ground, minor wear **550.00**

Ersari, West Turkestan, last quarter 19th C, 10' 6" x 6' 10", three columns of six octagonal gulli-gulls in midnight blue and navy blue, apricot and blue-green on red field, multicolored cruciform motif border, moth damage, small holes, several small patches and rewoven areas........................... **1,100.00**

Feraghan Sarouk

3' 3" x 4' 9", c1890, central black medallion with orange highlights, overall orange and black floral design ... **1,150.00**

3' 4" x 5', c1890, central star-shaped medallion in dark blue and light blue on beige and red ground, dark blue border **980.00**

Hamadan, Northwest Persia, second quarter 20th C

4' 1" x 5' 8", multiple ivory, blue, and tan borders, dark blue spandrels, ivory ground, wear............................ **325.00**

7' x 4' 8", indented diamond medallion, matching spandrels, overall Herati design in midnight and navy blue, ivory, rose, and dark green on red field, midnight blue turtle border........ **650.00**

Heriz, Northwest Persia

8' 10" x 11' 9", c1935, light blue central medallion, overall floral ground in shades of red and blue, moth eaten in one corner **900.00**

9' 1" x 11' 1", dark blue border, ivory spandrels, burgundy ground **750.00**

9' 4" x 3' 5", early 20th C, three hooked diamond medallions in midnight blue, red, camel, dark brown, ivory, and blue-green on light tan field, ivory floral meander border, slight end fraying, very small edge and corner gouges .. **1,100.00**

9' 4" x 12' 6", Azerbejan design, dark blue border, light rust ground, camel and green accents...................... **6,620.00**

9' 8" x 12' 9", wide dark blue border, green and ivory spandrels, tomato red ground **7,475.00**

11' 6" x 8', early 20th C, large gabled sq medallion surrounded by floral motifs in midnight and royal blue, rose, tan, and dark blue-green on terracotta red field, stepped ivory spandrels, midnight blue "turtle" border, small spots of wear, end fraying **1,300.00**

12' x 9' 2", late 19th/early 20th C, large gabled sq medallion with palmette pendants in midnight and navy blue, rose, camel, and blue-green on terracotta red field, large ivory spandrels, midnight blue rosette and serrated leaf border, areas of wear, end fraying...................... **2,585.00**

Jaf Kurd, Northwest Persia, early 20th C, bagface, 2' 7" x 2' 7", diamond lattice of hooked diamonds in midnight and navy blue, red, gold, brown, rust, aubergine, and blue-green, aubergine border, slight brown corrosion **530.00**

Karabagh, South Caucasus, last quarter 19th C

2' 1" x 4' 5", prayer, dated, ivory, orange, and pale blue borders, black abrash ground, minor edge wear **250.00**

3' 5" x 7', bittersweet border, ivory ground, edge wear, small repairs **2,175.00**

3' 10" x 7', ivory border, blue abrash ground, wear .. **500.00**

Karaja, 8' 2" x 10' 7", c1920, central medallion, red, dark blue, and light blue, floral borders, overall wear................ **1,495.00**

Kashan, 7' 8" x 12' 8", signature cartouche, midnight blue border, blue and ivory spandrels, deep burgundy ground......... **1,495.00**

Konaghend, Northeast Caucasus, late 19th/early 20th C, 6' x 4' 3", characteristic arabesque lattice in ivory, red, rose, royal blue, gold, and blue-green on black field, ivory border, some black corrosion **1,295.00**

Kuba, Northeast Caucasus, late 19th/early 20th C, 4' 10" x 3' 6", three diamond medallions, each radiating four serrated motifs and four small diamonds in red, red-brown, navy blue, ivory, orange, and blue-green, abrashed midnight blue field, navy blue border, areas of minor wear, slight dye runs, black corrosion, some glue to back **1,000.00**

Kurd, Northwest Persia, early 20th C, 9' 5" x 3' 9", column of five turkoman-style octagonal turret guls in red, sky blue, gold, aubergine-brown, olive, and blue-green, midnight blue field, dark red border, end fraying **900.00**

Lenkoran, Southeast Caucasus, last quarter 19th C, 10' x 4' 4", three large calyx medallions separated by two large rect medallions in red, navy blue, aubergine, ivory, apricot, light camel, and blue-green on dark brown field, ivory border, brown corrosion, even wear to center, creases **715.00**

Lesghi, Northeast Caucasus, last quarter 19th C, 4' 10" x 3' 9", column of four Lesghi stars in red, sky blue, ivory, tan-gold, and blue-green on navy blue field, two ivory borders, even wear, slight end fraying **1,300.00**

Luri, Southwest Persia, early 20th C, 7' x 4' 7", large gabled and serrated sq medallions flanked by six large rosettes in red, navy blue, apricot, gold, and dark blue-green on midnight blue field, ivory border, even center wear **765.00**

Malayer, Northwest Persia, second quarter 20th C, 4' 10" x 3' 6", overall design of flowerheads and blossoming vines in red, ice blue, camel, and olive on abrashed royal blue field, ivory border, outer guard stripes partially missing from both ends..................... **1,000.00**

Persian, $400.

Photo courtesy of Dotta Auction Co., Inc.

Qashqai, Southwest Persia, late 19th/early 20th C, 6' 9" x 4', large hooked hexagonal medallion inset with blossoming angular vines in red, navy blue, ivory, gold, brown, and blue-green, midnight blue field, brown border, slight wear to center, minor moth damage, small repair **1,100.00**

Sarouk, West Persia, second quarter 20th C

5' x 3' 4", overall floral sprays in midnight, navy, and ice blue, red, gold, and light blue green on rose field, narrow midnight blue floral border **500.00**

9' 1" x 12' 1", floral and checkered border with floral spandrels, pink, blues, and ivory on salmon ground, good sheen....................... **2,530.00**

Seraband, Northwest Persia, early 20th C, 19' 6" x 7' 7", staggered rows of small boteh in midnight blue, apricot, ivory, and blue-green on abrashed terra-cotta red field, three ivory and red floral meander borders, even wear to center, slight end fraying **3,000.00**

Shiraz, East Caucasus, late 19th C, 3' x 5', Caucasian type design, multiple borders, diagonal stripes in dark blue, red, ivory and gold......... **460.00**

Shirvan, East Caucasus, late 19th C

3' 10" x 5' 6", geometric and star designs in blue, burgundy, red, green, gold, and ivory, wear and small splits **920.00**

5' 10" x 3' 6", c1890, three medallions, shades of blue and red, minor border loss at ends........................... **950.00**

9' 6" x 5', three columns with stepped diamond and serrated diamond medallions in red, ivory, navy blue, black, gold, and abrashed blue-green on midnight blue field, narrow ivory border, slight moth damage **2,550.00**

Soumak, Northeast Caucasus, late 19th C, 9' 4" x 8' 6", four elongated diamond medallions flanked by half medallions in midnight blue, black, rose, red, and tan on maroon-brown field, black border, areas of slight wear **2,475.00**

South Caucasian, second quarter 20th C, 13' x 3' 8", column of eight radiating hexagonal medallions in navy blue, red, rust, gold, dark brown, and light blue-green on midnight blue field, narrow ivory rosette border, slight dye run in one corner........................... **1,175.00**

Tabriz, silk, 5' 11" x 4' 5", c1890, tree of life, deer, and floral borders, shades of brown, overall war, dry areas, missing one end border **1,265.00**

Sarouk, rust red ground, beige and blue floral designs, c1950, 8'5" x 2'10", **$500**.

Photo courtesy of Alderfer Auction Co.

Yezd, cranberry red floral sprays on cobalt blue ground, cranberry floral border, c1900, 4'7" x 7'2", **$850**.

Photo courtesy of Alderfer Auction Co.

Tekke Torba, West Turkestan, late 19th/early 20th C

4' 2" x 1' 4", Kejebe design in midnight blue, red, ivory, and dark brown on cochineal field, multiple borders of similar coloration, outer border partially missing from one end **450.00**

7' 5" x 11' 9", multiple borders, overall design, ivory, blue, orange, and red, brown/brown ground, minor pile wear **1,150.00**

Ushak, West Anatolia, late 19th C, 11' 10" x 8' 2", large crenellated hexagonal medallion and matching spandrels in tan-gold, ivory, and blue-green on red field, red rosette and flowering vine border, areas of wear, edge and end gouges, several patches and rewoven areas **950.00**

Yomud Chuval, West Turkestan, last quarter 19th C, 3' 4" x 2' 3", nine Chuval guls in midnight blue, red, ivory, and blue-green on dark aubergine field, ivory border, plain aubergine elem, small spots of slight wear, re-overcast **825.00**

ORIENTALIA

History: Orientalia is a term applied to objects made in the Orient, an area which encompasses the Far East, Asia, China, and Japan. The diversity of cultures produced a variety of objects and styles.

Additional Listings: Canton, Celadon, Cloisonné, Fitzhugh, Nanking, Netsukes, Rose

Medallion, Japanese Prints, and other related categories.

Bottle, porcelain base with diminished neck, underglaze blue decoration, metal fittings, band around foot rim, chain for hanging, Chinese or Japanese, 17th C, 7-1/4" h, neck ground down, **$175**.

Bowl, metal, archaic style, standing on three winged bat-like figures and two others sitting on flared rim, well with engraved inscription, China, 19th C, 10-5/8" d, 4-1/2" h to bowl rim, 5-3/4" h to tips of wings, **$850**.

Album, fan paintings, 11 works by various artists including, Ch'en Fang Ting, Hsu Lin Lu (b1916), Shao Ping Chang, Wu Hsi Tsai (1799-1870), Kuo Shang Hsien (1796-1820), Fei Shih Po, Wu Hua Yuan (1893-1972), Wang I Ting, Yang I, Wang I Ting, Hou Pi I (2)............ **600.00**

Altar cabinet, 35-1/2" w, 22" d, 34" h, Huang Hua Li wood, moon-shaped brasses, side flanges carved with chih lung dragons, Lung chih fungus, and clouds, China, 18th C, cracks to top, old repair to back feet, loss ... **2,235.00**

Architectural element

Capitals, 22" l, carved wood, foo dogs, gold lacquered surface, China, 19th C, price for pr **775.00**

Finial, 4-3/4" h, bronze, figural dragon, patina with azurite areas, Khmer, 13th C .. **850.00**

Basin, 7" d, bronze, low relief designs of stylized birds and trees, 18-character grass script poem on the base, Japan, 18th C or possibly earlier **300.00**

Bell, 19" h, bronze, lid surmounted by two kneeling figures, iron mount with two apsara figures, Burma, 19th C **400.00**

Box, cov, 5" d, lacquer, foliate form, maki-e of a woman with a fan, Raiden inlay, Japan, 19th C **2,115.00**

Bowl

6-1/2" d, nephrite, white and pale green, incised and gilt character inscriptions with four character reign mark on base, Qing Dynasty, 20th C, price for pr **920.00**

7-1/2" d, porcelain, dark blue ext. with gilt dragons, clouds, and pearls, white int., China, Ch'ien Lung six-character seal mark, 1736-95 ..... **600.00**

Brush pot, 6" h, bamboo, carved in high relief with sages in forest, rosewood base, China, 18th C **1,300.00**

Buddha

13" h, hardwood figure, seated on lotus throne, numerous coatings of lacquer, China, 18th C.............. **425.00**

16" l, 6" h, Bodhisttva, carved stone, reclining figure, left hand supporting head, right hand resting on bent knee, peaceful expression, Chinese, possibly Tang Dynasty **950.00**

17" h, Buddha Amida, lacquered wood, standing with his hands in "abeyance of fear" mudra, gold lacquered robes, eyes inlaid with crystal, Japan, 18th C **1,350.00**

Buddhist bell, 14" d, Japan, hammered brass with a lacquered design of a dragon and thunder meanders, late 19th/early 20th C............. **450.00**

Bust

7" h, bronze, Quan Yin, Chinese, Sung or earlier period, losses **1,200.00**

13-1/2" h, sandstone, head of divinity with jeweled crown, Eastern Thailand, Khmer period, 11th C.......... **8,820.00**

Cabinet

47-1/2" l, 17" d, 48" h, two part, persimmon wood veneer, two long drawers over two smaller drawers each flanked by sq compartment, ornate iron mounts, Japan, early 20th C **1,530.00**

56-1/2" l, 20" d, 35" h, Hung Mu wood, two drawers over single gate, moon-shaped brasses, China, 18th/19th C **1,560.00**

Cabinet on stand, 23-1/2" w, black lacquer, cabinet with pair of doors, fitted int. of doors and pigeonholes, central painted oval portrait of a beauty, 27" h square base, cabriole legs, decorated allover with gilt scrollwork and foliage, Chinese Export, c1840............... **2,500.00**

Candlesticks, pr, bronze, 10" h, deer form, each supporting candle holder on back, Chinese, 18th C **600.00**

Censer, 10" l, bronze, modeled as caparisoned shishi playing with ball, parcel-gilt accents, Japan, 18th/19th C **1,410.00**

Chair, side, pr, Huang Hua Li wood with cane seats, China, 18th C or earlier **18,800.00**

Charger, 18" d, hawk design, sgd by member of Li family in red seal characters, China, 19th C **1,175.00**

Censer, bronze, lobed sides, six panels with raised detail, foo dog form handles, tripod feet, traces of gilding, later carved and fitted wood lid and stand, China, 18th C, 7" h, **$1,100.**

Cup, Chinese, porcelain, engraved dragons under egg yolk yellow color, six-character underglaze blue Kuang Hsu mark, 1874-1908, possibly of the period **200.00**

Deity, 8-1/2" h, gilt bronze, sitting position, robes with chased dec, China, 17th C, wear to gilding **990.00**

Dish, 5-1/4" d, Tou Tsai, scalloped edge, design of dragons and flowers in green on yellow ground, six-character Ch'ien Lung seal mark (1735-96) **1,880.00**

Left: pair of bronze candlesticks, deer form, each supporting candleholder on back, Chinese, 18th C, 10" h, **$600**; right: gilt bronze Deity, sitting position, chased decoration on robes, China, 19th C, 8-1/2" h, wear to gilding, **$990.**

Ceremonial robe, pale peach, navy blue, ivory, etc., silk, fully lined with natural linen, elaborately embroidered with silk and gold metallic threads in butterfly motif, sea creatures, flowers, finely embroidered birds, riveted brass and small mirrors, central dragon with green glass eyes, ermine trimming, Chinese, late 1800s, some damage and loose threads, **$395**.

Embroidery, on silk

17" x 13", crane by flowering tree, Japanese, Meiji period, 1867-1912.................. **320.00**

28" x 20", courtesan in elaborate costume holding pole with suspended basket of flowers, Chinese, 19th C **345.00**

Fan, folding, China, 19th C
Ivory, shaped stays with numerous figures in garden scenes, fan painted with harbor scene, other vignettes of idyllic village scenes, black lacquer box with gilt butterflies and flowers **490.00**
Wooden stays with black lacquer and gold dec, fan of paper dec with figures in silk and ivory, reverse magenta with three reserves of country scenes, gold and black lacquer case............... **250.00**

Fan, folding, Japan, 19th C
All ivory stays dec with shibayama inlay of gold lacquer and semi-precious inlay of birds and flowers, 11-1/2" l, orig box..... **4,025.00**
Carved ivory stays with shibayama inlay, one side dec with landscape, other with children watching fireworks **775.00**

Embroidery on yellow silk, eagle perched on tree above flowering plants, inscription upper right corner, hanging rod along right edge, China, early 20th C, 35-1/2" l, 19" w, small stains and holes, **$120**.

Figure, Kilin, bronze, lying in curved position, some gold splashes, repaired dorsal fin, Chinese, 19th C, 10" l, 5" h, **$925**.

Figure

2-1/2" h, 2-7/8" d, carved rose quartz, sitting puppy, head turned slightly to the left, possibly China, 20th C . **100.00**

Figure, monkey and horse, bronze, sleeping horse lying on belly, monkey with human face asleep on horse's back, long right arm clutching horse's tail, dark patina, Chinese or Japanese, 18th or 19th C, 12-1/2" l, 6" h, **$650**.

5-5/8" h, carved quartz with mauve and white striations, green veining, longevity god or immortal, holding staff in left hand, ruyi scepter in right, fitted wood stand, China, 19th or 20th C **220.00**
15" l, elephant, bronze, sgd on foot, Japan, Meiji period (1868-1911)............... **500.00**
17-3/4" h, carved and painted ivory and horn, maiden holding fan in left hand, basket of flowers in right hand, carved and pierced horn rock beside her with lantern sitting on top, head carved separately and pinned to shoulder, China, 19th C, wear to paint surface.. **990.00**
40" h, Goddess, carved stone, gray schist image of Kuan Yin, China, 20th C.............. **285.00**

Fish bowl, porcelain, blue and white, design of phoenix in garden, scrolling at mouth, Ming period, probably Chia Ching period, 1522-1566, hairline **1,175.00**

Flower vessel, 9-1/2" l, 3-1/2" h, bronze, tightly curled lotus leaf resembling small boat, attached lotus flowers, seed pod, and crabs crawling to top, carved wooden stand, sgd on base with rect reserve, Japan, 19th C **2,225.00**

Foo Dog, 11" l, 10-1/2" h, carved wood, surface lacquered in red and gold, China, 19th C . **600.00**

Gong, 18" d, brass, dragons and tokugawa mons designs, Japan, early 20th C **325.00**

Guardian figure, 9" h, standing figure of Nio, bronze, Japan, Meiji period (1868-1911) **275.00**

Hanging scroll, ink and color on silk

37-1/2" h, 19-1/4" h, figure in boat amidst mountainous landscape, China **360.00**
44-1/2" l, 20" w, doves and blossoming rose bush, sgd, Japan, mounted on silk. **360.00**
49" l, 25-3/4" w, scholar in boat, river landscape, China **540.00**

Incense box, 2" x 2", Komei-style, iron inlaid with gold and silver, Japan, Meiji period (1868-1911)................................ **600.00**

Incense burner, 15" h, bronze, decorative elements of elephants in handles, tripod base and finial, floral elements, inlaid glass and semi-precious stones, China, 18th C .. **1,530.00**

Geisha, porcelain, sitting position, enveloped by kimono, decorated with maple leaves, holding fan, Japanese, 19th C, 6-1/4" h, scattered small firing cracks, slight loss to enamel, **$295.**

Inro, netsuke, ojime
2-1/4" h, 2-1/8" w, lacquer, three compartment, dragon amidst clouds, unsigned, 1-1/4" d carved wood manju netsuke of dragon with inlaid eyes, agate ojime bead, Japan, 19th C, some wear and edge losses, crack on neck of netsuke **900.00**
3-1/4" h, gold lacquer, four compartment, each side dec with hawk perched on railing, sgd "Igawa" lower right, 1-5/8" h carved ivory netsuke in form of shells, one with crab emerging from top, metal ojime with foo dog and peony, stylized signature on side, Japan, Meiji period.. **3,750.00**
Inro, Saya type, 3-1/2" h, lacquer, four compartment, dec with Kwannon, moon behind her head, reverse dec with trees and waterfall, removable sheath having small cartouches with dragons, base sgd "Koma Koryu" with kakihan, Japan, 19th C, slight losses............. **1,265.00**
Jar, cov
11" h, blue and white, design of cranes, deer, and pine trees, carved hardwood cover, K'ang Hsi period (1662-1722) **1,880.00**
25" h, baluster, blue and white dec of village by water, Foo dog finial, China, 19th C **2,350.00**
Kogo, 3-1/8" d, silver, chased and repousse dec of two phoenix birds among flowers,

applied enamel highlights, silver lined interior sgd on underside, Japan, Meiji period, dent on inside of lid.................. **1,725.00**
Libation cup, 2" h, 4-1/2" w, porcelain, applied chi dragons in relief, two forming handle, underglaze enamels, Chinese, 18th C, losses **115.00**
Officials' chairs, pr
20" h seat, 43" h back, mortised construction, serpentine crests, carved back splats, paneled seats, sq legs, relief carved and scalloped aprons, old red wash, Chinese, restorations **650.00**
20-1/2" h seat, 47" h back, 24-1/2" w, 18-1/2" d, Huang Hua Li wood with cane seats, sq sections with inward tapering carving, China, Ming period, 16th/17th C, ex-James I lightower **00,500.00**
Okimono, 3" l, ivory study of group of rats and lantern, horn inlay, 19th C **635.00**
Painting, oil on canvas, Chinese Export School, 19th Century, portrait of American clipper ship, gilt frame
The Almeda of Bath, Maine, 20" x 27", lined, "Shanghai China 1878, May 8," scattered retouch, craquelure . **9,990.00**
The Charles B. Kenney of New York, handwritten inscription on the stretcher reads "Shanghai China 1878,

May 8," 20" x 27", lined, scattered retouch, craquelure **9,400.00**
Painting table, 70" l, 32-1/2" w, 34" h, Huang Hua Li Hunah back braces, China, Ming period, 16th/17th C **44,650.00**
Palace urn, 24" h, bronze, elaborately dec with scenes of birds, Foo dogs, foliage, large applied dragons, rich chocolate brown patina, Chinese, c1900, price for pr **750.00**
Panel, 23" x 16", rosewood, deep relief carving of two peacocks on flowering tree, Chinese, early 20th C **125.00**
Pitcher, 12" h, Sumidagawa, monkeys, Japan, early 20th C, loss to one hand **400.00**
Plaque, 8" x 6", bronze, relief dec of Kuan Yin surrounded by attending deities, extensive inscription on back, China, 19th C **135.00**

Plaques, hard stone, engraved writing, well-figured detail, Chinese, 19th C, 5" x 3-3/8", 6-3/8" x 4-5/8", 8-1/2" x 4-1/8", price for set of three, **$525.**

Furniture: top: low cabinet, hardwood, five drawers, three small drawers over two long drawers, carved with prunus on front and sides, back is plain, four feet, China, c1900, 23-1/4" l, 13-3/4" d, 8-1/2" h, natural shrinkage, minor losses, **$250**; center: lacquered table, top painted with landscape, sides with flowers and tendrils, brown lacquered ground, China, c1900, 61-5/8" l, 17-1/4" d, 32" l, fitted with later electric light underneath, small chips and light cracks, **$1,100**; bottom: lacquered low table, openwork gallery with turned spindles, China, 19th C, 55" l, 13-1/2" d, 13-5/8" h, one piece of gallery missing, crack, separation on one side, **$175.**

O

Orientalia

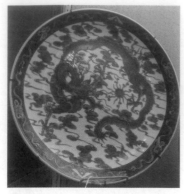

Plate, Chinese-style decoration, green enameled coiled dragon chasing flaming pearl, rose enamel border, Buddhist precious things, back signed in overglaze red "Tashiro," impressed square mark, Japan, c1900, 13-3/4" d, **$550**.

Plate, underglaze blue decoration, roundel painted with two phoenix in cavetto, border with six floral panels and geometric designs, Chinese, 18th or 19th C, 9-3/4" d, tight hairline, **$375**.

Rank badges, pr, K'o ssu work, white egret rank, China, 19th C, mounted as a tray **380.00**
Robe
Dragon, China, late 19th/early 20th C, loose threads . **360.00**
Informal, woman's, black ground, floral embroidery, China, late 19th/early 20th C **360.00**
Sagemo, basket cup holder, celadon porcelain netsuke of karako, 19th C................. **420.00**
Scepter, 13" l, ju-i, carved boxwood, lotus pod with movable seeds and single leaf, sgd, Japan, 19th C **420.00**
Screen
67" h, 37" w, "tagasode-byobu," two-fold, brocade with mounted ink, color, and

gold leaf on paper panel showing kimono over rack and accessories, Japan, Meiji period (1868-1912) **10,755.00**
94" x 18", six panels, finely detailed Buddhist and Taoist figures, checkered silk border, black lacquered frame, Japanese, c1750, accompanied by "Certificate of Antiquity" dated 1971 addressed to US Customs by David Kidd and Y. Morimoto of "Three Dynasties," Ashiya City, Japan, minor losses **1,450.00**
Sculpture, bronze
17" l, crayfish, fully articulated, Japan, Meiji period (1868-1911), loose............ **3,200.00**
24" l, scene of bull and farmer, carved fitted wood base, sgd, Japan, Meiji period (1868-1911) **1,300.00**
Seal case, four-compartment form with lacquer dec of warrior and courtier, crystal ojime, and netsuke sennin on horse, Japan, 19th C **775.00**
Shanxi cupboard, 57" w, 25-1/4" d, 69-1/4" h, gold and black Chinoiserie dec over dark red ground, mortised construction, paneled ends, two doors with brass hardware, removable int. shelf, wooden rod brackets, pieced restoration to moldings, touch-up **650.00**
Shrine
7" h, black lacquer case, gilt standing image of Amida Buddha, Japan, 19th C **395.00**
27" h, black lacquer, gold lacquered figure of Kshitagarba, inlaid eyes, Japan, 18th/19th C .. **3,200.00**
86" h, lacquered, structured as temple building, triple roof; ornately carved with shishi, dragons, and flowers, surface lacquered in gold, red, brown, and black, engraved gilt copper metal mounts, Japan, Meiji period (1868-1911) **1,250.00**
Stand, hardwood
31-3/8" h, 16-5/8" x 12" top, rect, two wooden shelves, red marble insert on top, carved flower and tendrils around top frieze an openwork gallery, ball and claw feet, China, 19th, natural fissues in marble **175.00**

39-3/4" h, 15" x 16-1/5" top, marble insert, round carved openwork sides, China, 19th C, light separation of joints, natural shrinkage........ **520.00**
Statues, pr, 53" h, granite, two officials from spirit way, Korea, Yi period, 18th C or earlier **9,400.00**
Stool for two, 40" w, 16" d, 19" h, Huang Hua Li wood, humpback stretchers, China, Ming to early Ch'ing dynasty, staining and cracking to top and legs **9,400.00**
Stupa, 6-1/2" h, bronze, four makala supports, stupa surmounted by four figures of Buddha, Nepal, 19th C ... **550.00**
Tankard, 8" h, blue and white, scholar in garden scene, Continental silver mounts with Dutch export hallmarks, China, Transitional period, c1620 .... **3,985.00**
Table, pr, 47" l, 15-1/4" w, 33" h, lacquered, Tzu Tan wood ornately carved with archaic scrolling, inlaid oval pale celadon jade plaques, carved resonance stones and archaic dragons, China, 18th C, cracks to both tops of both, lacquer wear **23,500.00**
Teapot
7-1/2" h, silver, Hira Arare, globular, hailstone pattern, cov surmounted with pierced sphere finial, base marked, Japanese Export, 16.65 oz **660.00**
8-1/4" h, globular, Fen tsai palette, design of flowers on brocaded blue ground, ju-i and stylized acanthus leaf borders, gilt accents, four-character seal mark within red square, China, 18th/19th C **13,000.00**
Tonkotsu, 4" w, 3" h, wood, applied lacquered ivory and mother-of-pearl dec of sea life, sgd on rect tablet, reddish-brown ojime bead, possibly ceramic, well carved 3-1/4" h netsuke of Ryujin's attendant standing and supporting his left hand on octopus straddling his shoulders, tentacles entwined around each other and the attendant's arms and robes, forming natural himotoshi, attending holding jewel in his right hand, skirt encrusted with shells, inlaid eyes in octopus, Japan, 18th or 19th C **46,000.00**

Trunk, 37-1/2" w, 21" d, 17" h, Hung Mu wood, moon-shaped handles, panels of archaic carving on top and front, China, 19th C, staining **715.00**

Vase, Shibayama, gold lacquer, diamond form, four sides decorated with birds among flowering plants, mother-of-pearl, coral, and stained ivory, unsigned, Japanese, Meiji period, 6" h, several rim and base chips, **$1,950**.

Vase, finely painted in black and brown on biscuit ground, dragon among clouds, carp leaping waterfall, Xuande six-character mark on recessed base, China, 19th or 20th C, **$225**.

Vase
8-1/2" h, enameled silver, pear shaped with jump rings, enamel dec of phoenix in flowering trees, sgd "Peking, Pure Silver," maker's mark, China, dated 1916 in extensive inscription, minor loss to enamel, some dents, price for pr **500.00**
12" h, stoneware, matte green celadon glaze, Art Deco style, Japan, c1930 .... **450.00**
14" h, bronze, hexagonal body with designs of high relief dragons, Japan, late 19th C **600.00**
15" h, bronze, relief dec of waves with dragon in round holding glass pearl, sgd "great Japan sei don sai," Japan, Meiji period .. **1,650.00**
20-1/2" h, Tsun-shape, Wu Tsai ware, birds and flowers dec, China, Transitional period, c1640 .... **2,000.00**
42" h, bronze, flared rim, paneled shoulder takers to base with flower petals, detailed peacock sits on flowering tree branch, peahen below, dark patina, peacock's crest missing **3,500.00**
Votive plaque, 7" d, gilt copper and bronze, a central image of the Buddha surrounded by the wheel of law, Japan, late 19th/ early 20th C **250.00**
Watercolor, 16-1/2" x 12", Hong Kong Harbor, watercolor and gouache on paper, unsigned, Chinese School, 19th C, octagonal oblong reserve depicting junks and side-wheeler moored in harbor before several buildings on waterfront, flanked by pen and ink apple and eggplant-shaped reserves painted with decorative artifacts, molded giltwood frame, creases, foxing, moisture stains . **5,875.00**
Wine ewer, 6-1/4" h, Hirado ware, form of Hoi tea, bag of wealth, underglaze blue, yellow, pale green, tan, and black accents, 19th C, cover missing **750.00**

OWENS POTTERY

History: J. B. Owens began making pottery in 1885 near Roseville, Ohio.

In 1891, he built a plant in Zanesville and in 1897, began producing art pottery. After 1907, most of the firm's production centered on tiles.

Owens Pottery, employing many of the same artists and designs as its two cross-town rivals, Roseville and Weller, can appear very similar to that of its competitors, e.g., Utopian (brown glaze), Lotus (light glaze), and Aqua Verde (green glaze).

There were a few techniques used exclusively at Owens. These included Red Flame ware (slip decoration under a high red glaze) and Mission (over-glaze, slip decorations in mineral colors) depicting Spanish Missions. Other specialties included Opalesce (semi-gloss designs in lustered gold and orange) and Coralene (small beads affixed to the surface of the decorated vases).

Three-tile frieze, decorated in cuenca, rural landscape in matte polychrome, stamped "Owens," one tile missing in sequence, some pitting to glaze, mounted in new rustic frame, 14-1/2" x 30", **$3,775**.

Photos courtesy of David Rago Auctions, Inc.

Bud vase, 6-1/4" h, 2-1/2" w, standard glaze, yellow roses, marked "#004," initials for Larry Robinson **165.00**
Ewer, 10" h, brown high glaze, cherry design **200.00**
Jug, 8" w, 4-1/2" w, standard glaze, ear of corn dec, marked and sgd "Tot Steele" **230.00**
Lamp base, 11-1/4" h, 5" d, Utopian, classically-shaped, painted yellow daffodils, unmarked, drilled, some glaze bubbles to back, hairline around neck **350.00**
Mug, 7-1/2" h, standard glaze, cherries, marked "#830," sgd "Henry R. Robinson," hairlines to int. **110.00**
Tankard
7" h, brown high glaze, Indian design, incised signature, restored **325.00**

6-1/2" h, 5" d, leathery green glaze, brown trim, stamped "OWENS 1228/XX," lines at base, repaired rim chip **220.00**

Vase

4" h, Lotus, bee flying above green blades of grass, ivory to blue ground, imp mark, artist initials **400.00**

4" h, 4" w, yellow chick surrounded by thinly painted grass, four feet, artist sgd **300.00**

6-3/8" h, Utopian Ware, silver overlay, flared rim on tapered oviform, glossy glaze, cream and brown rose blossoms and leaves, shaded brown ground, silver overlay imp "Utopian J. B. Owens 923" and "Phee F.N. Silver Co.," crazing, scratches, nicks **290.00**

7" h, fluted, Ida Steel, floral **625.00**

8" h, Aqua Verdi, green matte, textured surface, incised geometrics, four handles around neck, unmarked **550.00**

8" h, 8-1/2" w, ftd pillow, dark to light brown with yellow ground, Indian portrait, cream and red vest, blue in hair, imp mark, repaired top ... **1,100.00**

10" h, orange and yellow tulips, green leaves, brown ground, imp mark **250.00**

10" h, 5" w, standard glaze, marked "Owens #010" **210.00**

10-3/4" h, 5-3/4" d, sgraffito, orange and blue irises, dark brown ground, Henri Deux, unmarked, pea-sized burst bubble on shoulder ... **650.00**

12-1/2" h, pink poppy, green stems and leaves, pink, ivory, and light blue ground, artist initialed, imp mark **600.00**

12-1/3" h, 5-3/4" d, baluster, painted white chrysanthemums, shaded gray ground, stamped OWENS 1122/Artist's cipher, firing line, several base chips **350.00**

PADEN CITY GLASS

History: Paden City Glass Manufacturing Co. was founded in 1916 in Paden City, West Virginia.

David Fisher, formerly of the New Martinsville Glass Manufacturing Co., operated the company until his death in 1933, at which time his son, Samuel, became president. A management decision in 1949 to expand Paden City's production by acquiring American Glass Company, an automated manufacturer of bottles, ashtrays, and novelties, strained the company's finances, forcing it to close permanently in 1951.

Contrary to popular belief and previously incorrect printed references, the Paden City Glass Manufacturing Company had absolutely no connection with the Paden City Pottery Company, other than its identical locale.

Although Paden City glass is often lumped with mass-produced, machine-made wares into the Depression Glass category, Paden City's wares were, until 1948, all handmade. Its products are better classified as "Elegant Glass" of the era, as it ranks in quality with the wares produced by contemporaries such as Fostoria, New Martinsville, and Morgantown.

Paden City kept a low profile, never advertising in consumer magazines of the day. It never marked its glass in any way because a large portion of its business consisted of sales to decorating companies, mounters, and fitters. The firm also supplied bars, restaurants, and soda fountains with glassware, as evidenced by the wide range of tumblers, ice cream dishes, and institutional products available in several Paden City patterns.

For more information, see *Warman's Glass*, 4th edition.

Paden City's decorating shop also etched, cut, hand painted, and applied silver overlay and gold encrustation. However, not every decoration found on Paden City shapes will necessarily have come from the factory. Cupid, Peacock and Rose, and several other etchings depicting birds are among the most sought-after decorations. Pieces with these etchings are commanding higher and higher prices even though they were apparently made in greater quantities than some of the etchings that are less known, but are just as beautiful.

Paden City is noted for its colors: opal (opaque white), ebony, mulberry (amethyst), Cheriglo (delicate pink), yellow, dark green (forest), crystal, amber, blue, and great quantities of ruby (red). The firm also produced transparent green in numerous shades, ranging from yellowish to a distinctive electric green that always alerts knowledgeable collectors to its Paden City origin.

Rising collector interest in Paden City glass has resulted in a sharp spike in prices on some patterns. Currently, pieces with Orchid or Cupid etch are bringing the highest prices. Several truly rare items in these etchings have recently topped the $1,000 mark. Advanced collectors seek out examples with unusual and/or undocumented etchings. Colored pieces, which sport an etching that is not usually found on that particular color, are especially sought after and bringing strong prices. In contrast, prices for common items with Peacock and Rose etch remain static, and the prices for dinnerware in ruby Penny Line and pink or green Party Line have inched up only slightly, due to its greater availability.

Adviser: Michael Krumme.

Bowl, nappy

#215 Glades, 7" x 1-3/4", ruby **40.00**

#221 Maya 7" crimped, ruby **50.00**

#412 Crow's Foot Square, 7", Orchid etch, crystal **55.00**

Bowl, two-handled serving type

#210 Regina, Black Forest etch, green **125.00**

#215 Glades, Trumpet Flower etch, crystal **115.00**
#220 Largo, ruby **65.00**
#411 Mrs. B., Gothic Garden etch, crystal **45.00**
#412 Crow's Foot Square, cobalt **95.00**
#412 Crow's Foot Square, green **35.00**
#412 Crow's Foot Square, Ardith etch, yellow **50.00**
#412 Crow's Foot Square, Delilah Bird etch, black **130.00**
#412 Crow's Foot Square, Orchid etch, yellow **150.00**
#412 Crow's Foot Square, Sasha Bird etch, yellow **165.00**
#412 Crow's Foot Square, Trumpet Flower etch, ruby **165.00**
#412 Crow's Foot Square, Trumpet Flower etch, yellow **225.00**
#881 Gadroon, Rose & Jasmine etch, crystal **50.00**

Cake salver, footed
#191 Party Line, high footed, cheriglo **65.00**
#191 Party Line, low, etched & gold encrusted border, crystal **30.00**
#210 Regina, Black Forest etch, ebony or green **75.00**
#215 Glades, ruby **45.00**
#215 Glades, Spring Orchard etch, crystal **65.00**
#220 Largo, high footed, crystal **50.00**
#220 Largo, low footed, ruby **140.00**
#300 Archaic, Cupid etch, cheriglo **125.00**
#330 Cavendish, gold encrusted border etch with rose, crystal **60.00**
#411 Mrs. B, Ardith etch, green **85.00**
#412 Crow's Foot Square, 8-1/4" w, 4-1/2" h, cobalt **125.00**
#411 Mrs. B, Gothic Garden etch, amber **40.00**
#411 Mrs. B, Gothic Garden etch, cheriglo **50.00**
#412 Crow's Foot Square, Ardith etch, ruby **190.00**
#412 Crow's Foot Square, Delilah Bird etch, yellow **85.00**

Candleholders, pr
#210 Regina, Black Forest etch, ebony **95.00**
#220 Largo, light blue. **130.00**

#220 Largo, Garden Magic etch, light blue **90.00**
#300 Archaic, Cupid etch, cheriglo **115.00**
#411 Mrs. B, keyhole style, Ardith etch, ebony **50.00**
#411 Mrs. B, keyhole style, Ardith etch, green **80.00**
#411 Mrs. B., keyhole style, Gothic Garden etch, yellow **68.50**
#411 Mrs. B, keyhole style, no etching, ebony **25.00**
#412 Crow's Foot Square, mushroom style, no etching, yellow **30.00**
#412 Crow's Foot Square, keyhole style, Satin Rose etch, crystal **45.00**
#412 Crow's Foot Square, keyhole style, mulberry **50.00**
#412 Crow's Foot Square, keyhole style, ruby **55.00**
#412 Crow's Foot Square, keyhole style, Orchid etch, crystal **40.00**
#881 Gadroon, Irwin etch, crystal **75.00**
#890 Crow's Foot Round triple, ruby **125.00**
#895 Lucy double, crystal **145.00**

Candy box, cov, flat
#215 Glades, ruby **50.00**
#215 Glades, Spring Orchard etch, crystal, filigree base and finial **60.00**
#300 Archaic, Cupid etch, cheriglo **145.00**
#411 Mrs. B, Ardith etch, yellow **70.00**
#411 Mrs. B, Ardith etch, black **125.00**
#411 Mrs. B, Delilah Bird etch, cheriglo **240.00**
#412 Crow's Foot Square, Satin Rose etch, crystal **35.00**
#412 Crow's Foot Square, Orchid etch, crystal **60.00**
#412 Crow's Foot Square, Orchid etch, yellow **155.00**
#412 Crow's Foot Square, Orchid etch, cheriglo .. **230.00**
#412 Crow's Foot Square, filigree holder, Orchid etch, ruby **275.00**
#412 Crow's Foot Square, filigree holder, Delilah Bird etch, ruby **390.00**
#412-1/2, cloverleaf shape, Orchid etch, crystal, filigree holder, ruby **425.00**
#555 heart shaped, Ardith etch, crystal **45.00**

Candy dish, covered, flat, #701 Triumph, Ardith etch, **$125**.
All Paden City photos courtesy of Ken Slater.

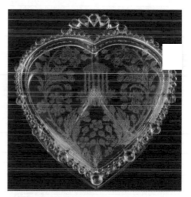
Candy dish, covered, flat, #555, heart shape, Utopia etch, **$95**.

Candy dish, cov, footed
#191 Party Line, green . **40.00**
#210/#503 Black Forest etch, ebony **225.00**
#444 Bridal Wreath etch, ruby **75.00**
#555 footed, light blue.. **35.00**
#555 footed, ruby **75.00**
#555 footed, wheel cut flowers, ruby **65.00**
#701/#503 base, cutting, green **30.00**

Cheese and cracker set
#210 Regina, Black Forest etch, green **100.00**
#210 Regina, Black Forest etch, amber **190.00**
#220 Largo, Garden Magic etch, crystal **30.00**
#221 Maya, dome lid style, light blue **75.00**
#411 Mrs. B, Ardith etch, cheriglo **125.00**
#412 Crow's Foot Square, Orchid etch, cheriglo .. **200.00**
#777 Comet, domed lid style, cutting, light blue **85.00**

Cigarette box, lid
#191 Party Line, footed jar, etched band of stylized roses, crystal **50.00**

#215 Glades, ashtray lid,
Spring Orchard etch, crystal
.... **125.00**

Cocktail shaker
#156 cobalt.................. **90.00**
#215 Glades, ruby, platinum
band dec **75.00**
#901 polished cutting, crystal
.... **40.00**
#901 Utopia etch, crystal
.... **130.00**

Cologne bottle
#191 Party Line, dauber
stopper, green **40.00**
#215 Glades, amber stopper
.... **20.00**
#215 Glades, black stopper
.... **30.00**
#502 dauber stopper, blue
.... **50.00**

Comport, footed, open
#210 Regina, 9-1/2" w, Black
Forest etch, green **100.00**
#211 Spire, Trumpet Flower
etch, crystal **50.00**
#215 Glades, 6-1/2" wide,
Forest Green................. **40.00**
#300 Archaic, turquoise blue
.... **45.00**
#300 Archaic, unusual flared
shape, Peacock & Rose etch,
green **115.00**
#411 Mrs. B, 4" h x 6" w,
Gothic Garden etch, cheriglo
.... **60.00**
#411 Mrs. B, 7" h x 7" w,
Gothic Garden etch, yellow
.... **35.00**
#412 Crow's Foot Square,
7" w, low footed, mulberry
.... **45.00**
#412 Crow's Foot Square,
7" w, low footed, Orchid etch,
yellow.......................... **75.00**
#412 Crow's Foot Square,
8" w, low footed, Ardith etch,
ruby............................ **175.00**
#412 Crow's Foot Square,
10" w, low footed, Orchid etch,
crystal **50.00**
#412 Crow's Foot Square,
5" w, cupped sides, two flared
sides, Delilah Bird etch, ruby
.... **300.00**
#412 Crow's Foot Square, 5" h
x 9" w, Orchid etch, crystal
.... **185.00**
#881 Gadroon, 6-1/2" h x 7" w,
Irwin etch, ruby **150.00**
#890 Crow's F Round, 6-1/2" h
x 7" w, ruby **40.00**
Nerva, 9-1/2" w, 6" high, Bridal
Wreath, crystal.............. **45.00**

Compote, footed, covered,
#211 Spire, 8-1/2" h, Loopie
etch, crystal **100.00**

Cordial decanter on tray, Ardith etch,
cheriglo, **$250.**

Creamer and sugar
#210 Regina, Black Forest,
ebony........................... **75.00**
#220 Largo, light blue .. **45.00**
#220 Largo, ruby **62.00**
#300 Archaic, cheriglo . **20.00**
#411 Mrs. B, amber or ebony
.... **20.00**
#411 Mrs. B, Ardith etch,
green **165.00**
#411 Mrs. B, Gothic Garden
etch, yellow.................. **90.00**
#412 Crow's Foot Square,
cobalt........................... **35.00**
#412 Crow's Foot Square,
mulberry **100.00**
#412 Crow's Foot Square,
opal.............................. **85.00**
#412 Crow's Foot Square,
Ardith etch, ruby **180.00**
#412 Crow's Foot Square,
Orchid etch, yellow..... **135.00**
#701 Triumph, Nora Bird etch,
crystal **80.00**
#881 Gadroon, Irwin etch,
crystal **40.00**
#881 Gadroon, Irwin etch,
ruby **150.00**
#991 Penny Line, cobalt
.... **40.00**
Nerva, Rose Cascade etch
.... **65.00**

Cup and saucer
#210 Regina, Black Forest
etch, cheriglo.............. **180.00**
#210 Regina, Black Forest
etch, ebony................. **100.00**
#210 Regina, Black Forest
etch, ebony, gold encrustation
.... **230.00**
#411 Mrs. B, Ardith etch,
yellow........................... **35.00**
#881 Gadroon, ruby **15.00**
#991 Penny Line, Black Forest
etch............................ **100.00**

Decanter
#191 Party Line, cordial size,
green **35.00**
#210 Regina, Black Forest
etch, green **450.00**
#994 Popeye & Olive, ruby,
orig ruby stopper........ **130.00**

Decanter set
#191 Party Line, five blown
whiskeys, cheriglo........ **75.00**
Oblong decanter, Ardith etch,
six shots, metal holder,
cheriglo...................... **275.00**

Egg cup
#210 Regina, Black Forest
etch, green **150.00**
#881 Gadroon, ruby **75.00**

Ice bucket, metal bail
#191 Party Line, Peacock &
Rose etch, amber **120.00**
#902, Peacock & Rose etch,
cheriglo **165.00**
#902, Eden Rose etch, green
.... **125.00**
#902, Cupid etch, cheriglo
.... **195.00**
#902, Lela Bird etch, green
.... **225.00**

Ice tub, tab handles
#191 Party Line, cheriglo
.... **30.00**
#300 Archaic, Cupid etch,
green **200.00**
#895 Lucy, Oriental Garden
etch, crystal **45.00**
#991 Penny Line, ruby **125.00**
#411 Mrs. B, Ardith etch,
yellow, liner and ladle ... **60.00**
#412 Crow's Foot Square,
Orchid etch, crystal **48.00**
#412 Crow's Foot Square,
Trumpet Flower etch, yellow
.... **125.00**
#881 Gadroon, Black Forest
etch, crystal, liner and ladle
.... **115.00**

Napkin holder, #210 Regina,
green **100.00**

Night set, pitcher, inverted
tumbler, #210 Regina, Black
Forest etch, green **450.00**

Pitcher, #191 Party Line 74 oz.
pitcher, green **75.00**

Plate, #220 Largo, forest green, 9" d, **$25.**

Plate
#210 Regina, 8", Black Forest
etch, cheriglo................ **40.00**

#220 Largo, 9", amber .. **10.00**
#220 Largo, 9", ruby **25.00**
#300 Archaic, 8-1/4", Nora Bird etch, green............ **35.00**
#411 8" plate, Ardith etch, yellow............................ **22.00**
#411 8" plate, Nora Bird etch, crystal **50.00**
#412 8" plate, Orchid etch, green **45.00**
#412 10" plate, Orchid etch, cobalt......................... **175.00**
#881 Gadroon, 8" plate, ruby **15.00**
#800 Crow's Foot Round, 9" mulberry **20.00**
#890 Crow's Foot Round, 10", Orchid etch, cheriglo ... **65.00**
Relish dish, #555 oblong, three parts, Gazebo etch, light blue **40.00**

Sugar pourer
#04 Bullet, screw-on metal base, green **145.00**
#191 Party Line, cheriglo **100.00**

Syrup pitcher
#185, amber **22.50**
#185, gold encrusted band etch, amber **40.00**
#185, cutting, green **45.00**
#185, w/underplate, cutting, cheriglo........................ **85.00**
#900 Emeraldglo, star cut, metal underplate........... **45.00**

Pitcher, #991 Penny Line, ruby, **$125.**

Tray, two handles
#220 Largo, ruby **25.00**
#411 Mrs. B Ardith etch green **100.00**
#412 Crow's Foot Square, hand painted tulips, opal **195.00**
#412 Crow's Foot Square, Orchid etch, crystal **40.00**
#412 Crow's Foot Square, Orchid etch, ruby........ **200.00**

#412 Crow's Foot Square, Peacock & Rose etch, yellow **100.00**
Tumblers and stemware
#191 Party Line, tumbler, Ardith etch, cheriglo **75.00**
#191 Party Line, banana split, flat, green............... **25.00**
#215 Glades, whiskey, Ardith etch, crystal **15.00**
#890 Crow's Foot Round, tumbler, amber **40.00**
#890 Crow's Foot Round, tumbler, cobalt.............. **70.00**
#991 Penny Line, whiskey, mulberry **5.00**
#991 Penny Line, tall stem goblet, ruby **20.00**
#994 Popeye & Olive, goblet, cheriglo........................ **20.00**
Vase
#61 8" hourglass shape, Zinnia & Butterfly etch, green **125.00**
#61 8" hourglass shape, Zinnia & Butterfly etch, cheriglo **175.00**
#61 8" hourglass shape, Zinnia & Butterfly etch, amber **325.00**
#61 8" hourglass shape, Zinnia & Butterfly etch, medium blue **400.00**
#180 12", Butterfly & Zinnia etch, green **200.00**
#180 12", Daisy etch, cheriglo or green **225.00**
#180 12", Daisy etch, gold encrusted Cosmos etch at top, cheriglo **225.00**
#180 12", Peacock & Rose etch, cheriglo **375.00**
#182 8" elliptical, ebony, silver overlay **65.00**
#182 8" elliptical, gold encrusted Utopia etch, ebony **250.00**
#182-1/2 5" elliptical, Ardith etch, crystal **80.00**
#182-1/2 5" elliptical, Frost etch, crystal **40.00**
#184, 8", bulbous, Gothic Garden etch, green ... **195.00**
#184, 8", bulbous, Rose with Jasmine etch, crystal.. **200.00**
#184, 10" bulbous, Eden Rose etch, red and gold encrusted **225.00**
#184, 10" bulbous, Gothic Garden etch, black..... **125.00**
#184, 10" bulbous, Orchid etch, ruby **365.00**
#191 Party Line, fan shape, cheriglo or green **35.00**
#191 Party Line, cuspidor shape, Ardith etch, black. **85.00**

#191 Party Line, 8" blown, hourglass shape, crimped top, cheriglo or green... **35.00**
#210 Regina 7", squatty, Harvesters etch, black **195.00**
#210 Regina 9", cylinder shape, Harvesters etch, ebony......................... **225.00**
#210 Regina, 10" bulbous bottom, Lela Bird etch, ebony **110.00**
#300 Archaic fan vase, Ardith etch, ebony................. **400.00**
#411 9" Gothic Garden etch, black...................... **125.00**
#411 9" Gothic Garden etch, yellow...................... **165.00**
#411 9" Gothic Garden etch, green...................... **435.00**
#411 9" silver deposit dec, crystal...................... **50.00**
#411 9" Utopia etch, cheriglo **250.00**
#412 Crow's Foot Square, 8" cupped rim, ruby...... **50.00**
#412 Crow's Foot Square, 8" flared rim, Irwin etch..... **55.00**
#503 dome footed fan vase, ruby **95.00**
#994 Popeye & Olive, 7", ruby **50.00**
Unknown #, 8", Frost etch **40.00**
Unknown #, paneled, 10-1/2", floral silver overlay, cobalt **90.00**
Unknown #, paneled, 10-1/2", Gothic Garden etch, green **300.00**
Unknown #, paneled, 10-1/2", silver overlay, opal **375.00**

PAIRPOINT

History: The Pairpoint Manufacturing Co. was organized in 1880 as a silver-plating firm in New Bedford, Massachusetts. The company merged with Mount Washington Glass Co. in 1894 and became the Pairpoint Corporation. The new company produced specialty glass items, often accented with metal frames.

Pairpoint Corp. was sold in 1938 and Robert Gunderson became manager. He operated it as the Gunderson Glass Works until his death in 1952. From 1952 until the plant closed in 1956, operations were maintained under the name Gunderson-Pairpoint. Robert Bryden reopened the glass manufacturing business in 1970, moving it back to the New Bedford area.

For more information, see *Warman's Glass*, 4th edition.

China

Chocolate pot, 10" h, cream ground, white floral dec, gold trim and scrolls, sgd "Pairpoint Limoges 2500 114" **675.00**

Gravy boat and underplate, fancy white china with scrolls, Dresden multicolored flowers, elaborate handle, Limoges, two pcs **175.00**

Plate, 7-3/8" d, hp harbor scene, artist sgd "L. Tripp," fuchsia tinted rim, gold highlights, back sgd "Pairpoint Limoges" **550.00**

Lamp, table

Candlestick type, 18" h, urn-shaped tops, electric sockets, clear cut columns with diamond designs, octagonal base with fine leaf detail, relief cast signatures on bases "Quadruple Plate," price for pr **550.00**

Orange Poppy, 21" h, 14" d, reverse painted mold blown puffy shade, silvered base, imp "Pairpoint 3085," shade damaged and repaired **1,500.00**

Reverse painted
16-1/2" d, shade dec with three floral and urn-form medallions separated by stylized circular medallions in pink, blue, and gold against black ground, three sockets, trapped bubble colorless glass standard, hexagonal green stone base..... **3,290.00**
21-3/4" h, 13-3/4" d dome shade of harbor scene with sailboats in mauve, peach, blue, and gold, sgd "C. Durand," two sockets, wooden vasiform standard with brass mounts, minor nicks at top aperture **1,645.00**

Metal

Lamp base
12" h, 8" d ring, patinated metal, quatrefoil wirework supporting shade ring, ribbed standard with applied foliate handles and feet, bronze patina on white metal, imp "Pairpoint Mfg Co.," "P" in diamond and "30031/2" on base, worn patina **400.00**
15" h, patinated metal, two-socket fixture, four-sided shaft and lobe base, bronze patina on white metal, imp "Pairpoint Mfg Co.," "P" in diamond, and "B3040" on base, patina wear **350.00**

Trophy, 7" d, 8-1/2" h, copper, two fancy handles, feather design, plaque inscribed "New Bedford Yacht Club Ocean Race won by Nutmeg for the fastest time, Aug. 5, 1909," base marked "Pairpoint Mfg Co.," "P" in diamond mark, numbered **400.00**

Sweetmeat, oval, pale green Mount Washington Glass insert, hp floral decoration, pierced Pairpoint stand with two rope twist handles, four curved feet, silver rim and lid, 7" l jar painted "3946" and "208," 9-1/2" l stand with stamped Pairpoint marks, style no. 3946, some wear to decoration, wear to finish on lid, **$200**.

Photo courtesy of Alderfer Auction Co.

Glass

Box, cov, 7-1/4" d, Russian pattern cut glass, silver mountings, sgd "Pairpoint" **410.00**

Candlesticks, pr, cobalt blue, controlled bubble sphere **450.00**

Compote, 7-1/4" d, 5-1/4" h, glass bowl painted with yellow and blue poppies against a rose-colored ground, gilt accents, attributed to Mount

Washington Glass Company, Pairpoint ribbed silver plated base with paw feet, sgd "Pairpoint" on base, dent **470.00**

Console set, three-pc set, 12" d bowl, matching 3" h candlesticks, Tavern glass, bouquet of red, white, and green flowers............. **575.00**

Dish, fish shape, teal blue, controlled bubbles dec, late **275.00**

Ferner, 8" w, elongated mold blown oval body, purple and crimson pansies dec, emb metal lid with two ring handles, numbered "5126-211" **400.00**

Perfume bottle, 6-3/4" h, amethyst, painted butterfly, teardrop stopper, "P" in diamond mark **375.00**

Pokal, cov, 14" h, Chrysopras, dark yellow-green, wheelcut grapes and leaves, finial wheelcut with eight-petaled flower **625.00**

Vase
5-1/2" h, 4-1/2" w, Tavern glass, bulbous, enameled floral dec of vase of flowers, base numbered **225.00**
14-1/2" h, flared colorless crystal trumpet form, bright-cut floral dec, gilt metal foliate molded weighted pedestal base, imp "Pairpoint C1509" **490.00**

PAPER EPHEMERA

History: Maurice Rickards, author of *Collecting Paper Ephemera*, suggests that ephemera are the "minor transient documents of everyday life," material destined for the wastebasket but never quite making it. This definition is more fitting than traditional dictionary definitions that emphasize time, e.g., "lasting a very short time." A driver's license, which is used for a year or longer, is as much a piece of ephemera as is a ticket to a sporting event or music concert. The transient nature of the object is the key.

Collecting ephemera has a long and distinguished history. Among the English pioneers were John Seldon (1584-1654), Samuel Pepys (1633-1703), and John Bagford (1650-1716). Large American collections can be found at historical societies and libraries across the country, and museums, e.g., Wadsworth Athenaeum, Hartford, CT, and the Museum of the City of New York.

When used by collectors, "ephemera" usually means paper objects, e.g., billheads and letterheads, bookplates, documents, labels, stocks and bonds, tickets, and valentines. However, more and more ephemera collectors are recognizing the transient nature of some three-dimensional material, e.g., advertising tins and pinback buttons. Today's specialized paper shows include dealers selling other types of ephemera in both two- and three-dimensional form.

Additional Listings: See Advertising, Catalogs, Comic Books, Photographs, and Sports Cards. Also see Calendars, Catalogs, Magazines, Newspapers, Postcards, and Sheet Music in *Warman's Americana & Collectibles*.

Calendar, 1941, K & L Lumber, shows bungalow styles, **$18**.

Calendars

1896, actors and actresses, one per month, sepia and white **125.00**

1897, pansy, each page with different litho of a pansy, scalloped edges, printed in Bavaria, designed in England, 6" x 4-1/4" **65.00**

1906, Christmas Belle, no calendar pad, 14" x 11" **200.00**

1908, fish, adv for Spicer & Beasley, Smithshire, IL, 15" x 9" **180.00**

1908, woman with red poppies, heavily emb, adv for J.I. Sawyel, General Merchandise, Smithshire, IL, full pad, 10" x 14" **270.00**

1912, Calumet Baking Powder, adv for H. J. Coffey Grocers, LaKemp, Oklahoma, print titled "Firelight," by G. Sether **220.00**

1918, Swifts Premium, for January, February, March, Haskell Coffin illus of "The Girl I Leave Behind Me," WWI soldier saying goodbye to pretty girl, 15" x 8-1/4" ... **90.00**

1922, lady in car, Hayes Litho Co., Buffalo, NY, 15" x 20-1/2" **100.00**

1926, Maxfield Parrish, Fountain of Pirene, orig 6" x 8" box, titled "Sunlit Road Calendar," Dodge Publishing Co., #5895 .... **125.00**

1930, Love is Blind, antique cars, service station, 22-1/2" x 14" **115.00**

1931, Midland Wood Products, Midland, Ontario, each page is different model home with floor plan on reverse, 9-3/4" x 5-1/2" **35.00**

1951, Puzzling Pups, Kinghon, 10" x 17" **60.00**

1952, Songbird Families, series 0, Dolly Carnes, watercolors by Roger Tory Peterson, published by Barton-Cotton Co. **12.75**

1960, Look for the Sign of Happy Motoring, Esso Gas, adv for R. Y. Foster, Johnson City, TN, 14-3/4" x 8-1/2" **48.00**

Checks

1863, State of Vermont Treasurer's Office, Rutland, state seal at left, brown on white, 2 cent US Internal Revenue bank check stamp, hand and punch canceled **40.00**

1865, National Bank of Commerce, New York, issued by Central Railroad Co. of NJ, red on white design, orange 2 cent US Internal Revenue Documentary and Proprietary stamp **20.00**

1869, First National Bank, New York, NY, bank building vignette, violet on white, orange 2 cent US Internal Revenue Documentary and Proprietary stamp **15.00**

1871, Pennsylvania Academy of the Fine Arts, Philadelphia, PA, Liberty, eagle, and shield, black on white **35.00**

1875, First National Bank of Chicago, issued by the office of Downer & Bemis Brewing Co., vignette of brewery, horse drawn carriages and people in street scene, black printing, olive security paper **45.00**

1875, Trenton Banking Co., Trenton, NJ, two vignettes, issued and canceled.... **12.00**

1882, National Park Bank, New York, NY, blue 2 cent US Internal Revenue Documentary and Proprietary stamp at left, "Iron Cliffs Company" stamped in red above signature line, payable to Third National Bank for $30,000 .... **20.00**

1898, Treasurer of Stanton Co., State of Nebraska, locomotive vignette at left, three horse heads at right, brown on sepia, hand stamp cancelled **30.00**

1903, Pittsburgh Brewing Co., Pittsburgh, PA, pale blue, red, gold, and black round logo, hand written, payee endorsement on reverse **6.00**

1911, First National Bank, Troutville, VA, vignette of bald eagle perched on rock, clutching arrows, olive branch, and US shield, black on orange, issued, canceled, printed by Kennedy Printing Co., Fredonia, Kansas.. **10.00**

1924, Baker Loan & Trust Co., gray vignette of bank entrance **7.50**

1957, Christmas Club, Anacostia National Bank, Washington, DC, Santa with open book, quill, ink bottle **7.50**

Cigar box labels

Alfonso Rigos & Co. **10.00**
Camel Brand Cigars, Arab man riding camel across desert **18.00**
Elektra, red, gold, and white, pretty girl...................... **15.00**
Royal Banner, allegorical lion with flag **15.00**

Deed, framed, Bechtelsville, Berks County, Pennsylvania, 1886, **$125**.

Document, indenture, between John Penn and Edmund Physick for tract of land in Philadelphia, dated Dec. 27, 1799, framed, 13" x 27-1/2", **$150**.

Photo courtesy of Alderfer Auction Co.

Documents

Appointment of administrator of estate, sgd by John Evans, Colonial Gov or PA, dated March 24, 1704, wax seal, some fold weakness, 9-1/2" x 15"................................ **500.00**
Appointment of Gideon Mumford Deputy Postmaster at East Greenwich, RI, dated April 19, 1796, foxing, fold weakness, 12-1/2" x 7-1/2" **75.00**
Bill of Exchange, written for Robert Robson, London, March 2, 1796, in Charleston, SC, two pgs, concerns exchange for 160 pounds sterling, 8-1/2" x 7" **50.00**
Indenture
13" x 27-1/2", vellum, John Penn and Edmund Physick, tract of land in Philadelphia, Pam, Dec. 27, 1799, framed **130.00**

15-1/2" x 29", vellum, between Samuel Jones and wife to John Stillwagon, tract of land in Philadelphia, PA, May 10, 1757, sgd on reverse by Charles Brockden, Justice for PA, folding, toning, foxing **60.00**
16" x 22", vellum, pre-printed royal seal, between Josiah Winter and wife to William Hambleton, tract of land in Solebury, PA, bordering Delaware River, Nov. 9, 1770, folding, slight toning, foxing **85.00**
21" x 24-1/2", vellum, Jonathon Jones and wife to Samuel Norcross, tract of land in Gloucester Twp, NJ, July 23, 1792, small hand drawn map on reverse, sgd by Thomas Rodman, Burlington County Judge, folding, toning, foxing, ink stains **50.00**
Legal deposition, involving litigation between Horace Day and Charles Goodyear, Aug. 29, 1851, concerning Indian rubber fabric, attached map of eastern US printed on Indian rubber fabric, reverse marked "Exhibit A4," damaged cover sheet, some soiling to sheets, 13" x 8" **350.00**
Ship paper, issued by port of Charleston, SC, for brig *Mary*, March 10, 1812, 8" x 11" **80.00**

Greeting cards

Easter Greetings, raised satin fabric with two cloth flowers, red bow, gold lettering, fringed edges, hand writing on back........................ **25.00**
Get Well, dachshund, 1950s, 4-1/4" x 4-1/4" **5.00**
Happy Birthday to a Sweet Daughter, Raggedy Ann, 4-1/2" x 6-1/2" **15.00**
Hawaii Greetings, with orig handkerchief, 1942, 6" x 5" **18.00**
Hearty Greeting, diecut, fold-out, emb red roses and dove, verse inside, scalloped edge, made in Germany, 3-1/4" x 4" **25.00**
Hearty Greeting, male hand and female hand clasping wreath of ivy and forget-me-nots, front panel unfurls to paper card

held in place with tasseled cord, "To Greet you and wish you a bright Christmas Day," with poem, published by Davidson Bros, London, printed in Saxony, c1900-10, 5-1/2" x 3-5/8" **35.00**
Pinocchio and Gepetto, mechanical, 1930s **35.00**
Romeo and Juliet, diecut, 3-3/4" x 7-1/2" **25.00**

Miscellaneous

Badge, Red Cross, Official Worker, 2-1/2" sq, 1934, sgd by Miss L Quinn............ **10.00**
Calling card, First Lady Florence Harding, orig envelope. **95.00**
Child's diecut book, *Dolly's Adventures*, McLoughlin Bros, heavy stock pages to color, pre-1920 .... **18.50**
Diary, Richard Tregaskis, *Guadal-Canal*, pictorial, 263 pgs, copyright 1945 ..... **12.00**
Ink blotter, 8-1/2" x 3-1/2", Lancaster Iron Works **8.00**
Ledger book, 9" x 5", Schuylkill Navigation Co., from Aug. 13, 1816 to Feb. 11, 1830, 250 pgs, binding loose, pages dry, spine damage **575.00**
Letterhead, Louisville & Nashville RR Co., 1913, typed message........................ **6.50**
Poster, Kennedy for President, Leadership for the US, red, white, blue, and black, 28" x 40", two folds **120.00**
Receipt, M. P. Norris Newspaper, Morristown, NJ, Nov 1, 1895 .... **12.00**
Tour brochure, Vermont Marble Co., Proctor, VT, 27 pgs, 4-1/2" x 6".............................. **24.00**
Tobacco label, Watson & McGill Tobacco Co., 14-1/8" x 7-1/4", 1872 copyright, multicolored stone litho, eagle, sailing ships, draped flags, topless woman **90.00**

Postcards

Advertising
Austro Fiat, artist sgd "Wilrab," left side with Austrian ships on Danube River, sailor and Fiat car, Fiat logo on back, 1920-30 . **48.00**
Munich Traffic Exhibition, Deutsche Verkehrsausstellung Muenchen, designed by Eugene O Sporer, man riding bicycle, first day cancellation, 1953 .... **60.00**

Postcards, assorted holidays, all with a bell theme, matted and framed, **$125**.

Art Deco

Lady smoking cigarette, hand colored, French **32.00**

Taifun – Wheel, amusement park, sent to Wien, Austria, 1929.............................. **28.00**

Blacks, Aint's I yo Honey?, 1907, hand written address **40.00**

Holiday

A Happy New Year 1908, heavily emb holly wreaths and snow, muted icy blue-gray, touch of red, icicles dangle at top, used........................ **10.00**

A Merry Christmas, 1906, letters outlined in sandy glitter, covered with starlets, black and white, used **10.00**

Humor

Always After New Business, rooster chasing chicken, Lustercomics #151, Tichnor Bros, Inc., Boston, MA, 3-1/2" x 4-1/2" **12.50**

"An Help Me to Forgive..." Mabel Lucie Attwell, #3696, copyright Valentine and Sons, Ltd., Dundee and London, 1900s, 3-1/2" x 4-1/2" **15.00**

"I Work and Worry, Scheme and Plan...," Lustercomics #132, Tichnor Bros, Inc., Boston, MA, 3-1/2" x 4-1/2" **12.50**

Let's Grow Old Together, Mabel Lucie Attwell, #3530, copyright Valentine and Sons, Ltd., Dundee and London, 1900s, 3-1/2" x 4-1/2" **15.00**

Old Maid, Lustercomics #143, Tichnor Bros., Inc., Boston, MA, 3-1/2" x 4-1/2" **12.50**

We're raising a big rumpus, Colourpicture Publication, Boston, MA, pre-1960..... **5.00**

Leather

Disguise our bondage As we will, Tis woman, woman Rules us still, Tom Moore, postmarked Dec. 22, 1906, 5-3/8" x 3-1/4" **45.00**

Look before you leap, There are two kinds of women, One that breaks you and one that makes you, hand written personnel message on front, postmarked April 1908, 5-3/8" x 3-1/4" **45.00**

Political, John F. Kennedy, NY Democratic State Committee, 1960, unused, with five Kennedy for President buttons **80.00**

Real photo

Geisshuebel, Sauerbrunn, Austria, sent to Union Hotel, Sinagore, 1902, black and white **110.00**

People digging for gold, black and white, c1910, printed in Germany, undivided back **36.00**

Roney's Boys Concert Co., Chicago, printed text "Henry B. Roney, Trainer and Manager, 2358 Indiana Ave, Photo by the Root Studio, Chicago, c1910, black and white **15.00**

Zeynard's Lilliputian Troupe, black and white **26.00**

Ship

Cunard *R.M.S. Lusitania-Mauretania,* New York harbor, Statue of Liberty at left, black and white illus, c1910 ... **30.00**

U.S.S. Battleship Virginia, #6507, c1907 .... **25.00**

Silk, WWI, butterfly design formed from flags of the Allies, c1917, 3-1/2" x 5-1/2" ... **95.00**

World War I, "And You? Sign in for War Bonds" WWI pilot, Germany, unused **32.00**

PAPERWEIGHTS

History: Although paperweights had their origin in ancient Egypt, it was in the mid-19th century that this art form reached its zenith. The finest paperweights were produced between 1834 and 1855 in France by the Clichy, Baccarat, and Saint Louis factories. Other weights made in England, Italy, and Bohemia during this period rarely match the quality of the French weights.

In the early 1850s, the New England Glass Co. in Cambridge, Massachusetts, and the Boston and Sandwich Glass Co. in Sandwich, Massachusetts, became the first American factories to make paperweights.

Popularity peaked during the classic period (1845-1855) and faded toward the end of the 19th century. Paperweight production was rediscovered nearly a century later in the mid-1900s. Baccarat, Saint Louis, Perthshire, and many studio craftsmen in the U.S. and Europe still make contemporary weights.

Lundberg Studio, butterfly, 1980, **$65**. *Photo courtesy of Joy Luke.*

Antique

Baccarat, France, 19th C, Double Garland, double trefoil garland of red and white canes centered by ring of blue canes, pink white and green cane, 3" d, 2" h, minor wear............................ **490.00**

Boston & Sandwich Glass Co., second half 19th C

Five large pears, four large leaves, four small vegetables, four small leaves, yellow, red, green, and rose, dew-like air traps, polished concave base, 1-1/2" h, 2-1/4" d **315.00**

Flower, 10 bright blue petals with central cane, deep green stem, three leaves, dew-like air traps, polished concave base, 2" h, 2-3/4" d **550.00**

Clichy, France, 19th C

Chequer, complex millefiori canes centered by pink and green Clichy rose, all divided by white latticinio twists, 2-3/4" d, 2" h **1,265.00**

Millefiori, complex millefiori canes set in colorless crystal, 1-3/4" d, 1-3/8" h **375.00**
Swirled, alternating purple and white pinwheels emanating from white, green, and pink pastry mold cane, minor bubbles, 2-5/8" d **2,200.00**

Degenhart, John, window, red crystal cube with yellow and orange upright center lily, one to window, four side windows, bubble in center of flower's stamens, 3-3/16" x 2-1/4" x 2-1/4" **1,225.00**

Gillinder, orange turtle with moving appendages in hollow center, pale orange ground, molded dome, 3-1/16" d **500.00**

Millville, umbrella pedestal, red, white, green, blue, and yellow int., bubble in sphere center, 3-1/8" d, 3-3/8" h **800.00**

New England Glass Co.
Apple form, deep rose to bright yellow, clear circular base, engraved "K. A. Osgood," second half 19th C, 2-1/2" h, 3" d **990.00**
Pink flower, striated pink five-petal flowers, millefiori cane center, pink bud on deep green leafy stem, white latticinio bed, 2-1/4" d, 1-3/4" h, minor wear... **690.00**

Pinchbeck, pastoral dancing scene, couple dancing before a group of onlookers, 3-3/16" d **650.00**

Vandermark, red flower, marked "FLC 1980," on lighted base, **$50**.
Photo courtesy of Joy Luke.

Sandwich Glass Co.
Dahlia, c1870, red petaled flower, millefiori cane center, bright green leafy stem, highlighted by trapped bubble dec, white latticino ground, 2-1/2" d, 1-3/4" h **650.00**

Poinsettia, double, red flower with double tier of petals, green and white Lutz rose, green stem and leaves, bubbles between petals, 3" d **1,200.00**

St. Louis, fruit basket, red and green ripening fruits, latticino base basket, central base cane, 3" d, 2-1/2" h .. **1,150.00**

Unknown maker, sulphide, silvery white figure of walking dog, polished base, late 19th or early 20th C, 1-3/8" h, 2-1/8" d, light scratching and pitting **110.00**

Val St. Lambert, patterned millefiori, four red, white, blue, pistachio, and turquoise complex canes circlets spaced around central pink, turquoise and cadmium green canes circlet, canes set on stripes of lace encircled by spiraling red and blue torsade, minor blocking crease, 3-1/2" d **950.00**

Modern, Rick Ayotte, two chickadees sitting on holly leaves, berries on ground of fallen snow, signed, dated 1990, 3-1/2" d, **$865**.
Photo courtesy of Alderfer Auction Co.

Modern
Ayotte, Rick, yellow finch, perched on branch, faceted, sgd and dated, limited edition, 1979 .... **750.00**

Baccarat, Gridel pelican cane surrounded by five concentric rings of yellow, pink, green, and white complex canes, pink canes contain 18 Gridel silhouette canes, lace ground, 1973 date cane, signature cane, sgd and dated, limited ed. of 350, 3-1/16" d .. **850.00**

Banford, Bob, cornflower, blue flower, yellow center, pink and white twisted torsade, "B" cane at stem, 3" d...... **550.00**

Bryden Pairpoint Glass Co., 2-1/4" h, 3-1/4" d, red rose, green leaves, cut diamond-point panel base, second half 20th C **210.00**

Kaziun, Charles, concentric millefiori, heart, turtle silhouette, shamrocks, six-pointed stars, and floret canes encircled by purple and white torsade, turquoise ground flecked with goldstone, K signature cane, 2-1/16" d **1,200.00**

Labino, free form, white, amber, and irid gold flower center, air bubbles, surrounded by green glass, sgd "Labino 1969," 2-1/2" d........... **210.00**

Orient and Flume, red butterfly with blue and white accents, brown and green vines, white millefiori blossoms over dark ground, 3-1/2" d, dated 1977, orig sticker and box... **235.00**

Parabelle, tightly packed multicolored millefiori canes, dark blue ground, attributed to Gary and Doris Scrutton, signature and date cane, orig paper label, 2-3/4" d.. **575.00**

Modern, Perthshire, central dark green seaweed, yellow coral and three fish, one facet on top, two rows of facets on sides, signature cane, dated 1998, 3-1/4" d, **$350**.

Perthshire, miniature bouquet, yellow flowers, pink buds, basket of deep blue canes, green and pink millefiori canes cut to form base, orig box and certificate, 2-1/2" d **160.00**

Rosenfeld, Ken, Monarch butterfly, leafy stem, red blossom with three buds, R signature cane, inscribed "KR 2001," 1-7/8" h, 2-5/8" h **350.00**

Salazar, David, compound floral, lavender six-petal poinsettia star blossom, three-leaf stem over green and red wreath, white ground, inscribed "David Salazar/ 111405/Lundberg Studios 1991," 3-1/4" d........... **225.00**

Modern, Saint Louis, spray of flowers lying on white base, yellow, pink, white, light blue, and cobalt blue flowers, green leaves, signed, dated 1988, 3-1/2" d, **$575**.

Photo courtesy of Alderfer Auction Co.

Modern, Paul Ysart, double-tiered pink and green flower, white millefiori center, green leaves, and curved stem, encircled by purple and white complex millefiori garland, translucent dark purple ground, "PY" signature cane in center of flower, 3" d, **$750**.

Photo courtesy of Alderfer Auction Co.

Stankard, Paul, morning glory, bee on hive in center of two blue morning glories, three orange berries, two yellow flowers, sandy ground, root figure and word canes "Moist" and "Fertile" beneath, inscribed "Paul J. Stankard V32 '97," 2-3/8" h, 3-1/4" d **2,875.00**

Tarsitano, Debbie, pansy, two central blue and yellow pansies flanked by three rose-pink blossoms, three yellow blossoms, green leafy stems, signature cane **475.00**

Trabucco, Victor, Buffalo, NY, magnum pansy, purple pansy blossom and bud, leaf stem, white lace cushion, inscribed "Trabucco 1998," 2-1/2" h, 3-1/2" d **635.00**

Whitefrairs, Star of David, five rows of tightly packed blue and white millefiori canes, 3" d **395.00**

Whittemore, Francis, two green and brown acorns on branch with three brown and yellow oak leaves, translucent cobalt blue ground, circular top facet five oval punties on sides, 20-3/8" d **300.00**

Ysart, Paul, green fish, yellow eye, yellow and white jasper ground encircled by pink, green, and white complex cane garland, PY signature cane **550.00**

PAPIER-MÂCHÉ

History: Papier-mâché is a mixture of wood pulp, glue, resin, and fine sand, which is subjected to great pressure and then dried. The finished product is tough, durable, and heat resistant. Various finishing treatments are used, such as enameling, japanning, lacquering, mother-of-pearl inlaying, and painting.

During the Victorian era, papier-mâché articles such as boxes, trays, and tables were in high fashion. Banks, candy containers, masks, toys, and other children's articles were also made of papier-mâché.

Cigar Store Indian, 8-3/4" l, 8-3/4" w, 42-1/2" h, painted, standing on wooden base, holding bundle of cigars in right hand, Indian pipe in decorated bag over left arm, Adams County, PA, late 19th C **7,150.00**

Doll, painted papier-mâché head, wooden arms and legs, stuffed cloth body, orig printed cotton dress, c1860 .... **5,600.00**

Fan, 15-1/2" l, domiluno, scalloped border, turned wooden handle, one side painted with variety of ferns on ochre ground, black japanning on other side, Victorian, late 19th C, price for pr **250.00**

Hat stand, woman's head, painted facial features, sgd "Danjard, Paris," 19th C, wearing later Amish straw hat **1,300.00**

Jewel box, 12" h, 10" w, 10" d, painted lit top, fitted int., two doors enclosing small drawers, Victorian, mid-19th, minor restorations **520.00**

Lap desk, 11-5/8" w, 9-1/4" d, 3-3/4" h, late 19th C, rect with bombe sides, sloped hinged lid with scalloped edge, painted and mother-of-pearl inlaid center with floral spray within gilt and inlay vines, opening to red velvet-lined

writing surface fronted by fitted compartments, and storage, Victorian, late 19th C **325.00**

Halloween lantern, black cat, **$65**.

Notebook, 11-1/2" x 9-1/2", black lacquered ground, dec with floral arrangement, mother-of-pearl vines, hand painted accents, int. with notebook with some sketches, blank pages **295.00**

Pip-squeak, 4-1/4" h, rooster, orig paint, yellow, orange, and black, recovered wooden bellows, faint squeak... **85.00**

Plate, 12" d, painted cat, marked "Patented August 8, 1880" **35.00**

Roly poly, 4-1/8" h, clown, orig white and blue polychrome paint, green ribbon around neck **65.00**

Snuffbox, 3-7/8" d, round, lid painted with interior genre scene of family with baby, interior lid painted with title "Die Tanzpuppen," painted mark "StabwassersFabrik in Braunschweig," German, late 19th/early 20th C **460.00**

Table, tilt-top, 24" h, hinged 20" d top painted with Continental city view, pedestal painted as stone tower, circular base with maritime scene, Victorian, stamped "J & B/Patent" for Jennens and Bethridge, Birmingham, England **7,475.00**

Tray, 32-1/4" w, 25" h, ovoid, ogee rim, painted black, hand painted center scene of children playing, thatched cottage, pigs, ducks, and hound, gold painted vine and butterfly surround, back imp "W. & P. Steele, 61 George Street, Edinburgh," Victorian, late 19th C **1,765.00**

Match safe with hinged lid, decorated with portrait of Kaiser Wilhelm II, metal push button latch, striker on bottom which shows considerable wear, commemorative piece from coronation, German, 1888, 2-1/2" x 1-7/16" x 9/16", **$250**.

Photo courtesy of Gamal Amer.

Tray and stand, English
18-1/4" l, 14-1/8" w, rect, black ground, large central scene of white haired gentleman on bobtail chestnut, five hunting dogs in open field, border gold painted with egg and dart design, 7-3/4" w, 4-1/4" d, 9" h mahogany stand...... **1,100.00**
30" l, 24" w tray, 11-1/4" w, oval, black ground, large central scene with two scarlet-coated huntsmen, one standing, other seated on bobtail chestnut with black foal on a hill, border with gilt transfer printed guilloche border, Mark Knowles & Son maker, English Registry mark for 1864, burl hardwood 6-1/4" d, 18-3/4" h stand......................... **1,250.00**
Traveling case, lady's, 11" w, 9" d, 9-1/2" h, black lacquer and polychrome, hinged front doors dec with portraits of Queen Victoria and Prince Albert, hinged top and sides with scenes from English landscapes, sewing compartment with some orig accoutrements, two doors open to jewelry drawers, fourth drawer with foldout writing desk and ink bottle, Victorian, mid-19th C **1,150.00**

PARIAN WARE

History: Parian ware is a creamy white, translucent porcelain that resembles marble. It originated in England in 1842 and was first called "statuary porcelain." Minton and Copeland have been credited with its development; Wedgwood also made it. In America, parian ware objects were manufactured by Christopher Fenton in Bennington, Vermont.

At first, parian ware was used only for figures and figural groups. By the 1850s, it became so popular that a vast range of items was manufactured.

Figure, Homer, partially draped adult male and youth figures mounted atop oval base, England, c1870, 13-1/2" h, **$1,000**.

Photos courtesy of Skinner, Inc.

Bust
8-3/4" h, maiden with ivy circlet, English, second half 19th C **250.00**
9-3/8" h, Apollo, English, second half 19th C **295.00**
10-1/2" h, Charles Dickens, printed quote from The Old Curiosity Shop on back, short socle, English, late 19th C **215.00**
10-1/2" h, Peabody, mounted on waisted circular socle, raised title, England, c1870 .... **250.00**
11-3/4" h, Classical Woman, with impressed "RC" mark at shoulder, English, second half 19th C **275.00**
12" h, Clytie, woman with Romanesque hair and draping bodice, with leaftip surround, England/France, late 19th/early 20th C, after the antique.................. **300.00**
20-3/4" h, Beethoven, titled, mounted on waisted circular socle, England, second half 19th C **1,880.00**
Creamer, 5" h, Tulip pattern, relief dec..................... **100.00**

Doll
18-1/2" h, Countess Dagmar, shoulder head, café au lait molded hair with side-swept wings to comb and curls in back, curls on forehead held by molded band, blue painted eyes, pierced ears, cloth body, brown leather arms, blue plaid wool dress, orig underwear, blue leather shoes, c1870 .... **250.00**
20" h, lady, bisque shoulder head, very pale coloring, center part blond hairstyle, 10 vertical curls, painted features, blue eyes, closed mouth, three sew holes, cloth body, kid arms, separate fingers, red cotton print jumper, white blouse with tucking and lace trim, leather slippers, Germany, c1870 .... **350.00**

Figure, Milton, standing figure, modeled leaning on pedestal topped with stack of books, England, c1870, 14" h, **$600**.

Figure, mother and first-born, by A. Carrier-Belleuse, incised artist and impressed mark, Minton, England, c1872, 12-1/4", **$1,775**.

Figure
13-3/4" h, Comedy modeled as woman adorned with flowers, seated on freeform rocky base, impressed year cipher, Minton, England, second half 19th C .. **1,200.00**

14-1/2" h, Una and Lion, unmarked, England, second half 19th C **1,115.00**
18-1/4" h, Lady with Lyre, modeled as draped woman, seated on rocky base, England, c1870, toe, finger, and lyre repair **765.00**
18-3/4" h, Vision of the Red Crosse Knight, John Rose & Co. later Coalport China, modeled by Josh Pitts, England, c1851 .... **2,235.00**
25 3/4" h, The Bather, scantily clad female figure modeled standing by tree stump, England, c1870, toe repair, footrim chip.............. **1,300.00**
Plaque, 6" d, relief, angels, brass frames, orig German labels, Boston retailers label, pr **275.00**
Sculpture, nude riding back of lion, early registry marks, c1860........................... **895.00**
Urn, cov, 20" h, classical shape, allegorical scene in low relief, three Graces, temples, revelers, and centaur, fish scale pattern on pedestal base, double scrolled handles, fruit finial, base marked with crown with ribbon and "FB" **250.00**
Vase, 10" h, applied white monkey type figures, grape clusters at shoulders, blue ground, c1850, pr....... **265.00**

PATE-DE-VERRE

History: The term "pate-de-verre" can be translated simply as "glass paste." It is manufactured by grinding lead glass into a powder or crystal form, making it into a paste by adding a two percent or three percent solution of sodium silicate, molding, firing, and carving. The Egyptians discovered the process as early as 1500 B.C.

In the late 19th century, the process was rediscovered by a group of French glassmakers. Almaric Walter, Henri Cros, Georges Despret, and the Daum brothers were leading manufacturers.

Contemporary sculptors are creating a second renaissance, led by the technical research of Jacques Daum.

For more information, see *Warman's Glass*, 4th edition.

Bookends, pr, 6-1/2" h, Buddha, yellow amber pressed molded design, seated in lotus position, inscribed "A Walter Nancy" **2,450.00**
Center bowl, 10-3/8" d, 3-3/4" h, blue, purple, and green press molded design, seven exotic long-legged birds, central multi-pearl blossom, repeating design on ext., raised pedestal foot, sgd "G. Argy-Rousseau" **6,750.00**
Clock, 4-1/2" sq, stars within pentagon and tapered sheaves motif, orange and black, molded sgd "G. Argy-Rousseau," clock by J. E. Caldwell.................. **2,750.00**
Dagger, 12" l, frosted blade, relief design, green horse head handle, script sgd "Nancy France" **1,200.00**
Jewelry, pendant, 2-1/4" d, round plaque, low relief molded rose blossom and branch, shaded rose, brown, and frosted glass, molded "G.A.R," (G. Argy-Rousseau), c1925........................... **700.00**
Paperweight, 3/4" w, 1-1/4" h, large beetle, green leaves, mottled blue ground, intaglio "AW" mark **6,800.00**
Sculpture, 9-5/8" l, crab in sea grasses, lemon yellow, chocolate brown, pale mauve, and sea green, sgd "A. Walter/Nancy" and "Berge/SC" **8,500.00**
Tray
5" d, molded as large moth, mottled blue, yellow, and emerald green, brown accents, emb "A. Walter," c1910....................... **1,150.00**
6" w, green to yellow ground, molded school of swimming fish, sgd "A. Walter Nancy, Berge" **1,450.00**

Vase, 5-1/2" h, press molded and carved, mottled amethyst and frost ground, three black and green crabs, red eyes, naturalistic seaweed at rim, center imp "G. Argy-Rousseau," base imp "France" **5,500.00**
Veilleuse, 8-1/2" h, Gabriel Argy-Rousseau, press molded oval lamp shade, frosted mottled gray glass, elaborate purple arches with three teardrop-shaped windows of yellow, center teal-green stylized blossoms on black swirling stems, imp "G. Arty-Rousseau" at lower edge, wrought iron frame, three ball feet centering internal lamp socket, conforming iron cover **6,900.00**

PATE-SUR-PATE

History: Pate-sur-pate, paste-on-paste, is a 19th-century porcelain-decorating method featuring relief designs achieved by painting layers of thin pottery paste one on top of the other.

About 1880, Marc Solon and other Sevres artists, inspired by a Chinese celadon vase in the Ceramic Museum at Sevres, experimented with this process. Solon emigrated to England at the outbreak of the Franco-Prussian War and worked at Minton, where he perfected pate-sur-pate.

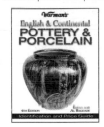

For more information, see *Warman's English & Continental Pottery & Porcelain*, 4th edition.

Box, cov, 5-3/4" d, round, white female portrait, blue ground, Limoges, France, late 19th C **690.00**
Centerpiece, 16" l, elongated parian vessel, molded scroll handles and feet, pierced rim, two brown reserves, white pate-sur-pate amorini, gilding, dec attributed to Lawrence Birks, marked "Minton," retailer's mark of Thomas Goode & Co., Ltd., London, c1889.......... **1,400.00**

Dresser jar, 3-3/4" d, ovoid, cobalt blue ground, lid with pate-sure-pate profile bust of classical woman, gilt banding, Meissen, Germany, early 20th C **1,955.00**

Lamp base, 10-1/4" h, Chinoiserie-style, black ground moon flask with pate-sur-pate and blue-printed dec of village scenes, mounted on gilt-metal beaded and scroll ftd base, 20th C, price for pr **490.00**

Medallion, 2-3/8" x 3-3/8", oval, blue ground, white relief cherub figure, unidentified factory mark on reverse, France, 19th C, edge ground **320.00**

Plaque
5-1/4" x 11-1/4", Victoria Ware, Wedgwood, rust ground, gilt florets, applied white figure of Adam, imp mark, c1880, rim chip, framed **2,200.00**
7-5/8" d, one with maiden and cupid spinning web, other with maiden seated on bench with whip in one hand, sunflowers stalked with humanistic snail on other, artist sgd "Louis Solin," both marked on back, framed, pr **2,500.00**
15" l, demi-lune shape, green ground, white slip, central figure of Venus holding mirror in each hand, fending off two groups of putti with their reflections, artist sgd Louis Solin, rosewood frame **9,200.00**

Plate, 9-1/8" d, deep brown ground, gilt trim, white dec of nude child behind net supported by two small trees, artist monogram sgd "Henry Saunders," printed and imp Moore Brothers factory marks, c1885 .... **750.00**

Tile, 7" l, 5" w, sword wielding warrior on horseback, cobalt blue ground, sgd "Limoges France" in gold script, mounted in antique frame **220.00**

Urn, 8" h, double handles, pedestal base, portrait medallion, pale green ground, ivory trim, gilt accents **250.00**

Vase
6" h, brown ground, white slip dec of cherubs flying among foliage, gilt trim rings and stylized foliate band at necks,

impressed George Jones marks, c1880, price for pr, one with slight glaze abrasion **5,000.00**
13-3/4" h, cov, dark brown ground, white slip of partially draped female figure holding flowering branch, shaped tripod base, gilt dec at rim, artist sgd Louis Solon, printed and imp marks, 1898, rim cover damage, minor gilt wear **2,300.00**
16-1/2" h, cov, deep green ground, circular panels dec in white slip, Psyche being carried heavenward by Mercury, maiden figures applied to shoulder, gilt trim, artist sgd Frederick Schenck, dated 1880, imp George Jones factory marks, cov damaged, hairlines to figures, light gilt wear **3,565.00**

PATTERN GLASS

History: Pattern glass is clear or colored glass pressed into one of hundreds of patterns. Deming Jarves of the Boston and Sandwich Glass Co. invented one of the first successful pressing machines in 1828. By the 1860s, glass-pressing machinery had been improved, and mass production of good-quality matched tableware sets began. The idea of a matched glassware table service (including goblets, tumblers, creamers, sugars, compotes, cruets, etc.) quickly caught on in America. Many

pattern glass table services had numerous accessory pieces such as banana stands, molasses cans, and water bottles.

Early pattern glass (flint) was made with a lead formula, giving many items a ringing sound when tapped. Lead became too valuable to be used in glass manufacturing during the Civil War, and in 1864, Hobbs, Brockunier & Co., West Virginia, developed a soda lime (non-flint) formula. Pattern glass also was produced in transparent colors, milk glass, opalescent glass, slag glass, and custard glass.

The hundreds of companies that produced pattern glass experienced periods of development, expansions, personnel problems, material and supply demands, fires, and mergers. In 1899, the National Glass Co. was formed as a combine of 19 glass companies in Pennsylvania, Ohio, Indiana, West Virginia, and Maryland. U.S. Glass, another consortium, was founded in 1891. These combines resulted from attempts to save small companies by pooling talents, resources, and patterns. Because of this pooling, the same pattern often can be attributed to several companies.

Reproduction Alert: Pattern glass has been widely reproduced. Items in the listing marked with an * are those for which reproductions are known to exist. Care should be exercised when purchasing such pieces.

Special Auction prices

Every year, Green Valley Auctions, Inc., sells hundreds of fine examples of Early American pattern glass. Here are a few examples for a few flint pieces it sold in 2004.

Bellflower, spooner, single vine, brilliant cobalt blue, 5-5/8" h **9,900.00**
Blaze, sugar, covered, 7-1/2" h **35.00**
Bull's Eye, spooner/spill, 4-1/2" h **45.00**
Bull's Eye with Diamond Point, goblet, 7" h .. **165.00**
Cable, goblet, 5-1/2" h **125.00**

Cleat, decanter, quart, 10-1/4" h, chip **220.00**
Comet, goblet, 6-1/4" h, in-the-making flake............ **100.00**
Horn of Plenty, butter dish, cov, Washington head finial, 5" h, minor roughness **1,100.00**
Magnet and Grape with Frosted Leaf, champagne, 5" h **255.00**
Morning Glory, tumbler/spooner, ftd, 4-3/4" h **125.00**
Ribbed Ivy, lemonade, applied handle, 2-3/4" h **135.00**

Additional Listings: Bread Plates, Children's Toy Dishes, Cruets, Custard Glass, Milk Glass, Sugar Shakers, Toothpicks, and specific companies.

Abbreviations:

ah	applied handle
GUTDODB	Give Us This Day Our Daily Bread
hs	high standard
ind	individual
ls	low standard
os	original stopper

Aegis

Bead and Bar Medallion, Swiss

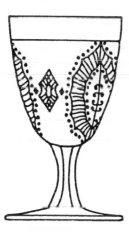

Made by McKee & Brothers Glass Company, Pittsburgh, PA, in the 1880s. Shards have been found at the site of the Burlington Glass Works, Hamilton, Ontario, Canada. Made in non-flint, clear.

Items	Clear
Bowl, cov, collared base, 6" d	15.00
Bowl, open, oval, flat	15.00
Butter dish, cov	35.00
Compote, cov, hs, 7" d	45.00
Compote, cov, ls, 8" d	40.00
Compote, open, hs, 6" d	20.00
Compote, open, ls, 8" d	25.00
Creamer	25.00
Egg cup	25.00
Goblet	30.00
Honey dish, flat, 3-1/2" d	7.00
Pickle, 5" x 7"	15.00
Pitcher, water, ah	55.00
Salt, master	15.00
Sauce, flat or footed	8.00
Spooner	20.00
Sugar bowl, cov	18.00

Barberry

Berry, Olive, Pepper Berry

Manufactured by McKee & Brothers Glass Company, Pittsburgh, PA, in the 1880s. Made in non-flint, clear. The 6-inch plates have been found in amber, canary, pale green, and pale blue and are considered scarce. The pattern has either nine berries in a bunch or 12 berries in a bunch.

Items	Clear
Bowl, cov, 6" d	48.00
Bowl, cov, 8" d	55.00
Bowl, open, oval, 6" l	24.00
Bowl, open, round, flat, 8" d	36.00

Items	Clear
Butter dish, cov	60.00
Butter dish, cov, flange, pattern on edge	95.00
Cake stand	110.00
Celery vase	48.00
Compote, cov, hs, 6" d, shell finial	66.00
Compote, cov, ls, 8" d, shell finial	75.00
Compote, open, hs, 7" d	36.00
Compote, open, ls, 8" d	42.00
Cordial	48.00
Creamer	36.00
Cup plate	18.00
Egg cup	110.00
Goblet	24.00
Honey dish, flat, round	18.00
Pickle	12.00
Pitcher, water, bulbous, half gallon	120.00
Salt, master, ftd	24.00
Sauce, flat	12.00
Sauce, footed	18.00
Spooner, ftd	36.00
Sugar bowl, cov	55.00
Syrup, orig top	18.00
Tumbler, ftd	30.00
Wine	30.00

Cordova

Manufactured by O'Hara Glass Company, Pittsburgh, PA. It was exhibited for the first time at the Pittsburgh Glass Show on Dec., 16, 1890. Made in non-flint, clear and emerald green. Toothpick holders have been found in ruby stained (valued at $45).

Item	Clear	Emerald Green
Almond dish, sq	20.00	-
Berry bowl, cov	30.00	-
Bowl, cov, 6" d to 8" d	25.00-30.00	-
Bowl, flared, 6" d to 9" d	20.00-25.00	-
Bowl, straight sides, 6" d to 9" d	15.00-20.00	-
Butter dish, cov, handle	50.00	-
Cake stand, hs, 10" d	45.00	-
Casserole, 6" d to 8" d	30.00-35.00	-
Catsup, cov, handle	75.00	-
Celery vase	45.00	-
Cheese dish	45.00	-
Cologne bottle	30.00	-
Compote, cov, hs, 6" d to 8" d	35.00-45.00	-
Compote, open, hs	35.00	-

Item	Clear	Emerald Green
Cracker jar, cov	45.00	-
Creamer, individual	30.00	-
Creamer, regular	35.00	45.00
Finger bowl	15.00	-
Inkwell, metal lid	50.00	-
Marmalade dish, handle, 5" d	15.00	-
Mug	20.00	35.00
Mustard jar, cov	45.00	-
Nappy, handle, 6" d	12.00	-
Olive, triangular	20.00	-
Pickle jar, cov	55.00	-
Pitcher, milk, quart, tankard	30.00	-
Pitcher, water, half gallon, tankard	60.00	-
Punch bowl	90.00	-
Punch cup	15.00	30.00
Salt, individual, flat	25.00	-
Salt shaker	20.00	-
Sauce, flat, 4" d or 4-1/2" d	10.00	15.00
Spooner	35.00	45.00
Sugar bowl, cov, regular	45.00	80.00
Sugar bowl, open, individual	25.00	45.00
Syrup, orig top	125.00	40.00
Toothpick holder	15.00	20.00
Tumbler	18.00	-
Vase, bud, 7" h to 9" d	15.00-20.00	-
Water tray	50.00	-
Wine	12.00	-

Drapery

Lace

Manufactured by Doyle and Company, Pittsburgh, PA, in the 1870s. Originally designed and patented by Thomas B. Atterbury, c1871. Reissued by the United States Glass Company, Pittsburgh, PA, after 1891. Shards have been found at Boston and Sandwich Glass Company, Sandwich, MA. Made in non-flint, clear. Pieces with fine stippling have applied handles. Pieces with coarse stippling have pressed handles. The finials are shaped as pinecones.

Items	Clear
Butter dish, cov	55.00
Compote, cov, hs, 7" d	65.00
Compote, open, ls, 7" d	55.00
Creamer, applied handle	36.00
Creamer, pressed handle	30.00
Dish, oval	36.00
Egg cup, ftd	30.00
Goblet	42.00
Pitcher, water, ah	85.00
Plate, 6" d	36.00
Sauce, flat, 4" d	12.00
Spooner	30.00
Sugar bowl, cov	48.00
Tumbler	36.00

Beaded Oval Window goblet and Paneled Forget Me Not pitcher, 8-1/4" h, both in amethyst. Goblet is **$150**; pitcher is **$275**.

Jacob's Ladder celery vase, blue, footed, **$295**.

Mitered Diamond sauce, footed, blue, 3-1/2" w, 2-3/8" h, **$18**.

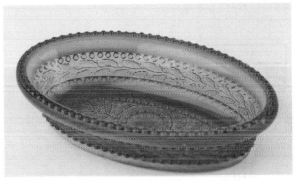

Holly Amber bowl, 7-3/8" l, 4-1/2" h, **$400**.

Beaded Oval Window sauces, left: blue, flat, **$150**; right: Vaseline, footed, 2" h, **$175**.

Eureka

Manufactured by McKee & Brothers Glass Company, Pittsburgh, PA, in the late 1860s. Made in flint, and non-flint, clear. Handles are applied and finials are shaped like buds.

Items	Flint
Bowl, oval, 7" l	36.00
Bowl, oval, 8" l	42.00
Bowl, round, 6" d	30.00
Butter dish, cov	72.00

Items	Flint
Champagne	42.00
Compote, cov, hs, 6" d to 8" d	75.00-115.00
Compote, cov, ls, 6" d to 8" d	85.00-110.00
Compote, open, hs, 6" d to 8" d	72.00-95.00
Compote, open, ls, 6" d to 8" d	60.00-85.00
Cordial	48.00
Creamer	55.00
Dish, oval, 6" l to 9" l	42.00-60.00
Egg cup	36.00
Goblet	36.00
Pitcher, water	115.00
Salt, master, ftd	36.00
Sauce, flat, 4" d	12.00
Spooner	48.00
Sugar bowl, cov	60.00
Tumbler, ftd	30.00
Wine	30.00

Feather

Cambridge Feather, Feather and Quill, Fine Cut and Feather, Indiana Feather, Indiana Swirl, McKee's Doric, Prince's Feather, Swirl, Swirl and Feather

Manufactured by McKee and Brothers Glass Company, Pittsburgh, PA, 1896-1901; Beatty-Brady Glass Company, Dunkirk, IN, c1903, and Cambridge Glass Company, Cambridge, OH, 1902-03. Later the pattern was reissued with variations and quality differences. Made in non-flint, clear, emerald green, and some amber stained. A chocolate water pitcher is documented.

Reproductions: The wine has been reproduced from a new mold and can be found in clear and clear with a pink stain, c1950. Reproduction goblets are known in amber, blue, and clear.

Items	Clear	Emerald Green
Banana boat, flat	75.00	190.00
Banana boat, footed	115.00	240.00
Bowl, oval, 8-1/2" l	30.00	-
Bowl, oval, 9-1/4" l	25.00	75.00
Bowl, round or sq, 4" d or 4-1/2" d	18.00	-
Bowl, round, 7" d	30.00	75.00
Bowl, round, 8" d	36.00	85.00
Bowl, square, 8" w	36.00	-
Butter dish, cov, flanged rim	72.00	172.00
Butter dish, cov, plain rim	55.00	180.00

Items	Clear	Emerald Green
Cake plate	65.00	-
Cake stand, hs, 8" d	48.00	130.00
Cake stand, hs, 9-1/2" d	60.00	142.00
Cake stand, hs, 11" d	85.00	155.00
Celery vase	42.00	85.00
Champagne	65.00	-
Cheese dish, blown domed lid	180.00	
Compote, cov, hs, deep bowl, 6" d	120.00	225.00
Compote, cov, hs, shallow bowl, 10" d	130.00	300.00
Compote, cov, ls, deep bowl, 6" d	110.00	240.00
Compote, open, ls, 8" d	42.00	135.00
Cordial	130.00	180.00
Creamer	48.00	85.00
Cruet, os	55.00	300.00
Dish, 7", d 8" d and 9" d	48.00	65.00
Goblet	55.00	180.00
Honey dish	18.00	36.00
Jelly compote, cov, ls, 4-1/4" d	120.00	180.00
Marmalade jar, cov	120.00	180.00
Pickle castor	155.00	-
Pitcher, milk	60.00	165.00
Pitcher, water, tankard	75.00	300.00
Plate, 10" d	42.00	75.00
Relish tray	24.00	48.00
Salt shaker	42.00	75.00
Sauce, 4" d or 4-1/2" d	15.00	30.00
Spooner	30.00	72.00
Sugar bowl, cov	55.00	95.00
Syrup, orig top	130.00	360.00
Toothpick holder	85.00	165.00
Tumbler, water, flat	55.00	85.00
Wine, scalloped border	48.00	-
Wine, straight border φ	30.00	-

Hamilton

Cape Cod

Manufactured by Cape Cod Glass Company, Sandwich, MA, c1860. Shards have been found at the site of the Boston and Sandwich Glass Company, Sandwich, MA. Other companies also may have made this pattern. Made in flint, non-flint, and clear. Rare examples found in color.

items	Flint	Non-Flint
Butter dish, cov	90.00	30.00
Castor set, four bottles, pewter standard	190.00	130.00
Celery vase, pedestal	72.00	24.00

Items	Flint	Non-Flint
Compote, cov, hs	115.00	42.00
Compote, open, ls, scalloped rim, 6" d	95.00	36.00
Creamer, ah	90.00	30.00
Creamer, ph	80.00	24.00
Decanter, os	160.00	60.00
Egg cup	60.00	18.00
Goblet	55.00	15.00
Hat, made from tumbler mold	130.00	-
Honey dish	18.00	12.00
Lamp, hand	105.00	42.00
Pitcher, water, ah, half gallon	190.00	130.00
Plate, 6" d	55.00	15.00
Salt, master, ftd	36.00	12.00
Sauce, 4 1/2" d	36.00	12.00
Spooner	42.00	15.00
Sugar bowl, cov	90.00	30.00
Sweetmeat dish, hs, cov	115.00	42.00
Syrup, ah, orig top	350.00	-
Tumbler, bar	105.00	42.00
Tumbler, water	95.00	36.00
Whiskey, ah	115.00	42.00
Wine	110.00	36.00

King's #500

Bone Stem, Parrot, Swirl and Thumbprint

Manufactured by King, Son & Company Pittsburgh, PA, in 1891. Continued by United States Glass

Company, Pittsburgh, PA, 1891-98, and made in a great number of pieces. Made in clear, frosted, and a rich, deep blue, known as Dewey Blue, both trimmed in gold. Values shown here are for pieces with very good gold trim. A clear goblet with frosted stem ($60) is known. Also known in dark green and a ruby stained sugar is reported ($115).

Items	Clear, gold trim	Dewey Blue, gold trim
Bowl, 7" d to 9" d	12.00-20.00	36.00-55.00
Butter dish, cov	80.00	130.00
Cake stand, hs	48.00	72.00
Castor set, three bottles	90.00	240.00
Celery vase	24.00	80.00
Cologne bottle, 1 oz or 2 oz	42.00	90.00
Cologne bottle, 4 oz or 6 oz	55.00	105.00
Cologne bottle, 8 oz	65.00	115.00
Compote, cov, hs, 8" d or 9" d	65.00	95.00
Compote, open, hs, deep bowl, 8" d or 9" d	42.00	60.00

Items	Clear, gold trim	Dewey Blue, gold trim
Compote, open, hs, saucer bowl, 9" d or 10" d	60.00	90.00
Cracker jar, cov	105.00	130.00
Creamer, bulbous, ah, individual	24.00	42.00
Creamer, bulbous, ah, table	36.00	60.00
Cruet	55.00	190.00
Custard cup	12.00	18.00
Decanter, locking top	120.00	-
Dish, cov, sq, flat, 7" w or 8" w	65.00	90.00
Dish, open, sq, flat, 7" w or 8" w	24.00	48.00
Finger bowl	18.00	42.00
Goblet	55.00	105.00
Lamp, hand	55.00	-
Lamp, stand	80.00	-
Pitcher, milk, three pints	60.00	240.00
Pitcher, water, half gallon, bulbous	90.00	240.00
Pitcher, water, half gallon, jug shape	105.00	224.00
Relish	24.00	36.00
Rose bowl	24.00	55.00
Salt shaker	18.00	48.00
Sauce, flat, 4" d	18.00	24.00
Spooner	36.00	85.00
Sugar bowl, cov, individual	24.00	48.00
Sugar bowl, cov, table	55.00	90.00
Syrup, orig top	65.00	270.00
Tumbler	30.00	42.00
Water tray, tab handles	55.00	115.00
Wine	42.00	80.00

Leaf and Star

Tobin, New Martinsville No. 711

Manufactured by New Martinsville Glass Manufacturing Company, New Martinsville, WV, c1910-15. Made in clear with gold trim, and ruby stained (add 100 percent). A toothpick holder (valued at $55) has been found in orange iridescent.

Items	Clear w/gold
Banana stand, ls, 8-1/2" d	55.00
Berry bowl, master, 7" d	110.00
Bon bon, turned up sides, 5" d	24.00
Bowl, scalloped rim, 8" d	24.00
Butter dish, cov	42.00
Celery tray, 11" l	24.00

Items	Clear w/gold
Celery vase	30.00
Creamer	210.00
Cruet, os	42.00
Custard cup	12.00
Dresser jar, metal top	110.00
Fruit bowl, crimped rim, 10" d	24.00
Goblet	24.00
Hair receiver, metal top	110.00
Humidor, orig silver plate top, 5" h, 4" d	55.00
Ice cream dish, 6" d	18.00
Jelly compote, open, hs	110.00
Nut bowl	18.00
Pitcher, water, ice lip, half gallon	65.00
Pitcher, water, plain lip, half gallon	60.00
Plate, 6" d or 8" d	12.00
Salt shaker, orig nickel-plated top	12.00
Sauce, flat	12.00
Sauce, footed, flared rim	18.00
Spooner	30.00
Sugar bowl, cov	36.00
Toothpick holder	18.00
Tumbler	24.00
Vase, 8-1/4" h	18.00
Wine	24.00

Medallion

Hearts and Spades, Spades

Manufacturer unknown, c1880. Made in non-flint, amber, apple green, blue, canary-yellow, and clear.

Reproductions: Imperial Glass Company, Bellaire, OH, has reproduced the butter dish. These reproductions can be easily detected: often the design is reversed, new colors are harsh, and the "I.G." monogram can be found on the base.

Items	Amber or Apple Green	Clear	Canary Yellow or Blue
Butter dish, cov φ	48.00	60.00	42.00

Items	Amber or Apple Green	Clear	Canary Yellow or Blue
Cake stand, hs, 9-1/4" d	55.00	65.00	30.00
Castor bottle	75.00	65.00	48.00
Celery vase	36.00	48.00	24.00
Compote, cov, hs	60.00	72.00	48.00
Compote, open, hs	48.00	60.00	36.00
Creamer	48.00	55.00	36.00
Egg cup	30.00	48.00	24.00
Goblet	42.00	55.00	24.00
Pickle	24.00	30.00	18.00
Pitcher, water	65.00	75.00	55.00
Relish tray	24.00	30.00	18.00
Sauce, flat or footed	18.00	24.00	15.00
Sugar bowl, cov	48.00	60.00	30.00
Tumbler	30.00	42.00	18.00
Waste bowl	40.00	55.00	24.00
Water tray	65.00	75.00	36.00
Wine	36.00	48.00	24.00

New England Pineapple

Loop and Jewel, Pineapple, Sawtooth

Manufacture attributed to Boston and Sandwich Glass Company, Sandwich, MA, or New England Glass Company, Cambridge, MA, in the early 1860s. Made in flint, and non-flint, clear, and opaque white. Rare in color.

Reproductions: Reproductions are known in clear, color, and milk glass with gilt trim. The Fenton Art Glass Company, Williamstown, WV, first started reproducing the goblet about 1950, and later included a sherbet, wine, and open compote with a ruffled trim. Glasscrafts and Ceramics, Inc., Yonkers, New York, made a reproduction goblet in 1953 in clear, non-flint.

Items	Flint	Non-Flint
Berry bowl, scalloped, 8" d	100.00	-
Butter dish, cov	260.00	-
Cake stand	142.00	-

Items	Flint	Non-Flint
Castor bottle	60.00	-
Castor set, four bottles	360.00	-
Champagne	190.00	-
Compote, cov, hs, 5" d to 8" d	190.00-230.00	-
Compote, open, hs or ls, 7" d to 8-1/2" d	110.00-130.00	-
Cordial	190.00	-
Creamer, ah, 6" h or 7" h	200.00	85.00
Cruet, ah, os, two styles	190.00	-
Decanter, os	230.00	-
Egg cup	60.00	42.00
Fruit bowl	90.00	-
Goblet, lady's	120.00	-
Goblet, regular φ	75.00	-
Honey dish, 3-1/2" d	18.00	-
Mug, ah	115.00	-

Items	Flint	Non-Flint
Pitcher, milk, ah, quart	660.00	-
Pitcher, water, ah, half gallon	360.00	-
Plate, 6" d	110.00	-
Salt, individual	30.00	-
Salt, master	55.00	48.00
Sauce, flat	18.00	12.00
Sauce, footed	30.00	-
Spill holder	72.00	-
Spooner	72.00	42.00
Sugar bowl, cov	180.00	115.00
Sweetmeat, cov, hs	230.00	-
Tumbler, bar	130.00	-
Tumbler, water	100.00	-
Whiskey, ah	155.00	-
Wine φ	180.00	-

Peerless #1

Lady Hamilton

Manufactured Richards & Hartley Company, Pittsburgh, PA, in 1875 and continued for a number of years. Made in a great number of pieces, many sizes of bowls, 22 compotes, five cake stands, and two types of goblets and creamers. Prices for similar items are all comparable to those listed. Made in clear.

Items	Clear
Bowl, 7" d	110.00
Bread plate, oval	30.00
Butter dish, covered	48.00
Cake stand	36.00
Castor set	90.00
Celery	30.00
Champagne	35.00
Compote, cov	60.00
Compote, open	36.00
Creamer	42.00
Dish	35.00
Egg cup, saucer base	35.00
Goblet	30.00
Pickle	18.00
Pickle jar, cov	48.00
Pitcher, water, ah, half gallon	75.00
Platter, oval	30.00
Salt, cov	42.00
Salt, open, individual	12.00
Sauce	10.00
Spooner	30.00
Sugar bowl, cov	48.00
Tumbler	35.00
Wine	30.00

Three Panel

Paneled Thousand Eye, Thousand Eye Three Panel, Richards & Hartley Pattern Line No. 25

Manufactured by Richards & Harley Company, Tarentum, PA, 1888, and by United States Glass Company, Pittsburgh, PA, in 1891, at Factory "E." Shards have been found at Burlington Glass Works, Hamilton, Ontario, Canada. Made in non-flint, amber, blue, clear, milk glass, and vaseline.

Items	Amber	Blue	Clear	Vaseline
Bowl, deep, 8-1/2" d	30.00	48.00	24.00	55.00
Bowl, flared, 8" d	36.00	55.00	30.00	60.00
Bowl, scalloped rim, 8" d	36.00	55.00	30.00	60.00
Butter dish, cov, flanged cover	55.00	60.00	48.00	60.00
Butter dish, cov, regular cover	48.00	55.00	45.00	55.00

Items	Amber	Blue	Clear	Vaseline
Celery vase, flared rim	60.00	72.00	36.00	60.00
Celery vase, plain rim	55.00	65.00	30.00	55.00
Celery vase, ruffled top	65.00	75.00	45.00	65.00
Compote, open, ls, 7" to 10" d	45.00-60.00	65.00-85.00	45.00-60.00	65.00-85.00
Creamer	48.00	55.00	30.00	48.00
Cruet, os	260.00	275.00	110.00	190.00
Goblet	45.00	48.00	30.00	45.00
Mug, large	45.00	55.00	30.00	45.00
Mug, small	36.00	48.00	24.00	36.00
Pitcher, milk, quart	118.00	145.00	115.00	124.00
Pitcher, water, half gallon	120.00	130.00	90.00	112.00
Salt shaker, orig top	65.00	72.00	36.00	65.00
Sauce, ftd	18.00	18.00	12.00	18.00
Spooner	42.50	55.00	36.00	48.00
Sugar bowl, cov	65.00	72.00	55.00	85.00
Tumbler	45.00	48.00	24.00	36.00
Wine	45.00	48.00	30.00	45.00

Valencia Waffle

Block and Star #1

Made by Adams & Company, Pittsburgh, PA, c1885. Reissued by United States Glass Company, Pittsburgh, PA, after 1891. Made in non-flint, amber, apple green, blue, clear, and vaseline.

Items	Amber or Vaseline	Apple Green	Blue	Clear
Berry bowl	25.00	35.00	30.00	20.00
Bread plate	42.00	45.00	42.00	35.00
Butter dish, cov	80.00	90.00	65.00	55.00
Cake stand, hs, 10" d	85.00	55.00	65.00	42.00
Celery vase	42.00	40.00	45.0	30.00
Castor set, complete	85.00	110.00	90.00	75.00
Compote, cov, hs, 7" d	85.00	110.00	110.00	75.00
Compote, cov, ls	55.00	75.00	85.00	42.00
Creamer, ph	45.00	-	65.00	42.00
Dish	30.00	-	35.00	15.00
Goblet	55.00	-	55.00	42.00
Pickle jar, cov	75.00	85.00	4000	42.00
Pickle dish	30.00	30.00	35.00	25.00
Pitcher, milk	75.00	85.00	80.00	55.00
Pitcher, water	90.00	85.00	80.00	55.00
Relish or Pickle	30.00	30.00	35.00	25.00
Salt, individual	45.00	-	-	-
Salt shaker	30.00	42.00	45.00	25.00
Sauce, flat, sq, 4" w	15.00	-	25.00	10.00
Sauce, ftd, sq, 4" w	20.00	-	20.00	15.00
Spooner	42.00	-	45.00	30.00
Sugar bowl, cov	55.00	-	75.00	45.00
Syrup, orig top	125.00	135.00	135.00	85.00
Tray, 10-1/2" l, 8" w	-	45.00	-	-
Tumbler	35.00	-	42.00	20.00

PAUL REVERE POTTERY

History:

S.E.G.

Paul Revere Pottery, Boston, Massachusetts, was an outgrowth of a club known as The Saturday Evening Girls. The S.E.G. was composed of young female immigrants who met on Saturday nights to read and participate in craft projects, such as ceramics.

Regular pottery production began in 1908, and the name "Paul Revere" was adopted because the pottery was located near the Old North Church. In 1915, the firm moved to Brighton, Massachusetts. Known as the "Bowl Shop," the pottery grew steadily. In spite of popular acceptance and technical advancements, the pottery required continual subsidies. It finally closed in January 1942.

Items produced range from plain and decorated vases to tablewares to illustrated tiles. Many decorated wares were incised and glazed either in an Art Nouveau matte finish or an occasional high glaze.

Marks: In addition to an impressed mark, paper "Bowl Shop" labels were used prior to 1915. Pieces also can be found with a date and "P.R.P." or "S.E.G." painted on the base.

Bowl, interior decorated with band of white flowers and buds, leafy green stems, yellow and light blue bands, green center, blue exterior, painted "S. E. G. 7-18," Boston, 1918, 8-3/8" d, 2-1/2" h, **$5,000**.

Photo courtesy of Skinner, Inc.

Bookends, pr, 4" h, 5" w, night scene of owls, 1921, ink marked "S.E.G./11-21," flat chip to one base..... **1,300.00**

Bowl
8-1/2" d, 2-1/2" h, cuerda seca dec, band of white rises on bright yellow ground, mkd "S.E.G./4-16," restoration to chip........................... **900.00**
11-1/2" d, 5" h, cuerda seca dec by Fannie Levine, white geese, bright yellow ground **35,000.00**

Cake set, Tree pattern, black outline scene, blue sky, green trees, 10" d cake plate, six 8-1/2" d serving plates, each marked "J.G., S.E.G.," three dated 7/15, three dated 1/4/15, one dated 3/15, price for seven-pc set...... **1,840.00**

Candle sconce, 7-3/4" h, 4-1/4" w, cuerda seca dec, mountainous landscape with tall trees and irises in foreground, mkd "SG/SEG/11-13," two tight lines from center edge **4,250.00**

Cereal bowl, 5-1/2" d, 2-1/2" h, cuerda seca dec, white swans swimming on blue water, S.E.G./A70.5.11/AS . **1,000.00**

Child's breakfast set, 3-1/2" h mug, 5-5/8" d bowl, and 7-3/4" d plate, dec with running rabbits, white, green, and blue, monogrammed "David His Mug," "His Bowl," "His Plate," potter's mark, two chips on mug........... **1,380.00**

Fruit set, green glaze with cream-colored border, incised and outlined in black, initialed "F. G." (Fanny Ginsburg) and "S. E. G." stylistic detail, large 8-1/4" d fruit bowl with artist's initials "I. G.," numbered "239.6.11," and "S. E. G."; and six 3-3/4" d smaller bowls with artist's initials "I. G.," sequentially numbered "196.6.11, 197.6.11, 198.6.11, 199.6.11, 200.6.11, 201.6.11" **1,880.00**

Goblet, 3-3/4" h, cuerda seca dec, band of white lotus, bright yellow ground, S.E.G./ 3.16/FL................... **850.00**

Humidor, cov, 6-1/4" h, 5-3/4" d, spherical, blue matte glaze, pink int., minute int. rim nick, sgd in slip "P.R.P. 3/36" **400.00**

Lamp base, 18-3/4" h, ovoid, yellow glaze, reticulated wooden base, unmarked **230.00**

Mug, 6" h, 4-3/4" d, cuerda seca dec, three fishing boats, sails monogrammed "C.R.S.," green, brown, blue, and ivory, mkd "AM/224-412/S.E.G." **2,300.00**

Pitcher
6-3/4" h, ovoid, applied handle, charcoal gray glaze, partial imp potter's mark, painted "4 26," artist's initials L.S., c1926, three rim chips........................ **70.00**
7-1/8" h, ovoid, applied handle, green glaze, painted "J.M.D. June 17, 1920 S.E.G. 5-20," by Josephine M. Davis, handle repaired **115.00**

Plate
6-1/2" d, incised white mice, celadon and brown band, ink mark "Dorothy Hopkins/Her Plate," 1911 .... **1,300.00**
7-5/8" d, incised geese in mottled green on speckled blue ground, painted "S.E.G. 6-13," artist's initials "I.G.," c1913......................... **490.00**
8" d, cuerda seca dec, white and blue geese and water lilies, green matte ground, marked "S.E.G./6-17/AM" **1,380.00**

Ring tray, 4" d, circular, blue-gray and green band of trees, blue-gray ground, marked "S.E.G./J.G." **275.00**

Teapot, 4-1/2" h, 9" d, brown and white wavy band of sailboats, yellow sky, 1918, restored **700.00**

Tile, 3-3/4" sq, Washington Street, blue, white, green, and brown, marked "H.S. S4 9/1/ 10," edge chips **420.00**

Trivet
4-1/4" d, medallion of house against setting sun, blue-gray ground, 1924, imp P.R.P. mark **425.00**
5-1/2" d, medallion of poplar trees in landscape, blue-green ground, 1925, imp P.R.P. mark.................. **600.00**

Vase
4-1/4" h, 4" d, ovoid, cuerda seca dec, band of green trees against blue sky, gunmetal black ground **2,400.00**
9-1/4" h, semi-matte ochre glaze, signed "P. R. P.," dated 1926........................... **265.00**

10-1/2" h, band of trees in blue and green glaze outlined in black, charcoal gray glazed body, imp pottery mark at center of base, dated "8-23," Brighton, MA, fine hairline at rim **1,300.00**

PEACHBLOW

History: Peachblow, an art glass which derives its name from a fine Chinese glazed porcelain, resembles a peach or crushed strawberries in color. Three American glass manufacturers and two English firms produced peachblow glass in the late 1880s. A fourth American company resumed the process in the 1950s. The glass from each firm has its own identifying characteristics.

Hobbs, Brockunier & Co., Wheeling peachblow: Opalescent glass, plated or cased with a transparent amber glass; shading from yellow at the base to a deep red at top; glossy or satin finish.

Mt. Washington "Peach Blow": A homogeneous glass, shading from a pale gray-blue to a soft rose color; some pieces enhanced with glass appliqués, enameling, and gilding.

New England Glass Works, New England peachblow (advertised as Wild Rose, but called Peach Blow at the plant): Translucent, shading from rose to white; acid or glossy finish; some pieces enameled and gilded.

Thomas Webb & Sons and Stevens and Williams (English firms): Peachblow-style cased art glass, shading from yellow to red; some pieces with cameo-type relief designs.

Gunderson Glass Co.: Produced peachblow-type art glass to order during the 1950s; shades from an opaque faint tint of pink, which is almost white, to a deep rose.

For more information, see *Warman's Glass*, 4th edition.

Marks: Pieces made in England are marked "Peach Blow" or "Peach Bloom."

Bowl
3-3/4" d, 1-1/4" h, New England, Wild Rose, satin finish, smooth pontil mark **495.00**
7-1/2" d, 8" h, acid finished, ftd, shaped trefoil fold down rim, soft pink shades to pale blue on bulbous rubbed body, three vertically ribbed feet, berry pontil, Mt. Washington, ex-Maude Feld **12,000.00**

Bride's basket, Mount Washington, shades of pink, replated Meriden frame **650.00**

Celery vase, 7" h, 4" w, New England, sq top, deep raspberry with purple highlights shading to white **785.00**

Claret jug
9-1/2" h, shape #322, Hobbs, Brockunier & Co., Wheeling, acid finish, applied reeded amber handle, ex-Maude Feld **5,500.00**
10" h, shape #322, Hobbs, Brockunier & Co., Wheeling, shiny finish, applied reeded amber handle, ex-Maude Feld **6,500.00**

Cologne bottle, 5" h, Webb, bulbous, raised gold floral branches, silver hallmarked dome top **900.00**

Cream pitcher
2-3/4" h, New England, satin finish **1,120.00**
3-1/4" h, Wheeling, applied amber handle **885.00**
4-1/4" h, #319, Hobbs, Brockunier & Co., Wheeling, shiny, applied amber handle **650.00**

Cruet
6-1/2" h, Wheeling, ball shaped, mahogany colored trefoil spout and neck, paper label from Maude Feld **2,475.00**
7" h, Wheeling, glossy, petticoat, applied amber handle, cut and faceted stopper, orig Maude Feld label, ex-Maude Feld.. **850.00**
7" h, Wheeling, satin, teepee shape, applied amber handle, replacement faceted clear glass amber stopper **1,950.00**

7-1/4" h, Hobbs, Brockunier & Co., Wheeling, ruby reeded handle, amber faceted stopper **800.00**

Decanter, 10" h, 5" w, Gundersen, Pilgrim Canteen form, acid finish, deep raspberry to white, applied peachblow ribbed handle, deep raspberry stopper **950.00**

Finger bowl, 4-1/2" w, 2-3/4" h, #93, Hobbs, Brockunier & Co., Wheeling, glossy, ovoid **275.00**

Goblet, 7-1/4" h, 4" d top, Gundersen, glossy finish, deep color, applied Burmese glass base **285.00**

Morgan vase, Wheeling, acid finish, shades from mahogany to custard, 10" h, original acid finish griffin holder, ex-Maude Feld, **$3,000.**

Photo courtesy of Early Auction Co.

Miniature, pitcher, 5" h, #319, Hobbs, Brockunier & Co., Wheeling, glossy, sq mouth, orig Maude Feld paper label, ex-Maude Feld **700.00**

Mustard, cov, Wheeling, SP cov and handle **475.00**

Pear, 4-1/2" h, New England, translucent, shading from white to pink **100.00**

Pitcher
5-1/2" h, Wheeling, Drape, squatty, mahogany shading to lemon yellow, sq mouth, applied clear reeded handle **350.00**

5-1/2" h, Wheeling, glossy finish, sq mouth, applied amber handle, orig Maude Feld label on int. of mouth, ex-Maude Feld................. **800.00**
5-3/4" h, Wheeling, acid finish, sq mouth, deep mahogany extends to lemon yellow, applied amber handle, orig Maude Feld label, ex-Maude Feld.......................... **1,200.00**
7" h, Wheeling, glossy, rect mouth, applied amber handle **1,050.00**

Punoh oup
Gundersen, acid finish **275.00**
Hobbs, Brockunier, 2-1/2" h **535.00**

Sugar shaker, 5-1/4" h, Wheeling.................. **3,025.00**
Toothpick holder, 2-1/2" h, Mt. Washington, dec, ex-Maude Feld....................... **15,680.00**

Tumbler
3-1/2" h, Wheeling, matte finish **200.00**
3-3/4" h, Gundersen, matte finish **275.00**
3-3/4" h, New England, satin finish **285.00**
3-3/4" h, New England, satin finish, deep raspberry red on upper third shading to creamy white **285.00**
3-3/4" h, New England, shiny finish **285.00**
3-7/8" h, Wheeling, glossy finish, shading from fuchsia to yellow......................... **200.00**

Vase, attributed to Thomas Webb & Sons, England, late 19th/early 20th C, narrow neck over bulbed base, cream-colored glass cased in red shading to pink, polished pontil, unsigned, 10-1/4" h, **$300**.

Photo courtesy of Skinner, Inc.

Vase
4" h, Wheeling glossy finish, sq mouth..................... **500.00**

4" h, Wheeling, shiny finish, sq mouth, shouldered body, mahogany shading to custard yellow, white opaque liner **550.00**
4" h, 6" d, Wheeling, rare lavender casing, ex-Maude Feld...................... **15,000.00**
6-3/4" h, New England, satin finish, lily, fades to white stem and wafer base........... **635.00**
7-1/4" h, ovoid, peaked rim, shading from soft pink to cream, camphor tooled base **250.00**
8" h, Wheeling, Morgan, shiny finish, deep red shading to butterscotch **850.00**
8" h, Wheeling, Morgan, shiny finish, three minute-in-the-making rim flakes **1,750.00**
9-1/4" h, tapering ovoid, raised enameled, Queens design dec, Mt. Washington, ex-Maude Feld **20,000.00**
10" h, Webb, cased deep crimson to pink, cascading green leafy branch, gold highlights **1,265.00**
10" h, Wheeling, Morgan, acid finish, shades from mahogany to custard, orig acid finish holder, ex-Maude Feld **3,000.00**

PERFUME, COLOGNE, AND SCENT BOTTLES

History: The second half of the 19th century was the golden age for decorative bottles made to hold scents. These bottles were made in a variety of shapes and sizes.

An atomizer is a perfume bottle with a spray mechanism. Cologne bottles usually are larger and have stoppers that also may be used as applicators. A perfume bottle has a stopper that often is elongated and designed to be an applicator.

Scent bottles are small bottles used to hold a scent or smelling salts. A vinaigrette is an ornamental box or bottle that has a perforated top and is used to hold aromatic vinegar or smelling salts. Fashionable women of the late 18th and 19th centuries carried

them in purses or slipped them into gloves in case of a sudden fainting spell.

Blue opalescent glass perfume bottle, ruffled sides, gold washed atomizer top, bulb missing, 7" h, **$70**.

Photos courtesy of Joy Luke Auctions.

Atomizer
Cambridge, 6-1/4" h, stippled gold, opaque jade, orig silk lined box..................... **140.00**
Cameo, Gallé, 8" h, lavender flowers and foliage, shaded yellow and frosted ground **1,250.00**
Moser, 4-1/2" h, sapphire blue, gold florals, leaves, and swirls, melon ribbed body, orig gold top and bulb................ **275.00**

Cologne
Baccarat, 5-7/8" h, colorless, panel cut, matching stopper **75.00**
Cameo glass
3-1/4" h, bulbous, crimson satin, opaque white floral cutting, hallmarked British Sterling cap **1,400.00**
4" h, citrine ground, white shaded star shaped blossoms, sterling mounts, English, c1900, very minor nick in foliage **1,495.00**
8" h, finely etched ground, citron cameo stemmed flowers, French, attributed to St Louis, faceted stopper, very minor chips on stopper and rim.............. **300.00**
Cranberry glass, 7" h, faceted, finely cut faceted stopper **175.00**
Cut glass, 7" h, cranberry cut to colorless, cane cut, matching stopper **250.00**
Malachite, 6-1/2" h, Ingrid Line, molded rose garden surrounds artistic medallions, Kurt Schlevogt, c1935......... **275.00**

Paperweight, 7" h, 5" d, double overlay, crimson red over white over colorless squatty bottle, five oval facet windows reveal concentric millefiore cane int., matching stopper **460.00**

Vaseline, 4-1/2" h, vaseline, attributed to New England Glass Co., flint, orig stopper **225.00**

Perfume bottle, emerald green, woman with arms outstretched embossed on base, Art Deco, original stopper, **$125**.

Perfume

Enamel, 3-1/4" l, pear shape, silvered metal lid with bale, green ground, two central cartouches of courting couples, Continental, late 18th/early 19th C **215.00**

Glass

3-7/8" l, Continental, early 19th C, latticino, tapered ovoid, clear, white, and yellow strands, ext. of bottle with horizontal ribbing, silver gilt floral engraved hinged lid, enclosing glass stopper **425.00**

4" h, French, late 19th/early 20th C, baluster form, blue opaline bottle, gilt metal floral overlay, foot, and neck mounts, hinged lid set with shell cameo of young man in feathered cap **200.00**

4-3/4" l, cut glass, colorless, pistol-form, etched silver-gilt mounts, short chain, spring-action trigger opens lid set with maker's medallion, French, late 19th/early 20th C **1,380.00**

Glass and silver, Victorian, London, 1885, fish-form flask, 6-1/4" l, green and metallic flecked blown glass body, gilt over enamel detailing of scales and eyes, engraved silver tail, retailed by W.Thornill & Co., fitted velvet lined case **1,500.00**

Porcelain

2-1/2" l, Continental, late 19th C, underglaze blue crossed swords mark, leg-form, garter and pale blue shoe, flat metal lid **250.00**

2-1/2" l, Meissen, Germany, late 19th C, courting couple, ivy covered tree trunk, enamel and gilt detailing, orig stopper **635.00**

3-1/4" l, Continental, late 18th/19th C, swaddled infant shape, enamel detailing, silvertone domed lid, tapered base........................... **325.00**

Silver gilt, 1-3/4" l, shield shaped, collet-set heart-shaped opal applied to front, surrounded by applied ropetwist, green and yellow enamel dec, back engraved with leafy scrolls, conical screw-in stopper, Hungarian, 20th C **115.00**

Silver plate, Victorian, London, 1885, 2-3/4" l, bud shape, engraved rim, all over repoussé reeding, glass int. **190.00**

Sterling silver

2-3/4" l, Victorian, London, 1885, bud shape, engraved rim, body with all over repoussé reeding, glass int. **175.00**

3-1/4" l, Birmingham, England, 1897, hinged heart-shaped case, domed lid, emb angel dec, gilt int. with heart-shaped green glass bottle, monogrammed, 2 troy oz **230.00**

Scent

1-3/4" h, free-blown, dolphin or mermaid, colorless, opaque white stripes, applied cobalt

blue rigaree, plain lip, possibly Boston & Sandwich Glass Co., 1825-50, some losses **80.00**

2-1/4" h, pattern molded, flattened ovoid, brilliant peacock green, 20 ribs swirled to right, plain rim, rough pontil mark, American or English, early to mid-19th C **265.00**

2-3/4" h, 1-1/2" d, blown molded, sunburst, brilliant sapphire shading to cobalt blue, shield shaped body, plain lip, rough pontil break, early to mid-19th C **495.00**

2-7/8" h, pattern molded, flattened tapering ovoid, deep brilliant amethyst, 26 ribs swirled to right, plain rim, rough pontil mark, American or English, early to mid-19th C **200.00**

2-7/8" h, pattern molded, flattened tapering ovoid, teal blue, red swirl, 24 vertical ribs, plain rim, rough pontil mark, American or English, early to mid-19th C **180.00**

3" h, free-blown, dolphin or mermaid, colorless, applied rigaree, engraved "Eliz-h Richardson" on one side, sprig on other side, American or English, mid-19th C, small rough spot on rigaree... **50.00**

3" h, pattern molded, flattened tapering ovoid, deep cobalt blue, light iridescence, 24 ribs swirled to right, plain rim, rough pontil mark, American or English, early to mid-19th C, rib flake, pinhead nicks **90.00**

3" h, pattern molded, flattened tapering ovoid form, pale yellow amber, 26 vertical ribs, plain rim, rough pontil mark, American or English, early to mid-19th C, tiny flake on lip **165.00**

3-5/8" l, silver, Japanese, late 19th/early 20th C, tear shape, molded dragon dec on stippled ground, attached silver chains, approx 1 troy oz **450.00**

3-3/4" h, ivory, figural, woman holding basket of flowers in one hand, fan in other, polychrome dec, Japan **90.00**

4-1/8" h, blown, colorless, cranberry and white stripes, white and gold metallic twist **95.00**

Vinaigrette

Cranberry glass, 2-1/4" x 1", rect, allover cutting, enameled tiny pink roses, green leaves, gold dec, hinged lid, stopper, finger chain................. **185.00**

Cut glass, 3-7/8" l, cobalt blue, yellow flashing, sterling silver overlay, emb sterling silver cap............................ **125.00**

English, silver

7/8" l, tooled purse shape, gilded int., John Turner, Birmingham hallmarks, 1792 .... **250.00**

1" w, 1-1/2" l, marker's mark "JT," Birmingham, c1845, rect, foliate engraved lid, base with molded scroll rims, gilt interior with pierced and engraved dec, approx 1 troy oz . **290.00**

European, silver, late 19th/early 20th C, 3" shaped as three squashes on vine, engine-turned textured dec, threaded bases, largest with pierced grate to interior, 1 troy oz **350.00**

Victorian, late 19th C, staghorn, 2-1/2" l rough-textured horn mounted with thistle-cast lid, quatrefoil neck band, horn with guilloche strapping, short link chain.................... **350.00**

PETERS AND REED POTTERY

History: J. D. Peters and Adam Reed founded their pottery company in South Zanesville, Ohio, in 1900. Common flowerpots, jardiniéres, and cooking wares comprised the majority of their early output. Occasionally, art pottery was attempted, but it was not until 1912 that their Moss Aztec line was introduced and widely accepted. Other art wares include Chromal, Landsun, Montene, Pereco, and Persian.

Peters retired in 1921 and Reed changed the name of the firm to Zane Pottery Company.

Marks: Marked pieces of Peters and Reed Pottery are unknown.

Left: dish, Moss Aztec, embossed dragonflies; rear: 4-1/2" h planter, Moss Aztec, embossed with pinecones; front: planter, Moss Aztec, banded decoration, unmarked, **$150.**

Photo courtesy of David Rago Auctions, Inc.

Vase, Chromal Ware, ovoid, unmarked, 4" d, 9-1/4" h, **$815.**

Photo courtesy of David Rago Auctions, Inc.

Bowl, 9" d, 3-1/4" h, closed-in rim, round tapering bowl, raised budding branches and berries in relief, matte green glaze, couple of chips on branch **175.00**

Doorstop, cat, yellow **375.00**

Ewer, 11" h, orange and yellow raised grapes dec, brown ground **50.00**

Jardinière, 9-1/2" d, 9" h, Moss Aztec, c1925, unmarked, few small chips to dec **200.00**

Mug, blended glaze **40.00**

Pitcher, 4" h, green and yellow raised fern leaves, gloss dark brown ground **65.00**

Vase, 4-1/4" d, 10-1/2" h, Moss Aztec, corseted, stylized flowers and leaves...... **230.00**

PEWTER

History: Pewter is a metal alloy consisting mostly of tin with small amounts of lead, copper, antimony, and bismuth added to

make the shaping of products easier and to increase the hardness of the material. The metal can be cast, formed around a mold, spun, easily cut, and soldered to form a wide variety of utilitarian articles.

Pewter was known to the ancient Chinese, Egyptians, and Romans. England was the primary source of pewter for the American colonies for nearly 150 years until the American Revolution ended the embargo on raw tin, allowing the small American pewter industry to flourish until the Civil War.

Note: The listings concentrate on the American and English pewter forms most often encountered by the collector.

Basin, American, Parks Boyd, Philadelphia, 1771-1819, touch mark on center interior, 9" d, **$275.**

Photo courtesy of Alderfer Auction Co.

Basin, "Love," attributed to John Andrew Brunstrom, Philadelphia, PA, 1781-93, round, flared sides, single-reed brim

6-11/16" d, touchmarks include partial circular mark with facing birds and "LOVE," "LONDON," and "X" and crown mark, [Celia Jacobs 16, 17] **650.00**

8-1/8" d, partial circular mark with facing birds and "LOVE," [Celia Jacobs 16], and "LONDON," 8-1/8" d ... **500.00**

9-1/8" d, partial circular mark with facing birds [Celia Jacobs 16], and "LONDON," minor wear.................. **530.00**

10-1/8" d, circular mark with facing birds and "LOVE," [Celia Jacobs 16], and "LONDON," 10-1/8" d, minor wear........................... **650.00**

11-1/2" d, circular mark with facing birds and "LOVE," "LONDON," "X" and crown mark, [Celia Jacobs 16, 17], minor wear.............. **2,250.00**

12-5/8" d, circular mark with facing birds and "LOVE," "LONDON," and two "X" and crown marks, [Celia Jacobs 16, 17], minor wear.. **2,820.00**

Basin, quart

7-7/8" d, Edward Danforth, Middletown and Hartford, CT, 1788-94, circular form, flared sides, single reeded brim, small touch mark with lion and "ED" [Carl Jacobs 82] **650.00**

8" d, Richard Austin, Boston, MA, c1790-1810, round bowl, flared sides, single reed brim, touchmark with dove and lamb, "RICHARD AUSTIN" in shaped oval [Celia Jacobs 230]............................ **750.00**

Beaker

3-1/8" h, Boardman & Hart, Hartford CT, second quarter 19th C, tapered cylindrical body, incised bands, "BOARDMAN & HART" "N-YORK" touch marks [Carl Jacobs 47], wear, scattered small dents and pitting **200.00**

5" h, Samuel Danforth, Hartford, CT, 1795-1816, tapered cylindrical body, incised bands, "SD," eagle and dagger marks, [Carl Jacobs 105]............. **1,765.00**

5-1/4" h, Timothy Boardman, New York City, 1822-24, tapered cylindrical body, incised bands, molded base, "TB&Co" and "X" quality mark, [Carl Jacobs 49]
.... **900.00**

Bud vase, 5" d, 10-1/2" h, Secessionist style, orig green glass insert, peacock feather emb, stamped "WMF" **865.00**

Butter plate, 6" d, American, unmarked...................... **70.00**

Candlesticks, pr, 6-1/4" h, Freeman Porter, Westbrook, ME, 1835-60, baluster stem, molded round foot, circular mark with "F. PORTER WESTBROOK," and "No. 1," [Laughlin text II p. 110], imperfections.............. **770.00**

Charger, 16-3/8" d, Samuel Ellis, London, monogrammed on back "MH," wear, knife, scratches, small rim repairs
.... **350.00**

Coffeepot

7-1/4" h, Rufus Dunham, Westbrook, ME, 1837-82, conical cover, flared cylindrical body, incised reeding, scrolled black painted handle, marked "R. DUNHAM," [Laughlin text II, p. 100], minor wear **500.00**

10-1/2" h, Issac C. Lewis, Meriden, CT, 1834-52, tapered body, tooled rings around base and rim, worn black paint on scrolled ear handle, interior of base raised, additional touchmark scratched out, touchmark for I.C. Lewis on base...... **260.00**

11" h, Freeman Porter, Westbrook, ME, 1835-60, ovoid, tooled ring at center, flared foot, and rim, domed lid, wafer finial, scrolled ear handle with later black paint, circular touchmark "F. Porter Westbrook No. 1," small hole at base of handle, restored dents.......................... **320.00**

Communion chalice, 6-1/4" h, unmarked American, handles removed, pr **200.00**

Creamer, 5-7/8" h, unmarked American, teapot shape
.... **250.00**

Chamberstick, American, second quarter 19th C, push-up form chamberstick, ring handle, 5-1/8" circular tray base, **$325**.

Photo courtesy of Alderfer Auction Co.

Charger, ringed rim, three indistinct impressed marks, impressed "AB," possibly English, 16-1/2" d, scattered pitting and scratching, **$320**.

Photo courtesy of Alderfer Auction Co.

Deep dish

6-1/8" d, Thomas Danforth III, Stepney (Rocky Hill), CT, c1790, circular form, rare eagle mark, [Laughlin 370]
.... **1,650.00**

11" d, S. Kilbourn, Baltimore, eagle mark............... **1,045.00**

Deep dish, "Love," attributed to John Andrew Brunstrom, Philadelphia, PA, 1781-93

11" d, round, single reed brim, circular mark with facing birds and "LOVE," crown and "X" quality mark [Celia Jacobs 16, 17] and "LONDON" stamped twice, minor wear **500.00**

13" d, circular, single reed brim, circular mark with facing birds and "LOVE," [Celia Jacobs 16] and "LONDON"
.... **1,000.00**

13" d, round, single reed brim, circular mark with facing birds and "LOVE," crown and "X" quality mark [Celia Jacobs 16, 17] and "LONDON" stamped twice **950.00**

Flagon, one quart, 9" h, Thomas D. and Sherman Boardman, Hartford, CT, c1815-20, disk finial, three domes, molded cover with "chair back" thumb piece above tapered cylindrical body with fillet, scroll handle with bud terminal, molded base, "TD & SB" in rectangle and "X" quality mark, [Celia Jacobs 150] **4,700.00**

Flagon, three quarts

13" h, Boardman & Hart, Hartford, CT, c1825-30, domed cover with "chair back" thumb piece, tapered cylindrical form, molded fillet and base, double scrolled handle with bud terminal, "BOARDMAN & HART," "N-YORK" and two round eagle touch marks, [Carl Jacobs 39, 47] **3,100.00**

14" h, Thomas D. and Sherman Boardman, Hartford, CT, c1815-20, urn finial, domed and molded cover with "chair back" thumb piece, tapered cylindrical body with molded fillet and molded base, double scroll handle with bud terminal, marked with "TD & SB," eagle, and "X" quality mark, [Celia Jacobs 64, 150]....... **4,000.00**

Inkwell, 1-3/4" h, small circular lid, four quill holes surrounding wide flat circular base, replaced glass receptacle, 19th C **225.00**

Ladle, 13" l, plain pointed handle, touch mark "WH" in oval, 19th C **65.00**

Lamp
5-3/4" h plus brass and tin whale oil burner, Putnam touch, James Putnam, Madison, MA, some splits in rim of base **315.00**
7" h plus fluid burner, unmarked American, attributed to Meriden, reeded detail on base, ear handle, light pitting **110.00**
8-1/2" h plus burner, Yale and Curtis, NY 1 touch, matching fluid burner missing, snuffers and one brass tube loose **190.00**

Measure
2-3/8" to 8" h, assembled set, bellied, English, minor damage **550.00**
5-3/4" h, John Warne, English, brass rim, battered, old repair, quart **100.00**

Mug
4-1/8" h, Robert Palethorp, Jr., Philadelphia (1817-22), 4-1/8" h **3,800.00**
4-1/2" h, Thomas D. and Sherman Boardman, Hartford, CT, c1815-20, pint, tapered cylindrical form, medial incised banding, S-scroll handle with bud terminal, molded base, "TD & SB" touchmark in rectangle [Celia Jacobs 150], minor wear, small dent on base edge **1,530.00**
5-7/8" h, Samuel Hamlin, Hartford, CT, late 18th C, quart, flared cylindrical form, everted lip, molded fillet, S-scroll handle with bud terminal, molded base, shaped "SAMUEL HAMLIN" touch, [Carl Jacobs 158], minor wear and pitting **4,200.00**
5-7/8" h, Samuel Hamlin, Hartford, CT, late 18th C, quart, tapered cylindrical form, everted lip, molded banding, S-scroll handle with bud terminal on molded base, shaped "SAMUEL HAMLIN" touch, [Carl Jacobs 158], minor wear **3,900.00**

5-7/8" h, Jacob Whitmore, Middletown, CT, c1750-75, flared cylindrical form with fillet, S-scroll handle with bud terminal, molded base, rare rose mark to interior base, round rose touch, [Laughlin 382], mug accompanied by 1997 note from John Carl Thomas commenting on it's fine quality and marks **9,400.00**
6" h, Joseph Danforth Sr., Middletown, CT, 1780-88, quart, flared cylindrical form with molded fillet, S-scroll handle with bud terminal, molded base, "ID" mark near rim and handle, [Celia Jacobs 164], 6" h, minor wear **4,700.00**
6-1/4" h, unknown maker, Boston, MA, last half 18th C, tapered cylindrical form, everted rim, molded band, scrolled strap handle with shell-like thumb grip, molded base, marked "CM" "S" and "CS" around rim **7,100.00**

Pitcher
6" h, Freeman Porter, Westbrook, ME, two quart **225.00**
6-1/2" h, Continental, swirl design, hinged lid, angel touch **85.00**

Plate, unmarked, American, 15" d, **$35**.

Plate
7-7/8" d, Richard Austin, Boston, MA, 1792-1817, circular, single reed brim, rare oval shaped touch mark with dove, lamb and "RICHARD AUSTIN" **250.00**
7-7/8" d, Thomas Badger Jr., Boston, MA, 1787-1815, round, single reed brim, arched left facing eagle mark and "BOSTON," [Laughlin 309, 287a], normal wear, price for pr **1,000.00**

7-7/8" d, Blakslee Barnes, Philadelphia, PA, 1812-17, eagle touchmarks and "BB," [Carl Jacobs #15], knifemarks, dents, some edge damage, set of six **980.00**
7-7/8" d, Thomas Danforth III, late 18th C, circular, single reed brim, oval lion touchmark with "TI" initials and four hallmarks [Laughlin 363a and 365], normal wear **650.00**
8" d, John Skinner, Boston, MA, 1760-90, round, single reed brim and hammered booge, partial lion touchmark and four hallmarks, [Carl Jacobs 249], normal wear **825.00**
8-1/4" d, Gershom Jones, Providence, RI, 1774-1809, circular, single reed brim, struck two lion in gateway touch marks, four small hallmarks, [Laughlin 339 and 340], normal wear.... **1,200.00**
8-1/2" d, John Skinner, Boston, 1760-90, round, hammered booge, left facing lion touchmarks, same owner's marks on all, [Laughlin 293], price for set of three, minor wear..... **1,880.00**
9-1/2" d, Thomas Danforth II, Middletown, CT, c1760-70, round, smooth brim, hammered booge, two lion in gateway touches, four small hallmarks, and "X" quality mark [Carl Jacobs 113] **3,175.00**

Platter, 28-3/4" l, Townsend and Compton, London, pierced insert, marked "Cotterell" **2,400.00**

Porringer, Westtown School, PA form, attributed to by Elisha Kirk, York, PA, plain tab handle with hole for hanging, 7-1/8" l, 5-1/4" d, **$700**.

Photo courtesy of Alderfer Auction Co.

Porringer
3-1/4" d, Thomas D. and Sherman Boardman, Hartford, CT, c1815-20, round, boss bottom, flowered handle, "TD & SB" in rectangle touchmark [Laughlin 428] **715.00**

Tankards, set of six, Victorian, lipped rims, turned bands on lower bodies, octagonal panel inscribed "T. Page Foresters Arms Tunbridge," top of handles inscribed with upper case "B," marked as quart size, hallmarks include rearing horse inside shield and crown above letters "V.R." (Victoria Regina) and "357," 6" h, one handle with soldered repair, minor wear and scratching, **$400**.

Photo courtesy of Alderfer Auction Co.

3-1/4" d, Richard Lee or Richard Lee Jr. Springfield, VT or unknown maker, late 18th C, round basin form, boss bottom, openwork handle with crescents and hearts, raised reversed "R" mark on handle back............................ **600.00**
4" d, Thomas D. and Sherman Boardman, Hartford, CT, 1810-30, circular form, boss bottom, Old English handle, "TD & SB" in rectangle, touch mark [Laughlin 428]... **470.00**
4-1/4" d, William Calder, Providence, RI, 1817-56, round basin form, boss bottom, openwork handle with partial round eagle touchmark [Carl Jacobs 67], dents, pitting.......................... **360.00**
4-1/4" d, Gershom Jones, Providence, RI, 1774-1809, round form, boss bottom, flowered handle, circular lion mark with "GI" initials on handle [Carl Jacobs 176], minor wear **2,350.00**
4-1/2" d, Samuel Hamlin Jr., Providence, RI, 1801-56, circular basin form, boss bottom, flowered handle, round mark with eagle and anchor, [Laughlin plate XLIX, fig. 337].................. **1,100.00**
5" d, Gershom Jones, Providence, RI, 1774-1809, round form, boss bottom, flowered handle, partial circular lion mark [Carl Jacobs 176 or 177].. **2,115.00**
5-1/4" d, Thomas D. and Sherman Boardman, Hartford, CT, 1810-30, circular form,

boss bottom, flowered handle, [Laughlin 428] **900.00**
5-3/8" d, Samuel Hamlin Jr., Providence, RI, 1801-56, circular basin form, boss bottom, flowered handle, engraved "LAH" monogram and date "1820" on bottom, round touch mark with eagle and anchor, [Laughlin plate XLIX, fig. 337] on handle **1,550.00**

Teapot, S. Simpson, baluster form, domed lid, scroll handle, impressed mark, 8-1/2" h, American, mid-19th C, dented, **$185**.

Photo courtesy of Alderfer Auction Co.
Soup plate, 8-7/8" d, unmarked Continental, angel touch **75.00**
Sugar bowl, 6" h, Ashril Griswold, Meriden, CT, eagle touch.......................... **490.00**
Tablespoon, rattail handle, heart on back of bowl, marked "L. B.," (Luther Boardman, MA and CT). set of six **330.00**
Teapot
6-3/4" h, Roswell Gleason, Dorchester, MA, eagle touch **495.00**

6-3/4" h, Ashbil Griswold, Meriden, CT, eagle touch, some battering and repairs **200.00**
7" h, Eben Smith, Beverly, MA, 1813-56, minor pitting and scratches.................. **375.00**

PHOENIX GLASS

History: Phoenix Glass Company, Beaver, Pennsylvania, was established in 1880. Known primarily for commercial glassware, the firm also produced a molded, sculptured, cameo-type line from the 1930s until the 1950s.
Ashtray, Phlox, large, white, frosted **80.00**
Bowl, 14" d, nude diving girl, white **495.00**
Creamer and sugar, Catalonia, light green **45.00**
Lamp shade, ceiling type, 12" d, pale pink, emb floral dec **115.00**
Umbrella stand, 18" h, Thistle, pearlized blue ground **450.00**
Vase
4-3/4" d, 4-3/4" h, Jewel, brown over milk glass**. 200.00**
8" h, Daisy, pearlized daisies, light green ground, orig label **360.00**
8-1/8" d, 11-3/4" h, Nude Scarf Dancers, light brown ground, cream figures, orig label **650.00**
10-3/4" h, Dogwood, green and white.................. **600.00**
11" h, Wild rose, blown out, pearlized dec, dark rose ground, orig label **275.00**

PHONOGRAPHS

History: Early phonographs were commonly called "talking machines." Thomas A. Edison invented the first successful phonograph in 1877; other manufacturers followed with their variations.

Adviser: Lewis S. Walters.

Angelica, cylinder, duplex horns **2,100.00**
Columbia
Graphaphone BS..... **7,700.00**
Graphaphone type Q **1,760.00**
HG cylinder player .. **2,400.00**
BQ cylinder player... **1,200.00**

Delpheon, mahogany stained case, **$650**.

Decca, Junior, portable, leather
case and handle........ **150.00**
Edison
Amberola Model A, upright
.... **6,050.00**
Fireside, K reproducer **850.00**
Gem, maroon........... **1,400.00**
Opera, Triumph horn **6,700.00**
Triumph, oak cygnet horn
.... **3,750.00**

Edison, brass plaque with name inside
top, table-top model, original, **$400**.

Edison, oak case, **$350**.
Photo courtesy of Dotta Auction Co., Inc.

Edison Amberola 50 cylinder
phonograph in mahogany case,
14-1/2" w, 20" d, 16" h, 47 Blue Amberol
cylinder records, **$400**.
Photo courtesy of Joy Luke.

Graphone
12.5 oak case, metal horn,
retailer's mark, cylinder
.... **450.00**
15.0 oak case with columns
on corners, nickel-plated
platform, metal horn,
stenciled cast-iron parts
.... **725.00**
Home Grand, oak case,
nickel-plated works, #6 spring
motor **1,300.00**
Harmony Deluxe, outside horn
.... **2,600.00**
Heywood-Wakefield, floor
model, wicker cabinet **750.00**
Kalamazoo, Duplex, reproducer,
original horns with decals,
pat. date 1904 .... **3,300.00**
Odeon Talking Machine Co.,
table model, crank wind,
brass horn, straight tone arm
.... **500.00**
Puck, talking machine **770.00**
RCA Victor, portable, John
Vassos (1898-1985), mid-

1930s, aluminum and various
other metals, 17-3/4" l,
15-1/2" w, 8" h **2,710.00**
Silvertone (Sears), two
reproducers **500.00**
Singing bird, mechanical
Single bird **3,245.00**
Three bird automata **6,600.00**
Two bird automata ... **4,950.00**
Sonora, Gothic Deluxe, walnut
case, triple spring, gold-
plated parts, automatic stop
and storage **400.00**
Starr, desk top **2,090.00**
Talk-O-Phone, Ennis disc
.... **1,000.00**
US Banner, cylinder, oak
grained papier-mache horn
.... **2,700.00**

Victrola, VV-XI-244, metal plaque
inside, refinished case with two sets of
doors, **$575**.

Victor
Victor II, humpback . **1,250.00**
Victor C **6,500.00**
Victor F, oak horn **1,825.00**
Victor Model D, oak spear tip
horn **4,000.00**
Victor Model M, rigid tone arm
.... **4,250.00**
Victor III **1,250.00**
Victor V, oak horn, record
cabinet.................... **5,100.00**
Victor V, oak horn, on Victor III
record cabinet **5,100.00**
Victor VI, mahogany horn
.... **7,000.00**
Victor Schoolhouse, brass bell
horn **3,000.00**
Zon-O-Phone, Grand Opera
table model.............. **8,250.00**

PHOTOGRAPHS

History: A vintage print is a positive image developed from the original negative by the photographer or under the photographer's supervision at the time the negative is made. A non-vintage print is a print made from an original negative at a later date. It is quite common for a photographer to make prints from the same negative over several decades. Changes between the original and subsequent prints usually can be identified. Limited edition prints must be clearly labeled.

Album

"A Souvenir of the Harriman Alaska Expedition, volumes I and II," 251 photographs, more than 100 by Edward Curtin, additional images by Edward H. Harriman, C. Hart Merriam, G. K. Gilbert, D. G. Inverarity, and others, silver prints, various sizes to 6" x 7-1/2", several with handwritten credit and date in negative, others with copyright, album disbound and defective, title pages and map laid in, prints generally in excellent condition, 1899, pr .. **21,850.00**

"Kodak," 104 photographs of Eastern and Midwestern U. S. by Wm Hoblitzell, prints document his train ride across country from MD to Missoula, MT, unposed glimpses of trains and local stations, Missoulan bicyclists and Native-Americans on horseback, handwritten captions and/or dates on mount rectos, mounted four per page recto and verso, oblong 4to, gilt-lettered morocco, spine and edges worn, pgs loose, photographer's handstamp on front and rear pastdowns, ties missing, 1890-91 .... **575.00**

Albumen print

Lincoln, Abraham **1,550.00**
View of the Oswego Harbor, arched top, 13" x 16-1/2", title, photographer, and date printed on label affixed below image, 1869............. **1,380.00**

Ambrotype, William Gannaway Brownlow, known as Parson Brownlow, the fightin' preacher, half plate.. **3,190.00**

Cabinet card

Early, Gen. Jabal A., sgd, 6-1/4" x 4-1/4" **1,840.00**
Garfield, J.A., sgd, 6-1/2" x 4-1/4" **1,495.00**
Lincoln, Abraham, lengthy inscription to Lucy Speed, 6-1/2" x 4-1/4"............. **1,840.00**
Sitting Bull, D. F. Barry, titled, copyrighted, dated, and Barry's imprint on recto, Bismarck D. T. imprint on mount verso, 1885, 7" x 5" **1,495.00**
Wilde, Oscar, age 32, Alfred Ellis & Wallery imprint on mounts recto and verso, period German inscription handwritten on mount verso, 1892, 5" x 4"............. **1,100.00**

CDV, carte de visite
Bill, Buffalo, long dark hair, wide lapel jacket, lighter overcoat with fur collar, light sepia color, 3-3/4" x 2-3/8", minor edge damage... **230.00**
Lee, Robert E., sgd, large bold signature, 3-3/4" x 2-1/2" **4,025.00**
Lincoln, Abraham, taken by Matthew Brady, 1864 .. **1,045.00**
Mrs. Lincoln, portrait with spirit of Abe behind her, Wm Mumler's Boston imprint on mount verso, c1869. **1,725.00**

Colotype, 18-1/2" l, 8-1/4" h, by L. A. Huffman, Plains view, several cowboys on horseback rounding up large herd of cattle, 24-1/4" l, 14" h, professionally matted and framed **750.00**

Portrait, unidentified conductor wearing uniform from Willow Grove Park, oval frame, **$200**.
Photo courtesy of Joseph P. Smalley, Jr.

Daguerreotype

Northern abolitionists, America, c1849, group of men believed to be five Northern abolitionists and a Southern politician, identified left to right as Joshua R. Giddings (1795-1864), John Adams Dix (1798-1879), John Alexander McClernand (1812-1900), Henry Alexander Wise (1806-1876), Levi Coffin (1789-1877), and John Parker Hale (1806-1873), quarter plate, 2-1/2" x 3-1/2" plate, 3-3/4" x 4-5/8" case, mounted in brass mat, black leather covered wood case with red velvet int., case with repaired spine **5,000.00**
Sell, John Todhunter, seated young child, tinted, sixth plate by M. A. Root, Philadelphia, stamped on matt, orig seal, some discoloration to mat, damaged leatherette case, c1840......................... **475.00**
Store front, four-story brick building, signage on building, crates pilled in front, man with top hat, unknown photographer, quarter-plate, image not sealed, plate marked "Chapman," leatherette case with some damage, c1850 .... **4,775.00**
Unknown gentleman, sixth-plate image by Robert Cornelius, orig brass Cornelius frame with repeating diamond pattern, orig seal, affixed yellow paper label on reverse "Daguerreotype Miniatures by R. Cornelius, Eighth Street, above Chestnut, Philadelphia," minor oxidation to image, slight mineral deposits on glass, c1840 .... **13,200.00**
Unknown gentleman, seated, sixth-plate image by W & F Langenheim, Philadelphia Exchange, re-sealed image, verdigris on mat, heavy tarnish halo at mat opening, leatherette case with photographer's name on pad, c1840......................... **425.00**
Unknown woman, seated, sixth-plate image by W & F Langenheim, Philadelphia Exchange, re-sealed image, verdigris on mat, heavy tarnish halo at mat opening, leatherette case with photographer's name on pad, c1840......................... **425.00**

Unknown woman, well dressed in dark taffeta dress, lace collar and cuffs, leather gloves, portrait brooch at neck, slight tint on cheeks, by Collins, 3rd & Chestnut St., Philadelphia, half-plate, orig seal, Collins paper label, full leatherette case, c1840-50 .... **450.00**

Magic lantern slides, group of 320 photographic images from 1920s and 1930s, Atlantic City views and events, yachting, fireboats, Mohonk (NY), Duluth (MN), etc. housed in four individual carrying cases, several slides cracked..................... **230.00**

Photograph
Aspens, New Mexico, 1958, by Ansel Adams, sgd "Ansel Adams" in ink on mount, identified on label from Boston gallery on reverse, 19-1/2" x 15-1/2", framed **6,325.00**
First Annual Round-Up, sgd in plate "Doubleday Photo, Wichita, Kan, 1920, First Annual Round-Up," 47 cowboys, cowgirls, workers, some on horseback, tipping hats, buildings and fences in background with advertising signs, 33-3/4" l, 8" h, 35-1/2" l x 9-1/2" black frame with worn paint........................... **550.00**
Portrait of Albert Einstein, c1938, by Lotte Jacobi, sgd "Lotte Jacobi" in pencil lower right, 9-3/4" x 7", framed **1,265.00**
Portrait of Marc Chagall and His Daughter in His Studio, by Lotte Jacobi, sgd "Lotte Jacobi" in pencil lower right, 6-3/4" x 5-1/2", framed **300.00**
Ten Mile Creek, detailed scene near mouth of Ten Mile Creek, Powder River, Montana, heard of cattle spread out in the valley, several cowboys on horseback, 20" l, 14-1/2" h, contemporary 21-1/8" l, 16" h frame.......................... **350.00**

Silver print, 13-3/8" l, 10-3/8" h, sepia tones, by Edward S Curtis, shows Indians riding horses in single file, signature and "L.A." lower right, glued down to thin card backing, 14" x 17" orig brown and black frame, sold with book *Portraits from North American Indian Life*, by Coleman and McLuhan.................. **1,150.00**

Tintype
Family, identified on mat "Marshall Kimpton," man wearing military coat, wife wearing elaborate hat, huge bow, daughter stands behind, ninth plate, cased, minor bends, case hinge has old taped repair **150.00**
Unidentified Union soldier with rifle and bayonet, 1/6th plate........................... **360.00**

PIANO BABIES

History: In the late 1900s, a well-decorated home had a parlor equipped with a piano, which usually was covered by a lovely shawl. To hold the shawl in place, piano babies were used. Piano babies are figures of babies, usually made of unglazed bisque. These "Piano Babies" range in size from three inches to more than 20 inches. They were made in a variety of poses—sitting up, crawling, lying on their tummies, and lying on their backs. Some babies were dressed, while others were nude.

Most piano babies were produced in Germany, England and France. There were more than 15 factories in Germany that produced this type of bisque ware. Among them Hertwig and Co., Julius Heubach, Royal Rudolstadt, Simon and Halbig, Kling and Co, and Gerbruder Heubach, were the most prolific. Ger. Heubach produced most of his wares for export, between 1914 and 1918. The Heubach company often produced several versions or sizes of the same Piano Baby. Many of these manufacturers also made dolls and carried the artistry required for fine doll making to their piano baby creations.

A large number of the piano babies found today were manufactured by the Heubach Brothers (1820-1945) in Germany, whose rising sun mark is well known. However, many pieces left factories with no mark. The Heubach factory is well known also for creating the same baby but in different sizes. The Heubach babies are well known for their

realistic facial features as well as their attention to minute details, such as intaglio eyes, small teeth looking out from lips, blond hair, blue eyes, etc.

Reproduction Alert: In the 1950s, US companies began importing bisque piano babies from Japan. They seem to be everywhere! Many of these were originally only marked with paper labels. They are not "true reproductions," as they do not truly duplicate earlier styles, but collectors should be aware that they are also not vintage bisque piano babies just because they aren't marked. Generally these types of piano babies will have a different type of painting, especially around the eyes and are usually not as detailed as the original piano babies, the quality of the bisque is usually inferior to that of genuine old bisque babies, and at times have the numbers on the base painted in red. Red mark numbers are not a sure sign of a reproduction as some antique piano babies were also marked in this way. Many reproductions also have a larger bisque-manufacturing hole in the bottom while older ones have a smaller hole. Because these Japanese bisque versions are from the 1950s and not the 1890s, their values should be considerably less than vintage German bisque piano babies.

Adviser: Jerry Rosen.

Two piano babies, both lying on tummies, front: dark haired boy with blue romper, back: blond girl with pink romper, **each $25**. These babies are modern Japanese imitations of vintage bisque piano babies.

2-3/4" h girl, lying down on tummy, looking upright, hands folded, crisp mold, Germany **75.00**

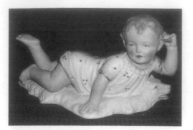

Baby boy laying on bear skin rug, 4-1/2" h, 8" l, **$195**.

3" h, 7" l girl, rosy cheeks, lying down holding lamb, bonnet with pink bow **150.00**

4" h, baby, seated, bottle in hands, white gown, gold beaded trim **200.00**

4" h, baby, seated, holding rattle, yellow floral trimmed nightgown with large bows and gold beading **250.00**

4" h, Occupied Japan, chubby baby, sitting down, wearing diaper, sour face expression **55.00**

4" h, 6" l, Hertwig, Pansy, baby girl, intaglio eyes, rosy cheeks, smiling lips, delicately pansy flowers painted around head .. **250.00**

4" h, 8" l, Gebruder Heubach, little boy holding his dog, blond, intaglio eyes, sunburst Heubach mark, model #11160 dep, Germany **560.00**

4-3/8" h, baby, sitting up, legs slightly crossed, rosy cheeks, brown hair, old fashioned one-pc shorty pajama, white with gold trim, tiny bisque beads **175.00**

4-3/4" h, Heubach, nude, angry looking expression, both hands fisted near face, intaglio blue eyes, rosy complexion, pouting red lips **350.00**

5" h, boy, arms at sides, in Dad's shoes **275.00**

5" h, baby, holding potty on head, white gown trimmed in gold.......................... **200.00**

5" h, child, crawling, open eggshell on back........ **300.00**

5" h, Heubach, sitting child with white dress and pink detailed flowered hat **155.00**

5" h, 10" l, baby holding ribbon from bonnet **145.00**

5-1/4" h, Heubach, Dutch boy and girl, standing back to back **125.00**

Baby in white gown trimmed in gold, 5" h, holding potty on head, **$200**.

6" h, Heubach, baby, foot close to mouth, green glazed tub **300.00**

6" h, Heubach, Flower Child, sitting, hands folded on lap, blue flower-shaped bonnet **400.00**

6" h, 8" l, crawling baby, holding basket, white shirt, pink trim, mkd "Germany 11649" **350.00**

6" h, 10" l, Andrea, by Sadak, 1950's crawling baby, pink bow on right arm, mkd "23/109" in red **100.00**

Crawling baby, 6" h, 8" l, white shirt with pink trim, holding basket, marked "Germany 11649," **$350**.

7" h, baby with left hand to ear, gold beading on gown **175.00**

7" h, 10" l, Heubach, crawling baby, yellow half egg on back, mkd **650.00**

8" h, German, sitting up, holding shoe in right hand **295.00**

8" h, 4" l Heubach, baby, sitting up, holding pocket watch, finger is pointing up, incised "13468 Germany" **840.00**

Boy, 6-1/2" h, 13" l, lying on tummy, stretched out, yellow gown with blue trim, blond hair, blue eyes, marked "5032 Germany" with crown and "R" in red, Meissen, **$650**.

9" h, baby, sitting up, arms raised, feet crossed, beautiful facial expression, Victorian white baby gown with pink detailing...................... **400.00**

9" h, baby, standing in boots, gown incised "6751" .. **475.00**

9" h, Heubach, boy, in rabbit suit, holding blue bisque egg **650.00**

Crawling baby with yellow half egg on back, 7" h, 10" l, Heubach mark, **$650**.

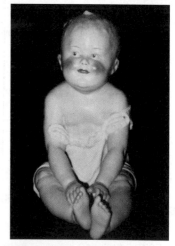

Heubach, 8" h, intaglio blue eyed molded baby wearing white gown with mint green trim, white raised dots along ruffling at top gown front, detailed dimples in knees, elbows and back, incised mark on back with Heubach sunburst marking, green #37 incised on mold on bottom, **$600**.

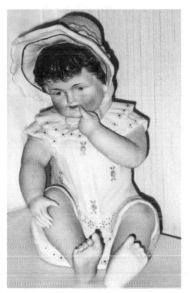

Girl in blue dress, 9-1/2" h, floppy hat, finger pointed to mouth, no mark, **$275**.

9-1/2" h, boy, sitting on chair, blue outfit, Shriners' cap with white tassel on back, pince-nez glasses in hand.... **295.00**

10" h, baby, crossed legs, holding pear in left hand, intaglio eyes **330.00**

12" l, baby, blond, crawling position, arms and hands away from body, blue intaglio eyes, white molded-on gown, pale yellow ruffle around top, pink bow on right shoulder, circle mark with smaller circle in center, "H" in circle . **300.00**

14" h, Heubach, bicycle figures, man and woman with light green bicycling attire holding metal bicycle **1,000.00**

PICKARD CHINA

History: The Pickard China Company was founded by Wilder Pickard in Chicago, Illinois, in 1897. Originally the company imported European china blanks, principally from the Havilands at Limoges, which were then hand painted. The firm presently is located in Antioch, Illinois.

For more information, see *Warman's American Pottery & Porcelain,* 2nd edition.

Bowl
6" d, Autumn Blackberries, sgd "O. Goess" (Otto Goess), 1905-10 mark **200.00**
9-1/2" d, 4-1/2" h, ftd, strawberries, white blossoms, and gooseberries dec, sgd "E. Challinor" (Edward Challinor), 1905-10 mark **300.00**
10" d, red and white tulips, gold dec, Limoges blank...... **230.00**

Cabinet plate
8-1/2" d, heavy gold enameled border, Limoges blank........................... **175.00**
9" d, lilies, gold background, artist sgd "Yeschek" ... **100.00**

Celery set, two-handled oval dish, five matching salts, allover gold dec, 1925-30 mark.......................... **125.00**

Chocolate set, 12" h chocolate pot, creamer, cov sugar, 11" tray, sgd "F. Lind" (Frederick Lindner), Pickard and various French and German back stamps, c1903........ **1,495.00**

Claret set, claret jug, five tumblers, 11-1/2" d tray, Deserted Garden pattern, sgd "J. Nessy" (John Nessy), 1912-18 mark **2,600.00**

Coffee set, Modern Conventional pattern, coffee pot sgd "Hessler" (Robert Hessler), 1910-12 mark, eight cups and saucers sgd "Hess & RH" (Robert Hessler), 1912-18 mark.................. **1,450.00**

Creamer, 5-1/4" h, Tulip Conventional, sgd "Tomash" (Rudolph Tomascheko), 1903-05 mark...................... **400.00**

Creamer and sugar
Deserted Garden pattern, sgd "J. Nessy" (John Nessy), 1912-18 mark **200.00**
White Poppies & Daisy, sgd, 1912-18 mark **250.00**

Demitasse cup and saucer
Gold Tracery Rose & Daisy pattern, green band, 1925-30 mark........................... **40.00**

Poppy pattern, sgd "LOH" (John Loh), 1910-12, price for pr **325.00**

Lemonade pitcher
Encrusted Honeysuckle pattern, 1919-22 mark **100.00**
Schoner Lemon pattern, sgd "Schoner" (Otto Schoner), 1903-05 mark **1,700.00**

Match holder, Rose & Daisy pattern, allover gold, 1925-30 .... **40.00**

Pin dish, violets dec **40.00**

Plate
8-1/2" d, blackberries and leaves, sgd "Beitler" (Joseph Beitler), 1903-15 .... **90.00**
8-1/2" d, Calla Lily pattern, sgd "Marker" (Curtis H. Marker), 1905-10 mark **225.00**
8-1/2" d, Gibson Narcissus pattern, sgd "E. Gibson" (Edward Gibson), 1903-05 mark........................... **300.00**
8-1/2" d, Lilium Ornatum pattern, sgd "Beulet" (F. Beulet), 1910-12 mark **100.00**
8-3/4" d, Florida Moonlight, sgd "E. Challinor" (Edward Challinor), 1912-18 mark **2,300.00**
9" d, Yeschek Currants in Gold pattern, sgd "Blaha" (Joseph Blaha), 1905-10 mark **110.00**

Punch bowl, 11" d, grape dec, sgd "Coufall" (John Anton Coufall) upper right, "T & V Limoges" and "Pickard" back stamps, c1905 .... **895.00**

Tankard, 10-1/4" h, red poppies, anonymous artist, "T & V Limoges" and "Pickard" back stamps, c1905 .... **1,150.00**

Tea set, cov teapot, creamer, cov sugar, Carnation Garden pattern, each sgd "Yeschek" (Joseph T. Yeschek), 1900-05 marks..................... **2,600.00**

Vase
8" h, Golden Pheasant pattern, sgd "E. Challinor" (Edward Challinor), 1919-22 mark........................... **500.00**
8-1/4" h, scenic, sgd "E. Challinor" (Edward Challinor), 1912-18 mark **425.00**
11" h, Calla Lily pattern, sgd "Marker" (Curtis H. Marker), 1905-10 mark **550.00**
13-1/2" h, Carmen, red poppies, sgd "J. Kiefus" (Jacob Kiefus) lower right, "D & C France" and "Pickard" back stamps, c1905... **595.00**

Vase, tapered cylindrical form, double gilt handles, rim, and foot, bands below rim in iridescent blue and yellow, decorated with floral motifs, vertical bands of cobalt blue with white floral decoration, textured gold body, mark obscured by paper label inscribed "Pickard China, Arno vase, Eg. G. Linear," Edith Arno, early 1900s, 7-1/4" h, **$325**.

Photo courtesy of Alderfer Auction Co.

Salt, open, embossed gold decoration, self handles, marked "Pickard China Made in USA, 241," **$35**.

PICKLE CASTORS

History: A pickle castor is a table accessory used to serve pickles. It generally consists of a silver-plated frame fitted with a glass insert, matching silver-plated lid, and matching tongs. Pickle castors were very popular during the Victorian era. Inserts are found in pattern glass and colored art glass.

For more information, see *Warman's Glass*, 4th edition.

Pickle castor insert, colorless, Little River pattern, original lid, **$90**.

Photo courtesy of Dotta Auction Co., Inc.

Pickle castor, colorless Zipper Block pattern insert, original silver plated lid, frame, and tongs, **$220**.

Amberina, melon ribbed IVT insert, SP lid, ftd frame, lid, tongs, c1875-95 .... **700.00**

Colorless, 11-3/4" h, diamond quilted pattern insert, silvered metal frame **200.00**

Cranberry, IVT insert, enameled blue and white florals, green leaves, shelf on frame dec with peacocks and other birds **325.00**

Crown Milano, 8-3/4" h, cylindrical hobnail insert shades from pink to opal, hand enameled dec, sgd "Pairpoint" silver plate flower emb holder, orig tongs **2,150.00**

Double, vaseline, pickle leaves and pieces, resilvered frame **800.00**

Mount Washington, 11" h, opalescent stripes with light and dark pink, Pairpoint #604 frame **850.00**

Opalescent, 11-1/2" h, cranberry, Daisy & Fern emb apple blossom mold, orig Empire frame, later tongs, Victorian...................... **500.00**

Pink, shiny pink Florette pattern insert, white int., bowed out frame **325.00**

POLITICAL ITEMS

History: Since 1800, the American presidency has been a contest between two or more candidates. Initially, souvenirs were issued to celebrate victories. Items issued during a campaign to show support for a candidate were actively being distributed in the William Henry Harrison election of 1840.

There is a wide variety of campaign items—buttons, bandannas, tokens, pins, etc. The only limiting factor has been the promoter's imagination. The advent of television campaigning has reduced the quantity of individual items, and modern campaigns do not seem to have the variety of materials that were issued earlier.

Reproduction Alert
Campaign Buttons

The reproduction of campaign buttons is rampant. Many originated as promotional sets from companies such as American Oil, Art Fair/Art Forum, Crackerbarrel, Liberty Mint, Kimberly Clark, and United States Boraxo. Most reproductions began life properly marked on the curl, i.e., the turned-under surface edge.

Look for evidence of disturbance on the curl where someone might try to scratch out the modern mark. Most of the backs of original buttons were bare metal or had a paper label. Beware of any button with a painted back. Finally, pinback buttons were first made in 1896, and nearly all made between 1896 and 1916 were celluloid covered. Any lithographed tin button from the election of 1916 or earlier is very likely a reproduction or fantasy item.

Additional Listings: See
*Warman's Americana &
Collectibles* for more examples.
Adviser: Theodore L. Hake.

Bookmark, McKinley, Pan-Am Expo,
McKinley portrait above image of
"Temple Of Music" exhibit, black olive
branch beneath portrait, colorful fan-
shaped design at bottom tip suspends
thread tassel, reverse marked
"Copyrighted," 10-1/2" l, 2-1/2" w, **$145**.

*Photo courtesy of Hake's Americana &
Collectibles.*

Ashtray, 3-1/2" sq, smoked
glass, "Thanks To A Key
Leader," facsimile signature
"Dick Nixon," 1960........ **15.00**
Badge
1-3/16", Wilson, diecut white
metal, name on bar at top,
portrait on six-pointed star
below, stickpin **65.00**
1-1/2" x 5", DNC Page, 1984,
black and brass luster
medals, red, white, and blue
fabric ribbon, 1-1/2" d bar pin
medal with raised image of
Golden Gate bridge and DNC
logo............................... **15.00**
4", Ike, red, white, and blue
fabric covering bar pin at top,
tiny brass flag accent
suspended below, 2" clear
plastic disk with name "Ike"
printed in gold lettering on
reverse.......................... **30.00**
Bandana, 30" sq, George
McGovern, red, white, and
blue, map, red star on each
state capitol, slogans
surround map **20.00**
Bank, 3" h, 3" d, New Deal Bank,
Chein, coin slot on solid red
painted top, red, white, and blue
stars and stripes, eagles, center
red band, c1930s **85.00**

Bar pin
3/4" l, Hoover, brass lettering,
whit enamel dec **5.00**
1-1/2" l, Theodore Roosevelt,
sterling silver, lettering on
stippled background **35.00**
Booklet, 9" x 12", "Our Patriotic
President, His Life in
Pictures," Theodore
Roosevelt, Columbia Press,
1904, bright red and blue on
tan cover with large black and
white photo, anecdotes,
sayings, principles,
biography, and photos . **25.00**
Brass shell
1-1/8", Blaine and Logan,
single sheet of cardboard with
photos surmounted by pair of
six-sided panels accented by
emb stars.................... **275.00**
1-1/8", Benjamin Harrison,
from 1888, Our Next
President, eagle atop
horseshoe surrounding
cardboard photo......... **165.00**

Cello with easel, McKinley, sepia, real
photo, reverse covered metal back,
small center stamp by "J. Abrahams
229 Bowery New York" plus 1896
patent date, two cutout notches holding
replacement easel wire. 3-1/2" d, **$290**.

*Photo courtesy of Hake's Americana &
Collectibles.*

Bust, 7" h, hollow cast metal,
Wm McKinley, black patina,
reverse stamped "G. B.
Haines & Co., Chicago" **70.00**
Button
7/8" d, William McKinley,
1896, black and white photo,
gold trim, diamond design
flanked by red, white, and
blue star and stripe motif,
bright gold outer motif .. **30.00**
1-1/4", For President Harry S.
Truman, black on cream
.... **60.00**
1-1/8" d, Adlai Stevenson,
white and dark blue litho,

"Volunteer for Stevenson"
.... **20.00**
1-1/2", No Roosevelt Dynasty,
blue on cream **15.00**
1-3/4", All The Way With
Kennedy For President,
slogan in blue, white
background, name in bright
red **75.00**
2-1/2" d, Adlai Stevenson,
celluloid, red, white, and
black, "I'm for Stevenson"
slogan around cartoon
portrait of Harry Truman with
lip buttoned, below "How
We'd Like Harry".......... **45.00**
3-1/2", Re-elect LBJ sepia
toned photo in center, white
background, red "Re-elect" at
top, blue "Johnson For
President" at bottom..... **25.00**
3-1/2", Willkie Our Next
President, black and white,
some scratches............ **20.00**
6", Humphrey Delegate, red,
white, and blue, 6" neck cord
attached to black cardboard
easel back.................... **20.00**

Elephant, cast iron, anti-FDR, 1936,
hollow iron figural GOP symbol, dark
red molded blanket with gold raised
slogan on both sides "Land-on
Roosevelt 1936," 90 percent original
paint, 90 percent original gold lettering
on one side, 50 percent on other side, 2-
1/2" x 5" x 3", **$495**.

*Photo courtesy of Hake's Americana &
Collectibles.*

Coin, 1-1/8" US one-cent coin,
Liberty head on front, date
1838, front stamped "Vote the
Land Free," issued in 1848 for
Martin Van Buren, reverse
lightly struck **135.00**
Electoral ticket, 1856, 10-1/2" x
18" linen-like fabric, black
printed text, cream-colored
ground, top reads "National
American Fillmore and
Donelson Ticket," various
elector names, some as-made
flaws, archival tape repair
.... **200.00**

Ferrotype, Stephan A. Douglas 1860, rim hole, brass lustered rim **275.00**

Flicker

2-1/2", Stevenson, Tucker, and 1956 Indiana governor candidate **40.00**

3" d, red tin litho frame holds full color cardboard photo of John F. Kennedy by Fabian Bachrach, suspended below is 5" gold on blue ribbon "I Was At The Inauguration of President Kennedy," date and city, mounted above text is 1-1/4" w full-color flicker which alternates between White House and US Capitol .. **35.00**

Flue cover, US for Ike, red, white, and blue shield with portrait, **$15**.

Hat, Bull Moose, Theodore Roosevelt caricature image, 1912 Progressive Party, dark blue felt, stenciled letters, image of Teddy in tan Rough Rider hat, red bandanna, white eyeglasses and teeth, 13" across base, 12" h, **$2,085**.

Photo courtesy of Hake's Americana & Collectibles.

Jugate

1-1/4", black and white photos of McKinley and Teddy Roosevelt, red, white, and blue accent bow, backpaper reads "National Equipment Co.," Whitehead and Hoag, 1900 .... **20.00**

1-3/8" color portraits on bluish-white, names in black

printed on yellow ribbon panel, red slogan above "Go Forward With Adlai Stevenson" 1952 .... **40.00**

1-3/4", JFK and LBJ, 1961, The New Frontier Inauguration, black and white photos against top panel in white, lower panel in light blue, red text, four gold stars **75.00**

3", Carter and Birch Bayh, 1976, bluetone photos and text, red stars, white background, "Bayh-Centennial" at top, names below **15.00**

3-1/2", Nixon, black and white photos outlined in gold against red, white, and blue background, for 1960 PA campaign **20.00**

3-1/2", Truman and Barkley, celluloid, sepia photos against cream background, names in red, red, white, and blue flag **325.00**

Lapel stud, William McKinley, black and white photo in center, dark blue and bright red stars on cream rim . **20.00**

Letter opener, 9" l, brass, Roosevelt, die-cut and raised FDR image handle, 1930s **45.00**

Mechanical pencil, 5-1/2" l, Ritepoint, red, white, and blue, black and white photos of Stevenson and Sparkman at top, "Win with Adlai Stevenson and John Sparkman" in blue and red **35.00**

Medalet

Grant Memorial, brass hanger with eagle perched on crossed cannons, cannonballs below, white metal, portrait name, reverse with wreath surrounding dates of birth and 1885 death, some fading to silver luster **18.00**

W. H. Harrison, 1-1/8" d, copper, portrait name and date of birth, log cabin and slogan "The People's Choice The Hero Of Tippecanoe" on back, silver finish worn off **35.00**

Lincoln, 1860, 1" d, bright luster, spread-wing eagle with slogan "Success to Republican Principles" on one side, other "Millions for Freedom Not One Cent For Slavery" **75.00**

Paperweight, 2-1/2" x 3", William McKinley, solid brass bust, c1896 .... **60.00**

Portrait button, Truman, 1948, cello, centered by black and white portrait circled by gold leafing, dark blue outer rim, crossed red white and blue flags, cardboard insert on back with bar fastener, 3-1/2" d, **$200**.

Photo courtesy of Hake's Americana & Collectibles.

Photograph

1" x 1-3/8", Garfield, cardboard, emb brass frame with bright luster, 1880 **225.00**

7-1/2" x 9-1/2" oval, 1903, browntone photo, "President Roosevelt and Family," orig owner's name inked on reverse, four raised ornamental designs on frame, slight damage to frame **35.00**

Pin, 7/8", plastic, donkey's head, white, Adlai Stevenson printed in blue panel between ears **15.00**

Plate, 7" d, milk glass, green and brown accent paint, center bear holds open book, left bear smokes pipe, right bear wearing pince-nez glasses, c1904, 50 percent paint loss **70.00**

Postcard, 3-1/2" x 5-1/2", bright red, white, and blue flag design, emb white oval frame at center surrounding browntone image of Teddy Roosevelt, musical notes above "Yankee Doodle" and slogan "Glory to the Union," printed in Germany, undivided back **35.00**

Ribbon

1-5/8" x 3-5/8", black on white silk, Garfield portrait, text for "Garfield Barbeque Oct. 21, 1880, Sacramento, Cal". **125.00**

2-1/2" x 7", William McKinley, 1896, "Our Standard" platform, black and white, cream ground, brass eagle and flags bar pin hanger at top **90.00**

Ribbon, George Washington, c1832, black on white silk, "Washington Association," "First In War, First In Peace, First In The Hearts Of His Countrymen," oval portrait surrounded by wreath, burst of black lines, miniature sword and quill pen immediately above portrait, some fold damage, 12" l, 1-3/4" w, 2" h inscription/portrait area, unlisted in Sullivan-Fischer reference, **$150**.

Photo courtesy of Hake's Americana & Collectibles.

Scarf, 13" x 58", George McGovern, red, white, and blue repeat pattern of "For President George McGovern," also repeat pattern "Truth, Unity, Peace, Honesty, Togetherness" **20.00**

Sheet music, *Sidewalks of New York*, tan, brown, and white, six pgs, "Complete with Campaign Choruses," 6" x 7-1/2" image of Al Smith with facsimile signature on cover **45.00**

Stickpin
7/8" d, narrow brass rim holding ferrotype with large image of beardless Lincoln, 1860, brass stickpin removed, replaced by 1" silver luster straight pin **700.00**
1-1/16" tall emb brass frame, bright luster, cardboard photo of Tilden and Hendricks, 1876, 1-1/4" l stickpin . **400.00**

Tie tack, 1" black luster frame with alternating black and white flicker images of Nixon and Lodge, needle post and brass clutch on back **15.00**

Window decal, 2-3/4" x 3", dark blue decal on pale blue sheet, button like design "Forward with President Truman "No Retreat," direction text on edge **45.00**

PORTRAIT WARE

History: Plates, vases, and other articles with portraits on them were popular in the second half of the 19th century. Although male subjects, such as Napoleon or Louis XVI, were used, the ware usually depicts a beautiful, and often unidentified, woman.

A large number of English and Continental china manufacturers made portrait ware. Because most was hand painted, an artist's signature often is found.

Cabinet plate, 8-1/4" d, classical woman and young girl, dark green border, set into 19" d bronze and gilt metal reticulated surround with six cartouches of cavorting cherubs, German, late 19th/early 20th C **560.00**

Charger, 18-3/4" d, Elizabethan style figures, polychrome enamel and gilt dec, artist sgd "G. Sieves 79," impressed Worcester Royal Porcelain Works factory marks, England, c1879, price for pr **4,460.00**

Dresser box, cov, 4" l, 3 1/4" w, 1 1/2" h, brass heart-shaped box, inlaid lid with hp portrait on ivory of women in formal dress, Florentine designs on box, portrait sgd "Brun" **350.00**

Medallion, 3-1/2" d, Le Pensee, sgd "Wagner," jeweled gilt bronze frame **975.00**

Plaque, German, titled "Odaliske," oval form, woman with long hair, bare breast, back stamped "Heubach Bros.," artist signed, 3-3/8" x 2-5/8" plaque, carved gilt wood frame of scrolled leaves, **$315**.

Photo courtesy of Alderfer Auction Co.

Plaque
3-1/2" x 2-3/4" porcelain, partially nude beauty, sgd "Wagner," ornate 8-1/2" x 9-1/2" gilt shadow box frame **1,035.00**
6" x 4", woman in white gown, pink drape, outstretched hand with flowers, gilt bronze frame, putti and garlands, minor scratches **725.00**

Plate, central portrait medallion with hand painted portrait of young woman with long brown hair, diaphanous white garment, one exposed breast, gilt border surrounded by white cartouches with pink rose sprays, gilt accents, titled "Unschuld," (the Ingenue), signed "Wagner," red German maker's mark, gilding around foot rim, 9-1/2" d, **$750**.

Photo courtesy of Alderfer Auction Co.

Portrait plate, Queen Louise, scarf around neck and head, unmarked, 10" d, **$95**.

Portrait plate, small, **$65**.
Photo courtesy of Dotta Auction Co., Inc.

Plate, Josephine, titled on edge of center design, ornate alternating pink and burgundy panels on border with gold embellishments, **$175**.

Plate

8" d, Napoleon, dated 1901, Knowles, Taylor & Knowles **100.00**
9-1/4" d, Empress Louise, central printed portrait, indistinctly titled and signed "L. Dgt," in gilt surround, paneled rim with scrolls, urns, and griffins, possibly Hutschenreuther, Bavaria, late 19th/early 20th C **115.00**
9-1/2" d, dark haired mother and child, deep olive green border, gold tracery, marked "Royal Vienna" **125.00**
9-1/2" d, Napoleon I, sgd "Wagner," cobalt blue and pale blue band, cornucopia and urn ornamentation, inscribed "Made for Mrs. John Doyle" verso, minor gilt loss **970.00**
9-3/4" d, octagonal shape, hp portrait of Psyche, blue Vienna beehive mark .. **490.00**
10" h, young woman with wreath of flowers in hair, marked "Royal Munich" **115.00**
12" d, young woman, gilt bronze-colored border, mounted in 15" x 17" walnut frame, German **300.00**
Tray, 9-1/2" sq, Napolean I, standing, looking left, left hand behind back exposing dress sword and medals, background of fine furniture and papers, gilt garland border, dark blue-green ground, fitted frame, sgd "Reseh," marked "Vienna, FD, Austria" **1,320.00**
Urn, cov, 15-1/2" h, double handles, "Mme de Montesson," central portrait of French woman wearing white

wig, floral designs, reverse with floral dec, marked "2912, S-2," illegible ring mark, restored lid................ **275.00**

Vase, Austrian, late 19th/early 20th C, slender ovoid body, acanthus molded neck, pair of openwork C-scroll handles, trumpet foot, body with central portrait of Ruth, signed "Graf" lower right, gilt surround, horizontal band of birds, strapwork, and stag in landscape, body with overall pattern of raised gilt quatrefoils offset with turquoise beads, 18-3/4" h, **$2,585**.

Photo courtesy of Skinner, Inc.

Vase

4-3/4" h, bulbous, titled "Ariadne," sgd "Wagner," maroon ground, gilt floral dec, Austrian beehive mark **850.00**
5-3/4" h, gold enamel framed portrait of Ruth, violet luster ground, blue beehive mark with "Germany" in script **435.00**
6-1/2" h, young beauty with basket of flowers in garden setting, artist sgd "Garnet," base imp "Made in France," enamel on bronze, c1900 .... **500.00**
7" h, young beauty in red dress, red roses in hair, finely enameled on bronze, tinted silver foil cartouche against translucent emerald green ground, French, c1900.. **865.00**
7-1/2" h, finely dec portrait of young man, natural colors, enameled bronze, tinted silver foil under sparkling crystal glaze, unmarked, attributed to Limoges, early 20th C **750.00**
8" h, hp portrait of young girl framed in gold enamel, violet luster ground, German, unmarked **375.00**

8-1/2" h, Clementine, sgd "N. Kiesel," Art Nouveau form, green-brown mirrored ground, heavily gilt acanthus leaves and vines, bearing mark of Richard Klemm........ **1,690.00**
12" h, woman holding yellow roses, opalescent ground in shades of green and purple, gilt floral design, Dresden, wear to gilding......... **1,570.00**

POSTERS

History: Posters were a critical and extremely effective method of mass communication, especially in the period before 1920. Enormous quantities were produced, helped in part by the propaganda role posters played in World War I.

Print runs of two million were not unknown. Posters were not meant to be saved; they usually were destroyed once they had served their purpose. The paradox of high production and low survival is one of the fascinating aspects of poster history.

The posters of the late 19th and early 20th centuries represent the pinnacle of American lithography. The advertising posters of firms such as Strobridge or Courier are true classics. Philadelphia was one center for the poster industry.

Europeans pioneered posters with high artistic and aesthetic content, and poster art still plays a key role in Europe. Many major artists of the 20th century designed posters.

Advertising

Clarenbach & Herder Ice Skate Manufacturers, Philadelphia, PA, large scene of ice skaters on Schuylkill River, Waterworks in background, mid-19th C, later archival backing, 17-1/4" x 23". **675.00**
Coffres-Forts Fichet, adv for French bank vaults, c1905, 68" x 23-1/2"............. **2,760.00**
Cycles Clement, Arthur Foache, Bourgerie, Paris, c1900, 53-1/2" x 37"............. **5,750.00**
Ferry's Seeds, full-color image of pretty young lass amid towering hollyhocks, light fold lines, restoration to edges, thin tears, 1925, 21" x 28" **325.00**

Entertainment, bright oranges, blue, copyright Gemini Enterprises, **$250**.

Photo courtesy of Gary Sohmers.

Fire! Fire! Fire!, "Chicago Lost But J. Dearman of Knoxville, Penna. Continues to Roll Up, Bundle Up, and Box Up As Many Goods As Ever!" red and black, some replacement to border, Oct. 15, 1871, 22" x 27" **225.00**

Maggi, Chocolat Menier, Firmin Bouisset, 1895, 54" x 38-1/4" **4,140.00**

Richfield Gasoline, race driver in car, c1930, 39" x 53" **1,100.00**

Royal Portable Typewriter, dark green detailed manual portable typewriter against leafed red and green ground, c1940, 24" x 36" **285.00**

Waterman's Ideal Fountain Pen, paper, Uncle Sam at Treaty of Portsmouth, early 1900s, 41-1/2" x 19-1/2" **950.00**

Art Nouveau

La Emeraude, Alphonse Mucha, 1900, 26" x 11" **9,775.00**

La Topaze, Alphonse Mucha, 1900, 26" x 11" **9,775.00**

Leslie Carter, Alphonse Mucha, Strobridge, Cincinnati, 1908, 83" x 31-1/2" **9,775.00**

Le Livre de Magda, Paul Berthon, Chaix, Paris, 1898, 25-1/4" x 19" **2,300.00**

Les Eglantines, Paul Berthon, Chaix, Paris, 1900, 19-1/2" x 25-1/2" **815.00**

Princezna Hyacintha, Alphonse Mucha, V. Neubert, Prague, 1911, 50-1/4" x 35-3/4" **18,400.00**

Vi Slet Vsesokolsky & Lide Cesky! Alphonse Mucha, V. Neubert, Smichov, 1912, 66" x 32" **14,950.00**

Exhibition

Bals Des Arts, Crane-Howard, Joseph W. Jicha, 1928, 37" x 23" **2,990.00**

Jazz at the Institute-5th Anniversary, Romare Bearden, offset color litho, sgd in white ink, published by Founders Society Detroit Institute of the Arts, Detroit, 1982, 29-/2" x 15-7/8" **410.00**

Kunst Im Handwerk, Vereinigte Druckereln und Kunstanstalten, Munich, Bruno Paul, 1901, 34-3/4" x 23-1/2" **5,635.00**

Midas, Whatsoever He Touches Might Be Gold, Continental Litho, Cleveland, Joseph W. Jicha, 1927, 37-1/2" x 25" **2,530.00**

Magazine

The Chap Book, Stone & Kimball, Chicago, Claude Fayette Bragdon, c1895, 21" x 13-1/2" **4,140.00**

The Idler, A. E. Forrest, 1898, J. M. Dent & Co, London, 29-3/4" x 20" **690.00**

Movie, Walt Disney's Mickey Mouse, "The Mad Doctor," Joseph M. Schenk, United Artists Picture, certificate of authenticity stating it is one of a kind, **$800**.

Entertainment, The Golddiggers, Stars of the Dean Martin Show, Boston, real photo of Golddiggers, blue and white ground, **$75**

Photo courtesy of Gary Sohmers.

Entertainment, Grateful Dead, April 1988, Centrum, Worcester, Massachusetts, hot pink and blue, **$50**.

Photo courtesy of Gary Sohmers.

Movie and theatrical

A Good Man Is Hard To Find, Union Label, New York, Ben Shahn, 1948, 46" x 30-1/4", expertly repaired tears in margins.................... **5,750.00**

Anatomy of a Murder, Columbia, Saul Bass design, 1959, 27" x 41"............ **125.00**

A Trip To Chinatown, Dangerfield Printing Co., London, Beggarstaff Brothers, James Pryde and William Nicholson, 1894, 117" x 89-1/2" **43,700.00**

Atlantic City, Republic, Constance Moore, Jerry Colonna in drag, by James Montgomery Flagg, 1941, 14" x 36" **250.00**

Bad Boy, James Dunn and Louise Fazenda, Fox, 1934, 27" x 41" **150.00**

Bringing Up Father, McManus, "Jiggs, Maggie, Dinty Moore-George McManus's cartoon comedy with music," early newspaper cartoon characters against New York skyline, c1915, 41" x 81" **425.00**

Chaussures Caoutchouc, Marque "Au Coq," Gus Bofa (Gustav Blanchot), c1907, 53-1/4" x 37-1/4" **3,220.00**

Dr. No, United Artist, Sean Connery, Ursula Andress, 1962, 27" x 41" **325.00**

Goodbye Mr. Chips, Robert Donat and Greer Garson, MGM, 1939, 27" x 41" . **450.00**

Mule Train, Columbia Pictures, Gene Autry, Champion, full-color portraits, 1950, 27" x 41" **150.00**

No No Nanette, Tony Gibbons, Theatre Mogador, Paris, European production of American musical, c1925, 15" x 22" **375.00**

Smoldering Fires, Pauline Frederick and Laura La Plante, Universal, 1925, 14" x 22" **125.00**

Political and patriotic

America Lets Us Worship As We Wish—Attend The Church Of Your Choice, for American Legion sponsored "Americanism Appreciation Month," full-color image of praying Uncle Sam, family at dinner table behind him, c1945, 20" x 26" **275.00**

Confidence, large color portrait of Roosevelt over yacht at sea, "Election Day was our salvation/Franklin Roosevelt is the man/Our ship will reach her destination/Under his command...Bring this depression to an end...," c1933, 18" x 25" **250.00**

Extra Post. Democratic Salt River Excursion, Incidents of the Annual Voyage to the Old Stamping Ground, Philadelphia, Tuesday, Oct.

10, 1871, comic details of Philadelphia political events, text and 9 vignettes, published by Philadelphia Post, later archival backing, 17-3/4" x 14-1/2" **200.00**

Give Us The Faith And Courage of Our Forefathers, dark and somber image of Uncle Sam, Howard Chandler Christy, Recruiting Publicity Bureau, US Army, 1950, 35-1/4" x 24-3/4" **1,265.00**

Kennedy for President, Leadership for the 60s, red, white, and blue, photo in center, 1960, 42" x 27", some restoration................ **2,530.00**

United Nations Day, blue and white U.N. banner waves over airbrushed stylized brown and yellow globe, minor edge crumple, 1947, 22" x 23" **250.00**

"I Want You for US Army," James Montgomery Flagg, American, 1877-1960, colored lithograph of Uncle Sam, c1917, 40" x 29-7/8", **$4,370**.
Photo courtesy of Pook & Pook.

Transportation

Air France—North Africa, Villemot, stylized imagery of mosques and minarets, lavenders, yellow, and blues against sky blue background, plane and Pegasus logo, c1950, 24" x 39" **225.00**

A Subway Poster Pulls, Edward McKnight Kauffer, 1947, 45" x 30".............................. **7,475.00**

Europe, The *SS United States*, *SS America*, United States Lines, Lester Beall, 30" x 22" **2,990.00**

Red Star Line, Antwerpen-Amerika, Henri Cassiers, Couleurs Berger & Wirth, Leipzig, 1899, 43-1/2" x 59-1/4" **5,060.00**

Royal Mail Atlantis, Padden, tourists in Royal mail motor launch approaching harbor village, mountains in background, c1923, 25" x 38" **675.00**

SS France, Bob Peak, launching of French ocean liner, champagne and confection in front of huge, night-lit bow of ship, 1961, 30" x 46" ... **450.00**

Travel

Boston—New Haven Railroad, Nason, full color, stylized montage of Historic Boston by day and night, faint folio folds, c1938, 28" x 42" **275.00**

Come to Ulster, Norman Wilkinson, sailboats and fishermen in front of lighthouse, full color, c1935, 50" x 40" **450.00**

Hawaii—United Air Lines, Feher, stylized wahini, island behind her, full color, c1948, 25" x 40" **650.00**

Paris, Paul Colin, doves floating above stylized Eiffel tower and Arc de Triumph, 1946, 24" x 39".............................. **600.00**

World War I

Call to Duty—Join the Army for Home and Country, Cammilli, recruiting image of Army bugler in front of unfurled banner, 1917, 30" x 40" **325.00**

Follow the Flag—Enlist in the Navy, James Daugherty, sailor plants flag on shore, 1917, 27" x 41".......................... **450.00**

Gee!! I Wish I Were A Man I'd Join The Navy, Howard Chandler Christy, 1918, 41-1/4" x 27"............ **1,955.00**

Give it Your Best, US Government Printing Office, Charles Coiner, red, white, and blue flag above slogan, 1942, 20" x 28" **575.00**

Give Us The Faith And Courage of Our Forefathers, dark and somber image of Uncle Sam, Howard Chandler Christy, Recruiting Publicity Bureau, US Army, 1950, 35-1/4" x 24-3/4" **1,265.00**

I Want You For The Navy,
Howard Chandler Christy,
Forbes, Boston, 1917, 41" x
26" **1,265.00**
Keep Him Free, War Savings
Stamps, bald eagle on edge
of nest, Charles Livingston
Bull, Ketterlinus, Philadelphia,
1918, 30" x 20" **575.00**
Put Strength in the Final Blow,
Buy War Bonds, Frank
Brangwyn, Avenue Press,
London, 1916, 60-1/2" x 40"
.... **815.00**
Save the Products of the Land,
Eat More Fish, Charles
Livingston Bull, Heywood
Strasser & Voit, NY, c1918, 30"
x 20-1/4" **750.00**
The Spirit of America, nurse
wrapped in American flag
calling on people to join Red
Cross, Howard Chandler
Christy, Forbes, Boston, 1919,
30" x 20" **1,150.00**
Treat 'Em Rough—Jon The
Tanks, A. Hutaf, window card,
electric blue-black cat leaping
over tanks in fiery battle, white
border, c1917, 14" x 22"
.... **900.00**
**Will You Supply Eyes For The
Navy?** Gordon Grant, "Navy
Ships Need Binoculars and
Spy-Glasses...Tag Each
Article with Your Name and
Address, Mail to Hon. Franklin
D. Roosevelt, Asst. Sec'y of
Navy,..." image of Naval
captain ready with blindfold
on stormy deck, gun crew at
ready behind him, 1918, 21" x
29" **625.00**

PRATT WARE

History: The earliest Pratt
earthenware was made in the late
18th century by William Pratt, Lane
Delph, Staffordshire, England.
From 1810 to 1818, Felix and
Robert Pratt, William's sons, ran
their own firm, F. & R. Pratt, in
Fenton in the Staffordshire district.
Potters in Yorkshire, Liverpool,
Sunderland, Tyneside, and
Scotland copied the products.

The wares consisted of relief-
molded jugs, commercial pots and
tablewares with transfer decoration,
commemorative pieces, and
figures and figural groups of both
people and animals.

Marks: Much of the early ware is
unmarked. The mid-19th century
wares bear several different marks
in conjunction with the name Pratt,
including "& Co."

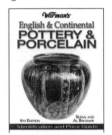

For more information, see *Warman's
English & Continental Pottery &
Porcelain*, 4th edition.

Bank, 5" h, figural, underglaze
enamel dec center chimney
house, male and female figure
to either side, Yorkshire, 19th
C, damage to chimney and
backside of roof **275.00**
Cow creamer, 7" l, sponge dec,
milkmaid dressed in yellow,
some edge damage, rebuilt
ear, lid missing **350.00**
Cradle, pearlware
4" l, underglaze polychrome
enamels, one molded with
baby sleeping, c1800, repairs
to hood and side of body
.... **100.00**
5-1/4" l, cradle, underglaze
polychrome enamel, c1800,
restored chip **100.00**
7-3/4" l, underglaze
polychrome enamels, oval
form molded as hooded
cradle with sleeping child,
c1800, restored to lower body
and under base, chip and
hairline to hood **600.00**
Cup plate, 3-1/8" d, Dalmatian,
white, black spots **95.00**
Figure
9-3/4" h lady with barrel,
pitcher at her feet, chips,
restorations **300.00**
10" h, gentleman feeding
black bird, sitting on tree
stump, chips, restorations
.... **310.00**
Flask, 4-1/8" l, pearlware, shell-
form, underglaze polychrome
enamels, c1800, slight glaze
blemishes **765.00**
Jar, cov, chromolithograph lid
3-1/4" l, rect, milkmaid,
damage, undersized lid
.... **150.00**

4" d, round, Dr. Johnson, three
men in parlor, flakes ... **150.00**
4" d, round, mother and
children playing hide and
seek, stains, flakes **95.00**
4-1/8" d, round, Albert
Memorial, mis-matched base,
stains, flakes **100.00**
4-1/8" d, round, man reading
the Times, stains, flakes
.... **115.00**
4-1/4" d, round, Dangerous,
ice skating man falling, stains,
flakes **125.00**
4-1/4" d, round, shrimpers
filling their nets, flakes and
stains **165.00**

Dish, multicolored border with white
flowers, yellow lilies, blue cornflowers,
and green leaves, center with milkmaid
and cow, 3-7/8" d, **$45**.

Jug, 8" h, molded leaves at neck
and base, raised and
polychrome painted hunting
scene on colored ground,
c1800 .... **750.00**
Mug, 4" h, colorful tavern scene
transfer **95.00**
Pitcher
5-5/8" h, molded figures on
sides, leaves at rim and base,
one side with Toby Philpots,
other with classical warrior
green, gold, dark brown, and
cobalt blue, flakes on base
and handle, short hairline on
spout **675.00**
12" h, medium blue transfer
scene on each side of "Swiss
Cottage," by J. & W. Pratt,
molded handle with man's
face at end, stains, hairline
.... **90.00**
Plaque, 6-1/4" x 7-1/4", Louis XVI
portrait, oval form, beaded
border, polychrome enamels,
c1793, rim nicks, glaze wear
.... **900.00**
Plate, 9" d, Haddon Hall,
classical figure border **120.00**

Pot lid, chromolithograph
   4" d, dogs overturning kettle of fish, flakes.............. **100.00**
   4-1/8" d, village wedding, flakes **100.00**
   6-1/2" d, View of Windsor Castle......................... **170.00**
Tea caddy, 6-1/4" h, rect, raised figural panels front and back, fluted and yellow trimmed lid, blue, yellow, orange, and green dec **350.00**

PRINTS

History: Prints serve many purposes. They can be a reproduction of an artist's paintings, drawings, or designs, but often are an original art form. Finally, prints can be developed for mass appeal rather than primarily for aesthetic fulfillment. Much of the production of Currier & Ives fits this latter category. Currier & Ives concentrated on genre, urban, patriotic, and nostalgic scenes.

Additional Listings: See Nutting, Wallace.

Will Barnet, (American, b 1911,) *Persephone,* 1982, edition of 250, published by Associated American Artists, printed by Fine Creations, Inc., New York, sgd and dated "© Will Barnet 1982" in pencil lower right, numbered "71/250" in pencil lower center, titled in pencil lower left, color screenprint on Arches paper, 34" x 16-1/2", unframed, wide margins, handling marks, creases, **$470.**

Photo courtesy of Skinner, Inc.

Reproduction Alert: The reproduction of Maxfield Parrish prints is a continuing process. New reproductions look new, i.e., their surfaces are shiny and the paper crisp and often pure white. The color on older prints develops a mellowing patina. The paper often develops a light brown to dark brown tone, especially if it is acid based or was placed against wooden boards in the back of a frame.

Size is one of the keys to spotting later reproductions. Learn the correct size for the earliest forms. Be alert to earlier examples that have been trimmed to fit into a frame. Check the dimensions before buying any print.

Carefully examine the edges within the print. Any fuzziness indicates a later copy. Also look at the print through a magnifying glass. If the colors separate into dots, this indicates a later version.

Apply the same principles described above for authenticating all prints, especially those attributed to Currier & Ives. Remember, many prints were copied soon after their period introduction. As a result, reproductions can have many of the same aging characteristics as period prints.

Arms, John Taylor, *Rodez/The Tower of Notre Dame*, etching on paper, edition of 120 plus six trial proofs, sgd and dated "John Taylor Arms-1927" in pencil lower right, inscribed "Arms 1926" and "Rodez 1926" in the plate, 11-7/8" x 4-7/8", framed **230.00**
Atkins & Nightingale, publisher, J. Cartwright, engraver, *Georgetown and Federal City, or City of Washington,* 1801, etching with aquatint and hand coloring on paper, 16" x 23-1/4", framed, few minor scattered stains, light toning **17,625.00**
Barlach, Ernest, Fluchende Alt, woodcut, sgd in pencil lower right, Ferdinand Roten Gallery, Baltimore, on back, 4" x 3" **920.00**

Barnet, Will, *Silent Seasons-Summer,* color litho, sgd, titled, and numbered 113/200 in pencil lower margin, 1975, 29" x 22-1/2"............... **920.00**
Bearden, Romare, *Girl in the Garden,* color litho, sgd and numbered 29/150 in pencil, lower margin, 1979, 22-1/8" x 16-1/8" **5,750.00**
Benson, Frank Weston, *Geese Alighting,* drypoint on paper, 1916, second of two published states, sgd "Frank W. Benson" in pencil lower left, dated in the plate lower left, numbered "44" in pencil lower right, 9-3/4" x 8" plate size, framed............ **1,035.00**
Benton, Thomas Hart, lithograph, sgd in pencil lower right, published by Associated American Artists, New York, edition of 250
   Goin' Home, 1937, 9-1/2" x 12" **1,840.00**
   Missouri Farmyard, 1936, 10" x 16"......................... **2,070.00**
   Old Man Reading, 1941, 10" x 12-1/8" **2,185.00**
   Planting, 1939, 10" x 12-1/2" **2,760.00**
Boileu, Philip, child, c1914, "The Associated Sunday Magazines" cover, Feb. 1, 1914, sgd lower right, 16" x 20" frame, grade 4.0..... **45.00**
Boydell, John, publisher, image by Benjamin West, engraved by John Hall, *William Penn's Treaty with the Indians, When He Founded the Province of Pennsylvania in North America in 1681*, hand colored engraving, c1775, 18-1/2" x 23-1/2", minor repairs to border...... **1,450.00**
Brundel, Carl Alexander, *Return from the Fields*, color woodcut on cream wove paper, sgd and inscribed "orig Holzchnitt Hand-" in pencil, c1930, 12-1/2" x 15-3/4" **460.00**
Calder, Alexander, color litho
   Composition with Mobile Forms, sgd in ink lower right, numbered 93/100 in pencil lower right, 19-3/4" x 25-1/4", very pale time stain . **1,840.00**
   Composition with Spirals, sgd in pencil lower right, 26" x 39" **1,840.00**

Alexander Calder (American, 1898-1976). *Blue Moon*, c1970, edition of 100, published by Associated American Artists, signed "Calder" in pencil lower right, numbered "66/100" in pencil lower left, identified on AAA label affixed to backing, color lithograph on paper, image/sheet size 23" x 30-1/2", framed, deckled edges, cockling, not examined out of frame, **$1,765**.

Photo courtesy of Skinner, Inc.

Cassatt, Mary, color drypoint
Margot Wearing a Bonnet, c1902, 9" x 6" **1,040.00**
Sara Smiling, c1904, 7-1/4" x 5" **1,725.00**

Chagall, Marc
De mauvais Sujets, color aquatint on Japon nacre, sgd and numbered 9/9 in pencil, printed by Lacourière and Frélaut, Paris, published by Les Bibliophiles de l'Union, Française, Paris, 1958, 13-5/8" x 10-1/2" **5,060.00**
L'Avare qui a perdu son Trésor, aquatint and etching, sgd and numbered 49 in pencil, printed by Maurice Potin, Paris, published by Tériade, Paris, 1927-30, 11-3/4" x 9-5/8" **1,265.00**
L'Âne et le Chien, aquatint and etching, sgd and numbered 88/100 in pencil, printed by Maurice Potin, Paris, published by Tériade, Paris, 1927-30, 11-3/4" x 9-1/4" **1,725.00**

Currier, Nathaniel, publisher, after Arthur Fitzwilliam Tait, *The Cares of a Family 1856*, lithograph with hand coloring heightened by gum Arabic on paper, identified in inscription in the matrix, Conningham, 814, 22" x 28", matted, unframed **2,990.00**

Currier, Nathaniel, publisher, Frances Flora Palmer, lithographer, lithograph with hand coloring on paper, identified in inscription in matrix

American Farm Series No. One, 1853, Conningham 134, 21-3/8" x 28-1/4", framed **2,185.00**
American Forest Scene, Maple Sugaring, 1856, Conningham 157, 24-7/8" x 32-5/8", label from Old Print Shop, NY on reverse, framed **19,550.00**
American Winter Scene, Evening, 1854, Conningham 207, 20-3/4" x 27", unframed **8,625.00**
The American Clipper Ship, Witch of the Wave, undated, Conningham 115, 13" x 16-1/2", framed, overall toning, scattered staining, fox marks, creases throughout **865.00**

Currier and Ives, publishers
A Scene on the Susquehanna, C#5415, farm on one side of river, flock of sheep, damage to modern gilt frame, repaired tears, 21-1/4" w, 18-1/4" h **175.00**
Fruit and Flowers No. 2, c1848, "Lith & Pub by N. Currier" lower left, "152 Nassau St. Cor. Of Spruce, NY" lower right, 8-1/2" x 12-1/2" print framed in 10" x 14" orig frame, grade 3.5 .... **165.00**
Meeting of the Waters, 14" x 10" orig frame, orig wooden backing, grade 3.0 ..... **75.00**
Scenery of the Upper Mississippi, An Indian Village, C#5422, trimmed, stained, matted, framed, 14" w, 10-1/4" h **300.00**

Eda Soest Doench, An Afternoon Caller, Gutmann & Gutmann Colonial print, pencil signed "Gutmann" lower right, titled lower left, marked "Gutmann & Gutmann" lower left on image, 14" x 11" period frame, c1916, **$75**.

Photo courtesy of Michael Ivankovich Auction Co., Inc.

Ensor, James, *La Cathédrale*, etching on imitation Japan paper, sgd and dated in pencil lower right, 1886, 9-1/2" x 7" **7,475.00**

Fox, R. Atkinson
A Perfect Melody, c1920-25, pseudonym sgd "DeForest" lower right, title lower center, 7" x 9" orig frame, grade 4.0 .... **50.00**
Clipper Ship, c1920-25, unsigned, 20" x 12" period frame, grade 2.75 .... **40.00**
Sunset Dreams, c1920-25, sgd "R. Atkinson Fox" lower right, "Copyright Borin Mfg Co., Chicago" lower left, 18" x 10" orig frame, grade 3.75 .... **370.00**
The Old Mill, c1920-25, unsigned, 9" x 12" frame, grade 4.0 .... **60.00**

Grimball, Meta M., *The Loving Cup*, c1909, sgd lower right, titled lower center, 10" x 8" period frame, grade 3.0, unusual six-sided double over mat **165.00**

Hundertwasser, Friedensreich, *Pacific Steamer*, color woodcut on paper, 1986, dated, numbered and inscribed "989/999 ©...868A Auckland 3 March 1986" in ink lower left, sgd with various chops lower right, 20-1/2" x 15-3/4" image size, framed, deckled edges **2,875.00**

Hyde, Helen, *Moon Bridge at Kameido*, color woodcut on paper, sgd "Helen Hyde" in pencil lower right, monogram and clover seals lower left, numbered "67" in pencil lower left, inscribed "Copyright, 1914, by Helen Hyde" in the block lower left, 13-1/4" x 8-7/8", framed **460.00**

Icart, Louis, *Sleeping Beauty*, color etching and aquatint, sgd in pencil, artist's blindstamp, 1927, 14-3/4" x 18-1/2" **1,495.00**

Kellogg & Co., hand-colored lithograph, *Napoleon*, four stages of life, *Subaltern to Exile*, yellow and orange painted frame, 15" w, 13" h, damage **150.00**

Kent, Rockwell
Diver, wood engraving on paper, 1931, edition of 150, sgd "Rockwell Kent" in pencil lower right, 7-3/4" x 5-1/4" image size, framed, 3/8" margins or more **1,120.00**

Resting, lithograph on paper, 1929, edition of 100, sgd "Rockwell Kent" in pencil lower right, 9-5/8" x 5-7/8" image size, framed, 3/8" margins or more **1,175.00**

Knight, Dame Laura Knight, *Gilding the Lily*, etching and aquatint on paper, edition of 35, sgd "Laura Knight" in pencil lower right, 11-1/2" x 7-1/2" plate size, framed, margins over 1".......... **750.00**

Lindenmuth, Tod, *Low Tide*, color woodcut on paper, sgd "Tod Lindenmuth" in pencil lower right, titled in pencil lower left, 15" x 14" image size, framed............. **1,600.00**

Lindner, Richard, *Man's Best Friend*, color lithograph on paper, c1970, edition of 250, sgd "R. Lindner" in pencil lower right, numbered "31/250" in pencil lower left on Arches cream paper with watermark, 27-3/4" x 21-1/2" sheet size, unmatted, unframed, minor handling marks, nicks, creases. **530.00**

Bertha Lum, Kites, color woodblock print, copyright 1918, pencil signed and dated, No. 87, matted and framed, 8" x 14-1/4", **$950**.

Photo courtesy of David Rago Auctions, Inc.

Marin, John, *La Cathedral de Meaux*, 1907, etching on Arches wove paper with watermark, sgd "...de J. Marin" in pencil lower center, sgd and dated within the plate, 8-1/2" x 6-1/8" plate size, matted, deckled edges on two sides............... **350.00**

Marsh, Reginald
Tattoo-Shave-Haircut, etching and drypoint, tenth state, 1932, 9-7/8" x 9-5/8". **9,775.00**
Three Girls on a Chicken, engraving, sgd in pencil lower right, second state of edition of 20, 1941, 8" x 9-3/4" **2,185.00**

Newell, J. P., lithographer and publisher, *Newport, R.I.*, identified in inscription in matrix, lithograph with hand-coloring on paper, framed, tear to margin upper right, toning, stains, foxing............. **1,175.00**

Maxfield Parrish, The Knave, 9" x 12" older frame, newer backing paper, c1925, **$100**.

Photo courtesy of Michael Ivankovich Auction Co., Inc.

Parrish, Maxfield
Chancellor and the King, c1925, orig 9" x 12" frame, grade 4.0 .... **65.00**
Dinky Bird, c1915, 5" x 7" frame, grade 4.0........... **55.00**
Hilltop, c1927, 6-1/4" x 10", framed in period 9" x 12" blue and gold frame, sgd lower left, titled lower center, "House of Art" lower right, grade 3.75 .... **195.00**
Lady Violetta in the Royal Kitchen, c1925, 9" x 12" orig frame, grade 4.0........... **65.00**
Prince Codadad, c1906, 9" x 11" print, orig 11" x 14" mat, orig blue and gold frame, "Copr P. F. Collier & Son" lower left, grade 4.0...... **70.00**
Rose Bower, c1920-25, unsigned, 10" x 15" period blue and gold frame, orig paper label preserved on back, grade 4.0............ **65.00**
Rubaiyat, c1917, 28-1/2" x 7" print in 33" x 11" orig brown and gold frame, "copyright 1917 C. A. Crane Cleveland" lower right, "Reinthal & Newman, New York" imp lower left, grade 4.0.... **250.00**

The Village Brook, c1940, sgd lower right, 16" x 20" period frame, grade 3.5......... **165.00**
Thy Templed Hills, c1930, 5" x 7" period frame, "Original painting by Maxfield Parrish, of Cornish, NY, courtesy of Brown and Bigelow" lower center, grade 4.0 .... **65.00**
Vegetables for the Meal, c1925, 9" x 4", grade 4.0 .... **65.00**

Picasso, Pablo
Deux Femmes Nues, etching on paper, 1930, edition of 125, sgd and numbered "34/125 Picasso..." in ink beneath image, label from Goodspeed's Book Shop, Boston, on reverse, 12-1/4" x 8-7/8" plate size, framed, scattered pale foxing **5,875.00**
La Guitare Sur la Table, etching with drypoint on paper, 1922, reprinted 1961, total edition of 70, stamped signature "Picasso" lower right, numbered "29/50" in pencil lower left, 3-1/8" x 4-3/4" plate size, framed **1,100.00**

Pressler, Gene, *Cinderella*, c1920-25, sgd lower right, titled, 8" x 11" orig metal frame, grade 4.0........... **45.00**

Remington, Frederick, *Indians in Canoe*, c1900, sgd lower left, 16" x 12" period frame, grade 2.75, damaged mat **35.00**

Ripley, Aiden Lassell, *Grouse on Pine Bough,* drypoint on paper, c1941, sgd "A Lassell Ripley" in pencil lower right, titled in pencil lower left, 8-3/4" x 11-7/8" plate size, framed, unobtrusive mat toning **1,100.00**

Roth, Ernest David, *Florentine Roofs*, Florentine, etching on laid paper with "G" watermark, sgd and dated "Ernest D. Roth 1912" in pencil lower center, titled dated and inscribed "Trial Proof" in pencil lower left, 10-1/2" x 10-3/8", matted, soiling, breaks to hinges......... **315.00**

Schille, H., Publisher, American, 19th C, *Panorama of the Catskills*, c1870, large folio, lithograph printed in colors with panorama and numerous vignettes, 21" x 27" **825.00**

Sloan, John

McSorley's Backroom, etching and drypoint, sgd, titled and inscribed "100 of 100," third state, 1916, 5-1/4" x 7" **2,530.00**

Patience, sgd, titled, inscribed "100 proofs" in pencil, sgd by printer Ernest Roth, in pencil lower left, fourth state, 1925, 5" x 4" **320.00**

Soyer, Raphael, *Bust of a Girl,*
lithograph in black, red and blue on paper, edition of 300, sgd "Raphael Soyer" in pencil lower right, numbered "86/300" in pencil lower left, image size 18-3/8" x 13-5/8", framed, over 1" margins **210.00**

Spence, R. S., publisher, printed
by William Robertson, NY, *American Hunting Scene,* four gentlemen with guns, dogs, and boat hunting waterfowl, hand colored lithograph, 22" x 28", framed, some foxing and waterstains at borders... **330.00**

J. Symington, chromolithograph, pencil signed "J. Symington" lower right beneath image, and "J. Symington" lower right within image, 15" x 20" original frame, original backing paper, c1900, **$45**.

Photo courtesy of Michael Ivankovich Auction Co., Inc.

Prang & Mayer, publishers, J.
F.A. Cole, delineator and lithographer, *New Bedford, Massachusetts,* identified in inscriptions in the matrix, hand coloring, 16" x 32" image size, framed, repaired tears and punctures, scattered fox marks, staining, light toning **865.00**

Toulouse-Lautrec, Henri
Carnival, color lithograph, fourth state, 1894, 9-7/8" x 6-1/2" **3,450.00**

Étude de femme, lithograph, third state, published by Henry Floury, Paris, monogram in stone lower left, 1893, 10-1/2" x 8"..... **1,265.00**

Ward, Lynd, *Giant,* wood
engraving on tissue-thin paper, sgd and dated in pencil, 1955, 15-7/8" x 6" **920.00**

Warhol, Andy, *Jimmy Carter III,*
screenprint, sgd and numbered 14/100 in pencil, printed by Rupert Jasen Smith, NY, published by the Democratic National Committee, Washington, DC, 1977, 28-1/4" x 20-1/2" **1,725.00**

Weidenaar, Reynold, *Bridge
Builders, Mackinac Straits,* mezzotint, trial proof, sgd and titled in pencil,1956, 12-7/8" x 6-7/8" **2,300.00**

Hutton Webster, Junior (American, 1910-1954), *Cactus Flowers,* signed "Hutton Webster, Jr." in ink lower center, color monotype on paper, image size 9-1/4" x 8-3/8", framed, margins 1/2" or more, soiling and foxing, rubs to sheet below image lower right, **$235**.

Photo courtesy of Skinner, Inc.

Whistler, James A. M.
Annie, Seated, etching and drypoint on antique cream laid paper, second state, 1858, 5-1/8" x 3-3/4" **2,070.00**

Fumette, etching on thin laid paper, fourth state, 1859, 6-3/8" x 4-1/4" **1,380.00**

Le Veille aux Loques, etching and drypoint, third state, 1858, 8-1/8" x 5-7/8" **1,495.00**

Wood, Grant, lithograph,
published by Associated American Artists, NY *In The Spring,* sgd in pencil lower right, 1939, 9" x 12" **4,600.00**

Seed Time and Harvest, sgd and dated in pencil, edition of 250, 1937, 7-3/8" x 12-1/8" **4,830.00**

Zorn, Anders, etching
The New Maid, sgd in pencil, sixth state, 1909, 11-3/4" x 8" **1,265.00**

Two Butlers, sgd in pencil lower right, 1910, 6-1/4" x 4" **1,035.00**

PRINTS, JAPANESE

History: Buying Japanese woodblock prints requires attention to detail and abundant knowledge of the subject. The quality of the impression (good, moderate, or weak), the color, and condition are critical. Various states and strikes of the same print cause prices to fluctuate. Knowing the proper publisher's and censor's seals is helpful in identifying an original print.

Most prints were copied and issued in popular versions. These represent the vast majority of the prints found in the marketplace today. These popular versions should be viewed solely as decorative since they have little monetary value.

A novice buyer should seek expert advice before buying. Talk with a specialized dealer, museum curator, or auction division head.

The following terms are used to describe sizes: chuban, 7-1/2 x 10 inches; hosoban, 6 x 12 inches; and oban, 10 x 15 inches. Tat-e is a vertical print; yoko-e a horizontal one.

Note: The listings below include the large amount of detail necessary to determine value. Condition and impression are good unless indicated otherwise.

Chikanobu, framed triptych of women by lake, c1890, good impression, somewhat faded **125.00**

Chinese, unidentified artist Landscape, Blue and Green style, numerous seals, 18th/19th C, 35" x 19" **1,880.00**

Scroll, ink and colors on silk, scene of two monkeys trying to gather honey, Chien Lung cyclical date but probably 19th C, 32" x 19" **1,530.00**

Sino Japanese War Poster, fair to good impression, color, and condition, some tears, creases, soiling, losses, framed **120.00**

Eiza, three prints, two kakemono-e of courtesans and one of samurai with a falcon, good impressions, color, stains, toning, fading and creases, framed .. **360.00**

Goyo, *Portrait of a Beauty*, Daioban, excellent impression, toned and matted to within image...................... **1,100.00**

Harunobu, pillar print of woman carrying bucket, framed, very good impression, horizontal creases and tears **345.00**

Hasui

A Farmer with Wagon in View of Tall Pines and Mt. Fuji, fine color, impression, and condition **650.00**

Mt. Fuji from Miho-No-Matsubara, excellent impression, stained and creased...................... **590.00**

Nezu Shrine in Snow, excellent impression, color, and condition, framed **775.00**

Rainy Season at Ryoshimachi, Shinagawa, excellent impression, color, and condition, framed........ **775.00**

Hiroaki Takahashi, *Village Below Mt. Fuji at Twilight*, c1930, fine impression, color, and condition, framed **300.00**

Hiroshige, harbor scene, **$195**.

Hiroshige, *An Island, Lake and Mountains in Rain*, from *Eight Views of Omi*, c1850, very good impression, color, and condition, some stains, not examined out of frame **360.00**

Hiroshige II, *Five Views of Edo*, c1862, set of five prints, very good impressions, color, and condition, one trimmed to image and laid down, others with soiling, stains, and creases **600.00**

Hiroshige III, *The Port of Yokohama with a Locomotive on a Stone Bridge and Western Steamships in the Harbor*, c1870, good impression and color, fading, toning, creases, and staining, framed **825.00**

Hokusai, *Kajikazawa in Kai Province*, from *Thirty-six Views of Mt. Fuji*, 20th C, good impression, color, and condition, some staining, soiling, and creases ... **200.00**

Japan, unidentified artist, scroll, figure of woman with lines of poetry, 18th C, very long **3,525.00**

Jaquolet, Paul, *An Elegant Chinese Lady Holding a Veil*, matted to image, very good impression, color, and condition, not examined out of frame **470.00**

Junichiro Sekino, portrait of actor Kichiemon, "il ne etat," printed signature and seal lower right within the image, pencil sgd, 13/50 in lower margin, 22" x 18"......... **920.00**

Kasamatsu Shiro, *Pagoda in the Rain on a Spring Evening*, fine impression, color, and condition, upper right corner crease...................... **200.00**

Kunisada, *Ladies Gathering in Springtime for Music and Poetry*, triptych, good impression, color, and condition, with toning, fading, and stains, framed...... **150.00**

Kunisada II, scene from a legend, good impression, color, and condition, not examined out of frame, framed **215.00**

Kuniyoshi

A Courtesan in Elegant Kimono Holding a Pipe, excellent impression and color with visible wood grain, slight staining and holes **190.00**

Ladies Feeding Carp from a Pleasure Boat, triptych, c1840, excellent impression, color, and condition, with some fading of the blue **950.00**

Kiyoshi Saito, color woodcut, *Daitoku-Ji, Kyoto*, signed lower right, dated 1959, numbered 14/100, sheet size 23-1/2" x 18", **$900**.

Photo courtesy of Sloans & Kenyon Auctions.

Okiie Hashimoto, *Village in the Evening*, sgd in pencil in margin, dated, Hashi seal, good impression, framed, 17" x 21-1/2" **250.00**

Sekino, *Bridge in Snow*, sgd in image, seal, good impression, 18" x 12-1/2"................ **200.00**

Shunga, *Couples Engaged in Lovemaking*, two double-page illustrations from album, mid-19th C, fine impressions, color, and condition, centerfolds and slight creases, framed **420.00**

Toyokuni, perspective print of busy shopping area and temple grounds, 1790s, framed, good impression, faded **260.00**

Toyokuni II, *Two Courtesans*, c1800, good impression, faded, trimmed, small hole, stains, and creases **150.00**

Toyokuni III, Pentaptcyh of people in boat feeding goldfish, iris garden, framed, very good impression, missing leaf, somewhat faded **230.00**

Utagawa Kuniyoshi, color woodcut triptych, *Ship Battle*, signed and sealed, c1837, *oban tate-e*, **$1,300**.

Photo courtesy of Sloans & Kenyon Auctions.

Utamaro, *Woman Washing Her Hair*, good impression, stained, rubbed, and faded, framed **725.00**

Utamaro II, three women in an interior, c1811, good impression, faded, soiled **175.00**

Yoshida Hiroshi, *Daibutsu Temple Gate,* signed in pencil, with Jizuri seal, excellent impression and color **490.00**

PUZZLES

History: The jigsaw puzzle originated in the mid-18th century in Europe. John Spilsbury, a London mapmaker, was selling dissected-map jigsaw puzzles by the early 1760s. The first jigsaw puzzles in America were English and European imports aimed primarily at children.

Prior to the Civil War, several manufacturers, e.g., Samuel L. Hill, W. and S. B. Ives, and McLoughlin Brothers, included puzzles in their lines. However, it was the post-Civil War period that saw the jigsaw puzzle gain a strong foothold among the children of America.

In the late 1890s, puzzles designed specifically for adults first appeared. Both forms—adult and child—have existed side by side ever since.

Prior to the mid 1920s, the vast majority of jigsaw puzzles were cut out of wood for the adult market and composition material for the children's market. In the 1920s, the die-cut, cardboard jigsaw puzzle evolved and was the dominant medium in the 1930s.

Interest in jigsaw puzzles has cycled between peaks and valleys several times since 1933. Mini-revivals occurred during World War II and in the mid-1960s, when Springbok entered the American market. Internet auction sites are impacting the pricing of puzzles, raising some (Pars, Pastimes, U-Nits, figure pieces), but holding the line or even reducing others (Straus, Victory, strip cut). As with all auctions, final prices tend to vary depending upon the time of year and the activity of at least two interested bidders.

Adviser: Bob Armstrong.

Note: Prices listed here are for puzzles that are complete or restored, and in good condition. Most puzzles found in attics do not meet these standards. If evaluating an old puzzle, a discount of 50 percent should be calculated for moderate damage (one to two missing pieces, three to four broken knobs), with greater discounts for major damage or missing original box.

Comical Animals Picture Puzzle, Parker Bros, **$90.**

Cardboard, pre-1950

Consolidated Paper Box

Indian Paradise, R. Atkinson Fox artist, 1930s, 13-1/2" x 10-1/4", 250 pcs, orig box **15.00**
Unwelcome Visitors, 1940-50, 13-3/4" x 10-1/4", 250 pcs, orig box **12.00**

Jaymar, untitled, tinkering with early auto, artist Norman Rockwell, 1940-50, 17-1/2" x 17-1/2", 500 pcs, orig box **15.00**

Tuco/Deluxe, Trouble on the Trail, 1930s, 19-1/2" x 15", 357 pcs, orig box **16.00**

Unknown maker, untitled, cowboy surprising bear family, artist McCallist, 1930s, 13" x 10", 54 pcs **10.00**

Wood and/or handcut, pre-1930

Ayer, Isabel, Picture Puzzle Exchange
News of Peach 1865, artist Clyde O. Deland, 1910s, solidwood, 15-1/2" x 11-3/4", 321 pcs, orig box **140.00**

Simple Simon, artist G. G. Wiederseim, c1909, solidwood, 10-3/4" x 12-1/2", 185 pcs, one replaced, orig box............................... **85.00**

Holtzapffel, English, The York Coach, artist Victor Venner, c1909, solidwood, 23-1/2" x 14-1/4", 600 pcs, two replaced **250.00**

Leisure Hour, Over the Fence and Away, c1909, solidwood, 6-1/4" x 8", 111 pcs, orig box **45.00**

Olive Novelty, Olive Picture Puzzle, Steady, c1909, plywood, 8" x 6", 121 pcs, orig box............................... **50.00**

Parker Brothers/Pastime
Afternoon Tea, artist P. Phillippi, 1920-30, 18-3/4" x 16-1/4", 516 pcs, 60 figures **220.00**
David Copperfield Bids Farewell, artist Ludovici, c1912, 19-1/2" x 11-3/4", 362 pcs, three replaced, 20 figures......................... **175.00**
Moses in the Bullrushes, artist Relyea, 1930s, 11-3/4" x 16-1/2", 354 pcs, 38 figures **150.00**

Unknown maker

Colonial Picture, Washington and colonists, 1910-20, plywood, 14-1/2" x 10-3/4", 380 pcs, one replaced **120.00**
Household Calvary, Thomson artist, c1909, solidwood, 18-1/4" x 12", 500 pcs, two replaced, orig box **220.00**
The People's Advocate, Lincoln, artist Griswold Fang, 1920s, plywood, 21-1/4" x 16, 540 pcs....................... **150.00**
Where Seconds Mean Minutes, Philip R. Goodwin artist, 1910-20, plywood, 15-3/4" x 11-1/2", 140 pcs **35.00**

Wood and/or handcut, 1930s-40s, plywood

Chad Valley

The Cenotaph, 1930s, 13-3/4" x 10", 200 pcs, orig box **40.00**
The Millhouse, artist Will Thompson, 1930-40, 15-1/2" x 19-1/2", 550 pcs, orig box **110.00**

Clark, Edward Leggett, Deer in Mountain Valley, 1930s, 22" x 16", 850 pcs, orig box... **250.00**

Make Me Jig, distributed to American Stores, original box, 200 pieces, complete, **$45**.

Clift, Lloyd/Miloy, George Washington's Ancestral Home, 20" x 16", 607 pcs, orig box, 14 figures............ **175.00**

Deltagram Puzzle Co., Treasure Ships, artist Hadlan, 1930s, 9-1/2" x 12-1/4", 100 pcs, orig box, 10 figures.............. **35.00**

Hayter/Victory
Sheep Shearing and Reaping, 1930-40, 18-1/2" x 14-3/4", 500 pcs, orig box, 27 figures **125.00**
Union with Scotland, 1930-40, 21-1/4" x 20-1/2", 1,000 pcs, orig box, 60 figures..... **170.00**

Hedger, Fred, Leigham Puzzle Club, England, Squire & His Daughter, 1930s, 10-1/2" x 7-3/4", 203 pcs, one pc replaced, orig box **65.00**

Jewel Puzzle Co., Over Field and Fence, 1930s, 10" x 8", 134 pcs, one replaced, orig box................................ **35.00**

Macy's, The Old Mill, 1930s, 8-3/4" x 11-3/4", 200 pcs, two replaced, orig box, 15 figures **70.00**

Madmar Quality Co.
Beautiful Garden of Dreams, 1930s, 10" x 12-1/2", 250 pgs, orig box......................... **65.00**
The White Horse Tavern, 1930s, 12-1/4" x 9-1/4", 200 pcs, three replaced, back papered **40.00**

McLellan, Phyllis, Lending Library, 1930s, The Invocation, 11-3/4" x 9-3/4", 280 pcs, orig box.......... **85.00**

Milton Bradley, #4216, Little Boy Blue Puzzle Box, three complete puzzles, original box, **$90**.

Milton Bradley, Premier Buffeting the Billows, 1930s, 8-1/2" x 11-1/2", 158 pcs, orig box, 13 figures, cutter #147 .... **50.00**
Oriental Traders in Venice, 1930s, 27-1/4" x 21-3/4", 1009 pcs, three replaced, orig box, 82 figures, cut by #71. **330.00**

Parker Brothers, Kohler's Puzzles, Mountain Train, 1930s, 18-3/4" x 12-1/2", 412 pcs, one replaced, orig box, 48 figures, Pastime cut **150.00**

Parker Brothers/Pastime
Bamboo Walk, 1930-40, 10" x 6-3/4", 108 pcs, orig box, cutter #757 .... **40.00**
Sunlight in Paris, 1930-40, 15-1/2" x 12", 257 pcs, orig box, 30 figures, cutter #756 **110.00**

Pulver Novelty Co., Idle-Hour
A Summer Afternoon, 1930s, 18-1/4" x 12-1/2", 366 pcs, five replaced, orig box **65.00**
Dairy Pride, 1930s, 18" x 12", 301 pcs, one replaced, orig box................................ **80.00**

Schwartz, F. A. O., Spec Cut, Tranquility, 1930-40, 11-3/4" x 8-3/4", 210 pcs, four replaced, orig box, 12 figures....... **40.00**

Parker Bros, Women on Beach, artist signed "R. Featherstone," color line cutting and figure pieces, 200 pieces, 11" x 16", no box, **$120**.

Parker Bros, O'Shaunessy Dam, color line cutting and figure pieces, 100 pieces, 8" x 10", complete, no box, **$65**.

Straus, Joseph K.
In Golden Hunting Grounds, artist Hintermeister, 1930s, 11-1/2" x 15-3/4", 300 pcs **35.00**
Pride of the Litter, 1930s, 19-1/2" x 15-1/2", 500 pcs, one replaced, orig box **60.00**
Peaceful Valley, artist M. D. Lee, 1940-50, 19-3/4" x 15-3/4", 500 pcs, orig box **65.00**
The King's Cavalier, artist Doheny, 1940-50, 21-3/4" x 27-1/2", 1,000 pcs, orig box, 21 figures..................... **200.00**

Tuck, Zag-Zaw, Derby Day, artist B. P. Smith, 1930s, 14-3/4" c 6-1/2", 211 pcs, orig box, 24 figures......................... **70.00**

Zig-Zag Puzzle Co., A Welcome Guest, 1930s, 16" x 20", 500 pcs, three replaced, orig box, "Cut by Bill" on box **135.00**

Unknown maker
Arriving at Grandfathers for Christmas, artist J. L. G. Ferris, 1930s, 14" x 8-3/4", 208 pcs, orig box **60.00**
Hunting Dog, 1930s, 8-1/4" x 9-1/2", 162 pcs, two replaced **35.00**
In Northern Climes, artist Grittefiem, 1930s, 11-3/4" x 9-1/2", 204 pcs, orig box **40.00**
Sunshine and Shadows, artist Weber, 1930s, 19-3/4" x 14-3/4", 467 pcs, three replaced, one figure ... **120.00**
The Happy Family, artist E. Zampighi, 1930s, 16" x 12", 443 pcs....................... **115.00**
Washington and His Birthplace, 1732-1932, artist Adelaide Hiebal, 1930s, 17" x 21-1/4", 716 pcs, three replaced, 25 figures, ornate border......................... **200.00**

Victory Jig-Saw Puzzle, Lee Shore, Ringstead Bay, 21" x 16", plywood, 600 pieces, original box, **$150.**

Victory Picture Puzzle, child's, animals in wagon pulled by duck, 30 pieces, 7" x 8-3/4" box, **$45.**

Wood and/or handcut, post 1950, plywood

Browning, James, U-Nit, Juawles Pius, artist Pablo Picasso, 1960s, 29-1/2" x 24", 1,000 pcs, orig box, 120 figures **375.00**

Hayter/Victory/Artistic, Summer Harvest, artist Shepherd, 1950-60, 19-3/4" x 13-3/4", 500 pcs, orig box, 28 figures **80.00**

Par Company, High Society, 24-3/4" x 17", 825 pcs, orig box, 27 figures, personalized, irregular edges **1,200.00**

Schribner, Louise, 1950-60 A Dessert of Fruit, Currier & Ives, 12" x 8-1/2", 246 pcs, orig box .... **60.00** Girl from Arizona, 7" x 12", 193 pcs, orig box .... **50.00** Winter Morning in the Country, Currier & Ives, 12" x 8-1/2", 127 pcs, orig box **25.00**

QUEZAL

History: The Quezal Art Glass Decorating Company, named for the quetzal—a bird with brilliantly colored feathers—was organized in 1901 in Brooklyn, New York, by Martin Bach and Thomas Johnson, two disgruntled Tiffany workers. They soon hired Percy Britton and William Wiedebine, two more Tiffany employees.

The first products, which are unmarked, were exact Tiffany imitations. Quezal pieces differ from Tiffany pieces in that they are more defined and the decorations are more visible and brighter. No new techniques were developed by Quezal.

For more information, see *Warman's Glass*, 4th edition.

Johnson left in 1905. T. Conrad Vahlsing, Bach's son-in-law, joined the firm in 1918, but left with Paul Frank in 1920 to form Lustre Art Glass Company, which copied Quezal pieces. Martin Bach died in 1924, and by 1925, Quezal had ceased operations.

Marks: The "Quezal" trademark was first used in 1902 and placed on the base of vases and bowls and the rims of shades. The acid-etched or engraved letters vary in size and may be found in amber, black, or gold. A printed label that includes an illustration of a quetzal was used briefly in 1907.

Bowl, 9-1/2" d, irid gold Calcite ground, stretch rim, pedestal foot, sgd "Quezal" **800.00**
Candlesticks, pr, 7-3/4" h, irid blue, sgd **575.00**
Ceiling lamp shade, 13-3/4" d, 21-1/2" l drop, radiating irid gold and green leaf dec, domed irid ivory glass shade supported by brass ring suspended from three ball chains, two-socket fixture, shade inscribed "Quezal," Brooklyn, NY, early 20th C **6,325.00**

Jack-in-the-pulpit vase, iridescent gold, stretched rim on narrow vessel widening at base, inscribed "Quezal T 565," 6-3/4" h, **$1,300**.

Photo courtesy of Skinner, Inc.

Left: Jack in the pulpit vase, green pulled feather decoration tipped in iridescent gold, alabaster body, shiny gold interior, signed "Quezal," 6-1/2" h, **$2,250**; center: vase, tri-fold flower form, random wintergreen loops over iridescent gold pulls, soft velvet gold iridescent interior, signed "Quezal," 5" h, **$1,750**; right: jack in the pulpit vase, green pulled feather tipped in iridescent gold, signed "Quezal," 6" h, very minor wear to gold interior, **$1,600**.

Photo courtesy of Early Auction Co.

Chandelier, 14" h, four elaborate gilt metal scroll arms, closed teardrop gold, green, and opal shades, inscribed "Quezal" at collet rim, very minor roughness at rim edge
.... **2,000.00**

Cologne bottle, 7-1/2" h, irid gold ground, Art Deco design, sgd "Q" and "Melba" **250.00**

Finger bowl and underplate, 4-1/2" d gold irid bowl, pontil sgd, 4-1/2" d ribbed underplate, sgd "Quezal" **300.00**

Jack-in-the-pulpit vase
6" h, green pulled feather tipped in irid gold, sgd "Quezal," very minor wear to gold int.................... **1,600.00**
6-1/2" h, green pulled feather dec tipped in irid gold, alabaster body, shiny gold int., sgd "Quezal"..... **2,250.00**

Lamp, desk, 14-1/2" h, irid gold shade with green and white pulled feather dec, inscribed "Quezal" at rim, gilt metal adjustable crook-neck lamp
.... **575.00**

Lamp shade
4-1/2" h, 2-3/16" d aperture, ribbed bell form, calcite exterior, gold iridescent int., sgd on rim................... **180.00**
4-3/4" h, 1-3/4" d aperture, irid gold, cylindrical, ruffled rims, signed, set of three..... **235.00**

Lampshade, green and gold leaf designs, gold threading, 4-3/4" h, **$150**.
Photo courtesy of Early Auction Co.

Low bowl, 4" d, irid gold, ribbed shallow bowl, polished pontil, sgd............................. **450.00**

Salt, open, 2-1/2" d, 1-1/4" h, shouldered, irid body, protruding ribs, pontil sgd "Quezal"...................... **200.00**

Sherbet, 4" h, irid gold body, blue coil dec, sgd "Quezal" **700.00**

Toothpick holder, 2-1/4" h, melon ribbed, pinched sides, irid blue, green, purple and gold, sgd **200.00**

Lampshade, egg shape, green and gold pulled feather design, 4-1/2" h, **$200**.
Photo courtesy of Early Auction Co.

Lampshade, green damascene dome shade, inscribed "Quezal," fitter rim chips, 7-7/8" d; bronze adjustable socket on harp arms and round base, impressed "TIFFANY STUDIOS NEW YORK 21601 TDCo," early 20th C, 11" h, **$4,700**.
Photo courtesy of Skinner, Inc.

Lampshade, feather-pull glass shade, signed, 5-1/4" h, **$175**.
Photo courtesy of David Rago Auctions, Inc.

Urn, cov, 13-1/2" h, shouldered form, marigold body, overall green King Tut swirl pattern, matching lid, irid gold foot, sgd "Quezal" in silver........ **5,500.00**

Vase
5" h, tri-fold flower form, random wintergreen loops over irid gold pulls, soft velvet

gold irid int., sgd "Quezal"
.... **1,750.00**
5-1/4" h, floriform, folded irid gold rim, green and gold leaf dec, sgd "Quezal S 651"
.... **2,350.00**
6" h, floriform, wide mouth with stretched ruffled rim, irid gold interior, irid green, gold, and white ext., sgd "Quezal S 594" **2,470.00**
10-1/2" h, tulip-form body, pinched rim, green and gold irid pulled feather dec, circular foot with folded rim, base sgd "Quezal" **18,800.00**

Whiskey taster, 2-3/4" h, oval, irid gold, four pinched dimples, sgd "Quezal" on base............................ **200.00**

QUILTS

History: Quilts have been passed down as family heirlooms for many generations. Each one is unique. The same pattern may have hundreds of variations in both color and design.

The advent of the sewing machine increased, not decreased, the number of quilts made. Quilts are still being sewn today.

Notes: The key considerations for price are age, condition, aesthetic appeal, and design.

Appliqué, Friendship Album, America, 1858, 48 blocks of red, blue, and green mostly solid color fabrics appliquéd to white ground, separated by red cotton grid, naturalistic, patriotic, geometric, and musical instrument motifs including flowers, fruit, butterfly, peacock, flag, violin, circles, stars, etc., larger central square with appliquéd lettering "TO SARAH ACCEPT OUR GIFT AND MAY IT PROVE THY FRIENDS ARE MANY WARM THEIR LOVE," with embroidered signature "Amanda Birdsell Apr 20th, 1858," many squares with embroidered and pen and ink signatures, mounted on wood frame, minor fading, 86" x 65-1/2", **$4,200**.
Photo courtesy of Skinner, Inc.

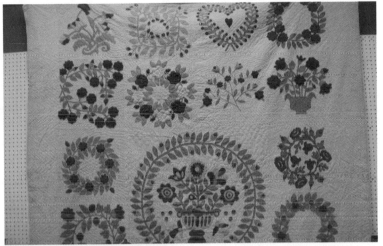

Appliqué, Baltimore album type, **$850.**

Appliqué, Whig rose, **$750.**

Appliqué

Eagle, red, green, and gold eagles, bordered nine block pattern, white ground, quilted in conforming eagle and geometric pattern, Missouri, 20th C, 83" x 77" **2,350.00**

Flower Basket, red, green, and yellow calico, white ground, toning, minor staining, fabric wear, 77-1/2" x 67" **885.00**

Grape vines, green and purple vines meandering between quilted stuffed grapes, hand quilted following pattern, minor stains, 66" x 82". **800.00**

Nine blocks, each with large red flower, pink and yellow center, blue leaves and vines, red buds, border of blue quarter boons and red stars, white quilted ground, signed with embroidery "Polly Matthias (heart) Lug March 1837," 84" x 84"......................... **1,750.00**

Oak leaf, red and green printed fabric vine border, white ground, late 19th C, 72" x 88", minor stains, marker lines **300.00**

Rose of Sharon, pieced scalloped border, red, green, pink, and yellow calico, white ground and backing, red binding, conforming floral pattern quilting, attributed to PA, c1840, 88" x 90". **1,530.00**

Tulips
Bright pink and green tulips, white ground, figure eight quilting in border, white back, 80-1/2" x 92" **300.00**
Pink and green tulips rising out of blue triangles, white ground with vining stem and leaf design quilted into it, white backing, 74 3/4" sq **350.00**

Twenty medallion blocks, blue, green, and red flowers and berries, surrounded by red, and green vining, two with pots of flowers flanking central ground dated "1849" near top, hand quilted, light staining, some damage to appliqué, 82" x 88"... **1,380.00**

Vine and Blackberry, 16 white blocks, each with appliqued aqua vine with pendant blackberries, separated by aqua grid also forming border, white cotton backing with intricate quilting, America, c1920, minor stain, 82" x 86" **4,000.00**

Appliqué and pieced

Album, red plaid separates squares with appliquéd polychrome prints, most are floral, some have deer or birds, two have Eastern scenes with camels and elephants, inked signatures,

dates in the 1850s, stains, 64" sq............................ **1,870.00**

Appliqué and pieced, whirled feathers, green and pale red calico on white, **$350.**

Embroidered, appliquéd, pieced cotton, 16 white blocks separated by diagonal red grid, each with floral sprigs and blossoms in solid red, yellow, blue and green accented with wool yarn and cotton embroidered buds and leaves, white backing, New England, late 19th C, losses and fading, 80-1/2" x 90" **1,410.00**

Nine floral medallions, red, yellow, and green, red and green sawtooth edging, hand quilted, feathering between medallions, scroll work along border, stains, 82" x 83" **1,430.00**

Tulips, pink, purple, and orange, green leaves and borders, hand quilted with flowers, feathering, and diamonds, dark black and blue pencil lines, light green edging, 70" x 82"............................. **770.00**

Chintz

Printed overall design of exotic birds drinking from urns hanging from trees, brown on white, printed gold, blue, green, and reddish-brown, brown floral backing, light stains, 94" x 116" **1,450.00**

Crazy

Pieced, many embroideries, including chenille goldenrod, owl at center of pin-wheeled fabrics, 1891............ **4,500.00**

Pieced, velvet and satin multicolored fabrics, embroidered seams, many embroidered embellishments, appliquéd flowers, burgundy velvet border, gold cotton backing, wear to binding, 79-1/4" x 81" **750.00**

Child's quilt, embroidered squares with animals, birds, children, blue edging, **$100**.

Crazy quilt, velvet, satin, silks, cotton prints and solids, some embroidery, **$75**.

Crazy quilt, velvet, satin, silks, center Log Cabin pattern blocks, **$350**.

Photo courtesy of Dotta Auction Co., Inc.

Pieced

Basket, 16 baskets composed of solid white and yellow cotton triangles, white ground with double yellow borders, white cotton backing, quilted with feather medallions, diamond and undulating feather border, possibly Mennonite, c1900, 79" sq **1,550.00**

Bow Tie, small green and red triangles, red zig zag border with green sawtooth edging, hand stitched four petal flower quilting, red edging, slight wear and facing, 74" sq **1,575.00**

Broken Star, orange, yellow, green, red, brown, blue, and white printed calico patches, red and white calico Flying Geese border, PA, 19th C, 80" x 76" **460.00**

Cathedral, multicolored diamonds within white circles, hand stitching, 90-1/4" x 105" **425.00**

Chinese Lanterns, green, red, blue, yellow, and white printed calico and solid patches, blue and white ground, red border, diamond and rope quilting, PA, late 19th C, minor staining, 82" x 84" **1,495.00**

Courthouse Steps, various silk colors, black border, highlighted by decorative embroidery, late 19th C, minor wear, 20" x 26-1/2" **260.00**

Diamond blocks, bands of calico alternating with bands of diamond blocks, shades of brown on white ground, scattered staining on front, small hole in backing, 102" x 107" **750.00**

Diamonds, polychrome calico bars forming concentric diamonds, white backing, white edge binding, quilting follows bars, 74" sq..... **300.00**

Eagles and sunburst, central teal and red sunburst surrounded by four teal and red eagles and shields, bright yellow ground, leaf motifs in corners, border with band comprised of red and yellow triangles, red band, yellow outer band with red binding, floral motif quilted into yellow ground, pink and yellow broad bands backing, 76" x 81-1/2", some fading on back, small stain................ **1,400.00**

Pieced and embroidered, baseball theme, center dated "1934 Al Simmons, Milwaukee, WI," other panels naming various teams, together with two matching pillowcases, **$350**.

Photo courtesy of Pook & Pook.

Flower Basket in Diamond design, red, yellow, pink, and red calico, 20th C, 89" x 87", 1" tear.......................... **450.00**

Four petal flowers in two shades of light yellow and pale green, white ground, border of arches with buds, hand stitched, princess feather medallions, fancy scrolls, and interlacing lines quilting, scalloped edge, light stains, 84" sq **495.00**

Irish Chain, pink, green, and peach calico, straight green and pink borders, brown calico backing, embroidered with red "B" in lower left hand corner, 6' 10" x 6' 11", very minor staining **225.00**

Log cabin, silk, satin, and velvet, bright colors, four thin borders surround 20 large blocks, hand and machine stitched, 58" x 74", small label attached says "Florida Quilt Heritage, #216 NQG #6, documented Florida quilt, Museum of Florida History" **320.00**

Martha Washington's Flower Garden, calicos and printed fabrics, predominately yellows, red and tan borders, hand stitched, minor wear, 66" x 86".......................... **300.00**

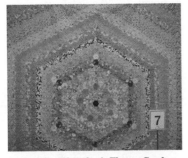

Pieced, Grandmother's Flower Garden, pieced cotton prints, purple center, double bed size, **$175**.

Pieced, bright red and white, zig-zag design, **$500**.

Moon and Stars, pieced wool, 10 full and three quarter circles composed of four pie-shaped wedges, shades or rust and green, tan twill binding, woven wool backing, 83" x 96", fading, stains, small holes **770.00**

Nine Patch, various colors, red grid, hand and machine stitched, backed and bound with red and white printed fabric, late 19th/early 20th C, minor fading, 79" x 71" . **230.00**

Nine Patch variant
Chintz squares edged with triangles, floral printed border, hand stitched, diamond and floral quilting, orig pencil marks, some stains, 82" x 83". **1,540.00**
Multicolored squares alternating with off-white, arranged diagonally in block and surrounded by red grid, sawtooth border, backed with white, red binding, minor imperfections, 81-1/2" x 75"
.... **460.00**

Philadelphia Pavements, blue, red, orange, and white square printed and solid patches, orange and red banded borders with feather and floral fine quilting, PA, late 19th/ early 20th C, 84" x 80". **825.00**

Pineapple corner elements with birds, central medallion, golden yellow on red, white green borders, burnt orange calico backing, hand stitched, 92" sq **725.00**

Pineapple Log Cabin, pieced calico, border of four bands, two yellow, green, and pink, backed with brown figured print, bound with green, Mennonite, Washington, PA, c1880, 96" x 84" **1,175.00**

Schoolhouse, red, orange, yellow, and tan buildings machine-stitched on white ground, several interesting quilting patterns, scallops, and zigzags on roofs, stars and geometric shapes in gable ends, birds and leaves on sashing, Midwest, late 19th C, 75-1/2" x 73-1/2" .. **1,060.00**

Serrated Square, corresponding border, pink and green calico, shell and diamond quilting, 82" x 84"
.... **320.00**

Spider Web, pink, red, blue, purple green, peach, and brown printed calico patches, wide purple calico border, diagonal line quilting, Mennonite, PA, late 19th C, some staining, 82" x 80"
.... **825.00**

Star, large eight-pointed star in pastels, white ground, white backing, repair at corner, 69" sq **200.00**

Pieced, rows of four squares forming diamond blocks, multicolored calicos, green sashing, brown and white border blocks on each row, full size, **$300**.

Pieced, Maple Leaf pattern, red and white, **$150**.

Photo courtesy of Pook & Pook.

Pieced, 16 eight-pointed stars, yellow, red and green calico, white ground, elaborately quilted in foliate and geometric designs, red, green and cream calico border, 103" l, 100" w, **$1,725**.

Photo courtesy of Alderfer Auction Co.

Starbursts inside latticework, eight-pointed starbursts, yellow and green calico blocks and bars form lattice, calico baking, 98" x 101-1/2", scattered light staining on front, small section of wear
.... **200.00**

Starbursts with blocks and bars, multicolored starbursts, pink blocks and bars, complex quilting, reverse stamped "M. A. Darby," paper tag states c1865, PA, scattered staining front and back, one star worn through, 82" x 90" **350.00**

Star of Bethlehem, purple, green, red, blue, and pink calico, white ground, early 20th C, toning, minor staining, fabric wear, 82" x 73-1/2"
.... **650.00**

Stars, eight-pointed green and pink calico stars, white calico ground, green and pink band on border with figure eight quilting, three broad pink bands on back, 72-1/2" x 80", two small stains **200.00**

Stars, 42 blocks of eight-point stars set on the diagonal in a variety of printed cotton fabrics separated by floral printed blocks, red, yellow, and black, triangle border, edged in same floral pattern, natural woven cotton backing, chevron and concentric diamond quilting stitches, America, circa 1870, minor stains, 80" x 90"........ **1,765.00**

Windmill, yellow, red, green, and blue printed calico patches, wide red calico with swag quilting, PA, late 19th C, 86" x 76" **690.00**

QUIMPER

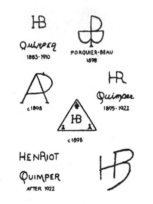

History: Quimper faience, dating back to the 17th century, is named for Quimper, a French town where numerous potteries were located. Several mergers resulted in the evolution of two major houses—the Jules Henriot and Hubaudière-Bousquet factories.

The peasant design first appeared in the 1860s, and many variations exist. Florals and geometrics, equally popular, also were produced in large quantities. During the 1920s, the Hubaudière-Bousquet factory introduced the Odetta line, which utilized a stone body and Art Deco decorations.

The two major houses merged in 1968, the products retaining the individual characteristics and marks of the originals. The concern suffered from labor problems in the 1980s and was purchased by an American group.

For more information, see *Warman's English & Continental Pottery & Porcelain*, 4th edition.

Marks: The "HR" and "HR Quimper" marks are found on Henriot pieces prior to 1922. The "Henriot Quimper" mark was used after 1922. The "HB" mark covers a long time span. Numbers or dots and dashes were added for inventory purposes and are found on later pieces. Most marks are in blue or black. Pieces ordered by department stores, such as Macy's and Carson Pirie Scott, carry the store mark along with the factory mark, making them less desirable to collectors. A comprehensive list of marks is found in Bondhus book.

Adviser: Al Bagdade.

Additional Terms:

A la touche border decor—single brush stroke to create floral

Breton Broderie decor—stylized blue and gold pattern inspired by a popular embroidery pattern often used on Breton costumes, dates from the Art Deco era.

Croisille—criss-cross pattern

Decor Riche border—acanthus leaves in two colors

Fleur de lys—the symbol of France

Vegetable bowl, 9" l, "HenRiot Quimper" mark, **$175**.

Ashtray, 4-1/2" l, 2-1/2" w, octagonal, male peasant in center, scattered four dot designs, typical florals, blue sponged border, indented rests, yellow striped base, "HB Quimper France C.D. 1154" mark **45.00**

Basket, 4-1/2" h, 5-1/4" w, lobed body, female peasant on int., sprigs of fantasy florals, four blue dash overlapped handles at top, yellow and orange flower center, ext. border of blue, green, and red single stroke florals, "HenRiot Quimper France" mark, c1935 .... **365.00**

Bell, 3-1/4" h, bagpipe-shape, frontal view of female peasant, yellow centered blue dot florals, red and green foliage, molded brown pipe, blue ribbon, bluets on reverse, Porquier Beau Normandy, hairline........ **85.00**

Biberon, 5" h, center band of red, yellow, green, and blue single stroke florals, concentric blue and yellow bands on base, blue dash handle and spout, unmarked **170.00**

Bookends, pr, 6" h, Modern Movement, standing peasant boy playing bagpipes, yellow trimmed black hat, cobalt blue jacket, light green trousers on one, seated little peasant girl, black jacket, orchid sleeves, yellow apron on other, "HB Quimper" marks **425.00**

Bowl, 5-3/4" h, bagpipe shape, frontal view of male or female peasant, traditional florals, molded blue ribbon on top, brown molded pipes form overhead handle, blue and orange striped rim, "HenRiot Quimper France" marks, price for pr **300.00**

Box, cov, 10-1/4" l, rect, seated male peasant playing horn, seated female holding basket, both under trees, orange outlined dark blue acanthus borders, blue striped foot, "HenRiot Quimper 148" mark **575.00**

Cache pot, 10" h, 11" d, seated female peasant holding basket facing seated male peasant with walking stick, reverse with large or orange single stroke daisies, green foliage, lower border of half chains, blue dots, blue and yellow striped border above, green sponged rim, yellow and blue dash ring handles, "HenRiot Quimper" mark **675.00**

Candlesticks, pr, 8" h, figural, standing male peasant, eggplant hat, cobalt blue coat, green vest, orange trousers on one, standing female with dark green blouse, white apron, cobalt blue skirt on other, each holding pot on head, green mound bases **1,375.00**

Chamberstick, 5" sq, male peasant with staff on one side, single branch of red tipped single stroke flowers on opposite, scattered blue dot designs, rolled blue streaked and orange rim, blue streaked ring handle... **170.00**

Charger, 15-3/4" w, octagonal, seated male peasant playing bagpipe, standing peasant blowing horn, blue acanthus on yellow border, "HB Quimper" mark **225.00**

Cheese dish, cov, 8-1/2" d, lightly fluted cover, seated male peasant playing bagpipes, red tipped yellow flowerheads, four blue dot designs, brown branch handle ending in yellow and green fruit, circular side with alternating red and blue crisscross designs, red tipped yellow flowerheads in orange and blue lined panels, lobed base with similar alternating panels on border, "HenRiot Quimper France" mark **800.00**

Coffeepot, 9-1/4" h, male peasant standing in front of brown fence, yellow ajonc flowers on reverse, orange rims, band of blue demi-circles, orange banded handle with blue dashes, "HR Quimper" mark **750.00**

Compote, 11" d, 5" h, HP yellow wild roses, green foliage, flying insect, pale blue ground, yellow outlined lobed rim, Porquier-Beau mark **2,875.00**

Dish, 11-1/2" l handle to handle, oblong octagonal shape, male and female peasant in

forest setting, borer of alternating local flora and fleur de lys, crest of Brittany, four small feet, blue insect on bottom, orange and green molded olive leaf handles, "HenRiot Quimper" mark **1,250.00**

Egg cup, 2-3/4" h, attached underplate, female peasant on cup, band of red, blue, and green foliage on base, blue lined wavy rim on cup, "HenRiot Quimper France" mark **175.00**

Figure
5-1/4" h, standing peasant woman, holding yellow-orange basket, cobalt blue vest, green blouse, yellow crossed sash, rose apron, green mound base titled "MARIK," mkd "HenRiot Quimper 29" **255.00**
9-1/4" h, sailor carrying sails, overall white glaze, mkd "EJB HenRiot Quimper"....... **595.00**
13" h, 16" w, bust of peasant woman, gold-orange vest and coif, metallic sleeves, "HB Quimper Porson" mark . **775.00**

Grill plate, 12-1/4" d, "HenRiot Quimper France" mark. **750.00**

Grill plate, 12-1/4" d, "HenRiot Quimper France" mark, $750.

Holy water font, 3-1/4" h, relief bust of Mary, standing infant Jesus, red outlined yellow cross at top, blue and green streaks on sides, blue relief "M" on bowl, red, green, and blue streaks, "HenRiot Quimper" mark **375.00**

Inkpot, 3" h, 4" w, three lobes, seated female peasant on front, scattered red and green foliage, blue and orange lined rims, blue button know, "Quimper Made in France" mark **295.00**

Inkstand, 8-1/2" l, 3-3/4" h, male and female peasants on top plate, scattered blue dot design, band of single stroke red florals, black ermine tails on base, yellow and gold fleur de lys and ermine tails on backplate, blue dash molded swirl borders, "HB Quimper" mark........................... **525.00**

Knife rest, 4" l, Modern Movement, reclining figural female peasant, head propped in hands, black dress, orange stripes, light blue apron, white coif, "C. Malllard, HenRiot Quimper" marks **130.00**

Menu, 5-1/2" h, 3-1/2" w, female peasant, basket of fish in lower corner, crest of Brittany at top, "Menu" top right, blue outlined wavy rim, Porquier Beau **1,100.00**

Mustard pot, cov, 3-1/2" h, 4" d, band of single stroke orange, red, blue, and green, foliage and flowers on cover and body, blue lined rims, blue dash applied arched handles, "HenRiot Quimper France" mark........................... **145.00**

Oyster plate, 8-3/4" d, center well with small blue flower, one well with male peasant, five wells with blue, red, and green florals, blue sponged rim, "HenRiot Quimper" mark **395.00**

Petite Dejeuner set, 11" l, ribbed, cup with female peasant, band of red, blue, and green florals, yellow and blue rim, sponged green wishbone handle, male peasant on base, cup space outlined with red chains, molded green and blue tab, "HR Quimper" marks .. **585.00**

Pipe, 5" l, female peasant on bowl with foliage, stem with alternating bands of blue interlocking circles, orange and blue dashes, "HB Quimper" mark **600.00**

Pipe rack, 10" l, 7-1/2" h, bagpipe-shaped backplate, male and female peasant, molded blue and orange ribbons at ends, crest of Brittany surmounted by yellow crown, green sponged openings, "HenRiot Quimper" mark **375.00**

Pitcher, 7" h, male peasant under spout, red, blue, or green single stroke half daisies, yellow ground **215.00**

Soup bowl, 6-1/2" d, pierced for hanging, "HenRiot Quimper France" mark, **$145**.

Plate
7-3/8" d, large yellow centered single stroke red daisy, blue and green foliage, border band of red single strokes alternating with two blue dots, blue lined rim, "HB" mark............... **195.00**
8-3/4" d, large blue stylized basket in center, yellow and red or blue and yellow flowerheads, border band of red two petaled flowers alternating with three blue dot designs, blue rim, "HB" mark...................... **100.00**
9-1/4" d, female peasant seated on rocks, blue acanthus or décor riche border, black and white crest of Brittany, Pouquier-Beau mark...................... **1,650.00**
9-3/8" d, male peasant in center, purple shirt, blue trousers, red and green vertical foliage, single stroke blue, yellow, and green foliage on border separated by four blue dot deigns, blue outlined shaped rim, "HR Quimper" mark **295.00**
9-1/2" d, walking peasant boy, goose flapping wings, green acanthus border, crest of Brittany, yellow scrolling rim, Porquier Beau.......... **1,295.00**
Porringer, 7-1/2" w handle to handle, male peasant in center, vertical foliage, yellow and blue striped border, blue sponged handles, "HB Quimper" mark **165.00**
Sauce boat, 8-3/4" l, 3-1/2" h, male peasant on side, female on reverse, scattered typical local flora, yellow shells

molded on borders, shell feet, scattered florals on interior, cobalt blue dolphin handle, blue streaked rim, "HR Quimper" mark **825.00**
Serving bowl, 11" w handle to handle, octagonal, crest of Quimper in center, red, yellow, and blue lambrequin and drape border, blue sponged roped handles, Porquier Beau mark......................... **1,000.00**
Snuff bottle, 3" h, bagpipe-shape, male peasant on front, green shirt, blue trousers, brown molded pipes, molded blue ribbon, typical foliage, "HenRiot Quimper" mark **495.00**

Sugar bowl, covered, male peasant with walking stick, **$265**.

Sugar bowl, cov, 5-1/2" h, 7" w handle to handle, traditional male or female peasant on side separated by green, red, and yellow centered blue vertical florals, orange outlined blue dash curled handles, orange fleur de lys knob, "HenRiot Quimper France" mark **265.00**

Teapot, 8" h, Breton Broderie pattern, bands of cobalt blue and raised orange chevrons, green enamel dots, white body, "HB Quimper" mark, c1930......................... **295.00**
Tea set, 8" h cov teapot, 4-1/2" h cream jug, 7-1/2" h cov sugar bowl, orange edged panels with female peasant holding distaff, or seated, alternating with demiflorals or blue crisscross designs, scattered four blue dot designs, blue flame knobs, orange dash handles, "HenRiot Quimper France" marks, hairline. **575.00**
Wall pocket
8" h, figural bagpipe-shape, typical male peasant, molded blue ribbon at top, brown pipe at side, yellow glaze, "HB Quimper" mark **110.00**
10" h, overlapped cone shape, standing male or female peasant, blue acanthus or décor riche borders, blue streaked cone tip, orange lined rim, pierced for hanging, "HenRiot Quimper" mark, price for pr.............................. **700.00**

RADIOS

History: The radio was invented more than 100 years ago. Marconi was the first to assemble and employ the transmission and reception instruments that permitted the sending of electric messages without the use of direct

This stunning display of vintage radios was offered by www.primeaumusic.com at the March 2004 Atlantique City Antiques show.

connections. Between 1905 and the end of World War I, many technical advances affected the "wireless," including the invention of the vacuum tube by DeForest. Technology continued its progress, and radios filled the entertainment needs of the average family in the 1920s.

Changes in design, style, and technology brought the radio from the black boxes of the 1920s to the stylish furniture pieces and console models of the 1930s and 1940s, to midget models of the 1950s, and finally to the high-tech radios of the 1980s.

Additional Listings: See *Warman's Americana & Collectibles* for more examples.

Adviser: Lewis S. Walters.

Freshman Masterpiece, three dial set, c1924, speaker not shown, **$95.**
Photo courtesy of Dotta Auction Co., Inc.

Ham radios bring in big prices

Outstanding prices were set for ham radios at a January 2004 Ohio auction, during which time the collection of late Russell Hanselman was sold by Richard Estes.

Chicago Radio Lab Z-nith, receiver, c1919-20, black metal panel, three knobs **16,000.00**

DeForest
SP 4 .... **3,100.00**
Type MP-100 .... **3,500.00**

Marconi Wireless Telegraph Co.
Type 294 receiver, c1918, mahogany case. **19,000.00**
Type 306 receiver, incomplete **15,000.00**

Mignon Wireless RLC 2 receiver, pine cabinet finished in dark stain **11,000.00**

Norden Hauck receiver **3,000.00**

Sodion DR6 receiver **2,400.00**

Western Electric
2-A tuner **2,850.00**
34-B amplifier **3,000.00**
4-C receiver **3,000.00**

Wireless Speciality IP-501-A receiver **8,000.00**

Admiral
Portable, #33-35-37 ..... **30.00**
Portable, #909, All World **85.00**

Y-2127, Imperial 8, c1959 .... **45.00**
Air King, tombstone, Art Deco **2,200.00**
Arvin
Mightymite #40 .... **75.00**
Rhythm Baby #417 ..... **225.00**
Hoppy with lariatenna. **585.00**
Table, #444 .... **80.00**
Table, #522A **75.00**
Tombstone, #617 Rhythm Maid **250.00**
Atwater Kent
Breadboard style, Model 9A **1,200.00**
Breadboard style, Model 10, with orig tags **1,200.00**
Breadboard style, Model 12 .... **1,250.00**
Cathedral, 80, c1931 .. **375.00**
Table, #55 Kell **225.00**
Tombstone, #854 .... **155.00**
Type R Horn **200.00**
Bulova, clock radio
#100 .... **30.00**
#120 .... **30.00**
Colonial "New World Radio" **1,000.00**
Columbia, table radio, oak **125.00**
Crosley
ACE V **170.00**
Bandbox, #600, 1927 .. **80.00**
Dashboard **100.00**
Gemchest, #609 .... **350.00**
Litfella, 1N, cathedral . **175.00**
Pup, with box **575.00**
Sheraton, cathedral **290.00**
Showbox, #706 .... **100.00**
Super Buddy Boy **125.00**
#4-28 battery operated **130.00**
#10-135 .... **55.00**
Dumont, RA346, table, scrollwork, 1938 .... **110.00**
Emerson
AU-190 Catalin Tombstone **1,200.00**

BT-245 .... **1,100.00**
Patriot **700.00**
Porcelain Dealer Sign **150.00**
#274 brown Bakelite.. **165.00**
#400 Aristocrat **525.00**
#409 Mickey **1,500.00**
#411 Snow White..... **1,200.00**
#570 Memento............ **100.00**
#640 Portable **50.00**
#888 Vanguard **80.00**
Fada
#43............................ **275.00**
#53............................ **750.00**
#60W **75.00**
#115 bullet shape....... **750.00**
#252............................ **575.00**
#625 rounded end, slide rule dial............................ **700.00**
#1000 red/orange bullet **750.00**
#L56 Maroon and White **1,750.00**
Federal
#58DX........................ **750.00**
#110 .... **700.00**
General Electric
#81, c1934................. **200.00**
#400, 410, 411, 414..... **30.00**
#515, 517 clock radio.. **25.00**
K-126.......................... **150.00**
Tombstone................. **250.00**
Grebe
CR-8 .... **700.00**
CR-9 .... **500.00**
CR-12 .... **700.00**
MU-1.......................... **250.00**
Service Manual............ **50.00**
Halicrafters
TW-600 .... **100.00**
TW-200 .... **125.00**
Majestic
Charlie McCarthy..... **1,000.00**
#59, wooden Tombstone **375.00**
#381........................... **225.00**
Treasure Chest **125.00**
Metrodyne Super 7, 1925 .... **220.00**

Motorola
#68X11Q Art Deco **75.00**
Jet Plane **55.00**
Jewel Box **80.00**
M logo **25.00**
Pixie **45.00**
Ranger, portable **60.00**
Table, plastic **35.00**
Olympic, radio with phonograph
.... **60.00**
Paragon
DA, two table **775.00**
RD, five table **775.00**
Philco
T-7, 126 transistor **65.00**
T1000 clock radio **80.00**
#17, 20, 38 Cathedral . **250.00**
#20 Cathedral **250.00**
#37, 62 table, two tone **100.00**
#40, 180 console wood
.... **150.00**
#46, 132 table **35.00**
#52, 544 Transitone **40.00**
#49, 501 Boomerang .. **475.00**
#60, Cathedral **125.00**
#551, 1928 .... **175.00**
Radiobar, with glasses and
decanters **1,000.00**
Radio Corporation of America–RCA
LaSiesta **550.00**
Radiola
#17 .... **120.00**
#18, with speaker **125.00**
#20 .... **165.00**
#28 console **200.00**
#33 .... **60.00**
#6X7 table, plastic **25.00**
8BT-7LE portable **35.00**
40X56 World's Fair ... **1,000.00**
Silvertone-Sears
#1 table **75.00**
#1582 Cathedral, wood
.... **225.00**
#1955 Tombstone **135.00**
#9205 plastic transistor **45.00**
Clock radio, plastic **15.00**
Sony, transistor
TFM-151, 1960 .... **50.00**
TR-63, 1958 .... **145.00**
Sparton
#506 Blue Bird, Art Deco
.... **3,300.00**
#5218 .... **95.00**
Stewart-Warner, table, slant
.... **175.00**
Stromberg Carlson, # 636A
console **125.00**
Westinghouse, Model WR-602
.... **50.00**
Zenith
#500 transistor, owl eye **75.00**
#500D transistor **55.00**

#750L transistor, leather case
.... **40.00**
Trans-Oceanic **90.00**
Zephyr, multiband **95.00**

RAILROAD ITEMS

History: Railroad collectors have existed for decades. The merger of the rail systems and the end of passenger service made many objects available to private collectors. The Pennsylvania Railroad sold its archives at public sale.

Notes: Railroad enthusiasts have organized into regional and local clubs. Join one if you're interested in this collectible field; your local hobby store can probably point you to the right person. The best pieces pass between collectors and rarely enter the general market.

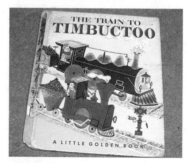

Little Golden Book, *The Train to Timbuctoo*, **$35.**

Ashtray, Soo Line, ceramic, track and car design border, "Denver Wright Co." backstamp, 7" d **25.00**

Badge pendant, gold luster finish thin metal rim holding color celluloid, showing steam engine during night run, lower center with red, white, and blue logo for Brotherhood of Locomotive Engineers, early 1900s **20.00**

Bond
Allegheny & Kinzua Railroad Co., NY & PA, $1000 first mortgage, 5 percent gold bond, train emerging from tunnel, green, Homer Lee Bank Note Co., 30 coupons attached **95.00**
Boston, Hartford & Erie Railroad Co., MA, $1,000 7 percent coupon bond, arched fancy "United States of

America" over old steam train at station, Columbia, eagle, and shield, green, three printed revenue stamps, sgd by John S Eldridge, President, National Bank Note Co., 50 coupons attached **125.00**
Chicago and North Western Railway Co., $1000 second mortgage, 4-1/2% convertible income bond series A, vignette Wheel of Progress, olive, American Bank Note Co. **35.00**
Cleveland, Cincinnati, Chicago & St. Louis Railway Co., $1,000 refunding and improvement, 4-1/2% mortgage bond, series E, vignette of two steam engines traveling thru tunnel, American Bank Note Co., 10 attached coupons **20.00**
West Shore RR, NY, $10,000 bond, brown and black, Hudson River panorama with trains, loading dock, steam ships, distant mountains, second vignette on reverse with bald eagle, canceled, American Bank Note Co. **15.00**

Book
1900 Chicago Rock Island & Pacific History, Biographical Publishing Co., 756 pages, CRIP and representative employees, beautiful tooled and gilt engine dec cover, gilt edges, center signatures are loose **260.00**
Southern Pacific Color Guide to Freight & Passenger Equipment, Vol. 1, Anthony Thompson, 128 pgs, hard cover **30.00**
Western Maryland Diesel Locomotives, P. Salem, hard cover **35.00**
Western Pacific Locomotives & Cars, Patrick C. Dorn, hard cover **35.00**

Booklet, *Quiz Jr Railroad Questions and Answers,* green and black, printed by Assoc of American Railroads, 1955 .... **10.00**

Brake gauge, Westinghouse, brass, two dial indicators, 140 lbs, 6-1/2" d **35.00**

Builders plate
Corps of Engineers U.S. Army 45-ton Diesel Electric Locomotive Manufactured by Vulcan Iron Works, cast bronze, dated 1941, 11" x 6"
.... **85.00**

Fairbanks-Morse, stainless steel, etched letters on enamel ground, 1955, serial #166-972, 17" x 8"....... **115.00**

Calendar
New York Central, 1922, illustration depicting travel in 1830 and 1920, timetables for various lines in margins, some minor losses, period oak frame, 18" x 30".......... **265.00**
Soo Line, 1930, illus, Lake Louise Alberta by R. Atkinson Fox, later oak frame and mat, overall 34" x 29" **230.00**

Calendar plate, Pennsylvania Lines, 1949, after a painting by Grif Teller, framed, 30" x 23" **35.00**

Check
Philadelphia & Erie RR Co., PA, 1902, drawn on Phila National Bank, fancy script bank title, black on white.................. **8.50**
Rocky Fork & Cooke City RR, Montana territory, March 1899, fancy script bank title, hand stamped in blue above bank title, cut cancel **18.00**

Pennsylvania Railroad items, top: pocket knife, yellow celluloid, **$15**; two PRR cast iron plaques, **each $45**; employee's pinback button, white ground, red logo, black lettering and employee number, **$35**.

Cap
Agent, Soo Line, pill box style, embroidered "Agent" and "Soo Line," labeled "Marshall Field & Co. Chicago," size 7" **50.00**
Brakeman's, open-weave crown, missing name plate, labeled "A. G. Meier & Co. Chicago," size 6-3/4" **35.00**

Railroad Conductors, labeled "A.G. Meier & CO. Chicago," size 7-1/4" **95.00**

Crimper, railroad seal, nickel plate, dies marked "CNS & M. R. R. Co.," handle emb "Porter Safety Seal Co.," 7" l **115.00**

Cuspidor
Missouri Pacific Railroad, white porcelain on metal, black "MOPAC" lettering, minor loss, 7-1/2" d..... **150.00**
Texas & Pacific Railroad, white porcelain on metal, blue lettering, minor loss, 8" d **260.00**

Date stamp, Atlantic Coast Line Railroad, c1940, Defiance Stamp Co., 4" h............. **35.00**

Depot clock, electric, patent date 1908, oak case, hinged face, marked "Property of the Ball RR Time Service St. Paul, Minn," 21" sq **210.00**

Depot sign, Rock Island System, reverse painted and mother of pearl, c1890, Chicago, Rock Island & Pacific 4-4-0 locomotive #476 pulling 11 cars, against tree-lined Midwest route, orig oak ogee frame with gilt liner, overall 50" x 22" **23,000.00**

Directory, *Soo Line Shippers Directory, Vol. III*, 1918-19, soft cover, 644 pgs, gilt, ads, illus, two-pg Soo Line map, four color maps of MI, MN, ND, WI **60.00**

Fire bucket, Missouri, Kansas & Texas Railroad, orig red paint, stenciled "Fire," emb "MK&T," 12" h............................ **60.00**

Flare and flag box, Gulf Mobile & Ohio, tin, stenciled letters, contains flag and fuses, 30" l **20.00**

Hollowware
Coffee pot, silver plate, Chicago & Eastern Illinois, 10-oz size, marked "Reed & Barton 086-H, C&E.I.RY.CO" on base, 7" h.............. **265.00**
Coffee server, silvered, Nashville, Chattanooga & St. Louis, applied emb "N.C.& St. L" logo on front, gooseneck spout, long wood handle, backstamped "Reed & Barton 482-32 oz, N.C. & St. L" **520.00**
Sauce tureen, silvered, Chicago Great Western Railway, two handles, lid, backstamped "C.G.W.R.R.– Reed & Barton," 8" l.... **125.00**

Sugar bowl, silvered, New York Central, imp "NYC" on hinged lid, 3-3/4" h **50.00**
Tea pot, silvered, Missouri Pacific & Iron Mountain, 10-oz size, front engraved "M.P.I.Mt.RY," backstamped "Missouri Pacific & Iron Mountain R. Wallace 03295," 4-1/2" h **230.00**

Illustration, Great Northern Railway, orig illus for cover of travel brochure, scenic marvel of America, Glacier National Park, c1920, full-color gouache on paper, detailed study, 9-1/2" x 14", 1/2" margins...................... **315.00**

Jug, Baltimore & Ohio, stoneware, brown cone top, one gal, 11-1/2" **210.00**

Kerosene can, Chicago & Northwestern, one gal, oxidized finish, emb "C&NRR," 13" h **25.00**

Lantern, D. L. & W. R. R., clear globe embossed "D.L. & W.," **$125**.
Photo courtesy of Dotta Auction Co., Inc.

Lantern, L.V.R.R., Adlake "Reliable" frame, dated 1931, ruby red globe embossed "L.V.R.R.," **$290**.
Photo courtesy of Dotta Auction Co., Inc.

Lantern

Adam & Westlake Co., Adlake Reliable, red 5-1/4" globe with P.R.R. stamped on top, Adlake #300 kero burner, orig wick.............................. **75.00**

Conger Lantern Co., Twin-Bulb, battery operated, chromed, bulbs missing **15.00**

Dietz

Fitzall, Inspectors, clear globe etched "NYC Lines," raised "Dietz Fitzall NYUSA".. **195.00**

Hi-Top, Vesta, clear globe, raised "US" and "Dietz Vesta" logo, bronze plated, rusted thru kero pot **48.00**

No. 999, NYC system, red Fresnel globe, Dietz convex kero burner, "NYCS" stamped on top............................ **95.00**

Letter opener, Southern Pacific, orig case, 7-3/4" l......... **30.00**

Locomotive nose plate, Frisco, black, heavy 1/8" stainless steel, 28" l **1,150.00**

Map

Chicago, Iowa, and Nebraska Railroad, color litho, published by J. Sage & Sons, Buffalo, NY, 1859, some discoloration and losses, mounted on linen, 26" x 23" **450.00**

Soo Line, Minneapolis, St. Paul, and Sault Ste. Marie RY, printed by Matthews, Northrup & Co. Buffalo, NY, c1890, 39" x 16" **130.00**

Williams Telegraph and Railroad Map of the New England States, dated 1852, by Alexander Williams, published by Redding & Co. Boston, printed table of construction costs for area railroads, hand-colored state borders, separated folds with later linen backing, some toning, 32" x 30" **60.00**

Name plate, Soo Line, cast aluminum, mounted on walnut back board, 24" l **95.00**

Operation manual, 4-1/2" x 7", New York Air Brake Co., 1909 .... **5.00**

Paperweight, Adlake Centennial, 1857-1957, extruded aluminum, 5" l **40.00**

Pass, PRR, 1940, black and red on blue........................... **5.00**

Plate, Missouri Pacific Lines, state flowers in panels on border, gold rim, $345.

Print, framed, Pennsylvania RR, #9604 locomotive, $125.

Photo courtesy of Dotta Auction Co., Inc.

Photo

Chicago, Rock Island & Pacific, Rocky Mountains, c1910, orig frame, 7" mat, 53" x 23" **920.00**

Denver & Rio Grande Railroad Depot, Canyon of the Rio Las Animas, Colo, hand colored black and white print, printed logo and title, "Copyright 1900 by Detroit Photographic Co.," orig oak frame, stains in margin, overall 33-1/2" x 27-1/2" **2,645.00**

Machinist Apprentices of the Chicago & Alton R.R., dated Sept. 5th 1908, depicting 34 apprentices posed on C & A R.R. locomotive #605, Stafford B. Cable photo, Bloomington, IL, orig frame and mat, 17" x 11" image size **490.00**

Soo Line, Lake Louise early 20th C, hand-colored black and white print, orig titled mat with Soo Line logo, orig oak frame, overall 25" x 21" ... **50.00**

Pinback button

Chesapeake & Ohio Railway Veteran Employees Assn, 21st annual meeting, Cincinnati Zoo, June 26, 1937 .... **20.00**

Division 241, American Assn of Street & Electric Railway Employees of America, purple and pink membership button **20.00**

Reading Lines, red image, white logo, green rim, c1930s **20.00**

Poster, 41-1/2" x 27-1/2", Greater Power, The New Haven Railroad, Latham Litho, Long Island City, Sascha Mauer, used to celebrate 50th anniversary and new locomotives **2,185.00**

Print, 7" x 10", *Loco-Erie Watering*, etching, Reginald Marsh, 1929, sgd in pencil **1,955.00**

Puzzle, paper covered wooden blocks, six scenes, $70.

Photo courtesy of Joy Luke Auctions.

Receipt

Baltimore and Ohio Assoc of Railways Surgeons, for membership dues, 1933 **5.00**

Baltimore and Ohio Railroad, 1884, freight bill, for shingles, sgd by agent W. L. Gross **12.00**

Steam whistle, brass

3" d, 8" h, single chime, lever control........................ **200.00**

5-1/2" d, 12" h, triple chime, manufactured by Crosby Steam, Gage & Valve Company, Boston, Pat. Jan. 30, 1877..................... **720.00**

Step ladder, ST.L.K& N-W Railroad, folding, wooden, four steps, stenciled "St.L.K&N-W" and "Mail Car 103" **270.00**

Step stool, Denver & Rio Grande Western RR, rubber no-skid top, 9" h......... **260.00**

Stock certificate

Buffalo, Rochester and Pittsburgh Railway Co., NY, train at station at left, miners working at right, 100 shares, common, red-brown design, ornate border, Franklin Bank Note Co., NY................. **30.00**

Cincinnati and Fort Wayne Railroad, IN, small train on left edge, common stock, .. **40.00**

Little Miami Railroad Co., Cincinnati, OH, vignette of Tom Thumb engine and cars with passengers and watchers, hole cancel, American Bank Note Co. **22.50**

Washington Railway & Electric Co., Washington, DC, vignette of trolley car in busy city, green, 100 shares, Western Bank Note Co., Chicago **24.00**

Ticket

1900, Niagara Gorge RR Co., Great Gorge Route, 2-1/4" x 1-5/16"........................... **12.00**

1903, International Railway Co., Buffalo, NY, stripe of five employee tickets, engraved title, Security Bank Note Co., Philadelphia, reverse with four digit number and "Not Good for Women or Children," 1-5/8" l, 11/16" w **18.00**

Steam whistle, brass and copper, mounted on keystone shaped wooden plaque along with cast iron railroad spike, **$95**.

Ticket cabinet, Soo Line, c1914, oak, locking tambour slant front, divided compartments for tickets, timetables, one drawer, stenciled "M.ST.P. & S.S.M.RY" on back, 21" x 35" x 16".............................. **460.00**

Timetable, 4" x 8-1/2"

Atlantic Coast, 1954 .... **2.50**

Delaware & Hudson, 1951 .... **2.50**

Lehigh Valley, 1951......... **3.50**

New York Central, 1946 .. **2.50**

Santa Fe, 1959 .... **2.50**

Seaboard, 1924-25......... **5.00**

Southern Pacific, 1912 ... **4.00**

Tray, Soo Line, Montana Success, map of Soo Line Route, tin litho, 10-1/2" x 15" **200.00**

Wax sealer

American Exchange Co., El Paso, Ill, brass die with wood handle, 3" l................. **150.00**

S.W. & B.V. RR, Agent-Bryan, Texas, one-piece brass die and handle, 2-1/2" l ... **550.00**

Toledo, Peoria & Western, Agent-El Paso, Ill, brass die, wood handle, 4" l **525.00**

RECORDS

History: With the advent of the more sophisticated recording materials, such as 33-1/3 RPM long-playing records, 8-track tapes, cassettes, and compact discs, earlier phonograph records became collectors' items. Most have little value. The higher-priced items are rare (limited-production) recordings. Condition is critical.

All records start with a master tape of an artist's or groups' performance. To make a record, mastering agent would play the master tape and feed the sound to a cutting lathe which electronically transcribes the music into the grooves of a circular black lacquer disc, known as an acetate. The acetate was played to determine if the sound quality was correct, to listen for defects or timing errors, order of presentation, etc. The finished acetate was then sprayed with a metal film. Once the film dries, the acetate is peeled away, creating a new "master" with a raised groove pattern. Another metallic compound is sprayed on the new "master" and after this compound is removed, a "mother" disc is created. The "mother" disc is then coated with another metallic compound, and when that is removed, a "stamper" is made. Pertinent production information is often written on the stamper before it

is pressed in the production process. Each two-sided record has two stampers, one for each side.

The material used for early 45s and LPs was polyvinyl chloride (PVC), and commonly called "vinyl." To make a record, hot PVC is pressed between the stampers using a compression molding process. Excess vinyl that is trimmed away after the pressing process is recycled. When this re-cycled material is reused, it may result in a record that looks grainy or pockmarked. Each stamper was good for about 1,000 pressings, then the whole process began again. Vinyl is still used for LPs, but polystyrene is now used for 45s. The production process for polystyrene is slightly different in that the base material is more liquid. Application of labels can be made directly to the polystyrene record, eliminating the label stamping process used with vinyl. To tell the difference between vinyl and styrene records, consider the following points:

Vinyl records are thicker and heavier.

7-inch vinyl 45s won't bend.

A label of one color with information "engraved" or spray painted in the center indicates a styrene record.

For more information, see *Warman's American Records, 2nd edition*; and *Warman's Records Field Guide*.

As with many types of antiques, a grading scale has been developed.

Mint (M): Perfect condition, no flaws, scratches, or scuffs in the grooves. The cardboard jacket will be crisp.

Near Mint (NM) or Mint-Minus (M-): The record will be close to perfect, with no marks in the grooves. The label will be clean, not marked, or scuffed. There will be no ring wear on the record or album cover.

Very Good Plus (VG+): Used for a record that has been played, but well taken care of. Slight scuffle or warps to the grooves is acceptable as long as it does not affect the sound. A faint ring wear discoloration is acceptable. The jacket may appear slightly worn, especially on the edges.

Very Good (VG): Used to describe a record that has some pronounced defects, as does the cover. The record will still play well. This usually is the lowest grade acceptable to a serious collector. Most records listed in price guides are of this grade.

Good (G): This category of record will be playable, but probably will have loss to the sound quality. Careful inspection of a styrene record in this condition may allow the viewer to see white in the grooves. The cover might be marked or torn.

Poor or Fair (P, F): Record is damaged, may be difficult to play. The cover will be damaged condition, usually marked, dirty, or torn.

Additional Listings: See *Warman's Americana & Collectibles* for more examples.

Note: Most records, especially popular recordings, have a value of less than $3 per disc. The records listed here are classic recordings of their type and are in demand by collectors.

Blues

Adkins, Katherine, Individual Blues, Okeh 8363 .... **45.00**

Alabama Jim, Crossin' Beale Street, Gennett 6905... **150.00**

Blind Blake, Early Morning Blues, Paramont 12387 **75.00**

Kelly, Willie, Big Time Woman, Victor 23270............... **165.00**

King, B. B., My Baby's Gone, RPM 318 .... **25.00**

Nighthawk, Robert, Return Mail Blues, Chess 1484........ **20.00**

Jimmy Rogers & His Trio, Going Away Baby, Chess 1442............................. **25.00**

Smith, Trixie, Trixie's Blues, Black Swan 2039 .... **25.00**

Washboard Sam's Band, Ocean Blues, Bluebird 5983 .... **85.00**

Children's

Dumbo, Disneyland, record and book, 1968, some wear .. **7.60**

Higitus Figitus, Walt Disney Productions, Little Golden Record, 1938 .... **8.00**

Partridge Family, Up To Date, Bell, 33-1/3 rpm, 1971 .. **15.00**

Star Wars, 24-page read-along book, 33-1/3 rpm record, Buena Vista................... **5.00**

The Adventures of Captain Midnight, set of eight numbered flexi-disk 33-1/3 records, each with 7"x 7" black and white sleeve, certificate, decoder **75.00**

Edison Records, box full of assorted titles, wax cylinders, each between **$5-$15.**

Country, LP

Allen, Jules, Jack O'Diamonds, Victor 21470................... **8.00**

Bunch, Sam, My Sarah Jane, Supertone 9372............. **8.00**

Choates, Harry, Hackberry Hop, Cajun Classics, 1007/1010 .... **12.00**

Delmore Brothers, Blue Railroad Train, Bluebird 5531 .... **12.50**

Kincaid, Bradley, The Old Wooden Bucket, Bluebird 5201............................. **10.00**

Lewis, Jerry Lee, All Country, 1969............................. **10.00**

Monroe Brothers, Roll in My Sweet Baby's Arms, Bluebird 6773............................. **12.00**

Puckett, Holland, Weeping Willow Tree, Gennett 614 .... **12.00**

Tweedy Brothers, Home Brew Rag, Champion 16048 . **18.00**

Wells, Kitty, Country Music Time, Decca DL 74554, black label with rainbow band through center **8.00**

Williams, Jimmie, Polecat Creek, Okeh V40240 .... **30.00**

Wynette, Tammy, Your Good Girl's Gonna Go Bad, Epic LN 26305, LP, stereo, 1967 .. **5.00**

Jazz, 78 RPM, 10" d

Alamana Harmony Boys, Chicken Supper Strut, Champion 15366........ **150.00**

Armstrong, Louis, I'm Gonna Gitcha, Okeh 8343 .... **75.00**

Dixie Jazz Band, Some of These Days, Oriole 413 .... **12.00**

Ellington, Duke, Jungle Nights in Harlem, Victor 23022 **20.00**

Gershwin, George, Someone to Watch Over Me, Columbia 812-D................... **15.00**

Goodman, Benny, Overnight, Melotone 12024........... **25.00**

Hayes, Clifford, Louisville Stompers, Bare-Foot Stomp, Victor 21489 .... **100.00**

Holiday, Billie, A Fine Romance, Vocalian 3333............... **15.00**

Martin, Dean, Oh Marie, Apollo 1088........................... **30.00**

New Orleans Jazz Band, Tiger Rag, Banner 6049 .... **10.00**

Oriole Orchestra, Honolulu Blues, Brunswick 2398 . **10.00**

Robinson, Elzadie, Houston Bound, Paramount 12420 .... **90.00**

Smith, Kate, Tell Me A Love Song, Columbia 2563-D **12.00**

Tennessee Music Men, Bugle Call Rag, Clarion 5461-C **25.00**

Trumbauer, Frankie, High Up On a Hill Top, Okeh 41128 .... **40.00**

Vallee, Rudy, Caressing You, Harmony 834-H **10.00**

Waters, Ethel, Stormy Weather, Brunswick 6564 .... **15.00**

Wilson, Duke, & His Ten Black Berries, Once or Twice, Perfect 15697 .... **20.00**

Zenith Knights, Eyes of Blue, QRS 1020 .... **12.00**

Rock

Beatles
Can't Buy Me Love, You Can't Do That, Capitol 4140, 1964, picture sleeve **200.00**
Help, I'm Down, Capitol 5476, 1965, with "A Subsidiary of Capitol" in white along perimeter **25.00**
I Wanna Hold Your Hand, Capitol 5112, 1964 .... **40.00**

Dean, James, A Tribute to James Dean, Columbia, 33-1/3 rpm, c1956 .... **18.00**

Golden Earring, Greatest Hits, Polydor 236228, Dutch imp, LP **10.00**

Four Beatles LP albums: Capitol T2385 "Beatles VI", Vee Jay VJP 1085 "The Beatles and Frank Ifield"; Capitol 2835 Mono, "Magical Mystery Tour" and Capitol ST 8-2047 "Meet the Beatles," all in original covers, **$150**.

Photo courtesy of Joy Luke Auctions.

Every record collector needs a place to store their records. This record case is similar to a stacking barrister type bookcase with glass front doors, with each unit having an identification numbering system, **$350.**

Lennon, John, Roots, Adam VII-A-80100, orig, LP ... **200.00**
Monkees, Valerie, Tapicoca Tundra, Colgems, 45 rpm, late 1960s **5.00**
Presley, Elvis
  Elvis, RCA Victor, 33-1/3 rpm, black label **30.00**
  Elvis Fun in Acapulco, RCA Victor, 1963 .... **45.00**
  Elvis Presley His Hand In Mine, RCA Victor, black label, 33-1/3 rpm **35.00**
  That's All Right, Blue Moon of Kentucky, Sun 209, 1954 .... **750.00**
The Hollies, Here I Go Again, Imperial LP-9265, 1964, black label with stars............. **25.00**

Tiny Tim, With Love and Kisses From Tiny Tim, Concerts in Fairyland, Bouquet, late 1960s........................... **12.00**
Wells, Mary, album, 20th Century Fox , #TFM3171B, 1965.............................. **5.00**

REDWARE

History: The availability of clay, the same used to make bricks and roof tiles, accounted for the great production of red earthenware pottery in the American colonies. Redware pieces are mainly utilitarian—bowls, crocks, jugs, etc.

Lead-glazed redware retained its reddish color, but a variety of colored glazes were obtained by the addition of metals to the basic glaze. Streaks and mottled splotches in redware items resulted from impurities in the clay and/or uneven firing temperatures.

Slipware is the term used to describe redwares decorated by the application of slip, a semi-liquid paste made of clay. Slipwares were made in England, Germany, and elsewhere in Europe for decades before becoming popular in the Pennsylvania German region and other areas in colonial America.

Charger, yellow four-line slip decoration, Pennsylvania, 19th C, chip, 12" d, **$350.**

Redware photos courtesy of Pook & Pook.

Birdhouse, 8" d, 10-1/2" h, incised banding dec, finial with hanging hole **470.00**
Bowl, 6-3/8" d, 1-1/2" h, mottled, orange glaze, unglazed exterior, attributed to Miller Pottery, minor chips, usage wear **440.00**

Egg cup, green and orange manganese decoration, attributed to by Bell Pottery, 19th C, 2-1/2" h, **$2,185.**

Crock
  3-1/2" d, 2-1/2" h, molded rim, manganese brown int. glaze **250.00**
  6" d, 4" h, molded rim, red-orange and green glaze **360.00**
Figure
  2" h, 2-1/4" l, 1-1/2" w, chicken on base, orange glaze, attributed to Jesiah Shorb, W Manheim Twp, York County, PA, restoration to front edge of base........................ **1,320.00**
  2-5/8" h, 2-3/4" l, 1-1/2" w, rooster on base, orange glaze, attributed to Jesiah Shorb, W Manheim Twp, York County, PA, restoration front edge of base **1,485.00**
  3-1/2" h, 2-3/4" l, 2" w, seated squirrel on base, eating nut, orange glaze, attributed to Jesiah Shorb, W Manheim Twp, York County, PA, tail restoration................ **1,715.00**
  4-1/4" h, 2-3/4" l, 2-1/4" h, seated begging dog on base, basket of fruit, incised fur, orange glaze, attributed to Jesiah Shorb, W Manheim Twp, York County, PA.......... **7,150.00**
  4-3/4" h, 3-1/2" l, 2" w, seated begging dog on base, incised, dark glaze, circular banding imp at base, attributed to Elia Swartzbaugh, Jefferson, York County, PA **2,970.00**
  5" h, seated dog, reddish-brown glaze, row of incised circles at base, attributed to Peter Bell, Shenandoah Valley, Waynesboro, PA **8,500.00**
  5" l, freestanding hound, yellow glazed, brown raised and incised ears and tail, attributed to Peter Bell................ **9,000.00**

5-1/2" h, 6-1/2" l, 2-3/4" w, dog carrying basket of fruit, green-orange glazing, base sgd "Ernst Beicher, the 8 1/3 Month 1862," provenance: possibly one of two known sgd examples, Eugene and Dorothy Elgin collection, Conestoga Auction, April 3, 2004 .... **44,000.00**

7-1/2" l, 8" w, poodle, standing, yellow, green, and brown, coleslaw clay to front half of body, leads and raised head, stepped orange oval base, incised "Anton Audon Ruppert May 1869" **20,000.00**

Finger bowl, 4" d, 1-3/4" h, orange ground, brown sponge dec, molded base, incised banding to rim, chips, small rim restoration ... **385.00**

Fireplace trivet, 6-14" sq, 2-1/2" h, scalloped edges, four feet, unglazed, sgd "S. Hiney" on base, wear . **635.00**

Flower pot, attached undertray, green and brown glaze over cream ground, Shenandoah Valley, 19th C, 7-1/2" d, 8" h, **$2,900.**

Flower pot, 5-5/8" h, mottled green and brown glaze, rust ground, crimped rim, attached saucer, attributed to John Bell **275.00**

Inkwell, 8" l, 3-1/2" w, 3-3/4" h, three inkwells, sander, two pen compartments, dark manganese glaze, PA, firing line on front **600.00**

Jar, cov, 7-5/8" h, 6" d, bear shape, button finial, orange-brown glaze **1,045.00**

Jar, open
5-1/4" h, 5" d, bulbous, flared rim, incised banding, red-orange ground, black sponge-dripped highlights **750.00**

6-3/4" h, 6" d, flared rim, three color slip dec of village, houses, pine trees, grass, festooned yellow slip border, found in Hanover, PA **9,350.00**

7" h, flared rim on sloped shoulder, brownish-green glaze with lighter spots and dark brown streaks, attributed to New England, late 18th/early 19th C, minor wear to glaze on rim **360.00**

7-1/2" h, barrel shaped, splotched dec, four ribbed and incised bands, dated "1766" **5,000.00**

11" h, ovoid, raised rim, lug handles, incised line on shoulder, brown streak deco, CT, early 19th C, minor shallow rim chips **1,530.00**

Jug
4-1/2" d, 5" h, bulbous, applied handle, brown manganese glaze, minor chips **415.00**

5-1/2" d, 6-1/2" h, bulbous, applied handle, incised banding on shoulder, manganese glaze, glaze chips **440.00**

5-3/4" d, 6-1/4" h, applied handle, incised banding at center, brown manganese glaze **200.00**

6" d, 7-1/8" h, bulbous, applied handle, molded spout, brown manganese glaze **250.00**

6-1/2" d, 9" h, bulbous, applied handle, formed spout, brown manganese glaze **220.00**

7" d, 8-3/4" h, bulbous, applied handle, brown manganese glaze **275.00**

7-1/4" d, 8-1/4" h, applied handle, brown manganese glaze, usage wear, base chips **210.00**

9" d, harvest, spout, mottled glaze, yellow and brown glaze, stamped "G. H. Baker" on side, (G. H. Baker, Hamilton Twp, Adams County, PA" **2,860.00**

Miniature
Jug, 2-1/2" w, 3" h, applied handle, brown and black mottled glaze, attributed to Jesiah Shorb, W Manheim Twp, York County, PA, handle broken and glued **110.00**

Turk's head, 3-3/4" d, 1-1/2" h, brown-orange glaze, PA **715.00**

Pie plate, 8-5/8" d, 1-3/4" h, slip dec, orange base glaze int., three double slip squiggle lines **1,375.00**

Pie plate, yellow slip decoration of three wave lines in center, straight lines on right and left, three branches on top and bottom, lead glaze, southeastern Pennsylvania, early to mid-1800s, 8" d, **$350.**

Photo courtesy of Gamal Amer.

Plate, sgraffito, showing Ben Franklin reading book, framed by Pennsylvania Dutch verse, dated 1779, 12" diameter, 2" deep, 19th C repair to glued crack, **$2,530.**

Photo courtesy of Bruce & Vicki Wassdorp.

Plate
8-7/8" d, 1-1/2" h, orange ground glaze, green and black slip tulip dec, attributed to Dryville Pottery, some discoloration **2,750.00**

10-3/4" d, 1-3/4" h, serrated rim, yellow slip dec of bird on branch, orange glaze, normal wear **8,525.00**

10-3/4" d, 1-3/4" h Sgraffito dec, centralized flower, German text banding rim, orange ground, yellow, blue, and green highlights to flower, dated 1846, translation of rim inscription "The Star that Looks Down on the Flask has Destroyed the Luck of Many," minor chips on rim ... **11,000.00**

Plate, yellow slip decoration, Pennsylvania, 19th C, chip, 5-3/4" d, **$415.**

11-3/4" d, Mary's Dish, squiggle lines and dots, interior flakes and chips **4,800.00**

Pot, 4-3/4" d, 3-7/0" h, Incised bands at rim and base, brown glaze **135.00**

Potter's brick, 4-1/2" l, 3" w, 2" h, orange glaze, inscribed "Solomon Miller, Reading Township, Adams Co. May 28," back with date 186?, wear from use as door stop **715.00**

Salt, open, master, 3-3/4" d, 2" h, incised banding, brown and black glaze, inscribed "Made by Solomon Miller," Adams Co., PA **2,310.00**

Shaving mug, reddish-brown glazed slipware, brown splotched dots and lines, two bands of incised lines, c1805-25, small scuttle container **3,300.00**

Smoking pipe, 3-1/2" w, 3-1/2" h, orange and brown mottled glaze **750.00**

Sugar bowl, cov
Open reticulated work on bowl and lid, rope twist handles, yellow-brown glaze, attributed to Jesiah Shorb, W Manheim Twp, York County, PA **9,900.00**
Two applied handles, molded rim, red-brown glaze, drip manganese brown dec, zigzag banding on lid with finial, 6-1/2" w, 5-1/4" h **1,595.00**

Vessel, 7-3/4" d, 5-3/4" h, tapered, incised banding, D-shaped cut-out handles, orange and green mottled glaze, Dover, York County, PA **880.00**

RED WING POTTERY

History: The Red Wing pottery category includes several potteries from Red Wing, Minnesota. In 1868, David Hallem started Red Wing Stoneware Co., the first pottery with stoneware as its primary product. The Minnesota Stoneware Co. started in 1883. The North Star Stoneware Co. was in business from 1892 to 1896.

The Red Wing Stoneware Co. and the Minnesota Stoneware Co. merged in 1892. The new company, the Red Wing Union Stoneware Co., made stoneware until 1920 when it introduced a pottery line that it continued until the 1940s. In 1936, the name was changed to Red Wing Potteries, Inc. During the 1930s, this firm introduced several popular patterns of hand-painted dinnerware, which were distributed through department stores, mail-order catalogs, and gift-stamp centers. Dinnerware production declined in the 1950s and was replaced with hotel and restaurant china in the early 1960s. The plant closed in 1967.

Marks: Red Wing Stoneware Co. was the first firm to mark pieces with a red wing stamped under the glaze. The North Star Stoneware Co. used a raised star and the words "Red Wing" as its mark.

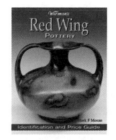

For more information, see *Warman's Red Wing Pottery.*

Bowl, Brush Ware, daisy type embossed decoration on exterior, green glazed interior, marked "Red Wing Union Stoneware, Red Wing, Minn," **$75.**

Bean pot, cov, "It Pays to Trade with Shors & Alexander Pocahontas, IA" **85.00**

Bowl
4" d, Spongeband **275.00**
6" d, Greek Key **115.00**
7" d, brown shoulder, bottom mkd **45.00**
7" d, sponge dec, cap shape **95.00**
8" d, Spongeband, "Merry Christmas from Weigolb & Nordby Stores, Mix With Us" **125.00**
9" d, Spongeband **145.00**
13" d, shoulder, mkd... **175.00**

Butter churn, two gallons, 2" wing and oval mark **250.00**

Butter crock
One gallon, "Polly Ann Boston Baked Beans"............. **175.00**
Three lbs, "Fresh Butter Model Dairy Inc." **75.00**
Three lbs, "North American Creameries, Inc., Meadowbrook Butter". **125.00**
Three lbs, "White & Mathers" adv.............................. **200.00**
Five lbs, "Goodhue County Co-ooperative Co.," minor nick on top edge **95.00**

Casserole, Spongeband, large **125.00**

Casserole, cov, 8" d, "Merry Christmas Hokah Co-Op Creamery" **195.00**

Chicken water, half gallon, "Oak Leaf Simmon's Hardware Co." **250.00**

Churn, four gallons
4" wing and oval mark **175.00**
Oval over birch leaf, hairline in bottom **145.00**
Salt glaze, lazy 8 and target dec **375.00**

Churn lid, 5/6 gallon **120.00**

Crock
One gallon, 2" wing **350.00**
Two gallons, 4" wing mark **90.00**

Three gallons, 2" wing and circle oval mark **90.00**
Three gallon, 2" wing, "Potteries" oval **65.00**
Eight gallons, 6" wing and oval mark, chip on base........ **75.00**
Ten gallon, 6" wing and oval mark, "10" and oval in black ink **125.00**
Twenty gallons, 6" wing and oval mark **125.00**
Crock, salt glaze
Two gallons, target, bottom mkd **100.00**
Three gallons, tornado, front stamped "Red Wing Stoneware Company," large chip at bottom............ **250.00**
Five gallons, birchleaf, Union label, chip on handle **55.00**
Six gallons, leaf dec ... **175.00**
Ten gallons, leaf, front stamped "Minnesota Stoneware," hairline.... **250.00**
Twenty lbs, butterfly, back stamped, hairlines **175.00**
Crock lid
One-gallon size............ **90.00**
Two gallons **225.00**
Fifteen gallons, nick where wire handle enters lid ... **65.00**
Custard, Spongeband
Large, tight hairline....... **65.00**
Small **85.00**
Funeral vase, Brushware . **65.00**
Hotplate, Minnesota Centennial, 1958............................. **45.00**
Jug
One-eighth pint, Michigan advertising **225.00**
One gallon, ball top shoulders, bottom mkd. **95.00**
One gallon, brown top shoulders, "The Banner Liquor Store, Winona, Minn" **175.00**
One gallon, brown top shoulders, wing mark . **195.00**
One gallon, "Fargo Creamery Supply House St. Paul, Minn" in oval, bottom marked **150.00**
One gallon, tomato, brown top, wing mark **395.00**
Three gallons, shoulder, 2" wing and no oval mark . **35.00**
Five gallons, Imperial, shoulder, 4" wing and oval mark.......................... **125.00**
Five gallon, shoulders, 4" wing and "Union" oval........... **80.00**
Five gallons, shoulder, "The Mason House & Mineral Springs, Colfax Iowa," shield and Union label **775.00**

Dinnerware set, Tampico, 80 pieces, **$500**.
Photo courtesy of Dotta Auction Co., Inc.

Koverwate
Three gallons, "3" on side with instructions **450.00**
Fifteen gallons, mkd "15," small nick................... **125.00**
Mug
Blue bands, "Certainly" **150.00**
Blue bands, "Good Luck Malt Syrup," hairline **135.00**
Blue bands, "I Came From Atlas Malt Products Co., Janesville, WI," hairline **115.00**
Blue bands, "Souvenir West End Commercial Club, St. Paul June 21-26, 1909" **185.00**
Spongeband.............. **575.00**
Nappy
Blue and white **120.00**
Saffronware, "Compliments of C. A. Habergarten & Co., Waconia, Minn" **195.00**
Pitcher
Blue mottled, large, minor bottom edge chips **200.00**
Cherry band, large **175.00**
Cherry band, small **195.00**
Spongeband, large..... **195.00**
Spongeband, small **335.00**
Sponge, mottled **165.00**
Refrigerator jar, small size, hairline **65.00**
Salt shaker, Spongeband, white glaze........................... **120.00**
Sewer tile **70.00**
Snuff jar, cov, North Star, Albany slip, minor chip under lid **125.00**
Spittoon, German-style, bottom edge chip **375.00**

Thrashing jug, five gallons, beehive, 4" wing and oval mark, six-sided spigot hole **1,650.00**
Water cooler, five gallons, 4" wing mark **350.00**

RELIGIOUS ITEMS

History: Objects used in worship or as expressions of man's belief in a superhuman power are collected by many people for many reasons.

This category includes icons, since they are religious mementos, usually paintings with a brass encasement. Collecting icons dates from the earliest period of Christianity. Most antique icons in today's market were made in the late 19th century.

Reproduction Alert: Icons are frequently reproduced.

Alms box, covered, hinged, carved and painted gesso figures, 12-1/2" x 6-1/4" x 10-3/4" h, **$400**.

Photo courtesy of Joy Luke.

Altar crucifix, 24" h, wood frame overlaid with repoussé copper, cabochons, paste stones, verso with compartment for relic . **550.00**

Architectural relief of saint, 16-1/8" w, 25-5/8" h, carved walnut, male figure holding pair of keys, standing in arched niche, traces of gilding, Continental, late 17th/early 18th C, set into velvet framed open shadow box **1,650.00**

Buddha
Coral, carved, sitting position, base carved flat and with sedimentary inclusions, two-character signature, China, 18th or 19th C **420.00**

Bronze
Young features, crane at his feet, Chinese, 19th C, slight wear to patina **850.00**
Amida in appeasement mudra, bronze, partial gilt, boxed, China, 19th C, 6" h **2,820.00**
Amytaus, gilt bronze, China, 18th C, 8" h **1,410.00**
Stone, bust, old tan color, 16-1/4" h, 12-1/4" w, 8" d **415.00**
Wood, carved, standing image of Amida, ornate throne, halo at back, gilt surface, Japan, 19th C, 21" h, losses........................... **650.00**

Bust
10-1/2" h, gilded metal Immaculate Heart of Mary and the Sacred Heart of Jesus, onyx pedestal with flared base, French, c1920, price for pr **320.00**
11-1/2" h, veiled Madonna, hand painted porcelain, Royal Worcester, 1863 .... **1,495.00**

Candlestick, 38-1/2" h, Ciborium-form, silver plated, quatrefoil crown-form sconce, over cathedral-form stem with pointed arches and flying buttresses, square section standard, base with clipped corners and recumbent lion-form feet, conforming marble plinth base, Gothic Revival, C. Nisini, Rome, late 19th C **650.00**

Chalice and paten
9" h, engraved and partial gilt sterling, French, c1920 .... **815.00**
9" h, sterling, c1920 .... **435.00**

9-1/4" h, heavy solid gilded silver, Gothic style, c1922 .... **1,065.00**
9-1/2" h, partial gilt sterling, c1920 .... **700.00**

Chausable, 40-1/2" l, Gothic Revival, silk, metallic embroidery, and stumpwork, cream silk ground, stitched central Gothic cross, centered by metal purl stumpwork agnes dei, flanked by scrolling gilt and gilt embroidered flowering vines, ending in metal spherule mounted grape bunches, metallic ribbon trim, late 19th C **600.00**

Corpus, 39" h, 23-1/4" w, carved wood, polychrome, gilt, detailed features, hand forged iron spike, European, 18th C, some repainting **2,300.00**

Crucifix
14" h, finely painted, overlaid with ornate repoussé, chased riza, Russian, 19th C **1,150.00**
28" x 23", finely carved, South German, 19th/20th C .. **520.00**

Deity
4-1/2" h, porcelain, seated on lotus pillow, Famille rose enamels, gilt body, Chinese, 18th or 19th C, chips to petals on crown, old repairs around neck **1,100.00**
6-3/8" h, Mahaka, bronze, deity standing on prostrated figure, double lotus base, polychrome highlights, Tibetan, 19th C **1,315.00**
7" h, Yamantaka Vajrabhairava, gilt bronze, buffalo headed deity in yabyum with his consort, trampling prostrated figures and animals, sealed lotus base with Sanskrit inscription, Tibetan, 18th C **5,260.00**

Figure
5-1/4" h, praying Madonna, Pattarino.................... **435.00**
5-1/2" h, Image of God of Literature, China, Ming period (1368-1644), bronze ... **500.00**
7" h, Goddess, Chola-style, bronze, Indian, late 19th C **325.00**
7" h, Lama, seated on double lotus throne, bronze, cold gold paste on the face, inscription on front ... **3,290.00**
12-1/4", St. Thomas Aquinas, carved and polychrome gilt wood, Spanish-Colonial, 19th C **750.00**

Ecclesiastical vestments, left: burgundy floral silk damask, trimmed with ivory and burgundy silk fringe, fully lined in tan linen, c1900, **$125**; right: rose and tan brocade with bird, urn and flower motif, trimmed with gold metallic lace, lined with yellow and green cotton, c1890, wear, **$115**.

Photo courtesy of Alderfer Auction Co.

14-1/2" h, Christ on the Cross, carved and polychromed wood, clad in loin cloth, blood dripping down body, metal crown of thorns, metal halo inserts, nailed on cross with plaque marked INRI, raised on stepped square base with two carved miniature angels at feet, Spanish, Colonial **360.00**
14-1/2" h, Madonna and sleeping Christ, Pattarino **1,495.00**
15-1/2", Image of Wish Bestowing Avalokitesvara, gilt bronze, Korea, 11th C, possible repair to the feet **5,875.00**
16" h, St Christopher carrying Infant Christ, carved and polychrome, glass eyes, silver halo and crown, 20th C **700.00**
16-1/2" h, Madonna and Child, Christ holding rosebud, delivering blessing, Pattarino **2,990.00**
18-3/4" h, Black Madonna and Child, Pattarino **3,450.00**
21-1/2" h, Madonna and Child, carved and polychrome gilt wood, Baroque style, South German, 20th C........... **815.00**

21-1/2" h, Madonna and Child, fully carved in the round, base inscribed "Oberamergare," South German, c1930........... **500.00**
22" h, Madonna and Child, finely carved and polychromed, Baroque taste, German, 20th C **575.00**
22" h, Madonna and Child enthroned, Pattarino **3,795.00**
25" h, Madonna and Child, carved polychrome and gilt wood, South German, late 19th/early 20th **1,900.00**

Funerary centerpiece, 45" x 31", beaded wire construction for casket top, French, c1890-1910............................ **300.00**

Icon, Buddhist, 32" x 21", mandala of Yamantakra surrounded by wrathful deities of ancient Bon faith, Tibet, 18th C **1,500.00**

Icon, Greek
11" x 14", The Evangelist St. Mark, c1700, finely painted on gold leafed ground **980.00**
25-1/2" x 34", The Mother of God, 18th C, sgd by iconographer lower right "Georgio Pandi".......... **865.00**
38" h, Bishop Saint, carved and polychrome wood, Provincial, French, 17th C
.... **460.00**

Choir robe, black, black velvet stripe details, large, **$45**.

Photo courtesy of Joy Luke.

Icon, Russian
10" x 12", The Birth of John the Forerunner, c1700 ... **1,265.00**
10-1/2" x 12", Mandylion, (The Not Made By Hand Image,) c1750......................... **835.00**
10-1/2" x 12-1/2", The Kazan Mother of God, c1775. **1,495.00**
11" x 9-1/4", The Lord Almighty, c1650 .... **3,220.00**
11" x 13", The Korsunskaya Mother of God, c1675-1725
.... **1,495.00**
22-3/4" x 12", The Archangel Gabriel, gold leaf and incised ground, c1890 .... **750.00**
32" x 19-1/2", The Sign Mother of God...................... **1,610.00**

Monstrance and lunette,
27-1/2" h Gothic-style gem set gilded silver and enamel monstrance on large sculpted circular base depicting four evangelists with their symbols, octagonal pillar with four sided shelter with column niches, each with saint, Gothic canopy, central exposition window set within open fretwork of scrolling grapevines resting on base set with horizontal row of guillouche enamel and four gilded silver bell drops, flanked by pair of Gothic shrines with spires, 16 individually sculpted saints, each set with champleve enamel, above window baldacchino set with intricate arches and spires, mounted with 82 rose cut garnets and four pearls, bezel surrounding central exposition set with 60 rose cut garnets, 19 diamonds, one synthetic diamond, 10 lbs, 2 oz, engraved lunette with 2-1/2" d luna, Madrid, after 1935, custom padded case
.... **9,450.00**

Mosaic, 24" x 30", Madonna and Child, more than 7,000 individually cut and placed colored stones, gilded frame, Byzantine style, early 20th C
.... **2,990.00**

Painting, oil on board, Ernst Christian Pfannschmidt, German 1868-1941, Angels Mourning the Crucified Christ, sgd lower right, dated 1898, 16" x 12".................... **2,070.00**

Painting, oil on canvas, Charles Bosseron Chambers, American, 1882-1964, Adoration of the Magi, sgd lower left, 32" x 26" .. **6,900.00**

Pendant, 18k gold rope frame centering two reverse painted images of Virgin Mary holding infant Jesus **265.00**

Plaque, pink luster border, black verse: "The loss of gold is great, The loss of health is more, But losing Christ is such a loss As no man can restore," **$95**.

Plaque, 5-1/4" x 4-1/8", Duomo from a Distance, pietra dura, showing roof of the Duomo in a distant landscape, with green and gold painted border, Italian, late 19th/early 20th C, set in gold painted frame **275.00**

Processional candleholders, pr, 15-1/4" d, 19-1/2" l, metal, single light, trumpet shaped, eight trefoil ribs ending in scrolls, band of acanthus, guilloche and trefoil labrequins at waist, candle nozzle set into wood lined interior, Renaissance Revival, Venetian, late 19th C, lacking poles **560.00**

Reliquary
3-1/4" h, gilded filigree and enamel, French........... **300.00**
12" h, ornate gilded filigree, relics of several saints and apostles **550.00**
12-3/4" h, ornate gilded, paste stones and cabochons, relic of St. Catherine Laboure
.... **700.00**
14-1/4", cross-form, gilded, relic of true cross..... **2,875.00**
15" x 15", elaborately framed, 18 relics **1,265.00**
17-1/2" h, bronze, relics of cross, apostles, and several saints **1,610.00**

Rosary beads, 18k gold and platinum crucifix, Sloan & Co., black hardstone beads suspending two sided medal, yellow gold crucifix with platinum Christ, 43.1 dwt, hallmark, missing one bead, chain detached, provenance: from estate of Reverend

Thomas Mary O'Leary (1875-1949), Bishop of Springfield **360.00**

Santos, 8-1/2" h, carved wood, well dressed shepherd carrying lamb, tin flag, orig red, blue, and yellow paint, trace of gilt, wear, Spanish **200.00**

Retablo, Spanish Colonial School, 19th C, Our Lady of Guadalupe with Juan Diego, paint decoration gesso on hand-adzed wood panel, 11" x 7-1/2", **$800**.

Photo courtesy of Skinner, Inc.

Santos, two monk form figures, losses, 10-1/2" h, 10-3/4" h, **$150**.

Photo courtesy of Abilene Antique Co

Still life, 25-3/4" x 29", mosaic, depicting fruit on a tabletop, Vatican Workshops, early 20th C, bearing paper label from the Mosaic Studios at San Pietro in the Vatican, artist name Cassio, 35-3/4" x 29" giltwood frame **7,050.00**

Tabernacle, 31" h, gilt bronze, removable dome lid for exposition, c1940 .... **980.00**

Tantric crown, 10" h, repoussè copper with parcel gilt, coral and turquoise inlays, Tibet or Nepal, 18th C or earlier **650.00**

Tapestry fragment, 118" x 81", Madonna enthroned, flanked by saints, other biblical scenes, Continental, 17th/18th C **6,465.00**

REVERSE PAINTING ON GLASS

History: The earliest examples of reverse painting on glass were produced in 13th-century Italy. By the 17th century, the technique had spread to central and eastern Europe. It spread westward as the center of the glassmaking industry moved to Germany in the late 17th century.

The Alsace and Black Forest regions developed a unique portraiture style. The half and three-quarter portraits often were titled below the portrait. Women tend to have generic names, while most males are likenesses of famous men.

The English used a mozzotint, rather than free-style, method to create their reverse paintings. Landscapes and allegorical figures were popular. The Chinese began working in the medium in the 17th century, eventually favoring marine and patriotic scenes.

Most American reverse painting was done by folk artists and is unsigned. Portraits, patriotic and mourning scenes, floral compositions, landscapes, and buildings are the favorite subjects. Known American artists include Benjamin Greenleaf, A. Cranfield, and Rowley Jacobs.

In the late 19th century, commercially produced reverse paintings, often decorated with mother-of-pearl, became popular. Themes included the Statue of Liberty, the capitol in Washington, D.C., and various world's fairs and expositions.

Today craftsmen are reviving this art, using some vintage-looking designs, but usually with brighter colors than their antique counterparts.

Sailing ship, windmill, original oval frame, **$95**.

Mirrors

12-1/4" w, 21" h, reverse painted panel with fenced house, attributed to John Rupp, Hanover, York County, PA, Federal period, molding and columns, yellow and red grain paint dec frame **3,575.00**

13-1/4" w, 22-1/2" h, reverse painted white house, red and yellow roof, mahogany and mahogany veneer on pine, orig dark finish, reeded lower corner blocks and center divider, applied rope twist pilasters, scalloped cornice, turned acorn drops, orig backboards, some flaking to reverse panel **260.00**

13-1/4" w, 25" h, reverse painted panel with two men in boat on lake, cottage in background, attributed to John Rupp, Hanover, York County, PA, Federal period, molding and columns, yellow and red combed grain paint dec frame.................... **1,870.00**

18-1/4" w, 33-3/4" h, Federal, primitive orig painting of houses with double chimneys near stream, mahogany frame with old reddish brown varnish, reeded pilasters, cove molded cornice and base........................... **375.00**

36-5/8" w, 38" h, reverse painted panel with British naval battle scene, inner walnut veneered surround, giltwood and composition mirror with shaped crest centered by female mask and flanked by scrolls, mid-Georgian-style **4,700.00**

Portraits

7-1/4" w, 8-1/4" h, Napoleon, military uniform, painted mat, cast plaster frame **200.00**

Portrait of Martha Washington, c1830, 23-1/2" x 19-1/2", **$250**.

Photo courtesy of Pook & Pook.

7-1/4" w, 9" h, George Washington, blue coat, ruffles, teal oval background, brown rect, white border, old burl walnut frame **690.00**

9" w, 12" h, Lafayette, gray hair, blue and red military uniform, fur collared green coat, titled "Lafajetty" in bottom border, orig frame, some flaking **825.00**

9-1/4" w, 11-1/2" h, Albert von England, military uniform with medal, sash, and epaulettes, titled in white bottom border, black painted frame, some flaking, damage to one corner **320.00**

11-1/2" w, 15-1/2" h, woman dressed white, blue shawl, seated outdoors, holding basket of flowers on bounder in front, minor wear with flaking edges, possibly orig backboard, later gilt frame with black repaint **920.00**

12" w, 15-3/8" h, young woman seated at tea table, holding white rose in hand, yellow skirt, blue jacket, white lace, white border mkd "Morgen," black painted frame, some flaking, corner cracked **175.00**

Church scene, mica highlights, framed, **$65**.

Photo courtesy of Dotta Auction Co., Inc.

Scenes

7" x 9", Perry's Lake Erie Victory, Sept. 10, 1813, naval battle scene **250.00**

8-1/4" w, 6-1/4" h, Mount Vernon, river, boat, and trees, old repainted frame **550.00**

10-1/2" h, 12-1/2" w, country house in winter, gold painted frame............................ **75.00**

10-1/2" h, 12-1/2" w, *Ohio*, side wheeler steamship, poplar frame, 10-1/2" h, 12-1/2" w **175.00**

ROCKINGHAM AND ROCKINGHAM BROWN-GLAZED WARES

History: Rockingham ware can be divided into two categories. The first consists of the fine china and porcelain pieces made between 1826 and 1842 by the Rockingham Company of Swinton, Yorkshire, England, and its predecessor firms: Swinton, Bingley, Don, Leeds, and Brameld. The Bramelds developed the cadogan, a lidless teapot. Between 1826 and 1842, the Bramelds developed a quality soft-paste product with a warm, silky feel. Elaborate specialty pieces were made. By 1830, the company employed 600 workers and listed 400 designs for dessert sets and 1,000 designs for tea and coffee services in its catalog. Unable to meet its payroll, the company closed in 1842.

The second category of Rockingham ware includes pieces produced in the famous Rockingham brown glaze that became an intense and vivid purple-brown when fired. It had a dark, tortoiseshell appearance. The glaze was copied by many English and American potteries. American manufacturers that used Rockingham glaze include D. & J. Henderson of Jersey City, New Jersey; United States Pottery in Bennington, Vermont; potteries in East Liverpool, Ohio; and several potteries in Indiana and Illinois.

Additional Listings: Bennington and Bennington-Type Pottery.

Bowl, 9-1/2" d, 3-1/4" h **65.00**
Casserole, cov, 12" l, 10-1/4" h, oval, fruit finial, applied handles **275.00**

Portraits, left: gentleman in black suit, standing in room with dark green drape, patterned carpet, SRC, "B. F. Ferguson," shaped frame, 16-1/4" w, 21-3/8" h, slight losses, **$200**; right: woman wearing royal blue gown, hook skirt, holding white fan and lace handkerchief, standing in room with pink drape, patterned carpet, S&DRC, "B. F. Ferguson 1867," shaped frame, stamp on reverse: "B. F. Ferguson Artist, S.W.Cor. 8th & Arch St., Philadelphia," 16-1/4" w, 21-3/8" h, **$250**.

Photo courtesy of Alderfer Auction Co.

Pitcher, hound handle, yelloware, relief design of eight columns of hanging game and fowl, relief eagle below spout, c1850, 9-1/2" h, minor hairline, **$125**.

Photo courtesy of Bruce & Vicki Wassdorp

Creamer, 6-3/4" h, cow-form, 19th C, minor chips **260.00**
Cuspidor, 6-5/8", 4" h, four sides, molded eagles, dark brown Rockingham glaze **330.00**
Figure, 12-1/2" h, molded seated spaniel, mottled brown glaze over yellow pottery, chips, flakes................ **615.00**
Flask, 8" h, molded floral dec, band **45.00**
Flower pot, 10-1/4" h, emb acanthus leaves, matching saucer........................... **45.00**
Inkwell, 4-1/8" l, shoe shape **60.00**
Mixing bowl, nested set of three, emb design **95.00**
Pie plate, Rockingham glaze, 10" d.............................. **80.00**
Pitcher, 12" h, Revolutionary War battle scene with George Washington **2,750.00**
Plate, 9" d, painted center with exotic bird in landscape, raised C-scroll border with gilt and painting, puce griffin and green number marks .. **650.00**
Potpourri vase, cov, 11" h, two handles, pink ground borders with central enamel dec floral bouquets, gilt foliage and trim, pierced neck, rim, and cov, printed griffin mark, c1835, slight gilt rim wear to vase, rim chips and hairline to cover........................... **290.00**
Scent bottle, 6" h, onion shape, applied garden flowers, gilt line rims, c1831-40, printed puce griffin mark........ **465.00**

Vase, 4-3/8" h, flared, painted view of Larington Yorkshire, figures and sheep, wide gilt border, dark blue ground, restored, c1826-30, iron red griffin and painted title **420.00**
Washboard, 24-1/4" h, 19th C, imperfections **350.00**

ROCK 'N' ROLL

History: Rock music can be traced back to early rhythm and blues. It progressed until it reached its golden age in the 1950s and 1960s. Most of the memorabilia issued during that period focused on individual singers and groups. The largest quantity of collectible material is connected to Elvis Presley and The Beatles.

In the 1980s, two areas—clothing and guitars—associated with key rock 'n' roll personalities received special collector attention. Sotheby's and Christie's East regularly feature rock 'n' roll memorabilia as part of their collectibles sales. At the moment, the market is highly speculative and driven by nostalgia.

It is important to identify memorabilia issued during the lifetime of an artist or performing group, as opposed to material issued after they died or disbanded. Objects of the latter type are identified as "fantasy" items and will never achieve the same degree of collectibility as period counterparts.

Reproduction Alert. Records, picture sleeves, and album jackets, especially for The Beatles, have been counterfeited. When compared to the original, sound may be inferior, as may be the printing on labels and picture jackets. Many pieces of memorabilia also have been reproduced, often with some change in size, color, and design.

Additional Listings: See The Beatles, and Rock 'n' Roll in *Warman's Americana & Collectibles* and *Warman's Flea Market Price Guide*.

Two autographed photos: one Yoko Ono, signed "To Billy, Love Yoko, NYC '89" and one black & white photo of Paul McCartney, **$50**.
Photo courtesy of Joy Luke Auctions.

Autograph, photo
   Chuck Berry................ **75.00**
   Mick Jagger............... **135.00**
   Harry James **35.00**
   Madonna **195.00**
   Paul McCartney......... **275.00**
Autograph, program, Wayne Newton, 1980s.............. **20.00**

Autograph, Elvis, poster, **$750**.
Photo courtesy of Gary Sohmers.

Backstage pass, cloth
   Aerosmith, Pump Tour '89, afternoon **10.00**
   Bon Jovi, NJ Guest **7.00**
   KISS, 10th anniversary, after show, unused **7.00**
   Cyndi Lauper, Crew '86-87 .... **6.00**
   Rolling Stones, American Tour '81 .... **15.00**
Book, *The Beatles Authorized Biography,* McGraw-Hill, copyright 1968, 32 glossy black and white photos **25.00**
Christmas card, The Partridge Family, color photo of family opening presents, Christmas tree, facsimile signatures, 5-3/4" x 8-1/2", matching red envelope, trimmed in dark gold, c1971 .... **15.00**

Counter display, Rolling Stones, "Made In The Shade," 1976, 21" x 19", 3-D cardboard, bowed diecut, with four previous LP covers at left and "Rolling Stones & Tongue" logo on silver at top right **250.00**

Drawing, pencil, 12-1/2" x 16" sheet of animation paper, 2-1/4" x 2-1/2" image of Jeremy the Bobb balancing on one foot, from Beatles Yellow Submarine, production notations, 1968 .... **150.00**

Drinking glass, Beatles, clear, images and text in black, 1960s, 6-1/2" h **20.00**

Drumsticks
Alice in Chains **25.00**
Black Crows, concerned used, logo **20.00**
Iron Maiden, 1985 .... **50.00**

Fan photo, 8" x 10"
Jackson Five, 1970s, full color **10.00**
James Dean, c1954, black and white glossy **15.00**

Magazine
Lennon Photo Special, Sunshine Publications, copyright 1981, 8" x 11" **15.00**
Life, Rock Stars at Home with Their Parents, Vol. 17, #13, Sept. 14, 1971 .... **5.00**
Post, Mamas and Papas article, March 25, 1967... **5.00**
The Rolling Stones Magazine, Straight Arrow Publishers, copyright 1975 .... **10.00**

Newsletter, Rolling Stones Fan Club, 5" x 8", four pgs, black and white, orig mailing envelope **15.00**

Pinback button
3" d, Led Zeppelin, group logo in center, blue and white lettering: Summerfest At The Stadium Presents An Evening With Led Zeppelin, Sat, Aug. 6, 1977, Buffalo, NY" ... **35.00**
3-1/2" d, Hey, Let's Twist, red lettering on white ground, striped peppermint candy design, c1961 .... **20.00**

Portrait, Elvis Presley, by Ivan Jesse Curtain, wooden frame, 1960s **125.00**

Poster
Beatles, four sheets, each with Richard Avedon stylized portrait, 1968, 79" x 29" **1,840.00**

Poster, Bruce Springsteen, Liberty Hall, March, 1974, blue tone photo, **$750**.

Photo courtesy of Gary Sohmers.

Family Dog, Oct. 6-8, 1967, art by Victor Moscoso, second printing **35.00**
Janis Joplin, Neon Rose, Matrix, San Francisco, Jan. 17-22, 1967, 13-3/4" x 20" **75.00**

Press kit, KISS, Casablanca, 1976, custom folder, three-page bio, one-page press clipping, five 8" x 10" black and white photos, orig mailing envelope with no writing or postage **500.00**

Scarf, Beatles, glossy fabric, half corner design, marked "The Beatles/Copyright by Ramat & Co., Ltd./London, ECI," 25" sq, c1964.... **160.00**

Sheet music
Jackson Five, *Mama's Pearl,* copyright 1971 Jobette Music Co. **5.00**
Michael Jackson, *We're Almost There,* copyright 1974 Stone Diamond Corp, browntone photo cover... **5.00**

Record, Beatles, "Sgt. Pepper's Lonely Hearts Club Band," framed, 11-1/2" d, **$45**.

Photo courtesy of Joy Luke Auctions.

Ticket
Beatlefest '82-LA **10.00**

Elvis, 9/88 .... **75.00**
The Beatles Again Movie, 2-1/4" x 5-1/2", 1976...... **20.00**
Yardbirds/Doors, 1967 .. **50.00**

Tour book
Depeche Mode, Devotional Tour 1993/94 .... **10.00**
KISS, 10th anniversary, Vinnie V in makeup............... **125.00**

Toy, Beatles car, battery operated tin, 1964 Ford Galaxie, vinyl Beatles-like group, "Los Yes-Yes" lithographed on hood, record inside car is bit garbled, but working, orig Rico (Spain) hand tag, orig box with insert, C.9 .... **850.00**

T-shirt, never worn
Bon Jovi, L, Slippery When **25.00**
Deep Purple, L, Perfect Str...'85 .... **25.00**
Rolling Stones, XL, Steel Wheels **20.00**

Watch, Elvis Presley, 1-1/4" d goldtone metal case, dial with full-color illus of Elvis in elaborate white jumpsuit, blue background, copyright 1977 Boxcar Enterprises, Unique Time Co., orig blue vinyl straps **45.00**

ROOKWOOD POTTERY

History: Mrs. Marie Longworth Nicholas Storer, Cincinnati, Ohio, founded Rookwood Pottery in 1880. The name of this outstanding American art pottery came from her family estate, "Rookwood," named for the rooks (crows) that inhabited the wooded grounds.

Though the Rookwood pottery filed for bankruptcy in 1941, it was soon reorganized under new management. Efforts at maintaining the pottery proved futile, and it was sold in 1956 and again in 1959. The pottery was moved to Starkville, Mississippi, in conjunction with the Herschede Clock Co. It finally ceased operating in 1967.

Rookwood wares changed with the times. The variety is endless, in part because of the creativity of the many talented artists responsible for great variations in glazes and designs.

Marks: There are five elements to the Rookwood marking system—the clay or body mark, the size mark, the decorator mark, the date mark, and the factory mark. The best way to date Rookwood art pottery is from factory marks.

From 1880 to 1882, the factory mark was the name "Rookwood" incised or painted on the base. Between 1881 and 1886, the firm name, address, and year appeared in an oval frame. Beginning in 1886, the impressed "RP" monogram appeared and a flame mark was added for each year until 1900. After 1900, a Roman numeral, indicating the last two digits of the year of production, was added at the bottom of the "RP" flame mark. This last mark is the one most often seen on Rookwood pieces in the antiques marketplace.

Bowl, Wax Matte, painted by Louise Abel, red blossoms on mustard ground, interior covered in mottled burnt sienna glaze, 1924, flame mark/XXIV/2757/artist's mark, 7-1/4" d, 2-1/4" h, $750.

Photo courtesy of David Rago Auctions, Inc.

Architectural tile, 17-1/2" sq, cuenca, tree landscape, blue, green, and tan matte glazes, mounted in Arts & Crafts frame, imp "Rookwood Faience".................. **3,450.00**
Bookend, 6-1/4" w, 5-3/4" h, elephant, semi-matte ivory glaze, production, 1920, flame mark/XX/244C, firing line to back, X'd for glaze drip **145.00**
Bowl, 6-1/2" d, Ombroso, carved and inlaid poppy pod dec around top, dec by Charles Todd, 1915............... **2,200.00**

Bud vase, 5-1/4" h, bulbous, flowers on brown to gold ground, flame mark/III/745C/CCL, by Clara Lindeman, 1903........................... **360.00**
Cabinet jug, 3-1/2" d, 4-1/2" h, by N. J. Hirschfeld, dec in Limoges-style, bamboo and butterfly, shaded brown, ivory, and blue-green ground, gilded details, stamped "Rookwood 1883 G 61," artist's cipher **410.00**
Cabinet vase, 3" d, 3" h, Tiger Eye, flame mark obscured by glaze, two very minor grinding base chips.................. **350.00**
Chamberstick, 3" h, Standard Glaze, painted by Jeannette Swing, yellow violets, flame mark, artist's cipher, 1894 .... **350.00**
Charger, 12-1/2" d, mauve and oohre gallon center, light blue splashed border, John Wareham, dated 1905 .... **1,500.00**
Chocolate pot, 10" h, standard glaze, oak leaves and across dec, shape #722, Lenore Ashbury, 1904........ **700.00**
Ewer, 14" h, 8" d, Standard glaze, painted by A. R. Valentein, branches of yellow cherry blossoms, 1890, flame mark/387A/S.A.R.V./I., minimal crazing, firing line to handle **1,100.00**
Figure, 7-1/2" d, 8" h, woman's head, matte white glaze, 1924, flame mark/XXIV/2026 .... **365.00**
Flower boat, 16" l, standard glaze, pansies dec, shape #3745, Matt A. Daly, 1890 .... **900.00**
Flower frog, #2251, 1915. **325.00**
Humidor, cov, 6" h, round, Standard Glaze, portrait of American Indian, Pueblo Man, painted by Grace Young, dated 1901 .... **3,750.00**
Jug, 3-1/2" d, 5-1/4" h, by Albert Humphrys, 1882, Limoges style, geese flying over bamboo thicket, stamped "ROOKWOOD 1882 A.H." with anchor **490.00**
Paperweight, 3-1/2" d, elephant, 1928........................... **250.00**
Pitcher
6" h, flowers on green to gold ground, flame mark/I/657D/FH, artist's initials FH, 1901 .... **270.00**

7" h, flowers on blue to white ground, flame mark/VI/907F/EN, by Eliza Lawrence, 1906 .... **300.00**
9-1/2" h, standard glaze, Kataro Shirayamadani, flowering tree branch, gold to brown ground, imp maker's and artist's mark on base, 1890........................ **1,000.00**
Planter, 8-3/4" h, 8-1/2" d, incised stylized leaves, frothy brown-green matte glaze, c 129 10, flame mark/XI/180C **500.00**

Plaque, Scenic Vellum, painted by Lenore Asbury, Cypress Trees, tall trees in snow peaked mountain landscape at dusk, 1926, 6-3/4" x 11-1/2" plaque mounted in period frame, corner chip to back, $8,000.

Photo courtesy of David Rago Auctions, Inc.

Plaque, scenic vellum
7-1/2" x 3-1/2", Ombroso, pr of Rooks flanking bowl and reverse RP symbol, 1915, minor edge flakes **6,000.00**
9-1/2" x 11-1/2", The Morning Hour, Venetian sailboats, painted by Carl Schmidt **6,500.00**
10-3/8" w, 13-5/8" h, End of the Woods, view of trees and distant view, soft greens, blues, and pink, sgd "FR," flame mark and date on reverse, dec by Frederick Rothenbusch, 1920, orig wood frame.............. **6,900.00**
11-1/2" x 9", winter scene, frozen lake at twilight, painted by Elizabeth F. McDermott, 1910........................ **7,500.00**

12" x 9-1/2", meadow and trees, painted by L. Asbury, 1922, orig frame **7,000.00**

2" sq, shade trees in foreground, lake and mountain in background, Arts & Crafts oak frame... **2,500.00**

14-1/4" w, 8-3/4" h, Penacock Lane, Concord, NH, view of lake through trees, sgd "ED," Rookwood flame mark and date on reverse, dec by Ed Diers, Cincinnati, OH, 1916, framed, crazing **8,625.00**

14-1/2" x 9-1/2", lake bordered by shade trees and mountain, painted by Ed Diers, 1919, orig frame **10,000.00**

Teapot, cov, 11", Turkish, frog fishing with pole and bobber on riverbank, painting attributed to Maria Longworth Nichols, dated 1833 .... **1,500.00**

Vase, vellum, painted by Carl Schmidt, blue arrowroot blossoms, green leaves, blue to green ground, 1914, flame mark/XIV/922B/V/CS, minor peppering, 5-3/4" d, 11" h, **$2,425.**

Photo courtesy of David Rago Auctions, Inc.

Vase, Jewel Porcelain, cylindrical, finely painted by Arthur Conant, branches of blossoms in pink, caramel, blue, and green, 1928, uncrazed, flame mark/XVIII/1873/P/C, 3-3/4" d, 5-1/4" h, **$2,300.**

Photo courtesy of David Rago Auctions, Inc.

Vase

4-3/4" h, bulbous, blue, turquoise, and magenta running glaze, flame mark/XXI/915F/LNL, by Elizabeth Lincoln, 1921 .... **475.00**

5" h, baluster, flowers on green to gold ground, flame mark/V/605E/GH, by Grace Hall, 1905 .... **300.00**

5-1/4" h, bulbous, flowers on brown to gold ground, flame mark/VII/654D/LEL, by Laura Lindeman, 1907 .... **330.00**

5-1/4" h, 3-3/4" d, Jewel Porcelain, Oriental landscape with sailboats and prunus trees on three panels, painted by Arthur Conant, 1919, flame mark/XIX/2103/C, uncrazed **4,500.00**

6" h, drip glaze, bulbous body, long neck, imp maker's mark and numbered "6363," 1949 .... **300.00**

6" d, 9-1/2" h, Wax Matte, by Jens Jensen, 1929, stylized yellow, red, and purple flowers, pink ground, flame mark/XXIX/2303/artist's cipher **1,610.00**

7" h, ovoid, flowers on blue to white ground, flame mark/VI/907F/EN, by Edith Nooan, 1906 .... **800.00**

7-3/8" h, artist sgd with initials for W. E. Hentschel, dated 1915, olive brown mat glaze above emb green, blue, and light gray flowers **1,775.00**

8" h, Standard Glaze, silver overlay of wild roses, poppies, and lily-of-the-valleys, painted nasturtiums, L. N. Lincoln, c1895. **5,750.00**

8" h, 10" d, Standard glaze, three handles, painted by Artus Van Briggle, woman's portrait, three champagne bottles, 1893, flame mark/659/W/AVB/L **1,700.00**

9" h, 3-3/4" h, Scenic vellum, stark landscape at sunset, painted by Sally Coyne, 1912, flame mark/XII/SEC/951D/V/G **3,500.00**

9" h, 4-1/2" h, Scenic vellum, river landscape, blue and apricot sky, painted by E. T. Hurley, 1931, flame mark/XXI/892C/E.T.H., uncrazed **2,700.00**

9-1/2" d, Iris glaze, decorated by Ed Diers, c1904, earth tone underglaze color at neck

shading to soft greens, mauve carnation with buds and trailing stems, marks include Rookwood logo, date, artist's monogram, "879D," paper label "133," crazing ... **1,530.00**

9-1/2" h, Later Tiger Eye, Empire Green, carved sea horse dec, by E. T. Hurley, 1923 .... **3,500.00**

Vase, vellum, bulbous, by Kataro Shirayamadani, brown crocus and green leaves on shaded yellow ground, 1934, flame mark/XXIV/S/X and artist's cipher, seconded mark for small black glaze spots, 4" d, 5-1/2" h, **$1,610.**

Photo courtesy of David Rago Auctions, Inc.

Vase, Scenic Vellum, painted by Fred Rothenbusch, trees by lake, pink and blue sky, 1924, flame mark/XXIV/926B/FR, 11" h, 6" d, **$6,500.**

Photo courtesy of David Rago Auctions, Inc.

9-1/2" h, Vellum glaze, Venetian harbor scene, dated 1922, Carl Schmidt signature stamp **3,450.00**

Vase, Vellum, painted by Carl Schmidt, purple irises on shaded ground, 1912, flame mark/XII/614B/artist cipher, high water mark around shoulder, glaze scaling to small area inside, short tight firing line, 15-1/2" h, 8" d, **$4,000**.

Photo courtesy of David Rago Auctions, Inc.

Vase, Wax Matte, painted by Elizabeth Lincoln, clusters of red flowers on green foliage, vermilion butterfat ground, flame mark/XXIX/2785/LNL, 1929, factory shaved foot ring, 13-1/4" h, 5-1/4" d, **$2,700**.

Photo courtesy of David Rago Auctions, Inc.

9-1/2" h, 3-3/4" d, matt, by O. G. Reed, pink roses with yellow centers, indigo-to-rose ground, 1906, flame mark/VI/907DD/O.G.R......... **11,000.00**

Vase, Wax Matte, lobed, flaring, painted by Elizabeth Lincoln, panels of red stylized flowers against pink and red butterfat ground, flame mark/XXIII/LNL, 1923, 7" h, 3" d, **$1,400**.

Photo courtesy of David Rago Auctions, Inc.

9-3/4" h, Iris glaze, possibly decorated by Rose Fechleimer, 1901, peach-colored underglaze shading to white near base, clusters of pendant flowers with wide green leaves and trailing stem, mkd with Rookwood logo, date, artist's monogram, incised "W" and "786C," paper label "257," crazing **1,530.00**
10-3/4" h, 5-1/2" d, Iris glaze, diaphanous white poppies, pearl gray ground, painted by A. R. Valentien, 1902, flame mark/II/922B/A. R. Valentien **2,100.00**
11" h, 6" d, Scenic vellum, trees by lake, pink and blue sky, painted by Fred Rothenbusch, 1924, flame mark/XXIV/926B/FR, uncrazed.................. **6,500.00**
11-1/4" h, 5" d, vellum, bulbous, blue irises, purple ground, painted by Fred Rothenbusch, 1908, flame mark/VIII/1659/FR/V . **1,800.00**
12-1/2" h, 3-3/4" d, bottle shape, sea green, painted blue bells, black to celadon ground, Sally Toohey, 1899, flame mark/742D/ST/G **5,500.00**
15" h, 6-1/2" d, Iris glaze, painted by A. R. Valentien,

two rooks on pine branch, shading from dark green to celadon to sky blue, flame mark/IV/S1766/A.R. Valentien, 1904, uncrazed...... **22,500.00**
17-1/2" h, 11" d, Standard glaze, bottle shape, painted by A. R. Valentien, orange nasturtium, 1897, flame mark/537B/A.R.V., shallow chip to int. of foot ring.......... **1,500.00**

ROSE BOWLS

History: A rose bowl is a decorative open bowl with a crimped, pinched, or petal top which turns in at the top, but does not then turn up or back out again. Rose bowls held fragrant rose petals or potpourri, which served as an air freshener in the late Victorian period. Practically every glass manufacturer made rose bowls in virtually every glass type, pattern, and style, including fine art glass.

For more information, see *Warman's Glass*, 4th edition.

Reproduction Alert: Rose bowls have been widely reproduced. Be especially careful of Italian copies of satin, Mother of Pearl satin, peachblow, and Burmese, and recent Czechoslovakian ones with applied flowers.

3" d, diamond quilted, amethyst and white **100.00**
3" d, 1-3/4" d, satin, crimped body, shading from medium to light blue, clear applied dec............................. **110.00**
3-1/2" d, 3-1/2" h, satin, diamond quilted mother of pearl, golden-brown to golden cream......................... **495.00**
3-3/4" h, satin, inverted crimped bulbous body shading from deep rose to pink, enamel floral dec, attributed to Thomas Webb & Sons **100.00**

Carnival glass, Swirled Hobnail, Millersburg, purple, **$265**.

Carnival Glass, Drapery pattern, white iridescent, **$250**.

Photo courtesy of Seeck Auctions.

4" d, cased blue and white, flowers and leaf dec **80.00**

4" d, cased yellow and white **75.00**

4" d, satin, blue **90.00**

4" d, satin, green **75.00**

4" h, bulbous ruffled top, pastel, frosted and opal vertical bands on body, English, Victorian...................... **125.00**

4-1/2" d, satin, green and white, leaf design.................. **115.00**

5" d, amethyst and white leaf design.......................... **90.00**

5" d, blue and white, pleated **95.00**

5" d, cased, orange and white satin **100.00**

Carnival Glass, Honeycomb pattern, peach opalescent, **$85**.

Photo courtesy of Seeck Auctions.

Lavender, applied clear glass rigaree flowers and leaves, **$190**.

Photo courtesy of Joy Luke Auctions.

Opalescent, Spanish Lace, large, **$125**.

5" d, cased, red and white satin **100.00**

5" d, green and white opalescent, ruffled rim.. **95.00**

5" d, spatter glass, orange and white **90.00**

5-1/2" d, red and white shell design......................... **110.00**

5-1/2" d, satin, green and white, shell design **125.00**

5-1/2" h, satin, blue, ruffled **100.00**

6" d, blue and white, shell design, floral dec........ **120.00**

ROSE CANTON, ROSE MANDARIN, AND ROSE MEDALLION

History: The pink rose color has given its name to three related groups of Chinese export porcelain: Rose Mandarin, Rose Medallion, and Rose Canton.

Rose Mandarin, produced from the late 18th century to approximately 1840, derives its name from the Mandarin figure(s) found in garden scenes with women and children. The women often have gold decorations in their hair. Polychrome enamels and birds separate the scenes.

Rose Medallion, which originated in the early 19th century and was made through the early 20th century, has alternating panels of figures and birds and flowers. The elements are four in number, separated evenly around the center medallion. Peonies and foliage fill voids.

Rose Canton, introduced somewhat later than Rose Mandarin and produced through the first half of the 19th century, is similar to Rose Medallion except the figural panels are replaced by flowers. People are present only if the medallion partitions are absent. Some patterns have been named, e.g., Butterfly and Cabbage and Rooster. Rose Canton actually is a catchall term for any pink enamelware not fitting into the first two groups.

Reproduction Alert: Rose Medallion is still made, although the quality does not match the earlier examples.

Rose Canton

Brush pot, 4-1/2" h, scenic, ladies, reticulated, gilt trim **275.00**

Charger, 13" d, floral panels, 19th C **215.00**

Platter, 16-1/2" l, 19th C, enamel and gilt wear **200.00**

Puzzle teapot, 6" h, Cadogan, painted birds and foliage, light blue ground, late 19th C, minor chips **150.00**

Umbrella jar, 24-1/4" h, 19th C, minor chips **805.00**

Urn, cov, 19-1/4" h, minor chips, cracks, gilt wear, pr . **2,990.00**

Vase, 14" h, four panels of birds and butterflies, rocks and tree peonies, applied molded gilded serpents and animals at neck and shoulder, converted to electric lamp, slight wear **320.00**

Rose Mandarin, vase, famille rose enamels, dragons, and foo dogs, 19th C, 25" h, $2,470.

Photo courtesy of Skinner, Inc.

Rose Mandarin

Bowl, 13-1/4" d, 5-1/2" h, exterior with continuous courtyard scene, multiple figures including horse and groom, musician, checkers players, scholars, int. with mandarin panels surrounding gilt fretwork, alternating images of fans, scrolls, and vases, rose, bird, and butterfly border, gilt ground, gilt details, orange peel glaze, wooden base **2,300.00**

Brush pot, 5-3/8" d, 6-1/4" h, continuous scene of empress on throne, surrounded by court ladies and maids, gilt trim, bright rose and butterfly border, small rim flakes and crow's foot in base **230.00**

Creamer, 3-1/2" h, continuous scene with figures indoors and in fenced yard, 100 Antiques border on int., gold accents **200.00**

Cup and saucer, courtyard scenes in center, kissing carp border alternating with scrolls and other fish, wear **350.00**

Dish, 8-1/4" x 10-1/2", kidney shape, courtyard scenes, bird and flower borders, orange peel glaze, wear **200.00**

Plate
7-3/4" d, man and four women seated in courtyard overlooking lake, border of butterflies and birds with two reclining deer, minor wear **350.00**
8-5/8" d, courtyard scenes, bird and flower borders **200.00**

9-3/4" d, brilliant blue fretwork borders with pink flowers, flower baskets, dark mustard yellow irid ground, detailed center with women and children in courtyard, man brandishing sword at woman, minor wear, price for pr **500.00**
10" d, detailed courtyard scene with fish pond, armored warrior with elaborate pheasant tail headdress, border of gourds, vases, and scrolls, gilt details, some wear **375.00**

Platter
10" x 13", multiple figures, scribe, and soldiers, border with birds chasing insects, butterflies, orange peel glaze **600.00**
14" x 17", 26 children, courtiers with large necklaces, man holding scepter, kissing carp border with alternating blue and green scrolls, dark gray silver oxide painted carp, faint orange peel glaze, minor wear **1,955.00**
14-1/2" x 16-1/2", court scene with 16 figures, borders with figures alternating with objects covered in Oriental calligraphy, gilt trim, orange peel glaze **2,100.00**

Shrimp dish, 10-1/8" x 10-1/4", bright butterflies, flowers, fruit on gilt border, gold trim and hair accents, orange peel glaze, minor wear, shallow rim flake **865.00**

Soup plate, 10" d, armorial, one with garden scene, other with man holding baby with three women in courtyard, borders with multiple butterflies, birds, tree peonies, and bamboo trees, each with European dolphin above belt with "Avis La Fin," monogram "RAK," gilt trim and accents, two minor flakes, price for pr.... **1,840.00**

Tray, 9-1/2" x 11", oval, scalloped edge, gilt and rose border, gilt highlighted figures in center, one with gilt robe, orange peel glaze, flake on table ring.................... **250.00**

Tureen, cov, matching underplate, 7-3/4" l, 6" h, continuous courtyard scene, gild accents, pink roses and white trailing flowers borders,

gilt finial and intertwined handles, well done professional restoration to lid and underplate **650.00**

Rose Medallion

Armorial plate, 9-5/8" d, exotic birds, butterflies, marbleized textures, gold hair accents, hand painted orange armorial device in center with belt surrounding sword and laurel wreath, "Fides Praestantior Auro," slight wear, price for pr **600.00**

Basket and undertray, 9-3/4" l, 7-1/4" w, 3-3/4" h, two handles, reticulated, China, 19th C, chips **325.00**

Boullion cup and saucer, cov, thinly potted, double handles **200.00**

Bowl, 10" d, 4" h, detailed panels with four figures and man at window alternation with roses and birds, wear **260.00**

Candlesticks, pr, 7-1/4" h, China, 19th C, one with a couple base edge repairs **600.00**

Charger
10-1/2" d, celadon, court scene within shaped One Hundred Antiques border, textured ground, gilt wear to rim.................................. **275.00**
13" d, celadon, court scene bordered with animals and floral trophies, textured ground, minor gilt wear **355.00**
15" d.......................... **225.00**

Dish, 9-1/4" d, scalloped rim, 19th C **275.00**

Lamp, 18" h vase, chi dragons around neck, foo dog handles, mounted on pierced wood stand, China, late 19th C **760.00**

Plate
8" d, alternating panels of men and women, birds and butterflies, faint gold dec **115.00**
8-5/8" d, light blue, yellow, and pink reticulated border **120.00**
9-1/2" d, alternating panels, gold trim, wear.............. **90.00**

Platter
12" x 15", oval, six alternating panels, orange peel glaze, faded colors................ **115.00**

14" x 18-1/4", six alternating panels, orange peel glaze, worn gilt trim, shallow rim flakes **350.00**

Punch bowl
13-1/2" d, Chinese Export, 19th C **825.00**
24" d, hp scenes, four with birds, fruits, clouds, and flowers, alternating with panels of village scenes, gilt rim and highlights **3,680.00**

Saucer, 6-1/4" d, figures dec, gilt, minor rim flakes, price for set of eight **250.00**

Serving dish, 10-3/4" l, 9-1/4" w, 1-3/4" h, oval, shaped rim, celadon, mid-19th C .. **400.00**

Soup bowl, 8-1/4" d, Mandarin scene, gilding **110.00**

Teapot, 8" h, domed cov, squatty, gilt floral embellishments on handle and spout.................... **765.00**

Tray, 9-1/8" sq, landscapes alternating with birds and flowers, hillside fort with multiple flakes, pagodas, fishing boats, orange peel glaze ext. **250.00**

Umbrella stand, cylindrical, China, 19th C,
23-5/8" h, cylindrical form, repaired cracks........... **400.00**
24-1/4" h.................. **1,880.00**

Vase
12" h, 19th C, truncated, mounted as a lamp, 19th C **400.00**
14" h, four panels with matching mandarin courtyard scenes, scalloped edge rims, applied molded serpents and animals on neck and shoulder with worn gilding, birds and butterflies, wear, wooden stand, price for pr **700.00**

Vegetable tureen, cov, oval underplate, 9-3/4" l, 8" h, figures with gilt trim, blue bats under two intertwined handles, orange peel glaze on base, molded gilt finial, minor wear **920.00**

ROSENTHAL

History: Rosenthal Porcelain Manufactory began operating at Selb, Bavaria, in 1880. Specialties were tablewares and figurines. The firm is still in operation.

Coffee service, three pieces, Dorothy Hafner, L Studio-Line, "Flash Frisco" pattern, black and white striped design against blue-green ground, impressed "Rosenthal/Studio-Linie/Germany," each piece also artist signed, **$300**.

Photo courtesy of David Rago Auctions, Inc.

Dinnerware set, Premier pattern, cream ground, gold band, 67 pieces, **$250**.

Box, cov, Studio Line, sgd "Peynet" **175.00**

Cake plate, 12" w, grape dec, scalloped ruffled edge, ruffled handles **75.00**

Candlestick, 9-1/2" h, Art Deco woman holding candlestick **275.00**

Chocolate set, San Souci pattern, six cups and saucers, cov pot, creamer and sugar, marked "Selb Bavaria," c1880, 15-pc set......... **425.00**

Creamer and sugar, pate-sur-pate type blue cherries dec **115.00**

Cup and saucer, San Souci pattern, white **20.00**

Demitasse cup and saucer, Marie pattern **25.00**

Design page, 6" w, 9-1/2" h, hand rendered, each page showing transfer printed and hand-tinted designs, most numbered or named, some on graph paper, 10 pages **230.00**

Figure, deer, spotted, light brown, marked on base, **$45**.

Figure
Band figure, male cello player, 5-1/4" h........................ **250.00**
Band figure, male clarinet player.......................... **250.00**
Band figure, male tuba player **285.00**
Man taking snuff, 8-1/2" h **295.00**
Middle Eastern child with scimitar **250.00**
Middle Eastern lantern lighter **200.00**
Middle Eastern man with urn **200.00**
Middle Eastern pipe smoker **230.00**

Luncheon plates, painted with flowers, gold swag border, 9" d, price for set of 10, **$150**.

Photo courtesy of David Rago Auctions, Inc.

Plaque, 9" x 7-1/2", titled "Die Falknerin," sgd "Hans Makart" **1,100.00**

Plate, 10" d, girl and lamb dec, multicolored **40.00**

Portrait plate, 9-7/8" d, bust portrait of lady, pale yellow and white ground, faux green, turquoise, blue, and red hardstone jewels......... **350.00**

Vase
7" h, modeled owls on branch **165.00**
11" h, hp, multicolored roses **125.00**

Pitcher, creamy ivory body, red rose bud decoration, green foliate, silvered base, marked, **$95.**

ROSEVILLE POTTERY

History: In the late 1880s, a group of investors  purchased the J. B. Owens Pottery in Roseville, Ohio, and made utilitarian stoneware items. In 1892, the firm was incorporated and joined by George F. Young, who became general manager. Four generations of Youngs controlled Roseville until the early 1950s.

A series of acquisitions began: Midland Pottery of Roseville in 1898, Clark Stoneware Plant in Zanesville (formerly used by Peters and Reed), and Muskingum Stoneware (Mosaic Tile Company) in Zanesville. In 1898, the offices also moved from Roseville to Zanesville.

In 1900, Roseville introduced Rozane, an art pottery. Rozane became a trade name to cover a large series of lines. The art lines were made in limited amounts after 1919.

The success of Roseville depended on its commercial lines, first developed by John J. Herald and Frederick Rhead in the first decades of the 1900s. In 1918, Frank Ferrell became art director and developed more than 80 lines

of pottery. The economic depression of the 1930s brought more lines, including Pine Cone.

In the 1940s, a series of high-gloss glazes were tried in an attempt to revive certain lines. In 1952, Raymor dinnerware was produced. None of these changes brought economic success and in November 1954, Roseville was bought by the Mosaic Tile Company.

Child's feeding dish, Sunbonnet decoration, **$225.**

Basket
Gardenia, green, raised mark, No. 618-15" **490.00**
Jonquil, pillow, unmarked, 10-1/2" d, 7-1/2" h **750.00**
Ming Tree, white, raised mark, No. 585-14" **425.00**
Poppy, green, raised mark, No. 347-10" **350.00**
Vista, unmarked, 4-3/4" d, 6-3/4" h **575.00**
Basket planter
Apple Blossom, green, asymmetrical rim, raised mark, No. 311-12" **490.00**

Iris, spherical, pink, imp mark, No. 354-8" **365.00**
Bookends, pr
Iris, book shape, blue, raised mark, No. 5, 5-1/4" w, 5-1/4" h **290.00**
Water Lily, model no. 14, molded open book form, water lily blossoms in relief, walnut brown glaze, raised "Roseville U.S.A." mark, 4-3/4" l, 5-1/4" d, 5-1/2" h, repair **200.00**
Bowl
Chloron, buttressed, unmarked, 4" x 8" **225.00**
Futura, "Aztec," faceted, unmarked, 4" x 8" **325.00**
Futura, "Balloons," unmarked, 3-1/2" x 8-1/2", touch-ups **150.00**
Imperial II, emb snail-like designs around entire body, pale green dripping glaze over pink ground, unmarked **2,000.00**
Mostique, two handles, bands of blue and white flowers, unmarked, 3" x 10" **350.00**
Bud vase
Orange blossoms, green ground, model no. 870, double reservoir, c1940, raised "Roseville U.S.A." mark, 6-1/4" h.............. **100.00**
Pine Cone, blue, raised mark, 5" d, 7-1/2" h, minute flake on base.......................... **400.00**
Candlesticks, pr
Blackberry, gold foil label, 4" d, 4-1/2" h **690.00**
Imperial II, orange and green mottled glaze, unmarked, 3" x 4-1/4"........................... **350.00**

Imperial II, pair of 4-1/2" h x 4-1/2" d candlesticks, covered in blue and yellow mottled glaze, black paper label and original price tag, **$900;** 12-1/2" d x 5" h flaring bowl, bright blue and yellow frothy glaze, unmarked, **$500.**

Sunflower, black paper label, 3-3/4" d, 4-1/4" h **800.00**
Wisteria, brown, unmarked, 4-3/4" d, 4-3/4" h **460.00**

Coffee set, cov coffeepot, cov teapot, creamer, cov sugar, Mock Orange, green, raised marks, 10-3/4" h coffeepot, minor spider lines to spout **490.00**

Compote, Donatello, 7-1/2" d **150.00**

Console bowl
Cremona, oval, pink, unmarked, 11" d, 2-1/4" h **95.00**
Ferella, ovoid, brown, black paper label, 13" l, 5-3/4" h **815.00**
Moderne, semi-matte ivory glaze, incised mark, No. 301-10" **230.00**

Console set
Fuchsia, brown, imp marks, No. 1133-5 and No. 350-8" **490.00**
Iris, pink, No. 360-10" oval centerbowl, pair of No. 1135-4-1/2" candlesticks, imp marks **375.00**
Thorn Apple, pink, low center bowl No. 307-6", pair of No. 1111 candlesticks, imp marks **290.00**

Cookie jar, cov
Clematis, No. 3-8, green ground **550.00**
Magnolia, No. 2-8, tan ground **450.00**
Water Lily, No. 1-8, gold shading to brown ground **555.00**
Zephr Lily, No. 5-8, blue ground **360.00**

Cornucopia vase
Pine Cone **140.00**
White Rose **95.00**

Ewer
Apple Blossom, green, raised mark, No. 318-15, minute fleck to body **630.00**
Carnelian I, pink and gray glaze, RV ink mark, 7" d, 12-1/4" h **345.00**
Freesia, green, raised mark, No. 21-15", two base chips **290.00**
Gardenia, brown, raised mark, No. 618-15" **490.00**
Mock Orange, No. 918-16, white blossoms, green leaves, pink ground, 16" h **310.00**
Pine Cone, brown, raised mark, No. 909-10" **690.00**

Left: two Creamware Dutch mugs, unmarked, **$45 each**; center: Aztec corseted vase decorated in squeezebag with white flowers and blue leaves, unmarked, minor glaze scaling, 4" d, 8-1/4" h, **$350**; right: Persian planter, fitted liner, unmarked, 6-1/4" d, 5" h, **$225**.
Photo courtesy of David Rago Auctions, Inc.

Floor vase
Fuchsia, brown, raised mark, No. 905-18" **750.00**
Pine Cone, brown, incised mark, No. 913-18", repair to rim and base **815.00**
Vista, bulbous, 18" h, unmarked, several bruises and chips **860.00**
Water Lily, green, raised mark, No.85-18" **630.00**

Flower pot and underplate, Iris, blue, raised marks, No. 648-5", 1" bruise to rim **365.00**

Hanging basket, Mock Orange, white blossoms, green leaves **375.00**

Jardinière, Bleeding Heart, orange ground, green leaves, lighter flowers, #651-6, 7" h, **$140**.
Photo courtesy of Joy Luke Auctions.

Jardinière
Baneda, pink, paper label, 4" x 5-1/2", small base nicks **250.00**
Cherry Blossom, pink, 6" x 8-1/2" **500.00**
Jonquil, spherical, unmarked, 9" d, 6" h, small stilt-pull chips **2,300.00**
Velmoss, broad leaves and buds, unmarked, 7" x 9-1/2" **1,100.00**

Jardinière and pedestal, Ivory Florentine, unmarked, 25" h overall, small nicks and chips, **$325**.
Photo courtesy of David Rago Auctions, Inc.

Jardinière and pedestal, Fuchsia, blue, #645-10" raised mark, very tight touch-up to base, **$2,800**.
Photo courtesy of David Rago Auctions, Inc.

Jardinière on stand

Freesia, No. 669, Delftware blue glaze, creamy yellow and white blossoms, raised "Roseville U.S.A." mark, stand marked "U.S.A.," c1945 .... **500.00**
Freesia, No. 669-8, molded florals, blue ground, base emb "Roseville, USA, 669-8, c1935 .... **865.00**
Moss, green **3,250.00**
Mostique **900.00**

Lamp base, Imperial II, bulbous emb band around rim, dripping pale green over pink glaze, factory drilled **1,400.00**

Low bowl

Blackberry, unmarked, 7-3/4" d, 3-1/4" h, minor glaze bubbles **345.00**
Sunflower, low shoulder, unmarked, 7-1/4" d, 4" h, burst bubble on one leaf **535.00**

Mug, Pine Cone, blue, imp mark, No. 960-4", price for pr **700.00**

Mostique, left: 10" h corseted vase with enameled yellow and green decoration; center: 12" h corseted vase with enameled yellow and green decoration; right: 7 1/2" d low bowl with Glasgow roses, unmarked, few flecks and nicks, **$300**.
Photo courtesy of David Rago Auctions, Inc.

Pitcher

Fuchsia, brown, imp mark, 8-1/2" d, 8" h, peppering to body **400.00**
Pine Cone, no. 415, green glaze, brown, and cream tones, raised "Roseville, U.S.A." mark, c1931, 9-1/4" h **750.00**
Rozane Olympic, Ulysees at the Table of Circe, signed and titled, 8-1/2" d, 7" h, restoration to 5" spider lines **1,495.00**

White Rose, pink, raised mark, No. 1324, 8" d, 7" h, glaze drip around rim . **275.00**

Planter

Blackberry, faceted, unmarked, 9-3/4" d, 3-1/2" h **435.00**
Florentine, brown, rect, 11-1/4" l, 5-1/4" h, few base chips **290.00**
Lily, squeezebag dec with water lilies and waves, orig liner, unmarked, 6" x 7-1/2" **800.00**
Persian, fitted liner, unmarked, 5" x 6-1/4", abrasion to rim **350.00**
Primrose, bulbous, pink, incised mark, No. 634-6", flecks to flowers and one handle **85.00**
Wisteria, blue, unmarked, 6-1/4" x 8-3/4", minor touch-ups **475.00**

Left: Dontalleo planter and fitted liner, unmarked, few flecks, small reglued chip, 7-1/2" d, 3-1/2" h, **$75**; right: Corinthian wall pocket, unmarked, 4-1/2"w, 9-1/2" l, **$250**.
Photo courtesy of David Rago Auctions, Inc.

Ivory Florentine, left: sand jar, #299-14", raised mark, base rim chip, **$250**; right: umbrella stand, #298-18", raised mark, rim fleck, flat chip on base, **$425**.
Photo courtesy of David Rago Auctions, Inc.

Planter bookends, pr, Columbine, blue, raised mark, 5" w, 5" d, 5-1/4" h **260.00**
Sand jar, Primrose, blue, 15-3/4" h, base chip and hairline **575.00**

Teapot, cov, Rozanne Della Robbia, hearts, cups, saucers, and Japanese fans dec, brown and celadon, Rozane Ware wafer, small lid nicks, 1" clay burst at rim **1,355.00**

Tea set, cov teapot, creamer, cov sugar
Freesia, blue, raised marks **415.00**
Peony, yellow, raised marks **415.00**
Snowberry, blue, raised marks **750.00**
White Rose, pink raised marks **490.00**
Wincraft, brown, raised marks, minor flaws **200.00**

Three vases, upper left: Blue Wisteria, bulbous, partial foil label, strong mold, pin-head size fleck on one leaf, 6-1/4" x 8-1/2", **$650**; front left: Baneda, bulbous, foil label, #235-5, 5-1/2" x 6-3/4", **$425**; right: Ferrella, bulbous, unmarked, 8 1/2" x 7-1/2", restoration to small area of base, **$850**.
Photo courtesy of David Rago Auctions, Inc.

Umbrella stand, Pine Cone, brown, raised mark, No. 777-20", minor scaling area at handle, 1" rim bruise **2,070.00**

Urn

Baneda, bulbous, pink, black foil label, 7-3/4" d, 10-1/2" h **1,355.00**
Carnelian I, pink and gray glaze, RV ink mark, 8-1/4" d, 9-1/2" h **375.00**
Iris, bulbous, pink, imp mark, No. 928-12" **460.00**
Moss, bulbous, buttressed base, incised mark, restorations to base and rim **200.00**
Pine Cone, blue, imp mark, No. 912-15", restoration to rim chip **2,185.00**
Velmoss, orange glaze, foil label, 8-1/4" x 6-3/4" ... **675.00**

Vase, Pine Cone, two handles, gold ground, **$225**.

Vase, Pine Cone, two low handles, blue ground, **$275**.

Vase, Brown Water Lily, 84-16, raised mark, **$375**.

Photo courtesy of David Rago Auctions, Inc.

Vase

Baneda, bulbous, pink, foil label, 5-1/2" x 6-3/4".... **450.00**
Blackberry, black paper label, 6-1/2" x 5-3/4"............. **550.00**
Cherry Blossom, two handles, sq base, pink, unmarked, 8-1/2" x 5".................... **700.00**
Earlam, tapering, ribbed, pink, unmarked, 8-1/2" x 6".................................... **450.00**
Falline, bulbous, blue, stepped neck, two handles, foil label, 7-1/4" x 6" . **2,300.00**
Ferella, bulbous, red, unmarked, 8-1/2" x 7", restoration to base...... **850.00**
Ferella, flaring, brown, paper label, 5" x 7" **500.00**
Futura, conical form, three stepped rect devices on sides, round disk base, semi-gloss terra cotta, blue, and green glazes, c1928, unmarked, 8" h............ **575.00**
Imperial II, bulbous, band of wave-like designs at rim, bright blue mottled glaze, paper label, tight 2" line from rim........................... **1,400.00**
Imperial II, flaring, mottled green and orange glaze, unmarked, 8-1/2" x 7" **3,250.00**

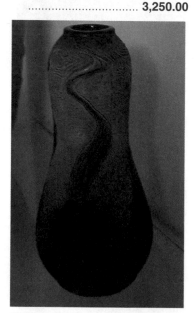

Vase, Fijiyama, bulbous, decorated with flowers and flowing leaves, stamped, mark, minor rim repair, 3" d, 6" h, **$475**.

Photo courtesy of David Rago Auctions, Inc.

Two Sunflower vases, left: ovoid, crisp mold, unmarked, 6" d, 10-1/4" h, **$2,500**; right: bulbous, crisp mold, unmarked, 6-1/2" d, 8-1/2" h, **$2,300**.

Photo courtesy of David Rago Auctions, Inc.

Vases, left: Orion, red, bulbous base, slightly flared neck, 4-3/4" d, 7-1/2" h, unmarked, **$300**; center: Orion, red, squat base, flared rim, unmarked, 8" d, 7-1/4" h, **$275**; right: Imperial II, ovoid, covered in blue and yellow mottled glaze, paper label, drill hole to underside, 7" d, 11-1/2" h, **$1,600**.

Photo courtesy of David Rago Auctions, Inc.

Imperial II, tapering, ribbed bands around body, pale green and gray mottled glaze, unmarked, 5-1/2" x 3-3/4"
.... **300.00**
Montacello, bulbous, brown, unmarked, 7-1/2" x 6-1/2"
.... **500.00**
Morning Glory, pillow shape, two buttresses at base, unmarked, 7" x 3-3/4".. **500.00**
Orion, cylindrical neck, red, unmarked, 7-1/2" x 4-3/4"
.... **500.00**
Rozane Royal Dark, tapering, by Hester Pillsbury, painted yellow wild roses, Roxane Ware wafer, 7" d, 8-3/4" h **475.00**
Rozane Woodland, corseted, enamel dec, white blossoms, green leaves, Rozane Ware/ Woodland wafer, 3" d, 10" h
.... **575.00**

Sunflower, double handles,
9" h............................. **1,300.00**
Velmoss, spherical,
unmarked, 6-1/2" x 8-1/2"
.... **350.00**
Vista, bulbous, unmarked,
7-1/2" d, 17-1/2" h ... **1,890.00**
Wisteria, blue, 10" h . **2,000.00**

Vessel
Imperial II, squat, yellow and
green glaze over matte blue-
gray ground, unmarked,
5-1/2"....................... **1,400.00**
Montacello, squat, green,
unmarked, 4-1/2" x 5".. **300.00**
Sunflower, squat, unmarked,
4-1/4" x 7-1/2".............. **700.00**
Wisteria, bulbous, blue, partial
foil label, 6-3/4" x 8-1/2", tiny
fleck to one leaf **650.00**
Wisteria, squat, blue,
unmarked, 4-1/2" x 6-1/2"
.... **450.00**

Wallpocket, Imperial II, triple, russet
and green, unmarked, tight line to
edge, **$460.**

Wall pocket
Blackberry, flaring, unmarked,
7-3/4" l...................... **1,610.00**
Cosmos, double, blue,
unmarked, silver foil label
.... **630.00**
Earlham, unmarked, 6-1/2" l
.... **920.00**
Imperial II, mottled green over
lavender glaze, paper label,
6-1/2" x 6-1/2".............. **800.00**
Moss, bucket, pink,
unmarked, 10" l, 1/2" chip,
small edge nick **520.00**
Pine Cone, triple, blue, raised
mark, 9" l **1,725.00**
Savona, blue, unmarked,
8-1/4" l........................ **630.00**
Silhouette, pink, ivy leaves,
raised mark No. 766-8"
.... **290.00**

ROYAL BAYREUTH

History: In 1794, the Royal Bayreuth factory was founded in Tettau, Bavaria. Royal Bayreuth introduced its

figural patterns in 1885. Designs of animals, people, fruits, and vegetables decorated a wide array of tablewares and inexpensive souvenir items.

Tapestry wares, in rose and other patterns, were made in the late 19th century. The surface of the piece feels and looks like woven cloth. Tapestry ware was made by covering the porcelain with a piece of fabric tightly stretched over the surface, decorating the fabric, glazing the piece, and firing.

For more information, *see Warman's English & Continental Pottery & Porcelain,* 4th edition.

Royal Bayreuth still manufactures dinnerware. It has not maintained production of earlier wares, particularly the figural items. Since thorough records are unavailable, it is difficult to verify the chronology of production.

Marks: The Royal Bayreuth crest used to mark the wares varied in design and color.

Ashtray, elk................... **225.00**
Bell, Musicians scene, man
playing cello and mandolin
.... **300.00**
Candleholder, basset hound,
dark body, unmarked.. **400.00**
Creamer
Bird of Paradise **225.00**
Cat, black and orange **200.00**

Creamer, elk, figural, brown and white,
marked, **$95.**

Crow, brown bill **200.00**
Duck **200.00**
Eagle.......................... **300.00**
Frog, green **225.00**
Lamplighter, green...... **250.00**
Pear **295.00**
Robin **195.00**
Water Buffalo, black and
orange **225.00**
Cup and saucer, yellow and
gold, purple and red flowers,
green leaves, white ground,
green mark **80.00**
Hatpin holder, courting couple,
cutout base with gold dec,
blue mark.................... **400.00**
Milk pitcher, butterfly.... **1,200.00**
Miniature, pitcher, portrait **95.00**
Portrait plate, 9" d, Arab and
camel, green back stamp
.... **125.00**
Ring box, cov, pheasant scene,
glossy finish **85.00**
Salt and pepper shakers, pr,
Elk **165.00**
Vase, 3-1/2" h, peasant ladies
and sheep scene, silver rim,
three handles, blue mark
.... **60.00**

Patterns

Conch Shell
Creamer, green, lobster
handles **125.00**
Match holder, hanging **225.00**
Sugar, cov, small flake .. **85.00**
Corinthian
Creamer and sugar, classical
figures, black ground.... **85.00**
Pitcher, 12" h, red ground,
pinched spout............ **225.00**
Vase, 8-1/2" h, conical, black,
blue mark.................... **225.00**
Devil and Cards
Ashtray....................... **650.00**
Creamer, 4" h, blue mark
.... **175.00**
Mug, large **295.00**
Salt, master................ **325.00**

Lobster
Ashtray, claw............. **145.00**
Celery tray, 12-1/2" l, figural,
blue mark.................. **245.00**
Pitcher, 7-3/4" h, figural,
orange-red, green handle
.... **175.00**
Salt and pepper shakers, pr
.... **150.00**

Nursery Rhyme
Bell, Jack and the Beanstalk
.... **425.00**
Planter, Jack and the
Beanstalk, round, orig liner
.... **225.00**
Plate, Little Jack Horner
.... **125.00**
Plate, Little Miss Muffet
.... **100.00**

Snow Babies
Bowl, 6" d................. **325.00**
Creamer, gold trim..... **110.00**
Jewelry box, cov........ **275.00**
Milk pitcher, corset shape
.... **185.00**
Tea tile, 6" sq, blue mark
.... **100.00**

Sunbonnet Babies
Bell, babies sewing,
unmarked.................. **425.00**
Cake plate, 10-1/4" d, babies
washing **400.00**
Cup and saucer, babies
fishing **225.00**
Dish, 8" d, babies ironing,
ruffled edge, blue mark
.... **175.00**
Mustard pot, cov, babies
sweeping, blue mark .. **395.00**
Nappy, Sunbonnet Babies,
Wash Day, blue mark, 6" l
.... **230.00**
Plate, Sunbonnet Girls, pair,
one washing, other sweeping
.... **290.00**

Tomato
Creamer and sugar, blue
mark........................... **190.00**
Milk pitcher **165.00**
Mustard, cov............. **125.00**
Salt and pepper shakers, pr
.... **85.00**

Rose tapestry

Basket, 5" h, reticulated **400.00**
Bell, American Beauty Rose,
pink, 3" h **500.00**
Boot............................ **550.00**
Bowl, 10-1/2" d, pink and yellow
roses **675.00**
Cache pot, 2-3/4" h, 3-12/4" d,
ruffled top, gold handles
.... **200.00**
Creamer........................ **250.00**
Dresser tray **395.00**

Hairpin box, pink and white
.... **245.00**
Nut dish, 3-1/4" d, 1-3/4" h,
three-color roses, gold feet,
green mark **175.00**
Pin tray, three-color roses
.... **195.00**
Plate, 6" d, three-color roses,
blue mark.................. **150.00**
Salt and pepper shakers, pr,
pink roses **375.00**
Shoe, roses and figures dec
.... **550.00**

Tapestry, miscellaneous

Bowl, 9-1/2" d, scenic, wheat,
girl, and chickens **395.00**
Box, 3-3/4" l, 2" w, courting
couple, multicolored, blue
mark........................... **245.00**
Charger, 13" d, scenic, boy and
donkeys **300.00**
Dresser tray, goose girl.. **495.00**
Hatpin holder, swimming swans
and sunset, saucer base, blue
mark........................... **250.00**

ROYAL BONN

History: In
1836, Franz
Anton Mehlem
founded a
Rhineland
factory that
produced
earthenware

and porcelain, including
household, decorative, technical,
and sanitary items.

The firm reproduced Hochst
figures between 1887 and 1903.
These figures, in both porcelain and
earthenware, were made from the
original molds from the defunct
Prince-Electoral Mayence
Manufactory in Hochst. The factory
was purchased by Villeroy and Boch
in 1921 and closed in 1931.

Marks: In 1890, the word "Royal"
was added to the mark. All items
made after 1890 include the
"Royal Bonn" mark.

Console set, 14" l oval bowl, pr
13-1/2" h vases, all over
painted scenes on tapestry
ground, gilt metal mounts
.... **2,990.00**
Cup and saucer, relief luster
bands, marked **40.00**

Charger, blue and white transfer
decoration of pastoral scene, rose
border, rim chip, overall crazing, light
staining, 15" d, **$65**.
Photo courtesy of Alderfer Auction Co.

Ewer, 10-1/8" h, red and pink
flowers, raised gold, fancy
handle........................ **75.00**
Portrait urn, cov, 35" h,
elaborate tooled gilt foliage
dec, portrait of woman on one
side, burgundy ground, sq
plinth, underglaze blue
beehive mark, c1900
.... **3,910.00**
Tea tile, 7" d, hp, pink, yellow,
and purple pansies, white
ground, green border, marked
"Bonn-Rhein" **35.00**
Urn, cov, 13" h, hp, multicolored
flowers, green, and yellow
ground, two gold handles,
artist sgd................... **120.00**

Vase, tapered vasiform body, sinuous
everted rim with short openwork loops,
sinuous spreading base with openwork
loops, glazed in maroon and green, body
hand-painted with roses, gilt accenting,
Franz Anton Mehlem Earthenware
Factory, Bonn, Germany, early 20th C,
12-3/8" h, **$300**.
Photo courtesy of Skinner, Inc.

Vase
18-3/4" h, blue ground, gilt
and enameled floral designs,
scrolled handles, printed and
imp marks, late 19th C
.... **400.00**
20" h, 5" d, hp multicolored
floral spray with raised gold
dec, link handles, ftd .. **240.00**

ROYAL COPENHAGEN

History: Franz Mueller established a porcelain factory at Copenhagen in 1775. When bankruptcy threatened in 1779, the Danish king acquired ownership, appointing Mueller manager and selecting the name "Royal Copenhagen." The crown sold its interest in 1867; the company remains privately owned today.

Blue Fluted, Royal Copenhagen's most famous pattern, was created in 1780. It is of Chinese origin and comes in three styles: smooth edge, closed lace edge, and perforated lace edge (full lace). Many other factories copied it.

Flora Danica, named for a famous botanical work, was introduced in 1789 and remained exclusive to Royal Copenhagen. It is identified by its freehand illustrations of plants and its hand-cut edges and perforations.

Marks: Royal Copenhagen porcelain is marked with three wavy lines, which signify ancient waterways, and a crown, added in 1889. Stoneware does not have the crown mark.

Figure, boy holding pig, 7" h, **$80**.
Photo courtesy of Joy Luke Auctions.

Bowl, reticulated blue and white **125.00**
Candlesticks, pr, 9" h, blue floral design, white ground, bisque lion heads, floral garlands **160.00**

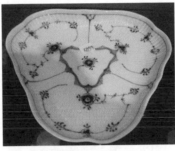

Dresser tray, triangular, blue decoration, **$45**.

Cream soup, #1812 .... **75.00**
Cup and saucer, 2-1/2" h cylindrical cup with angular handle, 5-1/2" d saucer with molded and gilded rim, hp floral specimen, 20th C **575.00**
Dish, reticulated blue and white **175.00**
Figure
    6-3/4" h, girl knitting, No. 1314 .... **350.00**
    7-1/2" h, 11" l, dachshund, blue wave mark **375.00**
    15-1/4" h, Nymph with Satyr, timid satyr kneeling at feet of nude female nymph, on naturalistic ovoid base, 20th C **1,100.00**

Figure, little girl and boy embracing puppy, **$85**.
Photo courtesy of Joy Luke.

Fish plate, 10" d, different fish swimming among marine plants, molded and gilt border, light green highlights, gilt dentil edge, crown circular mark, 10-pc set **8,250.00**
Inkwell, Blue Fluted pattern, matching tray **150.00**
Pickle tray, 9" l, Half Lace pattern, blue triple wave mark **70.00**

Figure, milkmaid and cow, **$80**.
Photo courtesy of Joy Luke.

Two figures, left: girl mending sock, right: boy whittling stick, **each $75**.
Photo courtesy of Joy Luke.

Plaque, oval, beaded rim surmounted by ribbon and bow decoration, depicting Fredensborg Castle, back marked "Prove," 5-3/4" w, 8" h, **$615**.
Photo courtesy of Alderfer Auction Co.

Plates, two 7-5/8" d, six 10" d, each with gilt serrated rim and central hp floral specimen, price for eight-pc set **2,990.00**
Platter, 14-1/2" l, #1556 .. **140.00**
Salad bowl, 9-7/8" d, Flora Danica, botanical specimen, molded gilt border, dentil edge, pink highlights, blue triple wave and green crown mark **825.00**

Teaset, teapot, sugar, and creamer, blue and white, floral decoration, **$395**.

Photo courtesy of Joy Luke Auctions.

Soup tureen, cov, stand, 14-1/2" l, Flora Danica, oval, enamel painted botanical specimens, twin handles, finial, factory marks, botanical identification, modern **5,750.00**

Tray, 10" l, Blue Fluted pattern **65.00**

Vase, 7" h, sage green and gray crackled glaze **150.00**

ROYAL CROWN DERBY

History: Derby Crown Porcelain Co., established in 1875 in Derby, England, had no connection with earlier Derby factories which operated in the late 18th and early 19th centuries. In 1890, the company was appointed "Manufacturers of Porcelain to Her Majesty" (Queen Victoria) and since that date has been known as "Royal Crown Derby."

Most of these porcelains, both tableware and figural, were hand decorated. A variety of printing processes were used for additional adornment. Today, Royal Crown Derby is a part of Royal Doulton Tableware, Ltd.

Marks: Derby porcelains from 1878 to 1890 carry only the standard crown printed mark. After 1891, the mark includes the "Royal Crown Derby" wording. In the 20th century, "Made in England" and "English Bone China" were added to the mark.

Bottle, 6" h, orig stopper, molded body, two handles, hp flowers, gold accents . **150.00**

Candlesticks, pr, bone china, Imari pattern, paneled baluster form, bulbous toes, brass nozzle **765.00**

Soup tureen, covered, stand, Kings pattern, oval, c1830, 10" x 17-1/2", **$2,300**.

Cup and saucer, 5" d saucer, Imari pattern, 20th C.... **70.00**

Dessert service, Pattern 1128, Imari pattern, bone china, twelve 8-1/2" d dessert plates; twelve 6-1/2" d bowls; twelve teacups and saucers **1,880.00**

Ewer, 6" h, Oriental-style gold enameled dec, soft coral ground, handle **200.00**

Luncheon plates, 9-1/8" d, dark Kelly green rim, gilt inner and outer rims, white faux jewelling applied to outer rim, c1898, price for set of 12.......... **470.00**

Jug, Imari palette, pink round, gold trim, c1885, pr ... **750.00**

Mug, grapes and vines dec, blue and gold **125.00**

Plate, 8" d, Daisy pattern, blue transfer print, gilt details, late 19th/early 20th C, price for set of 11........................... **260.00**

Soup plate, 9-7/8" d, inner band of gold jewelling with wide rim of gilt quatrefoils, grapevine, and leaf sprays, some leaves accented with bronze tone, shaped beaded edge, retailed by Tiffany & Co., early 20th C, price for set of 18....... **5,750.00**

Tea and coffee service, bone china, Pattern 1128, Imari dec, 9" h ovoid coffeepot, 7-1/4" h teapot, creamer, cov sugar, modern **950.00**

Urn, 12" h, squatty, double reticulated handles and finials, birds, butterfly, and floral designs, ivory ground, gilt accents, marked "Bailey, Banks, and Biddle," dripped for lamp, finials replaced, restoration to one handle, price for pr **1,325.00**

Vase, covered, England, c1894, globular shape, raised gold foliate decoration, deep cobalt blue ground, printed mark, chips to finial, hairline to cover insert, 15" h, **$2,585**.

Photo courtesy of Skinner, Inc.

Vase

7-1/2" h, enameled floral dec, gold encrusted lip....... **320.00**

13" h, ovoid, narrow neck, flared rim, serpent handle, cobalt blue and iron-red Imari type dec, gilt accents, hp floral panels, minor gilt loss, touch-up, price for pr.. **925.00**

ROYAL DOULTON

ROYAL DOULTON FLAMBE

History: Doulton pottery began in 1815 under the direction of John Doulton at the Doulton & Watts pottery in Lambeth, England. Early output was limited to salt-glazed industrial stoneware. After John Watts retired in 1854, the firm became Doulton and Company, and production was expanded to include hand-decorated stoneware such as figurines, vases, dinnerware, and flasks.

In 1878, John's son, Sir Henry Doulton, purchased Pinder Bourne & Co. in Burslem. The companies became Doulton & Co., Ltd. in 1882. Decorated porcelain was added to Doulton's earthenware production in 1884.

Most Doulton figurines were produced at the Burslem plants, where they were made continuously from 1890 until 1978. After a short interruption, a new line of Doulton figurines was introduced in 1979.

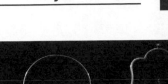
Dickens ware, in earthenware and porcelain, was introduced in 1908. The pieces were decorated with characters from Dickens's novels. Most of the line was withdrawn in the 1940s, except for plates, which continued to be made until 1974.

Character jugs, a 20th-century revival of early Toby models, were designed by Charles J. Noke for Doulton in the 1930s. Character jugs are limited to bust portraits, while Royal Doulton toby jugs are full figured. The character jugs come in four sizes and feature fictional characters from Dickens, Shakespeare, and other English and American novelists, as well as historical heroes. Marks on both character and toby jugs must be carefully identified to determine dates and values.

Doulton's Rouge Flambé (Veined Sung) is a high-glazed, strong-colored ware noted primarily for the fine modeling and exquisite colorings, especially in the animal items. The process used to produce the vibrant colors is a Doulton secret.

Production of stoneware at Lambeth ceased in 1956; production of porcelain continues today at Burslem.

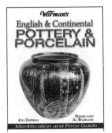

For more information, *see Warman's English & Continental Pottery & Porcelain,* 4th edition.

Marks: Beginning in 1872, the "Royal Doulton" mark was used on all types of wares produced by the company.

Beginning in 1913, an "HN" number was assigned to each new Doulton figurine design. The "HN" numbers, which referred originally to Harry Nixon, a Doulton artist, were chronological until 1940, after which blocks of numbers were assigned to each modeler. From 1928 until 1954, a small number

Biscuit jars, from left: gold and rust colored chrysanthemums, foliage in gray-greens and gold, c1894, **$995**; scrolled motif with white and pink passion flowers, gold trim, Doulton Burslem, 1891, **$895**; peach colored body with multicolored florals, gold foliage, Doulton Burslem, 1891, **$995**, Carlton Ware, tan ground with pink and white flowers, yellow centers, blue forget-me-nots, cobalt blue drapery panels at top alternating with beige, gold trim, c1894, **$1,250**.

was placed to the right of the crown mark; this number added to 1927 gives the year of manufacture.

Biscuit jar, covered, Many Kiss the Child For the Nurse's Sake, signed "Noke," blurred blue mark, **$195**.

Animal
Alsatian, HN117 .... **175.00**
Bull terrier, K14 .... **325.00**
Dalmatian, HN114 ..... **250.00**
English bulldog, HN1074 .... **175.00**
Irish setter, HN1055 ... **165.00**
Salmon, 12" h, flambé, printed mark **435.00**
Tiger, 14" l, flambé, printed mark **375.00**
Biscuit jar, earthenware
6-1/2" h, emb scrolled mold, polychrome florals, nickel silver mount, handle, and lid, green "Doulton Burslem England" backstamp .. **220.00**
6-3/4" h, stoneware, enamel decorated geometric designs

in relief, silver plated rim, handle and cover, imp Doulton Lambeth mark, 1882 .... **265.00**
9" h, silver plated lid and handle, floral dec, Doulton Burslem mark............. **200.00**
9-1/2" h, silver plated lid and handle, floral dec, Doulton Burslem mark............. **290.00**
Bowl, 9" l, 7-1/2" w, rect, farm scene, 1932 mark **115.00**
Cabinet plate, pink and yellow roses painted in center, lower left artist sgd "W. Slater," raised gilt border and rim, turquoise faux jewel accents, early 20th C **325.00**
Candlesticks, pr, 6-1/2" h, Walton Ware, Battle of Hastings, cream color earthenware ground, stamped mark, c1910, small base chip on one **290.00**
Chamberstick, 2" h, Walton Ware, fishermen dec, ivory earthenware ground, stamped mark, c1910, one of pair damaged **400.00**
Character jug, large
Cardinal **150.00**
Poacher, D6781 .... **350.00**
Character jug, miniature
Blacksmith **50.00**
Pickwick **65.00**
Character jug, small
Pearly King **35.00**
Toby Philpots **85.00**
Charger, 12-5/8" d, hp, allover incised leaf, berry, and vine border, central fruits and leaves, attributed to Frank Bragwyn, printed mark, c1930 .... **245.00**

Charger, Coaching Days, decorated with coach and horses, 15-1/4" d, **$180**.

Photo courtesy of Joy Luke Auctions.

Clock case, King's are, night watchman, c1905 ...... **450.00**

Cuspidor, 7" h, Isaac Walton ware, polychrome dec, transfer printed, fisherman on ext., verses on int. lip, printed mark............................ **325.00**

Dinner service, Rondelay pattern, service for eight, platter, tea set, 60 pcs **450.00**

Figure
Carolyn, HN 2112, 71/4" h, 3-1/2" d **335.00**
Fair Lady, coral pink, HN2835 .... **225.00**
Lady Charmain, HN1949 .... **225.00**
King Charles I, dark brown gloves, black flora at boots, imp date 1919......... **1,312.00**
Orange Lady, HN1758 **245.00**
Queen Mother's 80th Birthday, HN464, 1980.............. **750.00**
Priscilla, pantaloons showing beneath crinoline, HN1380, 1920-40...................... **288.00**
Sandra, HN2275......... **200.00**
The Leisure Hour, HN2055 .... **400.00**
Victorian Lady, HN1208, 1926-38...................... **355.00**

Fish plate, 9" d, swimming fish centers, pale yellow ground, gold bands and rims, sgd "J. Hallmark," 10-pc set ... **700.00**

Game plate, 9-1/2" d, bone china, each with gilt trim lines and polychrome enamel painted with shore birds in landscapes, artist sgd "C. Holloway," titled and factory marked on reverse, c1925, retailed by Tiffany & Co., set of twelve.................. **1,300.00**

Figure, man using plane, **$350**.

Figure, balloon seller, **$395**.

Humidor, 7-1/2" h, Walton Ware, Battle of Hastings, cream color earthenware ground, stamped mark, c1910. **365.00**

Inkstand, 3" h, stoneware, tapered cylindrical form molded with floral sprays, blue, ochre, and brown glazes, silver mounts, Doulton Lambeth, hallmarked London, 1901.......................... **215.00**

Jardinière, 4-1/2" h, Walton Ware, Battle of Hastings, cream color earthenware ground, stamped mark, c1910 .... **350.00**

Jug, 10-1/2" h, Regency Coach, limited edition, printed marks, 20th C **930.00**

Loving cup
9-3/4" h, Three Musketeers, limited edition, sgd "Noke, H. Fenton," orig certificate, 20th C **920.00**
10-1/4" d, King George V and Queen Mary, 25-year reign anniversary, c1935 ..... **750.00**

Milk pitcher, 7" h, sharkskin ground, cobalt blue flowers trimmed in gold, US patent **150.00**

Mug
4" h, gladiator, #D6553.. **300.00**
8-1/4" h, St. John Falstaff **125.00**

Pitcher
7-3/4" h, stoneware, dec by Florence Barlow, stippled ground with enameled pate-sur-pate design of birds in flight among tall marshy grass, incised artist monogram and imp Doulton Lambeth mark, c1884.......................... **1,000.00**
12-1/2" h, Walton Ware, fishermen dec, ivory earthenware ground, stamped mark, c1910, price for pr, one with bruise and restoration................... **400.00**

Plate, 8-1/2" d, English Garden series **115.00**

Gibson girl plate, titled "She contemplates the Choister," **$75**.

Photo courtesy of Dotta Auction Co., Inc.

Gibson girl plate, titled "She is disturbed by a vision...," **$75**.

Photo courtesy of Dotta Auction Co., Inc.

Gibson girl plate, titled "Some think she has remained in retirement too long, others are surprised she is out so soon," **$75**.

Photo courtesy of Dotta Auction Co., Inc.

Story plates, set of six, polychrome landscape scenes with figures, rims with flying birds and clouds, back of each plate printed with store depicted on front, and Royal Doulton marks, 10-1/2" d, **$350**.

Photo courtesy of Alderfer Auction Co.

Royal Doulton, platter, hunt scene, two riders walking horses, 10" l, back stamp, **$95**.

Platter, 9" l, 7-1/2" w, Dr. Johnson at Bootham Bar-York, registered in Australia. **120.00**

Service plate, 10-5/8" d, cream-colored ground, interior band of gilt anthemia, rim with gilt scrollwork over cream-colored ground, apple green reserves, gilt-shaped rim, mold date mark 1910, price for 18-pc set **5,465.00**

Spirits barrel, 7" l, King's Ware, double, silver trim rings and cov, oak stand, c1909 .... **1,200.00**

Sweet meat, 5" d, 3-1/2" h, sharkskin ground, applied flowers, silvered lid and handle, rosette mark artist sgd "Eleanor Tosen" ... **125.00**

Tankard, 9-1/2" h, hinged pewter lid, incised frieze of herons among reeds, blue slip enamel, imp mark, sgd, c1875 .... **1,600.00**

Teacup and saucer, cobalt blue, heavy gold dec **120.00**

Tea set, Walton Ware, cov teapot with underplate, creamer,

sugar bowl, Battle of Hastings, cream-colored earthenware ground, stamped mark, chip on spout, hairline on sugar lid ... **365.00**

Tobacco jar, 8" h, incised frieze of cattle, goats, and donkeys, imp mark, sgd, worn SP rim, handle and cover, dated 1880 .... **995.00**

Toby mug, large size, Falstaff, marked on base, **$245**.

Toby mug, large, pirate, green and yellow parrot for handle, black hat with white skull and crossbones, brown shirt, **$85**.

Toby jug
Beefeater, #D6206, 6" h **85.00**
Winston Churchill, #8360 .... **95.00**

Umbrella stand, 23-1/2" h, stoneware, enamel dec, applied floral medallions within diamond formed panels, framed by button motifs, imp mark, glaze crazing, c1910 .... **550.00**

Vase
6-1/2" h, Hannah Barlow dec, double handled, wide central panel with incised landscape

and horses grazing by sleeping hound, enameled bands of scrolled leaves and stylized stiff leaves to borders, artist signed and imp Doulton Lambeth mark, 1882 .... **1,765.00**
7-3/4" h, Titanium Ware, sq, hand painted enamel dec of birds below sunny sky, titled "Herring Gulls," artist signed Harry Allen, printed mark, c1925 .... **1,645.00**
11-3/4" h, emb tapestry dec, enameled scrolls, imp mark, Slaters patent, early 20th C, price for pr **2,250.00**

ROYAL DUX

History: Royal Dux porcelain was made in Dux, Bohemia (now the Czech Republic), by E. Eichler at the Duxer Porzellan-Manufaktur, established in 1860. Many items were exported to the United States. By the turn of the century, Royal Dux figurines, vases, and accessories, especially those featuring Art-Nouveau designs, were captivating consumers.

Marks: A raised triangle with an acorn and the letter "E" plus "Dux, Bohemia" was used as a mark between 1900 and 1914.

Bowl, 17-1/2" l, modeled as female tending a fishing net, oval shell-form bowl, imp mark, early 20th C **490.00**

Bust, 14" h, female portrait, raised leaves and berries on base, Czechoslovakia, early 20th C, unmarked, chips **290.00**

Compote, figural, 14-1/2" l, modeled as female atop shell-form bowl, another figure within the wave modeled freeform base, imp mark, early 20th C **750.00**

Figure
15" x 9-1/2" x 4-1/2", flamenco dancer, cobalt blue and white glaze, gold trim, pink triangle mark, stamped, numbered **1,250.00**
18" x 11" x 6", Pierrrot serenading lover, perched on harvest moon, pre-war "E" mark, price for facing pair **3,500.00**

Figure, male and female European pheasants, each marked on inner side of base, 21" h, **$750**.

Photo courtesy of Early Auction Co.

Figure, female bather, nude woman seated on rocky outcrop, drying her foot with gilt enameled cloth, oblong base, Czechoslovakia, early 20th C, 18-1/2" h, **$1,000**.

Photo courtesy of Skinner, Inc.

Figure, shepherd and shepherdess, lady standing holding staff, man seated playing an instrument, naturalistic ovoid base, indistinct initials OAP?, man lacking item from hands, Czechoslovakia, early 20th C, 22" h, **$825**.

Photo courtesy of Skinner, Inc.

21" h, male and female European peasant, sgd on inner side of base, price for facing pr **750.00**

Floor vase, 36-1/2" h, 37-1/4" h, date palm tree form, Middle Eastern woman and water urn on one, her suitor playing lute on other, matte finish flesh toned skin, cobalt blue clothing against white, gilt rims and highlights, ink labels "Royal Dux Bohemia" with acorn in triangle, glued unstable repairs to man, price for pr **5,225.00**

Tazza, 19-1/2" h, figural, putti and classically draped woman supporting shell, price for pr, one with hairline in base **880.00**

Vase, 11" h, Grecian, "E" mark **595.00**

ROYAL FLEMISH

History: Royal Flemish was produced by the Mount Washington Glass Co., New Bedford, Massachusetts. Albert Steffin patented the process in 1894.

1892

Royal Flemish is a frosted transparent glass with heavy raised gold enamel lines. These lines form sections—often colored in russet tones—giving the appearance of stained-glass windows with elaborate floral or coin medallions.

Advisers: Clarence and Betty Maier.

For more information, see *Warman's Glass*, 4th edition.

Biscuit jar, cov, 8" h, ovoid, large Roman coins on stained panels, divided by heavy gold lines, ornate SP cov, rim, and

bail handle, orig paper label "Mt. W. G. Co. Royal Flemish" **1,750.00**

Box, cov, 5-1/2" d, 3-3/4" h, swirled border, gold outlined swirls, gold tracery blossoms, enameled blossom with jeweled center on lid **1,500.00**

Ewer, oval, rope handle, ruffled spout, decorated with light purple and pink flowers, intricate gold enamel floral motif and lines on frosted glass, signed with red "FR," in diamond and "566," Boston, late 19th C, 13-3/4" h, **$3,290**.

Photo courtesy of Skinner, Inc.

Ewer, 10-1/2" h, 9" w, 5" d, circular semi-transparent panel on front with youth thrusting spear into chest of winged creature, reverse panel shows mythical fish created with tail changed into stylized florals, raised gold dec, outlines, and scrolls, rust, purple, and gold curlicues, twisted rope handle with brushed gold encircles neck, hp minute gold florals on neck, burnished gold stripes on rim spout and panels **4,950.00**

Vase, 6" d, 6-1/2" h, stylized scrolls of pastel violet sweep down two tiny handles and across body, realistically tinged sprays of violets randomly strewn around frosted clear glass body, gold lines define violet nosegays and frame scrolls, gold accents daubed here and there, sgd with Royal Flemish logo and "0583" **2,200.00**

ROYAL WORCHESTER

c.1876-1891   1891

History: In 1751, the Worcester Porcelain Company, led by Dr. John Wall and William Davis, acquired the Bristol pottery of Benjamin Lund and moved it to Worcester. The first wares were painted blue under the glaze; soon thereafter decorating was accomplished by painting on the glaze in enamel colors. Among the most-famous 18th-century decorators were James Giles and Jefferys Hamet O'Neale. Transfer print decoration was developed by the 1760s.

For more information, *see Warman's English & Continental Pottery & Porcelain,* 4th edition.

A series of partnerships took place after Davis' death in 1783: Flight (1783-1792), Flight & Barr (1793-1807); Barr, Flight, & Barr (1807-1813); and Flight, Barr, & Barr (1813-1840). In 1840, the factory was moved to Chamberlain & Co. in Diglis. Decorative wares were discontinued. In 1852, W. H. Kerr and R. W. Binns formed a new company and revived the production of ornamental wares.

In 1862, the firm became the Royal Worcester Porcelain Co. Among the key modelers of the late 19th century were James Hadley, his three sons, and George Owen, an expert with pierced clay pieces. Royal

Worcester absorbed the Grainger factory in 1889 and the James Hadley factory in 1905. Modern designers include Dorothy Doughty and Doris Lindner.

Dinner service, Evesham Vale, 10 each dinner plates, salad plates, bread plates, bowls, saucers; four lidded jars; cup; two covered casseroles; hors d'oeuvres tray; round tray; two round baking dishes, six ramekins, covered jam pot; covered butter dish; covered sugar; creamer; mug; three salt shakers; slotted spoon; two tab-handled bowls, **$450.**

Photo courtesy of Joy Luke Auctions.

Basket, 8-1/2" d, flaring pierced sides mounted with floral heads, pine cone and floral cluster int., blue and white transfer dec, first period, mid-18th C **550.00**
Biscuit jar, cov, 7-1/4" h, fluted body, raised spear head borders surrounding enamel floral design **550.00**
Bowl, 10" d, scalloped border, shell molded boy, fruit and floral spray, blue and white transfer dec, first period, mid-18th C **320.00**
Butter tub, cov, 4-1/4" d, 3-1/4" h, cylindrical, fully sculpted finial, painted floral sprays below geometric borders, first period, c1765 .... **450.00**
Demitasse cups and saucers, 4-3/8" d saucer, hand painted, painted fruits dec, gilt rims and handles, sgd "E. Townsend," retailed by the Goldsmiths and Silversmiths Company, c1936, orig boxed set includes set of six 4" l gold-washed silver spoons, London, 1931, maker's mark HJH **3,820.00**
Dessert plate
9-1/8" d, bone china, hand painted, center with peach

stem and bluettes, sgd lower right "E. Townsend," gilt rocaille inner rim, seafoam green fluted outer rim, c1941, set of 12 .... **900.00**
9-1/4" d, bone china, hand painted, center with flowers, gilt rim, labeled "Designed by A. H. Williamson, Royal Worcester, Made in England," set of 12 .... **375.00**

Ewer, white body, gold neck band and handle, multicolored floral decoration, crossed arrows mark, one of pair shown, **$400.**

Photo courtesy of Dotta Auction Co., Inc.

Ewer, 9" h, pale pink powder horn shape, gold stag horn handle, minor chip **150.00**
Figure
6-1/2" h, Welsh girl, shot enamel porcelain, sgd "Hadley," late-19th C .. **690.00**
7-3/4" h and 8-1/4" h, lady and gentleman, George III costumes, sgd "Hadley," pr **1,100.00**
8-3/4" h, Cairo water carrier, 1895 .... **635.00**
Fish plates, 9-1/4" d, bone china, hp fish, gilt lattice and foliage border, sgd "Harry Ayrton," printed marks, c1930, 13-pc set..... **2,300.00**
Fruit cooler, 6-1/4" h, cylindrical, Royal Lily pattern, stylized floral reserve, stepped circular foot, first period, c1800 .... **225.00**

Lamp base, 13-3/4" h, baluster vase form, slender gilt neck, two short Moorish-style gilt handles, hand-painted scene of gilt shipwreck on shore by lighthouse, reverse with small scenic roundel, gilt guilloche foot, electrified **325.00**

Mustard pot, 4" h, cylindrical, blue and white transfer, floral clusters, floral finial, first period, mid-18th C **325.00**

Pitcher
5-3/4" h, cream, gold enamel dec............................. **150.00**
5-3/4" h, Indian elephant head handle......................... **175.00**
5-3/4" h, tri-corner shape, blue and white overlapping circles, gold enameled pouring lip, c1860....................... **260.00**
6" h, 5" d, floral dec, gold handle........................ **230.00**

Plate
7" w, octagonal, landscape fan form reserves, cobalt blue ground, first period, 18th C, pr **350.00**
7-3/4" d, Blind Earl pattern, raised rose spray, polychrome floral sprays, scalloped border, first period, mid-18th C **1,100.00**

Salad bowl, 9" d, leaf molded, three handles, printed mark, c1899......................... **560.00**

Sauce boat, 4-1/4" h, geometric band above foliate molded body, painted floral sprays, oval foot, first period, c1765, pr **275.00**

Service plate, 10-1/2" d, hand painted, central roundel painted with dense spray of various flowers, sgd "E. Phillips," speckled green inner rim, gilt outer rim etched with laurel wreaths and husk swags, c1921, price for set of 12............................. **1,530.00**

Sweetmeat jar, 6" d, molded swirl base, thistles dec, silverplate lid, bail, and handle, marked "RW" with crown **200.00**

Tankard, 6" h, cylindrical, blue and white transfer dec of parrot among fruit, first period, mid-18th C...... **325.00**

Teabowl and saucer, painted chinoisiere vignette, blue border, first period, c1865 .... **185.00**

Teapot, cov, 6-1/2" h, globular form body, fully sculpted blossom finial, domed top, painted floral sprays, first period, c1765 .... **375.00**

Salver, round, wide band of underglaze blue transfer printed Middle Eastern-style flowers, inner and outer rim accented with gilt scrolls and linework, 1878, 14-1/2" d, **$300**.

Photo courtesy of Skinner, Inc.

Urn, cov, 11-1/2" h, pierced dome top, globular body, painted floral sprays, basketweave molded base, early 20th C **195.00**

Vase, 9-5/8" h, double handles, gilt and enamel dec, scene of birds by moonlit sky, printed mark, c1887 .... **715.00**

ROYCROFT

History: Elbert Hubbard founded the Roycrofters in East Aurora, New York, at the turn of the century. Considered a genius in his day, he was an author, lecturer, manufacturer, salesman, and philosopher.

Hubbard established a campus that included a printing plant where he published *The Philistine*, *The Fra*, and *The Roycrofter*. His most-famous book was *A Message to Garcia*, published in 1899. His "community" also included a furniture manufacturing plant, a metal shop, and a leather shop.

Ali Baba bench, 42-1/2" l, 11" w, 20" h, half-log top, flaring plank legs, keyed through tenon stretcher, carved orb and cross mark, minor loss to bark, orig finish **16,500.00**

Billfold, matching change purse, lady's, 3-1/2" x 6-3/4", tooled leather, emb foliate motif, monongrammed "RK," orig mirror, pencil, and notepad, orb and cross mark **425.00**

Andirons, pair, No. 069, curls and rivets, attached to each other with twisted links, unmarked, excellent condition, minor rusting to original black patina, 24" x 14-1/2", **$2,500**.

Photo courtesy of David Rago Auctions, Inc.

Bookcase, slab sides with keyed tenon construction, plate rail top, orig iron hardware, orb mark, refinished, 46" w, 16" d, 71" h **9,775.00**

Bookends, pr, 4-1/8" w, 3-1/4" d, 5-1/4" h, model no. 309, hammered copper, rect, riveted center band suspending ring, dark brown patina, imp Roycroft orb, minor wear **225.00**

Book
Old John Burroughs, by Elbert Hubbard, full levant, cover and inside covers incised and painted with blossoms, each hand made paper page with watercolor by Clara Schlegel and Richard Kruger, hand painted bookmark, 1901, 8" x 5-1/4"........................ **4,000.00**
So Here Then Is The Last Ride, by Robert Browning, half levant and marbleized paper, each page illuminated by Frances June Carmody, 1900, sgd and numbered, 8" x 5-3/4".......................... **650.00**

Box
1-1/2" x 4" x 4", tooled leather and suede lined, lid emb with poppy medallion, orb and cross mark, some scuffs and wear to corners........... **475.00**
3-1/4" x 13" x 10", "In" and "Out," from Roycroft Inn, one quarter-sawn oak, stenciled with letter "O," stamped "OF.336.S," other pine, stamped "P501," orig finish, branded orb and cross marks **600.00**

Bowl, 10-1/4" d, 4-1/8" h, hammered copper, rolled rim, shouldered bowl, three point feet, red patina, imp mark, traces of brass wash .. **450.00**

Box, covered, hammered copper, rectangular, hinged, lid embossed with quatrefoil, orb and cross mark, original dark patina, some wear to patina on top, 7" l, 3-1/2" w, 1-3/4" h, **$425.**

Photo courtesy of David Rago Auctions, Inc.

Bud vase, 10-1/2" l, wall hanging, hammered copper, cut-out frame **200.00**
Candle lamp, blue art glass, baluster form, flaring foot, stamped "Roycroft," electrified **175.00**
Candle sconce, 3-1/2" w, 10" h, hammered copper, riveted strap holder, imp backplate, orig dark brown patina, orb and cross mark, few scratches, price for pr **630.00**
Candlesticks, pr
3" x 8-1/4", hammered copper, triple light, curled bands, orig dark patina with some wear, orb and cross marks... **500.00**
6" x 6-3/4", hammered copper, double light, wood grain pattern, orb and cross marks **350.00**
7-1/2" h, Princess style, brass washed, good grain double shafts, faceted bases, stamped orb and cross mark, orig patina.................. **650.00**

Chair, straddle type, tacked-on new leather seat, original finish, orb and cross mark top front stretcher, 34-1/4" x 24" x 22", **$1,700.**

Photo courtesy of David Rago Auctions, Inc.

Side chair, four vertical backslats, Mackmurdo feet and replaced leather upholstered seat, original finish, orb and cross mark, 18" w, 17" d, 38" h, **$1,485.**

Photo courtesy of David Rago Auctions, Inc.

Chair, side, 37" x 16-1/2" x 16-1/4", ladderback, three horizontal back slats, leather covered cushions, carved orb and cross mark, refinished, price for pr **460.00**
Chandelier, from Roycroft Inn, 14-1/2" w, 10-3/4" h, copper, triangular strap support base with cut-out hearts and three pendant fixtures, each with enameled amber glass shade dec in stylized floral motif, triangular ceiling plate, hanging chains, orb and cross mark **1,955.00**
Desk lamp, 14-3/4" h, 7" d Steuben blown glass lustered glass shade, hammered copper, shaft of four curled and riveted bands, stamped orb and cross mark . **5,750.00**
Desk set, hammered copper, blotter corners, inkwell, letter holder, pen tray, perpetual calendar with cards, letter opener, orb and cross marks, orig dark patina **350.00**
Dresser, 62-3/4" x 45" x 21", pine and oak, two small drawers over four long drawers, hammered iron hardware, paneled sides, orb and cross die-stamped on each pull, from Roycroft Inn **1,500.00**
Frame, 8" x 5-3/4", hammered copper, emb with quatrefoils, orb and cross mark, and "Roycroft," orig dark patina **1,100.00**

Dresser, four drawers, integrated mirror, brass pulls, Mackmurdo feet, excellent original finish and condition, orb and cross mark, 43-1/2" l, 25-1/2" w, 61-1/2" h, **$10,450.**

Photo courtesy of David Rago Auctions, Inc.

Goody box, 23" l, 13" d, 10" h, mahogany, wrought cooper strap hardware, monogrammed "H," orig finish, carved orb and cross on top......................... **630.00**
High chair, child's, tacked-on leather seat, hand carved name "Silas," orig finish, carved orb and cross front center, seat and tacks replaced, 42" x 18-1/2" x 21-1/2".......................... **950.00**
Humidor, 4-3/4" w, 5-3/4" h, hammered copper, covered in brass wash, Trillium pattern, stamped orb and cross mark, minor wear to patina... **690.00**
Kitchen work table, 30" x 70" x 18-1/4", mixed woods, tacked-on zinc counter over two lower shelves, orig finish, unsigned, from Roycroft Inn...... **2,700.00**
Lamp, boudoir, 10-1/2" d faceted mica shade, brass washed hammered copper base, base stamped with orb and cross mark, wear and flakes to mica.............. **350.00**
Lamp, table
15" h, 10" d, hammered copper and mica, single socket, riveted heraldic shade, lined with band of mica, orig dark patina, orb and cross mark........ **3,500.00**
23" h, 18" d conical shade of lime green and purple leaded slag glass, classical hammered copper base, riveted bands, ring pulls, three sockets, orb and cross mark, replaced cord **35,000.00**

Magazine stand, 37-1/2" x 17-3/4" x 15-1/2", arched tapering sides, three shelves, orb and cross mark, orig finish, ... **5,550.00**

Marble bag, 8" l, laced suede, large orb and cross mark tooled to front panel.... **450.00**

Refectory table, chestnut, five shaped legs, curved end stretchers, carved orb and cross mark on leg, From Roycroft Inn, refinished, separation and scratches to top, metal brackets added underneath, 132-1/2" l, 42-1/4" w, 30" h, **$2,100**.

Photo courtesy of David Rago Auctions, Inc.

Morris chair, shaped arms and posts, laced leather covered foam cushions, four slats under each arm, carved orb and cross mark on front stretcher, arms refinished, replaced leather and cushions, 39-1/2" x 29-1/2" x 38".......................... **3,250.00**

Motto, orig Roycroft frame, matted
"Do Not Keep Your Kindness...," 17-1/4" x 12-1/2" **350.00**
"Happiness is a Habit, Cultivate It," 23" x 19".. **350.00**

Paper folio, six woodblock prints, Roycroft Inn pamphlet with photographs....... **750.00**

Smoking set, Trillium pattern, hammered copper, humidor, cigarette holder, cylindrical match holder, stacking ashtrays with matchbox holder, 14" x 9" rect tray **500.00**

Sugar bowl, cov, china, hp by Bertha Hubbard, sgd "B. C. Hubbard" **200.00**

Tray, 14-3/4" d, hexagonal, hammered copper, stitched border, two handles, orb and cross mark, orig dark patina **475.00**

Vase, 7" h, 2-1/2" d, hammered copper cylinder, emb with stylized quatrefoils on tall stems, stamped orb and cross mark and "KK" for Karl

Kipp, patina cleaned some time ago................... **1,600.00**

Vase, hammered copper, cylindrical, band of stylized quatrefoil under verdigris triangles, orb and cross mark, excellent new patina, 7" h, 2-1/2" d, **$1,000**.

Photo courtesy of David Rago Auctions, Inc.

Telephone, hammered copper and bakelite, inscribed "PROPERTY OF THE AMERICAN BELL TELEPHONE COMPANY," original wiring and patina, orb and cross mark, 12", **$8,100**.

Photo courtesy of David Rago Auctions, Inc.

RUSSIAN ITEMS

History:
During the late 19th and early 20th centuries, craftsmen skilled in lacquer, silver, and enamel wares worked in Russia. During the Czarist era (1880-1917), Fabergé, known for his exquisite enamel pieces, led a group of master craftsmen located primarily in

ВРАТЬЕВЪ
Baterin's factory
1812-1820

КорНИЛОВЫІХЪ
Korniloff's factory
c 1835

Moscow. Fabergé also had an establishment in St. Petersburg and enjoyed the patronage of the Russian Imperial family and royalty and nobility throughout Europe.

Almost all enameling was done on silver. The artist and the government assayer sign pieces.

The Russian Revolution in 1917 brought an abrupt end to the century of Russian craftsmanship. The modern Soviet government has exported some inferior enamel and lacquer work, usually lacking in artistic merit. Modern pieces are not collectible.

Enamels

Blood cup, 4" h, gilt and transfer dec, Imperial double headed eagle, cipher of Czar Nicholas II above date 1896...... **260.00**

Bonbonniere, 3-3/8" d, 2-3/16" h, orchid guillouche enamel on silver, cylindrical, cast silver bas-relief applied dec on cov and back, applied relief, monogram of Nicholas II set with precious stones, Henrik Wigstrom, workmaster, St. Petersburg, 1908-17, slight damage **4,225.00**

Cane, 35" l, 4-1/2" l x 3-1/4" tau handle dec with champleve style raised enamel, light blue, dark blue, green, white, and red, worn Russian hallmarks, heavy ebony shaft, 7/8" replaced brass ferrule, c1900...................... **2,350.00**

Cigarette case, 3-1/2" l, 2-1/4" w, 84 standard, silver gilt, robin's egg blue enamel, feathered guillouche ground, opaque white enamel borders, diamond chips on clasp, gilt in., Ivan Britzin, St. Petersburg, 1908-17, small losses and chips to enamel **1,200.00**

Coffee spoon, blue dot border in bowl, stylized polychrome enamel foliage, gilt stippled ground, twisted gilt stem, crown finial, G Tokmakov, c1890........................ **300.00**

Cup, 3" w, 2-1/4" h, silver-gilt and cloisonné enamel, Antip Kuzmichev, Moscow, dated 1895, marked "Made for Tiffany & Co.," price for set of four.......................... **4,025.00**

Egg, silver gilt and shaded enamel ware, two-pc construction, cabochon stone, maker's mark obliterated, 20th C, 3" h, ftd **700.00**

Kovsh, 3" h, silver, shaded enamel on moss green field, Pan Slavic style, hallmarked Moscow, 1907, Cyrillic "Faberge" under Imperial Warrant **2,875.00**

Matchbox holder, 2-1/4" l, silver gilt and cloisonné, hallmarked Moscow, c1900, indistinguishable makers mark **350.00**

Napkin ring, 1-3/4" x 1" x 1-1/2", enameled green, blue, pink, brown, white, light blue and maroon, Maria Semenova, Moscow, c1890 .... **700.00**

Spoon

7-1/4" l, silver-gilt and shaded enamel, back with colorful plumed bird on stippled ground, beaded border, Dmitri Nicholiaev, Moscow, c1900 .... **865.00**

7-1/2" d, round bowl, twisted handle ending in crown finial with enamel accents, obverse of bowl dec with hp portrait of woman surrounded by band of blue and green plique-a-jour in geometric design, illegible mark **1,760.00**

Sugar shovel, 4-3/4" l, silver gilt and enamel, Antip Kuzmichev, Moscow, 1899 .... **500.00**

Sugar tongs, 5-1/4" l, silver gilt and cloisonné enamel, Moscow, 1899, indistinguishable makers mark **250.00**

Vase, 11-1/2" h, champleve enamel, central cartouche on both sides, one with stylized double headed eagle, other side with roosters, Slavonic inscription at base rim, hallmarked Moscow, dated 1874, Cyrillic "P. Ovchinnikov" under Imperial Warrant **5,750.00**

Icon

7" x 5-3/4", The Kazan Mother of God, faux enameled background and borders, c1890 .... **300.00**

8-3/4" x 10-1/4", The Theodore Mother of God, overlaid with custom fitted silvered riza, attached gilded halos, late 18th C **1,350.00**

Icon, St. Nicholas, 1893, Moscow, silver gilt Oklad, richly enameled halo, 12-1/2" x 10-1/4", $1,900.

Photo courtesy of Sloans & Kenyon Auctions.

8-3/4" x 10-3/4", The Three Handed Mother of God, 19th C **435.00**

9" x 7", The Smolensk Mother of God, 19th C **1,035.00**

9" x 10", St. Nicholas, 19th C, cast bronze and champleve enamel **635.00**

9-3/4" x 11-1/2", The Tikhvin Mother of God, finely painted, overlaid with finely crafted riza, c1800-50 .... **1,380.00**

9-3/4" x 11-3/4", The Resurrection and Descent Into Hades, 1550-1600, attributed to Tver ... **10,350.00**

10" x 12", The Dormition, 19th C **2,070.00**

10-1/4" x 12", The Lord Almighty, c1700 .... **2,760.00**

10-1/2" x 12", Six Days, c1600 .... **2,070.00**

10-1/2" x 12-1/4", The Entry Into Jerusalem, borders and background gilded and finely incised, c1890 .... **2,185.00**

10-1/2" x 12-1/4", The Not By Hands Made Image of Christ-The Holy Napkin **1,725.00**

10-1/2" x 12-1/4", The Smolensk Mother of God, c1775-1825 .... **920.00**

10-3/4" x 13-1/2", John the Forerunner, c1575.... **8,625.00**

12" x 14", The Archangel Mikhail, 19th C **2,645.00**

12" x 14", The Holy Great Martyr Catherine, 20th C....... **920.00**

12-1/4" x 10-1/4", The Lord Almighty, 18th or 19th C **1,725.00**

12-1/2" x 11", The Vladimir Mother of God, c1700-1750 .... **1,725.00**

12-1/2" x 15-1/4", The Passion, c1650, central panel with elaborate scene of Christ descending into Hades, sixteen separate scenes **1,725.00**

13-1/2" x 11-3/4", The Tikhvin Mother of God, 18th C **815.00**

13-1/2" x 15-3/4", The Eucharist, c1550-1600, inscribed "Peite Ot Neya Siya Est Krov Moya" **13,800.00**

14-1/4" x 17-1/2", The Ascension of the Lord, 19th C **920.00**

15-1/2" x 23-1/2", The Apostle John and Prokhorus, 16th C **16,100.00**

17" x 12-1/2", The Mystical (Last) Supper, 18th C......... **3,335.00**

28" x 23", The Symbol of Faith, second half of 20th C **1,955.00**

31-1/2" x 22", The Terrible Judgment, Strashnuiy Sud, second half 20th C .. **2,645.00**

32" x 13-1/2", The Holy Martyr Paraskeva, c1750, full-length figure........................ **4,370.00**

35" x 28", Saint Tikhon of Amathus, Moscow workshop, c1890...................... **2,990.00**

Kovsh, silver-gilt and enamel, 1895, probably Moscow, typical shape, notched handle and band of trailing flowering branches in colors, 4-1/4" l, $675.

Photo courtesy of Sloans & Kenyon Auctions.

Metal

Bust, 10" h, Tsar Alexander Mikhailovich, Cyrillic foundry mark "F. Shopeen," dated 1867, bronze............ **1,250.00**

Cross, 47" x 22", Palekh or Mstera, 19th C, recessed edges (kovcheg), painted in classic 16th C style, top with Holy Napkin and Angels, center crossbeam with Mary and Apostle John, center with crucified Christ with implements of the passion, base with skull of Adam **4,600.00**

Samovar
14" h, cylindrical, orig bowl and undertray, 19th C. **400.00**
17-1/2" h, cylindrical, paneled body, 19th C **375.00**
22" h, cylindrical, front and rim stamped with profusion of awards, Kvana Kaprzina, Tula, c1905 .... **575.00**

Sculpture, bronze
12-1/4" l, 7" w, 7-1/2" h, couple being driven in troika, deep brown patina, sgd in base in Cyrillic "Gratchev" (Vasilil lakovelvich Gratchev, 1831-1905) and "Voerffel Foundry-St Petersburg" **2,875.00**
18-1/2" x 16-1/2" h, mounted Imperial soldier, dark brown patina, c1890, indistinguishably signed in Cyrillic on base **2,300.00**

Tray, 13-1/2" x 10-1/2", painted and lacquered metal, troika scene, verso sgd in Cyrillic "Lukutin," beneath Imperial Warrant, 19th C **690.00**

Powder box, lift-off lid, lacquer, miniature of man and woman sitting with priest at a table, dark brown background, interior marked "O.F. Vishnyakov & Sons Workshop, Fedoskino Russia," 1882, 2-1/2" d, 1-1/4" h, **$300.**

Photo courtesy of Gamal Amer.

Powder box, opened view, showing marks.

Miscellaneous

Box, 6-1/2" x 4-1/2", lacquer and transfer printed papier-mache, colorful foil backed transfer images of famous

Russian scenes on lid, lock and key, c1890, price for pr **460.00**

Card case, 3-1/2" l, nephrite and gold, cabochon thumbpush, hallmarked St Petersburg 1908, standard 56, makers mark "A. A." **4,890.00**

Charger, 15" d, carved in Pan Slavic style, borders carved relief inscription "To Her Imperial Highness Princess Yevheniya Maximiliyanova of Oldenburg," center with Imperial Russian coat of arms and Princess's coat of arms, relief carved "Housewarming from th Chertkov and Sverbeyev families 1887," verso with makers plaque in Cyrillic "F. Schilling, Moscow" **850.00**

Purse, 14k yg, curved frame gypsy-set with 11 old mine-cut and old European-cut diamonds, approx. total wt. 3.00 cts, further set with gypsy-set oval sapphires and circular-cut rubies, mesh body, trace link chain, 95.2 dwt, Russian hallmarks. **200.00**

Stool, 13-1/2" w, 9-1/4" d, 8-7/8" h, paint dec, geometric strapwork dec on top, turned tapered legs, early 20th C **125.00**

Porcelain

Cabinet plate, 9" d, cobalt blue, green, and red central rosette, gilt ground **275.00**

Cup and saucer, 4-1/2" h, blue glazed, honoring coronation of Nicholas II, 1878, M. S. Kuznetsov **250.00**

Dessert plate, floral rim, magenta ground, Islamic script, printed mark, I. E. Kuznetsov, 19th C, set of six **265.00**

Plate, 8-3/4" d, two soldiers, verso with underglaze Cyrillic P.S. beneath crown mark **750.00**

Portrait plate, 8" d, Empress Elizabeth, Safronov, early 19th C, hairline.................. **315.00**

Tankard, 8" h, figural, Turk's head, marked "F. Gardner, Moscow," 19th C, restored **1,210.00**

Tea service, 13 pcs, 9" w x 5" h cov teapot, creamer, sugar,

four cov cups, four saucers, two open cups, Kornilov Bros, c1910 .... **2,415.00**

Vase, 8" h, one green with medallion of Olga, other puce with medallion of Vladimir, allover gilt foliate dec, Gardner, 19th C, drilled, price for pr **250.00**

Silver, cigarette case, raised decoration of horse-drawn sleigh with figures, red stone cabochon on latch, gold wash interior, Russian standard marks, 4-3/4" l, 3-1/2" w, **$250.**

Photo courtesy of Alderfer Auction Co.

Candlesticks, pair, silver, 1838, Chernigov, chased with leaves and scrolls, 9-1/2" h, **$2,500.**

Photo courtesy of Sloans & Kenyon Auctions.

Caviar tub, silver, 1860, faux wood grain, vermeil reeded bands, locking cover, glass liner, 4" d, 10 oz, **$950.**

Photo courtesy of Sloans & Kenyon Auctions.

Silver

Box, 2-3/4" d, 2-1/8" h, cylindrical, enameled blue, green, white, and coral, star design on lid, panels of bird and scroll designs on sides, gilt int., marked "?84" and double-headed bird, crazing in white enamel band on lid **600.00**

Cordial set, 7-3/4" h, maker's mark "BC," early 20th C, stoppered ewer, six footed cordials, circular tray, engraved foliates and stylized houses, approx 15 troy oz **260.00**

Figural group, 8" d, 9" h, silver, mounted officer, saddle blanket embroidered with cipher of Tsar Nicholas II, polished granite base, Cyrillic makers mark "A.L.," hallmarked Moscow, c1908 .... **4,600.00**

Place setting, dinner fork, place spoon, dessert spoon, dinner knife, niello and silver gilt, Moscow, 1836, maker's mark "ST," all marked, some marks worn, 9.30 oz **240.00**

Punch ladle, 10" l, silver, bowl, stem, and handle finely enameled with scrolling foliage, red cabochon set in handle, Feodor Rückert, Moscow, c1899 .... **2,550.00**

Sugar scoop, 4-1/2" l, cloisonné enamel dec, hallmarked Moscow, dated 1891, maker's mark "G.K." for Gustav Klingert **300.00**

Tabernacle, 23" h, silver gilt, multiple piece, hallmarked Moscow, dated 1893, Cyrillic maker's mark "I.A." .. **3,300.00**

Teaspoon, 5" l, silver gilt and niello, twist handles with finial, monogrammed, Moscow, 1881, Cyrillic makers mark "S.D.S.," set of 12 .... **300.00**

SALT AND PEPPER SHAKERS

History: Collecting salt and pepper shakers, whether late 19th-century glass forms or the contemporary figural and souvenir types, is becoming more and more popular. The supply and variety is practically unlimited; the price for most sets is within the budget of cost-conscious collectors. In addition, their size offers an opportunity to display a large collection in a relatively small space.

Specialty collections can be by type, form, or maker. Great glass artisans, such as Joseph Locke and Nicholas Kopp, designed salt and pepper shakers in the normal course of their work.

Additional Listings: See *Warman's Americana & Collectibles* and *Warman's Flea Market* for more examples.

For more information, see *Warman's Glass*, 4th edition.

Art glass
(priced individually)

Cranberry, Inverted Thumbprint, sphere.......................... **175.00**

Hobnail, sapphire blue, Hobbs, Brockunier & Co., one orig metal top, 2-3/4" h **95.00**

Mt. Washington
2-1/2" h, egg shape, one with pink and blue daisies, other with red mums **120.00**
2-1/2" h, egg shape, stemmed flower dec **65.00**

Pairpoint
3" h, barrel shape, enameled flowers **55.00**
3" h, mold blown, faceted body, colored flowers ... **45.00**

Shell shape, colorless, two purple blossoms, spray of yellow daisies, green leaves **885.00**

Wave Crest, Erie Twist body, hp flowers, 2-1/2" h **185.00**

Salt and pepper shakers with napkin ring combination, loop handle on footed stand, silver plated, **$95**.

Figural and souvenir types (priced by set)

Bride and groom, pigs, nodders, marked "Made in Japan," c1950 .... **325.00**

Christmas, barrel shape, amethyst **165.00**

Ducks, 2-1/2" h, sitting, glass, clear bodies, blue heads, sgd "Czechoslovakia" **45.00**

Egg shape, opaque white body, holly dec, 23 red raised enameled berries, Mt. Washington................. **175.00**

Mammy and broom, orig "Norcrest Fine China Japan" foil labels, numbered H424, 4-1/4" h **395.00**

Strawberries, flashed amberina glass strawberry-shaped shakers, white metal leaf caps, suspended from emb white metal fancy holder, 2-3/4" h strawberries, 5" h stand, sgd "Japan," c1921-41 .... **285.00**

Opalescent glass
(priced individually)

Argonaut Shell, blue **65.00**
Fluted Scrolls, vaseline... **65.00**
Seaweed, Hobbs, cranberry **60.00**
Windows, Hobbs, blue, pewter top **55.00**

Left: Blue opalescent striped shaker with original top, **$65**; right: Creased Bale, peach colored fire-on decoration, white ground, original top, **$85**.

Opaque glass

(priced individually)

Bulge Bottom, blue **25.00**
Cathedral Panel, white.... **20.00**
Creased Bale, pink **20.00**
Fleur de Lis Scrolling, custard **20.00**
Heart, blue...................... **25.00**
Leaf Clover, blue............. **20.00**
Little Shrimp, white.......... **20.00**
Swirl Wide Diagonal, white **20.00**

Pattern glass

(priced individually)

Block and Fan, colorless, 1891 .... **20.00**
Franesware, Hobbs, Brockunier Co., c1880, hobnail, frosted, amber stained............. **45.00**
Lobe, squatty.................. **120.00**
Tulip............................... **100.00**

Silver

Figural, Oriental street merchant pushing cart that contains salt and pepper shakers, toothpick container, hallmarked "90 HM," 5-1/4" l **195.00**
Spratling, Mexico, 3-1/2" h, domed forms on angular wooden bases, maker's marks **500.00**

SALTS, OPEN

History: When salt was first mined, the supply was limited and expensive. The necessity for a receptacle in which to serve the salt resulted in the first open salt, a crude, hand-carved, wooden trencher.

As time passed, salt receptacles were refined in style and materials. In the 1500s, both master and individual salts existed. By the 1700s, firms such as Meissen, Waterford, and Wedgwood were making glass, china, and porcelain salts. Leading glass manufacturers in the 1800s included Libbey, Mount Washington, New England, Smith Bros., Vallerysthal, Wave Crest, and Webb. Many outstanding silversmiths in England, France, and Germany also produced this form.

Open salts were the only means of serving salt until the appearance of the shaker in the late 1800s. The ease of procuring salt from a shaker greatly reduced the use of and need for the open salts.

For more information, see *Warman's Glass*, 4th edition.

Note: Allan B. and Helen B. Smith have authored and published 10 books on open salts beginning with *One Thousand Individual Open Salts Illustrated* (1972) and ending with *1,334 Open Salts Illustrated: The Tenth Book* (1984). The numbers in parentheses refer to plate numbers in the Smiths' books. Another reference book that collectors refer to for salts was written by L. W. & D. B. Neal, *Pressed Glass Salt Dishes of the Lacy Period, 1825-50.*

Condiment sets with open salts

German silver, two castors, two salts, two salt spoons, Renaissance style with swan supports, c1900, marked ".800 fine" **800.00**
Limoges, double salt and mustard, sgd "J. M. Limoges" (388) **80.00**
Metal, coolie pulling rickshaw, salt, pepper, and mustard, blown glass liners, Oriental (461) **360.00**

Quimper, double salt and mustard, white, blue, and green floral dec, sgd "Quimper" (388) **120.00**

Chinese Export, porcelain, master, oval, scalloped rim, blue under-glaze decoration, hand-painted polychrome bird and foliage motif over the glaze, scalloped base decorated with blue under-glaze tea leaf accented with red over-glaze painting, ground has slight bluish tint, 3-1/2" l, 2-7/8" w, 1-3/16" h, **$920**.

Photo courtesy of Alderfer Auction Co.

Early American glass

Blown molded, 2-1/4" h, 2-3/8" x 2-1/2" d rim, 2" d base, hat shape, brilliant cobalt blue, inward folded rim, rayed type IV base, rough pontil mark, Boston & Sandwich Glass Co., 1825-35, McKearin GIII-23................................. **650.00**
Pressed, lacy
    Neal BF-1F, 2" h, 1-3/4" x 3", Basket of Flowers, fiery opalescent violet blue, four feet, Boston & Sandwich, unlisted color, extremely rare, slightly warped, small chips **1,100.00**
    Neal BS-2, 1-7/8" h, 1-7/8" x 3-1/8", Beaded Scroll & Basket of Flowers, colorless, Boston & Sandwich Glass Co., 1835-45, flakes on inner rim.............................. **135.00**
    Neal BS-2, 2" h, Beaded Scroll & Basket of Flowers, clambroth, Boston & Sandwich Glass Co., 1825-50 .... **375.00**
    Neal BS-2, 2" h, Beaded Scroll & Basket of Flowers, opalescent, Boston & Sandwich Glass Co, 1825-50 .... **400.00**
    Neal BS-3a, 2" h, Beaded Scroll pattern, violet-blue, Boston & Sandwich Glass Co, c1825-50, edge cracks and chips.......................... **360.00**

Neal BT-2, 1-1/2" h, 1-7/8" x 3-5/8", Pittsburgh Steamboat, colorless, emb on stern, Stourbridge Flint Glass Works, 1830-45, minor rim flakes **825.00**

Neal BT-4D, 1-5/8" h, 1-7/8" x 3-5/8", Lafayet Steamboat, deep cobalt blue, mkd "B & S Glass Co." on stern, "Sandwich" in int. base, Boston & Sandwich Glass Co., 1830-45, minor inner rim flaking **2,750.00**

Neal CT 1, 1 3/4" h, 2 1/8" x 2 7/8", chariot, mottled silvery opaque blue, scallop and point rim, Boston & Sandwich Glass Co., 1835-50, rim corner chip, mold roughness **1,265.00**

Neal EE-3B, 2-1/8" h, 2-1/8" x 3-1/4", fiery opalescent, four feet, Boston & Sandwich Glass Co., 1835-45, near proof, chip on interior of one foot **615.00**

Neal JY-2, 2" h, 2-1/8" x 3", light green, scallop and point rim, emb "Jersey" under base, Jersey Glass Co., c1835-50 .... **880.00**

Neal NE-6, 2" h, 2-1/8" x 2-7/8", light green, scallop and point rim, star under base, Jersey Glass Co. or New England Glass Co., 1835-50, two rim chips **245.00**

Neal OL-15, 1-3/4" h, Beaded Strawberry Diamond, brilliant deep purple blue, high and low point rim, Boston & Sandwich Glass Co., 1830-50 .... **495.00**

Neal OO-2, 1-1/2" h, Octagon, oblong, colorless, c1825-50 .... **195.00**

Neal OO-9, 1-3/8" h, Octagon, oblong, colorless, flat rim, possibly New England, 1835-50, minor inner flake ... **210.00**

Neal OP-8, 1-7/8" h, Oval Pedestal, amethyst tint, New England, c1825-50, imperfections **195.00**

Neal PO-1A, 1-1/2" h, Peacock Eye, oval, colorless, serrated table ring, Boston & Sandwich Glass Co., 1830-50, unlisted color **275.00**

Neal PO-4, 1-3/8" h, Peacock Eye, oval, dark blue, rayed base, Boston & Sandwich Glass Co., 1830-45, unlisted color **2,640.00**

Neal PO-5, 1-1/2" h, Peacock Eye, oval, colorless, c1825-50 .... **225.00**

Neal PR-1A, 1-1/2" h, Peacock-Eye, round, violet-blue, Boston & Sandwich Glass Co., 1825-50.... **425.00**

Neal RP-9, 1-1/2" h, Round Pedestal, colorless, c1825-50, imperfections.............. **165.00**

Neal SC-5, 1-7/8" h, Scroll, medium blue, c1825-50 .... **365.00**

Neal SD-7, 2" h, Strawberry Diamond, medium blue, Boston & Sandwich Glass Co., 1825-50 .... **365.00**

Neal SL-1, 1-3/4" h, Shell, red-amethyst, Boston & Sandwich Glass Co. c1825-50, minor edge roughness, few base chips.......................... **650.00**

Neal SL-4, 1-3/4" h, Shell pattern, dark amber, Pittsburgh area, c1830, edge chips **350.00**

Neal SL 11, 1-3/4" h, Shell pattern, peacock blue, Boston & Sandwich Glass Co., 1825-50............................... **295.00**

Neal SL 18, 2-5/8" h, Shell pattern, raised scroll pedestal, colorless, Boston & Sandwich Glass Co., 1825-50, edge chips, small base cracks........................ **715.00**

China, master salt and six individual oval serving salts, gold floral border and trim, marked "Nippon," **$30**.

Figurals

Basket, 3" h, 2-3/4" d, coral colored glass, SP basket frame, salt with cut polished facets.......................... **55.00**

Bucket, 2-1/2" d, 1-5/8" h, Bristol glass, turquoise, white, green, and brown enameled bird, butterfly and trees, SP rim and handle.......................... **75.00**

Sea horse, Belleek, brilliant turquoise, white base, supports shell salt, first black mark (458) **350.00**

Individual

Cameo, Daum Nancy, 1-3/8" h, cameo glass, bucket form, two upright handles, frosted colorless ground, cameo etched and enameled black tree lined shore, distant ruins, gilt rim, sgd "Daum (cross) Nancy" in gilt on base, small rim chips..................... **575.00**

Cut glass, 2" d, 1-1/2" h, cut ruby ovals, all-over dainty white enameled scrolls, clear ground, gold trim, scalloped top **60.00**

Moser, cobalt blue, pedestal, gold bands, applied flowers sgd (380)...................... **75.00**

Mount Washington, blue Johnny Jump ups, cream ground, raised gold dots on rim............................... **135.00**

Pattern glass
Fine Rib, flint................ **35.00**
Pineapple and Fan **25.00**
Three Face **40.00**

Purple slag, 3" d, 1-1/4" h, emb shell pattern.................. **50.00**

Russian, 1-1/4" d, 1-3/4" d, colorless glass liner, gold finished metal, red and white enamel scallop design, Russian hallmarks, c1940 .... **110.00**

Sterling silver, Georg Jensen, Denmark, porringer (238) **215.00**

Tray lot of open salts, all Nippon, each **$15**.

Masters

Coin silver, made by Gorham for retailer Seth E. Brown, Boston, ftd, gold washed int., monogrammed, pair in fitted case, two coin silver spoons by Jones, Ball & Poor, pr, approx 4 troy oz **375.00**

Cranberry, 3" d, 1-3/4" h, emb ribs, applied crystal ruffed rim, SP holder with emb lions heads......................... **160.00**

Tray lot of open salts, some pattern glass, some masters, intaglios, **each $5-$15**.

Cut glass, 2" d, 2" h, green cut to clear, SP holder **115.00**
Green, light, dark green ruffled top, open pontil (449) .. **90.00**
Mocha, seaweed band, yellow ware ground, 2" h **250.00**
Pattern glass
    Barberry, pedestal **40.00**
    Basketweave, sleigh (397)
    .... **100.00**
    Portland, branches handle
    .... **110.00**
    Snail, ruby stained **75.00**
    Sunflower, pedestal **40.00**

Tray lot, cobalt blue liners in silver holders, inkwell and mustard too, **each salt, $25-$45**.

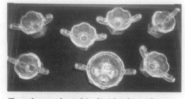

Tray lot, pedestal individuals and one larger Chippendale pattern, individuals, **$5-$15**, larger **$25-$35**.

Tray lot of 24 matching salts, pressed glass, clear, octagonal, paneled sides, price for set, **$65**.

Pearlware
    2-1/2" d, rounded form, medium blue rim band, vertical ribbed dark brown slip dec on white ground, England, early 19th C **590.00**
    2-3/4" d, rounded form, dark brown banding, dark brown dendritic dec on rust field, narrow green glazed reeded band, early 19th C, cracked, rim chip **590.00**
Pewter, pedestal, cobalt blue liner (349) **65.00**
Redware, 2-1/4" h, mottled brown alkaline glaze, c1850 .... **75.00**
Sterling silver, 1-3/4" h, Stieff Co., early 20th C, chased and emb allover floral pattern, applied floral rim, three scrolled shell feet, pr, 6 troy oz **260.00**
Vaseline, 3" d, 2-1/4" h, applied crystal trim around middle, SP stand **125.00**

SAMPLERS

History: Samplers served many purposes. For a young child, they were a practice exercise and permanent reminder of stitches and patterns. For a young woman, they were a means to demonstrate skills in a "gentle" art and a way to record family genealogy. For the mature woman, they were a useful occupation and method of creating gifts or remembrances, e.g., mourning pieces.

Schools for young ladies of the early 19th century prided themselves on the needlework skills they taught. The Westtown School in Chester County, Pennsylvania, and the Young Ladies Seminary in Bethlehem, Pennsylvania, were two institutions. These schools changed their teaching as styles changed. Berlin work was introduced by the mid-19th century.

Examples of samplers date back to the 1700s. The earliest ones were long and narrow, usually done only with the alphabet and numerals. Later examples were square. At the end of the 19th century, the shape tended to be rectangular.

The same motifs were used throughout the country. The name of the person who stitched the piece is a key factor in determining the region.

Sampler, silk on linen, wrought by "Susan E. Cutter aged 12," central alphabets within double sawtooth border surmounted by floral vines, New England, 16-1/4" x 15", **$2,300**.
Photo courtesy of Pook & Pook.

1799, Lydia Wood's sample Anno Domini 1799, stylized floral upper border above two alphabet panels over panel of flowering shrubs and birds, black, green, and pink silk threads, unframed, 15-1/4" x 10-1/2", fading, toning .. **715.00**
1801, Sally Clark, Aged 8 Years 1801, inspirational verse flanked by stylized vases of flowers, upper borders above birds on branches, landscape with thatched roof cottages, framed, 21" x 17", faded **890.00**

1803, "Fanny Chandler Born December the 15 1803," silk threads on linen ground, rows of alphabets over pious verse, centered with house flanked by flowering trees and baskets of flowers, grid with the initials of family members, molded wood frame, 15-1/2" x 19-1/2", fading **825.00**

1804, Elizabeth Willits, each corner with different flower in soft pale blue, ivory, and gold, central vining wreath with tulip drop encircles verse, numbers, and "Maidencreek, Elizabeth Willits 1804" all done in dark brown, loosely woven linen ground, modern frame, 13-1/4" x 14", minor stains **2,970.00**

1805, Adam and Eve, England, "Jane Harrison Vinnis is my name and with My Needle I did work the same that all the World may plainly see what care my Parents took of me, Finished at Mis Tucker Northfleet in Kent November the sixth one thousand eight hundred and five and in the twelve year of my age," floral symbols enclosed in panel above Adam, Eve, the tree, entwined serpent, flanked by various religious, animal, and floral devices, surrounded by stylized floral border, gray blue ground, framed, 15" x 19", imperfections **1,880.00**

1808, Abigail A Jenney, Plainfield, New Hampshire, three alphabets, trees, various devices, upper and lower borders, silk threads on linen ground, shades of green, yellow, and brown, 4-3/4" x 3-3/4" sight size, 6-3/4" x 5-3/4" frame....................... **2,585.00**

1809, Lucenda Bingham, MA, 1809, silk threads on woven green and blue Linsey-Woolsey ground, three alphabet panels over pious verse over lettering reading "Lucenda Bingham aged 11 years 1809 born August the 3 1798," floral, star, bird, and tree motifs enclosed in sawtooth border, framed, note on back of frame with family genealogy, 17-5/8" x 11-1/4", several unobtrusive losses to background **2,725.00**

1810, Anne Armstrong, Aged 11 Years Clones 1810, geometric bands in red, pink, green, blue, brown, purple, and yellow, row of trees, alphabets, and vowels, linen ground, verse by "C. Quigley," minor stitch loss, framed, 19" w, 18-1/4" h **1,265.00**

1810, Frances Croll 1810, England or America, basket of flowers over alphabet panels above pious verse, surrounded by floral dec bannor, worked in shades of red, blue, green, yellow, and blue threads, framed, 16-3/8" x 12-3/4", fading, scattered staining **825.00**

1811, Mary Brown, several alphabets, house topped by birds and flanked by trees and flowers in baskets, stitched in blue, green, and shades of brown, signed "Mary Brown, Sampler Made May 18, 1811, and Born November 18, 1796," 17" x 12" sight, framed, losses to stitching and period frame, **$5,750**.

Photo courtesy of Alderfer Auction Co.

1812, Elizabeth Thomas, homespun linen, alphabet and name, "Elizabeth Thomas, April 9, 1812," border by vine and floral motif, grain painted frame of yellow ground, red-brown highlights, 10-3/4" w, 12-3/4" h **5,280.00**

1816, American, Sawyer and Ryan families, border of vines and roses surrounding central image of two stylized trees, paper panels inscribed in ink with names of Ryan and Sawyer families and dates from 1795 to 1816, 17" sq **20,000.00**

1819, genealogy, "Wrought by Charlotte Perkins AE t 12 Years Aug. 12 1819," attributed to ME, silk threads on linen ground, listing the vital statistics of Ezekiel Cushing and Frances (McCobb) Cushing and their six children, and Benjamin Perkins and Frances (Cushing) Perkins and their five children, beginning in 1752 and ending in 1808, lower reserve with monument and weeping willow commemorating the deaths of two family members, next to house, figure with sheep and dog, town across the river in the distance, all enclosed by border of flowers, foliage and a bowknot, unframed, 24-1/4" x 21" toning, losses, stains **2,585.00**

1822, Lucy Parham, Tyngsboro, MA, 1822, silk threads on linen ground, centered alphabet panels over inscription "Lucy Parham born October 27, 1811, she wrought this in the 11th year of her age," above verse "When youth's soft season shall be o'er/And seasons of childhood charm no more/My riper year with joy shall see/ This proof of infant industry," flanked by two urns with flowers, wide borders with basket of flowers on top, sides with two urns issuing flowering vines, lower border with house, trees and deer, framed, 17" x 18", toning, scattered stains **27,025.00**

1823, Massachusetts, 1823, "Wrought by Mary D Kimme of Bolton 1823 (?) Aged 12 Years," verse and alphabets, house and floral symbols below, right-hand side appears to be unfinished, unframed, small areas of thread losses, some fabric loss to the linen ground, minor fading, 17-1/4" x 17-1/2" **890.00**

1826, E. J., homespun linen, vase of flowers, sawtooth border, initialed "E. J. 1826," pulled and frayed edges, red painted frame, 4" w, 4-1/2" h **2,090.00**

Sampler, 1838, silk on linen, wrought by "Mary Mercer...1838 Aged 12 years," alphabet and verse above floral sprays, potted flowers, peacock, turkey, meandering vine border, attributed to Pennsylvania, 19" x 17-1/4", **$1,840**.

Photo courtesy of Pook & Pook.

1843, Harriet N. Potter, New Providence, text "Iotham Pottery Born Oct. 3, 1781, Phebe Petit Born Dec. 23, 1791, Married May 6, 1810," listing of children's dates of birth, marriage, and death, verse "If they childrern (sic) will keep my covenant and my testimony that I shall teach them, their children shall also sit upon thy throne forevermore. 132nd Psalm, 12th Verse," elaborate border of grapes and leaves, 18" x 16" sight, framed, staining, losses at edges of old nail holes, **$350**.

Photo courtesy of Alderfer Auction Co.

1840, Isabella Lunds work Aged 16 AD 1840, inspirational verse, attached buildings, trees, vines, floral and animal devices surrounded by stylized floral border, 26-3/4" x 32-1/4", toning and fading **2,470.00**

1841, Ann Fuller, "Ann Eliza Fuller wrought in the 12th year of her age 1841," silk threads

on linen ground, flowering border surrounding seven rows of alphabet examples, verse and signature, framed, 17" sq, fading, stains .. **300.00**

Sampler, Victorian, wool on linen needlework, wrought by "Rebecca Pursel Age 11," figure and landscape, "We Hope to Meet," 12-1/2" x 12-3/4", **$300**.

Photo courtesy of Pook & Pook.

1850, Mary Jane Flint, aged 11 years, April 19, 1850, five alphabet panels, pictorial scene, Federal buildings, trees, bird and inspirational verse, framed, 22-1/2" x 19-1/2", fading, toning, staining **1,175.00**

1854, homespun linen, alphabet at top, house scene with dog, bird, fruit, trees, and pump, red, green, blue, and brown, "Work in the year 1854," grain painted frame with yellow ochre ground, red-brown highlights, 17-1/2" w, 20-1/4" h **4,620.00**

Late 18th C, Cynthia Taft, Uxbridge, Massachusetts, pink and green floral vine encloses verse worked in pink linen above pictorial lower half with garden, trees, flowers, birds, and grass, pink, green, and red hues, good coloration and condition, reframed, minor imperfections, 10-5/8" w, 12" h **4,115.00**

Undated

Rebecca Myers, homespun linen, three alphabets, name at bottom, sawtooth border, veneered frame with minor paint dec, 11-1/2" w, 14" h **1,100.00**

Caroline Wills, homespun linen, four alphabets, Roman numerals and house at base, "Paradise Tenant House," sgd

"Caroline Elizabeth Wills," tiger maple frame, 18-1/2" w, 20-3/4" h, fading and discoloration, photo on back of maker.................. **2,530.00**

Undated, unsigned, central basket with flowering plants above two baskets of strawberries, topped by peacocks, ladybugs, birds, and tree, strawberry and floral border, shades of green with colored accents, 20-1/2" x 17" sight, framed, slipped in frame, wrinkled, **$1,650**.

Photo courtesy of Alderfer Auction Co.

Undated, MM, several alphabets, central basket of flowers with birds and floral spray, verse oriented perpendicular to remainder of design "This work of mine my friends may have, When I am silent in my grave, Look on this Work and then u (sic) will see how Kind my Parents whare (sic) to me, William & Mary Moorehead," basket of flowers with initials "MM," 17" x 12", **$450**.

Photo courtesy of Alderfer Auction Co.

SANDWICH GLASS

History: In 1818, Deming Jarves was listed in the Boston Directory as a glass maker. That same year, he was appointed general manager of the newly formed New England Glass Company. In 1824, Jarves toured the glassmaking factories in Pittsburgh, left New England Glass Company, and founded a glass factory in Sandwich.

Originally called the Sandwich Manufacturing Company, it was incorporated in April 1826 as the Boston & Sandwich Glass Company. From 1826 to 1858, Jarves served as general manager. The Boston & Sandwich Glass Company produced a wide variety of wares in differing levels of quality. The factory used the free-blown, blown three mold, and pressed glass manufacturing techniques. Both clear and colored glass were used.

Competition in the American glass industry in the mid-1850s resulted in lower-quality products. Jarves left the Boston & Sandwich company in 1858, founded the Cape Cod Glass Company, and tried to duplicate the high quality of the earlier glass. Meanwhile, at the Boston & Sandwich Glass Company, emphasis was placed on mass production. The development of a lime glass (non-flint) led to lower costs for pressed glass. Some free-blown and blown-and-molded pieces, mostly in color, were made. Most of this Victorian-era glass was enameled, painted, or acid etched.

For more information, see *Warman's Glass*, 4th edition.

By the 1880s, the Boston & Sandwich Glass Company was operating at a loss. Labor difficulties finally resulted in the closing of the factory on January 1, 1888.

Bowl, Gothic paneled arches, hexagonal, clambroth. **150.00**

Butter dish, cov, colorless, flint, Gothic pattern............. **225.00**

Candlesticks, pr, pressed 9-1/4" h, yellow, petal form candle cups, columnar shaft, sq stepped base, c1850-65, chips to petals on one, base edge and corner chips on both **600.00**
9-7/8" h, translucent blue petal socket, clambroth dolphin standard, double-stepped sq base, c1845-70, few minor chips and cracks **1,530.00**
10" h, translucent light lavender alabaster/clambroth, petal sockets, dolphins, wafer construction, double step base, 1845-70 .... **3,300.00**

Champagne, Sandwich Star **850.00**

Compote, 10-1/2" w, 4-3/4" h, cranberry overlay, oval cuts, enameled birds and flowers on inner surface, c1890 .... **495.00**

Cologne bottle, stopper, blown molded, yellow, Star and Punty pattern, polished pontil, 1841-70, imperfections, 7-3/8" h, $450.

Photo courtesy of Skinner, Inc.

Creamer
4-1/4" h, Acanthus Leaf and Shield, colorless, plain rim, molded handle, octagonal even scallop foot, 1835-50 .... **315.00**
4-1/2" h, Heart and Scale, colorless, molded handle, circular foot, 1838-45.. **220.00**

Decanter, 11-1/2" h, blown-molded, quart, colorless, plain

base, rough pontil mark, replacement pressed wheel stopper, c1825-35, McKearin GV-17......................... **625.00**

Dish
5-7/8" x 8" x 1-3/4" h, Beaded Medallion and Urn, oval, colorless, shaped plain even scallop rim, 1835-45, chip under rim **90.00**
6-1/4" x 8-1/4" x 1-1/2" h, Pipes of Pan, octagonal oblong, colorless, plain scallop and point rim, rope table ring, 1930-40, corner rim spall **310.00**
7-3/8" x 7-3/4" x 1-1/4" h, Hairpin, colorless, scallop and point rim, c1830-40, near proof, shallow edge flake **7,700.00**
9-1/8" x 12-1/4" x 2" h, Double Peacock Eye, octagonal oblong, colorless, concave corners, variation with no background stippling on ends, plain cross bars in center, plain even scallop rim with interior beads, 1835-50, some loss to four corners.................. **360.00**

Lamp base, bright canary yellow, brass collar, wide paneled body, pedestal base, **$200**.

Fluid lamp
6-7/8" h, colorless, conical font with button stem attached to pressed Lee/Rose No. 32 cup plate base, cork tube whale oil burner, rough pontil mark, 1828-35, minute base chips and flakes **1,980.00**
8-3/4" h, circle and oval pressed fonts, pressed hexagonal baluster stem and base, clear, brass collars, base flakes, pr............ **250.00**

9-1/2" h, sapphire blue, font wafer attached to pressed hexagonal base, early brass #1 collar, 1840-60, top of one loop chipped and later polished **1,045.00**

9-3/4" h, cut overlay font of cobalt blue cut to clear, quatrefoil and punty cuts, brass columnar standard, sq marble base, 1840-65, minor base edge chips......... **950.00**

10-1/4" h, Bigler pattern, octagonal shaft, sq base, pewter collar, cobalt blue, 1840-65.................... **1,120.00**

Fruit basket, on stand

8-1/4" d rim, 4-1/2" d foot, 8-1/4" h, brilliant deep amethyst, basket with 32-point rim, 16 vertical openwork staves, 34-point star in sloping base, wafered to hexagonal knop and foot, 1840-55, possibly in-the-making shallow chip on knop...................... **17,600.00**

8-3/4" d rim, 4-1/2" d foot, 8-1/2" h, colorless, 32-point rim, 16 vertical openwork staves, 34-point star in sloping base, wafered to hexagonal knop and foot, 1840-55...................... **615.00**

11-3/4" h, cut overlay, triple dolphin base, font opaque white cut to colorless, connected to fiery opalescent base, heavily gilded dec on font, early #2 brass collar, brass connector, kerosene period, 1860-75 .... **7,150.00**

Goblet, colorless, flint, Gothic pattern, 12-pc set **650.00**

Inkwell, 2-9/16", cylindrical-domed form, colorless, pink and white stripes, sheared mouth, applied pewter collar and cap, smooth base **2,300.00**

Miscellaneous Sandwich glass, $200.
Photo courtesy of Joy Luke.

Miscellaneous Sandwich glass: toothpick holder, footed compote, jar, lidded jar, four berry bowls, punch cup, rectangular tray, salt dip, miniature cup (damaged), saucer, creamer and three plates, $380.
Photo courtesy of Joy Luke.

Nappy

4-1/8" d, 1-1/8" h, Plume and Acorn, medium amethyst, even scallop rim, small rim spall **100.00**

5-1/8" d, 1-1/4" h, Plume and Acorn, fiery opalescent, even scallop rim, minor flaking/mold roughness............ **55.00**

9-1/4" d, 1-1/2" h, Crossed Peacock Eye, colorless, rayed center with alternating clear and stippled panels, shaped rim with plain even scallops, 1835-50, loss to several scallops **150.00**

Paperweight, 3-1/2" w, 1-1/4" h, colorless and frosted, portraits of Queen Victoria and Prince Consort, 1851 .... **220.00**

Pitcher, 10" h

Amberina Verde, fluted top **525.00**

Electric Blue, enameled floral dec, fluted top, threaded handle...................... **425.00**

Plate, lacy design, $115.

Plate, 6" d, lacy, Shell pattern **175.00**

Pomade jar, cov

3-1/2" h, 2-1/2" d, drum, slightly translucent jade green, plain shield, cover missing, minor rim flake **360.00**

3-3/4" h, bear, deep amethyst, 1850-87, polished around edge of cover and base **135.00**

5" h, bear, clambroth, emb "J Hauel & Co., Phila" under base, 1850-87, large chip to back of one ear, flange chips **490.00**

Salt, open, pressed, lacy

1-3/4" h, Shell pattern, red-amethyst, c1825-50, Neal SL 1, minor edge roughness, few base chips.................. **650.00**

2" h, Beaded Scroll pattern, violet-blue, c1825-50, Neal Bs 3a, edge cracks and chips **360.00**

Sander, 2-3/4" x, 2-3/4" d rim, lacy, fiery opalescent, stippled rim with vertical chain of beads on body, rope-edge base, concentric circles under base, pewter cover missing **470.00**

Spooner/spill, 5" h, 3-3/4" d, Sandwich Star, slightly translucent electric blue, hexagonal foot, polished pontil mark............... **1,265.00**

Sugar, cov, 8-3/4" h, 5-1/4" d base, Star and Punty, colorless, octagonal, short paneled stem, circular foot, 1840-70, finial flake, roughness on rims...... **100.00**

Toddy, 5-3/8" d, brilliant dark amethyst, lacy, Roman Rosette, edge chips ... **330.00**

Tray, 6-1/8" x 9-1/8" x 1-3/8" h, oval, central butterfly and beaded bull's eyes, shoulder with fleur-de-lis, pinwheels, and fans, tiny even scallops on side rims, 1835-50, slight mold roughness.......... **235.00**

Vase

4" h, 3-3/4" d rim, 3-1/8" d foot, ruby stained, acid etched leaves and polished grapes, notch-cut circular foot with polished center, 1880-87, tiny rim flake..................... **145.00**

4-3/4" h, 3-1/2" d rim, elongated loop with bisecting lines, deep fiery opalescent/opaque, hexagonal foot, polished table ring, 1835-50 .... **1,265.00**

Vase, trumpet, amethyst and colorless, gauffered rim, slightly twisted eight-panel vase, pestle stem fluted on inside, square base, 1840-60, McKearin plate 195, couple minor small base cracks, 10-1/8" h, **$5,000**.

Photo courtesy of Skinner, Inc.

4-3/4" h, 3-1/2" d rim, elongated loop with bisecting lines, medium brilliant amethyst, hexagonal foot, polished table ring, 1835-50 .... **990.00**

9-3/4" h, pressed, tulip, dark amethyst, scalloped rim, octagonal base, c1845-65, very minor edge chips **4,600.00**

9-3/4" h, 5-1/2" d rim, 4-3/8" d foot, brilliant deep amethyst, panels continue to peg extension, wafered to octagonal base, 1845-65 .... **4,950.00**

10" h, pressed, tulip, amethyst, scalloped rim, paneled oval bowl, octagonal base, c1840-60, minor base chip **2,115.00**

10-1/4" h, pressed, tulip, dark amethyst, octagonal base, mid-19th C, price for pr, small chip on one petal, minor base chips **9,400.00**

Whiskey taster, cobalt blue, nine panels **175.00**

SARREGUEMINES CHINA

History: Sarreguemines ware is a faience porcelain, i.e., tin-glazed earthenware. The factory that made it was established in Lorraine, France, in 1770, under the supervision of Utzschneider and Fabry. The factory was regarded as one of the three most prominent manufacturers of French faience. Most of the wares found today were made in the 19th century.

Marks: Later wares are impressed "Sarreguemines" and "Germany" as a result of changes in international boundaries.

Fruit basket, white plate center with cobalt blue floral decoration, wire work frame, **$175**.

Basket, 9" h, quilted, green, heavy leopard skin crystallization **250.00**

Centerpiece, 14-3/4" h, 14-3/4" d, bowl with pierced ringlets to sides, supported by center stem flanked by sea nymphs either side, mounted atop circular base on four scrolled feet, polychrome dec, imp marks, chips, restorations, c1875.......................... **900.00**

Cup and saucer, Orange, majolica, crack to one cup, nicks, set of four **200.00**

Dinnerware service, white china, multicolored scenes, six luncheon plates, six bread and butter plates, six demitasse cups, six porringers, two platters, divided dish **150.00**

Face jug, majolica
  Suspicious Eyes, #3320 .... **550.00**
  Upward Eyes, #3257 .. **500.00**

Garniture, Art Nouveau faience, 10-3/4" h pr of vases, shouldered trumpet form, shaped oval centerpiece bowl, each with wide gilt band of foliage within diamond borders centered by decorative medallion, verte ground **350.00**

Plate, 7-1/2" d, dec with music and characters from French children's songs, 12-pc set **375.00**

Vases, pair, (one shown), earthenware, Aesthetic Movement, ovoid, body printed and enamel decoration with morning glories and butterflies on green ground, against vertical brown panels, quatrefoil borders, rim with band of butterflies, gilt accenting, early 20th C, 17" h, **$2,000**.

Photo courtesy of Skinner, Inc.

Tankard, cov, 11" h, stoneware, continuous country scene of dancing and celebrating villagers, branch handle, pewter lid with porcelain medallion and painted polychrome coat of arms, dated 1869 .... **325.00**

Urn, 31-1/4" h, gilt metal mounted majolica, baluster form, cobalt blue glazed, mounted with the figure of a crowned lion holding sword, lion and mask handled sides, pierced foliate rim, raised on four scrolling foliate cast feet, imp "Majolica Sarreguemines," second half 19th C **1,800.00**

SATIN GLASS

History: Satin glass, produced in the late 19th century, is an opaque art glass with a velvety matte (satin) finish achieved through treatment with hydrofluoric acid. A large majority of the pieces were cased or had a white lining.

While working at the Phoenix Glass Company, Beaver, Pennsylvania, Joseph Webb perfected mother-of-pearl (MOP) satin glass in 1885. Similar to plain satin glass in respect to casing, MOP satin glass has a distinctive surface finish and an integral or indented design, the most well known being diamond quilted (DQ).

The most common colors are yellow, rose, or blue. Rainbow coloring is considered choice.

For more information, see *Warman's Glass*, 4th edition.

Additional Listings: Cruets, Fairy Lamps, Miniature Lamps, and Rose Bowls.

Reproduction Alert: Satin glass, in both the plain and mother-of-pearl varieties, has been widely reproduced.

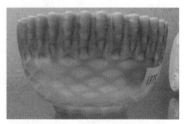

Bowl, shading from peach to white, crimped edge, crosshatched decoration, $55.

Bowl
4-1/2" d, 2-3/4" h, DQ, MOP, rainbow, crimped, sgd "Patent," orig Maude B. Feld label, ex-Maude Feld **1,100.00**
6" d, 1-1/2" h, DQ, MOP, ruffled, shading from white to peach............................. **80.00**
9-3/4" l, 6-1/4" h, DQ, MOP, rainbow, int. with fold down ruffled rim, four clear feet (slight roughness), berry pontil, mkd "Patent," ex-Maude Feld.............. **3,400.00**
10" d, Peacock Eye pattern, MOP, white, painted floral and ladybug dec, gilt highlights, scalloped................. **2,000.00**
Bride's basket, 15-1/2" h, deep rose, enamel swan and floral dec, heavy bronze holder with birds perched at top ... **450.00**
Celery vase, 5" h, MOP, cased blue, Herringbone pattern, waisted squared body .. **200.00**

Center bowl, DQ, MOP, rainbow, circular ovoid body, alternating bands of multicolored hues, heavily applied clear rigaree collar and thorn handles, clear stylized feet, ex-Maude Feld, 10" d, 9-1/2" h, **$7,750**.

Photo courtesy Early Auction Co.

Center bowl, 10" d, 9-1/2" h, DQ, MOP, rainbow, circular ovoid body, alternating bands of multicolored hues, heavily applied clear rigaree collar and thorn handles, clear stylized feet, ex-Maude Feld **7,750.00**
Cologne bottle, 3-1/2" d, 6-1/2" h, Verre Moire, pulled three-color dec, coral and chartreuse on opaque white body, satin finish, crown-like cap attached to delicate chain to collar, anchor stamps and "cs fs" on collar ... **750.00**
Cream pitcher
2-1/2" h, blue, gold lettering "1893 World's Fair," made and dec by Mt. Washington **435.00**
3-1/2" h, blue, DQ, MOP, camphor reeded handle **200.00**
Cruet, Rainbow, 7" h, pastel blue, pink, and yellow swirls from base to trefoil spout, molded-in bulging ribs, polished pontil mark, ribbed applied handle, cut glass stopper **975.00**
Cup and saucer, Raindrop MOP, pink to white, 3" h cup, 5" d saucer...................... **385.00**
Epergne, 13-3/4" h, 10" d, pink and white, hobnail bowl, resilvered base and lily vase holder **395.00**
Ewer
8-1/4" h, DQ, MOP, pink, fold over ruffled rim, applied rope handle, price for pr **100.00**

Ewers, yellow shading to white base, crimped rims, white birds perched on flowering branches, price for pair, **$165**.

9" h, glossy blue, tri-fold top, applied crystal twist handle, heat check in handles, price for pr **50.00**
12" h, DQ, MOP, dusty pink shades to pale pink, air trays cross over 24 vertical ribs of melon shaped body, ruffled and crimped mouth, frosted clear handle with thorns, Victorian...................... **350.00**
Fairy lamp, 4-1/4" h, blue shade and base, clear candle base insert, Victorian........... **225.00**
Lamp, 22" h, white satin body, matching font with air-trapped Flower and Acorn design, enameled Japanese cherry blossoms, bronze ftd base with lions' heads, burner marked "Hinks & Sons Patent" and "Sherwoods Limited," retailer's soldered tag "T. R. Grimes, New Broad St., London," some flakes under font lip...................... **1,260.00**
Mustard pot, 2-1/2" h, bright yellow, gold prunus dec, SP top, Webb.................. **450.00**
Rose bowl
3" h, 1-3/4" d, crimped body, shading from medium to light blue, clear applied dec **110.00**
3-3/4" h, inverted crimped bulbous body shading from deep rose to pink, enamel floral dec, attributed to Thomas Webb & Sons **100.00**
4" h, DQ, MOP, rainbow, trefoil shaped body, applied clear rigaree collar, berry pontil, three shaped clear feet, mkd "Patent," ex-Maude Feld **1,900.00**
5" h, Herringbone, blue MOP, crimped ruffled rim **50.00**
Salt shaker, 3-1/4" h, rose shaded to white, MOP, DQ, tapered barrel, orig two-pc lid **550.00**

Perfume bottle, Birmingham, England, c1895, narrow neck on bulbed vessel, pulled loop decoration in peach and yellow on white ground, mounted foliate silver lid and ring, struck with lion, anchor, and two maker's touchmarks "CS FS," 6-1/2" h, **$500**.
Photo courtesy of Skinner, Inc.

Spill vase, 10-1/8" h, pale green body, hand enameled dec, Victorian **110.00**
Sugar shaker, 5-1/2" h, Rainbow MOP, ex-Maude Feld **4,760.00**
Tumbler, 3-1/2" h, Rainbow, DQ, enameled floral dec, pr **375.00**

Pair pink satin glass vases, diamond quilted pattern, 8" h, **$150**.
Photo courtesy of Joy Luke.

Vase
4-1/2" h, ribbed body, flaring ruffled to, shades from mahogany to lemon yellow, acid finish **325.00**
5" h, stick, MOP, blue .. **125.00**
5-1/2" h, Pompeian Swirl, MOP, blue shading to pale blue at base, pale blue cased int., two shiny upward spiraling ribbons **500.00**
5-3/4" h, bulbous, DQ, MOP, pink, ruffled top, gilt design in center **150.00**

6" h, Herringbone, MOP, top ground **50.00**
6-1/2" h, DQ, MOPO, flaring conical body, deep azure shading to pearl, gold prunus dec, applied thorn handles, attributed to Thomas Webb and Sons **800.00**
7" h, DQ, MOP, blue, shouldered, quadrafold rim **150.00**
7" h, DQ, MOP, butterscotch shading to pearl **85.00**
7" h, DQ, MOP, light blue, ruffled top, floral dec .. **100.00**
7" h, DQ, MOP, rainbow, bulbous, cylindrical neck, crimped fold down rim **800.00**
7-1/2" h, DQ, peach MOP, bulbous, tight ruffled crimped rim **125.00**
10-3/4" h, gourd, DQ, yellow shading to white frost . **170.00**
Water pitcher, 8-1/2" h, MOP, cased, shading from rose to pink, Coinspot pattern, applied reeded handle, ground pontil **425.00**

SATSUMA

History: Satsuma, named for a war lord who brought skilled Korean potters to Japan in the early 1600s, is a hand-crafted Japanese faience (tin-glazed) pottery. It is finely crackled, has a cream, yellow-cream, or gray-cream color, and is decorated with raised enamels in floral, geometric, and figural motifs.

Figural satsuma was made specifically for export in the 19th century. Later satsuma, referred to as satsuma-style ware, is a Japanese porcelain also hand decorated in raised enamels. From 1912 to the present, satsuma-style ware has been mass produced. Much of the ware on today's market is of this later period.

Bowl
10" d, scene of figures before Mount Fuji, sgd, late 19th C **470.00**
12-1/4" d, 5-1/4" h, lobed body, scalloped rim, overall flowering peonies and chrysanthemums in red and gold, mkd on base, Meiji period, slight wear to gilding **2,000.00**

Bowl, lobed body, scalloped rim, allover flowering peonies and chrysanthemums in red and gold, base marked, Meiji period, 12-3/4" d, 5-1/4" h, slight wear to gilding, **$2,000**.

Cache pot, 6-1/2" h, figural and landscape scene **120.00**
Censor
3-1/2" h, ovoid, three cabriole legs, two shaped handles rising from shoulder, lid with large shishi seated on top, continual river landscape scene, patterned lappet border above, key fret border below, base sealed "Yabu Meizan," minor loss to one ear on shishi **2,990.00**
10-1/4" h, tapering rect form, lobed base, two squared handles, pierced domed lid, all-over dec or Arhats, Meiji period **635.00**

Censor, earthenware, ovoid, tripod, fu dog head form handles, floral decoration, Japanese, Meiji period, 5" h, **$500**.
Photo courtesy of Sloans & Kenyon Auctions.

Cup and saucer, bird and floral motif, cobalt blue border, Kinkozan **115.00**
Figure
4" h, God of Longevity, holding scroll, sgd **360.00**
12" h, Kannon, seated on rock throne holding lotus, 19th C, repairs **765.00**

Incense burner, 5" d, two reserves, one with sparrows and flowers, other of Mijo shrine, borders of brocade patterns, butterflies caught in net, and hanging jewels, sgd "Kinkozan," Meiji period, 1868-1911................ **5,500.00**

Jar, cov, 4" d, 6" h, two cartouche panels, one of Samurai, other with birds, insects, and flowers, one side ring missing **230.00**

Koro, pierced lid, 3" h, hexagonal, six bracket feet, each side with flowers blooming behind garden fences, domed lid, sgd with Shimazu mon **2,185.00**

Miniature cup, 2" d, interior painted with Bishamon and Hoi tei, ext. with dancing children, mille fleur borders, sgd with paulownia crest in gold, Meiji period, 1868-1911 .... **980.00**

Plate
9-1/4" d, One Hundred Birds design, early 20th C ... **650.00**
10-1/2" d, samurai design, monogram at top, sgd "Kinkozan" in gold on base, Meiji period (1868-1911) **345.00**

Seal paste box, 5" d, cobalt blue, gilt trim, reserve of children flying kites, sgd "Kozan," Meiji period, 1868-1911, minor int. chip .. **320.00**

Tea bowl, 4-3/4" d, dec with butterflies, powdered gold ground, sgd "Kinkozan," Meiji period, 1868-1911 ...... **350.00**

Tea cup and saucer, 1-3/4" h cup, 4-3/4" d saucer, colorful groups of flowerheads with scrolling gilt vines, minor gilt wear, sgd "Yabu Meizan" **900.00**

Doll tea set, decorated with flowers: tray, teapot, lidded sugar, creamer, two cups and two saucers, **$65.**
Photo courtesy of Joy Luke.

Tea set, 6-1/2" h teapot, creamer, sugar, six cups and saucers, 6 7-1/4" d plates,

paneled designs of courtesans in courtyard settings, c1900 .... **290.00**

Tray, 11-1/2" d, rounded form with indented edge, design of scrolls of birds, flowers, and women, cobalt ground with gold bamboo, sgd with imp seal "Kinkozan," Meiji period, 1868-1911 .... **1,650.00**

Urn, 37-1/2" h, dragon handles, geishas in landscape ... **295.00**

Vase, ovoid form, scene having many figures, reverse with floral decoration, unmarked, crazed, 7" h, **$100.**
Photo courtesy of Alderfer Auction Co.

Vase, gourd form hand painted butterflies, birds and floral designs, artist's signature signed on base, chipping on base, wear to gilt, 6" h, **$90.**
Photo courtesy of Alderfer Auction Co.

Vase
4-7/8" h, Samurai on horseback, fighting each other and tigers, price for pr **500.00**
6-1/2" h, cylindrical form, slight neck, mythological scenes with brocade and floral borders, sgd "Hakuzan," Meiji period (1868-1911) **2,235.00**

7" x 6", double handles, designs of dragons and various brocade patterns, sgd "Senzan" **1,410.00**

12" h, basketweave design with panels of prunus blossoms, sgd "Taizan," 19th C **360.00**

12" h, double handles, blue ground, pheasants, butterflies, flowers, sgd "Taizan," Meiji period (1868-1911) **530.00**

12" h, sq, blue and yellow panels, birds, flowers, and butterflies, sgd "Taizan," Meiji period (1868-1911)..... **650.00**

12-3/4" h, pr, double gourd earthenware body, enameled and gilt battle scenes, upper body with applied sinuous dragon, sgd, 19th C **1,000.00**

SCALES

History: Prior to 1900, the simple balance scale was commonly used for measuring weights. Since then, scales have become more sophisticated in design and more accurate. There are a wide variety of styles and types, including beam, platform, postal, and pharmaceutical.

Balance scale, floor model, brass, two pans, stamped "Day & Millward Birmingham," 52" w, 68" h, **$850.**
Photo courtesy of Alderfer Auction Co.

Advertising, Merchants Metal Spanish Tiles, Star Ventilator, Gothic Shingles, High Grade Roofing Plates, diecut multicolored tin litho, weighs up to 4 oz.................... **400.00**

Apothecary, 19-1/2" l, 15-3/4" h, walnut, fitted ivory dec... **250.00**

Balance

14" l, cast iron, orig red paint with black and yellow trim, nickel plated brass pans, marked "Henry Troemner, Phila. No. 5B, Baker's" **120.00**

26" h, J. L. Brown & Co., 83 Fulton St., New York, circular pans, baluster turned cast iron stand **690.00**

Gold, 9" l, Allender's Gold Scale, I. Wilson, New London, CT, cast brass rocker balance, slots and platforms for $1, 2-1/2, 5, 10, and 20, additional weight and instructions in shaped paper box, mid-19th C **490.00**

Health chart, trade stimulator type, black enamel base, tan and red top with chart, **$90**.

Letter scale, folding, unmarked, leather case marked "Letter Scale," **$45**.

Grain, 11" l, chonodrometer, brass, Fairbanks, arm graduated for "lbs per bush," "lb & oz," and "% of lb," sliding weight, bucket, and suspension ring **350.00**

Pamphlet, testimonials, Jones of Binghamton, NY, c1880, 32 pgs, illus price list of Jones

Scales, cuts of canal weight-lock scale, universal, portable platform, postal, counter, rolling mill, lever, truss scales, etc., 3" x 5-1/2" **55.00**

Hanson, white enamel body, red and black logo, measures in pounds, **$40**.

Photo courtesy of Joseph P. Smalley, Jr.

Platform, 63" h, Peerless Junior, Peerless Weighing Machine Co., porcelainized steel, tiled platform, gold lettering .. **350.00**

Pocket balance, 5-1/2" w, steel, silvered pans, silver mounted shagreen case, engraved plaque, velvet lined interior, two fitted circular weights and various others, 18th C **575.00**

Shop scales, Majolica central support, brass pans and chains, German, 45" h, **$1,450**.

Photo courtesy of Joy Luke Auctions.

Postal

4-1/2" h, 6-3/4" l, S. Mordan & Co., England, 19th C, plates with blue and white Wedgwood jasper neoclassical roundels in ropetwist surround, rect base with three weights **350.00**

7-3/4" h, candlestick-style, gilt metal, British, 1840s, for American market, circular pan with scrolled foliate borders,

red enameled stem, trellis work and C-scrolls, rate table with eagle dec, circular foot modeled in high relief with locomotive, steam clipper and farm implements interspersed with cornucopia **275.00**

Store type, Chatillon's Improved Circular Spring Balance to Weigh 30 lbs by ounces, brass face, some wear, **$165**.

Store type, Henry Troemner, original weights and brass pans, wrought iron base, gold pin stripe decoration, **$145**.

Store

6" x 14" x 10", Hanson Weighmaster, cast iron, gold case with ground, black lettering and indicator . **45.00**

15-1/4" h, 17-1/2" w, "Computing Scale Co., Dayton, Ohio" **225.00**

SCHLEGELMILCH PORCELAINS

History: Erdmann Schlegelmilch founded his porcelain factory in Suhl in the Thuringia region in 1861. Reinhold, his brother, established a porcelain factory at Tillowitz in Upper Silesia in 1869.

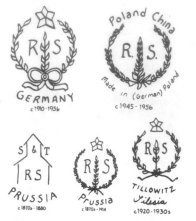

In the 1860s, Prussia controlled Thuringia and Upper Silesia, both rich in the natural ingredients needed for porcelain.

By the late 19th century, an active export business was conducted with the United States and Canada due to a large supply of porcelain at reasonable costs achieved through industrialization and cheap labor.

The Suhl factory ceased production in 1920, unable to recover from the effects of World War I. The Tillowitz plant, located in an area of changing international boundaries, finally came under Polish socialist government control in 1956.

Marks: Both brothers marked their pieces with the "RSP" mark, a designation honoring Rudolph Schlegelmilch, their father. More than 30 mark variations have been discovered.

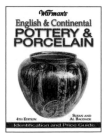

For more information, see *Warman's English & Continental Pottery & Porcelain*, 4th edition.

Reproduction Alert: Many "fake" Schlegelmilch pieces are appearing on the market. These reproductions have new decal marks, transfers, or recently hand-painted animals on old, authentic R. S. Prussia pieces.

Reproduction Alert: Dorothy Hammond in her 1979 book, *Confusing Collectibles*, illustrates an R. S. Prussia decal that was available from a china-decorating supply company for $14 a sheet. This was the first of several fake R. S. Prussia reproduction marks that have caused confusion among collectors. Acquaint yourself with some of the subtle distinctions between fake and authentic marks as described in the following.

The period mark consists of a wreath that is open at the top. A five-pointed star sits in the opening. An "R" and an "S" flank a wreath twig in the center. The word "Prussia" is located beneath. In the period mark, the leg of the letter "P" extends down past the letter "r." In the reproduction mark, it does not. In the period mark, the letter "I" is dotted. It is dotted in some fake marks, but not in others.

The "R" and the "S" in the period mark are in a serif face and uniform in width. One fake mark uses a lettering style that utilizes a thin/thick letter body. The period mark has a period after the word "Prussia." Some fake marks fail to include it. Several fake marks do not include the word "Prussia" at all.

The period mark has a fine center line within each leaf of the wreath. Several fake marks do not.

R. S. Germany, cheese keeper, white and yellow flowers, brown centers, green leaves, peach colored ground, gold trim, marked, **$115**.

R.S. Germany

Biscuit jar, cov, 6" h, loop handles, roses dec, satin finish, gold knob **95.00**

Bonbon dish, 7-3/4" l, 4-1/2" w, pink carnations, gold dec, silver-gray ground, looped inside handle **40.00**

Bowl
10-1/4" d, emb floral mold, red steeple mark **100.00**
10-1/2" d, lily mold, "S & T" steeple mark **165.00**

Bread plate, iris variant edge mold, blue and white, gold outlined petals and rim, multicolored center flowers, steeple mark **115.00**

Cake plate, deep yellow, two parrots on hanging leaf vine, open handles, green mark **235.00**

Celery tray, 11" l, 5-3/4" w, lily dec, gold rim, open handles, blue label.................... **120.00**

Chocolate pot, white rose florals, blue mark **95.00**

Cup and saucer, plain mold, swan, blue water, mountain and brown castle background, RM........ **225.00**

Demitasse cup and saucer, 3" h, pink roses, gold-stenciled dec, satin finish, blue mark...................... **90.00**

Dessert plate, 6-1/2" d, yellow and cream roses, green and rich brown shaded ground, six-pc set **135.00**

Ewer, 4-3/4" h, mold #640, green mark........................ **75.00**

Hatpin holder, 4-1/2" h, Art Deco mold, green mark **85.00**

Lemon plate, cutout handle shaped as colorful parrot, white ground, gold trim, artist sgd "B. Hunter" **60.00**

Napkin ring, green, pink roses, white snowballs **55.00**

Nut bowl, 5-1/4" d, 2-3/4" h, cream, yellow, roses, green scalloped edge **65.00**

Pitcher, 5-3/4" h, light blue, chrysanthemums, pink roses, gold trim **85.00**

Plate, 9-1/2" d, allegorical scene, sgd "Kaufmann," green mark **90.00**

Powder box, cov, green poppies, green mark **50.00**

Punch bowl, 17-1/4" d, 8" h, mahogany shading to pink, polychrome enameled flowers with gilt, imp fleur-de-lis mark with "J. S. Germany"... **275.00**

Tea tile, peach and tan, greenish white snowballs, RM over faint blue mark.... **165.00**

Toothpick holder, 2-3/4" h, Art Deco mold, green mark .. **80.00**
Vase, 6" h, crystalline glaze, orange and white **45.00**

R S Germany, relish dish, soft pastel yellow ground, four clusters of pale blue violets with green leaves, gold edges and handles, signed "S. Hemsher" in gold, blue wreath mark with star, **$45**.

R. S. Poland

Berry bowl, 4 1/2" sq, white and pale orange floral design, green leaves, small orange-gold border flowers, marked **45.00**
Creamer, soft green, chain of violets, applied fleur-de-lis feet, RM **110.00**
Dresser set, glossy, pink roses, pr 6-1/4" h candlesticks, 5" h hatpin holder, 13" x 9" tray **425.00**
Flower holder, pheasants, brass frog insert **675.00**
Vase
8-1/2" h, 4-3/4" d, large white and tan roses, shaded brown and green ground **195.00**
12" h, 6-1/4" d, white poppies, cream shaded to brown ground, pr **750.00**

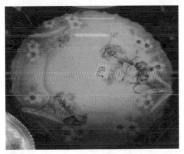

R. S. Prussia, plate, handkerchief type print with delicate white edging, green border, pink carnations, white edelweiss decoration, green wreath mark, 7" d, **$45**.

R. S. Prussia

Biscuit jar, cov
5-1/2" h, mold #501, unmarked **115.00**

7" h, mold #644, red roses, red mark **300.00**
9" l, clematis florals, red mark **225.00**
Bowl, 10-1/2" h, lily mold #29, ftd, red mark **275.00**
Box, cov, 4-3/4" h, 1-1/2" h, rect, detailed floral and gilt highlights, sgd **150.00**
Butter dish, cov, porcelain insert, cream and gold shading, pink roses, raised enamel, RM **715.00**
Cake plate, 11" d, reflecting lilies dec, red mark **165.00**
Celery dish, 12" l, mold #207, rose dec, red mark **85.00**
Chocolate pot, 9-1/2" h, mold #501, rose dec, red mark **150.00**

Creamer and sugar
Iris mold, Winter Portrait, red mark, very minor flake touch-up on creamer **275.00**
Mold #605, red mark, sugar lid finial reattached **125.00**
Pedestal form, florals, red mark **185.00**
Dresser tray, 11-3/4" l, mold #18, red mark **165.00**
Ferner, 7" d, mold 876, florals on purple and green ground, unsgd **165.00**
Hair receiver, green lilies of the valley, white ground, RM **95.00**
Milk pitcher, 5" h, Morning Glory mold, pink carnations dec **200.00**
Mustard, cov, 3-1/4" h, mold #511, red mark **50.00**
Plate
8-3/4" d, floral mold, red mark **115.00**
9" d, swans in lake, red mark **210.00**
Portrait bowl, 5-1/2" d, mold #18, dice player variant, red mark **275.00**
Portrait plate, 8-3/4" d, mold #32, Springtime, red mark, faint 1" hairline on back **375.00**
Shaving mug, 3-3/4" h, emb floral mold **85.00**
Spoon holder, 14" l, pink and white roses **200.00**
Syrup, cov, underplate, green and yellow luster, pink flowers **125.00**
Tankard
10-3/4" h, ftd, mold #642, red mark **275.00**

13" h, striped floral mold #525, red mark, small flake touch-up on lip **325.00**
14" h, mold #643, reflecting water lilies, red mark, repaired **165.00**
Toothpick holder, green shadows, pink and white roses, jeweled, six feet, RM **250.00**
Vase, 6-1/4" h, jeweled, rose floral dec, embedded opal jewels, sgd **275.00**

R. S. Prussia, pitcher, covered, white ground, light green panels, dark green panel with pink shaded rose around top, pink rose on light green shaded ground on lower section, green mark, gold trim, **$70**.

R. S. Prussia, chocolate set, chocolate pot, four cups and saucers, white ground, purple violets, green leaves, gold trim, **$295**.

R. S. Suhl

Coffee set, 9" h, coffeepot, creamer, sugar, six cups and saucers, figural scenes dec, some marked "Angelica Kauffmann" **1,750.00**
Pin tray, 4-1/2" d, round, Nightwatch **375.00**

Plate, 6-3/4" d, cherubs dec
.... **90.00**
Powder dish, cov, Nightwatch,
green shading **425.00**
Vase, 8" h, four pheasants,
green mark **275.00**

R. S. Tillowitz

Bowl, 7-3/4" d, slanted sides,
open handles, four leaf-
shaped feet, matte finish, pale
green ground, roses and
violets, gold flowered rim,
marked........................ **125.00**
Creamer and sugar, soft yellow
and salmon roses **65.00**
Plate, 6-1/2" d, mixed floral
spray, gold beading, emb rim,
brown wing mark **120.00**
Relish tray, 8" l, oval, hp,
shaded green, white roses,
green leaves, center handle,
blue mark..................... **45.00**
Tea set, stacking teapot,
creamer, and sugar, yellow,
rust, and blue flowers, gold
trim, ivory ground, marked
"Royal Silesia," green mark in
wreath **95.00**
Vase, 10" h, pheasants, brown
and yellow, two curved
handles...................... **125.00**

SCHNEIDER GLASS

For more information, see *Warman's Glass*, 4th edition.

History: Brothers Ernest and
Charles Schneider founded a
glassworks at Epiney-sur-Seine,
France, in 1913. Charles, the
artistic designer, previously had
worked for Daum and Gallé.
Robert, son of Charles, assumed
art direction in 1948. Schneider
moved to Loris in 1962.

Although Schneider made
tablewares, stained glass, and
lighting fixtures, its best-known
product is art glass that exhibits
simplicity of design and often has
bubbles and streaking in larger
pieces. Other styles include
cameo-cut and hydrofluoric-acid-
etched designs.

Marks: Schneider glass was
signed with a variety of script and
block signatures, "Le Verre
Francais," or "Charder."

Center bowl, 13-3/4" d, 7-3/4" h,
rose and caramel-colored
spattered glass, flared rim,
wafer joined to ftd base with
rolled lip, signed "Schneider"
on side of base **900.00**
Compote, 8" d, 3-7/8" h, shallow
round bowl, pedestal base,
mottled rose pink translucent
glass with internal bubbles,
shading to dark purple,
polished pontil, acid etched
"Schneider" on base, light
edge wear, minor scratches
.... **300.00**
Ewer, 10-3/4" h, elongated
spout, mottled purples, pink,
yellow, and orange splashes,
applied purple handle,
bulbed disk foot, acid stamp
"France" on base, c1925
.... **450.00**
Finger bowl and underplate,
4-1/2" d bowl, 7-1/4" d
underplate, mottled red, burnt
umber and clear, stamped
mark.......................... **350.00**
Tazza, 7-5/8" h, shallow white
bowl rising to mottled
amethyst and blue inverted
rim, amethyst double-bulbed
stem, disk foot, sgd
"Schneider," c1920.... **865.00**
Vase
3-1/8" h, gold spattered body,
coiled gold threading at
shoulder, sgd with a vase and
"Schneider" **215.00**
4-1/2" h, mottled orange
ground, cameo cut with blue
Art Deco design, candy-cane
signature, c1920......... **490.00**
8" h, corset shape, internally
dec, mottled amethyst and
yellow, three amethyst Art
Nouveau applied dec, sgd in
hourglass in script **700.00**
12-1/2" h, cameo dec, orange
and mottled green against
yellow body, base signature
"Verre Francais," later marks

"France Ovington New York"
.... **1,120.00**
14" h, tapering cylindrical,
baluster neck, orange overlay,
five clusters of pendant
grapes, geometric pattern cut
foot over yellow mottled
ground, inset cane at base
.... **650.00**
17-3/4" h, tapered form,
incurvate rim, shaded orange
overlaid in mottled brown,
cameo-etched and cut
cascading fruit and leaves,
pedestal foot inscribed "Le
Verre Francais," polished
pontil....................... **1,265.00**

SCRIMSHAW

History: Norman Flayderman
defined scrimshaw as "the art of
carving or otherwise fashioning
useful or decorative articles as
practiced primarily by whalemen,
sailors, or others associated with
nautical pursuits." Many collectors
expand this to include the work of
Eskimos and French POWs from
the War of 1812.

> **Reproduction Alert:** The
> biggest problem in the field is
> fakes, although there are some
> clues to spotting them. A very
> hot needle will penetrate the
> common plastics used in
> reproductions but not the
> authentic material. Ivory will not
> generate static electricity when
> rubbed, plastic will. Patina is not
> a good indicator; it has been
> faked by applying tea or
> tobacco juice, and in other
> ingenious ways. Usually the
> depth of cutting in an old design
> will not be consistent since the
> ship rocked and tools dulled;
> however, skilled forgers have
> even copied this characteristic.

Box, small inlaid pieces of ivory with
scrimshawed map type design with
sailing ships, seagulls, seals, coast line,
etc., velvet lined interior, **$45**.

Box, 2-1/4" d, 2" h, circular, engraved and stained, whaling scene, large whale surrounded by compass positions, late 19th C .. **225.00**

Busk
12-3/8" l, bone, scratch carved eagle, pinwheels, vining foliage, compass stars, and heart at top, black coloring with red in eagle's shield and one flower, small chip at top................... **550.00**
13-7/8" l, wood, dec with eagle, shield, lovebirds, and ship under sail, heart and foliate devices, inscribed "GC & EW," dated 1840 ..... **345.00**

Cane, American, c1864, 1-1/3" d x 1-1/8" h whale ivory knob handle, top with scrimmed spiral sunburst, baleen dot in center, highlighted in red, surrounded by feathery black-inked wreath with red berries, scrimmed around rim "U.S.S. Kearsarge, 1864," with tiny baleen dots, hand fashioned 1/4" ring brass collar on smooth and tapered whalebone shaft with oval brass eyelets, under collar inked scrimshaw "To Capt. John A. Winslow From His Crew," uniform yellow patina, 35-1/4" l, sold with engraved certificate from New York Chamber of Commerce to Captain Winslow and his crew **15,680.00**

Cribbage board, carved walrus tusk, late 19th C
11" l, carved in relief with Northwest fish and sea life, polychrome dec.......... **360.00**
23" l, carved on both sides, obverse, board in floral dec panel flanked by scenes of Northwest animals and fish, reverse with scenes of life in Northwest region, minor age splits **475.00**

Domino box, 6-7/8" l, bone and wood, shoe form, pierced carved slide top with star and heart dec, domino playing pcs, Prisoner of War, 19th C, cracks, minor insect damage **520.00**

Game box, 5-3/4" x 6-1/2", bone, pierced carved box with geometric dec, three slide tops, compartmented int., backgammon and other playing pcs, traces of paint

dec, Prisoner of War, 19th C, repair, warping to tops, very minor loses **690.00**

Jagging wheel, 7-1/4" l, dec with building flying American flag, berried vines, 19th C, very minor losses **520.00**

Obelisk, 13-3/8" l, inlaid mahogany, inlaid with various exotic woods, abalone and ivory in geometric and star motifs, 19th C, minor losses, minute cracks **815.00**

Plaque, 14-1/2" l, sailing ship, pencil inscription "Whale bone found in England by Mrs. Fred Rich," c1800 .... **13,000.00**

Salt horn, 5-1/2" l, engraved "John Snow March...1780 by S. H.," crosshatched borders enclosing reserve of ship, geometric, and foliate devices, insect damage **460.00**

Seal, carved and engraved ivory, America, 19th C, oblong form, engraved depiction of six American flags, shield over crossed cannon, inscribed "LIBERTY," sunburst on one side, three masted ship engraved on reverse, base carved with name "LOHN G. JESSEN," red and black highlights, 1-7/8" x 1-5/8", **$715**.

Photo courtesy of Skinner, Inc.

Seam rubber, 4" l, whalebone, geometric designs on handle, traces of orig paint, 19th C **850.00**

Snuff box, 5" l, horn, architectural and marine motifs, dated "AD 1853" and "William Sandilands Plumber," English....................... **950.00**

Swift, 16" h, all whale bone and ivory, copper pegs, yarn ties, nicely turned detail, pincushion socket on top, age cracks, minor edge damage, possible replaced section **900.00**

Walrus tusk
17-3/4" h, reserves of animals, courting couples, ships under sail, memorials, sailors and

armaments, later engraved brass presentation caps, "Presented by George M. Chase to Ike B. Dunlap Jan. 25th 1908," cracks, one restored, pr............. **2,530.00**
18-7/8" l, walrus, dec with two eagles, lady, Indian, and vulture, age cracks, 19th C **1,840.00**

Watch hutch, 11-7/8" h, bone, pierce carved floral and figural dec, brass backing, polychrome foliate highlights, Prisoner of War, 19th C, custom-made case, minor cracks, losses, repairs.. **750.00**

Whale's tooth, 19th C
4-3/8" l, dec with ship, woman resting on anchor holding flag, two potted plants, chips, minor cracks, 19th C .. **690.00**
6-5/8" h, historic landmarks, dec on both sides, very minor cracks and chips........ **865.00**
6-7/8" h, various ships under sail and young lady, cracks **1,380.00**

SEVRES

History: The principal patron of the French porcelain industry in early 18th-century France was Jeanne Antoinette Poisson, Marquise de Pompadour. She supported the Vincennes factory of Gilles and Robert Dubois and their successors in their attempt to make soft-paste porcelain in the 1740s. In 1753, she moved the porcelain operations to Sevres, near her home, Chateau de Bellevue.

The Sevres soft-paste formula used sand from Fontainebleau, salt, saltpeter, soda of alicante, powdered alabaster, clay, and soap. Many famous colors were developed, including a cobalt blue. Such famous decorators as Watteau, La Tour, and Boucher painted the wonderful scenic designs on the ware. In the 18th century, Sevres porcelain was the world's foremost diplomatic gift.

In 1769, kaolin was discovered in France, and a hard-paste formula was developed. The baroque gave way to rococo, a style favored by Jeanne du Barry, Louis XV's next mistress. Louis XVI took little interest in Sevres, and many factories began to turn out counterfeits. In 1876, the factory was moved to St. Cloud and was eventually nationalized.

Marks: Louis XV allowed the firm to use the "double L" in its marks.

Reproduction Alert.

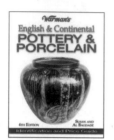

For more information, see *Warman's English and Continental Pottery & Porcelain*, 4th edition.

Box, cov
2-1/2" l, 1-1/4" w, 1-1/2" h, oval, cobalt blue ground, panels of putti dec, sgd "JB," chip on base.............. **425.00**
7" l, 4-1/2" w, 3-1/4" h, oval, hp, hinged lid, opalescent cranberry ground, gilt roses and scrolls, lid with painted scene of woman and putti, sgd "E. Carelle," int. dec with polychrome floral panels
.... **650.00**

Bud vase, 6" h, gilt ground, enamel Art Nouveau stylized leaf and flower design, printed mark **635.00**

Bust, 13" h, Marie Antoinette, bisque bust, gilt highlights, cobalt blue ground, molded porcelain socle with central garland and monogram, 19th C **650.00**

Café au lait cup and saucer, 6" h, ftd cup, cobalt blue enameled ground, gilt eagle roundel and torcheres, corresponding molded saucer, early 20th C.... **200.00**

Candelabra, pr, 18" h, painted scenes of winged cherubs, Bleu-celeste ground, foliate gilt border, figural gilt bronze cherubs holding branches of three candle sockets, c1900 .... **2,530.00**

Centerpiece, 17-1/2" l, 13-1/2" h, int. painted with scene of two lovers, Bleu-celeste ground, scrolled gilt border, bronze plinth, foliate gilt bronze handles, 19th C **2,990.00**

Clock, 17" h, emb metal case, five inset painted porcelain panels, three are scenic, frontal pc with young lovers, c1900.......................... **815.00**

Compote, 11-1/2" d, 9-1/2" h, int. painted with young beauty and cherub, sgd "Lote," Bleu-celeste ground, dec porcelain pedestal, bronze plinth, 19th C **2,760.00**

Cup and saucer, 3" h cup, cobalt blue ground, painted roundel depicting an 18th century couple playing with dog, gilt tooled surround, saucer with floral painted center, blue border with floral cartouches, late 19th C **815.00**

Dish, 14" d, 7" h, rim dec with flowers, reserve with portrait of lady, turquoise ground, gilt bronze stand with two handles cast with scrollwork, garlands of leaves and grapes, 19th C
.... **2,150.00**

Display tray, 14-5/8" h, round, short gilt handles, cobalt blue rim with rocaille scrolls, center painted with scene of courting couple, sgd E. Roy, early 20th C **400.00**

Ecuelle, cov, 8" d, panel florals, bright enamels, raised gilt cartouches, pink ground, round matching stand, c1860 .... **460.00**

Figure, 8-1/2" h, pair in Elizabethian dress, royal blue ground, gold accents, early
.... **640.00**

Inkwell, 11-1/2" l, 8-1/2" h, scene of winged cherub and florals against Bleu-celeste ground, foliage gilt borders, each ink receptacle supported by gilt bronze sphinx like young beauty, 19th C **1,150.00**

Lamp base, 21-1/2" h, urn shape, cartouches painted with allegorical female depictions of Spring and Autumn, surrounded by cherubs, gilt enamel surrounds, cerulean blue ground, landscape cartouches recto, mounted with vine wrapped reeded handles ending in Demetre masks, trumpet foot topped by turquoise molded beading, rect bronze base molded with swags, corners with swag centered patera, electrified, late 19th C, price for pr
.... **7,650.00**

Mantel urns, pr, 18" h, lidded teal blue tapered vases with horizontal gilt banding, oblong bases set with pair of kneeling bisque figures of semi-nude classical women, c1919, base chips... **2,500.00**

Mantel vase, cov, 19-1/2" h, painted with wide central band of courtiers on verandas in pastoral landscape, white and red faux jeweled borders, body with cobalt blue ground accented with gilt enameling, angular husk-draped ormolu handles, lids with inverted berry finials, late 19th C, price for pr **9,400.00**

Monteiths, pr, 12" w, scalloped rim flanked by two scroll handles, floral garlands and blue ribbon dec, white ground, blue interlaced L's mark, 19th C **960.00**

Patch box, cov, 3-1/4" l, shaped ovoid, green ground, hinged lid with hand painted scene of Napoleon on horseback, sgd lower right "Morin" **250.00**

Plaque, 10-1/2" l, 9-5/8" w oval format, Marie Antoinette, mauve gown, blue celeste border with gilt scrollwork, 10-3/4" x 13-5/8" giltwood and crème painted frame, late 19th C **550.00**

Portrait plate, 9" d, Lobelia portrait, surrounded by wreath, cobalt blue band border with gilt dec including Napoleonic crest and crowns, mounted in shadow box frame, gilt loss **150.00**

Solitaire, 6-1/4" h teapot, cup and saucer, cov sugar, tray, gilt scrollwork, reserves dec with flowers or fetes galantes, turquoise ground, 19th C
.... **1,135.00**

Tray, 18-1/2" x 13", six-sided oblong form, French allegorical park scene, ladies with parasols, Florentine gilt border, sgd "Bertien".. **525.00**

Urn
15" h, light blue body, hp elephant lady framed with gold medallion, overall random amethyst leafy stemmed flowers, gold gilt emb foot, metal handled collar, blue trademark, metal stamped "France" **950.00**

19" h, campana form, Napoleonic scenes painted reserves, green ground, sgd "L. Loreau," mounted on plastic base, fitted as lamp, 19" h......................... **1,195.00**

Urn, cov
14-1/2" h, dome cov, pine cone finial, neck dec with band of vitruvian scrolls and ram's heads, reserves dec with flowers, fluted socle and octagonal base, gilt metal mounts, 19th C **1,675.00**
10 1/2" h, finely painted French garden scene by L. Bertren within gilt foliate cartouche, cobalt blue ground, winged anthropomorphic bronze handles, verso with pastoral cottage and stream scene, bronzed acorn finial lid, mkd with Serves style cipher, c1900..................... **10,120.00**

Vase, 11" h, pink ground, oval cartouches with figural landscapes and ornaments, metal mount, pr........ **1,380.00**

Wine cooler, 10-1/4" h, Louis XVI style, circular tapering form, top section with gilded ram's heads over reeded band, base dec with ribboned garlands and entwined laurel, multicolored, white ground **2,300.00**

SEWING ITEMS

History: As recently as 50 years ago, a wide variety of sewing items were found in almost every home in America. Women of every economic and social status were skilled in sewing and dressmaking.

Iron or brass sewing birds, one of the interesting convenience items that developed, was used to hold cloth (in the bird's beak) while sewing. They could be attached to a table or shelf with a screw-type fixture. Later models included a pincushion.

Additional Listings: *Warman's Americana & Collectibles* for more examples.

Bodkins, whalebone and ivory, sealing wax inlaid scribe lines, 19th C, minor losses, nine-pc set................ **400.00**

Hanging cabinet, two drawers, **$100.**
Photo courtesy of Dotta Auction Co., Inc.

Book, *Fleisher's Knitting & Crocheting Manual*, S. B. & B. W. Fleisher, Inc., Philadelphia, PA, 1924, 112 pgs, 7" x 9-1/2", 21st edition **15.00**

Catalog, E. Butterick & Co., New York, NY, 1878, 32 pgs, 7-1/2" x 10", Catalog for Fall of Women's Clothing Patterns **38.00**

Folder, 8-3/4" x 14-1/4", Wm. R. Moore Dry Goods Co., Memphis, TN, three pgs, c1937, heavy weight, "Guaranteed Fast Color No. 10 Batfast Suitings," 10 tipped-in blue Batfast Suiting swatches, 19-1/4" x 2" colored swatches tipped in **28.00**

Etui, 3-1/2" l, tapered ovoid agate case, ormolu mounts, hinged lid, fitted interior with scissors, knife, pen, ruler, needle, pincers, and spoon, Continental, late 18th/early 19th C **700.00**

Hand book, Davis Sewing Machine Co., Watertown, NY, *Centennial Hand Book Presented at the Great Exhibition*, 12 pgs, directions to get around at Exhibition, info. on sewing machine, cabinets, etc............... **65.00**

Instruction book, *Singer Sewing Machines No. 99*, c1910, 32 pgs, 3-1/2" x 5-1/4" **16.00**

Magazine, *Home Needlework Magazine*, Florence Publishing Co., Florence, MA, 176 pgs, 1899, Vol. 1, No. 2, April **20.00**

Needle book, Rocket Gold Tipped Needles, cov illus of man and woman riding needle shaped like rocket, nighttime sky background, marked "Made in Japan," 1940s........................... **10.00**

Needle case, tri-color 18k gold, chase and engraved geometric and floral motifs, European hallmark **320.00**

Pin cushion
4" d, eight-sided star, brown and red cloth on one side, purple and blue cloth on other side, black ribbon hanging loop............................... **90.00**
4" l, 1-1/2" w, sewing bird shape, brown cloth, foliate pattern **200.00**
6" d, 1-1/2" h, doughnut shape, brown and black cloth on one side, light blue and dark blue cloth on other side, purple hanging loop **85.00**
6" sq, woolen, multicolored checkerboard pattern, black edges, brown velvet back, Amish, Centre County, PA, price for pr.................. **165.00**
9-1/2" h, felt and yarn cushion strawberry mounted on pattern glass finial, Amish, Lancaster County, PA.................. **3,080.00**

Sewing bird, 4-1/8" l, ivory, four side-mounted spools, geometric and heart exotic wood inlay, 19th C, inlay loss and replacements ... **1,150.00**

Sewing box, original sewing implements, thread, containers with buttons, button hook, lace making implements, fashionable ladies images decoupaged from Godey's or Peterson's Magazine on top, late 1800s, some loss to decoupage, 14" l, 10-1/2" w, 3-1/2" h, **$225.**
Photo courtesy of Alderfer Auction Co.

Sewing box, wallpaper covered 5-1/2" d, 5" h, eight-sided, ftd, yellow wallpaper with maroon floral dec, green and blue cloth edging, sgd "Eli Myers, December 1885" in English and German **3,850.00**
6" d, 5-1/2" h, round, nine paneled sides, dots and diamonds, orange, blue, green and white polychrome dec, under lid mkd "To Mother Ellin".........................**1,870.00**

Sewing box, wood
5-1/2" w, 3-1/2" d, 3-1/4" h, inlaid hearts, arrows, diamonds, and circles, one dovetailed drawer, turned pull, worn pin cushion top, minor edge damage at corner **275.00**
12-1/4" w, 7-1/4" d, 5-5/8" h, mahogany inlaid, hinged lid, center inlaid oval reserve with shell motif, ext. with inlaid borders and corners, int. lid centered with diamond motif, lift-out tray with several compartments, America, 19th C, minor imperfections.. **998.00**

Sewing egg, 2-1/2" l, walrus ivory, unscrews to reveal ivory spool, thimble, and needle case, 19th C **920.00**

Spinning wheel
34-1/2" h, upright, hardwoods, turned posts, iron fly wheel, ivory and ebonized wood details, old mellow refinishing, treadle with dec carving, old repair to cord belt **450.00**
35" h, upright, hardwoods, turned posts, wood and wire fly wheel, small turned ivory pegs alternating with wheel spokes, traces of black paint on wheel, base, and legs, German, worm holes, some edge damage, one finial glued, two spokes damaged **295.00**
38" h, upright, cherry, mellow refinishing, small ivory buttons, turned legs, tripod base, 9-1/2" d wheel, single flyer **350.00**

Stand, 12-3/4" h, carved and turned walnut, round, four-tiered, graduated stand, pin cushion mounted on top, two rotating discs, each having six ivory spool holders, four ivory ball feet, New England, mid-19th C **300.00**

Tape loom, 39-1/2" h, standing, floor type, turned wormy maple post, oak step down, cross bar base, loom pegged into post, replacements to loom and base **150.00**

Tape measure, advertising
General Electric Refrigerator, black and white beehive-style refrigerator on dark blue background, light blue rim, black and white name and text for local distributor on back.............................. **20.00**
Kiwanis Club, blue and white celluloid canister printed on both sides, one side with international emblem, "We Build" on reverse **15.00**
Lydia E. Pinkham, pale brown and white celluloid canister, sepia portrait of Lydia on one side, reverse with Vegetable Compound Blood Medicine tonics line **25.00**
Parisian Novelty Co., celluloid canister printed in blue, white ground, both sides with text promoting celluloid novelties **35.00**
Pillsbury's Family of Foods, celluloid canister, red, white, and blue flour sack printed on white, blue rim **25.00**

Spool cabinet, round, oak case, curved glass, refinished, **$725**.

Tape measure, figural, owl, metal, German.............. **45.00**

Thimble, brass, fancy band design.......................... **15.00**

Thimble holder, 5-3/4" h, fisherman holding large rod, beautifully detailed large fish on ground, bucket by fish, post in front of fisherman, rect base, marked "Miller Silver Co. Silver Plate" **350.00**

Thread and needle holder, 4" d, 7" h, turned wood, polychrome paint dec in yellow, red, and green banding, pin cushion on top with metal spool holders, opens to three compartments **2,750.00**

Thread cabinet
Clarks, white lettering, four drawers, some damage to case........................... **100.00**
Dexter Fine Yarn, oak, four drawers, 18-3/4" h, 18-5/8" w, 16" d **650.00**
Merrick's Spool Cotton, oak, cylindrical, curved glass, 18" d, 22" h **725.00**
Willimantic, four drawers, ornate Eastlake style case, 14-1/4" h **550.00**

Yarn or cord winder, 28" w, 16-1/4" d, 29-1/2" h, enameled steel and brass works, mahogany platform base, turned feet, signature plate "Goodbrand & Co. Ltd., Makers, Staleybridge" **550.00**

SHAKER

History: The Shakers, so named because of a dance they used in worship, are one of the oldest communal organizations in the United States. Mother Ann Lee, who emigrated from England and established the first Shaker community near Albany, New York, in 1784, founded this religious group. The Shakers reached their peak in 1850, when there were 6,000 members.

Shakers lived celibate and self-sufficient lives. Their philosophy stressed cleanliness, order, simplicity, and economy. Highly inventive and motivated, the Shakers created many utilitarian household forms and objects. Their furniture reflected a striving for quality and purity in design.

In the early 19th century, the Shakers produced many items for commercial purposes. Chairmaking and the packaged herb and seed business thrived. In every endeavor and enterprise, the members followed Mother Ann's advice: "Put your hands to work and give your heart to God."

Herb bentwood box, pine top and base, maple sides, fingered, lift-off lid initialed "BC," mid-19th C, 3-1/2" l, 2" w, 1-1/2" h, **$200.**

Photo courtesy of Gamal Amer.

Apothecary cabinet, 66" x 14", stained wood, rect, front fitted with 12 small drawers, molded white glazed porcelain handles, identification labels, drawer sides inscribed with various content titles, New England, 19th C **450.00**

Basket, 12" x 12" x 4-3/8" h, finely woven splint, sq shape, two delicate bentwood handles, minor damage, traces of old red stain. **360.00**

Blanket chest, 40-1/2" w, 18-1/2" d, 36" h, New Lebanon, NY, 1830-40, hinged rect breadboard lift top, nail construction well, two long scratch beaded drawers, tapering cut-out feet, all-over later grain paint to simulate exotic wood, old replaced pulls, surface imperfections **1,265.00**

Bonnet, dark brown palm and straw, black ribbons, 9" flounce, KY **395.00**

Book, *How the Shakers Cook & the Noted Cooks of the Country, Feature the Chefs and Their Cooking Recipes*, A. J. White, New York, NY, 1889, 50 pgs, 3-3/8" x 6-1/8", bust of men illus, dusted, chips **15.00**

Bottle, 9" h, aqua, emb "Shaker Pickles," base labeled "Portland, Maine, E.D.P. & Co." **90.00**

Box, cov, bentwood 5-1/2" w, 3-1/2" d, 2-1/8" h, finger construction, two fingers on base, one finger on lid, copper tacks, old green repaint, some wear on lid **850.00**
6-1/8" w, 4" w, 2" h, finger construction, two fingers on

base, one finger on lid, brass tacks, old green (black) repaint over traces of earlier green, minor wear **690.00**
7-1/2" w, 5-1/8" d, 2-1/2" h, finger construction, two fingers on base, one finger on lid, copper tacks, reddish stain **320.00**
9-1/2" w, 7" d, 3-3/4" h, finger construction, two fingers on base, one finger on lid, copper tacks, old blue paint, some wear **1,400.00**
12" w, 8-3/8" d, 4-3/4" h, oval, Harvard lap, copper tacks, mellow natural finish, remnants of paper label on one end **440.00**
20" w, oval, orig light green and cream paint sponged in leaf and feather patterned dec, seven fingers on side, one finger on lid, ex Elgin **26,000.00**

Carrier
9-1/4" l, 6-3/4" w, 8" h, oval, maple, three lapped fingers, swing handle, copper tacks, number "5" impressed on base, clear lacquer finish **425.00**
12-1/2" d, 1" h base, 6" h handle, round, single stapled finger, bentwood handle, some red stain remains, copy of old Currier & Ives hunting print in center, minor splits **250.00**

Chair, dining, 17" h seat, 25" h back, attributed to Canterbury, NH, c1835, birch and pine, concave rect back rail above turned stiles, four spindles, shaped seat, splayed turned tapering legs joined by stretchers, old red stain, missing right side stretcher...................... **825.00**

Chair, side, maple and hickory, old brick red paint, pegged construction, back with three arched slats, high turned finials, turned and tapered posts with eight rungs each, old striped tape seats, minor variations in turnings, old pieced restoration to one leg, 16" h seat, 37-1/4" h, price for set of four.................... **700.00**

Chest of drawers, 63" w, 17-1/2" d, 39-1/2" h, pine, eight graduated dovetailed drawers arranged in two banks of four, turned pulls, six

high feet with semi-curved cut-outs, old mellow refinish, replaced back boards, some pulls replaced........ **14,300.00**

Child's rocker, 7 3/4" h seat, 24" h back, production, Mt. Lebanon, NY, 1880-1930, incised "O" with decal on rocker, old varnished surface, replaced tape seat, minor imperfections........... **3,300.00**

Cloak
Adult's, pink wool, labeled "The Dorothy Shakers, East Canterbury, New Hampshire," c1880-1920 .... **1,195.00**
Child's, red wool, labeled "The Dorothy Shakers, East Canterbury, New Hampshire," c1880-1920 .... **1,195.00**
Infant's, white wool, pink silk lining, c1880-1920, shattering to lining **595.00**

Corner shelves, tiered, wooden, from West Family seed house, Enfield, NH, 19th C, 20" w, 9-1/8" d, 31-5/8" h, **$4,700.**

Photo courtesy of Skinner, Inc.

Dough scraper, 4-1/2" l, wrought iron................................ **40.00**

Dry sink, walnut, single double paneled door, shaped feet, Whitewater Shaker Meeting House **5,500.00**

Flax wheel, 33 1/2" h, various hardwoods, old dark brown finish, stamped "SR. AL," (Deacon Samuel Ring of Alfred, Maine 1784-1848), two pieces of distaff replaced **330.00**

Grain measure, 7-1/2" d, bentwood, stencil label "Shaker Society, Sabbathday Lake, Me," minor edge damage **160.00**

Hanger, 24" w, bentwood, chestnut...................... **65.00**

Linen cupboard, painted poplar and pine, red, black sponged dec, Whitewater Shaker Meeting House **21,000.00**

Mat, 14-1/4" d, braided, plush velvet-like fabric, multiple colors and white, Canterbury, NH................................ **80.00**

Recipe book, Laura Sarle, Canterbury, Shaker Village, New Hampshire, 1883-87, inscribed by author, recipes, brief autobiography, short play, housekeeping, records, knitting instructions, pen and ink on paper, mottled orange cardboard cover with black binding, wear to cover, few random annotations by later hand....................... **5,520.00**

Side chair, birch, Enfield, NH, c1830, elongated elliptical pommels, three arched and beveled slats above caned seat, turned legs, stretcher base, old surface and caning, very minor imperfections, 15-1/4" seat, 41" h, **$1,550**.

Photo courtesy of Skinner, Inc.

Rocker

#6, ladderback, old dark brown varnished surface, imp "6" on top slat, four arched back slats, elongated acorn shaped finials, later tan woven tape seat, curved arms with tapered rear posts, finely turned arm supports, splits at bottom of legs, restoration to one rocker, 15-1/2" h seat, 42" h back................... **350.00**

#7, Mt Lebanon, maple and birch, woven tape seat and back, shaped arms, domed caps, short acorn finials, imp "7" on upper slat, orig label remaining inside one runner, worn surface, 15-1/2" h seat, 42" h back................... **500.00**

Small, Mt. Lebanon, black painted finish, small acorn finials, old woven tape back panel and seat, orig decal

label inside one rocker, 14" h seat, 34" h back.......... **300.00**

Sewing box, cov, 15" l, 11-1/4" w, 11" h including upright handle, oval, pine lid with maple sides and lid rim, swing handle, five lapped fingers, int. lined with light blue padded silk, repair, wear **1,880.00**

Shoe last, 9" to 11" l, wooden, two with removable uppers, one with steel toe and heel, one with leather repair, Canterbury, NH, provenance: Lewis Noble Wiggins Shaker collection, price for set of four **150.00**

Trinket box, bentwood, three-finger construction, old red wash surface, late 19th C, 6" l, 2" h, **$865**.

Photo courtesy of Pook & Pook.

Table, 34-3/4" x 35-1/2" x 28", maple, drop leaf, rect top, hinged rect leaves, single drawer, sq tapering legs, first half 19th C **6,500.00**

Table swift, 29-3/4" d extended, 25" h, maple, 19th C .. **230.00**

Tea table, attributed to Mt. Lebanon, NY, c1830, birch, circular tilt top with bull-nose edge, tilts on platform, tapering turned pedestal, tripod cabriole legs, pad feet, old refinish, 34-1/4" d, 26-3/4" h **6,465.00**

Wash tub, 24" d, 16-1/2" h, New England, late 19th C, stave and lap fingered hoop construction, two handles, old red paint, imperfections **460.00**

SHAVING MUGS

History: Shaving mugs, which hold the soap, brush, and hot water used to prepare a beard for shaving, come in a variety of materials including tin, silver, glass, and pottery. One style,

which has separate compartments for water and soap, is the scuttle, so called because of its coal-scuttle shape.

Personalized shaving mugs were made exclusively for use in barbershops in the United Sates. They began being produced shortly after the Civil War and continued to be made into the 1930s.

Unlike shaving mugs that were used at home, these mugs were personalized with the owner's name, usually in gilt. The mug was kept in a rack at the barbershop, and it was used only when the owner came in for a shave. This was done for hygienic purposes, to keep from spreading a type of eczema known as barber's itch.

The mugs were usually made on European porcelain blanks that often contained the mark of "Germany," "France," or "Austria" on the bottom. In later years, a few were made on American-made semi-vitreous blanks. Decorators who worked for major barber supply houses did the artwork on mugs. Occasionally the mark of the barber supply house is also stamped on the bottom of the mug.

After a short time, the mugs became more decorative, including hand-painted floral decorations, as well as birds, butterflies, and a wide variety of nature scenes, etc. These are classified today as "decorative" mugs.

Another category, "fraternal mugs," soon developed. These included the emblem of an organization the owner belonged to, along with his name emblazoned in gold above or below the illustration.

"Occupational mugs" were also very popular. These are mugs that contained a painting of something that illustrated the owner's occupation, such as a butcher, a bartender, or a plumber. The illustration might be a man working at his job, or perhaps the tools of his trade, or a product he made or sold.

Of all these mugs, occupationals are the most prized. Their worth is determined by several factors: rarity (some occupations are rarer than others), size of mug, and size of illustration (the bigger the better), quality of artwork, and condition—although rare mugs with cracks or chips can still be valuable if the damage does not affect the artwork on the mug. Generally speaking, a mug showing a man at work at his job is usually valued higher than that same occupation illustrated with only the tools or finished product.

The invention of the safety razor by King C. Gillette, issued to three and one-half million servicemen during World War I, brought about changes in personal grooming—men began to shave on their own, rather than visiting the barber shop to be shaved. As a result, the need for personalized shaving mugs declined.

Note: Prices shown are for typical mugs that have no damage and show only moderate wear on the gilt name and decoration.

For more information, see *Warman's English & Continental Pottery & Porcelain*, 4th edition.

Fraternal

B.P.O.E., Elks, double emblem, Dr. title **300.00**

F.O.E., Fraternal Order of Eagles, eagle holding F.O.E. plaque **260.00**

IB of PM, International Brotherhood of Paper Makers, papermaking machine, clasped hands **275.00**

I.O.M., International Order of Mechanics, ark ladder **270.00**

Loyal Knights of America, eagle, flags, six-pointed star **275.00**

Loyal Order of the Moose, gold circle with gray moose head, purple and green floral dec, gilt rim and base, marked "Germany" **220.00**

United Mine Workers, clasped hands emblem flanked by crossed picks and shovels, floral dec, rose garland around top, marked "Germany" **125.00**

Dr. Franklin Bach, M.D., 1931, red rose and green leaves, slight wear to gold, **$125**.

Occupational

Electrician, hand-painted image of electrician wiring inside of electrical box, T & V Limoges, France, wear to gold lettering and trim, 3 5/8" d, 3-5/8" h **2,500.00**

Express wagon, 4" x 3-3/4", hp, man driving horse drawn wagon, word "Express" on side, floral springs, gold rim and name **400.00**

Fabric store, colorful hp shop int., owner waiting on well-dressed woman, gold trim and name, 3-5/8" x 4-1/2" **700.00**

General store, pork, flour, and whiskey barrels, I images, 4" x 4-3/4" **650.00**

Hotel clerk, clerk at desk, guest signing register **375.00**

House painter, detailed hand-painted image of man painting side of building, marked "Fred Dole" on bottom, light crack mark around top of handle, wear to gold lettering and trim, 3-1/2" d, 3-1/2" h **350.00**

Hunting
Duck hunting, 3-1/2" x 3-1/2", hp, duck hunter and dog in boat **275.00**
Ducks, 3-5/8" x 3-5/8", hp, two colorful ducks at water's edge, mkd "J. & C Bavaria" **100.00**
Hunting dogs, 4-1/8" x 3-3/4", hp, two hunting dogs, brown background, mkd "St Louis

Electronic Grinding Co., Barber Supplies," some wear to gold trim, crack in ring handle **120.00**
Rabbit hunting, 3-1/2" x 3-1/2", hp, large rabbits in foreground, hunter walking thru snow, factory in background **120.00**
Sportsman, 3-5/8" x 3-5/8", hp, caught fish, fishing rod, shot gun, leafy sprigs, scene of men fishing in background, name in scroll, V D Austria **130.00**

Ice man, 3-1/2" x 3-1/2", hp, horse drawn Palmer's Ice Co. delivery wagon, rim and name in gold, I & V France .. **825.00**

Mail wagon, 4" x 3-3/4", hp, postal worker driving horse drawn mail wagon, German, repair to top rim on back, gold trim linoc rodone **475.00**

Mover, detailed hand-painted image of two men in moving van, gold name and trim, Royal China Int'l, 3-7/8" d, 3-5/8" **1,400.00**

Oil derek, 3-5/8" x 3-5/8", hp, detailed oil well scene, T & V France **220.00**

Photographer, detailed hand-colored image of portrait photographer, marked "Webb Bros" in gold, wear to gold lettering and trim, 3-5/8" d, 3-1/2" h **700.00**

Railroad, detailed hand-painted image of two railway workers on hand car, wear to gold lettering and trim, 3-1/2" d, 3-5/8" h **650.00**

Shoemaker, hp, scene of shoemaker in shop, gilt foot and swags around name **225.00**

Three shaving mugs, all unmarked, left: burgundy surround, floral trim, name in gold; center: blue ground, dated 1913; right: pink ground, dated 1902, each **$75-$110**.

Soda fountain, 3-3/4" x 3-5/8", hp, serving clerk behind counter of soda fountain, well dressed woman sitting at counter on stool, name in gold, Germany **2,500.00**

Surveyor, 3-1/2" x 3-5/8", hp, detailed land surveying instrument in center, wear to gold name and trim, D & C **550.00**

Tugboat, boat in water, crew and captain........................ **750.00**

Veteran, 3-3/4" x 3-1/2", hp, US Civil War soldier holding American flag, name in gold **1,500.00**

Writer, black desk inkwell with sander, pen, and brass handle........................ **350.00**

Other

Drape and flowers, purple drape, pot of flowers, gold name........................... **85.00**

Fish shape, scuttle, green and brown.......................... **75.00**

Skull, white, gray, black, and cream, scuttle, marked "Bavaria".................... **135.00**

SHAWNEE POTTERY

History: The Shawnee Pottery Co. was founded in 1937 in Zanesville, Ohio. The company acquired a 650,000-square-foot plant that had previously housed the American Encaustic Tiling Company. Shawnee produced as many as 100,000 pieces of pottery a day until 1961, when the plant closed.

Shawnee limited its production to kitchenware, decorative art pottery, and dinnerware. Distribution was primarily through jobbers and chain stores.

Marks: Shawnee can be marked "Shawnee," "Shawnee U.S.A.," "USA #——," "Kenwood," or with character names, e.g., "Pat. Smiley" and "Pat. Winnie."

Console set, white speckled design, **$65**.

Photo courtesy of Joy Luke Auctions.

Bank, bulldog **50.00**
Basket, 9" l, 5-1/2" h at handle, turquoise glaze, relief flowers and leaves, USA 688... **45.00**
Batter pitcher, Fern........ **65.00**
Casserole, cov, Corn Queen, large **40.00**
Cookie jar, cov
  Cinderella, unmarked . **125.00**
  Drum major, marked "USA 10," 10" h **295.00**
  Jo-Jo the Clown, marked "Shawnee USA, 12," 9" h
  .... **300.00**
  Little Chef **75.00**
  Owl **110.00**
Creamer
  Elephant **25.00**
  Puss n' Boots, green and yellow...................... **65.00**
  Smiley Pig, clover bud **165.00**
Figure
  Gazelle **45.00**
  Squirrel **30.00**
  Rabbit **40.00**
Fruit bowl, Corn Queen .. **25.00**
Mug, Corn King **35.00**
Paperweight, Muggsy..... **65.00**
Pitcher
  Bo Peep, blue bonnet, yellow dress......................... **125.00**
  Chanticleer **75.00**
Planter
  Gazelle **25.00**
  Horse with hat and cart **20.00**
  Locomotive, black **60.00**
  Mouse and cheese, pink and yellow........................ **25.00**
  Wheelbarrow............... **20.00**

Salt and pepper shakers, pair of milk cans, cream, blue and red decoration, **$18**; owls, cream, red, green, and black decoration, one of pair shown, **$24**.

Salt and pepper shakers, pr
  Chanticleer, large, orig label **45.00**
  Dutch Boy and Girl, large
  .... **55.00**
  Milk cans **30.00**
  Mugsey, small............. **65.00**
  Puss n' Boots, small **30.00**
  Smiley, small **30.00**
  Watering cans............. **27.50**

Teapot
  Granny Ann, peach apron
  .... **125.00**
  Horseshoe, blue **65.00**
  Tom Tom, blue, red, and yellow........................ **175.00**
Utility jar, Corn King....... **50.00**
Wall pocket, bird house ... **25.00**

SILHOUETTES

History: Silhouettes (shades) are shadow profiles produced by hollow cutting, mechanical tracing, or painting. They were popular in the 18th and 19th centuries.

The name came from Etienne de Silhouette, a French Minister of Finance, who cut "shades" as a pastime. In America, the Peale family was well known for the silhouettes they made.

Silhouette portraiture lost popularity with the introduction of the daguerreotype prior to the Civil War. In the 1920s and 1930s, a brief revival occurred when tourists to Atlantic City and Paris had their profiles cut as souvenirs.

Marks: An impressed stamp marked "PEALE" or "Peale Museum" identifies pieces made by the Peale family.

George Washington, hand cut, gold ground, signed "B. Kendall," label verso, black wood frame, 3-1/2" x 2-5/8", sold with matching silhouette of Martha, price for pair, **$260**.

Photo courtesy of Alderfer Auction Co.

3-1/8" x 2-1/8", hollow cut and painted, possibly work of William Chamberlain, c1820, bust length profile portraits, one of a young woman identified by inscription on reverse as "Pamelia DeWolf, sister of T. K. DeW, born July 16, 1794, D 1862," other young man identified on note as "T. W. DeWolf/Brother," hollow cut head and area below shoulder with black painted detailing of hair, vest, collar, and ruffles, deep blue velvet, matted, molded giltwood frame, toning, stains, small tears, foxing...... **775.00**

3-1/2" x 2-1/2", watercolor, pen and ink, gouache and silk on paper, hollow cut, half-length portraits of woman wearing comb in upswept hair, black dress, ruffled collar set off with blue ribbon, and man with blue best, black jacket, holding red book, black silk lining, unsigned, indistinct penciled inscription on reverse of frame "Dudley, Oct.-1835," emb brass and wood frame, American School, 19th C, pr.... **2,235.00**

3-3/4" w, 5-1/4" h, cut-out portrait of matronly woman wearing bonnet, penciled eyelash, reeded frame with black paint and punched brass rosettes, minor edge damage to frame **220.00**

5-1/2" h, cut-out, gentleman, gold ink details in hair and coat, oval brass liner with convex glass, black painted frame.......................... **175.00**

Girl with sewing basket, girl wearing long lace-trimmed dress sitting beside sewing basket, Wallace Nutting, 1927, 4" x 5", **$40**.

Photo courtesy of Michael Ivankovich Auctions.

4-3/8" w, 5-3/4" h, hollow cut, portrait of boy under leafy branch, very faint name underneath, worn gilt frame, fold lines with minor damage **85.00**

4-1/2" w, 5-1/2" h, hollow cut, gentleman, stenciled frock coat, eglomise glass mat with yellow painted designs, black

velvet backing, black painted frame with traces of yellow on outer edge **475.00**

4-3/4" w, 5-5/8" h, hollow cut, boy, inked details, wrinkles, stains, partial typed label, pine frame **200.00**

4-3/4" w, 5-5/8" h, hollow cut, man, inked hair, scarf, and labels, eglomise mat, period gilt frame, wear, stains, minor edge damage............. **435.00**

4-3/4" w, 5-3/4" h, hollow cut, man, painted details, hair, scarf, and lapels, eglomise mat, period gilt frame, wear, repaint, stains **350.00**

4-7/8" w, 5-3/4" h, hollow cut, bust, lady with ornate hat, back marked "Mrs. Norman" and "Mrs. Norman, Henley on Thames," black lacquered case with gilded fittings, wear and stain **200.00**

5" w, 5-3/4" h, cutout, boy, rosewood frame with worn gilt liner............... **220.00**

5-1/4" w, 5-7/8" h, hollow cut, Edward Brook, aged 16, wearing top hat, eglomise mat, period gilt frame, wear, repaint, stains, minor edge damage **435.00**

5-3/4" w, 7-1/2" h, ink and watercolor on laid paper, British officer, red uniform jacket, gold epaulets and medal, sgd "de Mors," faint inscription on frame "Captain Robert Conig of His Majesty's 40th Regiment of Infantry...," orig gilt frame with damage **230.00**

5-3/4" w, 7-3/4" h, man with floral motif around head, cut-work backed with black textile, old typed paper on back "Isaac Darlington, the famous Ice Cream Maker, whose farm overlooked the Brandywine above Jeffrey Bridge. This was cut by a traveling artist who held the scissors with his toes. Bought from Mr. Mark Darlington, May 10, 1927," orig frame **1,430.00**

5-1/4" w, 6" h, hollow cut, man and woman, man with high collar, woman with hair comb, black cloth backing, molded gold frame, some foxing of paper, price for pair.... **440.00**

5-3/8" w, 6-3/8" h, young woman, hollow cut, cut detail at collar, pencil inscription "Sarah Sage," stains **200.00**

7-1/2" w, 7-1/2" h, hollow cut, man and wife, man with pigtail, wife with bonnet, laid paper, matching grain painted frames with gilt liners, stains, minor wear.................. **350.00**

7-1/2" x 10-1/4", Emily and Rosa, two girls playing, hand painted detailing, 1838 .... **600.00**

8" w, 9-7/8" h, full length cut-out, man identified in pencil as "Sir Walter Scott" writing at a table, attributed to Auguste Edoart, glued to page cut from book, hinged to mat, 12-5/8" w, 13-5/8" h frame **320.00**

8-1/2" x 7-1/2", girl with flower basket, jumping dog, titled "Miss Montague" **250.00**

9-1/4" w, 11-1/4" h, cutout three-quarters length portrait of minister speaking from pulpit, wearing spectacles, presentation note "Kings College Cam Apr 30 1836...," backing with notice for "Portrait, _ and Looking Glass Club...H. Flowers, carver and gilder...Southwark," bird's eye maple frame with worn gilt liner............... **500.00**

9-1/2" w, 7-5/8" h, boy and girl, full length, standing facing each other, hollow cut, gilt detail, bird's eye veneer ogee frame **725.00**

10" w, 6-1/2" h, man and woman, hollow cut, ink and watercolor details, framed together, sgd "Doyle," eglomise glass mat with two ovals, gilded frame **425.00**

10" x 9-3/8", Mrs. Rosanna Lamb, full length, sgd and dated "Aug.st Edouart fecit 1842 Boston U.S.," cut-out paper figure laid down on paper, graphite, ink, and watercolor genre scene in background, sitter identified in note affixed to reverse, framed, toning, staining.......................... **450.00**

SILVER

History: The natural beauty of silver lends itself to the designs of artists and craftsmen. It has been mined and worked into an endless variety of useful and decorative items. Pure silver is too soft to be fashioned into strong, durable, and serviceable utensils. Therefore, a way was found to give silver the required degree of hardness by adding alloys of copper and nickel.

Silversmithing in America goes back to the early 17th century in Boston and New York and the early 18th century in Philadelphia. Boston artisans were influenced by the English styles, New Yorkers by the Dutch.

American, 1790-1840

Mostly coin

Coin silver is slightly less pure than sterling silver. Coin silver has 900 parts silver to 100 parts alloy. Sterling silver has 925 parts silver. American silversmiths followed the coin standards. Coin silver is also called Pure Coin, Dollar, Standard, or Premium.

American, centerpiece, pierced motif with grape decoration, monogrammed, unmarked, 12" d, **$400**.

Photo courtesy of Wiederseim Associates, Inc.

Beaker, 3" h, 3" d, top and bottom molded rims, engraved, minor dents, Anthony Rasch, Philadelphia, 1807, 4 troy oz **490.00**

Cake server, 9-1/8" l, George C. Shreve, late 19th C, mark partially rubbed, shaped blade engraved with harbor scene within foliate cartouche, unfurling flag, engine-turned ground, fitted case, 3 troy oz **200.00**

Coffee spoon, John David Jr., Philadelphia, PA, 1795-99, made for Cooch family, monogrammed, one with damage, dents, wear, 5-1/4" l, price for set of eight, 4 troy oz **1,035.00**

Creamer, 6" h, ewer form, beaded detailing, marked "RH" **2,750.00**

Cup, 2-1/2" h, scroll handle, geometric banding at top and bottom, engraved sun motif,

inscribed "Awarded by the S.C.A.S. (Southern Central Agriculture Society) & Mechanical Ins of Georgia, Oct 19th, 1852, for the best half dozen pair of Brogan Shoes, marked "Pure Silver Coin, J. E. Caldwell & Co., Phila" **1,320.00**

Dessert spoon, William Hollingshead, Philadelphia, PA, 1754-85, marked "WH" in shaped stamp, twice on each handle, engraved "KIS," wear to bowls, imperfections, price for set of five, 9 troy oz **490.00**

Ewer, 12" h, ftd, repoussé vintage dec, vine form handle extending round shoulder and around base of both pieces, engraved, minor dents, William F. Ladd, New York City, 1828-45 .... **1,200.00**

Goblet, 6-1/2" h and 6-3/4" h, Simon Chaundron, Philadelphia, PA, 1812-15, marked "Chaundron" in banner, floriform, raised flutes at base of bowls, applied foliate band on bases, price for pr, 16 troy oz **3,750.00**

Jug, 7" h, J. B. Jones & Co. makers, 2nd quarter 19th C, inverted pear-shaped body, scroll handle and stepped neck, round stepped foot, name engraved under spout, 12 troy oz **700.00**

Mug, 4" h, John L. Westervelt, Newburgh, NY maker, mid-19th C, cylindrical, fine beading to foot and rim, scroll handle, central cartouche engraved with name and dated 1863, engraved Greek key border, allover engine turned ground, 6 troy oz **200.00**

Pitcher, 8" h, mid-19th C, bulbous, molded rim above engraved band, body with all-over repoussé strawberries and vines, weighted circular foot with emb dec, inscription on front and foot **290.00**

Salt, 1-1/2" x 3-1/2", oval form, four hoofed feet, repoussé floral and wreath dec at knees, gold wash bowls, minor dents, Ball, Black & Co., New York City, 1851-76, 7 troy oz, pr **290.00**

American, compote, Kalo, hammered, floriform, monogram "GSH," stamped "STERLING HAND WROUGHT KALO SHOP CHICAGO, U.S.A., CHRISTMAS 1929," 7" x 9", **$1,100**.

Photo courtesy of David Rago Auctions, Inc.

American, serving bowl, Tiffany & Co., Art Deco, footed, marked "23356," approximately 47.10 oz, 12-1/2" d, 4-1/4" h, **$1,150**.

Photo courtesy of Pook & Pook.

Snuff box, stamped "PP," flattened ovoid form, bottom inscribed "I trust this triffle in thy mind will favor find, 1791," imperfections, 1-1/2" x 3-1/2" x 2-5/8", 2 troy oz **1,100.00**

Soup ladle, Simon Chaundron, Philadelphia, PA, 1812-15, marked "Chaundron" in banner, English crest dec, 14-1/2" l, 10 troy oz **920.00**

Sugar bowl, cov, 8" h, Gorham, mid-19th C, squat baluster, stepped foot, wide band of engine-turning, one plain and one engraved cartouche, two serpentine handles, domed lid with flower form finial, 17 troy oz, minor dents... **175.00**

Tablespoon, 8" l, front tips, back engraved, bowl with emb scallop shell below short drop handle, minor dents, wear, Samuel Edwards, Boston, 1705-62, 2 troy oz **635.00**

Tea service, unmarked, 19th C, 9-1/2" h teapot with hinged lid, creamer, cov sugar, lids with floriform knob finials attached to circle of ribbing, above round form bowl with shaped shoulders having vertical ribbing on lower half of body, raised on round stepped bases, four ball feet, applied tooled banding at neck, shoulder, and base, foliate devices attached to hollow strap handles and spout, 60 troy oz **885.00**

American, 1840-1920

Mostly sterling

There are two possible sources for the origin of the word *sterling*. The first is that it is a corruption of the name Easterling. Easterlings were German silversmiths who came to England in the Middle Ages. The second is that it is named for the sterling (little star) used to mark much of the early English silver.

Sterling is 92.5 percent per silver. Copper comprises most of the remaining alloy. American manufacturers began to switch to the sterling standard about the time of the Civil War.

Basket, 9" d, 3" h, Whiting Mfg Co., late 19th C, reticulated, sides with scrolls and diapering, scroll rim, three scroll feet, fluted base, monogrammed, 11 troy oz **460.00**

Bowl, 5" d, 3-1/4" h, Arthur Stone, Gardner, MA, chased decoration on bowl, circular stepped foot, imp mark with initial "H" **1,410.00**

Bread plate, 0-1/2" d, Reed & Barton, banded dec, monogrammed, marked "Sterling 700," set of 12, 50 troy oz **450.00**

Butter chip, 3" d, Gorham, gadrooned border, engraved dragon with crown, monogram for Henredon Family, price for eight-pc set **150.00**

Castor, 5-3/4" h, S. Kirk & Sons, Baltimore, Egyptian Revival, 1861-1868, urn form, domed lid with repoussé leaves, bud form finial, body with three cast loop handles, all-over repoussé foliates, three cast sphinx feet, monogram, 4 troy oz **690.00**

Center bowl, 14-1/2" d, Frank W Smith Silver Co., Inc., late 19th C, retailed by Bigelow, Kennard & Co., ovoid,

engraved with quilted style pattern, edges reticulated with engraved leafy scrolls, edge with wide cast border of rocaille shells and C-scrolls, monogrammed center, 31 troy oz **1,840.00**

Challis, 7" h, 3-1/2" d at rim, presentation, engraved "Award by the G & A.A. Society to W. F. Fannin for the best collection of Southern made Plows, Oct 1852," inscription flanked by repousse wheat sheaves, reverse side with repousse plow **1,650.00**

Cigarette case, 4-1/2" h, Reed & Barton, 1" w 14k yg band running entire length and reverse, hinged gate stamped "14kt" and "Sterling R & B," 4.79 troy oz **300.00**

Silver, American, Stieff, after dinner coffee service, Baltimore Rose pattern, overall repoussé floral decoration, 10" h hinged coffeepot with floral finial, 5" h creamer, 6-1/2" h covered sugar, 14" d circular tray with polished surface, repoussé trim, and "sterling, W, hand chased, 700," **$3,500**.

Photo courtesy of Alderfer Auction Co.

Coffee set, Gorham, coffeepot, creamer, cov sugar, 16" tray, 73.05 troy oz **550.00**

Compote, 8-3/4" d, 4-1/2" h, Bigelow, Kennard & Co., late 19th C, Etruscan-style, bowl with central roundel of classical man holding grapes, seated woman with baby, dog, beaded surround, engraved anthemion and flowerheads, short stem with single rib to center, trumpet foot, plain flattened loop handles, applied Greek key rim, 22 troy oz **700.00**

Dish, 8" l, Howard & Co., quatrefoil form, filigree sides in fleur-de-pattern, applied ornamentation on rim of "C" and "S" scrolls and shells, marked "Howard & Co., New York, Sterling, 1903," 15 troy oz **300.00**

Dresser set, International Silver Co., Meriden, CT, early 20th C, cut glass powder jar, hair receiver, three dresser jars, all with sterling lids, pair of cut glass perfume bottles with silver mounted stoppers, hair brush, two clothes brushes, mirror, nail buffer, shoehorn, and nail file, all with engraved and banded rims, monograms **920.00**

Fish knives, Gorham, Providence, Aesthetic Movement, late 19th C, blades with ornate monograms and bright cut foliates, mixed metal Japanese-style Kozuka handles with molded dec, price for set of 12 .... **2,300.00**

Flask

4-1/4" l, late 19th/early 20th C, ovoid, emb foliates on textured ground, domed lid with attached chain, approx two troy oz **175.00**

9" h, Clarence Vanderbilt, New York, c1909-35, rect, overall textured finish, reeded circular screw cap, approx 10 troy oz **260.00**

Fruit bowl, 12-1/2" d, Dominick & Haff, late 19th/early 20th C, retailed by Shreve, Crump & Low, fluted int., wide reticulated edge with realistically modeled chrysanthemums and daisies, 21 troy oz **1,150.00**

American, ladle, Gorham, no monogram, **$275**.

Photo courtesy of Wiederseim Associates, Inc.

Ice cream slice, 10" l, George W. Shiebler & Co., late 19th C, hammered finish, handle with Roman style male medallion on end, engraved bands of classical style designs, gold washed blade with further classical style engraving, medallion to lower right, central horizontal band of further small medallions, monogrammed on back of handle, 6 troy oz **4,025.00**

Ice water pitcher
12-1/2" h, Jaccard & Co., 1870, emb and chased dec **210.00**
16-3/4" h, Rogers Smith & Co., c1872, tilting, pitcher stand, goblet, and tumbler all dec with emb scenic bands of walrus hunters in icy water, enameled lined pitcher **550.00**

Jug, Lewis E. Jenks, Boston, c1875, 10" h, vasiform, shaped lid with cast bird finial, lid and body with all over repoussé foliates, central monogrammed cartouche, spreading circular foot, 17 troy oz **635.00**

Kettle-on-stand, 13" h, bombe repoussé allover with flowers and leaves on fine stippled ground, hinged cover with similar dec, floral finial, fixed handle, circular base with conforming dec on four paw feet issuing from foliage, marked "S. Kirk & So., #101," c1903-24, burner marked "Jl sterling silver," 56 oz **2,500.00**

Mustard pot, 4-1/2" d, S. Kirk & Son, Baltimore, mid 19th C, vegetal finial, glass liner, 7 troy oz **150.00**

Perfume flask, Dominick & Haff, 9" l, tapered cylindrical, floral chased and emb at lid, neck, and base, wide band of horizontal fluting at center, monogrammed, 5 troy oz **490.00**

Platter, Dominick & Haff, oval, border repoussé with flowers and leaves on fine matted ground, monogrammed, 16 oz **475.00**

Punch bowl, 10-1/4" d, 6-1/8" h, circular stand with shaped rim, interior gold washed, chased and repousse with garlands, scallop-shells and swags, maker's mark "BSC" on base **750.00**

Roast platter, 20-5/8" l, 14-1/8" w, Gorham, early 20th C, Greek key border ... **750.00**

Salad serving set, spoon and fork, 9" l, Chambord pattern, Reed & Barton, monogrammed, 5 oz, 6 dwt **200.00**

Salt, open, 3-1/4" l, 1-3/4" h, Black, Starr & Frost, late 19th C, Classical Revival style, ovoid body, hoof feet terminating in lion's heads, red glass liner, 8 troy oz, four-pc set **450.00**

Salver, 9-3/4" d, Whiting M.F.G. Co., center chased with crab caught in a fishing net, monogrammed MLI, planished rim, shaped feet, 20.35 oz **1,195.00**

Sauce ladle, 6-3/4" l, Wood & Hughes, New York, second half 19th C, scalloped bowl, beaded handle with portrait medallion of classical warrior, monogrammed on reverse, 1 troy oz **320.00**

Serving dish, cov, 8-7/8" w, 11-5/8" l, Thomas Kirkpatrick, NY, third quarter 19th C, oval, domed lid with beaded band, cast stag finial, emb key pattern and beading on underside of rim, base with similar dec, some loses, 59 troy oz **1,035.00**

Tazza, 7-1/8" d, 2-1/2" h, Howard & Co., dated 1898, vessel with wide reticulated band and applied scroll rim, center monogram, applied scroll base, reticulated foot, pr, 19 troy oz **700.00**

Tea and coffee service, gadrooned border, chased with floral sprays and arabesques, monogrammed A.P.A., 15" h hot water kettle on lampstand, coffeepot, teapot, creamer, cov sugar, double handled waste bowl, all marked; together with silver plate tray, 164.05 oz **2,400.00**

Tea service
Ball, Black & Co., third quarter 19th C, tapered ovoid teapot, cov sugar, helmet-shaped open creamer, each with applied profile medallion and anthemion engraving, pendant handles, monogrammed, 36 troy oz. **2,185.00**

American, tea set, Dunkirk Silversmiths, coffeepot, teapot, creamer, double-handled covered sugar, and waste bowl, ovoid form, floral repoussè decoration, marked "Hand Chased/500/Sterling," approximately 72 troy oz, **$900.**

Photo courtesy of Alderfer Auction Co.

American, tea set, Gorham, 10" h coffeepot, teapot, creamer, double handled covered sugar, and waste bowl, ovoid form, acanthus leaf and beaded details, engraved with crown over "RR," monogrammed "MGD," wooden handles on tea and coffee pots, marked "2910/ Sterling," minor denting, approximately 74 troy oz, **$900.**

Photo courtesy of Alderfer Auction Co.

Gorham, made for Blanche M. Halle, Cleveland, OH, each pc stamped with her name, panels separated by ribs, dec with repousse and chased trumpet urns of fruit, lids with carved ivory pineapple finials, 10-1/2" h teapot, 11-1/2" h coffeepot, creamer, cov double handled sugar, waste bowl, 18-1/2" x 30" tray, 276 troy oz **4,675.00**
Gorham, Plymouth pattern, coffeepot, teapot, creamer, cov sugar, waste bowl, monogrammed, 55 troy oz, some dents to sugar lid . **875.00**
Shreve, Stanwood & Co., 1860, 16" h hot water urn on stand, creamer, cov sugar, open sugar, and 9" h teapot, ovoid, beaded detailing, lids with swan finials, domed stepped foot, urn with presentation inscription on side, burner and one sugar lid missing, 35 troy oz . **2,185.00**

Tea tray, 17-7/8" w, 25-3/4" l, Gorham, Providence, 1912, shaped molded rim, beaded band, pierced handles, monogrammed, 114 troy oz **1,725.00**

Tete-a-tete, Gorham, Providence, 1880, 4" h teapot, creamer, open sugar, cone shape, ball finial, reeded handles, banded necks, gilt interiors, monogrammed, 16 troy oz **320.00**

Travel clock, 3-5/8" l, 3-1/8" w, Wm Kerr & Co., late 19th C, plain rect case with rounded corners, eight-day movement, oct goldtone engine-turned face, black Roman numerals, silver surround with engine turning, engraved scrolls and floral sprays, monogrammed cover **200.00**

Tray, 10-1/4" w, 14-1/4" l, Reed & Barton, Taunton, MA, late 19th/early 20th C, rect, shaped molded rim with openwork and engraved band, monogrammed center, 24 troy oz **350.00**

Trophy pitcher, Whiting, New York, Harvard University, c1892, cylindrical, inverted rim, waisted body with inscription on front, circular base with molded scroll dec, 33 troy oz **1,380.00**

Vase
15-3/4" h, J. E. Caldwell & Co., late 19th/early 20th C, tapered baluster form with engraved laurel wreath on each side, one with monogram, everted rim with engraved band of lines and circles, trumpet foot with similarly engraved band, 34 troy oz **750.00**
20-1/2" h, Gorham, flared draped rim, scalloped edge, bulbous base, pedestal foot, engraved scroll, foliage, and floral urn designs, figural accents, monogrammed central cartouche, marked "1083L, Sterling," 99 troy oz **3,850.00**

Water pitcher
Dominick & Haff, New York, 20th C, 9" h, vasiform, molded rim, "S" scroll handle, molded base, 22 troy oz **375.00**
Gorham, Providence, 1885, 9-1/4" h, paneled vasiform, rim and base with beaded bands, handle with cast acanthus dec, octagonal molded base, monogrammed, 26 troy oz **635.00**

American, water pitcher, presentation type, Tiffany & Co., 1875-91 mark, baluster body, repoussè and chased with Bacchanal couple, medallions framed by scrolling grape vines and acanthus leaf tips, centering presentation tablet inscription 'Monmouth Park, July 12th 1879, Three Quarter Dash, Gentlemen Riders Won By Mr. W. C. Sanford's, Brg. Kadi by Lexington, Owner," wrapped anthemion-form handle rising from bacchanal mask, 38 oz 4 dwt., 8-3/4" h, **$5,350.**

Photo courtesy of Sloans & Kenyon Auctions.

American, water pitcher, unmarked, 7-1/2" h, **$395.**

Photo courtesy of Wiederseim Associates, Inc.

Continental

Generations have enjoyed silver created by Continental silversmiths. Expect to find well-executed forms with interesting elements. Most Continental silver is well marked.

Austria
Candlesticks, pr, 12-1/2" h, Rococo-style, late 19th C, paneled baluster stem and socket, scrolled weighted base, removable bobeche, lacquered **690.00**

Casket, 3-3/8" w, 5-1/4" l, mid/late 19th C, rect, lid with cast pear form finial, molded rim and foot, waisted body with silver mount on lock, 14 troy oz **575.00**

Order, 6" l, 1929-30, traces of gilt, inscribed "HM 1929/30," marked, 1.30 oz **120.00**

Continental
Asparagus server, 11-1/4" l, late 19th C, reticulated handles topped by crowned lion's head, flowerheads and scrolls, standing figure, ending in cherub face above floral basket flanked by cherub herms over reticulation, blades reticulated with C-scrolls and engraved with flowers and further scrolls, monogrammed, 9 troy oz **230.00**

Beaker, 17th C, silver gilt, tapering cylindrical form, circular gadrooned foot, upper body engraved with strapwork enclosing arabesques, base chased with two bands of bosses, 3.35 oz **3,850.00**

Candelabra, 21-1/2" h, three-light, shaped sq lobed foot with scroll and floral rim rising to fluted stem applied with similar dec, two scrolling foliate branches, central fixed sconce, detachable bobeches, convertible to candlestick, engraved with monogram below crown, weighted base **900.00**

Condiment jar, 4-3/4" h, late 19th/early 20th C, formed as sedan chair, stamped with scrolls and cartouches of dancing couples, hinged lid with quadripartite finial, cobalt blue glass liner, restorations, 5 troy oz **375.00**

Creamer, 5-1/2" l, 4-1/4" h, figural, horned cow, fly hinged lid, 19th C **800.00**

Oil lamp, 29" h, tapered ovoid form, chased overall with grapes and vines, associated pierced silvered metal shade **720.00**

Spoon, 6-1/4" l, possibly 17th C, figural terminal, pear shaped bowl chased on obverse with armorial crest, inscribed "MIS Df HS, ANNO 1642, WER-ALTID LYKLIG," verso inscribed "A," marked, 1.80 oz **420.00**

Tea and coffee service, foliate decorated handles and spouts, reeded decoration on rims, seven pieces in original fitted case, 6" h teapot, 8" h coffeepot, 11-1/2" h hot water kettle on stand, 5" h covered sugar, 4-3/4" h creamer, 3" h waste bowl, imp marks for Frank W. Smith Silver Co., Inc., and Bailey, Banks & Biddle Co., stamped "Sterling, 1259," late 19th or early 20th C, monogrammed "RPFC," 82 troy oz, mahogany case with upper compartment fitted for tea and coffee service, lower drawer for flatware, 23" w, 16" d, 16-1/2" h, scattered denting, some discoloration, box scratched, case and set married, **$1,200**.

Photo courtesy of Alderfer Auction Co.

Danish

Coffee service, Georg Jensen Silversmithy, 1933-44, Blossom pattern, 7-1/8" h coffee pot, mkd "no. 2B"; cream jug, mkd "no. 2A"; waste bowl, mkd "no. 2A"; 25.10 oz **2,650.00**

Compote, round bowl over round stepped standard, base imp "Denmark 300" at bowl center, 6-5/8" d, 5-3/8" h, price for pr **290.00**

Flatware service, Georg Jensen Silversmithy, post 1945, Acorn pattern, 12 each dinner forks, salad forks, oyster forks, dinner spoons, dessert spoons, cream soup spoons, demitasse spoons, dinner knives, butter knives; two serving spoons, one serving fork, 111 pcs, 119.55 oz **7,200.00**

Low bowl, 7-5/8" d, 2-1/8" h, circular foot, imp Georg Jensen, "G830s," in beaded oval, signed in script .. **1,645.00**

Water pitcher, 9-3/4" h, 20th C, tapered egg-shaped body, flared stem with beading to top, stepped foot, spout with curved reeding to underside, wooden handle with stylized floral terminal to top **750.00**

Wine coaster, 4-3/4" d, F. Hingelberg, 20th C, molded rim, twisted wire sides, composition base, price for pr **490.00**

Dutch

Bowl, 14-1/4" l, 3" h, 19th C, .833 fine, Dutch export mark, repoussé, lobed, reserves with chased and emb country scenes, two pierced handles with putto to top, central flowers flanked by putto riding dolphins, 15 troy oz **460.00**

Box, 2-5/8" w, 5-1/2" l, late 19th C, .833 silver, rect, shaped lid with engraved nativity scene within foliates, base with two biblical scenes, banded sides with engraved foliates, 8 troy oz **960.00**

Chatelaine, 12-1/8" l, c1890, cast brooch with scene of putti with goddess, medallion mounted chains supporting two boxes, cylindrical container, pair of scissors, stylized crown, 9 troy oz **600.00**

Coffeepot, 8" h, late 19th C, .833 fine, baluster form pot with all-over scroll and foliage repoussé, windmill vignette on one side, scroll cartouche topped by crown flanked by putto on other side, legs topped by crowned human masks, four ball and claw feet, turned wood handle set at right angle to ram-horned grotesque spout, flattened lid with vertical ribbing, rampant lion finial, 11 troy oz ... **800.00**

Pitcher, 5-1/2" h, late 19th C, .833 line, baluster form, neck with band of fluting, repoussé to lower section of foliage, birds and putti, domed foot with vertical ribbing, spout with putto, beaded serpentine handle, lid with vertical reeding, repoussé and vegetal finial, base engraved "Esther Cleveland," 6 troy oz, descended in family of Grover Cleveland **260.00**

French, .950 fine

Coffeepot, 9-1/4" h, third quarter 19th C, pear-shaped, cast quadripartite scroll embellished serpentine spout and handle, heat stops, domed lid with flower form finial, 22 troy oz **460.00**

Dish, cov, undertray, Paris, 1819-38, "C. P." maker's mark, cylindrical body with acanthus and flat leaf handles, rim with beading and flat leaf band, base with band of flat leaves, foot with band of laurel, lid with beaded edge, removable circular handle formed as cornucopia on leaf and flower base, fitted leather case, 30 troy oz **2,615.00**

Fish serving platter, 27-3/4" l, 11-1/2" w, oval, reeded rim, monogrammed, 66 troy oz **1,265.00**

Serving dish, 11-3/4" l, 2-1/4" h, third quarter 19th C, oval, two shell handles, vertical reeded border, 17 troy oz **490.00**

Sweetmeat dish, 5-1/2" l, 5" h, Odiot, Paris, maker, late 19th/ 20th C, shell form vessel drawn by sea creatures, reins held by two putti, flanking central standing putto poised as Neptune, holding trident-form fork, shaped rect base cast as water, 65 troy oz, pr **2,100.00**

Tureen, cov, 12-3/4" l, 10-1/2" h, third/fourth quarter 19th C, sprays of acorns and oak leaves to top, reeded rim, lid with flat leaf rim, stem with reeded shoulder, oval foot, flat leaf band, angular handles with flat leaf to bottom, stylized corn finial about flat leaf and lotus ground **1,840.00**

Continental, centerpiece, oval, foliate scroll and shell feet, sides pierced with guilloches, hung with ribbon-tied berried laurel swags between bands of vitruvian scrolls, pierced anthemion, open double scrolls handles, fitted with silver-plated liner, crowned A, crowned P and crowned fleur-de-lis marks, 27 oz, 14" h, **$1,100**.

Photo courtesy of Sloans & Kenyon Auctions.

German, .800 fine

Basket, 14" l, shaped oval, paneled sides pierced with flowers, garlands, and scrolling foliage centering four vacant cartouches, center repoussé with flowers, foliage, and three putti at play, 15 oz, 8 dwt **200.00**

Beaker, cov, 7-3/4" h, 18th C, silver gilt, chased with swags and tasseled drapery, highlighted with matting, marked on cover and base, 8.95 oz **2,400.00**

Box, 5-1/4" x 3-1/4" x 1-1/2", rect, hinged lid, Roman chariot scene in relief, beaded edge, reeded sides with vine accents, marked "800 Germany" **200.00**

Bread tray, 15" x 10-1/2", repousse, cartouches of courtship coono, imp Gorman hallmarks and "800," c1920 .... **920.00**

Kettle-on-stand, 16" h, compressed circular with lobed sides, four hoof feet, detachable cover with wooden finial, central swing partial wooden handle, multi-scroll stand with border, 48 oz, 8 dwt **325.00**

Sauceboat, 10-3/4" l, late 19th/early 20th C, shape of open-mouthed fish, emb and engraved scales, open back with molded rim, tail shape handle, supported by cast fins, glass eyes, 13 troy oz **1,495.00**

Serving dish, 12" d, 3-1/2" h, Wilhelm T. Binder, c1900, rounded trefoil shape, three handles, repoussé leaf bud and line dec, scalloped, ribbed glass insert, imp "WTB, 800 fine" **1,150.00**

Tankard, 5-1/4" h, 17th C, silver gilt, barrel embossed with strapwork enclosing male masks above dentilated band, double scroll handle, cover with baluster finial, marked on footrim and cover, 9.45 oz **5,750.00**

Wedding cup, 9" h, figural, beaded figure with chased and emb skirt, cup chased and emb with scrolls and grotesques, 15 troy oz **1,955.00**

Italian

Asparagus tongs, F. Broggi, Milan 20th C, 5-1/4" l, individual, plain, tapered form, set of six, 6 troy oz **115.00**

Punch bowl, 12-5/8" d, 10-1/2" h, late 19th/early 20th C, repoussé, bowl with band of flat leaves to base below further continuous hunt scene of men attacking various animals, domed foot with band of flat leaves below continuous hunt scene, removable liner, 146 troy oz **4,025.00**

Continental, salver, chased floral decoration, early hallmark with heart with P surmounted by crown, zigzag below, 7" d, **$375**.

Photo courtesy of Wiederseim Associates, Inc.

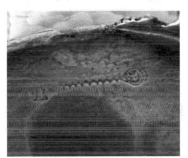

Close-up of hallmark, heart with P surmounted by crown, zigzag below.

Photo courtesy of Wiederseim Associates, Inc.

Portuguese, .833 silver

Bowl, 11-3/4" d, Oporto, 20th C, molded scroll and shell rim, band of chased dec, molded circular foot, 14 troy oz **230.00**

Chalice, 12-1/2" h, domed lid with applied openwork foliate band, engraved bands and cruciform finial, bowl with engraved band with Latin inscription, applied gothic style openwork mounts, stem with beaded and engraved knop, stepped circular base, int. gilt, 31 troy oz **690.00**

Ewer, 11-3/4" h, maker's mark "S&P," late 19th/early 20th C, bulbous, molded shaped rim, body with chased stippled dec, emb foliate, scroll, and shell band, cast scroll handle, molded circular foot with emb dec, 33 troy oz **815.00**

Kettle-on-stand, 14-1/4" h, maker's mark effaced, second half 19th C, inverted pear form, domed lid with cased foliates and wood urn finial, upright handle with cast silver acanthus mounts, body with all-over chased and engraved foliates and scrolls, circular stand with four scroll legs and shell feet, chased and engraved burner with turned wood handle, 54 troy oz **920.00**

Salver, 11 5/8" d, molded openwork scroll and foliate rim, bright cut foliate dec on face, three cast legs with shell feet, 25 troy oz **350.00**

Tray, 13-1/2" w, 22-5/8" l, maker's mark "QP," 20th C, rect, openwork raised rim with molded grape dec, cast foliate handles, face with engraved dec, 85 troy oz **1,265.00**

Swedish

Hot water kettle on lampstand, 14-3/4" h, maker's mark "AH," globular body with gadroon rim and cover, acorn finial, stand raised on s-scroll legs terminating in shell-form feet, marked on kettle base, cover and stand, base and stand with illegible English marks, 49.20 oz **850.00**

English

From the 17th century to the mid-19th century, English silversmiths set the styles which inspired the rest of the world. The work from this period exhibits the highest degree of craftsmanship. English silver is actively collected in the American antiques marketplace.

Basting spoon, 13-3/4" l, George I, London, 1714, Brittania Standard, rat tail/Hanoverian pattern, back of terminal inscribed with crest, mkd on back of stem, maker's mark illegible, 5.80 oz **2,155.00**

Basket, 6" d, 3-1/2" h, J. R. Hennell maker, London, 1884, Victorian, reticulated foliate pattern, circular banding, shaped edge with bead and flat leaf rim, four scroll and cylinder feet with husk swags, glass liner, 21 troy oz, pr **1,725.00**

Bowl, 5-1/4" d, 1-1/2" h, W. Comyns & Sons maker, London, 1902, Edward VII, shallow bowl emb with shield-shaped panels, hand-hammered surface, low flower form foot, 7 troy oz...... **435.00**

Candelabra, pr, 19" h, William Comyns & Son, 1908-09, Edward VII, silver gilt, in Neo-Classical taste, fluted domed base rising to fluted baluster stem hung with floral swags, removable branches with laurel leaf arms supporting candle sockets and vase shaped nozzles, each fully marked on exterior base and detachable nozzle, 232.05 oz **11,360.00**

English, candlesticks, pair, George II-style, square drip pans above stop-fluted column, stepped square weighted bases with gadrooned rims, spurious marks for London, 1846 and maker's mark ER, also bearing two illegible marks, possibly import marks, 11" h, **$2,125**.

Photo courtesy of Sloans & Kenyon Auctions.

Candlesticks, pr, Crichton Brothers, London, 1909-10, Charles II style, quadripartite shell-form base rising to smaller quadripartite shell-form drip pan, vase form standard rising above four open scrolls to fluted columnar sconce with shaped bobeche, each fully marked on base and underside of bobeche, stamped "Crichton Brothers, New York & London," 74.45 oz ... **3,700.00**

Castor, 5-3/4" h, Hester Bateman, London, 1788, George III, urn form, engraved pierced lid with cast urn finial, engraved bands at shoulder, waist, and spreading circular foot, 2 troy oz............................. **690.00**

Caudle cup, 6" h, 10-1/2" l, Samuel Wastell maker, London, 1704, William III, Brittania Standard, tapered cylindrical body with single applied molded band, cast ear-shaped handles, spreading domed foot, engraved on one side, heraldic device in rococo-style cartouche, 26 troy oz... **2,990.00**

Center bowl, 17" l, 5-1/2" h, Robert Garrard, London, 1811, George III, lobed ovoid body, two short scroll and acanthus handles, gadroon and shell border offset with two scroll details to each side, four cast paw feet topped by group of scrolls, 51 troy oz **4,325.00**

Chamberstick, 4" l, 1-3/4" h, W. Comyns maker, London, 1888, Victorian, chased and emb with flowers and scrolls, removable bobeche, handle with monogrammed thumb-piece, 2 troy oz.......... **115.00**

Charger, 11-3/4" d, Rebecca Emes and Edward Barnard, London, 1826, George IV, shaped edge, applied gadroon and shell border, engraved gartered heraldic device on rim, 29 troy oz **1,380.00**

Cigarette case, 4-1/2" h, c1944, engine turned ext., monogram, 5.29 oz **70.00**

Coaster, 4-3/8" d, "W.H.H." maker's mark, Birmingham, 1904, Edward VII, round, inset to center with George III Irish 10-pence bank tokens dated 1905, 4 troy oz, pr...... **115.00**

Coffeepot, 14-1/2" h, William Grundy maker, London, 1767, George III, baluster, spreading foot, scroll handle with ivory heat stops, serpentine spout with rocaille shell to base, flat leaf to spout, engraved monogram within foliate rococo-style cartouche, domed hinged lid with spiral reeded egg-shaped finial, 60 troy oz **5,750.00**

Compote, 12-1/2" d, 7" h, Benjamin Smith maker, London, 1845, Victorian, bowl with shaped edge and vertical ribbing, everted rim with applied grapevine dec, tree-trunk form base with twining grapevine, 36 troy oz.. **1,150.00**

Cream jug, 5-1/4" h, Hester Bateman, London, 1782, George III, vasiform, chased beaded rim, body with repoussé farm scenes surrounding central cartouche, trumpet foot with spreading rim, 3 troy oz, restoration................. **225.00**

Cup, 5-5/8" h, Samuel Godbeheve, Edward Wigan and J. Bolt makers, London, 1800, George III, baluster form, two handles, four drill holes in base, 11 troy oz **490.00**

Demitasse spoon, 5" l, John Wren maker, London, 1791, George III, bright cut engraved stem, fluted bowl, 3 troy oz, set of six........ **260.00**

Dish cross, 12" l, "BD" maker's mark, (Burrage Davenport), London, 1772, George III, pierced shell form feet and plate supports, burner with gadrooned rim, 15 troy oz **1,265.00**

Egg cup frame, Henry Nutting maker, London, 1800, George III, reeded central handle, four ball feet, six associated Sheffield egg cups, five associated demitasse spoons, 18 troy oz **550.00**

Entree dish, cov, 12-1/8" l, 5-3/4" h, "BS" makers mark, London, 1820, George IV, lid modified with later band of foliate repoussé and engraved with heraldic crest and monograms, base with gadroon and shell rim, removable leaf and shell handle, 67 troy oz.... **1,725.00**

Epergne, 10-1/2" l, 11-3/4" h, "GJ DF" maker's mark, London, 1913, George V, central stem below navette-shaped reticulated basket with applied border, flanked by smaller removable baskets on scrolled arms, ovoid reticulated base with applied scroll and shell border, four scroll feet, 76 troy oz **6,325.00**

Fish server, 11-1/4" l, attributed to John Neville, London, 1770, George III, reticulated blade with scrolling foliage, stem end with shell, handle, engraved with gadrooned edge, central heraldic device, 4 troy oz.................. **1,100.00**

Flatware service, partial, Spaulding-Gorham, London, 1938, George VI, six dinner forks, six lunch forks, six salad forks, six dinner forks, 18 fish forks, six dinner knives, 18 fish knives, six butter knives, 18 place spoons, six soup spoons, 18 cream soup spoons, 21 teaspoons, 18 five o'clock teaspoons, six demitasse spoons, 12 ice tea spoons, monogrammed MMR, 18 George VI/Elizabeth II fruit knives, maker's mark CWF, 1952, 189 pcs, 221.75 oz **3,150.00**

Flower bowl, George III, Paul Storr, classical design based on Warwick vase, hallmarked London, 1808 .... **4,700.00**

Goblet, 6-1/2" h, maker's mark partially obscured (attributed to Henry Greenway), London, 1775, George II, beaded collar, tapered round funnel bowl, beaded trumpet foot, engraved coat of arms in roundel, 16 troy oz, pr **1,955.00**

Hot water kettle on stand, 12" h, John Emes maker, London, 1807, George III, lid partially reeded with wood finial, pot with ovoid body partially reeded with gadrooned edging, on tapered circular foot, fluted tap, upright silver and wood handle, stand with gadrooned rim with burner and cover, flat leaf legs, four hairy paw feet with wooden ball supports, pot engraved with mottoed coat of arms, small heraldic device on pot lid, burner lid, and burner, 83 troy oz **2,100.00**

Jug, cov, 7-3/4" h, "C. W." maker's mark, London, 1769, George III, later Victorian adaptations, stamped bands flanking convex band at rim, ovoid body with twisted reeding and fluting to lower section, central cartouche flanked by C-scrolls, serpentine handle, domed foot, short spout, domed hinged lid with Victorian hallmarks, twisted reeding, fluting on urn finial, 18 troy oz **400.00**

Marrow scoop, 9" l, Richard Pargeter, London, 1737-38, George II, back engraved "BWM," mkd, 1.65 oz . **500.00**

Meat skewer, 12-3/4" l, Thomas Whipham & Charles Wright, London, 1761-62, George III, tapering, plain loop terminal, engraved "V," mkd, 3.90 oz **210.00**

Mirror, 14-1/4" h, 10" d, "JR SJ" makers, London, 1887, Victorian, rect, curved top, reticulated with scrolls and flowers, mask center at base, grotesque beasts on either corner, beveled edge mirror, easel stand on back ... **980.00**

Muffineer, 8-1/2" h, Charles Stuart Harris maker, Brittania standard marks, London, 1899, tapered paneled lid with engraving, baluster form finial, paneled baluster form, tiered foot, 14 troy oz **800.00**

Mug, Richard Beale, London, 1731, George II, cylindrical, cast "S" scroll handle, molded circular foot, engraved crest, 6 troy oz, 3-3/4" h **980.00**

Mustard pot, attributed to William Barrett II, 1827, George III, circular, disk finial, reeded rim and base, reticulated sides with engraved foliates and urns, associated glass insert, 3 troy oz, 2-1/2" h **290.00**

Porringer, cov, 4-3/4" d, 4" h, maker's mark II, London, 1691, William & Mary, tapered body, engraved armorial within baroque strapwork cartouche below cast scroll handles, raised cov with central fluted dec and baluster finial, mkd only on body, 10.80 oz **1,800.00**

English, punch ladle, bearing marks of William Gibson and John Langman, London, c1899, 13" l; together with English silver punch ladle, c1789, bearing mark of "T.S." (Thos. Shephard), 13-1/2" l, **$500**.

Photo courtesy of Pook & Pook.

Salt, open, 4" l, Walker & Hall, Sheffield, 1902-03, Edward VII, cobalt blue glass liner, mkd **180.00**

Salver
12-3/8" d, John Tuite maker, London, 1783, George II, shaped molded rim offset with shells, central engraved coat of arms in rococo cartouche, four scrolled leaf feet, 32 troy oz **2,185.00**
16-1/4" d, John Cotton & Thomas Head maker, London, 1813, George III, beaded and ribbed border, four beaded and ribbed feet, center engraved with mottoed coat of arms, 64 troy oz .. **3,750.00**
17-1/4" d, Mappin & Webb makers, London, 1946, shaped edge with bead shell border, four scrolled feet, 60 troy oz **1,610.00**
22-7/8" h, Robert Abercomby maker, London, 1750, George II, shaped edge, engraved with wide band of florals, fruits, shells, scrolls, and diapered cartouches, four paw feet topped by shells, engraved central Chinoiserie-style coat of arms, 156 troy oz **4,320.00**

Sauceboats, pr, 7-1/4" l, maker's mark "T. D. & S.," Birmingham, 1947, George III style, oval form, shaped borders, flying scroll handles, hoof feet with fluted shell headers, marked on bases, 15 oz **400.00**

Sauce ladle, 13" l, Hester Bateman, London, 1790, George III, Old English pattern, mkd on back of terminal, 4.30 oz **450.00**

Sauce tureen, cov, 9-1/4" l, 5 1/2" h, George Smith and Thomas Hayter makers, London, 1804, George III, domed lid with urn finial, boat shaped body with ribbed rim, loop handles, pedestal foot, lid and body monogrammed, 33 troy oz, pr **2,760.00**

Serving spoon, 11-3/4" l, William Eley and William Fearn, London, 1818, George III, engraved crest, 3 oz, 6 dwt **175.00**

Soup tureen, cov, 14-1/2" l, 10-1/4" h, William Elliott maker, London, 1819, George III, gadrooned rim, acanthus handles, four paw feet terminating in shell and acanthus leaves, lid with two bands of gadrooning and ribbed removable handle, engraved coat of arms on body and lid, 136 troy oz **7,475.00**

Spoon
6-1/8" l, illegible marker's mark, London, 1540-41, Henry VIII, maidenhead terminal with traces of gilding, crowned leopard's head mark very worn, 1.00 oz ... **5,750.00**
6-5/8" l, Elizabeth I, London, 1589-90, prick-dot engraved with initials "HRM" to back of bowls, lion Sejant Affronte terminal, traces of gilding, 2.90 oz, worn terminals, pr **5,750.00**

Standish, 11-3/8" l, 7-1/2" w, J. C. Vickery maker, London, 1906, Edward VII, rect, reeded border, two horizontal pen wells, two tapered inkwells with canted corners and hinged lids, central ovoid covered well, hinged lid fitted with eight-day clock, four ball and claw feet, some restoration needed, 32 troy oz **2,100.00**

English, sugar caster, $125.
Photo courtesy of Dotta Auction Co., Inc.

Sugar basket, 5-1/2" l, 3-1/2" w, Peter & Ann Bateman, London, 1798, George III, navette shape, molded banded rim and swing handle, engraved body with reticulated bands, banded oval foot, monogrammed, cobalt glass insert, 3 troy oz **920.00**

Sugar bowl, 6" l, 5-3/8" h, Georgian, marks rubbed, beaded rim, ovoid body with ribbon-tied floral sprays and swags, roundels on each side, heraldic device, spiraled loop handles, trumpet foot with bands of bright cut engraving, 5 troy oz **350.00**

Sugar tongs, Georgian, cast with shell, foliage, scrolls engraved with flowers, center vacant cartouche, 1 oz, 2 dwt **95.00**

Sweetmeat dish, 9-1/8" l, 5-5/8" w, 2-1/4" h, R & S Garrard maker, London, 1879, ovoid, flanked by male and female figure, auricular scroll and stylized shell handle, four periwinkle shell feet, 13 troy oz **1,495.00**

Tablespoon, 8-3/4" l, William Eley, London, 1826, George IV, fiddle pattern, monogrammed, pr, 6 troy oz **200.00**

Tankard, 7-3/4" h, John Longlands I maker, Newcastle, 1769, George III, tapered cylindrical form, plain body with engraved cartouche, serpentine handle with reticulated thumb-piece, gadrooned foot rim, slightly domed lid with gadrooned rim, engraved presentation inscription, lacquered, 26 troy oz **1,265.00**

Taperstick, 4" h, London, possibly early 18th C, octagonal base with urn-shaped stem rising from circular well to banded campana sconce, base engraved with crest, worn marks, maker's mark appears to be mark for Samuel Margas, 5.10 oz **2,160.00**

Tazza, pr, 16" h, two-tier, R. & S. Garrard, London, 1864-65, Victorian, in the Renaissance taste, domed base and baluster stem supporting two dishes pierced with shells and chased with interlaced strapwork, top dish engraved with crest, with an inscription reading "Presented to Viscount Cole BY THE TENANTRY OF THE ENNISKILLEN ESTATES, ON THE OCCASION OF HIS MARRIAGE 12th JULY 1869," both marked on underside of base and exterior base of smaller dish with maker's mark, duty mark, lion passant, and date letter, 144.50 oz **9,000.00**

Teapot
5" h, attributed to Augustus Le Sage, London, 1771, George III, cylindrical, disc finial,

wood ear handle, engraved antelope crest on lid and side, 13 troy oz **1,100.00**
6-1/4" h, George Smith & Thomas Hayter, London, 1796, George III, fluted ovoid, engraved domed lid, bone mushroom finial and handle, engraved foliates and central crest, 15 troy oz, restorations **525.00**
10-1/2" l, 4-1/4" h, Andrew Fogelberg & Stephen Gilbert, London, 1786-87, George III, oval form, chased with arabesques, floral garlands, cov surmounted with ivory finial, monogrammed, mkd, 14.25 oz **550.00**

Teapot stand, 7" l, Robert & David Hennell, London, 1795, Georgian, oval with beveled corners, molded rim engraved, face with engraved and bright cut foliate bands, central cartouche, four feet, 5 troy oz, 4-7/8" w **435.00**

Tea and coffee service, Rebecca Eames & Edward Barnard, London, 1814-15, George III, 8-3/4" h coffeepot with gadrooned pedestal, teapot, creamer, open sugar, sq bulbous form, emb lids with cast foliate finials, molded gadrooned rims, bodies with bands of spiral reeding, four ball feet, 73 troy oz **2,300.00**

Tea service
7-3/4" h teapot, Peter, Ann, and William Bateman makers, London, 1800, George III, ovoid teapot, helmet shaped cov creamer with angular handle, cov sugar with angular handles, all with partial vertical lobing, bands of bright cut engraving and engraved heraldic device, wooden pineapple finials, 33 troy oz **1,495.00**
9" h coffeepot, 16" h kettle on stand, Crichton Bros. makers, London, 1930, George V, coffee and teapots, kettle on stand, creamer, open sugar, cov sugar, all with ovoid body, arcaded and ribbed banding, teapot and coffeepot with wooden handles topped with silver flat leaves, lion's head roundels, reamer and sugar with curved handles terminating in lion's head roundels, 174 troy oz . **2,990.00**

English, tea strainer, shaped handle with shell motif, hallmarked, 4" d, **$500.**

Photo courtesy of Alderfer Auction Co.

Tea urn, 15" h, maker's mark "I. R.," London, 1778, lid with tapered egg-shaped finial, beaded tape with ivory handle, beaded loop handles, four ball feet with stepped rect base and beaded edge, bright cut engraving throughout with husks, cartouches, and floral swags, 37 troy oz **2,100.00**

Tray, 25" l, 16-1/4" w, "EB" makers mark, London, 1822, George IV, rect, gadrooned border, handles with shells and leaves, four paw feet flanked by floral roundels and stylized wings, engraved allover pattern of flowers and leaves, center with mottoed crest and later monogram, 120 troy oz **2,760.00**

Trefid spoon, 10-1/8" l, 1686-87, stem mkd with arm and sword emerging from crown mark, round terminal, traces of gilding, 3.75 oz **2,400.00**

Trump indicator, 2-3/4" x 2-1/4", hallmarked Birmingham, round base, celluloid suit indicators suspended from pair of loops **200.00**

Waxjack, 6-1/2" h, attributed to Augustus Le Sage, London, third quarter 18th C, George III, cast handles, attached snuffer, spindle with spirally reeded bud form finial, domed base with beaded rim, supported by three cast claw and ball feet, inscription on base, 4 troy oz **980.00**

Wine coaster, 5-3/4" d, 2-3/4" h, Joseph and John Angel makers, London, 1846,

Victorian, applied scroll and shell rim, reticulated sides, engraved to base with scrolls, shells, and central heraldic crest, pr **5,465.00**

Irish

Fine examples of Irish silver are becoming popular with collectors.

Candlesticks, pr, George III/IV, Dublin, attributed to John Laughlin, Jr., larger gadrooned knob over gadrooned knob below partially vertically reeded stem with single horizontal beaded band, well with applied stylized wheat or grass fronds, domed gadrooned base, vertically reeded sconce, removable nozzle with gadrooned rim, small heraldic crest engraved on foot and nozzle, 49 troy oz **7,475.00**

Caudle cup, cov, 7-1/4" h, Dublin, mid-18th C, marked for John Hamilton, domed lid topped by ovoid finial, body with single molded band, crabstock handles, lobed spreading foot, no date mark, 37 troy oz, pr **5,175.00**

Cup, 4-7/8" h, mid-18th C, marked for John Letabliere, tapered cylindrical body with leaf cut card work, band of foliate engraving, domed spreading foot, scroll handles topped with flat leaves, engraved on one side with cartouche, no date marks, 44 troy oz, pr **5,465.00**

Ladle, 7" l, chased floral and scroll designs on silver bowl, Irish hallmarks and maker's mark for Phineas Garde, Corke, c1815, baleen handle, minor battering on rim **320.00**

Salver, 6-1/2" l, George II/III, Dublin, William Townsend maker, shaped molded border, engraved center with heraldic crest in rococo cartouche, three pad feet with scroll legs, 8 troy oz. **1,100.00**

Snuffer tray, George III, Dublin, 1798, William Doyle maker, octagonal boat shape, base with bright-cut engraved husk drops, heraldic crest within roundel flanked by leaves, sides reticulated with arcading, paterae, 4 troy oz **700.00**

Scottish

Not to be outdone by their Irish and English neighbors, Scottish silversmiths also created fine objects.

Berry spoon, Edinburgh, 1820, George Fenwick maker **75.00**

Punch ladle
13-1/2" l, Edinburgh, 1789, maker's mark "CD," 6 troy oz **300.00**
14-1/2" l, Edinburgh, 1820, maker's mark "AH," ovoid bowl, twisted baleen handle, silver end cap **150.00**

Silver, bowl, oval, paneled sides, shaped rim, footed base, two curving handles, molded glass liner with conforming shaped rim and starburst motif on underside, hallmarked "800" beneath rim, 7-1/2" w, 5-1/2" h, 17" l handle to handle, **$425.**

Photo courtesy of Alderfer Auction Co.

Sheffield, English

Sheffield silver, or Old Sheffield Plate, has a fusion method of silver-plating that was used from the mid-18th century until the mid-1880s, when the process of electroplating silver was introduced.

Sheffield plating was discovered in 1743, when Thomas Boulsover of Sheffield, England, accidentally fused silver and copper. The process consisted of sandwiching a heavy sheet of copper between two thin sheets of silver. The result was a plated sheet of silver, which could be pressed or rolled to a desired thickness. All Sheffield articles are worked from these plated sheets.

Most of the silver-plated items found today marked "Sheffield" are not early Sheffield plate. They are later wares made in Sheffield, England.

Basket, 7-3/4" w, 13-3/4" l, S. Smith & Son, England, second half 19th C, oval, molded foliate rim, emb and reticulated sides, cast foliage handles, oval reticulated and engraved base, cobalt blue glass liner **460.00**

Biscuit box, 7" w, 7-1/2" h, oval, hinged lid, gadrooned trim, lion mask side handles, attached tray base on ball feet, late 19th C **120.00**

Carving set, 16-1/2" l, fork, knife, and steel, engraved image of Windsor Castle on knife blade, horn handles, silver plated crown finials, leathered case, late 19th C......... **350.00**

Claret jug, 11" h, cut glass body mounted at neck, hinged cover, baluster finial, multi-scroll foliate handle, c19435 .... **500.00**

Domed lid, 22" h, 11" l, engraved armorial whippet, oval handle, early 19th C **575.00**

Pitcher, 7-1/4" h, finely chased quatrefoil medallions and feathering, Sheffield hallmarks for 1857 by John Fred Fenton, ivory insulators on handle, minor damage **520.00**

Plate, 9-3/4" d, circular, gadrooned rim, engraved Carlill crest, George III, price for pr **175.00**

Platter and meat cover, 26" l oval tree platter, four ball feet, two wooden handles, gadrooned rim, armorials on both sides, dome cover with gadrooned rim, reeded handles, engraved armorials **2,750.00**

Serving dish, cov, England, first half 19th C, rect, gadrooned rim and lid, cast branch and maple leaf handle, engraved coat of arms, 11-1/2" l, 8-5/8" w **230.00**

Tantalus, England, late 19th/early 20th C, central casket with two engraved hinged lids below handle, sides supporting two cut and pressed glass decanters, pedestal base supported by four column legs, 5-3/4" w, 15" l........................... **490.00**

Tray, 18-1/2" x 7-1/2", kidney shape, gadrooned rim, pierced gallery of open lattice work, centered engraved lion crest, early 20th C **120.00**

Vegetable dish, cov, 13" l, plated, shaped rect, applied grapevine, scroll, and foliage handle, monogrammed **250.00**

Wine bottle holder, 16" l, wooden base, vintage detail, ivory casters **275.00**

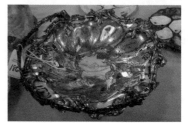

Silver-plated champagne bucket, rococo foliate border, two scrolling handles, footed, **$200**.

Silver, plated

Englishmen G. R. and H. Elkington are given credit for being the first to use the electrolytic method of plating silver in 1838.

An electroplated-silver article is completely shaped and formed from a base metal and then coated with a thin layer of silver. In the late 19th century, the base metal was Britannia, an alloy of tin, copper, and antimony. Other bases are copper and brass. Today, the base is nickel silver.

In 1847, Rogers Bros. of Hartford, Connecticut, introduced the electroplating process in America. By 1855, a number of firms were using the method to produce silver-plated items in large quantities.

The quality of the plating is important. Extensive polishing can cause the base metal to show through. The prices for plated-silver items are low, making them popular items with younger collectors.

Bacon warmer, George III style, rect, dentilated rim, turned wood handle, hinged cover with ivory finial, inscribed crest, 10-1/4" l............. **250.00**

Bun warmer, 12-1/2" l, oval, cover chased with flowers and foliage, beaded rim, paw feet, liner, two reeded handles **275.00**

Candelabra, pr, 12" h, Continental, three-light, tapering stem issuing central urn-form candle-cup and two scrolling branches supporting wax pan and conforming candle-cup, oval foot with reeded border, vertical flutes **150.00**

Candle lamp shade, Tiffany Studios, Grapevine pattern, domed, pierced grapevine design, imp "Tiffany Studios New York," 6-1/2" d, 2" d fitter rim, 3-3/8" h, minor dents, price for four **1,265.00**

Candlesticks, pr, 7-1/2" h, Wurtembergishe Metallwarenfabrik, sq base applied with bow-tie garlands and foliage, rim with stylized leaves and beads rising to Corinthian column stems, detachable bobeches with beaded rims **375.00**

Claret jug, 9-1/2" h, eagle-form, textured cranberry glass body with realistic silver plate head and feet, set with glass eyes, hinged at neck, clear draw handle, Continental, early 20th C **460.00**

Silver plate, centerpiece basket, center engraved armorial crest, scrolling foliate border, Victorian, **$200**.

Photo courtesy of Wiederseim Associates, Inc.

Coffee urn and stand, ovoid body, spout over reeded legs, paw feet joined to X-form stretcher raised on bun feet, cover surmounted with leaf and scroll finial, unmarked, 16" h........................... **300.00**

Egg cup, 2-3/4" h, England, early 20th C, stems formed as cast kangaroos resting in circular underplates, price for pr **100.00**

Epergne, 13-1/2" h, three pale blue patterned glass vases with central reeded shaft, tripod base, winged sea horses supports, marked "HW & Co.," top insert missing **450.00**

Silver plate, English, 19th C, epergne, four arms, cut glass centerpiece, four cut glass holders, all supported by pierced silver bowls, standard with central urn surrounded by garland swags and rams' head motifs, supported by pierced base with ribbon and garland decoration supported by four legs with scrolled feet, reeded curved arms rise from leaves at base, hallmarked on underside of top bowl, 18-1/2" d, 16-1/2" h, **$2,600.**

Photo courtesy of Alderfer Auction Co.

Fish set, English, late 19th C, six forks, six knives with engraved blades, mother-of-pearl handles, wood case **320.00**

Game platter, 16" h, 26-1/2" l, English, late 19th C, well and three-platter base with attached hot water pan, raised on four medallion-capped feet, associated domed cov with beaded bands and engraved wide border of entwined circlets, applied open handle surrounded by conforming engraved dec, body with engraved griffin **700.00**

Garniture, 6-1/4" h ftd compote with repoussé floral and foliate bands, each side pc with conforming dec, Tiffany & Co. **350.00**

Hot water kettle on stand, 13" h, rounded kettle, partially reeded sides, scrolled silver, wood handle, detachable warming stand, marked "Made in England, Hand Chased" **150.00**

Inkwell, 11-1/2" h, England or America, 20th C, fence form, central fence supporting two urn form candle sconces, ends with three stakes bearing square cut glass inkwells with silver plated lids **195.00**

Lamp, table, 20-1/2" h, paneled shade, conical base, openwork silverplate grape vine designs, five panels of green and white slag glass, cast leaf finial, engraved leaves on base, base marked "Made and Guaranteed by the MB Co. USA," electrified, five sockets **1,200.00**

Monteith cooler, attributed to England, late 19th C, oval, shaped rims and cast loop handles, 7-3/4" w, 13" l, price for pr **815.00**

Silver plate, muffinier, folding, Victorian, **$525**.

Photo courtesy of Wiederseim Associates, Inc.

Punch cup, Lavigne, 1881 Rogers **25.00**

Sandwich box, 5-3/4" h, 4-1/8" h, English, early 20th C, rect, loop handle, hinged lid monogrammed, gilt int., leather carrying case... **80.00**

Snuffbox, 2-3/4" l, English, late 19th C, foliate scroll engraved lid, set with central faceted purple stone, cowry shell body **300.00**

Teapot, 8" h, Derby Silver Co., emb floral motifs and arabesques, wear **60.00**

Toast rack, 7" l, 2-5/8" w, England, late 19th/early 20th C, oval, central ring handle above cast cricket ball, rack formed as crossed cricket bats, four ball feet **90.00**

Tray, 32" l, Victorian, oval, field engraved with floral and diaper medallions flanked by foliage with foliate garlands at intervals, beaded and geometrical design border and handles **350.00**

Tea and coffee service, five-piece set, **$300**.
Photo courtesy of Dotta Auction Co., Inc.

Sheffield

Englishmen G. R. Elkington and H. Elkington are given credit for being the first to use the electrolytic method of plating silver in 1838.

Candlesticks, pr, 24" h, ornate columns with composite capitals, pale blue blown glass hurricane shades with cut floral designs **425.00**

Entree dish, 11" x 8", shaped rect, gadrooned rim, detachable handle with gadroon dec **75.00**

Hot water urn, 22-3/4" h, early 19th C, Philip Ashberry & Sons makers, urn-form body with flat leaf engraving at base, wide central band of engraved anthemion, round domed base with beaded rim, trumpet foot with band of guillouche centered by flowerheads and accented with husks, angular handles terminating in flat leaves, anthemion handle on top, domed lid with flat leaf engraving and foliage baluster finial, inner sleeve **750.00**

Sauceboat with underplate, rim applied with grapevines **95.00**

Soup tureen, 16" l, 10-3/4" h, early 19th C, ovoid body with applied gadroon and shell border, two fluted handles with leaf terminals, four scroll and flat leaf feet, domed lid with reeded band, leaf-form finial, body and lid with let-in engraved heraldic device, fitted drop-in liner, restorations, rosing .. **1,725.00**

Tankard, 5" h, Hy Wilkinson & Co. makers, tapered cylindrical form, plain ear handle, gold washed int., fitted leather case, 10 troy oz **235.00**

Tea and coffee service,
baluster shaped coffeepot, 12-1/4" h kettle-on-stand, teapot, creamer, two handled open sugar, waste bowl, oval with canted corners, angular handles **425.00**

SILVER OVERLAY

History: Silver overlay is silver applied directly to a finished glass or porcelain object. The overlay is cut and decorated, usually by engraving, prior to being molded around the object.

Glass usually is of high quality and is either crystal or colored. Lenox used silver overlay on some porcelain pieces. Most designs are from the Art Nouveau and Art Deco periods.

For more information, see *Warman's Glass,* 4th edition.

Basket, 5-1/2" l, 6" h, deep cranberry body, allover floral and lattice design, sterling handle......................... **600.00**
Decanter, 11-1/2" h, molded, pinched oval bottle, surface bamboo dec overall, base disk imp "Yuan Shun/Sterling," faceted crystal hollow stopper **375.00**
Flask, 5" h, clear bottle shaped body, scrolling hallmarked silver, hinged cov....... **275.00**
Inkwell, 3-3/4" x 3", bright green ground, rose, scroll, and lattice overlay, matching cov, monogram **650.00**
Jug, 9" h, colorless glass, tapered baluster form, star-cut base, silver cased applied draw handle, overlay of twining grapes and grape vines, plain cartouche beneath spout, stylized cobweb overlay below, Alvin Mfg Co., late 19th/early 20th C **1,380.00**

Bottle, cordial, long neck, matching stopper, Art Nouveau-type foliate silver overlay, **$125**.

Perfume bottles, left: atomizer top, large petaled flower, sweeping foliage; right: scrolling Art Nouveau silver overlay, matching stopper, **each $75-$120**.

Perfume bottle
4" h, bulbed colorless glass bottle with engraved scrolled foliate silver overlay dec, initial "S" in cartouche, silver overlay on ball shaped glass stopper, Continental, wear, some loss to silver **75.00**
5" h, baluster, elongated neck, colorless glass, scrolling foliage overlay, central monogrammed cartouche **225.00**
Tea set, 8-3/4" h, Lenox porcelain body, Reed & Barton silver overlay, three-pc set **325.00**
Vase
5" d, 12-1/4" h, bronze, sterling silver overlay of trees, verdigris patina, Heintz **850.00**

Front: perfume bottle, round bottle, round body, scrolling Art Nouveau silver overlay, matching silver overlay ball stopper; **$95**, center: cruet, bell-shaped body, scrolling Art Nouveau silver overlay, faceted stopper with silver overlay decoration, **$85**; right: perfume bottle, Art Nouveau floral silver overlay decoration, matching ball stopper with silver overlay decoration, as found condition, **$125**.

Pitcher, cream-colored porcelain body, scrolling silver overlay, **$125**.

7" h, Art Nouveau free-form irid blue body, applied silver overlay in iris pattern.. **1,100.00**
8" h, bulbous stick, translucent green glass body overlaid with embossed floral Alvin........................... **450.00**
9-3/4" h, baluster porcelain body, cerulean blue ground, painted prunus stems, overlaid with silver detailing, silver neck and foot rims, Aesthetic Movement, French, late 19th C **470.00**
13-3/4" h, Art Nouveau ovoid cranberry glass body, flared rim supported by three applied clear glass handles, silver overlay on rim and body, waterlily and cattails design, marks obscured, minor losses to silver overlay **1,250.00**

Vessel, 6-1/8" h, Tiger Ware, bulbous stoneware body with ear handle, narrow neck mounted with strapwork engraved silver collar, engraved monogram "ISA" and date "1594," English... **4,410.00**

SMITH BROS. GLASS

History: After establishing a decorating department at the Mount Washington Glass Works in 1871, Alfred and Harry Smith struck out on their own in 1875. Their New Bedford, Massachusetts, firm soon became known worldwide for its fine opalescent decorated wares, similar in style to those of Mount Washington.

Marks: Smith Bros. glass often is marked on the base with a red shield enclosing a rampant lion and the word "Trademark."

Reproduction Alert: Beware of examples marked "Smith Bros."

Atomizer, 7" h, tan shading to cream opaque body, enameled amethyst and pink flowers, painted lion trademark, new hardware...... **260.00**
Biscuit jar
  6" d, melon ribbed body shading from white to blue, polychrome enameled flowers **150.00**
  7" h, opaque cream ground, sculptured diagonal swirl pattern, polychrome flower dec, red lion trademark **300.00**
  7" d, 7-1/4" h, melon ribbed cream body, fall colored oak leaves, gold acorns, metal lid stamped "S.B." **415.00**
  7" d, 8-1/2" h, green and pastel brown tendrils of ivy wind around melon ribbed body, gold plated fittings, sgd "405" **885.00**
Bowl
  3" d, lobed, pale pink ground, daisies dec, red rampant lion mark **150.00**
  6" d, 2-3/4" h, melon ribbed, two shades of gold prunus dec, beaded white rim **375.00**

9" d, 4" h, melon ribbed, beige ground, pink Moss Rose dec, blue flowers, green leaves, white beaded rim...... **675.00**
Bride's bowl, 9-1/2" d, 3" h bowl, 16" h overall, opal glass bowl, painted ground, 2" band dec with cranes, fans, vases, and flowers, white and gray dec, fancy silver-plated holder sgd and numbered 2117 **1,450.00**
Creamer and sugar, 4" d, 3-3/4" h, shaded blue and beige ground, multicolored violet and leaves dec, fancy silverplated metalware **750.00**
Humidor, 6-1/2" h, 4" d, cream ground, eight blue pansies, melon-ribbed cov **850.00**
Jar, cov, 4" h, melon ribbed cream body, white daisies dec, red lion trademark **150.00**
Mustard jar, cov, 2" h, ribbed, gold prunus dec, white ground **300.00**
Plate, 7-3/4" d, Santa Maria, beige, brown, and pale orange ship **635.00**
Ring vase, 9" h, hand painted floral motif on vase, bamboo and butterfly motif silverplate stand, stamped "Tufts" . **75.00**
Salt and pepper shakers, silverplate napkin ring center on platform base, white shakers with blue floral trim, marked "Rockford #29" **750.00**

SNUFF BOTTLES

History: Tobacco usage spread from America to Europe to China during the 17th century. Europeans and Chinese preferred to grind the dried leaves into a powder and sniff it into their nostrils. The elegant Europeans carried their boxes and took a pinch with their fingertips. The Chinese upper class, because of their lengthy fingernails, found this inconvenient and devised a bottle with a fitted stopper and attached spoon. These utilitarian objects soon became objets d'art.

Snuff bottles were fashioned from precious and semi-precious stones, glass, porcelain and pottery, wood, metals, and ivory. Glass and transparent-stone bottles often were enhanced

further with delicate hand paintings, some done on the interior of the bottle.

Agate, Chinese, flattened circular form carved as two men in garden, woman in background on one side, man and woman in garden on reverse, carved lizards on narrow sides, coral stopper, intact ivory spoon, 1-7/8" w, 2-3/8" h, **$1,035.**
Photo courtesy of Alderfer Auction Co.

Agate, carved
  2-1/4" h, amber, quatrefoil form, each side carved with bat and stylized ruyi design, Chinese, 19th C, tiny chip and slight wear on rim, slight fissure on shoulder **150.00**
  2-3/8" h, flat rect shape, carved sprig of peony, reverse dec with carved ruyi scepter, Chinese, 19th C **125.00**
  2-1/2" h, mottled brown, flattened round form, carved fisherman, reverse with cat looking up at a flying insect, red glass top, orig spoon, Chinese, 19th C **200.00**
  2-1/2" h, mottled gray, flattened oval form, well carved with three men mooring boat, flower, tree dec, Chinese, 19th C **575.00**
Amber, 4" l, landscape and figures, caramel inclusions, conforming id, Chinese, late 19th C **1,265.00**
Celadon, 2-1/4" h, light jade, flattened ovoid short neck **200.00**
Chrysoprase, 3" h, flattened ovoid, light green, conforming stopper **215.00**
Cinnabar lacquer, 3-1/4" h, ovoid, continual scene of scholars and boys in a pavilion landscape, dark red, conforming stopper... **230.00**
Cloisonné, auspicious symbols among clouds, yellow ground, lappet base border, ruyi head neck border, conforming stopper with chrysanthemum design, Qianlong four-character mark **185.00**

From left: carved jade, flattened oval form, carved pine tree on one side, obverse with man sitting under willow tree with fish on line, Chinese, 19th C, 3" h, **$450**; carved agate, flat rectangular shape, carved sprig of peony, reverse decoration with ruyi scepter, Chinese, 19th C, 2-3/8" h, **$150**; carved coral, asters, eagle finial, Chinese, 19th C, 2" h, **$195**; carved coral, peony in high relief, quail finial, Chinese, 19th C, 2" h, **$175**; carved coral, roses on diamond reserve, plain round finial, Chinese, 19th C, 1-3/4" h, **$125**; carved tiger's eye, flat oval form, one side carved with curled chi dragon design, 2" h, stopper missing, internal fissure, **$80**; carved glass, brown, amber, and green mottled body, flat oval form, rectangular projections on sides, 2-3/4" h, **$200**; carved glass, flat oval form, dark body, original coral stopper, 2-1/2" h, **$200**.

From left: porcelain, famille verte decoration, Chinese, 19th C, 3-3/8" h, loose cap, **$85**; porcelain, flattened round form, famille rose decoration, Chinese, 19th C, marked, 2-3/4" h, **$115**; porcelain, vasiform, famille rose decoration, Chinese, 19th C, 2-1/4" h, **$100**; porcelain, narrow cylindrical form, underglaze blue decoration, four-character mark on base, Chinese, 18th C, 3-1/4" h, **$200**; porcelain, underglaze blue, red, and yellow decoration, Chinese, 19th C, 3-1/4" h, **$175**.

Coral, 2-1/2" h, carved, tree trunk with foliage, carved flower stopper, China, 19th or 20th C, stopper glued to bottle............................ **320.00**

Glass
2-1/4" h, clear, flat rect shape, broad oval foot, stone stopper with eye design, Chinese, 19th C **125.00**
2-1/2" h, interior painted with three horned goats by tree, verso with inscription, sgd "Ma Shaoxian," China, no stopper **480.00**
3" h, opaque body, enameled peony blossoms, verso with two birds, three-characters on base, China **175.00**

Ivory, 3-3/4" l, curved ivory carved with bulrushes and crocodiles, flatleaf cap with ball finial, pebbled gilt-metal lid with glass-inset neck, mounted with short neck chain, Indian, late 19th/early 20th C **300.00**

Jade, carved
2-3/8" h, oval, carved butterfly near flowering branch, amber inclusions on one side, Chinese, 18th or 19th C, design incorporates natural fissure **875.00**
2-3/8" h, slender oval form, carved basketweave dec, tiger's eye stopper, Chinese, 18th C, dark inclusion at base, spoon broken.............. **450.00**
3" h, flattened oval form, carved sage and pine tree on one side, reverse with man sitting under willow tree, fish on line, Chinese, 19th C **435.00**

Lapis lazuli, 4" h, ovoid, relief carved, figures beneath tree, Chinese **125.00**

Malachite, 3" h, carved, gourd, Chinese **95.00**

Opal, 3" h, carved sage seated before gourd, Ch'ing Dynasty **125.00**

Overlay glass, seven colors, one side with floral designs in two archaic-form vases, reverse with immortal attending a crane and deer, bats flying above, each side with animal mask and ring handles, green, blue, mauve, coral, brown, and yellow, on white ground, 19th C . **520.00**

Peking glass, Snowflake
2-1/4" h, red overlay, flattened ovoid, one side with serpent and tortoise, other with frog sitting under lily pad **1,265.00**
2-1/2" h, blue overlay, each side with prancing deer, head turned with a lingchi branch in mouth, 19th C **490.00**

Porcelain
2-1/2" h, Famille Rose dec, vasiform, Chinese, 19th C, marked **125.00**
2-3/4" h, Famille Rose dec, flattened round form, Chinese, 19th C, marked **125.00**
3-1/8" h, Famille Rose dec, raised molded dec, iron-red sacred fungus and bat mark, gilt foot rim, coral stopper, China, 18th or 19th C, small chip, stopper glued to bottle **95.00**
3-1/4" h, gamboling lions among clouds, ruyi band on shoulder and base, carved wooden stopper and ivory spoon, gilt rims, iron-red Jiaqing four-character mark on base, China, 19th C, small chips............................ **320.00**
3-3/8" h, Famille Verte dec, Chinese, 19th C, cap loose **115.00**
3-3/4" h, Famille Verte dec, Chinese, 19th C **150.00**

Rock crystal, 3-1/2" h, carved dec of pine trees in mountainous landscape, inclusions of black crystalline in various lengths, carved coral stopper, Chinese, 19th C, spoon missing........ **375.00**

Rose quartz, 3" h, flattened ovoid, relief carved leaves and vines, Chinese...... **45.00**

Stag horn, 2-1/8" h, flattened ovoid, one side with inset ivory panel with two laughing figures, reserve with inset panel with gold archaic script........ **175.00**

Turquoise, high relief carving of children and prunus trees, China **235.00**

SOAPSTONE

History: The mineral steatite, known as soapstone because of its greasy feel, has been used for carving figural groups and designs by the Chinese and others. Utilitarian pieces also were made. Soapstone pieces were very popular during the Victorian era.

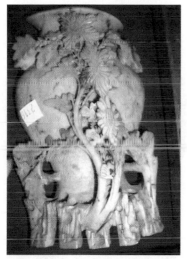

Vase, flat back, urn with cascading chrysanthemums, faux bamboo stand as base, **$35.**

Bookends, pr, 5" h, carved, block form, fu lion resting on top, Chinese **300.00**
Candlesticks, pr, 5-1/8" h, red tones, flowers and foliage **85.00**
Carving
　3" h, even white color, servant kneeling before woman holding fan, China, 19th C **115.00**
　4" w, 4-1/2" d, 3-1/2" h, dog's head, old darkened color, America, 19th C, chips, with stand **420.00**
　9-1/4" h, Buddha, seated, praying, carved stone base **60.00**
　12" h, woman, standing, wearing robe, restoration **120.00**
Hot plate, 16" l, 8-1/2" w ... **75.00**
Plaque, 9-1/2" h, birds, trees, flowers, and rocks **125.00**
Sculpture, 10-1/4" h, 4-1/2" w, kneeling nude young woman, Canadian **95.00**
Sealing stamp, carved dec, 5" h, 1" d, curved scroll ... **95.00**

Toothpick holder, two containers with carved birds, animals, and leaves...... **85.00**
Vase
　6-3/4" h, 9-1/2" l, four openings, red tones, Chinese, c1900 .... **125.00**
　15-1/2" h, carved peacock and chrysanthemums . **495.00**

SOUVENIR AND COMMEMORATIVE CHINA AND GLASS

History: Souvenir, commemorative, and historical china and glass includes those items produced to celebrate special events, places, and people.

　Collectors particularly favor China plates made by Rowland and Marcellus and Wedgwood. Rowland and Marcellus, Staffordshire, England, made a series of blue-and-white historic plates with a wide rolled edge. Scenes from the Philadelphia Centennial in 1876 through the 1939 New York World's Fair are depicted. In 1910, Wedgwood collaborated with Jones, McDuffee, and Stratton to produce a series of historic dessert-sized plates showing scenes of places throughout the United States.

　Many localities issued plates, mugs, glasses, etc., for anniversary celebrations or to honor a local historical event. These items seem to have greater value when sold in the region in which they originated.

　Commemorative glass includes several patterns of pressed glass that celebrate people or events. Historical glass includes campaign and memorial items.

Ashtray, New York City, china, blue and white transfer, Empire State Building, Statue of Liberty, Rockefeller Center, harbor scene, mkd "Fine Staffordshire Ware, Enco, National, Made in England" **20.00**

Plate, Souvenir of Plymouth Rock, MA, blue and white, marked "Old English Staffordshire Ware, Made in Staffordshire, (Jonroth England mark) England, Imported for Plymouth Rock Gift Shop, Plymouth, Mass, (Adams mark) Adams, est. 1657," **$20.**

Bust, Gillinder
　Lincoln, frosted　　**325.00**
　Napoleon, frosted and clear **295.00**
Creamer
　New Academy, Truro, multicolored image on white medallion, cobalt blue ground, gold and white dec **30.00**
　Wadsworth Atheneum, Hartford, CT, multicolored image on white medallion, lustered ground, 2" h, marked "Wheelock China, Austria" **18.00**
Cup, Entrance to Soldier's Home, Leavenworth, Kansas, multicolored, beaded dec, 2-1/2" h, marked "Germany," slight wear to gold dec. **18.00**
Cup and saucer
　Niagara Falls, cobalt blue ground, gold trim, 1-1/4" h x 1-3/4" d, 3-1/2" d saucer, scene of falls on saucer, marked "Made in Japan," matching wooden display stand **20.00**
　Souvenir of Edina, Missouri, white ground, rose dec, gold trim, 2-1/2" h x 3-3/4" w cup, 5-1/2" w cup, marked "Japan" **20.00**
　Washington and Lafayette, transfer print portraits on cup of George Washington and Lafayette, saucer with portrait titled "Washington His Country's Father," 1-3/4" h, creamware, England, early 19th C **490.00**

Demitasse cup and saucer

My Old Kentucky Home, 2" h x 2" w cup, 4" d saucer, marked "Handpainted, Made in Japan, NICO" **15.00**

Souvenir of Chicago, Ill, Victorian man and woman on inside of cup, 2" h x 2-1/2" w cup, gold trim, marked "Crest O Gold, Sabin, Warranted 22K" **17.50**

Plate, Souvenir of St. Augustine, Florida, Old City Gates in center, vignettes of other sights around border, blue transfer decoration, marked "Usina Brothers King St, St Augustine, Fla, Staffordshire, England," **$60**.

Dish

Beauvoir House, Jefferson Davis House, Biloxi, MS, 3-1/4" d, marked "Made by Adams, England for the Jefferson Davis Shrine" **20.00**

DeShong Memorial Art Gallery, Lester, PA, yellow luster ground, 3-3/4" x 3-1/4", marked "Made in Germany," wear to lettering and gold trim **12.00**

Dish, cov, Remember the *Maine,* green opaque glass .. **135.00**

Figure, souvenir of Atlantic City, two pigs having picture taken, green ground, marked "Germany" **150.00**

Goblet

G.A.R., 1887, 21st Encampment **100.00**

Mother, Ruby Thumbprint pattern **35.00**

Mug, Souvenir of Blairsville, ruby stained, applied clear handle **25.00**

Paperweight

Moses in Bulrushes, frosted center........................ **145.00**

Plymouth Rock, clear... **95.00**

Washington, George, round, frosted center **295.00**

Pitcher, 10" h, ironstone, shell molded oval form, wine-red ground, circular paneled sides enamel dec with landscape scenes, gilt trim, titled cartouche below spout "Senator Martin Wyckoff, of Warren County," imp mark "U Pottery," c1885, gilt wear **460.00**

Plate, Valley Forge, 1777-78, Washington's Headquarters in center, vignettes of other signs around border, blue transfer decoration, Rowland & Marcellus Co., Staffordshire, England, with poem by Gus Egolf, Dec. 19, 1910, Norristown, Pa, **$75**.

Plate, Martha Washington, shaded beige border, marked "Silesea" and "Tatler & Lawson, Trenton," **$60**.

Plate

Boston department stores, founders in border, blue transfer, white ground, Wedgwood, 9-3/4" d **35.00**

Hogg, James Stephen, first native born governor of Texas, brown print, Vernon Kilns, marked "Designed for Daughters of the Republic of Texas" **25.00**

Memorial, Garfield center, clear pressed glass, 10" d **75.00**

Oklahoma, Agricultural and Mechanical College, Vernon

Kilns, marked "Designed especially for Creech's Stillwater, Oklahoma".... **32.00**

Plymouth Rock, Plymouth, MA, brown and white, mkd "Old English Staffordshire Ware, Made in England, (Jonroth mark) (Adams mark) Imported Exclusively for Plymouth Rock Gift Shop, Plymouth, Mass".......... **25.00**

Remember the *Maine,* Spanish-American war, c1900, 8-1/2" d **240.00**

Sulphur Springs, Delaware, OH, light blue and black transfer, Staffordshire, NY retailer's label, 10-1/2" d, chip on table ring **200.00**

Washington, Bellingham, green print, Vernon Kilns **60.00**

Plate, B. F. Block & Bros., 25th Anniversary Opening, New & Greater Department Store, Norristown, Pa, Oct. 5th and 6th, 1928, multicolored portrait of Col. Lindbergh at top, black and white portraits of George and Martha Washington among multicolored florals on side borders, back marked "Limoges China Co., USA 1127," **$45**.

Tile, 4" d, Detroit Women's League, multicolored irid glass........................... **135.00**

Tumbler, etched Lord's Prayer................ **15.00**

Niagara Falls, Prospect Point, gold rim **20.00**

SOUVENIR AND COMMEMORATIVE SPOONS

History: Souvenir and commemorative spoons have been issued for hundreds of years. Early American silversmiths engraved presentation spoons to honor historical personages or mark key events.

In 1881, Myron Kinsley patented a Niagara Falls spoon, and in 1884, Michael Gibney patented a new flatware design. M. W. Galt, Washington, D.C., issued commemorative spoons for George and Martha Washington in 1889. From these beginnings, a collecting craze for souvenir and commemorative spoons developed in the late 19th and early 20th centuries.

Basiwgstoke, red, blue, and orange enameled shield, 5" l **15.00**

Boulder, CO, name in bowl, Indian head handle...... **40.00**

B. P. O. E. Elks #896, marked "Reed & Barton Klitzner RI," silverplate, 4-1/2" l **15.00**

Cawston Ostrich Farms, marked "Sterling," 3-1/4" l **15.00**

Denver, CO, sterling, gold washed bowl, acid etched pack mule, stem-end topped with winch with handle that turns, applied pick and shovel, stem entwined with rope, ending in bucket, opposed by modeled rock, 1 troy oz, late 19th C.... **85.00**

Fort Dearborn, 1803-1857, marked "Sterling, Hyman Berg," 6" l **20.00**

Golden Gate Bridge, San Francisco, CA, marked "Holland 90" and hallmark, 5" l **15.00**

Lancaster, city name engraved in bowl, sterling............. **30.00**

Memorial Arch, Brooklyn, NY, round oak stove **40.00**

Palm Springs, Aerial Tramway, SP, John Brown, marked "Antico"....................... **100.00**

Philadelphia, Independence Hall in bowl, SS............ **45.00**

Prophet, veiled.............. **135.00**

Richmond, MO, SS **30.00**

Royal Canadian Mounted Police, "Victoria, British Columbia" in bowl, marked "Made in Holland," 4-1/2" l **30.00**

Stratford on Avon, yellow enameled shield, 3-5/8" l, mkd "EPNS"......................... **15.00**

St. Paul, The Tower, Houses of Parliament, West Minister, each marked "L. E. P. A1" on back, set of four in orig box **42.00**

Thousand Islands, fish handle, engraved bowl, SS, Watson **45.00**

Vista House, Columbia River, OR, detailed handle, marked "Sterling"...................... **32.00**

SPANGLED GLASS

History: Spangled glass is a blown or blown-molded variegated art glass, similar to spatter glass, with the addition of flakes of mica or metallic aventurine. Many pieces are cased with a white or clear layer of glass. Spangled glass was developed in the late 19th century and still is being manufactured.

Originally, spangled glass was attributed only to the Vasa Murrhina Art Glass Company of Hartford, Connecticut, which distributed the glass for Dr. Flower of the Cape Cod Glassworks, Sandwich, Massachusetts. However, research has shown that many companies in Europe, England, and the United States made spangled glass, and attributing a piece to a specific source is very difficult.

For more information, see *Warman's Glass*, 4th edition.

Basket, 7" h, 6" l, ruffled edge, white int., deep apricot with spangled gold, applied crystal loop handle, slight flake **225.00**

Bride's bowl, 10-1/2" d, ruffled rim, yellow and white mottled ground, overall silver mica flakes, yellow stemmed blue daisies dec **90.00**

Candlesticks, pr, 8-1/8" h, pink and whit spatter, green aventurine flecks, cased white int. **115.00**

Creamer, 3-1/4" d, 4-3/4" h, bulbous, molded swirled ribs, cylindrical neck, pinched spout, blue ground, swirled mica flecks, applied clear reeded handle.......... **225.00**

Cruet, Leaf Mold pattern, cranberry, mica flakes, white casing, Northwood **450.00**

Ewer, 9-1/2" h, raspberry pink ext., white int., mica flecks, twisted applied handle, rough pontil......................... **250.00**

Bride's basket, ruffled yellow base with gold spangles, creamy white exterior, applied colorless bark handle, **$145**.

Basket, pink glass exterior, embedded mica flakes, opaque white interior, applied ribbed colorless glass bent handle with impressed design in ends, 5-1/4" w, 8" h, **$100**.

Photo courtesy of Alderfer Auction Co.

Jack-in-the-pulpit vase, 6-1/4" h, oxblood, green, and white spatter, mica flakes, c1900.......................... **125.00**

Pitcher, 8-1/2" h, white, and amber cased to clear, mica flakes, applied amber reeded handle........................ **550.00**

Salt shaker, cranberry, cased white int., molded leaf design, Hobbs, c1890............ **125.00**

Sugar shaker, cranberry, mica flakes, white casing, Northwood **115.00**
Toothpick holder, 2-1/4" h, alternating crimson and white mottled ground, gold mica, lattice stripes **65.00**
Tumbler, 3-3/4" h, pink, gold, and brown spatter, mica flecks, white lining **90.00**
Vase
6-3/4" h, glossy pink cased satin, silver mica, two applied crystal handles **75.00**
8-3/4" h, stick, cased satin glass alternating pink and blue panels, overall silver mica, crystal rigaree around neck **75.00**
Water set, 9-1/2" h tankard pitcher, Aventurine, pink and white mottled ground, yellow and blue accents, metallic flecks, four matching 3-3/4" h tumblers **350.00**

SPATTER GLASS

History: Spatter glass is a variegated blown or blown-molded art glass. It originally was called "end-of-day" glass, based on the assumption that it was made from batches of glass leftover at the end of the day. However, spatter glass was found to be a standard production item for many glass factories.

Spatter glass was developed at the end of the 19th century and is still being produced in the United States and Europe.

Reproduction Alert: Many modern examples come from the European area previously called Czechoslovakia.

Basket, tortoiseshell, cream, tan, yellow, white, and brown spatter, white lining, rect, tightly crimped edge, colorless thorn handle **120.00**
Berry set, master bowl and two sauces, Leaf Mold, cranberry vaseline...................... **300.00**
Bowl, 8-1/2" d, amber and brown mottled tortoiseshell **90.00**
Box, cov, cranberry ground, white spatter, clear knob finial **200.00**
Candlestick, 7-1/2" h, yellow, red, and white streaks, clear overlay, vertical swirled molding, smooth base, flanged socket **60.00**

Bowl, tortoise shell pattern, amber ground, brown and black striations, **$450**.
Photo courtesy of Wiederseim Associates, Inc.

Cologne bottle, 5-1/2" h, white spatter, enamel dec, orig stopper applicator, marked "Made in Czechoslovakia," price for pr **115.00**
Creamer, Leaf Mold, cranberry vaseline **250.00**
Cruet, 6-1/2" h, Aventurine, applied clear reeded handle, cut faceted stopper **375.00**

Cruet, white spatter over amber ground, applied amber handle, matching amber ball stopper, **$65**.

Darning egg, multicolored, attributed to Sandwich Glass **125.00**
Ewer, yellow ground, white spatter, tri-fold spout, flared applied clear handle, sharp pontil, 8-3/4" h.............. **85.00**
Finger bowl and underplate, 6" d, 3-1/4" d, tortoiseshell, ruffled........................ **275.00**
Jack-in-the-pulpit, 5" h, 3-1/2" d, Vasa Murrhina, deep pink int., clear ruffled top **115.00**
Pitcher, 6-1/2" d, 8" h, burgundy and white spatter, cased in

clear, ground pontil, clear reeded handle **395.00**
Rose bowl
Leaf Mold, cranberry ground, vaseline spatter **250.00**
Mt. Washington, pink, blue, and white spatter on colorless ground, white opalescent scalloped top............. **135.00**
Salt, 3" l, maroon and pink, white spatter, applied clear feet and handle....................... **125.00**
Sugar shaker, Leaf Umbrella pattern, cranberry **495.00**
Toothpick holder, 3" h, tubular design, crystal rigaree feet **60.00**
Tumbler, 3-3/4" h, emb Swirl pattern, white, maroon, pink, yellow, and green, white int. **65.00**

Water pitcher, dark red, cranberry, and white spatter, applied colorless reeded handle, **$95**.

Vase
4-3/4" h, Aventurine, tapering global body, short cylindrical neck, white opaque lining **125.00**
7" h, baluster shape, shades of blue, sgd "Czechoslovakia" **50.00**
Watch holder, 3-3/4" x 4-1/4" dish, ruffled rim, blue spatter, 7" h ormolu metal watch holder **175.00**

SPATTERWARE

History: Spatterware generally was made of common earthenware, although occasionally creamware was used. The earliest English examples were made about 1780. The peak period of production was from 1810 to 1840. Firms known to have made spatterware are Adams, Barlow, and Harvey and Cotton.

The amount of spatter decoration varies from piece to piece. Some objects simply have decorated borders. These often were decorated with a brush, requiring several hundred touches per square inch to achieve the spatter effect. Other pieces have the entire surface covered with spatter.

Marks: Marked pieces are rare.

Reproduction Alert: Cybis spatter is an increasingly collectible ware in its own right. The pieces, made by the Polishman Boleslaw Cybis in the 1940s, have an Adams-type peafowl design. Many contemporary craftsmen also are reproducing spatterware.

For more information, *see Warman's English & Continental Pottery & Porcelain*, 4th edition.

Notes: Collectors today focus on the patterns—Cannon, Castle, Fort, Peafowl, Rainbow, Rose, Thistle, Schoolhouse, etc. The decoration on flatware is in the center of the piece; on hollow ware, it occurs on both sides.

Aesthetics and the color of spatter are key to determining value. Blue and red are the most common colors; green, purple, and brown are in a middle group; black and yellow are scarce.

Like any soft paste, spatterware is easily broken or chipped. Prices in this listing are for pieces in very good to mint condition.

Bowl, 5-1/2" d, Morning Glory flowers, red spatter, purple flowers, light overall crazing, small table rim chip **65.00**

Charger
12-1/2" d, stick spatter, red, blue, green, and purple flowers, purple stick spatter border **125.00**

Stick spatter, plate, red stick border, center star shaped flower with additional red petals, small cobalt blue stick flowers, green leaves, English, 9" d, **$275**.

Photo courtesy of Wiederseim Associates, Inc.

Stick spatter, Snowflake pattern, cobalt blue decoration, white ground, 8-1/2" d plate, handle-less cup and saucer, **$200**.

Photo courtesy of Dotta Auction Co., Inc.

14-1/2" d, stick spatter, red and blue flowers, green leaves, purple stick spatter buds, mkd "Adams, England," minor staining **100.00**

Creamer
3-1/2" h, red and green rose, brown and black spatter, rim flake **650.00**
3-3/4" h, Morning Glory, blue and green flower, red spatter **2,750.00**
4" h, Rainbow Thumbprint, red, yellow, and blue peafowl, red, blue, and green spatter, damage and restoration **1,650.00**
5" h, red and green cockscomb design, blue spatter, paneled, stains on foot, minor flakes **860.00**
5-5/8" h, Peafowl, red, green, and blue, paneled, unusual squiggly branches, minor enamel flake in blue .. **770.00**

Cup, blue stick spatter looping pattern, red, green, and blue long tulip **75.00**

Cup and saucer, handleless Dark blue, green, and red pomegranate, yellow dots, blue spatter, light stains, crazed saucer **800.00**

Light brown spatter, red and blue spray with green leaves, hairlines **385.00**
Peafowl, light blue, mustard yellow, and green dec, red spatter, damage and repair to cup, flake and inpainting in saucer **150.00**
Rainbow, Drape pattern, red, yellow, and green, small rim repair on cup, minor stains on saucer..................... **3,080.00**
Red, mustard, and green six-pointed star, stains on cup, foot chip..................... **925.00**
Red, yellow, green, and blue tulip dec, blue spatter, cup has stained area, filled-in flakes, hairline............ **110.00**

Miniature, handleless cup and saucer
Blue spatter, blue, mauve, and green dahlia **300.00**
Blue spatter, light green yellow, and red peafowl **350.00**
Red spatter................. **200.00**

Pitcher, Peafowl decoration, red spatter, 8" w, 7" h, **$775**.

Photo courtesy of Joy Luke.

Pitcher
4-3/4" h, blue drape with bands on shoulder, rim, and handle, hairlines, some stains, in-the-making separation at handle........................ **460.00**
7-1/2" h, paneled sides, five-color rainbow spatter, handle cracked **5,500.00**
8-1/2" h, Acorns, yellow and teal green, green and dark brown leaves, purple spatter, paneled, bubbles in brown and yellow, stains, rim repair **3,650.00**

Plate
7-1/2" d, Peafowl, red, yellow, and green, blue spatter border, rim chips **110.00**
8-3/8" d, blue border, blue, red, and green dahlia pattern **350.00**

8-1/2" d, blue border, center red and green flower, light stains **150.00**

8-1/2" d, Peafowl, dark blue, green, and dark brown, long tail, red spatter, short hairline, in-the-making chip on table ring............................ **715.00**

8-1/2" d, Rainbow, light red, blue, and yellow border, rim flake **3,300.00**

8-5/8" d, Rainbow, red, yellow, and blue spatter, few minor knife scratches **3,250.00**

8-3/4" d, red border, red, blue, and green flowers, minor enamel imperfections, minor stains **110.00**

9-1/8" d, Black Beauty, black floral border, red, blue, and green floral center, transfer label "Wm. Adams & Co., Tunstall, England" **150.00**

9-1/2" d, Rainbow, purple and black, bull's eye center **1,500.00**

9-5/8" d, Rainbow, blue and reddish-purple, red Adams rose in center, stains, rim flake **450.00**

10-1/2" d, Rainbow, red, blue, and green border, scalloped edge, imp "Adams," filled-in rim chip........................ **385.00**

10-3/4" d, blue flowers, red and blue flowers green leaves **150.00**

Platter

8-1/4" x 10-3/4", Peafowl, red, blue, and dark brown, appears to have been scoured, two hairlines, and flake on rim underside **615.00**

Stick spatter, plate, red stick border, purple passion flowers with yellow centers, green foliage, red and blue feather design, English, **$200**.

Photo courtesy of Wiederseim Associates, Inc.

Stick spatter, plate, blue cog flowers, green leaves, red petals, English, **$250**.

Photo courtesy of Wiederseim Associates, Inc.

Plate, paneled, red, green, and blue rainbow spatter, 9-1/4" d, **$1,150**.

Photo courtesy of Pook & Pook.

10-1/2" x 13-3/4", red and green rainbow border, large red and blue tulip with green and black foliage, imp anchor mark, restorations, hairline **4,510.00**

12-3/8" d, 15-7/8" w, light blue borders, rect white center panel, oblong, scalloped corners, minor rim flakes **220.00**

13-3/4" x 17-1/2", dark brown eagle and shield transfer center, blue spatter border, octagonal, stains and hairline **295.00**

Soup plate, 8-3/4" d, blue border, red, green, and yellow stripes, floral center **195.00**

Sugar bowl, cov

5" d, 5" h, blue, green, and red designs, blue stripes, minor roughness on inside flange **250.00**

5-3/4" h plus lid, paneled, red school house, green spatter trees and grass, blue spatter, small crow's foot, restored

handles, lid blue transfer replacement **715.00**

Teapot

5" h, Rainbow, green and yellow with purple loops, black spots, stains, filled-in rim chip, restoration to handle, spout, and lid **5,060.00**

7-5/8" h, Cockscomb, red and green design, blue spatter, hairlines in base, restored replaced lid **550.00**

9" h, Peafowl, blue, green, and red, red spatter, small flakes **1,400.00**

Waste bowl, 6-1/4" d, 3-1/2" h, brown, red, and black Fort pattern, blue spatter, hairline **200.00**

SPORTS COLLECTIBLES

History: People have been saving sports-related equipment since the inception of sports. Some was passed down from generation to generation for reuse; the rest was stored in dark spaces in closets, attics, and basements.

Two key trends brought collectors' attention to sports collectibles. First, decorators began using old sports items, especially in restaurant decor. Second, collectors began to discover the thrill of owning the "real" thing. Sports collectibles are more accessible than ever before because of on-line auctions and several houses that dedicate themselves to that segment of the hobby. Provenance is extremely important when investing in high-ticket sports collectibles. Being able to know the history of the object may greatly enhance the value, with a premium paid for items secured from the player or directly from their estate.

Banner, Princeton, 1940, black and red felt, matching pennant, **$200**.

Baseball

Annual, 1963, *Official Baseball Annual,* Fawcett, color action photo of Los Angeles Dodgers Don Drysdale on cov **10.00**

Autograph
Brett, George, 8" x 10-3/4" magazine page with full color photo in Kansas City Royals uniform, sgd on shoulder, c1980 .... **20.00**
Carew, Rod, 11-1/2" x 14-1/2" four page folio segment from June 29, 1974 issue of Sporting News, bold signature **30.00**
Coveleski, Stanley, 3-1/2" x 5-1/2" Hall of Fame postcard, published for National Baseball Museum, Cooperstown, NY, showing player's bronze plaque, 1969 .... **30.00**
Spahn, Walter, 8" x 10" glossy full-color photo, Milwaukee pitcher's uniform, c1953 .. **25.00**

Bank, 6-1/2" h, All Stars, bobbing head, painted composition figure, orig string tag, 1960s **50.00**

Baseball, autographed, sgd by members of team
American League All-Star Team, 1937, Foxx, Gehrig, DiMaggio **7,000.00**
Boston, 1964, Herman, Yastrzemski **250.00**
National League All-Star Team, 1955, Musial **600.00**
New York, 1960, Stengel, Kubek, Maris, Howard, Berra, Ford **700.00**
Oakland, 1981, Martin, Henderson **200.00**

Baseball cap, autographed, game used
Bench, Johnny, 1970s Cincinnati Reds **450.00**
Jackson, Bo, 1994 California Angels **95.00**
Walker, Larry, 1995 Colorado Rockies **165.00**

Baseball card, issued by Cracker Jack, Ty Cobb, Detroit Tigers Hall of Fame **6,400.00**

Baseball glove
Ashburn, Richie **45.00**
Berra, Yogi **100.00**
Reese, Pee Wee **65.00**

Bobbing head
5-1/2" h painted composition figure, blue cap, painted white initial "M," white shirt trimmed in blue, gold tan trousers, holding yellow bat, 3" x 3-1/2" x 6" orig box, mkd "Made In Japan" **40.00**
6-1/2" h, New York, sq white base, 1961-63, professionally restored **65.00**

Dixie picture, Bob Feller, Cleveland Indians, 8" x 10" photo, four additional action photos on back, plus biography **90.00**

Emblem, 4" h, white plastic, on orig card, c1950
Pirates, black accents .. **12.00**
Reds, red accents **12.00**

Exhibit card, 3-3/8" x 5-3/8", sepia tone, facsimile signature
Drysdale, Don **25.00**
Killebrew, Harmon **20.00**
Mayes, Willie **35.00**
Mazeroski, Bill **15.00**

Hartland figure, 7-1/2" h, Roger Maris, 25th anniversary, orig 4" x 6" x 8-1/2" box **70.00**

Lunch box
6-1/2" x 8-1/2" x 3-1/2", Boston Red Sox, Ardee, 1960s, vinyl **50.00**
7" x 8-1/2" x 4", Toronto Blue Jay's, Canadian issue, late 1980s, blue vinyl **25.00**

Magazine
Baseball Monthly, Vol. 1, #4, June 1962 .... **5.00**
Complete Baseball Magazine, Sports Life editors, summer issue, 1950 .... **10.00**
Life, Aug. 1, 1949, black and white cover with close-up photo of Joe DiMaggio . **15.00**
Men Your Goodyear Dealer's Magazine, Mickey Mantle cover, 1957 .... **45.00**

Pennant, felt
Brooklyn Dodgers, Ebbert Field, blue, 1940s **190.00**
Cooperstown, blue, multicolored Braves style Indian head, 1940s...... **75.00**
Minnesota Twins A. L. Champs World Series, photo, 1965............................. **125.00**
New York Yankees, photo "M&M Boys Last Year Together!," 1966 .... **95.00**

Photograph, silver print, ladies baseball team wearing numbered uniforms, two hold bats, three with gloves, verso "Ladies baseball team 1900, Photo by Brown Brothers, New York City," 6" x 8", **$350.**

Photo courtesy of Historical Collectibles Auctions.

Photograph, 10" x 35" black and white stiff paper, Whiz Kids of 1950, The Fightin' Phillies, shows time lined up on field, holding hats and gloves, newspaper supplement **90.00**

Pinback button
Go-Go Mets, dark orange on navy blue, image of youthful batter in oversized batting helmet, late 1960s, 3-1/2" d **24.00**
Minnesota Twins, Western Division Champions, America League, 1987, red, white, and blue, 3-1/2" d **12.00**
Ted Williams, 1-3/4" d, black and white photo as youthful Boston Red Sox star, late 1930s............................. **40.00**
York White Roses, 1-1/4" d blue and white celluloid figural baseball suspending blue and white fabric ribbons with miniature plastic baseball, 1940s **15.00**

Plate, 7-1/4" d, Base Ball, Caught on the Fly, center transfer print, white glazed ground, c1850 .... **920.00**

Pocket tin, 4-1/8" x 3-1/2" x 1-1/8", Yankee Boy Plug Cut, Scotten, Dillion Co., tin litho, little boy slugger on shield shape, red and white check background **625.00**

Poster, 11-1/2" x 38", 1930 Chicago Cubs, photo and facsimile signature of each player, adv Blue Ribbon Malt Co., contemporary frame **250.00**

Presentation bat, 34" l, red painted bat, polychrome Odd Fellows symbols, incised in gold "West Lynn 15-3 Kearsarge West Lynn 23 East Lynn 5 Presented by H. W. Eastham, July 21, 1900, Aug. 18, 1900," (MA), with stand **4,025.00**

Program
All Star, Philadelphia, 1943 .... **495.00**
All Star, St. Louis, 1948 .... **325.00**
New York Yankees, 1937 .... **195.00**
New York Yankees, 1951 .... **195.00**
World Series, 1950, at Philadelphia **250.00**

Roster sheet, Pirates, 1927 .... **175.00**

Score counter, 2" x 3-1/4" cardboard panels, six diecut openings, red and blue printing on white, blank back, c1890 .... **25.00**

Tab
Jerome "Dizzy" Dean, St. Louis Cards **20.00**
Wally Berger, New York Giants **15.00**

Window sign, 10" x 13-1/2", Mike Higgins Savvy Skipper of the Red Sox, *Saturday Evening Post,* July 21, 1956 .... **30.00**

Yearbook
Famous Slugger, 1970, 4-1/2" x 6-1/2", published by Hillerich & Bradsby Co., make of Louisville Slugger bats **10.00**
Los Angeles Dodgers, 1968, 8-1/2" x 11" **15.00**
Mets, 1965, 8-1/2" x 11" **20.00**

Basketball

Autograph, basketball
Archibald, Nate.......... **100.00**
Bird, Larry................. **200.00**
Bradley, Bill.............. **150.00**
O'Brien, Larry **125.00**
Autograph, photograph, 8" x 10"
McGuire, Dick.............. **20.00**
Phillip, Andy.............. **20.00**
Thurmond, Nate............ **24.00**

Bobbing head, 7" h, Seattle Supersonics, painted composition, orig sticker: American Sports Sales Ltd., Made in Korea, late 1970s **25.00**

Magazine, *Sports Illustrated,* Feb. 1949, Ralph Beard, Kentucky cover............. **95.00**

Pencil holder, 6-1/2" h, 4-1/4" x 5-1/2" white base, high gloss ceramics, All American basketball dribbler, fleshtone body parts, black hair and shoes, pale blue shirt inscribed "Champ," white shorts, brown basketball hollowed out for pencils **20.00**

Pin, Chicago Americans Tournament Championship, brass, 1935.................. **75.00**

Program
Basketball Hall of Fame Commemoration Day Program, orig invitation, 1961 .... **75.00**
NCAA Final Four Championship, Louisville, KY, 1967.......................... **175.00**
World Series of Basketball, 1951, Harlem Globetrotters and College All-Americans **55.00**

Shoes, pr, game used, autographed
Drexler, Clyde, Avais .. **225.00**
Sikma, Jack, Converse **100.00**
Webber, Chris, Nikes.. **550.00**

Souvenir book, *Los Angeles Lakers,* with two records, Jerry West and Elgin Baylor on action cover........... **75.00**

Ticket
NBA Finals Boston Celtics at Los Angeles Lakers, 1963 .... **95.00**
San Antonio Spurs ABA Phantom Playoff, 1975, unused........................ **15.00**
St. Louis Hawks at San Francisco Warriors, Dec. 17, 1963............................ **50.00**

Yearbook
1961-62, Boston Celtics **150.00**
1965-66, Boston Celtics **85.00**
1969-70, Milwaukee Bucks **40.00**

Print, gravure, *Peter Jackson* by A. D. Baston, published by Cadbury, Jones & Co., London, 1894, black Australian boxer who held heavyweight titles for Australia and Britain, inducted into International Boxing Hall of Fame in 1990, professionally framed, 27-1/2" x 37-1/2", **$230**.

Photo courtesy of Historical Collectibles Auctions.

Boxing

Autograph
Baer, Max, 8" x 10" photo **180.00**
Foreman, George, 8-1/2" x 11" letterhead, upper torso photo in muscular pose, Humble, TX, post office box address, black ink signature, mailed fold creases.................. **35.00**

Badge, 4" d, Larry Holmes, black and white photo, red and black inscriptions, 1979 copyright Don King Productions **25.00**

Boxing gloves, 35 readable autographs **380.00**

Cabinet card, 4" x 6"
Corbett, James F., dressed in suit............................ **375.00**
Ryan, Paddy, full boxing post, dark brown border...... **395.00**
Sullivan, John L., dark brown border, "John L. Sullivan, Champion of the World" **495.00**

Dinner program, 6-1/4" x 9", Boxing Writers Association, January 1968............... **20.00**

Figure, 8" w, 20-1/4" h, carved fruitwood, fully carved figure throwing right jab, standing on continuation of trunk with tree bark intact, attributed to New Hampshire, c1900 .. **1,955.00**

Letterhead, 8-1/2" x 11", white stationery, printed in blue on upper quarter for "International Boxing Club," bluetone photos of Rocky Marcianio-Champion, Joe Walcott-Challenger, James D. Norris-President, designates presentation "For the Heavyweight Championship of the world" schedule for Chicago Stadium, Friday, April 10 (1953), unused **25.00**

Magazine
Foreman-Ali Zaire Fight, 8-1/2" x 11" l, 52 pgs, Oct. 30, 1974 .... **35.00**
The Ring, 8-1/4" x 11", March, 1965, cover photo of Emile Griffith **10.00**

Plaque, 12-1/2" w, 16-3/4" h, carved pine, polychrome, figure of John L. Sullivan carved in relief against landscape in horseshoe-form, inscribed at base "J. L. Sullivan," old darkened crackled painted surface, New York, late 19th C **2,185.00**

Pool table, together with accessories such as cue racks, cues, bridge, two sets of balls, brushes, score keepers, etc., 98" l, 50" w, 32" h, **$900**.

Photo courtesy of Sloans & Kenyon Auctions.

Football

Autograph, football
Bergey, Bill **70.00**
Ditka, Mike **125.00**
Flaherty, Ray **150.00**
Green, Roy **70.00**
Long, Howie **75.00**
Autograph, helmet
Aikman, Troy, Dallas Cowboys **265.00**
Dawson, Len, Kansas City Chiefs **250.00**

Elway, John, Denver Broncos **275.00**
Autograph, photograph, 8" x 10"
Bradshaw, Terry **40.00**
Brown, Jim **30.00**
Thomas, Thurman **25.00**
Bank, 4-1/2" h, high gloss black finish ceramic, helmet, orange stripes, white face, orange and black decal "Northampton Area Senior High School/Konkreet Kids," white sponsor decal "First National Bank of Bath," c1960 .... **20.00**

Cartoon, 15" x 22" white art sheet, 14" x 19" orig sgd art in black ink and pencil by cartoonist Williard Mullin, blue pencil title "Theory vs Practice," blindfolded "All American Selector" attempting to select ideal college team and geographically correct, large center character "Pro Draft" who simply points to smiling footballer while deciding "Me For You," 1950s **125.00**

Drinking glass, 6-1/4" h, 3" d, National Football Clinic Banquet, Atlantic City, painted football passer, March 23-26, names of Dr. Harry G. Scott, Executive Director and Kenneth McFarland, banquet speaker, reverse lists staff of 14 university football coaches **12.00**

Media guide, Philadelphia Stars, 1984, 5" x 7-1/2" paperback **15.00**

Pennant, felt, A.F.L.
Boston Patriots, white on red, multicolored Patriot **75.00**
Buffalo Bills, white on blue, pink buffaloes **95.00**
Houston Oilers, white on light blue **75.00**

Pinback button
Gustavus Homecoming, gold and black, cartoon art of Ole and Gus wearing football helmets while tugging at worm between them, 1929 .... **15.00**
Hail to Pitt, blue on yellow, cartoon of football player using coal bucket to catch football, inscribed "Scuttle The Lions," c1940 .... **15.00**
Philadelphia Eagles, green on white cello, orange suspended miniature football charm, c1950 .... **15.00**

Program
Army vs. Duke, at the Polo Grounds, 1946 .... **40.00**
Green Bay Packers, 1960 .... **30.00**
Heisman Trophy, 1957, John David Crow **30.00**
Rose Bowl, 1974, USC vs. Ohio State **40.00**
Soda bottle or can, unopened
Baltimore Colts, RC Cola, late 1970s **2.00**
Penn State Championship Season 1986, 9-1/2" h unopened Coke bottle.. **15.00**

Bing Crosby stand-up display, leaning on golf club, cardboard, **$200**.

Golf

Autograph, photo, sgd, Tiger Woods **60.00**
Drinking glass, USGA Tournament, set of four, 5" h, clear glass, green inscription "U.S.G.A 56th Open Championship" and "Oak Hill Country Club-Rochester, NY," images of golfers at 18th hole in brown and white **25.00**
Golf club cane, 37-1/2" l, known as "Sunday Stick," 3" l x 3-1/2" h handle fashioned as early driver, ivory foot held in place with four ebony pins, faux lead weight, marked "Addington" on top of handle, orig owner's initials, two ivory and one ebony separators, oak shaft, 7/8" burnished brass and iron ferrule, c1890 .... **1,075.00**
Magazine, *American Golfer,* June 1932 .... **10.00**

Noisemaker, 2-3/4" d, 6-1/2" l, litho tin, full-color image of male golfer, marked "Germany" on handle, 1930s **35.00**

Print, Charles Crombie, *The Rules of Golf Illustrated*, 24 humorous lithographs of golfers in medieval clothes, London, 1905 .... **1,265.00**

Program, Fort Worth Open Golf Championship, Glen Garden Country Club, Ft Worth, TX, 1945 .... **100.00**

Tournament badge
Henredon Classic, 1987, celluloid **12.00**
PGA Tour, 1999, diecut rigid plastic **7.50**
21st Bob Hope Desert Classic, Jan. 9-13, 1980, diecut rigid plastic **9.50**

Hockey

Autograph
Orr, Bobby, photograph, 8" x 10" **50.00**
Smith, Clint, photograph, 8" x 10" **12.00**
Thompson, Tiny, puck .. **50.00**
Worsley, Gump, sgd 1968-69 Topps card **15.00**

Hockey stick, game used, autographed
Beliveau, Jean, 1960s CCM, cracked **700.00**
Cashman, Wayne, Sher-wood, uncracked **175.00**
LeBlanc, J. B., Koho, cracked **50.00**

Jersey, game used, Wayne Gretzky, Rangers, autographed **415.00**

Magazine, *Sport Revue,* Quebec publication, Feb 1956, Bert Olmstead, Hall of Fame cov **15.00**

Program, Boston Bruins, Sports News, 1937-38 .... **250.00**

Stick, game used, autographed
Bondra, Peter, Sherwood **90.00**
Lindros, Eric, Bauer Supreme **295.00**

Tobacco tin, Puck Tobacco, Canadian, tin litho, detailed image of two hockey players on both sides, 4" d, 3-1/4" h **190.00**

Tournament badge, 4" d, celluloid, World Hockey Tournament, Canada, red, and white **8.50**

Hunting

Badge, Western Cartridge Co., plant type, emb metal, pin back, 1-3/4" x 1-3/8" ... **100.00**

Book, *The World of the White-Tailed Deer*, Leonard Lee Rue III, J. B. Lippencott, 1962, 134 pgs, black and white illus, dj **15.00**

Box, Peters High Velocity, two-pc cardboard shot gun shells, multicolored graphics, 25 16-gauge shells **250.00**

Calendar top, Winchester, paper, man atop rock ledge, hunting rams, artist sgd "Philip R. Goodwin," metal top rim, 20" x 14" **125.00**

Manual, *How To Be A Crack Shot,* Remington/Dupont, June 1936 .... **20.00**

Print
"Life in the Woods-The Hunters Camp," published by Lyon & Co., printed by J. Rau, NY, five gentlemen in camp, two more fishing in lake, framed, 22" x 28", some foxing, center line burn, water stains in borders **150.00**
"Rabbit Catching-The Trap Sprung," lithographed by Currier and Ives, NY, two boys approaching box trap, winter setting, framed, 10" x 13", some toning, water stains at borders **495.00**

Sign
Paul Jones Whiskey, game-hunting scene, orig gold gilt frame, 43" x 57" **750.00**
Remington UMC, diecut cardboard
15" x 14", oversized shell next to box of ammunition .. **200.00**
15-1/2" x 9", Nitro Club Shells, English Setter atop pile of Remington Shotgun Shells **100.00**
L. C. Smith Guns, paper, two setters pointing to prey, 14" x 14-3/4" **1,200.00**
Winchester, diecut, cardboard, stand-up, Indian Chief with Winchester shotgun in one hand, additional barrels in other hand, 24" x 60" **200.00**

Trophy, 10-1/2" h, silverplate teapot, engraved in German "2nd Prize of the First Shooting Festival in Cincinnati held the 29th and 30th of September 1867 and won by

Julius Lang," Eastlake style, some denting **295.00**

Watch fob, Savage Revolver, figural, metal **110.00**

Pocket flask, pottery, green glaze, black lettering, Beneagles Scotch Whiskey, Sportsman's Flask, Red Deer, $5.

Olympics

Badge
1-3/4" x 2-1/4", enamel on brass, Winter Olympics, Albertville, red and blue on white, colored Olympic rings **25.00**
4" d, red, white, and blue celluloid, 1966 Central America Games **10.00**

Brochure, 9-1/4" x 12-1/2", Official Pictorial Souvenir, 1932, issued by organizing committee, Los Angeles, stiff paper covers, lightly emb soft green cover design with silver and gold accents, 64 black and white pages **40.00**

Cartoon, 8-1/2" x 12-1/2", white art sheet centered by 6-1/4" x 12" orig art cartoon in black ink by Carl Hubenthal, Los Angeles Examiner, 1956, art and caption relate to first ever 7' high jump in Olympic trials by US athlete Charlie Dumas **45.00**

Key ring tag, 2" x 2-1/2", metal, finished in pewter silver luster finish, official emblem for 1980 Lake Placid Winter Olympics **15.00**

Photo album, 10" x 12-1/2", 1932 Summer Olympics hosted in Los Angeles, hardcover, printed in Germany, 142 pgs of mounted photos, German text with results and statistics, orig dj **95.00**

Poster, 22" x 30", Lake Placid Winter Olympics, full color, copyright 1978 Amy Schneider, tightly curled **20.00**

STAFFORDSHIRE, HISTORICAL

History: The Staffordshire district of England is the center of the English pottery industry. There were 80 different potteries operating there in 1786, with the number increasing to 179 by 1802. The district includes Burslem, Cobridge, Etruria, Fenton, Foley, Hanley, Lane, Lane End, Longport, Shelton, Stoke, and Tunstall. Among the many famous potters were Adams, Davenport, Spode, Stevenson, Wedgwood, and Wood.

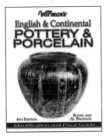

For more information, *see Warman's English & Continental Pottery & Porcelain*, 4th edition.

Notes: The view is the most critical element when establishing the value of historical Staffordshire; American collectors pay much less for non-American views. Dark blue pieces are favored; light views continue to remain underpriced. Among the forms, soup tureens have shown the largest price increases.

Prices listed here are for mint examples, unless otherwise noted. Reduce prices by 20 percent for a hidden chip, a faint hairline, or an invisible professional repair; by 35 percent for knife marks through the glaze and a visible professional repair; by 50 percent for worn glaze and major repairs.

The numbers in parentheses refer to items in the Armans' books, which constitute the most detailed list of American historical views and their forms.

Adams

W. ADAMS & SONS ADAMS

The Adams family has been associated with ceramics since the mid-17th century. In 1802, William Adams of Stoke-on-Trent produced American views.

In 1819, a fourth William Adams, son of William of Stoke, became a partner with his father and was later joined by his three brothers. The firm became William Adams & Sons. The father died in 1829 and William, the eldest son, became manager.

The company operated four potteries at Stoke and one at Tunstall. American views were produced at Tunstall in black, light blue, sepia, pink, and green in the 1830-40 period. William Adams died in 1865. All operations were moved to Tunstall. The firm continues today under the name of Wm. Adams & Sons, Ltd.

Adams, bowl, dark blue transfer printed decoration, villa at Regent's Park, London, difficult to read impressed mark, crazing, 10" d, **$150**.
Photo courtesy of Alderfer Auction Co.

Bowl, 11" d, 2-1/2" h, English scenes with ruins, dark blue transfer, yellowed repair on back............................ **155.00**
Creamer, 5 3/8" d, English scene, imp "Adams," dark blue............................ **175.00**
Pitcher, 5-3/4" h, Eagle, Scroll in Beak, blue and white transfer, illegible imp mark for William Adams, Stoke, 1827-31, glaze scratches................ **1,320.00**
Plate, 10-1/4" d, Mitchell & Freeman's China and Glass Warehouse, Chatham St, Boston, blue and white transfer, imp marker's mark and printed title on reverse **500.00**
Teapot, Log Cabin, medallions of Gen. Harrison on border, pink (458) **450.00**

Clews

From sketchy historical accounts that are available, it appears that James Clews took over the closed plant of A. Stevenson in 1819. His brother Ralph entered the business later. The firm continued until about 1836, when James Clews came to America to enter the pottery business at Troy, Indiana. The venture was a failure because of the lack of skilled workmen and the proper type of clay. He returned to England, but did not re-enter the pottery business.

Bowl, Landing of Lafayette, 9" d, ext. floral design, rim repair **410.00**
Cup plate, Landing of Lafayette at Castle Garden, dark blue **400.00**
Pitcher
6" h, Welcome Lafayette the Nation's Guest and Our Country's Glory, blue and white transfer, handle repair, int. staining **2,070.00**
6-3/4" h, States Border pattern, scenic country vista with mansion on hill, river in foreground, blue and white transfer dec, minor int. staining **980.00**

Clews, plate, America and Independence, States border, impressed mark, 10-1/2" d, **$175**.
Photo courtesy of Wiederseim Associates, Inc.

Plate
7-3/4" d, Landing of Gen Lafayette, blue and white transfer, imp maker's mark for James and Ralph Clews, c1819-36, minor wear. **500.00**
10" d, Landing of General Lafayette, imp "Clews," dark blue, very minor wear. **350.00**

10-1/2" d, America and Independence, States border, America wears Mason's apron, holds portrait of Washington, dark blue transfer, scalloped edge, imp "Clews, Warranted, Staffordshire" **825.00**
10-5/8" d, States series, America and Independence, fisherman with net, imp "Clews," dark blue, small rim flake **440.00**

Clews, plate, The Landing of General Lafayette at Castle Garden, impressed Clews mark, 10" d, **$375**.

Photo courtesy of Wiederseim Associates, Inc.

Clews, plate, America and Independence, States border, impressed mark, 9" d, **$275**.

Photo courtesy of Wiederseim Associates, Inc.

Platter

Landing of Gen LaFayette at Castle Garden New York 16 August 1824, 11-3/4" x 15-1/4", blue and white transfer, imp maker's mark, minor glaze scratches **2,200.00**
States Border, center with vista of river with two swans, two men, rowboat on river bank, large country house surrounded by trees in background, blue and white transfer, imp marker's mark of James and Ralph Clews, Cobridge, 1819-36, glaze scratches **2,530.00**
Winter View of Pittsfield Massachusetts, 14" x 16-1/2",

blue and white transfer, imp maker's mark, glaze scratches **3,450.00**

Soup plate

10-3/8" d, Winter View of Pittsfield, Mass, imp "Clews," dark blue **440.00**
10-1/2" d, Picturesque Views, Pittsburgh, PA, imp "Clews," steam ships with "Home, Nile, Larch," black transfer, chips on table ring **330.00**
Saucer, Landing of Gen. Lafayette, dark blue transfer, imp "Clews Warranted Staffordshire" **275.00**
Toddy plate, 5-3/4" d, Winter View of Pittsfield, Mass, scalloped edge, medium blue transfer, imp "Clews Warranted Staffordshire" **400.00**

J. & J. Jackson

J.&J. JACKSON

Job and John Jackson began operations at the Churchyard Works, Burslem, about 1830. The works formerly were owned by the Wedgwood family. The firm produced transfer scenes in a variety of colors, such as black, light blue, pink, sepia, green, maroon, and mulberry. More than 40 different American views of Connecticut, Massachusetts, Pennsylvania, New York, and Ohio were issued. The firm is believed to have closed about 1844.

Deep dish, American Beauty Series, Yale College (493) **125.00**
Plate, 10-3/8" d, The President's House, Washington, purple transfer **275.00**
Platter, American Beauty Series 12" l, Iron Works at Saugerties (478) **275.00**
17-1/2" l, View of Newburgh, black transfer (463) ... **575.00**
Soup plate, 10" d, American Beauty Series, Hartford, CT, black transfer (476) ... **150.00**

Thomas Mayer

In 1829, Thomas Mayer and his brothers, John and Joshua, purchased Stubbs' Dale Hall Works of Burslem. They continued to produce a superior grade of ceramics.

Cream pitcher, 4" h, Lafayette at Franklin's Tomb, dark blue **550.00**
Gravy tureen, Arms of the American States, CT, dark blue (498) **3,800.00**
Plate, 8-1/2" d, Arms of Rhode Island, blue and white transfer, eagle back stamp, 1829, minor glaze scratches **790.00**

Platter

8-1/4" l, Lafayette at Franklin's Tomb, dark blue......... **525.00**
19" l, Arms of the American States, NJ, dark blue (503) **7,200.00**
Sugar bowl, cov, Lafayette at Franklin's Tomb, dark blue (510) **850.00**

Mellor, Veneables & Co.

Little information is recorded on Mellor, Veneables & Co., except that it was listed as potters in Burslem in 1843. The company's Scenic Views with the Arms of the States Border does include the arms for New Hampshire. This state is missing from the Mayer series.

Plate, 7-1/2" d, Tomb of Washington, Mt. Vernon, Arms of States border.......... **125.00**

Platter

14-1/2" x 19-3/4", European view, light blue and white transfer, imp and printed maker's mark, c1843, hairline, light wear **365.00**
15" l, Scenic Views, Arms of States border, Albany, light blue (516) **265.00**
Sugar bowl, cov, Arms of States, PA, dark blue **350.00**
Teapot, 9-1/2" h, Windsor pattern, dark blue **200.00**

John & William Ridgeway, soup plate, dark blue transfer printed decoration, *Boston Octagon Church,* from Beauties of America series, floral medallion border, printed title and maker on the reverse, Hanley, England, 1814-30, 9-3/4" d, **$400**.

Photo courtesy of Skinner, Inc.

J. & W. Ridgway and William Ridgway & Co.

John and William Ridgway, sons of Job Ridgway and nephews of George Ridgway, who owned Bell Bank Works and Cauldon Place Works, produced the popular Beauties of America series at the Cauldon plant. The partnership between the two brothers was dissolved in 1830. John remained at Cauldon.

William managed the Bell Bank Works until 1854. Two additional series were produced based upon the etchings of Bartlett's American Scenery. The first series had various borders including narrow lace. The second series is known as Catskill Moss. Beauties of America is in dark blue. The other series are found in light transfer colors of blue, pink, brown, black, and green.

Plate
 7" d, American Scenery, Valley of the Shenandoah from Jefferson's Rock, brown (289) **120.00**
 10" h, Beauties of America, City Hall, NY, dark blue (260) **225.00**

Platter
 12-3/4" x 16-1/2", Beauties of America series, Alms House New York, blue and white transfer, printed title, scratches, scattered minor staining **1,265.00**
 19" l, Catskill Moss, Boston and Bunker's Hill, imp "William Ridgway Son & Co," medium blue, dated 1844, minor chips, knife marks, edge wear **525.00**

Relish tray, 5-3/8" x 8-1/4", Savannah Bank, Beauties of America Series, blue and white transfer, printed title, c1814-30, minor imperfections **750.00**

Soup plate, 9-7/8" d, Octagon Church Boston, imp "Ridgway," dark medium blue **330.00**

Wash bowl, American Scenery, Albany (279) **325.00**

Rogers

ROGERS

John Rogers and his brother George established a pottery near Longport in 1782. After George's death in 1815, John's son Spencer became a partner, and the firm operated under the name of John Rogers & Sons. John died in 1916. His son continued the use of the name until he dissolved the pottery in 1842.

Basket and undertray, 3" x 6-1/2" x 9-1/4", Boston State House, blue and white transfer, imp marker's mark for John Rogers and Son, Longport, 1815-50, hairline cracks **2,760.00**

Cup and saucer, Boston Harbor, dark blue (441) **650.00**

Cup plate, Boston Harbor, dark blue (441) **1,400.00**

Deep dish, 12-3/4" d, Boston State House, blue and white transfer, imp marker's mark for John Rogers and Son, Longport, 1815-42, minor glaze scratches **2,070.00**

Plate, 9-5/8" d, The Canal at Buffalo, lace border, purple transfer, int. hairline **55.00**

Platter, 16-5/8" l, Boston State House, medium dark blue (442) **1,000.00**

Sauce tureen, cov, undertray, Boston State House, blue and white transfer, imp maker's mark for John Rogers and Son, Longport, 1815-42 .... **2,900.00**

Waste bowl, Boston Harbor, dark blue (441) **850.00**

Stevenson

As early as the 17th century, the name Stevenson has been associated with the pottery industry.

R. S. W.

Andrew Stevenson of Cobridge introduced American scenes with the flower and scroll border. Ralph Stevenson, also of Cobridge, used a vine and leaf border on his dark blue historical views and a lace border on his series in light transfers.

The initials R. S. & W. indicate Ralph Stevenson and Williams are associated with the acorn and leaf border. It has been reported that Williams was Ralph's New York agent and the wares were produced by Ralph alone.

Bowl
 8-3/4" d, Park Theater New York, blue and white transfer, printed mark, Ralph Stevens and Williams, Cobridge, 1815-40, minute scratches . **2,530.00**
 11" d, Capitol Washington, blue and white transfer, printed mark, Ralph Stevens and Williams, Cobridge, 1815-40, glaze imperfections **2,645.00**

Cup and saucer, New Orleans, floral and scroll border . **95.00**

Jug, 8-1/4" h, dark blue print **750.00**

Pitcher, 10" h, Almshouse, Boston, reverse with Esplanade and Castle Garden New York, blue and white transfer, unmarked... **2,300.00**

Plate
 6-1/2" d, Catholic Cathedral, NY, floral and scroll border, dark blue (395) **1,650.00**
 7-1/2" d, Columbia College, portrait medallion of President Washington, inset View of the Aqueduct Bridge at Rochester, blue and white transfer, Ralph Stevens and Williams, Cobridge, 1815-40, minor scratches **8,625.00**
 8-1/2" d, Welcome Lafayette the Nation's Guest, portrait medallion of President Washington, City Hotel, New York, inset "entrance to the Canal into the Hudson at Albany," blue and white transfer, Ralph Stevens and Williams, Cobridge, 1815-40, minor scratches **4,600.00**
 9" d, Boston Hospital, blue and white transfer, stamped title, maker's initials, imp maker's mark, minor glaze scratches **350.00**
 10" d, Welcome LaFayette the Nation's Guest, Jefferson, Washington, Governor Clinton, Park Street Theater New York, vignette of View of Aqueduct Bridge at Little Falls, blue and white transfer, Ralph Stevens and Williams, Cobridge, 1815-40, minor scratches **3,740.00**

10-1/4" d, New York from Brooklyn Heights, printed title, imp maker's mark, A. Stevenson, Cobridge, 1808-29 .... **900.00**
10-1/4" d, View of Governor's Island, printed title, imp maker's mark, A. Stevenson, Cobridge, 1808-29 ..... **950.00**

Platter
7-1/4" x 9-1/4", Troy from Mount Ida, by W. G. Wallogy, landscape scene, floral border, blue and white transfer, back stamped with American eagle, marked "A. Stevenson Warranted Staffordshire" **1,550.00**
10-1/4" x 13", Battle of Bunker Hill, blue and white transfer, printed title, imp maker's mark, Ralph Stevenson, Cobridge, 1815-40, one scratch **8,625.00**
14-1/2" x 18-1/2", New York Esplanade and Castle Garden, blue and white transfer, printed title, imp maker's mark, Ralph Stevenson, Cobridge, 1815-40, minor glaze scratches **5,750.00**

Soup plate, 9" d, View on the Road to Lake George, printed title, imp maker's mark, A. Stevenson, Cobridge, 1808-29 .... **1,100.00**

Toddy plate, 4-7/8" d, American Museum, NY, dark blue transfer, mkd "Scudder's American Museum, R.S.W.," impressed Stevenson . **660.00**

Wash bowl, Riceborough, GA, lace border (388) **375.00**

Stubbs

In 1790, Stubbs established a pottery works at Burslem, England. He operated it until 1829, when he retired and sold the pottery to the Mayer brothers. He probably produced his American views about 1825. Many of his scenes were from Boston, New York, New Jersey, and Philadelphia.

Gravy boat, 4-1/4" h, Hoboken in New Jersey, Steven's House, blue and white transfer, printed title, Joseph Stubbs,

Burslem, 1790-1829, minor imperfections **550.00**
Pitcher, 6" h, Boston State House, reverse with City Hall New York, blue and white transfer, unmarked, small chip on handle **980.00**
Plate
6-1/2" h, City Hall New York, floral and eagle border, medium blue transfer, unmarked, minor wear and small repair **225.00**
9" d, Upper Ferry Bridge of the River Schuylkill, blue and white transfer, printed title, Joseph Stubbs, Burslem, 1790-1829, imperfections **950.00**
10-1/4" h, Fair Mount near Philadelphia, floral border with eagles, medium blue transfer, imp "Stubbs" **475.00**
Platter
12" x 14-3/4", State House Boston, blue and white transfer, printed title, marked "Joseph Stubbs, Burslem," 1790-1829, minor scratches and crazing **1,265.00**
13-3/4" x 16-3/4", Mendenhall Ferry, blue and white transfer, printed title, minor glaze scratches **2,185.00**
15-1/2" x 18-3/4", Upper Ferry Bridge over the River Schuylkill, well and tree, printed title on reverse, hairline **715.00**
Salt shaker, Hoboken in NJ, spread eagle border, dark blue (326) **700.00**
Wash bowl and pitcher, Upper Ferry Bridge Over the River Schuylkill, 12-5/8" d bowl, 10" h pitcher, blue and white, printed title, Joseph Stubbs, Burslem, 1790-1829 **1,840.00**

Unknown makers
Bowl, 11-1/8" d, 3-1/4" d, Franklin, scene of Ben flying kite, red transfer, minor wear **495.00**
Cup, handleless, dark blue transfer, Quadruped series, llama on both sides, floral border, scalloped rim . **115.00**
Fruit bowl, undertray, 10-1/2" l, 5" h, reticulated, blue and white transfer, figures, cows, and manors in rural landscape, floral borders **765.00**

Unknown maker, bowl, "A View Near Philadelphia," titled on back, 9-3/4" d, **$395**.

Photo courtesy of Wiederseim Associates, Inc.

Unknown maker, plate, "Fair Mount Near Philadelphia," titled on back, 10-3/4" d, **$375**.

Photo courtesy of Wiederseim Associates, Inc.

Unknown maker, plate, Library of Philadelphia, titled on back, 8" d, **$350**.

Photo courtesy of Wiederseim Associates, Inc.

Jug, 6-3/4" h, pearlware, brown transfer print, commemorating British Admiral Nelson, portrait, ship *Victory,* various nautical devices, orange enamel highlights on rim and edges of handle, minor imperfections **1,650.00**
Pitcher, 5-7/8" h, dark blue transfer, View of the Erie Canal, floral borders, transfer slightly blurred, repairs **715.00**

Plate

8" d, View from Coenties-slip, scene of Great Fire, City New York, light blue transfer, wear, small edge flakes........ **385.00**

8-1/2" d, Court House Baltimore, blue and white transfer, fruit and flower border, printed title on reverse, light wear, hairline.................. **470.00**

8-3/4" d, Nahant Hotel near Boston, dark blue transfer, wear, chips on table ring **200.00**

9" d, "The Residence of the late Richard Jordon, New Jersey," brown, minor wear and stains **250.00**

9-3/4" d, City Hall, New York, dark blue transfer, minor wear **275.00**

9-7/8" d, The Dam and Waterworks Philadelphia, blue and white transfer, fruit and flower border, printed title on reverse...................... **650.00**

10" d, Exchange Baltimore, blue and white transfer, fruit and floral border, printed title on reverse **390.00**

10-1/4", Fulton's Steamboat, blue and white transfer, floral border, minor scratches and rim chips **890.00**

Platter, 16-5/8" l, Sandusky, dark blue, very minor scratches **8,525.00**

Saucer, 5-7/8" d, scene of early railroad, engine and one car, floral border, dark blue.. **275.00**

Teapot, 8-1/4" h, The Residence of the Late Richard Jordan, New Jersey, brown transfer, small chip, stain and repair to lid **715.00**

Tea service, partial, Mount Vernon the Seat of the Late Gen Washington, blue and white transfer, floral border, three teapots, creamer, three cov sugar bowls, waste bowl, 13 tea bowls, 12 saucers, some with printed titles, imperfections **8,625.00**

Unknown maker, coffeepot, dark blue transfer printed decoration, wide floral and scroll border, English landscape scene with old woman and seated man, rim chip, lid broken, 9" h, **$390**.

Photo courtesy of Alderfer Auction Co.

Unknown maker, plate, dark blue transfer printed decoration, scalloped rim, centered with words of First Amendment of United States Constitution, border of eagles with American shields and four medallions; two with quotations from Constitution, third with pair of scales, fourth with Justice pardoning a slave, England, 19th C, 9-1/2" d, **$500**.

Photo courtesy of Skinner, Inc.

Wood

Enoch Wood, sometimes referred to as the father of English pottery, began operating a pottery at Fountain Place, Burslem, in 1783. A cousin, Ralph Wood, was associated with him. In 1790, James Caldwell became a partner and the firm was known as Wood and Caldwell. In 1819, Wood and his sons took full control.

Enoch died in 1840. His sons continued under the name of Enoch Wood & Sons. The American views were first made in the mid-1820s and continued through the 1840s.

It is reported that the pottery produced more signed historical views than any other Staffordshire firm. Many of the views attributed to unknown makers probably came from the Woods.

Marks vary, although always include the name Wood. The establishment was sold to Messrs. Pinder, Bourne & Hope in 1846.

Creamer, 5-3/4" h, horse drawn sleigh, imp "Wood," dark blue, minor hairline in base . **550.00**

Cup and saucer, handleless Commodore MacDonnough's Victory, imp "Wood & Sons," dark blue, pinpoints on cup table ring **355.00**

Ship with American flag, Chancellor Livingston, imp "Wood & Sons" **770.00**

Gravy boat, 7-1/2" l, Catskill Mountains Hudson River, blue and white transfer, printed title, minor imperfections **650.00**

Pitcher and basin, 4-1/2" d x 9-5/8" h pitcher, 12" d basin, Lafayette at Franklin's Tomb, floral and foliate borders, blue transfer dec, Burslem, England, 1819-46, repair on spout of pitcher **1,410.00**

Enoch Wood & Sons, plate, dark blue transfer printed decoration, titled *The Landing of the Fathers at Plymouth, Dec 22 1620,* border with medallions with ships and inscriptions, "America Independent July 4 1776," and "Washington Born 1732 Died 1799," impressed maker's mark, Burslem, England, 1819-46, 10-1/8" d, **$300**.

Photo courtesy of Skinner, Inc.

Plate

6-1/2" d, Cowes Harbour, blue and white transfer, shell border, imp maker's mark on reverse, light wear **245.00**

6-1/2" d, Mount Vernon, the Seat of the Late Gen'l Washington, blue and white transfer, imp maker's mark, 1819-46 .... **850.00**

6-1/2" d, Transylvania University, Kentucky, shell border, dark blue, label with eagle and banner and "E Pluribus Unim," imp "Wood" **775.00**

7-5/8" d, Commodore MacDonnough's Victory, shell border, blue transfer, printed titles on the front and impressed maker's marks on the reverse, c1819-46.. **325.00**

8-1/4" d, Dartmouth, ships in harbor, irregular shell border, medium blue transfer, unmarked, knife scratches, minor stains **350.00**

8-1/2" d, Boston State House, blue and white transfer, imp maker's mark, 1819-46.. **325.00**

9-1/8" d, Commodore MacDonnough's Victory, shell border, blue transfer, printed titles on the front and impressed maker's marks on the reverse, c1819-46. **300.00**

9-1/4" d, The Baltimore & Ohio Railroad, (incline), imp "Enoch Wood," dark blue........ **770.00**

10" d, View of Liverpool, shell border, blue transfer, printed titles on the front and impressed maker's marks on the reverse, c1819-46. **350.00**

10-1/4" d, Commodore MacDonnough's Victory, shell border, blue transfer, printed titles on the front and impressed maker's marks on the reverse, c1819-46. **300.00**

10-1/4" d, Pine Orchard House, Catskill Mountains, blue and white transfer, printed title, glaze scratches **575.00**

10-1/4" d, The Baltimore & Ohio Railroad, (straight), imp "Wood," dark blue, minor scratches **825.00**

10-3/8" d, Constitution and Guerriere, imp "Wood," dark blue minor scratches **1,760.00**

10-1/2" d, East Cowes Isle of Wright, shell border, blue and white transfer **765.00**

Platter

10" x 12-3/4", Highlands Hudson River, blue and white transfer, printed title, imp maker's mark, Enoch Wood & Sons, Burslem, 1819-46, minor roughness **3,335.00**

12-3/4" x 16-1/2", Lake George State of New York, blue and white transfer, printed title, partial imp marker's mark, c1819-46, minor glaze imperfections **2,585.00**

14-1/2" x 18-3/4", Christianburg Danish Settlement on the Gold Coast Africa, blue and white transfer, imp maker's mark, minor glaze imperfections. **3,220.00**

Sugar bowl, cov, 7" d, 6" h, Wadsworth Tower, blue and white transfer, scalloped shaped handles, minor imperfections **265.00**

Tea service, partial, Wadsworth

Tower, cov teapot, two large teacups, one large saucer, five teacups, six saucers, 15 plates, imperfections **2,645.00**

Toddy plate, 6-1/2" d, dark blue transfer, Catskill House, Hudson, imp "Wood," minor wear and stains **525.00**

Tureen, cov, 7" h, Passaic Falls, State of New Jersey, blue and white transfer, repairs, glaze wear **200.00**

Undertray, 8-1/8" l, Pass in the Catskill Mountains, blue and white transfer, imp maker's mark, printed title, repair to handle **200.00**

Waste bowl, 6-1/4" d, 3-1/4" h, Washington standing at Tomb, scroll in hand, blue and white transfer, unmarked, Enoch Wood & Sons, Burslem, 1819-40, minor imperfections **750.00**

STAFFORDSHIRE ITEMS

History: A wide variety of ornamental pottery items originated in England's Staffordshire district, beginning in the 17th century and still continuing today. The height of production took place from 1820 to 1890.

Many collectors consider these naive pieces folk art. Most items were not made carefully; some even were made and decorated by children.

The types of objects are varied, e.g., animals, cottages, and figurines (chimney ornaments).

For more information, *see Warman's English & Continental Pottery & Porcelain,* 4th edition.

Reproduction Alert: Early Staffordshire figurines and

hollowware forms were molded. Later examples were made using a slip-casting process. Slip casting leaves telltale signs that are easy to spot. Look in the interior. Hand molding created a smooth interior surface. Slip casting produces indentations that conform to the exterior design. Holes occur where handles meet the body of slip-cast pieces. There is not hole in a hand-molded piece.

A checkpoint on figurines is the firing or vent hole, which is a necessary feature on these forms. Early figurines had small holes; modern reproductions feature large holes often the size of a dime or quarter. Vent holes are found on the sides or hidden among the decoration in early Staffordshire figurines; most modern reproductions have them in the base.

These same tips can be used to spot modern reproductions of Flow Blue, Majolica, Old Sleepy Eye, Stoneware, Willow, and other ceramic pieces.

Note: The key to price is age and condition. As a general rule, the older the piece, the higher the price.

Breakfast set, Crown Staffordshire, turquoise blue ground, applied floral decoration, 11-piece set, **$175**.

Photo courtesy of Dotta Auction Co., Inc.

Bank, 5-1/4" h, cottage shape, repairs........................ **195.00**

Bust, 8-1/4" h, Empress Maria Theresa, England, lead glaze creamware, underglaze translucent enamels, half bust mounted atop waisted socle, pierced hole to one shoulder factory made and apparently for holding additional ornament, late 18th C, slight glaze chip **1,175.00**

Cake stand, blue and white transfer, Wild Rose pattern, crazing, 12" d, 2-1/2" h **400.00**

Candlestick, lead glazed creamware
11-1/4" h, underglaze translucent colors, free form tree with leaf molded sconce and applied florets, late 18th C, restorations **1,175.00**
11-3/4" h, underglaze translucent brown, green, and blue enamels, molded tree form with applied foliage and shells, bird perched on branch, male figure standing on flat platform in center, late 18th C, restorations **650.00**

Cheese dish, cov, 9-3/4" l, 7-1/2" h, figural, cow head, enamel and pink luster detailing, shaped undertray **265.00**

Chimney piece
7-1/4" h, castle with two towers, drummer, polychrome enamel dec, gilt, coleslaw foliage, minor edge damage **215.00**
9-1/8" h, multistoried house, coleslaw trim, pierced windows, topped with vining strawberries, some wear, hairlines **320.00**

Bust, George Washington, blue jacket, floral patterned vest, black cravat, simulated marble plinth, early 19th C, minor chip, retouch, 8" h, **$500**.

Photo courtesy of Skinner, Inc.

Creamer, 7" l, 2-1/2" h, cow, blue and dark red splotch polychrome dec, pearlware, early 19th C **235.00**

Cup and saucer, handleless, Gaudy floral design, blue, dark green, and gold, saucer imp "Clews Warranted Staffordshire," small rim flake on cup **250.00**

Cup plate
3-3/4" d, hand dec, polychrome floral wreath border, spring center, imp "TT"............................. **145.00**
3-7/8" d, two hunters, one seated, hunting dog, light blue, border with gun and bag, imp "D" **100.00**
3-15/16" d, Sheltered Peasants, dark blue, flower and fruit border, mkd with title **110.00**
4" d, Moses and the Ten Commandments, red, floral and shell border, indiscernible imp mark..................... **180.00**
4" d, Prunus Wreath, medium dark blue, imp "Rogers" **165.00**
4-1/8" d, Moral Maxim, red, two border reserves.... **125.00**
4-1/4" d, three unidentified vases, light blue, mkd "Smith & Pardee, Kingston, NY" ... **55.00**

Seated dogs, copper luster highlights, facing pair, 9" h, **$250**.

Photo courtesy of Joy Luke

Figure, polychrome enamel dec
7" h, sportsman, orange jacket, mounted on horse, hairlines **350.00**
7-5/8" h, spaniels, seated, red and white, yellow collars, pr................. **320.00**
8-1/8" h, The Lost Sheep, pearlware, shepherd wearing maroon coat, ochre striped vest and green breeches, carrying sheep with its legs tied to stick over his shoulder, rocky base and square plinth, England, 1750-85, small repair **530.00**

Figure, shepherdess, standing, blue skirt, jacket trimmed in yellow, holding lamb in one arm, early 19th C, 10-1/4" h, **$1,175**.

Photo courtesy of Skinner, Inc.

9-1/4" h, Scottish couple, matching green feathered caps, man wearing green and orange tartan, holding horn, woman holding basket **115.00**

10-3/4" h, Whippet holding rabbit in its mouth, Victorian, second half 19th C, price for pr, one with leg damage **425.00**

10-7/8" h, cow and calf with tree trunk vase, facing pair, Victorian, c1870.......... **470.00**

11" h, Templars, modeled as three officials, two women flanking bearded man, raised initials I.O.G.T. (International Order of Good Templars), Victorian, c1870.......... **200.00**

11" h, Turpin and King, titled bases, late Victorian, price for pr **400.00**

11-3/4" h, St. Patrick, standing, hand to heart, base titled, enamel and gilt dec, Victorian, c1860.......... **215.00**

12" l, Antony and Cleopatra, reclining, silver lustered armor, England, early 19th C, possibly Wood and Caldwell, slight footrim chips, price for pr **2,585.00**

12-3/4" h, King John Signing the Magna Carta, King John seated beneath tent, page to either side, Victorian, c1865, restored chip at tip of flag, pen chipped **300.00**

13-1/4" h, Prodigal's Return, two standing figures, raised title on base, gilt highlights, Victorian, c1880.......... **360.00**

13-3/4" h, male and female figures arm in arm, seated beneath arbor, Victorian, c1860, stained glaze .. **200.00**

13-3/4" h, Victoria and Victor Emmanuel II, modeled standing figures, man in military attire with hound by his feet, woman in formal dress, base titled "Queen & King of Sardinia," gilt trim, Victorian, c1855, crazing **200.00**

13-7/8" h, Charles Stewart Parnell, England, c1880, standing, holding shillelagh in one hand, flag bearing the Union Jack and Irish harp in other, raised title on base, Victorian, c1880, gilt wear **450.00**

14-3/4" h, William Wallace, standing, holding shield in one hand, sword in other, raised title to base, Victorian, c1860 .... **250.00**

15-1/2" h, Mary, standing, holding book, peasant garb, Victorian, c1860 .... **200.00**

15-1/2" h, Napoleon III, standing, military uniform, holding cocked hat, base titled "Louis Napoleon," enamel and gilt dec, Victorian, c1855 .... **200.00**

16-1/2" h, Gordon-Cumming, modeled standing by dead lion, titled "The Lion Slayer," c1860 .... **275.00**

Fruit basket and underplate, 12" l basket molded and reticulated with central guilloche band, 10" d underplate with matching rim, underglaze blue and pink floral sprays, gilt accenting, mid-19th C **235.00**

Figure, calico cat, seated on oval scroll decorated base, early 19th C, minor chips, 3-5/8" h, **$1,000**.

Photo courtesy of Skinner, Inc.

Hens on nests, three white with naturalistic colored beaks and eyes, seated on basketweave bases with polychrome decoration, small one in front with yellow, red, and white painted feathers with black and gray shading, black one in back with crack, **$650**.

Photo courtesy of Wiederseim Associates, Inc.

Hen on nest, 10-1/2" l, polychrome, good color, minor edge wear and chips on inner flange of base **715.00**

Jar, cov, 3-1/4" h, melon shape, alternating yellow and green stripes, cov with molded leaf, lead glaze, 18th C, hairline to cover, finial and rim chips **4,315.00**

Jug, 8-1/2" h, Fair Hebe, high relief, modeled as tree trunk, creamware, lead glaze, attributed to Yoyez, c1788, rim chip and repair **998.00**

Miniature, tea set, Gaudy pink and green rose dec, 4-1/4" h teapot, creamer, sugar, waste bowl, two cups and saucers, few flakes, repairs **425.00**

Mug, 3-3/4" h, pearlware, black transfer print of Hope in landscape scene, silver luster highlights, minor imperfections **60.00**

Pitcher, 4-7/8" h, mask, pink luster rim, glaze wear, hairline to spout **175.00**

Plate
5-7/8" d, New York, US, medium red, eagle and cornucopia mark **95.00**
7-7/8" d, Shannondale Springs, Virginia, US, medium red, eagle and cornucopia mark............................. **70.00**

Platter, 21" d, blue and white transfer, "The Italian Pattern," attributed to Spode, early 19th C, unmarked, glaze wear, scratches **575.00**

Sauce boat, 7-7/8" l, fruit and flowers, molded feet and handle, dark blue, rim chips **330.00**

Stirrup cup, 4-3/4" l, creamware, modeled as a stag and decorated in translucent brown and yellow enamels, lead glaze, England, 18th C, restorations **2,585.00**

Seated dogs, coleslaw coats, black noses, yellow eyes, facing pair, 6" h, **$350**.

Photo courtesy of Dotta Auction Co., Inc.

Teapot, cov, 9-3/4" l, black basalt, oval form, scalloped rim and classical reliefs centering columns with floral festoons, banded drapery on shoulder, incised brick banded lower body, unmarked, early 19th C, restored spout **360.00**

Toddy plate, 4-13/16" d, multicolored view of thatched cottage at foot of hill, surmounted by castle ruins, sepia butterfly border, imp "P" **90.00**

Tureen, cov, 10-1/4" l, stoneware, white, salt glazed, oval, press molded dot and diaper, star and diaper and basket pattern, three grotesque mask and paw feet, England, c1760, rim line, repaired chips to two feet **2,350.00**

Vegetable dish, cov, 10-3/4" d, 7-1/2" h, domed cover with ornately molded knop and handles, blue transfer flowers, fruit, and shells, sq foot, Longport, England, early 19th C, minor nick to knop and cover rim................. **1,410.00**

Waste bowl, 5-5/8" d, Forget Me Not, red transfer, edge roughness.................... **60.00**

Whistle, 3-1/2" h, overglazed enamel dec, modeled as bird perched on tree trunk, applied florets, c1820, tail restored **420.00**

STAFFORDSHIRE, ROMANTIC

History: In the 1830s, two factors transformed the blue-and-white printed wares of the Staffordshire potters into what is now called "Romantic Staffordshire." Technical innovations expanded the range of transfer-printed colors to light blue, pink, purple, black, green, and brown. There was also a shift from historical to imaginary scenes with less printed detail and more white space, adding to the pastel effect.

Shapes from the 1830s are predominately rococo with rounded forms, scrolled handles, and floral finials. Over time, patterns and shapes became simpler and the earthenware bodies coarser. The late 1840s and 1850s saw angular gothic shapes and pieces with the weight and texture of ironstone.

The most dramatic post-1870 change was the impact of the craze for all things Japanese. Staffordshire designs adopted zigzag border elements and motifs such as bamboo, fans, and cranes. Brown printing dominated this style, sometimes with polychrome enamel highlights.

For more information, *see Warman's English & Continental Pottery & Porcelain*, 4th edition.

Marks: Wares are often marked with pattern or potter's names, but marking was inconsistent and many authentic, unmarked examples exist. The addition of "England" as a country of origin mark in 1891 helps to distinguish 20th-century wares made in the romantic style.

Plate, Andalusia pattern, red and white transfer, name on back, impressed "Adams," **$76**.

Caledonia, Williams Adams, 1830s
Plate, 9-1/2" d, purple transfer, imp "Adams" **60.00**
Platter, 17" l **500.00**
Soup plate, two colors **175.00**

Canova, Thomas Mayer, c1835; G. Phillips, c1840
Plate, 10-1/2" d **95.00**
Pudding bowl, two colors **200.00**
Vegetable, cov **325.00**

Cheshire pattern, Burleigh Ware, cheese dish, cov, 9-1/4" l, 5" h, rect, sloped lid, underglaze blue ovoid finial, rect undertray, transfer printed green and blue **115.00**

Columbia, W. Adams & Sons, 1850
Creamer **115.00**
Cup and saucer **65.00**
Cup plate **65.00**
Plate, 10" d **60.00**
Relish **65.00**

Dado, Ridgways, 1880s
Creamer, brown **75.00**
Cup and saucer, polychrome **80.00**
Plate, 7-1/2" d, brown ... **35.00**

Dr. Syntax, James and Ralph Clews, Cobridge, 1819-36
Plate, 10-1/2" d, Dr. Syntax Disputing his Bill with the Landlady, blue and white transfer **125.00**
Platter, 14-1/4" x 19", Dr. Syntax Amused with Pat in the Pond, blue and white transfer, glaze scratches, scattered minor staining **1,840.00**

Coffeepot, blue transfer decoration, Oriental-type scene, **$350**.
Photo courtesy of Dotta Auction Co., Inc.

Place setting, maroon border with reserves of multicolored peacocks, gold trim, marked "Myott, Staffordshire, England," **$80**.

Undertray, 10" x 5-3/4", Death of Punch, Dr. Syntax literary series, blue and white transfer, crazing on reverse **85.00**

Marmora, William Ridgway & Co., 1830s
Platter, 16-1/2" l **325.00**
Sauce tureen, matching tray **350.00**
Soup plate **100.00**

Millenium, Ralph Stevenson & Son, 1830s, plate, 10-1/2" d **145.00**

Palestine, William Adams, 1836
Creamer and sugar **265.00**
Cup and saucer, two colors **135.00**
Cup plate **75.00**
Plate, 7" d **60.00**

Platter, 13" l **325.00**
Vegetable, open, 12" l. **200.00**
Quadrupeds, John Hall, 1814-32
Plate, 10" d, central medallion with lion, printed maker's mark, pattern mark in crown, price for pr **865.00**
Platter, 14-3/4" x 19", Quadrupeds pattern, central cartouche of elephant, printed maker's mark, pattern mark in crown, minor surface imperfections **4,315.00**

Pitcher, Tamara, polychrome decoration, purple transfer, **$125**.

Photo courtesy of Wiederseim Associates, Inc.

Shell pattern, Stubbs and Kent, Longport, 1828-30
Cream jug, 5" h, blue and white transfer, unmarked, imperfections **1,200.00**
Milk pitcher, 7" h, blue and white transfer, unmarked, imperfections **900.00**
Platter, 18-1/2" l, oval, blue and white transfer, imp maker's mark, repaired rim chip **1,955.00**
Soup plate, 10" d, blue and white transfer, imp maker's mark, wear, price for three
.... **750.00**
Tea bowl and saucer, 2-1/2" h, blue and white transfer, imp maker's mark **450.00**
Vegetable dish, 12-1/4" d, 2-1/2" h, oval, blue and white transfer, imp maker's mark, scratches, wear **1,150.00**
Union, William Ridgway Son & Co., 1840s
Plate, 10-1/2" d **70.00**
Platter, 15" l **165.00**

Vegetable bowl, green and white transfer decoration, center scene with elephant in garden, marked "Reproduction of Rogers 1780, Made in England, John Stevenson & Son, Burslem," **$25**.

The reproduction mark of the vegetable bowl, shown above.

Unknown pattern
Cup and Saucer, two dogs, flower and leaf border, imp maker's mark for James & Ralph Clews, Cobridge, 1817-34, 2-1/4" h, 5-3/4" h, minor light wear **150.00**
Tea Set, partial, blue and white transfer
Bird in oval reverse, floral border, two teapots, creamer, small bowl, waste bowl, imperfections **1,265.00**
Three figures in landscape, manor house in distance, teapot, creamer, and two cov sugar bowls **1,610.00**
Venus, Podmore, Walker & Co., 1850s, plate, 7-1/2" d ... **50.00**
Yorkshire, soup plate, 10" d, light blue, slight glaze lines
.... **200.00**

STAINED AND/OR LEADED GLASS PANELS

History: American architects in the second half of the 19th century and the early 20th century used stained- and leaded-glass panels as a chief decorative element. Skilled glass craftsmen assembled the designs, the best known being Louis C. Tiffany.

The panels are held together with soft lead cames or copper wraps. When purchasing a panel, protect your investment by checking the lead and making any necessary repairs.

Arched window, turquoise border, single flower above green foliage, gold trim, **$295**.

Stained glass panel, green and red heart pattern, framed, modern, 25" x 28", **$195**.

Photo courtesy of Joy Luke Auctions.

Leaded

Door, 28" w, 78" h, bench leaded, clear glass, elongated with ornate part beveled glass inserts
.... **1,450.00**
Fire screen, 32-3/4" h, leaded glass, tripartite, central square panel and two narrow side panels set with multicolored textured and

bull's eye glass pieces, brass surround, griffin-form trestle feet, Renaissance Revival, late 19th/early 20th C **1,100.00**

Panel, 96" h, 20" w, rect, rippled, and opaque glass, turquoise, white, and avocado, clear glass ground, stylized flowering plant motif, c1910, six panels................ **6,000.00**

Sketch for leaded glass window

Charcoal on paper, The Crucifixion, 26" d, America, c1920......................... **170.00**

Watercolor, garden scene, mother and child before Christ figure, sgd on mat "Louis Comfort Tiffany," 6-3/4" x 4-1/2"......................... **1,725.00**

Triptych, 34 3/4" h, 17-3/4" w, twining grapevines and grape clusters, green slag, textured purple and brown glass, amber border segments, textured colorless glass background, wood frame, cracks..................... **1,380.00**

Window

17-3/4" d int., 19-1/4" d outside, bull's eye, beaded gilt-metal frame, octagonal surround, central beveled colorless glass octagon, surrounded by beveled diamonds, price for pr **1,035.00**

29" h, 93" l, Henry Belcher, mosaic and chunk jewels, orig frame...................... **8,400.00**

36" h, 16-1/4" d, Prairie School, zinc caming, clear, white, green, and violet slag glass, stylized lilies and tulips, set of five, few minor cracks in glass **4,250.00**

44" x 33", crossed American flag and other fanciful flag **875.00**

Stained and leaded glass panel, waterlillies, framed, 23-3/4" x 36", $250.

Photo courtesy of Joy Luke Auctions.

Stained and leaded glass panel, red flowers, green leaves, jeweled, framed, 18-1/2" x 32", $175.

Photo courtesy of Joy Luke Auctions.

Stained

Panel

24" x 14", red, white, green, pink, and blue floral design, two layers of striated and fractured glass, green patinated bronze frame, stamped "Tiffany Studios New York" pr **2,400.00**

26" x 21", Richard the Lion-Hearted on horseback, 1883 .... **675.00**

Transom window, 59" x 17", arched form, amber, green, and red, later walnut frame, brass plaque "Illinois Traction System Car Number 523" **260.00**

Window

35-1/8" w, 15-1/2" h, rect, arched top, brown glass border, gold glass panels, central stain painted medallion of bush of classical male, sgd "Louis Shuys," scrolled leaf surround, late 19th/early 20th C **425.00**

36" w, 22" h, fruit and flower design, layered glass in ewer and some fruit, waffle texture ribbon, from west side Buffalo, NY, c1885 home **1,200.00**

61" l, 61-1/2" h, over entry door type, blue and orange shield and geometric design, c1920........................ **490.00**

STANGLE POTTERY BIRDS

History: Stangl ceramic birds were produced from 1940 until the Stangl factory closed in 1978. The birds were produced at Stangl's Trenton plant and either decorated there or shipped to its Flemington, New Jersey, outlet for hand painting.

During World War II, the demand for these birds, and other types of Stangl pottery as well, was so great that 40 to 60 decorators could not keep up with the demand. Orders were contracted out to be decorated by individuals in their own homes. These orders then were returned for firing and finishing. Colors used to decorate these birds varied according to the artist.

Marks: As many as 10 different trademarks were used. Almost every bird is numbered; many are artist signed. However, the signatures are used only for dating purposes and add very little to the value of the birds.

Adviser: Bob Perzel.

Note: Several birds were reissued between 1972 and 1977. These reissues are dated on the bottom and are worth approximately the same as older birds, if well decorated.

Cockatoo, yellow, $250.

3250, preening duck, natural colors........................ **125.00**
3273, rooster, 5-3/4" h..... **800.00**
3274, penguin................ **500.00**
3276, bluebird.................. **90.00**
3281, mother duck......... **600.00**
3285, rooster, 4-1/2" h, early blue green base **100.00**
3400, lovebird, old, wavy base **135.00**
3400, lovebird, revised leaf base **75.00**

3402, pair of orioles, revised
.... **115.00**
3402, pair of orioles, old . **300.00**
3404, pair of lovebirds, old
.... **400.00**
3404, pair of lovebirds, revised
.... **125.00**
3405, pair of cockatoos, revised,
open base................. **150.00**
3406, pair of kingfishers, blue
.... **165.00**

From left: small bird with yellow leaf,
$45; pair of small pink cockatoos, **$350**;
hummingbird, **$125**.

3407, owl......................... **350.00**
3430, duck, 22".......... **8,000.00**
3431, duck, standing, brown
.... **850.00**
3432, rooster, 16" h **3,500.00**
3443, flying duck, teal..... **250.00**
3445, rooster, yellow **185.00**
3446, hen, gray.............. **300.00**
3450, passenger pigeon
.... **1,800.00**
3451, William Ptarmigan
.... **3,500.00**
3453, mountain bluebird
.... **1,500.00**
3454, Key West quail dove,
single wing up **275.00**
3454, Key West quail dove, both
wings up **1,800.00**
3455, shoveler duck **2,000.00**
3457, walking pheasant
.... **3,500.00**
3458, quail **2,000.00**
3459, falcon/fish hawk/osprey
.... **6,000.00**
3490, pair of redstarts..... **200.00**
3492, cock pheasant **225.00**
3518, pair of white-headed
pigeons...................... **950.00**
3580, cockatoo, medium **150.00**
3580, cockatoo, medium, white
.... **600.00**
3581, group of chickadees,
black and white **300.00**
3582, pair of green parakeets
.... **225.00**

Red cockatoo, **$250**; blue jay, **$900**; evening grosbeak, **$150**; pair of blue parakeets, **$200**.

3582, pair of blue parakeets
.... **250.00**
3584, cockatoo, large **275.00**
3590, chat **165.00**
3591, Brewers blackbird. **160.00**
3595, Bobolink **150.00**
3596, gray cardinal.......... **80.00**
3597, Wilson warbler, yellow
.... **55.00**
3599, pair of hummingbirds
.... **325.00**
3625, Bird of Paradise, large,
13-1/2" h **2,500.00**
3634, Allen hummingbird.. **90.00**
3635, group of goldfinches
.... **215.00**
3717, pair of blue jays . **3,500.00**

Rooster, **$1,000**; pair of yellow and
green birds, **$270**; cockatoo, **$250**.

Rooster, **$1,000**; pheasant, **$175**.

3746, canary, rose flower **250.00**
3749, scarlet tanager..... **425.00**

3750, pair of western tanagers
.... **500.00**
3751, red-headed woodpecker,
pink glossy **300.00**
3752, pair of red-headed
woodpeckers, red matte
.... **550.00**
3754, pair of white-winged
crossbills, pink glossy **425.00**
3755, audubon warbler .. **475.00**
3756, pair of audubon warblers
.... **600.00**
3758, magpie jay **1,400.00**
3810, blackpoll warber .. **185.00**
3811, chestnut chickadee
.... **145.00**
3812, chestnut-sided warbler
.... **150.00**
3813, evening grosbeak . **150.00**
3814, blackthroated green
warbler........................ **165.00**
3815, western bluebird... **440.00**
3848, golden crowned kinglet
.... **125.00**

Yellow warbler, **$150**; Mountain
bluebird, **$2,100**; black and white
chickadee, **$145**; nuthatch, **$145**.

3852, cliff swallow.......... **170.00**
3853, group of golden crowned
kingfishers **780.00**
3868, summer tanager .. **750.00**
3921, yellow-headed verdin
.... **1,700.00**
3922, European finch... **1,200.00**
3924, yellow-throated warbler
.... **680.00**
Bird sign **2,500.00**

STEIFF

History: Margarete Steiff, GmbH, established in Germany in 1880, is known for very fine-quality stuffed animals and dolls, as well as other beautifully made collectible toys. It is still in business, and its products are highly respected.

The company's first products were wool-felt elephants made by Margaret Steiff. In a few years, the animal line was expanded to include a donkey, horse, pig, and camel.

By 1903, the company also was producing a jointed mohair teddy bear, whose production dramatically increased to more than 970,000 units in 1907. Margarete's nephews took over the company at this point.

Newly designed animals were added: Molly and Bully, the dogs, and Fluffy, the cat. Pull toys and kites also were produced, as well as larger animals on which children could ride or play.

Marks: The bear's-head label became the symbol for the firm in about 1907, and the famous "Button in the Ear" round, metal trademark was added.

Notes: Become familiar with genuine Steiff products before purchasing an antique stuffed animal. Plush in old Steiff animals was mohair; trimmings usually were felt or velvet. Unscrupulous individuals have attached the familiar Steiff metal button to animals that are not Steiff.

Bear, large, white mohair, rare size, **$2,500**; holding small lidded basket with leather strap, **$125**.

Bear
5" h, blond mohair, rattle, no button, black shoe button eyes, fully jointed, embroidered nose and mouth, overall wear, stains, rip on arm, working rattle, excelsior stuffing, no pad style, c1910 .... **415.00**
8 1/2" h, golden mohair, shoe button eyes, embroidered nose, mouth, and claws, fully jointed, excelsior stuffing, no pad arms, c1915, moth damage to foot pads. **1,380.00**
12-1/2" h, light apricot, ear button, fully jointed, shoe button eyes, embroidered nose, mouth, and claws, excelsior stuffing, felt pads, c1905, fur loss, lower back and back of legs, slight moth damage on pads **1,610.00**
14" h, golden mohair, ear button, black embroidered nose and claws, mouth missing, black shoe button eyes, squeaker, fully jointed body, excelsior stuffing, original felt pads, c1905, one-inch fabric tear right front arm joint, very minor fur loss, overall soil **1,955.00**
14" h, light golden mohair, underscored ear button, black shoe button eyes, center seam, black embroidered nose, mouth, and claws, fully jointed, tan felt pads, c1905, holes in hand pads . **4,890.00**
17" h, One Hundredth Anniversary Bear, ear button, gold mohair, fully jointed, plastic eyes, black embroidered nose, mouth, and claws, peach felt pads, excelsior stuffing, certificate no. 0904, orig box **200.00**
20" h, cinnamon mohair, swivel head, black shoe button eyes, cotton floss stitched nose with vertical stitching, stitched mouth, center seam body and head, no button in ear, rig felt pads on paws **9,500.00**
30" h, blond mohair, script ear button, glass eyes, embroidered nose, mouth, claws excelsior stuffed, fully jointed, mid-19th C, felt feet pads have scattered moth holes, break at sides . **1,955.00**
Beaver, 6" l, Nagy, mohair, chest tag, post WWII **95.00**

Bison, 9-1/2" l, mohair, ear button, chest tag, post WWII **200.00**
Boxer, 16-1/2" l, 15-1/2" h, beige mohair coat, black trim, glass eyes, leather collar marked "Steiff," head turns, minor wear, straw stuffing.... **165.00**
Boxer puppy, 4-1/4" h, paper label "Daly".............. **135.00**

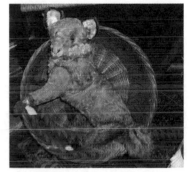

Fox, well loved and played-with condition, **$275**.

Cat, 14" l, pull toy, white mohair coat, gray stripes, glass eyes, worn pink ribbon with bell, pink felt ear linings, button, cast iron wheels **1,980.00**
Cocker spaniel, 5-3/4" h, sitting, glass eyes, ear button, chest tag, post WWII **125.00**
Cocker spaniel puppy, 4-3/4" h, button **90.00**
Dalmatian puppy, 4-1/4" h, paper label "Sarras" ... **145.00**
Dog, 15-1/2" l, 14" h, pull toy, orange and white mohair coat, glass eyes, steel frame, cast iron wheels, one ear missing, button in remaining ear, voice box does not work **280.00**
Frog, 3-3/4" l, velveteen, glass eyes, green, sitting, button and chest tag **125.00**
Goat, 6-1/2" h, ear button **150.00**
Gussy, 6-1/2" l, white and black kitten, glass eyes, ear button, chest tag, post WWII . **125.00**
Horse on wheels, 21" l, 17" h, ear button, glass eyes, white and brown, wear and breaks to fabric, on solid metal wheels, non-functioning pull-ring, c1930 .... **215.00**
Kangaroo and joey, 20-3/4" h mohair mother, 4" h velveteen baby both with glass eyes, embroidered nose, and mouth, ear button and tag **395.00**

Koala, 7-1/2" h, glass eyes, ear button, chest tag, post WWII **135.00**

Lion, 21" l, 18" h, pull toy, worn gold mohair coat, glass eyes, worn streaked mane incomplete, no tail, ring pull voice box, steel frame, sheet metal wheels with white rubber treads marked "Steiff" **500.00**

Monkey, 7-1/2" h, Jocko, 1950s, C.8+ **100.00**

Owl, 4-1/2" h, Wittie, glass eyes, ear button, chest tag, post WWII **95.00**

Poodle, black, $75; and tan cow, $45.

Parakeet, 6-1/2" h, Hansi, bright lime green and yellow, airbrushed black details, plastic eyes, button tag, chest tag, plastic beak and feet **115.00**

Rabbit, 9-1/2" h, unmarked, wear **220.00**

Soldier, 14" h, c1913, slight moth damage, hat and equipment missing **460.00**

Turtle, 7" l, Slo, plastic shell, glass eyes, ear button, chest tag, post WWII **85.00**

Walrus, 6-1/2" l, Paddy, plastic tusk, glass eyes, ear button, chest tag, post WWII .. **145.00**

STEIN, LEA

History: Lea Stein, a French-trained artist born in Paris in 1931, began making her whimsical pieces of jewelry in 1969, after her husband, Fernand Steinberger, came up with a process of laminating layers of rhodoid (cellulose acetate) sheets with interesting textures and colors. The layers were baked overnight with a secret component of his creation and then cut into shapes for various designs of pins, bracelets, earrings, and shaped decorative objects. Some pieces have as many as 20 layers of cellulose bonded together.

In 1957, Stein started her own company and continued in the textile business until 1965. From 1965 to 1967, she made buttons. In 1967, she began to make buttons in rhodid, which is the cellulose acetate that is associated with her jewelry. The skills she developed as a button maker were put to use when she began producing jewelry in 1969. From that time until 1981 is the vintage period of her jewelry production. She then employed as many as 50 works and was mass-producing her jewelry. However, an influx of Asian competition caused the company to fail. An American dealer in New York bought a big part of her remaining stock and began selling her jewelry in the US. After running a computer business in the late 1980s, Stein returned to jewelry making. Every year since 1988, she has created a new piece for her collection, after putting much time and research into each design. New designs include: Porcupine, 2000; Goupil, 2000; Cicada, 2001; Penguin, 2001; Christmas Tree in 2001, Sacha, 2002, Quarrlesome the Cat, 2003, Pouf the Pup, 2003; Tom the Bear, 2004; Leo, a stylized tiger, 2004.

The most easily recognizable Stein pin is the 3-D fox, produced in a myriad of colors and designs. Often, lace or metal layers were incorporated into the celluloid, which produced an astounding number of unique textures. The 3-D fox's tail is looped from one piece of celluloid.

Many different styles of cats, dogs, bugs, bunnies, birds, ducks, and other creatures were introduced, as well as Art Deco-styled women, mod-styled children, flowers, cars, hats, purses, gold-encased and rhinestone encrusted designs, and lots of little "things," such as stars, hearts, rainbows, and even pins resembling John Travolta and Elvis Presley. In addition, collectors can find many bangles, rings, cuffs, earrings, barrettes, and rarer boxes, mirrors, and cigarette cases. The designs seem endless and to a Lea Stein collector, the ability to collect one of everything is almost impossible, because so many pieces were one of a kind.

These "vintage" pieces of jewelry were made from 1969 until 1981 and are identified by a V-shaped pin back, which is heat mounted to the back of each piece, as are the pin backs on her newer pieces. The pin back is always marked "Lea Stein Paris." Some of the later issues have riveted backs, but all of them are marked in the same way. At one time the age of a pin could be determined by the pin back, but because of many newly released pieces in the past few years, that no longer is always the case. Stein's workshop is still producing jewelry. While some of the vintage pieces are rare, it is virtually impossible to tell the difference between old and new releases, except with the knowledge of which designs were created at what time in Stein's career. Whether old or new, her jewelry is quite collectible.

Adviser: Judy Smith.

Bracelet, bangle, dark green and red swirled peppermint stick swirls **95.00**

Earrings, pr, clip, bright green swirls on pearly white, stamped on back, 1-3/8" d **95.00**

Pins, all with signature Lea Stein-Paris V-shaped pin back Attila the Cat, standing, magenta lace, faux-mother-of-pearl ears and eyes, 3-3/4" l, 1-3/4" h **65.00**

Bacchus, cat's head, pearly silver and black, 2-3/8" w, 1-1/8" h **65.00**

Bee, transparent wings with gold edge, faux ivory body and head, topaz-colored glass edge eye, 2-3/8" wingspan **80.00**

Blueberries, transparent faux-tortoise berries and leaves with beige crackled lace leaves, 2-7/8" l **65.00**

Cicada, irid red wings, striped body and head, 3-3/8" l, 1-1/4" w **85.00**

Double Totie, Scottish terriers, left in white lace, dark blue bow around neck with bright blue nose, right magenta lace, black neck bow and nose, 2-1/4" w, 1-5/8" h **100.00**

Pin, bowling pin, shades of beige, faux-tortoise, and faux-ivory, V-shaped Lea Stein Paris clasp, 2-5/8" w x 7/8" h, **$75**.

Pin, Joan Crawford, also known as "Carmen" in Europe, gray tinged waved brown lace hair, creamy skin, bead earring, pearly purple dress with striated beige and gray collar, V-shaped Lea Stein Paris clasp, 2-1/8" w, 1-3/4" h, **$100**.

Edelweiss, coral flowers, white and marbled green stem, 3-3/8" h **70.00**
Flamingo, pink, 1-7/8" w, 2-3/8" h **55.00**
Golden Raptor, translucent blue body, golden overlay, topaz colored glass bed eye, 2-1/8" w, 2-1/4" h **80.00**
Mistigri Kitty, caramel, 4" 2, 3-7/8" h **85.00**
Oriental girl, shades of blue and white, transparent light blue hat, faux-ivory face, transparent light blue eye, 2" w, 2-1/8" h **90.00**
Panther
3-1/2" w, 1-1/8" h, beige and red lace, early design... **55.00**
4-1/4" w, 1-3/4" h, early ivory harlequin, medium faux tortoiseshell, modern version **65.00**
Penguin, dark red brocade body and head, yellow lace beak, eye, neck, and feet, pearly harlequin lace body, 1-3/4" w, 3-1/8" h **85.00**
Porcupine, irid gold and dark red body with black accents, black face and paws, dark red eye and nose, 3" w **85.00**
Ric, Airedale Terrier, pearly ivory harlequin pattern, shiny black ears, nose, eye and collar **65.00**

Sailor, faux ivory face, neck, hands and feet, pearly purple suit and cap, pearly gray collar, 1-5/8" w, 2-3/8" h 60.00
Swallow, pink and white lace wings, 2-3/4" w, 1-3/8" h 80.00
Swan, silvery glitter neck, black beak and a faux-coral seashell body, 1-7/8" w, 2-7/8" h **85.00**
Three ducks, orange lace bodies, dark royal blue heads, dark blue wings, 1" w, 2-1/4" h **85.00**

STEINS

History: Steins, mugs especially made to hold beer or ale, range in size from the smaller 3/10 and 1/4 liter to the larger

1892-1921

1, 1-1/2, 2, 3, 4, and 5 liters, and in rare cases to 8 liters. A liter is 1.05 liquid quarts.

Master steins or pouring steins hold 3 to 5 liters and are called krugs. Most steins are fitted with a metal-hinged lid with thumb lift. The earthenware character-type steins usually are German in origin.

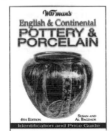

For more information, *see Warman's English & Continental Pottery & Porcelain*, 4th edition.

Character
Beethoven, half liter, porcelain, lire on side of body and on porcelain inlaid lid, E. Bohne & Sohn **570.00**
Frederick III, in uniform, 1/2 liter, porcelain, porcelain lid, Schierholz, chips on lid repaired, int. color yellowing **1,735.00**
Monk, 1/3 liter, design by Frank Ringer, marked "J.

Reinemann, Munchen" on underside of base, inlaid lid, 5" h **580.00**
Pug dog, Mettlach, #2018, 1/2 liter, character, pug dog, inlaid lid **1,100.00**
Singing pig, 1/2 liter, porcelain, Schierholz, inlaid lid ... **580.00**
Skull, 1/3 liter, porcelain, large jaw, inlaid lid, E. Bohne & Sohn, pewter slightly bent **550.00**

Copper luster, cream-colored ground, **$120**.

Faience
Thuringen, 1 liter, 9-1/2" h, hp, floral design on front, purple trees on sides, pewter top rim and lid, pewter base ring, 18th C, tight hairline on side **1,155.00**

Glass
9-1/2" h, 1 liter, blown, wedding type, hp floral design and verse, pewter lid with earlier date of 1779, pewter brass ring, c1850 .... **925.00**
15-1/4" h, 6-1/2" d, amber, encased in fancy French pewter frame, ram's heads around stein, hinged top lid **495.00**

Ivory, hand carved, c1850-70
11-1/2" h, elaborate battle scene with approx. 100 figures, carving around entire body, silver top with figural knight finial, cherub bases and fruit in repousse on lid, figural handle of man in armor, silver base with touch marks, discoloration to ivory **6,700.00**

Colorful scene titled "Heidelberg 1620," pewter lid, base marked "Made in Western Germany," **$55**.

13-1/2" h, elaborate hunting scene, four men on horseback, 15 dogs, ivory lid with various animals carved around border, 3-1/2" h finial of man blowing trumpet with dog, figural handle of bare breasted woman with crown, dog head thumb lift, left arm and trumpet missing **11,550.00**

Gesetzlich, scene of waiter and man with open purse, pewter top with extended thumb rest, sterling foam scraper, **$95**.

Porcelain and pottery

Delft, 1/2 liter, elaborate scene of two people playing lawn tennis, porcelain inlaid lid of sail boat, marked "Delft, Germany" **1,390.00**

Meissen, 1 liter, 7" h, hp, scene of three people in forest, floral design around sides, porcelain lid with berry finial and painted flowers, closed hinge, cross swords and "S" mark, c1820, strap repoured **3,100.00**

Mettlach

#1896, 1/4 liter, maiden on one side, cherub face on other, grape dec, pewter lift handle **350.00**
#2007, 1/2 liter, etched, black cat, inlaid lid **660.00**
#2057, 1/2 liter, etched, festive dancing scene, inlaid lid **325.00**
#2580, 1/2 liter, etched, Die Kannenburg, conical inlay lid, knight in castle **695.00**
#2755, 1/4 liter, cameo and etched, three scenes of people at table, Art Nouveau design between scenes, inlaid lid **560.00**

Salt glaze

11-1/2" h, blue and brown accent of man and woman drinking at table, thread relief blue accented vine design on back, orig pewter lid, mold mark #6 .... **180.00**
11-1/2" h, pouring type, imp "Fort Edward Brew Co." along base with blue accents, relief and blue accented man with cane on one side, man and woman reading on opposite side, heavy orig pewter lid, mold mark #3 .... **1,100.00**
13-1/2" h, relief and blue accented man and woman drinking at table, thread relief blue accented vine design on back, orig pewter lid, gargoyle thumb lift, mold mark #6 .... **150.00**

Unknown maker, 1/4 liter, transfer and enameled, color, Ulmer Splatz!, The Bird from the City of Ulm, pewter lid **115.00**

Regimental, 1/2 liter, porcelain

2 Schwer. Reit. Regt. Erzh. Fz, Ferd u. Osterr-Este Esk Landshut 1899-02, named to Friederich Schmidt, two side scenes, lion thumb lift, old tear on lid repaired, minor scruffs, 11-1/2" h......... **675.00**

11 Armee Corps, Mainz 1899, names to Res. Doring, two side scenes, plain thumb lift, strap tear repaired, lines in lithophane, 10" h........ **485.00**
123 Grenadier, Ulm 1908-10, named to Grenadier Schindler, four side scenes, roster, bird thumb lift, open blister on int. base, finial missing **550.00**

Wood and pewter, Daubenkrug

1/2 liter, 6-1/2" h, pewter scene of deer, vines and leaves on sides, pewter handle and lid, c1820, some separations to pewter...................... **925.00**
1/3 liter, 5-1/2" h, floral design on sides, oval with crown on front, pewter handle and lid, 18th C, splints in pewter and wood **1,270.00**

STEUBEN GLASS

History:
Frederick Carder, an Englishman, and Thomas G. Hawkes of Corning, New York, established the Steuben Glass Works in 1904. In 1918, the Corning Glass Company purchased the Steuben company. Carder remained with the firm and designed many of the pieces bearing the Steuben mark. Probably the most widely recognized wares are Aurene, Verre De Soie, and Rosaline, but many other types were produced.

1903–32

The firm is still operating, producing glass of exceptional quality.

Acid cut back

Lamp, table, 22" h, ovoid shouldered form, blue Aurene cut to yellow jade, emb metal foot and collar......... **2,000.00**
Vase
9-1/2" h, shape #5000, shouldered form, Green Jade over Alabaster, perched songbirds on leafy stems, sgd **2,000.00**
10" h, catalog #7391, shouldered form, Green Jade, acid cut stemmed peony flowers and branches cut back to Alabaster **3,250.00**

Animals

Colorless, NY, 20th C, inscribed "Steuben"
Donkey, standing, 10-1/2" h **980.00**
Dove, on stand, 12-1/8" h, abrasion to side of dove **635.00**
Eagle, 4-3/4" h, imperfections **350.00**
Elephant, raised trunk, 8" h, script sgd **100.00**
Frog, sitting, 4-1/4" l, minor base wear **230.00**
Preening Goose, #8344, and Gander, #8355, clear, 5-1/4" h, both sgd by artist Lloyd Atkins, orig box and pamphlet, price for pr. **250.00**
Seal, resting on flippers, 8-1/2" l **375.00**
Shore Bird, 8-3/8" l, light scratches to base **115.00**
Snail, 3-5/8" l, base scratch **115.00**
Squirrel, 4-1/8" h **350.00**

Aurene, compote, gold, catalog No. 2642, rounded bowl raised on slightly bulbed stem, disk base, inscribed "Aurene 2642," 8" h, **$1,175**.
Photo courtesy of Skinner, Inc.

Aurene

Atomizer, 6" h, amber, gold irid finish, c1920, atomizer bulb missing **415.00**
Bowl, 10" d, calcite int., remnants of orig paper label **450.00**
Bud vase, 3" d base, 10" h, blue, gold highlights, sgd "Steuben Aurene 2556" **700.00**
Candlesticks, pr, 10-1/8" h, catalog #686, amber, twist stems on applied disc foot, strong gold luster, sgd "Aurene 686," c1920 .... **1,100.00**
Chandelier, 40" h overall, 17" w, five-light, gold Aurene ribbed bell-shaped shades, burnished bronze metal holder, five chain drop, dec griffin fleur-de-lis, refurbished and rewired, three shades sgd with fleur-de-lis mark, some damaged to fitter ring of one **1,250.00**
Compote, 7" h, shape #2604, gold, twist stem, applied cabochons, sgd "Aurene" **1,600.00**
Darner, 5-1/2" l, 2-1/4" d, gold, some nicks and scratches from use **850.00**
Goblet
6" h, gold twist, stem, gold irid circular foot, sgd "Aurene 2361" **250.00**
6" h, gold, twist stem, sgd "Aurene 2861" **250.00**
Grotesque bowl, 5" h, shape #7276, blue, strong coloring, sgd on bottom of one foot **1,100.00**
Lamp base, 22" h overall, 8-1/2" h shouldered form insert, pink, dec with gold Aurene random internal threading, acanthus leaf carving at stem, club shaped ftd base, dye stamped "Crest & Co." **3,000.00**
Lamp shade, 5" h, irid green and gold drag loops ... **225.00**
Low bowl, 12" d, blue, three prunt feet, sgd "Aurene 2586" **550.00**
Perfume, 6" h, amber, irid gold finish, sgd "Aurene 1818," c1915 .... **650.00**
Planter, 12" d, blue, inverted rim, three applied prunt feet, engraved "Aurene 2586" **775.00**
Sherbet, 3-1/4" h, gold, stemmed, sgd "Aurene 2960" **150.00**
Sherbet and underplate, 6" d, 4-1/2" h, gold, stemmed, sgd "Aurene 2680" **250.00**

Aurene, vase, gold, catalog No. 2683, flared rim, shouldered bulbous form, inscribed "Steuben," 8" h, **$1,175**.
Photo courtesy of Skinner, Inc.

Aurene, vase, iridescent blue, unsigned, 8" h, some scratches to finish, **$500**.
Photo courtesy of Alderfer Auction Co.

Vase, colorless, irregularly faceted sides, small opening to capsule-form cavity, etched "Steuben" on underside, original fitted box, 6-1/4" h, **$980**.
Photo courtesy of Alderfer Auction Co.

Vase
5" h, shade form, vertical ribbing, blue, sgd **900.00**
5-1/2" h, squatty shouldered form, irid gold over calcite, sgd "Aurene F. Carder" **475.00**
5-3/4" h, shape #599, Style J, gold, leaf, vine, and millefiori dec, inscribed "Aurene" on bottom **3,750.00**
5-3/4" h, shouldered ovoid, rich turquoise irid, dec with striated scrolling lappits, rich amber/pink irid, inscribed "Aurene 655" **17,000.00**
5-7/8" h, flared rim, conical body, circular foot, rough pontil, gold, sgd "Steuben Aurene 2909" **825.00**

Aurene, vase, blue, catalog No. 7447, flared rim, ribbed body, double bulb at waist, inscribed "Steuben," 6" h, **$1,175.**

Photo courtesy of Skinner, Inc.

6" h, flaring scalloped rim, blue, sgd "Aurene 727" **900.00**

6" h, shape #2683, shouldered, gold, sgd "Steuben".................... **800.00**

7-1/4" h, shape #2604, corset shape, gold................ **350.00**

10" h, shape #2683, shouldered, blue, sgd "Steuben Aurene," numbered **1,600.00**

10-1/4" h, shape #2683, shouldered, gold irid, brilliant pink and blue highlights, orig factory aperture filled **950.00**

Calcite

Bowl
8" d, ftd, opal, gold Aurene int., c1915 .... **230.00**
10" d, ftd, irid gold int. ... **350.00**
Compote, 8" h, amber bowl and foot, red and gold irid finish, irid blue rope twisted stem with gold finish **1,880.00**
Finger bowl and underplate, 6" w, 2-1/2" h, gold Aurene int. **200.00**
Lamp shade, 5" h, dome, etched horizontal leaves **125.00**
Low bowl
10" d, gold irid int........ **350.00**
12" d, rolled rim, irid gold int., c1915......................... **460.00**
Parfait and underplate, 4-1/2" h, 5-1/4" d underplate, gold, partial paper label **625.00**
Sherbet and underplate, 6" d, stemmed, bright blue Aurene int. **450.00**

Celeste Blue

Candlesticks, brilliant blue, applied foliate form bobeche and cups, bulbed shafts, c1920-33, set of four .. **2,300.00**

Center bowl, 16-1/4" d, 4-1/4" h, catalog #112, swirled optic ribbed broad bowl, rolled rim, applied fluted foot, partially polished pontil, c1925 **400.00**
Finger bowl, underplate, catalog #2889, 5" d flared bowl, 6-1/2" underplate, swirled ribbed design, c1925, set of 12, some chips . **600.00**
Iced tea goblet, 6-1/2" h, catalog #5192, blue, flared, light ribbon, c1918-32, set of eight **400.00**
Juice glass, 4-1/2" h, catalog #5192, blue, flared, light ribbon, c1918-32, set of eight **375.00**
Luncheon plate, 8-1/2" d, molded blue body, Kensington pattern variant, engraved border of leaves and dots, c1918-32, set of 12 .... **550.00**
Sherbet, 4-1/2" h, optic ribbed body, crystal stem **95.00**
Vase, 10" d, 12-1/4" h, clear glass handles **1,700.00**
Wine glass, 4-3/4" h, optic ribbed body, crystal stem **95.00**

Cluthra

Bowl, 5-1/2" h, squatty shouldered form, pink shading to opal........... **600.00**
Lamp base, 12-1/2" h, ovoid, creamy white cluthra acid-etched Art-Deco flowers, acid-etched fleur-de-lis mark near base, orig gilded foliate bronze lamp fittings, c1925 .... **2,070.00**
Vase, 8" h, catalog #2683, rose, acid stamp script mark **2,600.00**
Wall pocket, 15-1/2" w, 8" h, half round flared bowl, black and white cluthra, cut and mounted to foliate gilt metal framework, polished pontil, c1930, slight corrosion to metal......................... **490.00**

Crystal

Bowl, 11-1/4" d, basket shape, form #8079, inscribed "Steuben" on base, orig Steuben sock.............. **150.00**
Calyx bowl, 9-1/2" d, 3-3/8" h, floriform oval, solid foot, inscribed "Steuben" ... **230.00**

Candlestick, 10" h, shape #3178, green etched rim **150.00**
Center bowl, cov, 9" d, 12" h, dolphin and wave finial on cov, round bowl, applied wave motif on base, inscribed "Steuben," base scratches **690.00**
Cocktail set, 15" h cocktail shaker, six matching 2-1/2" h glasses, two applied red cherries, wheel-cut leaves, and stems on shaker, ruby stopper, same dec on glasses, some with fleur-de-lis marks, slight damage to stopper **3,700.00**
Goblet, 7-1/16" h, flared cylindrical vessel, knobbed stem, sq base, small "S" inscribed on base, designed by Arthur A. Houghton, Jr., 1938, Madigan catalog #7846, set of six, two with small chips **260.00**
Paperweight, 2-1/2" d, sphere with randomly imp heart motifs, late 20th C....... **115.00**
Vase, 7-3/8" h, catalog #SP919, flared wing form, pedestal base, inscribed "Steuben" on base........................... **330.00**

Crystal seagull, wooden base with light, **$185.**

Grotesque

Bowl, 11-1/2" l, 6-1/4" h, blue jade, Frederick Carder design, minor int. surface wear, fleur-de-lis mark **3,850.00**
Vase
9-1/4" h, amethyst, catalog #7090, pillar molded floriform body, ruffled rim shaded to colorless crystal at applied disk foot, acid script "Steuben" mark in polished pontil, c1930.............. **525.00**

11" h, ftd, cranberry at rim shades to clear, foot chipped **75.00**

Jade

Bowl, 8" d, 6" h, two-line pillar, ftd, alabaster int., fleur-de-lis acid stamp mark **800.00**

Bud vase, 7-3/4" h, green trumpet form vase with ruffled rim, supported on scrolled tripod hammered silver mount over round base, engraved "RAP" monogram, imp "Black Starr & Frost 7050 Sterling" on base **460.00**

Candlesticks, pr, 10" h, No. 2956, jade candle cup and base, alabaster shaft, gold foil labels **550.00**

Compote, 10" h, yellow, ftd **1,450.00**

Goblet, 4-3/4" h, alabaster foot **95.00**

Lamp base, 13" h flared double gourd shaped dark amethyst body cased to alabaster int., overlaid with amethyst, cameo etched in Chinese pattern, double etched with scrolling design, gilt metal fittings with three scroll arms, shallow chip under fixture **1,850.00**

Parfait, 6" h, applied alabaster foot **350.00**

Rose bowl, 7" d, 7" h, spherical, smooth jade crystal ... **350.00**

Vase, 3-1/2" d base, 8" h, catalog #1169, alabaster int., floral design **2,450.00**

Miscellaneous

Bowl, 6-1/2" h, Old Ivory, catalog #7307, pillar ftd, applied raised foot, c1930 .... **435.00**

Candlestick, 3 1/2" h, shape #7564, Ivrene, ruffled collar, sgd "Steuben" **200.00**

Center bowl, 14" d, 8" h, ftd, topaz body, celeste blue rims, eight swirl cabochons **375.00**

Compote, 7" h, stemmed, translucent body, translucent green rim, etched floral dec **175.00**

Cordial, 6" h, optic ribbed body, gray blue, amber twisted stem, price of set of seven **450.00**

Finger bowl and underplate, 7" w, optic ribbed amethyst body, turquoise lip wrap, bowls acid etched "Steuben" in block letters with fleur-de-lis mark, price for five matching sets **525.00**

Goblet

6-1/4" h, translucent, random bubbles, amber threading **115.00**

8" h, French blue, bubbles and reeding, corkscrewed stem, price for set of five **650.00**

Lamp base, 10-1/4" h, catalog #8023, urn form, swirled purple, blue, and red moss agate, gilt-metal lamp fittings, acanthus leaf dec, purple glass jewel at top, needs rewiring **2,415.00**

Paperweight, Excalibur, designed by James Houston, 1963, catalog #1000, faceted hand-polished solid crystal embedded with removable sterling silver sword, 18k gold scabbard, base inscribed "Steuben" **1,955.00**

Serving plate, 14-1/4" d, 2" h, catalog #3579, Bristol Yellow, board convex and folded rim, slight optic ribbing, wear scratches **200.00**

Sherbet and underplate, 5-1/2" h, peach ground, intricately engraved, sgd in block letters **375.00**

Vase

6-1/2" h, Cintra, ftd ovoid, yellow, fleur-de-lis signature **850.00**

7" h, Green Silverina, ftd, translucent green, internal diamond quilted silver flecks **325.00**

8" h, Ivrene, flaring ruffled rim **425.00**

10" h, Bristol Yellow, swirled **175.00**

Wine glass, 12" h, colorless, white air twist stems, script sgd, price for pr **300.00**

Oriental Poppy

Goblet, 5-3/4" h, opalescent foot **325.00**

Wine glass, 5-3/4" h, rose body, opalescent bands, vaseline tinted and opal rimmed foot, unmarked **320.00**

Pomona Green

Candlestick, 3-1/2" h, ornamental stem, acid block letters signature **200.00**

Vase, 7-1/2" h, crystal, faint quilting, Pomona Green threading at top, shape #6980, acid stamped factory signature **325.00**

Rosaline

Bowl, 8" l, 7" w, 3-1/4" h, one end folded in, other pinched spout, inscribed "F. Carder Steuben 723" on edge of polished pontil **350.00**

Compote, 4" h, ruffled, alabaster stem and foot **275.00**

Goblet, crystal foot **90.00**

Perfume, 5-3/8" h, catalog #6412, teardrop shape, cloudy pink, applied alabaster glass foot, c1925, pr... **435.00**

Table setting, 7-1/2" h, four goblets with translucent rose bowl, clambroth foot, four matching 8-1/2" d plates **1,260.00**

Selenium, goblet, red, engraved grapevines, deep ruby red ground, etched "Steuben" in block letters, 5-7/8" h, **$325**.

Photo courtesy of Garth's Auctions, Inc.

Selenium Red

Goblet, 4-1/2" h, ftd, fleur-de-lis framing family crest **200.00**

Plate, 8-3/8" d, acid etched factory mark and Carder post-production signature .. **200.00**

Spanish Green

Cordial, 5-3/4" h, lead glass, applied ornamental stem, threading, random bubbles, acid stamped signature, set of six, one professionally repaired **475.00**

Pitcher, 9" h, catalog #6665, slightly ribbed oval, flared mouth, applied angled handle, raised disk foot, acid fleur-de-lis mark **460.00**

Sherbet, 4" h, lead glass, applied ornamental stem, threading, random bubbles, acid stamped block letter signature, set of six **225.00**

Water goblet, 7-1/2" h, lead glass, applied ornamental stem, threading, random bubbles, acid stamped signature, set of four ... **325.00**

Wine, 7-1/2" h, lead glass, applied ornamental stem, threading, random bubbles, acid stamped signature, set of four **325.00**

Verre De Soie

Bonbon, 6" h, compote form, overall irid surface, swirled celeste blue finial, twisted stem **850.00**

Finger bowl and underplate, 6" w, 2-1/2" h, etched floral motif **175.00**

Lamp shade, 3-1/2" d, dome shape, price for pr **80.00**

Perfume, 4-1/2" h, catalog #1455, ribbed body, celeste blue flame stopper, c1915 .... **400.00**

Vase
6-3/4" h, ftd, lime green body, Verre de Soie irid finish **250.00**
10" h, classic form, notched rim, all over floral motif .. **450.00**

STEVENGRAPHS

History: Thomas Stevens of Coventry, England, first manufactured woven silk designs in 1854. His first bookmark was produced in 1862, followed by the first Stevengraphs, perhaps in 1874, but definitely by 1879 when they were shown at the York Exhibition. The first portrait Stevengraphs (of Disraeli and Gladstone) were produced in 1886, and the first postcards incorporating the woven silk panels in 1904. Stevens offered many other items with silk panels, including valentines, fans, pincushions, and needle cases.

Stevengraphs are miniature silk pictures, matted in cardboard, and usually having a trade announcement or label affixed to the reverse. Other companies, notably W. H. Grant of Coventry, copied Stevens's technique. Their efforts should not be confused with Stevengraphs.

Collectors in the U.S. favor the Stevengraphs with American-related views, such as "Signing of the Declaration of Independence," "Columbus Leaving Spain," and "Landing of Columbus." Sports-related Stevengraphs such as "The First Innings" (baseball), and "The First Set" (tennis) are also popular, as well as portraits of Buffalo Bill, President and Mrs. Cleveland, George Washington, and President Harrison.

Postcards with very fancy embossing around the aperture in the mount almost always have Stevens name printed on them. The two most popular embossed postcard series in the U.S. are "Ships" and "Hands across the Sea." The latter set incorporates two crossed flags and two hands shaking. Seventeen flag combinations have been found, but only seven are common. These series generally are not printed with Stevens name. Stevens also produced silks that were used in cards made by the Alpha Publishing Co.

Stevens' bookmarks are longer than they are wide, have mitered corners at the bottom, and are finished with a tassel. Many times his silks were used as the top or bottom half of regular bookmarks.

Marks: Thomas Stevens's name appears on the mat of the early Stevengraphs, directly under the silk panel. Many of the later portraits and the larger silks (produced initially for calendars) have no identification on the front of the mat other than the phrase "woven in pure silk" and have no label on the back.

Bookmarks originally had Stevens' name woven into the foldover at the top of the silk, but soon the identification was woven into the fold-under mitered corners. Almost every Stevens' bookmark has such identification, except the ones woven at the World's Columbian Exposition in Chicago, 1892 to 1893.

Note: Prices are for pieces in mint or close-to-mint condition.

Bookmarks

Assassination, Abraham Lincoln **395.00**

Centennial, USA, 1776-1876, General George Washington, The Father of Our Country, The First in Peace, The First in War, The First in the Hearts of Our Countrymen!, few small stains **125.00**

Forget-Me-Not, Godden #441 .... **350.00**

I Wish You a Merry Christmas and a Happy New Year **85.00**

Lord Have Mercy **400.00**

Mail Coach **225.00**

Mother and Child, evening prayers, 10-1/2" l, 2" w, 1-1/2" silk tassel **400.00**

Mourning, Blessed Are They Who Mourn, 9-1/2" l, 2" w, 2" silk tassel **450.00**

My Dear Father, red, green, white, and purple **200.00**

Old Armchair **150.00**

Prayer Book Set, five orig markers attached with small ivory button, cream-colored tape fastened to orig frame, Communion, Collect, Lesson I, Lesson II, Psalms, gold lettering, gold silk tassels, orig mount, c1880-85 .... **3,400.00**

The Old Arm Chair, chair, full text, musical score, four color, 2" w, 11" l **125.00**

The Star Spangled Banner, U.S. flag, full text and musical score of song, red tassel, seven color, no maker's mark, 2-1/2" w, 11" l **185.00**

To One I Love, Love me little, love me long is the burden of my song, Love that is too hot and strong, burneth soon to waste, Still I would not have thee cold, not too backward or too bold; Love that lasteth till this old fadeth not in haste **175.00**

Postcard

RMS *Arabic*, Hands Across the Sea **465.00**

RMS *Elmina* **225.00**

RMS *Franconia* **225.00**

RMS *Iverina* **215.00**

USMS *Philadelphia* **225.00**

Stevengraph

Betsy Making the First United States Flag, Anderson Bros., Paterson, NJ, 5" x 8-1/2" **80.00**

Buffalo Bill, Nate Salsbury, Indian Chief, orig mat and frame, 8" x7" **500.00**

Chateau Frontenac Hotel,
Quebec, silver filigree frame
.... **95.00**
Coventry, 7-1/4" x 13", framed
.... **100.00**
Death of Nelson, 7-1/4" x 2-1/2"
.... **200.00**
Declaration of Independence
.... **375.00**
For Life or Death, fire engine
rushing to burning house, orig
mat and frame **350.00**
Good Old Days, Royal Mail
Coach, 5-3/4" h, 8-1/2" l, orig
frame........................... **200.00**
Kenilworth Castle, 7-1/4" x 13"
framed 120.00
Landing of Columbus ... **350.00**
President Cleveland **365.00**
Oxford, Cambridge, Are You
Ready, 5-3/4" h, 8-1/2" l, orig
frame........................... **300.00**
The Water Jump **195.00**

STEVENS AND WILLIAMS

History:
In 1824, Joseph Silvers and

19th C

Joseph Stevens leased the Moor
Lane Glass House at Briar Lea Hill
(Brierley Hill), England, from the
Honey-Borne family. In 1847,
William Stevens and Samuel Cox
Williams took over, giving the firm
its present name. In 1870, the
company moved to its Stourbridge
plant. In the 1880s, the firm
employed such renowned glass
artisans as Frederick C. Carder,
John Northwood, other Northwood
family members, James Hill, and
Joshua Hodgetts.

Stevens and Williams made
cameo glass. Hodgetts developed
a more commercial version using
thinner-walled blanks, acid
etching, and the engraving wheel.
Hodgetts, an amateur botanist,
was noted for his brilliant floral
designs.

Other glass products and
designs manufactured by Stevens
and Williams include intaglio ware,
Peach Bloom (a form of
peachblow), moss agate,
threaded ware, "jewell" ware,

tapestry ware, and Silveria.
Stevens and Williams made glass
pieces covering the full range of
late Victorian fashion.

After World War I, the firm
concentrated on refining the
production of lead crystal and
achieving new glass colors. In 1932,
Keith Murray came to Stevens and
Williams as a designer. His work
stressed the pure nature of the glass
form. Murray stayed with Stevens
and Williams until World War II and
later followed a career in
architecture.

Additional Listings: Cameo Glass.

For more information, see *Warman's
Glass*, 4th edition.

Basket, 8-1/2" h, tapering ivory
body, inverted ruffled rim,
appliqué of flowers and
leaves, amber twist handle,
Victorian **175.00**
Biscuit jar, cov, 7-1/2" h,
5-1/2" d, cream opaque, large
amber and green applied
ruffled leaves, rich pink int., SP
rim, lid, and handle **300.00**
Bonbonniere, 3-3/4" d, 2" h,
matching 4-3/4" d underplate,
satin finish, swirling ribbon
like air traps on exterior of
bowl and upper side of plate,
crimson shading to golden
pink at frilly edges, piecrust
crimped edge underplate,
bowl with robin's egg blue
interior, underplate with oyster
white underside **1,485.00**
Bowl, 5" d, Osiris, mauve
ground, swirling threaded
dec, cased **1,430.00**
Box, cov, 4-1/2" d, 2-1/2" h,
hinged, aventurine, green and
red spatter, green metallic
flakes, white lining, polished
pontil **250.00**
Calling card receiver, 10" l,
applied amber handle, rolled
edge, translucent opalescent
ground, three applied berries,
blossoms, and green leaves,
three applied amber feet
.... **750.00**

Ewer, 8-1/2" h, 5" w, Pompeiian
Swirl, deep rose shading to
yellow, off white lining, frosted
loop handle, all over gold
enameled wild roses, ferns,
and butterfly **1,500.00**
Jardinière, 6-1/2" d, 10" h, pink
opalescent, cut back, two
spatter flowers and
sunflowers, three applied
opalescent thorn feet, leaves,
and stems, minor damage
.... **350.00**

STIEGEL-TYPE GLASS

History: Baron Henry Stiegel
founded America's first flint-glass
factory at Manheim, Pennsylvania,
in the 1700s. Although clear glass
was the most common color
made, amethyst, blue (cobalt),
and fiery opalescent pieces also
are found. Products included
bottles, creamers, flasks, flips,
perfumes, salts, tumblers, and
whiskeys. Prosperity was short-
lived; Stiegel's extravagant lifestyle
forced the factory to close.

It is very difficult to identify a
Stiegel-made item. As a result, the
term "Stiegel-type" is used to
identify glass made during the
time period of Stiegel's firm and in
the same shapes and colors as
used by that company.

Enamel-decorated ware also is
attributed to Stiegel. True Stiegel
pieces are rare; an overwhelming
majority is of European origin.

Reproduction Alert: Beware of
modern reproductions, especially
in enamel wares.

Bottle, blown
5-3/8" h, brilliant deep
peacock green, 15 diamonds,
pot stone in neck **440.00**
5-7/8" h, hexagonal, colorless,
enameled white dove, red
rose, scroll work, red, blue,
yellow, and white floral
designs, flared lip **175.00**
6" h, flattened octagonal,
colorless, bright polychrome
dec of deer on obverse, "1763"
on reverse, floral dec on sides,
flaring polished lip, kick up
base, small flake **60.00**

Bride's or cordial bottle
4-3/4" h, 2-1/8" d x 2-1/2", colorless, polychrome enamel floral dec, orig pewter collar with protruding threads, rough pontil mark, late 18th or 19th C **315.00**
6-1/8" h, blue, "VIVAT, es leben alle miller 1764," (long live all Miller's) central floral motifs surrounding folklore symbols **3,100.00**

Flip glass, free-blown,
polychrome enamel dec, colorless, rough pontil mark, late 18th or 19th C
3-1/8" h, 2-1/2" d rim, 1-5/8" d base, bird perched on heart and foliage................... **440.00**
3-1/4" h, 2-3/4" d rim, 1-7/8" d base, building, three tower wings, foliage............. **425.00**
3-1/2" h, 3-1/4" d rim, 2-1/8" d base, bird perched on bright blue heart, above "3" and foliage......................... **385.00**
4-1/2" h, 3-3/4" d rim, 2-1/2" d base, bird perched on heart and foliage................... **420.00**
4-3/4" h, 3-3/4" d rim, 2-1/2" d base, two double steepled buildings and foliage .. **315.00**
8" h, 6" d rim, 3-3/4" d base, front dec with bold tulip, back with stylized flower...... **220.00**

Salt, master, cobalt blue, molded diamond quilted pattern, double ogee bowl, short stem, circular foot, tooled rim, pontil scars, 3-1/4" h, **$200**; non-Stiegel perfume in background, **$90**.

Flask
4-3/4" h, amethyst diamond and daisy..................... **495.00**
5" h, amethyst, globular, 20 molded ribs, minute rim chip **1,380.00**

Jar, cov, 10-1/2" h, colorless,
engraved sunflower and floral motifs, repeating dot and vine dec on cov, applied finial, sheared rim, pontil scar, form similar to McKearin plate 35, #2 and #3.................... **750.00**

Tankard, handle, cylindrical,
applied solid reeded handle, flared foot, sheared rim, pontil scar, form similar to McKearin plate 22, #4
5-1/2" h, milk glass, red, yellow, blue, and green enameled dec of house on mountain with floral motif, old meandering fissure around body of vessel **150.00**
5-3/4" h, colorless, engraved with bird in elaborate sunburst motif........................... **500.00**

Tumbler, 2-7/8" h, colorless,
paneled, polychrome enameled flowers **220.00**

STONEWARE

History: Made from dense kaolin and commonly salt-glazed, stonewares were hand-thrown and high-fired to produce a simple, bold, vitreous pottery. Stoneware crocks, jugs, and jars were made to store products and fill other utilitarian needs. These intended purposes dictated shape and design—solid, thick-walled forms with heavy rims, necks, and handles and with little or no embellishment. Any decorations were simple: brushed cobalt oxide, incised, slip trailed, stamped, or tooled.

Stoneware has been made for centuries. Early American settlers imported stoneware items at first. As English and European potters refined their earthenware, colonists began to produce their own wares. Two major North American traditions emerged based only on location or type of clay. North Jersey and parts of New York comprise the first area; the second was eastern Pennsylvania spreading westward and into Maryland, Virginia, and West Virginia. These two distinct geographical boundaries, style of decoration, and shape are discernible factors in classifying and dating early stoneware.

By the late 18th century, stoneware was manufactured in all sections of the country. This vigorous industry flourished during the 19th century until glass fruit jars appeared and the use of refrigeration became

widespread. By 1910, commercial production of salt-glazed stoneware came to an end.

For more information, *see Warman's American Pottery & Porcelain*, 2nd edition.

Advertising
Butter crock, 1 lb size, "Western Dairy Company Pasture Queen Butter, Chicago, Ill," hairline **90.00**
Jug, 9" h, unsigned, half gal, Bristol glaze, stenciled under glaze "This Jug Not To be Sold Registered," blue script "Hollander Bros., 1-3-5 Main St, Paterson, NJ," c1880, glaze flakes throughout, glaze chipping at spout **440.00**
Jug, 10-1/2" h, J. Fisher, Lyons, NY, c1870, 1 gal, blue script on front "Collins & Jordan 351 Elk St Buffalo, NY, minor wear and staining from use.............................. **315.00**

Batter pail, four quarts, N White & Co., Binghamton, original bail handle, brush blue accents at ears, handle, spout, and impressed name, c1860, 8-1/2" h, minor surface chip under spout, **$415**.
Photo courtesy of Bruce & Vicki Wassdorp.

Preserve jar, 12-1/2" h, S. Hart, c1875, 3 gal, imp and blue accents," Crawfords & Murdock, Dealers in Dry Goods Groceries, Clothing Crokery & Hardware, Pulaskie, NY," blue script "3" surrounded by brushed plumes below store mark, professional restoration to rim chip at front................. **385.00**
Rolling pin, cobalt blue wildflower dec, "John Quast & Son Furniture, Pianos-Undertaking, Buffalo Lake, Minn".......................... **665.00**
Rolling pin, "Mix with Us and Save Dough, H. D. Bryam & Son General Mdse & Drugs," blue bands................. **485.00**
Batter jug, Cowden and Wilcox, Harrisburg, PA, scrolling floral dec, orig bail handle, tin spout, tin spout cover, 8-1/2" h **7,000.00**

Beanpot, covered, cobalt blue "Boston Baked Beans" and floral decoration, $450.

Batter pail
6" h, unsigned, attributed to White's, Utica, c1865, six quarts, imp "6," oak leaf design under spout, orig bale handle, short tight hairline **330.00**
8-1/2" h, N. White & Co., Binghamton, c1860, blue brush accents at ears, handle, spout, and impressed name, orig bail handle, surface chip under spout **415.00**
9" h, unsigned, attributed to Whites, Utica, c1865, one gal, cobalt blue slip leaf below spout on front, orig bail handle........................ **615.00**
10" h, unsigned, attributed to Whites, Utica, c1865, six

quarts, navy blue hollyhock dec, professional restoration to rim chips and lug handle **360.00**
Bottle
9-1/2" h, imp and blue accented "C. F. Washburn," minor crow's foot at shoulder **35.00**
10" h, imp and blue accented "B. F. Haley California Pop Beer 1889," glaze drip at shoulder to right of imp name **135.00**
Butter churn
16" h, Whites, Utica, c1865, four gal, ribbed orchid dec, possible fire damage on left side, ear missing **330.00**
17-1/2" h, White & Wood, Binghamton, NY, c1885, five gal, dasher guide, top to bottom paddletail dec, double flower branch, fully filled bird's body, long surface chip at front worn smooth from use **8,800.00**
18" h, H. M. Whitman, Havana, NY, c1860, five gal, dasher guide, top to bottom iris dec, blue at name and gallon designation, long in-body thru line that runs thru design on left side **2,200.00**
19" h, J Norton & Co., Bennington, VT, c1861, six gal, orig dasher guide, flowering cornucopia of flowers, some very minor staining, 3" very tight lie on side.......................... **8,250.00**
19" h, West Troy NY Pottery, c1880, six gal, stoneware guide, blue dec, bird perched in large tree stump, restoration to glaze flaking **1,020.00**
20" h, J Burger Jr, Rochester, NY, c1885, six gal, dotted bird on stump dec, blue accent at maker's mark, professional restoration **1,210.00**
Joshua J. German, Muskingum County, Ohio, five gal, imp "5" capacity mark, raised initials "JJG" hidden in the mark that was filled in with raised dots, incised owl, stenciled C. C. Rankin, (Newark, OH grocer), badly cracked, wide metal band and wire around rim to stabilize it, ex-Clark Garrett **4,800.00**

Butter churn, five gallons, New York Stoneware Co., Fort Edward, NY, bull's eye stylized flower design, c1880, 17-1/2" h, **$330**.
Photo courtesy of Bruce & Vicki Wassdorp.

Cake crock, four gallons, unsigned, attributed to New York state, bold flower and leaf decoration, c1870, 9-1/2" h, some staining from use, 2" clay separation the base that occurred in the making, **$275**.
Photo courtesy of Bruce & Vicki Wassdorp.

Cake crock, cov
8" d, 4 3/4" h, salt glazed, stamped "John Bell, Waynesboro" under lid and handle.................... **3,850.00**
12" d, 7-1/2" h, J. & E Norton, Bennington, VT, c1855, two gal, dotted reclining deer with fences, pine tree, tree stump, ground cover, two extremely tight hairlines at back of right ear **18,700.00**
13" d, 7-1/2" h, salt glazed, applied handles, stamped under handle, cobalt blue floral dec, attributed to Peter Hermann, Baltimore. **1,925.00**

Canning jar, 9-1/2" h, unsigned, c1850, 1 gal, four wide accent stripes across front, stack mark, glaze burns on left side **110.00**

Chicken waterer, 11" h, unsigned, probably PA origin, c1840, 1 gal, imp "1" at shoulder, brushed blue accents at button top and inner and out rim of watering hole **415.00**

Cream pot
7-1/2" h, Roberts, Binghamton, NY, c1860, 1 gal, bird on branch, ext. rim chip on back **770.00**
8-1/2" h, Brady & Ryan, Ellenville, NY, c1885, 6 quarts, singing bird on dotted branch, imp "6" below maker's name, extensive glaze flaking at rim and spots on back **180.00**
10-1/2" h, T. Harrington Lyons, c1865, two gal, brushed wreath surrounding gallon designation, couple of minor surface chips at rim in back **330.00**

Crock, cov
Three gal, floral cobalt blue banding, "No. 3" stamped on side, two handles, 11" d, 14-1/2" h.................. **1,155.00**
Four gal, straight sided, two handles, "No. 4" stamped on side, copious cobalt blue floral dec, line repair on side **2,420.00**

Crock
4-3/4" d, 4-3/4" h, salt glazed, attributed to Pfaltzgraff, York, PA, bulbous, flared rim, incised banding at top, cobalt blue dec tulip, int. brown glaze, small line at top rim **3,960.00**

Crock, E. Norton, late 19th C, five gallons, large cobalt blue stylized flower, impressed "E. Norton & Co., Bennington, VT," 12-1/2" h, **$250**.

Photo courtesy of Pook & Pook.

Crock, small, marked "A. Conrad, New Geneva, PA," **$250**.

7" h, unsigned, attributed to Macquoid & Co. Pottery Works, New York city, c1870, 1 gal, Victorian style woman's profile on front, minor staining, 3" tight hairline **4,620.00**
8" h, D. Mooney, Ithaca, NY, c1862, pail shape, brushed blue dec, somewhat overglazed in the firing **330.00**
9" h, Brady & Ryan, Ellenville, NY, c1885, two gal, singing bird on plume, professional restoration.................. **550.00**
9" h, Lyons, c1860, two gal, double tulip dec, blue accents at name and ears, stained from use **165.00**
9-1/2" h, J. Clark & Co., Troy, c1826, two gal, ovoid, simple brushed design, blue at deeply imp maker's mark, blue accents under ears, couple of surface chips at rim **360.00**
9-1/2" h, Paul Cushman, Albany, c1807, approx 1-1/2 gal, brush blue accents, deeply impressed name, blue accent at handles, three petal lightly brushed flower on back, deeply tooled diamond and leaf pattern all around extended rim, cinnamon clay color in the making .. **2,530.00**
10-1/2" h, E & L P Norton, Bennington, VT, c1880, three gal, bird on plume dec, small stong pin in design **360.00**
10-1/2" h, F. B. Norton & Co., Worcester, Mass, c1870, three gal, chicken pecking corn design, blue at maker's mark and imp gallon designation, thick blue cobalt application **3,850.00**
10-1/2" h, Whites Utica, c1865, three gal, standing stag among ground cover, dry glaze in the making . **3,190.00**

11" h, Troy NY Pottery, c1870, four gal, large dotted and stylized leaf and floral design, some glaze flakes....... **360.00**
11" h, Paul Cushman Stoneware Factory, c1807, 1 gal, deeply impressed unusual maker's mark, blue handles, large stone ping thru name, restoration to full-length hairline on back **1,980.00**

Crock, N. White & Co., Binghamton, two gallons, cobalt blue floral decoration, ear handles, **$375**.

Crock, unsigned, attributed to New York state, brushed and sponge blue horse design below gallon mark, c1870, 8" h, **$4,400**.

Photo courtesy of Bruce & Vicki Wassdorp.

12-1/2" h, N. A. White & Son, Utica, NY, c1870, five gal, flying bird dec, floral wreath, artistically shaded tail feathers, professional restoration............... **3,960.00**
12-1/2" h, Weston & Gregg, Ellenville, NY, c1869, six gal, large bird on detailed plume, blue accent at deeply imp maker's mark, Y-shaped through line extending along bottom **1,155.00**

13" h, J Fisher Lyons NY, c1880, five gal, "Lyons" in artistic script across front, some surface roughness at rim, age spider line **275.00**

13" h, N York Corlears Hook Commeraws, c1805, two gal, ovoid, applied open handles, deep incised and blue accented clam shell swag design all along shoulder, deep signature impression, stack mark and kiln burn on one side, minor surface wear at base **5,390.00**

13" h, unsigned, attributed to Crolius, NY, c1800, three gal, ovoid, thick blue draped design all around shoulder, blue accents at open handles, overall stained from use, old age cracks **500.00**

Two gal, D. C. Milburn, Alexandra, VA, sunflower and flourishes **3,520.00**

Three gal, Eagle Pottery, eagle stencil **1,765.00**

Three gal, ovoid, freehand dec of cat-like face **19,000.00**

Three gal, 10" h, America, early 19th C, salt glazed, cylindrical form, brown Albany slip interior, applied lug handles, impressed cow motif filled with cobalt blue .. **900.00**

Three gal, Wedding Proposal, NY **10,450.00**

Face jug, black man, caricatured features, 6-1/2" h, imperfections **4,600.00**

Flask, 6-1/2" h, unsigned, c1810, brushed blue tree dec, design repeated on both sides, incised reeded accents at neck, minor surface wear at base, stack mark **2,630.00**

Jar

9-1/4" h, attributed to New York or New Jersey, c1797, salt-glazed, wide-mouth ovoid, applied open loop handles, cobalt blue inscriptions around shoulder, (some indistinct) "Mark PBH N???29 1797," minor chips **3,100.00**

10-1/2" h, N. Clark & Co., Lyons, one gal, ovoid, stoneware lid, brush blue lollipop flower, blue accents at ears and maker's mark, minor surface chip................ **690.00**

Jar, Burger Bro's & Co., Rochester, NY, four gallons, deep blue tulip with "4," also impressed "Rochester, N. Y.," double handles, spider hairlines, good contrast with bubbling in the decoration, 15-1/2" h, $425.

Photo courtesy of Garth's Auctions, Inc.

Jug, America, 19th C, ovoid form, applied strap handle, stylized cobalt blue floral and leaf decoration, minor rim chips and hairlines, 8" h, $600.

Photo courtesy of Skinner, Inc.

Jug, embossed New York, S & Co., Fort Edward, NY, cobalt blue flourish, strap handle, $395.

Jug

11-1/2" h, Whites, Utica, c1865, one gal, long tailed bird, blue at maker's mark, very tight lie in handle, short clay separation line at base **880.00**

12-1/2" h, Whites, Binghamton, c1860, two gal, dotted double poppy dec, professional restoration to tight line **275.00**

13" h, America, early 19th C, imp "2" below top, cobalt blue bird with high comb and long bill perched on large leaf, light staining **420.00**

13-1/2" h, J Fisher & Co, Lyons, NY, c1880, two gal, bee stinger dec, minor glaze burning, large glaze drips at shoulder and back **180.00**

13-1/2" h, Lyons, c1865, two gal, large brushed leaf design, some over glazing at shoulder...................... **165.00**

13-1/2" h, S Hart Fulton, c1875, three gal, signature double love birds, staining from use, long J-shaped glued crack on back .. **500.00**

13-5/8" h, America, early 19th C, salt glazed, ovoid, applied strap handle, cobalt blue stylized head of an animal, minor base chip....... **1,100.00**

14" h, J & E Norton, Bennington, VT, c1855, two gal, peacock dec, minor stone ping at back near handle..................... **4,950.00**

14" h, N. A. White & Son Utica, NY, c1870, two gal, paddletail bird, ribbed wings, head, and beak, kiln burn, stone ping **1,595.00**

14-1/2" h, J. Clark & Co., Troy, c1827, two gal, brushed blue flower dec, blue at maker's mark, stack mark at top **220.00**

15" h, Humiston & Stockwell, S. Amboy, NJ, c1830, three gal, ovoid, large brushed flower design, pin head size flake at top of lip, stack mark on side..................... **1,890.00**

15-3/8" h, America, 1833, salt-glazed, ovoid, applied strap handle, cobalt blue "1833," few minor rim chips **600.00**

16" h, J & E Norton, Bennington, VT, c1855, three gal, compote of flowers, thick glassy cobalt, professional restoration, some staining from use..................... **550.00**

16" h, W. Hart, Ogdensburgh, c1860, four gal, horse-head design, blue at name, minor stone pings in the making **17,325.00**

18-1/2" h, N. Clark Jr., Athens, NY, c1850, five gal, double handled, brushed blue bird with dotted wing perched on flowering branch, blue at maker's mark, very tight jagged hairlines extends down from rim and thru pottery's mark **935.00**

Jug, Cowden and Wilcox, Harrisburg, PA, late 19th C, cobalt blue foliate decoration, impressed name, 11-1/2" h, **$375**.

Photo courtesy of Pook & Pook.

Jug, Remmey Pottery, PA, inscribed "Turned on wagon at the Constitutional Centennial Celebration Sept. 15th 1889, Richard C. Remmey," cobalt blue floral decoration, 7-3/4" h, **$13,800**.

Photo courtesy of Pook & Pook.

Keg, unmarked, ovoid, incised bands, painted cobalt blue pinwheels, stars, and leaves, molded relief dec of man's head, 13-3/4" h, ex-Clark Garrett.................... **10,000.00**

Milk pitcher, 17" h, unsigned, Shenandoah Valley origin, attributed to Remmey factory, c1850, three gal, brushed blue floral design fills entire front, professional restoration to handle, partially replaced **1,210.00**

Mug, 4-1/2" h, 4-1/4" d, Shenandoah Valley, incised banding, single cobalt blue flower and leaves on each side, bottom initialed "L. B.," attributed to Levi Dice Bell **2,090.00**

Pitcher

7" h, ovoid, applied handle, brushed cobalt blue flower with long leaves, three flourishes around rim at handle, interior with grown glaze, hairline at base **675.00**

10" h, Whites Binghamton, incised line around middle, raised rim, cobalt blue polka dot floral dec **615.00**

10-1/2" h, unsigned, attributed to Lyons, NY, factory, c1860, 1 gal, wreath surrounding floral design, blue accent at handle, cobalt blue has bled because of heavy application by potter, surface chip at spout may be in the making **330.00**

11" h, J. Burger, Rochester, NY, c1880, 1 gal, blue accents at handle and imp name, bow tie dec **615.00**

Plaque, 5" x 6", emb with Daniel and the lion **1,800.00**

Preserve jar

1-1/2 gal, J. Norton & Co., Bennington, VT, c1861, stylized flower design, blue at deeply imp maker's mark, 11" h......................... **2,420.00**

1-1/2 gal, unknown maker, military general, orig lid **18,700.00**

Two gal, A. O. Whittemore, Havana, NY, c1870, squat, blue flower design, blue "2" and blue at maker's mark, couple of short hairlines, 10 " h........................... **310.00**

Pitcher, maidens carrying water jugs, intricate tooled top and bottom bands, applied handle, unmarked, **$350**.

Pitcher, kissing Dutch children, **$195**.

Pitcher, America, 19th century, spouted ovoid form, applied ribbed strap handle, stylized floral and linear cobalt blue decoration, 16-1/2" h, **$1,000**.

Photo courtesy of Skinner, Inc.

Two gal, J & E Norton, Bennington, VT, c1855, peacock on stump design, short clay separation lines that occurring in the making **635.00**

Two gal, T. Harrington Lyons, c1850, bull's eye wreath design, two blue "2"s, light blue at maker's mark, professional restoration to surface chips around rim and full-length hairline at back.............. **415.00**

Two gal, W. Hart Ogendsburg, c1860, orig lid, signature horse head design, cinnamon clay color, dry glaze in the making, chips, surface wear, staining from use, hairline at rim at back............... **3,300.00**

Three gal, J & F Norton, Bennington, antlered and spotted deer in landscape with trees and fences, ex-Clark Garrett, surface edge chip to handle........ **16,000.00**

Four gal, Buffalo, NY, rooster, orig lid, c1870, few hairline cracks **34,100.00**

Five gal, freehand dec of Colonial-era soldier, long coat, broad rimmed hat, holding riffle, handle, 15-3/4" h................. **14,000.00**

Five gal, freehand dec of standing woman in long dress, tulips on either side, circled "V" **9,000.00**

Five gal, freehand dec of woman holding garment, standing between two trees above standing peacock and two more trees, 15-3/4" h **19,000.00**

10" h, Little West, 12th St. N. Pottery Works, c1870, 1 1/2 gal, double dropping flower design, two short clay separation lines at rim probably occurred in making **495.00**

Pitcher, attributed to Remmey Pottery, Pennsylvania, late 19th C, cobalt blue floral decoration, 6-1/2" h, **$1,725**.

Photo courtesy of Pook & Pook.

11" h, F. Stetzenmeyer & G. Goetzman Rochester, NY, c1857, two gal, blue dec ribbed leaf and flower bud design, long glaze spider on side............................ **990.00**

11" h, Harrington & Burger, Rochester,c1853, two gal, bowed wreath design, script blue in canter of wreath, blue at name, int. short clay separation line at rim occurred in making..... **330.00**

11-1/2" h, John Burger, Rochester, c1865, two gal, orig stoneware lid, triple fern design surrounds large "2," minor crow's foot glaze spider on side...................... **580.00**

11-1/2" d, N. Clark & Co., Rochester, NY, c1850, two gal, stoneware lid, finely executed floral design, c1850, int. lime staining, couple of surface chips at rim, stone ping on side............. **1,760.00**

12" h, Brady & Ryan, Ellenville, NY, c1885, two gal, fitted stoneware lid, bushy tailed bird on dotted plume dec in bright blue, surface chip on lid, mottled clay color in the making **470.00**

12" h, Cortland, c1850, three gal, brushed plume design, blue accent at name, minor surface chips from use **165.00**

13-1/2" h, N. A. White & Son, Utica, NY, c1868, three gal, wide paddletail bird, very minor design fry to thick blue **3,520.00**

Water cooler

11" h, Gates City, patented May 25, 1886, six quarts, stoneware lid, orig spigot, cobalt blue bird dec ... **935.00**

15" h, Somerset Potters Works, c1870, three gal, elaborate incised double bird dec, blue accents at ears, maker's mark, blue dabs and brush blue leaf designs at rim and front, brushed, potted, double flower design on back, kiln burn on front, glued crack, chip out of bung hole frame that may have occurred during the making ... **3,960.00**

Water cooler, three gallons, Somerset Potters Works, elaborate incised double bird decoration, blue accents at ears, maker's mark, blue dabs and brush blue leaf designs at rim and front, c1870, 15" h, **$3,900**.

Photo courtesy of Bruce & Vicki Wassdorp.

15-1/2" h, J & F Norton, Bennington, VT, c1855, six gal, barrel shape, incised and blue accented horizontal lines frame dotted centerpiece floral design, additional blue dotted accents at bung hole, X-shaped spider line to left of design...................... **1,760.00**

12 gal, Henry Dilts, Ohio, two handles, elaborate tree emblem and Masonic compass, incised "12," ex-Clark Garrett, handles and some lip missing.... **11,000.00**

Whimsy, slide of watermelon, orig paint, c1900, 7" l, ex-Clark Garrett **5,500.00**

Whistle, figural, Rockingham glaze, c1870

1-1/2" h, bird, chips in glaze **90.00**

3-1/2" h, owl on stump .. **220.00**

3-3/4" h, seated poodle **250.00**

STRING HOLDERS

History: The string holder developed as a useful tool to assist the merchant or manufacturer who needed tangle-free string or twine to tie packages. The early holders were made of cast iron, with some patents dating to the 1860s.

When the string holder moved into the household, lighter and more attractive forms developed, many made of chalkware. The string holder remained a key kitchen element until the early 1950s.

Reproduction Alert: As a result of the growing collector interest in string holders, some unscrupulous individuals are hollowing out the backs of 1950s figural-head wall plaques, drilling a hole through the mouth, and passing them off as string holders. A chef, Chinese man, Chinese woman, Indian, masked man, masked woman, and Siamese face are altered forms already found on the market.

Figural wall lamps from the 1950s and 1960s also are being altered. When the lamp hardware is removed, the base can be easily altered. Two forms that have been discovered are a pineapple face and an apple face, both lamp-base conversions.

Cast iron, suspended type, scrolling acanthus leaf design, two piece, some rust, **$25**.

Advertising
Chase & Sanborn's Coffee, tin, 13-3/4" x 10-1/4" sign, 4" d wire basket string holder insert, hanging chain . **825.00**
Dutch Boy Paints, diecut tin, Dutch Boy painting door frame, hanging bucket string holder, American Art Sign Co., 13-3/4" x 30".......... **2,000.00**
Es-Ki-Mo Rubbers, tin, cutout center holds string spool, hanging boot moves up and down on sign, 17" x 19-3/4" h **2,500.00**
Heinz, diecut tin, pickle, hanging, "57 Varieties," 17" x 14".......................... **1,650.00**
Figural
Ball of string, cast iron, figural, hinged, 6-1/2" x 5" h... **100.00**
Black man and woman, chalkware, matched pair **275.00**

Cat face, white, pink and black trim, Holt Howard, **$95**.

Bonzo, blue, chalkware, 6-1/2" h **185.00**
Boy, top hat and pipe, chalkware, 9" h **125.00**
Bride, ceramic, marked "Made in Japan," 6-1/4" h **145.00**
Carrots, chalkware, 10" h **225.00**
Cat, red rose on top of face, green bow under chin, chalkware **165.00**
Chef, multicolored, chalkware, 7-1/4" h **165.00**
Chipmunk, ceramic, 5-1/8" h **135.00**
Dog, chalkware, 7" h... **155.00**
Dutch girl, chalkware, 7" h **100.00**
Gourd, green, chalkware, 7-1/2" h **135.00**
Indian, chalkware, 10-1/4" h **295.00**
Jester, chalkware, 7-1/4" h **195.00**
Mammy, yellow blouse, blue apron, scissors in pocket, chalkware, 6-1/2" h **385.00**
Mammy, white dress, ceramic, 6-1/2" h **225.00**
Parrot, chalkware, 9-1/4" h **235.00**
Pineapple, face, chalkware, 7" h........................... **165.00**
Porter, chalkware, 6-1/2" h **220.00**
Rose, red, green leaves, chalkware, 8" h **175.00**
Senorita, chalkware, 8" h **275.00**
Shirley Temple, chalkware, 6-1/4" w, 6-3/4" h....... **395.00**
Strawberry, chalkware, 6-1/2" h **115.00**
Terrier, chalkware, gray and white, 8-1/2" h **195.00**
Woody Woodpecker, chalkware, copyright Walter Lantz, 9-1/2" h............. **345.00**

SUGAR SHAKERS

History: Sugar shakers, sugar castors, or muffineers all served the same purpose: to "sugar" muffins, scones, or toast. They are larger than salt and pepper shakers, were produced in a variety of materials, and were in vogue in the late Victorian era.

Glass
Amber, 4-1/4" h, Paneled Daisy, Bryce Bros./US Glass Co. **275.00**
Amethyst, 4-1/2" h, nine panel, attributed to Northwood Glass Co. **180.00**
Apple green, 5-3/4" h, Inverted Thumbprint, tapered... **160.00**
Blue, 5" h, Inverted Fern. **325.00**
Bristol, 6-1/4" h, tall tapering cylinder, pink, blue flowers and green leaves dec .. **75.00**
Cobalt blue, 4-3/4" h, Ridge Swirl **375.00**
Cranberry glass, 4-1/2" h, molded fern pattern.... **150.00**
Custard, 4-3/4" h, Paneled Teardrop, Tarentum Glass Co. **110.00**
Cut Glass, Russian pattern alternating with clear panels, orig SS top **375.00**
Emerald Green, 4-1/4" h, Hobnail, US Glass Co. **170.00**
Green, 5-3/4" h, four blown molded panels, diamond and cross design, rib between each panel, lid mkd "E. P.," open bubble on surface **100.00**
Light blue, 4-1/4" h, Paneled Daisy, Bryce Bros./US Glass Co. **375.00**
Milk glass, 4-1/2" h
Apple Blossom, Northwood Glass Co. **160.00**
Quilted Phlox, white, hand painted blue flowers, Northwood Glass Co./Dugan Glass Co. **100.00**
Mt. Washington
2-3/4" h, tomato shape, cream ground, raised white and blue flowers **230.00**
4" h, melon ribbed, rose colored hues, raised blue and rust colored berries, emb metal lid **300.00**
4" h, 3-1/4" d, fig shape, opalescent body, pansy dec, orig top **1,200.00**

Hand painted, pale blue ground, autumn flowers, embossed pewter top and handle, **$65**; rose satin, clear applied handle, shiny silvered top, **$75**.

Photo courtesy of Dotta Auction Co., Inc.

4-1/4" h, egg shape, yellow ground, blue, yellow, and amethyst mums, sgd, molded patent............................ **200.00**

5-1/2" h, ribbed pillared body, enameled cascading Shasta daisies, emb metal lid. **355.00**

7" h, light blue to white, enameled flowers, Pairpoint metal caddy, paper label from Mt Washington Art Glass Society Annual Convention **950.00**

Opalescent glass

3-1/2" h, Beatty Honeycomb, white, Beatty & Sons... **110.00**

4-1/2" h, Daisy & Fern, cranberry **230.00**

4-1/2" h, Spanish Lace, blue, roughness to fitter rim. **200.00**

4-1/2" h, Windows pattern, blue, roughness to fitter rim **250.00**

4-3/4" h, Bubble Lattice, blue **325.00**

4-3/4" h, Chrysanthemum Base Swirl, blue, Buckeye Glass Co. **275.00**

4-3/4" h, Coin Spot, bulbous base, blue, Hobbs, Brockunier & Co./Beaumont Glass Co. **160.00**

4-3/4" h, Reverse Swirl, white, Buckeye Glass Co./Model Flint Glass Co. **120.00**

5" h, Poinsettia pattern, blue, roughness to fitter rim. **375.00**

5-1/4" h, Swirl, cranberry **425.00**

Opalware, 4-1/2" h, Gillinder Melon, light blue shading to white, satin finish, hand painted multicolored floral dec, Gillinder & Sons.. **180.00**

Opaque

3" h, Little Shrimp, ivory, Dithridge & Co. **100.00**

3-3/4" h, Challinor's Forget-Me-Not, white, Challinor, Taylor & Co. **90.00**

4-1/2" h, Alba, pink, Dithridge & Co. **190.00**

4-1/2" h, Parian Swirl, green, hand painted floral dec, Northwood Glass Co **175.00**

4-1/2" h, Quilted Phlox, light green, cased, Northwood Glass Co./Dugan Glass Co. **210.00**

4-1/2" h, Rings & Ribs, white, hand painted floral dec **50.00**

4-1/2" h, Utopia Optic, green, hand painted floral dec, Buckeye Glass Co./ Northwood Glass Co. .. **300.00**

5" h, Acorn, blue, Beaumont Glass Co. **230.00**

5-1/4" h, Cone, blue, Consolidated Lamp & Glass Co. **140.00**

Polka Dot, blue opalescent, original top, **$85**.

Photo courtesy of Dotta Auction Co., Inc.

Satin

4" h, Leaf Mold, light blue, Northwood Glass Co. . **325.00**

4-1/2" h, Leaf Umbrella, blue, Northwood Glass Co. . **425.00**

Slag, Creased Teardrop, brown shading to green, 4-3/4" h **275.00**

Smith Bros

5" h, blue body, polychrome flowers **125.00**

5" h, melon ribbed, enameled flowers **250.00**

Spatter

4-1/2" h, Leaf Umbrella, cased cranberry, Northwood Glass Co. **350.00**

4-3/4" h, Ring neck, cranberry and white **140.00**

Unidentified maker, 4-3/4" h, opal glass body, blue stemmed flowers, Victorian **100.00**

Wavecrest, 5" h, conical, polychrome fern dec .. **335.00**

Silver

6-3/4" h, Continental, 18th C, pierced fruit-form cover, baluster body molded with leaftips, circular foot, marked "C.G N," 7 troy oz **265.00**

7" h, Victorian, W. Comyns maker, London, 1891, pierced pear-shaped lid with flame finial, inverted pear shaped body, trumpet foot, lid and body with diagonally curved lobing, 7 troy oz. **250.00**

8-1/4" h, Edward VII, maker's mark M & Co., Birmingham, 1904, waisted baluster form, fluted base, short spreading foot, lid with stylized flowerhead and foliage piercing, urn finial, 8 troy oz. **250.00**

SWORDS

History: The first swords used in America came from Europe. The chief cities for sword manufacturing were Solingen in Germany, Klingenthal in France, and Hounslow and Shotley Bridge in England. Among the American importers of these foreign blades was Horstmann, whose name is found on many military weapons.

New England and Philadelphia were the early centers for American sword manufacturing. By the Franco Prussian War, the Ames Manufacturing Company of Chicopee, Massachusetts, was exporting American swords to Europe.

Sword collectors concentrate on a variety of styles: commissioned vs. non-commissioned officers' swords, presentation swords, naval weapons, and swords from a specific military branch, such as cavalry or infantry. The type of sword helped identify a person's military rank and, depending on how he had it customized, his personality as well.

Following the invention of repeating firearms in the mid-19th century, the sword lost its functional importance as a combat weapon and became a military dress accessory.

Note: Condition is key to determining value.

Basket hilted, steel basket hilt cast with roundels of Romaine heads, grotesque figures, military trophies, similarly styled pommel over spiral-carved wooden grip, blade marked for Andrea Ferrara, 43-3/4" l, **$1,550**.
Photo courtesy of Skinner, Inc.

Sword

Artillery, 25" l, Ames, 18-3/4" blade stamped with faint signature, U. S. and inspectors' markings, brass hilt with fish scale design, relief eagle **440.00**
Artillery officer's saber, 33" l, 27-1/2" l curved blade, wide fuller, eagle head pommel and hilt show most of orig fire gilding, replaced wooden handle, early 19th C ... **330.00**

Calvary saber

41" l, 35-1/2" l import blade with later date stamp of 1851, brass three branch hilt missing leather and wire wrapping, with scabbard
.... **220.00**
41-1/2" l, Civil War, 35-3/4" blade stamped "Ames Mfg. Chicopee Mas, U.S.J.R. 1857," brass three-branch hilt with good patina, part of wire wrap and most of leather remains, iron scabbard
.... **700.00**
42-3/4", Model 1860, Emerson & Silver, Trenton, NJ, signature on ricasso, inspector's initials and 1863 on other side, brass three

branch hilt with good patina, dark leather wrapped handle missing its wire, browned steel scabbard.......... **825.00**
43" l, 1840, stamped "U. S. 1862," brass three branch hilt with leather and wire wrapped handle, steel scabbard
.... **660.00**

Continental rapier, lobed grip with crosshatched pommel, faceted quillions, cup pierced and engraved with scrolls, long wavy textured blade, 58-1/2" l, **$750**.
Photo courtesy of Skinner, Inc.

European

Broadsword, 36" l, 31" blade, 1-1/2" wide blade with floral motif, leather covered wooden grip, brass guard, brown pommel cap, provenance descended from Gen George Meade family, early 19th C, some rusting, some dryness to leather, no scabbard
.... **650.00**
Court type, 38-1/2" l, 33-1/2" blade, thin triangular blade with floral etching, hand engraved steel cross guard, bone grip, provenance descended from Gen George Meade family, early 19th C, some rusting, loss to grip, no scabbard or chain guard
.... **350.00**
French, artillery saber, 40" l, brass single branch hilt, wire and leather cov handle, 32" l curved blade with engraving along top edge, steel scabbard, drag reshaped
.... **350.00**
Indonesian, long blade carved with figures, scrolling leaf motifs and script, handle carved with figures, bulbous pommel, wooden scabbard, 35" l............................. **300.00**
Infantry officer, Model 1850, Ames, 30-1/4" l etched and engraved blade with

"Chicopee, Mass" address, cast hilt wash with open work, leather scabbard with brass bands and drag, engraved "Lt. Geo. Trembley, 174th N.Y.S.I.," 36-1/4" l.... **1,980.00**

Japanese

20" l, Wakizashi, orig scabbard **250.00**
34" l blade, Koto period, No dachi type, mokume grain, choji temper line, single mekugi ana, silver habaki, scabbard and hilt of negoro lacquer **5,600.00**

French, late 19th C, gilt bronze, grip with flowering vines on stippled ground, ending in leopard's mask, short reeded quillions, red morocco sheath topped by gilt cartouche of hound seated by tree suspending snared hare, scroll engraved endcap, mounted with metallic stitched waist sash, watered steel blade etched and gilded with cartouches of game, scrolls, and military trophies, 24-1/2" l, **$3,000**.
Photo courtesy of Skinner, Inc.

Officer

39" l, non-regulation, Civil War, 32" blade with fine etching including "U.S." eagle, and banner on opposite side, steel hilt with pierced "U.S." and detailed eagle with "E. Pluribus Unum," sharkskin cov grip with orig copper wire remaining, steel scabbard with minor pitting **1,200.00**
40" l, 19th C, import, 34" blade, sgd "Sargent & Son, Manufacturer to the East India Company," cast brass three-branch hilt with leaf designs, handle retains orig sharkskin and wire wrapping...... **150.00**
Russia, 38-1/4" h, dress, Nicholas II, engraved in Cyrillic lettering on partial basket hilt, further engraved with device of nobility above monogram, leathered sheath
.... **4,120.00**

Staff and field sword, Model 1860, 37" l, 31" thin blade with floral motif, wood grip with double brass wire twist, brass guard with eagle motif, guard bent with slight break, provenance descended from Gen George Meade family missing reverse clamshell and drag to scabbard, some rusting to blade and scabbard, no maker's name **650.00**

Tibetan, scabbard mounted with coral and turquoise, 36-3/4" l, possibly 19th C **720.00**

Turkish, yataghan, curving blade inlaid in silver with Arabic inscriptions, handle and pommel chased and filigree in silver, chased and filigree silver mounted leather scabbard, 1" l **850.00**

TEA CADDIES

History: Tea once was a precious commodity and stored in special boxes or caddies. These containers were made to accommodate different teas and included a special cup for blending.

Around 1700, silver caddies appeared in England. Other materials, such as Sheffield plate, tin, wood, china, and pottery, also were used. Some tea caddies are very ornate.

English, mahogany veneer, mahogany drawer fronts, hinged lid opening to interior top compartment, eight interior drawers, wallpaper interior, minor veneer bubbling, 11" w, 6-1/2" d, 12" h, **$750**.

Photo courtesy of Alderfer Auction Co.

Fruitwood, Georgian, late 18th C, apple shaped, realistically turned, small wood stem, small iron escutcheon, traces of foil in interior, 5" h, **$3,525**.

Photo courtesy of Skinner, Inc.

Famille Rose, 5-1/2" h, Mandarin palette, arched rect form, painted front, figures and pavilion reserve, c1780 .... **550.00**

Ivory tusk, 4-1/4" w, 5" h, formed as section of tusk, silver-plated mountings, flat hinged top with foliate finial, engraved scrolls, beaded and waved rim bands, 19th C **460.00**

Papier-mâché, 9-1/4" l, 6-3/4" d, 6" h, Regency Chinoiserie-style, rect case with canted corners, ornately dec with figural reserves within flower blossoms bordered by wide bands of gilding, conforming hinged lid opening to int. fitted with two removable pewter tea canisters with dec chasing **950.00**

Quillwork, 8-3/8" l, 4-3/4" d, 5-1/4" h, hexagonal, inlaid mahogany frames, blue and gilt quillwork panels covered with glass, floral vintage and leaf designs with crown and "MC 1804," two int. lidded compartments, replaced foil lining, English **2,750.00**

Silver, 7" h, lobed hexagonal form, lobed lid with filigree finial, all-over Eastern style bird and foliate enamel dec, mounted with semi-precious stones, gilt int., approx 17 troy oz, Europe, late 19th/early 20th C **500.00**

Treen, ovoid, fruitwood, late 18th C, 5" h, missing finial and internal hasp............ **1,400.00**

Wood

7-1/2" w, 4" d, 4-3/8" h, mahogany veneer, banded and string inlay, oval fan inlay in lid, front panel with oval inked flower basket medallion that matches another inside, two lidded interior

compartments with replaced foil lining **320.00**

7-1/2" w, 4-1/2" d, 5-3/4" h, rosewood veneer, line inlay around edges, canted sides, brass feet, bone or horn inlaid diamond keyhole escutcheon, two lidded interior compartments with ivory knobs, traces of foil lining, red paper lined lid **300.00**

Lacquered, Chinese Export, 19th C, eight-sided oblong box, hinged lid, brass swing handles, top and sides gilt decorated with reserves, painted figures in courtyard, surrounded by floral and foliate borders and dragons on black ground, interior fitted with two canisters engraved with figures, scroll, and foliate designs, 12" w, 9" d, 5-3/4" h, **$940**.

Photo courtesy of Skinner, Inc.

Mahogany, oblong octagonal form, veneered body with line inlay and monogrammed cartouche, ebonized accents, minor losses to moldings, 6" l, 4" d, 5" h, **$165**.

Photo courtesy of Alderfer Auction Co.

Sterling silver, James T. Woolley, Boston, early 20th C, shouldered footed vessel, monogrammed "VH" on lid, impressed "WOOLLEY STERLING," 7 troy oz, 4-3/4" h, **$500**.

Photo courtesy of Skinner, Inc.

8-3/4" w, 5-1/4" d, 5-3/8" h, mahogany, hinged rect box, cove molded top, brass bail, ivory diamond-shaped escutcheon, bracket feet, opening to three compartments, repairs, England, late 18th C ... **360.00**
9-5/8" w, 5" d, 6" h, mahogany, banded inlay, inlaid diamond keyhole escutcheon, bracket ogee feet, brass bale handle, two lined int. compartments with later red paper, edge damage, small pieced repairs **350.00**
12-1/4" w, 6-1/4" d, 6-1/2" h, rosewood, rect box, sloped sides, inlaid hinged lid and front with brass scrollwork, sides with flush handles, int. fitted with two hinged and inlaid lidded wells flanking area for mixing bowl, int. of lid with velvet ruching, Georgian-style, late 19th C **450.00**
12-1/4" w, 6-1/2" d, 7-3/4" h, burled veneer, satinwood banding, brass claw and ball feet and ring handles, lion face plates, paneled lid with raised medallion at center, divided interior with two cov containers and well for glass canister, restorations to one foot and back of lid..... **635.00**
12-3/8" w, 8" h, rosewood , ivory escutcheon, sarcophagus shape, two lidded, foil-lined wells, colorless glass mixing bowl, interior of lid lined with ruched velvet, flattened ball feet, Regency, early 19th C **400.00**

TEAPOTS

History: The origins of the teapot have been traced to China in the late 16th century. Early Yixing teapots were no bigger than the tiny cups previously used for drinking tea. By the 17th century, tea had spread to civilized nations of the world. The first recorded advertisement for tea in London is dated 1658 and called a "China drink…call Tcha, by other Nations Tay, alias Tee…" Although coffee houses were already established, they began to add tea to their selections.

From the very first teapots, figural shapes have always been a favorite with tea drinkers. The Victorian era saw a change from more utilitarian teapots toward beautiful, floral, and Rococo designs, yet figural pots continued to be manufactured.

Early American manufacturers mimicked Oriental and British designs. While the new land demanded sturdy teapots in the unsettled land, potteries were established steadily in the Eastern states. Rockingham teapots were produced by many companies, deriving this term from British companies manufacturing a strong, shiny brown glaze on heavy pottery. The best known is from the Bennington, Vermont, potteries.

By the 1800s and the turn-of-the-century, many pottery companies were well established in the U. S., producing a lighter dinnerware and china including teapots. Figural teapots from this era are highly desired by collectors, while others concentrate on collecting all known patterns produced by a company.

The last 20 years has seen a renewed interest in teapots and collectors desire not only older examples, but also high-priced, specialty manufactured teapots or individual artist creations commanding hundreds of dollars.

Reproduction Alert: Teapots and other ware with a blurry mark of a shield and two animals, ironstone, celadon-colored body background, and a design made to look like flow blue, are new products, possibly from China. Yixing teapots have been reproduced or made in similar styles for centuries.

Basalt, 9-3/4" l, black, oval form, scalloped rim and classical relief centering columns with floral festoons, banded drapery on shoulder, incised brick banded lower body, unmarked, England, early 19th C, restored spout **360.00**

Cloisonné, panel with butterflies and flowers, Chinese, late 19th C **450.00**

English pottery, figural lady finial, ruffled skirt forms teapot base, green base with pink highlights, marked "DainTee Lady Teapot, Regd No. 824 S41, Made in England," **$95**.

Earthenware, 7" h, brown and green speckled ext., matching lid, c1880.... **420.00**
Flow blue, Scinde pattern, Alcock, octagonal, 8-1/2" h **950.00**
Graniteware, large teapot with pewter handle, lid and spout, Manning Bowman & Co. Manufacturers, called Perfection Granite Ironware, West Meriden, Connecticut **325.00**
Ironstone, Mason's Ironstone, Vista pattern, red and white scenic dec, matching trivet **195.00**
Majolica, fish, multicolored, Minton, no mark, late 1800s **2,000.00**
Pratt, 6" h, pearlware, underglaze polychrome enamels on oval forms molded with ribbed bodies and central medallions of classical reliefs, swan finial, slight flake and line to cover, chipped spout **450.00**

Oriental teapot with original basket, Famillie Rose decoration, **$95**.

Rockingham glaze, 4-3/8" h, brown glaze, tree trunk form body, molded fruiting vines, branch handle, twig finial, imp Wedgwood, England, mark, c1870, chip to cover collar **520.00**

Silver, 5-3/4" h, Hester Bateman, London, 1786, oval, domed lid with beaded rim, engraved bands, body with engraved bands and central cartouche, wood ear handle and finial, approx 13 troy oz..... **3,450.00**

Wedgwood, 7-1/4" l, Rosso Antico, Egyptian, applied black basalt hieroglyphs, crocodile finial, imp mark, early 19th C, slight chips to rim and spout........... **1,100.00**

Yang-Tz-u, 8-1/4" h, enameled, hexagonal, bright polychrome painted mountainous landscapes on each panel, imitation famille rose and jaune dec top and borders, Chinese export, 19th C, professional repairs on spout, lid, and handle............ **250.00**

TEDDY BEARS

History: Originally thought of as "Teddy's Bears," in reference to President Theodore Roosevelt, these stuffed toys are believed to have originated in Germany. The first ones to be made in the United States were produced about 1902.

Most of the earliest teddy bears had humps on their backs, elongated muzzles, and jointed limbs. The fabric used was generally mohair; the eyes were either glass with pin backs or black shoe buttons. The stuffing was usually excelsior. Kapok (for softer bears) and wood-wool (for firmer bears) also were used as stuffing materials.

Quality older bears often have elongated limbs, sometimes with curved arms, oversized feet, and felt paws. Noses and mouths are black and embroidered onto the fabric.

The earliest teddy bears are believed to have been made by the original Ideal Toy Corporation in America and by a German company, Margarete Steiff, GmbH. Bears made in the early 1900s by

other companies can be difficult to identify because they were all similar in appearance and most identifying tags or labels were lost during childhood play.

Notes: Teddy bears are rapidly increasing as collectibles and their prices are rising proportionately. As in other fields, desirability should depend upon appeal, quality, uniqueness, and condition. One modern bear already has been firmly accepted as a valuable collectible among its antique counterparts: the Steiff teddy put out in 1980 for the company's 100th anniversary. This is a reproduction of that company's first teddy and has a special box, signed certificate, and numbered ear tag; 11,000 of these were sold worldwide.

5" h, Schuco, perfume, gold mohair, black shoe button eyes, black floss nose and mouth, jointed at shoulders and hips, head lifts off to reveal small bottle for perfume **375.00**

8" h, unjointed gray mohair, replaced shoe button eyes, black floss nose, vertical stitching, eyes high on head, felt paw pads, mounted on unmarked cast iron wheels, brown leather collar **500.00**

8" h, brown mohair, brown glass eyes, black cotton floss nose with horizontal stitching, floss mouth, hump on back, excelsior stuffing, brown leather collar with decorative metal studs, wheels mounted on metal housed in mohair covered legs, some mohair missing **325.00**

10" h, ginger mohair, fully jointed, black steel eyes, black embroidered nose, mouth, and claws, felt pads, Steiff, blank ear button, spotty fur loss **1,150.00**

10" h, light yellow short mohair pile, fully jointed, excelsior stuffing, black steel eyes, embroidered nose, mouth, and claws, felt pads, Ideal, c1905, spotty fur and fiber loss, pr...................... **920.00**

11" h, blond mohair, fully jointed, excelsior stuffing, black steel eyes, open composition

mouth with full set of teeth, c1908, fiber wear around mouth and nose, some fur wear at seams **750.00**

12" h, yellow mohair, fully jointed, glass eyes, embroidered nose and mouth, excelsior stuffing, felt pads, Schuco, early 1920s, moth damage, spotty fur loss **350.00**

13-1/2" h, saffron rayon plush, fully jointed, excelsior stuffing, glass eyes, embroidered nose, mouth, and claws, felt pads, some fur loss, and fiber damage, c1930 .... **115.00**

16" h, ginger mohair, fully jointed, excelsior stuffing, glass eyes, long arms, shaved muzzle, vertically stitched nose, felt pads, arrow ear button, Bing, c1907, very slight fur loss, head disk broken through front of neck............. **2,300.00**

16" h, golden yellow mohair, fully jointed, glass eyes, brown still nose, embroidered mouth, excelsior stuffed, light fur loss, felt pads damaged, probably American, c1920 ...... **260.00**

16-1/2" h, ginger mohair, fully jointed, black steel eyes, black embroidered nose, mouth, and claws, beige felt pads, excelsior stuffing, American, c1919, patchy fur loss, felt damage **800.00**

TERRA-COTTA WARE

History: Terra cotta is ware made of hard, semi-fired ceramic. The color of the pottery ranges from a light orange-brown to a deep brownish red. It is usually unglazed, but some pieces are partially glazed and have incised, carved, or slip designs. Utilitarian objects, as well as statuettes and large architectural pieces, were made. Fine early Chinese terra-cotta pieces recently have sold for substantial prices.

Architectural element, 22" w, 22" h, foo lion, scribed character on sides, fish scale design on bodies, small saddles carry filled bags, flat base, price for pr, base and edge chips **425.00**

Bowl, 6" d, 2" h, glazed **30.00**

Bust, Marie Antoinette, France, late 19th C, applied sepia toned finish, gray marble socle, 25-1/2" h, **$1,175**.

Photo courtesy of Skinner, Inc.

Bust, 10-1/2" w, 10" h, good detail, dark red patina, hollow interior, firing separation noticeable from underside, nose restored.............. **125.00**

Figure
7-1/2" h, Aphrodite, dressed in tunic, open back, South Italian, third century B.C. **345.00**
11" h, St. Joseph, wearing long loose robes, black hat, polychrome dec, Spanish, 19th C **600.00**
18-3/4" l, reclining male figure with dog, inscribed "Claude Janin"........................ **400.00**

Pedestal, 7" sq top, 24" h, price for pr **400.00**

Planter, 10-1/4" h, garland and mask motif **100.00**

Portrait plaque, 4-1/2" d, Benjamin Franklin, circular shape, self-framed with raised title "B. Franklin Americain" surrounding portrait in relief, sgd "Nini" (for Jean Baptiste Nini) dated 1777, unidentified impressed fleur-de-lis mark, France, mounted in ebonized wood frame, shallow rim nicks **1,410.00**

Statue, 55" h, Minera, woman in draped toga, grape and cable head dress, holding wine cup **2,000.00**

Tray, 9" x 7", hp, pilgrims resting, gilt dec, 1920................ **85.00**

Urn, 29-1/2" h, molded putti and foliage dec, green glaze, waisted neck, two handles, circular base............... **395.00**

Water pitcher, 13" h, c1810, base chip................... **325.00**

TEXTILES

History: Textiles is the generic term for cloth or fabric items, especially anything woven or knitted. Antique textiles that have survived are usually those that were considered the "best" by their original owners, since these were the objects that were used and stored carefully by the housewife.

Textiles are collected for many reasons—to study fabrics, to understand the elegance of a historical period, for decorative purposes, or to use as was originally intended. The renewed interest in antique clothing has sparked a revived interest in period textiles of all forms.

Bedspread
Embroidered candlewick, by Eliza Spink, (1807-77), Auburn, NY, white on white embroidered dec, central cartouche with floral urn, medallion above name and date surrounded by grapevine border, further framed by grapevine and tulip border, central floral urn, 108" x 112", small holes, light staining, repairs **1,840.00**
Printed cotton toile, New England, late 18th/early 19th C, Cupid and several allegorical female figures in scenes of love, hand sewn, pieced and quilted in diamond pattern, backed with white homespun fabric, extended center panel, two pillow gussets, side drops, scalloped border on three sides, white binding, minor repair to backing, 109-1/2" l, 52-1/2" w center panel, 31-1/2" l side drops.. **1,295.00**

Braided rug
17-1/2" d, round, blue green, and pink...................... **180.00**
28-1/2" l, 23" w, oval, multicolored, predominately pink............................ **200.00**
33" d, round, multicolored, hooked star in center, small repair **660.00**
36-1/2" d, round, shades of green, red, and blue... **125.00**
39" d, round, blue, red, and green **190.00**

Child's seat, 9-1/2" sq, woven, flame stitch saw tooth pattern, green, pink, and black . **200.00**

Coverlet, damask, two pcs, red, blue, and green on white ground, rose and star design, marked "made for P. Matthias by W. H. Gernand Damask Coverlet Manufacturer Westminster Carroll County, MD, 1871," 89" x 90".. **1,125.00**

Coverlet, jacquard, one pc, Bierderwand, broad loom Mustard, dark salmon, and navy blue stripes on natural, corner block "William & Rachel Guthrie" with poppy, overall floral designs, tulip-like medallions, added fringe, 84" x 96".......................... **385.00**
Natural, dark navy blue, burgundy, and olive, "Latest Improvent P. Warranted M. by H. Stager, Mount Joy" on edge, star medallion with tulip center, surrounded by rose branches, Greek key and rose branch border, corner block with bird in tree branch, worn areas, fringe loss, some edge damage, 69" x 77" **300.00**

Coverlet, jacquard, red, blue and green, eagle border, made for Elisabeth Rischel, 1836, **$350**.

Photo courtesy of Pook & Pook.

Coverlet, jacquard, two pcs, Biederwand
Natural and navy blue, corner block "Daniel Lehr, Dalton, Wayne County, Ohio, 1847," leaf medallions, borders with backwards looking birds with tulips, minor stains and wear, some fringe loss, edge backed with blue cloth, 70" x 76"..................... **450.00**
Natural and soft salmon, tan, and gold, corner block "Made by W. Moore 1848," (Newark, OH), rose medallion, grape vine border, another small diamond border, minor wear, fringe loss, some edge damage, two halves don't line up at center seam, 78" x 86" **250.00**

Natural, navy blue, and tomato red, corner block "H. Petry, Canton, Stark County, Ohio, 1840," floral medallions with borders of potted tulips, eagles with trees and stars, fringe loss, minor stains, small hole, stitched repairs, 70" x 72" **425.00**
Natural, navy blue, red, and golden olive, corner block "T. M. Alexander, Wayne County, S.C.T. Ohio 1845," floral motif, lions and sunbursts, borders of backwards looking birds with roses, grape vines, and diamonds, few stains, fringe loss, small hole, unbound top edge, 72" x 88" **650.00**
Natural, navy blue, salmon red, and olive brown stripes, corner block with four oak leaves "Peter Hartman, Wooster, Ohio, 1843," connected mirror images of potted flowers, alternating with bunches of grapes, border with eagles with shields sitting on grape vines and roses, wear, few stains, some repair, fringe loss, 77" x 90" **300.00**
Navy blue, red, and olive green stripes, natural ground, corner block labeled "Gabriel Rausher, May 10, Delaware, Ohio, 1854," floral medallions, two vining floral borders, bottom border has backward looking parrots, one rolled edge, minor wear and fringe loss, some stitched repairs, 58" x 86" **440.00**
Navy blue, tomato red, and mixed green and yellow stripes with natural, corner block with fancy tulip and "F. Yahraus, Knox County, Ohio 1864," stars with flower and star medallions, one border with backward looking birds and flowers, two borders with grape vines, wear, small repair, edge damage, 74" x 88" **500.00**
Tomato red and navy blue bands on foundation of natural threads individually dyed light blue, border labeled "1848 Wove by J.S. for F.L.T.," quatrefoil corner block with bird under tree, diamonds alternating with wavy leaves, double borders of berry vines, worn edges with traces of blue calico binding, 74" x 90" **385.00**

Coverlet, jacquard, two pcs, double weave
Blue and white, attributed to Duchess County, New York, unidentified weaver, Agriculture & Manufactures are the Foundations of our Independence, floral medallions bordered by buildings, American eagle flanked by Masonic columns, monkeys, and small human figures, 78" x 82", some stains and edge damage **865.00**
Blue and white, attributed to James Alexander (1770-1870), Orange County, New York, second quarter 19th C, cotton and wool, woven in two lengths with an interior of six large floral medallions on polka dotted background, border designs of Independence Hall flanked by eagles with overhead stars, and eagles with Masonic compass and square and columns, name "PHEBE HULSE OCT. 14 1824" woven in corner blocks, minor toning, stains, 94" x 79" **3,410.00**
Blue and white, New York State, 1841, central star and floral medallions, side borders of birds, undulating grapevines, and pine trees, lower border with eagles and willow trees over name "DEWITT," corner blocks with flower in vase, flanked by "SA" and "C" over "N.Y. 1841," toning, 86" x 82" **500.00**
Dark tomato red, navy blue, and natural, unusual geometric overshot type pattern, minor fringe loss, 68" x 78" **425.00**
Natural, navy blue, and salmon, conch shell corner block for Samel Balantyne, 1808-1861, Lafayette, IN, flowers in grid, borders of urns and pineapple with internal hearts, fringe missing some wear, edge damage, 75" x 86" **365.00**
Natural, salmon, and navy blue, sunflower corner blocks, thistle medallions surrounded by roses, borders with grape vines, wear, minor stains, 72" x 78" **600.00**
Natural, tomato red, and dark green, corner block with

pinwheel and "Jas McLD" for James McLeran, Columbiana County, OH, after 1848, flower and leaf medallions on speckled background, pots of strawberries on border, bound edges, few areas of wear, 72" x 76" **425.00**
White and dark navy blue, geometric pattern, pine tree borders, overall light stains, one edge rebound with blue calico, 76" x 84" **220.00**

Coverlet, double weave, red, green, gold, and natural, eagles in corners, feathered spokes with tulips in center, maker's identification, "Henry Dannert, Allentown, P" across edge, **$325**.

Pair of pillow cases and top sheet, white linen, red cross-stitch monograms "C. M." and lace trim on each, early 1900s, **$125**.

Cover or wall hanging, attributed to Bangladesh, early to mid-1900s, cotton/linen and silk plain weave, piecing, appliqué, and embroidery in running, seed, and outline stitches, shades of tan, blue, darker blue, gold, etc., 100" x 91", **$195**.
Photo courtesy of Alderfer Auction Co.

Coverlet, overshot

One piece, broadloom, intricate optical pattern, natural, purple, and cinnamon, 74" x 106" .. **495.00**
Two piece, optical pattern, natural, pink-red, and navy blue, some fringe trimmed, 68" x 78" **450.00**
Two piece, tightly woven, natural, navy blue, and dark red, added red fringe, 80" x 90" **250.00**

Coverlet, single weave, two pc,

brick red, navy blue, medium blue, and some green on natural, striped designs, tree borders, most orig fringe, small areas of moth damage, 75" x 93" **300.00**

Coverlet, summer/winter, one pc, broad loom

Centennial, red, green, and navy blue stripes on natural, central medallion with star surrounded by flowers and eagles with shields in each corner, bound edge with checkered design, worn areas, fringe loss, 80" x 87" **125.00**
Hunter green and tomato red, central floral medallion surrounded by triangles, wide border with capitol building in center flanked by grape vines and flower urns, small stitched repair with minor damage at one of bound ends, 78" x 84" **450.00**
Natural, medium green, blue, and tomato red, corner block "Ettinger and Co. Arronsburg, Centre Co., 1865," central acanthus leaf medallion with floral corners, multiple borders including stars, diamonds, and grape vines, minor stains, one end cut down and rebound, 78" x 81"
.... **350.00**
Natural, navy blue, red, dark green, corner block "Made by J. Hausman in Lobachsville for John Bechtol 1842," minor wear and stains, 76" x 100"
.... **400.00**
Natural, red, blue, and yellow stripes, corner block "Emanuel Ettinger, Aaronsburg, Centre Co. 1846," quatrefoil leaf medallions alternating with stars and diamonds, tulip border, 76" x 91" **200.00**
Tomato red and natural, central sunburst surrounded

by acorn and oak leaf wreath, eagle corners, wide floral borders with paisley scrolls in corners, minor stains, 76" sq
.... **230.00**

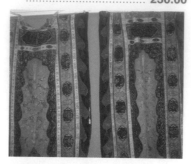

Draperies or hangings, pair, wool piercing and appliqué, complex intricate satin embroidery, predominately floral motifs, lilac, cream, blue, green, gold, green, and ivory silk and cotton, mandarin orange, black, cream, and aqua wool, backed in heavy purple velvet, late 1800s, 49" x 78", **$350**.

Photo courtesy of Alderfer Auction Co.

Draperies, Fortuny, early 20th C, four 19-1/4" w by 54" l panels, three 40" l by 54" l panels, large green fleur-de-lis patterns on taupe ground
.... **2,990.00**

Foot rest, 15" d, braided, round, padded, hanging loop, multicolored, stuffed with rags, wear **110.00**

Fragment

42" x 66", linen and cotton toile, red printed designs on natural white, George Washington guiding leopard drawer chariot, Franklin, Goddess of Liberty, and soldiers, old but not orig edge binding, stains, torn typewritten paper label stitched to front **320.00**
52-1/4" x 49", crewel work, wool yarn, colorful bird perched in flowers tree, edges with later stitching, minor stains **215.00**

Handkerchief, printed on cotton, Democratic Party, donkeys from Jefferson to Truman, 1949 .... **230.00**

Hooked mat

8" x 8-3/4", sailing ship, labeled "Grefell Labrador Industries, Hand Made in Newfoundland & Labrador," minor edge damage ... **200.00**

Embroidered verse, "Hope and Fear," made by "Ann Maddy 1834," some wear, framed, 14" square, **$250**.

Photo courtesy of Joy Luke Auctions.

Framed needlepoint and petit point panel, two children playing with cats, walnut frame, 20-1/2" x 23-1/2" overall. **$325**.

Photo courtesy of Joy Luke.

12" d, round, gray, brown, red, and blue turkey on pale green ground, multiple borders
.... **160.00**

Hooked rug

21" x 21-1/2", center reclining cat, multicolored, blue ground, black cloth border
.... **3,300.00**
25" x 18", center gray rabbit, flanked by red tulips in each corner on dark background, scalloped pink-lavender fabric border **690.00**
26" x 44-1/2", multicolored angled line borders, olive green corner blocks, horse's head center, burgundy, red, and brown center ground, mounted to stretcher, areas of loss and wear **260.00**
27" x 11-1/2", rect, center cat with whiskers, multicolored, border, cloth backing. **1,210.00**
31-1/2" x 20", theorem type, basket of multicolored flowers, black ground, red scalloped border **1,155.00**

35" x 20", multicolored, central blue elephant with black legs, eye, ear, and trunk... **1,320.00**
36" x 20", full figure red and black Indian holding tomahawk, standing on rock dated 1917, light background, multicolored striped border **5,775.00**

Hooked rug, folk art type scene of rooster standing on back of sheep, farm setting, America, 20th C, **$195**.

36" x 22", multicolored, geometric pattern, cloth bound edges **935.00**
38-1/2" x 85", three stars surrounded by flowers and concentric diamonds, borders of diamonds and triangles, rect, multicolored, predominantly wool strips hooked onto burlap backing, America, 19th C, minor imperfections **2,235.00**
39" x 24", center running horse, surrounded by butterflies and birds, multicolored **1,710.00**
39" x 30", center lying dog, multicolored, hooked crazy quilt background, initialed "E.G.M." **7,150.00**
40" x 28", two central black horses, red background, blue, green, yellow, and red floral vines on top and bottom, vivid orange ground, white panel "M.H." in black script (Mary Hull,) other white panel "1897," later printed cloth backing, provenance: purchased from Hull family estate, Dover, York County, PA **7,700.00**
41" x 33", central gray dog, flanked by salmon butterflies, red five-pointed stars, two pink sassafras leaves at top, red and green vine with leaves and flowers at bottom, multicolored scalloped border **2,750.00**
42-1/2" x 39", center dog, surrounded by hearts, elves,

and geometric designs, multicolored, date "1921" woven into background, repairs...................... **2,530.00**
54" x 37", eagle motif, rope border **1,000.00**
Welcome, semi-circle, Cape Cod origin **1,750.00**

Mourning picture, framed, silk threads, silk ground, central weeping willow tree, tombstone, obelisk, church in far left ground, never embroidered with names, 16-1/4" x 22", minor losses, deterioration of silk ground **600.00**

Needlepoint picture, woolwork, rooster and two chickens in landscape, multicolor floral border, America, 19th C, 24-3/8" x 21-3/8", **$275**.

Needlework genealogy, silk on linen, wrought by "Eliza Jordan 1828," floral border, American, 15-1/2" x 16-3/4", **$1,100**.

Photo courtesy of Pook & Pook.

Needlework picture
8-1/2" x 7-3/8", Mrs. Saunders and Miss Beach's Academy, Dorchester, Massachusetts, 1807, silk threads on silk ground, flowers and fruit in urn, pen and ink inscriptions below reading "Wrought at Mrs. SAUNDER'S & Miss BEACHES Academy

Dorchester 1807, by Miss June Withrington," stains, laid down........................... **780.00**
13-5/8" x 13", silk threads on silk ground, watercolor highlights, shepherdess seated while inscribing the letters "TANCRED" on nearby tree, two sheep in foreground, distant mountain, in an oval enclosed by meandering flowering vine, by "Maria Billings M.E. and A. Sketchley's Boarding School, Poughkeepsie," unframed, thread loss, color runs, couple of tears........................ **775.00**
17-1/2" x 14-1/4", wool embroidery, allegorical scene of man casting out young woman and boy, French knotted trees, painted silk ground, bird's eye maple frame, Victorian, late 19th C **360.00**
22-5/8" x 17", densely chain and couch stitched allegorical scene of couple espied by nobleman and woman in castle, painted faces, accented with French knots, faux pearls, and gold metal chain, matted, 29-1/2" x 23-1/2" frame, England/France, mid to late 19th C **1,300.00**

Penny rug
37" x 23", round discs, black background, yellow, blue, and red **1,210.00**
57" x 32", six-sided, appliquéd felt pennies, yellow birds, red berries on stems, green leaves, orange daisies with yellow centers, light background, decorative scalloped border **2,100.00**

Pillow, 15" h, 14" l, beadwork, central demi lune beaded panel, white, gray, pink, and blue floral scene, gray velvet ground, blue, gray, and maroon silk trim, late 19th C **200.00**

Pocketbook, 4-5/8" x 7-5/8", America, 1740-90, crewel embroidery, rect containing initials "ZS," various flowers and foliage in shades of red, yellow, green, and gold issuing from urn set against black ground, green twill woven taped edging, blue glazed wool int. lining with two compartments, imperfections **10,575.00**

Rag runner
2' 10" x 10' 9", blue, rainbow
stripes, yellow predominate,
PA, stains **125.00**
3' 1" x 12' 11", brown, tan,
blue, and orange stripes
.... **85.00**

Show towel
14-1/2" w, 40" l, strong blue
and dark pink cross-stitch
geometric design, "Susanna
Johnson 1839" **200.00**
15-3/4" w, 54" l, homespun,
pink and two shades of blue
cross-stitch needlework, urns
of flowers, one with birds,
hearts, diamond, and fretwork
lines, "Elisabeth Schli 1810,"
fringed, few small holes, some
repaired **440.00**
19" w, 62" l, homespun, dark
brown finely stitched urns of
flowers, one urn is heart
shaped, "Betz Huhn 1808,"
woven decorative bands with
pulled work and fringe at end,
one end is bound........ **250.00**
19-1/2" w, 58" l, red, pale blue,
pink, and yellow yarn crewel
work flowers, potted tree, dark
blue cross-stitched "ER
1840," decorative woven
bands, wear to yarn border,
stitch loss, very minor stains,
added fringe **385.00**

Shawl, all over paisley design in
greens, roses, reds, blues, etc., black
center, three sides with short fringe,
late 1800s, 70" x 72", **$225**.

Photo courtesy of Alderfer Auction Co.

Paisley shawl, woven with cashmire
motifs, 126" x 58", **$425**.

Photo courtesy of Sloans & Kenyon Auctions.

Shawl, paisley, sheer wool, shades of
mandarin orange, red, blue, gold, black,
and mustard, black center, short fringe
on two sides, late 1800s, 70" x 70",
$275.

Photo courtesy of Alderfer Auction Co.

Table cloth, 16' 6", banquet size,
damask, banded foliate
border with panels of classical
subjects, central Portland
vase designs, Wedgwood,
England, 20th C **235.00**
Table mat, braided
4" d, round, brown and blue,
price for pr **200.00**
6-3/4" d, round, brown and
green, cloth backing, price for
pr **220.00**
15" d, round, purple.... **200.00**
21" w, 34-1/2" l, oval, tan,
maroon, and pink........ **275.00**
24" w, 41" l, oval, multicolored
.... **470.00**
Table runner, 19" l, 10-1/4" h,
homespun linen, brown,
white, and blue checkered
pattern, frayed ends, price for
pr **440.00**

Tablecloth and matching napkins,
white linen damask, original box and
paper tags reading "Pure Irish Linen
Damask, Made in Ireland," 64" x 84"
tablecloth, eight 16" square napkins,
original gift card included, late 1930s or
early 1940s, unused, **$175**.

Photo courtesy of Alderfer Auction Co.

Tablecloth and matching napkins,
cream rayon and cotton damask,
labeled "Cotton & Rayon, Made in
Scotland," late 1930s or early 1940s,
unused, **$150**.

Photo courtesy of Alderfer Auction Co.

Tapestry, Aubusson-style, 60" x
36", shore bird in landscape
of trees and flowering plants,
tears and repairs **2,000.00**

TIFFANY

L.C. Tiffany-Favrile

History: Louis Comfort Tiffany (1849-
1934) established a glass house in
1878 primarily to make stained glass
windows. In 1890, in order to utilize
surplus materials at the plant, Tiffany
began to design and produce "small
glass," such as iridescent glass
lampshades, vases, stemware, and
tableware in the Art Nouveau
manner. Commercial production
began in 1896.

Tiffany developed a unique
type of colored iridescent glass
called Favrile, which differs from
other art glass in that it was a
composition of colored glass
worked together while hot. The
essential characteristic is that the
ornamentation is found within the
glass; Favrile was never further
decorated. Different effects were
achieved by varying the amount
and position of colors.

Louis Tiffany and the artists in his studio also are well known for their fine work in other areas—bronzes, pottery, jewelry, silver, and enamels.

Marks: Most Tiffany wares are signed with the name "L. C. Tiffany" or the initials "L.C.T." Some pieces also are marked "Favrile," along with a number. A variety of other marks can be found, e.g., "Tiffany Studios" and "Louis C. Tiffany Furnaces."

For more information, see *Warman's Glass*, 4th edition.

Reproduction Alert: Tiffany glass can be found with a variety of marks, but the script signature is often faked or added later. When considering a purchase of Tiffany glass, look first to the shape, the depth of the iridescent coloring then the signature.

Bronze

Bookends, pr, 4-3/4" w, 6" h, Zodiac, dark brown and green patina, imp "Tiffany Studios New York 1091" **490.00**

Box, cov
2-1/2" h, 5" d, circular, enameled stylized spray flowers in irid gold, blue, and green, on bronze ground, script signature, "Louis C. Tiffany 9151" **24,000.00**
6-1/2" l, etched metal grape vine pattern, imp "Tiffany Studios New York 816," c1900, three Favrile panels damaged, hinge detached **550.00**

Candelabra
9-1/8" h, two arms supporting cups with seven green and gold irid glass "jewels," brown and green patina, imp "Tiffany Studios New York" ... **2,760.00**
2-1/2" h, four bulbous cups with blown green Favrile glass

on four curved arms, base with sixteen green "jewel" inserts around platform base, imp "TG & D Co., Tiffany Studios New York D 887," corrosion, missing bobeches **2,100.00**

Candlestick, 8" d, 24" h, tripod shaft, circular base, prong-set bobeche with flaring rim, orig dark verdigris patina, stamped "Tiffany Studios, New York, 1211" **4,315.00**

Cigar box, 6-1/2" l, 6" d, 2-1/2" h, rect hinged box, Zodiac pattern, multicolored enameling to each medallion, partial cedar liner, base stamped "Tiffany Studios New York 1655" **1,610.00**

Clock, mantle, Pine Needle pattern, sgd "Tiffany Studios New York, #2246," 9" w, 6" d, 13" h......................... **3,585.00**

Desk accessories, inkwell, pen holder, stamp box, ten Favrile panels, secret drawer hidden within central drawer, 8-3/4" l, 4-1/2" h **23,000.00**

Desk box, 7-3/4" d, 2-1/2" h, Pine Needle pattern, polished, stamped Tiffany Studios mark and numbered "824"
Caramel slag glass..... **825.00**
Green slag glass **1,000.00**

Frame, gilt, easel back, 10-1/4" w, 12" h, cast Heraldic pattern, lower recessed finished in patinated brown, imp mark "Louis C. Tiffany Furnaces Inc. 61"............................. **1,035.00**

Glove box, 13-1/2" l, 4-1/2" d, 3-1/8" h, Grapevine pattern, striated green slag glass inserts, ball feet, imp "Tiffany Studios, New York" **980.00**

Lamp base, 22" h, three sockets, hexagonal standard, circular base, base stamped "Tiffany Studios New York 534" **3,820.00**

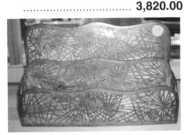

Bronze, letter holder, Pine Needle pattern, green slag glass inserts, $1,200.
Photo courtesy of Dotta Auction Co., Inc.

Letter opener, Grapevine pattern, green slag glass **450.00**

Letter stand, 6-1/2" l, 5-1/4" h, etched metal grape vine pattern, Favrile panels, brown and mottled verdis gras patina, imp "Tiffany Studios New York, c1910 ..... **1,100.00**

Magnifying glass, 8-7/8" l, gilt bronze, rosette pattern on handle, imp "Tiffany Studios 1788," imperfections .. **750.00**

Paperweight, 1-1/2" h, 2-1/4" l, sphinx, orig patina, some gilt, stamped "Tiffany Studios New York" **275.00**

Pen tray, Grapevine pattern, green slag glass, numbered "1004" **650.00**

Plate, 9-3/4" d, 1" h, ftd, relief arts and crafts block designs around rim, sgd "Tiffany Studios New York, 1744" **475.00**

Plate, bronze, gilt wash, Greek Key design border, marked "Tiffany Studios/New York/1743," 8" d, **$220**.
Photo courtesy of Alderfer Auction Co.

Stand, 31-1/2" d, circular top centered by medallion relief-decorated with classical figures, three ribbed legs, base accented with scroll and leaf dec, imp Tiffany & Co. mark, and numbered "0297," maker's "7725 M," one ornamental finial missing **1,175.00**

Thermometer, 8-3/4" h, Grapevine pattern, beaded border, green patina, green slag glass, easel stand, imp "Tiffany Studios New York" on reverse, minor corrosion **1,495.00**

Tray, 9-7/8" d, circular with extended rim and handles, etched, enameled blue, pink, and green floral cloisonné dec on handles, imp "Louis C. Tiffany Furnaces Inc., Favrile 512" under handle...... **460.00**

Left: plate, amethyst pastel, translucent body with opalescent ribs radiating from pontil to the ruffled edge, signed "L. C. Tiffany Favrile," 8-1/2" d, ex-Maude B. Feld, with inventory label, **$600-$900**; center: candlestick, baluster, iridescent blue, King Tut pattern, gold interior, attributed by Christian Revi in *American Art Nouveau Glass* as "blue luster glass candlestick with damascene decoration in gold luster: Tiffany Furnaces, CA 1910," accompanied by book page, 10" h, **$1,100**; right: center bowl, royal blue stretch border shading to quilted opalescence, intaglio cut leaf and vine decoration, mounted on scrolled foliate bronze base, stamped "Louis C. Tiffany Furnaces Inc., Favrile," 12" d, 5-1/4" h, **$3,500-$4,500**.

Photo courtesy of Early Auction Co.

Twine holder, 3" h, Bookmark pattern, hexagonal form, hinged lid, reddish patina in lower recesses, imp "Tiffany Studios New York 905," minor spotting **1,035.00**

Glass, all Favrile

Bowl
5-3/4" d, pastel, flattened flaring rim, yellow pastel body, opalescent feathering, stretch border, sgd around pontil "L.C.T. Favrile #1925" . **250.00**
6" d, irid gold, sgd "L.C.T." **100.00**
8-1/8" d, flared rim, diamond quilted pattern, aqua, polished pontil, sgd "L.C. Tiffany Favrile," numbered "1926" **1,000.00**

Bowl and flower frog, 10" w, irid gold, intaglio green lily pad and random green vines, double chain looped flower frog sgd "7127L L.C. Tiffany Favrile" **3,900.00**

Bud vase
6" h, flared rim, tapering cylindrical form, gold favrile, pulled blade dec, rough pontil, sgd "L. C. Tiffany - Favrile, Inc.," numbered "1504" **825.00**
8" h, ftd, irid gold, green pulled feather dec, sgd "1501 1980 LC Tiffany Favrile" **1,000.00**

Candle lamp shade, 5-1/2" h, yellow pastel opal, pulled green and silvery irid feather dec, inscribed "L.C.T., N 841," c1900 .... **1,955.00**

Candlestick, 10" h, baluster irid blue, King Tut pattern, gold int., attributed by Christian Revi in *American Art Nouveau Glass* as "blue luster glass candlestick with damascene decoration in gold luster: Tiffany Furnaces, CA 1910," accompanied by book page **1,100.00**

Carafe, 11" h, pinched ovoid body, elongated neck, topped with pinched and beaded stopper, ambergris, overall strong gold irid, polished pontil, base sgd "L. C. Tiffany Favrile 430," slight wear to rim **1,035.00**

Center bowl, 10" d, 3-3/4" h, deep blue irid swirling ribbed body, sgd "L.C.T. Favrile," orig paper label on pontil **1,700.00**

Compote, floriform
4-1/2" h, gold body, opal overlay, pulled green feathers, irid gold onion skin rim, inscribed "L.C. Tiffany Favrile 2648L," c1917 .... **1,495.00**
4-3/4" h, gold body, pinched ruffled rim, sgd "1504C L.C. Tiffany-Favrile" **1,000.00**

Cordial, 3" h, cylindrical flaring form, irid gold, sgd "L.C.T." **300.00**
Cup, 2-1/4" h, gold, green arrowroot dec around the body, applied handle, sgd "L. C. Tiffany – Favrile," numbered "7246D" **650.00**
Decanter set, 11" h decanter with bulbous stopper, irid gold, fine horizontal band of grapes dec, six matching 4-1/4" h cordials, each sgd **5,500.00**
Dish
5-1/4" d, 1-1/2" h, extended ruffled rim, round form, blue, inscribed "L. C. Tiffany Favrile 1034-1595m" **490.00**
5-7/8" d, round rim, irid gold, inscribed "L.C.T.," paper label, polished pontil .. **215.00**
Finger bowl, 4-1/4" d, pigtail prunts dec, sgd "L.C.T. T8919" **475.00**
Finger bowl and undertray, gold favrile
4-1/8" d bowl with ruffled rim sgd "L. C. T.," 5-5/8" d undertray sgd "L. C. T." and numbered "R3491"..... **500.00**
6" w, 3" h, bright blue hues, pigtail prunts, sgd "L.C.T. M9115" **450.00**
Flower frog, 1-1/2" d, irid blue, two tiers of loops, sgd "L.C. Tiffany Inc. Favrile," numbered "488N"....... **400.00**
Goblet, 7" h, irid gold, sgd "LCT Favrile"........................ **550.00**
Lamp base, 25" h, bulbous shaped body, gold Cypriote finish, doré foot, metal collar, foot die stamped "Cassidy Company Inc. New York," glass body sgd "Louis C. Tiffany Favrile" **4,500.00**
Lamp shade, 5" h, irid gold, inscribed "L.C.T. Favrile," c1900.......................... **575.00**
Low bowl, 8" d, fold-over rim, optic ribbed body, irid gold, sgd "1883 L.C. Tiffany Favrile," paper label ... **550.00**
Nut dish
2-3/4" d, ruffled rim, irid gold, sgd "L.C.T. Favrile"..... **175.00**
3" d, gold swirled rib form, polished pontil, numbered "1401 L.C.T. Favrile" ... **450.00**
Punch cup, 2-1/4" h, irid gold, dec with intaglio band of grapes and leaves, applied handle, sgd "L.C. Tiffany Favrile"....................... **400.00**

Rondel, 17-3/8" d, circular disk, irid gold glass within metal rope-turned frame with loop handle, polished pontil, unsigned, minor wear . **940.00**

Rose bowl, 3-3/4" h, 10-ribbed form, ruffled rim, cobalt blue, overall blue irid luster, polished pontil sgd "L. C. Tiffany Favrile 1103-7725K," some scratches **865.00**

Salt, open
2-1/2" d, gold, pinched inverted rim, polished pontil, paper label **300.00**
2-1/2" d, gold, ruffled rim, polished pontil, sgd "L.C.T. Favrile" **265.00**
3-1/2" h, irid gold, four pronged feet, sgd "L.C.T." **450.00**

Tazza, 5-3/4" d, 6" h, pastel, aqua bowl, flattened stretch border, opalescent feathering, green tinted translucent stem, raised irid disc, sgd around pontil "L.C.T. Favrile 1702" **650.00**

Toothpick holder
2-1/4" h, gold, trailing prunts, sgd "L. C. T.," numbered "D7626" **250.00**
2-3/8" h, gold, trailing prunts, sgd "L. C. T.," numbered "-3599" **500.00**

Vase, Favrile, trumpet shape, short knopped stem, domed base, signed "L. C. Tiffany Favrile, 1905-9850L," 9-7/8" h, **$790.**

Photo courtesy of Sloans & Kenyon Auctions.

Vase
3-1/2" h, tapering ribbed body, irid waves, special order, sgd "L.C.T. o8136" **1,200.00**
4-1/4" h, bulbous stick, flared rim, irid gold, sgd "2240J L.C. Tiffany Favrile" **450.00**

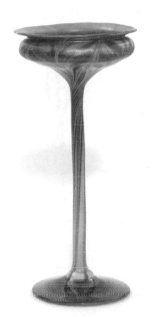

Vase, floriform, wide circular opalescent glass cup with iridescent interior, ruffled edge, exterior decorated with green striated leafage continuing to cylindrical stem, amber iridescent circular foot, unsigned, Corona period, 13-1/4" h, **$3,000.**

Photo courtesy of Early Auction Co.

4-1/2" h, flower form, gold int., green pulled feather on alabaster body, sgd "4749G L.C. Tiffany Favrile," 3" crack extends from rim into body **200.00**
4-3/4" h, tapering, irid gold, intaglio butterfly and insect dec, sgd around pontil "L.C. Tiffany Inc. Favrile 7924N" **750.00**
5" h, flared amber Favrile glass oval body, 25 tiny white cane blossoms among emerald green leaf leaves, amber stems, overall irid luster, inscribed "LCT Tiffany Favrile 2889C" around button pontil **2,415.00**
5-3/8" h, cameo, etched colorless body, white and pale yellow overlapping petals emerging from transparent green base, ftd, rolled base rim, rough pontil, sgd "L.C. Tiffany Favrile," numbered "4053D" **11,200.00**
5-1/2" h, narrow mouth, bulbous body, blue, vertical tone on tone stripes, button pontil, sgd "L.C. Tiffany Favrile 7548H" **1,880.00**

5-3/4" h, ovoid form, irid gold, covered in molded lily pad motif, conical pedestal, sgd "L.C. Tiffany-Favrile" ... **950.00**
6" h, floriform, blue, white and green hearts and vines dec, foot marked "5090 L. C. Tiffany Favrile" **4,800.00**
7" h, gold, high rounded shoulders with irid opal dec, marked "L. C. T. O1105" **3,250.00**
7-1/2" h, translucent green, striking gold drips over rows of cascading irid drops, sgd "L.C.T. A214" **2,500.00**
8-1/4" h, wide mouth and shoulder, irid green, lower body shading to purple, polished pontil, sgd "L. C. Tiffany-Favrile," numbered "3525 L" on base, imperfections........... **1,880.00**

Vase, ribbed floriform, gold Favrile, engraved "L. C. Tiffany-Favrile 1298 G," 9-1/4" h, **$1,100.**

Photo courtesy of David Rago Auctions, Inc.

8-3/8" h, ovoid tapering body, cylindrical neck, gold, covered in molded branch and leaf design, raised disc base, mkd "L.C. Tiffany Favrile 1559, 506P". **1,500.00**
8-1/2" h, protruding ribs, scalloped rim, irid gold, sgd "L.C. Tiffany Favrile #N5986," orig paper label on pontil **1,150.00**
8-7/8" h, colorless, alternating vertical bands of white opal, interior iridized in rich shaded azure blue, inscribed "L.C. Tiffany Favrile 1882". **1,265.00**
9" h, swollen body tapering to bulbed stem, amber, dec with trailing vines and heart leaves, applied dark foot, sgd

"L. C. Tiffany - Favrile 5603G," bubbles below surface **1,840.00**

9-1/2" h, gourd form, random pulled designs in gold over yellow irid body, wafer pontil inscribed "LCT H1230" **2,500.00**

10" h, bulbous stick vase, flaring inverted rim, irid gold body dec with undulating white wave and gold zipper pattern, button pontil, sgd "A1493 L.C.T." **1,750.00**

10" h, trumpet, knopped stem, elongated irid gold body, flared rim, sgd "1509-9850L L.C. Tiffany-Favrile" . **1,300.00**

10-1/4" h, 10-ribbed gourd form, flared and ruffled rim above bulbed top, round disk foot, blue irid, inscribed "L. C. Tiffany Favrile 1089-68201" **1,495.00**

11-3/4" h, flared rim, long cylindrical form, irid blue, sgd "L. C. T. Favrile," raised on pair of unsigned brass dolphin-form candlesticks, price for pr **2,235.00**

12-3/4" h, ribbed floriform body, ruffled rim, circular foot, irid gold, sgd "L. C. Tiffany Favrile," numbered "66D" **2,710.00**

13" h, floriform, translucent green and variegated opal, pulled in feather design, slender stem, bell shape foot, inscribed "L.C.T. R 9927" **7,130.00**

13-1/4" h, floriform, wide circular opalescent glass cup with irid interior, ruffled edge, exterior dec with green striated leafage continuing to cylindrical stem, amber irid circular foot, unsgd, Corona period **3,000.00**

Vessel, 3-5/8" h, gold, flared rim and shoulder on ribbed body, raised on circular foot, sgd "L. C. T. 63B" **1,175.00**

Wine, 3-3/4" h, irid gold, faceted stems, price for set of three **475.00**

Lamps

Boudoir, 15-1/2" h, dome shade, restored oviform base, irid gold glass dec with intricate intaglio carved green leaves, trailing budded vines, both sgd "L. C. Tiffany Favrile," shade also marked "5594L" **9,775.00**

Lamp, desk, 13" h, bronze, three gold iridescent ribbed lily shades, each inscribed "L.C.T.," bronze base stamped "Tiffany Studios New York 319," 13" h, crack and hole in one shade, **$2,500**.
Photo courtesy of Early Auction Co.

Candlestick, 12" h, 7-1/2" d shade, 2-1/2" aperture size, quilted blue shade with stretched rim, ribbed and swirled base fitted with green and white pulled feather standard, aperture rim nicks **2,235.00**

Desk, 13" h, bronze, three gold irid ribbed lily shades, each inscribed "L.C.T.," bronze base stamped "Tiffany Studios New York 319," crack and hole in one shade **2,500.00**

Floor, 52-1/2" h, counterbalance, gold doré finish, base stamped "Tiffany Studios New York 681," unsigned 9-3/4" d shade with four rows of fourteen panels **3,055.00**

Mantel lamp, 8" h, slight octagonal form, cream colored glass rising to bulbed top, caramel and gold pulled petal design, fitted gilt bronze and wood base **1,150.00**

Table lamp, green damascene Favrile dome shade inscribed "L. C. T. Favrile," double-curved arm and ball on stepped base, brown patina, base impressed "Tiffany Studios New York 417," shade 7-1/8" d, 14-3/4" h, **$11,200**.
Photo courtesy of Skinner, Inc.

Table lamp, green leaded glass geometric shade, faceted bronze base, marked "Tiffany Studios New Ork," original verdigris patina, lines to eight glass pieces, reproduced cap, 30-1/2" h, 22" d, **$22,500**.
Photo courtesy of David Rago Auctions, Inc.

Table lamp, dome shade of green and white leaded glass in floral and geometric pattern over footed converted oil font base with single socket, shade and font stamped "TIFFANY STUDIOS," normal wear to original patina, few small breaks to glass panel, 16" d, 22" h, **$10,925**.
Photo courtesy of David Rago Auctions, Inc.

Table

12-1/2" h, Nautilus, adjustable shell-form shade of striated green and white leaded glass segments, supported on bronze standard and cushion base, raised leaf dec, reddish-brown patina, base imp "Tiffany Studios New York 25891" and "Tiffany Glass and Decorating Company" mark, c1892-1902, 12-1/2" h **8,625.00**

21-1/2" h, 15-5/8" d, linenfold, 10 panels of pleated amber glass, doré metalwork, lower edge slightly lipped, stamped "Tiffany Studios New York 1957, PAT APPL'D FOR," three sockets, gold doré standard, base stamped "Tiffany Studios New York 533" **10,575.00**
22" w, 15-1/2" h, bronze, double branch, each branch with three irid glass shades, central bronze stem hollowed to one side to accept separate candle snuffer (missing), base imp "Tiffany Studios 10456" on each glass shade, sgd "LCT" minor roughness on base of shades **12,500.00**
24" h, 16" d, Crocus, four inverted clusters of spring green flowers with stems, mottled white ground, lower geometric border, stamped metal tag on shade rim, standard with three sockets, knob with seven cabochon jewels, base plate stamped "S216 437 Tiffany Studios New York" **18,800.00**
24" h, 20" d, Dragonfly, conical shade, seven blue-bodied dragonflies with red eyes, caramel-gold colored ground with twenty-one oval gold jewels and doré metalwork, shade stamped "Tiffany Studios New York 1495," three-socket standard base in turtle back design with verdigris doré finish, base plate stamped "Tiffany Studios New York 587" **44,650.00**
28-1/2" h, 22-1/2" d leaded glass globe shade, mottled green geometric slag glass segments progressively arranged, stamped "Tiffany Studios" on rim, four socket bronze standard, domed, stepped, circular base, stamped "Tiffany Studios New York 532" on base . **19,550.00**

Silver

After dinner coffeepot, 11" h, elongated handle and spout, flip lid with leaf finial, ftd, sgd "Tiffany & Co." **300.00**
Bowl
5-3/4" d, 3" h, incised banding, everted rim, low

domed foot, c1907-38, 11 troy oz **200.00**
9-1/4" h, 4-1/4" h, ftd, shaped edge with applied flowerhead and fern rim, stylized pad and paw feet with scrolled legs topped by acanthus leaves, center monogram, 1891-1902, 24 troy oz **1,610.00**
10-1/4" d, scalloped rim, foot ring marked "Tiffany & Co., Makers Sterling 23844, 26 troy oz **660.00**
Bread basket, 7" w, 10-3/4" l, oval, molded rim, center monogram, 1925-47, approx 12 troy oz **215.00**
Cake pate, 13-1/4" d, circular, shaped rim with molded foliate edge, face with reticulated and engraved bands, domed circular foot with engraved and reticulated dec, center monogram, c1908-1947, approx 47 troy oz **1,955.00**
Candelabra, 12-1/4" h, three-light, cornucopia shoulder and central sconce, flanked by reeded scroll candle arms and further cornucopia sconces, plain columnar stem, foliate cornucopia and shell edge, round floral repoussé foot, removable beaded nozzles, sq base, 1902-07, 26 troy oz.. **1,150.00**
Cigarette case, 3-3/8" x 2-1/4", rect, rounded corners, gold-washed ovoid push button clasp, gold-washed interior, engraved on front with name and date, suspended from silver link chain, c1907-38, 4 troy oz **90.00**
Cocktail set, 6-3/8" h cocktail shaker, six 4-1/8" cordial glasses, tapered ovoid shaker with hammered surface, engraved initials and date in base, glasses with conical bowl, baluster stem, plain foot, monogrammed, c1875-91, 26 troy oz **865.00**
Coffee and tea service, 14" h coffeepot, creamer, hot water pot on ftd warming stand, cov sugar, waste bowl, each pc chased with band of ivy leaves, circular bases with bracket form feet, pinecone finials, each stamped "Tiffany & Co., 550 Broadway Quality 925-1000, 1375-3139 MM," late 19th C, 171.47 troy oz **7,475.00**

Dresser set, 10 pcs, three brushes, comb, covered jar, receiving jar, hand mirror, shoe horn button hook, rect box, floral and scroll acid etched dec, gold-washed int. on jars and boxes, monogrammed, c1907-38, 23 troy oz................ **1,850.00**
Flower basket, flattened bell shape, flared sides, engraved husk drops and floral swags, reticulated to rim in guillouche pattern, overhead handle engraved with further husks, oval foot, 1907-38, pr, 26 troy oz **2,645.00**
Iced tea spoon, 8" l, Bamboo pattern, molded bamboo form handles, set of four in Tiffany & Co. blue cloth bag in Tiffany box, mid-20th C.......... **175.00**

Fountain pen and pencil set, sterling silver, relief decorated with raised putti, floral swags, monogrammed medallion "M. V. P.," impressed "Tiffany & Co. Sterling," minor wear, 7" l, 7-3/4" l, **$265**.
Photo courtesy of Skinner, Inc.

Kettle on stand, 11-1/2" h, bulbous, domed lid, reeded bud finial, cast upright handle with leather mount, body with engraved band, circular stand with openwork skirt, three cast scroll legs with shell feet, 1916-47, 59 troy oz... **1,495.00**
Ladle, 11" l, Wave Edge, marked "Tiffany & Co., Sterling Pat 1884 M," 6 troy oz **320.00**
Muffiner, 7-1/2" h, 1891-1902, urn form body with bat's wing fluting below applied stylized leaf banding, spiral reeded stem, sq base, screw-in domed lid with paneled ball finial, 12 troy oz **635.00**

Pitcher, 8-1/2" h, repoussé, waisted baluster form, ear handle, short spout, chased and emb all over with flowers and leaves, 1891-1902, 32 troy oz **3,220.00**

Serving dish, 11-1/8" l, 5-1/2" h, crenelated banding, lid with ovoid handle flanked by anthemion, c1854-70, 41 troy oz **1,150.00**

Strawberry set, 11 strawberry forks, one sugar sifter, all gilt, twisted openwork handles and strawberry finials, early 20th C **1,800.00**

Stuffing spoon, 12-1/2" l, Chrysanthemum pattern, monogrammed, 8 troy oz **750.00**

Tray, 11" w, ovoid, reticulated border, emb flowers and shells, sgd "Tiffany & Co.," monogrammed **500.00**

Vase, cov, 16-3/4" h, flared rims, incised lines, stepped round bases, cov with wafers, elongated tear shaped finials, marked "Tiffany & Co. Makers, Sterling Silver," 65 troy oz, price for pr **2,550.00**

TIFFIN GLASS

History: A. J. Beatty & Sons built a glass manufacturing plant in Tiffin, Ohio, in 1888. On January 1, 1892, the firm joined the U. S. Glass Co. and was known as factory R. Fine-quality Depression-era items were made at this high-production factory.

c1960

From 1923 to 1936, Tiffin produced a line of black glassware called Black Satin. The company discontinued operation in 1980.

For more information, see *Warman's Glass*, 4th edition.

Marks: Beginning in 1916, wares were marked with a paper label.

Bell, June Night, crystal ... **65.00**
Bud vase, Fuchsia, crystal, 11" h **100.00**
Candlestick, June Night, duo, crystal **75.00**
Celery, Flanders, pink **140.00**
Champagne
 Cherokee Rose, crystal **20.00**
 June Night, #17358, crystal **30.00**
 Palais Versailles, #17594, gold encrusted **135.00**
 Plum, #17762............... **35.00**
Cocktail
 Byzantine, yellow.......... **15.00**
 Cerise, crystal............... **28.00**
 Fuchsia, crystal **20.00**
 June Night, #17538, crystal **30.00**
Compote, cov, #17523, Wisteria, crystal Cellini foot, two minute rim nicks **395.00**
Console bowl, Fuchsia, crystal, flared, 12-5/8" d **135.00**
Cordial
 Cordelia, crystal **10.00**
 Flanders, pink............. **150.00**
 Melrose Gold, #17356, crystal **125.00**
 Persian Pheasant, crystal **45.00**
 Westchester Gold, #17679, crystal **95.00**

Lamp, figural, basket of fruit, $250.

Cornucopia, Copen Blue, 8-1/4" **90.00**
Creamer, Flanders, pink, flat **230.00**
Cup and saucer, Flanders, yellow.................. **100.00**
Decanter, Byzantine, crystal **600.00**
Goblet
 Cherokee Rose, crystal. **28.00**

June Night, #17358, crystal **35.00**
Palais Versailles, #17594, gold encrusted **150.00**
Pink Rain, #17477, wisteria **55.00**
Plum, #17662................ **35.00**
Iced tea tumbler
 Cerise, crystal.............. **28.00**
 June Night, #17358, crystal **35.00**
 Pink Rain, #17477, wisteria **55.00**
 Plum, #17662................ **35.00**
Juice tumbler
 Bouquet, gold encrusted, Killarney green **75.00**
 June Night, #17358, crystal **30.00**
 Palais Versailles, #17594, gold encrusted **125.00**
Lamp, 8-1/2" h, 5" d, owl, rewired **500.00**
Martini glass, 4-1/2" d, 3" h, Shawl Dancer, set of four **150.00**
Perfume bottle, 4" h, parrot, slate gray painted finish, enamel dec, orig label **125.00**
Pickle, Flanders, yellow.... **55.00**
Plate, Flanders, pink, 8" d **35.00**
Rose bowl, 5-1/2" x 5", Swedish Optic, citron green, c1960, mold #17430............... **145.00**
Salad plate, June Night, crystal, 7-1/2" d **22.00**
Seafood cocktail, liner, Palais Versailles, #17594, gold encrusted **175.00**
Sherbet
 Cherokee Rose, crystal, tall **24.00**
 Ramblin' Rose, crystal, low **23.00**
Sherry
 June Night, crystal........ **30.00**
 Shawl Dancer, crystal... **55.00**
Sugar
 Cerice, crystal **25.00**
 La Fleure, yellow........... **40.00**
Vase
 7-3/8" d, 14" h, crystal, artist sgd **400.00**
 8" h, Dahlia, cupped, Reflex Green, allover silver overlay **225.00**
 8-3/4" h, dark amethyst satin, poppy like flowers **200.00**
Wall pocket, 9" l, 3-1/4" w, ruby **175.00**
Water set, cov 12" h pitcher, Classic etch, Nile green handle, lid and foot, 11 8" h goblets with Nile green stem and foot, etched cameos of dancing girl **1,750.00**

Wine

Byzantine, crystal **18.00**
Cherokee Rose, crystal **40.00**
Mirabelle, #17361, crystal,
6-1/4" H **48.00**
Mystic, #17378, crystal, 5-5/8" h
.... **45.00**
Palais Versailles, #17594,
gold encrusted **150.00**

TILES

History: The use of decorated tiles peaked during the latter part of the 19th century. More than 100 companies in England alone were producing tiles by 1880. By 1890, companies had opened in Belgium, France, Australia, Germany, and the United States.

Tiles were not used only as fireplace adornments. Many were installed into furniture, such as washstands, hall stands, and folding screens. Since tiles were easily cleaned and, hence, hygienic, they were installed on the floors and walls of entry halls, hospitals, butcher shops, or any place where sanitation was a concern.

Notes: Condition is an important factor in determining price. A cracked, badly scuffed and scratched, or heavily chipped tile has very little value. Slight chipping around the outer edges of a tile is, at times, considered acceptable by collectors, especially if a frame can cover these chips.

It is not uncommon for the highly glazed surface of some tiles to have become crazed. Crazing is not considered detrimental as long as it does not detract from the overall appearance of the tile.

Art pottery, 6" h, 12" w, landscape with birds and moose in foreground, dark green high gloss glaze
.... **175.00**
Arts & Crafts, 10" x 5-1/2", framed, scene of salt marsh landscape, blues, greens, and white, c1907 ..... **2,100.00**

Batchelder, 6" h, 18" l, beige bisque clay with blue engobe, stamped "Batchelder/Los Angeles"
Bouquet of flowers and birds, slight abrasion to surface
.... **375.00**
California desert landscape, abrasion to a few spots . **850.00**
California Art, 8" h, 12" l scene of California court yard with fountain, restored color and varnish, imp mark, mounted in Arts & Crafts frame .. **1,600.00**
Cambridge Art Tile, Covington, KY, 6" x 18"
Goddess and Cherub, amber, pr **250.00**
Night and Morning, pr .. **500.00**
Claycraft
6" x 12", horizontal, English thatched roof cottage next to foot bridge, semi-matte polychrome, mounted in period ebonized Arts and Crafts frame, covered stamp mark **1,610.00**
7-3/4" x 4", molded lone tree rising over ocean, matte polychrome glazes, stamped "Claycraft," mounted in new Arts & Crafts frame **815.00**
13-1/4" h, 35" l, five tile faience panel, molded landscape of Mediterranean houses by sea, marks hidden by contemporary Arts & Crafts frame **2,400.00**
Grueby, 6-1/4" sq, mottled matte green glaze, mustard yellow blossom, ftd copper frame, raised indecipherable mark on base **1,100.00**
J. & J. G. Low, Chelsea, MA
4-1/4" sq, putti carrying grapes, blue, pr **75.00**
6" d, circular, yellow, minor edge nicks and glaze wear
.... **35.00**
6" sq, woman wearing hood, brown **95.00**

Gilliot & Cie (Hemixem), fireplace surround, 18 6" tiles embossed with frieze of oak branches in brown, celadon, and ivory, each stamped "H," minor nicks and lines, **$275**.

Photo courtesy of David Rago Auctions, Inc.

Grueby, embossed putto playing cymbals, ivory matte glaze over dark blue-gray ground, unmarked, small chip to two corners, 6" square, **$400**.

Photo courtesy of David Rago Auctions, Inc.

KPM, 5-3/4" x 3-3/8", portrait of monk, titled "Hieronymous of Ferrara sends this image to the prophet to God," small nicks to corners **245.00**
Lowe, Chelsea, Massachusetts, late 19th/early 20th C, architectural, glossy taupe glaze, including forty-eight undecorated bricks, thirty-four scroll and leaf pattern, two pairs of framed tiles, one depicting winged dragon, the other warriors faces in mottled cream-color and brown glossy glazes, some with pottery marks.............. **360.00**
Marblehead, 4-5/8" sq, ships, blue and white, pr **125.00**
Minton China Works
6" sq, Aesops Fables, Fox and Crow, black and white .. **75.00**
8" sq, Rob Roy, Waverly Tales, brown and cream **95.00**
Minton Hollins & Co.
6" sq, urn and floral relief, green ground **45.00**
8" sq, Morning, blue and white
.... **100.00**
Moravian
10" x 7-1/4", Tempus, Father Time, blue and ivory glaze, red clay showing through, unmarked, small glaze flake on one edge **1,150.00**
18" d, 1-1/2" h, Autumn, young man picking apples, basket at his feet, stamped "MR," made for Old Wicker Art School, Detroit, MI, 1920s, custom made wrought iron museum stand **5,750.00**
Mosaic Tile Co., Zanesville, OH
6" sq, Fortune and the Boy, polychrome.................... **80.00**
8" sq, Delft windmill, blue and white, framed............... **55.00**

Moravian, Persian Antelope, ivory and blue glaze, red clay showing through, stamped "MORAVIAN," minor firing nicks to edges, 6-3/4" x 5-3/4", **$400**.

Photo courtesy of David Rago Auctions, Inc.

Pardee, C.
4-1/4" sq, chick and griffin, blue-green matte **175.00**
6" sq, portrait of Grover Cleveland, gray-lavender **125.00**

Providential Tile Works, Trenton, NJ, round, stove type, hold in center, flowered **20.00**

Rookwood Faience, 8" h, emb pink, ochre, and green geometric floral pattern, Arts & Crafts frame, stamped "RP," chips to corners.......... **325.00**

Sherwin & Cotton
6" sq, dog head, brown, artist sgd.............................. **100.00**
6" x 12", Quiltmaker and Ledger, orange, pr...... **145.00**

Unmarked, cat motif, light green glaze, $35.

Photo courtesy of Wiederseim Associates, Inc.

Trent, 6" sq, head of Michelangelo, sea green glaze, sgd by Isaac Broome, imp mark..................... **115.00**

U. S. Encaustic Tile Works, Indianapolis, IN, 6" x 18", panel, Dawn, green, framed **150.00**

Wedgwood, England
6" sq, calendar, November, boy at seashore, peacock blue.............................. **95.00**
8" sq, Tally Ho, man riding horse, blue and white ... **85.00**

TINWARE

History: Beginning in the 1700s, many utilitarian household objects were made of tin. Because it is nontoxic, rust resistant, and fairly durable, tin can be used for storing food; and because it was cheap, tinware and tin-plated wares were in the price range of most people. It often was plated to iron to provide strength.

An early center of tinware manufacture in the United States was Berlin, Connecticut, but almost every small town and hamlet had its own tinsmith, tinner, or whitesmith. Tinsmiths used patterns to cut out the pieces, hammered and shaped them, and soldered the parts. If a piece was to be used with heat, a copper bottom was added because of the low melting point of tin. The industrial revolution brought about machine-made, mass-produced tinware pieces. The handmade era had ended by the late 19th century.

ABC plate, alphabet embossed around rim, plain center, use wear, **$30**.

Anniversary top hat, 11" d, 5-3/4" h, 19th C **1,150.00**

Candle lantern
10" h, 5-7/8" d, conical, removable base, circular handle, banded pierce work, PA **5,390.00**
12" h, round removable base, glass panels in sides, cone shaped top with crimped dec, ring carrier, price for pr, one with pitted surface **400.00**

Cheese mold, heart shaped, punched circular design in base, applied handle and three feet, 4" w, 4-3/4" d, 2-7/8" h, **$210**.

Photo courtesy of Alderfer Auction Co.

Candle mold
5" h, 4-1/4" w, three-tube, handle........................ **715.00**
10" h, 6-1/4" l, 12-tube, applied handle, hanger ring, two wick holders......... **250.00**
10" h, 6-1/2" d, 12-tube, round, crimped pie plate top and base, C-shaped handle **990.00**
10-3/4" h, 72 tubes, sq, applied tin handles, both resoldered **320.00**
15-3/4" h, 6-1/4" d, 12-tube, round, ring handle and base **1,650.00**

Candlestick
3-1/2" h, 5-3/8" w, triangular base, push-up, ring handle, remnants of japanned finish **580.00**
6" h, 4-1/4" d, adjustable push-up, scallop grip ring handle, round base **330.00**
18-1/4" h, 6" d, push-up, scalloped base, adjustable, cone-form sand-filled base with rod for candle adjustment, attributed to William Smith, Dillsburg, York County, PA **3,740.00**

Cheese mold, 3" h, 7-1/4" w, pierced stylized geometric pattern, three tin conical feet, wire hanger, PA........ **2,420.00**

Coffeepot, 11" h, 8" w, conical, gooseneck spout, padded handle, finial, punched birds and flowers, made by William Resser, East Berlin, Adams County, PA, early 20th C **715.00**

Cookie cutter, hand made, 19th C
4-3/4" h, 2-1/2" w, 7/8" w, man in the moon, mounted on flat back plate................... **385.00**
5-1/4" h, 4-1/2" w, 1" d, eagle on nest, mounted on back plate with raised post for eye **165.00**

5-5/8" h, 4-3/4" w, 1" d, standing rooster, mounted on flat back plate **1,320.00**
6" h, 3" w, 1" d, crowing rooster, mounted on flat back plate with crimped edges **330.00**
6" h, 6-1/2" l, 1" d, swan, mounted to flat back plate **880.00**
7" h, Indian holding tomahawk **2,700.00**
8" h, man and woman dancing **3,900.00**
8" h, 4" w, 1" d, parrot, mounted to flat back plate **1,100.00**
8" h, 5" w, 1-1/8" d, Uncle Sam profile, mounted on flat back plate, unusually shaped handle with thumb rest **770.00**
8" h, 10" l, 7/8" d, moose, mounted on back plate with crimped edges **1,210.00**
12-1/2" h, 10-1/2" l, 7/8" d, George Washington on his horse, illegible center stamp attributed to Germantown, PA maker **13,200.00**
Creamer, 4" h, polychrome spray of yellow, green, and red flowers beneath spout, attributed to New York, mid-19th C, minor paint loss **200.00**

Comb case, wall hanging type, old light green paint, some rust, **$15**

Dust pan, 13-1/2" w, 16-1/2" l, bell shaped, crimped molding, compass wheel and various stamps, anniversary type, wooden handle .. **440.00**
Foot warmer
8-3/4" x 7-3/4" x 6" h, punched panels with heart in circle design, mortised wooden frame with turned posts and incised lines, wire bale handle, refinished **315.00**
9" x 7-1/2" x 5-5/8" h, punched panels with heart in circle design, mortised wooden frame with turned posts, old red stain, wire bale handle,

traces of rust, penciled note inside **200.00**
Grater, 9-1/8" l, 4" w, pierced, tapered sides, reinforced back **310.00**
Lamp
Grease, 1-5/8" h, colorful glaze **165.00**
Petticoat, 4" h, orig whale oil burner, orig black paint **65.00**
Skater's, 6-3/8" h, light teal-green globe **225.00**
Lantern, 17-1/2" h, hanging, old dark green repaint, rococo detail, six panes of glass with reverse painted dec, candle socket in base, attributed to Ohio, one pane with corner missing **420.00**

Squirrel cage, "Lehigh" stamped into side under gable, rotating cage, **$250**.
Photo courtesy of Dotta Auction Co., Inc.

Mold
7-3/4" w, 7" l, 1-3/4" d, heart shape, wire crimped rim **300.00**
9-1/2" w, 1-3/4" d, star shape, wire crimped rim **385.00**
Quilt pattern
7-3/4" d, six-sided star, central hole, names in pencil . **200.00**
9-3/4" d, compass wheel in plumed wreath **990.00**
13-1/2" d, eight-sided star, central hole **275.00**
Spice box, dome lid, punched floral dec, molded banding, ring feet, leaf form hasp support, int. spice grater, three compartments **1,320.00**
Tea bin, 8-3/4" w, 8" d, 10" h, painted red, litho portrait of pretty young lady, stenciled gold dec, America, 19th C, minor paint loss, price for pr **750.00**
Tea kettle, 5" h, 5-1/2" h, swing handle, copper brackets, straight spout, base finial **525.00**

Wall sconce, punched decoration, radiating sun motif in center, cutwork edges and details, **$195**.

Wall sconce
9" h, 3-1/2" w, tapered back, crimped dec.............. **500.00**
11" h, 6-3/4" w, oval, scalloped edges, crimped edge reflector **1,045.00**
12" h, 4" w, rect, scalloped roof, D-shaped base .. **330.00**
12" h, 6" w, roof, crimped dec reflector, scalloped roof, crimped band on candleholder base **880.00**
12-1/4" h, 3-3/4" w, rect, japanned black, half circle roof, candleholder base **110.00**
15" h, 9" w, oval, crimped and scalloped edges......... **990.00**
Weather vane pattern
11" h, 15" l, running horse **20.00**
11" h, 19-1/2" l, running horse **385.00**

TINWARE, DECORATED

History: The art of decorating sheet iron, tin, and tin-coated sheet iron dates back to the mid-18th century. The Welsh called the practice pontypool; the French, töle peinte. In America, the center for tin-decorated ware in the late 1700s was Berlin, Connecticut.

Several styles of decorating techniques were used: painting, japanning, and stenciling. Both professionals and itinerants did designs. English and Oriental motifs strongly influenced both form and design.

A special type of decoration was the punch work on unpainted tin practiced by the Pennsylvania tinsmiths. Forms included coffeepots, spice boxes, and grease lamps.

Note: Some record setting prices for decorated toleware were achieved during the auction of the collection of Eugene and Dorothy Elgin, at Conestoga Auction Company, Inc., in April of 2004. Those items are noted as "ex-Elgin."

Toleware, basket, Federal, crescent form, reticulated, swing handle, oval base, red paint decoration, hand-painted gilt and black accents, paint loss, splint in handle, 8" l, 5-1/2" d, 8-1/2" h, **$330.**

Photo courtesy of Alderfer Auction Co.

Box, cov, 13-3/4" l, 8-3/4" d, 9" h, dome top, wire and turned wooden handle on lid, yellow scrolled foliate designs, box with red and white swags, yellow leaf embellishments, black ground, America, 19th C **765.00**

Bun tray, 12-5/8" d, 3-5/8" h, elliptical, pierced handles, off-white rim band dec with yellow, red, green-blue, green, and black flowers, asphaltum ground, crystallized in interior, America, late 19th/early 20th C, paint losses **500.00**

Canister, cylindrical, 6-1/4" h, 6" h, red cherries, green leaves, white border, yellow stylized leaves and swag borders, lid centered with leaf dec, red japanned ground, minor scratches **400.00**

Chamberstick, 6-1/4" d, 2" h, applied handle, japanned ground, polychromed floral dec, yellow, red, green, and white, yellow banding, ex-Elgin **22,000.00**

Coffeepot, cov

10-1/4" h, orig red and yellow pomegranate dec, yellow foliage, brown japanned ground worn and alligatored, orig construction with pieced triangle below handle, wear **1,495.00**

10-1/2" h, 6-1/4" d, gooseneck spout, dome top, japanned ground, central medallion, white, orange, red, green, blue, and yellow fruit, floral and foliate dec, ex-Elgin **38,500.00**

10-1/2" h, 6-3/8" d, 9-1/2" w, gooseneck spout, red ground, central medallion with floral motifs, yellow, black, blue, green, and tan, ex-Elgin **55,000.00**

10-3/4" h, hooked spout, hinged lid, bands of red and yellow flanking bands of yellow flowers and foliage, asphaltum ground, America, late 18th/early 19th C, paint wear, minor dents **1,530.00**

Cream pitcher, cov, 3" d, 4" h, applied handle, triangular spout, japanned base, yellow floral and band dec, red, yellow, green, and white highlights, ex-Elgin **5,500.00**

Deed box, dome top

6-3/4" w, 3-1/8" d, 3-5/8" h, orig dark brown japanning, white band on front panel, green leaves, red cherries, yellow border dec, wire bale handle, tin latch, slight wear **660.00**

8" w, 4" d, 4-3/4" h, black ground, yellow swags and lines, front with fruit, yellow, and green foliate, wire bale handle, tin hasp, minor wear, mostly to lid edges **250.00**

Document box, 11-1/2" w, 5" d, 6-1/4" h, dome top, brown japanning, red draped swags, yellow leaves, wavy lines, tin hasp, brass bale handle, int. lined with remnants of glue-on leaves, minor touch-up on front of lid and some edges, some wear **990.00**

Tole, teapot, from Oliver Filley Tinsmiths, yellow bird and fruit decoration, inscribed on underside "H. Case, April 1824," Pennsylvania, paint loss, 11" h, **$1,725.**

Photo courtesy of Pook & Pook.

Match holder, hanging, 4-3/4" w, 1-5/8" d, 7-1/2" h, scalloped crimped edge, triangular pocket, black base, yellow, orange, and green floral banding, paint flaking, ex-Elgin............................ **420.00**

Milk can, 8-1/2" h, black japanning, stenciled red and gold stylized floral design.................... **200.00**

Spice box, 7-1/4" d, round, seven int. containers, worn orig brown japanning, gold stenciled labels **175.00**

Sugar bowl, cov, 4" d, 3-3/4" h, scrolled finial, japanned base, floral polychrome, yellow, green, red, and white band dec, ex-Elgin **11,550.00**

Tea caddy, 8-1/4" l, dark ground, worn stenciled bronze powder dec, int. lift-out tray fits over two lidded compartments, orig emb brass handle, minor damage **220.00**

Toy, 11-1/2" h, dancing man with top hat, arm and leg movement, polychrome dec, wooden handle........... **615.00**

Toleware, tray, oval, double handles, hand-painted barroom scene with sailors and dancing woman, paint loss, discoloration, 14-1/2" d, 21-3/4" l, **$450.**

Photo courtesy of Alderfer Auction Co.

Tray

8-3/4" l, 6-1/4" w, eight-sided, black base painted red ground, polychrome floral design, leaves, yellow banding, wire rim edge, minor paint flaking **990.00**

12-1/2" l, 8-3/4" w, eight-sided, japanned base, polychrome floral banding, crystallized center, yellow banding to sides with white, blue, yellow, orange, and red highlights, wire rim edge, ex-Elgin **17,050.00**

12-1/2" l, 8-3/4" w, eight-sided, japanned base, crystallized center, yellow, blue, and green floral banding on white ground, wire rim edge, attributed to Adams County, PA, ex-Elgin **9,350.00**

29-5/8" l, 24" w, oblong, scalloped edge, polychrome paint dec, centered scene of three masted ship, possibly U.S. frigate *Independence,* in coastal waters, enclosed by gilt stenciled leaf and scroll borders, black ground, metal hanging rack, America, early 19th C, imperfections **2,000.00**

Urn, cov

13-1/4" h, slender stem, ovoid foot, gilt florals, birds, and butterflies, 19th C, pr.. **1,725.00**

Two handles, acorn finials, dec with floral sprays and birds, scalloped floral and repeating gilt leaf borders, weighted base, French, 19th C, some paint loss, minor dents, pr **575.00**

TOBACCO JARS

History: A tobacco jar is a container for storing tobacco. Tobacco humidors were made of various materials and in many shapes, including figurals. The earliest jars date to the early 17th century; however, most examples seen in the antiques market today were made in the late 19th or early 20th centuries.

Bear with beehive, 6-1/2" h, majolica, Continental .. **770.00**

Blackamoor, 6" h, majolica, marked "DEP" in circle, c1900, some restoration **330.00**

Boy, kerchief around head and neck, green tea leaf poking out at forehead, red bow tie, eyes glancing to the side, unmarked, **$145**.

Photo courtesy of Joseph P. Smalley, Jr., Auctioneer.

Glass, deep amber paneled base, quadruple plate lid with pipe finial, **$125**.

Photo courtesy of Joy Luke.

Black boy, red hat with tassel, majolica, repainted, nicks **275.00**

Bull dog, porcelain, German **275.00**

Creamware, 9" h, 6" d, plum colored transfers on side, one titled "Success to the British Fleet," striped orange, blue, and yellow molding, domed lid **900.00**

Crystal, 7" h, hammered copper top, Roman coin dec, sgd "Benedict Studios" **250.00**

Dog's head, with pipe and green hat and collar, majolica **375.00**

Dwarf in sack, 8" h, terra cotta, multicolor dec, marked "JM3478," chips, wear **255.00**

Indian, 5-1/2" h, black, majolica **330.00**

Jasperware, raised white Indian chief on cov, Indian regalia on front, green ground..... **195.00**

Indian chief, multi-colored head dress, red head band, red beads at neck, unmarked, **$185**.

Photo courtesy of Joseph P. Smalley, Jr., Auctioneer

Majolica, 6" h, barrel shape, cobalt blue, green, gold, and brown, Doulton, Lambeth, England, #8481, artist's initials **225.00**

Mandarin, papier-mâché.. **95.00**

Man with pipe, large bow tie, with match holder and striker, rim chips, hairline **165.00**

Man with top hat, majolica, Sarreguemines, hairline in base.................................. **165.00**

Moose, porcelain, Austrian **200.00**

Owl, 11" h, majolica, brown, yellow glass eyes **825.00**

Royal Winton, hp relief scene, marked "Royal Winton, England" **195.00**

Stoneware, 5" d, 6" h, applied Egyptian motif, brown ground, c1890........................ **130.00**

Cut glass, floriform and foliate decoration, starburst on base, American Brilliant Period, late 19th/early 20th C, shelf scratching to base, small chips on lid, 7" h, **$350**.

Photo courtesy of Alderfer Auction Co.

Treenware, turned and painted poplar, lid with turned finial 4" d, 9-1/2" h, ftd base, incised banding, painted brown, spitting, chips . **600.00**
4-3/4" d, 7-1/4" h, incised banding, salmon base paint, black banding............ **990.00**
5-1/2" d, 7" h, incised banding, stained in multiple colors, varnished **770.00**
5-3/4" d, 9-1/4" h, incised banding, red, black, and green polychrome dec **2,475.00**
8" d, 8" h, finger grained paint dec on yellow base, brown highlights **5,500.00**
Wave Crest, 5" sq, white opaque body, SP fittings **450.00**
Wood, 7" l, 6-1/2" h, hand-carved walnut, knotty tree trunk, foreground of foliage, rabbit exiting his lair, flowering trumpet fine encircling vase, side inscribed "Viv Le Vin Lamour et le Tabac 1871," fitted lid with carved branch finial **320.00**

TOBY JUGS

History: Toby jugs are drinking vessels that usually depict a full-figured, robust, genial drinking man. They originated in England in the late 18th century. The term "Toby" probably is related to the character Uncle Toby from Tristram Shandy by Laurence Sterne.

Reproduction Alert: During the last 100 years or more, tobies have been copiously reproduced by many potteries in the United States and England.

Bennington type, 9-1/2" h, standing...................... **175.00**
Delft, 11-1/4" h, man seated on barrel, green hat, green and black sponged coat, blue and yellow pants, old cork stopper, c19th C **365.00**
Luster ware, 6-1/2" h, blue coat, spotted vest, 19th C ... **175.00**
Majolica, 8-3/4" h, monk. **165.00**
Minton, 11-1/4" h, majolica, Quaker man and woman, polychrome dec, imp mark, pr **4,600.00**
Portobello pottery, 10" h, standing, spatter enamel dec, orig cov, c1840 .... **275.00**

Left: seated man, brown hat, brown and white striped jacket, mustard colored breeches, white mug in one hand; right: seated woman with black hat, violet jacket with black decoration, yellow skirt, holding apple in hand, basket over arm, **$400.**

Photo courtesy of Wiederseim Associates, Inc.

Pratt
9-1/4" h, pearlware glaze, typical blue, brown, and ochre palette, hat inset, small chips **425.00**
10-3/4" h, Hearty Good Fellow, blue jacket, yellow-green vest, blue and yellow striped pants, blue and ochre sponged base and handle, stopper missing, slight glaze wear, c1770-80 .... **1,500.00**

Royal Doulton, gent in black top hat, maroon coat, gold braid trim, **$125.**

Royal Doulton
2-3/4" h, The Fortune Teller **500.00**

4-1/2" h, Sam Weller, #d6265, "A" mark **190.00**
6-1/2" h, stoneware, blue coat, double XX, Harry Simson **395.00**
8-1/2" h, Falstaff, designed by Charles Noke, D6062, 1939-91................................. **175.00**
9" h, Winston Churchill, DT6171 .... **175.00**
Shaker, 5" h, polychrome dec, standing figure, yellow hat, blue coat, and red breeches with pink luster highlights, England, 19th C.......... **150.00**
Shorter Son, Ltd., England, Long John Silver, 9-3/4" h **375.00**
Staffordshire
5-1/4" h, 4-1/4" h, seated, holding jug in one hand, glass in other, cobalt blue jacket, plaid vest, orange trousers, yellow hat, c1850........ **235.00**
9" h, pearlware, seated figure, sponged blue jacket, ochre buttons, ochre and lavender speckled vest and trousers, brown hair and hat, green glazed base, shallow flake inside hat rim, attributed to Ralph Wood, c1770-80 .... **1,950.00**
9-7/8" h, cobalt blue coat, red breeches, gilt accented vest, standing on green sponged ground, minor wear to gilding **300.00**
9-1/4" h, Martha Gunn, translucent brown and ochre glazes, pearl body, brim repaired at hairline... **1,265.00**
Whieldon, 9-1/2" h, pearlware, seated figure, yellow greatcoat, green vest, blue trousers, holding brown jug in left hand, raises foaming glass of ale towards mouth, lid missing, c1770-80 ... **1,600.00**
Wilkinson
10" h, Marshall Joffre, modeled by Sir Francis Carruthers Gould, titled "75mm Ce que joffre," printed mark, c1918, hat brim restored **345.00**
10-3/4" h, Field Marshall Haig, modeled by Sir Francis Carruthers Gould, titled "Push and Go," printed marks, c1917.......................... **460.00**
11-3/4" h, Winston Churchill, multicolored, designed by Clarice Cliff, black printed marks, number and facsimile signature, c1940......... **825.00**

Yorkshire-Type, 7-3/4" h, caryatid form handle, Pratt palette dec, sponged base and hat brim int.......... **750.00**

TOOLS

History: Before the advent of the assembly line and mass production, practically everything required for living was handmade at home or by a local tradesman or craftsman. The cooper, the blacksmith, the cabinetmaker, and the carpenter all had their special tools.

Early examples of these hand tools are collected for their workmanship, ingenuity, place of manufacture, or design. Modern-day craftsman often search out and use old hand tools in order to authentically recreate the manufacture of an object.

Assorted molding planes, well used, prices range from **$25 to $45**.

Auger, E. C. Stearns, No. 4, adjustable, hollow, 70% japanning....................... **60.00**

Axe head, ship builder's, Campbell's, XXX, New Brunswick, 6" w............. **55.00**

Bicycle wrench, Billings & Spencer Co., made for Pope Mfg Co., patent Jan. 15th 1895, adjusting screw on side, 5-1/2"................... **95.00**

Brace
P. S. & W., No. 1202, 12" sweep, Samson patent ball bearing chuck, 1895 patent date, rosewood handle. **40.00**
Stanley, No. 923-8, 8" sweep **55.00**
Yankee, No. 2101-10, 10" sweep **65.00**

Chamfer knife, cooper's, L & I. J. White, laminated blade **65.00**

Chisel
Buck Bros, 3/8" bevel edge, cast steel **45.00**
Stanley, No. 750, 5/8" bevel edge, mkd "Stanley, D, Made in USA," 9-1/4" l **35.00**

Clapboard marker, Stanley, No. 88, 80% nickel remains **25.00**

Doweling machine, Stanley, No. 77, 3/8 cutter **375.00**

Draw knife
C. E. Jennings's, pattern maker's type, black egg-shaped handles, 4"....... **40.00**
Whitherby, Winstead, CT, folding handles, 8"........ **70.00**

Fret saw, Miller Falls Co., No. 2, deep throat, extra blades, orig box, 12" l..................... **175.00**

Hammer
Claw, Stanley, 7 oz, bell face **25.00**
Magnetic tack, Stanley, No. 601, orig decal **40.00**

Hand drill
Miller Falls, No. 353, ratchet, three-jaw chuck, solid steel frame, 11" l.................... **50.00**
North Bros, Yankee No. 1530A, right and left hand ratchet movement, remnants of orig decal, orig box **175.00**

Jeweler's vice, Stevens Patent, c1900, 2" jaws **175.00**

Jointer and raker gauge, Simonds, No. 342, adjustable **30.00**

Machinist's toolbox, Gerstner, walnut, 11 drawers, 26" w, 9" d, 15-1/2" h, **$390**.
Photo courtesy of Joy Luke Auctions.

Nippers, W. Schollhorn, Bernard's patent, Pat. Oct 24, 1899, 90% nickel plating **25.00**

Nut wrench
Boos Tool Corp, Kansas City, MO, screw adjust, orig box, 6" l................................ **85.00**
Boston Wrench Co., Boston, MA, quick adjust nut, patent Oct. 2, 1906, 6" l......... **195.00**

Pipe wrench
Balin Tool Co., Los Angeles, CA, patent no. 2210274, spring-loaded jaw, 10" **165.00**
Eaton, Cole & Burnham, Franklin patent, July 20, 1886 .... **135.00**

Plane
Preston & Sons, miniature, beech, 4" l.................... **95.00**
Record, No. 050, "Improved Combo," metallic, Sheffield, England, orig cutters, orig wood box, 9" l............ **185.00**
Stanley, No. 3, c1950, made in USA logo, rosewood handle **100.00**
Stanley, No. 4, type 11, three patent dates cast in bed, dark rosewood handle........ **115.00**
Stanley, No. 5, Jack, 1910 patent date cast in bed, dark rosewood handle, tall knob **135.00**
Stanley, No. 9-1/2, block, adjustable throat and cutter **40.00**
Stanley, No. 20, Circular, '92 patent date on cutter, locking screw **225.00**
Stanley, No. 72, chamfer, 1886 patent date on cutter, cast cap screw, brass star-wheel date, rosewood handle and knob............................ **395.00**
Stanley, No. 271, router, 3" l **65.00**

Pliers, W. Schollhorn, Bernard's patent, parallel jaws, top nippers, blued, 6-1/2" l. **25.00**

Putty knives, Stanley, Handyman, cocobolo handles, six-pc set, orig box **95.00**

Ratchet brace, Stanley No. 2101, Yankee, 14" l **75.00**

Rip saw, Henry Disston & Sons, No. 12, London Spring steel, 1896-1917 medallion, four-screw apple wood handle with early wheat carving, 28" l **145.00**

Saw jointer, Atkins **30.00**

Saw set, Stanley, No. 43, pistol-grip, orig box **60.00**

Saw vise, Sears, Roebuck & Co., No. 4920, Dunlap, orig box, 11" l....................... **55.00**

Screwdriver, spiral ratchet, North Bros Mfg Co., Philadelphia
Yankee No. 30A, three orig straight bits, orig box.... **50.00**
Yankee No. 35, one orig bit, 12" l............................ **35.00**

Ship caulking mallet, oak head, 15-1/2" l........................ **85.00**

Shipwright's slick, L. H. Watts, NY, 2-1/2" size, 22-1/2" l **245.00**
Slide rule, boxwood, c1800, 24" l **395.00**
Socket gouge, Zenith, 1/4", 12-1/2" l **30.00**
Spoke pointer, Hargrave, Cincinnati Tool Co., No. 343, 90% enamel remains **65.00**
Sweep gouge, J. B. Addis & Sons, No. 9, 5/8" medium sweep, rosewood handle **30.00**
Swivel vice, North Bros, Yankee No. 1993, quick adjusting swivel base, cam-action lock, 2-3/4" jaws **115.00**
Tap and die set, Greenfield No. AA-4, two-pc adjustable die screw plate **45.00**
Yard rule, Stanley, No. 41, maple, 36" l **45.00**
Wire gauge, Starrett Co., L. S., Athol, MA, No. 283, US standard, 3-1/2" l **15.00**

TOOTHPICK HOLDERS

History: Toothpick holders, indispensable table accessories of the Victorian era, are small containers made specifically to hold toothpicks.

They were made in a wide range of materials: china (bisque and porcelain), glass (art, blown, cut, opalescent, pattern, etc.), and metals, especially silver plate. Makers include both American and European firms.

By applying a decal or transfer, a toothpick holder became a souvenir item; by changing the decal or transfer, the same blank could become a memento for any number of locations.

For more information, see *Warman's Glass*, 4th edition.

Bisque, skull, blue anchor-shape mark **65.00**
China
   Royal Bayreuth, elk..... **120.00**
   Royal Doulton, Santa scene, green handles.......... **75.00**
   R. S. Germany, Schlegelmilch, MOP luster................... **40.00**

Three toothpick holders: two peachblow style, one satin glass decorated with ferns and flowers, **$160**.
Photo courtesy of Joy Luke.

Mt. Washington
   1-3/4" h, Burmese, tri-fold, ruffled rim, diamond quilted body,........................... **200.00**
   2" h, ribbed pillar, blue flowers on leafy stem dec **175.00**
   2-1/4" h, 10-lobe, crimson and blue floral dec............. **225.00**
   2-1/2" h, Burmese, flared painted blue rim, mold-in ferns motif, scrolls at base, white blossoms with yellow dot centers **1,085.00**
   2-1/2" h, Burmese, sq mouth toothpick holder, orig gilt, white, and yellow daisy dec, silvered plated Victorian frame mkd "James W. Tufts, Boston" **1,000.00**
   2-1/2" h, Peachblow, sq mouth toothpick holder, shading from soft pink to soft blue, orig gilt dec and hp yellow daisies, silver plated Victorian holder mkd "James W. Tufts, Boston" **9,500.00**
   2-3/4" h, Burmese, sq mouth, matte finish, diamond quilted, yellow rim................... **325.00**
Pattern glass
   Arched Fleur-De-Lis...... **45.00**
   Daisy and Button, blue . **75.00**
   Fandango, Heisey **55.00**
   Hartford, Fostoria.......... **85.00**
   Jewel with Dewdrop **55.00**
   Paneled 44, Reverse, platinum stain **75.00**
   Truncated Cube, ruby stained **75.00**
   US Coin, colorless, frosted Morgan one dollar coin, c1892........................... **290.00**

White teddy bear seated in front of green and white shaded top hat, glazed ceramic, no marking, **$35**.
Photo courtesy of Dotta Auction Co., Inc.

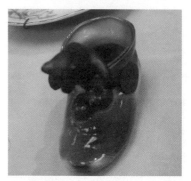

Brown bear crawling out of green shoe, red bow trim, glazed ceramic, no marking, **$35**.
Photo courtesy of Dotta Auction Co., Inc.

Satin glass, 2-3/8" h, 3" d at top, 2" d base creamy white diamond quilted mother of pearl satin glass holder with tightly crimped top edge, polished pontil, 7-3/4" l, 4" w, 3-1/8" h hallmarked silver plated stand **750.00**
Spatter glass, 3" h, tubular design, crystal rigaree feet **60.00**

TOYS

History: The first cast-iron toys began to appear in America shortly after the Civil War. Leading 19th-century manufacturers include Hubley, Dent, Kenton, and Schoenhut. In the first decades of the 20th century, Arcade, Buddy L, Marx, and Tootsie Toy joined these earlier firms. George Brown and other manufacturers who did not sign or label their work made wooden toys.

Nuremberg, Germany, was the European center for the toy industry from the late 18th through the mid-20th centuries. Companies such as Lehman and Marklin produced high-quality toys.

Today's toy collectors have a wonderful assortment to choose from. Many specialize in one company, time period, or type of toy, etc. Whatever their motivation, their collections bring joy. Individual collectors must decide how they feel about the condition of their toys, whether they prefer mint-in-the box or gently played with examples or perhaps even toys that have been played with extensively. Traditionally, the toys in better condition have retained their values more than those in played with condition. Having the original box, instructions, and/or all the pieces, etc., adds greatly to the collectiblity, and therefore the value.

Toy collectors can find examples to add to their collections at most of the typical antique and collectibles marketplaces, from auctions to flea markets to great antique shows, like Atlantic City, and even shows and auctions that specialize only in toys.

Additional Listings: Characters, Disneyana, and Dolls. Also see *Warman's Americana & Collectibles* and *Warman's Flea Market* for more examples.

Notes: Every toy is collectible; the key is condition. Good working order is important when considering mechanical toys. Examples in this listing are considered to be at least in good condition, if not better, unless otherwise specified.

Arcade, cast iron, Greyhound bus, #385, 7-3/4" l, $90.

Photo courtesy of Joy Luke Auctions.

Arcade, USA

Auto, cast iron
Chevrolet, sedan, 1925, 7" l
.... **450.00**

Arcade, auto transport, painted cast iron, green cab, red truck body, two coups and two sedans, each with original Arcade labels, **$3,600**, for the entire transport.

Photo courtesy of Dotta Auction Co., Inc.

Desoto, sedan, painted gray, nickeled grill and bumper, decal on trunk reads "Sundial Shoes," rubber tires, 4" l
.... **130.00**
Ford coupe, Model A, No 106, rumble seat, 1928, 6-3/4" l **295.00**
Pontiac sedan, 1932, 6-1/2" l
.... **360.00**
Dump truck, cast iron, International Harvester, painted green, red chassis, yellow pressed steel dump body, 11-1/4" l............ **275.00**
Fire trailer truck, red, blue fireman, detachable trailer, hose reel and ladder turntable, 16" l, ladders missing, paint loss **325.00**
Ice truck, cast iron, Mack, railed open bed body, rear platform, rubber tires, emb sides, painted blue, 6-7/8" l .. **275.00**
Milk truck, cast iron, Borden's, painted green, classic milk bottle design, rubber tires
.... **1,430.00**
Pick-up truck, cast iron, "International" decals on door, painted bright yellow, black rubber tires, 9-1/4" l, some rust on left side **330.00**
Racer, Bullet, cast iron, classic bullet-shaped body, painted red, nickeled driver and mechanic, side pipes, and disc wheels, emb "#9" on side
.... **550.00**
Stake truck
Chevrolet, 1925, 9" l.... **800.00**
Ford Model T, 1927, 9" l
.... **600.00**
Mack, No. 246X, 1929, 12" l
.... **1,400.00**
Tank, cast iron, camouflage painting, large metal wheels, 7-1/4" l........................ **330.00**
Taxi, cast iron, painted blue, black trim, emb luggage rack, seated driver and passenger, rubber tires, 8-1/4" l .. **660.00z**

Arcade, close up of one car from the photo above, showing original Arcade label.

Arcade, two door car, painted cast iron, blue, 5" l, 2-3/4" h, **$100**.

Photo courtesy of Joy Luke.

Thresher, McCormick-Deering, gray and cream wheels, red lining, chromed chute and stacker, 12" l **320.00**
Tractor, cast iron
Farmall, "A", No. 7050, 1941, 7-1/2" l........................ **475.00**
Fordson, No. 273, 1928, 3-7/8" l........................ **95.00**
McCormick-Deering, No. 10-20, 1925, 6-3/4" l **300.00**
Trolley, Greyhound, New York World's Fair, blue and orange, nickel driver, decals, three cars with tinplate canopies, black tires, 16" l, some chipping and scratching **635.00**
Wrecker, cast iron
Ford Model T, 11" l, 1927
.... **700.00**
Mack, No. 255, 1930, 12-1/2" l
.... **1,500.00**
Plymouth, No. 1830, 1933, 4-3/4" l........................ **350.00**

Arnold, USA

Motorcycle, civilian, litho tin wind-up, mkd "Made in US Zone Germany," tin wheels mkd "Union Cord," 7-3/4" l, C.8+............................ **400.00**

Ocean liner, twin funnels, white
superstructure, black and red
hull, tinplate, clockwork motor,
lg, 13" **460.00**
Satellite, remote control, tin and
plastic, orig box with
graphics, 7" d, C.9 ...... **100.00**

Bing, Gebruder,

Germany

Auto, tin, clockwork, center door
model, black, seated driver,
radiator cap ornament, spare
tire on rear, 6-1/4" l **385.00**
Garage, litho tin, double doors,
extensive graphics, houses
sedan and roadster **550.00**
Limousine, litho tin wind-up,
red, maroon and orange
striping, orig driver, c1910,
5-1/4" l **690.00**
Open tourer, four seater, litho
tinplate, gray-green, black
and yellow lining, red button
seats, black wings, front
steering, orange and gray
wheels, twin lamps,
windscreen frame, hand-
brake operated clockwork
motor, c1915, 12-1/2" l,
chauffeur missing, lamps
detached **2,400.00**
Union ferry boat, hand-painted
tin, clockwork, red hull, brown
open deck, white deck
housing, railing on side,
window cut-outs on both
sides, stack on roof, 12" l
.... **1,200.00**

Buddy L, USA

Airmail truck, black front, hood
fenders, enc cab, red body
and chassis, 1930, 24" l
.... **675.00**
Airplane, four-engine transport,
monoplane, green wings,
yellow fuselage and twin tails,
1949, 27" wingspan **200.00**

Buddy L, fire truck, pressed steel, repainted, white ladders, gold decal letters
"B.L.F.D.," **$225**.
Photo courtesy of Dotta Auction Co., Inc.

Auto
Flivver coupe, black, red
spoke wheels, aluminum tires,
1924, 11" l **775.00**
Jr Camaro, metallic blue
body, white racing stripes
across hood, 1968, 9" l. **50.00**
Cement mixer truck, red body,
white side ladder, water tank,
mixing drum, 1965, 15-1/2" l
.... **75.00**
Dump truck
Husky, yellow hood, chrome
one-pc wraparound bumper,
1969, 14-1/2" l **75.00**
Hydraulic Construction,
medium blue front, large
green dumper, 1967, 15-1/4" l
.... **50.00**
Jr Dumper, avocado cab,
tiltback dump section, 1969,
7-1/2" l **335.00**
Utility, done-tone slant design,
red front, gray chassis, royal
blue dump body, yellow seat,
1940, 25-1/2" l **175.00**
**Electric Emergency Unit
wrecker,** white pressed steel,
rear hoist, 16-1/2" l, paint wear
and staining **215.00**
Express Line delivery truck,
black pressed-steel, front
steering and rear doors, 24" l
.... **750.00**
Fire truck
Aerial truck, red, nickel
ladders, 1925, 39" l..... **850.00**
Extension ladder, rider, duo-
tone slant design, white front,
red hood top, cab, and frame,
red semi-trailer, white ladders,
1949, 32-1/2" l **150.00**
Ladder truck, red, bright
metal grille and headlights,
two white ladders, 1939, 24" l
.... **100.00**
Greyhound bus, pressed steel,
clockwork, bright blue and
white, "Greyhound Lines" on
sides, rubber tires, 16" l
.... **275.00**

Outdoor railroad, No. 1000
4-6-2 locomotive and tender,
No. 1001 caboose, No. 1003
tank, No. 1004 stock, No.
1005 coal cars (one with orig
decal), 121-1/2" l, repainted
.... **1,840.00**

Buddy L, steam shovel, pressed steel,
red roof, black body, **$275**.
Photo courtesy of Dotta Auction Co., Inc.

Steam shovel, No. 220, black,
red corrugated roof and base,
cast wheels, boiler, decal and
winch, 14" h, surface rust,
paint crazing on roof .. **115.00**
Telephone maintenance truck,
No. 450, two-tone green,
ladder, two poles, orig
maker's box **350.00**
Tractor
Husky, bright yellow body,
large rear fenders, black
engine block, 1966, 13" l
.... **50.00**
Ruff-n-Tuff, yellow grille, hood,
and frame, black plastic
engine block, 1971, 10-1/2" l
.... **50.00**
Wrecker, orig condition . **3,950.00**

Cast iron, unknown

American makers

Dump truck, green Mack style
front, C-cab, red bed with
spring lever, spoked nickel
wheels, 7-3/4" l **490.00**
Gasoline truck, blue, Mack-
style front, C-cab, rubber
tires, one tire missing. 7" l
.... **200.00**
Milk wagon, black cast-iron
horse, gilt harness, yellow
wheels, blue steel wagon
body, 6-3/4" l **150.00**
Stake truck, Ford Model A, red,
7" l............................... **200.00**

Champion

Auto, cast iron, coupe, painted
red, nickeled grill and
headlights, rumble seat,
rubber tires, spare mounted on
trunk, 7" l, repainted **250.00**

Gasoline truck, cast iron, painted red, Mack "C" cab, tanker body, emb on sides, rubber tires, 8-1/8" l **385.00**
Panel truck, cast iron, enclosed panel van, cast spare tires and headlights, traces of orig blue paint, spoked metal wheels, 7-1/2" l, poor condition **180.00**
Racer, cast iron, painted red, silver trim, wind deflector on rear, separately cast driver painted blue, nickeled disc wheels, 8-1/2" l **1,815.00**
Stake truck, cast iron, painted red, Mack "C" cab, stake side body, nickeled spoke wheels, 7" l **660.00**
Truck, cast iron, "C" Mack cab, blue body, 7-3/4" l, replaced wheels **195.00**
Wrecker, cast iron, red C-cab with crane, nickel plated crank and barrel, rubber tires, 8-1/4" l **330.00**

Chein, tin litho windup, dump truck, Mack, **$175.**

Photo courtesy of Dotta Auction Co., Inc.

Chein

Barnacle Bill, litho tin wind-up, some loss of paint, C.7 .... **350.00**
Bass drummer, litho tin wind-up, orig box missing end flap, 8-3/4" h, C.9 .... **275.00**
Disneyland ferris wheel, clockwork motor, bell, six gondolas, litho Disney characters and fairgrounds scenes, 16-3/4" h, distortion and paint loss **350.00**
Hercules ferris wheel, clockwork motor, bell, six gondolas, litho children and fairground scenes, 16-1/2" l **325.00**
Popeye, in barrel, litho tin wind-up, 7" h, C.8 .... **725.00**
Roller coaster, litho tin wind-up, orig box, 19" l, 10" h, C.8-9 .... **650.00**
Wagon, horse-drawn, "Fine Groceries," tinplate, 12" l **290.00**

Converse, USA

Heffield Farms delivery wagon, articulated horse, 21-1/2" l, considerable wear and paint loss **320.00**
Klondike Ice Co. delivery wagon, tinplate on wood, two litho horses, 17" l, paint poor **175.00**
Trolley, open sides, pressed steel, blue and mustard, stenciled dec, marked "City Hall Park 175" on both ends, reversible benches, large clockwork motor, 16" l, paint poor, destination boards missing **260.00**

Corgi

Ambulance, Chevrolet Superior, white body, orange roof, Red Cross decals, 4-3/4" l.... **30.00**
Auto
Buick Riviera, #245, MIB **100.00**
Chevrolet Caprice, #325, MIB **55.00**
Circus, land rover and animal trailer, #30, MIB.......... **220.00**
Citreon DS 19, #210S, MIB **70.00**
Ford Consol Saloon, #200M, MIB **100.00**
Ford Zephyr Estate Car, light blue, 3-7/8" **30.00**
Jeep CJ-5, dark metallic green body **10.00**
Mercedes-Benz 220 SE coupe, #230 .... **75.00**
Monkee Mobile, #277, MIB **250.00**
Porsche Carrera 6, white body, red or blue trim ... **30.00**
Volkswagen 1200 Driving School........................... **25.00**
Camera van, Commer Mobile, metallic blue body, black camera on gold tripod, cameraman, 3-1/2" **60.00**
Car transporter, Bedford, black diecast cap, 10-1/4" l.. **100.00**
Character cars
Batmobile, glossy black body, gold tow hook **200.00**
Captain Marvel Porsche, white body, 4-3/4" l **20.00**
Hardy Boys Rolls-Royce, red body, yellow hood......... **70.00**
James Bond Aston Martin, metallic silver body, diecast base, red int., two figures, working roof hatch, ejector seat............................ **100.00**

Popeye's Paddy Wagon **195.00**
Saint's Volvo P-1800, white body, silver trim **55.00**
Tank truck, Mack Exxon, white cap and tank, red tank chassis, 10-3/4" l **15.00**
Taxi
Austin, London, black, yellow plastic int. **35.00**
Thunderbird Bermuda, white body, 4" l **50.00**
Tractor, Ford 5000, blue body, yellow scoop arm and controls, chrome scoop, 3-1/8" l.......................... **55.00**

Dayton Friction Co.

Patrol wagon, pressed metal and wood, friction driven, painted red, stenciled "Police Patrol" on front panel, seated driver on open bench seat, spoke wheels. 10" l..... **200.00**
Touring car, pressed metal, painted red, gold spoke wheels, open sides, friction driver, 12" l................. **470.00**

Fliver car, stripped and ready for restoration, **$75.**

Dinky

Airplane
Autogyro, gold, blue rotor, 1934-41 .... **90.00**
Bristol Beinhem, 1956-63 .... **20.00**
Douglas DC3, silver, #60t, 1937-41 .... **125.00**
Lockheed Constellation, #66b, 1940 .... **70.00**
Percival Gull, camouflaged, #66c, 1940................. **100.00**
Twin Engine Fighter, silver, #70d/731, 1946-55 .... **10.00**
Ambulance
Range Rover, #268, 1974-78 .... **60.00**
Superior Criterion, #263, 1962-68 .... **50.00**
Auto
Austin Somerset Saloon, #161, MIB **70.00**
Cadillac Eldorado, #131, 1956-62 .... **60.00**

DeSota, Diplomat, orange, F545, 1960-63.............. **70.00**
Ford Fairlane, pale green, #148, 1962-66............. **30.00**
Jaguar XK 120, white, #157, 1954-62...................... **120.00**
Mercury Cougar, #174, MIB **95.00**
Plymouth Stockcar, #201, MIB **50.00**
Studebaker Commander, F24Y, 1951-61.............. **65.00**
Triumph TR-2, gray, #105, 1957-60...................... **60.00**
Volkswagen 1300 sedan, #129, 1965-76.............. **20.00**
Bulldozer, Blaw Knox, #561 .... **45.00**

Bus
Routemaster, #289, 1964-80 .... **75.00**
Silver Jubilee, #297, 1977 .... **25.00**

Fire truck
Airport fire tender, #276, MIB **90.00**
Fire chief's land rover, #195, MIB **50.00**

Motorcycle
A. A. Motorcycle patrol, #270/44B, 1946-44 .... **30.00**
Police Motorcycle Partol, #42B, 1946-53 .... **30.00**

Police car
Citroen DS19, #F501, 1967-70 .... **75.00**
Plymouth, #244, 1977-80 .... **25.00**

Taxi
Austin, #40H, 1951-52.. **60.00**
London, #284, MIB **50.00**
Plymouth Plaza, #266, 1960-67......................... **60.00**

Tractor
David Brown, #305 .... **35.00**
Field Marshall, #37N/301 .... **60.00**
Massey-Harris, #27A/300 .... **50.00**

Truck
Austin Van, Nestle's, #471 .... **60.00**
Brink's, #275, MIB......... **65.00**
Coles Hydra, #980, MIB **100.00**
Foden Mobilgas tanker, #941 .... **145.00**
Leland Tanker, Shell/BP, #944 .... **125.00**
Telephone service van, #261, MIB **100.00**
Willeme log truck, #F36A/987 .... **75.00**

Fisher Price, USA

American Airlines plane, paper litho over wood, bright orange and blue, extensive graphics, two propellers, 20" wingspan **500.00**

Gunther, (attributed to) tin litho motorcycle with sidecar, male driver, female passenger, original windshield, side door marked "GK," side marked "Germany," **$12,100**.

Photo courtesy of Dotta Auction Co., Inc.

Donald Duck Xylphone, play wear **65.00**
Jack n Jill TV Radio, #148, 1956 .... **55.00**
Katy Kackler, #140, 1954. **45.00**
Merry Mousewife, #473, 1949 .... **45.00**
Mickey Mouse, drummer . **60.00**
Mother Goose Cart, #784, 1955 .... **35.00**
Pony Express, #733, 1941 .... **60.00**
Pushy Elephant, #525, 1934 .... **350.00**
Rock-A-Bye Baby Cart, #627, 1960............................ **15.00**
Sleepy Sue, #632, 1960... **30.00**
Streamline Express, #215, 1935 .... **350.00**
Sunny Fish, #420, 1961... **25.00**
Teddy Drummer, #775, 1936 .... **300.00**
This Little Pig, #910, 1963 .... **25.00**
Uncle Timmy Turtle, #437, 1942 .... **100.00**
Wiggily Woofer, #640, 1957 .... **40.00**
Ziggy Zilo, #737, 1958 ..... **50.00**

Hot Wheels, Mattel,

vintage, MIP
American Hauler, redline, 1976 .... **70.00**
American Tipper, redline, 1976 .... **65.00**
Baja Bruiser, #8258, orange, 1974............................ **75.00**
Beach Bomb, green......... **75.00**

Hot Wheels, collector's case, blue, holds 24 vehicles, Mattel, played with condition, **$25**.

Blazer 4 x 4 .... **60.00**
Boss Hoss, #6406, 1971 . **75.00**
Buzz Off, redline, 1973 .. **500.00**
Captain America, #2879, white, 1979........................ **175.00**
Cement Miser, #6452, 1970 .... **60.00**
Chevy, '57, Ultra Hots, #47 .... **110.00**
Circus Cats, #3303, white, 1975 .... **75.00**
Classic '36 Ford Coupe, redline, 1969............ **60.00**
Custom Police Cruiser, #6269, 2969........................... **200.00**
Datsun 200XS, #3255, maroon, Canada, 1982............. **175.00**
Dune Daddy, #6967, light green, 1975........................ **75.00**
Earthmover, #16 .... **85.00**
El Rey Special, #8273, light blue, 1974............... **1,200.00**
Emergency Squad, #7650, red, 1975........................... **65.00**
Fire Engine, redline, 1970 .... **100.00**
Flat Out 442, green, Canada, 1984............................ **150.00**
Fuel Tanker, #6018, 1971 .... **200.00**
Heavy Chevy, #6408, 1970 .... **200.00**
Hood, redline................. **110.00**
Hot Heap, #6219, 1968 .... **65.00**
Ice T, redline, 1971........ **200.00**
Jet Threat, #6179, 1976 ... **60.00**
Light My Firebird, redline, 1970 .... **75.00**
Lotus Turbine, #6262, 1969 .... **60.00**
Mantis, #6423, 1970 .... **60.00**
Maxi Taxi, #9184, yellow, blackwall, 1977............ **60.00**
Mongoose Funny Car, redline, 1970.......................... **160.00**
Moving van, redline, 1970 .... **125.00**
Neet Streeter, #9510, chrome, 1976............................ **40.00**

Olds 442, #6467, 1971 ... **800.00**
Poison Pinto, #9240, green,
  blackwall, 1977 .... **30.00**
Police Cruiser, #6963, white,
  1973 .... **550.00**
Porsche 911, #6972, orange,
  1975 .... **65.00**
Probe Funny Car, #84,
  Motorcraft **30.00**
Race Ace, #2620, white, 1968
  .... **75.00**
Red Baron, #6963, red,
  blackwall, 1977 .... **25.00**
Rig Wrecker, #45 .... **225.00**
Road Roller, #55, yellow .. **25.00**
Rock Buster, #9088, yellow,
  blackwall, 1977 .... **15.00**
Sand Crab, #6403, 1970 .. **60.00**
Scooper, redline, 1971 ... **325.00**
Silhouette, #6209, 1979... **90.00**
Sir Sidney Roadster, #8261,
  yellow, 1974 .... **90.00**
Snake II, redline, 1971.. **275.00**
Super Van, #9205, chrome,
  1976 .... **40.00**
Sweet 16, #6422, 1970..... **75.00**
Tail Gunner, #29 .... **75.00**
Team Trailer, redline, 1971
  .... **225.00**
Tow Truck, #6450, 1970 ... **55.00**
T-Totaller, #9648, brown,
  blackwall, 1977 .... **40.00**
Turbo Streak, #104 .... **75.00**
Vega Bomb, #7654, green, 1975
  .... **800.00**
Volkswagen, #7620, orange,
  bug on roof, 1974 .... **60.00**
Warpath, #7654, white, 1975
  .... **110.00**
Whip Creamer, redline, #1870
  .... **60.00**
Z Whiz, #9639, gray, redline,
  1977 .... **70.00**

Hubley, Lancaster, PA

Airplane, cast iron
  American Eagle, WWII fighter
  11" wingspan **150.00**
  Lindy Glider, painted red,
  yellow wings, driver seated on
  front, emb wings, 6-1/2" l
  .... **1,210.00**
  Navy fighter, DC, moving
  propeller, retractable landing
  gear, folding wings, orig box,
  8-3/4", C.9 .... **125.00**
  Sea Plane, orange, and blue,
  two engines **35.00**
Auto, cast iron
  Chrysler Airflow, battery
  operated lights, 1934
  .... **1,250.00**
  Coupe, 1928, 8-1/2" l.. **600.00**

Lincoln Zephyr and trailer,
  painted green, nickeled grill
  and bumper, 13-1/2" l. **825.00**
Sedan and trailer, painted red
  sedan, trailer painted silver
  and red, rubber tires, factory
  sample tag, 9-1/2" l..... **715.00**
Streamlined Racer, 5" l **400.00**
Bell telephone, cast iron
  8-1/4" l, painted green, silver
  sides, emb company name,
  Mack "C" cab, nickeled
  ladders, long handled
  shovels, pole carrier, spoked
  wheels, repainted **250.00**
  9-1/4" l, painted green, winch,
  auger, nickel water barrel on
  side, ladders, and pole
  carrier, fatigued rubber tires
  .... **660.00**
Boat, cast iron, painted red,
  emb "Static" on sides, sleet
  form, seated driver, hand on
  throttle of attached motor,
  chromed air cleaner, painted
  orange, three tires, clicker, 9-
  1/2" l, over painted... **1,650.00**
Bus, cast iron, new tires, 5-3/4" l
  .... **125.00**
Cement mixer truck, cast iron,
  red and green, nickel tank,
  rubber wheels, Mack, 8" l,
  restored **1,760.00**
Delivery truck, Merchants,
  1925, 6-1/4" l **400.00**
Fire truck, cast iron
  Fire Engine, 5" l, 1930s . **75.00**
  Fire Patrol, 7-men, 1912, 5" l
  .... **3,575.00**
  Hook and ladder, 1912, 23" l
  .... **1,850.00**
  Ladder truck, 5-1/2" l **40.00**
Gasoline truck, cast iron,
  painted silver, red spoked
  wheels, cast figure, round
  tank body, rear facets, c1920,
  6" l **495.00**
Milk truck, cast iron, painted
  white, emb "Borden's" on side
  panel, rear opening door,
  nickeled grill, headlights, and
  spoke wheels, 7-1/2" l,
  repaired headlights . **1,980.00**
Motorcycle, cast iron
  Harley-Davidson, 1932,
  7-1/2" l **300.00**
  Hill Climber, 1936, 6-1/2" l
  .... **375.00**
  Indian Four Cylinder, 1929,
  9" l **1,700.00**
  Motorcycle cop with sidecar
  .... **700.00**
  Patrol Motorcycle, green,
  6-1/2" l **275.00**
  Parcel post, 90% orig paint,
  10" l **1,900.00**

Hubley, cast iron, pumper with rubber
tires, red body, #2167, **$250.**
Photo courtesy of Joy Luke Auctions.

Panama steam shovel, cast
  iron, painted rd and green,
  large scale, nickeled shovel,
  cast people on trailer, dual
  rubbers on rear, 12" l .. **935.00**
Pull toy, Old Dutch Girl, cast
  iron, white and blue dress,
  holding yellow can of
  cleanser, rubber tires, c1932,
  9" l, repaired stick, orig
  checker floor............ **4,100.00**
Racer, cast iron
  Painted blue, painted red
  articulated pistons, seated
  driver, black tires, spoked
  wheels, 10-1/2" l **1,760.00**
  Painted green, red emb "5" on
  sides, hood opens on both
  sides to show extensively cast
  engine, disc wheels, seated
  driver, replaced hood doors,
  9-1/2" l...................... **1,100.00**
  Painted red, seated driver,
  emb "#1" on sides, rubber
  tires, 7-3/4" l **385.00**

Japanese

Haji, 8" l, car with boat trailer,
  friction powered, blue Ford
  convertible, red and cream
  Speedo motor boat with
  friction-powered motor, red
  trailer, orig packing and
  maker's box **400.00**
Occupied Japan, Plymouth
  1942, litho tin wind-up, nickel
  trim, 6" l, orig box, C.8+
  .... **135.00**
SY, flying man robot, litho tin
  wind-up, orig box, 6" x 3"
  base, 11" h, C.9 .... **350.00**
T.N.
  Dump Truck, 11" l, friction
  powered tinplate, red and
  cream, automatic side dump
  action, orig maker's box
  .... **150.00**
  Great Swanee Paddle
  Wheeler, 10-1/4" l, friction
  powered tinplate, whistle
  mechanism, orig maker's box
  .... **175.00**

Koko the Sandwich Man, 1950s, orig box, 7" h, C.8 .... **95.00**

TPS
Circus parade, tin litho wind-up, clowns and elephants, orig box, 11" l, C.9 ...... **275.00**
Moon patrol, tin, battery operated, tin astronaut driver, plastic dome, bump and go action, 8" l, C.9............ **350.00**

Yone, swinging baby robot, litho tin wind-up, orig box, 4" x 4" base, 12" h, C.9 .... **350.00**

Yonezawa
Missle launching tank, litho tin, battery operated, four targets, orig box, 6" l, C.10 .... **125.00**
Happy n' sad magic face clown, battery operated, orig box, 10-1/2" h, C.9 ...... **150.00**

Keystone, litho tin fire station, red, white, green, and gold, **$650**.

Keystone, air mail airplane, pressed steel, **$400**.
Photo courtesy of Dotta Auction Co., Inc.

Keystone Mfg. Co., Boston

Air mail plane, olive green, three propellers, 25" **1,600.00**
Ambulance, canvas cover and stretcher, 27-1/2" l.... **1,000.00**
Bus, Coast to Coast, blue, 31-1/4" l.................... **1,200.00**
Fighter plane, "Ride 'Em," silver pressed-steel, red wings, propeller and seat, 25" l **520.00**

Moving van, black cab, red body, rubber tires, 26-1/4" **1,000.00**
Packard ride-on water tower, tower, nozzle, tank, and seat, lg. 32" l.................... **1,035.00**
Police patrol truck, decals, 27-1/2" l........................... **700.00**
Steam shovel, 20-3/4" l.... **75.00**

Kilgore, Canada

Airplane, cast iron, Seagull, painted red, nickeled wheels and wing mounted propeller, 7-3/4" l...................... **880.00**
Auto, open roadster, 1928, cast iron, painted blue, nickeled wheels and driver, decal reads "Kilgore, Made in Canada," 6-1/8" l **825.00**
Delivery truck, cast iron, Toy Town, painted red, emb on side panels, gold highlights, silver disc wheels, 6-1/8" l, repainted **360.00**
Dump truck, cast iron, painted blue enclosed cab, red dump body, lever to lift, nickeled disc wheels, 8-1/2" l.... **330.00**
Ice cream truck, cast iron, enclosed cab painted blue, orange body, emb "Arctic Ice Cream" on sides, disc wheels, 8" l............................... **420.00**

Lehmann, Dare Devil Galop Zebra Cart, tin litho windup, working, **$495**.
Photo courtesy of Dotta Auction Co., Inc.

Lehmann, Ehe & Co. truck, tin litho windup, good, working condition, **$365**.
Photo courtesy of Dotta Auction Co., Inc.

Lehmann, Germany

Beetle, spring motor, crawling movement, flapping wings, maker's box, one leg detached, but present, early Adam trademark......... **230.00**
Catalog, *Patent Lehmann Spielzug*, 1881, 21 pgs, orig order blank, 6" x 9", minor insect damage........... **315.00**
Heinkel-Blitz He 70, tin, orig string, instructions, plane with Nazi swastika, orig box, 4-1/2" l, C.10.............. **575.00**
Na-Ob, red and yellow cart, blue eccentric wheels, gray donkey, marked "Lehmann Ehe & Co.," 6" l, front wheel missing **145.00**
Oh-My Alabama coon jigger, lithograph tinplate, clockwork motor, 10" h................. **460.00**
Sedan, EPL No. 765, litho tin wind-up, some edge and tire wear, 5-1/2" l, C.7+ **150.00**
Truck, tinplate, cream, red, and yellow, blue driver, fixed steering, clockwork motor, marked "Lehmann Ehe & Co.," 6-3/4" l................ **435.00**
Tut Tut motor car, white suited driver, horn, front steering, bellows, coil springs, paint loss, rust spotting, 6-1/2" l..... **635.00**

Linemar, Japan

Cabin cruiser, litho tin, battery operated, detailed interior, fabric covered seats, orig box, 12" l, C.9 .... **250.00**
Clarabell Clown, tin mechanical action, 6-1/2" h, C.8.... **210.00**
Donald Duck, Walt Disney's mechanical tricycle, celluloid Donald Duck riding tin wind-up, box with illus of Mickey riding tricycle, 3-3/4" x 4" x 2-1/2" box **325.00**
Feeding birdwatcher, litho tin and plush, battery operated, orig box, 7-1/2" h, C.9.. **365.00**
Mickey Mouse
Moving van, litho tin friction, wear, 1950s, 13" l, C.7 **300.00**
Rocking on Pluto, litho tin wind-up, replaced ears and tail, 5-1/2" h, C.7 .... **850.00**
Roller skating, litho tin wind-up, pants faded, orig ears, 5-1/2" h, C.7+ **525.00**
Music box, cowboy dancing to music, tin and plastic, battery operated, orig box, 5" h, C.9 .... **175.00**

Prehistoric animal, T-Rex, litho tin wind-up, 9" l, 6" h, orig box **230.00**
Rocket express, litho tin wind-up, train and space ship, orig box, 5-1/2" sq, C.9 ...... **575.00**
Smoking Popeye, tin, battery operated, orig box, C.7+ **2,100.00**
Superman tank, tin, battery operated, orig box, © 1958, 5" h, C.9 .... **3,150.00**

Lineol, Germany

Armored car, litho tin clockwork, camouflage colors, revolving turret with gun, opening doors, spring lever for gun, wire guard covers vehicle, rubber tires, 10" l, symbols repainted, minor paint loss **935.00**
Cannon, 88MM, litho tin, camouflage colors, stabilizer arms, elevation cranks, four-tire open frame, tow hook, 14-1/2" l **935.00**
Motorcycle with side car, composition figures, tin fenders, disc wheels, 4-1/2" l **300.00**

Marx, Louls & Co., NY

Airplane
American Airlines, flagship, pressed steel, wood wheels, 1940, 27" wingspan **200.00**
Bomber, metal, wind-up, four propellers, 14-1/2" wingspan **100.00**
Floor Zeppelin, 1931, 9-1/2" l **225.00**
Lucky Stunt Flyer, litho tin wind-up, 1928, 6" l **150.00**
Military litho tin wind-up, orig box, mounted to orig insert, 13" l, 18" wing span, C.9 .... **260.00**
Pan American, pressed steel, four engines, 1940, 27" wingspan **90.00**
Pursuit Plane, one propeller, 1930s, 8" wingspan **125.00**
Skybird flyer, litho tin wind-up, plane and zeppelin circling tower, orig box with wear, 26" w, 10" h, C.8 .... **350.00**
Trans-Atlantic Zeppelin, litho tin wind-up, 1930, 10" l **225.00**
Auto
Army car, battery operated **65.00**
Crazy Dan car, litho tin wind-up, 1930s, 6" l **375.00**

Marx, Amos & Andy coupe, tin litho windup, complete, excellent working condition, **$600**.
Photo courtesy of Dotta Auction Co., Inc.

Marx, Old Jalopy, tin litho friction, 5" l, **$175**.
Photo courtesy of Dotta Auction Co., Inc.

Dippy Dumper, celluloid Brutus, litho tin wind-up, 1930s, 9" l **350.00**
Jalopy, tin driver, friction, 1950s **150.00**
Leaping Lizzie, litho tin wind-up, 1927, 7" l **250.00**
Queen of the Campus, four college students, 1950 **250.00**
Siren police car, 1930s, 15" l **75.00**
Speed racer, 1937, 13" l **250.00**
Streamline Speedway, two litho tin wind-up racing cars, 1936 .... **175.00**
Auto transport, plastic cab and cars, orig box, professional repairs, 23" l, C.9 .... **225.00**
Battleship, *U.S.S. Washington,* tin friction, orig box, 14" l, C.9 .... **275.00**
Bulldozer/tractor, gold body, rubber treads, plow and farmer driver, blue and red stake wagons, hitch, two discs, plow, corn planter, harvester.................... **230.00**
Drummer boy, litho tin wind-up, minor edge wear on drum, 7-1/2" h, C.7+ **310.00**
Dumbo, the acrobatic elephant, litho tin wind-up, Disney, 1941, orig box, 4" h, C.9 .... **725.00**

Jazzbo Jim, litho tin wind-up, orig box, 9" h, C.9 .... **575.00**
Lone Ranger, range rider, litho tin wind-up, 1938, 11" l, 9" h, C.9 .... **350.00**
Merrymakers Band, tinplate, one dancer missing.... **575.00**
Pluto, litho tin wind-up, Walt Disney Productions, orig box, 6-1/2" h, C.9 .... **600.00**

Marx, Range Rider, tin litho windup, original box, **$495**.
Photo courtesy of Dotta Auction Co., Inc.

Royal Bus Lines, litho tin wind-up, 1930s, 10-1/4" l **135.00**
Set
Bulldog tractor, aluminum, litho wind-up, 1940, 9-1/2" l tractor **250.00**
Sleeping Beauty, Prince Phillip, Samson the Horse, hard plastic, all accessories, orig box, 12" l, C.8+.... **150.00**
Super Power Tractor and Trailer, litho tin wind-up, 1937, 8-1/2" l tractor **125.00**
Truck
Dump truck, yellow cab, blue bumper, red bed, 1950, 18" l **100.00**
East-West Coast Van, tin litho, ten wheeler, tin balloon tires, adv graphics, 18" l, orig box, C.9 .... **320.00**
Gravel truck, pressed steel cab, red tin dumper, 1930, 10" **100.00**
Jalopy pickup, litho tin wind-up, 7" l......................... **60.00**
Mack towing truck, dark green cab, wind-up, 1926, 8" l **175.00**
Pet shop truck, plastic, six compartments with vinyl dogs, 11" l.................... **125.00**
Royal Oil Co., Mack, dark red cab, medium green tank, wind-up, 1927, 8-1/4" l........... **200.00**
Searchlight, toolbox behind cab, 1930s, 10" l......... **150.00**

Stake bed, pressed steel, wooden wheels, 1936, 7" l **65.00**

TV and radio station, battery operated, orig box, 27" l, 10" w, 8" h, C.8-9......... **300.00**

Zippo the climbing monkey, multicolored litho tinplate, pull-string mechanism, 10" l **60.00**

Matchbox, England

Austin Taxi, #17, 1960, MIB **60.00**

Atlantic Trailer, tan body, six metal wheels, 1956....... **15.00**

Atlas truck, metallic blue cab, orange dumper, labels on doors, 1975..................... **8.00**

Benford Ton Tipper, gray cap, 1961............................ **10.00**

Blue Shark, #61, 1971, MIB **10.00**

Caterpillar Tractor, No. 8, 1955 .... **40.00**

Chevrolet Impala, taxi, orange, 1965............................ **10.00**

Citroen DS19, #66, 1959 . **30.00**

Daimler ambulance, #14, 1955 .... **25.00**

Disney car, Donald Duck, 1989 .... **45.00**

Ferrari Berlinetta, metallic green body, 1965.......... **10.00**

Fiat 1500, 1965................. **10.00**

Foden Ready Mix concrete truck, orange body, 1961 .... **65.00**

Ford Customline Station Wagon, yellow body, 1957 .... **20.00**

Ford Zephyr 6, 1963 .... **38.00**

Fork lift truck, red body, yellow hoist, 1972 .... **5.00**

Harta tractor shovel, orange, 1965............................ **20.00**

Honda, motorcycle with trailer, 1968............................ **24.00**

Horse drawn milk flat, orange body, 1954..................... **25.00**

Jaguar XK 140 coupe, #32, 1956, MIB **55.00**

Lambretta TV 175 motor scooter and sidecar, metallic green, 1961 .... **25.00**

Land Rover Fire Truck, 1966 .... **10.00**

Leyland Royal Tiger Coach, silver-gray, 1961 .... **10.00**

London Bus, #5, 1954, MIB **45.00**

Mark Ten Jaguar, #24 ...... **65.00**

Maserati, 1958 .... **10.00**

Mercedes Benz Coach, white, 1965............................ **30.00**

MGA sports car, #19, 1969, MIB **70.00**

Military scout car, #61, 1959, MIB **32.00**

Morris Minor 1000, dark green, 1958............................ **20.00**

Pontiac convertible, #39, 1962, MIB **65.00**

Rolls-Royce Phamton V, 1964 .... **15.00**

Scaffolding truck, silver body, green tinted windows, 1969 .... **5.00**

Setra Coach, #12, 1970..... **5.00**

Snowtrac Tractor, red body, silver painted grille, 1964 .... **10.00**

Swamp Rat, green deck, plastic hull, tan soldier, 1976...... **5.00**

Taxi Cab, Chevrolet Impala, #20, 1965, MIB **35.00**

Thames Wreck, red body, 1961, 2-1/2" **15.00**

Volkswagon 1500 Saloon, #15, 1968, MIB **25.00**

Weatherhill Hydraulic Excavator, decal, 1956 **20.00**

Nylint, tin, Pepsi Cola truck, scratches to original paint, **$40**.

Photo courtesy of Joy Luke Auctions.

Pratt & Letchworth

Dray wagon, cast iron, open bed wagon, single slat slides, wooden floor, standing figure, red spoke wheels, one horse, 10-1/4" l...................... **175.00**

Hook and ladder truck, cast iron, horse drawn, one red and one white horse, black frame with red detailing, spoked wheels, seated front driver, seated rear steerer, two wood ladders and bell, 23" l **460.00**

Surrey, cast iron, open carriage, low splash board, two full width seams with arm and back rests, emb upholstering mounted on two prs of spoked wheels, pulled by one horse, c1900, 14" l................. **990.00**

Schoenhut, piano, painted white, **$65**.

Schuco, trademark of Schreyer and Co., Germany

Acrobat bear, yellow mohair, glass eyes, embroidered nose and mouth, turns somersaults when wound, orig key, 1950s, 5" h............................ **575.00**

Ambulance, Mercedes 408 Servo, plastic, orig box, 12-1/2" l, C.7+............. **125.00**

Mercedes Simplex, wind-up, 8-1/2" l............................ **125.00**

Monkey bellhops, Yes/No monkey with painted metal face, metal eyes, ginger mohair head and tail, red and black felt outfit and hands, Acrobatic monkey with painted metal face, metal eyes, ginger mohair head, red and black felt outfit and hands, winds by rotating arms, oak Mission style settee, 1930s, 8-1/2" h, moth damage on both **435.00**

Porsche microracer, No. 1037, red, key missing **55.00**

Racing kit, BMW Formula 2, tin and plastic, unassembled, orig box, 10" l, C.10.... **145.00**

Set, Highway Patrol, squad car, 1958............................ **100.00**

Tank, keywind................... **40.00**

Teddy bear on roller skates, wind-up, beige mohair head, glass eyes, embroidered nose and mouth, cloth and metal body and legs, cotton shirt, felt overalls, hands, and boots, rubber wheels, marked "Schuco, U. S. Zone, Germany," clothes faded, key not orig **490.00**

Teddy bear on scooter, friction auction, yellow mohair bear, black steel eyes, embroidered nose and mouth, black felt pants, blue litho scooter, 1920s, 5-3/4" h......... **1,035.00**

Tumbling monkey.......... **100.00**
Van, battery operated, 4" l... **75.00**

Structo, machinery hauler, pressed steel, orange, original decals, **$250**.
Photo courtesy of Dotta Auction Co., Inc.

Structo, tow truck, pressed steel, black and white, door reads "Structo Power Wrecker, You Bend 'em, We Mend 'em, EW1-1000, **$300**.

Structo

Bearcat Auto, 16" l, 1919 .... **850.00**
Cement mixer truck, 18-1/2" l, 9" h............................. **150.00**
Climbing military tank, green, 1929........................... **450.00**
Contractor truck, orange dump truck, 1924.................... **525.00**
Emergency van, blue and white, 1962........................... **100.00**
Fire insurance patrol, 18" l, 1928........................... **250.00**
Fire truck, hydraulic hook and ladder, pressed steel, red, 3" l **175.00**
Hydraulic dumper **65.00**
Lone Eagle airplane, monoplane, spring drive motor, 1928................. **600.00**
Motor dispatch, blue, decals, 1929, 24"..................... **850.00**
Sky King airplane, blue, gray wings, 1929 .... **900.00**

Tinplate, unknown makers

Clown violinist, stilt-legs, striped trousers, clockwork motor, 9" h, poor condition **60.00**
Delivery carriage, litho, black, red, yellow, and pink, flywheel drive, 4-1/4" l............... **150.00**

Strauss, Jennie, the Balking Mule, tin litho windup, good to excellent working condition, **$300**.
Photo courtesy of Dotta Auction Co., Inc.

Horse-drawn omnibus, attributed to Francis, Field and Francis, Philadelphia, 1850s, two white horses, black painted harnesses, wheel operated trotting, dark green roof with black fleur-de-lis and lining, emb gilt foliate surround, emb rear steps, door surround, driver's rear rest, emb window frames with painted curtains, front, rear upper section, lower half with hand-painted polychrome floral and foliate dec, over blue-gray, ochre int. with ochre vis-a-vis bench seating along sides, wheels, 23" l, overall paint flaking, wheels detached, one window frame partially detached.. **48,300.00**
Locomotive, attributed to Fallows, clockwork motor, cast wheels, high wings, cow catcher and bell, old repaint, 10" l............................ **460.00**
Locomotive, Victory, red boiler, bell, black and gilt stack, red and blue cab with green roof, silver stenciled windows, yellow chassis, spoked wheels, 4-3/4" l, one wheel damaged, scratches and paint loss **990.00**
Porter and trolley, clockwork motor in hinged trunk, blue uniform, red and orange electric-type trolley, 4-1/2" l **145.00**
Steamer, three funnels, hand painted, red, cream, and gray hull, cream superstructure, 10" l............................ **350.00**
Two-seater tourer, litho, red, yellow, and cream, driver, fly-wheel drive, 3" l **400.00**

Tonka

Airlines tractor, set of two baggage carts, C.9 .... **150.00**

Boat transport, 1960, 38" l **250.00**
Construction
Bulldozer, #0300, 1962. **35.00**
Dump truck, #0180, 1949 .... **100.00**
Dump truck and sand loader, #0616, 1963............... **100.00**
Hydraulic dump, #0520, 1962 .... **45.00**
Road grader, #0012, 1958 .... **75.00**
Fire truck
Aerial ladder truck, 1957 .... **200.00**
Rescue Squad, 1960.. **100.00**
Suburban pumper, #0046, 1960........................... **100.00**
Mini
Camper, #0070, 1963... **75.00**
Jeep pickup, #0050, 1963 .... **35.00**
Livestock Van, 1964, 16" l **50.00**
Stake truck, #0056, 1963 .... **35.00**
Truck
Air Express, #0016, 1959 .... **350.00**
Car Carrier, #0040, 1960 .... **100.00**
Carnation Milk delivery van, #0750, 1954............... **200.00**
Deluxe Sportsman, #0022, 1961........................... **100.00**
Farm state truck, 1957 **190.00**
Green Giant Transport semi, 1953........................... **150.00**
Minute Maid Orange Juice van, #0725, 1955........ **275.00**
Service truck, #001, 1960 .... **100.00**
Wrecker truck, #0018, 1958 .... **100.00**

Toonerville Trolley, tin litho windup, copyright 1922 by Fontaine Fox, **$475**.
Photo courtesy of Dotta Auction Co., Inc.

Tootsietoy

Airplane
Aero-Dawn, 1928.......... **20.00**
Beechcraft Bonanza, orange
.... **10.00**
Curtis P-40, light green . **120.00**
Navy Jet, 1970s, red..... **10.00**
P-38, WWII blue props **225.00**
Stratocruiser **30.00**
Transport plane, orange, 1941
.... **40.00**

Auto
Andy Gump Car............ **75.00**
Bluebird Daytona Race Car
.... **20.00**
Buick LaSabre, 1951 .... **25.00**
Buick Touring Car, HO series,
1960............................. **10.00**
Cadillac Coup, blue and tan
.... **40.00**
Chevrolet Roadster....... **20.00**
Corvette **12.00**
Ford Fairlane Convertible, red
.... **10.00**
Ford V-8 Hotrod, 1940 .. **15.00**
International Station Wagon,
red and yellow, 1939 .... **15.00**
Lincoln **20.00**
Oldsmobile 98, red, 1955
.... **20.00**
Packard, white, 1956.... **25.00**
Plymouth, dark blue, 1957
.... **10.00**
Pontiac Fire Chief, red, 1959
.... **20.00**

Boat
Battleship..................... **10.00**
Destroyer **10.00**
Transport...................... **15.00**
Yacht............................ **10.00**
Doodlebug, diecast, 4" l, orig
paint
Green, C.8 .... **65.00**
Red, C.9....................... **75.00**
Set, fire department, 1947 Mack
pumper, Mack fire trailer, Pontic
fire chief sedan, 1950 Chevy
panel truck ambulance, orig
box, 1950s, C.9 .... **250.00**

Unknown maker, American

Nine-pins, knockdown type, set
of Indians, each with different
polychrome paint, 9" h to
10-1/2" h................... **4,700.00**
Squeeze type, clown plays
tambourine, wood limbs, head
loose, 7" l **375.00**
Wooden crank, six soldiers on
horses, move when handle is
turned, orig polychrome paint,
19th C litho paper base,
8-1/2" l..................... **3,700.00**

Unknown maker, drum, litho, red sides
with parading children, white top, **$50**.

German U.S. Zone, painted tin toy key-
wind monkey on tricycle, original box,
$95.

Photo courtesy of Joy Luke Auctions.

Wyandotte, USA

Airplane
Army bombing plane, 8-1/2"
wingspan **25.00**
Defense bomber, 9-1/4" l
.... **70.00**
Stratoship mystery plane,
4-1/4" l......................... **10.00**
Ambulance, painted pressed
steel, nickeled grill, operating
rear door, minor scratches,
11" l............................ **150.00**
Car and trailer, painted pressed
steel, red, streamlined auto
and travel trailer with
operating rear door, replaced
white rubber tires, paint worn,
chips, and scratches, 25" l
.... **215.00**
Circus truck and wagon, red
and yellow, cardboard
animals, 19" l **650.00**
Hoky & Poky, litho tin wind-up,
play wear, 6-3/4" l, C.7 **195.00**
Humphrey mobile, litho tinplate,
fixed steering, clockwork
motor, rear door, moving hat
and arm, 9" l, some
scratching................... **350.00**
Pan Am clipper, painted
pressed steel, red and white,
brass engines, nickeled
propellers, 9" l............. **275.00**

Rocket racer, 6" l............. **50.00**
Streamlined Wagon, rubber
wheels, 5-1/4" l **25.00**
Zephyr roadster, rubber
wheels, 13-3/8" l **400.00**

TRAINS, TOY

History: Railroading has always
been an important part of childhood,
largely because of the romance
associated with the railroad and the
prominence of toy trains.

The first toy trains were cast
iron and tin; wind-up motors
added movement. The golden age
of toy trains was 1920 to 1955,
when electric-powered units and
high-quality rolling stock were
available and names such as Ives,
American Flyer, and Lionel were
household words. The advent of
plastic in the late 1950s resulted in
considerably lower quality.

Toy trains are designated by a
model scale or gauge. The most
popular are HO, N, O and standard.
Narrow gauge was a response to
the modern capacity to miniaturize.
Today train layouts in gardens are all
the rage and those usually feature
larger scale trains.

Additional Listings: See
*Warman's Americana &
Collectibles* for more examples.

Notes: Condition of trains is
critical when establishing price.
Items in fair condition and below
(scratched, chipped, dented,
rusted, or warped) generally have
little value to a collector. Accurate
restoration is accepted and may
enhance the price by one or two
grades. Prices listed are for trains
in very good to mint condition,
unless otherwise noted.

> **Train layout sold**
> A wonderful, custom-built
> model train layout, covering
> 1,500 square feet, was sold in
> late 2003. This layout was
> designed by Dick Kughn, and
> included 11 standard gauge
> trains on five different levels,
> hundreds of period Lionel
> accessories and rolling stock.
> The layout was formerly housed
> at the Carail Museum, Detroit,
> MI. It was sold by RM Auction,
> Sept. 20-21, for $218,000.

Front: unidentified maker, early cast iron locomotive and four passenger cars, search light and crossing light, **$100**; rear: Marx, Stream Line Steam Type Electric Train, six pieces, original box with cars, tracks, and original transformer, **$250**.

Photo courtesy of Dotta Auction Co., Inc.

American Flyer

Boxcar, #33514, HO gauge, Silver Meteor, brown **45.00**

Caboose, #935, S gauge, 1957, brown **60.00**

Circus pullman, #649, S gauge, minor wear to orig box, C.9 .... **650.00**

Flat car, #24558, S gauge, 1959-60, Canadian Pacific, Christmas tree load **145.00**

Gondola
#941, S gauge, 1953-57, Frisco **10.00**
#33507, HO gauge, D&H, brown, canister load **60.00**

Handcar, #742, S gauge, some wear to orig box and insert, C.0 .... **65.00**

Locomotive
#345, S gauge, steam, 1954, Silver Bullet, Pacific, 4-6-2 .... **200.00**
#425, decals and paint chipped, 426 tender, decals chipped, C.5 .... **75.00**
#435 locomotive, 433A tender, unnatural wear to drivers, C.7-8 .... **220.00**
#3020, O gauge, electric, 4-4-4, c1922-25 .... **375.00**
#3307 locomotive, 3189 tender, decals chipped, C.5 .... **90.00**
#3322 locomotive, 3199 tender, C.4-5 .... **110.00**

Set, O gauge
Freight, #476 gondola, #478 boxcar, #480 tank car, #484 caboose **130.00**
Passenger, Railway Post Office car, Paul Revere coach, Lexington observation, orange **115.00**

Set, standard gauge
#12 locomotive, painted cast iron, working clockwork, 120 tender, 1119 cattle car, 1109 gondola, 1111 IC caboose, tunnel, track, switches, C.4-5 .... **350.00**
#20 locomotive, 1131 tender, 1126 hopper, 1113 hopper, two 1223 coaches, C.4-5 .... **75.00**
#423 locomotive, 426 tender, 415 searchlight car, 416 wrecker, 410 tank car, 408 box car, 407 gondola, C.5-7 .... **190.00**
#434, 282 loco and tender, 500 combine, 501 coach, 502 vista dome, 503 observation, worn orig boxes, C.8-9 .... **2,000.00**
#3315 locomotive, 3319 tender, 3380 combine, 3382 observation, C.5-6 ...... **240.00**
#3322 locomotive, 3180 tender, two 3208 box cars, 3206 lumber car, 3211 caboose, C.5-6 .... **160.00**
#4644 locomotive, rewheeled, 4151 coach, 4152 observation, Eagle train, C.6 .... **350.00**
#K5364W Silver Rocket, 474 and 475 Rocket AA, three 962 vista domes, 963 observation, orig boxes with some wear, C.6-8 .... **1,550.00**
#20305, 21800-355 Baldwin diesel, 702 box of track, orig boxes, C.8-9 .... **420.00**
#20740 Defender, 234 logo, 24557 Navy flat with Jeeps, 25056 USM box car and rocket launcher flat car, 24549 searchlight car, 24631 caboose, C.6-8 .... **700.00**

Tank car, #24323, Baker's Chocolate, S gauge, gray tank ends, minor wear to orig box, C.8 .... **550.00**

Bing, German

Locomotive, O gauge, pre-war Clockwork, cast iron, no tender, headlight missing **70.00**

Live steam, 0-4-0, minor fire damage, no tender **815.00**

Set, O gauge, passenger, litho, #2395 combine, Winnegago coach, Lakewood observation, green with brown roofs **130.00**

Set, #1 gauge, passenger, litho, dark maroon, lettered "Pennsylvania Lines," combine #1250, coach #1207 .... **435.00**

Ives

Baggage car
#50, 1908-09, O gauge, four wheels, red litho frame, striped steps, white/silver body, sides marked "Limited Vestibule Express, United States Mail Baggage Co." and "Express Service No. 50," three doors on both sides, one on each end, black roof with celestory............. **150.00**
#70, 1923-25, O gauge, eight wheels, red litho body, simulates steel, tin roof with celestory stripe, sliding center door, marked "The Ives Railway Lines, Express Baggage Service, 60, U. S. Mail"............................. **30.00**

Caboose, #67, 1918, O gauge, eight wheels, red litho body, sliding door on each side, gray painted tin roof with red cupola, "The Ives Railway Lines"........................... **45.00**

Gravel car, #63, 1913-14, O gauge, eight wheels, gray litho, rounded truss rods, marked "63" on sides ... **35.00**

Livestock car, #65, c1918, O gauge, eight wheels, orange-yellow litho body, type D trucks, gray painted roof with catwalk, sides marked "Livestock Transportation, Ives RR" **27.50**

Locomotive
#19, 1917-25, O gauge, 0-4-0, black cast iron boiler and cab, two arched windows and "IVES No. 19" beneath, cast-iron wheels, NYC & HR No. 17 tender **225.00**
#25, 1906-07, O gauge, 4-4-2, black body, boiler tapers towards front, four separate boiler bands, three square windows on both sides of cab, gold frames and stripes, tin pony wheels, four-wheel L.V.E. No. 25 tender.............. **275.00**

#3200, 1911, O gauge, 0-4-o, cast iron S-type electric center cab, green body, gold trim, cast iron six-spoke wheels, center door flanked by two windows, raised lettering "Ives" and "3200" below windows **250.00**

Lionel, O gauge, #292 set, 153 locomotive, two #629 cars, one #630, original track and transformer, original box, **$400**.

Photo courtesy of Dotta Auction Co., Inc.

Lionel

Baggage car, #2602, O gauge, 1938, red body and roof **100.00**

Boxcar
#00-44, OO gauge, 1939 .... **45.00**
#HO-874, HO gauge, 1964, NYC **25.00**
#6464-375 Central of Georgia, unrun, minor wear to orig box, C.7 .... **120.00**

Caboose
#217, S gauge, 1926-40, orange and maroon **150.00**
#HO-841, HO gauge, 1961, NYC **10.00**

Cattle car, #213, S gauge, 1926-40, cream body, maroon roof **450.00**

Coal loader, #397, coal shield broken, minor wear and tape on orig box, C.6-7 .... **70.00**

Derrick, #219, S gauge, C.7 .... **240.00**

Dump, #218, S gauge Mojave end plates, minor wear to orig box, C.7 .... **270.00**

Hopper, #516, S gauge, coal loads, minor chips, incomplete orig box, C.6-7 .... **270.00**

Horse car, #3356-2, unrun, separate sale orig box, C.9 .... **400.00**

Locomotive
#8, S gauge, rewheeled, replaced headlights, minor touchup, C.6 .... **170.00**
#156, O gauge, electric, 4-4-4, dark green, c1917-23 .... **265.00**
#256 locomotive, RS, C.6 .... **440.00**
#258 locomotive, 257T tender, wear to paint, C.5-6 .... **165.00**
#265E, 265W tender, scratched, C.5 .... **120.00**

Observation car
#322, S gauge, 1924 .... **95.00**
#754, O gauge, 1934, streamliner **70.00**

Pullman
#35, S gauge, c1915, orange **65.00**
#607, O gauge, 1926 ... **45.00**

Refrigerator car, #214R, Standard gauge, 1929-40, ivory body, peacock roof **400.00**

Set, O gauge
Passenger, #252 electric locomotive, #529 coach, #530 observation, olive green, c1926 .... **175.00**
Passenger, Union Pacific, #752E power unit, #753 coach, #754 observation, silver, c1934 .... **350.00**

Set, S gauge
#8 loco, rewheeled, replaced headlamps, 337 coach, 338 observation, C.7 .... **240.00**
#218 SF Alco AA, dummy with crack, 3428 milk car, 2414 coach, two 2412 vista domes, 2416 observation, C-6 **360.00**
#225E locomotive, 265W tender, three restored 3659 dump cars, 2657 caboose, C.5-8 .... **245.00**
#254E locomotive, replaced headlamps, restored frame, two 610 coaches, 612 observation, C.5 .... **150.00**
#380 locomotive, 320 baggage, 319 coach, 322 observation, restored, C.8 .... **300.00**

TRAMP ART

History: Tramp art was an internationally practiced craft, brought to the United States by European immigrants. Its span of popularity was between the late 1860s to the 1940s. Made with simple tools—usually a pocketknife, and from scrap woods—non-reusable cigar box wood, and crate wood, this folk-art form can be seen in small boxes to large pieces of furniture. Usually identifiable by the composition of thin-layered pieces of wood with chip-carved edges assembled in built-up pyramids, circles, hearts, stars, etc. At times, pieces included velvet, porcelain buttons, brass tacks, glass knobs, shards of china, etc., that the craftsmen used to embellish his work. The pieces were predominantly stained or painted.

Collected as folk art, most of the work was attributed to anonymous makers. A premium is placed on the more whimsical artistic forms, pieces in original painted surfaces, or pieces verified to be from an identified maker.

Box, rose-colored fabric insert panel on front, unlined, 8" x 12" l, **$150**.

Bottom of small hanging box, showing how boxes were reused to create tramp art.

Dresser box, lidded, multi-layered pyramids, **$190**.

Photo courtesy of Dotta Auction Co., Inc.

Bank, 6" h x 4" w x 4" d, secret access to coins **335.00**

Box, cov
4-1/4" w, 3" d, 1-3/4" h, hinged cover, dove, heart, and anchor dec **200.00**
14" l, 7-1/8" d, 8-1/4" h, hinged top, cast brass pull, mounted pincushion on base, two concealed short drawers, painted blue and gold, c1890-1910 .... **815.00**

Cabinet, building shape, two towers, steeple roofline, small shelves..................... **3,600.00**

Chest of drawers, 40" h x 29" w x 20" d, scratch built from crates with four drawers, 10 layers deep............. **2,400.00**

Clock, mantel, 22" h x 14" w x 7" d, red stain with drawers at base........................... **475.00**

Comb case, 27" h x 17" w x 4"d, adorned with horseshoes, hearts, birds, two drawers and mirrors **700.00**

Crucifix, 16" h x 7" w x 4-1/2" d, wooden pedestal base, wooden carved figure. **195.00**

Document box, 14" h x 9-1/2" w x 9" d, diamond designs, sgd and date **375.00**

Picture frames, left: applied roundels and diamonds, **$45**; right: carved American eagle, stars, and laurel motif, **$95**.

Picture frames, larger one with natural finished wood and blue velvet banding, **$225**; smaller darker intricate design frame, **$195**.

Frame
9" h, 6-3/4" w, photograph of maker, signed and dated "1906" **275.00**
13" h x 12" w, horseshoe shape, light and dark wood **465.00**
14" h x 24" w, double opening frame with oval opening for photos........................ **325.00**
26" h x 24" w, velvet panels and sq corners **350.00**

Jewelry box
6" h x 11" w x 6" d, covered with hearts painted silver over gold, velvet lined **595.00**
9" h x 11-1/2" w x 7" d, large, dated "1898," metal lion pulls **300.00**

Lamp, table, 24" h, 10" w, 10" d, double socket............. **550.00**

Medicine cabinet, 22" h x 18" w x 10" d, light and dark woods **675.00**

Miniature
Chair, 8" h x 6" w x 5-1/2" d, crown of thorns **245.00**
Chest of drawers, 14" h x 5" w x 4" d, made of cigar boxes **375.00**

Music box, 3" h x 7" w x 6" d, velvet sides................. **425.00**

Night stand, 37" h x 22" w x 14" d, dark stain, drawer on top and cabinet on bottom, no losses **1,600.00**

Pedestal with lidded box, two birds on finial, 10" h, **$750**.

Photo courtesy of Joy Luke.

Pedestal
14 1-2" h x 12" w x 8" d, multi-level, six draws **675.00**
16" h x 7" w x 4-1/2" d, polychromed in green and black paint.................. **950.00**

Plant stand, 22" h x 11" w x 11" d, painted gold, heavily layered........................ **675.00**

Pocket watch holder, 9" h x 6-1/2" w x 5-1/2" d, ftd . **375.00**

Spice box, hanging type, painted black, white porcelain knobs, six small drawers over one longer drawer, ornate carved crest, **$175**.

Small hanging box with four drawers, made from cigar boxes, **$150**; inside pair of domed top picture frames, **$175**.

Sewing box, 8-1/2" h x 11-1/2" w x 8-1/2"d, velvet pin cushion on top **265.00**

Vanity mirror, 26" h, 14" d, 10" d, table top, heart on top and drawer **375.00**

Wall pocket
8" w, 3-1/2" d, 14" h, three pockets, hearts on crest, diamond and circle dec, trim and dec painted orig medium blue and goldenrod.... **275.00**
14" h x 11" w x 7"d, painted with hearts and stars, pr **700.00**

TRUNKS

History: Trunks are portable containers that clasp shut and are used for the storage or transportation of personal possessions. Normally "trunk" means the ribbed flat- or domed-top models of the second half of the 19th century.

Early trunks frequently were painted, stenciled, grained, or covered with wallpaper. These are collected for their folk-art qualities and, as such, demand high prices.

Camel back, medium size, as found, **$75**.
Photo courtesy of Dotta Auction Co., Inc.

Camel back, as found, **$120**.
Photo courtesy of Dotta Auction Co., Inc.

Dome top

6" l, 3-1/2" w, 2-5/8" h, paper-covered box green and red sponge dec, blue line and dot patterned paper-lined int., brass ring and iron latch, America, 19th C, wear **265.00**

11-1/2" h, 28" w, 14" d, paint dec, black painted ground, central vined pinwheel bordered by meandering floral and arched vines, front with tassel and drape border, central MA, early 19th C
.... **1,035.00**

19" l, fabric on wood, worn painted dec in ivory and green, red border designs and flowers, interior lined with green marbleized paper, worn
.... **425.00**

28-1/4" l, 13-3/4" w, 13-1/2" h, arched top with "L G" in scripted yellow paint, nail construction box, all grain painted to simulate mahogany, and outlined in yellow striping with yellow floral device centered under the lock, imperfections and repairs, New England, early 19th C **235.00**

33-1/4" w, 16-1/4" d, 18-3/4" h, black japanned brass mounts, gilt Chinoisiere dec of figures in garden landscape, side handles, late 18th/early 19th C, restoration **750.00**

44-1/2" w, 22-3/4" d, 19-1/2" h, hinged top, dovetailed box, white painted vine, floral and leaf dec over black painted ground, int. papered with early 19th C Boston area broadsides, attributed to MA, 19th C, some later paint **1,035.00**

Dome top trunk, wood stays, paper covering with lithographed straps, original hardware, **$65**.
Photo courtesy of Sky Hawk Auctions.

Dovetailed, 41-3/4" w, 24-3/4" h, 27-1/2" h, old dark brown finish, finely painted panels with Chinoiserie vases and planters of flowers in red, tan, and green on front and sides, wrought iron handles on ends, large brass hasp and moon escutcheon on front.... **320.00**

Flat top

14" x 8", Chinese, pigskin, red, painted Oriental maidens and landscapes within quatrefoils, brass loop handles and lock, 19th C **125.00**

15-1/4" l, tooled leather on pine, iron straps, brass buttons and lock, lined with worn newspaper dated 1871, hinged replaced, some edge damage **385.00**

24" w, 14" d, 11" h, poplar, old black paint, tacks border sides, top, lock, and handles, initials "P.L." on top, leather straps beneath tacks, worn cloth lining, age splits... **150.00**

30-1/2" w, 16-1/2" d, 17-1/2" h, copper and iron, Arts & Crafts strapwork and pyramidal tack mounts, black paint, hinged slant lid revealing rect box
.... **200.00**

Painted early wooden trunk with iron banding, decorated with flowers and scrolls, with painted names and dates "JTD – 1801" and "Johanes Larssen Roorvig 1853", 39" l, 18" d, 17" h, **$350**.
Photo courtesy of Joy Luke.

Striped exterior, original hardware, **$95**.
Photo courtesy of Dotta Auction Co., Inc.

Louis Vuitton trunk, John Wannamaker label, early 20th C, 20" w, 20" h, **$1,725**.
Photo courtesy of Pook & Pook.

Military, 21-3/4" w, 17" d, 12-1/2" h, brass bound camphor wood, hinged rect top, storage well, brass bail handles, English, second half 19th C **200.00**

Vuitton, Louis, early 20th C, wardrobe, rect, wooden strapping, leather handles on ends, brass corners and clasps, int. with hanger bars, eight Vuitton hangers, 21-1/2" d, 15-1/2" d, 40-1/2" h
.... **1,100.00**

VAL ST.-LAMBERT

History: Val St.-Lambert, a 12th-century Cistercian abbey, was located during different historical periods in France, Netherlands, and Belgium (1930 to present). In 1822, Francois Kemlin and Auguste Lelievre, along with a group of financiers, bought the abbey and opened a glassworks. In 1846, Val St.-Lambert merged with the Société Anonyme des Manufactures de Glaces, Verres à Vitre, Cristaux et Gobeletaries. The company bought many other glassworks.

Val St.-Lambert developed a reputation for technological progress in the glass industry. In 1879, Val St.-Lambert became an independent company employing 4,000 workers. The firm concentrated on the export market, making table glass, cut, engraved, etched, and molded pieces, and chandeliers. Some pieces were finished in other countries, e.g., silver mounts were added in the United States.

Val St.-Lambert executed many special commissions for the artists of the Art Nouveau and Art Deco periods. The tradition continues. The company also made cameo-etched vases, covered boxes, and bowls. The firm celebrated its 150th anniversary in 1975.

For more information, see *Warman's Glass*, 4th edition.

Bowl, colorless, cut design, **$45.**

Compotes, colorless, shallow, paneled stems, price for pair, **$65.**

Ashtray, 6" w, hexagon, colorless crystal............ **35.00**
Candlesticks, pr, 9-1/2" h, colorless crystal, orig paper labels **250.00**
Cologne bottle, 4-3/8" h, frosted cylindrical body, cameo cranberry floral relief, cut faceted stopper **175.00**
Cordial Glasses, set of six, 4-5/8" h, bowls cased in cobalt blue, cut with band of circles over paneled flutes, single knopped stem, spreading foot **250.00**
Epergne, 10-1/2" h, five 6" h etched cameo cylindrical flower holders, stylized naturalistic brass frame **1,800.00**
Figure, 3-1/2" d base, 7-1/4" h, parrot perched on bell, light cranberry, sgd "Val St Lambert, Belgique" **275.00**
Paperweight, 4" h, apple, colorless crystal, acid etched script signature............. **85.00**
Presentation vase, 14" h, green ground, cameo cut chrysanthemums, maroon enameling, c1900 .... **500.00**
Vase
8-3/4" d, 12" h, emerald and colorless crystal.......... **550.00**
11-1/2" h, cobalt blue ground, overlaid in copper, all over emb rosettes, emb "Val St Lambert Belgique," c1910 .... **575.00**

VALENTINES

History: Early cards were handmade, often containing both handwritten verses and hand-drawn pictures. Many cards also were hand colored and contained cutwork.

Mass production of machine-made cards featuring chromolithography began after 1840. In 1847, Esther Howland of Worcester, Massachusetts, established a company to make valentines that were hand decorated with paper lace and other materials imported from England. They had a small "H" stamped in red in the top left corner. Howland's company eventually became the New England Valentine Company (N.E.V. Co.).

The company George C. Whitney and his brother founded after the Civil War dominated the market from the 1870s through the first decades of the 20th century. They bought out several competitors, one of which was the New England Valentine Company.

Lace paper was invented in 1834. The golden age of lacy cards took place between 1835 and 1860.

Embossed paper was used in England after 1800. Embossed lithographs and woodcuts developed between 1825 and 1840, and early examples were hand colored.

There was a big revival in the 1920s by large companies, like R. Tuck in England, which did lots of beautiful cards for its 75th Diamond Jubilee; 1925 saw changes in card production, especially for children with paper toys of all sorts, all very collectible now. Little girls were in short dresses, boys in short pants, which helps date that era of valentines. There was an endless variety of toy types of paper items, many companies created similar items and many stayed in production until World War II paper shortages stopped production both here and abroad.

Adviser: Evalene Pulati.

Animated, large
Felix, half tone, German.. **25.00**
Jumping Jack, Tuck, 1900
.... **65.00**
Bank True Love note, England, 1865.............................. **75.00**
Bank of Love note, Nister, 1914
.... **38.00**
Charm string
Brundage, three pcs..... **45.00**
Four hearts, ribbon **45.00**
Comic
Sheet, 8" x 10", Park, London
.... **25.00**
Sheet, 9" x 14", McLoughlin Co., USA, 1915 .... **20.00**
Woodcut, Strong, USA, 1845
.... **25.00**
Diecut foldout
Brundage, flat, cardboard
.... **25.00**
Cherubs, two pcs **40.00**
Clapsaddle, 1911 .... **60.00**
Documentary
Passport, love, 1910..... **45.00**
Wedding certificate, 1914
.... **45.00**
English Fancy, from "Unrequited Love Series"
8" x 10", aquatint, couple, wedding...................... **135.00**
8" x 10", aquatint, girl and grandmother **95.00**
Engraved
5" x 7", American, verse **35.00**
8" x 10" sheet, English, hand colored.......................... **55.00**
Handmade
Calligraphy, envelope, 1885
.... **135.00**
Cutwork, hearts, 6" x 6", 1855
.... **250.00**
Fraktur, cutwork, 1800 **950.00**
Pen and ink loveknot, 1820
.... **275.00**
Puzzle, purse, 14" x 14", 1855
.... **450.00**
Theorem, 9" x 14", c1885
.... **325.00**
Woven heart, hand, 1840
.... **55.00**
Honeycomb
American, kids, tunnel of love
.... **48.00**
American, wide-eyed kids, 9"
.... **40.00**
German, 1914, white and pink, 11" **75.00**

Folk art, scherenschnitte, Pennsylvania, 19th C, circular, heart cutouts, 6-3/4" d, **$575**.
Photo courtesy of Pook & Pook.

Simple, 1920, Beistle, 8"
.... **18.00**
Lace paper
American, B & J Cameo Style
Large **75.00**
Small, 1865 .... **45.00**
American, layered, McLoughlin Co., c1880 **35.00**
Cobweb center, c1855 **250.00**
English, fancy
3" x 5", 1865 .... **35.00**
5" x 7", 1855 .... **75.00**
8" x 10", 1840 .... **135.00**
Hand layered, scraps, 1855
.... **65.00**
Layered, in orig box
1875, Howland **75.00**
1910, McLoughlin Co. .. **45.00**
Simple, small pc, 1875 . **22.50**
Whitney, 1875, 5" x 7" ... **35.00**

Mechanical, diecut light brown and white puppy with bee, "I'll Bee Your Valentine," head moves, marked "Made in USA," manufacturer's mark in lower corner, **$20**.

Novelty, American Fancy, c1900
5" x 7-1/2", mat, fancy corners, parchment, orig box
.... **32.50**
7-1/2" x 10", rect, panel with silk, celluloid, orig box.. **45.00**
10-1/2" x 10", star shape, silk rusching, orig box **55.00**
16" x 10-1/2", oblong, satin, celluloid, orig box **65.00**
Pulldown, German
Airplane, 1914, 8" x 14". **175.00**
Auto, 1910, 8" x 11" x 4"
.... **150.00**
Car and kids, 1920s **35.00**
Dollhouse, large, 1935 . **45.00**
Rowboat, small, honeycomb paper puff.................... **65.00**
Seaplane, 1934, 8" x 9". **75.00**
Tall Ship, 8" x 16" **175.00**
Silk fringed
Prang, double sided, 3" x 5"
.... **24.00**
Triple layers, orig box ... **38.00**
Standup novelty
Cupid, orig box............. **45.00**
Hands, heart, without orig box
.... **35.00**
Parchment, violin, large, boxed **125.00**

VALLERYSTHAL GLASS

History:
Vallerysthal (Lorraine), France, has been a glass-producing center for

centuries. In 1872, two major factories, Vallerysthal glassworks and Portieux glassworks, merged and produced art glass until 1898. Later, pressed glass animal-covered dishes were introduced. The factory continues to operate today.

For more information, see *Warman's Glass*, 4th edition.

Animal dish, cov
Hen on nest, opaque aqua, sgd.............................. **95.00**
Rabbit, white, frosted.... **85.00**
Swan, blue opaque glass
.... **110.00**
Butter dish, cov, turtle, opaque white, snail finial.......... **120.00**
Candlesticks, pr, Baroque pattern, amber.............. **75.00**
Compote, 6-1/4" sq, blue opaque glass............... **75.00**

Two painted milk glass strawberry-shaped lidded dishes with snail finials, 4-1/2" l, 5-1/2" h, **each $60**.

Photo courtesy of Joy Luke.

Dish, covered, cabbage shape, green opaque, original round paper label on base, **$195**.

Mustard, cov, swirled ribs, scalloped blue opaque, matching cover with slot for spoon............................ **35.00**
Plate, 6" d, Thistle pattern, green
.... **65.00**
Salt, cov, hen on nest, white opal
.... **65.00**
Sugar, cov, 5" h, Strawberry pattern, opaque white, gold trim, salamander finial .. **85.00**
Toothpick holder, hand holding ribbed vessel, opaque blue
.... **30.00**
Vase, 8" h, flared folded burgundy red rim, oval pale green body, matching red enamel berry bush on front, inscribed "Vallerysthal" on base........................... **490.00**

VAN BRIGGLE POTTERY

History: Artus Van Briggle, born in 1869, was a talented Ohio artist. He joined Rookwood in 1887 and studied in Paris under Rookwood's sponsorship from 1893 until 1896. In 1899, he moved to Colorado for his health and established his own pottery in Colorado Springs in 1901.

The Art Nouveau schools he had seen in France heavily influenced Van Briggle's work. He produced a great variety of matte-glazed wares in this style. Colors varied.

Artus died in 1904. Anne Van Briggle continued the pottery until 1912.

Marks: The "AA" mark, a date, and "Van Briggle" were incised on all pieces prior to 1907 and on some pieces into the 1920s. After 1920, "Colorado Springs, Colorado" or an abbreviation was added. Dated pieces are the most desirable.

Reproduction Alert: Van Briggle pottery still is made today. These modern pieces often are mistaken for older examples. Among the glazes used are Moonglo (off white), Turquoise Ming, Russet, and Midnight (black).

Basket, blue, marked with box mark and "Van Briggle, Colo. Spgs," **$165**.

Advertising plaque, 11-1/2" l, 5-3/4" h, green and blue matte glaze, emb "VAN BRIGGLE POTTERY/COLORADO CLAY," 1/3" corner chip, few smaller edge chips .. **2,300.00**
Bowl, 5" x 10", shade-shaped leaves, frothy green and purple matte glaze, robin's egg blue ground, buff clay showing through, mkd "AA Van Briggle/Colo Spgs/737," 1908-11, 2-1/2" hairline from rim........................... **1,690.00**
Cabinet vase, 2-1/2" d, 4-1/4" h, emb flowers in curved panels, covered in dark teal matte glaze, incised AA/Van Briggle/190?/186, with XXII/IV/33188 in ink, 1904 .... **1,610.00**

Chamberstick, 5-1/2" h, molded-leaf shape, hood over candle socket, green glaze
.... **115.00**
Figure, 7" h, female nude holding shell, matte Persian blue glaze, incised "Van Briggle"...................... **250.00**
Lamp base, 9" h, emb stylized florals under maroon glaze with blue over-spray, orig factory fittings, incised varnished bottom with logo, name, and Colo. Sprgs, c1920......................... **115.00**

Pitcher, #452, 1906, matte gray glaze, marked and dated, 4-3/4" h, **$520**.

Van Briggle photos courtesy of David Rago Auctions, Inc.

Low bowl
6-1/2" h, shape no. "689," emb arrow root design, under matte green glaze, incised with logo, varnished bottom, Colo Sprgs, c1920...... **260.00**
8-3/4" d, 2-3/4" h, Dragonfly, closed-in rim, four molded dragonflies around rim, deep mulberry matte glaze, incised cipher, incised Van Briggle U.S.A., c1922-29 .... **350.00**
Mug, 6" h, feathered matte green over blue glaze, 1908-11, overfired, burst bubbles, crack in handle........... **175.00**
Night light, 8-1/2" h, figural, stylized owl, bulb cavity, light refracting glass eyes, turquoise blue matte glaze, unsgd **425.00**
Tile, 18" x 12", six tile frieze, cuenca with stylized trees against blue sky, framed
.... **250.00**
Vase
4-3/4" h, 4" d, bulbous, crisply molded, spade-shaped leaves, sheer frothy light turquoise glaze, clay showing through, AA Van Briggle, 1908
.... **800.00**

Vase, 1908-1911, embossed blossoms, unusual lavender to chartreuse matte glaze, marked, 1" line from rim, 3-3/4", **$250**.

4-3/4" h, 5-1/4" d, squat, emb spade-shaped leaves, stylized blossoms, mustard and olive green dead matte glaze, 1904, AA/Van Briggle/ 1904/151 .... **1,300.00**
5-1/2" h, shape no. 833, molded stylized flowers, under brown glaze with green over-spray, dirty bottom with incised logo, name and Colo Sprgs, c1920 .... **230.00**
5-1/2" h, 5-1/4" d, bulbous, emb panels of stylized flowers and heart-shaped leaves in purple and green, matte blue ground, incised AA/Van Briggle/1905/?09/X, small glaze scale to one stem
.... **2,760.00**
6" h, incised and molded stylized flowers, under blue/ gray glaze with turquoise over-spray, "dirty bottom" incised with logo, name, and date "20," c1920......... **375.00**
7-3/4" h, 3" d, emb tulips, purple to periwinkle matte glaze, 1903, AA/Van Briggle/ 1903/II/141 .... **2,000.00**
8" h, figural, Native American Indian with pottery vase, incised "Van Briggle Col. Spgs D.R." **360.00**
8-1/4" h, 2-3/4" d, bulbous, crisply emb spade-shaped leaves, covered in mottled purple dripping over green matte glaze, incised AA/Van Briggle/Colo. Spgs./804/18/7, c1907-11, 3/4" rim bruise
.... **1,100.00**
8-1/2" h, 7" d, bulbous, emb panels of berries and leaves, covered in caramel, amber, and indigo matte glaze, incised AA/Van Briggle/1904/ V/164........................ **6,900.00**

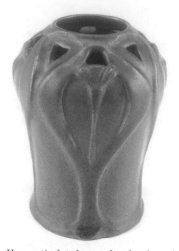

Vase, reticulated, carved and embossed with stylized papyrus blossoms, frothy indigo and olive green glaze, 1907-11, mark obscured by glaze, 6-1/4" h, 5" d, **$2,600**.

Photo courtesy of David Rago Auctions, Inc.

9" h, 6" d, bulbous, cupped rim, two loop handles, emb leaves around base, covered in rare purple and green matte glaze, incised AA/Van Briggle/1903/III/232 . **3,775.00**
9" h, 6" d, bulbous, emb poppy pods, rare dark blue-green leathery matte glaze, incised AA/Van Briggle/1903/ III/18........................ **4,890.00**
10-1/4" h, 4-1/4" d, tapering, emb tobacco leaves, covered in matte ochre and umber glaze, incised AA, die-stamped 1915 and 45
.... **1,380.00**
11-1/4" h, 4" d, tapering, emb peacock fathers, covered in charcoal and chartreuse matte glaze, incised AA/Van Briggle/1905/III/174 . **5,750.00**

Vessel, flat shoulder, 1908-1911, yellow and light green matte glaze, marked, 4", **$350**.

Vessel, squat, embossed butterflies, Persian Rose glaze, marked, 4", **$125**.

Vessel, squat, embossed leaves, Mountain Craig Brown, 1930s, marked "AA Van Briggle/Colo. Spgs," 5" d, 4-1/4" h, **$175**.

Vessel, 4-1/4" h, 5-1/2" d, bulbous, molded poppies, fine indigo and teal green frothy glaze, 1908-11, AA Van Briggle, Colo Spgs mark
.... **1,000.00**

VENETIAN GLASS

History: Venetian glass has been made on the island of Murano, near Venice, since the 13th century. Most of the wares are thin walled. Many types of decoration have been used: embedded gold dust, lace work, and applied fruits or flowers.

Reproduction Alert: Venetian glass continues to be made today.

Bowl, 7-1/2" w, 6-1/8" w, deep quatraform bowl, applied quatraform rim, blue, clear internal dec, trapped air bubble square, circles, and gold inclusions, c1950 . **360.00**
Candlesticks, pr, 8-3/8" h, white and black glass, formed as coat on twisted stem coat rack on tripod base, black domed foot, 20th C..... **275.00**

Centerpiece set, two 8-1/2"
baluster ftd ewers, 8-1/2" ftd
compote, red and white
latticino stripes with gold
flecks, applied clear handles
and feet, three-pc set . **150.00**

Compote, cov, 7-1/2" d, dusty
amber body, blue lip wrap,
floral finial...................... **70.00**

Compote, open, 7-7/8" h, pale
green glass body, five gold
metallic and colorless glass
loop ornaments, early 20th C,
price for pr **600.00**

Decanter, 13" h, figural clown,
bright red, yellow, black, and
white, aventurine swirls, orig
stopper **250.00**

Ewer, 6" h, pinched sided,
alternating green and opal
panels, chain dec **65.00**

Goblet, 6" h, shamrock shape,
translucent, dec with pictorial
medallions, intaglio cut gilt
scrolling and flowers,
Lobmeyer, price for pr **275.00**

Sherry, amber swirled bowls,
blue beaded stems, eight-pc
set **495.00**

Table garniture, two 14-1/4" h
clear glass dolphins on white
diagonally fluted short
pedestals, six 5-3/4" h to
7-3/4" h clear glass turtle,
bird, seahorse, dolphin, two
bunches of fruit in bowls,
figures on similar white
pedestals, including 20th C
.... **550.00**

Vase, 8" h, handkerchief shape,
pale green and white pulled
stripe, applied clear base,
base, attributed to Barovier,
1930s **65.00**

Wine, 3-7/8" h, alternating dec
panels **75.00**

VILLEROY &
BOCH

History:
Pierre Joseph
Boch
established a
pottery near
Luxembourg,
Germany, in
1767. Jean

Francis, his son, introduced the
first coal-fired kiln in Europe and
perfected a water-power-driven
potter's wheel. Pierre's grandson,

Eugene Boch, managed a pottery
at Mettlach; Nicholas Villeroy also
had a pottery nearby.

In 1841, the three potteries
merged into the firm of Villeroy &
Boch. Early production included a
hard-paste earthenware
comparable to English ironstone.
The factory continues to use this
hard-paste formula for its modern
tablewares.

Stein, 1/2 litre, stoneware, dancing
figures, King of Hops, #1909, pewter
lid, **$100**.

Photo courtesy of Joy Luke Auctions.

Beaker, quarter liter, couple at
feast, multicolored, printed
underglaze **115.00**

Bowl, 8" d, 3-3/4" h, gaudy floral
dec, blue, red, green, purple,
and yellow, marked "Villeroy &
Boch," minor wear and stains
.... **50.00**

Charger, 15-1/2" d, gentleman
on horseback, sgd "Stocke"
.... **600.00**

Dish, cov, triangular, orange and
black dec, marked "Villeroy &
Boch, Mettlach," and "Made
in Saar-Basin," molded
"3865," c1880-1900.... **125.00**

Ewer, 17-3/4" h, central frieze of
festive beer hall, band playing
while couples dance and
drink, neck and foot with
formal panels between leaf
molded borders, subdued
tones, c1884, imp shape
number, production number
and date codes **900.00**

Figure, 53" h, Venus, scantily
clad seated figure, ribbon tied
headdress, left arm raised
across chest, resting on rock,
inscribed "Villeroy & Boch,"
damage to foot and base
.... **1,900.00**

Platter, 9-1/4" l, 8" w, white
basketweave ground, blue
fish and aquatic plants dec,

marked "Villeroy & Boch,
Delphin, Mettlach, Ceschutzt"
.... **110.00**

Stein, three litre, stoneware, verse,
figure of lady holding goblet, pewter lid,
$200.

Photo courtesy of Joy Luke Auctions.

Stein, #2942, half liter, pewter
lid, brown ground, beige
earthenware cartouche
"Braun ist meine Maid,
Schaumt uber jeder-zeit,"
Jewish Star of David on
reverse, marked "Villery &
Boch/Mettlach, 7 02" .. **275.00**

Tray, oval, blue flowers and vines,
white ground, metal rim, handles, **$50**.

Photo courtesy of Joy Luke Auctions.

Tray, 11-1/4" d, metal gallery with
geometric cut-outs, ceramic
base with border and stylized
geometric pattern, white
ground, soft gray high gloss
glaze, blue accents, base
marked **200.00**

Tureen, cov, 11" w, Burgenland,
dark pink transfer, white
ground, marked "Mettlach,
Made by Villeroy & Boch"
.... **195.00**

Vase, 15" h, bulbous, cylindrical,
deep cobalt blue glaze,
splashes of drizzled white,
three handled SP mount cast
with leaves, berries, and
blossoms, molded, pierced
foot, vase imp "V" & "B," "S"
monogram, numbered, c1900,
price for pr................. **2,750.00**

WATCHES, POCKET

History: Pocket watches can be found in many places—from flea markets to the specialized jewelry auctions. Condition of movement is the first priority; design and detailing of the case is second.

Descriptions of pocket watches may include the size (16/0 to 20), number of jewels in the movement, whether the face is open or closed (hunter), and the composition (gold, gold filled, or some other metal). The movement is the critical element, since cases often were switched. However, an elaborate case, especially if gold, adds significantly to value.

Pocket watches designed to railroad specifications are desirable. They are between 16 and 18 in size, have a minimum of 17 jewels, adjust to at least five positions, and conform to many other specifications. All are open faced.

Study the field thoroughly before buying. There is a vast amount of literature, including books and newsletters from clubs and collectors.

Pocket, gentleman's

Aurora, Size 18, Roman numeral dial, lever set 15 jewel gilt movement #38691, Grade 3 1/2 Guild, second model, yellow goldfilled hunting case #5161726 .... **200.00**

Ball, Size 16, Arabic numeral dial, lever set 17 jewel nickel movement #134015, Official Standard, Waltham model, white goldfilled Illinois hunting case #51032 .... **500.00**

Borel, Size 19, Roman numeral dial, lever set 20 jewel gilt movement #15110, Minute Repeater, chronograph, 14 karat yellow gold hunting case #6947 .... **2,650.00**

Burlington, Size 16, open face Arabic numeral dial, lever set 17 jewel nickel movement #3447536, Illinois, yellow goldfilled case #5001237 .... **100.00**

Elgin

Size 6, Roman numeral dial, pendant set 7 jewel nickel movement # 10652232, first model, yellow goldfilled Wadsworth hunting case # 316391 .... **120.00**
Size 12, Arabic numeral dial, pendant set 17 jewel nickel movement #16472602, yellow goldfilled Dueber hunting case #9305829 .... **120.00**
Size 12, open face Arabic numeral dial, pendant set 19 jewel nickel movement #25254082, C.H. Hulburd 431, platinum case #103820 .... **1,100.00**
Size 16, open face Arabic numeral dial, lever set 19 jewel nickel movement #21235315, B.W. Raymond, yellow goldfilled case #8048 .... **215.00**

English, brass, key-wind, swing-out case, orig paper retailer's label "Thomas Harrison Silver-Smith Danville KY Clock and Watch Maker," iron forged chain and key, early 19th C **1,700.00**

Hamilton

Size 16, Arabic numeral dial, lever set 21 jewel nickel movement #776560, Grade 993, yellow goldfilled Illinois engraved hunting case #2922269 .... **330.00**
Size 16, open face Arabic numeral dial, lever set 21 jewel nickel movement #324343, Grade 960, model 960, 14 karat yellow goldfilled case # 5721 .... **570.00**
Size 18, open face Arabic dial, lever set 17 jewel nickel movement # 8023, Grade 936, silverode Keystone case # 9158568, for American Jewelry Co., Leadville, CO. **180.00**
Size 18, Roman numeral dial, lever set 17 jewel nickel movement #157179, Grade 925 The Union, yellow goldfilled hunting case **175.00**

Hampden

Size 16, Arabic numeral dial, lever set 17 jewel nickel movement #1890116, William McKinley, BRDG, in a yellow goldfilled hunting case #6028660 .... **165.00**
Size 16, open face Arabic numeral dial, lever set 23 jewel nickel movement #2801029, Grade 104, Bridge model, glass back nickel case **350.00**
Size 18, Roman numeral dial, lever set 17 jewel nickel movement #1332191, Adjusted, silverine Dueber hunting case #2942431 **90.00**

Howard

Size 12, open face Arabic numeral dial, pendant set 17 jewel nickel movement #1092624, Series 8, 14 karat yellow gold monogrammed case #121454 .... **360.00**
Size 16, open face Arabic numeral dial, lever set 21 jewel nickel movement #1361149, RR Chronometer Ser, white goldfilled Keystone case #1554922 .... **300.00**

Watch, pocket, Tiffany, hunting case, sterling silver, **$250.**

Photo courtesy of Joy Luke Auctions.

Illinois

Size 16, open face Arabic numeral dial, pendant set 17 jewel nickel movement #3136048, Texas Special, yellow goldfilled case #6287230 .... **120.00**
Size 16, open face Arabic numeral dial, lever set 21 jewel nickel movement #5036076, Bunn Special 60 HR 69, first model, 14 karat gold filled Bunn, special case by Wadsworth #7736676 .... **660.00**
Size 18, Roman numeral dial, lever set 11 jewel nickel movement #231676, yellow goldfilled hunting case #143231 .... **150.00**
Size 18, Roman numeral dial, lever set 15 jewel gilt movement #1165542, Grade 60, second model, for Sommer and Pierik, yellow goldfilled Philadelphia Watch Co. hunting case #4825167 .... **100.00**

Montgomery Ward

Size 18, open face Roman numeral dial, lever set 21 jewel nickel movement #1448074, Grade 61, sixth model, 10 karat yellow rolled gold plate Illinois case #7769495 .... **175.00**

Size 18, open face Roman numeral dial, pendant set 11 jewel nickel movement #757650, 20th C, silverine Dueber case #4280 ...... **75.00**

Waltham

Size 14, Roman numeral dial, pendant set 13 jewel nickel movement #3127180, Chronograph, first model, coin silver American hunting case #21280 .... **150.00**

Size 16, open face Arabic numeral dial, lever set 21 jewel nickel movement #20142536, Crescent St.U-D, model 1908, with wind indicator, yellow goldfilled case #9308103 .... **900.00**

Size 18, open face Arabic numeral dial with 24 hour time, lever set 21 jewel nickel movement #10559638, Crescent St., first model, yellow goldfilled American case #405850 .... **215.00**

Watches, pocket, ladies, hunting cases; first designed with decorated circular dial with Roman numerals and "Louis XIV hands," within engraved scenic case set in 18k yellow gold, key, wind and set; second designed with white circular dial with Roman numerals, "spade" hands, set in 14k yellow gold, **$450**.

Photo courtesy of Sloans & Kenyon Auctions.

Pocket, lady's

Betsy Ross, Size 0, open face Arabic numeral dial, pendant set 7 jewel nickel movement #861180, yellow goldfilled Keystone case #8186017 .... **100.00**

Elgin, Size 0, Roman numeral dial, pendant set 15 jewel nickel movement #8773791, first model, yellow goldfilled Wadsworth hunting case #667982 .... **120.00**

Meylan, C. H., 18k gold and enamel, openface, white enamel dial with black Arabic numerals, fancy scrolled hands, gray guilloche enamel bezel, cover enameled with gold flowers set with diamonds, suspended from platinum and purple guilloche enamel baton link chain, crystal replaced, minor enamel loss **850.00**

Unknown maker, retro, pink gold, hinged rect cover surmounted by rubies and diamonds, similarly set scroll and geometric shoulders, snake link bracelet, 6-1/4" l **750.00**

Vacheron & Constantin, 18k gold, hunting case, white enamel dial, Roman numerals, gilt bar movement, cylinder escapement, sgd on cuvette, engraved case, 10 size **350.00**

Waltham, 14k yg, hunting case, white enamel dial, Arabic numeral indicators, subsidiary seconds dial, Lady Waltham jeweled nickel movement by A.W.W. Co., floral engraved case no. 224709, 0 size, gold ropetwist chain **300.00**

Whipperman, A. J., Idaho Falls, Idaho, 14k yg, hunting case, white enamel dial, black Arabic numeral indicators, subsidiary seconds dial, 15 jewel nickel movement by Rode Watch Co., floral engraved case dec with pale pink guilloche enamel, old mine-cut diamond in center, signed Gruen, dust cover inscribed, "Father to Elsie 1914," 0 size, fancy 14k yg curb link and pink enamel baton link chain **180.00**

WATCHES, WRIST

History: The definition of a wristwatch is simply "a small watch that is attached to a bracelet or strap and is worn around the wrist." However, a watch on a bracelet is not necessarily a wristwatch. The key is the ability to read the time. A true wristwatch allows you to read the time at a glance, without making any other motions. Early watches on an arm bracelet had the axis of their dials, from 6 to 12, perpendicular to the band. Reading them required some extensive arm movements.

The first true wristwatch appeared about 1850. However, the key date is 1880 when the stylish, decorative wristwatch appeared and almost universal acceptance occurred. The technology to create the wristwatch existed in the early 19th century with Brequet's shock-absorbing "Parachute System" for automatic watches and Ardien Philipe's winding stem.

Shoppers at Atlantique City who specialized in collecting pocket watches might have been tempted to add this interesting trade sign to their collection for **$650**.

Gentleman's

Boucheron, dress tank, A250565, white gold, reeded bezel and dial, invisible clasp, black leather Boucheron strap, French hallmarks, orig leather pouch **2,150.00**

Bueche-Girod, 18 k yg, gold curved dial, black Roman numerals, 17 jewel movement, integrated textural mesh bracelet; dial, movement, case back and clasp all signed "Bueche-Girod," 39.80 dwts **360.00**

Cartier, 18k hg, rect convex white dial, black Roman numerals, round gold bezel, black leather strap... **1,380.00**

Concord, Delirium, 18k gold, round goldtone dial without indicators, flat rect bezel, quartz movement, Swiss hallmarks, 9" l orig crocodile band **1,265.00**

Garsons, 14k gold, sq goldtone dial with simulated jewel indicators, 17-jewel nickel movement, subsidiary seconds dial, 8-1/4" l integrated mesh band **345.00**

Hamilton, 18k yg, silverized rect dial, applied Arabic numerals, subsidiary seconds dial, nineteen jewel movement, black leather strap.................
.... **180.00**

Jurgensen, Jules, dress, 14k white gold, Swiss movement, silvertone brushed dial, abstract indicators, diamond-set bevel, black faux alligator strap.......................... **290.00**

Le Coultre, Futurematic, goldtone dial, subsidiary seconds dial, power reserve indicator, 10k yg-filled mount, lizard strap, 1950s **425.00**

Longines, pale green rect dial, applied diamond set platinum Arabic numerals with small round and baguette cut diamonds, fifteen jewel adjusted movement #3731402, case back engraved and dated 1935
.... **2,035.00**

Nardin, Ulysse, 14k yg, chronometer, goldtone dial, luminescent quarter sections, applied abstract and Arabic numeral indicators, subsidiary seconds dial, lugs with scroll accents, leather strap, discoloration and scratches to dial............................ **290.00**

Omega, 18k yg, round cream dial, goldtone Arabic numeral and abstract indicators, heavy mesh bracelet, mild soil to dial, 44.80 dwt **460.00**

Patek Philippe, 18k yg
Round ivory tone dial with stick indicators, later 18k gold band, c1960 .... **2,700.00**
Silvertone metal dial with gold abstract numeral indicators joined by curved lugs to brown leather strap, replaced closure **2,820.00**

Wristwatch, gentleman's, Hamilton, gold-filled shield shape case, 17 jewels, leather band, **$350**.

Wristwatch photos courtesy of Joy Luke Auctions.

Silvertone metal dial with raised indicators, subsidiary seconds dial, movement #977714, reference # 2470, triple sgd, leather strap, c1949..................... **6,230.00**

Rolex, Oyster Perpetual
14k yg, goldtone dial, abstract indicators, sweep second hand, ostrich strap, slight spotting to dial .. **850.00**
Stainless steel, Air King, silvertone dial, applied abstract indicators, sweep second hand, oyster bracelet with deployant clasp, discoloration to dial, scratches to crystal **575.00**

Vacheron & Constantin, 18k gold, white round dial, abstract numeral indicators, 17-jewel nickel movements, 7-1/4" l associated 18k gold brickwork band........ **1,495.00**

Wristwatch, gentleman's, Raymond Weil double dial, rectangular case, leather band, original fitted case, **$395**.

Lady's

Bulova, small round dial with Arabic and baton numerals, 17 jewel movement, 14k white gold case and bracelet set with single cut and baguette cut diamonds weighing approx 1.50 carats total
.... **750.00**

Cartier, Tank Francaise, 18k yg, rect ivory tone dial with Roman numeral indicators, gold band with integral clasp
.... **5,875.00**

Chanel, 18k yg, black and white dial with Roman numeral indicators, onyx cabochon winding stem, enclosing Swiss quartz movement, adjustable black alligator band and 18k gold clasp, sgd
.... **1,300.00**

Elgin, platinum, rect ivory tone dial with Arabic numeral indicators, 17 jewel movement, bezel, lugs, and bracelet set with single-cut and baguette diamonds, 6-1/2" l..................... **1,410.00**

Gruen, Art Deco, platinum, rect silvertone dial, black Arabic numerals, bezel enhanced with 32 circular-cut diamonds, mesh strap edged by box-set single-cut diamonds, highlighted by diamond-set floret shoulders, 6-1/4" l..................... **4,225.00**

Hamilton, platinum, rect ivory tone dial with Arabic numeral indicators, 17 jewel movement, bezel and lugs with single-cut and baguette diamonds, joining cord band. missing winding stem. **300.00**

Helbros Watch Co., 17 jewels, Art Deco, combination of old European and single cut diamonds, approx 1 ct, case hinged to allow better contour when worn, calibre French cut sapphires, curved crystal, platinum setting **995.00**

Movado
18k yg, rect gold tone dial with arabic numeral and dot indicators, 15 jewel movement, 14k gold link band
.... **765.00**
Stainless steel, yg, mother-of-pearl dial, diamond set bezel containing thirty-six round brilliant cut diamonds weighing approx 0.72 carat total, quartz movement, deployment buckle..... **550.00**

Patek Philippe & Co., rect gold metallic enamel dial, Arabic and dot numerals, movement #940981, case # 509109; dial, movement, 18k yg, case and bracelet sgd "Patek-Phillipe & Co Geneve," c1940, 8-1/2" l, 46.60 dwt............... **3,350.00**

Rolex, Oyster Perpetual, stainless steel, round blue dial with stick indicators, date aperture, original band with integral clasp, boxed, crystal scratched............... **1,530.00**

Swiss, 18k yg, Swiss movement, manual wind, domed bezel, goldtone dial, black Roman numerals, hallmark, leather strap............................ **920.00**

Tiffany & Co., Art Deco, platinum and diamond, rect ivory-tone dial with Arabic numeral indicators, 17 jewel International Watch Company movement, bezel and lugs with bead-set diamond melee, engraved accents, black cord band, 7" l, case with Krementz hallmark **940.00**

WATERFORD

History: Waterford crystal is high-quality flint glass commonly decorated with cuttings. The original factory was established at Waterford, Ireland, in 1729. Glass made before 1830 is darker than the brilliantly clear glass of later production. The factory closed in 1852. One hundred years later it reopened and continues in production today.

For more information, see *Warman's Glass*, 4th edition.

Bowl, 9-3/4" d, Kileen pattern **260.00**

Cake plate, 10" d, 5-1/4" h, sunburst center, geometric design............................ **85.00**

Cake server, cut-glass handle, orig box........................ **80.00**

Champagne flute, 6" h, Coleen pattern, 12-pc set **450.00**

Decanter set, decanter, four tumblers, fitted wooden tray with brass trim, **$195**.

Christmas ornament, Twelve Days of Christmas Series, crystal, orig box, dated bag, orig sticker, brochure
1982, Partridge in Pear Tree **450.00**
1985, second, two turtle doves.......................... **250.00**
1987, four calling birds **200.00**

Compote, 5-1/2" h, allover diamond cutting above double wafer stem, pr **400.00**

Creamer and sugar, 4" h creamer, 3-3/4" d sugar, Tralee pattern **85.00**

Decanter, orig stopper, 12-3/4" h, allover diamond cutting, monogram, pr.. **300.00**

Honey jar, cov **75.00**

Lamp, 23" h, 13" d umbrella shade, blunt diamond cutting, Pattern L 1122.............. **450.00**

Napkin ring, 2" h, 12-pc set **225.00**

Tumbler, Colleen, set of six, orig box.............................. **400.00**

Vase, 6" h, diamond pattern, wreath around center, sgd **225.00**

WAVE CREST

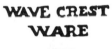

History: The C. F. Monroe Company of Meriden, Connecticut, produced the opal glassware known as Wave Crest from 1898 until World War I. The company bought the opaque, blown-molded glass blanks from the Pairpoint Manufacturing Co. of New Bedford, Massachusetts, and other glassmakers, including European factories. The Monroe company then decorated the blanks, usually with floral patterns. Trade names used were "Wave Crest Ware," "Kolva," and "Nakara."

Biscuit jar, cov, unmarked
5-1/2" d, 5-1/2" h, pink and white background, melon ribbed, hp flowers **250.00**
6-1/2" d, Helmschmied swirl opaque white and tan body, red enameled flowers . **460.00**
8" h, white ground, fern dec **200.00**

Bonbon, 7" h, 6" w, Venetian scene, multicolored landscape, dec rim, satin lining missing........... **1,200.00**

Box, cov
3" d, Double Scroll, aqua blue tint, hp florals, sgd, no lining **275.00**
5-3/4" l, ormolu feet and handles, red banner back stamp, c1890.............. **225.00**

Lismore pattern, 12 5-1/8" h sherry glasses, **$350**; 11 4-1/8" h champagne/tall sherbet glasses, **$265**; 23 3-3/8" h old fashioned tumblers, **$525**; 12 4-1/8" h cocktail/liquor glasses, **$200**; 11 3-1/2" h cordial glasses, **$250**; 12 5-7/8" h claret wine glasses, **$325**; eight 6-7/8" h water goblets, **$250**; three 4-3/8" h double old fashioned glasses, **$95**.
Photo courtesy of Alderfer Auction Co.

6" d, heart-shape, opaque tan glass body, dec with red and yellow mums, Belle Ware, #4625/10 .... **460.00**

7" w, pink florals, fancy ormolu fittings **800.00**

7-1/4" d, 3-3/34" h, Baroque Shell, Moorish Fantasy design, raised pink-gold rococo scrolls, fancy Arabic designs of pale turquoise and natural opaque white, lace-like network of raised white enamel beads, satin lining missing **1,250.00**

Cigar humidor, 8-3/4" h, blue body, single-petaled pink rose, pink "Cigar" signature, pewter collar, bail, and lid, flame-shaped finial, sgd "Kelva" **685.00**

Letter box, decorated with pink flowers, brass trim, 5-1/2" w, 4" h, **$350**.

Photo courtesy of Joy Luke.

Collar jar, opaque white, molded scrolls, hand-painted purple and white chrysanthemums, light beige silk lining, stenciled label on bottom "Wavecrest Trademark," 9" d, 6" h, **$525**.

Photo courtesy of Garth's Auctions, Inc.

Cracker jar, 5-1/4" d, 10-1/2" h, blue and white hp florals, green and brown leaves, white Johnny jump-ups, puffy egg crate mold **700.00**

Creamer and sugar, 4-1/2" h, Helmschmeid pattern, pink stemmed flowers **350.00**

Dresser box, cov

4" d, six-sided form, beaded enameling, unmarked, c1890 .... **250.00**

4-1/4" d, enameled violets, red banner back stamp, c1890 .... **185.00**

5-3/4" d, swirl mold, enameled florals, red banner back stamp, c1890 .... **230.00**

5-3/4" l, egg crate mold, enameled florals, unmarked, c1890 .... **245.00**

6-3/4" sq, 3-3/4" h, egg crate mold, hp florals, orig lining, red banner back stamp **320.00**

6-3/4" w, 6-3/4" h, egg crate mold, hp mums, shaded amber ground, ormolu mounted feet, reticulated shoulder, red banner back stamp, c1890 .... **2,425.00**

7" h, swirl mold, enameled florals, red banner back stamp, c1890, hairline in lid **210.00**

7" h, swirl mold, hp florals, unmarked, c1890 .... **260.00**

7-1/2" h, rococo mold, hp florals, orig interior, black block mark, c1890 ...... **525.00**

8" d, florals, blue ground, mkd "Nakara C.F.M. Co.," c1890 .... **900.00**

Dresser jar, silver-plated lid, apricot colored ground, white and blue flowers, scrolls, **$190**.

Photo courtesy of Joy Luke Auctions.

Ewer, lavender, figural woman on handle, ornate base **225.00**

Ferner, 6-3/4" d, egg crate mold, enameled blue flowers, four lion emb feet, orig liner **520.00**

Mustard jar, cov, spoon, green ground, floral dec, unmarked **140.00**

Pin dish, open
3-1/2" d, 1-1/2" h, pink and white, swirled, floral dec, unmarked **35.00**
4-1/4" d, 2" h, pink and white, eggcrate mold, blue violets dec, marked **80.00**
5" d, 1-1/2" h, white, scrolls, pink floral dec, marked. **80.00**

Plate, 7" d, reticulated border, pond lily dec, shaded pale blue ground **750.00**

Portrait box, cov, 4-1/4" d, swirl mold, painted florals and cupid, block mark, c1890 .... **250.00**

Salt and pepper shakers, pr Swirled, light yellow ground, floral dec, unmarked **75.00**
Tulip, brown and white ground, birds and floral dec **70.00**

Sugar shaker, 5" h, conical, polychrome fern dec .. **335.00**

Syrup pitcher, Helmschmied Swirl, ivory-colored body, blue and white floral dec, smoky-gray leafy branches, SP lid and collar.................... **485.00**

Tray, 4-1/2" d, 1-3/4" h, flattened circular form, molded scrolled designs, hp floral dec In reserves, emb collar with openwork handles, sgd, discoloration to metal ... **45.00**

Trinket dish, 1-1/2" x 5", blue and red flowers........... **175.00**

Urn
6-1/2" h, egg shaped body, short pedestal, two ornate handles, centered raised gold, floral bouquet, pale green tinted ground, gold patina on metal fittings **445.00**
6-1/2" h, horn shape over acorn shaped body, short pedestal, two ornate handles, centered raised gold, floral bouquet, sea foam green tinted ground, gold patina on metal fittings **445.00**

Vase
7-1/2" h, rococo mold, hp florals, ormolu ft base, red banner back stamp, c1890 .... **275.00**
7-1/2" h, swirl mold, ftd ormolu base, red banner back stamp, c1890......................... **250.00**
12-1/2" h, white wild rose blossoms, scattered sprays of gray rose buds, cobalt blue ground, gilt ormolu handles **2,450.00**

Tobacco jar, opaque white, yellow diagonal bands alternating with white bands, hand-painted pink roses and "Tobacco," brass collar, red label on bottom "Wavecrest" on flag, 5-1/4" h, **$365**.

Photo courtesy of Garth's Auctions, Inc.

12-1/2" h, white orchid blossoms with blue-gray shading, cobalt blue ground, gilt ormolu handles .. **2,450.00**

Vase ornament, 6-1/4" h, light blue, detailed hand enameled dec, fine ormolu mounts **150.00**

WEATHER VANES

History: A weather vane indicates wind direction. The earliest known examples were found on late 17th-century structures in the Boston area. The vanes were handcrafted of wood, copper, or tin. By the last half of the 19th century, weather vanes adorned farms and houses throughout the nation. Mass-produced vanes of cast iron, copper, and sheet metal were sold through mail-order catalogs or at country stores.

The champion vane is the rooster—in fact, the name weathercock is synonymous with weather vane—but the styles and patterns are endless. Weathering can affect the same vane differently; for this reason, patina is a critical element in collectible vanes.

Reproduction Alert:
Reproductions of early models exist, are being aged, and then sold as originals.

Cow, America, 19th C, cast zinc head on molded copper full-body figure, painted rust color with traces of gilt, raised on iron rod and wood shaft with cast iron directionals, imperfections, figure 42-1/2" l, 25" h, 94-1/2" h shaft, **$14,100**.

Photo courtesy of Skinner, Inc.

Allen, Ethan, molded and gilded copper, attributed to J. F. Fiske & Co **68,500.00**

Arrow
31" l, 17" h, copper, sphere finial, old gilded surface, wear, minor dents **590.00**
36" l, 16" h, gilt copper, ball finial, weathered gilt surface, no stand, dents **360.00**
60" l, 29" h, copper, spire and belted ball finial, verdigris surface, no stand, dents, several bullet holes **950.00**

Banner
15-3/4" l, 37" h, sheet iron, iron ball finial on shaft above banner, heart and oval cutouts, weathered black paint, stand.............. **1,645.00**
31-1/4" l, 49-1/2" h, sheet copper scrolled banner with pierced "1921," cut-out bird perched on end, copper directionals, America, c1921, sq white painted wooden plinth, verdigris surface, minor imperfections........... **2,350.00**

Bird and fish, 18-1/2" w, 19" h, molded metal, full bodied, bird flies with aid of propellers above fish, marble eyes, unpainted weathered gray surface, Illinois, early 20th C, tall stand **1,150.00**

Cow, full bodied, molded metal **1,475.00**

Deer, running, green patinated copper, hollow body, 19th C, 33" l, missing one antler **32,000.00**

Eagle
15-1/2" l, 14-3/4" w, 9-1/8" h, gilt copper, outstretched wings perched on belted sphere over arrow directional, old gilt-copper verdigris surface, no stand, small loss on arrow feather **1,100.00**
21" wing span, 18-1/2" h, copper, full bodied, cast zinc feet, wooden base, one foot loose, arrow bent........ **250.00**

Eagle, America, 19th C, copper, repairs, leaning against table leg, **$950**.

Photo courtesy of Wiederseim Associates, Inc.

Fire wagon, 40" l, 29-1/4" h, painted copper, two horses, driver, steam fire engine, iron supports on underside, red, black, and gold paint, attributed to I. W. Cushing & Sons, Waltham, MA, late 19th C, including stand, imperfections......... **15,275.00**

Fish
12-3/4" l, 3-1/4" h, carved wood, full bodied, tail wrapped with lead sheeting, tacked button eyes, Midwestern U.S., late 19th C, remnant of post, minor losses, with stand **2,645.00**
26" l, 6-1/2" h, white painted carved wood and sheet metal, America, mid-20th C, tall stand........................ **1,495.00**
27" l, 6" h, carved and painted wood, salmon orange, chamfered edge, tin reinforced carved bracket, Wakefield, MA, 19th C, inscribed "this set on a cedar tree near our farm before the Civil War," with stand **1,150.00**

Gamecock, 17-1/2" l, 18-1/2" h, molded copper, emb sheet copper tail, weathered gilt surface, no stand, repair on neck, bullet hole on breast **4,995.00**

Heart and feather, 76-3/4" l, 13-1/4" h, sheet iron, found in New York state, late 18th C, fine rust and overall pitting, with stand **4,900.00**

Heron, molded copper **39,950.00**

Horse

17-3/4" h, running, copper, verdigris patina, traces of gilt, America, late 19th C, includes copper sphere, no stand, dents, small seam separations, 17-3/4" h **2,350.00**

24" l, 18-1/2" h, zinc torso, copper ears, legs, and body, corrugated copper tail, attributed to J. Howard & Co., West Bridgewater, MA, third quarter 19th C, old surface with vestiges of gilt, no stand, old repair on one leg, wear, minor dents **7,650.00**

29" l, 14" h, running, molded copper and cast zinc, verdigris surface, attributed to A. L. Jewell & Co., Waltham, MA, 1850-67, no stand, minor dents, seam separation **4,625.00**

32" l, 17" h, running, painted copper, flattened full bodied, older darkened putty painted surface, traces of gilt, no stand, dents, bullet hole repairs **1,410.00**

34" l, 25-1/2" h, prancing, molded copper, weathered gilt surface, vestiges of sizing, with stand, imperfections **4,115.00**

38-1/4" l, 24-1/4" h, running, sheet iron, one side with gilt surface, other side gilt with black painted details, late 19th/early 20th C, including stand, minor wear **3,100.00**

41-1/2" l, 21" h, running, copper head, hollow molded full body, no stand, gilt wear, minor dent................ **4,115.00**

61-1/2" l, 23-5/8" h, running, full-bodied, zinc, mounted on a hollow zinc rod with vestiges of gilt in the recesses, black metal stand, minor separations, repaired bullet holes, America, 19th C **8,815.00**

Horse and jockey, 31-1/2" l, 22-3/4" h, copper, old yellow sizing surface, no stand, minor dents on ears and jockey's head **9,400.00**

Horse and rider, molded sheet iron, hollow body, orig mustard painted surface, wear, cracks **6,465.00**

Polo player, molded copper **193,000.00**

Quill, copper **4,950.00**

Pig, 32" l, 20-1/4" h, molded copper, weathered dark verdigris surface, traces of gilt, stand, late 19th C, imperfections **32,300.00**

Plow, 38-1/4" l, 13-1/2" h, iron and bronze, old surface, no stand........................ **3,415.00**

Pointing hand, 23" l, 35-1/4" h, sheet iron and wood, two wood finials on iron shaft, hand and sunburst sheet iron motif, no stand, imperfections **2,235.00**

Rooster, Hamburg, molded copper, attributed to L.W. Cushing & Sons, Waltham, Massachusetts, late 19th C, flattened full-body figure, verdigris patina with traces of gilt, repairs, bullet holes, dents, 29" l, 28" h, **$25,850**.

Photo courtesy of Skinner, Inc.

Rooster

Cast iron, 24" w, 23" h, two pc cast iron body, sheet steel tail feathers, old red paint, good detail, on later notched wooden base needs re-welding **6,670.00**

Molded copper, L. W. Cushing & Sons **41,125.00**

Schooner, 39" l, 23-3/8" h, wooden, hull painted red and black, cream colored sail, wire rigging, America, 20th C, wooden stand, wear ... **275.00**

Sloop, gaff-rigged, molded copper, verdigris surface, America, early 20th C, no stand........................ **4,415.00**

Stag, leaping

20" l, 19" h, molded copper, zinc antlers, old gilt surface, black metal stand, America, 19th C **8,225.00**

21-1/2" l, 17-3/4" h, molded copper, old regilded surface, mounted on wooden stand **5,290.00**

55-1/2" l, 41-5/8" h, molded copper, full body, attributed to A. I. Harris & Son, Waltham, MA, including stand, regilded old surface............. **12,925.00**

Steam locomotive, molded copper, unknown American maker, late 19th C.. **237,000.00**

WEBB, THOMAS & SONS

For more information, see *Warman's Glass*, 4th edition.

History: Thomas Webb & Sons was established in 1837 in Stourbridge, England. The company probably is best known for its very beautiful English cameo glass. However, many other types of colored art glass were produced, including enameled, iridescent, heavily ornamented, and cased.

Biscuit jar, cov, 6" d, 7-1/4" h, white cameo dec, single petaled blossoms, leafed branch, ruby red ground, silver plate fittings.... **2,950.00**

Bowl

2" h, Burmese, lilac, prunus dec **6,000.00**

4-1/2" d, Burmese, silver rim, sgd "Thomas Webb & Sons" **110.00**

5" d, alabaster, ruffled rim, hp silver and gold foliage and butterfly, turquoise int. **250.00**

Bride's bowl, 10" d, hobnail, creamy opal body, rose int., ruffled rim **325.00**

Cabinet vase, 2" h, rose ground, cameo carved white flower and butterfly, rim roughness **400.00**

Cane handle, 3-1/2" h, globular form, cameo carved, intricate Moorish design **800.00**

Cologne bottle, 5" h, Peachblow, bulbous, blue and white daisies, leafy green branches, two amethyst butterflies in flight, hallmarks on threaded ovoid cap **950.00**

Cream pitcher

3-1/4" h, sepia to pale tan ground, heavy gold burnished prunus blossoms, butterfly on back, gold rim and base, clear glass handle with brushed gold **385.00**

3-3/4" h, 2-1/2" d, bulbous, round mouth, brown satin, cream lining, applied frosted handle **210.00**

Epergne, canary yellow center inverted pyriform vase with everted rim and rigaree collar, flanked by two peachblow apples, four downward curving vaseline leaves with amber stems, 10-3/4" h, shaped mirrored plateau, ex-Maude Feld, **$18,000.**

Photo courtesy of Early Auction Co.

Epergne

10-3/4" h, canary yellow center inverted pyriform vase with everted rim and rigaree collar, flanked by two peachblow apples, four downward curving vaseline leaves with amber stems, shaped mirrored plateau, ex-Maude Feld............ **18,000.00**

11-1/2" h, Burmese, Hawthorne pattern, central post insert and three ruffled rim inserts, metal four-ftd base and holder, small chip **900.00**

Ewer, 9" h, 4" d, satin, deep green shading to off-white, gold enameled leaves and branches, three naturalistic applies, applied ivory handle, long spout, numbered base **425.00**

Figure, 3" l, 1-1/2" h, pig, solid Burmese body, pink tint to hind quarters, curly tail, four feet, ears, and snout, Webb **750.00**

Flask, 11-5/8" h, fish shape, lemon yellow glass overlaid in white, wheel carved features, sterling silver fish tail screw lid, cameo carved "Rd. 15711," lid imp "Sterling," hairline and cameo loss at mouth...................... **9,500.00**

Lamp, kerosene, 15" h, Burmese shade and base hand dec in Woodbine pattern, base with stamped trademark **4,250.00**

Perfume bottle, lay down style 2-3/4" h, circular, ivory, overall cameo flowers, emb flip lid, orig stopper **1,700.00**
10" l, cameo carved leafy ferns and butterfly on reverse, monogrammed silver lid **1,650.00**

Plate, Burmese, gold prunus blossom decoration with butterfly, scalloped edge, price for pair, **$325.**

Rose bowl, 2-1/4" h, 2-1/2" h, Burmese, amethyst flowers, green and brown foliage, price for pr **690.00**

Salad fork and spoon, 12" l, ivory ground, cameo carved garden of stemmed flowers, hallmarked "F & Co." with crown and shield **700.00**

Scent bottle

3" d, 3-3/4" h, Burmese, brilliant gold dec, restored gold cap **1,235.00**

Sweetmeats jar, ivory body, molded trailing branches, traces of red paint, silver-plated bale handle and lid with spoon opening, molded signature in banner "Thomas Webb & Sons," 3 3/4" d, 3" h, plus handle, **$425.**

Photo courtesy of Garth's Auctions, Inc.

3" d, 4" h, Peacock Eye MOP, pearl white ground, sterling silver fittings, screw on cap mkd "T. W. & S," hallmarks for 1902, "RD 58374" inscribed in base, minute dents in cap **950.00**

Sociable, 8-3/4" h, Burmese, center crimped rim vase, three round covered dishes, delicate shading and dec, gilt metal ftd base.......... **9,000.00**

Sugar shaker, 6-1/2" h, herringbone MOP, tapering ovoid body shades from citron to pearl, British sterling silver cap with hallmark, acid stamped signature on base **500.00**

Vase, peachblow, raised rim of rounded bowl of opal glass cased to shaded peach, gilt flowering vines, two insects, signed "TIFFANY & CO. PARIS EXHIBITION 1889 THOMAS WEBB & SONS," 4-1/8" h, **$560.**

Photo courtesy of Skinner, Inc.

Vase

2-3/4" h, Alexandrite, honeycomb.............. **2,700.00**
5-1/4" h, peachblow, tapering body, short everted neck, shades from deep cranberry to satin opal, allover applied coralene dec **200.00**

Vase, cameo, Japanese form, large blossoms, single butterfly in white, martelé ground, shading from orange at base to red, neck with Japanese style border, unmarked, 9-1/2" h, **$3,000.**

Photo courtesy of David Rago Auctions, Inc.

6-1/4" h, bulbous stick, opal body, cinnamon iced crystal overlay, hand enameled gold flowering vine, numbered "1095-4P5aa" **225.00**

7" h, shouldered, body shades from lime green rim to opal base, hp butterfly framed with leafy branch, mkd with registration number 676/5 R167 .... **350.00**

7" h, tapering ovoid, Prussian blue body, cameo carved opaque white floral cutting, cameo rings at top and base, butterfly on reverse, sgd **1,700.00**

7-1/2" h, bulbous baluster, gold ground, carved white geraniums, carved white coral bells on reverse, sgd "Webb" **1,750.00**

7-1/2" h, shouldered, deep crimson, enameled song birds perched on ginkgo flowering branches, numbered "893/7 P268," slight scratching on reverse **250.00**

7-3/4" h, bulbous stick, tightly scalloped crimped rim, ivory ground, cascading honey-suckle dec, butterfly on reverse, sgd with half moon

"Thos Webb and Sons" **1,000.00**

8-1/4" h, Burmese, trumpet, pink petaled rim shades to satin yellow, imp trademark **350.00**

9" h, white blossoms and buds, carved pink folds and veins, frosted clear ground, butterfly on reverse, imp "Thomas Webb & Sons Cameo" **3,450.00**

16" h, peachblow, bulbous body extends to knopped conical neck, crimson to pink shading, enameled bird, butterfly, stylized flowers, gilt scrolls **1,200.00**

WEDGWOOD

History: In 1754, Josiah Wedgwood and Thomas Whieldon of Fenton Vivian, Staffordshire, England, became partners in a pottery enterprise. Their products included marbled, agate, tortoiseshell, green glaze, and Egyptian black wares. In 1759, Wedgwood opened his own pottery at the Ivy House works, Burslem. In 1764, he moved to the Brick House (Bell Works) at Burslem. The pottery concentrated on utilitarian pieces.

Between 1766 and 1769, Wedgwood built the famous works at Etruria. Among the most-renowned products of this plant were the Empress Catherina of Russia dinner service (1774) and the Portland Vase (1790s). The firm also made caneware, unglazed earthenwares (drabwares), piecrust wares, variegated and marbled wares, black basalt (developed in 1768), Queen's or creamware, and Jasperware (perfected in 1774).

Bone china was produced under the direction of Josiah Wedgwood II between 1812 and 1822 and revived in 1878.

Moonlight luster was made from 1805 to 1815. Fairyland luster began in 1920. All luster production ended in 1932.

A museum was established at the Etruria pottery in 1906. When Wedgwood moved to its modern plant at Barlaston, North Staffordshire, the museum was expanded.

Miscellaneous, dinnerware set, cream colored, service for eight plus serving pieces, **$495.**

Photo courtesy of Alderfer Auction Co.

Agate ware

Candleholder, 6-1/2" h, surface agate, applied creamware drapery swags, black basalt base, wafer Wedgwood & Bentley mark, c1775, restored chip to socle **1,495.00**

Vase, cov, 9-1/2" h, solid agate, creamware sibyl finials, traces of gilding, black basalt base, imp wafer Wedgwood & Bentley marks, c1770, gilt rim wear, covers with rim chips, nicks to bases, pr **7,500.00**

Artist designed

Bowl, 8-1/8" d, Norman Wilson "Unique Ware" design, moonstone ground exterior, interior with translucent green glaze shading to blue center, impressed mark, England, 1930-60 .... **400.00**

Inkstand, Keith Murray design, 10-1/8" l, rect form pen tray with shallow wells and central cov box supporting two inkpots, matte green ground, imp and printed marks, c1936, slight chip under cover's rim **590.00**

Basalt, black, tea set, covered teapot (finial missing), creamer and sugar, $195.

Jug, 8" h, Keith Murray design, celadon slip, cream colored ground, imp and printed marks, c1940............... **210.00**
Vase, Keith Murray design 6" h, globular, engine turned banding, imp and printed marks, c1935.............. **650.00**
7-1/4" h, straw glaze, horizontally turned body, printed mark, c1940 ... **765.00**

Basalt

Bough pot, cov, 7" h, scrolled handles terminating in ram's heads, pierced disc lid with removable candle nozzle, imp mark, mid-19th C, restored nozzle and one handle **1,265.00**
Bowl, 10-1/8" d, engine turned dec, imp mark, early 20th C **230.00**
Bust, 14" h, Horace, mounted on waisted circular socle, titled on reverse, impressed Wedgwood & Bentley marks to bust and base, c1775 .... **3,100.00**
Candlestick, 11-1/2" h, Ceres, modeled holding cornucopia form candle sconce and mounted to stepped circular base, imp title and mark, 19th C, restored candle nozzle, rim nicks to base **1,265.00**
Canopic jar, cov, 10" h, bands of hieroglyphs and zodiac symbols in relief on jar, cover modeled as Egyptian head, impressed marks, c1867, price for pr, restored **3,820.00**
Cream jug, 4-3/8" h, Encaustic dec, green, black and white enamels, leaf and berry swags terminating at ribbon bows, below gilt trimmed band of foliage, impressed mark, early 19th C ... **1,800.00**

Crocus pot and tray, 9-3/4" l, hedgehog shape, imp marks, c1800, repaired chips **920.00**
Cup and saucer, 5" d saucer, iron red and white banded palmette borders, Encaustic dec, imp lower case mark, late 18th C, slight enamel flake to saucer rim ... **1,265.00**
Figure
9-1/2" h, Venus, standing nude woman modeled by tree trunk on circular base, impressed title and mark, 19th C **950.00**
11-1/2" h, Rousseau, standing figure modeled holding bunch of flowers in one hand and walking stick in other, impressed upper-lower case mark, late 18th C, chip to end of flower bunch, stick possibly replaced **4,000.00**
12-1/4" h, Adonis, standing nude male modeled with cloth over his shoulder, impressed mark, 20th C **2,235.00**
Hanging flower vase, 7-3/8" h, bottle shape, overhead loop handle, impressed mark, early 19th C **1,765.00**
Inkstand, 2-1/4" h sq shaped inkpot with insert, relief of classical figures bordered in oak leaves, gilted and bronzed, impressed marks, c1875, corner footrim nick, wear to gilt at top rim **5,875.00**
Jug, 7-1/4" h, central putti-relief between bands of engine turning, mask head to handle terminal, metal mounts, imp lower case mark, late 19th C **2,875.00**
Lamp, 8-3/8" h, vestal and reading, cov, female figure seated on oval lamps, applied acanthus leaves and

bellflowers, imp marks, 19th C, slight flake to book of reading lamp, ball finial reglued, finial and pitcher missing on vestal lamp, rim chip repair, price for pr **920.00**
Miniature, bust, 1-3/4" h, Zeus, half-bust modeled wearing crown, 19th C, impressed mark, mounted to silver collar with screw thread **500.00**
Model
2-3/4" h, bulldog, glass eyes, by Ernest Light, imp mark, c1915, imp nick to ear **345.00**
11-1/4" h, Sphinx, female figure, lion body, stepped rect base, imp mark, early 19th C, chips to footrim and headdress **865.00**
Plaque
4-1/4" l, oval, classical figures in relief depicting seasons, impressed marks, 19th C, price for pr, mounted to velvet lined wood frames **825.00**
5" x 6-1/4", self-framed, oval, relief representing Day and Night, impressed marks, 19th C, mounted in gilt wood frames, price for pr..... **765.00**
5" x 6-1/2", self-framed, oval, relief representing Day and Night, impressed marks, early 19th C, mounted in velvet lined painted wood frames, price for pr.................. **450.00**
6-1/2" x 8-1/2", oval, relief depicting groups of three Graces, impressed marks, 19th C, price for pr **900.00**

Miscellaneous, plate, Ben Franklin, embossed portrait medallion and laurel garland, back stamped "Univ of PA Bicentennial, 1740-1940, The Young Franklin, drawn by Roy F. Carson, '23, Wedgwood, Etruria, England," Boston importer's stamp, **$125.**
Photo courtesy of Wiederseim Associates, Inc.

Portrait medallion, oval 2-1/2" x 3-1/4", Martin Heinrich Klaproth, German chemist, black basalt, applied rosso antico bust above an impressed title, impressed mark, c1815 .... **650.00**
3" x 3-3/4", Oliver Cromwell, black basalt, relief bust above impressed title, scooped back, impressed mark, Wedgwood & Bentley mark, c1779, slight edge nick **650.00**
3-1/8" x 4", Captain Cook, black basalt, relief bust above impressed title, scooped back, self-framed, impressed Wedgwood & Bentley mark, c1779, shallow back edge chips **4,410.00**
Potpourri, cov, 13" h, globular, upturned loop handles, enamel and gilt dec tropical bird and flowers in famille rose style, impressed mark, c1820, finial possibly re-cemented at join, inner disc lid missing **3,055.00**
Slave Medallion, 1-1/8" x 1-1/4", oval, slave relief centering verse "Am I not a man and a brother?" imp mark and date, c1891 .... **635.00**
Rum kettle, 5-3/4" h, body with bacchanalian boys in relief above engine turned band, shaped bale handle, Sybil finial, imp lower case mark, late 18th C, restored chip on cov rim and finial **600.00**
Tankard, 4-1/4" h, cylindrical form, applied classical figures in relief, imp mark, restored rim chip, 19th C **360.00**
Tea cup and saucer, Iris Kenlock Ware, enamel dec floral design, imp mark, c1895 .... **815.00**
Teapot, cov, 3-3/4" h, oval, molded arabesque floral body, sunflower finial, imp mark, early 19th C, rim nick to cover, tip of spout slightly ground **290.00**

Carrara

Bust, 14-3/4" h, Stephenson, mounted on waisted circular socle, impressed mark, title, publish date and sculptor, E.W. Wyon. F, c1858 ... **900.00**
Figure, 20-1/4" h, Venus Victrix, seminude figure modeled standing on freeform base,

inscribed title, imp mark, mid-19th C, shallow chip and nick to base **1,450.00**

Carrara, figure group, "The Interpretation," modeled by William Beattie, Joseph before the Pharaoh, unmarked, c1860, 19" h, **$3,525**.

Photo courtesy of Skinner, Inc.

Vase, cov, 7-1/2" h, trophy relief between floral festoons terminating at ram's heads, foliate borders, bronzed and gilt, imp and printed marks, c1900, cover restored **1,495.00**

Cream ware

Bowl
7-1/2" d, scalloped edge, cut-out design, imp "Wedgwood" **600.00**
8-1/8" l, reticulated, molded fiddleback ladle, imp "Wedgwood," stains, edge chip **160.00**
Plate, 9-1/8" d, scenic, little girl and mother buying buns from the Bun Man, back titled "Buns!, Buns!, Buns!," 1863

mark and artist sgd "Lessore" **335.00**
Vase, 6" h, molded grape vines and foliage, painted band of strawberries, mid-19th C **250.00**

Drabware

Club jug, 7-3/8" h, molded body, hunt subject, applied white fruiting grapevine border, imp mark, c1830, shallow rim chip **490.00**
Potpourri, cov, 10" h, upturned loop handles, bulbous middle applied with band of blue foliage, pierced cover, acorn finial, solid insert disc lid, impressed mark, c1825 .... **1,650.00**
Tea set, 6-1/2" h cov teapot (slight chips to spout and sibyl finial), 4-1/4" h creamer (rim chip), 5" h cov sugar, imp marks, c1830 .... **575.00**

Jasperware, bowl, blue, white classical figures, 10" d, **$75**; ashtray, blue, white center, gold trim, **$30**.

Photo courtesy of Dotta Auction Co., Inc.

Jasperware, two dark blue candleholders, white trim, #45; brown jug with white classical figures, **$65**; stack of small plates with statesmen portraits, each **$35**; kidney-shaped covered box, **$40**; stein with buildings, **$65**.

Photo courtesy of Dotta Auction Co., Inc.

Jasper

Barber bottle, 10" h, three color, solid white body, applied bacchus heads at shoulder, classical relief, green foliate and lilac ground medallions, ram's heads and berries, impressed mark, mid 19th C, cover married **1,775.00**

Biscuit jar, cov
5-1/4" h, three color dip, applied white classical figures in relief on black ground bordered with yellow ground bands, silver plated rim, handle and cover, impressed mark, late 19th C, needs replating.................. **1,000.00**
5-1/4" h, three color dip, applied white relief with classical figures and floral festoons terminating at ram's heads on green ground, bordered in lilac with foliate borders, silver plated rim, handle and cover, impressed mark, mid 19th C, footrim nick, repaired chips to trim rings, needs replating
.... **600.00**

Bough pot, 6-3/8" h, solid light blue, sq shape with arched recesses to paneled sides, applied white relief figures representing four seasons within palm framed corners, impressed mark, late 18th C, missing lid, restored foot
.... **1,175.00**

Bowl, cov, 5-1/8" d, crimson dip, applied white classical figures in relief within foliate framed panels, acanthus leaves on cover, impressed mark, c1920
.... **1,880.00**

Bowl
6-5/8" d, solid blue, basketweave body, imp mark, early 19th C **1,380.00**
7-1/8" d, dark blue dip, applied white Dancing Hours relief, imp mark, mid-19th C
.... **920.00**
10" d, black dip, applied white Dancing Hours figures in relief, running laurel and berry and acanthus leaf borders, impressed mark, c1959
.... **720.00**

Brooch, 1" x 1-1/4", octagonal, three-color, applied white classical relief on green ground, solid light blue medallion, gold mounted

frame, imp mark, 19th C
.... **490.00**

Cache pot, undertray, 5" h, dark blue dip, pot with applied white classical relief, band of flowers on tray, impressed marks, 19th C, price for pr
.... **1,100.00**

Jasper, cache pot, green, floral garland around rim, body decorated with leaf and grape motif swags emanating from lions' heads, cartouches featuring classical figures, imp marks on bottom, "WEDGWOOD Made in England 5 W 71," 5 d, 4-1/2 h, **$115.**
Photo courtesy of Alderfer Auction Co.

Jasper, compote, crimson dip, white classical acanthus borders on bowl and pedestal base, **$65.**

Candlesticks, pr

4-1/4" h, black dip, applied white classical relief within bands of foliage and arabesque floral design, impressed mark, early 20th C, one with edge nick **715.00**
7-3/4" h, yellow dip, applied black classical relief and arabesque floral banded border, impressed marks, c1930, stain in drip dish
.... **1,100.00**

Candy dish, cov

2-1/4" h, three-color dip, dark blue ground with applied yellow zigzags and white florets, foliage, and diamond border, silver plated rim, handle, and cov, imp mark,

c1881, slight foot rim chip repaired **550.00**
2-5/8" h, lilac dip, applied white classical relief figures, silver plated rim, handle, and cov, imp mark, imp mark, c1877, light crazing, slight pitting to surface........ **690.00**

Jasper, cheese stand and cover, blue, classical white frieze, 19th C, lid handle reglued, 7-1/2" x 10-1/2", **$435.**
Photo courtesy of David Rago Auctions, Inc.

Goblet, 5-7/8" h, dark blue dip, applied white stiff leaves, impressed mark, 19th C
.... **500.00**

Hair receiver, 4-3/8" d, crimson dip, applied white classical relief and foliage designs, imp mark, c1920, slight loss to one figure **1,265.00**

Humidor, cov, 9-3/8" h, solid light blue, applied white relief with classical figures and urns framed within palm tree panels, banded arabesque floral dec, engine turned dome cover with Diana finial, limited edition in Masterpiece series, numbered 59 in edition of 200, printed and impressed marks, c1985.............. **720.00**

Inkstand, 6-7/8" h, solid pale blue, sarcophagus form supporting two pots, applied white relief with central medallion of The Sacrifice to Hymen within drapery enclosure, impressed mark, late 18th C, missing covers, crazing throughout, old restorations to pots, backside of stand, and scrolled foliate relief........................ **1,495.00**

Jam jar, cov, 3-3/4" h, three-color dip, central light green ground band bordered in lilac, applied white classical figures below floral festoons and foliate border, silver plated rim, handle, and cov, imp mark, mid-19th C. **650.00**

Jasperware, left: black covered jar, white classical figures, $75; center: lilac dip vase, white classical figures, $95; right: light blue covered jar, white classical figures, $65.

Jardinière

5-1/4" h, three-color, solid white ground, applied green floral festoons and foliate borders, lilac ram's heads and trophy drops, imp mark, 19th C **1,035.00**

7-1/8" h, black dip, applied white classical relief, impressed mark, early 20th C, price for pr, one with rim repair, marks partially removed....................... **825.00**

8" h, olive green dip, applied white classical Muses in relief below fruiting grapevine festoon terminating at lion masks and rings, impressed mark, c1920............... **400.00**

Jewel box, cov, 4-1/2" h, dark blue dip, oval, classical subject medallion mounted to three of paneled sides, larger medallion set on hinged lid, gilt brass mountings, 19th C **1,100.00**

Jug

3-7/8" h, crimson dip, barrel shape with applied white classical Muses in relief within foliate framed panels, trophy below spout, impressed mark, c1920....................... **1,530.00**

6-1/2" h, crimson dip, applied white classical relief below border of floral garlands, impressed mark, c1920, shallow chip to side of spout **940.00**

7-1/4" h, three color, solid white body, applied pale lilac trophies terminating at ram's heads, green floral festoon, oak leaf bands and acanthus leaves, impressed mark, mid 19th C, shallow footrim chips, some discoloration to white jasper....................... **1,650.00**

Miscellaneous, pitcher, green glaze, mottled grapes and grape leaves, "Made in England" mark, $65.

Photo courtesy of Joseph P. Smalley, Jr., Auctioneer.

Mustard pot, cov, 4" h, yellow dip, attached underplate, applied black fruiting grapevine relief, pot with lion masks and rings, silver plated cover, impressed mark, c1930, rim chip, stained interior, dish rim restored **325.00**

Necklace, 21" l, lilac dip, 21 assorted beads, each with applied relief, 14 teardrop-shaped with classical subjects, seven oval with stars and stiff leaves, unmarked, 19th C **920.00**

Oenochoe jug, 11" h, dark blue dip, applied white classical relief, scrolled handle terminating at female mask head, impressed mark, early 19th C **3,100.00**

Oil lamp, 5-1/4" l, dark blue dip, applied white classical relief, Zodiac signs border, imp mark, early 19th C ... **1,265.00**

Perfume bottle, 1-7/8" d, solid light blue, applied white relief portraits of George III on one side, reverse with Queen Charlotte, each bordered by floral festoons, unmarked, late 18th/early 19th C, repair, chips to neck **490.00**

Plaque

2-1/2" x 7-1/4", green dip, rect, applied white relief of children at play, impressed mark, England, 19th C, gilded and ebonized wood frame **1,120.00**

3" x 8-1/4", black dip, rect, applied white relief depictions of Domestic Employment from design by Lady Templetown, impressed mark, England, 19th C, painted wood frame **765.00**

4" x 9", black dip, rect, applied white relief of children with fruit, reading and playing musical instruments, impressed mark, mid 19th C **1,300.00**

Plate, blue and white transfer print, Vassar College, 1929, Taylor Hall, identification, importer's mark, and Wedgwood mark on back in blue, $95.

Portrait plaque, 8" d, green dip, Ariadne, oval, applied white relief, inscribed title and impressed mark, 19th C, giltwood frame............ **650.00**

Potpourri, cov, 2-1/2" h, solid light blue, squat cylindrical shape, applied white stiff leaves below running laurel border, impressed mark, 19th C................................. **825.00**

Salad bowl

5-3/4" d, dark blue dip, applied white classical relief below floral festoons terminating in ram's heads, foliate borders, silver plated rim, imp mark, 19th C . **375.00**

10-3/8" d, three-color dip, dark blue ground with applied relief alternating as bands of yellow trellis and white scrolls, silver plated rim, imp mark, c1882, old repairs to rim and foot rim chip................ **460.00**

Salad set, 7-1/2" d bowl, dark blue dip, applied white classical relief, silver plated rim, 11" l silver plate fork and spoon servers with dark blue handles, applied foliate relief, late 19th C **350.00**

Salt, open, 2-7/8" d, solid light blue, applied white Dancing Hours in relief, imp marks, 19th C, one with rim chip, other with relief loss to figure, price for pr **750.00**

Slave medallion, 1" x 1 1/4", solid white, raised verse surrounding applied black figure in relief, partial impressed mark, late 18th C, lacquered wood and brass frame........................ **1,765.00**

Spill vase, 3" h, three-color dip, light blue ground, engine turned fluting below lilac ground medallions, applied white classical relief above floral festoons terminating at ram's heads, imp mark, mid-19th C **1,035.00**

Sugar bowl, cov, crimson dip, applied white classical relief, imp mark, c1920, restored chip on cover collar and two areas of relief **290.00**

Syrup jug
6-1/4" h, dark blue dip, applied white birds in relief below oak leaf banded border, silver plated insert cov, imp mark, early 20th C **550.00**
7-3/4" h, three-color dip, dark blue ground with applied vertical bands of yellow trellis and white scrolls, hinged pewter lid, imp mark, late 19th C, restored **350.00**

Tea bowl and saucer, solid pale blue, applied white relief, children playing above band of engine turning on cup, 5" d saucer with acanthus and stiff leaves bordering engine turned center, imp mark, late 18th C **980.00**

Tea service, dark blue dip, 4-1/2" h cov teapot, 6" d waste bowl, twelve 6-1/8" d plates, seven 5-1/2" d tea cups,

seven saucers, each with applied white grass and foliate border, impressed marks, 19th C, few rim chips **1,765.00**

Jasper, urn, blue dip, white classical figures, two handles, late, **$35**.

Vase, cov
6-1/2" h, dark blue dip, applied white bacchus head handles and Dancing Hours in relief, foliate framed borders, impressed marks, late 19th C, price for pr, one handle simply reglued **1,880.00**
7-1/4" h, dark blue dip, bottle shape with applied white classical figures in relief within foliate frames, impressed marks, early 19th C, price for pr **1,765.00**
8-1/2" h, green dip, applied white relief with Dancing Hours, foliate borders, bacchus head handles, impressed marks, mid 19th C, price for pr, one finial reglued, one handle repaired, chip to socle rim **2,115.00**
9-1/2" h, dark blue dip, upturned loop handles, applied white classical relief, acanthus leaf borders, impressed marks, mid 19th C, price for pr **1,530.00**
11" h, crimson dip, upturned loop handles, applied white classical relief and foliate borders, impressed mark, c1920, cover with hairlines, restored finial **3,525.00**

Vase
3" h, three color dip, green ground, applied lilac medallions, white portraits in

relief between drapery swags, imp mark, 19th C, rim and foot rim chips **435.00**
5-1/2" h, yellow dip, applied blue relief with classical figures within foliate framed panels, fruiting grapevine and stiff leaf borders, impressed mark, 19th C, missing disc lid, chips restored below base **940.00**
6-3/4" h, solid light blue, applied white relief with columnar framed panels of floral festoons and classical medallions below band of vine and scrolled ribbon, impressed mark, 19th C, slight discoloration to foot **825.00**
8" h, light blue dip, bottle shape, applied white classical relief within foliate framed panels, neck with floral festoons terminating at ram's heads, impressed marks, c1867, price for pr... **1,000.00**
15" h, black dip, applied white relief with classical muses below fruiting festoons terminating at lion masks and rings, trophies to shoulder, fruiting grapevine and acanthus leaf borders, impressed mark, late 19th C **2,585.00**

Fairyland Luster, pair of tall vases, **$3,000**; small bowl with blue ground, **$400**.

Lusters

Bough pot, cov, 10" l, Moonlight, wall pocket modeled as nautilus shell, pierced insert grid, impressed mark, c1815, cover repaired, slight chip to spine **940.00**

Box, cov, 4" x 7", Dragon, pattern Z4829, mottled blue glaze, mother-of-pearl int., printed mark, c1920 **1,850.00**

Bowl

3-1/8" d, Oriental motifs, mottled green/black ext. with dragon, mother of pearl int., printed mark, c1920 ... **400.00**

4" d, fish dec, mottled blue ext., mother of pearl int., printed mark, c1920 ... **350.00**

7-1/8" d, Dragon, octagonal, mottled blue ground ext., mother of pearl int., Z4829, printed mark, c1920, slight glaze scratches **470.00**

7-3/4" d, Fairyland Lustre, octagonal, exterior with "Moorish" design on black ground, interior with "Smoke Ribbons" on daylight sky, Z5125, printed mark, c1920 .... **5,875.00**

9" d, Fairyland Lustre, octagonal, exterior with "Castle on a Road" on deep blue shaded sky, interior with "Fairy in a Cage" with daylight sky, Z5125, printed mark, c1920, slight wear to center **3,820.00**

Chalice bowl, 10-5/8" d, Fairyland Lustre, exterior with "Twyford Garlands" on flame ground, interior with "Fairy Gondola" on flame sky, Z5360, printed mark, c1920, stem restored, hairlines to base.......................... **6,500.00**

Coffeepot, cov, 5-1/2" h, Moonlight, imp mark, c1810, small chips to spout and cover.......................... **690.00**

Cup, 2" h, three handles, Dragon, blue ext., gilt reptiles, eggshell int. with central dragon, printed mark, c1920 .... **275.00**

Dish, 4-3/4" d, Dragon, Daisy Makeig Jones marks, Z4831, c1914-31..................... **675.00**

Imperial bowl

10" d, Fairyland Lustre, exterior "Poplar Trees" on night sky, interior "Feather Hat" on daylight sky, Z4968, printed mark, c1920, center gilt wear **5,000.00**

10-1/2" d, Fairyland Lustre, exterior with firbolg design on red ground, mother of pearl interior with Thumbelina center, Z5275, printed mark,

c1920, light glaze scratches to exterior................. **2,250.00**

Malfrey pot, cov, 8-1/4" h, Fairyland Lustre, "Candlemas" pattern, Z5157, printed mark, c1920, vase rim regilded **3,820.00**

Punch bowl, 11" d, Butterfly, ruby lustre exterior with butterflies and insects, mother of pearl interior with butterflies, Z4827, printed mark, c1920............. **2,820.00**

Teapot, cov, 3" h, Moonlight, drum form, imp mark, c1810, rim chips restored, nicks to spout rim..................... **575.00**

Vase

8-1/2" h, Hummingbird, mottled blue exterior, orange/ red mottled interior, Z5294, printed mark, c1920 **1,175.00**

8-1/2" h, paneled Daventry design, pale plum ground, Z5418, printed mark, c1920 .... **3,300.00**

8-3/4" h, Fairyland, exterior with "Firbolgs" on deep ruby ground, interior rim dec with fish from Thumbelina motifs on mother of pearl ground, printed mark, c1920 **2,590.00**

9-3/4" h, Fairyland, black, trumpet, shape 2810, Z4968, Butterfly Women, printed marks, c1920, pr **4,000.00**

11" h, Dragon, pattern Z4829, mottled blue ext., mother-of-pearl int., Chinese pagoda panels, printed mark, c1920 .... **1,150.00**

Wall pocket, 10" l, Moonlight, nautilus shell, c1810, restorations, pr............ **575.00**

Dragon Lustre, bowl, pattern Z4829, mottled blue exterior with dragon, mother-of-pearl interior with Chinese landscape cartouches to cell border, center dragons, printed mark, c1920, diameter is 9-1/8", **$650**.

Photo courtesy of Skinner, Inc.

Majolica

Barber bottle, cov, 11" h, cobalt blue ground, molded body with festooning fruiting grapevines

between Bacchus mask heads applied to shoulder bordered in laurel and berries, imp mark, c1869, cover collar restored **1,840.00**

Biscuit jar, cov, 5-1/2" h, jar with molded dec of elephants within floral framed cartouches flanked by elephant masks, silver plated rim, bale handle and cover, imp mark, c1867, cover possibly married...... **1,250.00**

Bowl, 11" d, cauliflower, multicolored, cobalt blue, rim nick on back............... **495.00**

Compote, 16" h, bowl molded as nautilus shell, base molded as two dolphins with entwined tails, impressed mark, c1866, possibly married, base chips **1,100.00**

Crocus pot, 6" h, hedgehog, oval shaped pierced body, green glaze, impressed mark, c1865, missing undertray, slight footrim chips **400.00**

Fish platter, 25-1/4" l, Argenta, oval, scalloped rim, molded in relief with large fish atop vegetation, impressed mark, c1878, staining........... **825.00**

Floor urn, 26" h, cobalt blue, ladies seated at top of bulbous vase, drapes of laurel wreaths and ladies head at base, turquoise, yellow, white, brown, green, and pink, repair to one base, minor nicks and repair to feet of ladies, pr **5,500.00**

Jug, 8-3/4" h, applied central fruiting grapevine band, imp marks, c1868, one with slight relief loss, price for pr **1,300.00**

Oyster plate, brown basketweave and shell **1,210.00**

Pitcher, 7" h, sunflower and urn, turquoise..................... **770.00**

Plate

8-3/4" d, mottled, reticulated **165.00**

9" d, crane **690.00**

Salt, open, 5-1/2" h, modeled as scantily clad boy holding basket, freeform base, imp mark, c1889, slight hairlines to rim, glaze flakes, restored base chips.................. **350.00**

Sugar, Argenta, bird and fan, repair to lid, hairline in base **125.00**

Umbrella stand, 24" h, Argenta Fan, hairlines **1,760.00**

Vase, 10" h, bottle shape, raised bands of foliage, flowers and fruiting festoons surrounding oval medallions, impressed mark, c1870 .... **900.00**

Pearlware

Candlesticks, pr, turquoise glaze, modeled as classical female holding cornucopia form base, supporting leafy sconce, imp mark, c1872, glaze wear, nicks to glaze surface **1,380.00**

Fruit basket, 10-5/8" one stand, oval, basketweave molded center, pierced gallery, green enamel trim, imp mark, early 19th C, some damage to strapping of basket, glaze wear on stand **320.00**

Platter, well and tree, gaudy cobalt blue and rust Chrysanthemum pattern, c1800, repaired **595.00**

Potpourri vase, pierced cov, blue ground, white relief floral swags, band above engine-turned fluting, imp mark, c1800, body restoration, married cover **230.00**

Tea tray, 18-1/8" l, rect, cut corners, red/pink transfer printed border, c1886.. **200.00**

Vase, 12 0/4" h, upturned loop handles, red ground with gilt trimmed blue transfer printed floral and bird design,

impressed mark, mid 19th C, cover missing, repaired handle......................... **500.00**

Queen's Ware

Basket, 9" l, oval, twisted overhead handles, molded basketweave body, pierced rim, enamel and gilt dec, impressed marks, early 19th C, price for pr **1,175.00**

Bidet, 21-1/2" l, fitted mahogany stand with cov, imp mark **425.00**

Bough pot, cov, 6" h, sq form, paneled sides, relief alternating with two figures representing Seasons and two urns, foliate molded sq disc lid and center insert, imp mark, mid-19th C, old repair to hairline on disc lid **460.00**

Box, cov, 3-3/4" d, flat cylindrical form, gilt trim to green transfer printed foliate design, imp mark, c1882, light wear **500.00**

Dish, 5-1/8" d, diamond shape, enamel painted Emile Lessore dec cherubs, artist sgd, impressed mark, c1860 .... **600.00**

Flemish jug, 8-1/4" h, molded body with majolica glazes, blue incised designs, relief portrait of Queen Victoria below spout, brown banded neck and foot, imp mark, 1877 .... **375.00**

Orange bowl, cov, 9-1/2" h, low pedestal foot, wide lobe-fluted flaring rim, high domed pieced cover with long tapering ovals framed by molded scroll lattice and floral designs, imp mark, 20th C **635.00**

Plate, 8-3/4" d, molded border, enamel dec center with Cupid and Psyche, artist sgd "E. Lossore," imp mark, c1870 .... **635.00**

Platter, 15-3/4" x 20-3/8", oval, polychrome bird and floral dec in Chelsea style, imp mark, 1871 .... **375.00**

Sauceboat, 8" l, molded trellis and scroll pattern after 19th C salt glaze stoneware model, imp mark, 19th C **460.00**

Soup ladle, 11-1/4" l, bowl with yellow ground banding, black enamel foliate vine dec, imp mark, early 19th C **320.00**

Commemorative plate, Queen Elizabeth II visit to Philadelphia, July 1976, light blue with arched and flowers on rim, swags, ribbons, and rams' heads surrounding classical figures in white, yellow, lavender, and green, central bust of Elizabeth, gold inscription "Royal Visit to America, Philadelphia, July 1976," impressed Wedgwood marks on underside, also inscription in gold indicating this is No. 4 of limited edition of twelve, 8-5/8" d, original packaging, Certificate of Authenticity, newspaper articles relating to visit sold with plate, **$300**.

Photo courtesy of Alderfer Auction Co.

Rosso Antico

Bowl

6-3/4" d, applied black basalt relief, fern dec, imp mark, early 19th C **850.00**

7-7/8" d, Egyptian, applied black basalt meander band above stylized foliate molded body, imp mark, early 19th C **1,300.00**

Dinnerware, Philadelphia pattern, Queen's Ware, cream ground, black decoration, retailed by John Wanamaker, price for 108-piece set, **$950**.

Box, cov, 3-1/2" d, flat cylindrical form, enamel painted flowers, imp mark, c1860, base rim chip.............................. **175.00**

Bust, 7-1/4" h, Matthew Prior, mounted on raised circular base, imp mark and title, restorations **420.00**

Candlesticks, pr, 7" h, polychrome floral sprays, imp mark, mid-19th C, each sconce restored.......... **415.00**

Club jug, 6-1/4" h, polychrome floral sprays, imp mark, mid-19th C **520.00**

Cream jug, 2-1/4" h, hexagonal form, banded Greek key relief, imp mark, early 19th C **450.00**

Inkstand, 4" h, applied black basalt leaf and berry border on stand, supported by three dolphin feet, central pot insert, imp mark, early 19th C, foot rim restored **550.00**

Jug, 5-1/8" l, oval, molded lobed body, foliage, stem, and flower relief, imp mark, early 19th C, restored spout rim chip............................. **675.00**

Tray, 8-1/2" l, oval, Egyptian, applied black basalt hieroglyphs in relief, imp mark, early 19th C .. **1,100.00**

Vase, cov, 8" h, tripod, applied black basalt Egyptian relief with central hieroglyph band, impressed mark, early 19th C, repair to one leg and finial **1,880.00**

Transferware, plate, blue, central portrait of George Washington, rim decorated with floral garland, inscription on reverse in tribute to Washington, stamped and impressed marks on reverse indicate manufacture in 1907, 9-1/4" d, **$200**.

Photo courtesy of Alderfer Auction Co.

Stoneware

Bough pot, cov, 4-3/4" h, D-shape, mottled green and white relief floral swags, acanthus, stiff leaves, England, c1785, impressed mark, chip to pot back corner and interior edge, cover as is **775.00**

Crocus basket, cov, 6-1/2" h, pierced and engine turned body with overhead bow handle, dark blue dip dicing, impressed mark, early 19th C **2,585.00**

Dish, 9-3/8" l, leaf form, white, enamel floral sprays, imp mark, early 19th C, very slight rim nick **230.00**

Mortar and pestle, 7-1/2" d mortar with spout, 10-1/4" l pestle with wood handle, vitrified, impressed marks, early 19th C, wear, chip on head **360.00**

Vase, 5-7/8" h, goblet shape, sponged brown and blue underglaze enamels, raised black basalt base, England, c1775, wafer Wedgwood & Bentley mark, slight flake to base, missing cover ... **600.00**

WELLER POTTERY

History: In 1872, Samuel A. Weller opened a small factory in Fultonham, near Zanesville, Ohio. There he produced utilitarian stoneware, such as milk pans and sewer tile. In 1882, he moved his facilities to Zanesville. Then in 1890 Weller built a new plant in the Putnam section of Zanesville along the tracks of the Cincinnati and Muskingum Railway. Additions followed in 1892 and 1894.

In 1894, Weller entered into an agreement with William A. Long to purchase the Lonhuda Faience Company, which had developed an art pottery line under the guidance of Laura A. Fry, formerly of Rookwood. Long left in 1895, but Weller continued to produce Lonhuda under the new name "Louwelsa." Replacing Long as art director was Charles Babcock Upjohn. He, along with Jacques Sicard, Frederick Hurten Rhead,

and Gazo Fudji, developed Weller's art pottery lines.

At the end of World War I, many prestige lines were discontinued and Weller concentrated on commercial wares. Rudolph Lorber joined the staff and designed lines such as Roma, Forest, and Knifewood. In 1920, Weller purchased the plant of the Zanesville Art Pottery and claimed to produce more pottery than anyone else in the country.

Art pottery enjoyed a revival when the Hudson Line was introduced in the early 1920s. The 1930s saw Coppertone and Graystone Garden ware added. However, the Depression forced the closing of the Putnam plant and one on Marietta Street in Zanesville. After World War II, inexpensive Japanese imports took over Weller's market. In 1947, Essex Wire Company of Detroit bought the controlling stock, but early in 1948, operations ceased.

Additional Listings: See *Warman's Americana & Collectibles* for more examples.

Bowl, Ardsley, flaring, figural Kingfisher flower frog, stamped mark, 16" d, 9-1/2" h, few minute flecks to base of frog, **$800**.

Photo courtesy of David Rago Auctions, Inc.

Bowl, Muskota turtle, built-in flower frog, unmarked, 9" l, 4" h, **$850**.

Photo courtesy of David Rago Auctions, Inc.

Bowl

Ardsley, flaring, stamped mark............................. **265.00**
Coppertone, perched frogs and lilypads, stamped mark **550.00**
Glendale, flaring, birds and waves crashing over rocks dec, stamped mark, few minor firing separations **350.00**

Cabinet jug, 3-3/4" x 2-3/4", Louwelsa, small yellow blossoms, silver overlay, imp mark......................... **1,000.00**

Candlestick

0 3/8" h, round rim, sq pyramid form, reticulated arches near base, raised flowers and berries on vine, matted brown glaze, pink, blue, and highlights, one imp "Weller" on base, late 1920s, price for pr.................. **150.00**
13-1/2" h, Glendale, owl dec **520.00**

Console set, 7" d, 3-1/2" h three-sided bowl, pr candlesticks, green, Tutone, stamped marks.......................... **250.00**

Ewer, Jap Birdimal, finely decorated by Rhead in squeezebag, trees and geisha, incised "Weller Faience Rhead G580," 10-3/4" x 7", pinhead size fleck to spout, **$3,000**.

Photo courtesy of David Rago Auctions, Inc.

Ewer, Jap Birdimal, squeezebag trees and geisha dec by Rheadin, incised mark **3,000.00**

Flower frog, Brighton bluebird, fleck to one wing, restoration, unmarked, 9" x 4 1/2", **$375**.

Photo courtesy of David Rago Auctions, Inc.

Figure, 2-1/2" x 6", turtle, Coppertown, unmarked **450.00**

Frog tray, 15-1/2" l, oval, raised edge, frog and water lily on one side, lily pads on other, blotchy semi-gloss green glaze, "Weller Pottery" ink stamp......................... **635.00**

Hanging basket

7-3/4" x 3-1/2", Forest, unmarked **300.00**
9-1/4" x 5-3/4", Parian, conical, unmarked...... **125.00**

Garden ornament, swan, ivory glaze, 20" x 18", minor flakes **6,500.00**

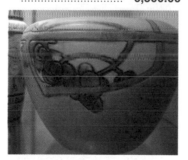

Jardinière, etched matte, branches of grapes and leaves, unmarked, 6-1/2" x 8-1/2", **$225**.

Photo courtesy of David Rago Auctions, Inc.

Jardinière

Aurelian, brown glaze, painted fruit, sgd "Frank Ferrell" **1,100.00**

Sicard, sunflowers, emerald green and gold on deep purple ground.......... **2,900.00**

Jardinière, Burntwood, carved roosters, impressed mark, 2" line from rim, 9-1/2" d, 8-1/2" h, **$225**.

Photo courtesy of David Rago Auctions, Inc.

Lamp base

5" d, 11-1/4" h, Forest, unmarked, 2" chip next to hole at base...................... **460.00**
10" d, 13-1/4" h, Louwelsa, by Hattie Mitchell, gourd shape, painted yellow cherry blossoms, stamped "Weller Louwelsa," sgd "H. Mitchell" on body **460.00**

Mug, Dickensware, dolphin handle and band, sgraffito ducks......................... **250.00**

Pedestal, Zona, panels of cattails, stamped mark, 9" d, 20" h, **$325**.

Photo courtesy of David Rago Auctions, Inc.

Zona pitcher, kingfisher and cattails decoration, impressed mark, 8-1/2" x 9", **$275**.

Photo courtesy of David Rago Auctions, Inc.

Pitcher

8" h, 8" d, Marvo, pink, unmarked **250.00**

9" h, 8-1/2" d, Zona, kingfisher and cattails, imp mark, glaze nick at base **250.00**

Planter

Rosemont, 7-1/2" x 9-1/2", unmarked, several lines **350.00**

Woodcraft, applied squirrel climbing up tree, 2" tight line **375.00**

Vase, Sicard, lobed, chrysanthemum decoration against nacreous purple, green, red, gold, and blue glaze, signed "Weller Sicard," impressed "38," 4-3/4" x 7", minor restoration to interior rim, **$750**.

Photo courtesy of David Rago Auctions, Inc.

Vase

4-1/4" h, 3-3/4" d, bulbous, Burntwood, band of flowers, unmarked **100.00**

6-1/2" h, 6" d, gourd shape, twisted handles, Silvertone, yellow flowers, ink stamp mark **275.00**

Vase, Hudson, bulbous, two handles, blue flowers on shaded pink ground, painted by Timberlake, stamped and impressed marks, artist's signature, 5-1/2" d, 6-1/2" h, **$325**.

Photo courtesy of David Rago Auctions, Inc.

Vases, three Adsley flaring vases, two marked, two 7-1/2" h, one 9" h, **$300**.

Photo courtesy of David Rago Auctions, Inc.

6-3/4" h, 6-1/2" h, bulbous, Hudson, painted band of white blossoms and leaves, Timberlake, stamped mark, artist's signature **500.00**

8" h, 3-1/2" d, cylindrical, Silvertone, pink and white flowers, ink stamp mark **300.00**

9" h, 5-1/2" h, bulbous, Silverton, pink chrysanthemums, ink stamp mark **395.00**

9" h, 9" d, Baldin, blue, imp mark, glaze nick at rim **475.00**

9-1/2" h, 4" d, tapering, Aurelia, berries and leaves, imp mark **300.00**

9-1/2" h, 8-1/2" w, pillow, L'Art Nouveau, one side with maiden in profile, other with shell, stamped mark partially obscured **450.00**

Vase, Creamware, Ethel, flaring, 9" h, **$195**.

Photo courtesy of David Rago Auctions, Inc.

Vase, Hudson, blue and yellow irises painted on both sides by Pillsbury, stamped mark, artist's signature, 1" blue glaze run next to iris on one side, 7" d, 15-1/2" h, **$1,700**.

Photo courtesy of David Rago Auctions, Inc.

10" h, 4-1/2" d, bulbous, flaring rim, Rosemont, imp mark **450.00**

10" h, 4-1/2" d, Warwick, unmarked **200.00**

Vase, Woodcraft, tree-shaped, built-in flower frog, figural owl perched on branch, stamped mark, tight 1" line to rim, chip on branch, 6" d, 15-1/2" h, **$1,700**.

Photo courtesy of David Rago Auctions, Inc.

10" h, 5 1/2" d, Silvortono, two angular handles, pink and white flowers, Silverton and Weller paper labels..... **300.00**

10" h, 8" d, shell shape, Art Nouveau, painted maiden and flowers, imp mark, 1" line, two minor glaze flakes....... **450.00**

10-1/2" h, 4-3/4" d, bulbous, Hudson, painted pink tulips, imp mark..................... **425.00**

10-1/2" h, 5-1/2" d, ovoid, Louwelsa, gooseberries and leaves, imp mark, fleck to rim, few shallow scratches **100.00**

11" h, 4" d, trumpet shape, Hudson, painted berries and leaves, imp mark **400.00**

11-1/2" h, 7" d, flaring, Greora, etched mark................ **450.00**

11-3/4" h, 5" d, flaring, Silvertone, calla lilies dec, ink stamp mark.................. **375.00**

12" h, 3-1/4" h, bulbous, Louwelsa, orange and yellow carnations, imp mark, few short shallow scratches **100.00**

14" h, 5-3/4", Fru Russet, emb flowers, pale blue-gray and green glaze, imp mark **2,600.00**

From left: vase, twisted form, wild roses painted by Shoemaker, unmarked, 11" h, bruise to rim, **$100**; center: Louwelsa cabinet jug, yellow painted blossoms, silver overlay, impessed mark, 3-3/4" w, 2-3/4" h, **$1,000**; right: Louwelsa vase, painted rises, impressed mark, tight 1" line from rim, 13" h, **$175**.

Photo courtesy of David Rago Auctions, Inc.

Vase, Woodcraft, double, owl perched on top, impressed mark, 14" x 7-1/2", **$550**.

Photo courtesy of David Rago Auctions, Inc.

19" h, Aurelian, singing monk playing the mandolin in earthtone glazes, mkd "Aurelian" on base, numbered, decorator's signature for R. G. Turner on side, c1904, crazing **1,530.00**

20-3/4" h, Louwelsa, vasiform body, yellow rose stems on brown ground, decorator's signature on side for Hattie Mitchell, imp maker's mark on base, numbered "466" and "1," c1900, minor glaze loss **1,880.00**

21" h, Eoccan, short rim on cylindrical form, thistle plants in pink, maroon, and cream, green stems on brown to green to cream-colored ground, incised "Eocean Rose Weller," numbered "547," letter "Y" on base, artist's initials on side for Eugene Roberts, c1907, crazing and areas of glaze roughness................ **1,880.00**

Wall pocket

12" h, Glendale, imp mark, restoration................... **250.00**

12-1/4" h, Suevo, conical, unmarked, minor wear to glaze........................... **250.00**

WHITE-PATTERNED IRONSTONE

History: White-patterned ironstone is a heavy earthenware, first patented under the name "Patent Ironstone China" in 1813 by Charles Mason, Staffordshire, England. Other English potters soon began copying this opaque, feldspathic, white china.

All-white ironstone dishes first became available in the American market in the early 1840s. The first patterns had simple Gothic lines similar to the shapes used in transfer wares. Pattern shapes, such as New York, Union, and Atlantic, were designed to appeal to the American housewife. Motifs, such as wheat, corn, oats, and poppies, were embossed on the pieces as the American prairie influenced design. Eventually, more than 200 shapes and patterns, with variations on finials and handles, were made.

White-patterned ironstone is identified by shape names and pattern names. Many potters only identified the shape in their catalogs. Pattern names usually refer to the decorative motif.

Butter dish, cov, Athens, Podmore Walker, c1857 **95.00**

Cake plate, 9" d, Brocade, Mason, handled.......... **180.00**

Chamber pot, cov, emb Fleur-De-Lis & Daisy on handle, 1883-1913, marked "Johnson Bros." **165.00**

Coffeepot, cov
Laurel Wreath.............. **275.00**
Wheat and Blackberry, Clementson Bros. **220.00**

Compote, ftd, Taylor & Davis, 10" d, 6" h.................... **220.00**

Creamer
Fig, Davenport.............. **95.00**
Wheat in the Meadow, Powell & Bishop, 1870 .... **85.00**

Creamer and sugar, Scroll pattern, E. Walley, repaired finial, luster dec **170.00**

Coffeepots, oval garland medallion, fluted base, rope twist motif handle, price for pair, **$250**.

Coffeepot, paneled body, fruit finial on domed lid, scrolling leaf decoration on handle and shoulder, **$175**.

Cup and saucer
Acorn and Tiny Oak, Parkhurst **35.00**
Grape and Medallion, Challinor **40.00**
Wheat, Brockhurst, handleless, luster dec .. **25.00**

Ewer, Scalloped Decagon, Wedgwood **150.00**

Gravy boat
Bordered Fuchsia, Anthony Shaw........................... **75.00**
Wheat & Blackberry, Meakin **65.00**

Milk pitcher, Leaf, marked "Royal Ironstone China, Alfred Meakin, England," 9" h **245.00**

Nappy, Prairie Flowers, Livesley & Powell **20.00**

Pitcher
Berlin Swirl, Mayer & Elliot **120.00**
Japan, Mason, c1915 . **275.00**
Syndenhaum, T. & R. Boote **195.00**
Thomas Furnival, 9" w, 9-1/2" h **220.00**

Pitcher, embossed corn and foliate at neck, marked "Royal Patent Ironstone, Turner, Goodard & Co." with lions and crown mark, **$225**.

Two pitchers, left: milk pitcher, Corn pattern, embossed rope around top, **$115**; right: water pitcher, plain top, paneled base, squared off handle, **$95**.

Plate
Ceres, Elsmore & Forster, 8-1/2" d **15.00**
Corn, Davenport, 10-1/2" d **20.00**
Fluted Pearl, Wedgwood, 9-1/2" d **15.00**
Laurel Wreath, 10", set of 13 .... **325.00**
Prairie, Clemenston, Hanley, 6-5/8" d **15.00**
Scroll pattern, E. Walley, 8" d **55.00**
Wheat and Clover, Turner & Tomkinson.................... **24.00**

Platter
Columbia, 20" x 15" **125.00**
Laurel Wreath, three graduated sizes.......... **325.00**
Wheat, Meakin, 20-3/4" x 15-3/4" **95.00**

Punch bowl
Berry Cluster, J. Furnival **175.00**
Rosettes, handles, Thomas Furnival & Sons, c1851-90, 9-1/2", 6" h..................... **315.00**

Relish
Laurel Wreath, diamond shape........................... **25.00**
Wheat, W. E. corn **30.00**

Sauce tureen, cov
Columbia, underplate, Joseph Goodwin, 1855 .... **315.00**
Prize Bloom, T.J. & J. Mayer, Dale Hall Pottery......... **320.00**
Wheat & Blackberry, Clementson Bros. **275.00**

Soap dish, Bordered Hyacinth, cov, insert, W. Baker & Co., 1860s........................ **150.00**

Soup plate, 10-sided, unmarked, **$20**.

Sugar bowl, cov
Hyacinth, Wedgwood . **145.00**
Fuchsia, Meakin **140.00**
Livesley Powell & Co., registry mark, 8" h.................... **295.00**

Teapot, cov, T & R Boote, Burslem, registry mark for Nov. 26, 1879, 9-1/2" h **240.00**

Sugar bowl with embossed leaves at handle, **$115**; Corn pattern creamer, **$135**; teapot, **$225**; both with embossed rope trim, marked "Elsmore Foster" with lion mark.

Toothbrush holder
Bell Flower, Burgess **50.00**
Cable and Ring, Cockson & Seddon **40.00**
Tureen, cov, underplate, Grape, matching ladle, chips . **135.00**

Wash bowl and pitcher set, large pitcher, bowl, small pitcher, shaving mug, covered soap dish, covered chamber pot, blue band with thin gold bands, marked "Ironstone China, W. & E. Corn, Burslem," embossed English registration mark, **$350**.

Vegetable, cov
Blackberry **95.00**
Lily of the Valley, pear finial **110.00**
Vegetable, open, Laurel Wreath, pr **200.00**
Waste bowl, Laurel Wreath **45.00**

WILLOW PATTERN CHINA

History: Josiah Spode developed the first "traditional" willow pattern in 1810. The components, all motifs taken from Chinese export china, are a willow tree, "apple" tree, two pagodas, fence, two birds, and three figures crossing a bridge. The legend, in its many versions, is an English invention based on this scenic design.

By 1830, there were more than 200 makers of willow pattern china in England. The pattern has remained in continuous production. Some of the English firms that still produce it are Burleigh, Johnson Bros. (Wedgwood Group), Royal Doulton (continuing production of the Booths' pattern), and Wedgwood.

By the end of the 19th century, production of this pattern spread to France, Germany, Holland, Ireland, Sweden, and the United States. Buffalo Pottery made the first willow pattern in the United States beginning in 1902. Many other companies followed, developing willow variants using rubber-stamp simplified patterns, as well as overglaze decals. The largest American manufacturers of the traditional willow pattern were Royal China and Homer Laughlin, usually preferred because it is dated. Shenango pieces are the most desirable among restaurant-quality wares.

Japan began producing large quantities of willow pattern china in the early 20th century. Noritake began about 1902. Most Japanese pieces are porous earthenware with a dark blue pattern using the traditional willow design, usually with no inner border. Noritake did put the pattern on china bodies. Unusual forms include salt and pepper shakers, one-quarter pound butter dishes, and canisters. The most desirable Japanese willow is the fine quality NKT Co. ironstone with a copy of the old Booths pattern. Recent Japanese willow is a paler shade of blue on a porcelain body.

The most common dinnerware color is blue. However, pieces can also be found in black (with clear glaze or mustard-colored glaze by Royal Doulton), brown, green, mulberry, pink (red), and polychrome.

Marks: Early pieces of Noritake have a Nippon "Royal Sometuke" mark. "Occupied Japan" may add a small percentage to the value of common tablewares. Pieces marked "Maruta" or "Moriyama" are especially valued.

> **Reproduction Alert:** The Scio Pottery, Scio, Ohio, currently manufactures a willow pattern set sold in variety stores. The pieces have no marks or backstamps, and the transfer is of poor quality. The plates are flatter in shape than those of other manufacturers.

Note: Although colors other than blue are hard to find, there is less demand; thus, prices may not necessarily be higher priced.

Set, assorted Japanese makers, grill plates, four sizes plates, cups, saucers, mugs, serving pieces, **$175**.
Photo courtesy of Alderfer Auction Co.

Berry bowl, small
Blue, Homer Laughlin Co. **6.50**
Pink, marked "Japan"..... **5.00**
Bowl, 9" d, Mason **45.00**
Cake plate, Newport Pottery Ltd., England, SP base, c1920.......................... **300.00**
Charger, 13" d **55.00**
Coffeepot, cov, 10" h, 3" h warmer stand............. **165.00**
Creamer, round handle, Royal China Co. **12.00**
Cup and saucer
Booths **30.00**
Buffalo Pottery **25.00**
Homer Laughlin **10.00**
Japanese, decal inside cup, pink.............................. **25.00**
Shenango **15.00**
Dinner plate
Allerton, 10" d **25.00**
Buffalo Pottery, 9" d **20.00**
Johnson Bros., 10" d **15.00**

Grill plate, divided sections, marked "Made in Japan," **$24**.

Egg, transfer printed pattern on ceramic body, early 20th C
4-1/2" l, gray ground **95.00**
5" l, white ground **90.00**
5-1/2" l, light blue ground
.... **85.00**

Platters, blue and white transfer, 13-1/2" l, underglaze blue mark for Ridgway Co.; 15-1/2" l, marked "W Adams"; 17-1/2" l, marked "W. Adams," all from late 19th C, minor rim roughness, **$225**.

Photo courtesy of Alderfer Auction Co.

Child's tea set, two teapots, two creamers, covered sugar, platter, four cups and saucers, six plates, most pieces marked "Japan," **$95**.

Platter, 19" x 14-1/2", marked "Copeland, Made in England," c1940 .... **195.00**
Sugar, cov, Allerton **65.00**
Tea cup and saucer, scalloped, Allerton **45.00**
Tea set, 5" h hexagonal teapot, creamer, cov sugar, tray, seven cups, six saucers, 20-3/4" d round tray with scalloped rim, gilt foo dog lid finials, gilt handles and rims, pattern registered January, 1879, printed at rim with quotation from Robert Burns' "Auld Lang Syne," Spode, late 19th C, retailed by Tiffany & Co., price for 17-pc set
.... **950.00**
Toby jug, 6" d, overall crazing
.... **930.00**
Wash bowl and pitcher, 7-1/2" h pitcher, 12" d bowl, Adderlys Ltd., Staffordshire, c1906, age crack in pitcher **375.00**

WOODENWARE

History: Many utilitarian household objects and farm implements were made of wood. Although they were subjected to heavy use, these implements were made of the strongest woods and well cared for by their owners. Today collectors and decorators treasure their worn lines and patina. Collectors often consider their hand-made wooden items as

folk art, elevating what once might have been a common utilitarian item to a place of honor.

Bowl, burlwood, lid with trapezoidal handle, crack in bowl, 5" d, **$935**.

Photo courtesy of Alderfer Auction Co.

Apple tray, 10" l, 10" w, 3-1/2" h, pine, dovetailed and sq nail construction, painted yellow ground, green stylized foliate motif, wood separation in base **6,050.00**
Bag stamp, 5" h, pine, relief carved tulip in heart-dec urn, PA, c1750 .... **2,100.00**
Bank, 4-1/2" w, 3-13/16" d, 3-5/8" h, rect, carved gardenia blossoms and leaves on top and sides, dark blue painted ground **525.00**
Bas-relief carving
5" w, 6-3/4" h, woman holding bird, found in Iowa **525.00**
6-1/8" l, 4-1/8" h, basket of fruit, repaired **435.00**
Basket, 10-3/4" l, 5-3/4" h, carved freeform burl, America, 19th C **1,120.00**
Bowl, 7-1/4" d, 3-1/2" h, cigar box construction, ten paneled cut-out floral and circle designs, cigar label base, painted red ground, yellow, red, and green highlights to cut-outs **715.00**
Bowl, burl
9" d, 2-1/2" h, good figure, dark patina, turned rim and foot **1,380.00**
9-3/8" d, early red paint
.... **11,500.00**
22-3/4" d, 28-1/2" h, dark brown finish, raised band around rim, turned foot, age split **200.00**

Box, cov

5-1/4" d, 3-3/8" h, oval, bentwood, single finger construction with opposite directions on lid and base, iron tacks, old dark green paint shows lighter under lid, minor wear to paint .. **2,420.00**

5-3/4" w, 4" d, 1-3/4" h, book shape, spruce, inland bands, star, crescent boon, hearts, and leaves, one end with sliding lid, minor alligatoring to varnish, short age cracks **200.00**

6-3/8" w, 3" d, 1-7/8" h, book shape, Frisian carved, made from solid piece of wood, sliding lid, overall geometric carving, matching patterns on front and back, hearts and pinwheel on spine, good patina, int. with ivory paint, yellowed varnish, minor edge damage, few worm holes **220.00**

8-1/4" w, 6-1/4" d, 4-1/4" h, oval, bentwood, single finger on lid, overlapping seams on base, steel tacks, old medium blue paint, wear to lid **495.00**

12" w, 6-1/4" d, 5-3/4" h, pine and poplar, orig red paint, applied molding on lid, dovetailed case, molded base, int. slotted for divider (missing) **550.00**

Bucket, 9-1/2" d, 10-1/4" h, oak, slat, tapered, metal band, lid with porcelain finial, painted salmon **880.00**

Busk, 12" h, carved maple, engraved with Indian smoking pipe, chip-carved geometric compass designs, attributed to New England, early 19th C, stand **980.00**

Butter paddle, figured maple, open heart terminal . **2,500.00**

Book rack, sterling silver ends with scrolling decoration and monograms, **$170**.

Photo courtesy of Dotta Auction Co., Inc.

Candle mold, 16" h, 21-1/2" l, 9-1/2" w, twenty-four pewter tubes, old brown paint with spattered white, sq cut nail construction, old edge chips and splits **590.00**

Canoe cup, 5-3/4" l, 2-1/4" h, cup with elongated bowl, carved beaver, New England, 19th C, with stand **520.00**

Chandelier shaft, 20-1/2" l, 2-3/4" d, turned, acorn finial, painted in dry red and green, 18th C, never used **385.00**

Compote, turned, orig painted dec, initials "M.H.D.H." on base, 6" h **1,500.00**

Cookie board, walnut, 10" x 12"
Carved man and women in Victorian dress **3,000.00**
Carved soldier holding sword, tent, American flag, drum, stack of cannon balls **3,750.00**

Figure, carved and painted
2-3/4" l, 1" w, 3" h, standing bird, white gesso with red and black highlights **385.00**
2-3/4" l, 1-1/4" w, 3-5/8" h, seated Doberman with collar, shellacked, aged patina **495.00**
3-1/4" l, 2-1/4" w, 1-7/8" h, frog, pine, applied metal eyes, painted dark green, red mouth **495.00**
3-1/2" l, 1-1/2" w, 3-5/8" h, standing duck, pine, incised wings and tail, natural wood finish, black and yellow paint highlights **420.00**
4" l, 1-1/4" w, 3-1/2" h, standing Scottie terrier, incised lines for fur, painted black, painted black paws, carved "C. S." for Carl Snavely **200.00**

Firkin
9" d base, 7" h, staved construction, four wooden bands, hand forged iron bail handle, wooden stopper, painted red, America, early 19th C, minor wear **265.00**
12" d, 12-1/2" h, staved construction, green lapped bands, swing handle fastened with pegs, painted red, "Cassia" inscribed in white letters, matching cover, America, mid-19th C, wear **530.00**

Flax wheel, 45" h, upright type, mixed hardwoods, four turned legs, single treadle, double flyers with bobbins, single

wheel at top with turned spokes, few replacements **250.00**

Fruit, grouping of carved, gessoed, and polychromed fruits, grapes, apples, citrus, bananas, and cantaloupe, attributed to Adams County, PA **6,050.00**

Fruit bowl, 9-1/2" w, 4-/4" h, hardwood, sample-type, six-sided, dovetailed, pegged turned feet, painted yellow ground with brown highlighted grain painting, each panel with different graining, rag sponged interior with finger dot pattern **2,860.00**

Herb drying rack, pine, old brown surface, mortised construction, later added old shoe feet, 29-1/2" w, 48-1/2" h **115.00**

Thacher's Calculating Instrument, for performing arthimetical calculations, original instruction sheet, 22" l, some loss to paper overlay, **$350**.

Photo courtesy of Alderfer Auction Co.

Perpetual calendar, round, **$95**.

Photo courtesy of Dotta Auction Co., Inc.

Jar, cov

3-1/2" d, 6" h, Peaseware, bulbous, shaped finial, incised ring dec on lid and body, low foot **325.00**

8-3/4" d, 9" h, treenware, fan shaped sponged vinegar dec in red over mustard, wide sloping rim and base, glued repair, edge damage on lid flange, age crack **1,210.00**

Letter holder, 13" l, fretwork, demilune form, central handle, the sides and dividers fret-carved with scrolling ivy leaves, Victorian, early 20th C **250.00**

Mask, carved

11" l, plain, well handled form, Nepal, 19th C or earlier **360.00**

11" l, wild boar, red, black, green, white, and orange **470.00**

12" l, face painted red, early 20th C **715.00**

13" l, turbaned man, face painted black.............. **765.00**

14" h, man wearing an ornate turban, brown stained face, red lips, Nepal, 19th C **940.00**

14-1/2" l, divinity, pronounced teeth and eyes, painted white, yellow, red, black, and green, Nepal, 19th C.............. **825.00**

Measuring device, carved and inlaid shoe-form, carved head of gentleman, ivory inlaid eyes, inlaid metal buckle, two ivory inlaid panels each dec with two engraved shoes, Holland, late 18th C, minor losses, wear, crack **920.00**

Mortar and pestle, 7" h, burl, flame graining, tapered sides, incised ring dec, lignum vitae pedestal, age splits **375.00**

Pantry box, 6-1/4" d, 2-1/4" h, round, painted black, top carved with central star within medallion and leafy border, cross hatch swags on side, int. lined with partial advertising lithographs, New England, mid-19th C, minor imperfections.............. **715.00**

Cage for bird or small animal, rounded top, sliding side opening, original perch and feed containers, **$75**.

Photo courtesy of Dotta Auction Co., Inc.

Pewter rack, hanging, 35" w, 3-3/4" d, 29-3/4" h, oak, dark finish, two shelves, stylized lion finials on tops, wire nail construction, English .. **150.00**

Picture frame

13-3/8" w, 15-1/2" h, stenciled and painted, rect, gold floral dec on black ground, remnants of paper label on reverse...................... **375.00**

13-3/4" w, 17-5/8" h, painted pine, black half round frame, meandering fruited vine and plant border, 19th C, finish alligatored.................. **520.00**

19-5/16" w, 22" h, rect, reticulated scalloped edge, compass star corner rosettes, painted black, 19th C, finish alligatored.................. **550.00**

Quilt rack, folding

34-3/4" w, 64" h, two sections, pine, old natural finish, three cross pcs mortised into frame **95.00**

108" w, 66" h, three sections, each fitted with three cross pcs mortised into frame, cast iron hinges, old putty colored paint............................ **120.00**

Saffron cup, 2-1/2" d, 4-7/8" h, Lehnware, blue ground, strawberry motif, blue, green, red, and salmon highlights, minor base chips..... **3,080.00**

Salver, 10-3/4" d, mahogany, molded pie-crust edge, America, 19th C, staining, edge loss................. **2,820.00**

Scoop, 9-3/4" l, carved, America, 19th C.......... **210.00**

Scrub box, wall type, 7-1/2" w, 11-3/4" h, pine, painted green, America, 19th C, wear **715.00**

Shelf, hanging

20-1/2" w, 6-5/8" d, 25-1/4" h, walnut, pine secondary wood, scalloped ends, three graduating shelves with molded edges, brass pulls on two small base drawers, ... **1,495.00**

21-1/2" w, 7-1/2" d, 26-1/2" h, softwood, scalloped and scrolled cut-outs, painted black and red **1,650.00**

22" w, 6-3/4" d, 29-1/2" h, walnut, four graduated shelves, rope suspended through hole in top of both side supports............. **990.00**

Shoe horn, tiger maple, carved clasped hand terminal, 1826 .... **4,000.00**

Slate board, 11-1/4" w, 4-1/2" h, tiger maple frame, slate on both sides................ **1,980.00**

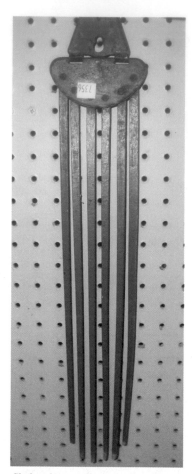

Clothes dryer, wall mounted type, six arms, **$200**.

Spoon rack, hanging, 10" w, 20" h, butternut or walnut, old faint blue-green graining on black ground, red bird's claw shaped dec, three racks hold six spoons each, pierced arch crest, triangular shaped scalloping across base, nailed splits, one scallop repaired **300.00**

Sugar bowl, cov, 5-3/4" h, burl, pedestal, ex-Clark Garrett **4,500.00**

Sugar bucket, cov

13-3/4" h, stave construction, copper tacks, bent hickory wood handle, minor wear and edge chips **460.00**

21" h, old blue-gray paint over earlier colors, tapered sides, copper tacks in staves, bottom painted green, arched bentwood handle, old chips on lid........................... **490.00**

Spoon, carved, seafarer's profile, polychrome decoration, **$45.**

Photo courtesy of Joseph P. Smalley, Jr., Auctioneer.

Tobacco jar, cov, 6-1/2" d, 7-1/2" h, treenware, turned and painted poplar, round, finger grained paint dec on yellow base, brown highlights **1,430.00**

Toddy ladle, 14-1/4" l, carved, notched handle, round bowl, dark brown patina, America, early 19th C, wear **440.00**

Trencher, hand carved, oval form, ends shaped to form handles, old black paint on exterior, minor shrinkage cracks, 23-1/2" l, 14" d, 4 1/4" h, **$185.**

Photo courtesy of Alderfer Auction Co.

Trencher, 23" l, 10-3/4" w, 3-1/4" h, rect, canted sides, rough hewn from pine, good patina............................ **65.00**

Trivet, 4-1/4" x 7-7/8" x 4-3/8" h, pine, wire nails, cut-out feet and ends on apron, old robin's egg blue with red stripes, hand painted decoupaged print of Mt. Vernon on top, minor flaking, multiple nail holes in one area **350.00**

Trump indicator, 4" h, pencil holder, barrel shape, rotates, brass pointers, 4 orig pencils **35.00**

Tub, 3-5/8" d, 2-1/2" h, Treenware, chip carved edge, two handles, heart cut-outs, dark green (black) ext., yellowed ivory paint int., split **1,375.00**

Ventriloquist's head, mounted on later stand 5" w, 6" d, 8" h, carved pine, natural surface, America, c1930, eyes missing... **375.00**
5-1/2" w, 5" d, 8-1/2" h, carved yellow pine, fixed eyes, spring-activated mouth with pull string, old patina, attributed to southern U.S., last quarter 19th C... **1,150.00**

Wall pocket, Victorian, walnut, carved female head and leaves, 17" w, 22" h, **$195.**

Photo courtesy of Joy Luke Auctions.

Wall shelf, 38-1/2" l, 6-1/2" d, 16" h, bird's eye maple, carved, shaped and slightly bowed top shelf with incised front on pierced, shaped, scrolling supports, each with three circular bosses joined by incised medial bar, lower shaped shelf, old finish, New England, mid-19th C, minor imperfections............. **920.00**

Watch hutch, 8" h, c1780, mahogany, early bracket clock shape, brass finial, tooled interior panel, and feet, ex-Clark Garrett **10,000.00**

WORLD'S FAIRS AND EXPOSITIONS

History: The Great Exhibition of 1851 in London marked the beginning of the World's Fair and Exposition movement. The fairs generally featured exhibitions from nations around the world displaying the best of their industrial and scientific achievements.

Many important technological advances have been introduced at world's fairs, including the airplane, telephone, and electric lights. Ice cream cones, hot dogs, and iced tea were first sold by vendors at fairs. Art movements often were closely connected to fairs, with the Paris Exhibition of 1900 generally considered to have assembled the best of the works of the Art Nouveau artists.

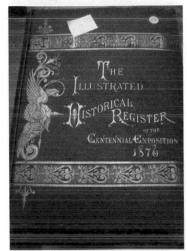

Book, *The Illustrated Historical Register of the Centennial Exposition, 1876,* gold trim on black leather cover, illustrated, **$250.**

Centennial, 1876

Bank, still, cast iron, Independence Hall, 9" h x 7" w **350.00**

Glass slipper, Gillinder, clear **35.00**

Handkerchief, 29-1/2" x 33", silk, dark golden background, black printed designs of Memorial Hall Art Gallery, Horticultural Hall, Machinery Hall, Agricultural Hall, Main Exhibition Building, large eagle and shield at top with "Fairmount Park, Philadelphia, 1776-1876" at bottom, stitched to cloth covered backing board, framed, small holes and staining **435.00**

Centennial Exhibition Puzzle Blocks, George Chinnock Co., five puzzles and illustration, 1875, original box, **$300**.

Medal, wooden, Main Building, 3" d................. **60.00**

Scarf, 19" x 34", Memorial Hall, Art Gallery colorful...... **100.00**

New Orleans World's Industrial and Cotton Expo, 1885, program, cover stamped "April 1885".................. **45.00**

Bird's eye view, Centennial, **$150**.
Photo courtesy of Alderfer Auction Co.

Columbian Exposition, 1893

Album, 5-3/4" x 9", hardcover, gold emb "World's Fair Album of Chicago 1893".......... **50.00**

Book, *History of the World's Fair Being A Complete Description of the World's Colombian Exposition from Inception,* Major Ben C. Truman, illus, 592 pgs......................... **60.00**

Cup, 2-1/2" h, peachblow glass, double handles, ribbed, shading from pink to white, gilt dec "World's Fair-1893

Chicago," minor crack at handle......................... **300.00**

Medal, 1-1/2", brass luster finish white metal, bust portrait of Christopher Columbus on one side, other side "400th Anniversary of The Discovery of America," 1492-Oct-1892 .... **20.00**

Mug, 4-3/4" h, salt glazed stoneware, imp, blue accents "World's Fair Chicago 1893" **165.00**

Photo booklet................. **25.00**

Souvenir spoon.............. **25.00**

Salt and pepper shakers, pr, 2-1/2" l, lay down, verse, dated 1893, Mt Washington **125.00**

Sugar bowl, open, 5-1/2" w, 2-3/4" h, peachblow, rose-colored walls, pronounced off-white ribs, satin finish, two applied opaque white glass handles, smooth pontil mark, made by Mt Washington Glass Co., sold by Libbey Glass Co., signature with flourishes **485.00**

Ticket............................. **30.00**

Watch case opener, Keystone Watch Case Co............. **15.00**

Cake plate and server, fair logo in center, gold border, tab handles, **$45**.
Photo courtesy of Sky Hawk Auctions.

Pan American, 1901

Cigar case, hinged aluminum 2-1/2" x 5-1/2" **35.00**

Frying pan, pictures North and South America, 6" long . **75.00**

Medallion, bright luster brass, profile of buffalo between "Souvenir" and "1901," reverse marked "Pan-American Exposition/May-November Buffalo, NY". **15.00**

Pinback button

Swifts Pig, multicolored plump pig seated in frying pan, tiny inscription "Pan-American Souvenir," black lettering "Swift's Premium Hams and Bacon-Swift & Co., U.S.A." **25.00**

Temple of Music, multicolored art view of building exterior **25.00**

Plate, frosted glass, three cats painted on dec, 7-1/2" d **35.00**

Poster, Pan American Exposition, Buffalo, May 1-November 1, 1901, based on painting "Spirit of Niagara" by Evelyn Rumsey Carey, 47-1/2" x 24-3/4"................ **12,650.00**

St. Louis, 1904

Match safe and cigar cutter, 2-3/4" w, 1-1/2" h, detailed drawing of Palace of Varied Industries on one side, picture of Gardens and Terraces of States on other, tarnished **150.00**

Medal, silvered brass, 2-3/4" d **60.00**

Photo album, eight pgs, 15 orig photos........................... **45.00**

Pinback button, KY home, multicolored exhibit building of Kentucky against upper half gold background, inscribed "Ky. Home World's Fair," bottom margin inscription "It's Part Mine" **25.00**

Plate, 7-1/4" d, scene in center, lacy border **25.00**

Stamp holder, aluminum, 1-1/8" x 1-3/8"......................... **35.00**

Souvenir mug, bronze, emb scene of Palace of Electricity, 6" h............................. **115.00**

Souvenir plate, 7" d, Festival Hall, Cascade Gardens **55.00**

Tumbler, 4" high, copper plated base, metal, shows Louisiana Purchase Monument, Cascades, Union Station and Liberal Arts Bldg.......... **35.00**

Panama-Pacific, 1915

Pocket watch, official, silver plated, 2" d **300.00**

Postcard........................... **5.00**

Pan-Am, 1915, calendar plate, cobalt blue border with gold trim, flags, calendar pages, map of Panama Canal, Klopp & Kalbach, North Heidelburg, PA, address on front, $25.

Panoramic view of Panama-Pacific International Exposition, San Francisco, 1915, period frame, $75.

Photo courtesy of Dotta Auction Co., Inc.

Century of Progress,

Chicago, 1933

Employee badge, round medallion with "A Century of Progress" around perimeter, "International Exposition Chicago 1933" and employee number below **55.00**

Menu, Walgreens **45.00**

Pinback button
I Was There, red, white, and blue **20.00**
New York Visitor, red, white, and blue **20.00**

Playing cards, full deck, showing views of the fair, all different, black and white **45.00**

Ring, adjustable, silvered brass, miniature exhibit building on blue enamel background, inscribed "Chicago, 1934" **25.00**

Souvenir key, bright silver luster brass, sponsored by Master Lock Co., "Master Laminated Padlocks Sold All Over the World," opposite side with miniature form image of exhibit buildings and "World's Fair 1933," tiny horseshoe and four-leaf clover, inscribed "Keep Me For Good Luck" **28.00**

Gaucho hat, Golden Gate International Expo, San Francisco, 1939, black, hand-painted text, top of rim with brown, blue, gray, and green silhouettes of buildings, Golden Gate Bridge, mountains, top of crown has fair building in white brown accents, brown and blue spotlights in background, bottom of crown has brown and yellow silhouettes of fair buildings and spotlight accents on back, yellow and brown attached cord, white painted text "Patent Applied For Sinbeck," crazing, 15-1/2" d, 3-1/2" h, $45.

Photo courtesy of Hake's Americana & Collectibles.

Tape measure, silver, blue, and white official logo, other side with black and white photo of Paris replica village exhibit **32.00**

Toy wagon, red, white wheels, decal of Transportation Bldg in middle approx 3-1/2" l **175.00**

Golden Gate, 1939

Bookmark, typical view, 4" l **20.00**

Match book, orig matches, pictures Pacifica **10.00**

Token, shows Sun Tower and Bridge, 1-1/8" d **15.00**

Ashtray, New York, 1939, Art Deco, space for four cigarettes, blue and tan stylized fair logo showing Trylon and Perisphere. 5/8" x 2-1/2" x 3-1/2", $25.

Photo courtesy of Hake's Americana & Collectibles.

New York, 1939

Bookmark, 3-3/4" l, diecut and silvered thin brass spear page marker and letter opener, applied metal disk with blue and dark orange accents on silver luster "New York Worlds Fair, 1939," plus images of Trylon and Perisphere... **20.00**

Candy tin, miniature, by Bagatele, very colorful, 4-1/4" x 6-1/2" **65.00**

Folder, 6-1/4" x 12", printed paper, blue, white, and orange, one side with three images of Borden's Elsie, Trylon, and Perisphere, reverse with blue and white printing, pictorial family endorsement, recipe, and text relating to Borden's Chateau cheese, August 1939 publication date............ **20.00**

Pencil sharpener, bakelite **45.00**

Pinback button, 1-1/4" d, gold and blue cello, blue fabric ribbon inscribed in gold for May 1, 1939 event, Revolutionary War soldier behind inscription "New Haven Advertising Club, Inc./ Vigilance," outer rim inscribed "New Haven Day-New York World's Fair"................ **125.00**

Pocketknife, 2" l steel knife based on each side by pearl-like plastic panels, one with tiny blue Trylon and Perisphere, plus inscription "New York World's Fair 1939," two steel blades **40.00**

Postcard, photo type.......... **6.00**

Ring, adjustable, silvered brass, inscribed "World's Fair" over "NY," flanked by numeral "19" on one left, "39" on right **25.00**

Souvenir spoon, 7" l, Theme Building on front, "Pat. Pend., Wm Rogers Mfg. Co."... **25.00**

Plate, embossed potter at wheel, turquoise glaze, backstamp "Joint Exhibit of Capital and Labor, The American Pottery, New York World's Fair," $25.

Photo courtesy of Sky Hawk Auctions.

New York, 1964

Dime, circular plastic case with 1946 Eisenhower dime in center, reads "NY World's Fair, 1964-1965 Neutron Irradiated Dime," back reads "Atomic Energy Commission, United States of America," 2" d **40.00**

Fork and spoon display, 11" l, mounted on wooden plaque, Unisphere decals on handles **45.00**

Hat, black felt, Unisphere emblem, white cord trim, feather, name "Richard" embroidered on front **25.00**

Lodge medallion, bronze luster finish, image of Unisphere and two exhibit buildings, brass hanger loop, inscribed "The Grand Lodge I.O.O.F. of the State of New York" .. **15.00**

Paperweight, panoramic scenes **40.00**

Postcard, 10 miniature pictures, 20 natural color reproductions, unused . **20.00**

Salt and pepper shakers, pr, Unisphere, figural, ceramic **50.00**

Souvenir book, *Official Souvenir Book of the New York World's Fair,* 1965 .... **25.00**

Yo-yo................................ **45.00**

YARD-LONG PRINTS

History: In the early 1900s, many yard-long prints could be had for a few cents postage and a given number of wrappers or box tops. Others were premiums for renewing a subscription to a magazine or newspaper. A large number were advertising items created for a store or company and had calendars on the front or back. Many people believe that the only true yard-long print is 36 inches long and titled "A Yard of Kittens," etc. But lately collectors feel that any long and narrow print, horizontal or vertical, can be included in this category. It is a matter of personal opinion.

Values are listed for full-length prints in near-mint condition, nicely framed, and with original glass.

Reproduction Alert: Some prints are being reproduced. Know your dealer.

Note: Numbers in parentheses below indicate C. G. and J. M. Rhoden and W. D. and M. J. Keagy, *Those Wonderful Yard-Long Prints and More,* Book 1 (1989), Book 2 (1992), Book 3 (1995), book number and page on which the item is illustrated, e.g. (3-52) refers to Book 3, page 52.

Advisers: Charles G. and Joan M. Rhoden and W. D. and M. J. Keagy.

Animals

A Yard of Puppies, ten puppies playing, one with foot in feeding dish (Bk 1-50) **450.00**

Ducklings, by W. M. Carey, baby ducks playing around a pool of water (Bk 3-22) **400.00**

Our Feathered Pets, by Paul DeLongpre, twelve birds sitting on lattice work fence (Bk 3-19) **400.00**

Spring is Here, by Cambril, c1907, The Gray Litho Co., New York (Bk 2-18) **325.00**

Tug of War, seven kittens and seven puppies playing tug of war (Bk 2-28) **400.00**

Twenty-one birds, sitting on a wire, c1899 (Bk 3-20) . **400.00**

Yard of Dogs, copyright 1903, eight adult dogs, one with bird in mouth, one with bandage on head covering eye (Bk 2-21) **325.00**

Yard of Kittens, eleven kittens playing, one climbing on box (Bk 2-23) **400.00**

Calendar

1095, Swift's Premium, four beautiful ladies showing four seasons (Bk 3-112) **400.00**

1906, Pabst Extract, Indian, by C. W. Henning, "Hiawatha's Wooing" poem on back of print (Bk 2-101).......... **575.00**

1907, Metropolitan Life Ins Co., showing four stages of life (Bk 3-111) **475.00**

1915, Seiz Good Shoes, lady and child on swing (Bk 2-102) **575.00**

1917, by Knowles Hare Jr., lady in pink hat and dress (Bk 3-88) **500.00**

1919, Clay, Robinson & Co., Live Stock Commission, advertising and picture of bull, Merry Monarch, on back (Bk 3-106) **500.00**

1925, Seiz Good Shoes, lady with walking stick **800.00**

Flowers and fruits

A Yard of Cherries, by Guy Bedford, c1906 (Bk 2-69) **300.00**

A Yard of Chrysanthemums, by Maud Stumm (Bk 2-33) **300.00**

A Yard of Wild Flowers, artist sgd in lower left corner (Bk 3-39) **300.00**

Bridal Favors, by Mary E. Hart (Bk 2-65) **300.00**

Dogwood and Violets, Paul DeLongpre, sgd (Bk 3-28) **350.00**

Lilacs and Lillies, artist sgd in lower right corner (Bk 3-31) **300.00**

Study of Sweet Peas, by Grace Barton Allen, copyright 1900 (Bk 2-62) **300.00**

Yard of Assorted Fruit, basket of cherries, plate of fruit on book (Bk 2-73)............ **300.00**

Long ladies

At the Gate, lady in pink by garden gate (Bk 3-82) **500.00**

Beautiful lady, holding vase of red roses (Bk 3-93)..... **500.00**

Beautiful lady, standing by table, holding open basket, vase of yellow roses on table (Bk 2-88)..................... **700.00**

Butterick Pattern Lady, copyright 1930 (Bk 3-42) **600.00**

Indian Maiden, holding basket of flowers (Bk 3-89)..... **500.00**

The Girl with the Laughing Eyes, copyright 1910 by F. Carlyle, lady in long off-shoulder gown, holding paper lantern (Bk 2-92) **500.00**

The Girl with the Poppies, by B. Lichtman (Bk 3-125) ... **500.00**

Wynette Lady, standing by large vase of yellow roses (Bk 3-80) **500.00**

For more information, *see Warman's American Pottery & Porcelain*, 2nd edition.

YELLOWWARE

History: Yellowware is a heavy earthenware which varies in color from a rich pumpkin to lighter shades, which are more tan than yellow. The weight and strength varies from piece to piece. Although plates, nappies, and custard cups are found, kitchen bowls and other cooking utensils are most prevalent.

The first American yellowware was produced at Bennington, Vermont. English yellowware has additional ingredients that make its body much harder. Derbyshire and Sharp's were foremost among the English manufacturers.

Bowl, rolled rim, three brown stripes, 9" d, **$95.**

Bowl, brown and cream striping, 9-1/2" d, 4-1/2" h, **$100.**
Photo courtesy of Alderfer Auction Co.

Bank, 3-5/8" h, house shape, molded detail highlighted in black, roof marked "For My Dear Girl," firing crack at chimney **660.00**

Bean pot, cov, 6-1/2" h, three white slip accent bands, bands repeated on orig matching lid, relief lines on both, Watt pottery logo on base, orig lid has been broken and reglued, bowl has some staining from use **165.00**

Bottle, slip dec attributed to Rudolph Christ, NC Moravian, early 19th C **9,900.00**

Bowl, 8-1/2" d, 4" h, minor age crazing to glaze............ **35.00**

Butter tub, twist handles, lead and manganese glaze, sgd "John Bell" **6,050.00**

Candleholders, pr, 2-1/2" h, Rockingham glaze, attributed to Bennington, replaced glass chimneys, c1850 .... **615.00**

Canning jar, 6-1/2" h, relief draped design, some crazing to glaze, rim surface chips **125.00**

Coffeepot, covered, top pot with pierced holes in base, covered, **$315.**

Coffeepot, 8-1/2" h, Rockingham glaze, relief of woman snorting snuff on one side, man smoking pipe on other side, matching lid, c1850 .... **50.00**

Creamer, 4-3/4" h, brown stripes, white band, blue seaweed dec, shallow flake on inside edge of table ring **440.00**

Figure, recumbent lion, 8" l Incised "Buck" on front **4,000.00**
Plain front, chip........ **2,600.00**

Flask, 7 3/4" h, book shape, Rockingham glaze, c1850, two unglazed spots on one side **275.00**

Food mold
3-3/4" d, 1-1/4" h, miniature, Yellow Rock, Phila mark **185.00**
7-1/2" d, 2-3/4" h, turk's head **145.00**

Foot warmer, 9" h, Rockingham glaze, relief scroll design at shoulder, c1850 .... **440.00**

Mixing bowl, thin cobalt blue stripes, 10" d, **$110.**

Mixing bowl, folded rim, green and white stripes, some wear from use, 10" d, **$85.**

Lamp base, 8-1/2" h, prominent rings, running brown and yellow/green glaze, partial lamp parts **115.00**

Measure, 5-3/4" h, 6-1/2" d, Spearpoint & Trellis..... **300.00**

Miniature, chamber pot, 1-1/2" h, cream and blue spongeware glaze, c1900 .... **90.00**

Mug

3" h, relief flower designs, ochre accented tooled band at rim and handle, stained from use.......................... **80.00**
3-3/4" h, adv, red stencil on one side: "Fenton's Pekin Buffalo, NY," black stencil on reverse: "If drinking interferes with your business, give up business," two gilt-relief accent bands............... **95.00**

Mug, band of cream and blue dec, hairline crack, chip in handle, 5" d, 4-1/2" h, **$125**.

Photo courtesy of Alderfer Auction Co.

Nappy, 9-1/2" d, 2-3/4" h, applied copper luster design in Pennsylvania-style floral design, c1860, very light 1" hairline extending from rim, overall wear to copper luster at int. rim **275.00**
Pepper pot, 4-1/2" h, blue seaweed dec, band dec **475.00**
Pie funnel, 2-1/2" h, unmarked **125.00**
Pie plate, 10" d, unmarked **90.00**

Pitcher, white mid band, applied strap handle, **$225**.

Photo courtesy of Joseph P. Smalley, Jr., Auctioneer.

Pitcher, 9-1/2" h, hound handle, Rockingham glaze, relief

design of columns of hanging game and foul, relief eagle design under spout, c1850, minor hairline in bottom **125.00**

Rolling pin, wooden handle through central bore, 15" h, **$315**.

Photo courtesy of Alderfer Auction Co.

Rolling pin, 8" l, very minor glaze age crazing....... **470.00**
Spittoon, 8" d, Rockingham glaze, overall relief vine pattern **30.00**
Storage jar, ovoid, slip dec attributed to Rudolph Christ, NC Moravian, early 19th C **24,200.00**
Sugar bowl, cov, 4-1/2" h, Rockingham glaze, relief vine and floral design........... **65.00**
Teapot, 5" h, applied brown/green sponged glaze, orig lid, small glaze flake......... **110.00**
Washboard, 25" h, brown Rockingham glaze, c1880, minor glaze wear **550.00**
Wash bowl and pitcher, 9-1/2" d bowl, 7-3/4" h pitcher, brown and blue sponged dec, brown stripe on pitcher **335.00**
Wine glass, 4" h, Rockingham glaze, darker accents at rim, c1870.......................... **275.00**

ZANE POTTERY

History: In 1921, Adam Reed and Harry McClelland bought the Peters and Reed Pottery in Zanesville, Ohio. The firm continued production of garden wares and introduced several new art lines: Sheen, Powder Blue, Crystalline, and Drip. The factory was sold in 1941 to Lawton Gonder.

Bowl

5" d, brown and blue **45.00**
6-1/2" d, blue, marked "Zanesware" **35.00**
Figure, 10-1/8" h, cat, black, green eyes................. **500.00**
Jardinière, 34" h, green matte glaze, matching pedestal,

artist sgd "Frank Ferreu" **375.00**

Vase

5" h, green, cobalt blue drip glaze............................. **30.00**
7" h, flowing medium green over dark forest green ground **85.00**
8" h, ivory glaze, emb flowers and leaves **75.00**
Wall pocket, Moss Aztec, 8-1/4" l **95.00**

ZANESVILLE POTTERY

LA MORO

History: Zanesville Art Pottery, one of several potteries located in Zanesville, Ohio, began production in 1900. At first, a line of utilitarian products was made; art pottery was introduced shortly thereafter. The major line was La Moro, which was hand painted and decorated under glaze. The firm was bought by S. A. Weller in 1920 and became known as Weller Plant No. 3.

Marks: The impressed block-print mark "La Moro" appears on the high-glazed and matte-glazed decorated ware.

Vase, baluster, speckled matte green glaze, unmarked, 12" h, **$230**.

Photo courtesy of David Rago Auctions, Inc.

Bowl, 6-1/2" d, fluted edge, mottled blue glaze........ **65.00**
Coffeepot, cov, 8" h, stoneware, Bodine Pottery Co., sand colored, unglazed ext., Albany slip int., tin wire straps, handle, spout, lid, and wire bale handle, c1880.. **1,020.00**

Jardinière
7-1/8" h, 8-1/2" d, waisted cylindrical form, landscape scene, blue, green, and maroon matte glaze, c1908 .... **175.00**

8-1/4" h, ruffled rim, cream to light amber peony blossoms, shaded brown ground .. **75.00**

Plate, 4-1/2" d, applied floral dec **25.00**

Vase, Standard Glaze, wild rose decoration, marked "SO," factory-drilled, 4" d, 8-1/4" h, **$175**.

Photo courtesy of David Rago Auctions, Inc.

Vase
8-3/4" h, cone shaped top, bulbous base, La Morro, marked "2/802/4" **350.00**

10-1/4" h, light gray horse portrait, light olive green to blue-green ground, matte ext., glossy brown int., sgd "R. G. Turner" **825.00**

ZSOLNAY POTTERY

History: Vilmos Zsolnay (1828-1900) assumed control of his brother's factory in Pécs, Hungary, in the mid-19th century. In 1899, Miklos, Vilmos's son, became manager. The firm still produces ceramic ware.

The early wares are highly ornamental, glazed, and have a cream-colored ground. Eosin glaze, a deep rich play of colors reminiscent of Tiffany's iridescent wares, received a gold medal at the 1900 Paris exhibition. Zsolnay Art Nouveau pieces show great creativity.

Marks: Originally, no trademark was used; but in 1878 the company began to use a blue mark depicting the five towers of the cathedral at Pécs. The initials "TJM" represent the names of Miklos's three children.

Note: Zsolnay's recent series of iridescent-glazed figurines, which initially were inexpensive, now are being sought by collectors and steadily increasing in value.

Figure, musician, seated, traditional dress, earthenware, green and gold luster glaze, ovoid base with indistinct title/signature beside seat, Hungary, 20th C, 9" h, **$500**.

Photo courtesy of Skinner, Inc.

Bowl, 6-1/2" l, 2-1/2" h, sea shell shape, hp florals, gold highlights and edging, blue mark "Zsolnay Pecs," castle mark, "Patent," imp factory mark and numbers **160.00**

Cache pot, 13" d, young girls dance holding hands around stylized tree form, blue, pale silver, and pale lilac glazes **4,250.00**

Chalice, 6" h, 4 flower stems as handles attached to upper body, flowers and berries in relief as terminals, green and blue Eosin glazes, red int., form #5668, c1899, millennium factory mark, ext. rim chip repaired **1,650.00**

Coffee set, 8-1/2" h cov coffeepot, creamer, sugar, cake plate, six cups, saucers, and dessert plates, cobalt blue and gold trim, white ground **600.00**

Compote, 11" d, ribbed, four caryatids molded as angels supports, blue-green irid glaze **1,100.00**

Creamer, 6-1/2" l, fierce dragon handle **250.00**

Figure, nude woman standing with bathing urn and robe at her side, iridescent green-gold finish, marked "Zsolnay Hungary Hand Painted," 10-1/2", **$360**.

Photo courtesy of Skinner, Inc.

Figure, small girl feeding hen, iridescent green-gold glaze, gilt maker's stamps, Hungary, 20th C, 4-1/4" h, **$125**.

Photo courtesy of Skinner, Inc.

Figure
Bears, pair, emerald green glaze, 7-1/2" l, 5" h **695.00**

Mallard ducks, 7" l, 7" h **195.00**

Spaniel, artist sgd, 5" h ... **95.00**

Woman, 9-3/8" l, 4-3/4" w, 5-1/2" h, irid blue and green glaze, brown manufacturer's stamp "Zsolnay PECS Made in Hungary," repaired base chips............................ **460.00**

Garden seat, 18-1/2" h, form #1105, c1882, wear to top surface, repairs to applied dec **1,850.00**

Jardinière, 16" l, ovoid, multicolored florals, protruding pierced roundels, cream ground, blue steep mark............................ **450.00**

Jug, 10-1/2" h, yellow glaze, worn gilt highlights, form #109, c1882............... **500.00**

Pitcher, 7-1/2" h, form #5064, red/maroon metallic Eosin ground, cream and pale brown flower dec, c1898, millennium factory mark **750.00**

Jug, earthenware, Japonesque, ovoid, short spout, dragon handle, mauve glazed ground, enamel decorated peonies, Hungary, late 19th C, 10-1/4" h, **$300**.

Photo courtesy of Skinner, Inc.

Pitcher, reticulated lid, handled cylindrical vessel, floral and foliate designs in gold, pink, blue, green, cream-colored glossy glaze, impressed and stamped marks, 12-1/2" h, crazing, **$600**.

Photo courtesy of Skinner, Inc.

Puzzle jug, 6-1/2" h, pierced roundels, irid dec, cream ground, castle mark, imp "Zsolnay" **195.00**

Vase

9" h, tapering reeded baluster, gold and cobalt blue irid finish **225.00**

9-1/4" h, quatrefoil rim, elongated neck, figure of woman wearing diaphanous dress seated on shoulder, irid gold, green and blue shaded glaze, irid stamped mark "Zsolnay PECS Made in Hungary" **460.00**

11" h, 5" d, classic shape, flaring rim, nacreous chartreuse glaze, stylized suns and flowers, gold stamp mark........................... **495.00**

AUCTION HOUSES

The following auction houses cooperate with *Warman's* by providing catalogs of their auctions and price lists. This information is used to prepare *Warman's Antiques and Collectibles Price Guide*, volumes in the Warman's Encyclopedia of Antiques and Collectibles. This support is truly appreciated.

Sanford Alderfer Auction Company
501 Fairgrounds Road
Hatfield, PA 19440
(215) 393-3000
Web site:
www.alderfercompany.com

American Bottle Auctions
2523 J. St.
Suite 203
Sacramento, CA 95816-4848
(800) 806-7722
Web site:
www.americanbottle.com

Andre Ammelounx
The Stein Auction Company
P.O. Box 136
Palantine, IL 60078
(847) 991-5927

Arthur Auctioneering
RD 2, P.O. Box 155
Hughesville, PA 17737
(717) 584-3697

Auction Team Köln
Jane Herz
6731 Ashley Court
Sarasota, FL 34241
(941) 925-0385

Auction Team Köln
Postfach 501168 D 5000
Köln 50, W. Germany

Bear Pen Antiques
2318 Bear Pen Hollow Road
Lock Haven, PA 17745
(717) 769-6655

Bertoia Auctions
2141-F Demarco Dr.
Vineland, NJ 08360
(856) 692-1881

Bonhams & Butterfields
Jon E. King, VP, business
development, NY
San Francisco
220 San Bruno Ave.
San Francisco, CA 94103
(415) 861-7500
Web site: www.butterfields.com

Buffalo Bay Auction Co.
5244 Quam Circle
Rogers, MN 55374
(612) 428-8440
Web site:
www.buffalobayauction.com

Cerebro
P. O. Box 327
East Prospect, PA 17317
(717) 252-3685

W. E. Channing & Co., Inc.
53 Old Santa Fe Trail
Santa Fe, NM 87501
(505) 988-1078

Chicago Art Galleries
5039 Oakton St.
Skokie, IL 60077
(847) 677-6080

Christie's
502 Park Ave.
New York, NY 10022
(212) 546-1000
Web site: www.christies.com

Cincinnati Art Galleries
635 Main St.
Cincinnati, OH 45202
(513) 381-2128
Web site:
www.cincinnatiartgalleries.com

Mike Clum, Inc.
P.O. Box 2
Rushville, OH 43150
(614) 536-9220

Cohasco Inc.
Postal 821
Yonkers, NY 10702
(914) 476-8500

Collection Liquidators Auction Service
341 Lafayette St.
New York, NY 10012
(212) 505-2455
Web site: http://www.rtam.com/coliq/bid.html
e-mail: coliq@erols.com

C. Wesley Cowan Historic Americana
673 Wilmer Ave.
Cincinnati, OH 45226
(513)-871-1670
Fax: (513) 871-8670
e-mail:
info@HistoricAmericana.com;
wescowan@fuse.net

Decoys Unlimited, Inc.
P.O. Box 206
West Barnstable, MA 02608
(508) 362-2766
Web site:
www.decoysunlimited.inc.com

DeWolfe & Wood
P.O. Box 425
Alfred, ME 04002
(207) 490-5572

Martin G. Denlinger
RR3, Box 3775
Morrisville, VT 05661
(802) 888-2775

Dixie Sporting Collectibles
1206 Rama Road
Charlotte, NC 28211
(704) 364-2900
Web site: www.sportauction.com

Dorothy Dous, Inc.
1261 University Drive
Yardley, PA 19067-2857
(888) 548-6635

Dotta Auction Company, Inc.
330 W. Moorestown Road
Nazareth, PA 18064
(610) 759-7389
Web site: www.dottaauction.com

William Doyle Galleries, Inc.
175 E. 87th St.
New York, NY 10128
(212) 427-2730
Web site:
www.doylegalleries.com

Early Auction Co.
123 Main St.
Milford, OH 45150
(513) 831-4833

Fain & Co.
P.O. Box 1330
Grants Pass, OR 97526
(888) 324-6726

**Ken Farmer Realty
& Auction Co.**
105A Harrison St.
Radford, VA 24141
(703) 639-0939
Web site: http://kenfarmer.com

Flomaton Antique Auction
P.O. Box 1017
320 Palafox St.
Flomaton, AL 36441
(334) 296-3059

Fontaine's Auction Gallery
1485 W. Housatonic St.
Pittsfield, MA 01201
(413) 488-8922
Web site:
www.fontaineauctions.com

Freeman's
1808 Chestnut St.
Philadelphia, PA 19103
(215) 563-9275
Web site:
www.freemanauction.com

Garth's Auction, Inc.
2690 Stratford Road
P.O. Box 369
Delaware, OH 43015
(740) 362-4771

Green Valley Auction Inc.
Route 2, Box 434
Mt. Crawford, VA 22841
(540) 434-4260

**Hake's Americana &
Collectibles**
P.O. Box 1444
York, PA 17405
(717) 848-1333

**Gene Harris Antique Auction
Center, Inc.**
203 South 18th Ave.
P.O. Box 476
Marshalltown, IA 50158
(515) 752-0600
Web site:
www.harrisantiqueauction.com

Norman C. Heckler & Company
Bradford Corner Road
Woodstock Valley, CT 06282
(203) 974-1634

High Noon
9929 Venice Blvd
Los Angeles, CA 90034
(310) 202-9010
Web site: www.High Noon.com

**Historical Collectibles
Auctions**
24 NW Court Square #201
Graham, NC 27253
(336) 570-2803
Web site: hcaauctions.com

Randy Inman Auctions, Inc.
P.O. Box 726
Waterville, ME 04903
(207) 872-6900
Web site:
www.inmanauctions.com

**Michael Ivankovich
Auction Co.**
P.O. Box 1536
Doylestown, PA 18901
(215) 345-6094
Web site: www.nutting.com

**Jackson's Auctioneers &
Appraisers**
2229 Lincoln St.
Cedar Falls, IA 50613
(319) 277-2256
Web site:
www.jacksonauction.com

James D. Julia Inc.
Rt 201 Skowhegan Road
P.O. Box 830
Fairfield, ME 04937
(207) 453-7125
Web site: www.juliaauctions.com

**Lang's Sporting
Collectables, Inc.**
31 R Turthle Cove
Raymond, ME 04071
(207) 655-4265

Joy Luke
The Gallery
300 E. Grove St.
Bloomington, IL 61701
(309) 828-5533
Web site: http://www.joyluke.com

**Mapes Auctioneers &
Appraisers**
1729 Vestal Pkwy
Vestal, NY 13850
(607) 754-9193

Martin Auctioneers Inc.
P.O. Box 477
Intercourse, PA 17534
(717) 768-8108

**McMasters Harris Doll
Auctions**
P.O. Box 1755
Cambridge, OH 43725
(614) 432-4419

**Gary Metz's Muddy River
Trading Company**
P.O. Box 1430
Salem, VA 24135
(540) 387-5070

William Frost Mobley
P.O. Box 10
Schoharie, NY 12157
(518) 295-7978

William Morford
RD #2
Cazenovia, NY 13035
(315) 662-7625

Neal Auction Company
4038 Magazine St.
New Orleans, LA 7015
(504) 899-5329
Web site: www.nealauction.com

**New Orleans Auction St.
Charles Auction Gallery, Inc.**
1330 St. Charles Ave.
New Orleans, LA 70130
(504) 586-8733
Web site:
www.neworleansauction.com

**Norton Auctioneers of
Michigan Inc.**
50 West Pearl at Monroe
Coldwater, MI 49036
(517) 279-9063

Old Barn Auction
10040 St. Rt. 224 West
Findlay, OH 45840
(419) 422-8531
Web site: www.oldbarn.com

**Richard Opfer
Auctioneering Inc.**
1919 Greenspring Drive
Timonium, MD 21093
(410) 252-5035
Web site: www.opferauction.com

Past Tyme Pleasures
PMB #204, 2491 San Ramon
Valley Blvd, #1
San Ramon, CA 94583
(925) 484-6442
Fax: (925) 484-2551
Web site: www.pastyme.com
e-mail: Pasttyme@excite.com

Pook and Pook
463 East Lancaster Ave.
P.O. Box 268
Downington, PA 19335
(610) 269-4040
Web site:
www.pookandpookinc.com

Postcards International
2321 Whitney Ave., Suite 102
P.O. Box 5398
Hamden, CT 06518
(203) 248-6621
Web site: www.csmonline.com/
postcardsint/

Poster Auctions International
601 W. 26th St.
New York, NY 10001
(212) 787-4000
Web site:
www.posterauction.com

Profitt Auction Company
684 Middlebrook Road
Staunton, VA 24401
(540) 885-7369

David Rago Auctions, Inc.
333 S. Main St.
Lambertville, NJ 08530
(609) 397-9374
Web site: www.ragoarts.com

Lloyd Ralston Toy Auction
350 Long Beach Blvd
Stratford, CT 06615
(203) 375-9399
Web site:
www.lloydralstontoys.com

James J. Reeves
P.O. Box 219
Huntingdon, PA 16652-0219
(814) 643-5497
Web site:
www.JamesJReeves.com

**Mickey Reichel Auction
Company**
18350 Hunters Ridge
Boonville, MO 65233
(660) 882-5292
Web site: www.awk-shn.com

Sandy Rosnick Auctions
15 Front St.
Salem, MA 01970
(508) 741-1130

Seeck Auctions
P.O. Box 377
Mason City, IA 50402
(641) 424-1116
Web site:
www.seeckauction.com

L. H. Selman Ltd
761 Chestnut St.
Santa Cruz, CA 95060
(408) 427-1177
Web site. www.selman.com

Skinner Inc.
Bolton Gallery
357 Main St.
Bolton, MA 01740
(978) 779 6241
Web site: www.skinnerinc.com

Skinner, Inc.
The Heritage on the Garden
63 Park Plaza
Boston, MA 02116
(978) 350-5429
Web site: www.skinnerinc.com

Sloans & Kenyon
4605 Bradley Blvd
Bethseda, MD 20815
(301) 634-2330
Web site:
www.sloansandkenyon.com

Joseph P. Smalley Jr.
2400 Old Bethlehem Pike
Quakertown, PA 18951
(215) 529-9834

Smith & Jones, Inc., Auctions
12 Clark Lane
Sudbury, MA 01776
(508) 443-5517

Sotheby's
1334 York Ave.
New York, NY 10021
(212) 606-7000
Web site: www.sothebys.com

Southern Folk Pottery Collectors Society
220 Washington St.
Bennett, NC 27208
(336) 581-4246

Stanton's Auctioneers
P.O. Box 146
144 South Main St.
Vermontville, MI 49096
(517) 726-0181

Michael Strawser
200 N. Main St., P.O. Box 332
Wolcottville, IN 46795
(219) 854-2859
Web site:
www.majolicaauctions.com

Swann Galleries Inc.
104 E. 25th St.
New York, NY 10010
(212) 254-4710
Web site:
www.swanngalleries.com

Swartz Auction Services
2404 N. Mattis Ave.
Champaign, IL 61826-7166
(217) 357-0197
Web site: http://www/
SwartzAuction.com

The House In The Woods
S91 W37851 Antique Lane
Eagle, WI 53119
(414) 594-2334

Theriault's
P.O. Box 151
Annapolis, MD 21401
(301) 224-3655
Web site: www.theriaults.com

Tradewind Antiques & Auctions
P.O. Box 249
Manchester-by-the-Sea, MA
01944-0249
(987) 526-4085
Web site:
www.tradewindsantiques.com

Treadway Gallery, Inc.
2029 Madison Road
Cincinnati, OH 45208
(513) 321-6742
Web site: http://
www.a3c2net.com/
treadwaygallery

Victorian Images
P.O. Box 284
Marlton, NJ 08053
(609) 985-7711
Web site: www.tradecards.com/vi

Bruce and Vicki Waasdorp
P.O. Box 434
10931 Main St.
Clarence, NY 14031
(716) 759-2361
Web site: http://www.antiques-stoneware.com

Wiederseim Associates, Inc.
P.O. Box 470
Chester Springs, PA 19425
(610) 827-1910
Web site: www.wiederseim.com

Woody Auction
Douglass, KS 67039
(316) 746-2694

Jim Wroda Auction Co.
5239 St. Rt. 49 South
Greenville, OH 45331
(937) 548-2640
Web site:
www.jimwrodaauction.com

York Town Auction, Inc.
1625 Haviland Road
York, PA 17404
(717) 751-0211
e-mail:
yorktownauction@cyberia.com

INDEX